WHAT WE NOW KNOW ABOUT JEWISH EDUCATION

Perspectives on Research for Practice

Edited by Roberta Louis Goodman, Paul A. Flexner and Linda Dale Bloomberg

Torah Aura Productions

ISBN 10: 1-934527-07-6

ISBN 13: 978-1-934527-07-8

Torah Aura Productions • 4423 Fruitland Avenue, Los Angeles, CA 90058

(800) BE-Torah • (800) 238-6724 • (323) 585-7312 • fax (323) 585-0327

E-MAIL <misrad@torahaura.com> • Visit the Torah Aura website at www.torahaura.com

MANUFACTURED IN THE MALAYSIA

Dedication

We dedicate this work to those who came before us,
who instilled in us the inspiration to pursue our Jewish learning:

Israel Friedlaender (1876–1920)
Israel Lippert (1902–1974)
Julia Esther Lippert (1906–1997)
Marian Gugenheim Flexner (1914–1987)
Rosalind Anne Diamond (1941–1978)

And to the next generations, our children and grandchildren,
in the hope that our commitment to Jewish education
will inspire them and their children:

Carla, Brent and Adam Bloomberg
Shoshana and Evan Goodman
Charles and Leah Rosenthal

Contents

CONTEXTS

PLANNING AND CHANGE

CLOSURE

What We Now Know about Jewish Education

Foreword

I remember sitting in my home in Berkeley editing the first volume while smelling smoke from the fire that was burning in the Oakland hills. The year was 1992, and the windows were closed, but the pungent odor was everywhere. Now, fifteen years later, much has changed in Berkeley and in Jewish education. Then thirty-two authors contributed. They were most of the names associated with research about Jewish education in this country. Now sixty-six authors are included. Of great interest is that only ten contributed to both. To what is this stunning growth in the number of researchers attributable? And, more important, how has Jewish education changed, matured or remained constant? In this new edition there are new subjects that are explored and new categories that have been added. Do these developments reflect a new field of inquiry that was not in evidence in 1992—or merely an attempt to be more complete?

A more interesting question stems from the original intent of the book, which was "to provide a useful tool for both practitioners and policy makers." Did this original focus meet its goal? Throughout the years many individuals have told me how useful the essays were—but the comments have been general at best. In what ways have research findings about Jewish education actually impacted those to whom they are addressed? Have these essays truly bridged the gap between the lay and the professional communities?

About a year after the publication I formulated five generalizations that, I believe, may still be relevant (or at least need further exploration):

1. Competition for "Jewish time" is ferocious.

2. Research that focuses on only one variable invariably does not adequately portray the whole, which may simply be impossible to do.

3. Formal education is out; non-formal education is in.

4. The plateau myth suggests that all day school education is the same or that all congregational Jewish education is the same. This is simply not true.

5. Not enough research is being conducted.

My estimate in 1992 was that the shelf life of the book would be five to ten years—at which point the book would move from the realm of sociology to that of history. The essays provided a snapshot of the state of Jewish education at least in North America at the beginning of the 1990's. The degree to which things have changed, matured, or stayed the same is for you, the reader, to judge. All I can offer is my deep gratitude to Paul Flexner, Roberta Goodman and Linda Bloomberg for providing another snapshot of Jewish education. May these volumes continue so that those who follow may glimpse the state of the field at periodic intervals and build on what we have learned.

Stuart Kelman
Berkeley, California
Pesa<u>h</u> 5767

Preface

Roberta Louis Goodman

When *What We Know about Jewish Education* was published in 1992, it was the first significant review of research related to and about Jewish education collected in a single place. At that time Jewish education was emerging as a Jewish communal priority. The Mandel Commission on Jewish Education in North America's Think Tank report, *A Time to Act* (1990), called for urgent and radical reform to Jewish education concentrating on personnel, lay leadership and funding. Shortly following that publication, the 1990 National Jewish Population Study claimed an intermarriage rate of 52% for recently married Jews, prompting a focus on Jewish education as *the* way to address Jewish continuity and to revitalize, strengthen, and deepen the knowledge and commitment of Jews to Judaism. *What We Know about Jewish Education* was written to help inform the deliberations about and initiatives in Jewish education. The book's intended audience included Jewish decision makers—institutional, communal, continental, and even international (primarily Israelis)—as well as Jewish educators in formal and informal settings involved in meeting the challenges of the 1990s.

Since Stuart Kelman's initial volume, the amount of research in Jewish education, the interest in that research and even the number of people conducting the research has grown exponentially. The result is that this volume is far more extensive than the original. We have included many new topics that were barely on the horizon as issues in Jewish education. We have also turned to many new researchers (while including a number of those from the previous edition) who have entered the field during these fifteen years. Thus the contents of this volume incorporate a level of research that is reflective of Jewish education as we approach the end of the first decade of the 21st century.

How is the term "research" understood? The emphasis in this book is on empirical studies with a focus on how something works, combined with several philosophical and historical studies. Research comes in many forms, including evaluation and needs assessment. Perhaps the main distinction between "classical" research studies on the one hand, and evaluation and needs assessments on the other, is their purpose. Research studies are conducted to increase our knowledge of an aspect of a phenomenon (e.g., recruitment, funding, teaching text). Evaluation studies are done on behalf of a particular entity (institution, organization or group) to measure how well a program or person has succeeded. Similarly, an organization or institution will conduct a needs assessment to help inform its work. Even though the generalizability of evaluation and needs assessments may be limited, since the scope and population studied may be narrow or small, this type of investigation contributes to the overall knowledge of a phenomenon (e.g., recruitment, funding, teaching text). The authors draw upon studies that were primarily conducted as research, evaluation and needs assessments. Therefore, throughout this book the word "research" will be used to refer to any type of study that contributes to our knowledge of a phenomenon, inclusive of evaluation and needs assessments.

This preface has three objectives: 1) to explore the ways that research in Jewish education can aid and enhance the field, 2) to examine the growth of research in Jewish education since the initial volume and 3) to present the organization and thinking behind the structure of the book and its contents.

ROLE OF RESEARCH IN JEWISH EDUCATION

What are the ways that Jewish education research advances the field of Jewish education? On a basic level, research contributes to knowledge about Jewish education in particular, and about the

North American Jewish experience overall. It raises and answers a wide range of questions about how Jewish education informs Jewish identity and commitment and the ways in which Jewish educational practice makes a difference for educators and learners. This research only contributes significantly to the field if policy makers, planners, funders, educators, and students of Jewish education are familiar with it and apply it to their decision making processes and educational practice. Policy makers and funders may use this knowledge to inform the direction in which a community, institution or foundation allocates resources and implements a vision for its constituents. Practitioners may turn to this information to strengthen their practice and help them grow as professionals.

Research is a tool that contributes to lay leaders and professionals being both well informed and critically reflective. Knowledge produced by research serves as a balance to intuition and experience. Research often introduces new ideas and perspectives, challenging a person's or group's assumptions and presenting different ways of thinking. Research also confirms and reaffirms previously held notions of how things can or should be. Reviewing research has the potential to overcome individual or institutional isolation by connecting the reader to a larger framework and creating an awareness of what others have learned in a variety of places.

Examining research is part of the quest for pursuing quality and excellence in Jewish education. Educational research, whether philosophical or empirical, presents theories and explores practices, often creating the link between the two. Research is often conducted by recognized experts—both theoreticians and practitioners—in a particular area. The reports, books and articles that these researchers write provide people in the field with many of the most important ideas, concepts, theories, and approaches of a particular era. While many theoreticians and practitioners tend to look for materials that identify best practices, all thinking needs to be analyzed and applied to the specific context or situation in order to improve it. Research adds to what we know and augments familiarity of Jewish education with the understanding that results are subject to interpretation.

GROWTH OF RESEARCH IN JEWISH EDUCATION

Many indicators attest to the growth of research in Jewish education. Two are used here to illustrate this expansion—the professionalization of researchers in Jewish education and the financial security of a serious publication for Jewish educational research in North America. First, in the early 1980s, the then Coalition for Alternatives in Jewish Education (now the Coalition for the Advancement of Jewish Education) started a network that focused on research in Jewish education. The attendees at the first network pre-conference could easily fit into one classroom. Now, over two decades later, the Network for Research in Jewish Education is an independent organization with nearly two hundred active members. Second, the Network has assumed the ownership of the *Journal for Jewish Education* and recently secured funding from the Mandel Foundation for its continued publication. The *Journal* provides an important vehicle for sharing significant research in Jewish education both for the members of the Network and for the community at large.

What do we NOW know about Jewish education that we did not know when Kelman edited the initial volume? What has changed about research in Jewish education and in Jewish education overall? What has remained the same? In order to answer these questions, a range of other questions about research in Jewish education need to be addressed:

- Why is research being conducted?
- Who is doing the research?
- What is the focus of the research?
- Who is sponsoring or funding research?
- What are the challenges of conducting research?
- What are the challenges in applying the knowledge learned from the research to the field at large?

WHY IS RESEARCH IN JEWISH EDUCATION BEING CONDUCTED?
WHO IS DOING RESEARCH IN JEWISH EDUCATION?

The days when research in Jewish education was primarily the domain of graduate students writing master's theses or doctoral dissertations in order to obtain degrees as Kelman intimates in 1992 are over. In the 21st century, research is conducted by consultants to address particular issues or evaluate programs locally or nationally and by academics who are well positioned to formulate theories and guide practice. Graduate students, perhaps even more than in 1992, also continue to write theses and dissertations and publish articles based upon their work. Others hold positions that include conducting research in Jewish education and communal life.

The connection between the significant increase in funding for Jewish educational programs and organizations and the demand for accountability by their funders has contributed significantly to the growth in research. As a result, research and evaluation are now viewed as integral rather than additional or non-essential parts of planning, policy making and program implementation. With the research often driven by these new funding sources, it is focused primarily on outcomes, a popular way of assessing the merit of an investment by its impact on the intended target population. Other purposes of research and evaluation include surveying a particular topic, conducting a needs assessment and contributing to program improvement. Many of these studies become reports or papers that are widely circulated through the Internet and are intended to inform local and/or national work.

The new funders, whether they are federations or philanthropists, are, in many ways, the driving force behind the expansion of research through their grant processes. Built into many grants is the requirement for an evaluation of the project or program with some including designated funds to cover the added expense. These evaluations increase our knowledge about the practice of Jewish education and have the potential for influencing practice in the field. The only major limitation to the influence of these evaluations is that they are often not publicly shared. It is imperative that this limitation, which is a prominent theme throughout this volume, be addressed in the near future.

A major side benefit of the changing role of research and evaluation is the growth of full-time research and evaluation staff, either experts in the field or program officers, within the larger organizations and foundations. The greatest growth is in the number of people commissioned to conduct research and evaluation projects either as independent consultants or as staff members of research centers. They include individuals who primarily work in Jewish communal life, or university settings or who do most of their work outside the Jewish community.

Another factor contributing to the increase of research is the growth of university programs and centers, both Jewish and secular, offering degrees or certificates in Jewish education on the bachelors, masters, and doctoral levels. This expansion of university programs has led to more students matriculating and writing about Jewish education. With this expansion of programs, new faculty positions in Jewish education have been created, which in turn leads to additional research in Jewish education.

Finally, there are a growing number of academic positions in related areas, such as Judaic studies, general education, religion, history and sociology. Often these academics have an expertise in Jewish education. The emergence of faculty members who connect their areas of primary research with Jewish education is an indicator of the value placed on Jewish education for understanding the larger American experience.

The overall growth of faculty with an academic interest in Jewish education impacts the amount of research conducted and published, as these efforts are often connected to promotion and tenure. This research is often supported through research grants that are obtained from foundations both within and outside of the greater Jewish community. Thus, the study of Jewish education within the university is an indication of the new role that it is offering to the creation of knowledge in related fields.

WHAT IS THE FOCUS OF THE RESEARCH? WHO IS SPONSORING OR FUNDING RESEARCH IN JEWISH EDUCATION?

Over the last two decades research has expanded to cover a wide spectrum of topics in Jewish education. It is difficult today to think of a topic or area that has not been studied or evaluated. While these studies have been conducted and some of the results have been disseminated, our knowledge in some areas remains relatively limited.

To a great extent, the topics of research studies are a result of the interests, demands and agendas of the funders and organizations paying for the research. While researchers have recommended creating a comprehensive or coordinated research plan that fills the gaps of knowledge and expands on what is known for either all of Jewish education or a particular area, this has yet to happen in a meaningful way. In fact, several studies sponsored by different organizations have tapped the same respondents or population groups on a similar topic within the same time frame. This replication of effort is an unfortunate by-product of the lack of a coordinated effort to create a research agenda that will have impact on the entire field.

WHAT ARE THE CHALLENGES TO CONDUCTING RESEARCH IN JEWISH EDUCATION? WHAT ARE THE CHALLENGES IN USING THE RESEARCH PRODUCED?

There are three main barriers related to conducting and utilizing research: sources of funding, publishing and the lack of a Jewish education database.

Even though funding for Jewish education has increased, there remain a limited number of organizations and foundations willing to invest in research, with much of the research being supported by the same few funders. This is in contrast to the R&D—research and development—initiatives that are common to much of corporate America as well as to many fields in the social services sector. Thus support for research in Jewish education remains sparse, especially among the foundations outside the Jewish world. Second, many of those who fund research in Jewish education fund research for the part of the system that they care about most passionately, and not the field as a whole. Third, many research and evaluation projects are underfunded due to the limited size of the programs that require evaluation. Many organizations are forced to get by on what they can afford rather than on what a thorough research project really warrants.

The barriers to publishing and disseminating results are the second issue. The Internet has greatly improved the diffusion of information and ideas across all disciplines. For research in Jewish education the Internet provides an inexpensive and readily accessible dissemination route and is frequently the method of choice. Yet many studies are not shared at all, and others appear in such a poor format, in terms of both writing style and graphics, that they are difficult to understand and digest. Not enough attention and finances are devoted to preparing studies in a readable and usable manner that would appeal to a broad range of readers. To address this weakness, funds need to be allocated to engage editors and graphic designers to prepare executive summaries and design reports to have greater impact on the field. The few reports where there has been funding for design and distribution have demonstrated the value of the investment through their significant impact on Jewish education.

In addition to the formal research reports mentioned above, shorter, more focused articles published in one of the many Jewish magazines add to the knowledge base for the field and the community as a whole. This is particularly true of evaluation studies where there is a distinction between the information required by the sponsoring organization to improve the program and the knowledge gained that would be most helpful and useful to a larger audience of policy makers and practitioners. Only rarely do the researchers receive the time or funding to translate their work into articles for publication. Also, although there are many publications serving general readers in the Jewish community, there are only a few that focus specifically on the results of research and evaluation. As a result, many institutions, organizations and researchers are now turning to the Internet rather than print media in order to share these "second tier" writings. Unfortunately, for many readers, publication on the Internet carries less status than being included in an official publication. For the foreseeable future, we need to turn to both the print and electronic media for distribution, as is the case in most fields of scholarship in North America, if we wish to reach the widest audience.

Finally, the lack of a database for Jewish education affects the researcher, the programmer and the wide array of readers. Search engines on the Internet facilitate locating research and evaluation reports, but they do not replace the usefulness of a rich and detailed database devoted to Jewish education. Some organizations have attempted to create electronic "libraries" or "collections" of research either in a particular delivery area or for Jewish education as a whole. These efforts have yet to fulfill the role of a database whose purpose is to collect and annotate the wide range of research and evaluation reports and studies for researchers, educators and policy makers to access.

RATIONALE FOR AND ORGANIZATION OF THE BOOK'S STRUCTURE AND CONTENT

The purpose of this book is to present the latest empirical and to some extent philosophical research that informs a wide range of Jewish educational topics. Our target audience includes lay leaders, professionals, policy makers, planners, funders, practitioners, students, researchers, evaluators and anyone with an interest in or role connected to Jewish education. Authors were asked to present the key research on a topic in Jewish education as well as any relevant research and literature from sources outside of Jewish education that were significant in terms of understanding the issues involved. The authors were asked to select the key studies conducted primarily in the time since the initial Kelman volume appeared. The authors are essentially the filters through which the research was selected and reviewed.

The overall organization of the chapters and the content within each chapter are patterned after the original Kelman volume.

Since this book is a collection of chapters written by multiple authors, having a format that each author followed was important in the creation of a consistent experience for the reader. The similarity of format for the chapters in all but the initial section helps the reader compare and contrast the accomplishments, issues and challenges for the wide variety of areas covered. The chapters follow an internal organization that includes setting the context, review of the key research, implications and policy recommendations, additional research questions, future directions for the field, a conclusion followed by bulleted highlights, placement of the topic in a larger context and finally an annotated bibliography of the most significant resources and references.

The book is divided into six sections. Four of those sections come from Schwab's four commonplaces of learning—learner, teacher, curriculum and milieu—which was used in the Kelman volume. While Schwab uses the term "milieu" to refer solely to the classroom environment, we, like Kelman, view the "milieu" of Jewish education as being the context both within and beyond the formal classroom, including the entire school system, informal educational settings such as camps and Jewish trips and the larger organizational and communal structures and factors affecting Jewish education in North America. Moreover, we extend the reach of the context in several directions. This volume adds a chapter on Jewish education in Australia as an attempt to inform and create dialogue beyond this continent, multiple perspectives on the role of Israel as an educational setting and a chapter that relates Jewish education to the broader field of religious education.

The two new sections are significant expansions of and departures from Schwab's framework. First the introductory section, entitled "Issues in Jewish Education," was added, providing a backdrop to some of the larger issues that frame and influence all of the commonplaces of Jewish education. Second, we have added an entire section on planning and changing Jewish education. This section speaks to how the delivery system in Jewish education has evolved over the last fifteen years or so. Many initiatives have focused on institutional, communal and even continent-wide Jewish educational planning. Other initiatives emphasize changing and improving the delivery system for Jewish education, including the lay leaders, educators, institutions and funding. The rise of new types of Jewish educational institutions, the expansion of other institutions and other shifts in the field make a section on planning and change important to understanding Jewish education in the 21st century.

Finally, a special addition to this volume is the final chapters by two of the book's editors. Linda Bloomberg's chapter analyzes and synthesizes the key research issues that emerge from this volume's chapters. Paul Flexner's chapter discusses Jewish educational topics. These closing chapters serve to capture the lessons learned about Jewish education to date and the implications thereof and in so doing provide a platform for launching the sequel to this volume. Indeed, with the rapid pace of change and development that is occurring and the explosion of new research and evaluation studies that are being conducted, Jewish education would certainly benefit from a third volume of *What We Know about Jewish Education* within the course of the next decade.

THE AUTHORS

The increased number of chapters in this volume from the original work is another indicator of the growth of research in Jewish education and the increase in the number of researchers. Many, but not all, of the key personalities conducting research and evaluation in Jewish education have authored chapters in this volume. We attempted to include the "veteran" or "well-known" researchers as well as some of the emerging researchers who will take the field in different directions in the future. Many of the authors wrote for the Kelman volume. Interestingly, only a very few revised chapters on the same topic for this volume.

A special note of thanks to the authors must be included here. We are grateful for the time and commitment that each so generously gave. The book took an inordinate length of time to complete. Many contributors were patient in waiting to see their chapters in print, and others were kind enough to write quickly under time constraints as chapters were added at later stages to enrich the book. What all of the chapter authors share is the sense of importance that this volume contributes not just to the research and evaluation endeavors, but to the field of Jewish education as a whole. Hopefully, what is presented to you, the reader, is a critical and helpful, yet compassionate and passionate, rendering of the field.

THE PUBLISHER

While we as the editors are wishing that this book makes a big splash, that it is read by more than just our own graduate students, Torah Aura deserves its own acknowledgement for the desire to further research in Jewish education. Primarily a publisher of curricular materials, Torah Aura has an understanding of the significance of research to quality Jewish education and a vibrant Jewish community. We are appreciative of the academic freedom that they afforded us, as no constraints were placed on either authors or editors. To Joel, Jane, Alan, and all who are part of Torah Aura, we as the editors are grateful for your support, patience and dedication.

THE EDITORS

In undertaking this project we officially called ourselves Moadon Ha'Yanshuf—the Night Owl Club (of course, we all have our mascot owls, too), since in order to accommodate one another's schedules our telephone meetings would typically begin late at night and continue into the wee hours of the morning. We designed the book together, sharing responsibilities and sometimes splitting roles as well. Paul was the expert editor of the text and Linda the expert editor of the references and annotated bibliographies. We identified and solved issues together, always looking to strengthen the book. We remain colleagues and friends upon completing this book as well!

For the most part, we share three educational institutions that have formed and informed our work. All three of us are graduates of the AEGIS doctoral program in adult and continuing education at Teachers College/Columbia University. All three of us teach for the Siegal College of Judaic Studies, where Linda was previously a student in the program with Roberta as her advisor and teacher and Paul as one of her teachers. Two of us received graduate degrees in Jewish education from Hebrew Union College–Jewish Institution of Religion, Paul in New York and Roberta in Los Angeles, where Stuart Kelman was an advisor, teacher and inspiration to her. We are grateful to all our colleagues and students who have in some way shaped our journeys and our own Jewish education.

THE READERS

To you, the reader, we hope that these chapters will inform your thinking, inspire you and impact your activities in the field of Jewish education. We hope that you, like us, will be impressed with the growth of research in Jewish education and recognize how it has made and continues to make a difference in the design and delivery of Jewish education, and that you will carry forward even further the multiple ways that this research can contribute to the field. In line with the view that research is an ongoing conversation, we always are open to your reactions, suggestions, feedback and comments! We are reachable through the publisher!

Issues in Jewish Education

The Current Moment
in Jewish Education:
An Historian's View

Jack Wertheimer

The field of Jewish education has undergone significant transformation over the past two decades. Broad new social trends have remade the larger environment of Jewish communal life and have also complicated the task of delivering a strong Jewish education. In response to altered social circumstances, a number of creative programs and bold champions have emerged to lead the field in new directions. Innovative thinking has enlivened the discourse about Jewish education. And some communities are addressing Jewish educational needs in a far more purposeful fashion.

Viewed within the longer historical trajectory since 1945, the extent of change is even more dramatic. After enjoying a period of expansive growth (particularly in its supplementary sector) and much optimism in the post-war decades, the field of Jewish education suffered from declining morale in the late 1970s and early 1980s due to a sharp decrease in enrollments and severely critical reports about the inadequacy of the synagogue school (see Wertheimer, 1999, 37–42). It did not help matters that despite promises of increased funding for Jewish education, neither the federation world nor Jewish philanthropists invested seriously in the field. But in the mid-1980s a new mood took hold. The Jewish Community Center movement began to focus more attention on Jewish education; family education came into vogue; a few pioneering federations engaged with local educational needs in a more concerted fashion; and the first glimmerings of new funding materialized.

Once the 1990 National Jewish Population Study riveted communal attention on the so-called "Jewish continuity" crisis, the momentum for change accelerated. Day schools attracted new champions, and greater numbers of parents outside the Orthodox world enrolled their children in such schools. Most medium and large city federations created a "continuity commission" to engage in planning for the improvement of local educational work. Funders conceived of a series of new initiatives to strengthen Jewish education. And various agencies devised programs to reach under-served populations and Jews-at-risk. Though it is too early to gauge the long-term impact of these efforts, it is possible to discern the contours of change and the important new initiatives in the field.

THE SOCIAL CONTEXT OF JEWISH EDUCATION

We begin with recent social trends that have reshaped the work of Jewish education, with perhaps none more apparent than the surging incidence of intermarriage. Both the 1990 and 2000–2001 National Jewish Population studies tracked the massive growth of this phenomenon over the last third of the twentieth century, demonstrating that nearly half of all Jews who wed in the late twentieth century married a non–Jew. One consequence of this new reality is a decline in the number of children enrolled in Jewish educational institutions of any kind, because the large majority of intermarried families do not provide their children with a Jewish education, although one study suggests that intermarried Jewish women tend to the Jewish education of their children in rising numbers (Phillips 1998; Saxe, Kadushin & Phillips 2006, p. 23; Cohen, Ukeles & Miller 2006). Still, even with these losses, an unprecedented number of children from intermarried homes are now enrolled in Jewish educational institutions. (Approximately 18% of intermarried families enroll their children, mostly in one-day-a-week synagogue-based programs [NJPS 2000–01]). This novel social reality has created new dilemmas: for example, should a synagogue school enroll a child who simultaneously attends a church school? More broadly, it has necessitated a rethinking of the language and categories employed in classes. Non–Jewish parents often approach religious education with a very different set of expectations than do parents who were born Jewish. Whereas the latter tend to think of Judaism largely as a matter of family and festivals, the former place a far greater emphasis on faith and feelings (Wertheimer 2005). Parents may not necessarily be in synch with the outlook and goals of the school or with one another, thereby adding further pressures to the work of educators.

The 1990 NJPS also demonstrated the growing extent of Jewish geographic dispersal (Goldstein & Goldstein 1996). The consequences of this mobility for Jewish education are considerable. New schools are springing up in locations that previously had small Jewish populations. Who would have imagined the extent of day school growth in the San Francisco Bay area, Las Vegas, Atlanta and southern Florida? And who would have expected some of these burgeoning communities to be at the forefront of educational experimentation, while institutions with venerable histories in long-established communities of the Midwest and Northeast are losing ground? Equally noteworthy, Jewish mobility is dispersing the population *within* communities at ever greater distances from local educational institutions. This complicates the delivery of Jewish education, for either young people must travel a long way to study or satellite schools must be built in the far-flung exurbs.

Still a third social development reshaping Jewish education is the high level of labor force participation by women (Hartman & Hartman 1996). In the postwar era stay-at-home mothers made themselves available for carpooling duties; but with the high incidence of dual-income families, parents are hard-pressed to deliver their children to congregational schools. These time constraints of *parents* are one in a series of pressures accounting for the reduction of school hours in supplementary settings. Parents are simply not available to drive their children to the synagogue several times a week. To be sure, other factors also account for the contraction of school hours in the supplementary system, such as the high priority many parents place on their children's involvement with sports and other extracurricular activities. All of these family considerations are serving to pressure supplementary schools to cut back on their hours, which, in turn, is forcing tough decisions affecting the use of reduced class time: Should schools give *priority* to teaching about the liturgy in order to enable children to participate in religious services, to preparing young people for their bar/bat mitzvah celebrations, to building Hebrew language skills, to fostering identification with the Jewish people or to providing positive Jewish experiences?

The labor force participation of Jewish women has also depleted all kinds of Jewish educational institutions of personnel. In the past, Jewish women were available for part-time teaching jobs or for volunteer work in schools. This is far less likely today as Jewish women seek full-time employment and substantial levels of remuneration. Undoubtedly they do so both for reasons of financial necessity and out of a desire to engage in full-time rather than part-time work. But for the field of Jewish education, with its limited resources and inability to offer competitive rewards, the consequences have been dire. Schools must scramble to insure teacher recruitment and retention, and in the process they often compete with one another to attract personnel from the shrinking pool of available educators and school directors (see also Aron, Zeldin & Lee 2005, pp. 160–163; Shevitz 1988).

On a more positive note, changing social attitudes are prompting greater parental involvement in children's Jewish education, from the selection of schools to playing an active role in reinforcing school lessons. Whereas Jewish parents at mid-century enrolled their children in the closest synagogue school, today's families are more apt to insist on just the right fit between *each* child and the type of schooling they choose to deliver that education. Thus it is hardly unusual for parents to enroll one child in a day school and a second child in a supplementary school and then to hire a tutor for their third child. This approach reflects the consumer orientation of today's parents and also their greater insistence on quality.

Parents are also far more engaged today in programs of Jewish family education and, more recently, in adult education. Whereas studies of the mid-century synagogue school portrayed a parent body dropping their children off at the curb outside the synagogue building, today's affiliated parents are far more likely to partake of some forms of Jewish education themselves and to enter the portals of Jewish education (see Fishman, Kress, Pomson & Prell in Wertheimer 2007a; Wertheimer 2007b; NJPS 2000–2001). Thus, even as educational programs struggle to cope with evolving social patterns, they often benefit from heightened parental participation and concern.

RETHINKING THE DELIVERY OF JEWISH EDUCATION

The field of Jewish education has worked hard to address the new realities of the American Jewish community. To begin with, the field has diversified the types of schools and programs that educate Jews about their religious civilization. The 1990s, for example, witnessed an expansion in day school options. Where once such schools were almost exclusively the domain of the Orthodox community, the Conservative movement now runs fifty-seven Solomon Schechter schools, some of which have expanded into high school education over the past decade. There are now nineteen day schools under Reform auspices; their umbrella organization is called PARDeS. A spurt of growth in the communal or so-called "pluralistic" sector has resulted in a total of ninety-five such schools, surpassing the combined number of day schools in the Conservative and Reform movements. Collectively, day schools now educate approximately 205,000 students, almost as many as are enrolled at any given moment in supplementary schools. To be sure, Orthodox day schools educate eighty percent of the day school pupils, but many more school choices are now available (see Schick 2004).

New options have also come into existence in the supplementary school sphere. Congregations are experimenting with various configurations to accommodate the needs and interests of families. Symptomatically, the educational arm of the Conservative movement identified six alternative ways for its synagogue schools to deliver an education (see "A Framework for Excellence"... 1998). Reform temples have also rethought the time allocated to schooling, many requiring Saturday attendance so as to teach synagogue skills. These options, in turn, are supplemented by a growing number of schools sponsored by the Chabad-Lubavitch movement, which runs several hundred supplementary schools offering great flexibility of hours and in settings outside of the synagogue community. By the early 21st century attention has shifted to the post-bar and bat mitzvah years as communities and synagogues experiment with new models for engaging their teenagers in both formal and informal Jewish activities. Thus providing more options for parents is a guiding principle in the supplementary school enterprise.

Equally important, the sphere of informal education has received a new infusion of funding and attention. One important outcome of the continuity commissions was expanded funding by federations of synagogue-based teen programs, teen trips to Israel or Jewish summer camping (Sales & Saxe 2002 and 2004; Keysar & Kosman 2004). (Communities generally did not add additional funds to all three.) The underlying assumption guiding investments in these programs was that exposure to informal Jewish education during the teen years was particularly beneficial for nurturing long-term Jewish commitments. Indeed, research in the 1990s highlighted the important role of peer relationships during adolescence in solidifying lifelong Jewish engagement (Phillips 1998, pp. 35–40).

Informal educational programs were given an important boost when the 1990 National Jewish Population Study demonstrated the enduring effects of multiple Jewish exposures on later Jewish participation. Adults who had participated in a combination of informal educational experiences in addition to their formal schooling tended to be involved with Jewish life far more intensively than those with fewer educational exposures (Cohen 1995; Cohen & Kotler-Berkowitz 2004; Kosmin & Keysar 2004). Moreover, adults who had been enrolled in informal educational programs were inclined to replicate the experience for their children by sending them to the kinds of summer camps they themselves had attended or signing them up for teen trips to Israel (Wertheimer 2005, pp. 8–11). This research, in turn, encouraged funders to invest in informal education far more than had been the case prior to the 1990s.

Jewish philanthropists have also taken more notice of college-age students. Hillel, the Jewish campus organization, went through a remarkable expansion in the 1990s, garnering serious funding to house its programs in sparkling new facilities and involving Jewish campus youth in new types of programs. The Hillel network now operates in a far more deliberate fashion to nurture a new generation of Jewish leaders. Allied to these efforts is Birthright Israel, a ten-day trip to Israel provided free of charge to young Jews between the ages of eighteen and twenty-six. Designed to introduce Israel to young people who have never taken an educational trip there, birthright tours intentionally seek to raise the Jewish consciousness of young Jews and to strengthen their identification with the Jewish State and their own Jewishness (Saxe, Kadushin, et al. 2004).

Rounding out the multiplication of Jewish educational options are a series of new national initiatives in the realm of adult Jewish education. Educators have long debated whether much of significance can change in the field without serious parental involvement. The role model parents can provide their children as engaged learners is invaluable in demonstrating the seriousness of Jewish education. Moreover, the well-educated parent, it has been argued, might serve as a powerful advocate for higher educational standards. Anecdotal reports suggest that the investment in adult education is in fact leading to enhanced parental participation in their children's schooling (Shuster & Grant 2003; Grant et al. 2004).

Leading the way, the Florence Melton Adult Mini-School was created on the premise that a two-year intensive study program would make a difference in the lives of Jewish adults. Over the last twenty years thousands of adults in communities across the continent have graduated the program, with many continuing their study beyond the initial two-year curriculum. At the same time, the Wexner Heritage Foundation organized intensive two-year seminars of adult Jewish education in communities around the country—albeit for a hand-picked group of potential "Jewish leaders." More recently, the Meah program was developed at the Hebrew College in Boston with support from the federation and the central agency to serve as a gateway program into more intensive Jewish learning within the congregational structure. The Meah program is expanding to other communities as a way to engage more adults in Jewish study. Graduates of these programs are now serving as leaders in local and national efforts to improve Jewish education for children.

THE ALTERED ROLE OF JEWISH EDUCATION IN JEWISH FAMILY AND COMMUNAL LIFE

Collectively, these efforts suggest a new approach to Jewish educational thinking now gaining currency. One key idea is that Jewish education must be understood as a life-long enterprise if it is to engage children and if adults are to regard Jewishness as an organizing principle of their lives. Rather than view each program as discrete, communities are supporting education for Jews of all ages and are encouraging multiple forms of engagement with Jewish education. This is most evident in the expansion of adult educational curricula taught by Jewish studies professors, rabbis, and communal professionals for the Melton and Meah programs. At the other end of the life continuum, early childhood education is now benefiting from new thinking and investment. The larger agenda is to enrich such programs and use them as portals of entry into Jewish life for both children and their parents. But there is also new thinking about how the time in early childhood programs can be used: two remarkably innovative efforts are an immersion program in Hebrew to encourage language acquisition pioneered by the Jewish Theological Seminary and the adaptation of the Florence Melton Adult Mini-School to the needs and interests of parents of pre-school children in order to create a parallel learning track for both generations (Lipman 2006).

With more intensive Jewish learning taking place among the very youngest and adult learners, new initiatives aim to remake schooling for those in between. Nowhere is this more evident than in supplementary schools, which are housed mainly in synagogues. Over the past decade several new considerations have reshaped attitudes about such schools:

1. Synagogue revitalization efforts have spurred new understandings of how the synagogue school ought to function in the life of the congregation. Rather than segregate the synagogue into a sanctuary and a separate school wing, efforts are underway to integrate all activities within the congregation.

2. Today's parents are also more likely to demand more of the synagogue school. Contrary to the folk wisdom that parents tell their children "We suffered in Hebrew school and expect you,

our kids, to suffer through it, too," in many synagogues parents are insisting on better Jewish education for their children.

3. There has been a sea change in how supplementary education is defined. When the mission was mainly the acquisition of skills and knowledge, supplementary education was always found wanting. Today the rules of the game have changed. Schools are valued not only for the cognitive knowledge they impart, but also for the good experiences children have, the Jewish memories schools create, how much good fun parents and children have in the school preparing for celebrations and the like. This orientation has opened new avenues for supplementary education to compete more effectively with other Jewish and non–Jewish activities.

4. The new emphasis on wholesome fun has also raised morale within schools. Observers frequently comment on the improved spirit within schools among children, their parents, and the teachers. "It's far easier to do good things," claims one long-time educator.

These and other factors have prompted several new initiatives to re-create the supplementary school (Wertheimer 2007). Some projects seek nothing less than "systemic change," which will involve the entire congregation in restructuring the way it delivers Jewish education to learners of all ages. The most sustained of such projects has been the Experiment in Congregational Education, a national initiative, based at the campus of the Hebrew Union College in Los Angeles (Aron 2000). Two local community initiatives to spur such change are NESS and La'Atid, sponsored by the central agencies for Jewish education in Philadelphia and Hartford, respectively. On the denominational level, both the Reform and the Conservative movements have issued new curricula to upgrade the quality of learning in synagogue schools within their movements, the former known as the Chai curriculum and the later as Etgar. These national initiatives have been matched by equally innovative efforts within individual congregations to rework their schooling by reconfiguring hours, setting new goals, or adopting the model of informal education and even creating synagogue schools along the lines of camping models (Reimer 1997). Each of these initiatives is partially the result of a dramatic reduction over the last two or three decades in the time that children and families spend in the school and synagogue.

None of these approaches would have been possible without the infusion of new capital and prodding by philanthropists. The latter have created new umbrella bodies to link particular sectors within the field of Jewish education—the Partnership for Excellence in Jewish Education for day schools, the Foundation for Jewish Camping, the Jewish Early Childhood Education Initiative (JECEI), and the Partnership for Congregational Education. Day schools in several communities have received multi-million-dollar gifts from local benefactors to build impressive new facilities, substantially boost their compensation packages, offer across-the-board tuition reduction or in other ways upgrade their programming. Further enhancements of the field have come as several foundations such as the Avi Chai and Jim Joseph foundations have embraced Jewish education as their primary mission; others of greater and lesser size, such as the Shusterman Foundation, the Jewish Life Network, the Covenant Foundation, the Wexner Foundations and others, channel a portion of their largess to Jewish educational causes. The new Jewish philanthropy embodied by these foundations has transformed the financial landscape in which Jewish educational institutions operate.

For all these significant strides, the field of Jewish education continues to struggle with several perennial dilemmas.

1. While it is true that new types of funding are now available for national and local initiatives, the funds directed by philanthropists to Jewish education are still woefully inadequate. Although it is true that some champions of Jewish education with deep pockets have surfaced in particular communities, benefactors in general have not taken on the challenge of insuring a successor generation by directing their resources to improving the quality of Jewish education for all.

2. Jewish educational institutions are contending with a growing shortage of trained personnel due to the low wages paid to Jewish educators, inadequate benefits in the area of health, retirement and life insurance, and the relatively low status of the profession within the Jewish

community. An upwardly mobile Jewish population will find it hard to recruit educators unless the monetary and status rewards it offers are substantially upgraded.

3. The field of Jewish education is weakened by its highly diffuse organizational structure. Remarkably scant attention is paid to the task of channeling families from one educational option to the next in their home communities. On a national level, no agency has the authority or financial clout to set goals for the field. Even more globally, the voluntary nature of American society impedes attempts at coordination and instead fosters diffusion.

These factors and the erosion of commitment to Jewish life make it difficult to project the long-term future of Jewish education in North America. Still, developments over the past two decades attest to the dynamism of the field and its responsiveness to a changing community. Much has been accomplished; much more remains to be done.

Key factors influencing the changing nature of Jewish education:

- Jewish education operates in a social environment that poses many new challenges.
- These challenges have forced a rethinking of how Jewish education is delivered.
- In an age of choice, the field of Jewish education now offers many new options; day schools have proliferated, as have new models of supplementary schooling.
- Informal education assumes a greater role in the field, as does adult education.
- Jewish education is now seen as a life-long enterprise, involving the very youngest early childhood pupils, students in formal and informal educational programs, teens, college students, and adults.
- The field has benefited from new philanthropic investment and from the prodding of donors.
- Several endemic problems persist, including an insufficiency of funding, a dearth of champions who advocate on behalf of Jewish education, a shortage of personnel, and the wide diffusion of energy.

As it attends to the needs and challenges of the new century, the field of Jewish education has much reason to celebrate its recent achievements. A significant infrastructure of schools and programs has been put in place, new ideas have emerged to improve the delivery of Jewish education and some new champions have embraced Jewish education as a cause, insisting that Jewish communal leaders attend to the needs of the next generation. Still, important challenges remain. Even as schools are seeking to improve, a large gap remains between the school and the synagogue—with many families, including day school families, remaining aloof from the latter. New evidence also suggests that graduates of various types of programs absent themselves from organized Jewish activities from their entrance into university until they marry and bear children, a hiatus of at least fifteen to twenty years, which increasingly lasts a lifetime. And one of the most important concerns of Jewish educational programs—building a strong sense of connection between the individual Jew and the collective needs of the Jewish people—also seems to be an uphill struggle in an age when the social glue holding together most sectors of American society appears to be weakening. All of these factors suggest a gap between what Jewish educational programs seek to impart and the actual engagement of their students with Jewish life. For all the important strides made in the field, Jewish education in the coming years will have to pay far greater attention to moving Jews of all ages from embracing Jewish learning to active Jewish living.

ANNOTATED BIBLIOGRAPHY

Aron, I. (2000) *Becoming a Congregation of Learners*. Woodstock, VT: Jewish Lights. Isa Aron has directed a national effort to lead synagogues on a voyage of systemic transformation. Arguing against a partial fix that addresses only the school environment without remaking the broader congregational context for Jewish education in the synagogue, Aron lays out an ambitious plan for remaking the synagogue as a congregation of learners for Jews of all ages. Her influential book provides a guide to what she has learned from the Experiment in Congregational Education and includes some how-to material for those wishing to introduce her model of change.

Cohen, S.M. and Kotler-Berkowitz, L. (2004) *The Impact of Childhood Jewish Education upon Adults' Jewish Identity: Schooling, Israel Travel, Camping and Youth Groups*. United Jewish Communities Report Series on the National Jewish Population Survey 2000–01, Report 3, *www.ujc.org/njps*. Based on the National Jewish Population Study of 2000–2001, this report analyzes the long-term impact of various types of Jewish educational exposures. The authors correlate childhood educational experiences with the later identification of adults with different aspects of Jewish life. The report concludes with a series of policy prescriptions to maximize the impact of clusters of Jewish education, Israel experiences, and other successful educational exposures.

Reimer, J. (1997) *Succeeding at Jewish Education: How One Synagogue Made It Work*. Philadelphia: Jewish Publication Society. Employing the perspective and vocabulary of an ethnographer, Joseph Reimer studies a single synagogue school. Though hardly starry-eyed from the "successes" of the school, Reimer nonetheless portrays a school that has worked hard to create an environment for children and their parents to engage in Jewish learning and serves as a setting for enacting the drama of Jewish learning.

Sales, A.L. and Saxe, L. (2004) *How Goodly Are Thy Tents: Summer Camping as Jewish Socializing Experiences*. Lebanon, NH: University Press of New England. As the Jewish community has come to appreciate the critical role played by summer camps as living laboratories of informal Jewish education, the authors of this study take the measure of how Jewish education works in a camp environment. This book has played an influential role in bolstering camping as a valuable tool in the Jewish socialization of young people.

Schick, M. (2004) *A Census of Jewish Day Schools in the United States*. New York: Avi Chai Foundation. The 1990s witnessed a growth spurt in the number of Jewish day schools not under Orthodox auspices. Marvin Schick has painstakingly collected data on the number of those schools, their enrollment patterns, and the extent to which their graduates continue on to day high schools. The large number of day schools, nevertheless, remains under Orthodox auspices and his study sheds light on the relative demographic strength within different sectors of the Orthodox world.

Wertheimer, J. (1999) "Jewish Education in the United States: Recent Trends and Issues," *American Jewish Year Book*. New York: American Jewish Committee. This study surveys the major trends in Jewish education at the end of the 20th century. It contrasts these trends with the state of the field in the post–World War II era and traces the dynamism of the field as bold initiatives, new funding and thoughtful planning have propelled Jewish education into the consciousness of Jewish communal leadership. The study also highlights ongoing sources of weakness and tension.

Wertheimer, J. (2005) *Linking the Silos: How to Accelerate the Momentum in Jewish Education Today*. New York: Avi Chai Foundation. Based on a team project initiated by the Avi Chai foundation, this summary report situates Jewish education within the context of changing familial and communal norms. It analyzes how families in the early 21st century relate differently to Jewish education than did their predecessors. And it argues for a self-conscious program of creating linkages within communities between the various forms of Jewish education, between educators, between formal and informal Jewish education, and between families and the network of educational programs.

REFERENCES

"A Framework for Excellence in the Conservative Synagogue School: A Report of the Blue Ribbon Task Force on Standards for Conservative Jewish Education," (1998). *http://www.uscj.org/Blue_Ribbon_Report6668.html*

Aron, I. (2000). *Becoming a Congregation of Learners*. Woodstock, VT: Jewish Lights.

Aron, I., Zeldin, M. & Lee, S. (2005). "Contemporary Jewish Education," *The Cambridge Companion to American Judaism*, Dana Evan Kaplan, ed., Cambridge and New York: Cambridge University Press, pp. 145–68.

Cohen, S.M. (1995). "The Impact of Varieties of Jewish Education upon Jewish Identity: An Inter-Generational Perspective." *Contemporary Jewry 16*, 68–96.

Cohen, S.M. and Kotler-Berkowitz, L. (2004). *The Impact of Childhood Jewish Education upon Adults' Jewish Identity: Schooling, Israel Travel, Camping and Youth Groups*. United Jewish Communities Report Series on the National Jewish Population Survey 2000–01, Report 3, *www.ujc.org/njps*

Cohen, S.M., Ukeles, J. & Miller, R. (2006, December 8). "Read Boston Study on Intermarriage with Caution," *Forward*, www.forward.com/articles/read-boston-study-on-intermarriage-with-caution/

Grant, L., Schuster, D.T., Woocher M. & Cohen, S.M. (2004). *A Journey of Heart and Mind: Transformative Jewish Learning in Adulthood*. New York: Jewish Theological Seminary Press.

Goldstein, S. & Goldstein, A. (1996). *Jews on the Move*. Albany: SUNY Press.

Hartman, M. & Hartman, H. (1996). *Gender Equality and American Jews*. Albany: SUNY Press.

Keysar, A. & Kosmin, B. (2004). *Research Findings on the Impact of Camp Ramah: A Companion Study to the "Eight Up" Report*. NY: Ramah Camps *http://www.campramah.org/news/keysar_kosmin_2004_reserach_findings.pdf*

Kosmin, B. & Keysar, A. (2004). *Eight Up: The Jewish Engagement of Young Adults Raised in Conservative Synagogues, 1995–2003*. New York: Jewish Theological Seminary Press.

Lipman, S. (2006, January 13). "All Hebrew, All the Time," New York: *Jewish Week*.

"National Jewish Population Survey 2000–2001: Adult Jewish Education." New York: United Jewish Communities. *www.ujc.org/njps*

Phillips, B. (1998). *Re-examining Intermarriage: Trends, Textures and Strategies*. New York: American Jewish Committee.

Reimer, J. (1997). *Succeeding at Jewish Education: How One Synagogue Made It Work*. Philadelphia: Jewish Publication Society.

Sales, A.L. & Saxe, L. (2002). *Limud by the Lake: Fulfilling the Educational Potential of Jewish Summer Camps*. New York: Avi Chai Foundation.

Sales, A.L. & Saxe, L. (2004). *How Goodly Are Thy Tents: Summer Camping as Jewish Socializing Experiences*. Lebanon, NH: University Press of New England.

Saxe, L., Kadushin, C. et al. (2004). *Evaluating Birthright Israel: Long-term Impact and Recent Findings*. Waltham, MA: Cohen Center, Brandeis University.

Saxe, L., Kadushin, C & Phillips, B. (2006, November 17). "Boston's Good News on Intermarriage," New York: *Jewish Week*.

Schick, M. (2000). *A Census of Jewish Day Schools in the United States*. New York: Avi Chai Foundation.

Shevitz, S. (1988). "Communal Responses to the Teacher Shortage in the North American Supplementary School," *Studies in Jewish Education*, Janet Aviad, vol. 3. Jerusalem:Hebrew University.

Schuster, D.T. & Grant, L.D. (2003). *The Impact of Adult Jewish Learning in Today's Jewish Community*. New York: United Jewish Communities.

Wertheimer, J. ed. (2007a). *Family Matters: Jewish Education in an Age of Choice*. Lebanon, NH: University Press of New England.

Wertheimer, J. (2007b). *Recent Trends in Jewish Supplementary Education*. New York: Avi Chai Foundation.

Wertheimer, J. (2001). *Talking Dollars and Sense about Jewish Education*. New York: Avi Chai Foundation.

Vision-Guided
Jewish Education

Daniel Pekarsky

I

The role of guiding visions in advancing the cause of quality education has been a prominent theme in recent discussions of Jewish education. At work in these discussions is the principle that more money, higher-quality educators, more informal education, more intensive forms of Jewish education and/or other variables that have been suggested as the key to improvement are insufficient to produce high-quality education in the absence of another critical ingredient. This critical ingredient is the presence in an educating institution of a vision that is inspiring to a critical mass of stakeholders and that is also concrete enough to give guidance to practice.

Unfortunately, discussions of the role of vision in education are confused by vague and sometimes competing interpretations of what "vision" refers to. In the literature on Jewish education this problem has been remedied by a number of attempts to specify the meaning of the concept of vision and its relevance to educational deliberation, practice, and evaluation. In this discussion "vision" will be understood in two senses. First, an *existential vision* refers to the conception of the kind of person and community that are to be cultivated through the education process. An educating institution's existential vision answers the question: What outcomes would we count as success? What kind of person and community are we hoping to foster through the educational process? Second, an institution's *educational vision* includes not just the existential vision at its core but also those ideas that jointly define its approach to the effort to actualize this vision under real-world conditions. These will include, but not be limited to, ideas about human nature, motivation, learning and development, as well as ideas about the cultural background and communal context out of which learners and teachers come.

Against this background a vision-guided institution can be described as one that is informed both by an existential vision and by a stance toward the best way, everything considered, to actualize this vision in the circumstances in which we find ourselves.[1] Whether we find the educational vision that is at work in a practice, program, or institution compelling will thus depend on our assessment of its guiding existential vision and of the assumptions and theories that inform its efforts to actualize this existential vision. A corollary of this is that as our ideas about what is desirable and about the ways to achieve what is desirable change, our educational vision is, over time, also likely to change.

Those, including the author, who believe in the importance of existential vision in education typically hold that vision is indispensable in three ways. First, the presence of a clear, shared, and inspiring vision affords the stakeholders who carry forward an educational initiative a powerful motivation to continue in their work in the face of all the obstacles that confront anybody who seeks to change the status quo in significant ways. Second, having such a vision is an invaluable tool in the effort to make non-arbitrary decisions concerning such diverse matters as specific goals, curriculum, pedagogy, hiring and budgeting priorities. As an example, if my aspiration is to cultivate "labor-Zionist" types, or Buberian Jews who privilege I/Thou relations, or individuals who believe Gmilut Hesed is at the heart of a well-lived Jewish life, my calculations and decisions along these various

---

[1] A less stringent definition of a vision-guided institution does not insist on coherence between vision and practice; but it does require that, although there may be substantial weaknesses, the institution is committed to an existential vision and is seriously engaged in efforts to use this vision as a guide to its practice.

fronts are likely to vary in substantial ways. Third, the presence of a guiding vision offers educators a non-arbitrary basis for educational evaluation—i.e., for deciding what would count as success (as opposed to relying on the criteria announced by external testing bodies or the social conventions of the community).

Against this background, we are in a good position to identify some of the critical questions in this domain.

- First, what criteria must an adequate existential vision satisfy? For example, how inspiring, how concretely specified, how widely shared (and by whom) must it be?

- Second, how do such visions arise, and, related to this, who is to decide what guiding vision should inform the work of an educating institution? More specifically, are visions the product of charismatic leaders? Are they the result of an educational/social process that members of an educating community go through? To what extent should these visions arise through a relatively democratic process of collective values clarification? To what extent should the process incorporate learning activities—and what kind?

- Third, what communal arrangements encourage and discourage the emergence of vision-guided practices?

- Fourth, there are questions from the skeptic. For example, is it really true that educational effectiveness requires the presence of guiding existential visions? And might it be the case that designing educational arrangements around a guiding vision of the kind of person to be cultivated might be indoctrinatory, manipulative or otherwise ethically problematic? If so, are there ways to guard against such possibilities?

II

My own interest in the place of vision in education grows out of my work in the philosophy of education. Though it would be a serious mistake to believe that philosophers universally embrace the idea that education should be guided by a self-consciously articulated, inspiring vision that identifies an educating community's core aspirations, this idea sits very comfortably at the center of the educational theories of a number of philosophers and philosophers of education. The most important of these is Plato, whose *Republic* identifies not only an existential vision with individual and social dimensions that should inform education, but also a broader educational vision that includes a constellation of systematically integrated beliefs concerning human nature and growth that jointly move Plato toward a conception of the educational process. That is, Plato's *Republic* offers us an example not just of an existential vision but also of an educational vision. Educational philosophers like Jean-Jacques Rousseau, the author of *Emile,* also offer us examples of educational visions. More popular examples of vision-guided institutions can be found in books like A. S. Neill's *Summerhill,* B. F. Skinner's *Walden II,* and Aldous Huxley's *Island.*

Persuaded by the arguments for vision in this tradition of philosophy, and having come to the view that Jewish education is a field in which vision is under-represented both in discourse concerning education and in educational decision-making at communal and institutional levels, I have come to believe that this state of affairs needs remedying. For this reason, my own research and more practical efforts in Jewish education have increasingly focused on remedying this problem.

It may be relevant to add that my interest in vision has also come to influence the research and teaching I do in general education, especially the work I do in the University of Wisconsin's educator-preparation program. Having discovered that those preparing to be educators are typically asked to pay very little attention to the larger purposes of education and to the relevance of such purposes to educational planning and practice, I have sought to remedy this problem by introducing educators-in-training to a range of powerful but often competing ideas concerning the whys and wherefores of education. Among the challenges I put to them are the following: What differences in practice does it make if I choose this guiding idea rather than that one? If I choose E. D. Hirsch or John Dewey or Nel Noddings as my guide, what practical difference does it make? More fundamentally, which if any of these guiding ideas—or what combination of these ideas—seems most reasonable for communities and educators to adopt? What criteria should govern this selection? What individuals or body (e.g., parents, educators, the youngsters that will be affected, the State, etc.) should be empowered to make such decisions on behalf of the children of the community, and why?

III

I mentioned earlier that there is a tradition dealing with the role of guiding visions in education that stretches all the way back to Plato's *Republic*. But as already intimated, in both general and Jewish education there have been significant stretches of time in which educational theorists, teacher-educators, and practitioners have skirted questions of vision, as though the enterprise of education and the training of educational leaders and front-line educators could proceed without making decisions concerning guiding purposes. In the view of some, this has resulted in educational institutions that embody an unproductive mish-mash of this and that. Prominent among those who have expressed this view are Powell, Farrar, and Cohen, whose *Shopping Mall High School* (1985) embodies a powerful discussion of the failure of American high schools to make decisions at the level of basic purposes; instead, they argue, American secondary schools solve the problem of deciding basic purposes by claiming to embrace a great many of them—with the result that they make little progress on any of them. The authors urge that little progress is likely to be seen in American education until this situation is rectified. In their own words:

> By promising to do everything well for everyone, educators have contributed to the growing sense that they can do nothing well for anyone.

> There is one last, unhappy reason that educators have not pointed to certain misdirections. In the current crop of reforms: one cannot point to an incorrect direction without some sense of the correct one. But American school people have been singularly unable to think of an educational purpose that they should not embrace.

> ...High schools seem unlikely to make marked improvement...until there is a much clearer sense of what is more important to teach and learn, and why...If educators could agree on such purposes, they would be better armed for debating about education and for deciding that some things cannot be done because others are more important (1985: 305–307).

The view of these authors was foreshadowed in a well-known article by the former dean of the Harvard School of Education, Patricia Graham entitled, "Schools: Cacophony about Practice, Silence about Purpose." According to Graham:

> In the absence of a coherent and audible message about the rationale or purpose of education from today's professional educators, the governing educational philosophy on which practice is implicitly based remains the remnants of progressive education, which was the explicit message of a previous generation of educators. I will argue that the time has come for educators to emerge from this dark night of the soul, to find their voice, to join that discussion, and to argue, as only they can, what they believe that schools ought to do and how they ought to do it (1984, pp. 31–32).

Another former dean of Harvard's Graduate School of Education, Theodore Sizer, shares the view advanced by the authors of *The Shopping Mall High School* that American high schools are unlikely to be successful unless they make thoughtful decisions concerning those few important things that they have a good chance of doing well and then set about doing them. Guided by this idea, Sizer launched a movement called "the Coalition of Essential Schools", made up of institutions that have agreed to identify their mission with a particular set of core aspirations and to work with one another on their achievement. This movement continues to exist today.

One might ask whether the insistence of those calling for vision in general education is more than blind faith. The answer is that, in addition to the support of common sense, there is a measure of empirical evidence behind the claim that vision has the potential to enhance educational quality. As an example, in an important article entitled "Systemic School Reform," Smith and O'Day (1991) suggested, based on empirical evidence, that one of the major differences between successful and unsuccessful schools is that successful ones are suffused down to their very details with a vision that is shared by the various stakeholders.[2]

Not everyone shares the view of Powell, Farrar, and Cohen that there is no coherent conception of the aims of education at work in American schools. According to others (for example, Jules Henry [1963] and Philip Cusick [1983], as well as some Marxist educational theorists), beneath the appearance of incoherence there is a logic to the design of existing educating institutions in the United States as if by an invisible hand, they are guided by the ideal of preparing materialistic, competitive individualists to meet the needs of the American economy. Though Americans may be loath to acknowledge that this is what they want their youngsters to become, such thinkers argue that their educational institutions bear witness to these (perhaps unconscious) aspirations.

Under any interpretation, there is widespread agreement that American educating institutions are not informed by clear, coherent, inspiring ideals and aspirations, sufficiently concrete to give guidance to practice, that are also the product of thoughtful educational deliberation. There are, of course, exceptions. A famous vision-guided institution is the one developed by John Dewey near the end of the 19th century in Chicago. The Dewey experiment is described in compelling ways in his own writings, as well as in a wonderful book entitled *The Dewey School,* authored by two sisters, Mayew and Edwards (1966), who taught in the school for many years. More recent examples of educating institutions informed by strong visions—indeed very different visions—can be found in Sarah Lawrence Lightfoot's *The Good High School* (1983). Another example is offered in Deborah Meier's account of East Central Park School in New York City in *The Power of Their Ideas* (1995). This example is particularly important because it is situated in the world of public schools, an arena that, in the view of many, is singularly uncongenial to the emergence of vision-guided practice.

IV

The account offered thus far has emphasized research on vision and education that has been going on in general education; but it is now time to turn our attention to important work in this area that has been going on in Jewish education. This is especially important, because although it is sometimes the case that Jewish education follows in the wake of trends in general education, in this case, research in Jewish education has in fact been substantially ahead of, and may indeed be influencing, the work in general education.

That this is true is largely due to the wisdom and insistence of one individual, the late Seymour Fox (may his memory be a blessing). Through his work at the Jewish Theological Seminary, later as dean of the School of Education at the Hebrew University, and then for many years, until his death, as the guiding spirit of the Mandel Foundation's educational agenda, Fox was consistently a strong catalyst for important research and educational initiatives that have energized the field of Jewish education over the last half-century. More than thirty years ago Fox pointed disparagingly to the pareve quality of Jewish education and began urging those in the field to begin addressing larger questions of purpose. Fox's impact is to be seen in many arenas, including a variety of leadership-development programs and, increasingly, various educational initiatives being undertaken in local Jewish communities around the world. In the present context I focus not on these lines of influence but on the research that his work has spawned.

More specifically, Fox's pioneering work on the role of vision in education has catalyzed important kinds of research, especially in the last ten years. Most important of all is a volume edited by him, Israel Scheffler, and Daniel Marom entitled *Visions of Jewish Education* (2003). This book contains a number of different strands that illuminate the nature of vision and vision-guided education. At the center of the

[2]Note, though, that for Smith and O'Day, "vision" refers not to a guiding existential vision, i.e., to a conception of the kind of person we hope to cultivate, but to an institutional vision, to a coherent conception of what an institution at its best will look like. Moreover, their conception of success lays heavy emphasis on success with standardized achievement tests. In contrast, the concept of vision that I am emphasizing is that of existential vision, with the suggestion that our understanding of "success" needs to be based on the ideas in this vision that identify qualities of heart and mind, as well as community, that we should be striving to achieve.

book are a number of articles written by individuals who represent very different conceptions of the aims of Jewish education, as well as some important ideas concerning the way these aims are likely to be achieved. In addition to offering illustrations of what guiding existential visions of Jewish life are, the existential visions represented by these authors as well as their efforts to situate them in the context of more general educational conceptions offer readers a wealth of ideas to wrestle with as they attempt to clarify their own ideas about the larger purposes of Jewish education. These articles are accompanied by other important pieces. Especially worthy of note is an article in which Fox addresses the complex challenges of translating guiding visions into educational practice and highlights the ways in which differences in conception give rise to different approaches to practice (2003: 253–295). There is a also a powerful, empirically based account of a Jewish elementary day school that is struggling, with the aid of the article's author, Daniel Marom, to clarify its own guiding vision and to more effectively embody it in practice (2003: 296–331).

Since its publication *Visions of Jewish Education* has attracted considerable attention, especially within the field of Jewish education. Levisohn (2005) provided a thoughtful discussion and review, which was followed by a series of essays further commenting on the concept of creating a vision for Jewish education (Cohen, E.R.S. et al., 2005). Levisohn's discussion and those of the various respondents succeed in bringing out many important insights, as well as questions in need of further examination.

Other research has been inspired by the work pioneered by Fox and his colleagues in the Mandel Foundation's *Visions of Jewish Education* project. In making the case for vision-guided practice, Pekarsky (1997, 1998) clarified the concept of vision by drawing a distinction between existential, institutional and strategic visions. Simply put, existential visions refer to conceptions of the kind of person one hopes to cultivate; institutional visions refer to conceptions of what, at their best, educating institutions look like; and strategic visions refer to conceptions of what needs to be done to advance from current reality to institutional arrangements that show promise of achieving our favored existential vision. More recently, as a result of conversations with Fox, Marom, and Scheffler, Pekarsky (2006, 2007) has drawn explicit attention to the distinction between existential and educational visions and to the relationship between visions in these two senses. Pekarsky's (2006) study of a vision-guided school in New York complements other recent portraits of vision-guided Jewish educating institutions—notably, Marom's study in *Visions of Jewish Education*, referred to above, and Fox's study of Camp Ramah, *Vision at the Heart* (1997). Such studies exhibit what vision-guided educating institutions are and are a rebuttal to the skeptic's view that such institutions cannot be developed under real-world conditions.

There is, of course, a need for continuing research relating to vision and Jewish education. First—although, as indicated above, we already have documented examples of vision-guided institutions that thrive in the real world—it would be useful to document examples and analyses of educating institutions that have *transformed themselves* into vision-guided institutions, as well as to analyze the conditions, activities, and personnel that have facilitated this transformation. Studies of this kind are important not just because they might offer practical guidance to those who would reform Jewish education, but also because they would respond to the concern of skeptics who believe that it's impossible to significantly change existing institutions (and that therefore those interested in creating vision-guided institutions need to build them from scratch).

Second, it would be important to document examples of vision-guided education in settings other than camps and day schools. In particular, it would be useful to find, write up, and analyze vision-guided congregational schools (i.e., "Hebrew schools" or "religious schools"), with attention to their emergence and their impact (as compared with the standard fare).

Third, the field of Jewish education would benefit from the development of additional existential visions—that is, of additional conceptions of the agenda/aims of Jewish education that might inspire and/or challenge contemporary Jews in North America, Israel and elsewhere as they struggle to identify the kind of existential vision that is appropriate for their particular educational institutions. Fourth, there is a need for research that focuses in a more systematic way on the relationship between an existential vision and educational practice. In the belief that we tend to radically oversimplify what needs to be taken into account in the effort to move from conception to practice, Seymour

Fox was, before his death, deeply immersed in an effort to address this problem. It continues to be a pressing need today.

V

If, as those who have contributed to the literature I have been discussing have suggested, progress in Jewish education depends on a willingness to tackle questions of vision, then it is important to develop strategies that will result in putting the challenges relating to vision at the center of the Jewish community's educational agenda. But it's also important to note that some progress in this direction has already been made. For example, readings and questions relating to vision and education are presently part of the curriculum for Jewish educators at the major training institutions—places like Brandeis, Hebrew Union College, the Jewish Theological Seminary, the Mandel Leadership Institute, the Melton Centre for Jewish Education at the Hebrew University, Siegal College in Cleveland, and the University of Judaism. Related to this, the Mandel Foundation has convened a group of teacher-educators from these institutions to discuss issues relating to the teaching about vision-guided education in professional development programs. Another index of the importance that the theme of vision has come to occupy in the landscape of Jewish education is its place on the agenda of national and local conferences for Jewish educators and lay leaders.

For those interested in the advancement of vision-guided Jewish education, these developments are to be applauded but offer no good reason for complacency. The current interest in vision within the field of Jewish education could, after all, only represent the latest in a series of fads, after which attention will focus on some other promising ways of improving the field. The present interest in vision is perhaps best viewed as a window of opportunity during which the potential of vision-guided practice to enhance educational quality and the possibility of growing vision-guided institutions can be demonstrated.

Beyond demonstrating such things, advancing the cause of vision-guided education also requires another important ingredient. At a time when congregations, schools and camps appear to be more interested in thinking about larger questions of purpose and the relevance of such matters to their educational practice, it is essential that ways be found to help institutions and communities make progress in this area. If the stakeholders of such institutions come together to struggle with questions of vision and find themselves bewildered about how to proceed or overwhelmed by their diversity of opinion; or if their months of deliberation lead them no further than where they were before they started, or to a laundry list of aspirations that is pie-in-the-sky; or if, having struggled meaningfully with questions of vision, they have no idea about how to think about the implications of their thinking for practice—if such are the outcomes of their deliberations, the effect may be worse than "no progress".

These considerations make it important for those who believe in the power of guiding visions to improve Jewish education to develop tools (literature, documented processes and other resources) that will give institutions and communities that want to make progress in this arena the necessary scaffolding. Especially useful would be the development within the Jewish world of a cadre of individuals who have been trained to help facilitate the process of developing vision and vision-guided practice in different kinds of educating arenas. Such individuals could be brought in by interested communities to help them with their work. Alternatively (or perhaps in addition), short-term educational programs designed to pass on useful skills and resources might be developed for those individuals who have been designated by their communities to lead a process of becoming more vision-guided. In the absence of such developments, it may, unfortunately, be naïve to think that the unguided efforts of educating institutions are likely to bear fruit, though this may happen on occasion.

VI

Several key points developed in the preceding discussion are worthy of emphasis in this concluding section:

- An existential vision—i.e., a conception of the kind of person and community that the process of education should strive to realize—must be genuinely inspiring to the relevant community of stakeholders, as well as sufficiently clear and concrete to give real guidance. When it satisfies these conditions it offers an indispensable and powerful basis for educational planning and decision-making as well as evaluation.

- While the presence of an existential vision is critical, it is not sufficient to give rise to a vision-guided educating institution. Also needed is a constellation of ideas that jointly define a conception of the way the process of education should be organized to realize the ideals identified in the vision with the particular populations that are to be educated, given cultural, economic, and technological realities. This conception, which includes but is broader than what is identified in the existential vision, is what I earlier called an educational vision.

- A body of research has developed that a) explains the concept of vision and the case for vision-guided practice and b) offers examples of vision-guided institutions that thrive in the real world. But there is a need for additional kinds of research—research that identifies and seeks to understand institutions that have evolved into vision-guided institutions; research that examines instances of vision-guided practice outside the world of camps and day schools (for example, in congregational schools); and research that helps us to better understand the complex steps that mediate the relationship between vision and educational practice.

- There is a need to develop human and other kinds of resources that will be available to educating institutions (schools, camps, congregations, etc.) that are interested in becoming more vision-guided than they now are. Otherwise there is a risk that the recent surge in interest in the place of vision in Jewish education will dissipate with little to be shown for it.

In conclusion, it must be emphasized that, although attending to the challenge of vision is essential if we are to make substantial progress in the field of Jewish education, addressing this challenge adequately is neither easy nor a panacea. Achieving clarity about what, as communities and educators, we should be striving for is a challenge quite apart from the difficulties that accompany the effort to build bridges between our ideas about the aims of education and our practice. It is difficult because it requires us to give serious, honest thought to what we, as individuals and as a community, think the enterprise of Judaism and Jewish life is fundamentally about. The difficulties being substantial, it may be that we will end up making only limited progress in this arena; but this may be an instance in which the old saying applies, "The perfect is the enemy of the good." That is, even a little bit of clarity at the level of vision may be sufficient to make a world of practical difference.

Turning briefly to the second point, let us suppose that we achieve clarity of existential vision and have some reasonably good ideas concerning how they can meaningfully inform educational practice. Although this is a significant and important achievement, it is not sufficient to make for quality education. Human, financial and technological resources will still be necessary, as will the serious engagement of relevant stakeholders, including the families whose children are being educated. More generally, though it is a critical ingredient in an effective educational reform mix, successfully addressing the challenges of vision is not a magic bullet.

ANNOTATED BIBLIOGRAPHY

Fox, S. (1973). Towards a General Theory of Jewish Education. In D. Sidorsky (ed.), *The Future of the Jewish Community in America* (260–270). New York: Basic Books. In this seminal, oft-cited article Seymour Fox identifies the absence of inspiring ideas about the purposes of Jewish education as one of the critical issues that the field needs to address. This article established the foundation for future work addressing the need for and the nature of vision in Jewish education.

Fox, S., & Novak, W. (1997). *Vision at the Heart: Lessons from Camp Ramah on the Power of Ideas in Shaping Educational Institutions.* New York and Jerusalem: Council for Initiatives in Jewish Education and the Mandel Foundation; Pekarsky, D. (2006). *Vision at Work: The Theory and Practice of Beit Rabban.* New York: Jewish Theological Seminary Press. These volumes describe vision-guided Jewish educating institutions that exist in the real world. The first is Fox's study of the Ramah summer camp movement. In the second, the author offers an example of a vision-guided Jewish day school that is informed by ideas that are at once traditional and progressive. Jointly, the institutions painted in these texts offer what has been called an "existence proof" to the question, Can vision-guided institutions come into being in the real world?

Fox, S., Scheffler, I., & Marom, D. (eds.). (2003). *Visions of Jewish Education*. New York: Cambridge University Press. This seminal volume is a treasure trove for those interested in questions relating to vision and Jewish education. At the center of the book are several articles, each of which explains a different conception of the vision around which Jewish education should be organized. The book also includes a study of Marom's efforts to work with an extant Jewish day school around the clarification and deepening of its guiding vision and its reflection and practice, as well as a masterful discussion by Fox of the complex challenges of translating a vision into educational practice.

Huxley, A. (1962). *Island*. New York: Bantam Books; Plato (1992). *The Republic*. translated by G. M. A. Grube, Indianapolis: Hackett Publishing; and Skinner, B.F. (1948). *Walden II*, New York: MacMillan. These books paint utopian vision-guided educating institutions.

Levisohn, J. (2005). "Ideas and Ideals of Jewish Education: Initiating a Conversation on *Visions of Jewish Education*." *Journal of Jewish Education* 71 (1), 53–66. In successive issues of the *Journal of Jewish Education* Levisohn develops a thoughtful review of Fox, Marom, and Scheffler's *Visions of Jewish Education*, and a number of individuals variously associated with the field of Jewish education respond to Levisohn's discussion (and through this, to the book itself). Jointly these authors succeed in bringing out many important insights, as well as questions in need of further examination.

Mayew, K. and Edwards, A. C. (1966). *The Dewey School*. New York: Atherton Press; Meier, D. (1995). *The Power of their Ideas*. Boston: Beacon Press. Two important examples of vision-guided institutions in the world of general education. The first is an extraordinarily rich account, written by two sisters who taught there, of the school founded by John Dewey in Chicago at the end of the 19th century. In the second, Meier describes a vision-guided school that came into being in a *public* educational setting.

Pekarsky, D. (1997). "The Place of Vision in Jewish Education Reform." *Journal of Jewish Education*, 63 (1–2), 31–40; Pekarsky, D. (2007). Vision and Education: Arguments, Counter-arguments, Rejoinders. *American Journal of Education*, 113 (3), 423–450. In these articles the author attempts to offer succinct explanations of the concepts of vision-guided education, to explain the rationale for vision-guided approaches to Jewish and general education, and to evaluate objections to such approaches.

Powell, A. G., Farrar, E. & Cohen, D. K. (1985). *The Shopping Mall High School*. Boston: Houghton Mifflin. This book eloquently discusses the problems that flow out of the failure of American secondary schools to address questions of educational purpose (or what I have been calling the challenge of vision). Though written twenty years ago, it is, unfortunately, still very much on the mark.

REFERENCES

Cohen, E.R.S. et al. (2005). Responses to 'Ideas and Ideals of Jewish Education: Initiating a Conversation on *Visions of Jewish Education*.' *Journal of Jewish Education*, 71 (2), 219–250.

Cusick, P. (1983). *The Egalitarian Ideal and the American Public School*. New York: Longman Books.

Dewey, J. (1944). *Democracy and Education*. New York: Free Press.

Fox, S. & Novak, W. (1997). *Vision at the Heart: Lessons from Camp Ramah on the Power of Ideas in Shaping Educational Institutions*. New York and Jerusalem: Council for Initiatives in Jewish Education and the Mandel Foundation.

Fox, S., Scheffler, I., & Marom, D. (eds.) (2003). *Visions of Jewish Education*. New York: Cambridge University Press.

Graham, P. (1984). "Schools: Cacophony about Practice, Silence about Purpose." *Daedalus*, 113 (4), 29–57.

Henry, J. (1963). *Culture against Man*. New York: Vintage Books.

Hirsch, E.D. (1987). *Cultural Literacy*. Boston: Houghton-Mifflin.

Huxley, A. (1962). *Island*. New York: Bantam Books.

Levisohn, J. (2005). "Ideas and Ideals of Jewish Education: Initiating a Conversation on *Visions of Jewish Education*." *Journal of Jewish Education*, Volume 71 (1), 53–66.

Lightfoot, S. L. (1983). *The Good High School*. New York: Basic Books.

Mayhew, K. & Edwards, A. C. (1966). *The Dewey School*. New York: Atherton Press.

Meier, D. (1995). *The Power of Their Ideas: Lessons for America from a Small School in Harlem*. Boston: Beacon Press.

Neill, A. S. (1992). *Summerhill School: A New View of Childhood*. New York: St. Martin's Press.

Noddings, N. (1984). *Caring*. Berkeley, CA: University of California Press.

Pekarsky, D. (1997). The Place of Vision in Jewish Educational Reform, *Journal of Jewish Education*. 63 (1-2), 31–40.

Pekarsky, D. (1998). "Vision and Education" in H. Marantz (ed.), *Judaism and Education: Essays in Honor of Walter Ackerman (277–292)*. Be'er-Sheva, Israel: Ben Gurion University, 227–292.

Pekarsky, D. (2006). *Vision at Work: The Theory and Practice of Beit Rabban*. New York: Jewish Theological Seminary Press.

Pekarsky D. (2007). Vision and Education: Arguments, Counter-arguments, Rejoinders. *American Journal of Education* 113(3), 423–450.

Powell, A. G., Farrar, E., & Cohen, D. K. (1985). *The Shopping Mall High School*. Boston: Houghton Mifflin.

Sizer, T. (1984). *Horace's Compromise: The Dilemma of the American High School*. Boston: Houghton-Mifflin.

Sizer, T. (1992). *Horace's School*. Boston: Houghton-Mifflin.

Skinner, B.F. (1948). *Walden II,* New York: MacMillan.

Smith, M. & O'Day, J. (1991). Systemic School Reform. In S. H. Fuhrman and B. Malen (eds.),*The Politics of Curriculum and Testing: 1990 Yearbook of the Politics of Education Society*. Philadelphia: Falmer Press, 233–267.

Jewish Education in the Age of Google

Jonathan S. Woocher

Type the words "Jewish education" into Google and you will get—the header tells us—approximately 34,800,000 results. (This amounts to around two and a half web links for every Jew in the world.) "Torah" is somewhat less popular, apparently, yielding only 7,020,000 hits. "God" does better—176,000,000 results—though not as well as "Israel"—250,000,000—the interpretation of which I will leave to the reader.

In one sense, this is nothing more than a curious exercise. Yet in another, the ease with which I conducted the searches, the speed with which I received the results (less than a tenth of a second), the incredible variety of listings to peruse under each heading, the time it would take (years) to pursue all of the links (and the fact that they would change again and again while I was doing so) and your immediate comprehension of what I am talking about all tell us much that is highly relevant to any effort to understand the state of Jewish education today, its future and the challenges it faces.

The last quarter century has seen the world change dramatically for everyone, and perhaps even more so for Jews. The number, scope and implications of these changes—geo-political, socio-cultural, economic, technological, and religious—far exceed what could be catalogued, much less fully assessed, in a short paper. But consider just a few examples:

- In 1981 the United States was locked in a Cold War with the "evil empire" of the atheistic Soviet Union and its bloc of vassal states, and as Jews we struggled to help our fellow Jews trapped in the USSR escape to freedom. Today our enemy is global terrorism fueled by religious, largely Islamic, extremism, while as Jews we celebrate the renewal of Jewish life in the FSU and Eastern Europe even as Israel and our own communities have been transformed by the millions of Jews (and non–Jews) who have migrated from the FSU over the past decades.

- In 1981 baby boomers were in their peak years of child rearing, and the millions of Jews among them were enjoying the fruits of their and their parents' successful passage into the mainstream of American life. Today Jewish baby boomers' children are forming families of their own, families that include non–Jews, partners of the same gender, and children from diverse racial and religious backgrounds far more often than those of their parents.

- Since 1981 America and its Jews have been through a complex journey of simultaneous secularization and spiritual renewal. Individualism, multi-culturalism, universalism and neo-tribalism shape a generational culture among young Jews today that both celebrates and downplays difference and that elevates personal choice and non-judgmentalism to the summit of its value system.

- And underlying or overarching the changes in politics and in social, cultural, and religious norms and mores is a quarter century of technological change that only science fiction authors could have dreamed of. In 1981, personal computers had barely spread beyond groups of techno-hobbyists; today, they are ubiquitous and link together billions of users around the globe via the Internet. Fewer than 5,000 Americans had cell phones in 1981 (they were available in only three cities); today you can not only call anyone anywhere on phones smaller than your hand, you can browse the web, download your email, listen to music and watch TV. In 1981 cable television had just reached the point where its first true non-broadcast network, HBO, felt it worthwhile to offer programming twenty-four hours a day, seven days a week. Today cable and satellite bring us hundreds of programming choices every minute of every day, and On Demand services and DVRs have placed us in virtually complete control of what we see, when.

Amid such changes, and a host of others that could be listed, Jewish education has hardly been static. It has responded primarily to two broad changes in American Jewish identity over this period: first, the perceived weakening of Jewish identification and of traditional forms of Jewish expression that came to be called the "crisis of Jewish continuity"; and second, the simultaneous growth of a segment within the Jewish population that is open to and even actively seeking a more intensive relationship to their own Jewishness. These two phenomena complemented each other and encouraged those guiding Jewish education to promote the expansion of intensive educational experiences as the key to strengthening Jewish identity. The results of this effort may be seen in the growth of Jewish day schools, in the drive to get more young people to Israel that has culminated in Birthright Israel, in expanded investment in Jewish summer camping and in the rapid spread of new programs like Melton, Meah and Wexner that expose adults to high-level Jewish learning on an ongoing basis.

At the same time, persistent voices have reminded the Jewish community that these intensive educational experiences still reach only a minority of Jews. Although the debate over how much effort and resources to put into "outreach," especially to intermarried families, has continued to agitate the community, nearly everyone agrees that initiatives to engage Jewish families early on and to try to re-engage young adults on campus or post-college must also be part of any viable "continuity" strategy. Hence the expansion of Jewish early childhood education, the revitalization of Hillel and the spread of Jewish studies and (to a lesser extent) the launching of a variety of other endeavors targeted at Jews in their 20s and 30s and at interfaith families have also won attention and support from educational activists and funders.

The landscape of Jewish education clearly has changed over the past quarter century, and for the better. But has it changed enough? There are disquieting as well as encouraging elements in the over-all portrait of North American Jewish education today. Enrollment in part-time Jewish education is declining, and not all of the decrease can be attributed either to defections to day school or reduced cohort sizes. A majority of teens continue to exit the educational system between bar/bat mitzvah and high school graduation. And though solid research is lacking, there is good reason to believe that the quality of Jewish education in nearly every setting, though improving, remains inconsistent, with pockets of excellence co-existing alongside expanses of mediocrity.

Should we tie these persisting weaknesses to a failure to respond fully and appropriately to the changes of the past quarter century? It's difficult to say. On the one hand, Jewish education has certainly responded to some of the events and trends of the era by trying to incorporate new content into its curricula, whether relating to the role of women in Jewish life or to the changing relationship to Israel. Yet at the same time, most of what is taught today is similar to what was taught twenty-five years ago—updated and often improved, but essentially the same. Pedagogically, Jewish education has hardly ignored the technological revolution (recall those millions of web links). All manner of multimedia and distance learning is now available. Yet again, the times, places, and ways in which Jewish education is delivered remain primarily those that were dominant twenty-five years ago. New technologies have been a "gloss" added to a system that remains fundamentally unchanged.

This inherent conservatism is not necessarily a bad thing. For a thirty-five-hundred-year-old enterprise to rush to redefine its fundamentals based on a quarter century of not unambiguously positive change would be, at the very least, hasty. Yet there is an equal danger in assuming that the changes of the past twenty-five years can be accommodated *without* rethinking at least some of these fundamentals. Jewish education has spent insufficient time reflecting deeply, critically, and self-critically on the developments of the last quarter century, at least some of which may present far more profound challenges and opportunities with respect to how Jewish education is designed and delivered than has been generally appreciated. Google is not just a neat search engine or a symbol for a new technological age. It is a signpost pointing toward new realities in how the world operates, in how knowledge is defined and delivered and in how people live and control their lives.[1] Jewish education ignores these deeper changes at its peril. And if it can tap into the new sensibilities and habits of behavior that Google and its like both foster and feed upon, Jewish education may discover new ways to expand its impact and effectiveness.

So what are some of the most salient characteristics of the "age of Google," and what might they mean for Jewish education?

IN THE AGE OF GOOGLE, INFORMATION IS PLENTIFUL AND EASY TO ACCESS (BUT NOT NECESSARILY EASY TO ASSESS).

Information, slews of it, is literally at our fingertips today. For teachers and students both, the ubiquity and ease of accessing hundreds or thousands of sources and resources on virtually any topic calls for a fundamental rethinking of how learning is designed and implemented. Learners are liberated from their dependence on a handful of textbooks or what teachers are able to tell them under the pressure of limited time. The democratization of learning that the ancient rabbis first promoted and that the printing press made imaginable has come to fruition in the age of the Internet and multimedia technology. Learning literally can become an adventure as both the number and types of resources available to students (and teachers)—and the pathways through them—multiply exponentially.

At the same time, however, the challenges of determining what information from what sources is truly reliable and worth knowing multiply as well. The call from educational theorists for transforming the teacher's role from that of "the sage on the stage" to "the guide on the side" preceded the age of Google. But now this is no longer simply desirable; it is a necessity. The shift from defining teaching primarily as the transmission of content to a definition that sees teaching as the facilitation of enthusiastic, adventurous, but responsible and discerning self-guided learning is not an easy one to make pedagogically. For Jewish education it is perhaps equally challenging philosophically. Our tradition of learning places great value on accurately transmitting (and then elaborating upon) the teachings of one's predecessors. This tradition need not be lost; in fact, the availability and ease of searching the canon of traditional texts that DVDs and the Internet have made possible can open up these texts to today's students in manifold ways that were previously unthinkable. But the processes and premises of learning and teaching are changing. Teachers will not hold a monopoly on determining what is worth knowing in a world where Amazon and Epinions encourage users to provide their own reviews to complement those of the "experts," and the former are often more trusted than the latter.

Can Jewish education adapt to a world where every student (and parent) has access to the equivalent of a university library in her or his bedroom or den? Can we take advantage of the possibilities this opens up and learn how to re-craft our programs and pedagogy accordingly? We have begun to answer these questions, but there is still more to be done before we can confidently respond in the affirmative.

IN THE AGE OF GOOGLE (AND DELL AND AMAZON), "CUSTOMERS" EXPECT TO BE ABLE TO GET WHAT THEY WANT, WHEN THEY WANT IT AND AT A GOOD PRICE.

If the industrial age was the era of mass production and consumption, the age of Google—the age of information—is the era of re-customization[2]. We expect today that producers and sellers will deliver the products that we want, when and where we want them, and that the purchase itself will

---

[1]Indeed, a colleague suggested that "living in the age of Google means that SEARCHING is a legitimate, life-encompassing activity!" (personal communication from Renee Rubin Ross). Whether there is a correlation between the ease and ubiquity of computer searching and the apparent popularity of more existential and spiritual questing, I do not know. But we should not quickly dismiss the possible links between our daily and our religious habits and dispositions.

[2]The term often used today is "mass customization"—the use of sophisticated information technology to create personally tailored messaging and to give customers options to customize their purchases, within carefully prescribed limits, while preserving the efficiency of operation that true customization cannot achieve.

be simple, efficient, and a bargain to boot. In the commercial world, and increasingly in nonprofit settings as well, the provider who can deliver the best "customer experience" wins more often than not.

We are beginning to learn this lesson in Jewish education, but there is still a considerable distance to go before we can honestly say that we have put the customer at the center of the educational experience. Part of the challenge is in the products we offer, and part lies in our modes of delivery. In both respects, despite the large number and variety of providers, Jewish education remains largely a "take what we give you, when and where we offer it" proposition. Programs are packaged by the provider, with few opportunities for the consumer to select the components or change the time and place of delivery. Most congregational schools offer similar curricula, and these are determined far less by what congregants want than by a top-down view of what their children need. The ability to construct one's own educational experience by mixing and matching the offerings of many providers is severely constrained by a lack of information regarding what is available (a sharp contrast to going on Amazon and finding a list of customized suggestions for books to buy based on your last order) and the need to "join" many institutions in order to access their programs (rewarding customer loyalty makes sense; requiring a pledge of loyalty in advance seems counterproductive).

The exceptions to these general propositions prove the rule. Chabad, which emphasizes responding directly to what its customers want and asking for little up front, is thriving as an educational provider for children, families, and adults. Youth groups are moving from membership-based models to more open frameworks for programming. And cultural events—film festivals, concerts, plays, exhibits—are drawing crowds of Jews who are not prepared to make extended commitments to institutions and programs.

Of course, the reality is far more complex than the picture sketched above. Institutions cannot survive on intermittent patrons, and the Jewish community cannot possibly offer every potential configuration of content, method, time, and location that prospective learners may seek. Customization in the marketplace is driven by large volumes and vast databases that allow diverse customer needs to be met efficiently—but as anyone who has dealt with impossible-to-navigate phone menus and interminable waiting times can testify, we confuse such customization with true personal attention at our peril. The marriage of marketing and education is inevitably a problematic one. Is good education nothing more than giving consumers what they want? Most educators, including Jewish ones, would argue vociferously that it is not. Education is about learning important things, and it requires effort and commitment. Though we cannot impose contents or methods upon unwilling recipients, we abdicate our responsibility both to them and to the institutions and tradition we represent if we turn Jewish education into nothing more than an exercise in customer satisfaction.

Still, it is easy and increasingly dangerous to underestimate the extent to which those whom we seek to serve are legitimately asking more of us. We can do a far better job of lowering the barriers to Jewish educational experiences, of providing useful guidance to those who are uncertain about what modes of learning are available to them and what they can expect from these. We can provide more differentiated offerings and a greater variety of options and opportunities to try these. And we can make the entire experience of Jewish education more responsive to what people are seeking as well as to what we so earnestly want to give them. A Jewish education that is more customer-centric and customer-friendly is a necessity today; else the very people on whom we pin our hopes for the future will turn elsewhere.

IN THE AGE OF GOOGLE (AND XBOXES AND IPODS) LEARNING IS A MULTISENSORY, MULTIDIMENSIONAL EXPERIENCE.

In the fall of 2005, the hottest holiday shopping item was the Xbox 360—Microsoft's latest effort to best Sony and other rivals in the arena of video game playing devices. The introduction of the Xbox was accompanied by a spate of articles in the popular media describing the video gaming culture that now includes millions of young and not-so-young people around the world. Lest we be tempted to dismiss this as a pop culture story without educational significance, we should note that at the same time as purchasers began scrambling to get their scarce Xboxes, one prominent educational periodical led its issue with an article on "Video Games and the Future of Learning" that claimed that such games "give a glimpse into how we might create new and more powerful ways to learn in schools, communities, and workplaces."[3]

Though the notion that video game parlors will replace classrooms anytime soon surely constitutes hyperbole, both the observations and the reasoning on which the article is based deserve to be taken seriously. Video games aside, the past quarter century has seen a revolution in learning theory that focuses on the diverse ways in which we use our multiple senses and multiple intelligences to make sense of the world. As Jews we proudly wear the mantle of People of the Book, but learning no longer comes from the written word alone. We may not be ready to abandon the study of traditional texts for interactive gaming where avatars play out complex scenarios in syn-worlds. But Jewish education surely must adjust to a world in which multisensory and experiential learning is becoming the norm.

Again, this is a process that to some extent has already begun. Certainly the concept of "experiential" or "informal" education has entered the mainstream of Jewish educational thinking and practice. So too have we seen an expanded interest in the use of the arts as a vehicle for serious Jewish learning (viz. projects like Avodah Arts or Storahtelling). And of course, the technological revolution has not passed Jewish education by: Increasingly sophisticated use is being made of technology's ability to bridge time and space by making it possible for students to encounter in their classrooms and homes cultural artifacts, historical events and personages that once could only be read about in textbooks or seen in museums.

Still, the larger challenge remains. In an era of constructivist learning, multiple intelligences, and diverse learning styles, can Jewish education keep pace with an educational environment that is rapidly generating new types of materials and new modes of teaching and learning? It is fair to say that what has been achieved in this regard thus far demonstrates the potential for redesigning Jewish education as an encompassing set of experiences of touching, seeing, hearing, feeling, making and doing, as well as listening, reading, speaking and writing. But, this potential is still far from fully realized. To do so will require a major investment not only in programs or materials, but in people. This is now underway in domains like camping and youth work where experiential education has long been the norm. But in other areas like the use of arts and technology, the serious work of preparing a generation of adept educators has barely begun.

Someday soon—if not already—our children, and some of us, will be carrying devices that operate as cell phones, PDAs, MP3 players, PlayStations or Xboxes, Wifi Internet devices, DVD players and TV receivers all in one. Perhaps these devices will even emit pre-selected odors to accompany whatever one is seeing, hearing or doing. For certain, our children will be expecting the education they receive to be as rich, inviting and diverse a sensory experience as the rest of their lives. We had better be prepared to deliver.

IN THE AGE OF GOOGLE (AND INSTANT MESSAGING AND FRIENDSTER), CONNECTIONS CAN BE FORMED READILY ACROSS MULTIPLE BOUNDARIES, AND "VIRTUAL" COMMUNITIES CAN COMPLEMENT AND SUPPORT "REAL" ONES.

Anyone who has watched teenagers for any length of time—including observing them from the back of a classroom—knows that alongside whatever visible and purposeful activity is taking place, one can often detect a stream of silent communication flowing. Whether it is instant messages from "buddies" popping up on the computer screen or text messages whipping back and forth on cell phones, distance and time no longer serve as barriers to immediate connection with whomever one wants, whenever one wants. From a larger socio-cultural standpoint, this immediacy of communication reinforces the rise to prominence of networks as primary vehicles for organizing human activity and relationships, both as a supplement to and a substitute for more formal types of organization. Such networks, both "virtual" and "real," not only strengthen existing ties, but open up connections that might otherwise never be made and allow for the emergence of new types of community among individuals otherwise unlikely to come into contact.

[3] David Williamson Shaffer, Kurt R. Squire, Richard Halverson, and James P. Gee, "Video Games and the Future of Learning," *Phi Delta Kappan*, 87:2, October 2005, pp. 104–111.

In a networked world of easy and immediate communication, the social dimensions of education can be dramatically expanded to encompass many more individuals. For Jewish education in particular this is a boon of enormous potential. As a group both few in numbers (comparatively speaking) and widely dispersed, Jews are in a position to make especially good use of the power of communications technology to create virtual connections and communities to complement face-to-face ones.

Such efforts are being made. In a bold move to re-position both itself and the entire domain of Jewish youth group activity, BBYO has launched a website called b-linked, billed as a "BBYO online community." The site functions as a Jewish version of Friendster, allowing teens to register their profiles and connect via the web with other teens based on mutual interests rather than geography. It also includes a variety of "portals" that allow teens to blog, get help with college admissions, post photos, find out about events in their areas and who is signed up for them and connect with Israel and their "spiritual side." B-linked follows on the considerable efforts to build similar electronic connections for young adult alumni of Birthright Israel through its website. Other recent innovative technology-based projects include efforts to connect Jews here in North America with counterparts in Israel and other parts of the Jewish world (e.g., a project called Bavli-Yerushalmi sponsored by an Israel-based organization called Kolot, in which groups of Jews in North America and in Israel study common texts and share their insights via email).

Yet even these notable efforts constitute only small down payments on what eventually could and should be invested to take advantage of the new networked world we live in. Computers, cell phones, wireless email and instant messaging are wonderful tools. But for Jewish education, networking is not ultimately about technology. It is about expanding Jewish conversations, creating a context in which communication among Jews flows freely and individuals can find others with whom to carry on discussions that are personally meaningful and culturally generative. It is about building communities around discovered shared interests and using a variety of modes of communication, both face-to-face and electronically mediated, to create and re-create connections, some temporary, some enduring.

The re-emergence of informal "Jewish salons" in several communities over the last few years, the success of ventures like Reboot and Kol Dor that connect Jewish young adults from diverse backgrounds, together with phenomena like b-linked and Birthright Israel, are perhaps the harbingers of a new era of Jewish "networking." In such an era, Jewish education should be re-imagining itself as a global enterprise for facilitating a myriad of Jewish connections and conversations using all means available. If this spirit of open and free-flowing discussion were really to take root, perhaps instead of IM'ing their friends in the next row about this weekend's party, we might even imagine students IM'ing friends in distant cities to share opinions about the latest events in Israel or ideas on how to interpret a particularly knotty piece of text. In such an environment teachers might even forgive the occasional ringing cell phone.

IN THE AGE OF GOOGLE (AND LINUX AND WINDOWS), GOOD PLATFORMS CAN BE EVEN MORE POWERFUL (AND PROFITABLE) THAN PROGRAMS.

Since its debut as a search engine for the web, Google has spawned a slew of spin-offs and extensions that allow users to search their own hard drives, look for academic articles in journals, read a customized version of the day's news, view satellite pictures of one's neighborhood, shop and, it is promised, access the collections of some of the world's great libraries. Microsoft's Windows dominates the world of personal computer operating systems because thousands of programs—most not authored by Microsoft—run on this platform. Its chief rival today, Linux, goes Windows one better. As "open source" software, it has mobilized an army of programmers to continuously improve the platform itself in a remarkable self-sustaining, self-policing collaborative effort that in turn makes possible an ever-expanding array of programs that many claim are better than anything that runs on Windows.

The lesson in these endeavors is that building a great platform, one that can grow and xpand and that draws out the talents of others, is even better than creating a great program. This is a lesson that Jewish education would do well to heed. Too often educational institutions think only about how to design and implement new and better programs. But if these institutions—e.g., synagogues—saw themselves as platforms and sought success by attracting as many other talented programmers as possible to make use of their platform, the entire ecosystem of Jewish education might function dramatically differently, and with far greater effectiveness.

A successful platform does a few fundamental things very well and meshes seamlessly with other programs that do specific tasks far better than the platform itself could alone (ever tried to write a paper with Windows' Wordpad?). A good platform makes it easier for programmers to write good programs, and good programs in turn make the platform far more valuable to its users. Jewish education by and large does not emulate this formula. Institutions try to do too much on their own (sometimes for fear of sharing and possibly losing their users, sometimes because they simply don't know what is or could be available). Creative individuals or groups with excellent programs have difficulty breaking into the marketplace. The result is wasted energy and resources and a product that is not nearly as good as it could be.

How can Jewish education learn better how to build both strong platforms and dynamic programs? One possible answer is to introduce more of the free-enterprise model into its operation. Birthright Israel used what is in essence an "open sourcing" model, allowing a wide variety of program providers to develop specific trips (the programs) within a framework of well-codified, detailed standards (the platform) and then to compete in the marketplace for participants.

A second key is to take seriously the idea that Jewish education is (or could be) a true system in which the individual parts support one another and each contributes to the viability and vitality of the whole. Combining the concept of platforms with that of organizational networks, in which smaller, more flexible and adaptable organizations mesh their talents and do not try to do everything by themselves, is a spreading strategy for increasing both productivity and quality. In such a systemic approach, information about clients, critical success factors, and prior experiences ("source code") would be shared, not hoarded. Interfaces would be smooth (imagine synagogues, camps, and JCCs working together to provide families with full-service, year-round educational experiences). And, "bug fixes" and regular updates would ensure that the quality and usability of the product improved continuously.

A new focus on building strong platforms as well as programs would also mean investing seriously in those platforms for the long term. In the nonprofit world generally today there is a growing awareness that supporting endless streams of new programs without building the capacity of the institutions that must operate these programs to sustain themselves and to generate successive generations of new initiatives is a bad investment. (Jim Collins talks of the distinction between "telling time" and "building clocks.") For Jewish education this would mean ensuring that institutions like synagogues, JCCs, camps and day schools that should be the platforms for a continuing flow of creative programming have the wherewithal to do the fundamental tasks that they must, tasks such as building close, enduring relationships with those who pass through their doors or gates. Investments in "infrastructure," whether for adequate staff or for systems of knowledge-sharing, are notoriously difficult to sell to many funders. Yet if we are to have great platforms for great programs, such investments are vital, even as we ask the institutions themselves to become far more focused in what they do and far more open to bringing in others to add to their talent pools.

CONCLUSION

I have tried to suggest a number of ways in which Jewish education in the age of Google will need to look and work differently than it does today. The lessons I have tried to draw and the proposals I have made are hardly the only ones we might imagine emanating from the changes we have experienced over the past quarter century. I have concentrated heavily on technological changes and their social, cultural, and educational accompaniments. Some readers may disagree with my analysis and recommendations; others may cite changes in other aspects of our experience that are far more consequential than those I have pointed to and that call for different strategies to maximize Jewish education's reach and impact.

What is critical for Jewish education is not the specific menu of recommendations that I or others may produce. Rather, it is that we take seriously that the world *has* changed, and that Jewish education has not changed fast enough or far enough to keep pace with these changes. Being *au courant* or even "relevant" is, of course, not a sufficient goal in its own right. As noted above, Jewish education, like all education, serves best when it incorporates a strong element of conservatism (with a small "c").

Nonetheless, the times challenge us to not rest on the good efforts of the past, not to assume that what worked then will still work now and not to reject all new ideas and approaches as either faddish or disruptive. We do live in the age of Google, and much more. And it is an age that offers us possibilities for realizing old visions that our predecessors could never have dreamt of but might well have grasped enthusiastically. Our task, as Rav Kook argued nearly a century ago, is simple, yet endlessly challenging: It is to renew the old and sanctify the new. Jewish education deserves no less.

Jewish Education in the World of Web 2.0

Brian Amkraut

SNAPSHOTS OF CONTEMPORARY CULTURE

1. For the Super Bowl in February 2007, Pepsi-Cola took the unprecedented step of outsourcing, or more accurately "crowdsourcing," the creation of an advertisement for Doritos tortilla chips to be aired during the game. Consider for a moment the company's willingness to put a thirty-second spot, for which they paid $2.5 million, in the hands of amateurs, or more shockingly in the hands of you and me. Not only was the creative content generated by a non-professional end user, but the decision regarding which ad to run was put in the hands of the online user population, who could vote for their favorite spot. The creator of the winning ad received thirty seconds of glory (and perhaps a future career in advertising) and Pepsi-Cola saved millions of dollars in the cost of creative content generation while pre-screening its Super Bowl investment to ensure viewer popularity.

2. The starting point for research today, for students young and old, invariably begins in one of two places: Google or Wikipedia. Most likely the results from the Google query will send the student to Wikipedia. Whereas Google depends on a mathematical algorithm to provide a list of the websites most responsive to the user query, Wikipedia provides a forum bringing the concept of "user-generated content" to the realm of the encyclopedia. Whether or not you think the collective wisdom that informs Wikipedia is a legitimate reference, that model reflects both a new reality and an important trend in terms of authority.

3. To kick off her run for the 2008 presidential nomination, Hillary Clinton adopted the slogan "Let's begin the conversation." While Hillary clearly has no intention of personally engaging the many millions that may join that dialogue, her campaign hopes to respond to the trend of interactive discourse, perhaps most clearly manifest in cyberspace, where millions literally do join the discussion. Whether or not one supports Hillary ideologically, this campaign strategy attempts to tap into the social culture of interactivity.

4. The March issue of *614*, an electronic magazine (Ezine) published by the Hadassah-Brandeis Institute, asked a number of female Jewish authors to comment on recently published works that changed their thinking about being a Jewish woman. Yet instead of taking the advice of these "experts," 21st-century readers frequently receive guidance from reviews and suggestions posted on or generated by Amazon.com.

CHALLENGE OF WEB 2.0

That technology is rapidly transforming the very fabric of American society is no doubt an understatement. In a world in which broadband access and open-source software facilitate file sharing, streaming media, and the development of user-generated content, Web 2.0 represents merely the latest stage in this consistently fluctuating environment. The challenge for Jewish education—and all education, for that matter—rests not merely with ever changing technological developments—both the explosion of information available and the ability to access that information—but more significantly on the individual's changing attitude towards authority and empowerment. The collaborative, interactive, and user-generated world of the new Internet enabled by Web 2.0 reflects a social and an intellectual culture in which the individual end user has the ability and is even encouraged to shape and create the frame of reference for Jewish life in the 21st century.

Jews today, both young and old, but more often young, define Judaism on their own individually generated terms, regardless of whether their perceptions coincide with the "establishment" of organized Jewish life. This phenomenon challenges the long-standing approach to Jewish life in which conceptions of community were defined by geographical parameters, and religious and cultural standards were determined by authoritative figures, most often rabbinic but occasionally otherwise. While "legitimate" Jewish authorities clearly dismiss such unauthorized attempts to redefine Jewishness, isn't it possible that this user-generated Judaism represents the latest step in a chain that includes such revolutionary but ultimately significant challenges as the havurah movement, Kaplan's call for reconstruction, Zionism, early Reform and even Hasidism? In every stage of modernity, Jews have developed interpretations and understandings of their tradition as a response to the challenge of new circumstances, and these reactions quite often build on contemporary trends in social and intellectual culture.

RESPONSES

What responsibilities do Jewish educators have in the environment where anyone can blog on Judaism's significance, Google provides the most popular answers to Jewish questions and a wiki-Judaism could soon represent a new type of religious denomination? Must our teachers and educational institutions serve, as Jonathan Woocher suggests, as a conservative force amid a sea of unrestrained individualized challenges to communal authority? While Woocher (see previous chapter) quite accurately assesses the concerns that emerge in the "age of Google," the development and proliferation of Web 2.0's infrastructure and software may already make some of those observations academic. Shouldn't we also ask whether trying to restrict or repress the individualized expressions that are helping define the age of Web 2.0—in venues such as MySpace and YouTube—is either possible or even desirable? In the minds of the champions of the information revolution, access, not merely to information, but also to the tools of production and authority, represents nothing less than the most current manifestation of freedom. When parents genetically screen embryos, are they playing God or exercising their God-given right to shape their own future? The cover of *New York* magazine from February 2007 calls the perception of freedom embraced by 21st century youth "the greatest generation gap since rock and roll."

When the landscape of Jewish life is shaped by mainstream American Jewish educators calling for conservatism, and social scientists like Cohen and Sheskin continue to measure Jewish identity almost exclusively by the yardsticks of intermarriage and affiliation, then Jewish leaders don't address the many and varied ways that 21st-century Jews are using today's cultural tools to express themselves and redefine what Judaism means for them. Cohen and others see the rejection of denominational models largely as an issue confronting Conservative Judaism, where the engaged and more educated segment of that movement feels increasingly uncomfortable in their synagogues. In a recent response Eisen, the new chancellor of the Jewish Theological Seminary, began an articulation of a clear Conservative outlook for the movement.

Cohen has also hypothesized that American Jewry can already be classified as bifurcated between the "inmarrieds" and the "intermarrieds." Yet Cohen and others ignore the fact that 21st-century adherents increasingly relate to their faith or other aspects of identity in individualized and often innovative terms. Using the many resources available, including the Internet, cable television, and even books, to chart an expression of Jewishness, they respond to their personal needs and world outlook regardless of what "organized Judaism" presents as normative. Anecdotally, a significant proportion of the "user community" posting on the many Jewish websites calls for Jewish unity rather than denominational and political factionalism.

Not surprisingly, unconventional forums allow increasing opportunities for communication and connection among Jews sharing attitudes and interests they feel are underrepresented in the mainstream Jewish establishment. While, statistically speaking, only a slim minority of young Jews currently participate in the social networks, blogs, and other venues for "user generated Judaism," the impact belies their numbers. As one colleague suggests, the historical legacy of the 1960s counter-culture was not shaped by a majority, but rather by the active and engaged minority. We should not quickly dismiss the new attitudes toward Jewish community, Jewish identity and Jewish religion simply because most Jews do not yet share or even respect these innovative approaches. What is radical and revolutionary today may prove to be normative in the not-too-distant future.

E-KEHILLOT?

Jewish communal life faces numerous challenges in early 21st-century America. Judaism is a way of life in so many ways dependent on the physical presence of others to form communal institutions, so how does the phenomenon of online social networking and virtual community impact on Jewish notions of congregation or *kehillah?*

The changing nature of the individual's relationship to the collective combined with ongoing technological and economic developments demands a redefinition of the concept of community. In Jewish tradition the word community, *kehillah* in Hebrew, has deep significance and is frequently included in the title of institutions of organized Jewish involvement, such as JCCs, federations, and synagogues. But community today has new meanings with the parallel developments of globalization and virtual reality. Although contemporary trends might indicate a challenge to the conventional concept of community, the conclusions need not be pessimistic. In fact, the proliferation of new communication technologies and young Jews' facility with technology may contribute to communal strengthening, if Jewish leadership is willing to embrace new definitions. Even as people become more removed from one another physically, as survey data seem to show, the web of communication will bring people closer together, albeit in virtual space. For many Americans today an online social network does in fact represent a collection of very real relationships.

Whether an electronic *kehillah* can ever replicate the organized community of the past is to some extent irrelevant. The question is whether virtual communities can become real enough to serve the needs of Jews in the 21st century and beyond. Think back to the experimental models of the 20th century, especially the kibbutzim of all stripes as examples of innovation designed to establish new communities. With the plethora of online varieties of Jewishness in the marketplace already, 21st-century Jews are in the process of constructing their own innovative "real world" communities as well.

USER-GENERATED JEWISHNESS—ONLINE AND "REAL WORLD"

This phenomenon of user-generated Jewishness has been called, among other things, Jew-it-yourself, Jew 2.0, and Jewtube. The directions that end users take when they harness new media to serve their own Jewish needs run the entire spectrum of Jewish identification and engagement. Trying to obtain a comprehensive picture of what cyberJudaism and other innovative expressions of Jewishness look like is a monumental task, with the numbers of sites and postings expanding geometrically. Perhaps the clearest proof of the growing importance of the online community today is the number of federation websites that hope to occupy this space. (In April 2007, six of the top ten sites on a Google search for "online Jewish community" were the federations for Cleveland, Chicago, Philadelphia, Toronto, Denver, and Richmond.) In general, though, these websites represent access to information and not innovative content and probably do not appeal to a new generation that does not readily recognize either Jewish federations or synagogues as the central address for Jewish communal life.

WHAT IS OUT THERE

In both virtual and concrete space, 21st-century Jewish communities are taking on new directions and filling unconventional needs. A quick glance at a few will highlight the changing nature of this universe. But first, established Jewish social networks such as *jdate.com* are old news. Other examples, like the new ḥavurot, while often innovative, still use well-established formats. (Please note that the following websites and activities, while active when this article was first written, may no longer be operative, or the focus and content may have shifted over time.)

Now five years old, the magazine *Zeek*, available online for free, proclaims both "its independence and its expansive definition of Jewish cultural and spiritual life." What counts for "Jewish" in this environment is loosely and broadly defined. "We welcome the heretical, honor the sincere and are generally bored by in-jokes, apologetics and irony. We value independence, courage and thoughtfulness, and publish stories which say something new about that which is meaningful. Above all, we believe that an intelligent, articulate Jewish sensibility is one that speaks from its place of particularity in a far wider conversation—and true conversation requires both a fearlessness to create and an openness to change" (*www.zeek.net/masthead*—accessed May 30, 2007). An example of the type of people taking leadership roles with these groups includes British comedian Sacha Baron Cohen of *Borat* fame, who is on the advisory board.

There are sites devoted to free expression that emerge from the world of ultra-Orthodoxy, such as *thelockers.net*, a virtual community for yeshiva teens, whose self-description includes the following: "The Lockers has no agenda. It is not here to convince anyone to be observant, or to love Israel, or to *daven* every day. We will never tell you whether or not you should touch someone of the opposite sex, or whether or not it's cool to party. Not because we don't believe in observant Judaism (we do), but rather because we realize that you can't ever love anything by force." The issues raised in this environment—questions about faith, relationships, school, and self-esteem—are no different than in previous eras, but the forum is now public, and the users who post questions are turning not to a set rabbinic authority (of any denomination) but rather to the virtual community. For example, an April 2007 posting by a high school junior/senior in an all-girls Orthodox school posed the dilemma:

> Okay, so here's my problem. I want to cover my hair when I'm married and I want to be shomer negiah now. But at the same time I don't want to be. I want to be able to make out with my bf, and i want to be able to go to the mall when I'm married without always weaing a hat (im not into the sheitel thing). I don't know what to do, on the one hand I am obligated to keep the Mitzvoth but on the other hand I feel that there are somethings that I am just not capable of doing. so yeah, there's my dilemna. Any thoughts? (syntax errors in original)

The "cyber-she'elah" does not demand a rabbinic response but allows the full community of users to contribute to the discussion.

A UK website, *Jewtastic.com,* calls itself "the home of Jewish pop culture covering music, TV, film, food, fashion and more." And the Jewishness of those who get to determine that culture is defined broadly. To help users navigate the site, they provide guidance, "Seen an acronym on Jewtastic when we reference someone? Don't have a clue what it means? Well, if it's an OJO, then it's someone Of Jewish Origin." How authentic is the Jewish culture that emerges from those pages? Perhaps my personal sensitivities reject the very notion, but these resources are clearly accessible and not only informing but accurately reflecting the opinions of a significant segment of the Jewish world.

On the blog *Yoyenta.com*, part of the Jmerica.com network, Yoyenta defines herself as a "clueless, winging-it-as-I-go Jew." In researching the difficulty in obtaining kosher-for-Passover Coca-Cola she provides the perfectly accurate explanation as to why certain foods known as *kitniyot*, including sodas made with corn syrup, are not technically forbidden, according to biblical and rabbinic law. Linking Ashkenazic Jewry's ban on legumes during Passover to the authority of Moses Isserles in 16th-century Poland, Yoyenta challenges its relevance for today's Jews. Questioning the need for continuing to avoid *kitniyot* is not revolutionary, but the fact that Yoyenta, an anonymous blogger, enjoys a forum that might impact Jewish practice reflects the new virtual community enabled by Web 2.0. Should young Jews be taught in school to avoid Yoyenta because she has no standing in the Jewish world? Should the next Jewish blogger be discouraged to comment on Jewish law and practice if he or she has no rabbinic ordination? Most likely, a generation being reared in this environment will not accept any curtailment of its freedom to both navigate the Internet and create the content therein.

Moishe House, funded by the Forest foundation (whose mission is fostering young leaders committed to social action based on the concept of Tikkun Olam), is a network of homes throughout North America and beyond that serves "as a hub for young adult Jewish community." The homes allow "eager, innovative young adults to live in and create their vision of an ideal Jewish communal space." While the concept resonates with echoes of early kibbutzim, the Moishe House communities have no preconceived vision of Jewish communal life while allowing the residents to develop their own unique outlook. As of February 2007 there were seven such homes in the United States and three elsewhere, serving not only as residences, but also as innovative communal centers. (Information available at www.theforestfoundation.net)

The website *Jewlicious.com* hosts a broad range of blogs and videos with Jewish content—the subtitle on the site reads "100% kosher" next to a girl sporting an "I (heart) Hashem." The site hosts postings including a heavy metal rendition of *Ha-Tikvah*, h̲assidic and kabbalistic commentary from "Rabbi Yonah," and an Israeli clip from YouTube that appears to be a party sponsored by *Playboy* in Israel. Jewlicious.com allows users to vote for their favorite Jewish postings in the following categories: Best Group Blog, Best Jewish Culture Blog, Best Pro–Israel Advocacy Blog, Best Slice of Life in Israel Blog, Best–Designed Blog, and Best Contribution/Blog That Made a Difference.

The blog site *Jewschool.com* describes itself as "an open revolt…Offering the latest and greatest from the bleeding edge of Jewish cultural and communal life." Among its many blogs the site includes a posting from "Y-Love" titled "Generation Moschiach" that states the following: "At the nexus of brand marketing and contemporary Torah Judaism you will find this blog [thisbabylon. net], where I ask the question, 'Who is Moshiach's target market?' Jewish tradition is replete with phrases regarding the generation to which Moshiach will come. The generation to experience the Messianic transition is to be '(brazen-) faced as a dog', is to 'thirst for the words of G-d', and so on. Today our classification systems are less likely to offer an animal analogy than they are to rely on psychographic, consumer research, or demographic data. I proffer that Web 2.0, social networking, and social marketing—buzzwords that are becoming the lifeblood of the new marketing arena—provide a uniquely pro–Messianic environment. So who is Moshiach destined for? The collaborators, the individualists, or the workaholics? The 'early adopters' or the 'echo boomers'?" In the ongoing quest to define 21st-century youth, Y-Love sees them as the Messianic generation.

CONCLUSIONS?

Can any of us reach significant conclusions regarding the nature of Jewish life and Jewish education in the future based on the ever-expanding possibilities for Jewish expression? Perhaps the most important response by educators to the engagement of Jewish youth with the interactive world of Web 2.0 is not to apply a corrective or "authentic" view of Judaism, but rather to become conversant with user-generated Judaism and become personally familiar with the media, digital or otherwise, that enables such extensive individual engagement. Should we give any weight to a possible "Long Tail" of Judaism that allows all of us to provide our "recommendations" for Jewish life, in the style of Amazon.com and Netflix? On the other hand, whether or not the "Jewishness" that flows from these sources corresponds to late-20th-century normative patterns pales in comparison to the very fact that 21st-century Jews, many of them unaffiliated and removed from serious discussions of Jewish life, some raised in interfaith or faith-less homes, now actively engage with some aspect of their Jewish identity. Even if their opinions, behaviors, and religious beliefs fail to conform to standards deemed acceptable by communal leadership, they are creating their own dialogue while attempting to participate in the larger communal discussion. In large measure the culture of Web 2.0 is merely the latest means, and perhaps the most powerful, of continuing the 3,000-year-old conversation that is Judaism.

IMPLICATIONS FOR EDUCATORS

Considering the broad ideological and religious spectrum that Jewish educators represent, detailed policy recommendations to respond to the technologically enabled social culture seem inappropriate. Of course, some institutions do attempt to control the flow of information available to their students, but this approach hardly appears realistic. The following brief list suggests action steps Jewish educators may take on their own and collaboratively to respond to the constant changes in the 21ˢᵗ-century learning environment.

- Become familiar with the increasingly popular genres of technological and communal activity that currently engage children of all ages, including social networking, online gaming and user-generated content. (You might have fun while learning a bit about your students.)

- Assess how students use technology as an information source. They will continue to Google and rely on Wikipedia, so the informed educator should understand in general terms both the mathematical and advertising basis for Google and other frequently used search engines and the communal "wisdom" that creates wikis of all sorts.

- Continually update your literacy in this space. The constant flow of information and rapidity of technological innovation means that year to year, if not more frequently, significant change will likely appear.

- Don't go it alone! Take advantage of the many resources that provide virtual community for Jewish educators to share their concerns, experiences, and suggestions for navigating this brave new world. And if you are uncomfortable with what you find, create your own and expand the conversation even further.

ANNOTATED BIBLIOGRAPHY

These volumes, some dating back to the year 2000, address the cultural changes facilitated by the digital revolution. While not always shedding direct light on the Jewish experience, they are useful references for the broader transformations afoot that are shaping the contemporary Jewish experience.

Greenberg, A. (2006) *Grande Soy Vanilla Latte with Cinnamon, No Foam: Jewish Identity and Community in a Time of Unlimited Choices*, Rebooters.net. The statistically organized study seeks to understand the changing identities of Gen-Y and Millennial Jews, recognizing that they inhabit an environment of increasing customization. Builds on the previous rebooters.net study titled *OMG! How Generation Y is Redefining Faith in the iPod Era* (2005).

Howe, N. & Strauss, W. (2000) *Millennials Rising: The Next Great Generation*. New York: Vintage Press. This book analyzes so-called Generation Y and their successors, dubbed *millenials* as they come of age in the 21ˢᵗ century. According to the authors, this cohort marks a sharp break from Gen-X trends because as a generation they have received more concern and attention than any others in quite some time.

Nakamura, L. (2002) *Cybertypes: Race, Ethnicity, and Identity on the Internet*. London: Routledge. While accepting the possibility of virtual anonymity offered by the Internet, Nakamura argues that racial identities, politics, and stereotypes follow users into cyberspace, in many respects conditioning online activity to the human and communal relationships of the "real" world.

Surowiecki, J. (2004) *The Wisdom of Crowds: Why the Many are Smarter Than the Few and How Collective Wisdom Shapes Business, Economics, Societies, and Nations*. New York: Doubleday. As the name implies, Surowiecki examines ways that the collective intelligence of the masses significantly impacts important sectors of contemporary civilization. He even argues that given an effective mechanism for harnessing the "wisdom of crowds," the general population more often than not will outperform the "so-called experts."

Turkle, S. (2002) "E-Futures and E-Personae," in *Designing for a Digital World*, N. Leach (ed.). UK: Wiley-Academy (31–36). Turkle addresses the anonymity enabled by the Internet and demonstrates how users can adopt distinct online personae, seemingly contradictory in many ways to their "real life" characters, but nevertheless reflecting genuine elements of their individual identities.

SOME ADDITIONAL INTERESTING WEBSITES OF ONLINE USER-GENERATED JEWISH CONTENT:

http://www.jewcy.com

http://www.abigjewishblog.blogspot.com

http://jlearn20.blogspot.com

http://www.e-kehillah.org

http://www.opensourcejudaism.com/

The Place of Israel in North American Jewish Education: A View from Israel

Rachel Korazim

…Each bus queue can easily catch fire and turn into a stormy seminar, with total strangers arguing not only about strategy, economy and family, but about the essence of history, the importance of morality, theology, the connection between nation and God, and metaphysics. But even while disputing their moral viewpoint it doesn't stop them from elbowing their way to the head of the line.

Amos Oz

One evening I took a walk with my wife on the Tel Aviv beachfront. I noticed a board bearing the words "אֵין מַצִּיל," "no savior," which translates in Modern Hebrew to "no lifeguard". But my archaic Hebrew imparted theological significance to the board: "Oy gevalt, there is no savior". Perhaps, in order to save a nation from exile, one must believe that there is no other savior. This is not what I believe. I believe that we are partners with the Almighty in Creation and in the process of Redemption.

Rabbi Jonathan Sacks, Chief Rabbi of Britain

In May 2001 The Lainer Chair at Bar Ilan University held a seminar entitled Israel: Visions and Reality. The event brought together two thinkers: Rabbi Jonathan Sacks, Chief Rabbi of Great Britain, and Israeli writer Amos Oz. The debate focused on the Zionist idea and the Zionist dream. These two brief excerpts serve as the entrance point to our deeper understanding of Israel in the lives of North American Jews today. Both touch on the tension between the ideal or spiritual approach to Zion and the practicalities of everyday life in Israel.

This is the real challenge for the 21st-century Jew in North America. Whether we look at the gap between the ideal image of Israel and its ever-changing realities or at a critical reading of Israel education programs for North American Jewish audiences, we will deepen our understanding of the interconnectedness of the two countries and peoples.

IMAGES OF AN IDEALIZED ISRAEL

The land of longing and prayers, compounded by the romantic portrayal of its early years, often clashes with the less-than-perfect reality of recent years. In my professional life, working for the Jewish Agency—Education Department, I frequently visit North American Jewish communities. When asked to discuss Israeli education, I often choose to do so through the literary and artistic works of Israeli writers. In hundreds of meetings with thousands of educators, students, and lay leaders I reiterate the same message: Israel has many voices; it is complex, sometimes painful, at times not so pleasing. As a general rule these sessions involve a great deal of discussion and questions, which sometimes lead to angry words. This kind of encounter with Israel with many conflicting voices and shades is not easy. I often feel that my audiences would prefer it to be less complex. Perhaps it would be easier, if only it were possible, to draw a clear and unequivocal picture of a righteous, victorious, delightful Israel where one is secure in the knowledge that it exists, shining with the glow of the brilliant Zionist enterprise.

My overall impression is one of sadness, even lamentation—a sense of a situation gone awry, a new generation who, unlike their parents and grandparents, is not connected to Israel. There used to be a time when things were different; the watershed events of the Holocaust followed by the birth of the state of Israel created a sense of living in miraculous times. The reunification of Jerusalem followed by the wonderful rescue at Entebbe continued a seemingly uninterrupted sequence of glory. Two generations were raised on these images. Israel, on the shores of the distant Mediterranean, was the answer to the prayers for Zion. It offered a safe haven for the persecuted and lived up to the dreams and expectations. North American Zionists could focus on clear causes and support them wholeheartedly. When my interlocutors address themselves to the other side of the equation, the youth and adults of today, they deplore the state of those too young to have witnessed the historical events that shaped bygone Israel. They are describing a void, a lack of content as compared to the past. This lacuna is always offered as the win-all explanation for the current situation, where there is no connection and very little interest in connecting to Israel.

Less attention is paid to the possibility that we may not be dealing with a void but rather with a different series of events, to some extent as powerful as the previous ones. The euphoria of the hope for peace was created by images: Palestinian kids offering olive branches to Israeli soldiers and handshakes of former enemies on the White House lawn. Unfortunately, these were swiftly followed by images of exploding human bombs, the assassination of Yitzhak Rabin and a bewildered, shattered Israeli society.

There has been little real effort to deal with the impact of the more recent images of Israel. Much more energy is invested in attempting to deal with the loss of the earlier idealized ones. This impression is further strengthened when I take a closer look at what has really transpired in Israel education in the last eighteen years (1990–2008).

For ten of these years the American Jewish educational community successfully invested tremendous energy and resources in building what we refer to as "The Israel Experience." From short-term trips for teens, families, and young adults to full-year programs at yeshivot and universities, a framework was created that placed Israel firmly at the heart of an educational process geared at strengthening Jewish identity by connecting to the land and its people. By so doing, an underlying message emerged very strongly: a real connection **to Israel** can happen only **in Israel**.[1]

Planning, recruiting and delivering Israel experience programs could not happen in an ideological vacuum. A raison d'être was developed to frame the educational value of the trips. It was suggested that the trip may provide, for participants who were far removed from the Holocaust and the birth of the State of Israel, an exciting encounter with historical sites, breathtaking views of the desert and experiences that cement a sense of belonging to something greater than one's own family and community. However, it seems that in planning these voyages, Israel, the real place, was not necessarily the goal. The trips aimed at something else—American Jewish identity would be enriched, strengthened and made more meaningful by connecting to a carefully crafted series of experiences in Israel. Group or family rituals at the Kotel, on top of Massada or at Yad Vashem are an integral part of the trip, no less important than the accompanying text study sessions guided by experienced educators who assist in processing and meaning making of the tour (Grant 2001).

It may be important to note that many of the trips included a stop in Prague or Poland, reiterating the message that Israel has to be experienced in the context of the miraculous Holocaust-to-Redemption cycle.

These Israel Experience programs had an impact on Israel as well. Thousands of people—providers of services, tour guides, counselors, paramedics, guards, bus drivers and educators—encountered North American Jewish youth and their staff. As the programs developed, the need to take the participants out of the glass bubble of their air-conditioned buses and allow them to interact with Israeli youth fostered the creation of The Bronfman Mifgashim program. Mifgashim was not just another

---

[1]This remark is not meant to diminish the importance of the trips, but it may point to a lesser investment in local, U.S. based Israel education programs in those years.

item on the tour. It demanded a clear articulation of how to create this intercultural encounter in which Israelis were equally engaged in learning and experiencing rather than merely serving as a resource for the Americans.

Further consequences followed from another Israeli insight. In the mid-90s Israeli political figures addressing the topic of Israel–Diaspora relations suggested that American Jewish funds might be better spent in giving American Jewish youth the gift of a trip to Israel. Yossi Beilin promoted this concept at the General Assembly of the Council of Jewish Federations (now the United Jewish Communities—UJC) in 1994 when he said, "I suggest that we make this a national project: to offer every young Jew in the world a free ticket to Israel and a variety of programs for a ten -day visit. After their visit I suggest we should maintain contact with each one of them. This way we can reach almost every Jewish youngster and can reduce the chances of losing them."

With the inception of Birthright Israel in 1998 as a partnership between major donors, Jewish federations and the Israeli government, we are presented with a well structured concept implying that even if one did not have a solid Jewish education as a child, a ten-day trip to Israel in early adulthood could still perform the miracle of creating a sense of belonging to the Jewish people.[2] At the beginning of 2007 more than 100,000 young adults have benefited from a Birthright Israel experience.

A second and equally powerful initiative, Partnership 2000, created during these years, linked dozens of North American Jewish communities to real places in Israel—not only mythical Jerusalem or fun-filled Tel Aviv, but Sderot, Beit Shemesh, and Hatzor. These partnership programs, based on direct involvement between North American Jewish communities and their Israeli counterparts, brought together educators and students in mutual visits to homes, schools and local places of interest. Fresh knowledge was gleaned at the cost, sometimes, of the loss of enchantment. Israelis became real, sometimes uncouth individuals, not necessarily always enthusiastic about life in Israel, and frequently ignorant of their own Jewish heritage.

A new language is in the process of being developed. There is a need to frame and articulate that which is happening: encounters with a land and its people that are meant to impact the life of Jewish communities in a distant land. *Peoplehood, Mifgash, and sites as texts* are but a few of the terms that have become codes to describe actions and meanings in this newly developing educational territory.

While well-meaning American and Israeli Jewish educators were busy creating these programs in Israel, the advent of the Internet bridged the information gap and made everyday Israel only two mouse clicks away.

Information about Israel is now abundant, readily accessible and unabridged.

Gone are the days of the exclusivity of well-edited texts with carefully selected sets of images. The information highways leave very little to the imagination.

It is not surprising that alongside these developments a need was felt to create an educational text that met the challenge of formulating a conceptual framework. In 1994, JESNA, in conjunction with the Bronfman Foundation, initiated the creation of the "Israel in Our Lives" series. This series was not the first attempt to create educational materials about the 'real' Israel.

Prior to "Israel in Our Lives" (1994), the organizing principle of most Israel education programs was either historical, from the beginning of modern Zionism to the second half of the 20th century, or geographical, from the Galil to the Negev. Rarely if ever did these programs connect to Humash or Navi classes: neither did they provide a framework for dealing with current events or understanding what all this information was supposed to mean to the student's life in America.

Thus one could wonder whether students realized that the land they were told about in Lekh Lekha, the place where the pioneers had danced hora and the city in which a bomb had exploded from the previous night's TV news program was one and the same place. "Israel in our Lives" presented a totally different text and context. It looked at the place of Israel in North American Jewish education and life from philosophical, existential and theological points of view. It addressed a large variety of Jewish educational frameworks, from early childhood to adult learners and from formal to informal. The suggestions for activities sprang from the philosophical framework. The units were

---

[2]The question of the lasting impact of Birthright Israel programs is still too early to evaluate. It will have to be studied in years to come.

written and evaluated by both Israelis and Americans, thus making yet another important and innovative statement. For the first time Israeli and North American educators collaborated on a joint curricular project.

The opening chapter of "Israel in Our Lives" by Eisen and Rosenak (1994) is, to this very day, one of the most important documents written in the field. Its uniqueness lies in its being one of the very few attempts to create an Israel education theoretical-pedagogical baseline, in contrast to most of the literature, that focuses on methodology and content rather then addressing the issue of the Why? and What For? of teaching Israel in North America.

Examining the role of Israel in North American Jewish educational frameworks today, one may hasten to interpret the changes as a direct result of the most recent events of the Intifada and Israel's often-criticized methods of dealing with terror. While this may well be the case, there may be other factors at work. The late 90s brought to Israel–Diaspora relations at least two additional texts. Neither was entirely new, yet both acquired added dimensions. With the growing numbers of non–Jews among the new immigrants from the F.S.U, discussions in Israel about the legalization of non–Orthodox conversions brought to the surface dissent and anger among all Jewish denominational circles in North America. Issues of state, religion and pluralism (or rather its absence) in Israel were openly and critically discussed.

Many could and did read this as a rejection or disregard of the State of Israel toward Reform and Conservative Judaism. At the same time Israel was moving in new socioeconomic directions. Free-market policies increased the gap and deepened the poverty of an ever-growing number of Israelis, particularly senior citizens and children. Needy Israel was brought to the forefront as donors were asked to support hungry children. During a visit to the United States in those years, I recall a huge poster that welcomed me in the entrance lobby of a large federation building. Under the picture of a two-year-old girl, the caption read: "She is not Reform, she is not Conservative—she is two and she is hungry". The message was clear. American Jews were called upon to disregard Israel's shortcomings and respond to its needs. A new image was now added to the ones we have previously considered—that of condescending acceptance of a poor relative.

The year 2000 was the best in living memory in terms of the number of North American Jews visiting Israel, and then came the second Intifada.

Horrific images of bombed buses, pubs and schools followed one another in rapid succession. Short-term programs in Israel came to an almost complete halt while the long-term programs continued with diminished numbers.

From my own perspective, dealing at the time with professional development programs in Israel for overseas Jewish educators, I saw an interesting phenomenon. Educators did not stop coming. Numbers remained steady, with some increase in the Orthodox sector. This became the subject of a research study conducted by JAFI's Education Department. The question was, Why did they continue to come? Since central agencies for Jewish education and other community organizations make educators' seminars happen, we looked into the reasons organizers brought educators to Israel. In other words, what did the organizers believe could better be achieved in terms of professional development for educators, during a ten- to twelve-day seminar in Israel, that could not be done at home?

In most cases the main objective was to give educators their own Jewish experience of Israel. Programs were not intended to provide educational skills or tools to deal with Israel-related issues. It was felt that the educators needed a firsthand experience of Israel. Another reason was the notion that for certain subjects, "the great teachers" were in Israel, and so they came to study with them. Third was the desire to express solidarity with Israel in difficult times. Finally, with the students not going, educators felt it was their obligation to visit and share their experiences.

Israel education programs developed in North America and in Israel in the years following the Intifada address similar needs. They deal with expressions of solidarity, supporting the Israeli economy and providing tools to deal with Hasbara (Israel advocacy) issues. Two examples out of many may illustrate this: "From Matzah to Matzav" (2002), an Internet site created by CAJE, provided a variety of resources for educators who may need help in addressing the complexity of Israel-related issues now requiring attention. The second is the case of "Ambassador", a web-based distance learning course created as a joint project between Israel's Ministry of Foreign Affairs and the Jewish Agency's Contact Center. It is geared toward students on university campuses and provides four weeks of intensive training by Hasbara expert Neil Lazarus. An informative article about the course appeared in the *Jerusalem Post* on the eve of Shavuot 2002. By the following week over two hundred students had registered. The number grew to more than three thousand in just over two years. These two examples reflect both the need and the sense of urgency to deal with the immediate.

Not surprisingly, focusing on the urgent and the immediate did not eliminate the big questions of Israel education. On the contrary, when addressing a recent event the question is almost always: "How far back in history does one need to go in order to understand it?" Grappling for words when dealing with a questionable act of the Israeli government, people always tread the thin line between solidarity and critical commitment. This situation makes North American Jews re-examine their ability to identify with Israel, while Israel needs to redefine its expectations from North American Jews.

In 2003, almost a decade after "Israel in Our Lives", the North American Coalition for Israel Education (NACIE) was established to pilot new projects for expanding Israel education in North America. In 2006 NACIE was renamed *Makom*. It is a joint project of the UJC/Federation community of North America and The Jewish Agency for Israel. NACIE was started as an endeavor to create both organizational and philosophical infrastructures. During a retreat for leading philosophers, educators and lay leaders, a document was drawn up to reflect a new conceptual framework, one that would embrace the challenges and the complexity of relationships with Israel:

> One opinion was that we ought to embrace the world of "high stakes"—all successful Jewish educational initiatives turned up the heat on the difficult issues. By working in this way, people are brought into the real conversation, rather than a synthetic one. An alternative perspective offered was that the challenge may be to think through and re-convey the tension between this real conception of Israel, and the notion of Israel as a tourist destination where Jews can live a normal and happy life. (Boyd & Moskovitz-Kalman 2003)

Reading these lines, one may be reminded of a text we all carry in our hearts.

After the first exile from Zion we were given the lines:

עַל נַהֲרוֹת בָּבֶל שָׁם יָשַׁבְנוּ גַּם־בָּכִינוּ בְּזָכְרֵנוּ אֶת־צִיּוֹן.

"On the rivers of Babylon, where we sat and wept as we remembered Zion."

These words coined the kind of longing to Zion that is rooted in suffering. Jerusalem's glory is remembered in contrast to exile's misery.

Many centuries later the poet Yehuda Halevi coined the phrase:

לִבִּי בְמִזְרָח וַאֲנִי בְּקָצֵה מַעֲרָב.

"My heart is in the east while I am at the end of the west."

This time it is beautiful Toledo that has to be abandoned for the sake of ruined Jerusalem.

None of these phrases, which have served Jews so well for centuries, captures the essence of the issues we are facing today. America is not a miserable exile, neither is Jerusalem in ruins. We are in search of a paradigm, one that will capture the heart and the imagination, one that will include commitment and critique and may find expression in both liturgy and honest dialogue.

What may the future hold for the two largest centers of Jewish life in the 21st century, as each is grappling with the meaning of the existence of the other for itself?

• We need a better understanding of the term so frequently used these days: *Jewish peoplehood*. It demands from American as well as Israeli Jews the ability to articulate a sense of belonging to a club much larger than the one delineated by one's state or congregation.

- We need to reopen the discussion about the place of Hebrew in North America. Israel, both the ideal and the real, is related to, prayed for and expressed in Ivrit. If we want to have a shared language of codes and meaning connected to our classical common heritage, we cannot afford to keep Hebrew at the level at which it is taught in North America these days.

- We will need to continue creating the conceptual framework for the role of Israel in North American Jewish life, not stopping before the contextual framework is filled with texts to suit the variety of possible approaches. Spiritual center? Homeland? The road not taken?

- We need to accept the uniqueness of the times we live in, not wishing back bygone days but rather embracing that which is in its full potential, recognizing the dynamic developments of a living organism that will keep calling on us to revisit, reframe and rearticulate an old connection, forever young and changing.

REFERENCES

The Ambassador Course (2003). http://www.mfa.gov.il/MFA/MFAArchive/2000_2009/2003/4/Ambassador

Boyd, J. & Moskovitz-Kalman, E. (2003, September). Exploring the Place of Israel in the Lives of American Jews. North American Coalition for Israel Education—The Philosophers' Retreat.

Eisen, A. & Rosenak, M. (1994). Teaching Israel: Basic Issues and Philosophical Guidelines. New York and Jerusalem: The CRB Foundation.

"From Matzah to Matzav" (2002). *http://www.caje.org/learn/israel_curriculum.htm*

Grant, L.D. (2001). "The Role of Mentoring in Enhancing Experience of a Congregational Israel Trip." *Journal of Jewish Education* 67(1/2), 47–60.

Israel in Our Lives (1994). *http"//archive.jesna.org/cgi-bin/ilive.php3*

The Jewish Message as Medium: Jewish Education in the Information Age

Joel Lurie Grishaver

HIS MASTER'S VOICE

When I was eleven or so I visited Shlomo Pincas' living room and saw his father's wondrous device that we could only dream of using; we weren't even allowed to touch it. This amazing technology was a recording phonograph, one that literally cut records. Shlomo's father, known as Mr. Pincas, was the bar mitzvah tutor at the large Conservative synagogue in the neighborhood. His machine allowed him to "cut records" of Torah and Haftarah portions. A year later my father borrowed a home tape recorder, one the size of a small suitcase, and my tutor, Mr. Horowitz, recorded the pieces I needed on a reel-to-reel tape for me. Only a few years later, when I was working as a bar mitzvah tutor, I got to make cassette recordings for my students.

In the article "Making Your School a Technology Friendly Place" in the Spring 2007 *Jewish Education News,* Terry Kaye informs us that the thing to do today is to post the bar mitzvah material on a website and attach an MP3 file. That reveals another progression. Mr. Pincas cut apart one (or perhaps two) *Tikkunim* a year (books containing the Torah portion with vowels and without vowels in Torah script), giving each student a printed version of the bar mitzvah material in a folder. My family, because Mr. Horowitz was not the standard tutor for my synagogue, bought a *Tikkun* that is still in my library. The other option was to go to the town library and pay a dollar a page for a white-on-black photocopy. Since then Xerox entered the business and lent its trade name to a technological process, just like iPod. Since that time generations of students have received CDs of their bar mitzvah portion, along with photocopies of all they have to learn, which were covered in endless pencil marks for pauses and became stained and rumpled from endless trips in backpacks, to mark the path to reach their majority. All this, we are told, is no longer "technology friendly."

Marshall McLuhan taught us that "the medium is the massage." (Yes, that playful pun was actually the title of his book.) He taught such simple lessons as "A typewriter is a means of transcribing thought, not expressing it" and the contradictory "Mass transportation is doomed to failure in North America because a person's car is the only place where he can be alone and think." The tool and the medium become a major part of the learning.

On one hand, a recording is a recording, a tool that allows a student to parrot and master the required portion. But the tool makes a difference. With Mr. Pincas' custom-made records there was no going back. One listened to the whole thing, because at that time "scratching" was not yet an art form. The tape recorder allowed students to stop, start and review, to learn the material as a series of smaller elements. When the bar/bat mitzvah moved to the iPod a different change took place: the ear buds. Up to now the recording media had essentially used speakers for reproduction. Headphones did exist, but the recordings were normatively played for everyone. Today listening has become a private experience. When I prepared to become bar mitzvah my whole family could chant the entire thing because they had been subjected to the endless repetitions. In an MP3-player world, students listen on their iPods, making preparation a private process.

One can trace the same progression in the printed text. Once families had to own "the book." It became a permanent part of the family library. Then, for convenience, books were cut apart (and could be written on). Photocopying further privatized and desanctified the text. The requirement of Jewish law to safeguard or bury any copy of the divine name extends to all of the b'nai mitzvah folders that have ever existed. In our new, privatized world we have had to adapt the old ways to meet the new. God's name on a computer screen is not sacred; otherwise you would never be able to change the screen or turn it off if God's name came up. Several legal authorities have allowed the electronic destruction of a sacred name on our screens because it is no longer printed—it has been broken down to a series of dots, and dots can be erased.

"SPARKS" AND "IT"

Kabbalistic teaching suggests that the world is a combination of *nitzatzot* (sparks) and *klipot* (broken pieces of the containers that were supposed to hold the light that became the sparks). For a Kabbalist, *tikkun olam* (world repair) happens when individuals find, collect and share the sparks of divine light (wisdom). Martin Buber, a twentieth-century philosopher, took this model and recreated it as his classic *I and Thou*. He said that there are three kinds of relationships in the world. There is I–It, where I relate to things or relate to people as if they are things. There are I–Thou relationships, where people relate on a soul-to-soul basis. (Buber did write that people can have an I-Thou relationship with a tree, but that is another story.) Finally, Buber wrote that there is an I–THOU relationship in which, via our I–Thou relationships, we connect with God or whatever Greater Power we want to acknowledge. Buber's I–Thou is an expression of the *nitzatzot*. His I–It is another manifestation of *klipot*. And the gathering and sharing of sparks becomes the I–THOU relationship.

Let's ask a Kabbalistic, Buberian question: "What is idolatry?" In this framework it is actually easy to explain. It is mistaking a "piece of shell" for a "spark." It is thinking that an "It" is a "Thou." There is a great attempt in our society to deify technology, to believe that it is inherently redemptive. Simultaneously technology is seen as evil. Educators often blame their own technology gaps for their growing exile from their students. The simple truth is this: (1) Technology is a set of tools. (2) Tools shape the way we create and communicate. (3) Technology is not who we or our students are. Technology is an "it."

A simple story. I have a fine-motor coordination problem. Strange problem for a cartoonist, but the truth is that I basically draw and don't write my letters. When I was in seventh grade my parents gave me a great birthday present: a week at secretarial school to learn how to type. It had two benefits. First, I became a writer. That is something that could never have happened without the typewriter. By hand I could never get down on paper the things that were in my mind. My handwriting was too slow. The typewriter released the words. It made certain kinds of communication possible. It shaped the way I work. I began writing blank verse because of the carriage return, but the feelings, the words, the expression were all mine. The second benefit was spending a week surrounded by seventeen- to nineteen-year-old women. A perfect pre-bar mitzvah experience.

My process of writing changed with an electric typewriter and shifted again when I began word processing. The tool shapes the way I work, but it is not the work. "A typewriter is a means of transcribing thought, not expressing it."

COMMUNITY AS A SECOND LANGUAGE

As I was reflecting on this article I went to the graduation ceremony at the Los Angeles campus of the Hebrew Union College. There Deborah Tuttle, the student speaker, clarified my thoughts. She said:

> …recent research by Steven Cohen and Arnold Eisen observes that the "first language" many Jews speak is one of profound individualism. Community, they say, has become a "second language". Our "mother tongue" has become a private one; we shop online, we dial in to conference calls, we have fewer business lunches and more home offices. In this brave new world we keep to ourselves. We don't know our neighbors, and our communities are too often virtual rather than actual. We

build individual realities where we control the environment, the content and the interactivity.

With this as our baseline, the question of learning a communal language seems as foreign as the grammatical structures of high-school Latin. How do we create and sustain courageous communities when much of the American Jewish population feels that their community connection is lost in translation?

Years ago Christopher Lasch wrote *The Culture of Narcissism: American Life in an Age of Diminishing Expectations*. In it he says, "Experiences of inner emptiness, loneliness, and inauthenticity are by no means unreal or, for that matter, devoid of social content.... They arise from the warlike conditions that pervade American society, from the dangers and uncertainty that surround us, and from a loss of confidence in the future...now a desperate concern for personal survival, sometimes disguised as hedonism, engulfs (us)..."

If we are going to describe the millennial child, we know a few things. First come all the things we have said for a long time: under parental pressure, overscheduled, spending lots of time interacting with media and the like. Some of the things that are new are a de-emphasis of dating and a replacement with group experiences. We have "friends with benefits." and sex has become a "casual experience". There is a down-spiral in group membership (kids bowl alone, too) and an upturn in service learning (read: social action projects) because life is now a résumé rather than a résumé that reflects our life. All of this speaks to the truth that like their boomer grandparents, like their boomlet parents, this generation has made another turn toward narcissism and isolation. Or, in the words of Deborah Tuttle, "Community is now a second language."

Here is what we know. Technology did not create the isolation and alienation we sense in the privatization that seems evident in our students today. It may well serve and amplify that loneliness, but it is not its source. Its source is in fear and uncertainty, in a shrinking of hope, in the rise of hedonistic, self-protective reactions. Texting does not destroy communication. Rather, texting is a manifestation of less time to spend together. The electric guitar did not destroy the Grand Old Opry—rather, it took country music to a new level. Our students abandoned the news and focused on "surreality television" not out of laziness, not out of a collapse of intelligence, but as an act of survival.

Here are two simple truths: (1) Technology is not the enemy. (2) Technology is not the solution. E-mail has moved from instant communication to a glut of Viagra ads. Once Torah Aura ran exciting list-serves for middle school and high school kids. Then kids moved to IMs, texts, MySpace, and a lot of other communication formats that didn't get bogged down in the tedium of advertisements. It wasn't only because it was faster; it was also less invasive, more defensive. As more Jewish schools move to e-mail they will not only save paper, they will also escalate non-communication.

THE TWINKIE DEFENSE

I am doing a parenting session at a synagogue. In the midst of my talk a father stands up and says, "My eleven-year-old son has a busy week, he has school and sports, yada yada yada, he begs me to sleep in on Sunday, and I want to know why I should make him get up and go to Hebrew school." I have an epiphany, and I tell him: (1) Because Hebrew school is the only place he is going to learn how to heal death. (2) Because Hebrew school is the only place he is going to find his part in the redemption of the world. (3) Because Hebrew school is the one place where he is going to gain tools to turn himself into the best person he can be. And (4) because Hebrew school is the place he is going to find the connection between him, Israel, and the rest of the Jewish people. The father sits down and says "Thank you." Another father stands up and says, "If this school taught those things, my son would be here every single week." I have never forgotten that morning.

Here are some of the things I think I know.

- As Jewish educators we see our job as "Judification." We are not trying to inform our students about their Jewish skills or provide them with Jewish information. Instead we have taken the responsibility to create (or at least significantly deepen) their Jewish identification.

- We use three or four tools in order to do this. (1) We start early, because we want to build Jewish feelings. That is why preschool is so big on the agenda. (2) We try hard to make our schools either short or fun or both—because we accept the guilt that the previous generation of Jewish schools is responsible for the level of assimilation caused by the previous generation of students not feeling good about going to them. (3) We emphasize home and family not as process, but as the core context. We try to train our students to hold Shabbat, Passover, and Ḥanukkah at home, and we empower them to have privatized life-cycle rituals like Havdalah b'nai mitzvah ceremonies. And (4) we worship at the altar of memory rather than the altar of meaning. We operate on the assumption that if our students have enough photographs of enough positive Jewish moments, these good feelings will create the inertia needed to keep them moving in Jewish directions.

- The majority of our client families are consumers, but they have no brand loyalty. They will buy that which is most convenient, cheapest, or easiest. They are narcissists in the sense that Christopher Lasch described in *The Culture of Narcissism*. They are ruled by "The Sovereign Self" as described by Eisen and Cohen in *The Jew Within*. It is much easier and less long-lasting to help them feel good about being Jewish. Most important, recent studies show that it is completely possible to "feel positive about one's Jewish heritage" and to completely disengage one's self from the Jewish future. To succeed we should start in preschool building Jewish experiences and feelings, but if we don't make it to adulthood with a Judaism that is vocational—that offers positive contributions to Jewish life—little is gained. This next generation is not going to tell their children, "I went to Hebrew school and hated it, so you will go to Hebrew school and hate it." Instead it will be "Hebrew school wasn't worth my time, so we will not make you bother with it."

- We are in an era of post-ethnic chic. Judaism is now a Protestant religion. The bagel is now "The Great American Bagel." "You don't have to be Jewish to love Levy's rye bread." Holocaust guilt is not going to motivate late-bearing Boomers, Gen X-ers and Gen Y-ers to send their kids to Hebrew school. Neither is Grandma's Passover dinner. Judaism has got to make their lives richer, more meaningful. It has got to be vocational and productive, or it will drop away. We all know how to order Thai food, dim sum, tapas, sushi, Indian, Mexican, and the like. The deli is no longer our home, if we can even find one in our communities.

Here is my simple truth. Jewish education is going to fail unless (1) we instill a Judaism and a Jewish practice that is meaningful to adults; (2) we build a bridge from b'nai mitzvah observance to college and then another from college to adult Jewish life; (3) we make sure that our students have Jewish friends as well as Jewish memories. Unitarians can look at their old photos, too. This means that just like teachers writing objectives, we must focus on the final behaviors we are seeking before we plan our lessons and activities. Good memories alone are a meal made of Twinkies. The four questions—the ones about death, world repair, self-improvement and Jewish connection—are the ones we have to help our students answer. These are questions of meaning, not resolved by facts, not really touched by good memories. Anything less, however, is empty calories.

JUDAISM AS A MEDIUM

My rabbi, Mordechai Finley, likes to critique Hebrew schools as places that train docents for the Museum of Former Jewish Life. They are like guides in the orchestra section who can identify the oboe, the viola and the kettle drums but cannot tune or play any of them. I suspect the same is almost equally true of day schools. We teach about Judaism; we don't teach Judaism as a life process.

The solution part of this article is simple, perhaps naïve. The best possible future is when we begin to teach Judaism and do so in a Jewish way. Judaism is lot of things that transcend bar/bat mitzvah, that have a greater life impact than a *kametz katan*, that are more transformative than being able to dance *Ma Navu*. The truth is that Judaism is a lot of three things that should be familiar: God, Torah, and Israel. They are inner meaning, a sense of direction and a sense of connection. We make no impact until we get past learning about and get to learning how.

We need a Jewish education that makes a difference, that impacts the loneliness and alienation of millennial life. We need one that brings a sense of purpose and connection. That involves a lot more than knowing the festival *Kiddush*. To get there, how we teach makes a huge difference.

> Every person you meet deeply desires to be treated with respect. If you listen carefully, you will hear their cry: "Please consider me an important person." "Don't embarrass or insult me." "Please listen to me when I speak."
>
> Rabbi Yeruchem Levovitz, Da'at Hokhmah u'Mussar, vol. 3, p. 68

Jewish teaching begins with listening. It begins with respect and caring. It begins with a commitment to building community. Technology and our students' technological nature have a possibility of being useful in this endeavor, but electronics will not do the job for us. Tools never will. No overhead transparency ever made the impact of a teacher listening to students with great respect and appreciation. The truth is that Jewish life takes a community, and community starts with individual friendships. And luckily enough, Judaism believes in teaching through friendships.

> A friend is someone you eat and drink with.
> A friend is someone with whom you study Torah (God's word)
> and with whom you study Mishnah (ethics and laws).
> A friend is someone who sleeps over
> or at whose house you can spend the night.
> Friends teach each other secrets,
> the secrets of the Torah
> and secrets of the real world, too. (*Avot d'Rabbi Natan*)

The secret to successful Jewish teaching hasn't changed much, and technology makes little impact on the fact that pre-schoolers sometimes cry when their parents leave them for the first time; that fourteen-year-olds are angry at not being old enough; that third graders like to get the right answers. We teach students with human needs, and as we meet those needs we build connection and begin community. The truth is that rather than believing we can use technology to open the heart of the Jewish tradition, we can use the Jewish tradition to open our students' hearts and heal their brokenness in a way that technology never can.

REFERENCES

Buber, M. (1970). *I and Thou*. New York: Charles Scribner's Sons.

Kaye, T. "Making Your School a Teacher-Friendly Place." *Jewish Education News* 28 (1), 16–17

Lasch, C. (1991). *Culture of Narcissism: American Life in An Age of Diminishing Expectations*. New York: W. W. Norton & Company.

Eisen, A. & Cohen, S. (2000). *The Jew Within: Self, Family, and Community in America*. Bloomington, IN: Indiana University Press.

Learners

The Demography of Jewish Learners

Bruce Phillips

Demography and education are intimately linked. When the population of children grows, school districts have to find ways to accommodate them. Children from middle class families have to be taught differently than children from low-income families. Many urban school districts in the West and Southwest face the special challenge of children who are not native speakers of English. While the field of Jewish education does not face these types of challenges, Jewish demography is no less important for Jewish education than for education in general. This chapter will examine the implications of Jewish demography for Jewish education.

As both a sociologist and a demographer with over three decades of experience, I have conducted and/or analyzed over a dozen local Jewish population surveys and served on the National Technical Advisory Committee for both the 1990 and 2000 National Jewish Population Surveys. The principal area of my research since 1990 has been intermarriage, which is a growing phenomenon that impacts all aspects of Jewish life, including Jewish education. "Jewish demography" as a field encompasses more than just the classical demographic variables such as fertility, family formation, divorce, and migration. "Jewish demography" has come to mean the quantitative study of American Jews, including non-demographic subjects such as Jewish identity, affiliation, friendship networks, and religious observance.

Tobin's chapter on Jewish demography in *What We Know about Jewish Education* (Kelman 1992) was limited to data from local studies. This time we have the benefit of national data from the National Jewish Population Survey conducted in 2000–2001 (referred to as "NJPS"). This chapter draws heavily on national data from the NJPS while also looking at important findings from several local Jewish population studies. The first section of this chapter reviews the analyses done on the Jewish education of respondents with an emphasis on changing patterns over the past few decades and the impact of Jewish education on adult Jewish behaviors and Jewish identity. The second section examines the NJPS data on Jewish education for children under eighteen years of age, including a revised estimate of enrollment in different types of Jewish education based on methodological considerations. The third section focuses on the impact of intermarriage on Jewish education.

THE JEWISH EDUCATION OF ADULTS IN THE NJPS

THE NATIONAL JEWISH POPULATION SURVEY

The 2000–2001 National Jewish Population Survey was a telephone survey of over 4,500 respondents randomly selected to represent the entire United States Jewish population (Kotler-Berowitz, Cohen et al. 2003). For the NJPS report, a Jew was defined as a person:

- whose religion is Jewish, OR
- whose religion is Jewish and something else, OR
- who has no religion and has at least one Jewish parent or a Jewish upbringing, OR
- who has a non-monotheistic religion and has at least one Jewish parent or a Jewish upbringing.

The NJPS has been criticized for its low response rate, including specific problems with regard to Jewish education, which are discussed below. Nonetheless, even its sharpest critics agree that the NJPS 2000 is a valuable tool for examining the interrelationships among variables (Kadushin, Phillips et al. 2006). That, of course, includes looking at factors associated with Jewish education.

CHANGING TRENDS IN JEWISH EDUCATION

Cohen's analysis of the Jewish educational background of adults provides an encapsulated overview of changing patterns of Jewish education over recent decades (Cohen 2004). Cohen analyzed NJPS respondents who reported that at least one of their parents was partially Jewish and/or reported some evidence of having been raised Jewish. By dividing adult respondents into five age cohorts (18–34, 35–49, 50–64, 65–74, and 75+) Cohen was able to reconstruct the history of Jewish education enrollment over several decades. For example, a 50-year-old respondent in the NJPS would have been 13 years of age in 1963, a 65-year-old respondent in 1948, and a 75-year-old in 1938. By comparing older with younger cohorts Cohen produced a longitudinal narrative of change. The three most dramatic changes Cohen found were that: 1) Differences between men and women gradually disappeared so that the Jewish education of men and women ages 18–34 are virtually the same; 2) Day school attendance increased for both genders; but 3) The proportion of male respondents with no Jewish education increased over time even as it decreased among women.

Jewish education patterns vary by region and denomination. Jews living in the Northeast have the strongest Jewish education backgrounds and Jews living in the West the weakest. Jews living in the Northeast report day school attendance at twice the rate of those living in the Midwest, South, and West. Mirroring the lower affiliation rates overall, a greater proportion of Jews living in the West than in the three other regions had no Jewish education at all.

Denominational patterns of Jewish education are consistent with historical emphases of the three major movements. Respondents raised Orthodox attended day school at far higher rates than those raised Conservative or Reform. Respondents raised Conservative reported the highest rates of education in a 2–3 day/week school, and those raised in the Reform movement attended 2–3 day/week and one day/week schools equally. The vast majority (over 90%) of respondents raised in a denomination reported some kind of childhood Jewish education. Conversely, respondents raised in no denomination were the most likely to report no Jewish education at all.

THE IMPACT OF JEWISH EDUCATION

Cohen and Kotler-Berkowitz (Cohen & Kotler-Berkowitz 2004) examined the impact of childhood Jewish education on adult Jewish identification, observance, affiliation, and intermarriage among respondents born after 1951. They found that a day school education was more strongly predictive of in-marriage and Jewish identification than the 2–3 day/week program, which in turn was more predictive than a one-day-a-week school. Informal Jewish education such as camping, youth groups and trips to Israel also increased in-marriage and Jewish identification.

Phillips found a similar but slightly different result for intermarriage controlling for generation and Jewish parentage rather than age. For respondents with two American-born Jewish parents, the type of education was less important than continuing beyond the age of bar/bat mitzvah. Respondents with two American-born Jewish parents who ended their Jewish education at the age of bar/bat mitzvah intermarried at essentially the same rate regardless of the type of Jewish education received (31% for day school, 32% for 2–3 day/week school, and 33% for 1 day/week school). Moreover, this rate was the same as for respondents with no Jewish education at all (33%). By contrast, respondents with two American-born Jewish parents who continued beyond bar/bat mitzvah intermarried at much lower rates: 2% for day school and 22% for congregational school (1 day or 2–3 days/week). Similar but less dramatic results were found for foreign-born respondents and respondents with at least one foreign-born parent because they intermarry at lower rates to begin with.

CONTINUING BEYOND BAR/BAT MITZVAH

Jewish educators are painfully familiar with the phenomenon of "post-bar/bat mitzvah dropping out." Phillips and Zeldin measured its extent twenty years ago using local Jewish population surveys (Phillips & Zeldin 1987), but there has been no statistical analysis of the issue since that time. The 2000–2001 NJPS provides an opportunity to see if the situation has changed. Adopting the approach taken by Cohen described above, the NJPS questions on the Jewish education of respondents can be used to examine the cessation of Jewish education at the age of bar/bat mitzvah over several decades. The dropout rate decreased over time, but not by much, from 56% among 65–74-year-olds to 44% among 18–34-year-olds. If only respondents with two Jewish parents are considered, the picture looks a little better: the dropout rates falls from 54% to 39% for these same age cohort comparisons.

Looking at all respondents, day school graduates were the most likely to continue formal Jewish schooling beyond bar/bat mitzvah (84%) as compared with no more than half for respondents who attended 2–3-day-a-week or one-day-a-week schools. The vast majority (82%) of respondents raised Orthodox continued beyond bar mitzvah as compared with 54% for respondents raised in the Conservative movement and 48% for respondents raised in the Reform movement.

JEWISH EDUCATION OF CHILDREN UNDER 18

The NJPS publication on the Jewish education of children (Kotler-Berkowitz 2005) contained very good news about Jewish education for children. Kotler-Berkowitz reported that 72% of Jewish children whose religion is Judaism, who are being raised Jewish or who are considered Jewish are currently receiving a Jewish education and that: "The type of program with the largest current enrollments is day school/yeshiva… (27% of the total)…." He further noted that "When parents are in-married (i.e., married to another Jew), children are highly likely (86%) to be receiving some kind of Jewish education, including nearly 40% at day schools…" (page 16). The 27% of Jewish children receiving a day school education represents a 10 percentage–point increase over the 18% of adults 18–34 who reported receiving a day school education. The Partnership for Excellence in Jewish Education quickly relayed this "exciting evidence of day school growth" (PEJE 2003). Unfortunately this encouraging finding appears to be an overestimate because of missing data about Jewish education.

METHODOLOGICAL ISSUES IN THE NJPS THAT AFFECT JEWISH EDUCATION DATA

Jewish education questions in population surveys are typically asked about each child in the household, but this was not done in the NJPS 2000–2001. The NJPS conserved resources by asking Jewish education questions about a randomly selected child in the house. This child is referred to as the "selected child." The analysis is weighted by the total number of children in the household to compensate for the children not included in the Jewish education questions. The rationale for this unusual approach was that the NJPS sample was so large that there would be ample cases for analysis.

There were four categories of missing data (Table 1). The first was a contradiction between answers to two different questions. Early in the questionnaire the respondent was asked the type of schooling the child was receiving, and much later the Jewish education questions were asked. There were 22 interviews in which the respondent stated that the child was in public school but later said that the child was enrolled in a full-time Jewish day school or yeshiva. These 22 cases (representing almost 22,000 children) account for 4% of children being raised in Judaism. They were dropped from the Jewish education analysis because of this contradiction. If it is assumed that they were either not receiving a Jewish education or receiving some other kind, the percent in day school would drop to 25% from 27%.

The second category of missing data is that the child was being raised in an Eastern/New Age religion or in no religion and not being raised Jewish or considered Jewish. Jewish education questions were not asked about such children on the assumption that the answer would be no. The third category of missing data is that the respondent refused to answer either the Jewish education questions or the religion question that qualified the child for the Jewish education questions. There were only a small number of such cases, and all surveys experience some refusals to individual questions.

The fourth category of missing data is that the Jewish education questions were skipped for children who might have qualified for them. A programming error discovered after the survey was in the field caused some Jewish education questions to be skipped, but the questions analyzed here were not reported to be among those affected (NJPS 2004). One reason the Jewish education questions were skipped was that the respondent was classified a "Person of Jewish Background" (PJB). These respondents (almost all of whom were raised in an intermarried family) identified either with an Eastern or New Age religion or as a Christian (Phillips 2005). In response to a follow-up question these respondents said that they did not "consider" themselves Jewish, although they may have interpreted "Jewish" to mean "Judaism" specifically. Another reason the Jewish education questions were skipped was that the child was being raised either as nothing or in a New Age/Eastern religion, and the rationale for considering the selected child was not considered sufficient to warrant asking the Jewish education questions. There were multiple questions regarding how the child was being raised and considered Jewish (if not being raised in Judaism), but not all positive answers were considered sufficient. These mostly apply to children of intermarried parents (Phillips & Kotler-Berkowitz 2007). If a more liberal criterion were applied, the total number of "Jewish" children would have increased, and the percentage in day school would thereby decrease. In many cases it is not clear why the Jewish education questions were skipped for seemingly eligible children. Whatever the reason, these children were not included in the Jewish education figures. If it is assumed that such children were not in day school (since they were not considered Jewish enough to have been included in the Jewish education section of the questionnaire), then the percentage enrolled in day school drops to 20%. In an independent analysis of the NJPS and the Avi Chai study, Saxe of the Steinhardt Social Research Institute at Brandeis University similarly concluded that "it is unlikely that the day school population is as large a proportion as suggested by NJPS" (Saxe, Tighe et al. 2007).

Table 2 compares my revised estimates with those published in the NJPS report. The NJPS estimates regarding the absolute number of children were compared with a Jewish education census conducted in 2000 for the Avi Chai Foundation (Schick 2000). The estimated number of children currently enrolled in each form of Jewish education was remarkably similar in the NJPS and the Avi Chai study (UJC nd). The percentage adjustments result from categorizing the children for whom data were not collected either in congregational Jewish education (in the case of contradictory day school answers) or as not enrolled (children not being raised in Judaism). In other words, the number of children in day school remains the same, but I have increased the total number of children used as the basis for the percentages from 500,000 (Kotler-Berkowitz 2005) to 683,000. The children I have added to the total are the children of intermarried parents who are being raised in no religion (or in an Eastern/New Age religion). Adults of partial Jewish parentage who identified with "no religion" or an Eastern/New Age religion were included in the Jewish population count, and I have merely applied the same criterion to children in the household. There are about 200,000 such children over all and 183,000 between the ages of 6 and 17. As a result of adding these children to the total, the percentage enrolled in both formal Jewish education and day school declines.

Table 1: Missing Data for by Religion of Selected Child (Children Ages 6–17)

Religion of the selected child	Category of missing data				
	Contradictory answers to day school questions	Respondent refused to answer	Selected child not raised Jewish, question not asked	Jewish education questions skipped	Total missing data
Jewish or Judaism	4%	1%	0%	7%	11%
Dual Religion*	0%	0%	0%	9%	9%
No religion, child raised/considered Jewish	0%	0%	0%	16%	16%
Jewish and Eastern/New Age religion, child raised/considered Jewish	0%	0%	0%	0%	0%
Eastern/New Age religion, but not raised/considered Jewish	0%	0%	100%	0%	100%
No religion—but not raised/considered Jewish	0%	0%	100%	0%	100%
Christian—not raised/considered Jewish	0%	0%	99%	0%	99%
Refused religion questions	0%	0%	0%	100%	100%
All selected children ages 6–17	2%	<½%	47%	6%	54%

*This category includes children being raised in Judaism and Christianity as well as children raised Christian but considered Jewish or partially Jewish by the respondent.

Table 2: Jewish Education of Children Ages 6–17 Being Raised as Jews–Revised vs. Reported

Jewish Education—Current Enrollment	Revised	NJPS Report

Enrolled in any type of Jewish education	**62%**	**72%**
1/week program	19%	20%
2+/week program	16%	22%
A full-time Jewish day school or yeshiva	20%	27%
Tutoring or other	3%	3%
Inconsistent answer to day school question, assumed to be in some other form of Jewish education	3%	excluded
Not enrolled in any type of Jewish education	**39%**	**28%**
Not Enrolled	31%	28%
Questions not asked, probably not enrolled	8%	excluded
TOTAL	100%	100%

Table 3 presents data from five communities that conducted population surveys within a few years of the 2000–01 NJPS to illustrate the wide range of inter-communal differences. Jewish education enrollment overall is highest in New York (77%), followed closely by Baltimore (66%) and Chicago (64%). Enrollment is considerably lower in Tucson (39%) and San Francisco (35%). Day school enrollment varies even more dramatically by community. In New York, day school is by far the predominant form of Jewish education; two-thirds of all Jewish children and 86% of all currently enrolled children were receiving a day school education. In Baltimore 36% of all Jewish children and 55% of all currently enrolled children were in day school. In Chicago, however, day school was somewhat less prevalent: 17% of all Jewish children and 27% of currently enrolled Jewish children were receiving a day school education. In Tucson and San Francisco, less than 10% of Jewish children were enrolled in a day school, but this low figure is somewhat misleading, since enrollment was relatively low in both these communities. The impact of day school in these two communities becomes more apparent when only enrolled children are considered. Almost one out of four (23%) currently enrolled children in San Francisco and Tucson was receiving a day school education.

Identifying the factors that explain communal differences is beyond the scope of this analysis, but such a list would probably include the size of the Orthodox population, the number and diversity of existing day schools and communal support for day schools. Jewish educators and federation planners should be aware that national data do not necessarily apply to their own communities and should study local population surveys where available.

Table 3: Jewish Education of Children Ages 6–17 Being Raised as Jews in NJPS and Selected Communities

	NY 2002	Baltimore 1999 **	Chicago *	Tucson 2002 ***	San Francisco 2003 *
Enrolled in any type of Jewish education	**77%**	**66%**	**64%**	**39%**	**35%**
Jewish Full Time Day School Now	66%	36%	17%	9%	8%
Supplementary Jewish Education Now	12%	30%	46%	29%	27%
Not enrolled in any type of Jewish education	**39%**	**33%**	**36%**	**61%**	**65%**
Jewish Education in Past	19%	23%	22%	Not available	30%
No Jewish Education	16%	11%	14%		35%
TOTAL	**100%**	**100%**	**100%**	**100%**	**100%**

(Ukeles, Miller et al. 2001)   * Data run by author   * (Sheskin 2002) % calculated from reported

PREDICTORS OF JEWISH EDUCATIONAL ENROLLMENT

Even with the problem of missing data, it is still possible to examine who gives their child a Jewish education. Kotler-Berkowitz examined factors associated with the current enrollment of Jewish children (Kotler-Berkowitz 2005). Three important demographic factors emerged:

- The higher the parents' income, the higher the rate of current enrollment.
- Single parents are significantly less likely to have children enrolled in Jewish education than "intact" couples.
- Jewish education enrollment is lowest in the West.

The likelihood that a child will receive a Jewish education is strongly influenced by the Jewish education of his or her parents. Respondents with a day school education were the most likely to give their children a Jewish education, followed (in order) by those who had a 2–3 day/week education, a one day/week education, and no Jewish education. Respondents who continued beyond the age of bar/bat mitzvah were more likely to enroll their children in a Jewish school than those who had not.

GENERATIONAL CHANGES IN JEWISH EDUCATION

Cohen's analysis of adult Jewish education (2004) discussed above-grouped respondents by age to reconstruct changing Jewish education patterns over the past six decades. I take a similar but alternative approach using Cohen's basic logic. Rather than look at age cohorts, as Cohen has done, Table 4 presents a three-generation profile comparing the Jewish education of current children with that of their parents and grandparents. The child generation consists of the randomly selected child age 6–17 in the household. The parental generation consists of respondents between 25 and 59. This age cutoff was used because virtually all the parents with a biological or adopted child in the household were 59 or younger. The "grandparent" generation consists of respondents 60 years of age and older. To be consistent with Cohen's study, the same criteria were used here. The analysis was restricted to respondents "who reported that at least one of their parents was at least partially Jewish and/or reported some evidence of having been raised Jewish (or Jewish and another religion)." As Cohen notes (page 4), this criteria covers 95% of all the respondents. Table 4 includes two categories for the "parents" generation. The first category, "parent of selected child," refers to the actual parents of children in Table 2. The second category consists of the parental generation (i.e., all respondents aged 18–59), whether or not they have children in the household.

Unlike Table 2, which reported *current* enrollment, Table 4 reports the highest form of Jewish education *ever* received. This variable adds the previous type of Jewish education received for children not currently enrolled to make the question comparable with the adult data. Table 4 shows that today's Jewish children are both more and less educated than their parents and grandparents. They are more educated in terms of day school. Only 5% of the grandparents' generation and 9% of the parents' generation received a day school education. For reasons beyond the scope of this analysis, the actual parents of children ages 6–17 were more likely than all respondents under 60 to have received a day school education (13% vs. 9%). Nonetheless, their own children were more likely than they to have received a day school education (23% vs. 13%). The increase in day school enrollment becomes more apparent as a percentage of all Jewish education enrollments. A third (32%) of current Jewish children who have ever been enrolled have received a day school education (either currently or in the past), more than double the rate for their actual parents (15%). The increase in day school enrollment, then, has been at the expense of supplementary school enrollment. The percentage receiving no Jewish education decreased from the grandparents' generation to the parents' generation (26% to 18%), but it increases again among current children to 27%. As will be demonstrated later, this is the result of intermarriage.

Table 4: Jewish Education by Generation

	GENERATION			
		PARENT		
Highest Jewish education received	CHILD*	Parent of se-lected child	All Respondents (18–59)	GRANDPARENT (60+)
Day School	23	13	9	5
Supplementary or other	50	72	73	69
None	27	16	18	26
Total	100	100	100	100
% of all ever enrolled who have attended day school	32%	15%	11%	7%

* Based on Selected Child age 6–17

The growth of day schools in the NJPS is also evident in enrollment statistics. The number of students enrolled in Jewish day schools tripled between 1962 and the end of the century (JESNA 2003). Eighty new day schools opened their doors in the five years between 1998 and 2003, and enrollment grew by 11% in this time period alone (Schick 2005).

Beyond day schools, another important indicator of the growing intensity of Jewish education for the most committed is the correspondence between adult Jewish education and enrollment of their own children. Half the respondents with children currently enrolled in Jewish education reported participating in some kind of adult Jewish education during the previous year as compared with only 13% of respondents whose children were not currently enrolled (data not shown). This speaks of the parents' commitment to Jewish education and suggests interesting possibilities for family education.

THE ECONOMICS OF DAY SCHOOLS

Day schools, despite their dramatic growth, remain costly, and some recent studies have examined the impact of cost on day school enrollment. In the spring of 2003 Schick (2003) surveyed 88 day schools to assess the impact of the recent economic downturn. He reported that "The responses show clearly that schools feel that they have been hurt. Only four of the 88 schools said that there had been little or no impact. Furthermore, fully 60% said that the impact of the economic situation was 'considerable.'" Wertheimer has similarly observed that "Due to budgetary constraints, day schools often skimp on upgrading salary and benefit packages for faculty and staff, developing effective curricula, providing faculty enrichment, and purchasing and maintaining technology" (Wertheimer 2001).

The cost of day schools is strongly related to enrollment. In San Francisco, for example, parents earning above the median income for Jewish households were more than ten times as likely to enroll their children in a day school as those earning below the median income. Further, one out of five parents earning less than the median Jewish income reported that cost had been an obstacle to sending a child to a day school (data not shown).

Although parental commitment to Jewish education is a strong motivation underlying day school enrollment, day schools operate in a competitive environment and should also be understood from the perspective of "school choice." The San Francisco Jewish Population Survey (Phillips 2005) looked at consumer choices with regard to day school. Respondents who did not have children in day school were asked what factors led them to enroll their children in private or public schools. Many respondents rejected day schools out of hand, mostly because they were ideologically committed to public schools or to diversity. Among those respondents who were not ideologically opposed to day schools, cost was the number one consideration cited, but a "school choice" factor was equally important. Respondents were just as likely to cite the perceived academic quality of day schools as a reason for not considering them. An analysis of the 1997 Los Angeles Jewish

Population Survey demonstrated the impact of the competitive environment (Phillips 2006). Parents living in the City of Los Angeles, with its notoriously poor school district, were more likely to choose either day school or private school over public school than parents who live in better school districts. Economics, then, impacts day school growth in three demonstrable ways:

- Difficult economic periods strain day school resources.
- Lower-income households are less able to afford day school.
- Day schools compete with both public and private schools, especially among the non–Orthodox.

THE CHALLENGE OF INTERMARRIAGE

Intermarriage has now become the norm, at least as far as Jewish children are concerned. More Jewish children under age 18 have one non–Jewish parent than have two Jewish parents (51% vs. 49%), and only two of five Jewish children (39%) currently live with two Jewish parents (Table 5). In other words, what once was the "typical" Jewish family consisting of two Jewish parents living together with their children is now the exception rather than the rule. As will be seen shortly, there are important differences between currently intact and dissolved intermarriages. The focus here is on the current family status. Looking at patterns of remarriage (e.g., in-married Jews who divorce and remarry non–Jews) is beyond the scope of this analysis.

Table 5: Family Situation of Jewish Children (all children under 18 years of age)

Jewish parent is:	%
Currently in-married	39
Previously in-married*	10
Currently intermarried	39
Previously intermarried	12
Total	100

* and currently single. Some currently in-married parents may have been previously intermarried and vice versa.

HOW CHILDREN ARE RAISED

Much of the debate about the impact of intermarriage has focused on the ambiguities of how children are being raised (Cohen 2006). The impact of intermarriage on the Jewish future is typically discussed in terms of how many of the children are "raised as Jews." The NJPS asked in what religion each child in the household was being raised. If the child was not being raised in Judaism, the respondent was asked if the child was considered Jewish, and on what basis. Thus there are multiple criteria for deciding whether or not a child is being "raised as a Jew." In this analysis only children being raised in Judaism are considered as being raised Jewish because children being raised in no religion, even if the parent considers them Jewish in some way, will not receive a formal Jewish education (data not shown). Thus the number of such children being raised in Judaism will decide the future size of the Jewish school population.

Virtually every child with in-married parents is being raised in Judaism, as are most children with a previously in-married Jewish parent (Table 6). Although more than a third of children with a currently intermarried Jewish parent are being raised "as Jews" in some way, less than a quarter are being raised specifically in Judaism. Intermarried Jewish mothers are more likely than intermarried Jewish fathers to report raising their children in Judaism, and Jewish mothers divorced from a non–Jewish father are more likely to report raising a child in Judaism than currently intermarried Jewish mothers (43% vs. 29%). Overall less than two-thirds (60%) of all Jewish children (i.e., all children considered Jewish in some way) are being raised in Judaism.

Table 6: Children being raised in Judaism by gender of Jewish Parent and Current Marital Status (adopted and biological children only).

Gender and Current Marital Status of Intermarried Jewish Parent	Child being raised in Judaism
Currently in-married	96%
Previously in-married*	95%
Previously Intermarried Jewish **mother**	43%
Currently Intermarried Jewish **mother**	29%
Previously Intermarried Jewish **father**	18%
Currently Intermarried Jewish **father**	*
All biological and adopted children	60%

* too few cases because the mother apparently has custody of the child.

INTERMARRIAGE AND ENROLLMENT

Raising children in Judaism generally translates into Jewish educational enrollment, but with important variations. Table 7 reports the percentage of children receiving a Jewish education according to how they are raised and the intermarried status of the parents. The first column reports whether or not the parents are intermarried. The second column reports the religion in which the child is being raised. The third column gives the percentage currently enrolled. Virtually all in-married parents raise their children in Judaism (Table 6), and most of those children (81%) receive a Jewish education (Table 7, row 1). A minority of intermarried couples were raising their children in Judaism: 29% of intermarried Jewish mothers and 18% of intermarried Jewish fathers did so (Table 6), but they are serious about it: two-thirds (68%) of children being raised as Jews in an intermarriage were enrolled in a Jewish school (Table 7, row 2). By contrast 17% of children being raised Jewish and Christian and only 4% of children being raised outside of Judaism were enrolled in a Jewish school .

Children of single parents were less likely to receive a Jewish education than children from intact families. Among in-marriages, only half (51%) of children with two divorced Jewish parents were receiving a Jewish education as compared with 81% of children from intact in-marriages. Among intermarriages, children being raised in Judaism by a previously intermarried single parent were less likely to be enrolled in a Jewish school than children being raised in Judaism in families where the non–Jewish spouse was present (55% vs. 68%). Divorce seems to bring about a return to Judaism for children raised in two religions. A previously intermarried Jewish parent who was raising a child in two religions is twice as likely as currently intermarried parents to give that child a Jewish education (38% vs. 17%). While the religion of the Christian ex-spouse is apparently honored in how the child is raised, the custodial Jewish parent (who almost always is the mother) has apparently returned the child to Judaism via Jewish education as a result of the divorce; it may be that the divorce was the result of the religious differences.

Jewish educators should be sensitive to these potential family dynamics as they affect the child. It is noteworthy and even encouraging that between 17% and 38% of dual-religion children were receiving a Jewish education. On the other hand, the dual-religion child presents unique challenges to the teacher in the classroom and to the Jewish school. Jewish educators need to be aware of such children in their classrooms and the tensions inherent in being raised in two faiths.

Table 7: Jewish Education of Selected Child by Religion of Child and Intermarriage (adopted and biological children only).

Jewish parent is:	Religion of Child	% receiving a Jewish education
Currently in-married	Judaism	81%
Currently Intermarried	Judaism	68%
Previously Intermarried	Judaism	55%
Previously in-married	Judaism	51%
Previously Intermarried	Jewish & Christian	38%
Currently Intermarried	Jewish & Christian	17%
Currently Intermarried	Raised Jewish, but not in Judaism	4%

FOUR TYPES OF INTERMARRIAGE

Based on the religious commitments of the respective parents, there are four types of intermarriages. As Table 8 details, the respective religious commitments of intermarried Jews and non–Jews have a profound impact on how the children are raised and whether they will receive a Jewish education. Religion was specified in a question on current religion. Judaism means that the respondent specified Judaism as his or her current religion. Conversely, "Christian" means that the respondent named a specific denomination or church, such as Roman Catholics, Eastern Orthodox Catholics, Presbyterians, Methodists, Episcopalians, Baptists, Nazarenes, and so on. "Secular" means that the respondent or spouse indicated they were an atheist, agnostic, or had "no religion." Included in the "secular" category are the few cases in which either respondent or spouse identified with an Eastern or New Age religion. There were too few such cases to form a discrete category. Logically they could be combined with Christians in an "other religion" category, and this is how they were handled in the NJPS 1990. They differ from Christian Jews in three important ways. First, Christians were raised as such, and New Age persons (Jews and non–Jews alike) either abandoned the religion they were raised in or (more commonly) were raised secular. Second, the Eastern and New Age religions in the NJPS lack an established institutional structure. Pagans, Wiccans, and Earth worshippers do not have the organizational structure of Episcopalians, Methodists, and Catholics. These typical New Age religions are as much life styles and philosophies as they are ecclesial. Like secularists, New Age Jews and non–Jews are *outside* the religious mainstream of American society. Finally, when it comes to Christian religious observance, New Age and Eastern religion Jews are much closer to seculars than they are to Christians. At any rate, there were too few such cases to have much statistical impact on the analysis.

The four types of intermarriage are: 1) The "Judaic" intermarriage is comprised of a Jew by religion married to a secular non–Jew. In the "Judaic" intermarriage, Judaism is the only religion in the household. 2) The "Dual Religion" intermarriage consists of a Jew by religion married to a spouse identified as a Christian. 3) In the "Secular" intermarriage neither partner identifies with any religion, but the Jewish partner identifies as a Jew in terms of ethnicity, parentage, or ancestry. 4) The "Christian" intermarriage consists of a secular Jew married to an identified Christian.

The intermarried are less likely than the in-married Jews to raise their children in Judaism or to provide them with a Jewish education, but the patterns differ according to the type of intermarriage. "Judaic" intermarriages (Jews by religion married to secular non–Jews) are the most likely both to raise their children in Judaism and to give their children a Jewish education. One might expect the Christian spouse in a "Dual Religion" intermarriage to require equality in how the children are raised, but this was not the case. Almost as many children in "Dual Religion" intermarriages were receiving a Jewish education (34%) as in "Judaic" intermarriages (37%). A parent who is Jewish by religion is the important predictor of how children were being raised. Children with a secular Jewish parent were only rarely raised in Judaism or given a Jewish education, regardless of whether the non–Jewish spouse was secular or a practicing Christian. Only 2 percent of children with a secular Jewish parent married to a secular non–Jew were raised in Judaism. This is hardly different than the secular Jews married to Christians, none of whom raised their children in Judaism. This pattern is entirely consistent with the respondent's professed religious outlook. Why would parents raise a child in a religion not their own? Secular Jews, after all, have "no religion."

Table 8: Religion and Jewish Education of Child by Religion of Each Parent (adopted and biological children only)

Type of Intermarriage	Religion of Jewish Parent	Religion of non–Jewish Parent	Child being raised in Judaism (all children)[1]	Child being raised in Judaism (selected child)	% receiving a Jewish education (selected child)
JUDAIC	Judaism	Secular[2]	53%	53%	37%
DUAL RELIGION	Judaism	Christian	41%	47%	34%
SECULAR	Secular	Secular	3%	2%	2%
CHRISTIAN	Secular	Christian	0%	0%	0%

The discussion so far has looked at the national level. Local studies provide a different vantage point for understanding the children of intermarried parents. Consistent with the NJPS, the recently completed San Francisco Jewish population study found that the children of intermarriages were much less likely to receive a Jewish education than the children of in-marriages. Of all children ages 6–17, 78% of those with in-married parents had received some kind of Jewish education as compared with only 39% of those with intermarried parents (Phillips 2005). However, when the analysis is restricted to only those children being raised in Judaism, the picture changes (Table 9). Fully 82% of children with a non–Jewish parent had received a Jewish education at some point if they were being raised in Judaism (slightly higher than the 78% of children with in-married Jewish parents).

Unfortunately, the children of intermarriages left Jewish education earlier, even if they were being raised in Judaism. Children of intermarriages raised in Judaism between the ages of 6 and 8 were equally as likely as children with two Jewish parents to be receiving a Jewish education. Comparing the 6–8 and 9–12 age categories, enrollment increases from 48% to 62% for children with two Jewish parents but declines from 50% to 44% for children with one Jewish parent. The contrast is even more striking for the 13–17 age cohort: 37% of children with two Jewish parents were enrolled in Jewish education as compared with only 2% of children with one Jewish parent. It is not known why the children of intermarried parents left Jewish education earlier, but it is possible that either their parents were giving Jewish education a try or were using formal Jewish education to give their children at least a minimal exposure to Judaism. Because affiliation is lower in Western Jewish communities such as San Francisco, these findings are particularly salient. The children of intermarriage being raised in Judaism do appear in Jewish schools, but as they get older they are less likely to be found there. The challenge is less how to get these children into Jewish schools than it is to keep them there.

Table 9: Current Enrollment in Jewish Education for <u>Children Raised in Judaism</u> by Age of Child and Intermarriage of Parents, San Francisco, 2004 (% currently enrolled)

Age of Child	Jewish Parent Is Currently	
	In-married	Intermarried
6–8	48%	50%
9–12	62%	44%
13–17	37%	2%

THE IMPACT OF INTERMARRIAGE ON THE NUMBER OF CHILDREN RAISED IN JUDAISM

Two Jews married to each other make one family, but two Jews married to non–Jews create two families. Thus intermarriage has the potential to increase the number of Jewish children. A sense of this change can be inferred by dividing children in the household into two 8-year cohorts, 0–9 and 9–16 (Table 10). Comparing the younger to the older cohort can be used as an indication of changes taking place in the composition of the Jewish population. The total number of children increases by 20% from the 9–16 age cohort to the 0–8 cohort, but the number of children raised or considered Jewish by the respondent increases by only 4%. This is due to the increase among children considered Jewish but not being raised in Judaism from 102,000 in the 9–17 cohort to 137,000 in the 0–8 cohort.

As shown above, it is only children raised in Judaism that are at all likely to appear in a Jewish school, and intermarriage will slowly reduce the size of this population. The number of children raised in Judaism decreases by 4% from 367,000 in the older cohort to 351,000 in the younger cohort. The potential market for Jewish education will thus decrease steadily unless at least one of three changes occurs:

1. More intermarried parents raise their children in Judaism.

2. Intermarried parents raising their children "as Jews" but not in Judaism choose to provide them with a Jewish education (almost none do this currently).

3. More intermarried parents already raising their children in Judaism choose to give them a Jewish education.

Of these three scenarios, increasing enrollment among children being raised in Judaism has the greatest chance of success. Since almost a third of the children currently or previously enrolled in congregational Jewish schooling have a non–Jewish parent (data not shown), much can be learned from these families as to why and how they made this choice. The second scenario raises an interesting question: Can and should Jewish educators create programs for Jewish children being raised in no religion who are nonetheless considered Jewish in some way by their Jewish parent?

Table 10: Comparison of Children in Two Equal Age Cohorts, NJPS 2000

How child is regarded by parent	Religion of child	Age of child		Absolute difference	% growth or decline
		0-8	9-16		
Considered Jewish	Jewish or Judaism	350,999	366,570	-15,571	-4%
	Secular, but considered Jewish	76,721	61,804	14,917	24%
	Jew + Christian	60,096	40,360	19,736	49%
	Subtotal-Not Jewish by religion	136,817	102,164	34,653	34%
	Subtotal, children considered Jewish	487,816	468,734	19,082	4%
Not considered Jewish		482,032	342,334	139,698	41%
Total children		969,848	811,068	158,780	20%

LOCAL GEOGRAPHY AND INTERMARRIAGES

Local studies show that intermarried families have distinct residential patterns with important implications for Jewish schools. In the Los Angeles, Chicago, and San Francisco metropolitan areas, intermarried families with children were concentrated in the newer (and less expensive) suburbs farther away from the established Jewish population centers. In Chicago, for example, they were most concentrated in the newer "Northwest suburbs" adjacent to the older, more expensive, and more Jewishly engaged " North Shore" suburbs (Phillips nd). In Los Angeles, intermarried couples with children were dispersed throughout areas of low Jewish density such as the Conejo, Simi, and Santa Clarita valleys (Phillips 2007). In the San Francisco metropolitan area, more than 80% of children in Marin and Sonoma counties had intermarried parents (Phillips, 2005). Thus Jewish schools will be affected by intermarriage in different ways, depending on where they are located.

IMPLICATIONS AND POLICY RECOMMENDATIONS

SOURCES OF DATA

There is little chance that the United Jewish Communities will sponsor another National Jewish Population Survey in 2010 or anytime thereafter (Berkman 2006). Thus future demographic research on Jewish education will have to come from local studies. Jewish educators in communities contemplating such studies should be prepared to lobby for more extensive Jewish education questions than are currently the norm for such studies. Furthermore, researchers interested in quantitative data about the extent of Jewish education should be prepared to work with local studies. Fortunately, these studies are available through the North American Jewish Data Bank at the University of Connecticut (*www.Jewishdatabank.org*).

TODAY'S JEWISH PARENTS ARE DIFFERENT

The parents of children enrolled in Jewish schools today have a better Jewish educational background than their own parents. Studies indicate that a significant proportion of parents are furthering their own Jewish education as adults, a trend that runs counter to previous generations. Thus the decision to provide a child with a Jewish education includes a greater degree of Jewish commitment than was the case fifty years ago. Jewish educators should find out more about the Jewish backgrounds of their parent populations and explore ways to involve these parents in the Jewish education of their children.

THE DROPOUT RATE AND POST- BAR/BAT MITZVAH JEWISH EDUCATION

The post-bar/bat mitzvah dropout rate in Jewish education has declined in recent decades, but it has not been a steep decline. Given the importance of Jewish experiences in the teenage years, holding on to Jewish youth should be given a higher and specific priority. One such strategy, in the words of Wertheimer, is to "link the silos" of various Jewish educational experiences (Wertheimer 2005).

INTERMARRIAGE

The Jewish family has undergone a fundamental change. Students in Jewish schools are as likely to have a non–Jewish parent as two Jewish parents. This extends even to single parents whose ex-spouse is more likely to be a non–Jew than a Jew. The non–Jewish spouse of an enrolled student from an intermarried family is likely to be a Christian wishing to pass on some of his or her own "heritage." Jewish educators need understand these dynamics better (through more research) and develop strategies to meet the challenges presented to the school.

Although it is only the children of intermarriages raised in Judaism that are likely to be seen in Jewish schools, Jewish educators might consider whether they have a role to play in outreach to the intermarried population. For example, can Jewish educators have an impact on the Jewish identity of a child "raised Jewish" but not in Judaism? There is no immediately obvious answer to such questions, but they beg to be explored.

FUTURE RESEARCH

Over the past 30 years, much of the focus of survey research about Jewish education has been concerned with "outcomes," particularly the long-range impact of Jewish day school. That Jewish education has important impacts on Jewish identity has been credibly established. While there is still more work that might be done on statistically disaggregating the impact of the school from that of the family that sent the child, it is more urgent that researchers, practitioners and funders contemplate new questions that emerge from recent demographic trends:

- What influences parents to keep their children in Jewish education past bar/bat mitzvah?
- What factors influence parents to choose a day school education? How do they evaluate days schools vis-à-vis the "competition"?
- What can be learned from day school education that might be applicable to the congregational school?

- What are intermarried Jewish parents looking for from Jewish education?

- How does Jewish education take into account the presence of a non–Jewish parent, especially one that may be a practicing Christian?

- Do we need a new structure and curriculum for congregational schools in suburbs and exurbs with large intermarried populations?

- Given the high cost of Jewish day schools, are there feasible alternatives on the horizon such as Jewish charter schools or Jewish home-school networks?

- How do non–Jewish spouses regard Jewish education, and how do they influence the family's decision?

- How do the children of intermarriage think about and experience Jewish education?

MOVING THE DEMOGRAPHIC RESEARCH FORWARD

With regard to Jewish education, researchers who conduct local Jewish population studies should pay more attention to Jewish education.

- Because the 1990 and 2000 National Jewish Population Surveys included basic research questions of Jewish education, researchers conducting local studies have in many cases left out detailed questions on Jewish education. In the absence of future national studies, local communities should be prepared to take up the slack, and Jewish educators in local communities should actively lobby on behalf of Jewish education research.

- Local studies should be encouraged to include questions on enrollment, when Jewish education began and ended, and questions on informal Jewish education. This ideally should be asked both for the respondent and for all children in the household.

- Much can be learned from intermarried families who have chosen to enroll their children in Jewish education. Small-scale research in this regard could have great potential value.

- Foundations interested in Jewish education should partner with local Jewish communities to do small-scale studies on Jewish education by periodically surveying parents of enrolled students on their future plans. One such study would be on the decision making process regarding post-bar/bat mitzvah Jewish education.

Jewish education research in the 21st century will depend on local studies. Jewish educators and other communal leaders need to become an advocacy group for Jewish education research. One advantage of this challenging situation is that Jewish education questions can garner a larger share of the interview than has been the case over the past decades.

HIGHLIGHTS

- There have been important gains made in Jewish education over the past thirty years, including higher levels of Jewish education for women and a dramatic increase in day school enrollment.

- Because intermarriage is the single most important social force shaping the Jewish community today and because Jewish experiences in the teen years affect intermarriage, new emphasis should be given to post-bar/bat mitzvah Jewish experiences.

- A third of the students in Jewish congregational schools already have a non–Jewish parent. Jewish educators need to openly address the challenges this presents.

- Jewish social research should actively engage in studies of intermarried families and their children.

CONCLUSION

The suburbanization of Jewish America in the decades following the Second World War was a watershed period for American Jewry. It was brought about by major shifts in Jewish population characteristics and resulted in the transformation of the Jewish institutional landscape. Jewish education was taken for granted. Half a century later the American Jewish population is experiencing even more dramatic changes, with Jewish education increasingly understood to be crucial for shaping the Jewish community that will emerge.

ANNOTATED BIBLIOGRAPHY

Sheskin, I. M. (2002). *How Jewish Communities Differ: Variations in the Findings of Local Jewish Population Studies.* North American Jewish Data Bank (www.Jewishdatabank.org). The noted Jewish demographer has compiled 45 of the best studies in one book, with more than 120 easy-to-understand tables and commentary on a number of topics, including Jewish education.

Cohen, S.M. (2004). *Jewish Educational Background: Trends and Variations among Today's Jewish Adults.* New York: United Jewish Communities. One of the publications from the NJPS 2000–2001. This provides an excellent overview of changes in Jewish education over the past 30 years as well as a Jewish education profile of today's Jewish parents. It is available online from the North American Jewish Data Bank (*www.Jewishdatabank.org*) and the United Jewish Communities (*www.ujc.org*).

Cohen, S.M. & Kotler-Berkowitz, L. (2004). *The Impact of Childhood Jewish Education on Adults' Jewish Identity: Schooling, Israel Travel, Camping and Youth Groups.* New York: United Jewish Communities. One of the publications from the NJPS 2000–2001. This report provides evidence that Jewish education (both formal and informal) does indeed make a difference. It is available online from the North American Jewish Data Bank (*www.Jewishdatabank.org*) and the United Jewish Communities (*www.ujc.org*).

Kotler-Berkowitz, L. (2005). *The Education of Jewish Children: Formal Schooling, Early Childhood Programs and Informal Experiences.* New York: United Jewish Communities. One of the publications from the NJPS 2000–2001. This report is summarized in this chapter but deserves a complete reading for the additional detail and discussion it contains.

Wertheimer, J. (1999). "Jewish Education in the United States: Recent Trends and Issues." American Jewish Year Book 97: 3–92. Philadelphia: Jewish Publication Society. The American Jewish Year Book periodically publishes definitive essays on American Jewish life. This is the definitive conceptual overview of Jewish education in America.

REFERENCES

Berkman, J. (2006). "Amid renewed debate over numbers, UJC may drop population study." New York: Jewish Telegraphic Agency.

Cohen, S. M. (2004). *Jewish Educational Background: Trends and Variations among Today's Jewish Adults.* New York: United Jewish Communities, 19.

Cohen, S. M. (2006). *A Tale of Two Jewries: The "Inconvenient Truth" for American Jews.* New York: HUC-JIR.

Cohen, S. M. &. Kotler-Berkowitz, L. (2004). *The Impact of Childhood Jewish Education on Adults' Jewish Identity: Schooling, Israel Travel, Camping and Youth Groups.* New York: United Jewish Communities, 19.

JESNA (2003). *Spotlight on Jewish Day School Education.* New York: JESNA.

Kadushin, C., Phillips, B.T. et al. (2006). "National Jewish Population Survey 2000–01: A Guide for the Perplexed." *Contemporary Jewry* 25, 1–32.

Kelman, S. L. (1992). *What We Know about Jewish Education: A Handbook of Today's Research for Tomorrow's Jewish Education.* Los Angeles: Torah Aura Productions.

Kotler-Berkowitz, L. (2005). *The Education of Jewish Children: Formal Schooling, Early Childhood Programs and Informal Experiences.* New York: United Jewish Communites, 39.

Kotler-Berowitz, L., Cohen, S. M. et al. (2003). *The National Jewish Population Survey, 2000–2001: Strength Challenge, and Diversity.* New York: United Jewish Communities, 31.

NJPS (2004). *National Jewish Population Survey/National Survey of Religion and Ethnicity 2000–01 study Documentation.* Last Revised August 2, 2004. New York: United Jewish Communities.

PEJE (2003). *NJPS 2000–01: Day School Enrollment on the Rise.* PEJE Newsletter.

Phillips, B. & Zeldin, M. (1987). "Jewish Education as a Communal Activity: Patterns of Enrollment in Three Growth Communities." *Journal of Jewish Communal Service* 63, 123–136.

Phillips, B. A. (1997). *Re-examining Intermarriage: Trends, Textures and Strategies.* Boston: Wilstein Instittute of Jewish Policy Studies and the American Jewish Committee.

Phillips, B. A. (2005). *Jewish Community Study of San Francisco, the Peninsula, Marin and Sonoma Counties: Full Findings*. San Francisco: Jewish Community Federation of San Francisco, the Peninsula, Marin and Sonoma Counties.

Phillips, B. A. (2006). Is Synagogue Membership a Rational Choice? Applying Rational Choice Theory to the Jewish Community. Paper presented at the Association for the Study of Religion, Economics, and Society, Portland, Oregon.

Phillips, B. A. (2007). Faultlines: The Seven Socio-Ecologies of Jewish Los Angeles. *The Jewish Role in American Life: An Annual Review, 5*. B. Zuckerman and J. Schoenberg, Ashland, OH: Purdue University Press.

Phillips, B. A. (nd). "Lakeville Revisted: Suburbanization and Jewish Identity in the Chicago Metro Area." Unpublished paper.

Phillips, B. A. & Kotler-Berkowitz, L. (2007). *Intermarriage in the National Jewish Population Survey 2000–2001*. New York: United Jewish Communities.

Saxe, L., Tighe, E. et al. (2007). *Reconsidering the Size and Characteristics of the American Jewish Population: New Estimates of a Larger and More Diverse Community*. Waltham MA: Steinhardt Social Research Institute.

Schick, M. (2000). *A Census of Jewish Day Schools in the United States*. New York: Avi Chai Foundation.

Schick, M. (2003). *The Impact of the Economic Downturn on Jewish Day Schools*. New York: Avi Chai Foundatation.

Schick, M. (2005). *A Census of Jewish Day Schools in the United States 2003–2004*. New York: Avi Chai Foundation.

Sheskin, I. M. (2002). *The 2002 Tucson Jewish Community Study, Main Report*. Tucson: Jewish Community Foundation of Southern Arizona.

UJC (nd). Enrollment Estimates in Selected Types of Jewish Education: NJPS and the Avi Chai Foundation. *http://www.ujc.org/content_display.html?ArticleID=84103*, New York: United Jewish Communities.

Ukeles, J. B., Miller, R. et al. (2001). *Jewish Community Study of Greater Baltimore*. Baltimore: Jewish Community Federation of Baltimore.

Wertheimer, J. (2005). *Linking the Silos: How to Accelerate the Momentum in Jewish Education Today*. New York: Avi Chai Foundation.

Wertheimer, J. (2001). *Talking Dollars and Sense about Jewish Education*. New York: Avi Chai Foundation.

Identity and Jewish Education

Steven M. Cohen

Jewish identities in the United States, as elsewhere, are constantly undergoing change. The dynamics of how American Jews conceive of and express their diverse ways of being Jewish inevitably pose new challenges, constraints, and opportunities for Jewish education. Accordingly, an understanding of the changing configurations of American Jewish identity should inform the theory and practice of Jewish education.

To be sure, the implications of any analysis of Jewish identity for Jewish education are far from straightforward. The same findings can lead to dramatically different policy conclusions, given that policy-makers' values and resources inevitably come in to play. For example, understanding the impact of intermarriage on Jewish continuity leads some analysts and advocates to argue for increased investment in educationally targeting the intermarried and their children, those Jews most likely to abandon their sense of being connected to Judaism. In contrast, the same appreciation for the impact of intermarriage leads others to argue for a focus on the "moderately affiliated" as an effective way of building stronger Jewish communities that can appeal to Jews of all levels of engagement (Cohen 1985; Wertheimer et al. 1996).

Nonetheless, research on Jewish identities in America since 1997 (the focus of this chapter) points to several developments that are relevant to educators and policy makers, the most significant of which may be gathered under five rubrics that bear elaboration:

- Declining Social Ties and Weaker Collective Identity
- Intensified Religiosity, Spirituality, and Education
- The Rise of the Sovereign Self
- Younger Adults Crossing Boundaries in People, Culture, and Space
- Entrepreneurial Younger Adults in Culture, Social Justice and Spirituality

A WORD ABOUT "IDENTITY"

In common parlance, "identity" has come to be understood as related primarily to intra-psychic feelings—the attitudes and sentiments felt within. It connotes ideas about the self, such as the importance one attaches to being Jewish or the meaning associated with this label. But in truth, Jewish identity extends (or ought to extend) beyond the affective. Being an "identified Jew" is not just about feeling Jewish, but about expressing Jewish belonging and undertaking identifiably Jewish behaviors. For good reason sociologists of religious identity speak of the three B's: Belief, Behavior, and Belonging. As Marshall Sklare observed in his pioneering investigation of Jewish identity (Sklare & Greenblum 1967), Judaism is a "sacramental religion." It values the performance of certain behaviors, generally in interaction with others. Paraphrasing Ben-Gurion's remark originally made about Gentiles and Jews, "What matters is not what the Jews say, but what the Jews do."

If Jewish Beliefs (or attitudes and affect) and Jewish Behavior are constituent elements of Jewish identity, so too is Jewish Belonging, expressed in the full complex of social ties that link Jews with one another. Jews' social ties, or what Goldscheider (1986) refers to as Jewish social cohesion, are at the heart of any assessment of Jewish identities in America.

Not only is Jewish identity itself rich, ever-changing, variegated and contested, so too is the study of Jewish identity. Before the 1990s much of the research in the field used quantitative methods, a trend that has been abetted by the large number of population studies funded by the federation system both locally and nationally. At the same time, recent years have seen a broadening of methods, entailing such qualitative techniques as participant observation, ethnography, and depth interviews that co-exist or sometimes intertwine with quantitative data collection. No review of the literature can possibly encompass all the richness and variety of research in the field. Any review is inevitably influenced by the expertise and interests of the reviewer. Certainly, such is the case here, as I focus both upon the research with which I am personally most familiar (my own included) and upon those research questions and perspectives (or biases) that I find most compelling and intriguing.

DECLINING SOCIAL TIES AND WEAKER COLLECTIVE IDENTITY

Recent years have witnessed a decline in Jewish Belonging, the extent to which Jews maintain social ties with other Jews. Jewish Belonging is not simply a means to a stronger Jewish identity; it is inherently a piece of Jewish identity. A Jew with Jewish spouse, children, friends, neighbors and co-workers is, ipso facto, Jewishly identified. Conversely, few but the most committed Jews in modern America can sustain strong Jewish identities in near-isolation, without the social networks that make Jewish living possible and plausible.

In this regard, the decline in Jewish social ties over the last several years is of great consequence. Intermarriage (Kotler-Berkowitz et al. 2003) is but one feature of this phenomenon, but Jewish social ties extend beyond marriage. As compared with ten or twenty years ago, not only do fewer Jews today have Jewish spouses; fewer also have Jewish friends, neighbors, and co-workers. Among older Baby Boomers, roughly two-thirds report mostly Jewish friends; among those their children's age, only one-third report likewise.

The consequences of intermarriage for identity have been rather thoroughly explored (Beck 2005; Fishman 2004; Phillips 1997, 2005a, 2005b, 2005c; Phillips & Fishman forthcoming). Less well-appreciated is that Jewish in-group friendship is correlated with many measures of Jewish identity, including celebrating holidays, practicing rituals, belonging to synagogues and other institutions, supporting Israel, marrying Jews, bearing Jewish children and providing children with Jewish educational experiences. Jewish friendship circles are also critical to Jewish socialization and education (Fishman forthcoming). Cause and effect are impossible to disentangle, but the centrality of Jewish friendship for a wide complex of Jewish behaviors cannot be denied, and these social ties have been on the wane.

Jewish ties have diminished in the institutional domain as well (Cohen & Wertheimer 2006). For years, Jewish mass-membership organizations have seen fewer young recruits, resulting in aging and shrinking memberships. In 1990–2000 the total number of Jews affiliated with such organizations declined nearly 20%. The Jewish federation movement has been witnessing similar changes. Over the past 25 years inflation-adjusted giving has declined by more than half a percent a year. From 1990 to 2000 the percentage of Jews claiming to have made a gift to a local UJA-federation campaign shrank by a third, with younger donors far scarcer (Cohen 2004). Those born after World War II are increasingly unlikely to donate to federation, even as they maintain their support of other Jewish causes and, relatively speaking, increase their support for non–sectarian causes.

Related to and stemming from the decline in Jewish social and institutional ties is a weakening attachment to Israel and the Jewish people. Declining engagement with Israel dates back at least to the late 1980s (Cohen & Wertheimer 2006). Fewer Jews now than in the past care deeply about Israel or feel attached to the Jewish State. Similar trends can be seen when comparing younger adults with their older counterparts. Those who have been to Israel, old or young, maintain high rates of attachment; but among those who have not been to Israel, younger adults score lower on every available measure of Israel attachment than do their elders. We find similar patterns with respect to feeling a sense of belonging to the Jewish people. Taken together, these declines—in social ties, in institutional affiliation and in affective ties to the collective as embodied in Israel and the Jewish people—constitute a decline in Jewish ethnicity and collective Jewish identity.

INTENSIFIED RELIGIOSITY, SPIRITUALITY AND EDUCATION

While American Jews' ethnicity has declined, they have sustained, if not increased, most levels of religiosity, producing a pattern of "Religious Stability and Ethnic Decline" (Cohen 1998) or, as Charles Liebman (1999) observed, as transition from "ethnic to privatized Judaism." Over the last ten to fifteen years, measures of synagogue affiliation, ritual observance, service attendance and belief in God have held steady. So too have the overall numbers of Jews belonging to congregations, even amid a numerical reshuffling among the major denominations (Cohen 2006a). Moreover, all three major denominations have become, each in its own way, more observant and more Jewishly educated over time. Not only has Orthodoxy been "Sliding Right" (Heilman 2006), but so too have Conservatism (Cohen 2000) and Reform.

One can also make a case for an expanded interest in Jewish spirituality, as manifest in the numerous spiritually oriented publications, with at least one entire publishing house (Jewish Lights) dedicated to books on Jewish spirituality and related sensibilities. On social surveys, most American Jews regard themselves as spiritual. Interest in the study of Jewish spiritual texts and practices has caught on both with celebrities such as Madonna and with a noticeable number of the not-so-famous. Dozens of rabbis now participate in the activities of the relatively well-funded Jewish Spirituality Institute—itself a sign that at least some funders and rabbis now highly value Jewish spirituality.

In parallel with these trends, participation in many venues of Jewish education, itself often a reflection of Jewish religious commitment, has also been on the rise. Over the last ten to fifteen years participation grew or held steady in Jewish pre-schools, day schools (both Orthodox and otherwise), camping, Israel travel, Jewish studies on college campuses and adult Jewish education (inter alia, see Goldberg 2001; Grant et al. 2004; Heilman 2001; Kirshenblatt-Gimblett 2001; Sales & Saxe 2004; Saxe et al. 2004). At the same time, enrollment in supplementary schools declined, and more Jewish children are receiving no Jewish schooling whatsoever. In the last decade the Internet emerged as a new Jewish education delivery vehicle, providing news, information, events, graphics, videos, humor, social networking, music, blogs, classes, and more. The explosion in Jewish content on the Internet is palpable. As I write, Google reports over 187 million web pages for "Israel", 76 million for "Jewish," 7 million for "Torah," 4 million for "Passover," and over 3 million for "Talmud."

American Jews' vigor in the religious sphere is all the more striking when arrayed against the opposite trends in the ethnic sphere noted above. At a time when fewer Jews are maintaining ties with one another, their ability to maintain, if not increase, aggregate levels of religious involvement and productivity is truly remarkable. If in-group marriage and friendship are so closely allied with religious involvement (as indeed they are), then how is it that Jewish religiosity, spirituality and education have been holding steady or growing as the number of in-married Jews and Jews with mostly Jewish friends have been shrinking?

One reason lies with the growing proportion of Orthodox Jews in the American Jewish population, a figure that is likely to grow even further over time (Ukeles et al. 2006). The Orthodox make up about 8% of Baby Boomer Jews but comprise about 18% of Jews under the age of 18. Another reason for the stability in religiosity and related domains lies in the more intensive involvement of in-married Jews with children, a group comprised of all denominations. As compared with their parents' generation, such families have become relatively more active in so many ways: more observant of Jewish ritual, more likely to affiliate with synagogues, and more likely to send their children to day schools, to take just a few relevant indicators.

The in-married today are a more Jewishly selected group. When intermarriage was rare and Jews had few opportunities to marry non–Jews, then no special commitment was necessary to marry a Jew—the ethnic social enclave within which most Jews lived until the middle of the twentieth century made it only natural for Jews to marry one another. But when intermarriage became prevalent, Jewish commitment became more of a prerequisite for in-marriage. As a result, the in-married and the intermarried now constitute "Two Jewries" (Cohen 2006b) with vastly different levels of Jewish socialization and education, and even vaster differences in practice, association, affiliation, and child-rearing.

These patterns point to the difficulty of assessing the overall direction of Jewish identities in the United States. Some indicators are rising, others falling and still others holding steady. Moreover, different sub-populations are growing or shrinking, and their levels of Jewish involvement are moving, at times, in different directions. Adding to the complexity are shifts in the cultural environment and correlative changes in the understanding of what it means to be Jewish and how it is to be expressed.

THE RISE OF THE SOVEREIGN SELF

Since at least the 1980s social scientists have been observing Americans adopt a more independent, individualist stance toward institutions in general and toward religious life in particular (Bellah et al. 1985). Americans more readily redefine their identities, move between several identities, blend cultures and sample and assemble themselves repeatedly. The very titles of some of the major relevant monographs convey this thinking. Thus Americans are said to maintain only "Loose Connections" (Wuthnow 1998) to family, job, party, hometown, and religious identity. For some, the metaphoric phenomenon of "Bowling Alone" (Putnam 2000) has come to embody the idea that Americans experience less community than in the past. In the religious sphere they have moved from the dogmatic, communal and institutional to the autonomous, personal and private (Wolfe 2003). A "Generation of Seekers" goes shopping for religious experiences in the "Spiritual Marketplace" (Roof 1993, 1999). Even with respect to ancestral identity, seemingly an immutable given, Americans display the readiness to fashion their own "Ethnic Options" (Waters 1990), where they choose the group with which to be identified and invent the content of their ethnicities. In so doing they create ethnic meaning in very personal terms, arriving at what Gans termed (only) "Symbolic Ethnicity" (1979) and then "Symbolic Religiosity" (1994). European-Americans have entered "The Twilight of Ethnicity" (Alba 1986, 1990) in which ethnic identities, though still perceptible, are fading.

American Jews have proceeded along paths resembling those of other European-origin groups in the United States. Their Jewish identities moved inward from the communal and public domain to the personal and private spheres (Cohen & Eisen 2000). They embark upon personal Jewish journeys in which they not only experience rises and falls in the salience of their Jewish identities but also continually re-fashion the meaning of their Judaism (Horowitz 2000).

As described in *The Jew Within* (Cohen & Eisen 2000), we are witnessing the emergence of the Sovereign Jewish Self, in which American Jews feel perfectly comfortable deciding for themselves whether, when, where, why and how they will be Jewish. This notion encompasses six thematic observations on contemporary American Jewish identities.

1) It embraces an assertion of the *inalienability of being Jewish*. Jews are in effect saying, "No matter what I do or don't do, no matter what I believe or don't believe, I'm still a Jew, and a good Jew—and no one can alienate me from my valid claim to identify as a Jew." This stance contrasts markedly with previous generations who believed that certain acts (e.g., intermarriage) or behaviors (failing to support the community) in effect placed one outside the boundaries of the Jewish family or community.

2) The Sovereign Jewish Self asserts a strong measure of *voluntarism*: Each Jew may choose how, when and where to be Jewish. While Jews have made such choices for years, the voluntarism of our time means that Jews make their choices with less guilt than did their parents, acting with a greater sense of entitlement to make such choices without the constraints imposed by tradition or others. As one respondent in *The Jew Within* remarked, "I elect to observe it as I elect to observe it. If something is potentially annoying, I avoid it."

3) These choices are marked by a new emphasis on *autonomy,* which values serious reflection and informed choice, as opposed to a more traditional notion of compliance with religious law or conventional custom. Not coincidentally, Jewish education moves increasingly toward a stance of helping students make the Jewish choices that are right for them, as opposed to advocating fixed norms. As one respondent said about her connection to ritual observance, "I have to feel like it's coming inside out, and isn't just somebody else's idea of a ritual."

4) Jews today make such choices motivated by that which is personally meaningful, referred to as "personalism," a term coined by Charles Liebman. Personal feelings provide the rationale and legitimacy of action (or inaction), as illustrated by this respondent's remarks: "Yom Kippur—and every other ritual occasion, for that matter—is a very personal holiday. So if you're not feeling very connected to it, it's hard to observe it."

5) Sovereign Jewish Selves are *anti-judgmental*—they claim no basis for judging others' Jewish choices. In drawing upon a cultural resource, a religious and ethnic option, there is no right or wrong choice, representing a tremendous shift. Traditional Jews conceived of Judaism as a system of God-given obligations governing their relationships with God and with others. Jewish religious law is detailed, and, at times, quite demanding. Over time, Jews' conception of Judaism evolved from a system of Divine laws enforced by human sanction to a voluntarily accessed cultural resource for providing personal meaning. Consistent with Judaism that is more a matter of aesthetics than of norms, one that allows for multiple religious paths, rabbis and educators come to employ the rhetoric of inclusiveness, one that emphasizes "welcoming" and feeling "comfortable" with one's Jewishness.

6) The last component of the Sovereign Jewish Self refers to the expectation that individuals and institutions will accept, support, and nourish one another's highly individualized Jewish journeys—an expectation that constitutes "journeyism" (yet another neologism). As Horowitz (2000, 2002) amply demonstrates, Jews experience twists and turns in their relationship to being Jewish (as do others; see Wuthnow 1999), and they expect others to recognize and accept the contours of their journey. In speaking about his expectations of a wife, one single young man in *The Jew Within* gave voice to this notion: "I have been in a state of flux and learning. I certainly realize that I am not going to rest somewhere where I can easily say, 'This is the kind of Jew I am and therefore I need this kind of person.'... I am always going to be in exploration, so it will be difficult to do that with someone who does not identify with that in some respect."

Inalienability, voluntarism, autonomy, personalism, anti-judgmentalism, and journeyism—while all different and all of a single piece—combined to make for a very individual approach to being Jewish among the Baby Boomers, as contrasted with their parents. The next generation—Gen Xers and Yers—have both moved further along the paths charted by their parents and charted their own course and begun to leave their own imprint upon the ever-changing contours of Jewish identity in the United States (Cohen & Kelman 2006a, 2006b; Greenberg 2004, 2006; Ukeles et al. 2006).

YOUNGER ADULTS CROSSING BOUNDARIES IN PEOPLE, CULTURE AND SPACE

In one crucial respect, Jews differ from all other major American religious and ethnic groups. As Glazer (1972) observed, in their pre–American environs, Jews were the only immigrant group who experienced systematic exclusion from the larger society, exercised communal autonomy and developed a group-survivalist ideology. Irish, Italian, and Polish immigrants may have been poor, uneducated, and oppressed in their home countries. But they were part of larger societies—in fact, they were the larger society. They spoke its language, participated in and shaped its culture, and practiced its religion. In all these respects, Jews—especially East European Jews—were different and apart.

Thus Jewish immigrants not only proceeded along the modernization track "from fate to choice" (Berger 1979: 11) as did everyone else. They also proceeded along a uniquely Jewish track, one that led them from segregation to integration, from exclusion to inclusion, and from dwelling on the margins of society to participating in its mainstream. As Liebman observed, "The Ambivalent American Jew" (1973) struggled to resolve the tension between integrating in the larger society and surviving as a distinct group.

The growing integration into American society, with its increasing acceptance of non–Jews and by non–Jews, underlies an emerging feature of Jewish identity among American Jews born in the last quarter of the twentieth century. As several recent studies demonstrate (Cohen & Kelman 2006a, 2006b; Greenberg 2004, 2006; Ukeles et al., 2006), Jews now in their twenties and thirties often view their parents' generation's institutions as exceedingly "divisive." They criticize their apparent tendencies to divide Jews from non–Jews, Jews from Jews (along denominational lines), Jewish culture from other culture, and Jewish space from non–Jewish space. In short, they are bothered by seemingly exclusive group boundaries maintained by today's middle-aged institutionally mainstream American Jews.

Instead, they prefer to cross all these boundaries as they do in events and institutions organized by their generation. They seek Jewish programs that draw into and welcome their non–Jewish friends and that appeal to Jews of varying denominational persuasions. They deride attempts to define certain cultural elements as either authentically Jewish or definitively non–Jewish; instead they construct a Jewish culture that is infused with a contemporary aesthetic, combining elements whose origins may lie in several cultural traditions. Last, they tend to prefer events and programs that occur in bars, nightclubs, concert halls, and performance spaces—that is, in places other than explicitly Jewish venues (Cohen & Kelman 2006a).

Parallel trends in interpersonal relations have proceeded apace as well. Jews have become not merely increasingly comfortable with non–Jews, but increasingly uncomfortable with excluding them—even in overtly "Jewish" contexts. The shift over four generations has been both massive and remarkable. Around the turn of the twentieth century, East European Jewish immigrants—with their quasi-Orthodox upbringing, Yiddish language, and working-class status—could hardly have been expected to socialize much with non–Jews. Their Depression-era children, notwithstanding their social mobility and migration to the suburbs, experienced limits on intimacy with their non–Jewish acquaintances, associates, friends, neighbors and co-workers (Gans 1958; Ringer 1967). In contrast, their children—the Baby Boom generation—with their educational success, professional achievement and leaps in intermarriage—felt far more comfortable among non–Jews than did their parents or grandparents. Their increasing comfort was in large part due to sharp declines in anti–Semitism and increasing acceptance (Silberman 1985). Ivy League schools went from restricting the admission of Jews as students to selecting Jews to serve as presidents at every such distinguished institution of higher learning. Baby Boomers sharply reduced the extent to which they held contrary stereotypes of Jews and "Gentiles," the source of much ironic Borscht Belt humor. The fading of these stereotypes testifies to the fading of inter-group boundaries that once more sharply separated Jews from others (Liebman & Cohen 1990).

Today's young adults take the process of boundary-crossing and boundary-blurring several steps further. Like their parents, they are certainly comfortable in the presence of non–Jews. But when almost half may have non–Jewish parents, when nearly half of young Jews marry non–Jews (and presumably even more have had at one point non–Jewish romantic partners), they feel it makes little sense to curtail or distort their friendship or family relationships to participate in Jewish life. Rather, they seek to "do Jewish" in the presence of non–Jews. Some young Jews today even report that the presence of non–Jews ignites their Jewish identities, giving them opportunities to comfortably share or even proudly display their Jewishness. Obviously, it remains to be seen whether the next generation will take the process of boundary-blurring and boundary-crossing much further. But certainly younger adult Jews today often expect to live their Jewish lives in open, and often intimate, contact with non–Jews—a circumstance their parents, to say nothing of their grandparents, could not have imagined.

ENTREPRENEURIAL YOUNGER ADULTS IN CULTURE, SOCIAL JUSTICE AND SPIRITUALITY

Starting perhaps as early as 2002, younger adults have been organizing a wide variety of endeavors, initiatives, projects and communities (for examples, see *Slingshot '05* and *'06*). They include nearly two dozen independent minyanim; cultural endeavors in music, filmmaking, drama and other art forms; initiatives to promote human rights or social justice causes; and diverse learning initiatives, be they festival-like encampments, classes, or stand-alone programs.

At the heart of most of these endeavors are passionate and dedicated social entrepreneurs who energize a small coterie of supportive friends, who in turn engage a wider circle of supporters and participants (Cohen & Kelman 2006a, 2006b). These individuals are marked by a degree of earnestness and a search for authenticity as well as more than a touch of healthy iconoclasm that serves to differentiate their endeavors from the Judaism of their elders (witness *Heeb* magazine as an exemplar). They aim to inspire engagement, if not commitment, while studiously avoiding the coercive character, in their view, of the Jewish institutions with which they have been most familiar.

These initiatives, in reflecting the next round of shifts in Jewish identity and community in America, set themselves apart from and even challenge prevailing communal forms. At the same time, they are forging new alternatives to existing structures and customs, providing the next generation with new choices of how, when, where and why to be Jewish. In observing a young leader of a vibrant spiritual community, a middle-aged federation professional remarked, "She's good, but she's only a niche phenomenon." At which point another of his generation commented, "You don't get it. It's all about niche phenomena."

IMPLICATIONS FOR POLICY AND PRACTICE

This highly selective review of recent research on American Jewish identities had to make do with a few sweeping generalizations. It could not take into account variations by region (Sheskin 1999), by class and gender (Prell 1999), or by marital status. Cohen (2005), for example, argues for "segmenting the market" by marriage patterns—in-married, intermarried, and unmarried—while Ukeles et al. (2006) advocate including the Orthodox as a distinctive fourth major segment . The glossing over of these and other variations notwithstanding, this analysis leads to several policy- and practice-relevant implications.

First, the decline of ethnic tissue and of collective identity sets before Jewish educators a new explicit objective: to build the social ties between Jews that make Jewish education possible and plausible. In this day and age, the promotion of Jewish friendships and marriage is not the fortuitous by-product of Jewish education. It is, or ought to be, an inherent objective of Jewish education. Effective Jewish educators must also function as community-builders, be it in the classroom, camp or congregation, or by connecting their learners to others, by "Linking the Silos" of Jewish education (Wertheimer 2005).

Second, the vitality in religiosity and spirituality points to opportunities for Jewish education. Obviously, Jewish educators (be they in the role of rabbis, parents, or classroom teachers) have been investing more effort in helping their learners (be they congregants, children, or students) find personal meaning in religious and spiritual practice and study. Effective Jewish education today must, perforce, incorporate the provision of personal meaning in the context of well-functioning social networks and community, suggesting that community-building may now constitute an integral part of Jewish education, and we may need to start regarding community-builders as a new breed of Jewish educators.

Third, with this said, educators need to guard against "over-playing the religious card"; they need to avoid placing nearly exclusive emphasis on educating for the religious life, using primarily religious themes and lexicon. American Jews remain the least religious of all American religious groups and still the most ethnically cohesive of all major European-origin ethnic groups. The Protestant religious milieu that has re-shaped the meaning of being Jewish has not in the least transformed Jewish group identity into exclusively (or even primarily) a religious group identity. Jews are prone to say, "I'm cultural, but not religious." The meaning of "cultural" is not all that clear. But it does suggest a realm of Jewish identity, community and interest that extends beyond prayer, observance, faith, theology, and sacred texts. And it is an area where Jewish education in America, as a discipline, has failed to pay much attention, in part because so much Jewish education takes place under religious auspices, and so many Jewish educators are religiously trained and religiously committed.

These considerations immediately lead to a fourth and final implication: Increasingly, Jewish education is taking place outside of traditional educational contexts. The Internet, newspapers, social justice activities (witness the success of American Jewish World Service), music, films, and all manner of cultural events and pursuits provide the venue for many Jews—especially younger Jews—to express their Jewish interest and, perforce, engage in Jewish learning and Jewish education. In good measure, conventional Jewish educators have, as yet, failed to turn their attention to these domains.

In every generation, the key objectives in Jewish education have shifted in line with the changing needs and interests of students, community and society. As this research demonstrates, these needs and interests continue to change, creating both new demands on education and new opportunities. In particular, areas of weakness in the complex tableau of Jewish identity point to areas where Jewish educators must devote special efforts. The rebuilding of Jewish social ties is one such area today, as is the weakened connection with Israel. At the same time, areas of growth or strength point to opportunities for Jewish educational intervention, growth, and creativity. The signs of interest in spirituality, culture, social justice, the Internet, and entrepreneurial Jewish organizing suggest areas where Jewish educators—and all who are committed to strengthening Jewish life—need to devote additional attention and creative thinking.

HIGHLIGHTS

- Jewish identity consists not just of feelings, but also of behaviors and acts of belonging.
- Jewish social ties (marriage, friendship, neighbors, institutional belonging, attachment to Israel and the Jewish people) are in decline, as is, more generally, Jewish ethnicity and collective identity.
- The religious dimension of Jewish identity seems to be stable, if not growing, along with most forms of Jewish educational participation.
- Jewish identity takes the form of the Sovereign Self marked by inalienability of being Jewish, voluntarism, autonomy, personalism, anti-judgmentalism, and individual Jewish journeys.
- In response to what they see as the excessive divisiveness of their parents' generation ways of being Jewish, younger adults are engaging in the crossing of group boundaries—those that divide Jews from non–Jews, Jews from Jews, Jewish turf from non–Jewish turf, and Jewish culture from non–Jewish culture.
- More and more Jewish initiatives are being led by individual Jewish social entrepreneurs creating projects, endeavors and communities that differ from those of the previous generation.

ANNOTATED BIBLIOGRAPHY

Cohen, S. M. & Kelman, A. Y. (2006a). *Cultural Events and Jewish Identities: Young Adult Jews in New York*. New York: National Foundation for Jewish Culture. This study explores the meaning and potential of Jewish cultural engagement for Jewish identity today. A quantitative analysis of Jewish cultural participation nationally finds that cultural participation constitutes a larger share of the Jewish engagement of the less engaged and relatively unaffiliated than it does for the more Jewishly engaged. At the same time, a qualitative analysis of younger Jews attending Jewish cultural events in New York demonstrates that these events enhance Jewish social networks, incubate and develop Jewish leaders, and nurture newer forms of Jewish life with implications for established institutions and identities. Younger adult Jews are often "unaffiliated but engaged," with an interest in expressing their Jewish attachments in ways that are ironic, iconoclastic, entertaining, aesthetic, non-coercive and non-divisive.

Horowitz, B. (2000). *Connections and Journeys: Assessing Critical Opportunities for Enhancing Jewish Identity*. New York: UJA-Federation of Jewish Philanthropies. This study, combining original survey research of 1,500 adult respondents under the age of 52 with 100 in-depth interviews conducted in the New York area, found "evidence of ongoing psychological commitment, even when measures of organizational involvement were declining…The study uncovered a large number of people who have active interests in and commitments to Jewishness, but not necessarily in the ways expected by the American Jewish communal-organizational world….The study captured the complex, journey-like aspect of identity."

Cohen, S. M. & Wertheimer, J. (2006, June). "Whatever Happened to the Jewish People?" *Commentary* 121 (6), 33–37. This article argues that changes in several measures of Jewish engagement point to declining attachment to the Jewish people. Fewer Jews than in the recent past have Jewish spouses, friends, neighbors and co-workers. Fewer belong to Jewish organizations or contribute to Jewish federations, whose campaigns have not kept pace with inflation and whose allocations have shifted dramatically from overseas to local needs. Fewer feel attached to Israel or to the Jewish people. Taken singly, any one of these trends bears several explanations; taken together, they point to a broad-gauged decline in ethnicity and Jewish collective identity.

Fishman, S. B. (2004). *Double or Nothing? Jewish Families and Mixed Marriage*. Dartmouth, NH: Brandeis University Press/University Press of New England. Based on interviews with 254 mixed married family members in several locations, this study explores how such families negotiate their religious and group identities. Placing these personal narratives in a larger cultural context, the analysis underscores the fluidity of religious identities today, the thin connections of most intermarried families with Jews and Judaism and the enduring power of Jewish education and parental socialization to influence decisions regarding identity, practice, and child-rearing.

Liebman, C. S. & Cohen, S.M. (1990). *Two Worlds of Judaism: The Israeli and American Experiences*. New Haven: Yale University Press. This monograph examines what being Jewish means to Israeli and American Jews, and how each group has reinterpreted a common Jewish tradition. Jews in both societies share a familial sense of peoplehood and a common past. Yet they differ dramatically in so many ways. Judaism in the U.S. is conducted more in the private sphere than the public domain. Americans Jews value plural approaches to being Jewish. They live amid non–Jews who are their friends, family, spouses and children. Israeli Judaism remains more ritualistic and collectively oriented than its American counterpart.

Phillips, B. (2005). "Assimilation, Transformation, and the Long Range Impact of Intermarriage." *Contemporary Jewry 25:* 50–84. This study is one of Phillips' several complementary analyses of the impact of intermarriage upon Jewish identity of spouses and their children. Using the 2000–01 National Jewish Population Study, this study explores the variety of intermarried families (and Jews, including "Christian Jews") and demonstrates how tenuous are the ties of intermarried families to all manner of Jewish engagement, as well as the grave implications for the demographic future of American Jewry.

Prell, R.E. (1999). *Fighting to Become Americans*. Boston: Beacon. Drawing upon a wealth of cultural evidence over the decades, this work demonstrates how gender, social class, and American Jews' struggle to enter the larger society shaped images of themselves and of the other. It demonstrates the power of deeply rooted stereotypes of Jewish men and women and how they reflect and derive from Jews' interaction with the larger society.

Ukeles, J. B., Miller, R. & Beck, P. (2006). *Young Jewish Adults in the United States Today*. New York: American Jewish Committee. Drawing upon local community studies and several national studies, this study of Jewish young adults argues for the analytic and policy-oriented segmentation of this population into four groups: the Orthodox, non–Orthodox in-married, non–Orthodox non-married, and the intermarried. It demonstrates that "substantial numbers of young Jewish adults are being Jewish in ways that are quite different from the ways of connecting of their predecessors. For the younger Jewish generation, Jewish ties seem to be: more personal, more informal, more episodic."

REFERENCES

Alba, R. (1986). *Italian Americans: Into the Twilight of Ethnicity*. Englewood Cliffs, NJ: Prentice-Hall.

Alba, R. (1990). *Ethnic Identity: The Transformation of White America*. New Haven: Yale University Press.

Andrea & Charles Bronfman Philanthropies. (2005). *Slingshot '05*. New York: ACBP.

Andrea & Charles Bronfman Philanthropies. (2006). *Slingshot '06*. New York: ACBP.

Beck, P. (2005). *A Flame Still Burns: The Dimensions and Determinants of Jewish Identity Among Young Adult Children of the Intermarried*. New York: Jewish Outreach Institute.

Bellah, R. N., Madsen, R., Sullivan, W.M., Swidler, A. & Tipton, S.M. (1996). *Habits of the Heart: Individualism, Commitment in American Life*. Berkeley: University of California Press.

Berger, P. (1979). *Heretical Imperative: Contemporary Possibilities of Religious Affirmation*. New York: Doubleday.

Cohen, S. M. (1985). "Outreach to the Marginally Affiliated: Evidence and Implications for Policy-makers in Jewish Education," *Journal of Jewish Communal Service* 62 (2), 147–157.

Cohen, S. M. (1998). *Religious Stability and Ethnic Decline: Emerging Patterns of Jewish Identity in the United States*. New York: The Florence G. Heller/JCC Association Research Center.

Cohen, S. M. (1978). "Will Jews Keep Giving? Prospects for the Jewish Charitable Community." *Journal of Jewish Communal Service* 55, 59–71.

Cohen, S. M. (2000). "Assessing the Vitality of the Conservative Movement," in Jack Wertheimer (ed.), *The Jews in the Center: Conservative Synagogues and Their Members*. New Brunswick, NJ: Rutgers University Press.

Cohen, S. M. (2002). "Relationships of American Jews with Israel: What We Know and What We Need to Know," *Contemporary Jewry* 23, 132–155.

Cohen, S. M. (2004). *Philanthropic Giving among American Jews: Contributions to Federation, Jewish and Non–Jewish Causes.* New York: United Jewish Communities Report Series on the National Jewish Population Survey 2000–01, Report 4, *www.ujc.org/njps.*

Cohen, S. M. (2005). "Engaging the Next Generation of American Jews: Distinguishing the In-married, Inter-married, and Non-married," *Journal of Jewish Communal Service* 81 (1/2), 43–52.

Cohen, S. M. (2006a). *Members and Motives: Who Joins American Jewish Congregations and Why.* Los Angeles: S3K Synagogue Studies Institute. *www.synagogue300.org*

Cohen, S. M. (2006b). *A Tale of Two Jewries: The "Inconvenient Truth" for American Jews.* New York: Jewish Life Network/Steinhardt Foundation.

Cohen, S. M. & Eisen, A. (2000). *The Jew Within: Self, Family, and Community in America.* Bloomington: Indiana University Press.

Cohen, S. M. & Kelman, A. Y. (2006a). *Cultural Events and Jewish Identities: Young Adult Jews in New York.* New York: National Foundation for Jewish Culture.

Cohen, S. M. & Kelman, A. Y. (2006b). *Cultures and Conversations: New Modes of Jewish Connection and Community in North America."* New York: Andrea and Charles Bronfman Philanthropies.

Cohen, S. M. & Wertheimer, J. (2006) "Whatever Happened to the Jewish People?" *Commentary* 121 (6), 33–37.

Fishman, S. B. (2004). *Double or Nothing? Jewish Families and Mixed Marriage.* Dartmouth, NH: Brandeis University Press/University Press of New England.

Fishman, S. B. (2007). "Generating Jewish Connections: Conversations with Teenagers, Parents of Teenagers, Jewish Educators and Thinkers," in *Family Matters: Jewish Education in America,* Jack Wertheimer (ed.). Waltham: Brandeis University Press.

Gans, H. (1958). "The Origins and Growth of a Jewish Community in the Suburbs: A Study of the Jews of Park Forest." In *The Jews: Social Patterns of an American Group,* Marshall Sklare (ed.). New York: The Free Press, 205–248.

Gans, H. (1979). "Symbolic Ethnicity: The Future of Ethnic Groups and Cultures in America." *Ethnic and Racial Studies 2,* 1–20.

Gans, H. (1994). "Symbolic Ethnicity and Symbolic Religiosity: Towards a Comparison of Ethnic and Religious Acculturation." *Ethnic and Racial Studies* 17, 577–591.

Goldberg, H. (2001). "A Summer on a NFTY Safari (1994): An Ethnographic Perspective." In Barry Chazan (ed.), *The Israel Experience: Studies in Jewish Identity and Youth Culture.* Jerusalem: CRB Foundation, 23–142.

Glazer, N. (1972). *American Judaism.* Chicago: University of Chicago Press.

Goldscheider, C. (1986). *Jewish Continuity and Change.* Bloomington: Indiana University Press.

Grant, L, Schuster, D.T., Woocher, M. & Cohen, S. M. (2004). *A Journey of Heart and Mind: Transformative Jewish Learning in Adulthood.* New York: Jewish Theological Seminary Press.

Greenberg, A. (2004). *OMG! How Generation Y Is Redefining Faith in iPod Era. www.rebooters.net.*

Greenberg, A. (2006). *Grand Soy Vanilla Latte with Cinnamon, No Foam: Jewish Identity and Community in a Time of Unlimited Choices. www.rebooters.net.*

Heilman, S. (2001). "A Young Judaea Israel Discovery Tour: The View from Inside." In Barry Chazan (ed.), *The Israel Experience: Studies in Jewish Identity and Youth Culture.* Jerusalem: CRB Foundation, 143–265.

Heilman, S. (2006). *Sliding to the Right: The Contest for the Future of American Jewish Orthodoxy.* Berkeley: University of California Press.

Horowitz, B. (2000). *Connections and Journeys: Assessing Critical Opportunities for Enhancing Jewish Identity.* New York: UJA-Federation of Jewish Philanthropies.

Horowitz, B. (2002). "Reframing the Study of Contemporary American Jewish Identity." *Contemporary Jewry* 23.

Kirshenblatt-Gimblett, B. (2001). "Learning from Ethnography: Reflections on the Nature and Efficacy of Youth Tours to Israel." In Barry Chazan (ed.), *The Israel Experience: Studies in Jewish Identity and Youth Culture.* Jerusalem: CRB Foundation, 269–331.

Kotler-Berkowitz, L., Cohen, S. M., Ament, J., Klaff, V., Mott, F. & Peckerman-Neuman, D. (2003). *The National Jewish Population Survey 2000–01: Strength, Challenge and Diversity in the American Jewish Population.* New York: United Jewish Communities.

Liebman, C. S. (1973). *The Ambivalent American Jew.* Philadelphia: Jewish Publication Society.

Liebman, C. S. (1999). "Post-war American Jewry: From Ethnic to Privatized Judaism." In E. Abrams and D. Dalin (eds.), *Secularism, Spirituality and the Future of American Jewry.* Washington, D. C.: Ethics and Public Policy Center, 7–17.

Liebman, C. S. & Cohen, S. M. (1990). *Two Worlds of Judaism: The Israeli and American Experiences.* New Haven: Yale University Press.

Medding, P. Y., Tobin, G., Fishman, S.B.; & Rimor, M. (1992). "Jewish Identity in Conversionary and Mixed Marriages." *American Jewish Yearbook* 92: 3–76.

Phillips, B. & Fishman, S.B. (forthcoming). "Causes and Consequences of American Jewish Intermarriage," *Sociology of Religion.*

Phillips, B. (1997). *Re-examining Intermarriage: Trends, Textures, and Strategies.* Boston and New York: Wilstein Institute and American Jewish Committee.

Phillips, B. (2005a). "American Judaism in the 21st Century" in Dana Kaplan (ed.), *The Cambridge Companion to American Judaism.* New York: Cambridge University Press.

Phillips, B. (2005b). "Catholic (and Protestant) Israel: The Permutations of Denominational Differences and Identities in Mixed Families" in Eli Lederhendler (ed.), *Studies in Contemporary Jewry Annual, Vol. XXI.*

Phillips, B. (2005c). Assimilation, Transformation, and the Long Range Impact of Intermarriage. *Contemporary Jewry* 25, 50–84.

Prell, R. E. (1999). *Fighting to Become Americans.* Boston: Beacon.

Putnam, R. (2000). *Bowling Alone.* New York: Simon & Schuster.

Ringer, B. (1967). *The Edge of Friendliness.* New York: Basic Books.

Roof, W. C. (1993). *Generation of Seekers.* San Francisco: Harper.

Roof, W. C. (1999). *Spiritual Marketplace.* Princeton: Princeton University Press.

Saxe, L., Kadushin, C., Hecht, S., Phillips, B., Kellner, S. & Rosen, M. I. (2004) *Birthright Israel: Evaluation Highlights.* Waltham, Mass.: Cohen Center for Modern Jewish Studies, Brandeis University.

Sales, A. L. & Saxe, L. (2004) *"How Goodly are Thy Tents:" Summer Camps as Jewish Socializing Experiences.* Lebanon, NH: Brandeis University Press/University Press of New England.

Sheskin, I. (1999). *How Jewish Communities Differ: Variations in the Findings of Local Jewish Population Studies.* New York: North American Jewish Data Bank.

Silberman, C. (1985). *A Certain People: American Jews and Their Lives Today.* New York: Summit Books.

Sklare, M. & Greenblum, J. (1979/1967). *Jewish Identity on the Suburban Frontier.* Chicago: University of Chicago Press.

Tobin, G. A. (2001). *The Transition of Communal Values and Behavior in Jewish Philanthropy.* San Francisco: Institute for Jewish & Community Research.

Ukeles, J. B., Miller, R., & Beck, P. (2006). *Young Jewish Adults in the United States Today.* New York: American Jewish Committee.

Waters, M. C. (1990). *Ethnic Options: Choosing Identities in America.* Berkeley: UC Press.

Wertheimer, J. (1997). "Current Trends in American Jewish Philanthropy." *American Jewish Year Book* 97: 3–92.

Wertheimer, J., Liebman, C. S. & Cohen, S. M. (1996). "How to Save American Jews," *Commentary* 101 (1), 47–51.

Wertheimer, J. (2005). *Linking the Silos: How to Accelerate the Momentum in Jewish Education Today.* New York: Avi Chai Foundation.

Wolfe, A. (2003). *The Transformation of American Religion: How We Actually Live Our Faith.* New York: Free Press.

Wuthnow, R. (1998). *Loose Connections: Joining Together in America's Fragmented Communities.* Cambridge, MA: Harvard University Press.

Wuthnow, R. (1999). *Growing Up Religious: Christians and Jews and Their Journeys of Faith.* Boston: Beacon Press.

Outreach and Jewish Education

Kerry Olitzky & Paul Golin

Interfaith families and their children represent the fastest-growing segment of the North American Jewish community. Interfaith marriage is not a new phenomenon in the history of Jewish civilization, particularly as the Jewish people have been dispersed in communities throughout the world. However, the extent to which interfaith marriage has become commonplace is indeed a relatively new occurrence. And the advocacy for more welcoming attitudes toward these families has helped to change our relationship to them over the last twenty years. This new posture promises to be even more important in the decades ahead as the number of interfaith families continues to increase. Most significantly, the "them" has become "us." There are few families in the Jewish community, regardless of background or affiliation, that have not felt the impact of interfaith marriage.

As detailed below, married households where only one spouse is Jewish will soon make up the majority of Jewish family households throughout North America and may already do so in the United States. Whether we are motivated by a moral imperative ("The stranger that lives with you shall be to you like the native, and you shall love him [or her] as yourself; for you were strangers in the land of Egypt" [Lev. 19:34]) or by simple demographic insights (the only feasible method for stemming demographic decline and increasing the size of the Jewish community is outreach to the intermarried and their children), we have an obligation to respond to the needs of this population and to work with them. As a result, we have to consider the implicit and explicit challenges in Jewish education relevant to serving this population in ways that previous generations were able to avoid. Questions we need to address include: What changes have to be made in the classroom ecology for this population? In particular, what images have to be considered in textbooks and in study materials? What changes in language have to be made? What assumptions about "Jewish memory" have to be changed? What myths about interfaith families have to be disabused? And finally, how does the "Who is a Jew?" question impact on teaching and reaching this population, especially when the non–Jewish adult member of the family is the mother and the children have not formally converted to Judaism?

At the Jewish Outreach Institute (JOI), founded in 1987 as a research institute at the CUNY Graduate Center and committed to research and investigation as one of its cornerstones, we continue to be devoted to the exploration of all relevant aspects of interfaith marriage, especially as it impacts the Jewish education and identity of children. Since JOI believes that interfaith marriage is the most critical domestic issue facing the North American Jewish community, it is clear that the way in which the Jewish community responds to this megatrend—particularly through the education of children—will help determine the future shape of our community for generations to come and most especially the next one.

Egon Mayer served as the founding director of JOI. His early research into the phenomenon of intermarriage laid the groundwork for most other research in the field and provided the impetus for much of the growth of the organization, which had already started several years before his untimely death in 2004. In 2000 Olitzky took on the leadership mantle of JOI as executive director in order to grow it into a national organization and oversee its expansion, along with Golin, associate executive director. The organization now provides programs and other direct services to intermarried families; advocates for the inclusion of the intermarried in all aspects of Jewish communal life; does research into various aspects of Jewish communal life in order to better understand and respond to the phenomenon of intermarriage; and trains a core of Jewish communal professionals and volunteer leaders. As a result, the authors are intimately familiar with the issues surrounding interfaith marriage.

THE CONTEXT

Understanding the magnitude of the intermarriage phenomenon is important for Jewish educators who want to share their teachings with the Jewish people *in its entirety* and also want to help in growing the community. The 2001 National Jewish Population Study (NJPS) found an intermarriage rate of 47% for Jews who married between 1996 and 2001. That 47% is the new number burned onto the communal agenda, replacing the 52% found by the 1990 National Jewish Population Study (the study that launched a thousand continuity initiatives). Regardless of whether the intermarriage rate is near, at or above 50%, looking at the intermarriage rate alone does not paint a full picture, because it does not tell us the impact or results of that rate (United Jewish Communities 2003, p. 16).

In anticipation of the release of the 2001 NJPS, JOI issued a report called "The Coming Majority" (Golin 2003) to address how the intermarriage rate translates into real households. The report explained that the number of intermarried households created is much higher than the individuals' rate quoted by NJPS reports. A 50% rate of intermarriage in the last five years actually means that the number of intermarried households created in those years is *double* that of in-married households, because it only takes one Jew to create an intermarried household but two Jews to create an in-married household. Thus if you have eight Jews and they intermarry at a rate of 50%, it means the four who intermarry create four intermarried households while the four who in-marry create only *two* in-married households because they're marrying each other.

When United Jewish Communities released the 2001 study, it provided the full data set for anyone adept at using the advanced sociological data software SPSS. For the rest of us the UJC issued a report that omitted the total number of intermarried households or their ratio to in-married households (United Jewish Communities 2003, p. 17). The missed story of the 2001 NJPS is that due to the cumulative effect of the rising intermarriage rate, there will soon be more intermarried than in-married households, regardless of when those intermarriages took place. Only by examining the raw data set does it become clear that the NJPS identified that nearly half of all currently-married households containing a Jewish spouse are already intermarried households (B. A. Phillips 2004, p. 63). Today, six years later, the "coming majority" may have already arrived, with the number of intermarried households surpassing in-married households.

More importantly for Jewish educators, the number of children from intermarried households has already far outpaced the number of children from in-married households (United Jewish Communities, p. 18). According to the raw data, 60% of married households created in the 1990s were intermarriages compared to only 40% in-marriages (B. A. Phillips 2004, p. 63; also see Phillips chapter on Demography in this volume). Almost every new local community demographic study confirms that for the youngest age cohorts, there are more children in intermarried households than in-married households (see, for example, recent studies completed in Ottawa and San Francisco) (B. A. Phillips 2004, p. 64).

Of course, the mere existence of children in intermarried households does not make them Jewish. The official NJPS Report states that 96% of children in households with two Jewish spouses are "being raised Jewish" compared to only 33% of children in intermarried households (United Jewish Communities 2003 p. 18). This is a highly deceptive oversimplification of a complex and nuanced question—or questions. The 96% found for in-married households allows for their understanding of raising Jewish children to include ethnic as well as religious identity. For intermarried respondents, Jewish ethnicity becomes a much more difficult question to answer than for in-married households, where it can serve as the default answer for those who may not otherwise be doing anything Jewish.

On the other side of this equation, the 2001 NJPS report issued by UJC does not tell us how the other 67% of intermarried households are raising their children if not Jewish. Based upon the work of Miller and Mayer, Bruce A. Phillips, and others, these 67% are not all raising Christian children (Miller & Mayer 2001 p. 2; B.A. Phillips 2004). The 2001 NJPS report lumped together those raising children in both religions with those raising them in another religion (i.e., they were not included in the 33% "raised Jewish" rate above). The nuances of what it means to raise children in two religions have yet to be explored in a quantitative study.

More importantly, the 1990 study found that 24% (B.A. Phillips 1997) of interfaith households are raising their children in no religion at all, which—for those who refuse to give up on the inherent value of any Jewish household—represents an important future growth potential for our community (and may also represent the lack of a decision made by intermarried parents with very young children). One analysis of the 2001 NJPS data (B. Phillips and Chertok 2004) breaks down the upbringing of children of intermarriage as 32% Jewish (Religion), 10% Jewish (Secular), 8% No Religion, 11% Jewish and Other, 35% Christian, and 4% Other. The fact that the NJPS Report chose to show only a partial picture when reporting on this highly important population segment perhaps speaks more to the agenda of the report writers than to the scientific study of the population—especially when the 33% NJPS reported rate of intermarried families raising Jewish children is seemingly contradicted elsewhere within the very same study; the 2001 NJPS found that 45% of college students age 18–29 who identify themselves as Jewish come from intermarried homes.

Whatever the actual percentages are at any given time (and nobody can ever get an exact count), an attainable goal for each community should be to encourage and help more than half their intermarried households to raise their children as strongly identified Jews. It is also a goal that, when reached, will produce overall population growth despite the lower-than-average birthrate among Jewish parents. This is a tantalizingly achievable goal that received a major boost from the findings of the recent Boston community study that indicated 60% of intermarried families were raising their children Jewish and stated "it is likely that the increase [in Boston's Jewish population] is a result of improved survey methodology, growth in the total population of Greater Boston and the phenomenon of a majority of children in intermarried households being raised as Jews" (Saxe et al. 2006, p. 12).

The fact that Boston, together with San Francisco (which in a recent local Jewish demographic study also showed higher-than-NJPS levels of interfaith families raising Jewish children), has some of the best-coordinated, best-funded, longest-standing interfaith outreach programs was not lost on outreach advocates. Much was made of the budget provided for interfaith outreach by the Combined Jewish Philanthropies of Greater Boston (the local federation), which, at about 1.2% of its overall budget, reportedly represents the highest rate of outreach allocation in the United States (though still a small percentage considering the number of households in the cohort). A few vocal opponents, however, criticized the study on its methodology and suggested that even if the statistics about intermarried households raising Jewish children are true, it is because of the strong Jewish educational institutions in Boston, not because of outreach. Of course, they defined neither "education" nor "outreach" in their criticisms, and this speaks to a central problem not only in understanding the Boston study but in resolving the so-called outreach debate: outreach *is* education in much of its practice. And, education can be outreach. The reason the Boston Jewish community succeeds in reaching more intermarried households is not because of its education *or* its outreach, but because of its education *and* its outreach. Many of Boston's world-class Jewish educational institutions are integrally involved in and connected to its outreach efforts (Saxe et al. 2006, p. 17).

Outreach means understanding and reaching Jews on the periphery who are not currently involved in the community, including a disproportionately large percentage of intermarried households. While we speak of interfaith families as a whole, there are actually subsections of this population that are important to consider somewhat independently, especially because Jewish education will undoubtedly impact them differently. While sociologists may use different categories, we are defining the population in three loose categories:

- interfaith families raising Jewish children;

- interfaith families who are raising their children in "American civil religion" with a smattering of religious culture from both religions (which usually means a secular celebration of Hanukkah and Christmas and sometimes Easter and Passover); and
- interfaith families who are attempting to raise their children in both religions or solely as Christians.

For the most part, formal Jewish educational institutions serve only the first segment of this population—that is, those who have already made the decision to raise Jewish children and generally under the rubric of family education. Moreover, the programs of these educational institutions often focus on the children themselves without helping the household create Jewish memories for these children. One program, JOI's "Mothers Circle" (for women of other religious backgrounds raising Jewish children), targets parents rather than children and fits best under the broad category of adult education. Often, programs that exist outside of formal Jewish institutions have a much wider impact on the population. Local and national demographic studies suggest that most interfaith families, even those who have made a decision to raise Jewish children, are not being greatly impacted by the educational institutions in the Jewish community (Beck 2005). Informal Jewish education programs, especially in the form of "Public Space Judaism"—a signature program model of the Jewish Outreach Institute (discussed below)—have the potential to influence these intermarried subgroups, especially the large second subgroup of those who raise their children primarily in American civil religion (and who may be incorrectly grouped into the third category—actively raising children in both or another religion—by some in the Jewish community).

The so-called "conversionary marriage"—in which one adult partner has formally converted to Judaism—may look just like an in-marriage to an outsider. However, a number of the issues that emerge relevant to education for interfaith families will also present themselves in these families. In both cases, half of the extended families come from religious heritages other than Judaism and may be actively practicing a different religion. In addition, there are educational programs specifically designed for segments of this population that can be seen as part of the continuum of interfaith marriage (even when conversion takes place without the complement of an impending or existent marital relationship). Only recently have the formal Jewish religious movements started to understand this phenomenon. For converts affiliated with the Reform movement, the Union for Reform Judaism trains support group leaders as part of its "Outreach Fellows" certification program. These facilitators lead "New Beginnings" support groups for recent converts at their synagogues (http://urj.org/outreach/classes/workshops/). The Conservative movement has a new initiative to encourage conversion (under the rubric of the Edud Initiative—http://www.uscj.org/Beyond_Keruv_to_Edud6908.html). From a different perspective, JOI's Empowering Ruth program is designed for women who have recently converted to Judaism. Its design grew out of the reality that most Introduction to Judaism classes—which are generally required of conversion candidates—are primarily didactic in nature. Empowering Ruth is more experiential as a result.

RESEARCH OVERVIEW

Two types of research should be of most interest to Jewish educators and educational policy-makers: research about the target population itself, and research about programs to reach the target population. The challenge with the latter is that the field is so new that few programs have been fully evaluated, and there is little research that has studied the impact of the programs. The challenge with the former is that much of the research on intermarriage reflects the strong perspectives of the researcher and/or the sponsors based upon their positions as advocates, whether sociologists or trained in other fields. These studies are used as vehicles to determine which aspects of education (or which educational programs) can "prevent" interfaith marriage. They assume that intermarriage is the direct result of poor Jewish education, and therefore it can be prevented with better, more intensive methods of Jewish education. Yet no researcher has proven a *causal* relationship between higher levels of Jewish education and increased in-marriage.

For example, in the previous section we detailed one instance of selective presentation in the 2001 NJPS Report that creates a particularly bleak view of Jewish childrearing in intermarried families compared to in-married families. Cohen, a principal author of that report, has spent nearly two decades producing papers that discount the Jewish potential of intermarried households. His recent publication, "A Tale of Two Jewries: The Inconvenient Truth for American Jews" (2006), appears on its surface to be a boon for Jewish educators, seemingly *proving* that Jewish educational experiences in and of themselves reduce intermarriage. While he strongly recommends day schools, summer camps, Israel trips, student groups, and adult education as programs to enhance the quality of Jewish life, he does not mention the need to include intermarried families in those programs. The inherent educational and experiential values of these programs should appeal to the intermarried families as much as to the in-married. Higher levels of Jewish education *correspond* to lower levels of intermarriage but are not causal. There are simply too many other factors involved.

Cohen could have dissected the community by any number of variables and found alternative factors that "cause" in-marriage. For example, he did not compare religious practices between those who in-marry and those who intermarry while holding education levels constant; if he had, he could have easily claimed that simply keeping kosher—in and of itself—prevents intermarriage. Why not promote kashrut? Ignoring some corollary factors in favor of others points to his bias toward an ethnocentric rather than religious view of Judaism. Likewise, in a rare and too-brief nod to the larger trends of life in America, he admits that "Zip code may in fact be more predictive of in-marriage than Jewish education in that people still date and marry those they live near." In other words, intermarriage (and therefore in-marriage) is more an accident of demographics than a failing of Jewish education. Intermarriage is a byproduct of Jewish acceptance into the mainstream of non–Jewish America (about 98% of all Americans), and the spreading out from traditional Jewish neighborhoods and cities into the expanding suburbs and exurbs.

Alba (2003) is among the foremost contributors to studies on assimilation in American society, regardless of religious or ethnic background. His argument—that intermarriage in the Jewish community is an American phenomenon rather than a Jewish phenomenon—has proven to be a very important asset in our understanding of interfaith marriage. Research in this area will continue to help us discern population challenges that are uniquely Jewish and those that are simply Jewish reflections of the American whole. Alba suggests that that the blurring of lines of distinction between Jews, Christians and the nonreligious is both the result of intermarriage and that which has allowed for it in an open American society. Young American Jews today, in particular, have a seamless experience in which religious and ethnic boundaries don't seem relevant at all. But what is unique about the contemporary experience of Jewish assimilation is that while assimilation is usually one-sided, with the minority culture becoming totally absorbed by the majority culture, in the case of the Jewish community, Jews have influenced American culture out of all proportion to our numbers. Today most Jews feel both 100% Jewish and 100% American without conflict. In fact, in our experience, "integration" is more appropriate terminology for much of the current American Jewish experience than is "assimilation."

We must also keep in mind that neither the intermarried nor the in-married are monolithic groups. Practitioners on the ground, including countless Jewish educators, see intermarried families every day who are virtually indistinguishable from in-married families in their home practices and desire to educate their children as Jews. We would imagine that the overwhelming majority of educators want to help shape young Jewish minds regardless of whether those minds are the product of one or two Jewish parents (or single or married parents, for that matter). While it is easier for two Jewish parents to raise strongly identified Jewish children than for just one to do so, the danger in painting an entire group with one brushstroke—as when Cohen declares intermarried families as an entirely different "Jewry" than in-married families—is the license it gives others to completely write them out of the community.

The innovative research of Horowitz (2000/2003) examines a mode of Jewishness showing mixed patterns of Jewish engagement, between the two supposed extremes "that the American Jewish future is a forced choice between assimilation and Jewish distinctiveness." In fact, a majority of Jews move in and out of Jewish engagement and affiliation over the course of a lifetime. Through a combined qualitative/quantitative study, she found that "The people who have mixed patterns of Jewish engagement are not indifferent about being Jewish, but their ongoing Jewish involvement depends on it both being meaningful and fitting in with their lives. The people who subscribe to this third form of Jewishness experience their Judaism as a set of values and historical people-consciousness rather than as a mode of observance."

She summarizes her findings by pointing out: "For Jewish institutions, it is crucial to learn that 60% of the people in the study experienced changes in their relationship to being Jewish over time, suggesting that Jewish identity is not a fixed factor in one's life but rather a matter that parallels personal growth and personal development. There are critical periods and moments in people's lives that offer potential opportunities for Jewish institutions to play a role, if only these institutions can be open and available to individuals in a way that meets their changing needs and concerns." While Horowitz's research does not directly address intermarried Jews or their children, we know anecdotally—as an organization engaged in direct service—that this kind of "Jewish journey" is absolutely embarked upon by intermarried families, especially because lifecycle events like marriage, childbirth, and *brit milah* prompt Jewish challenges that many in-married couples do not have to address.

Among the children of intermarriage, three studies are instructive in determining, first, that Jewish continuity does not necessarily end with the intermarriage of their parents, and second, that there are points of contact with Judaism that educators can use to encourage such Jewish journeys.

Benjamin Phillips and Chertok (2004) evaluated the data set from the 2001 NJPS to determine that intermarriage—in and of itself—is not an "event horizon," a black hole of Jewish identity whereby all children of intermarriage disappear from the organized community. They determined that "the environment in which a person grows up plays a much greater role than simple heredity" and found that the Jewish identity of children of intermarriage parallels that of children of in-marriage (though still not as high) when those children of intermarriage have the same Jewish experiences. Those Jewish experiences are, in order of importance: parents who raise them Jewish; having Jewish friends; receiving Jewish education (the more intensive, like day schools, the better); and Jewish ritual practices. In speaking to the importance of Jewish education, the authors warn that "To the extent that these institutions screen out children from intermarriages who are being raised as Jews—whether by policy or attitude—they reinforce intermarriage as a black hole for Jewish identity from which no return is possible."

Bruce A. Phillips, who conducted the most detailed analysis of the 1990 NJPS in regard to intermarriage (1997) and reached bleak conclusions, nevertheless finds some rays of hope in the Jewish identity of the adult children of intermarriage in a recent analysis (2005). He finds high levels of Jewish identity among children of intermarriage *on some measures*, most strikingly when responding to two statements: "I have a strong sense of belonging to the Jewish people" (71% of children of intermarriage agreed compared to 87% of children of in-marriage); and "How important is being Jewish in your life?" (74% of children of intermarriage answered very or somewhat important compared to 85% of children of in-marriage).

He also found that "Most important to both groups was celebrating Jewish holidays: 81 percent of Jewish parentage respondents and 73 percent of mixed parentage respondents said that this was involved in how they were Jewish. The similarity between Jewish and mixed parentage respondents is all the more impressive when it is recalled that most of the mixed parentage respondents were not raised in Judaism and did not identify themselves as Jewish by religion." However, these celebrations appeared to be more cultural than religious. "Mixed and Jewish parentage respondents were also in close agreement that attending synagogue was the least salient aspect of how they were Jewish (47 percent of the former and 55 percent of the latter)." Phillips concludes by suggesting that "Given the movement away from Judaism [as a religion] associated with children of mixed marriage, the potential membership pool for synagogues and Jewish organizations will diminish and the institutions that have come to define the American Jewish community will become less numerous and less visible. *Whether other associational forms will emerge from this transformation remains to be seen* [emphasis added]" (1997).

A similarly strong desire to retain identification with the Jewish people, though not religiously, was one of the key findings of extensive interviews conducted by Beck on behalf of the Jewish Outreach Institute for its recent qualitative study of young adult children of intermarriage (2005). The respondents expressed comfort with their dual identity, with many volunteering that they identified themselves as "half and half" and most (64%) expressing a desire to "transmit a Jewish ethnic identity to their children" even as they indicated that having a Jewish partner is not important to them (78%). Despite their general lack of knowledge regarding Jewish laws and practices, respondents were cognizant that traditional Judaism considers only the offspring of Jewish mothers to be fully Jewish. Jewish people with whom they came into contact often reinforced this idea. For this reason and no doubt a variety of others, 64% of children with Jewish mothers celebrated their bar/bat mitzvah while only 37% of children with Jewish fathers celebrated their bar/bat mitzvah. Grandparents also played a pivotal role in determining many respondents' Jewish identities and in helping to instill a strong sense of culture and family history in their grandchildren.

A large proportion of respondents in the Beck study mentioned Jewish identity development through popular culture, especially being taken to see "Fiddler on the Roof" and/or "Schindler's List," or reading the diary of Anne Frank, and experiencing them as a "Jewish experiences." At the same time, possibly as a result of popular consciousness, over 80% currently believe that "opposing anti-Semitism" is somewhat or very important. Several respondents described how their Jewish consciousness was enhanced by actual or perceived anti–Semitic experiences directed at them. In many interviews the importance of Holocaust remembrance emerged as an essential component of our respondents' Jewish identity.

Nearly one-third of those interviewed by Beck indicated that they received some formal Jewish education, although limited in nature and perhaps only in an early childhood setting. On the other hand, 37% reported that they had enrolled in Jewish studies courses in college, and of those, the majority (59%) had no prior Jewish education. Of respondents with no prior Jewish education, slightly more enrolled in Jewish studies courses in college (33%) than attended a Hillel event (20%). This is also true of respondents who did have prior Jewish education: 48% enrolled in Jewish studies courses compared to 41% who participated in a Hillel-sponsored event. As for religious education, less than one-quarter of those interviewed had a bar/bat mitzvah when growing up; however, 90% of those who did so currently consider themselves exclusively "Jewish" by religion, while this is true for only 13% of those who did not. 85% of those who had a bar/bat mitzvah compared with 61% who did not said that being Jewish was "somewhat" or "very" important to them.

Overall, the research on intermarried households continues to paint a picture of disengagement from traditional measures of Jewish identity, while at the same time indicating that those who do engage are capable of raising strongly identified Jewish children, and that many more intermarried households retain aspects of Jewish identification and even practice that are not being fully exploited by the organized Jewish community for deeper engagement. The implication for educators is that to reach this growing (and soon to be majority) population, we may need to think further "outside the box." And in this case, the box may be our traditional institutions. That is what the programming of the Jewish Outreach Institute has attempted over the last nine years, and the evaluative study of our first three years of programming (Miller and Mayer 2001) is one of the few publicly accessible program evaluations relevant to education and outreach.

JOI obtained a list of past participants from eleven outreach programs operating throughout North America between 1998 and 2000. The programs varied in mission, target population and size (from a handful to literally thousands per program), but all shared the goal of reaching unaffiliated Jewish households. Prior to program contact, 51% of all 735 survey respondents identified themselves as either "Not at All Involved" or "Minimally Involved" in Jewish life. After program participation, that percentage fell to 34%. This shows that the outreach programs studied were effective in both (a) attracting unaffiliated Jews to participate and (b) increasing their level of Jewish involvement. Among intermarried survey respondents, those identifying as "Moderately Involved" in Jewish life rose from 30% prior to program contact to 47% at the time of survey completion. Those interfaith households identifying as "Highly Involved" increased nearly four-fold, from just 3% prior to program contact to 11% at the time of survey completion.

Among all program participants responding to the survey (40% from intermarried households and 60% representing single or in-married households), about half agreed that the outreach program had an impact on their Jewish home life, and an overwhelming majority agreed that the program both was "Helpful" and "Inspired Jewish Life Involvement." Among intermarried survey respondents, more than half agreed that the outreach program had "Some Impact" (35%) or "Considerable Impact" (19%) on their Jewish home life, and of those who had not been members of a synagogue prior to program participation, 35% joined one after program participation, and another 25% were still considering membership at the time of the survey. Overall, synagogue membership among interfaith respondents increased from 32% prior to program participation to 46% at the time of the survey. The majority of intermarried families who were attracted by the outreach programs were young couples with small children. Their primary interest was in family-oriented programming. Outreach worked most effectively in programs that took place in low-threshold public settings and provided a sense of an alternative Jewish community.

Most program-specific evaluations are internal and have not been released publicly. But in general, outreach efforts that make it past pilot stage are effective in impacting participants. JOI has conducted internal evaluations of its own programs, including The Mothers Circle, and for other organizations, including one of the longest-standing outreach programs in the country, "Interfaith Connections" in San Francisco. The challenge for outreach programs based in intensive learning is more about getting large numbers to participate. For those who participate, we know that intensive small-group programs do make a valuable impact.

JOI has also conducted "Jewish Community Environmental Outreach Scans" in nine North American communities of varying sizes over the past five years that demonstrate the challenges most Jewish institutions face in welcoming all newcomers, not just intermarried families. Through lengthy interviews with professionals at Jewish institutions (over 500 to date), plus "secret shopper" anonymous phone calls and blind emails, we've learned that traditional institutions such as synagogues and Jewish Community Centers rarely train their frontline staff to properly handle inquiries from the unengaged, even though these are cases where people on the periphery are "running toward us" rather than requiring us to go find them. Before we can educate, we must welcome in and make comfortable, and JOI's institutional research indicates that the community is losing opportunities with that very first step.

IMPLICATIONS AND/OR POLICY RECOMMENDATIONS

Because of the vast numbers involved, the research on children who have been raised in interfaith families necessarily has to impact the construct of future educational institutions and their programs. However, the widely debated analysis of this research and its concomitant population depends on attitudes that emerge out of ideological positions that precede the research and are often independent of it. The "tipping point" is beginning to emerge due to sheer numbers, with the hope that the community can come together around a single focus: helping all households—whether intermarried, in-married or unmarried—raise Jewish children.

Bringing more of the unaffiliated intermarried households inside the Jewish community requires an expansion of traditional pathways into Jewish identity. Research shows that intermarried households engage with Jewish institutions less frequently and for shorter lengths of time than in-married households. This is supported consistently by recent local community demographic studies, as well as by the National Jewish Population Studies of 1990 and 2001. The answer to why that happens is something about which we can currently only speculate. Certainly, disinterest or a competing faith may play a role. But some of the other reasons might include such factors as hesitancy to enter Jewish establishments when not all family members are Jewish (or raised as Jews); anticipation that they don't know enough to participate; and prior rejection or expectation of rejection due to their intermarried status. Certainly, sweeping attitudes about intermarried families held and transmitted by educators can sour the Jewish experiences of those very individuals who are among us, and this must be taken into consideration when creating a conducive classroom (or informal educational program) ecology. We recommend a more nuanced approach that takes into account the knowledge that individuals (including many from interfaith families) move in and out of Jewish affiliation and engagement over the course of a lifetime.

Each of these "barriers to participation" must be identified and then addressed if our institutions hope to remain relevant in the future. This is especially true because variations on each of these barriers exist for *all* underrepresented populations within the community, such as single-parent, LGBT, multiracial, disabled, and any other unengaged households.

Educators must try to see their programs through the eyes of the unaffiliated intermarried in order to identify the barriers and work around them to meet the needs of this population. Make sure your educational programs allow for students to join mid-stream or catch up separately and quickly, because sometimes when the "silos" are linked too tightly, those who did not begin at an early age feel too left behind to join later. For example, children of intermarriage may approach the community when they near their thirteenth birthday because their attendance at the *b'nai mitzvah* of their peers may have been a significant first encounter with Judaism that sparked their own desire to also be recognized as *b'nai mitzvah*. Can we then provide this transformative experience to them on a much-condensed timetable? Or is our only answer that they must study for three years and have their celebration when all their peers have moved on to Sweet Sixteens?

In trying to reach those who may not have benefited from a strong Jewish education, remove high-barrier language from your marketing materials; Hebrew words remind the less literate of their educational shortcomings and should be avoided or at least translated in program titles.

It is a growing imperative that we as educators come together more regularly to identify the barriers to participation, and to determine what works best in helping individuals over and around those barriers. More resources for Jewish educators to learn outreach methodology must be created so that we can engage the *majority* of the Jewish community, especially those who are currently not participating in our organizations.

Children of intermarriage are not yet participating in formal Jewish educational programs in numbers proportional to the size of their population. Most formal programs of Jewish education demand an extensive commitment on the part of the child and his/her family. This commitment is generally reflected in time and expense. In addition, these programs are often held in high-barrier institutions, many of which barriers the interfaith family finds difficult to surmount. Children who come from interfaith families primarily access Jewish "education" through secular means and mainstream culture. Thus the Jewish community needs to reach these families and children through their secular environments outside of the Jewish institutions. Currently, the "outside" face of the Jewish community to the at-large society is still very much shaped by a response to anti–Semitism and the Holocaust even as the "inside" of the community moves toward more joyous expressions of Jewish life. Holocaust remembrance and fighting anti–Semitism resonate surprisingly highly with the adult children of intermarriage and can be used as programmatic elements to reach them. At the same time, the Jewish community must do a better job of promoting additional facets of Jewish life within the secular mainstream, because Judaism in popular culture has a powerful impact on the Jewish identity of unaffiliated and intermarried households. Making our programs more accessible by placing them in secular venues is one way to address this. For example, if the choice of venue for an author reading is between a synagogue and a Barnes & Noble, you will get a less affiliated, more intermarried audience at the Barnes & Noble. Doing so is part of JOI's Public Space Judaism^{SM} model but would not be considered "outreach" unless participants were also greeted personally and had their names captured for individualized follow-up in order to provide relevant next steps into deepening Jewish engagement.

For Jewish educators and education policy makers, the move away from Jewish religiosity among the children of intermarriage suggests the need for more venues of Jewish identity through non-religious means. For example, college-age children of intermarriage are willing to study Judaism as a religion when it's presented in the non-threatening confines of a secular university class setting, but they will not walk into a synagogue for the same information. The fact that this is mirrored by children from in-married households should make this suggestion non-controversial. Jewish organizations can create joint programming with Jewish studies programs at secular universities to find and serve this population.

The demography of our community has changed dramatically during the past twenty years. We believe in the spark of Jewish identity within today's Jewish youth. The question: Can and will our institutions adapt to the change?

ADDITIONAL RESEARCH QUESTIONS

- What is the benefit to children being raised as Jews in an interfaith family? (Why should they bother?)
- What benefits can the adult partner from another religious heritage enjoy who is part of the Jewish community as a result of his or her marriage to a Jewish person?
- How do barriers limit access to informal and formal programs of Jewish education?

FUTURE DIRECTIONS

- Currently there are no formal training programs in institutions of higher Jewish learning for those who work in outreach education. It is important that tracks be added to existing training programs that emphasize the application of new research as it emerges about outreach to interfaith families and individuals.
- Continuing professional development needs to be added to the agenda of existing educational enterprises to better prepare educators in the field to plan outreach education programs.
- New opportunities to network must be accelerated if we are to meet the growing needs in the community. An example is JOPLIN: Jewish Outreach Professionals Log-In Network as a website (joplin.joi.org) and listserve to connect communal professionals across denominational and institutional lines around the issues of outreach best practices and programming.

CONCLUSION

Like it or not, interfaith marriage—an American phenomenon more than solely a Jewish one—is here to stay. The children who live in intermarried families already outnumber those who live in in-married households and will eventually comprise the majority of children who consider themselves Jewish—if the community embraces them. Thus, unless we are prepared to "write them off", we have no alternative but to reckon with the challenges implicit in working with this population—and then make whatever adjustments are necessary in our educational institutions and programs to serve their needs.

The approach to reaching this population does not have to mean that we are "diluting" the Jewish educational system. When barriers exist, they must be lowered while simultaneously making sure that every student has easy access to the tools necessary to climb over those barriers or at least build a ramp to approach them. It is not an "either/or" approach to Jewish education that is being advocated. Rather, it is a "both/and" position that will be necessary, provided both approaches are offered without value judgments or punitive measures, and that we do so within a supportive environment with equal access to all.

HIGHLIGHTS

- Interfaith marriage is the most critical domestic issue currently facing the North American Jewish community.
- The wisdom with which we respond to this challenge will determine the future of the North American Jewish community.
- Interfaith marriage has become the unfortunate "litmus test" for successful Jewish educational/ identity-building programs.

- Whether and *how* we educate the children of interfaith families is critical to the future growth and expansion of the North American Jewish community.

- The little research that has been done is primarily polemical in nature and has generally focused on Jewish continuity and identity.

- More research is indicated, since this population is the fastest–growing segment of the community and will soon be the largest segment.

LARGER CONTEXT

It is difficult to imagine any discussion about Jewish education in the 21st century without an in-depth conversation about the "elephant in the room": interfaith marriage. It is becoming so commonplace that there are large communities where the number of interfaith families outnumbers the number of in-married families. Moreover, nearly 50% of students who identify Jewishly on the college campus come from interfaith homes. While we may define what constitutes an interfaith family from a variety of perspectives, one thing is clear: It will remain the defining issue for Jewish identity for several generations to come. How the Jewish community, and particularly its educational institutions, responds will determine the extent to which the Jewish community is willing to reach out and welcome this population and—most importantly—its children. This chapter reviews the limited research on this target population, as well the policy implications of such research.

ANNOTATED BIBLIOGRAPHY

It is important to note that while the research listed below is not solely dedicated to the field of educational research under discussion, salient elements are indeed relevant to the subject of this chapter and are thus included. Since Jewish identity is intimately related to Jewish education, studies on identity are relevant.

Beck, P. (2005). *A Flame Still Burns: The Dimensions and Determinants of Jewish Identity Among Young Adult Children of the Intermarried*. New York: Jewish Outreach Institute. This study looked at a small number of young adult children of intermarriage (ages 24–30) in Chicago, San Francisco and Boston in an attempt to identify trends among this population. It is particularly helpful in disabusing certain myths about the population and making program recommendations for children of intermarriage before they reach the age of the cohort under scrutiny. The study also includes important recommendations that emerge from the study for the development of educational programs of outreach for young adult children of the intermarried, particularly on the college campus.

Fishman, S.B. (2004). *Double or Nothing*. Waltham, MA: Brandeis University Press. This book is based on a study of a small number of subjects and has been used by advocates of "in-marriage" to show the so-called "disastrous" results of interfaith marriage as it impacts on the future Jewish identity and ethnicity of children, as defined by the parameters set by the author.

Phillips, B. & Chertok, F. (2004). *Jewish Identity among the Adult Children of Intermarriage. Cohen Center for Modern Jewish Studies*. Waltham, MA. This presentation recommends a combination of outreach to the intermarried and identity-building programs (particularly day schools and teen trips to Israel) as prophylaxis for future interfaith marriage. The authors contend that such an approach "increases the Jewish capital of those who choose to intermarry" and positively impacts the children of the intermarried.

Phillips, B. A. (1997). *Re-examining Intermarriage: Trends, Textures, and Strategies*. Boston, Los Angeles and New York: Susan and David Wilstein Institute of Jewish Policy Studies and American Jewish Committee. In this approach to studying the population of those who have intermarried, the researcher interviewed both Jewish and non–Jewish partners. The study also challenges the common polar approach to intermarriage: either embrace outreach exclusively or reject it entirely. Most importantly, it provides a classification structure of intermarriages and a set of policy directions that suggest areas for further investigation.

Sales, A. L. & Saxe, L. (2004). *How Goodly Are Thy Tents*: Summer Camps as Jewish Socializing Experiences. Lebanon, NH: Brandeis University Press. This study shows the important influence of Jewish summer camps as a peer development mechanism in the development and nurturing of Jewish identity among children. One thing that is clear from this study and from other similar studies is that peer bonding is more significant than is identity development in programs such as summer camps. It is this peer bonding that is the more significant limiting factor in future interfaith marriage among members of the peer group.

Saxe, L., Kadushin, C., Kelner, S., Rosen. M.I. & Yereslove, E. (2002). *A Mega-experiment in Jewish Education: The Impact of Birthright Israel*. Waltham, MA: Cohen Center for Modern Jewish Studies. This study evaluates what is clearly one of the boldest endeavors in Jewish educational programming of the late 20th–early 21st century. As a surprise to many educators, this research indicates that even intensive programs of short duration such as the trips to Israel under the auspices of Birthright Israel have a lasting impact on the Jewish identity of its participants. However, it is a diminishing asset that requires follow-up to sustain its impact into the future. Of interest to this chapter, the report chose not to break down its findings between children from in-married homes and children from intermarried homes, even though we know that Birthright Israel has experienced moderate success in reaching large numbers of children of intermarriage.

REFERENCES

Alba, R. & Nee, V. (2003). *Remaking the American Mainstream: Assimilation and Contemporary Immigration*. Cambridge: Harvard University Press.

Beck, P. (2005). A *Flame Still Burns: The Dimensions and Determinants of Jewish Identity Among Young Adult Children of the Intermarried*. New York: Jewish Outreach Institute.

Cohen, S. M. (2006). *A Tale of Two Jewries: "The Inconvenient Truth" for American Jews*. New York: Jewish Life Network/Steinhardt Foundation.

Golin, P. (2003). *The Coming Majority: Suggested Action on Intermarried Households for the Organized Jewish Community*. New York: Jewish Outreach Institute.

Horowitz, B. (2000, revised 2003). *Connections and Journeys: Assessing Critical Opportunities for Enhancing Jewish Identity. A report to the Commission on Jewish Identity and Renewal*. New York: UJA-Federation of New York.

Jewish Outreach Institute. (2005). Jewish Outreach Scan of the San Francisco Bay Area, Jewish Outreach Institute. (Additional studies and material online at joplin.joi.org)

Mayer, E., Kosmin, B. & Keysar, A. (2001). *American Jewish Identity Survey*. New York: Center for Jewish Studies, The Graduate Center of the City University of New York.

Miller, R. & Mayer, E. (2001). *The Impact of Jewish Outreach on the Intermarried and Unaffiliated: A study of participants in outreach programs sponsored by the Jewish Connection Partnership, a program of the Jewish Outreach Institute*. New York: Jewish Outreach Institute.

Phillips, B. & Chertok, F. (2004). *Jewish Identity among the Adult Children of Intermarriage*. Cohen Center for Modern Jewish Studies, Brandeis University, presented to the 36th Annual Conference of the Association of Jewish Studies, Chicago, IL.

Phillips, B. A. (2004). *Jewish Community Study of San Francisco, the Peninsula, Marin and Sonoma Counties*. Jewish Community Federation of San Francisco, the Peninsula, Marin and Sonoma Counties. Online at www. sfjcf.org

Phillips, B. A. (1997). *Re-examining Intermarriage: Trends, Textures, and Strategies*. Boston; Los Angeles; and New York: Susan and David Wilstein Institute of Jewish Policy Studies and American Jewish Committee.

Phillips, B. A. (2005). "Assimilation, Transformation, and the Long Range Impact of Intermarriage." *Contemporary Jewry*: The Journal of the Association for the Social Scientific Study of Jewry 25, 50–74.

Quets, G. (2002). *The Outreach Potential of Jewish Film Festivals*. New York: Jewish Outreach Institute.

Saxe, L., Phillips, B., Kadushin, C., Wright G. & Parmer, D. (2006). *The 2005 Boston Community Survey: Preliminary Findings*. Boston: Steinhardt Social Research Institute, Brandeis University for Combined Jewish Philanthropies of Boston.

Ukeles, J. (2006). *Jewish Community Centennial Study of Atlanta*. Atlanta: Jewish Federation of Greater Atlanta.

United Jewish Communities (2003). *National Jewish Population Study 2000–01 Report*. New York: United Jewish Communities. *www.ujc.org/njps*

A "Who-ness" and a Wholeness: Optimizing the Learning and Development of Elementary Children

Michael Ben-Avie, Ph.D.

At each developmental level the child addresses the matter of identity anew. Identity is a pattern of organization superimposed on the ego to combine its various elements and identifications into an integrated and functional whole. To form an identity, the self musters these elements according to some inner template and gives them coherent form. Once established, identity confirms for the child a sense of being a distinctive person, of possessing a *who-ness* and a *wholeness* that are characteristically his or her own (Erikson, 1950). A composite structure emerges from the blending of many substructures, all fitted together and superimposed on one another. Thus, the child has a certain identity as a member of a particular family, as a member of a specific religious or ethnic group, as a representative of a given gender, as an aspirant perhaps toward certain career choices, as a bearer of particular ideals or values, and so on.

Excerpt from a chapter on "The Early Grade-School Child" by Joseph D. Noshpitz, Chesapeake Youth Centers, and Robert A. King (1991), Yale Child Study Center

A WHOLENESS

In optimal circumstances, children's development is balanced. There is a "wholeness" to their development because a meshing or coordination occurs among six pathways that are critical to academic learning. James P. Comer, M.D., associate dean of the Yale School of Medicine and founder of the Yale School Development Program, talks about six developmental pathways to characterize the lines along which children mature—physical, cognitive, psychological, language, social, and ethical (Comer, Ben-Avie, Haynes, & Joyner 1999, p. 3). Consider the power of the metaphor of "wholeness" as a method for understanding balanced and uneven development:

> This metaphor of balanced development is helpful in understanding how a bright child can also be socially awkward. The same child who can remember every algebraic formula might also be the one who can't remember to call his grandmother to say thank you for a gift. How is it that the bodybuilder can't manage to carry the laundry basket up the stairs? The child who has no problem telling you what you've done wrong somehow cannot seem to say, "You look tired. I'll do it" (Ben-Avie, 2004, p. 87).

Balanced development relies on children's self-regulation. Maholmes (2004), our colleague at the Yale School Development Program, writes: "Students should not be passive bystanders in their own development" (p. 50). Learning and development are not spectator sports. Children who engage in educationally purposeful activities and put forth the effort to enhance their growth along all the pathways will experience balanced development. In this way they will develop a "wholeness".

A WHO-NESS

Paying attention to students' development does not detract from student learning. In fact, promoting the highest levels of development among students seems to be what helps them reach high academic goals and form a sense of "who-ness" (Ben-Avie et al. 2003). With youth development as the aim of Jewish education, success has been achieved when students attain a "who-ness" that (1) is consistent with the goals and objectives of Jewish formal and informal educational programs and (2) will be sustained beyond students' participation in the program(s). For example, a sense of adherence to the Jewish people, past and present, is a developmental outcome of Jewish informal and formal educational programs. This sense of adherence is an "outcome" in its own right, and as an outcome it is not valued merely as a stepping stone or "process" leading to students' mastery of the Jewish sacred texts.

Of course, the interaction between the curriculum and the child is critical. On one side of the equation is an immeasurably large curriculum; on the other side of the equation is an elementary school-aged child. With development as the aim of education, we say that it is not sufficient for children merely to learn Jewish academic material cognitively; it is also essential for children to form an emotional attachment to the learning and to engage in actions or behaviors that are consistent with their learning. More than this, for children to completely form their "who-ness" they need to see themselves as members of the Jewish people. Thus indicators of success in promoting the development of young people in Jewish formal and informal educational programs are framed in terms of cognitions, emotions, actions, and partaking of community.

EXPERIENCES AND EDUCATION

Our interest in trying to figure out the relationship between youth development and student learning has led our Jewish Educational Change team to study educational and psychological interventions. The team's research among Jewish elementary school-aged students indicates that when children develop well, they learn well. This research is informed by the ongoing work of the Yale Child Study Center's School Development Program, fondly known as the "Comer process" in honor of its founder, James P. Comer. Ben-Avie and Comer (2005) articulate how research instruments developed at the Yale Child Study Center were customized for Jewish schools. Among these research instruments are the *Learning and Development in Jewish Schools Student, Educator, and Parent Surveys.* The *Educator Survey* is at the heart of our Educators in Jewish Schools Study (EJSS), a North American study of educators as adults in the workplace. The Student Survey comprises the core of our study of Jewish Educational Experiences and Happiness.

This chapter presents findings from research among Jewish elementary school-aged children that was conducted during the formation stage of the Jewish Educational Experiences and Happiness Study. In this study, young people's experiences in Jewish educational programs are measured by four constructs that have been scientifically demonstrated to impact adult quality of life:

- **Connectedness.** Connectedness refers to a psychological sense of community, relationships with others within and beyond the family; and complementary socializing systems (family, neighborhood, school, youth group, camp, etc.).

- **Successful Intelligence.** Successful intelligence is defined as the skills and knowledge needed for success in life, according to one's own definition of success. Successful intelligence is demonstrated through a balance of analytical, creative, and practical abilities. This construct is based on the work of Robert Sternberg (2001, 2003, 2004).

- **Social and Emotional Competence** refers to the ability to accurately perceive, appraise, monitor, express, and regulate emotion; social awareness and interpersonal skills such as communication; responsible decision making that leads to the avoidance of "risk taking" behaviors; and the ability to apply all of these in real-life social situations.

- **Meaning and Purpose.** Meaning and Purpose are defined as living a meaningful life, which in turn *comes from* living ("doing") a purpose whose goal is bigger than oneself and the moment (David Gordon, personal communication, 2005).

The developmental understanding of this study has already informed a national survey of the North American Federation of Temple Youth (NFTY).

Moreover, research is presented in this chapter from a study that was conducted at the Yale Child Study Center in six Jewish day schools (Ben-Avie & Comer 2005). This research was guided by the powerful idea that child development, and not learning theory, should be the foundational science of education. It is not that learning theory doesn't work; schools are built around behavior modification (if children are good, they receive an "A" grade; if not, they receive an "F"). The problem with this foundational science is that it does not adequately take into account the whole fabric of the environment.

THE WHOLE FABRIC OF THE ENVIRONMENT

To investigate the impact that Jewish educational programs have on the developmental trajectories of young people, the whole fabric of the child's environment needs to be considered.

> I walked with my son to the shul. He held my siddur [prayer book] that was once my great-grandmother's and my tallit [prayer shawl], which I had received from my dad when I married. He had wanted to hold them, to "help" me. We entered into the building. At one table, three men were in a heated argument over the meaning of a passage from the Talmud. One man had already started to daven [pray]. In the corner, a teenager held a tikkun and was chanting quietly; most likely he was to be the Torah reader today. Two young men were rolling the Torah scroll in their search for the day's reading. My friend from the next bungalow over waved to me to join him at his table. In his grasp was the book that we had been discussing yesterday. As Jochai and I sat down, it struck me that Vygotsky was talking about this world, the social plane, in his research. As I listened to the argument over the Talmud and to one of the young men explaining to the other what to look for when searching the Torah scroll, I thought to myself, so this is what the zone of proximal development means (Ben-Avie, "Summer Reflections," 1993).

Vygotsky (1978) focuses our attention on using the whole fabric of children's environments to promote their future, balanced development. It is in this way that children's "who-ness" as adherents to the Jewish people emerges. Thus it makes sense for Jewish schools to engage in the level of educational change that is known as "whole school reform."

As a result of what we (Ben-Avie and Kress) are learning through our Educators in Jewish Schools Study (www.JewishEducationalChange.org), we believe: "In well-functioning schools, educators thrive and stay and, in turn, the students learn and develop well." Hence the focus in "whole school reform" initiatives is on changing the underlying "operating system" of schools, and not on one specific curricular initiative or one aspect of development. For example, our Yale Child Study Center's School Development Program improves the way that adults interact and work with one another in order to change the whole fabric of the school community on behalf of young people's balanced development.

Consider Zephyr Jewish day school (pseudonym). Zephyr is one of six day schools studied in order to determine whether young people's formation of a strong adherence to the Jewish people, past and present, would differ based on the nature of the relationships among students, teachers, and parents in their school communities (Ben-Avie & Comer 2005). Zephyr students had the highest scores on the scale Complementary Configuration of Education. The term Complementary Configuration of Education (Cremin 1976) refers to the support and involvement of the Jewish community in the life of the school and the extent to which the Judaic learning of the students is reinforced by the parents and the Jewish community. They also had high scores on the scale that measures Adherence to the Jewish People. The relationship between the variables that measured these two areas was observed to be in the moderate high range. Moreover, among the schools surveyed, Zephyr's parent involvement level was the highest, according to the assessments of students, teachers, and parents. An identical mean (4.1 out of a possible 5) was found for both the parents and teachers on the Complementary Configuration of Education scale.

Windscent (pseudonym) Jewish day school, another of the six day schools in the study, is comparable to Zephyr. The students' motivation to achieve was identical at Windscent and Zephyr. It could have been expected that the students' formation of a strong relationship to the Jewish people would also be identical. However, this was not the case. The Windscent students' trend most closely paralleled the trend observed in the Yale School Development Program's 1993–1994 national study of relationships in public and private schools: The younger the student, the more positive the perceptions of the quality of relationships. At Windscent, the younger elementary school-aged children had positive assessments of the Complementary Configuration of Education and relative high scores on their Adherence to the Jewish People. By sixth grade, both of these assessments were low.

If we had only Windscent's scores, we could have thought that maturation was the best explanation. As students advanced through elementary school they experienced a steady downward slope of assessments of the quality of relationships within the school community. The strength of their formation of a relationship with the Jewish people also decreased, with the notable jump in scores around bar/bat mitzvah age that is not sustained. When we added Zephyr's scores to the equation, a different picture emerged. Whereas the configuration of education at Zephyr pulled up the scores on the scale that measured the strength of the students' adherence to the Jewish people, the configuration at Windscent pulled the scores down. Thus, it is not given that elementary school-aged children will necessarily experience decreases. Formation of a strong adherence to the Jewish people, past and present, is not a natural unfolding like the physical transformation of children from childhood to adolescence. Setting makes a difference.

At Zephyr and Windscent, the students were in the same developmental stages. Their trends should have been similar. Yet they were not. Zephyr was special among the schools studied.

- Zephyr had the highest score on Complementary Configuration of Education. This variable on the Educator Survey measures the support and involvement of the Jewish community in the life of the school and the extent to which the Judaic learning of the students is reinforced by the parents and the Jewish community.
- The Zephyr students had the highest mean on Parent Involvement among all the students in the sample. This variable measures the frequency of parent participation in school activities.
- The Zephyr students had the highest mean on Student-Teacher Relations of all the students in the sample. This variable measures the level of caring, respect, and trust that exists between students and teachers in the school.

How was the complementary configuration of education that supported the students' development at Zephyr created?

Relationships, relationships, relationships. The Zephyr teachers had the highest level of collaborative decision-making among the schools that participated in the study. The teachers also had the highest level of fairness and equity. Moreover, the teachers had the highest level of expectations for the students' learning and development. The "sparks" that move their development forward are the interactions that they have with others. The whole fabric of the environment promotes children's and adults' healthy learning and development—or not (Comer, Haynes & Joyner 1996, p. 1). Changing the school community to promote children's learning and development ensures that the scientific study of child development becomes the foundational science of education.

CHANGING THE SCHOOL COMMUNITY ON BEHALF OF STUDENTS' LEARNING AND DEVELOPMENT

When development is uneven, there is an overemphasis on one aspect to the detriment of overall development in the present and, possibly, in the future. For example, if students' cognitive development has been overemphasized to the detriment of their social development, they may be at grade level in their learning of math and Judaic sacred texts but may be unable to successfully engage in teamwork and group problem solving; this may ultimately impact their success at higher levels of learning. The research presented above suggests that students' underdevelopment along the social pathway may be exacerbated by the nature and quality of relationships among the educators and between the educators and parents.

To illustrate uneven development among children in Jewish schools, examples were reported by Ben-Avie and Comer (2005), who found high-quality relationships between teachers and students but tension-laden relationships among students. Two additional noteworthy fault lines were observed: (1) home–school relations and (2) teachers' interpersonal relations. One possible interpretation of these findings is that students will tend not to collaborate well with each other in a school characterized by low levels of collaboration between the teachers and between the teachers and the parents. This interpretation is grounded in Comer's (1995) analysis that "The climate provides a setting that allows the adults to become meaningful authority models in the minds of the children. Every incident in the school becomes an experience in which the students become carriers of the climate's value-system." Fault lines become tension-laden due to intense stress. As with any ecosystem, intense stress on one part of the system influences the functioning of the whole system. The outcome is that Jewish educational programs may exacerbate children's uneven development.

Because balanced development is not a natural unfolding, some young people will not develop the level of self-regulation required to take advantage of opportunities offered to them. Other children will present themselves to schools and educational programs with uneven development: They may have high levels of cognition but be underdeveloped in terms of the ethical developmental pathway. Thus they may engage in acts of bullying and other aggressive behaviors. Some children may not have a well-developed sense of who-ness and, therefore, be easily swayed by others (often to their detriment). The *Student Learning and Development in Jewish Schools Survey* (Ben-Avie, Kress, Brown & Steinfeld 2005) was administered in a recent study. By analyzing the data, Ben-Avie and Kress were able to see barriers that young people must overcome in order to develop in a healthy and balanced manner.

In one of our studies of elementary school-aged students in several different Jewish day schools (*N* = 262):

- 22 percent agreed that "During this school year, another student has bullied me."
- 25 percent agreed that "This school could really use help in making sure that students are not targeted by other students for any reason."

Aligned with the topic of bullying is peer pressure:

- Only 60 percent agreed that "I separate myself from a group of people my age if they are doing something I don't want to do."
- Only 48 percent agreed that "At school, if some other kids are going to do something harmful, I tell someone who can help."

Jewish schools and educational programs have a tremendous power to impact the developmental trajectory of the young people. However, given the prevailing sentiment in this country that cognitive learning should be the primary focus of schooling, addressing students' developmental needs is harder today than ever before.

Many schools throughout the country believe that they are taking youth development into account by teaching a "developmentally appropriate" curriculum. Ben-Avie et al. (2003) have found that merely packaging a curriculum in terms of "ages and stages" does not actually address the true developmental needs of students. In our data interpretation workshops with schools, we encounter teachers who tell us that it is not their responsibility to promote students' development. A teacher will say, for example, "I teach math." To this we respond, "No, you teach children." To these educators we need to demonstrate over and over again that student learning and youth development are inextricably linked.

In order to demonstrate the link between students' interpersonal relationships and academic learning, we constructed two scales from items on the *Learning and Development in Jewish Schools: Student Survey*—Menschlichkeit and Intellectual Engagement. The relationship was observed to be strong. This means that the higher the students' scores on Menschlichkeit, the higher their scores on the scale that measures Intellectual Engagement.

Whether the students are developing empathy is a youth development issue of great importance, because it indicates if their development is balanced, uneven, or constrained. Thus it is noteworthy that 36 percent agreed that "It often happens that I think people are angry, but they tell me they're not." In terms of their emotional life in school, the students in the study indicated healthy patterns. Nonetheless, 21 percent agreed that "At school, I try to hide my feelings from everyone." Students' emotional life at school or at a Jewish educational program will either impede or facilitate their learning of academic content.

One way of investigating whether students are developing a "who-ness" as Jews is to look at not only their cognitions and emotions but also their behaviors. Consider whether students follow the kosher dietary laws when outside of the house (for example, at a friend's house). For elementary school-aged students, this is a good indicator because (1) it is one of the few arenas in which they are able to demonstrate their personal Jewish practice and (2) *not* to follow the dietary laws can be a real temptation. (This question was relevant to the students in these schools because 66 percent indicated that they keep kosher at home.) Of the students, 35 percent indicated that they "always" keep kosher outside their homes. Another critical indicator of whether they are developing a "who-ness" is their self-reflections on their behavior. For example, 37 percent agreed that "There are times when I feel uncomfortable about something I've done because the person I think I am wouldn't do that." Feeling uncomfortable about an action raises the topic of self-regulation, the focus of the next section. The section highlights the way that Jewish educational programs may impact young people's cognitions, emotions, actions, and partaking of community: through concepts that create a "mindfulness" to Jewish ways of living in the world.

SELF-REGULATION

When youth development is considered the foundational science of education, it is critical to articulate the psychological principles that inform all the work of the educational program. Again, from a developmental perspective "success" is measured by students' thoughts, emotions, actions, and sense of community. Thus one who is able to decode Jewish sacred texts but does not behave in ways espoused by the sacred texts or is indifferent to Judaism is not a successful graduate of a Jewish school or educational program. A developmental approach expects far more from the students than cognitive development. Hence the importance of promoting students' self regulation.

Children regulate their behavior through self-talk. The nature of this self-talk ("egocentric speech") is at the heart of Vygotsky's approach in psychology. Lev Vygotsky rose up to challenge Pavlov in the early days of psychology. Vygotsky asked: What do we care about dogs salivating when they hear a bell? Our focus should be on that which makes humans unique, that is, human consciousness. As a Russian Jew, Vygotsky considered how forces external to individuals—for example, pogroms, wars, and the then-new Soviet Revolution—impact the development of their higher psychological processes and compel them to act.

To understand Vygotsky's contribution to our understanding of the development of self-regulation among elementary school-aged children, it is worthwhile for a moment to widen the frame to consider Piaget's view. In *The Development of Self-Regulation through Private Speech*, Zivin (1979) describes Piaget's focus on the inability of children in the early grades of elementary school to select their words and tone to fit the informational needs and social appropriateness of their audience (p. 18). This egocentric speech has no direct or indirect effect on elementary school-aged children's behavior, Piaget maintained. During the elementary school years, this self-talk disappears as children learn to adapt their speech to others' communicative needs. By way of contrast, Vygotsky held that this egocentric speech does not disappear. Children continue to use egocentric speech to initiate, sustain, and modify voluntary acts. (In adults, self-talk comes to the surface when they are faced with difficult tasks. They tend to talk to themselves aloud to encourage themselves to persist or to think through potential next steps.)

As children progress through the elementary school years a "wholeness" emerges, according to Vygotsky, due to an intertwining of two different developmental lines: thought and language. Whereas cognitions are processes that are within individuals, language comes from the outside to reorganize these processes. In this way, "Man makes use not just of physically inherited experience: throughout his life, his work and his behavior draw broadly on the experience of former generations, which is not transmitted at birth from father to son. We may call this historical experiences" (Vygotsky cited in Kozulin 1990, p. 81). Children are thereby able to go beyond their own personal experiences and "literally live in the experiences of others." Language becomes an instrument of the "external" regulation of individual behavior (Kozulin p. 83).

Thus Vygotsky was keenly interested in the process of concept formation among elementary school-aged children. Max Kadushin (1965), who came from the same Jewish cultural milieu as Vygotsky, used a more nuanced term: value-concepts. A loose analogy may clarify the intent of the term: *Democracy* and *liberty* are complex ideas compacted into words. Democracy and liberty are ideas that are shared by almost all U.S. citizens. People hold these ideas "warmly"; rhetorical or political use of these terms has the potential to excite people. In the United States the concepts of democracy and liberty are associated with another concept, capitalism. Kadushin would see that "In its cultural role, the value-concept—actually, the entire complex of concepts tends to permeate the mental and psychic make-up of the individual. It functions as a kind of 'mental habit,' shaping and guiding the life-outlook of the person who is part of the culture" (Steinberg 1980, p. 24). Without value concepts, the bearer of ideas from the past, the development of the minds of young Jews is impossible.

Education is the interaction between (1) everyday concepts that children learn on their own through experience and (2) value concepts that are embedded in the informal and formal curriculum of Jewish schools and educational programs (these latter concepts are known as "scientific" or "academic" concepts because they are derived from academic study). The interaction of everyday concepts learned in schools and educational programs is critical to the process of learning. To illustrate, children learn that the closer they move their hands to a source of heat, the hotter their hands become. This is an "everyday" concept because they learn it through everyday experiences. They therefore have a hard time comprehending in class when they are taught that the earth is not closer to the sun during summer. The latter is an example of a "scientific" concept that is embedded within academic content. According to Vygotsky, children reframe their everyday, unsystematic, unconscious concepts under the rubric of scientific concepts. This reframing of their everyday concepts changes their self-talk.

What are the "academic" value concepts that young people learn in Jewish educational programs? What is the impact of this study? For children studying value concepts embedded within Jewish sacred texts, their selective attention to ideas and events compels action. A key action of the Jewish people is the study of sacred texts. An analysis was conducted on data collected from 1,010 students in Jewish day schools (Ben-Avie & Comer 2005) in order to see the strength of the relationship between:

1. the extent to which teachers facilitate students' concept formation
2. the extent to which the students' behavior reflects Judaism's teachings on:
   • The obligations between people
   • The obligations between people and G-d

A moderately strong relationship was found between concept formation and behavior. Through the action of the study of sacred texts, the individual becomes "a reflection of the community," to borrow a phrase from Bruner (1990, p. 11).

Jewish schools and educational programs encourage elementary school-aged children to become "reflections" of the community through promoting their study of Jewish sacred texts and behaviors derived from these texts. However, study does not always directly cause behavior. The psychological process that mediates between study and religious observance may be termed "mindfulness," to employ Ellen Langer's (1994) term. The more one studies a subject, the more likely it is that one's mind will be occupied with topics relating to that subject. Moreover, the very method of study and the symbolic systems employed impress upon individuals' ways of thinking.

To illustrate, embedded within the sacred texts of the Jewish sociocultural community are value concepts that contain information of past generations. Through the study of the community's sacred texts, children's cognitive structures develop, "which select and categorize information, and serve as reference frames for thinking and acting" (Pepitone & Triandis 1987, p. 481). Studying the concept of *tzedekah* awakens children's selective attention to events and individuals in the environment that compel a *tzedekah* action. In other words, one might say that one undertook an ethical action because *tzedekah* required it. The study described in Ben-Avie and Comer (2005) explains that among 921 parents of students enrolled in Jewish schools, the relationship between thought and language was observed to be moderately strong. The more people's speech contains these Jewish concepts and topics, the more (1) their relationships are framed by Jewish thought and (2) they can articulate the values that guide their fundamental decisions.

It is this resulting "mindfulness" that promotes self-regulation. This mindfulness is not devoid of emotions. Rather, this mindfulness is a blend of cognitions and emotions that compels action. When Jewish schools and educational programs impact students on the intimate, internal level of self-regulation, the students are more likely to engage in actions informed by Jewish ways of living in the world and partake of the life of the community. The students' who-ness becomes a reflection of the Jewish people.

PROMOTING STUDENTS' DEVELOPMENT OF "WHOLENESS" AND "WHO-NESS"

One way in which to implement a Jewish educational program that promotes positive developmental experiences among elementary school-aged children is through using a framework for decision making that is built around balanced development. Within our Yale Child Study Center's School Development Program, we use the metaphor of six developmental pathways as a framework for decision making (see the *Field Guide for Comer Schools in Action* by Comer, Joyner & Ben-Avie 2004). Again these six developmental pathways characterize the lines along which children mature—physical, cognitive, psychological, language, social, and ethical. For Jewish schools and educational programs there is an additional nuance to the pathways. As discussed above, experiences that were unique to the Jewish people became embedded in our languages. Children's active use of the unique language(s) and speech patterns of the Jews facilitate their self-regulation and formation of a strong adherence to the Jewish people, past and present.

The metaphor of the six developmental pathways is not a theory of development but rather a method for checking to make sure that our programs promote all aspects of development. The chart on youth development that appears below graphically displays the pathways. If children do not develop well along any of the developmental pathways, development along others may be adversely affected. It is not enough for children to be articulate if they have nothing to say. It is not enough for them to care about the community—they need experience in coordinating efforts with others (Ben-Avie 2004, p. 88).

The metaphor of the six developmental pathways is closer to a theory of change than to a theory of development. Within school reform movements today there is an increasing focus on articulating a theory of change that describes the lifecycle of the change process: what is expected to happen at each stage. For example, the first stage of a change process may feel painful to many as issues that were once discussed only in the parking lot are now discussed in school-wide meetings. While undergoing this stage, it is reassuring to know that positive outcomes will result during the next stage. A theory of change by itself, however, will not result in positive outcomes. It may guide the implementation of the change process, but the change process requires a foundational science to channel the energies of all those who have a stake in the life success of the young people. (Our Yale School Development Program advocates child development as the foundational science of education.)

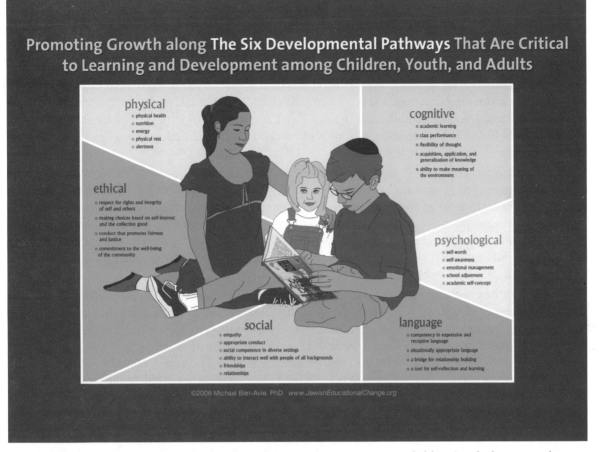

Thus for Jewish schools and educational programs to promote children's wholeness and sense of who-ness, both a suitable foundational science and a theory of change are essential. Educational change is not for the faint of heart. Yet Jewish educational programs will benefit if they change their underlying "operating system" and document the results of the change. This is especially important given the accountability movement that is becoming entrenched in this country and given the sophistication of today's parents, who expect the attainment of measurable outcomes. The whole operating system has to be changed because simply "dropping" a new initiative on a school will not result in meaningful change. In fact, it may cause harm (Zeuli & Ben-Avie 2003). The story of Zephyr narrated above indicates that the relationships at a school are able to pull up the scores on the scale that measures the strength of the students' adherence to the Jewish people. In other words, it's all about relationships.

IMPLICATIONS AND POLICY RECOMMENDATIONS

The Yale Child Study Center's School Development Program (SDP) is one of the country's largest educational change initiatives. SDP works with schools throughout the world to promote both healthy relationships in school communities and students' high academic achievement. According to *Review of Educational Research,* SDP's process meets "the highest standard of evidence" for comprehensive school reforms that improved student achievement (Borman, Hewes, Overman & Brown 2002). SDP changes the whole underlying "operating system" of the school to benefit students' learning and development.

The Comer process helps school communities organize themselves into three teams:

- The School Planning and Management Team (SPMT), which coordinates all the different initiatives in the school by developing a Comprehensive School Plan. The SPMT is not the school board or school leadership team. It is comprised of members of all the different constituent groups (administrators, teachers, parents, child development specialists, community members) and meets twice a month to ensure that all the activities of the school are aligned with the goals and objectives embedded within the Comprehensive School Plan (CSP). The CSP is the mechanism through which the SPMT transforms the entire fabric of the school community. The result is an *intentionality* in all aspects of the school's work.

- The Parent Team (PT), whose members function as a resource for other parents. The Parent Team is not the PTA or PTO. Typical activities of the Parent Team include workshops on such topics as standardized testing and the new math curriculum, social events to encourage parents' identification with the school (e.g., "I am a Cold Spring School Parent"), and enhancement of the school for all the students (e.g., for children who have qualified as being in need of special services).

- The Student Services Team (also known as the Student and Staff Support Team), which engages in global preventive planning to ensure students' healthy development and to manage individual cases. The team usually comprises such specialists as school psychologists and guidance counselors, an administrator, and one or more community members who are also professionals in the field of child development. Parents who are concerned that their children are not thriving socially and emotionally, for example, turn to the team; together, the team members and the parents address the developmental needs of the children.

When the three teams meet, a fundamental goal guides all their work: "All decisions are made in the best interest of children." (In fact, in many schools a placard sits on the table during team meetings to remind members of this goal.) In addition, three guiding principles structure the interactions of the team members: consensus, collaboration, and no-fault. In this way, the work of the teams focuses on child development topics and not on adult agendas. The three primary activities of the teams are writing the Comprehensive School Plan; organizing professional development activities that are aligned with the goals and objectives of the plan; and continually assessing the implementation of the plan's goals and objectives, making modifications as needed.

It is recommended that Jewish educational programs consider implementing a "whole school reform" process. To learn more about the work of the Yale School Development Program, please see Comer, Joyner and Ben-Avie's (2004) *Six Pathways to Healthy Child Development and Academic Success* and Joyner, Ben-Avie and Comer 's (2004) *Transforming School Leadership and Management to Support Student Learning and Development*.

ADDITIONAL RESEARCH QUESTION

The primary question for additional research is whether students' learning and development are most effectively promoted when school communities collaborate with Jewish camps and youth groups.

FUTURE DIRECTIONS

- Theory-based evaluations of Jewish educational programs that take into consideration not only demographic information (e.g., number of students enrolled) but also how the programs promote students' "whole child" development.

- Research that takes into consideration the whole fabric of the environment in which the young people live, learn, and develop. For example, to understand young people's development, researchers need to consider the parents' influence in conjunction with the educational program's influence.

- Research that is on the level of the individual young person. Within the research "tool kit," there are various research strategies for conducting individual assessments of children and adolescents that include behavioral projective techniques, the posing of moral dilemmas, social network mapping, and the administration of psychosocial and learning evaluations.

- Research that includes analyses of subgroups within individual educational programs to examine whether Jewish educational programs have a differential impact on subgroups of students (e.g., Do students with special needs derive the same benefits as do non-special-needs students?).

CONCLUSION

The developmental understanding underlying this chapter is that aspects of adult quality of life have childhood roots. If straight lines could be drawn from aspects of healthy child development to aspects of healthy mature development, what would these lines connect? Consider successful intelligence in adults. During the last several years the public scandals of prominent people in the financial and political arenas have raised the question of how smart people could be so stupid. Sternberg (2004) discusses the theory of successful intelligence in a manner that emphasizes its malleability (by way of contrast, physical development is not malleable by education). He writes:

> This theory defines successful intelligence as the skills and knowledge needed for success in life, according to one's own definition of success, within one's sociocultural context. One acquires and utilizes these skills and this knowledge by capitalizing on strengths and by correcting or compensating for weaknesses; by adapting to, shaping, or selecting environments; and through a balance of analytical, creative, and practical abilities (p. 326).

In addition to its malleability, successful intelligence may be seen as a precursor of a positive development outcome in adulthood. Sternberg uses the term *successful* intelligence "to underscore the importance of understanding intelligence not just as a predictor of academic performance...but as a predictor of success in life" (p. 326). Thus Jewish schools and educational programs should focus on those aspects of development that are malleable through education and are predictors of adult quality of life.

It is therefore worthwhile for us to consider whether there are developmental experiences in Jewish schools and educational programs that promote healthful cognitions, emotions, behaviors, and sense of community. It could very well be that Jewish schools and educational programs provide students with *saychel* (successful intelligence) as well as *menschlichkeit* (the qualities of a good person). And if parents value these qualities as outcomes, sending their children to Jewish schools and educational programs provides added value.

HIGHLIGHTS OF THE CHAPTER

- Children's development may be balanced or uneven. In optimal circumstances, children's development is balanced. There is a "wholeness" to their development as an interlocking occurs among six pathways that are critical to academic learning.
- With development as the aim of education, success has been achieved when students attain a "who-ness" that (1) is consistent with the goals and objectives of Jewish formal and informal educational programs and (2) will be sustained beyond students' participation in the program(s).
- Vygotsky's ideas focus our attention on using the whole fabric of children's environments to promote their future balanced development. Thus it makes sense for Jewish schools to engage in the level of educational change that is known as "whole school reform."
- To investigate whether children are developing a "who-ness" and a "wholeness," it is important to look at their thoughts, emotions, actions and (1) the extent to which and the way in which they become part of their community; and (2) the extent to which and the way in which they both contribute to and are supported by their community.

THE CHAPTER IN A LARGER CONTEXT

The *process* through which young people become members of religious communities has been a research topic in several academic disciplines, most notably in anthropology, sociology, and psychology. For example, researchers of urban societies developed an explanatory theory for how a member of a subgroup switches between subgroup and larger group self-identification. Goodenough (1971) described the process of code-switching: "In the conduct of his affairs a person must choose from the several cultures in his repertoire the one he regards as most suitable for his purposes on any given occasion. The one he chooses is his operating culture for the occasion" (p. 289). A code is any behavior within a group that conveys information, including situational use of language, clothing, and adherence to dietary laws. When interacting with another member of the same group, the individual will tend to employ the group's codes. Code-switching is introduced in an interaction when a code of another group becomes part of the same interaction. Code-switching can be either planned or spontaneous. A Jew *planning* to attend an event organized by the synagogue may decide to wear a head covering. In this case, the head covering is part of the Jewish group code because it conveys information to those who understand the code in question. In contrast, the following example illustrates spontaneous code-switching: Two Jews are having a conversation. In the course of their conversation about events taking place in the local Jewish community they intersperse their English with Hebrew or Yiddish words and phrases. When a non–Jew joins the conversation, the two Jews deliberately code-switch and speak only in standard English while he is present.

Anthropology describes the process of code-switching but does not concern itself with the process by which a member of a subgroup *learns* the codes of the group in tandem with the codes of the larger society. Demographic studies conducted by sociologists may discern subtle differences among subgroups in their practice of the codes and in how many are in each subgroup. At this juncture it is worthwhile to turn to psychology. Psychology provides a developmental perspective that helps to explain and predict how the educative process may either promote or impede group membership and the learning of the group's codes. Thus developmental psychology provides information that is actionable by Jewish schools and educational programs as they engage in reform to enhance young people's learning and development.

ANNOTATED BIBLIOGRAPHY

Comer, J. P., Joyner, E. T. & Ben-Avie, M. (2004). *Six Pathways to Healthy Child Development and Academic Success: The Field Guide to Comer Schools in Action*. Thousand Oaks, CA: Corwin Press. Today, schools are primarily guided by "ages and stages" of development, behavior modification, and learning theory. Implementing the Comer process changes the discourse about the purpose of schooling: Whole child development becomes the aim of education, and the scientific study of child development becomes the foundational science of education.

Joyner, E. T., Comer, J. P. & Ben-Avie, M. (2004). *Transforming School Leadership and Management to Support Student Learning and Development: The Field Guide to Comer Schools in Action*. Thousand Oaks, CA: Corwin Press. This volume of the three-volume field guide describes the everyday nuts and bolts of whole school reform.

Kozulin, A. (1990). *Vygotsky's Psychology: A Biography of Ideas*. New York: Harvester Wheatsheaf. Many books on Vygotsky mention that he was Jewish but do not explore the impact of his Jewishness on his ideas. To understand Vygotsky's ideas, it is worthwhile to consider what it was like to be a Russian Jew at the dawn of the Soviet Revolution.

REFERENCES

Ben-Avie, M. & Kress, J. (2008). *A North American Study of Educators in Jewish Day and Congregational Schools. Analytic Report of the Educators in Jewish Schools Study*. New Haven: Yale Child Study Center.

Ben-Avie, M. & Comer, J. P. (2005). "Philosophy and empirical evidence: Achieving vision through research". *Journal of Jewish Education*, 71, 67-94.

Ben-Avie, M., Kress, J., Brown, W. T. & Steinfeld, T. R. (2005). *Learning and Development in Jewish Day Schools: Parent, Educator, and Student Surveys*. New Haven: Impact Analysis and Strategies Group.

Ben-Avie, M. (2004). Children need healthy adults. In J. P. Comer, E. T. Joyner & M. Ben-Avie (eds.), *Six Pathways to Healthy Child Development and Academic Success: The Field Guide to Comer Schools in Action*. Thousand Oaks, CA: Corwin Press, 87–88.

Ben-Avie, M., Haynes, N.M., White, J., Ensign, J., Steinfeld, T. and Sartin, L. (2003). Youth development and student learning in math and science. In N. M. Haynes, M. Ben-Avie & J. Ensign (eds.), *How Social and Emotional Development Add Up: Making Gains in Math and Science Education*. New York: Teachers College Press.

Ben-Avie, M. *Summer Reflections* (unpublished). New Haven: Yale Child Study Center.

Borman, G. D., G. M., Overman, L. T. & Brown, S. (2003). "Comprehensive school reform and student achievement: A meta-analysis." *Review of Educational Research*, 73(2), 125–230.

Bruner, J. (1990). *Acts of Meaning*. Cambridge: Harvard University Press.

Comer, J. P., Joyner, E. T., & Ben-Avie, M. (2004). *Six Pathways to Healthy Child Development and Academic Success*. Thousand Oaks, CA: Corwin Press.

Comer, J.P., Ben-Avie, M., Haynes, N.M. & Joyner, E. (1999). *Child by Child*. New York: Teachers College Press.

Comer, J. P. (1995). Address to the School Climate Special Interest Group. Annual Meeting of the American Education Research Association.

Comer, J. P., Haynes, N. M. & Joyner, E. T. (1996). The School Development Program. In J. P. Comer, N. M. Haynes, E. T. Joyner and M. Ben-Avie (eds), *Rallying the Whole Village: The Comer Process for Reforming Education*. New York: Teachers College Press, 1–26.

Cremin, L.A. (1976). *Public Education*. NY: Basic Books, Inc.

Goodenough, W. (1971). *Culture, Language, and Society*. Addison-Wesley Module Publications, no. 7 (44 pp).

Gordon, D. (2004, October). Meaningful Existence Model. Seminar presented at The NLP Center of New York.

Joyner, E.T., Ben-Avie, M. & Comer, J.P. (2004). *Transforming School Leadership and Management to Support Student Learning and Development*. Thousand Oaks, CA: Corwin Press.

Kadushin, M. (1965). *The Rabbinic Mind* (2nd ed.). New York: Blaisdell Publishing Company.

Kozulin, A. (1990). *Vygotsky's Psychology: A Biography of Ideas*. New York: Harvester Wheatsheaf.

Langer, E. (July 1994). The mindful education. Keynote Address at The Sixth International Conference on Thinking, Massachusetts Institute of Technology.

Maholmes, V. (2004). Promoting youth leadership development in Comer schools. In J. P. Comer, E. T. Joyner & M. Ben-Avie (eds.), *Six Pathways to Healthy Child Development and Academic Success: The Field Guide to Comer Schools in Action*. Thousand Oaks, CA: Corwin Press.

Moll, L. C. (1990). Introduction. In L. C. Moll (ed.), *Vygotsky and Education: Instructional Implications and Applications of Sociohistorical Psychology*. Cambridge: Cambridge University Press.

Nicholl, T. (1998). Vygotsky. Retrieved on November 23, 2006 from *http://www.massey.ac.nz/~alock//virtual/trishvyg.htm*.

Noshpitz, J. D. & King, R. A. (1991). *Pathways of Growth: Essentials of Child Psychiatry* (Volume 1, Normal Development). New York: John Wiley & Sons, Inc.

Pepitone, A. & Triandis, H. C. (1987). "On the universality of social psychological theories." *The Journal of Cross-Cultural Psychology 18*, 471–498.

Steinberg, T. (1980). "Max Kadushin's contribution to the study of Jewish thought and its implications for Jewish education." *Jewish Education* 48 (4), 21–27.

Sternberg, R. J. (2004). "Culture and intelligence." *American Psychologist* 59 (5), 325–338.

Sternberg, R. J. (2003). "What is an 'expert student?'" *Educational Researcher 32* (8), 5–9.

Sternberg, R. J. (2001). "Why schools should teach for wisdom: The balance theory of wisdom in educational settings." *Educational Psychologist*, 36 (4), 227–245.

Zeuli, J. & Ben-Avie, M. (2003). Connecting with students on a personal level through in-depth discussions of mathematics. In N. M. Haynes, M. Ben-Avie & J. Ensign (eds.), *How Social and Emotional Development Add Up: Making Gains in Math and Science Education*. New York: Teachers College Press.

Zivin, G. (1979). *The Development of Self-regulation through Private Speech*. New York: Wiley.

Vygotsky, L. S. (1978). *Mind in Society*. Cambridge: Harvard University Press.

"A Moment of Developmental Triumph?" Adolescents in Jewish Education

Michael Ben-Avie

A study of 1,010 young people in six Jewish day schools (Ben-Avie & Comer 2005) focused on 14 factors related to adolescent learning and development. Among the most interesting findings of the study was that the three most important predictors in whether these adolescents were forming a strong relationship to the Jewish people, past and present, were: (1) the students' engagement in learning and their motivation to achieve, (2) their tendency to seek adult guidance, which is one manifestation of high-quality relationships between educators and young people, and (3) their parents' being their partners in education. A central theme unites these three factors: It's all about relationships.

Our Jewish Educational Change team administers surveys to children and adolescents, educators and parents/guardians that have been informed by our understanding of the relationship between learning and development. The *Learning and Development in Jewish Schools* surveys (Ben-Avie, Kress, Brown & Steinfeld 2005) are derivatives of surveys for Jewish day schools that were developed at the Yale Child Study Center (see Ben-Avie & Comer 2005). These "Quality of Life Outcomes" surveys measure all aspects of the school community that impact the life paths of young people (for a full description of the surveys, please see *www.JewishEducationalChange.org*). The current versions of the parent, educator, and student surveys are the *Learning and Development in Jewish Schools* surveys that satisfy many accreditation requirements, provide outcome data to funders, set goals and priorities for school reform, create opportunities for informed dialogue and partnership among constituencies (educators, students, parents, funders), set a model for the students of a spirit of self-reflection and growth and enable the school community to reflect on the impact of previous programs and initiatives.

THE FIRST TWO FACTORS: STUDENTS' MOTIVATION TO ACHIEVE AND HIGH-QUALITY RELATIONSHIPS BETWEEN EDUCATORS AND ADOLESCENTS

The first two important factors or "predictors" of whether adolescent students forge a strong relationship to the Jewish people are (1) the students' engagement in learning and their motivation to achieve and (2) their tendency to seek adult guidance, which is one manifestation of high-quality relationships between educators and young people.

Adolescents develop the motivation to achieve in school and in life through their interactions with adults as they navigate through school, home, work, and recreational activities. However, not all learning is constructive—consider Dewey's (1938) famous example of the individual who starts out on a career of burglary and through practice becomes a highly expert burglar (p. 36). Hence the importance of a student's personal engagement with educators. The educator is able to frame the learning and reframe young people's energy from negative to positive, outcome-oriented thoughts, feelings, and behavior. James Comer, associate dean of the Yale School of Medicine and founder of the Yale School Development Program, has remarked that once young people have internalized the value of academic learning — once they have made the learning their own—they derive three rewards: personal fulfillment, a sense of achievement and competence, and knowledge that is useful in the world. Until adolescents make learning their own, they need to be engaged with one or more educators who value learning. The relationship is important because it fosters adolescents' emotional attachment to the knowledge.

To understand the implications of the findings from our research among Jewish adolescents, it is worthwhile to broaden the frame for a moment to consider the relationship between learning and development.

When adolescents develop well, they learn well, according Comer (Comer, Ben-Avie, Haynes & Joyner 1999). The kind of learning he is speaking about consists of continually increasing one's cognitive ability, knowledge base, understanding, mastery, and sense of well-being, all of which, in turn, promote future interest in more learning. This kind of learning can be about any subject, whether or not that subject has traditionally been part of the educational program's formal academic curriculum. (In Comer's approach, such topics as learning how to resolve tough social situations and social and emotional learning fall under the category of "youth development" and not "student learning"). When explaining youth development to parents and educators, Comer employs the idea of six developmental pathways — physical, cognitive, psychological, language, social, and ethical. The idea of the "pathways" is a concrete metaphor that enables everyone in school communities, including the students, to look at themselves and their efforts through the lens of youth development. Through learning about how to promote the development of the young people, educators and parents themselves grow. In this way school communities become centers that also promote adult development and, in turn, the increasingly healthy and successful life paths of the adolescents.

Activities provide entry points and structures through which adults can impact the development of adolescents. Thus the most effective way to promote adolescents' development is to align curricular units with youth development. How can we achieve this alignment in formal and informal Jewish educational programs? Imagine a matrix designed to promote the involvement of young people in *tefillah* (prayer). The matrix enables the educators to make sure that all aspects of development are addressed in the curricular unit. The six developmental pathways are written on the first column on the left-hand side. Across the top of the matrix appear the ages and stages of development. Within each cell of the matrix the educators will describe how the activity will spark thought, emotion, action, and partaking of the life of the community. In adolescence—indeed, in every stage of development—we learn knowledge, develop attitudes as we think through what we have learned, experience emotional arousal when learning (this is what makes the learning "stick") and participate in the life of the community. Thus, in a matrix that deals with *tefillah*, for example, in the cell that represents the cross between the psychological pathway and adolescence, the following learning theme may appear: "God, the Jewish people and me." Under this learning theme the educators specify the most desired outcomes of the activity. The outcomes are framed in terms of thoughts, emotions, actions, and a sense of community.

Throughout our lives our understanding about how the world works and our place in the world entwine with our sense of our own emotional and behavioral capacity and habits, as well as with our sense of community. Together these are essential contributions to a sense of Being (or "spirituality"). (In a religious community, many will feel that the essential ingredient in one's Being and sense of Being is the presence of G-d; thus "essential contributions.") The matrix described is an example of a framework that educators may use to specify the most desired outcomes of educational activities. Its use would facilitate the development in each student of a sense of Being informed by *tefillah*.

Consider curricular units and activities that are designed to spark development along the social pathway. One can make the case that the most global desirable outcome of the social pathway is a sense of connectedness that leads to actions that support the healthy development and functioning of the community and of oneself in the community. Given this desirable outcome, what thoughts, emotions, actions, and experience of participation in community typify connectedness among adolescents? Are there positive developmental experiences in Jewish formal and informal educational programs that promote healthful cognitions, emotions, and behaviors along adolescents' social pathway? For the sake of providing an example, the following concepts that we have received as a cultural inheritance from past generations of our people are discussed in reference to adolescents' social development. An emphasis in Jewish educational programs on *middot* (virtues) may lead to young people's mastery of social and emotional competencies. An emphasis on covenant in Jewish educational programs may lead to young people's development of a Jewish sense of meaning and purpose in their adult lives. The Jewish concept of *tikkun olam* (literally, the fixing of the world), which is often embedded within the formal and informal curriculum of Jewish educational programs, discourages self-absorption and encourages awareness of people's interdependence (Robinson 2004).

Activities are the spark, but the stretching of adolescents' future orientation (defined as the ability to conceive of one's own future development) emerges through the relationships that adolescents have with others. Knowledge of youth development enables us to see that supportive relationships enhance students' engagement and motivate students to continue to study and learn. When instructional activities become too abstract, whenever students become disinterested and disillusioned, the generative relationships that students have with others—and with their own selves—have the power to sustain them in the learning process. Gradually they can reorganize their everyday experiences under the framework of our people's religious and sociocultural inheritance (see Vygotsky 1978), incorporating ever-more-abstract notions in this incremental way.

The outcome of development is adult quality of life (which is itself an ongoing process, rather than a "thing" to be achieved). People forge a relationship with the Jewish religious and sociocultural group as a byproduct of developing a framework by which to judge their lives and measure, as it were, their fullness or emptiness (Taylor 1989, p. 16). Quality of Life is measured by four constructs that have been scientifically demonstrated to provide youth with tools to make positive developmental transitions (Ben-Avie & Kress 2005). These four Quality of Life constructs are:

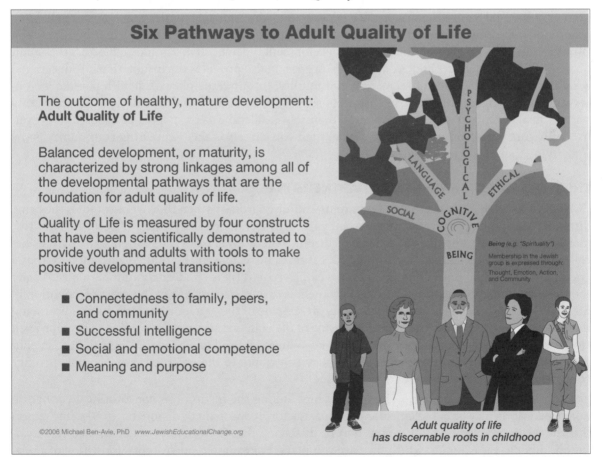

• **Connectedness to family, peers and community.** Connectedness refers to a psychological sense of community, relationships with others within and beyond the family; and complementary socializing systems (family, neighborhood, school, youth group, camp, etc.).

• **Successful intelligence.** Successful intelligence is defined as the skills and knowledge needed for success in life, according to one's own definition of success. Successful intelligence is demonstrated through a balance of analytical, creative, and practical abilities. This construct is based on the work of Robert Sternberg (2001, 2003, 2004).

- **Social and emotional competence** refers to the ability to accurately perceive, appraise, monitor, express, and regulate emotion; social awareness and interpersonal skills such as communication; responsible decision making that leads to the avoidance of "risk taking" behaviors; and the ability to apply all of these in real-life social situations.

- **Meaning and purpose.** Meaning and purpose are defined as living a meaningful life, which in turn *comes from* living ("doing") a purpose whose goal is bigger than oneself and the moment (David Gordon, personal communication 2005).

How did we arrive at these constructs? Each one meets the following three criteria: (1) The construct must have a discernable root in youth; that is, the quality must be present in youth and adulthood. (2) The construct must be malleable by Jewish formal and informal education. (3) Jewish educational programs endeavor to promote the construct through either the formal or the informal curriculum. In addition to providing meaning and value to everyday experience, the Quality of Life constructs are also protective factors during developmental transitions (e.g., going to college).

Taking a developmental perspective means looking at the potential outcomes of development and then designing curricular units in the here and now to impact the trajectory of the adolescents' life paths. If, for example, we know that the number one reason young people drop out of college is that they do not seek adult guidance when they get into trouble, what educational activities should we design when the adolescents are still in high school? When taking youth development into consideration, we would realize the importance of designing educational activities that emphasize helping others and other educational activities that emphasize that seeking help is a problem solving strategy (Brown 2006, personal communication). A developmental perspective reminds educators that adult quality of life has roots in childhood and adolescence. It also provides the insight that all educational activities are in the service of recreating community. In our research with Jewish parents we observed that 30 percent either refused to accept support when it was needed or accepted support only with difficulty. Only 27 percent considered themselves able to accept support graciously. However, in a fully functional community, if you give, then you can also take. Recreating community is the underlying theme of the next section.

THE THIRD FACTOR: PARENTS AS PARTNERS IN EDUCATION

As close as adolescents were to their parents and/or guardians when they were young is the same distance that they must move away from their parents to set out on their journey of becoming healthy, mature adults. It is ironic that as adolescents distance themselves from their parents, the parents become increasingly concerned about their education. This is due to the middle class anxiety that a good education is the only thing that parents can pass onto their children as an inheritance. When their children enter high school, parents become increasingly cognizant of the great competition in life that is known as college admissions. Thus on one side of the equation adolescents are distancing themselves from their parents. On the other side of the equation parents are seeking to become even closer to their adolescents (at least in order to keep them focused on college). Where do Jewish educational programs fit into this dynamic? Do they contribute to the emergence of a complementary configuration of education or to a dissonant one?

Cremin (1976) observed that "The relationships among the institutions constituting a configuration of education may be complementary or contradictory, consonant or dissonant" (p. 31). One reason that the relationship among institutions may be dissonant, that Cremin does not mention is that institutions differ in the extent to which they are voluntary. For example, adolescents' formation of a relationship to the Jewish people, past and present, is promoted or constrained by whether their parents voluntarily decide to buy into the attitudes, values, and behavior of the Jewish community. Moreover, parents' voluntary associations with Jewish organizations shape the home environment their adolescents experience. Another reason is that in a complex society, individuals may buy into some *aspects* of the institutions but not others. If parents are not whole-hearted about their adolescents' participation in Jewish informal and formal educational programs, then the configuration of education radiating toward the adolescents will be tension-laden. Moreover, the dissonance in the configuration of education will be exacerbated if the educators act in ways that discourage parents' partnership with them. If the relationships among the educators and the parents are stressful, a seamless web of authority may not emerge.

Society and culture also may hinder the emergence of a seamless web of authority among parents and educators. The educator who is charged to initiate the young into a relationship with a group in one setting faces the constraint that youth are simultaneously being persuaded to enter other relationships elsewhere. Moreover, educators and parents are up against the prevailing sentiment of individualism in North American culture and society. Because of the sentiment of individualism, adolescents are expected to form their own relationships with groups as they grow up. The individual in contemporary North America has the freedom to "buy into" the Jewish cultural inheritance or reject it completely. Instead of forming strong relationships with groups, many adolescents become alienated from adults and estranged from the groups that these adults represent. The result is either adolescents' lack of close identification with any group or their weak allegiances to many groups that may conflict with one another.

A *complementary configuration of education* emerges through "recreating community." In a functioning community there is a common language that is shared among educators and parents of adolescents that enables educational program designers, administrators, parents, and community members to align activities and curricular units with the aspects of development that they most desire to promote. This common language derives from knowledge of youth development. For example, in some congregations education is a holistic effort with one overall committee to coordinate all the informal and formal educational programs for youth as well as family education programs. Members of this overall coordinating committee include community members who are professionals in health and human services, school psychologists or guidance counselors, educators, parents, and others who bring knowledge of youth development with them to the work of the committee. In this way the congregation is able to immerse the adolescents in a learning environment that (1) supports their social and emotional development and (2) promotes the adolescents' formation of a strong relationship with the Jewish people, past and present. In another example, Jewish communities differ in the extent to which the congregational schools and the youth movements collaborate, the camps and the youth movements complement each other, and formal and informal Jewish educational programs are coordinated. Whether adolescents experience a "conspiracy on their behalf" depends on (1) which aspects of youth development parents desire Jewish educational programs to promote among their adolescents and (2) the efficacy of the educators in promoting these aspects of development.

When parents turn to Jewish educational programs for help in raising their adolescents, are there specific aspects of development that concern them? We asked 230 parents in one of our Jewish day school studies (Ben-Avie & Kress 2005) to reflect on what aspect of meaning and purpose they would most like the school to promote among their children. The parents were provided with four options:

- To be guided by an internal compass when making decisions about navigating in a complex society
- To be passionate about an activity or topic
- To have a purpose that is bigger than oneself
- To often experience a sense of awe, wonder, and joy

Fifty-five percent indicated "to be guided by an internal compass when navigating in a complex society." It was unexpected that the parents would so strongly indicate that they desired the school to promote among the children "being guided by an internal compass" and that parents did not select at all "having a purpose that's bigger than myself and the moment." We also asked the parents whether they attribute their own development of an internal compass to their schooling or their family when growing up. Seventy-five percent indicated "family." According to their responses, however, their own children do not see that they (the parents) are guided by an internal compass. Parents were asked whether their children are aware of their tendency to demonstrate the different aspects of quality of life. Being guided by an internal compass for navigating in a complex society ranked the lowest. One possible interpretation is that demonstrating to one's adolescent how to be guided by an internal compass for navigating in a complex society—although a meaningful skill—is a difficult thing to teach and to learn to do. Therefore, parents may be indicating that they desire the assistance of their children's educational programs to promote this aspect of development.

The development outcome of a complementary configuration of education is impressive. Students who feel that many adults care about them tend to have the highest levels of development and the fewest interpersonal relationship challenges. This statement is based on a survey of 2,232 public high school students in a Connecticut city (Ben-Avie 2004). One of the 125 items in the *Learning and Development Inventory* (Ben-Avie, Brown, Steinfeld, Ensign 2004) asked students to indicate approximately how many adults in their lives (at home, at school, in the community) care about what happens to them. Students who indicated "zero adults" had significantly lower scores on overall development than students who indicated a number greater than zero. Students who indicated either "13–25 adults" or "more than 25 adults" reported the fewest interpersonal relationship challenges, significantly differing from the other students. The May 2006 administration of the *Learning and Development Inventory* to a cohort of students who had also participated in the 2004 survey (*N* = 1,436 students) found similar results: Those students who indicated that more than 25 adults in their lives (at home plus at school plus in the community) care about them had the highest levels of development.

In a study among 247 Jewish adolescents in day schools (Ben-Avie and Kress 2005) the same item was asked, and the results were very encouraging. In response to this item only one adolescent indicated that "zero adults" care about him or her, 2 indicated "one adult," 13 indicated "2–5 adults," 35 indicated "6–12 adults," 44 indicated "13–25 adults," and 152 indicated "more than 25." The findings suggest that a well-functioning complementary configuration of education is radiating toward these adolescents.

IMPLICATIONS AND POLICY RECOMMENDATIONS

Jewish educational programs are voluntary communities. To attract members to our communities we need to articulate the "whole child" benefits of our programs. These benefits are the product of an alignment between youth development and curricular units. The take-home message is that this alignment cannot be left up to the ad hoc initiative of a single educator; the camp, youth group, school, and synagogue need to make a coordinated effort. In order to create a complementary configuration of education, all those who have a stake in the life success of the adolescents will need to change the way they work and interact with one another. For some it may be the first time that educators from day schools and educators from congregation-based youth groups sit together to talk about what types of positive developmental experiences to promote among adolescents so that the community as a whole benefits. A developmental framework creates a common language that reduces contradictory messages to the adolescents. This common language enables educators who work with different age groups and educators who work in different types of programs to engage in long-term planning.

To see whether the configuration of education radiating toward the adolescents is complementary or contradictory, it is worthwhile for Jewish congregational and day schools to undergo an accreditation process. To understand this point, it is worthwhile to widen the frame for a moment. Accrediting agencies not only look to see whether schools are meeting regional or national standards; they also look to see whether the individual school is meeting its own standards. Thus if a school aims to promote among the students a high level of adherence to the Jewish people, the accrediting agency will seek evidence that it is achieving this educational outcome. Undergoing an accreditation process benefits the school because it compels the school community to take a sober-eyed look at all the relevant data and then develop a comprehensive plan for educational improvement. In this way educational programs are able to (1) pinpoint what is really important, (2) know whether their efforts are on track to enact high-quality curricula in formal and informal educational programs, and (3) have a positive and effective impact on the life paths of the adolescents. Thus when undergoing an accreditation process, it is critical to administer parent, student, and educator surveys as well as individual assessments of the students to see the nature of the configuration of education.

Of course, the type of accreditation described here exists today primarily among early childhood programs and day schools that undergo accreditation as independent schools. It is recommended that policy makers encourage early childhood programs and day schools to seek accreditation. It is further recommended that new accrediting agencies within the Jewish community be established to provide accreditation to congregational schools, camps, and other educational programs that do not have national or regional accrediting agencies. In this way Jewish informal and formal educational programs will be able to demonstrate their quality.

ADDITIONAL RESEARCH QUESTIONS

If the impact of a Jewish education on adolescents' future quality of life could be clearly and scientifically demonstrated, then (1) Jewish parents would be more likely to enroll their children in Jewish educational programs, significantly improving the prospects for greater and more rapid growth in enrollment, and (2) there would be an increase in the number of foundations, federations, and individuals who would be willing to financially support Jewish education. Thus the primary questions for additional research are:

- whether Jewish educational programs provide their students with an advantage over their same-age peers not attending these programs
- whether these advantages are discernable at points across the lifespan, including adulthood

FUTURE DIRECTIONS

- Restructure the governance of Jewish educational programs to promote complementary educational systems. Fortunately, national educational change initiatives that have honed their skills in the public schools arena have a great deal of experience with implementing such governance structures as the Planning and Management Team, Parent Team, and Student Services Team.
- Implement a data-driven, both quantitative and qualitative process, of making decisions in Jewish education.
- Develop a cadre of facilitators who have the attitudes, skills, and knowledge to help Jewish educational programs translate research findings into educational practice.

CONCLUSION

Developmental experiences are the building blocks of adolescents' competencies. They are characterized by (1) cognitive processing that leads to a sense of well-being that in turn promotes future interest (Comer 1998) and (2) a reorientation of the self into a larger context. Even though the process may at first be painful, developmental experiences eventually produce a sense of psychological pleasure as the individual realizes that he or she can deal with conflict and/or handle the increased choices of how and what to think and feel, and how to behave in this larger context.

Adolescents may also have negative developmental experiences—those that limit choices for thoughts, emotions, and actions. Examples of negative developmental experiences are being told to mouth the words instead of being taught how to carry a tune or being told to go home and study longer and harder instead of being taught specific strategies for studying more effectively and efficiently. These experiences lead to world views in which others can sing but "I am tone deaf," or others can do math, but "I am stupid," each of which is an identity label that tends to limit future positive development (Ben-Avie et al. 2003). We learn certain thoughts, emotions, actions, and approaches toward community when we are young...and they matter when we are older.

A developmental experience—the reorientation toward oneself and the subject matter—can come in a sudden upwelling of insight, or it can be a slower or different type of development that virtually assembles itself before the adolescent or educator becomes consciously aware of the change. The way our educational programs are organized, adolescents tend to be rewarded primarily for quick and sometimes incomplete responses. Consider, for example, the stubborn fact that standardized tests are timed. Opportunities for the slower (and often richer) responses are rare. This is but one example of how our educational programs are not designed to take into account the fact that *youth development is individual.*

One notable desired developmental outcome of Jewish education is the adolescents' formation of a strong relationship with the Jewish people, past and present. The outcome of this relationship is membership in the Jewish group as expressed by the knowledge that we have learned and continue to learn, the attitudes we have developed and continue to develop, the emotional arousal we experienced and continue to experience when learning and participating and our continual partaking of the life of the community. Through forging a relationship with the Jewish people adolescents develop a framework by which to judge their lives and measure their fullness or emptiness. Our Jewish educational programs have the power to impact the developmental trajectories of adolescents. Optimizing this power requires changing the way we work and interact with one another on behalf of the adolescents. Educational change is not for the faint of heart—yet, as the sages teach in *Pirke Avot,* "It is not our task to complete the work, but neither are we free to desist from it."

HIGHLIGHTS OF THE CHAPTER

- The three most important predictors of whether adolescents are forming a strong relationship to the Jewish people, past and present, are (1) the students' engagement in learning and their motivation to achieve, (2) their tendency to seek adult guidance, which is one manifestation of high-quality relationships between educators and young people, and (3) their parents' being their partners in education.

- Whenever instructional activities become too abstract, whenever students become disinterested and disillusioned, the generative relationships that students have with others—and with their own selves—have the power to sustain them in the learning process.

- Activities provide entry points and structures through which adults can impact the development of adolescents. Thus the most effective way to promote adolescents' development is to align curricular units with youth development.

- Jewish educational programs are voluntary communities. To attract members to our communities, we need to articulate the "whole child" benefits of our programs.

- When adolescents develop well, they learn well.

THE CHAPTER IN A LARGER CONTEXT

Jewish education has only reluctantly, at best, learned from the country's educational change initiatives. Yet the great debates about education and how to translate research findings into educational practice are taking place within the initiatives. The Yale Child Study Center's School Development Program (SDP) is one of the largest educational change initiatives. According to *Review of Educational Research,* SDP meets "the highest standard of evidence" for comprehensive school reforms that improved student achievement (Borman, Hewes, Overman & Brown 2002). This chapter reflects SDP's emphasis on relationships as well as the unique understanding that youth development should be the foundational science of education. Moreover, this chapter underscores SDP's approach to assessment: Measure only what we truly value.

ANNOTATED BIBLIOGRAPHY

Bruner, J.S. (1977). *The process of education.* Cambridge, MA: Harvard University Press. Bruner discusses the act of learning and notes that learning a subject seems to involve three almost simultaneous processes: (1) Acquisition of new information—often information that runs counter to or is a replacement for what the person has previously known implicitly or explicitly; (2) Transformation—the process of manipulating knowledge to make it fit new tasks; and (3) Evaluation—checking whether the way we have manipulated information is adequate to the task.

Comer, J.P.; Ben-Avie, M.; Haynes, N.M. & Joyner, E. (1999). *Child by Child*. New York: Teachers College Press. James P. Comer, M.D., associate dean of the Yale School of Medicine and founder of the Yale School Development Program, joins parents, teachers, administrators, community members, and students in relating their personal narratives of how they had to change in order to promote young people's learning and development.

Cremin, L.A. (1976). *Public Education*. New York: Basic Books, Inc. In an age in which our educational systems are fragmented, Cremin provides timeless wisdom about the importance of providing young people with configurations of education that are complementary. By involving all the forces of society to promote, rather than erode, the development of children, we change society itself.

Dewey, J. (1938). *Experience and Education*. New York: Macmillan. In this book Dewey addresses a topic that is especially relevant to Jewish education. While we are teaching our young people the skills to decode Jewish texts, our focus needs to be on what the young people are experiencing in the here and now, and not only on the "educational utility" of the learning in the future.

Joyner, E.T., Ben-Avie, M. & Comer, J. P. (2004). *Dynamic Instructional Leadership to Support Student Learning and Development*. Thousand Oaks, CA: Corwin Press. Meaningful educational change is not for the faint of heart. Fortunately, there are national school reform initiatives that have paved the way for Jewish education. In this field guide the leaders of the Yale School Development Program describe "tried and true" strategies for effective school governance and instructional leadership.

Kozulin, A. (1990). *Vygotsky's Psychology: A Biography of Ideas*. New York: Harvester Wheatsheaf. One of Lev Vygotsky's first major works was an analysis of the play *Hamlet*. Kozulin's book enables us to understand Vygotsky as a Jew and what the play must have meant for Vygotsky as he considered how external societal forces compel us to act.

Taylor, C. (1989). *Sources of the Self: The Making of the Modern Identity*. Cambridge, MA: Harvard University Press. Frameworks help define the demands by which people judge their lives and measure, as it were, their fullness or emptiness. However, people today generally do not have one framework that can be taken for granted as *the* framework. Taylor's analysis enables the reader to think through the implications.

Wozniak, R. & Fischer, K.W. (1993). *Development in Context*. Lawrence Erlbaum Associates, Inc. To investigate the potential life paths of young people, it is not useful to focus only on such dyads as child–mother or child–teacher interactions; the whole fabric of the child's environment needs to be taken into account.

REFERENCES

Ben-Avie, M. (2004). *Learning and Development among Adolescents in a Connecticut City*. New Haven: Yale Child Study Center.

Ben-Avie, M., Brown, W., Steinfeld, T. & Ensign, J. (2004). *Learning and Development Inventory*. New Haven: Yale Child Study Center.

Ben-Avie, M. & Comer, J. P. (2005). "Philosophy and empirical evidence: Achieving vision through research." *Journal of Jewish Education*, 71:67–94.

Ben-Avie, M. & Kress, J. (2005). Jewish Day School Education and Quality of Life. Unpublished paper. Yale Child Study Center and the Jewish Theological Seminary.

Ben-Avie, M, Kress, J., Brown, W. T. & Steinfeld, T. R. (2005). *Learning and Development in Jewish Schools: Educator Survey, Parent Survey,* and *Student Survey*. New Haven and New York: Learning and Development Initiative for Jewish Educational Change.

Ben-Avie, M., Haynes, N.M., White, J., Ensign, J., Steinfeld, T. & Sartin, L. (2003). Youth development and student learning in math and science. In N. M. Haynes, M. Ben-Avie & J. Ensign (eds.), *How Social and Emotional Development Add Up: Making Gains in Math and Science Education*. New York: Teachers College Press.

Borman, G. D., Hewes, G. M., Overman, L. T. & Brown, S. (2002). Comprehensive School Reform and Student Achievement: A Meta-Analysis. Center for Research on the Education of Students Placed at Risk (CRESPAR), 59, November 2002 (retrieved from *http://www.csos.jhu.edu*).

Brown (2006). Personal communication.

Coleman, J.S. & Hoffer, T. (1987). *Public and Private High Schools: The Impact of Communities*. New York: Basic Books.

Comer, J.P., Ben-Avie, M., Haynes, N.M. & Joyner, E. (1999). *Child by Child*. New York: Teachers College Press.

Cremin, L.A. (1976). *Public Education*. New York: Basic Books.

Dewey, J. (1938). *Experience and Education*. New York: Macmillan.

Gordon, D. (2005). Personal communication.

Joyner, E.T., Ben-Avie, M. & Comer, J. P. (2004). *Dynamic Instructional Leadership to Support Student Learning and Development*. CA: Corwin Press.

Robinson, B. (2004). Personal communication.

Sternberg, R. J. (2004). "Culture and intelligence." *American Psychologist* 59(5), 325–338.

Sternberg, R. J. (2003). "What is an 'expert student'?" *Educational Researcher*, 32(8), 5–9.

Sternberg, R. J. (2001). "Why schools should teach for wisdom: The balance theory of wisdom in educational settings." *Educational Psychologist*, 36(4), 227–245.

Taylor, C. (1989). *Sources of the Self: The Making of the Modern Identity*. Cambridge, MA: Harvard University Press.

Vygotsky, L.S. (1978). *Mind in Society*. Cambridge: Harvard University Press.

Special Education in the Jewish Community

Sandy Miller-Jacobs

Richard Lavoie, a special education consultant with years of experience in teaching and administration, tells a story about a group of students waiting to get into their school during a snowstorm. The custodian is busily shoveling the steps, and the students are waiting to enter the school. A young boy in a wheelchair approaches the custodian and asks, "Can you shovel the ramp so I can get in?" The custodian, who's working as fast as he can in order to finish before the bell rings, says he will do the ramp as soon as he finishes the steps for the other children. When the boy repeats the question, the custodian, clearly annoyed, tells the boy to wait. The little boy looks at the custodian and says, "But if you shovel the ramp, we can all go in."

This story frames some of the most important issues facing the education of children with special learning needs in our Jewish schools. First, it paints a picture of inclusion. Sometimes creating an inclusive school necessitates changing our paradigm about schools, classrooms, teaching and learning, and our students. Second, it highlights the idea that all children can benefit from the special accommodations and instructional strategies used for those with special learning needs. While all children are special, not all children have special learning needs. Children with special learning needs require special teaching strategies and accommodations to learn, but these same approaches are beneficial for all children. Third, it shows the importance of advocacy. Unfortunately, students and parents still need to advocate for special education in Jewish schools.

INCLUSION—LEGAL AND MORAL OBLIGATIONS

The famous federal court case of Brown *v.* Board of Education of Topeka (1954) found that segregating students based on race and placing students in separate schools did not provide equal education. This "separate is not equal" decision sparked the thinking of parents of children with disabilities moving them to question placement of their children in separate schools. A series of court cases changed the country's thinking and made the education of those with disabilities a civil right. In 1975 Congress passed the Education for All Handicapped Children Act (PL 94-142), which has been reauthorized with slight changes five times. Currently the reauthorized law is the Individuals with Disabilities Education Improvement Act of 2004 (IDEA 2004). The purpose of this law has always been to ensure that all children with disabilities receive a free and appropriate public education that meets their learning needs while providing and guaranteeing parental rights.

The following six major principles underlie all the reauthorizations since PL 94-142 (Heward 2006; Kirk, Gallager & Anastasiow 2003):

1. Zero Reject—No child regardless of type or severity of disability may be excluded from public education from age 3–21. All children with disabilities are thereby ensured a free and appropriate public education (FAPE).

2. Nondiscriminatory Evaluation—Every student must receive a complete evaluation prior to receiving special education services, and the tests must be appropriate for the child's native language and culture.

3. Individualized Education Plan (IEP)—Each child receiving special education must have an education program developed by a team of professionals and parents and approved by parents (or the student if over 18). Included in the IEP are the child's current performance, educational goals (academic and functional), special education services to be received, and evaluation procedures. Included in the child's current performance level is information about how the student's disability affects his/her participation in the general curriculum and how progress will be measured. Beginning when a child is 14, transition plans are included in the IEP.

4. Least Restrictive Environment—The student must be educated in regular classrooms with non-disabled peers to the maximum extent possible.

5. Due Process—Legal procedures ensure that parents' voices are heard and respected. Evaluations cannot be done without parental consent. All evaluations, meetings, and reports must be completed within specified time limits.

6. Parental Participation—Parents are seen as partners in the IEP process. Parents have the right to disagree with the IEP developed and may reject it. They also have the right to obtain an outside evaluation.

While IDEA is the federal law that ensures that children attending public schools obtain the academic and related services (delivered by speech/language therapists, occupational therapists and physical therapists) to succeed in school, each state has specific regulations regarding the rights of parents who place their child in a private school, including Jewish day schools. Parents may request services from the public school whose personnel are responsible for evaluations, development of the IEP and delivery of services. Each state also has its own regulations about how they provide services and use their federally allocated funds, so it is important for parents to investigate their legal rights. All services provided by the public school are free.

Some Jewish day schools employ their own support staff or hire support staff through an agency or organization (e.g., Matan, NY; Gateways: Access to Jewish Education for All, MA). Again, parents should contact both the day school and the local school district to determine how best to meet their child's learning needs, weighing the advantages and disadvantages of each of their options for services.

IDEA strongly supports inclusion (i.e., educating children with special needs in the regular classroom as much as possible). Inclusion assumes the child is part of the general classroom and receives accommodations and services there. It is different from mainstreaming, which assumes the child starts in a special education setting and is moved into the mainstream (i.e., general classroom) as much as possible. In a fully inclusive classroom, special education is provided directly in the classroom. Schools supportive of the inclusive model may still pull the child out of the classroom for individual or small group direct instruction. Inclusion necessitates collaboration between the special educator and the classroom teacher who work together to jointly plan, share information, and co-teach (i.e., the special educator provides additional support such as notes, redirection, and visual cues throughout the teacher's lesson).

In 2001 the U.S. Office of Special Education organized a Learning Disabilities Summit in response to the increasing number of children identified with learning disabilities. However, only about 50% of students receiving special education services are labeled as learning disabled (Wright & Wright 2005). Becoming labeled is traditionally the result of the student's failure to achieve according to their ability or IQ; this discrepancy model involves waiting for the student to show an inability to make adequate progress or to fail in the classroom. IDEA 2004 strongly recommends a new model, Response-to-Intervention (RTI). The RTI approach suggests implementing effective research-based interventions with periodic measurements of the children's progress leading to early intervention when a child initially shows academic problems. Using a continual cycle of intervention, measurement of the student's response, and analysis of the data to determine the next level of intervention, RTI shows real promise for finding and remediating problems as soon as they appear (NCLD, 2004; Heward, 2006; Wright & Wright 2005). This approach works well in Jewish day schools where support teams seek to offer services when difficulties arise, often prior to a diagnosis. In New York the Board of Jewish Education is working with several day schools to use RTI for reading, measuring progress by using Dynamic Indicators of Basic Early Literacy Skills (DIBELS) in early grades in Project Success In Reading (Project SIR). DIBELS has been translated for use with Hebrew reading, also achieving success in pilot programs (PEJE, 2006).

In 2001 Congress passed No Child Left Behind (NCLB), a reauthorization of the Elementary and Secondary Education Act. Its goal is to improve student achievement by requiring teachers to be highly qualified and to implement effective curriculum and teaching strategies. Setting the expectation that students should be competent in all subject areas, many states have implemented high-stakes testing that requires students to exhibit mastery of the content whether the student has learning disabilities or not. Currently Jewish day schools are exempt from this process.

Section 504 of the Rehabilitation Act of 1973 prevents discrimination against people with disabilities in education, social and employment arenas. Any school receiving federal assistance, public or private, must provide accommodations for students with special needs (Baumel 2002). Students who have 504 plans (also called accommodation plans) generally have less severe disabilities than those receiving IEPs, commonly Attention Deficit/Hyperactivity Disorder (AD/HD) and mild learning disabilities. Success in school is achievable when proper accommodations such as the environment (e.g., physically accessible classroom, quiet space), time (e.g., extended time), format of presentation (e.g., less text on each page, change in reading level of text), and response (e.g., use of laptop, providing a scribe, answering only even-numbered problems) are a part of the school programs (Deschenes et. al. 1994). As private schools, Jewish day schools are required to comply if they seek to receive any type of federal funding.

While public schools are legally obligated to provide an education for students with disabilities, Jewish schools are morally obligated to do so. Just as God gave the Torah to all children, we must educate all children, including those with special needs. "One who denies a child knowledge of our religious heritage steals the child's inheritance" (Sanhedrin 91b). Regardless of the child's learning style or special learning needs, every child deserves a Jewish education.

Jewish schools have been slow to respond to this moral imperative. Parents seeking a quality education for their children in public schools are less vocal about placing demands on congregational and day schools. Jewish schools do not reach out to find students with special needs in their communities, perhaps concerned about the costs of providing schooling or about disenfranchising parents who fear their child's education will be diluted by the addition of children with special needs. Day schools hide behind their difficult dual curriculum. Congregational and day schools offer programs for students with visible disabilities. Students with invisible disabilities (i.e., children whose special needs are not readily apparent to the naked eye) remain invisible in the Jewish world.

With the increasing identification of learning disabilities, including attention deficit disorders, mood disorders, and autism spectrum disorders, Jewish schools recognize that students with these diagnoses are already sitting in their classrooms. Teachers acknowledge that there are students in their classes who do not learn as readily as others, who are unable to sit still and who act out and are disruptive in class. Recognizing these realities and providing the appropriate programs in Jewish schools is increasingly becoming a component of Jewish education delivery systems.

INCLUSION—THE CHANGING PARADIGM

As public schools become more inclusive, Jewish schools have increasingly responded to this initiative as well. Parents now have different expectations of Jewish schools, especially when they see how well the public schools educate and include children who have learning needs similar to their children (Miller-Jacobs & Koren 2003; Miller-Jacobs & Koren 2003a). Parents indicate that regardless of the type or severity of disability, they want their children to receive a Jewish education in their own community, whether that involves a congregational or a day school. They believe their children with special needs should attend the same school as their siblings. Many parents are not content to have their children with special needs at a different synagogue or day school, even if the program might be a better match for their child's learning. They want their children to feel comfortable in their own environment and want other parents and children in their community to know and interact with their children. Synagogues, in particular, sometimes refer a child to a private tutor and encourage participation in less formal school activities rather than send the family to another school and risk losing the family's membership. If the children are included in the local public school, parents want them to also be included in the congregational school, interacting with the children from their public school. Similarly, the children don't understand why they are in class during the day with their peers and then must be segregated for religious school.

The inclusion paradigm has broad implications. First, parents even at the preschool level must be willing to share information about their child's learning needs. They must feel comfortable that the shared information will not result in their child being labeled, resulting in non-acceptance to the program or in being counseled to leave. Second, many parents of preschoolers are not aware that their child has special needs until school professionals bring it to their attention. As they begin to learn about their child's special needs, they need time to adjust to the diagnosis and expect their Jewish community to be a supportive environment for them and their child. Unfortunately, this is not always the case, especially when the proper supports such as skilled special educators, early intervention specialists or therapists (e.g., speech/language, occupational, physical) are not on staff. In the Boston area, where funding is provided for professionals with the appropriate background in the Jewish preschools, major changes have resulted in attitudes toward and understanding of special needs as these professionals provide individual help and coaching for regular classroom teachers.

The situation is similar at the congregational school, where parents must be willing to share information about their children's learning needs. They need to know that the staff is capable of reading and understanding reports and translating the information into action in the classroom. For many parents there is a belief that the child's IEP relates only to the public school curriculum, therefore having little if any relevance for the congregational school. Many parents also want one place where their child is not seen as the "sped kid on meds"; they are less concerned about the actual learning, especially learning to read Hebrew, than the social connections they want for their child.

Research by Miller-Jacobs and Koren (2003a) of the Bureau of Jewish Education of Greater Boston examines the experiences of parents of children with special needs in day schools. After administering 52 completed surveys through synagogues, day schools, and parent groups, they held three focus groups with parents who all wanted day school education for their children. Nineteen parents participated, representing children with learning disabilities, multiple disabilities, attention deficit/hyperactivity, Asperger's syndrome, pervasive developmental disorder and/or autism, cerebral palsy, and emotional issues. From the families of the focus group participants, twelve children were counseled out or left the day school they attended, five children remained with adaptations, and seven families never considered a day school, although they wished it had been an option for their children. All the parents who attended the focus groups wanted the day schools to include children with special learning needs so that their children or others who wanted a day school education could successfully receive one. Parents of children with significant special needs who opted to not send their children to a day school knew that the appropriate support systems were not available. Parents whose children attended the day school found that support services were available and school personnel made accommodations. Despite their general satisfaction with the education, many still questioned whether their decision had been the right one. The group whose children were counseled out or chose to leave the day school generally between the second and fourth grades talked about the pain of this experience. One parent described the feeling of being excluded from this community with the words "I must have cried for a year because of this. It was—I've never felt so much pain in my life" (p.10). The parents' pain relates to the discovery of a learning issue, the exclusion of their children from their social, Jewish and academic community, and their own exclusion from this community. Surprising to some parents was the recognition that they were not alone when they learned that other children in the public school had also been at the day school and left under similar circumstances.

Jewish day schools are reluctant to be seen as "special needs schools" and therefore often hide the support services they provide. Schools tell their stories in a variety of ways on their websites, including how their graduates attend the best colleges, their students score well on SAT exams and win academic, music and science awards. With this information, parents who suspect or know their child has a special learning need are hesitant to apply, and if they choose to apply, they are reluctant to provide information about their child's learning needs for fear the child will not be accepted. A few schools (e.g., Manhattan Day School, Hebrew Academy of Cleveland, South Area Solomon Schechter School in Massachusetts) highlight their inclusion programming for students with special needs. The Partnership for Excellence in Jewish Education (PEJE), in collaboration with the BJE of Greater Boston, interviewed twenty programs providing special education, compiling the information in the fourth volume of *Noteworthy Practices in Jewish Day School Education: Serving Diverse Learners in Jewish Day Schools* (2006). Only the Hebrew Academy of Cleveland offers a complete range of least restrictive options for children with special needs. Another program, at the Charlotte Jewish Day School in North Carolina, is specifically tailored to meet the educational needs of children with emotional and behavior issues.

> *We are schizophrenic in the way we offer services but deliberately choose to ignore it on our web page.*
>
> Headmaster

Although most parents want an inclusive program, many are willing to give up this goal in order for their child to receive a Jewish education. Several congregational schools offer self-contained classes for children who are failing to progress; often these classes are much smaller, with perhaps as few as three students. Some schools have joined together to offer a regional program to provide services to children with special needs. These regional programs may provide self-contained classes, pull-out programs, or tutors and/or consultants to the synagogue schools. In some cities parents have organized programs when they believe the synagogue schools have not been able to meet the needs of their children whose needs are more significant or more specialized (e.g., on the autism spectrum) and may need specific methodology not provided by the synagogue school. Kulanu in New York (*www.kulanukids.org*) and the Sudbury Valley Jewish Special Education Initiative in Massachusetts are examples of communities joining together to educate and support children with special needs and their families.

Day schools are also not always totally inclusive. Some schools provide more of a resource room model, where students leave the classroom to work on specific skills with a special educator, either individually, in a small group. Another major approach to service delivery in day schools is a program with self-contained classes run autonomously from the day school, but located in the building with mainstreaming opportunities. These schools (e.g., Keshet, Chicago; Orot, Philadelphia; Sulam, Maryland; Amit, Atlanta) tend to serve the needs of students with more significant special needs and provide a different or modified curriculum, although they include students with moderate special needs as well. The teachers may be paid for and/or supervised by the central agency or the program itself.

ALL CHILDREN BENEFIT FROM SPECIAL EDUCATION

In assessing the field of Jewish special education, the first question asked is, "How many children with special needs attend our schools (preschool, congregational schools, and day schools)?" A subsequent question is "How many children with special needs are Jewish and not attending our schools?" These questions are extremely difficult to answer. In the public school setting, only children with an evaluation and a documented special need receive special services through an IEP or a 504 accommodation plan. As schools move to implementing the RTI approach, students will receive supports prior to evaluation. This approach is consistent with Jewish schools that offer support services without documentation of a special need, leaving questions about the number of students with special needs either unanswered or incompletely met.

While students with special needs require special instructional strategies to learn, many of these strategies are also helpful to students without special needs. Howard Gardner's research on multiple intelligences (1983) highlights different abilities of all children and, for educators, emphasizes the importance of teaching in a variety of ways (see chart).

Intelligence	Description
Linguistic	Strength in spoken and written language
Logical-mathematical	Strength in mathematics and science, logical thinking
Spatial	Strength in visual-spatial thinking, seeing patterns
Bodily-kinesthetic	Strength in athletics, dance and movement
Musical	Strength in musical performance and appreciation
Interpersonal	Strength in understanding and working with people
Intrapersonal	Strength in understanding one's own feelings and styles
Naturalistic	Strength in recognizing and categorizing objects in the natural environment

Gardner's research aligns with our knowledge of learning styles (i.e., children learn based on auditory, visual and/or kinesthetic input). Educators thus have a clear message to plan learning activities for children who learn in different ways. For example, in teaching about the holiday of Sukkot the teacher presents biblical texts that describe the holiday (linguistic), creates dimensions for sukkot that would fit in different spaces (logical-mathematical), presents pictures of the objects used on the holiday (visual), has children work in groups to create a diorama of a sukkah (spatial and interpersonal), has the class create a dance for a Sukkot party (bodily-kinesthetic), has a concert for the holiday (musical), asks the children to compare and contrast the different leaves found in the lulav (naturalistic), and has students talk about the holiday's personal meaning (intrapersonal). This kind of approach enables all students to expand their abilities and, if choices are given, enables them to choose an area of interest. While this is a simple example, by adding more depth to the questions and activities it can be used as a template for all grades. The children use their own learning style as they create their projects with written notes and pictures (visual), music (auditory) and movement (kinesthetic). While all the children will enjoy these varied projects, children with special learning needs must have different ways to gather the information and to show what they have learned.

Other teaching strategies for children with special needs include the use of graphic organizers, previewing information, and providing direct instruction. Graphic organizers are visual representations of information that are especially helpful for students with special learning needs. They provide visual clues, help children organize their thoughts, and support recall. There are many graphic organizers readily available on the internet (e.g., *www.graphic.org*; *www.eduplace.com/graphicorganizer/index.html*), and they can be adapted and used for any subject, Judaic and general studies. The following chart is an example of a graphic organizer.

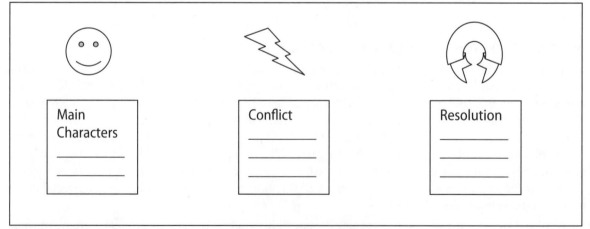

Another approach, differentiated instruction, enables teachers to tailor the classroom to meet the learning needs of all students, respecting students' capabilities and appropriately challenging them. Originally developed for gifted students, it is currently used by teachers to educate children in their class who possess a wide variety of learning styles, needs, and capabilities. Teachers differentiate the content being taught, enabling all students to access information, the process or learning activities in which the students engage, and the products that enable students to show their mastery of learning. Differentiation is based on the students' learning profile, readiness, and interests. Teachers provide tiered assignments and offer flexible grouping and choices (Heacox 2002; Tomlinson 1999). Differentiated instruction is increasingly being used in day and congregational/community schools.

ADVOCACY—STILL A NEED

Although special education laws have been in effect for over thirty years, people with special needs still have to advocate for themselves or have a parent or guardian advocate for them. Parents advocate for their child to be seen as a whole person, not by the label given to the disability that affects the learning. Parents may need to advocate for the appropriate sharing of key information with teachers, provision of appropriate services, and social as well as academic inclusion. For children with invisible disabilities, especially emotional and behavior issues, parents still have to advocate for services. There are many examples of schools advising parents that their children should receive private tutoring, be placed in more informal and social programs and other types of situations despite the fact that less structured and social situations are often a problem for children with special needs. Many schools also offer a one-to-one aide to maintain the child in the school, but often these aides lack special education training. And some schools still tell parents they do not offer support for "this kind of problem." In these situations parental advocacy is the appropriate response for providing the best Jewish education for their children.

FUTURE RESEARCH AGENDA

The field of Jewish special education is extremely new, and there are numerous questions for further research.

- Will the use of intake forms enable the open and honest sharing of information about a child's special learning needs?
- What methods of teaching Hebrew as a second language, especially for students with language processing learning disabilities, are the most successful?
- What are the instructional strategies that work at all levels (preschool through high school) and for different types and severity of special needs for teaching Hebrew and Judaics?
- What are noteworthy practices for school, family education, camp, Shabbat services, youth activities, Israel trips?
- What are the implications, challenges and benefits of inclusion for families of children with special needs *and* other members of the synagogue and school community?
- How do we measure the acceptance of disabilities within the school and synagogue community?

FUTURE DIRECTIONS

To move the agenda of providing Jewish education for all students ahead there are many practical ideas that can be implemented.

- In an effort to openly disclose special education services offered by schools, information should be placed on websites and in parent handbooks. Statements should be made suggesting that parents who are concerned about their child's learning progress or social interactions talk with a designated member of the school support services team. Such information should be kept confidential so as to encourage parents to share information.
- Parents of children with special needs often seek advice from educators who know their child's strengths and challenges. This is especially true as parents make decisions about school placement, including options for Jewish education, be it a day, congregational or community-based

school. It is important that the educational community know what services are available in Jewish schools to provide parents with the most accurate information and guidance.

- Each Jewish school should examine their formal and informal programming for children and youth through the lens of special education, asking questions such as: Is the physical environment appropriate? Is sufficient structure provided? Can all students have success with the learning tasks offered? How much and what kind of support is needed for a specific child, and does it match the support the school currently provides or is capable of providing?

- Parent meetings that address issues particularly relevant for students with special needs provide support and help eliminate the isolation felt by parents of children with special needs. Specific concerns of parents of children with special needs (e.g., inability to complete long-term assignments, need for improved social skills, ways to make smooth transitions more easily) are frequently of interest to many parents whose children do not have disabilities.

- Professional development must be provided to all teachers on topics such as multiple intelligences, differentiated instruction, classroom management, and providing accommodations for students with learning problems. While professional development is usually built into day school schedules, congregational and preschool staff should also be provided with opportunities to improve their knowledge and skills. All professional development activities should be ongoing, giving teachers the opportunity to learn together, experiment with new approaches and reflect on their impact on students with special needs.

- While there are many strategies for teaching secular subjects to students with learning disabilities and other special needs, Jewish special educators need to develop and share ways in which they have adapted or created programs and strategies for teaching Hebrew, Tanakh, and other Judaic studies. These methods should be shared through local and national conferences as well as on the web.

CONCLUSION

The field of Jewish special education is a relatively new and rapidly growing area of education in the Jewish community, with many programs emerging in just the past ten to fifteen years. Day schools want students in their school to succeed while retaining students with special needs; congregational schools want to provide education to all members' children. Jewish preschools play an important role, as this may be the first places someone raises concerns about the child's development. In all, discussions with parents about their child's learning issues lays the foundation for the parents' feelings about their acceptance within the Jewish community. There is more at stake in Jewish special education than just a child's education; it also affects the family's connection to their Judaism.

HIGHLIGHTS OF THE ARTICLE

- While Jewish schools are not bound by federal laws regarding students with special needs, they are morally obligated to service these children. Laws support the concept that the education of children with disabilities is a civil right.

- Many of our special needs programs are the result of advocacy by parents.

- Jewish schools—day, congregational and early childhood—are responding to special learning needs by hiring special educators, support staff and consultants to help students with special needs receive a Jewish education. Teachers are providing accommodations and are making modifications to help students be successful in the classroom.

- Schools in many Jewish communities offer a variety of programs, from inclusive to self-contained classes, with support personnel hired by the schools, by the central agency and/or by autonomous programs.

- Schools servicing students with special needs appreciate the multiple intelligences of their students by implementing specific instructional strategies developed for those with learning disabilities and cognitive challenges. Direct and differentiated instruction are used in many schools as a way for teachers to help all children with special learning issues, including the gifted, to learn together in inclusive classrooms.

• Teachers of Hebrew and Judaic studies have adapted special education strategies developed for general studies as they work with students with a variety of learning problems.

• Professional development for teachers has become increasingly important to help teachers develop the knowledge, skills and attitudes needed to teach students with special needs.

• Despite improvements in our schools, there are still students who are not able to receive the support needed to be successful and are still being counseled out; this is especially true for students with behavior disorders.

• Jewish schools continue to be quiet about their support services, making it difficult for parents to come forward with important information about their child's special learning needs.

LARGER CONTEXT

While public schools are legally required to provide a free and appropriate education for children with special needs, Jewish schools realize that they have a moral obligation to provide education for these students. Jewish special education is now a growing component of the knowledge that Jewish educators must learn to be effective in their roles. Of particular importance are special education laws, current strategies, approaches to educating students with disabilities, and ways to adapt these instructional practices to the teaching of Judaic content and Hebrew reading. To change the culture of our schools so that we are more accepting and responsive to the special learning needs of students, schools need to provide learning opportunities for teachers, administrators, parents and lay leaders. Teachers need to learn how to make accommodations and to create differentiated lessons; administrators need to recognize the benefits of inclusive education for students without disabilities; and lay leaders need to be spokespeople for the importance of providing special education programming for students who need it. Within our schools, systems need to be established for diagnosing learning problems, for delivery of services, and for referring students in need of support services. Schools need to be open about the services available so that parents feel welcomed and included. Developing and maintaining partnerships between schools and parents will provide the optimal experience for students with special needs.

ANNOTATED BIBLIOGRAPHY

_____, (2000). *Al Pi Darco/According to Their Ways: A Special Needs Educational Resource Manual.* New York: Union of American Hebrew Congregations. This publication provides basic information about disabilities and ways to interact with people with disabilities and ties this information to a Jewish perspective. A first stop in looking at the field of Jewish special education.

Heacox, D. (2002) *Differentiating Instruction in the Regular Classroom: How to Reach and Teach All Learners, Grades 3–12.* Minneapolis, MN: Free Spirit Publishing. This book contains a good summary of differentiated instruction and also gives practical ideas and examples. Teachers will find it quite helpful if they are creating a differentiated classroom. Teachers of Hebrew and Judaic studies will have to adapt this work, since the book addresses secular schools.

Heward, W. (2006) *Exceptional Children: An Introduction to Special Education* (8th Ed.) Upper Saddle River, NJ: Pearson Merrill Prentice Hall. This book is a typical introductory special education text that covers all the varieties of disabilities, including a chapter on autism. Examples from schools and excerpts from teachers are included, leading to easy reading. This text is filled with information about disabilities, methods of teaching students with disabilities, living with those with disabilities, and current issues in the field of special education.

"How Difficult Can This Be? F.A.T. City," video by Rick Lavoie, PBS (DVD released 2005). An excellent simulation of learning disabilities, this video has become a classic for teaching about learning disabilities and the effect learning disabilities can have on a child's self-concept. Many types of learning disabilities are demonstrated, and types of teacher responses are shown. Humorous and enjoyable to watch, the video provides a lot of information and is useful for professional development of staff and disability awareness for the community.

Miller-Jacobs, S. & Koren, A. (2003a) Research Report #12: Special Learning Needs in Day Schools: Parent and Community Responses, BJE of Greater Boston. This research report is one of the first done on the parent's perspective on having a child with a disability and how that impacts a child's education and a family's experience at a day school. Participants in focus groups talk openly about their experiences in Boston day schools. The parents fall into three groups—those who never approached the day school, those who left or were counseled out and those who remained. The introduction provides background on Jewish views toward educating those with special needs.

_____. (2006) *Noteworthy Practices in Jewish Day School Education, Vol. IV: Serving Diverse Learners in Jewish Day Schools.* Boston: PEJE. Available on the web at *www.peje.org* this is a first descriptive listing of twenty programs for students with special needs in Jewish day schools. Information is given about the program, types of children served, types of services, and contact people. The introduction provides an overview of Jewish views of special education, with a matrix that organizes the programs so that you can find programs based on type of disability, location or age of student.

Tomlinson, C. (1999) *The Differentiated Classroom: Responding to the Needs of All Learners.* Alexandria, VA: ASCD. Considered the guru of differentiated instruction, Carol Tomlinson is worth reading. This first book clearly outlines the theory of differentiated instruction and provides classroom examples. Also worth considering are the many videos she has created for the Association for Supervision and Curriculum Development.

Wright, P. & Wright, P. (2005, December 6) Wrightslaw: IDEA 2004, "Discrepancy, Response to Intervention and Learning Disabilities," pp. 135–137, (URL: *www.wrightslaw.com*). This website provides accurate and up-to-date information about legal issues. Information related to federal laws should be examined in light of state regulations that may take precedence.

REFERENCES

_____. (2006) *Noteworthy Practices in Jewish Day School Education, Vol. IV: Serving Diverse Learners in Jewish Day Schools.* Boston: PEJE.

Baumel, J. (2002, October) "Section 504—Federal Civil Rights Law" *www.schwablearning.org (downloaded 3/28/2006).*

Deschenes, C., Ebeling, D. & Sprague, J. (1994) *Adapting Curriculum and Instruction in Inclusive Classrooms: A Teacher's Desk Reference.* Bloomington, IN: Indiana University.

Gardner, H. (1983) *Frames of Mind: The Theory of Multiple Intelligences.* New York: Basic Books.

Heacox, D. (2002) *Differentiating Instruction in the Regular Classroom: How to Reach and Teach All Learners, Grades 3–12.* Minneapolis, MN: Free Spirit Publishing.

Heward, W. (2006) *Exceptional Children: An Introduction to Special Education* (8th Ed.) Upper Saddle River, NJ: Pearson Merrill Prentice Hall.

Kirk, S., Gallagher J. J. & Anastasiow, N. J. (2003) *Educating Exceptional Children* (9th Ed.). Boston: Houghton Mifflin.

Miller-Jacobs, S. & Koren, A. (2003) "Inclusion of Children with Special Needs in Day Schools: Parent Experiences." *Jewish Education News* 24 (3), 56–59.

Miller-Jacobs, S. & Koren, A. (2003a) Research Report #12: Special Learning Needs in Day Schools: Parent and Community Responses. Boston: BJE of Greater Boston.

NCLD (2005, June) IDEA 2004 Parent Guide: Response-to-Intervention, Part II. www.ncld.org/content/view/903/456087 (downloaded 5/15/2006) National Joint Committee on Learning Disabilities, "Responsiveness to Intervention and Learning Disabilities".

Tomlinson, C. (1999) *The Differentiated Classroom: Responding to the Needs of All Learners.* Alexandria, VA: ASCD.

Wright, P. & Wright, P. (2005, December 6) Wrightslaw: IDEA 2004, "Discrepancy, Response to Intervention and Learning Disabilities," 135–137, (www.wrightslaw.com).

www.jgateways.org

www.kulanukids.org

www.matankids.org

WEB RESOURCES

Children and Adults with Attention Deficit Disorders *www.chadd.org*

Council for Exceptional Children *www.cec.sped.org*

Learning Disabilities Resources *www.ldonline.org*

National Information Center for Children and Youth with Disabilities (NICHCY): *www.nichcy.org.*

Jewish Learning on the University Campus

Clare Goldwater

It is an accepted notion that the years spent at colleges and universities provide young people with opportunities to explore their own identities and commitments and to be immersed in a world of ideas that can broaden their horizons and open their minds. It is also the case that more than 80% of Jewish young people between the ages of 18 and 25 spend at least three years in an institution of higher education. This is the only thing that Jewish young people do in such high numbers. Yet despite this disproportionately high number, the expansion of research in the areas of Jewish education over the past decade reflected in other chapters in this volume, and the growth of Jewish communal interest in this population, we still know remarkably little about the Jewish education that goes on during the college years. What happens to these Jewish students during their college years? What opportunities do they have to grow Jewishly? What are their interests? How do their previous Jewish experiences impact their Jewish college life and influence their general college experience? How can we exploit the college setting (the atmosphere of study, the time to think and experiment) in order to encourage them to explore their Jewish identities and expand their Jewish horizons?

Of course, most Jewish students are not studying in Jewish institutions, nor studying Jewish subjects. They are studying liberal arts, the humanities and sciences, with the rest of their American peers. They are engaged in a wholly American, secular cultural experience. Yet at the same time the university years are full of Jewish educational possibilities of all kinds, and it is our interest in this chapter to consider what these are and to reflect on what we know, and what we would like to know, about them.

Before we do this we must first briefly define what we will refer to as "Jewish education" in this context. We will be referring to both formal and informal Jewish learning[1]. For our purposes, formal refers to the academic teaching of Jewish content that aims to inculcate knowledge, stimulate intellectual curiosity and, in the academy, promote research. Informal refers to learning that takes place in non-academic settings, in communal experiences of a religious or cultural nature, in opportunities for leadership and active engagement in Jewish life on campus, broadly defined.

As the director of the Joseph Meyerhoff Center for Jewish Learning at Hillel, I am an informal educator with an interest in the broadest Jewish educational possibilities for college students. Hillel: the Foundation for Jewish Campus Life is the largest Jewish organization on campuses in North America and elsewhere and is committed to the provision of non-academic Jewish experiences for students[2].

---

[1]The terms "formal" and "informal" education are slippery to define. This is not the place to debate the terms and the merit of the argument that "informal education" is just another way of referring to "good" education. For our purposes it is helpful to use the terms broadly to refer to the "academic" and the "non-academic" settings respectively, while we recognize that this may ignore some of the complexity inherent in both "types" of education. For a suggested definition of Jewish informal education (and other excellent material on informal education in general) see the *www.infed.org* website, especially Barry Chazan—*http://www.infed.org/informaljewisheducation/informal_jewish_education.htm*. Also see the chapter in this volume on Jewish Experiential Education by Reimer and Bryfman.

[2]Hillel supports 251 affiliated foundations, program centers and Jewish student organizations that serve students at 513 campuses throughout North America. Hillel Foundations, of which there are 105 in North America, generally serve more than 500 Jewish students and have more than one full-time professional. Some Hillel Foundations serve multiple campuses. There are also 46 Hillel Program Centers that have fewer than 500 Jewish students and only one full-time professional. See *www.hillel.org* for Hillel activities and a directory of all Hillels.

THE CONTEXT

Unlike the fields of day school or adult Jewish education, the world of the Jewish college student (all college students, in fact) is notoriously difficult to define, pin down and research. Students are hard to find, to track and, within the secular academy, to identify as Jewish. We have very little information, and often that which we have is disputed. Research in this area tends to become obsolete very quickly given the inherently short life span of college experience and the accelerating pace of change in youth culture. In the following section I will provide a survey of the most important research that relates to the Jewish education available to students on campus and the main lessons we can learn from it.

NUMBERS

The National Jewish Population Survey (NJPS) of 2000–01 identifies 271,000 undergraduates and 88,600 graduates between the ages of 18 and 29 currently in colleges and universities in the United States. They are scattered in a wide range of institutions and geographic locations, although the majority (45%) are in the northeast. While the overwhelming majority can be found in large numbers in a relatively small number of colleges, 25% of all students served by Hillel are studying in institutions with fewer than 800 Jewish students (most of these have significantly fewer) and very limited Hillel infrastructure in terms of staffing and resources.

MOTIVATIONS AND RESPONSIVENESS TO JEWISH EDUCATION

As has already been noted, although a very high proportion of Jews go to college, they do not go primarily, if at all, to learn about being Jewish. On the contrary, Jews go to college to participate as full members of American society. The college years are not a time for intentional Jewish education. Indeed, according to "America's Jewish Freshmen", a study that extracted Jewish-related data from the Cooperative Institutional Research Program (CIRP) Freshman Study at the Higher Education Research Institute at UCLA (Sax, 2002), they come to college with a wide range of motivations, of which "to learn about things that interest me", "to gain a general education and appreciation of ideas" and "to prepare myself for graduate or professional school" are the most important.

In addition, the CIRP study shows that the main reason that Jewish students choose to enroll at a particular college is the academic reputation of that college and the perceived advantages for graduates when it comes to finding jobs. At the same time, "Eight-Up: The College Years" (Keyser & Kosmin, 2004), a study commissioned by the Ratner Center for the Study of Conservative Judaism at the Jewish Theological Seminary, asked students whether the Jewish facilities at a college influenced their choice and found that for over 60% of the respondents the presence of other Jews *was* an important factor, and a slightly lower number said that a strong Jewish institutional presence, such as a Hillel program, played a role in their choice of college. In other words, more than half of Jewish students in the study appear to be interested in Jewish life on campus, whether social or educational. Although the "Eight-Up" study is not representative of Jewish students as a whole, and is focused on the cohort of young adults raised in Conservative synagogues, who are relatively more engaged and educated than many, we can extrapolate that a significant proportion of young Jews (less than 60% but still significant) are interested in some Jewish experience, social and/or educational, during their college years.

These figures provide us with a somewhat complex picture of the Jewish educational motivations of college students. On one hand, they are going to college for avowedly secular purposes. More than a quarter choose to go in order "to get away from home", perhaps to experiment and break away from family commitments. They are highly motivated to study and succeed academically. They are pressured academically and highly involved in sports, fraternities and sororities, and political organizations. Their life goals include "being very well off financially" (72.8%), "raising a family" (78.6%) and "helping others who are in difficulty" (63.5%), and their college years are the first step in the direction to these goals (Sax 2002). In addition to this, large numbers have paying jobs, as testified to by 71% of respondents in the "Eight Up" survey.

At the same time, other responses point to potential for meaningful Jewish education during the college years. Jewish students are interested in ideas and in exploring new things. At a higher level than their non–Jewish counterparts they profess interest in "learning more about things that interest me" (80%), and more than half see college as an opportunity "to make me a more cultured person". They appear to be looking for an expansion of their horizons and for new ideas. Half declare that they are interested in "developing a meaningful philosophy of life", and almost a third want to "integrate spirituality into my life". They are also more interested than non–Jewish students in areas of political concern, such as "keeping up to date with political affairs" (43.7%), "helping to promote racial understanding" (35.4%) and "influencing the political structure" (22.5%) (*Ibid.*). Hillel professionals also testify to the thirst for learning among many students and their openness to creative, relevant and inspiring opportunities. All these responses indicate that a significant number are potentially open to learning experiences that could be integrated into a Jewish context.

JEWISH EDUCATIONAL OPPORTUNITIES ON CAMPUS

The opportunities for Jewish educational experiences on college campuses are myriad and vary widely from university to university and from region to region. They break roughly into two major categories: academic and non-academic. The academic opportunities to study Jewish subjects exist within the formal university system and further the aims of the academy. The non-academic opportunities, usually focused around a Hillel center on campus, offer students informal educational opportunities of a social, religious, cultural and political nature. We will look at these categories in turn and identify what we know and what we would like to know about them.

ACADEMIC JEWISH STUDIES

The growth of Jewish studies in the university in the past three decades has revolutionized the opportunities for Jewish education on campus. Although there are no data on the exact numbers and types of courses available, it is clear that there exist hundreds, if not thousands, of courses in Jewish studies across North America, which are taken by a wide range of Jewish and non–Jewish students, usually as single courses and not part of a major or minor concentration. The courses range across the disciplines, from religious studies to sociology, history to literature, cultural studies and more.

Sales et al. (2005), in their recent study "Jewish Life on the American College Campus: Realities and Opportunities", find that by the time they are seniors, almost half of all Jewish students (45%) have taken at least one Jewish studies class, although there is great variation across institutions, depending on the quality of the course offerings on any given campus. Not surprisingly, the stronger a student's Jewish upbringing and involvement, the more likely he or she will be to take a Jewish studies course. Sales et al. found that 61% of student leaders have taken such courses, as opposed to 26% of the unengaged and 43% of the engaged.

Sales et al. point out that students' motivations for taking Jewish studies classes are complex. Primary motivations are to satisfy course requirements, with Jewish studies courses often fulfilling requirements for courses in non–Western civilization or in some kind of minority studies. In addition, because of the interdisciplinary nature of Jewish studies, courses can be found in many departments, allowing students with a wide range of major and minor concentrations to have access to them. The study also notes that some Jewish students choose these courses because they think, sometimes mistakenly, that they will get an easy "A".

Researchers and faculty anecdotes also point to secondary motivations that show that taking Jewish studies courses is also an act of Jewish identification. For student leaders and those with engaged Jewish backgrounds, this is fairly obvious. For them Jewish studies is an academically acceptable way to extend the possibilities for Jewish engagement and growth and fits into the university context extremely well. Perhaps more surprisingly, Sales and her colleagues found that 25% of students in these classes are not involved with any other kind of campus Jewish activity. For them it appears that academic study of Judaism is a "safe" way to explore and learn without the pressure to fit into a religious setting or to conform to some kind of acceptable behavior. Jewish studies, because of its integration into the university context, academic status and significant proportion of non–Jewish students, provides the less affiliated Jewish student with a place to learn in an arena that minimizes feelings of Jewish insecurity and has no stigma of ghettoization.

THE EFFECTS OF ACADEMIC JEWISH STUDIES

It is difficult to determine the effects of taking Jewish studies courses on the individual student. More research is needed in this area. Sales et al. do show, however, that there is a significant difference in changes of Jewish observance between those who have taken Jewish studies courses and those who have not. For those who have, 30% become more observant over their time at college. For those who have not, 18% become more observant. While cause and effect cannot be determined, this figure is interesting in itself and consistent with the findings that show higher levels of knowledge and engagement for those who have taken these courses.

THE TENSION BETWEEN THE "HEAD" AND THE "HEART"

Jewish studies is a secular, academic enterprise that serves the goals of the academy. Indeed, its expansion in the past decades is a function of this fact. As such, its goals, assumptions and measures of success, while not necessarily in opposition, are very different from those of the non-academic Jewish organizations on campus. The academic discipline of Jewish studies is focused on the intellectual and the "objective," while the non-academic Jewish activities on campus are concerned with Jewish growth, transformative experiences and Jewish leadership. This inherent tension has led to a lack of integration and sometimes even tension between the academic and the non-academic Jewish worlds on campus.

NON-ACADEMIC JEWISH OPPORTUNITIES

Theoretically, non-academic Jewish opportunities on campus provide students with a set of Jewish experiences to complement their academic studies. These include informal classes of all types, lectures, social gatherings, Jewish ritual celebrations, opportunities to volunteer and become involved in social and political activism and educational trips to Israel. As we have noted, these activities provide students with experiential opportunities to learn through interaction with peers, engagement with new ideas and places and active involvement in causes and campaigns.

On most campuses these activities are centered around a Hillel, which functions as a central convener of Jewish life on campus. As Sales et al. (2005) point out, there has been an expansion in Hillel activities across the country in the past fifteen years. Most Hillels, except the very smallest, offer regular classes, opportunities for leadership development, access to national student conferences, trips to Israel and many more informal learning opportunities. They are usually staffed by full-time professionals, and many have well-located buildings that provide space for activities including religious services, and often kosher dining facilities.

There has been growth in recent years in the number of Orthodox Jewish outreach programs on college campuses looking to provide students with more possibilities for Jewish learning. They include the Jewish Learning Initiative, which operates in cooperation with the Orthodox Union and Hillel on approximately ten campuses, the Maimonides Program, currently on approximately thirty campuses and the Jewish Awareness Movement on several campuses in California. In addition, Chabad is well established on campus, with sixty-five full-time rabbis offering classes and opportunities for group and individual Jewish learning and growth.

Despite the growth of these educational opportunities, there has been very little research about their impact. Not only is there a need for more detailed information about the range and types of these learning experiences, but we also need to understand more about their nature and quality as well as the impact that they have on students and their Jewish identities. The exception to this general lack of information is the Taglit-Birthright Israel program, which has been extensively researched since its inception. The results shed some light on the nature of informal Jewish education for college students, especially as this is the largest, most intensive Jewish experience that many Jewish students will have during their university years.

TAGLIT–BIRTHRIGHT ISRAEL

Since 1999 approximately 100,000 Jewish young adults of college age from North America have traveled to Israel on a free ten-day Israel experience provided by Birthright Israel (see www.birthrightisrael.com). The overwhelming majority of these participants were in college at the time of their trip. As most had not previously been to Israel and therefore were much less likely to be among the engaged group of Jewish students, they made up the most diverse Jewish population of any other Jewish activity on campus. Thirty percent participated in campus-based trips organized by Hillel, with the rest traveling with a wide range of other providers.

The Birthright Israel phenomenon and the accompanying research point to a number of important facts about college students and Jewish education. First, large numbers of Jewish students are open to this avowedly educational experience and are highly motivated learners. While they are certainly attracted to participate because of its reputation of being a fun experience (78%) and because it is free (63%), they also report that they participate because they have always wanted to see Israel (78%) and they want to learn more about Judaism (33%). The qualitative data also point to the openness of the students to learning experiences during the trip and to the variety of ways in which the participants construct their own learning experiences from their expectations and previous knowledge. The Cohen Center for Modern Jewish Studies at Brandeis University is responsible for most of the research on Birthright Israel (www.cmjs.org).

After the trip 80% of participants say that they found it personally meaningful, and 75% say that it was highly educational. It is clear that we are looking at a significant educational experience. If so, what are these students actually learning? The students report they are learning Jewish history (91%), about themselves (81%), their own Jewish directions (80%), about Judaism (78%) and about the Israeli-Palestinian conflict (77%).

The first five years of Birthright Israel research focused on the measurable impact of the trip on the students. While the exact nature of the impact is still unclear and, of course, more time is needed in order to measure long-term results, it is clear that the program has had significant impact on the attitudes, if not the behaviors, of the participants. The immersive group nature of the experience and the subject matter have left participants with a stronger relationship to Israel, a greater sense of belonging to the Jewish people and a greater knowledge of Israeli and Jewish history than non-participants. The Birthright Israel research also finds that there is a positive influence on the number of students who take Jewish studies courses following their Israel experience, indicating that there can be a positive, mutually reinforcing connection between the academic and non-academic.

Future research will expand its focus to pay more attention to the nature of the educational experience itself and shed more light on the role played by the educator and the group.

IMPLICATIONS AND POLICY RECOMMENDATIONS
INFORMATION

Despite the recent studies cited above and the gradual accumulation of data about Jewish college life in general, there is still very little knowledge about the nature of Jewish educational experiences for college students. How many students are exposed to Jewish education during college? What is the nature of these experiences? What is the relative balance between group and individual learning experiences? How do the academic and non-academic learning interact? As a result of our lack of knowledge, policy decisions are often made without a nuanced and rich understanding of the variety of Jewish students and their interests or without a clear picture of how they learn.

Therefore, there is a need to expand and collaborate on qualitative and quantitative efforts to understand these students, their interests, their needs and what is already working well for them. It would be helpful to continue collaboration with the Higher Education Research Institute (www.gseis.ucla.edu/heri) and to use data that is already available. In addition, more research should be commissioned, perhaps by a central body that can coordinate the interests of all the interested parties, in order to develop further research questions and to facilitate collaboration in the use of the data. Possible directions for research are described later in this article.

OPENNESS TO LEARNING

Contrary to the stereotype that students just want to party, we see that there is an openness and willingness to learn among Jewish students. Granted, we must recognize that their primary concern is their college experience, and that Jewish education will probably be only a secondary interest. However, if it can be integrated into their college agenda and exploit their interests and predilections, Jewish education, both the academic and non-academic, can find fertile ground during the college years.

More attention must be focused on the trends prevalent in the university setting, in general, and ways they can be used and expanded to provide complementary Jewish educational opportunities that can be successful in this context.

JEWISH STUDIES

The expansion of Jewish studies has a significant role to play in the development of Jewish student life. Because it is part of the university context it provides the easiest and safest way for students to learn more and expand their Jewish horizons. At the same time we have already noted that this may not necessarily result in the identity building or leadership development that interests the Jewish community.

As Sales et al. have also noted, there is a very strong need to create greater dialogue between the academic and the non-academic Jewish campus opportunities. On the campuses where the Hillel and the Department of Jewish Studies see themselves as complementary, and have built channels of joint activity and communication, the possibilities for Jewish student life are richer and are bound to be mutually advantageous. There are many potential models for productive Hillel–Jewish Studies relations; these must be studied, developed and nurtured in order to enrich Jewish campus life as a whole.

BIRTHRIGHT ISRAEL

Birthright Israel has become the largest single Jewish educational experience available to college students and is probably the most intense Jewish experience that they will have during their time in college. It is clear that the core educational messages students are receiving are concerned with Jewish peoplehood, expressed in Israeli and Jewish history, filtered through an intense group experience. This is significant because it is in contrast with the way that most synagogue and religious schools focus on the religious and spiritual aspects of Judaism. Often the first time students encounter a meaningful Jewish experience, it focuses on the cultural, the political and the historical sides of Judaism rather than the religious. In the long run this may serve to counteract the often negative messages that these students received during their childhood Jewish education. We must capitalize on this new understanding and consider the implications for learners and teachers alike.

All the research about Birthright Israel points to the potential for meaningful follow-through with the participants. It also points to the difficulties with this follow-through and the relatively small rate of involvement in follow-up activities. There is a need to continue developing creative ways for students to move from the Birthright experience to other Jewish educational opportunities.

In addition, lessons from Birthright Israel can be expanded and applied to other intensive Jewish travel experiences such as "alternative spring breaks". These are intensive, service-based trips that students are organizing locally and finding to be very powerful in terms of experiential learning and identity formation. The growth of "alternative spring breaks" and other forms of educational travel are bound to grow and are a significant form of educational experience.

ADDITIONAL RESEARCH QUESTIONS

Research in the following areas will shed light on some of the gaps in our current knowledge.

- How can we better define the categories of "leaders", "engaged" and "unengaged" developed by Sales et al.? Who are these different students? Where are the nuances and complexities in this categorization? Are there other ways of categorizing Jewish students' attitudes and behaviors?

- What is the impact of students with interfaith backgrounds? An estimated 45% of students have one parent who was not born Jewish (see NJPS 2000/01). This number will almost certainly grow in the future. Who are these students, and what is the nature of their Jewish identities? What are their Jewish interests? What can we do regarding language, accessibility of content and general inclusivity to encourage them to participate in Jewish experiences on campus?

- How many Jewish students are taking Jewish studies courses and why? What are they most interested in? What are their expectations regarding their academic Jewish study, and how does this study affect their Jewish identities, if at all? What is, or should be, the role of the Jewish professor in this learning process?

- What are the current models of good relations between Hillels and Jewish Studies departments? How can these models be extended or developed more widely? How can Jewish life on campus be enriched by the synergy between these two, and how can we measure this enrichment?

- How do leadership opportunities and political activism impact the Jewish identities of students? What are the lessons they are learning about the Jewish and non-Jewish worlds, and how can they be nurtured and developed?

FUTURE DIRECTIONS—PRACTICAL IDEAS FOR MOVING THE FIELD AHEAD

As has been indicated, the field of Jewish education for the university student requires more research and more careful strategic planning. It also requires the following elements:

- The establishment of a better structure for cooperation between Hillels and Jewish Studies programs. A national summit and ongoing dialogue on the national level will contribute to the development of better relationships between the formal and the non-formal branches of Jewish education on campus.

- As is recognized in other areas of Jewish communal life, talented and committed Jewish professionals are crucial to meaningful Jewish educational experiences. Hillel has recently embarked on a new initiative to recruit more aggressively in the Jewish community and develop new models for staff development and retention. This needs to be further developed and expanded to include the Jewish Studies faculty.

- Cooperation and collaboration between all the interested parties involved in Jewish education on campus needs to be expanded. Important stakeholders include students, campus ministries, university administrations, faculties of Jewish studies, Hillel staff and their lay leadership on a local and national level, the campus departments of the major religious denominations, outreach organizations such as Chabad, and the major funding organizations.

CONCLUSION

College life is extremely rich and full of promise and potential, both for students and for those interested in the long term of the North American Jewish community. Much has been done, especially in the last two decades, with much still remaining to be done in this complex, challenging and fast-moving field. We hope that by the time the next version of this book is written the field of university Jewish education will have continued moving forward, leading the Jewish community as a model for creative and powerful Jewish education that will impact the community as a whole as well as individuals themselves.

HIGHLIGHTS

- Going to college is an experience shared by approximately 80% of young Jews, but for most it is not a time for intentional Jewish education.

- Jewish students are primarily concerned with their academic studies and their future careers, but there is also a clear indication that they are open to Jewish educational experiences that are inspiring, relevant and integrated into the academic context.

- The academic and the non-academic may sometimes be in tension but can also be seen as complementary.
- The field of academic Jewish studies has grown enormously in the past two decades and now reaches an estimated 45% of Jewish students.
- Birthright Israel is the largest single Jewish education endeavor on campus today as well as the most intensive. It has the potential to change the face of Jewish education on campus.

ANNOTATED BIBLIOGRAPHY

Keysar, A & Kosmin, B. (2004). *Eight Up, The College Years: The Jewish Engagement of Young Adults Raised in Conservative Synagogues, 1995–2003*. New York: The Jewish Theological Seminary.The third stage of a longitudinal study tracking young Conservative Jews in the bar/bat mitzvah class of 1994–5. The study looks at why these students chose their colleges and how their time in college is shaped by their Jewish identities, as well as how they connect to Jewish life.

National Jewish Population Survey 2000-01 *http://www.ujc.org/content_display.html?ArticleID=60346*. The largest American Jewish population study. The methodology and results have been questioned, but the data on college students is useful, and much of it is not found elsewhere.

Sales, A. L., Saxe, L., Chertok, F., Hecht, S., Tighe, E., de Koninck, I. (2005). *Particularism in the University : Realities and Opportunities for Jewish Life on Campus*. Waltham, MA: Cohen Center for Modern Jewish Studies, Brandeis University. The most recent and comprehensive study of Jewish college life, including data on all aspects of college life, with recommendations for future research and expansion of academic and non-academic opportunities.

Sales, A. & Saxe, L. (2005). Engaging the Intellect: Jewish Studies on the College Campus in *Contact, the Journal of the Jewish Life Network*/Steinhardt Foundation. This article is also available at: *http://cmjs.org/files/Contact.winter_2005_Engaging%20the%20Intelect.pdf*

Sax, L.J. (2002). *America's Jewish Freshmen: Current Characteristics and Recent Trends among Students Entering College*. Los Angeles: Higher Education Research Institute, UCLA. The annual survey of freshmen was mined for variables relevant to Jewish students. Contains some good data and interesting comparisons between Jewish and non–Jewish students.

Saxe, L., Kadushin, C., Hecht, S., Rosen, M.I., Phillips, B. & Kelner, S. (2004). *Evaluating Birthright Israel: Long-Term Impact and Recent Findings*. Cohen Center for Modern Jewish Studies, Brandeis University. The most recent study of Birthright Israel, including data on the winter 2003-4 cohort of participants as well as a continuation of the long-term longitudinal study. This study and other Birthright Israel research can be found at www.cmjs.org

REFERENCES

Keysar, A & Kosmin, B. (2004). *Eight Up, The College Years: The Jewish Engagement of Young Adults Raised in Conservative Synagogues, 1995–2003*. New York: The Jewish Theological Seminary.

National Jewish Population Survey 2000–01. New York: United Jewish Communities, available in various formats at *http://www.ujc.org/content_display.html?ArticleID=60346*

Sales, A. L. et al. (2005). *Particularism in the University : Realities and Opportunities for Jewish Life on Campus*. Waltham, MA: Cohen Center for Modern Jewish Studies, Brandeis University.

Sax, L.J (2002). *America's Jewish Freshmen: Current Characteristics and Recent Trends among Students Entering College*. Los Angeles: Higher Education Research Institute, UCLA (http://www.gseis.ucla.edu/heri/heri.html).

Saxe, L. et al., (2004). *Evaluating Birthright Israel: Long-Term Impact and Recent Findings*. Waltham, MA: Cohen Center for Modern Jewish Studies. Brandeis University.

Jewish Family Education

Jo Kay & Evie Rotstein

Jewish family education is a field that has undergone considerable change over the last fifteen to eighteen years, continuing to evolve as the Jewish family continues to change. In guiding our analysis of this evolving field, four questions will serve as our guide: 1) What do we mean by Jewish family education today, and how has it changed over the years? 2) How has the change in the Jewish family affected the work of Jewish educators? 3) Who are our family educators? and 4) How do we enable both adults and children to find meaningful connections in Jewish learning and to bring that learning into their lives? We believe that looking through the "lens of family" can support systemic change in Jewish institutions.

The authors, Professor Jo Kay and Dr. Evie Rotstein, are currently involved in teaching future Jewish professionals (rabbis, cantors and educators at HUC-JIR) as well as congregational and communal professionals about family education through their work at the College Institute and with the Leadership Institute for Congregational School Principals (LICSP). Jo Kay, who has spent more them thirty years in day school and congregational school education, is a faculty member and consultant for the former Whizin Institute, today the Consortium for the Future of the Jewish Family: Expanding the Work of Whizin, and created the PACE (Parent and Child Education) Family program. Evie Rotstein, a congregational school principal for twenty-six years and the current director of LICSP, has developed family learning programs throughout her career. She has recently completed her dissertation on "Connections, Commitment and Community: What Motivates Teenagers from Interfaith Families to Continue Post Bar/Bat Mitzvah Jewish Education." Both authors have spent many years working in summer camps, and they understand and appreciate the value of learning outside the formal classroom and how that relates to working with families.

Through an examination of the research in the four key areas, greater insight will be developed into the context for Jewish family education and how it impacts the quality of the family and of Jewish educational programs.

WHAT DO WE MEAN BY JEWISH FAMILY EDUCATION TODAY, AND HOW HAS IT CHANGED OVER THE YEARS?

To define Jewish family education, experts have focused on the threefold nature of the term. What is *Jewish* about the lesson or program being developed? What does Jewish tradition say about the subject we are teaching? What authentic Jewish experience can be included in the development of the program or experience for families? What new Jewish skill or teaching will the parents and children learn as a result of this program?

Jewish family education places equal emphasis on the *family*. How does a program or experience support the positive growth and development of the family? What opportunities exist for parents and children to interact, to talk to one another, to share ideas and opinions? What opportunities exist for parents to speak with other parents (or for children to have conversations with other children) and share expertise or experiences? How can parents support one another through the developmental stages that all children experience?

Education refers to teaching and learning that leads to some change in behavior or some new way of thinking. This happens when the subject holds meaning for the learner; and when the learner has an opportunity to reflect on, interact with, and practice the learning. It is the single piece of all programs that will determine whether the experience will be enduring in ways that will affect future decisions and actions. It is why we work with families in the first place.

Those engaged in the work of Jewish family education have understood this from the beginning. However, this is not how the field developed. In most cases, rabbis and educators recognized the value of bringing parents and children together mostly within the context of the synagogue. However, the *educational piece* was not always considered. For learning to be enduring and transformational, it needs to be on going, lifelong and filled with personal meaning. It needs to go well beyond having fun with children and developing beautiful Jewish mementos. It also needs to address the adults as learners.

HOW HAS CHANGE IN THE JEWISH FAMILY AFFECTED THE WORK OF JEWISH EDUCATORS?

Today, there is an even greater challenge for family educators who are seeking to reach beyond the classroom into the homes of all of our learners, adults and children, to create a desire for these learners to engage in lifelong Jewish learning and living. Who are the learners? In essence, they are everyone we meet both inside and outside our Jewish settings. The adults have often had little if any Jewish education since childhood, although they may be quite accomplished in other areas of their lives. The children, on the other hand, are active participants in the school and other education programs of the congregation. Family educators must help bridge the gap between the *reality* of the lives and needs of today's Jewish families, and the image of the traditional Jewish family of the past.

Family educators, looking at their students through the lens of family, no longer concern themselves with the learner alone, but rather view the "family" as the entity they are trying to reach. Whether our learners are children and parents engaged in family educational experiences, together or apart, or adults learning without a connection to a "family education" program (rather in an adult learning course), all are members of families. It is also important to recognize that today's family bears little resemblance to the "traditional Jewish family" of the past. Jewish family educators find themselves teaching divorced families, interfaith families, interracial families, adoptive families, gay and lesbian families and single-parent families, to name only a few of the new family forms. They must approach these families with understanding and sensitivity to their stresses and their needs.

WHO ARE OUR FAMILY EDUCATORS?

Although there are many family educators and program coordinators working in Jewish educational settings, it is clear that all our professionals (rabbis, cantors, educators and communal professionals) are engaged in educating families. Some have had limited training in family dynamics and family counseling, but it is far more common for them to use their intuition and adapt their training in other areas when working with family cohorts. Working with families over a period of time often requires the combined skills of social workers, clergy and educators. Therefore, the more these professionals see themselves as part of a collaborative team, working together toward the positive growth and development of Jewish families, the more successful they will be. In general, all those working with families need to continually be learning about how today's Jewish family is changing and to be involved in continual professional development.

HOW DO WE ENABLE BOTH ADULTS AND CHILDREN TO FIND MEANINGFUL CONNECTIONS IN JEWISH LEARNING AND TO BRING THAT LEARNING INTO THEIR LIVES?

The family educator must meet their students *where they are*. Research in general education has taught us that learning must be meaning-centered. It must "make sense" for the learner. We must begin by asking: "What do you know or think you know? What do you want or need to know? What have you learned?" This classic teaching strategy is referred to in educational literature as K-W-L (What do I Know? What do I Want to know? What have I Learned? (Ogle 1986). This strategy asks that we enable students to find relevance in the learning for their own lives: Why should I learn this? Why is this important for me to know? How is it related to my life? And finally, they need an opportunity to reflect on the learning and ultimately to apply the learning in a context or setting (home, school, synagogue, camp, college, etc.) in which they function. Unless educators working with families or with adults or children independently address the learners' need to find meaning in their studies, learning cannot be enduring or transformative.

OVERVIEW OF RESEARCH

During the last decade Jewish family education has evolved as an integral component of religious education in both the congregational school and the day school. Woocher (2003) claims that "Family education has become almost normative as a complement to the schooling of young children" (p. 29). To better understand the field of family education we suggest three domains of research that can offer insight.

FAMILIES—THE SOURCE OF RELIGIOUS AND CULTURAL TRANSMISSION

Current research about religious and cultural transmission places the family at the center. The family is the place where we learn about who we are and how to interact with the world. Parents are the primary agents for transmitting religious beliefs and cultural values. Parents shape these beliefs, values and practices through the selection of a congregation and the intensity of their Jewish involvement (Keysar, Kosmin & Scheckner 2000, Parker & Gaier 1980). Parents make choices regarding Jewish education and Jewish ritual that determine the level and type of Jewish engagement in the family. In addition, parents direct their children to social settings that contribute to their overall Jewish involvement. So does the extended family; grandparents and others play an integral role in determining the religious socialization of children (Cohen & Eisen 2000). One of the goals of Jewish family education is to effectively influence the values, beliefs and practices of the parents, thereby having an impact on the family.

The National Study of Youth and Religion conducted research on the religious and spiritual lives of American adolescents from 2001–2005 at the University of North Carolina. Smith and Denton (2005) found that teenagers are far more influenced by the religious beliefs and practices of their parents and other adults integral to their lives than is commonly thought. Through nationwide telephone surveys of 3,370 teens and their parents, as well as 267 in-depth personal interviews, they also found that teenagers "feel good about the religious congregations they belong to and that faith provides them with guidance and resources for knowing how to live well" (p. 4). This body of research about adolescents indicates that for adolescents, belonging to a religious community and learning from parents as well as other adults who share common values, beliefs and behaviors is important. Knowing this makes a difference in how we approach Jewish family education.

In his recent article *Linking the Silos: How to Accelerate the Momentum in Jewish Education Today*, Wertheimer reports "that adults and their children mutually reinforce each other's Jewish engagements" (2005, p. 2). It is this notion that Pomson (2004) investigates when he considers how day schools can shape the lives of Jewish parents and their sense of Jewish community. Pomson observes three significant changes in the parents' lives. He suggests that the school has the potential to impact the parents' Jewish knowledge, their commitment to community, and their sense of safety. He refers to the concept of "intergenerational closure," in which children live and learn among parental networks that are connected socially, economically, geographically and religiously. To be effective, Jewish family education is about building a community that connects learning to real-life experiences in the context of a community of practice.

The role of parents in Jewish education is yet another element to be considered. Conventional wisdom informs us that parental involvement in our schools can be a source of great support. Roy (2006) emphasizes the importance of building partnerships with parents. She claims that family involvement influences student achievement and greatly enhances learning. Roy explains that schools need to cultivate family involvement by "increasing parenting skills, establishing open communication, encouraging volunteer opportunity, and building a community of shared decision making" (*www.nsdc.org/library/publications*). These are the principles necessary for Jewish family learning to be long-lasting and effective.

JEWISH FAMILY EDUCATION

The impact and effectiveness of Jewish family education programs during the last ten years is not well documented. Very little evaluation or research has been conducted to ascertain their success or impact. Three studies offer us limited information and insight.

During the early 1990s "*Sh'arim* Gateways to Jewish Living: The Family Educator Initiative," funded by Boston's Commission on Jewish Continuity, launched an extensive Jewish family education project. It began with eight sites in 1993, expanded to seventeen sites in the year 2000, and presently supports thirty sites. The initiative provided new personnel and programmatic resource to enable synagogues, community centers and day schools to engage the family to become effective partners in the education of their children. *Sh'arim's* stated goals included:

1. Involve family members in their children's Jewish education so that the whole family can support and enhance the children's learning.

2. Establish programs for joint family involvement in Jewish learning, thereby providing families with "quality time" together in Jewish pursuits and creating shared Jewish memories.

3. Build community among families in order to strengthen their connection to each other and to their Jewish institution.

4. Adapt Jewish learning to the home by empowering family members to become Jewish models and teachers for their children. (Sales, Koren & Shevitz 2000, p. 4).

With careful documentation from eleven of the participating institutions, which included parent surveys and focus groups, reports from the family education teams, and data collected from the congregation professionals and family educators, the impact of the initiative was examined from different perspectives. The results of the study indicated important consideration for future endeavors:

- There was a significant increase in parents' participation in Jewish education and in their attendance at worship services.

- Parents' sense of connection to the congregation increased only slightly during the three- year study.

- *Sh'arim* did not have a widespread impact on the Jewish quality of families' lives at home and in the community.

In short, the study found minimal increase in parent Jewish engagement and connection to the community or congregation; on the other hand, parents indicated that they would like to practice Judaism more. The result was that "there is little evidence that *Sh'arim* has had widespread impact on families' Jewish lives at home and in the community" (p. 35).

Results were more positive in a study conducted of the Jewish family education programs in Chicago under the direction of Vincent. In the fall of 1999 close to 2,000 parents from 38 synagogue schools completed the CFJE Family Education Survey, which documented the effectiveness of Jewish family education programs. Seidman and Milburn explored the outcomes of family education both in the improvement of participants' emotional connection to Jewish organizations and practices, and the increase of Jewish knowledge and understanding. Eighty-five percent of respondents believe that Jewish family education is an effective way to pass Jewish values and practices on to their children. Seventy-three percent believe that family education enhanced their Jewish connection to the Jewish community. Seventy-nine percent expressed the positive impact of Jewish family education through the joint participation of parents and children. The analysis reveals that a smaller percentage of respondents (68%) indicated that Jewish family education enhanced holiday observances for the family and that fewer respondents saw Jewish family education as a way to persuade parents to take part in their own Jewish studies (54%) (2000).

In a somewhat different context, a study done in one congregational setting in Penn Valley, Pennsylvania looked at the impact of a family Shabbat–centered religious school model in which parents were complete partners in all of the weekly learning experiences. Following is the description of the program.

The Shabbat-Centered Synagogue Community works to make Judaism—the traditions, values, and education—an important part of each member's daily life. Congregants, with the guidance of their leaders, develop the synagogue's "distinctive Torah," which will be taught consistently throughout the synagogue, fostering a common language for learning and living Jewishly. Through the ideal of the "distinctive Torah" and advancing teacher development, classes were added Shabbat mornings, engaging everyone in the congregation (wishing to be involved) to concentrate on how the Torah, its values and its content relate to each person (*www.jesna.org/j/pdfs/coaches/Synagogue_Change.pdf*).

The Philadelphia federation gathered data from families both in this program and in traditional religious school programs. In a baseline interview protocol fifty families, twenty-five from each setting, were asked to identify their personal beliefs, and their Jewish education goals for their children and for the family and to describe their religious practice, their ritual and their level of community participation. Two years later those families who participated in the Shabbat-centered program indicated that the experience each week enabled them to connect their Jewish learning to their work and home life in significant ways. They also shared that being part of a Jewish community was one of the most meaningful outcomes of the program (Margolius & Weissman 2002). This was not the case for the families that continued to participate in the traditional model.

FAMILY EDUCATION—LEARNING WITHIN COMMUNITY CONTEXT

In order for children to experience successful Jewish learning and to acquire the skills, values and behavior that we identify as critical to the goals of Jewish education, the learning needs to take place within the context of a community of learners. Students find their learning more relevant when they observe adults engaged in the discovery and exploration of Jewish knowledge as well. Instruction at all levels and in all content areas needs to happen as part of a community that supports the purpose of the learning.

The notion that children learn best when there is support from the adults around them has been the focus of the Penn Literacy Network for the Pennsylvania Department of Education. The framework includes four lenses through which powerful learning transpires. The first lens involves the centrality of meaning-making during the learning experience. The second lens explores the concept that learning is inherently social and that meaningful learning emanates from the broader context of family, neighborhood and community. We make meaning in collaboration with others; shared experiences result in changes in individual behavior. The third lens emphasizes that learning must be authentic in nature and relate to real-life situations using language as the system of transfer. The fourth lens focuses on learning as human; as learners we bring prior knowledge and our unique belief systems to the task (Lytle & Botel 1996).

Building on this framework, the American Psychological Association's Center for Psychology in Schools and Education offers a number of principles intended to focus holistically on learners in the context of real-world learning situations. These principles are intended to apply to all learners—from children to teachers to parents and community members. They provide a framework for Jewish family education as a process of meaningful learning that can be connected to real-life experience within the context of a larger community.

- **Nature of the learning process.** The learning of complex subject matter is most effective when it is an intentional process of constructing meaning from information and experience.
- **Goals of the learning process.** The successful learner, over time and with support and instructional guidance, can create meaningful, coherent representations of knowledge.
- **Construction of knowledge.** The successful learner can link new information with existing knowledge in meaningful ways.
- **Context of learning.** Learning is influenced by environmental factors, including culture, technology, and instructional practices.
- **Motivational and emotional influences on learning.** What and how much is learned is influenced by the learner's motivation. Motivation to learn, in turn, is influenced by the individual's emotional states, beliefs, interests and goals, and habits of thinking.

- **Social influences on learning.** Learning is influenced by social interactions, interpersonal relations, and communication with others.
- **Developmental influences on learning.** As individuals develop there are different opportunities and constraints for learning. Learning is most effective when differential development within and across physical, intellectual, emotional, and social domains is taken into account (*http://www.apa.org/ed/lcp2/lcp14.html*).

The efforts to provide a variety of learning experiences is one of the key components of transformative Jewish family education. We must include learners of all ages throughout all stages of development. Kelman (1992) suggests that "the purpose of a good Jewish family education program is to provide the help the family needs to cross the stream" (p. 14). She refers to the "stream" as a continuum of the specific kinds of knowledge and experience, from novice to expert, needed to support Jewish family learning. We meet the social needs of families by including opportunities for family members to engage with one another and with other families. By focusing program topics on issues confronting families today, we address motivational and emotional needs. Taking into consideration the nature and context of the learning process can foster stronger connections to the Jewish community and to a Jewish tradition that values each individual in a caring, nurturing environment.

IMPLICATIONS/POLICY RECOMMENDATIONS

1. Jewish family education provides opportunities for community building and meaning making.
2. Jewish family education immerses parents and children in the context of the learning, linking Jewish learning to Jewish life.
3. Jewish family education that seeks to promote behavioral changes must be ongoing and must engage both adults and children in meaningful learning activities.
4. Clergy and educators need professional development in order to work effectively with the continually evolving nature of the Jewish family.
5. Jewish family education assists parents in acknowledging and supporting the critical role they play in shaping the Jewish lives of their children and their families.
6. More funding for evaluation and research is needed to fully understand the accomplishments and challenges of Jewish family education.

ADDITIONAL RESEARCH QUESTIONS

1. What kind of Jewish family learning has proven to be transformational?
2. What types of families should be targeted for Jewish family education?
3. What programs and initiatives are most appropriate for the diversity of Jewish families?
4. What kind of professional development is necessary to support clergy and educators in their work with today's Jewish families?
5. How can Jewish family education continue to respond most effectively to the needs of the changing Jewish family?
6. What is the impact of the changing Jewish family on Jewish family education?

FUTURE DIRECTIONS

1. The Jewish community needs to explore new venues and structures to reach out to those families that are not connected to a Jewish institution.
2. Today's Jewish adults have demonstrated a desire for serious Jewish learning opportunities (Schuster 2003). Jewish family education must address the needs of parents' learning as well as children's.
3. Jewish institutions must consider looking at education through the lens of the Jewish family as a way of supporting systemic change.

4. Greater cooperation and collaboration between Jewish educational venues (synagogues, day schools, JCCs, Jewish camps, etc.) must be encouraged and supported by every Jewish community that is seeking to transform Jewish lives and Jewish living.

5. Family education must consider experiential learning in real time (Shabbat and holiday learning communities) due to the impact it can have on the life of the Jewish family.

6. Jewish family education must encourage lifelong Jewish learning for each member of the family.

HIGHLIGHTS

• Making the connection between knowledge, belonging to a community and living with values supported by the community will strengthen the case for transformative Jewish family education.

• Parents are the primary agents for transferring religious beliefs and cultural values to their children, and thus the entire family must be part of Jewish learning experiences.

• Family educators looking at their students through the lens of family no longer concern themselves with the children alone but rather see the family as the students they are trying to reach.

• There is minimal reliable research to document the impact of Jewish family education programs. More funding is needed to conduct studies that will provide information for future directions.

CONCLUSION

More and more adults are seeking serious and meaningful Jewish learning opportunities for themselves and their families. They want these learning opportunities to be available when they are available, in real time. Currently the traditional synagogue school model may not be poised to meet their needs. Creative thinking and visionary leadership are required to find new venues, new structures and new training (professional development experiences) for all those who find themselves working with families. Planning for serious and meaningful learning for families must include authentic Jewish experiences, community building for adults and children, support for family growth, opportunities to apply new learning and reflect on it and opportunities for the families to share their learning with other families.

The Jewish community has the greatest chance for successfully engaging adults and children in serious ongoing Jewish study and involvement in Jewish living if it will support and encourage collaborative efforts among the many venues and agencies currently trying to reach families today. Collaboration within institutions must also be encouraged. Supporting the growth and development of Jewish families must be seen as the work of all Jewish professionals. Partnership and teamwork will bring together the talent, skills and resources needed for this visionary work.

ANNOTATED BIBLIOGRAPHY

Bank, A. & Wolfson, R. (1998) (eds.). *First Fruit: A Whizin Anthology of Jewish Family Education*. Los Angeles, CA: The Shirley and Arthur Whizin Institute for Jewish Family Life. This edited book includes thirty-six articles by authors involved with the Whizin Institute and Jewish family education. Each contributor has extensive experience in the field and shares the challenges and struggles involved in his/her work with families.

Brodie, R. & Kelman, V. (eds.) (2002). *Jewish Family Education: A Casebook for the Twenty-first Century*. Los Angeles, CA: Torah Aura Productions. A series of ten case studies that represent the challenges and concerns involved in the work of Jewish family education. Text study and commentary from experts in the field are included.

Fishman, S. B. (1999). *Jewish Life and American Culture*. Albany, NY: State University of New York Press. Fishman investigates the lives of American Jews and their connection to religion and ethnicity, demonstrating how they have created a hybrid form of Judaism merging American values with Jewish tradition.

Keysar, A., Kosmin, B.A. & Schenckner, J. (2000). *The Next Generation: Jewish Children and Adolescents*. Albany. NY: State University of New York Press. Utilizing the results of the 1990 National Jewish Population Survey, the authors provide a comprehensive analysis of the critical issues facing the future of the Jewish community's next generation.

Kress, J. S. & Elias, M. J. (1998). "It takes a *kehilla* to make a *mensch*: Building Jewish identity as part of overall identity." *Jewish Education News, 19(2),* 20–24. The *kehilla*-centered approach offers a guide to understand the ecology of a particular community and its major contexts of influence; namely the Jewish family and the educational setting.

Schein, J. & Schiller, J.S. (eds.) (2001). *Growing Together: Resources, Programs, and Experiences for Jewish Family Education.* Denver, CO: A.R.E. Publshing. A resource of many varied programs and experiences that bring families together to learn, to celebrate and to function as Jewish families.

Smith, C. & Denton, M. L. (2005). *Soul Searching: The Religious and Spiritual Lives of American Teenagers.* Oxford: Oxford University Press. In one of the largest and most comprehensive studies about religion and adolescence, this book shares the findings of the National Study of Youth and Religion. This important research explores the role of religion and spirituality in the lives of contemporary American teenagers of all religions.

REFERENCES

Cohen, S. M. & Eisen, A. M. (2000). *The Jew Within; Self, Family and Community in America.* Bloomington, IN: Indiana University Press.

Kelman, V. (1992). *Zones and Scaffolds: Toward a Theory of Jewish Family Education in Jewish Family Retreats.* New York and Los Angeles: Melton Center for Jewish Education, JTSA and the Shirley and Arthur Whizin Instutute for Jewish Family Life.

Keysar, A., Kosmin, B.A., Schenckner, J. (2000). *The Next Generation: Jewish Children and Adolescents.* Albany, NY: State University of New York Press.

Lytle, S. L. & Botel, M. (1996*). The Pennsylvania Framework for Reading, Writing and Talking across the Curriculum.* Harrisburg, PA: Pennsylvania Department of Education.

Margolius, M. J. & Weissman, C.B. (2002). "Creating a Shabbat-Centered Community." *Shema,* March.

Ogle, D. S. (1986). K-W-L group instructional strategy. In A. S. Palincsar, D. S. Ogle, B. F. Jones, & E. G. Carr (eds.), *Teaching Reading as Thinking.* Alexandria, VA: Association for Supervision and Curriculum Development.

Parker, M. & Gaier, E.L. (1980). "Religion, religious beliefs, and religious practices among conservative Jewish adolescents." *Adolescence, xv* (58), 361–374.

Pomson, A.D.M. (2004). "Day school parents and their children's schools." *Contemporary Jewry,* 24, 104-123.

Roy, P. (2006, February). The heart of instructional leadership: Developing quality teaching. *The Learning Principal* 1 (5).

Sales, A. L., Koren, A. & Shevitz, S. L. (2000). *Sh'arim: Building Gateways to Jewish Life and Community.* Boston, MA: Commision on Jewish Continuity.

Schuster, D. T. (2003). *Jewish Lives, Jewish Learning: Adult Jewish Learning in Theory and Practice.* New York: UAHC Press.

Seidman, L. & Milburn, S. (2000). *Family Education Survey.* Chicago. Community Foundation for Jewish Education of Metropolitan Chicago.

Smith, C. & Denton, M. L. (2005). *Soul Searching: The Religious and Spiritual Lives of American Teenagers.* Oxford: Oxford University Press.

Wertheimer, J. (2005). *Linking the Silos: How to Accelerate the Momentum in Jewish Education Today. http://www. avi-chai.org/Static/Binaries/Publications/Linking%20The%20Silos_0.pdf#search=%22linking%20the%20silos% 22.* Retrieved August 2006.

Woocher, J. S. (2003). Jewish Education in the Twenty-First Century: Framing a Vision. In N. Skolnik Moskowitz (ed.), *The Ultimate Jewish Teacher's Handbook.* Denver, CO: ARE Publishing.

Learner-Centered Psychological Principles *http://www.apa.org/ed/lcp2/lcp14.html.* Retrieved September 2006.

The Jewish Education
of Parents

Betsy Dolgin Katz & Mitchell Parker

The education of parents of school-age children is rapidly becoming a primary focus of both schools and the field of adult education. As a result, important differences are emerging in the nature of the parent as learner as we gain more experience and become more familiar with these enthusiastic students. These insights have led to the examination of demographics, motivation of learners, best practices in teaching and specialized content. Since this is a new focus in Jewish education, there remain significant unexplored questions for further research and study.

The authors, Betsy Dolgin Katz and Mitchell Parker, are presently involved in creating and administering the Florence Melton Adult Mini-School's Parent Education Program. Katz has worked as a family, parent, and adult educator throughout her career. Parker, a psychologist, worked for over twenty years as the coordinator of a small havurah in Buffalo, N.Y. In that position he was responsible for both parent and family education for the group. Currently he is the director of the Parent Education Program of the Florence Melton Adult Mini-School and is involved in parenting in his private practice devoted to the families of children with developmental disabilities, behavioral and learning disorders.

KEY QUESTIONS

WHY IS THERE A SPECIAL CATEGORY WITHIN JEWISH ADULT LEARNING IN WHICH THE EDUCATION OF PARENTS IS ADDRESSED?

When addressing the needs of the Jewish adult population, parents of school-age children stand out as a group that has unique issues and concerns. Although they are very busy individuals, their interest in Judaism and how it relates to their family life is often a high priority.

Two of the factors that motivate adults to participate in learning are the implications of this stage of life and the transitions they and their children experience. In the Jewish world, parents become more aware of their own Jewish identity when they have children, when these children enter school and when the children approach their bar or bat mitzvah. Sometimes this is accompanied by questions about the family's relationship to Judaism and an awareness of their lack of Jewish knowledge. Beginning when the children first enter a Jewish preschool, parents commonly focus on their Jewish home life and their relationship to their synagogue and community. They want to know specifically what they can do, how they can enhance their children's Jewish lives, and how they can share Judaism with their children. As a flyer inviting preschool parents to participate in learning asks, "When your children ask the four questions, do you have the answers?" For many parents of children in Jewish preschools, their initial experience as learners and their involvement with the program will shape their entry as adults into the Jewish community.

WHAT ARE THE CHARACTERISTICS OF PARENTS OF SCHOOL-AGE CHILDREN?

One of the difficulties in accurately describing the characteristics of parents of school-age children is their wide age span. Although some upper-middle-class couples in their twenties and early thirties are having children, it is not uncommon to become a parent late in the fourth or even the fifth decade of life. For many young adults in the Jewish community, it is a common occurrence to pursue careers in their twenties and early thirties, which leads to delays in both marriage and having children. In addition, medical advances have made childbirth safer for women in their late thirties and early forties. In research on the demographics of the Jewish preschool, Pearl Beck indicates that the average age of a parent of preschool children in the Jewish community, considering both the father and the mother, is forty (Beck 2002). Thus for any age group, a classroom of "parents" could include adults spanning three decades, whether in the preschool or later in the educational process.

When we look for qualities of parents of school-age children we have to consider issues that are much broader than just those that are age-related. Other demographic information reported by Beck that impacts on parent education throughout children's school experience includes:

- The overwhelming majority of the fathers (93%) were engaged in full-time work. In contrast, 27% of the mothers reported having full-time employment, and 31% reported working part-time. This translates into 42% of the mothers not being employed outside the home.

- Approximately 25% of the sample consisted of families who were either intermarried (17%) or families in which one parent had converted to Judaism (8%).

- On one important measure of Jewish identity, visiting Israel, parents whose children attend a Jewish preschool had traveled to Israel at a rate 50% higher than that of the general American Jewish population (31%).

WHAT IS THE CONTENT OF THE EDUCATION OF PARENTS, AND HOW IS IT DIFFERENT FROM PARENTING EDUCATION?

The goal of parent education, as we are using the term, is the learning of Jewish content relevant to being a parent. It encompasses general Jewish knowledge as well as responses to the specific questions that are relevant to this demographic group and that would not be addressed in typical adult education classes. Knowing that much of Jewish knowledge shapes our lifestyles and the homes and communities in which we live, some of the information is directly applicable to Jewish family life while other knowledge shapes us more subtly. No matter what an instructor teaches, learners will shape the content to fit their lives. Because their parenting role is a top priority, the questions that arise naturally out of their learning are ones that relate to their chief concerns as mothers and fathers. This includes such questions as: What can we learn from Torah about relationships between generations? What does Judaism say about parents' responsibility to teach their children? What are the ideas, practices and values we can convey to our children? Why should we observe Jewish holidays and Shabbat as a family? What makes a home a Jewish home? What is the role of the synagogue in Jewish life today? What is the role of the synagogue in Jewish family life?

In contrast, "parenting education" encompasses the "how-to's" of Jewish life. It is learning how to raise children in a way that reflects Jewish values. This encompasses becoming aware of the Jewish perspectives that arise from the challenges that children present and includes such questions as: How do we set limits for our children in a Jewish way? What do we do if our children lie to us? What does Judaism say about the language children use? How do we observe Shabbat and holidays so they are meaningful to us and to our children? In recent years many books have been published, workshops organized and websites created to educate parents on how to discipline their children, how to solve eating problems, and how to teach children honesty and generosity in Jewish ways.

THE CONTEXT OF PARENT EDUCATION
NORTH AMERICAN JEWISH COMMUNITY

A generation ago there was a strong emphasis on synagogue education for children. Many parents dropped off their children and left it to the Jewish professionals to provide just enough knowledge to inform them about what Judaism was in the past and what it could offer them in the future. There was little participation of parents, and little was expected of them. For most, bar or bat mitzvah and/or Confirmation was the goal. This meant that Jewish learning was less likely to be integrated into life. Synagogue membership was for the most part tied to children's education. There were, however, exceptions to the trend. The Conservative Movement created a parent education program in the late

1960s that touched many lives, and beginning in the 1970s family education provided a bright light that led us to where we are now in terms of recognizing the importance of parent education.

The 1990 National Jewish Population study uncovered a high level of intermarriage and consequent assimilation. It sounded an alarm that led to a dramatic increase in new initiatives directed toward stemming the flow of young adults out of the Jewish community, including efforts to educate our adult population under the rubrics of Jewish continuity and renaissance and renewal. Ten years later, when the 2000/01 National Jewish Population Study was released, only minor changes in rates of assimilation were noted. During these years greater emphasis was placed on sustained education, with particular concern being given to teaching adults. At the same time, Birthright Israel was created to encourage college-age youth and young adults to travel to Israel on a free trip where they would be inspired to establish Jewish homes and raise Jewish children (NJPS 2000/01).

Parallel to these activities, the demand and support for quality Jewish education has grown in a number of directions. Day school enrollments are growing significantly, so larger numbers of children are receiving a strong basic Jewish education. Jewish summer camps are also thriving. The result is that the Jewish knowledge and the involvement of children who attend day schools and children who attend Jewish camps often exceeds that of their parents.

All of this is taking place as a result of partnerships between professionals and funders. The generosity of North American philanthropists who have made Jewish education their priority is at the heart of the strengthening and continuity of the American Jewish community. With this increased interest in strengthening the system on the part of philanthropists, the quality of Jewish education has taken on a new level of priority for the entire community.

Adult learning is one of the beneficiaries as it grows in popularity. The combination of leadership's awareness of the importance of adult Jewish learning and the increasing awareness of the adults themselves of the need to learn is creating, in Jonathan Sarna's (2005) words, "a reawakening in adult learning". As a result, the number of adult learners is expanding (Katz 1999), as seen by the proliferation of programs like the Florence Melton Adult Mini-School, Meah, CLAL, the Wexner Heritage program, the Jewish Learning Institute and Derech Torah. Congregations are also expanding their programs, with a number of larger institutions now engaging adult educators as full members of their professional staff. In addition to the philanthropic support for adult learning, a number of federations under the leadership of the UJC are investing both time and resources in the field. Finally, a new professional network of professionals engaged in adult Jewish learning activities, The Alliance for Adult Jewish Learning, was established to facilitate greater sharing among those most heavily involved in adult learning.

At the same time there is a growing awareness of how the education of parents strengthens children's educational experiences and influences the choices parents make for the Jewish education of their children.

PARENT EDUCATION

Given impetus provided by the success of family education and higher quality children's education, parent education classes are proliferating. For instance, in the past few years the American Jewish community has seen the establishment of classes for young parents by the Florence Melton Adult Mini School (Parent Education Program) and Meah (Ikarim). The Jewish Early Childhood Education Initiative (JECEI) is also creating a parent education program to accompany its pre-school curricular objectives. Each of these initiatives is targeting parents of young children in preschool and kindergarten to encourage them to attend classes to learn about Judaism. In some settings the school is being strengthened in ways that allow it to take on the education of parents as well as children. This is a significant change from the days when institutions would fulfill the traditional responsibility of parents for teaching the children. More and more parents are no longer willing to relinquish this responsibility. To be effective in fulfilling this new role, parents recognize the need to learn about Judaism on an adult level. This is in contrast to the typical family education experiences of the past, where parents and children learning together translated into all learning being on the child's level.

One of the basic characteristics of young adults today is that they continue to seek out expert information long after their formal education is concluded. Products of the age of information, they do not tolerate their own ignorance. With access to the Internet, parents can find answers to any questions they may have. When they want to find answers to Jewish questions they can look on the Internet, read books, or attend classes. In all of these areas quality is essential. Where high level learning is offered, classes taught by outstanding teachers are filled. Used to turning to experts on all aspects of childrearing, including tutors, social workers, and therapists, parents are turning to excellent Jewish educators to provide them with the knowledge to become better Jewish parents for their children.

OVERVIEW OF RESEARCH

DEMOGRAPHICS: JEWISH LEARNING AND IDENTITY TODAY

A. **Learning:** Adult Jewish education in North America is flourishing. Wertheimer (1999) reports that more than one million adult Jews are involved in some form of Jewish education today. Sixty percent of the students are women (Cohen & Davidson 2001). As suggested in the *Adult Jewish Education Handbook* (Goodman & Katz 2004), the umbrella of Jewish learning has expanded beyond the denominational movements, creating more providers of adult Jewish education in the United States than at any previous time. A new vocabulary of Jewish learning is emerging: mini-school, Elderhostel Shabbaton, and online learning. Melton, Wexner and Me'ah programs are proliferating. While the absolute numbers are increasing, there is still considerable room for growth. However, approximately 75% of the adult Jewish population in North America still does not engage in any form of Jewish learning.

B. **Identity:** Bethamie Horowitz, in her study *Connections and Journeys* (2000), suggests that among adult Jews today the range of emotion about being Jewish has shifted from acceptance versus rejection to meaningfulness versus indifference. Jews aren't running away anymore, but they are also not being drawn in. Seventy percent of the participants in this study show low or declining ritual observance, while 63% report high or increasing levels of subjective Jewish attachment. Horowitz suggests that American Jewish identity is not necessarily declining but changing and becoming more personal and interior.

C. **Age Differences:** There are significant differences between young adults and their older peers. A report from the United Jewish Communities based upon the 2000–2001 Jewish population survey suggests that at the present time younger Jews appear to be marginally increasing their practice of some rituals, including keeping kosher in their homes and lighting Shabbat candles. The use of the Internet for Jewish purposes is another example, reflecting both a greater technical proficiency among younger adults and their readiness to access new forms of Jewish engagement that technological advances bring. However, younger Jews tend to give less to charitable causes than do their older counterparts; they have fewer close friendships with other Jews and marginally fewer affiliations with Jewish organizations beyond synagogues and JCCs. Younger adults also report less frequent endorsement of two critical attitudes related to Jewish ethnicity, the importance of being Jewish and feeling emotionally attached to Israel. Similar to older adults, approximately 28% of young adults report participating in some form of Jewish education.

PARADIGMS FOR ADULT LEARNING

A. **Acquisition:** This is the traditional model of learning. The goal of education is to provide new knowledge and skills. Most commonly we assume that that the cognitive domain is the most important. Students enroll in classes to obtain information and understanding. However, the affective or social-emotional domain is equally vital. Making interpersonal connections and addressing the emotional needs of students is essential. Research by Goleman (1995) and others on emotional intelligence has shown us that life success is intricately intertwined with this second set of skills.

B. **Interaction:** The first paradigm suggests that the teacher provides the information and the student stores it. The relationship between student and teacher is incidental. Vygotsky (1926/1997), on the other hand, suggests that learning takes place in a social context. The interaction is essential. He contends that the nature of the relationship between teacher and student is essential. The teacher determines what the student knows and then guides him or her with only the most essential level of assistance to the next level. This type of assistance is sometimes known as scaffolding.

C. **Life Story:** Marsha Rossiter (1999) suggests that adults develop stories of their lives. These stories have heroes, themes, plots and crises. These narratives are shaped contextually, interpreted subjectively and modified over time. They have explanatory and predictive properties. Adult education involves a transformation or a re-storying process where the teacher is first a character, then a keeper of the story, then a critic and editor and then a co-author. The teacher can become a critical player and partner in the development, evaluation and restructuring of student narratives.

Taken together, these three paradigms have several implications for adult (Jewish) education.

1. Learning is more than the summative accumulation of facts.

2. The social-emotional component of learning is vital.

3. Learning takes place within a social context.

4. Education represents a partnership between student and teacher.

5. Teachers should provide their students with support so they can become independent learners.

6. The teacher is first a character in the life story of the student. Ultimately the teacher can become an agent for change.

THE CHARACTERISTICS OF (JEWISH) LEARNING IN YOUNG ADULTHOOD

While the nature of learning is largely the same for all adults, what is important for adults to learn changes as they age or as they move from one life stage to another? The social context of learning is an integral component in the process. *What* is important for parents to learn and *how* they apply this learning is often quite unique.

Erikson (1963) was one of the first developmental theorists to consider the stages of adult development important. He suggested that young adults are involved in developing loving and sexual relationships. They then move into a new stage, Generativity versus Stagnation, where they develop a sense of the need to contribute to the continuity of life.

Schaie (1994) proposes that in early adulthood people enter an Achieving stage in which intelligence is applied to specific situations involving the attainment of long-term goals regarding careers, family and societal contributions. During this stage the decisions that adults make have implications for the rest of their lives. People then move into the Responsible Stage, the major concerns of which include protecting and nourishing spouses, families and careers. Similarly, Gould (1978) suggested that in the 35–44 age range adults enter a period of urgency to attain life's goals.

Young adults are driven by needs to promote their careers and provide for themselves and their families. What they choose to learn and study must be at the service of these goals. Older adults have different social needs. For instance, Schaie (1994) suggests that sometime in middle adulthood many people enter the Executive Stage. They stop focusing only on their own lives and become interested in nourishing and sustaining societal institutions. Later they enter the Reintegrative stage, focusing on acquiring knowledge as a means of solving potential problems, but they learn things that particularly interest them. Young adults are interested in practical learning; older adults study for information and insight.

Fowler (1981) suggests that spiritual understanding and learning also evolve through experience. He posits that there are five stages of religious development, only two of which will be mentioned here. Fowler's fourth stage, Individuative-Reflective Faith, often emerges when young adults come into contact with other value systems. The meanings behind symbols and rituals become important. Individuals at this level construct systems or theories of belief that must be explicit, internally consistent and defensible. They can become overconfident in critical thought and the power of the rational mind. Middle age or older adults are often in Fowler's fifth stage—the Conjunctive stage. They display a new openness to experiment with ritual and learning. Some become comfortable with ambiguity and uncertainty, while others become inactive and passive.

In the field of adult Jewish education the learning differences between younger and older adults have been demonstrated in the research conducted on the Florence Melton Adult Mini-School. In their book *A Journey of Heart and Mind*, Grant et al. (2004) have shown that the typical Melton student, who is over forty years of age and female, graduates from the school with an increased commitment to and understanding of Judaism but demonstrates little change in ritual or practice. A conceptual but not a practical transformation has occurred. Conversely, the students who participated in Melton's Parent Education Program (PEP), which is geared for the parents of children in preschools, increased their level of ritual observance at home (Chertok & Saxe 2004). The study indicates that parents were eager to take what they had learned in class and apply it to their homes. The typical or core Melton students appeared to be pretty much set in their ways and comfortable with their Jewish lifestyles. The PEP parents, in contrast, were interested in learning concrete ways in which Judaism could enhance their Jewish family life. Unlike the adults interviewed by Horowitz (2000), mentioned earlier, these younger adults are increasing not only their attachment but their practice as well. In addition, they tended to be more likely than peers who did not participate in PEP to enroll their children in day schools following their Melton experience.

Anecdotal reports from the teachers and administrators suggest that the PEP students are more enthusiastic, vocal learners than their core Melton counterparts. They are eager to share their family stories and experiences with their peers. Thus the affective component of the learning experience becomes very important to them.

IMPLICATIONS/POLICY RECOMMENDATIONS

- Parents of children enrolled in Jewish schools are a group of potential learners whose needs should be addressed.
- Day schools, JCCs and congregations should provide support for families entering the Jewish community and expanding their involvement in it.
- School professionals, directors and teachers need to know more about Judaism.
- Schools require staff that has the ability to relate to and teach adults, requiring quality professional opportunities for school personnel in the area of adult development and learning.
- Curriculum for families must be created that is a sequential, systematically organized series of learning experiences for parents involved with a synagogue, day school, or JCC.

ADDITIONAL RESEARCH QUESTIONS

There is need for additional research, professional development and curriculum to support the field, as well as the funding to insure its success. Important questions that need to be addressed include:

- What constitutes literacy for a Jewish parent?
- Who is attending the parent classes today? Who is not?
- What is the impact of educating parents of children of varying ages in a variety of settings?
- What are the best strategies for attracting parents to enroll in Jewish learning programs based upon the ages of their children and the settings in which their children are learning?

- What can we learn through research about parents of all groups that would be similar to that recently conducted on the Florence Melton Parent Education Program?

FUTURE DIRECTIONS

- In addition to the research suggested above, creating a culture of sharing information among those involved in adult learning, parent education, family education, and teacher education will further the Jewish community.
- Synagogues, JCCs, preschools, and camps need to make parent education a specific part of their mission by raising their capacity to offer Jewish learning programs to parents of the children whom they now see as their primary target group.
- It is important to build on the "teachable moments" in Jewish life and expand the number of parents participating in Jewish learning.
- Despite the high cost of education for children, a case for funding quality parent education should be made to federations and philanthropists. To increase accessibility to adult learning opportunities, parents should be provided with vouchers for participation in adult learning. Finally, institutions should receive funding specifically designed to provide classes for parents as part of an overall strategy for increasing Jewish engagement.

CONCLUSION

One of the strongest motivations throughout the life cycle is the need to do something for one's children. It cannot be denied that a parent's Jewish learning benefits a child's life and has profound and lasting implications for that child as he/she develops toward adulthood.

With the need having been identified, it is imperative that more successful models be developed to move the effort forward. This has been accomplished in the area of education for parents of young children, and there is potential for other successful programs to meet the needs of parents of older children. With an awareness of the fact that the challenges for each parent group will vary, the benefits of the investment of time, energy and financial resources will certainly far outweigh the costs.

HIGHLIGHTS

- Parent education is a growing field that has differentiated itself from adult learning.
- Parents of children in any particular age group vary in terms of their age and whether they are inborn, converted or non–Jewish.
- As children learn more about Judaism, parents today want to learn how to share that Judaism with them in their homes and in the community.
- Parent education is the learning of Jewish content relevant to being a parent. Parenting education is about how to raise Jewish children in a way that reflects Jewish values.
- While still in a nascent phase, parent education is beginning to enjoy the support of Jewish professionals, researchers, and philanthropists. Schools of all types are beginning to see their mission as educating parents as well as children. This is an area of Jewish education that is deserving of further systematic exploration.

THE LARGER CONTEXT

This new emphasis on parent education complements and reinforces other current initiatives in Jewish education. It is not an add-on; instead, parent education serves as a strong and vital supplement to and support of other educational services by showing that Jewish education is not only a lifelong activity but one that creates interconnections among the generations.

- Parent education either compensates for the knowledge these students did not acquire in earlier years or provides them with new ways to understand this knowledge as adults.
- Parent education opens new gateways to the Jewish world.

- Parents realize that Jewish learning is not just for kids. They become role models for their children. "Mom and Dad go to Jewish school just like me."
- Parents learn that our Jewish sources have important information to offer about parenting and enhancing family life.

ANNOTATED BIBLIOGRAPHY

Beck, P. (2002). *Jewish PreSchools as Gateways to Jewish Life: A Survey of Jewish PreSchool Parents in Three Cities.* New York: Ukeles Associates, Inc. This survey collected information on the characteristics of parents of preschool children. Among other topics, it looks at what motivates them to select preschools and what their expectations of these schools are.

Chertok, F. & Saxe, L. (2004). *The Florence Melton Parent Education Program.* Waltham, MA: Cohen Center for Modern Jewish Studies. This article reviews the findings from the original Parent Education Program pilot study. It suggests that the graduates are more likely to send their children to day schools than their non–PEP peers and that they show more behavioral changes than typical Melton students.

Goodman, R.L. & Katz, B.D. (2004). *The Adult Jewish Education Handbook.* Denver: ARE Publishing. This is a guide to adult Jewish learning in a variety of settings. Responding to the growth of opportunities in the field, the authors provide tools, knowledge and language used in adult education and adult Jewish education. They enable readers to participate in the ongoing conversation about adult learning as reflective practitioners, lay leaders and learners.

Horowitz, B. (2000). *Connections and Journeys: Assessing Critical Opportunities in Enhancing Jewish Identity.* New York: UJA-Federation of Greater New York. This report presents Horowitz's ground-breaking work that provides insight into the Jewish population by looking at Jews' psychological, interior understanding of themselves and not just their actions.

NJPS 2000–1: Strength, Challenge and Diversity in the American Jewish Population. A United Jewish Communities Report. New York: United Jewish Communities. The National Jewish Population Survey (NJPS) 2000–01 is a representative survey of the Jewish population in the United States sponsored by United Jewish Communities and the Jewish federation system. You can find more information about the survey at *www.ujc. org.*

Parker, M. (2006). "Creating New Transmission Lines." *Jewish Education News* 27 (1). This article reviews the progress of Melton's Parent Education Program in its first three years and details findings concerning marketing, recruitment, instruction and curriculum development.

Schaie, K. (1994). "The Course of Adult Intellectual Development." *American Psychologist,* 49: 304–313. For a long time researchers assumed that developmental changes in how people learn did not take place beyond adolescence. Schaie suggests that how and what people learn is affected by their stage of life.

Ukeles, J., Miller, R. & Beck, P. (2006). *Young Adults in the United States Today.* New York: American Jewish Committee. A review of the interests, affiliations and ideologies of contemporary young Jewish adults

REFERENCES

Beck, P. (2002). *Jewish PreSchools as Gateways to Jewish Life: A Survey of Jewish PreSchool Parents in Three Cities.* New York: Ukeles Associates, Inc.

Chertok, F. & Saxe, L. (2004). *The Florence Melton Parent Education Program.* Waltham, MA: Cohen Center for Modern Jewish Studies.

Cohen, S. & Davidson A. (2001). *Adult Jewish Education in America.* New York: JCC Association Research Center.

Erikson, E. (1963). *Childhood and Society.* New York: Norton.

Fowler, J. (1981). *Stages of Faith: The Psychology of Human Development and the Quest for Meaning.* San Francisco: Harper and Row.

Grant, L. et al. (2004) *A Journey of Heart and Mind: Transformative Jewish Learning in Adulthood.* New York: JTS Press.

Goleman, D. (1995). *Emotional Intelligence.* New York: Bantam.

Goodman, R.L. & Katz, B.D. (2004) *The Adult Jewish Education Handbook.* Denver: ARE Publishing.

Gould, R. (1978). *Transformations.* New York, Simon and Schuster.

Horowitz, B. (2000). *Connections and Journeys: Assessing Critical Opportunities in Enhancing Jewish Identity.* New York: UJA Federation of Greater New York.

NJPS 2000–1: Strength, Challenge and Diversity in the American Jewish Population. A United Jewish Communities Report. New York: United Jewish Communities.

Parker, M. (2006). "Creating New Transmission Lines: Teachers to Parents to Children." *Jewish Education News* 27 (1).

Rossiter, M. (1999). "A Narrative Approach to Development: Implications for Adult Education." *Adult Education Quarterly* 50 (1), 56–71.

Schaie, K. (1994). "The Course of Adult Intellectual Development." *American Psychologist 49,* 304–313.

Vygotsky, L. (1926/1997). *Educational Psychology.* Delray Beach: St. Lucie Press.

Ukeles, J., Miller, R. & Beck, P. (2006). *Young Adults in the United States Today.* New York: American Jewish Committee.

Wertheimer, J. (1999). Jewish Education in the United States: Recent Trends and Issues. *American Jewish Year Book, pp. 3–115.*

Adult Jewish Learning

Diane Tickton Schuster & Lisa D. Grant

KEY FRAMING QUESTIONS

Adult Jewish learning is a flourishing part of the contemporary American Jewish landscape. When we enter into even a relatively small Jewish community today we are likely to see and hear about a wide variety of learning opportunities. Some of these programs and classes are led by rabbis and other teachers, while some are independent groups that meet without a professional Jewish educator. Some take place in synagogues and others at retreat centers, downtown offices, or Jewish community centers, through travel, and even in cyberspace. Programs range in length and venue. Some are linked to holidays or specific topics; others are geared to a particular audience, such as women, parents of young children, or senior citizens.

Consider just a sampling of potential offerings:

- On a Shabbat morning seventeen adults gather to study the weekly Torah portion. Each session is led by a fellow layperson who shares a range of classical and contemporary commentaries to explore the deeper meaning of the text.
- On a Monday evening twenty-three adults come together to study the Jewish calendar as part of a two-year program of adult Jewish literacy.
- Tuesdays at noon ten attorneys gather in a colleague's conference room to study Talmud with a rabbi.
- Every other Wednesday six men meet to study Mussar, a contemplative practice in Jewish ethics aimed at self-improvement.
- Thursday nights an adult b'nai mitzvah class of eleven women and two men meets to study Hebrew and learn about the Shabbat morning service.
- Sunday mornings a group of parents meet with a teacher to study the same curriculum as their children in religious school, but at an adult level.
- Once a month a dozen women join together for a hands-on "Cooking with the Rabbi" study program about Jewish food.
- Each year, after spending several weeks studying the book of Kohelet, twenty senior adults write a wisdom text that they share with fellow congregants during Sukkot services. This same congregation holds an annual Shabbat retreat for parents and their school-age children at an area Jewish summer camp.
- Every other year twenty to thirty congregants travel to Israel with their rabbi for a ten-day study tour.

This sampler opens us to considering a series of questions about the purposes, processes, and programs that fall within the broad rubric of what we call adult Jewish learning. Who are the adults who populate these adult Jewish learning classrooms and other settings? What do they expect of their learning? How does the learning affect their lives and the lives of their families? Do different types of learning programs and experiences have different impacts? Why don't more people join in on this exciting enterprise?

For the past dozen years Grant and Schuster have been exploring these questions. Together and separately we have conducted much of the contemporary research on adult Jewish learning (Schuster & Grant 2005). We also have a broad range of experience in professional development for Jewish adult education and directly as teachers of Jewish adults. In this chapter we review what we know about the learners, the pedagogy, the content, and the impact of adult Jewish learning programs. But first we begin by setting the context for the current popularity of and excitement about adult Jewish learning.

CONTEXT

Adult Jewish learning is valued as normative Jewish behavior. It is embedded in Jewish tradition and even elevated to sacred status. One of first prayers of the daily liturgy is the blessing for the commandment to study Torah. This is followed shortly by passages of rabbinic texts, including the familiar dictum that enumerates the deeds for which we are to benefit in this world and the world to come, with the study of Torah being greater than them all (Shabbat 127a). Jewish study deepens the meaning and understanding of Jewish beliefs and practices. It provides the language of Jewish discourse, which in turn, allows learners of all types to shape a personal "Jewish narrative." Without study Jews lack the ability to teach the next generation, which is a central obligation of the tradition. Indeed, without study Judaism's meaning becomes diluted, and practice remains shallow.

While Jewish study has been a consistent and integral component of Orthodox Jewish life among men, and more recently among women as well, the engagement in Jewish learning among the liberal strands of American Judaism follows a more cyclical pattern (Sarna 2005). For most of the twentieth century adult study was a low priority on a communal agenda that was more focused on rescue and resettlement of immigrants and refugees, supporting Israel, and other "civic" expressions of Jewish belonging. Over the last twenty-five years, however, as concerns have grown about Jewish "continuity" there has been a surge in interest in adult Jewish learning. Starting in the 1980s and increasing at a dramatic rate after the wake-up call of the 1990 National Jewish Population Study, adult Jewish learning emerged at the center of the religious and communal agenda for the revitalization of contemporary American Jewry. This is manifest both in the widening variety of learning venues and programs and in the integration of Jewish study into organizational life within the Jewish communal world. Today there is a widespread belief among Jewish communal leaders that increasing Jewish literacy and learning will lead to more meaningful involvement in Jewish practices, philanthropy, and communal life. Indeed, many communal leaders appear to have implicit faith in the Talmudic pronouncement that "study leads to action" (Kiddushin 40b).

This communal support and attention has led to the burgeoning growth of adult Jewish learning opportunities throughout the Jewish community. Educators and communal leaders celebrate the creativity of program development and are excited about the learners who participate in this enterprise. Yet they also express increasing concern that enrollments remain relatively low and that the same people "come over and over again." Scholarship about adult development and adult Jewish learning provides insights into why this dichotomy may exist and also suggests new directions for program planners who wish to enhance the quality and expand the reach of adult Jewish learning activities.

REVIEW OF RESEARCH

The need for research about adult Jewish learning was established in the early 1990s by a task force of the Jewish Education Service of North America (JESNA). The task force published the *Adult Jewish Learning Reader,* a series of papers about adult Jewish learners, their learning needs, and strategies practitioners might use to more effectively reach Jews at midlife. Individual contributors to that collection noted that all too often Jewish educational programs focus on children (Fishman), overlook the distinctive characteristics of adult learners (Frankel;, Wasserman), fail to empower learners to become self-directing (Lipstadt) and lack appropriate curricula and experiential learning components (Lipstadt, Zachary). In the introduction to these papers the editors acknowledged the absence of reliable data about adult Jewish learner motivations and outcomes and asserted that the community needed research that would "describe the adult Jew in terms that would be useful for planning Jewish learning experiences" (JESNA, 1993, i).

During the past decade a number of researchers have endeavored to address questions about adult Jewish learning patterns and interests, adult learner characteristics, the qualities of effective Jewish adult educators, and the scope of contemporary adult Jewish learning programs.

ADULT JEWISH LEARNING PATTERNS AND INTERESTS

The first broad-scale survey of Jewish adult learning patterns and interests was conducted in 2000. Based on questionnaires from 1,302 households, Cohen and Davidson reported that:

1. Although most Jewish adults (78%) regularly read about Israel or some aspect of Judaism or Jewish life, a much smaller percentage (25–40%) participate in leisure activities with a Jewish theme (such as going to a movie with Jewish content, playing Jewish music, reading Jewish fiction, visiting a Jewishly oriented website or chat room). Even fewer (10–20%) engage in "structured Jewish learning activities" (such as attending a lecture, taking a class, going to a study group, or studying Jewish texts).

2. Regardless of employment status, women surpass men in their frequency of participation in Jewish learning activities.

3. Jewish learning activity rises with increases in education. Thus Jewish adults who have post-graduate degrees participate in Jewish adult education with significantly greater frequency than do those with BA or high school degrees. Correspondingly, Jewish adults who feel competent as learners overall are disposed to seek out educational activities throughout their lives.

4. In-married Jews (Jews married to other Jews) who have children at home have the highest rate of participation in some form of Jewish learning. Correspondingly, intermarried Jews have the lowest level of adult Jewish learning participation.

5. There is a strong relationship between denomination and Jewish learning. Orthodox Jews participate in learning activities more than Conservative Jews, with Reform and non-denominational Jews studying less. However, across the denominational spectrum, affiliation with a synagogue increases the likelihood of systematic engagement in learning.

6. The most popular topics for adult Jewish learning are (in descending order): cooking, the Holocaust, Jewish history, holidays, Jewish values and ethics, and Israel. The study of texts, Hebrew, and prayer attract fewer people. However, an interest in the full range of Jewish topics increases when an individual becomes involved in Jewish learning activities. In other words, the more a Jewish adult learns, the more she or he wants to learn about more aspects of Judaism and Jewish life.

7. Although the major motivation for participation in Jewish learning activities is to "grow as a Jew," the appeal of Jewish learning frequently derives from the opportunity the learner has to come together with other Jews and to feel socially connected to a Jewish community.

8. Jewish learning programs range in length from one-time lectures and workshops to multi-session classes to longer-term structured study programs. The most preferred format for enrollment is the three-session class. However, formal long-term study programs have become increasingly popular in recent years.

WHAT CHARACTERIZES CONTEMPORARY ADULT JEWISH LEARNERS?

In many ways, adult Jewish learners are quite similar to their non–Jewish counterparts, as demonstrated by the literature on adult development, adult learning, and adult religious education. Studies in these domains are useful for contextualizing the analyses of the most salient aspects of the adult Jewish learning experience.

Adulthood as a time of change and new learning. Contemporary adults understand adulthood as a time of change and transitions, rather than continuity and sameness (Sheehy 1996; Tennant &

Pogson 1995). Many expect their lives to be marked by geographical relocations, career changes, new family configurations, shifts in lifestyle, and periodic acquisition of new skills or world views (Schlossberg 1989; Kegan 1994). They adapt to the reality that adult life may compel them to live in diverse settings, develop several "possible selves" and cultivate more than one "identity" (Markus & Nurius 1986). As members of a society in which participation in lifelong learning has become normative, they regard education as a resource for helping them to adapt to change and to achieve successful self-reinvention (Aslanian & Brickell 1980; Tennant & Pogson 1995).

Adult Jews repeatedly describe how changes and transitions lead them to seek new Jewish learning and to redefine the meaning of Judaism in their lives (Schuster 1995, Grant et al. 2004). They associate Jewish learning with times of personal growth and personal loss. Their narratives reveal shifts in Jewish identity as they negotiate varying life demands and move in and out of Jewish learning experiences. In this respect adult Jewish learners likely mirror other Jewish adults (such as those studied by Horowitz [2000] and Cohen and Eisen [2000]) for whom Jewish identity tends to "ebb and flow" throughout adult life.

Self-direction and generativity. Adult learners tend to bring an intrinsic motivation to decrease their dependence on teachers and to become "self-directing" in the acquisition of knowledge (Knowles 1980; Brookfield 1991). As adults increase the scope of their knowledge and become critical consumers of what they are studying, some develop the confidence to teach what they have learned to others (Belenky et al. 1986). Such motivation to transmit knowledge and wisdom to others conforms with Erik Erikson's description of adult life as a time of "generativity" (McAdams & de St. Aubin 1998).

In her review of adult Jewish learning in theory and practice Schuster (2003a) describes many such self-directed learners and shows how teachers who support learner growth are especially valued by contemporary Jewish adults. Teutsch (2004) reports that learners in an advanced class for "alumni" of a two-year study program are motivated to build on their growing Jewish knowledge and to make connections between their "learning and doing." To date no studies have focused on the long-term developmental experiences of adult Jewish learners, but there is anecdotal evidence (*Jewish Education News* 2002, Grant in press, Grant et al. 2004) that once engaged, learners become eager to continue their Jewish education and to share their knowledge and insights with others.

Learning orientations. Studies of learner motivation show that adults bring diverse attitudes and expectations to their learning experiences. Houle (1961) points to three "orientations": a *goal-orientation* in which education is seen as leading to a change in work or personal status; an *activity-orientation* in which participants' social interactions are especially valued; and a *learning-orientation* in which a love of learning underlies the learner's engagement and participation.

Recent research on participants in adult Jewish learning programs (Grant et al. 2004; Grant 2003; Schuster 2003a) identifies learners whose motivations conformed to Houle's typology, as well as a fourth group: *spiritually oriented* learners who seek new meaning and perceive education as the starting point for thinking in new ways. When describing their experiences as learners, students consistently express appreciation for teachers who anticipate the needs of learners who bring differing learning orientations.

Women as learners. Research on women as learners (Hayes & Flannery 2000; Belenky et al. 1986) shows that when women are helped to know their own histories as learners and are validated for their subjective wisdom, their self-esteem increases and their confidence to develop their authority as knowers improves.

Studies of women who become adult b'not mitzvah consistently demonstrate that this adult Jewish learning experience not only helps women to affirm their connection and commitment to Judaism, but also enables them to claim what they perceive to be their legitimate place in public ritual expression (Cousens 2002; Grant 1999/2000, 2003; Schoenfeld 1992). Furthermore, while their educational preparation is largely a process of mastering normative ritual practice, for many adult b'not mitzvah the experience leads to a profound transformation in their personal definition, as well as changes in participation and leadership in their synagogue communities (Grant 2003; in press).

Learning as perspective transformation. Transformational learning occurs when adults are guided to critically reflect on the assumptions, values, feelings, and cultural paradigms that have shaped their sense of self and the world (Mezirow 1991, 2000; Brooks 2000). This critical reflection, generally deepened through dialogue with others, results in a reframing and expansion of meanings. The "transformation" that occurs is frequently seen as a change in perspective, in which learners describe shifts in their "inner experience of knowledge" rather than in terms of specific changes in outward behaviors or amount of information acquired.

In a study of adults who attended the Florence Melton Adult Mini-School, a two-year Jewish literacy program that has served upwards of 20,000 adults in 65 locations (Grant et al. 2004), participants report that learning leads to significant changes in their inner Jewish lives. Through a broadened understanding of Jewish texts, history, and values they *make new meaning* about the Jewish behaviors they already perform. Their learning sharpens the Jewish lens through which they view their everyday Jewish lives and increases their overall commitment to Jewish education for themselves and others in the Jewish community. At the same time, few Mini-School learners report specific, immediate changes in behavior; because most of these learners are already active participants in Jewish communal life, they tend to seek learning more as a means for personal understanding than as a vehicle for change.

Communal responsibility and the toleration of difference. According to adult religious education experts, when adults join together to probe issues of meaning and religious faith their collaborative learning leads to an increased sense of communal responsibility and a greater willingness to tolerate difference (Vogel 1991; English & Gillen 2000).

The aforementioned study of the Melton Mini-School learners (Grant et al. 2004), confirms these insights. Melton students especially value the opportunity to study with classmates from diverse backgrounds and to build a safe community within which to explore serious Jewish questions and cultivate meaningful friendships. For example, after studying together about Jewish mourning rituals Mini-School learners typically feel responsible for one another at times of loss and strive to provide sensitive support during *shiva* visits. Because they study together over a period of time, many are inclined to include one another in Jewish holiday celebrations and family *simchas*.

With respect to tolerating difference, the Mini-School learners report that learning from diverse teachers who encourage a pluralistic view of Judaism results in their appreciating Jews whose approach and theologies differ from their own. This finding parallels Brown's (2003) observations about a group of women from across the denominations (Orthodox, Conservative, Reform, and unaffiliated) who study together in a non-judgmental, respectful, intellectually rich learning environment. Their collaborative learning experiences enable this diverse sample to interact openly and to develop a sense of community both inside and outside the classroom.

WHAT CHARACTERIZES EFFECTIVE ADULT JEWISH EDUCATORS?

The teacher as facilitator. More than eighty years ago the philosopher Franz Rosenzweig wrote about the need to create a Jewish adult education movement with "conversation" at the center. By this he meant that teachers must be both masters and learners. They must listen carefully to their learners' spoken and unspoken needs, because it is through such conversation that people become conscious of being a "Jewish human being" (Rosenzweig 1955). More contemporary scholars of adult learning also recognize that adult learners thrive in educational settings in which the teacher creates a democratic atmosphere that is enlivened by discussion, experiential learning, and collaborative inquiry (Brookfield 1986; Belenky et al. 1986; Maher & Tetrault 2001; Taylor et al. 2000). In this type of adult learning classroom teachers see themselves as facilitators who help others to acquire mastery and find their own authority as "knowers". Such teachers encourage learners to reflect critically on their ideas and to engage in dialogue with other learners (Brookfield 1987). They understand that dialogic learning includes not only discourse with others, but also internal dialogue and reflection that lead to greater self-awareness and ultimately to more independent decision making (Taylor et al. 2000).

By no means do all successful teachers of adults follow this dialogical approach, nor do all adult Jewish learners prefer it. Indeed, the teacher-centered lecture model is a common feature of a great many adult Jewish learning experiences, both for beginning learners who may feel too far outside the Jewish textual "conversation" to be legitimate participants and for more knowledgeable learners who feel more substantive and authentic learning can be obtained by sitting "at the feet of a master." Likewise, those learners who seek to develop skills and competencies such as Hebrew language or tools to enhance their abilities to interpret classical texts may benefit from a more teacher-directed learning experience.

Yet a more learner-center approach that encourages dialogue and reflection has profound potential to enhance the learner's sense of personal mastery and authority. Two studies of adult Jewish learners illustrate the importance of this approach. In an analysis of the experiences of synagogue leaders who were newcomers to text study, Aron and Schuster (1998) report that, despite their high levels of competence in other domains, many newcomers initially believe themselves to be inadequate and even unauthentic as knowledgeable Jews; however, once such learners are exposed to collaborative text study methods, many aspire to develop skills for engagement in thoughtful analysis and discourse. Similarly, in her ethnographic study of students in the Melton Mini-School classroom, Woocher (2004) observes that dialogue and social connection dramatically affect the learners' ability to make meaning of the texts under consideration and also increase students' commitment to support one another both intellectually and spiritually.

The teacher as mentor and guide. As adults redefine themselves, their goals and their meaning structures, they benefit from the support of mentors who can provide information and insights appropriate to their new challenges or life situations (Daloz 1999; Taylor et al. 2000).

Schuster (2003a) explores the impact of mentors on adult Jewish learners, noting that contemporary students seek coaches and tutors who can help them to compensate for inadequate Jewish educational background information. In studying adults on synagogue-sponsored family trips to Israel, Grant (2001) reports that a form of mentoring called spiritual direction greatly enhances how the participants critically reflect on their Israel experiences and how they reshape their Jewish beliefs and behaviors upon returning home. Likewise, there are countless anecdotal reports of rabbis, cantors, and other Jewish educators who fill such mentoring roles on adults' spiritual and learning journeys.

Teacher credibility and authenticity. Brookfield (1991) argues that adult learners attach great importance to how their teachers demonstrate subject matter expertise (credibility), as well as trustworthy behaviors that show that they are "human" and respectful of the learners' experience (authenticity). Based on their extensive action research about how teachers "develop" learners, Taylor et al. (2000) conclude that adults expect their teachers both to model the process of learning and to establish that like the learners, they are engaged in a continual process of making new meaning. Studies of feminist pedagogy (Belenky et al. 1986; Maher & Tetrault 2001) show that women students "come to voice" when they are helped by educators who value interpersonal connection and help learners to see how their lives and learning are interrelated.

Research about the competencies and pedagogical approaches of Jewish adult educators is just beginning. Schuster's (2003a) account of the characteristics of "connected teachers" points to how adult Jewish learners value educators who understand their insecurities and questions and yet encourage their capacity to grow intellectually as individuals and as groups. The characteristics of Melton Mini-School teachers conform to the desiderata of credibility-plus-authenticity described by Brookfield and others; Mini-School hiring policies reflect a commitment to selecting teachers who understand how to create a supportive and nurturing atmosphere while still providing substance and intellectual challenge (Grant et al. 2004).

Teacher development. Providing opportunities for teachers to reflect on their practice is understood as one of the core purposes of professional development (Feiman-Nemser 2001). As Shulman (1987) argues, content knowledge alone does not make for good teaching practice. The knowledge base of teaching is a complex combination of subject matter expertise, understanding of learners' needs and interests, and the ability to artfully represent subject matter in a way that is accessible, relevant, and meaningful to students. This means teachers need ongoing and substantive opportunities for what McDonald calls "reading teaching" and what others describe as reflective practice (Brookfield 1991; Palmer 1998; Schön 1990).

As Schuster (2003b) points out, the need for well-prepared Jewish adult educators is pressing. While we have reports of what constitutes good teaching of Jewish adults from the perspective of the learners and teachers (Grant et al. 2004; Goodman & Katz 2004; Schuster 2003a), there is virtually no research that explores this topic. To date there are no doctoral programs that offer a specialization in adult Jewish learning, although several seminaries and universities are beginning to recognize the need for systematic training in this area. More often than not, adult education is not the primary occupation of the scholars, rabbis, and other educators who teach adult Jewish education. Many of these teachers are superb subject matter experts but may lack a substantive understanding of the developmental needs of the Jewish adults who attend their classes. Programs such as the Melton Mini-Schools and Me'ah have recognized this shortcoming and offer faculty development opportunities through seminars, coaching and other forms of ongoing support.

THE "WHERE" AND "WHAT" OF ADULT JEWISH LEARNING

As we saw at the beginning of this chapter, adult Jewish learning can take place in a wide variety of settings. However, the 2000–01 National Jewish Population Study reports that the predominant locale remains the synagogue, with 63% of adult Jewish learning occurring there. The many other settings for adult Jewish learning include Jewish community centers, national programs such as the Wexner Heritage Institute and the Florence Melton Adult Mini-School, community-based initiatives such as the Lehrhaus Judaica in the San Francisco-Bay Area, Limmud Northwest in Seattle, the Foundation for Jewish Studies in Washington, D.C., and the Dawn Schuman Institute of Metropolitan Chicago. In addition, there are movement-based programs such as the Union for Reform Judaism's summer Kallah, the Wagner Institute at the Jewish Theological Seminary in New York, Chabad Lubavitch's Jewish Learning Institute, and Eilat Chayim, a retreat center associated with the Jewish Renewal movement. We also see a range of exciting partnership initiatives such as Me'ah, a two-year program of Jewish literacy developed by the Hebrew College in cooperation with the Boston federation that partners with over fifty different synagogues, or Limmud NY, an organization started by six lay people and supported substantially by the New York federation, that has the goal of bringing over five hundred participants together for three days of Jewish learning and culture.

One area of adult Jewish learning that may not be fully captured by survey research is the amount of time individuals spend reading, listening to taped lectures, taking distance learning classes, or exploring the Internet in the pursuit of Jewish knowledge. In addition, there are many informal venues such as book groups, study circles, and retreats that are privately organized outside of any Jewish institutional auspices that may attract a different group of people than those more likely to attend a synagogue or community-based program.

The content of learning offered in this rich array of settings is diverse and ever-expanding. As we have seen, adults are looking for meaning in Jewish study, and they most often find meaning by connecting their own life experience to the texts and content of Jewish study.

While some beginning learners are attracted by the intellectual challenge of text study, for many the relevance of Jewish texts to their lives is not immediately apparent. As Rosenzweig (1955) noted, Jewish educators must teach from "life to Torah and then back to life again." Even as advanced learners grow more comfortable with text study, they, too, still look to find personal relevance in these ancient sources. For example, Cohen's (2002) account of a long-established Talmud study learning circle shows that members engage in meaning making through rigorous study of the text but almost always "contemporize" the text by contextualizing it through analogies drawn from their own life experiences.

Programs can be short or long-term, devoted to a particular topic or of a more general nature. They can focus on building skills such as learning to chant Torah or write a d'var Torah, or they can be more open-ended discussions such as a weekly *parshat ha-shavua* class or a monthly Rosh Hodesh group. Some programs have a seasonal focus such as spiritual preparation for the High Holidays or deepening one's knowledge of the haggadah before Pesach. Some programs deal with contemporary and cultural issues; others consider how ancient texts or practices relate to modern lives. Many programs are also more experiential in nature such as Jewish meditation, writing workshops, Jewish parenting programs and Jewish cooking. The list of topics and venues seems endless!

FUTURE DIRECTIONS FOR RESEARCH AND POLICY

As the preceding discussion reveals, we do indeed know much about adult Jewish learning. We have a good understanding of who the learners are, what motivates them, and how learning may transform the meaning of Judaism in their lives. We also have some knowledge of what constitutes good teaching and the range of content offered in a wide variety of programs and settings.

However, many philosophical and practical questions about adult Jewish learning remain.

To date, Jewish communal leaders have not articulated what the *purposes* of adult Jewish learning should be. Moreover, we are still lacking an overview of Jewish adult education offerings and of participation rates in different kinds of learning activities. We do not know whether learning impacts behavior or leads to change in Jewish communal life, although Aron's (1995, 2000, 2002) discussions of "congregations of learners" help to frame many issues about the role adult learning can play in the transformation of synagogue practice. And while thousands of contemporary Jewish adults now seek to acquire Jewish literacy and participate in meaningful learning experiences, as yet there are inadequate data on which to base program planning or policy.

Presently research is needed about specific learning populations (e.g., parents, young adults, study group participants, converts and non–Jewish partners, Jewish communal leaders); synagogue initiatives (e.g., study groups, learning retreats, scholars-in-residence, family education); community-based adult education programs; informal Jewish education events (e.g., book and film festivals, travel programs, museum activities, retreats); and the long-term impact of adult Jewish learning on learners, family members, and communal institutions. Such information will assist communal leaders in making more informed decisions about how to meet the needs of Jewish adults and how to increase the literacy and intellectual well-being of the contemporary Jewish adult population.

Program planners, communal leaders, rabbis, and teachers of Jewish adults articulate many different goals for a vast array of programs that are described as adult Jewish learning. They hope such programs will:

- Build Jewish community through strengthening synagogues and other Jewish communal institutions.
- Enhance Jewish literacy by developing the competencies of those already engaged in Jewish life and Jewish learning.
- Strengthen Jewish identity.
- Increase Jewish practice.
- Inspire more people to take on leadership roles within the Jewish community.
- Infuse more Jewish content into the ways communal leaders set priorities and make decisions.
- Increase philanthropic giving to the Jewish community in general and Jewish education in particular.
- Inspire ongoing Jewish study.

Currently we can only speculate about how these community leaders should determine the best means for achieving these laudable goals. Dialogue among scholars, practitioners, curriculum writers, program planners, and policy makers will help to clarify objectives and values. Ongoing evaluation and research that probes the relationship between different types of adult Jewish learning activities, the instructional philosophies and curricula that support these activities, and the long-term impacts on learners and communities will provide much-needed information to guide responsible planning.

HIGHLIGHTS

- Adult Jewish learning is valued as a normative Jewish behavior.
- Since the 1980s adult Jewish learning has increased at a dramatic rate throughout the Jewish community.
- A 2000 survey of adult Jewish learning patterns and interests found a high correlation between Jewish communal affiliation and Jewish learning. Jewish adults participate in a plethora of activities including classes, lectures, reading books and magazines or watching films with Jewish content, and visiting Jewish sites and museums. Only about 16% of Jewish adults indicate they participate in formal classroom learning, and their preferred duration is three sessions or fewer. These adults are attracted to classes that help them grow as Jews and interact with other Jews.
- Other research reports that adult Jewish learners are motivated by changes in their personal lives and shifts in Jewish identity; seek to increase their knowledge and self-direction as learners and teachers of others; prize opportunities to make meaning about Judaism and themselves as Jews.
- Studies of high-quality adult Jewish learning programs indicate that participants increase their sense of communal responsibility to other learners and become tolerant of ideas and people different from their own. Such programs accommodate a range of learning orientations and expectations and empower learners to feel more authoritative as Jews.
- Effective Jewish adult educators facilitate learners' development through dialogue, mentoring, and authentic engagement with learners. To become and remain effective, such teachers need professional development opportunities to help them understand the learners, plan appropriate content, develop a range of pedagogical approaches, and reflect on their practice.
- Venues and formats for adult Jewish learning are highly varied. In addition to formal programs offered by Jewish communal institutions, many Jewish adults learn independently and informally. Research is needed to document the full range of program offerings, learner preferences, and rates of participation.
- The content of adult Jewish learning is wide-ranging and must be designed to reach learners from diverse backgrounds, levels of preparation, learning styles and interests.
- Many questions remain about the purposes and goals of adult Jewish learning, the populations that should be served, and what the impact of learning will be on the Jewish community.

THE LARGER CONTEXT

Jewish study is an essential act of Jewish self-expression. While there is an unbroken chain of lifelong learners from the Rabbinic era until today, most American Jews do not make Jewish study a regular part of their lives. Over the past several decades, however, increasing numbers of Jewish adults have been engaged in a seemingly ever-growing variety of Jewish learning—in classrooms, on their own, with other family members, and in the company of other Jews. Both internal and external influences on the Jewish community account for this current renaissance in adult Jewish learning. The well-documented turn inward toward individual personal searches for meaning has prompted a burgeoning adult learning industry for the broader American society. Within the Jewish community the wake-up call of the 1990 National Jewish Population Study that pointed to an unprecedented high rate of intermarriage pushed a massive shift of communal priorities toward a "continuity" agenda that had and continues to promote Jewish education as a key component. The assumption holds that as more and more people engage in quality Jewish education, learning will become a normative aspect of Jewish life for more and more Jews. And as Jewish learning increases, so too will the quality of Jewish life. What we know from the current research is that adult Jewish learning holds the possibility to transform the lives and outlooks of individual Jews and to have a positive impact on the Jewish community overall.

ANNOTATED BIBLIOGRAPHY

Aron, I. & Schuster, D. T. (1998). "Extending the Chain of Tradition: Reflections on the Goals of Adult Text Study." *Journal of Jewish Education* 64 (1/2), 44–56. Based on a study of newcomers to text study, this article sets forth five goals for teaching text: making it enjoyable, helping adults to find personal meaning, stimulating adults to think about the role of Torah in their lives, promoting textual literacy and familiarity with multiple interpretive lenses, and encouraging participation in communities of learners.

Cohen, S. M. & Davidson, A. (2001). *Adult Jewish Learning in America: Current Patterns and Prospects for Growth.* New York: Heller/JCCA Research Center. To date, this is the only national survey that focuses exclusively on adult Jewish learning patterns among American Jews. The report profiles demographics, motivations, interests, and activities of contemporary Jewish adults.

Grant, L. D. Schuster, D. T., Woocher, M. & Cohen, S. M. (2004). *A Journey of Heart and Mind: Transformative Jewish Learning in Adulthood.* New York: JTS Press. This book provides an in-depth analysis of the impact of learning at the Florence Melton Adult Mini-School, a two-year program of adult Jewish literacy. How and why this impact occurs is contextualized by an examination of the program's philosophy, curriculum, and teaching methods. The authors also consider the broader social and educational context for adult Jewish learning. An executive summary of the book is available at *http://ujc.org/content_display.html?ArticleID=95891*

Goodman, R. L. & Katz, B. (2004). *The Adult Education Handbook: Planning, Practice and Theory.* Denver: A.R.E. Publishing. This guide to the practice of adult Jewish education addresses theories of adult development and learning, the professional development of adult educators, curriculum planning, program design, and the use of technology in adult Jewish learning. Also included is an historical overview of adult Jewish learning in America.

Jewish Education News (2001, Winter). New York: Coalition for the Advancement of Jewish Education. This special issue on adult education brings together insights from eighteen leaders in the field of adult Jewish learning. Topics include text study as a religious experience, rabbinic models of lifelong learning, new adult learning program initiatives and models in synagogues and communities, teaching Hebrew to adults, guidelines for adult educators, and personal journeys of adult learners.

Schuster, D. T. (2003). *Jewish Lives, Jewish Learning: Adult Jewish Learning in Theory and Practice.* New York: UAHC Press. Using stories of learners and teachers as well as theories of adult development and learning, this book guides teachers and planners to design meaningful learning opportunities for contemporary Jewish adults. Included are practical tips and guidelines for structuring, teaching, and evaluating adult Jewish learning activities.

Schuster, D. T. & Grant, L. D. (2004). Teaching Jewish Adults. In Nachama Moscowitz (ed.), *The Ultimate Jewish Teachers Handbook,* 140–159. Denver: ARE Publishing. Drawing on Jane Vella's twelve principles of effective adult education practice and themes in adult development, the authors offer guidelines for teachers of Jewish adults. Included is a discussion of the many venues in which today's Jewish educators find themselves and a "theory-to-practice" chart that outlines key findings about what helps Jewish adults to learn.

Schuster, D. T. & Grant, L. D. (2005). "Adult Jewish Learning: What Do We Know? What Do We Need to Know?" *Journal of Jewish Education* 71, 179–200. This article describes the emergence of the field of adult Jewish learning and the need for research on this burgeoning aspect of contemporary Jewish life. The authors review existing research about adult Jewish learners, learning experiences and teachers, and identify questions for future research.

Teutsch, David (2004). "Building Bridges: From Learning to Living." *Journal of Jewish Communal Service* 80 (2/3), 180–188. This paper assesses the structure and impact of a year-long program for "graduates" of the Florence Melton Adult Mini-School that was designed specifically to promote change in the participants' spiritual lives and personal Jewish practices. The author discusses how the program helped learners to grow without disrupting their relationships with family members who were not as engaged with learning.

REFERENCES

Adult Jewish Learning Reader. (1993). New York: JESNA.

Aron, I. (1995). From the Congregational School to the Learning Congregation: Are We Ready for a Paradigm Shift? In I. Aron, S. Lee and S. Rossel (eds.), *A Congregation of Learners*, 56–77. New York: UAHC Press, 56–77.

Aron, I. (2000). *Becoming a Congregation of Learners.* Woodstock, VT: Jewish Lights.

Aron, I. (2002). *The Self-Renewing Congregation.* Woodstock, VT: Jewish Lights.

Aron, I. & Schuster, D. (1998). "Extending the Chain of Tradition: Reflections on the Goals of Adult Text Study." *Journal of Jewish Education,* 64 (1/2), 44–56.

Aslanian, C. B. & Brickell, H. (1980). *Americans in Transition: Life Changes as Reasons for Adult Learning.* New York: College Board.

Belenky, M. F., Clinchy, B., Goldberger, N. & Tarule, J. (1986). *Women's Ways of Knowing.* New York: Basic Books.

Brookfield, S. (1986). *Understanding and Facilitating Adult Learning.* San Francisco: Jossey-Bass.

_____. (1987). *Developing Critical Thinkers.* San Francisco: Jossey-Bass.

_____. (1991). *The Skillful Teacher.* San Francisco: Jossey-Bass.

Brooks, A. K. (2000). Transformation. In E. Hayes & D. D. Flannery (eds.), *Women as Learners: The Significance of Gender in Adult Learning.* San Francisco: Jossey-Bass

Brown, E. (2003). "An Intimate Spectator: Jewish Women Reflect on Adult Study." *Religious Education* 98 (1), 65–81.

Cohen, B. I. (2002). An Accidental Teacher Researcher Looks at a Synagogue Talmud Study Circle. In Burton I. Cohen and Adina Ofek (eds.), *Essays in Education in Honor of Joseph S. Lukinsky.* New York: The Jewish Theological Seminary Press, 81–96.

Cohen, S. M. and Davidson, A. (2001). *Adult Jewish Learning in America: Current Patterns and Prospects for Growth.* New York: Heller/JCCA Research Center.

Cohen, S. M. and Eisen, A. (2000). *The Jew Within: Self, Family, and Community in America.* Bloomington: Indiana University Press.

Cousens, B. (2002). *Adult Bat Mitzvah as Entree Into Jewish Life for North American Jewish Women.* Waltham, MA: Hadassah International Research Institute on Jewish Women.

Daloz, L. (1999). *Mentor: Guiding the Journey of Adult Learners.* San Francisco: Jossey-Bass.

English, L. M. & Gillen, M. A. (2000). A Postmodern Approach to Adult Religious Education. In Arthur L. Wilson and Elisabeth R. Hayes (eds.), *Handbook of Adult and Continuing Education.* San Francisco: Jossey-Bass, 523–538.

Feiman-Nemser, S. S. (2001). "From Preparation to Practice: Designing a Continuum to Strengthen and Sustain Teaching." *Teachers College Record* 103 (6), 1013–1055.

Grant, L. D. (2001). "The Role of Mentoring in Enhancing Experience of a Congregational Israel Trip." *Journal of Jewish Education* 67 (1/2), 46–60.

Grant, L. D. (2003). "Transitions and Trajectories Post Adult Bat Mitzvah." *Journal of Jewish Education* 69 (2), 34–50.

Grant, L. D. (1999/2000). "Adult Bat Mitzvah: An American Rite of Continuity," *Courtyard,* 1, 142–171.

Grant, L. D. (In Press). Finding Her Right Place in the Synagogue: The Rite of Adult Bat Mitzvah, in Riv Ellen Prell, ed., *Women Remaking Judaism.* Detroit: Wayne State University Press.

Grant, L. D., Schuster, D. T., Woocher, M. & Cohen, S. M. (2004). *A Journey of Heart and Mind: Transformative Jewish Learning in Adulthood.* New York: JTS Press.

Goodman, R. L. & Katz, B. (2004). *The Adult Education Handbook: Planning, Practice and Theory.* Denver: A.R.E. Publishing.

Hayes, E. & Flannery, D. (2000). *Women as Learners: The Significance of Gender in Adult Learning.* San Francisco: Jossey-Bass.

Horowitz, B. (2000). *Connections and Journeys: Assessing Critical Opportunities for Enhancing Jewish Identity.* New York: UJA-Federation of Greater New York.

Houle, C. (1961). *The Inquiring Mind.* Madison, WI: University of Wisconsin Press.

Jewish Education News (2001, Winter). New York: Coalition for the Advancement of Jewish Education.

Kegan, R. (1994). *In Over Our Heads: The Mental Demands of Modern Life*. Cambridge, MA: Harvard University Press.

Knowles, M. S. (1980). *The Modern Practice of Adult Education: From Pedagogy to Andragogy*, 2nd ed. Chicago: Follett.

Markus, H. & Nurius, P. (1986). "Possible Selves". *American Psychologist 41*, 954–969.

Maher, F. & Tetrault, M. K. (2001). *The Feminist Classroom: Expanded Edition*. Lanham, MD: Rowman and Littlefield.

McAdams, D.P. & de St. Aubin, E. (eds.) (1998). *Generativity and Adult Development*. Washington, D.C.: American Psychological Association.

McDonald, Joseph. (1992). *Teaching—Making Sense of an Uncertain Craft*. New York: Teachers College Press.

Mezirow, J. (1991). *Transformative Dimensions of Adult Learning*. San Francisco: Jossey-Bass.

Mezirow, J. & Associates (eds.) (2000). *Learning as Transformation: Critical Perspectives on a Theory in Progress*. San Francisco: Jossey-Bass.

NJPS 2000–01: Strength, Challenge, and Diversity in the American Jewish Population: A United Jewish Communities Report. http:\\www.jewishdatabank.org/default.asp

Palmer, P. (1998). *The Courage to Teach*. San Francisco: Jossey-Bass.

Rosenzweig, F. (1955). Towards a Renaissance of Jewish Learning. In N. Glatzer (ed.), *On Jewish Learning*. New York: Schocken, 55–71.

Sarna, J. D. (2005). The Cyclical History of Adult Jewish Learning in the United States. *The Jewish Role in American Life, Volume 4*. Los Angeles: Casden Institute, University of Southern California.

Schlossberg, N. (1999). *Overwhelmed: Coping with Life's Ups and Downs*. New York: Lexington Books.

Schoenfeld, S. (1992) Ritual and Role Tradition: The Use of Adult Bat Mitzvah as a Successful Rite of Passage. In J. Wertheimer (ed.), *The Uses of Tradition*. New York: Jewish Theological Seminary, 349–376.

Schön, D. (1990). *Educating the Reflective Practitioner: Toward a New Design for Teaching and Learning in the Professions*. San Francisco: Jossey-Bass.

Schuster, D. (1995, June). Jewish Lives/Jewish Learning: From Life to Torah in Contemporary America. Paper presented at Annual Meeting of the Network for Research in Jewish Education, Palo Alto, California.

_____. (2003a). *Jewish Lives, Jewish Learning: Adult Jewish Learning in Theory and Practice*. New York: UAHC Press.

_____. (2003b). "Placing Adult Jewish Learning at the Center." *Agenda: Jewish Education* 16.

Schuster, D. & Grant, L. D. (2005). "Adult Jewish Learning: What Do We Know? What Do We Need to Know?" *Journal of Jewish Education 71*, 179–200.

Sheehy, G. (1996). *New Passages: Mapping Your Life Across Time*. New York: Ballantine.

Shulman, L. (1987). Knowledge and Teaching of the New Reform. *Harvard Educational Review 57*, 1–22.

Taylor, K., Marienau, C. & Fiddler, M. (2000). *Developing Adult Learners*. San Francisco: Jossey-Bass.

Tennant, M. & Pogson, P. (1995). *Learning and Change in the Adult Years: A Developmental Perspective*. San Francisco: Jossey-Bass.

Teutsch, D. (2004). "Building Bridges: From Learning to Living." *Journal of Jewish Communal Service,* 80 (2–3) 180–188.

Vogel, L. (1999). *Teaching and Learning in Communities of Faith: Empowering Adults Through Religious Education*. San Francisco: Jossey-Bass.

Woocher, M. L. (2004). "Texts in Tension: Negotiating Values in the Adult Jewish Learning Classroom." *Journal of Jewish Education 70* (1/2), 22–31.

Jewish Spirituality and Adult Spiritual Development

Linda Rabinowitch Thal

"God talk" and the acknowledgement of Jews' hunger for spiritual connection are much more explicit than they were a dozen years ago when the first edition of this book was published. Books and classes on Kabbalah abound; adult education programs include meditation retreats and mussar courses; two-year distance-learning programs have been developed to train worship leaders, meditation teachers, and spiritual directors. Many of the students enrolled in these intensive training programs are rabbis, cantors, and Jewish educators as well as lay "seekers."

The larger context for the renewed interest in Jewish spirituality is the resurgence of general interest in spirituality in the United States over the last twenty years. We see this reflected in studies with titles such as *A Generation of Seekers* (Roof 1994), *The New American Spirituality* (Lesser 1999), *The Spiritual Marketplace* (Roof 1999), *Shopping for Faith* (Cimino & Lattin 1998), *and The Jew Within* (Cohen & Eisen 2000). Most scholars view this phenomenon as part of a worldwide response of disillusionment with, or reaction against, modernity's sacred–secular split. In addition to being part of these wider movements and trends, Jews have played out their own special versions of response to modernity and the distinctive ways that it has affected them through emancipation, the enlightenment, the secularization of messianic aspirations in the forms of socialism and Zionism, emigration from Europe to America, the Holocaust, and the establishment of the State of Israel. Modernity gave birth to a new category, the secular Jew, a Jew whose Jewish identity and commitments are based on ethnicity, culture, and ethics but not religiosity or relationship to God.

During the 1990s the communal Jewish agenda shifted somewhat from primary pre-occupation with institution-building, defense and survival to one that also embraced renewal, celebration and response to Jewish multicultural diversity. At the same time, increasing rates of intermarriage and assimilation signaled by the 1990 National Jewish Population Study provided stimulus for and helped define the community's "continuity agenda." As the continuity agenda promoted attentiveness to adult learning, adult educators quickly became aware of the transformational elements of Jewish study. Adult learning moved away from the *Wissenschaft de Judentums* model and toward one that began to privilege meaning-making. Nevertheless, the mission of adult learning is rarely considered to be spiritual or religious growth (Grant, Schuster, Woocher & Cohen, 14–15, pp. 233–234). There are a number of reasons for this:

- Many adult education programs define themselves as non-denominational or trans-denominational, making teachers cautious to avoid the appearance of advocacy or prescriptiveness in discussions of theology and practice.
- Most adult education programs define their mission in terms of Jewish literacy with a resultant commitment to Jewish identity and communal participation rather than spiritual or religious growth.

• Many teachers and directors have not explicitly examined their own spiritual commitments, developed fluency and ease with spiritual language, or been introduced to ways of understanding and fostering spiritual development in others.

EDUCATIONAL CONTEXTS

Adult learning and Jewish spirituality meet in two different educational contexts. The first consists of settings or programs that have explicitly adopted a spiritual agenda. Such programs can be found, to a limited extent, as components of a synagogue's overall adult educational offerings. Programs of greater intensity and/or duration tend to be conducted by special institutes on both local and national levels (for a sample survey see Thal 2005). The total number of students served by these more intensive programs, however, is quite small. The second context encompasses most extant adult learning programs. Here the spiritual component that does or could exist is implicit (as when educators adopt the assumption that adult learning is inherently spiritual).

This chapter begins with a brief overview of three pertinent literatures: adult learning, religious education, and Jewish spirituality. The first is particularly useful for settings in which spirituality is not the explicit curriculum. The second and third may contribute to, but do not adequately address, the need that we have for an integrated body of wisdom that can help us talk about, let alone teach toward, the goal of Jewish spiritual development. This is a field that is only now emerging. Consequently, much of this chapter is devoted to framing some of the key rubrics and issues that educators, researchers, policymakers and funders will need to consider as they move into this arena.

Adult Learning Literature: Congruent with the societal trends mentioned above, the secular literature of adult learning reflects renewed interest in spirituality. Intrigued with the idea of transformative learning (Mezirow 1991, 2000; Brookfield 1990, 1991; Cranton 1994), but disappointed by its focus on critical thinking to the exclusion of other ways of knowing (Boyd & Myers 1988; Tisdell 2003b), some in the field have claimed that spirituality is an integral part of adult learning and development (English et.al. 2003; Tisdell 2001; Astin 2004). Indeed, Palmer (2003) and Lauzon (2001) suggest that adult education should be understood as a process of "spiritual formation." This literature treats spirituality as distinct from religion, both because it presumes a student population that encompasses practitioners of multiple faith traditions (or no tradition at all) and because it, like so much of contemporary spiritual literatur,e assumes a common ground of inner experience (spirituality) in spite of the vastly different exterior practices, beliefs and institutional structures of particular faith traditions (Tacey 2004; Lesser 1999; Wuthnow 1998).

Much of this literature focuses on meaning-making (Hunt 2001, Vella 2000), self knowledge [including cultural identity (Tisdell 2001)], nurturing the soul (Dirkx 1997), and developing a sense of wholeness (Tisdell 2001). Less frequently authors mention connection to others or the interconnectedness of all things, the growth of compassion (Kristeller 2005), and connection to a higher power, the Lifeforce, or God (Tisdell 2003a).

Palmer (2003), more than most, makes an explicit connection between spirituality and the practice of traditional spiritual disciplines, calling for the study of sacred texts, the practice of contemplation as a learning modality, and the "gathered life of the community," something that Jewish educators will recognize as tantamount to Torah, *avodah* and *gemilut hasadim*. Similarly, he freely uses language of the spirit, calling for a healing of the Cartesian split between mind and matter, and suggesting that the ultimate goal of education is the unification of the known, the knower and the knowing, a goal that often takes us through the route of paradox. Miller, asserting that he "believe[s] that there is yet another level beyond [Schon's] reflection-in-action," requires his education students to meditate and to journal on their meditation as a way of fostering "contemplation-in-action" and a quality of "Presence" (Miller 1994).

Religious Education Literature: Grant, Schuster et al.   (2004), in their recent study of the Florence Melton Adult Mini-School, noted that although Talmud Torah is often considered the most elevated of religious activities, the literature of adult Jewish learning makes "no mention of a 'religious education agenda' among either teachers or learners." This body of literature is largely Christian. In spite of frequent references to shared Biblical texts or to Jewish thinkers, its goals and assumptions are often stated in ways that carry little resonance for Jewish ears. For Jewish educators who can read past or make the translation from both explicit and more subtle Christian language, this literature can stimulate new questions about our practice.

Jewish Spirituality: The growth of a popular literature on Jewish spirituality over the past twenty years has been nothing short of astounding. The genres range from spiritual autobiographies to theologies, guides for practice, aids and examples for finding personal meaning in Jewish texts, application of Kabbalah to growth and healing, and book-length explorations of the meaning of Jewish spirituality. In addition, growing numbers of traditional Hasidic and mystical texts are being published in English for the first time, often with commentary.

This new literature provides educators with incredible resources for both their own and their students' use. Nevertheless, these books address the individual reader, and, unlike the religious education literature, provide little help with pedagogic content knowledge (Shulman, 1987).

Consequently, there are few sources to which a Jewish educator can turn for a synthetic overview of or guidance in education for Jewish spiritual development. Spiritual development does seem to happen in the course of some forms of adult Jewish learning, but it occurs somewhat serendipitously. Grant et al. (2004) have documented learners' testimonies about changes (often intensification) in practice, identity (both individual and communal) meaning making, and for a "significant minority…some measure of interest in matters of faith and the divine." It nevertheless remains true, in the words of one of the teachers they interviewed, that "The goal is not to teach theology or make them into religious Jews. It is to make them *informed* Jews" (79, 233). Interestingly, in her study of Jewish women who had engaged in Jewish text study, Brown (2003) notes that several of the women reported that their study "did not contribute to their spiritual development, and some wrote that their intellectual development actually impaired their spiritual growth, [leading] them to be more critical and experience less religious connection."

In short, there is a great gap in our research-based knowledge about what we might call Jewish religious education or Jewish spiritual formation. To date there are only a few studies that examine programs of Jewish learning in which spirituality is the focus of either the teaching or the research.

FOUNDATIONAL ISSUES AND RUBRICS

WHAT IS JEWISH SPIRITUALITY?

What do we mean by spirituality? Is it behavior—mitzvot? Is it feeling and intentionality—*kavanah*? Is it belief—*emunah*?

The term "spirituality" itself is often considered problematic in Jewish discourse. Central to the contemporary Jewish discomfort with the notion of spirituality is the perception that *ruchaniyut* privileges the inner, non-material dimension over the worldly, action-oriented dimension of life lived in obedience to the commandments. The arguments employed by critics of the current surge of interest in Jewish spirituality range from the sentiment "It's not Jewish" to the accusation that spirituality is "privatized and narcissistic." Others argue that it caters to market forces and substitutes warm fuzzies for "submitting to God's will."

While spirituality may have its superficial and individualistic manifestations, genuine spirituality is about depth of connection to God (The Ground of Being, the Ultimate, the Sacred), and its result is self-transcendence. Green (1992), basing his definition of spirituality on Psalm 27, captures both elements: Spirituality is "seeking the face of God, striving to live in His presence and to live a life of holiness appropriate to God's presence." Transpersonal theoretician Evans (1992) offers a comparable definition:

> Spirituality consists primarily of a basic transformative process in which we uncover and let go of our narcissism so as to surrender into the Mystery out of which everything continually arises (p. 4). [Mystics tend to agree that any authentic spiri-

tual transformation] involves a shedding of narcissism, self-centeredness, self-separation, self-preoccupation, and so on (p. 158).

Theologian Gillman proposes that we define spirituality

> … as that which, according to the believer, God demands above all. God demands many things, forms of behavior, emotions, a set of beliefs or intellectual formulations…By spirituality we are trying to get at that form of religious expression which the believer considers indispensable. It is the ultimate focus of his religious energy, that dimension on which he places supreme emphasis. It defines the authentic believer at his best (1997, 12).

Gillman's definition acknowledges the difficulty of finding a single way of talking about or pointing to either spirituality or spiritual development.

PARADIGMS OF SPIRITUAL DEVELOPMENT

Indeed, many different paradigms for discussing spiritual development can be identified in the literature on spirituality; five are briefly introduced in this section.

- **Faith development, with its parallel to cognitive development.** Extending the content focus of earlier work by Piaget and Kohlberg (on moral development), Fowler (1981) introduced the idea of faith development, proposing that there is a natural pattern of spiritual maturation that roughly parallels cognitive development. The six stages he proposed can be clustered as pre-conventional (the embedded and mythic thinking of children); conventional (synthetic and individuative-reflective) and post-conventional (conjunctive and universalizing). Fowler related faith to the inherently human need to find or make meaning; accordingly, faith orders and orients an individual's life and values.

  The appeal of Fowler's approach is that, because he places emphasis on the structures rather than the contents of faith, religious educators of diverse traditions can identify with the dynamics of the theory and use it to match the ways they teach narratives, symbols, practices and theology to the competencies of each stage. Similarly, understanding the potential for stage unfolding, educators could more skillfully devise scaffolding of support and challenge. Among the critiques of faith development theory is that, because it deals with differences in worldview or ways of knowing, it has little to do with the way religious traditions self-define (Dykstra 1986). Others caution against giving too much credence to levels of spirituality, suggesting that, at best, they should be loosely held (May 1982a, p. 22).

- **Spiritual dynamics.** In the literature of Christian spirituality one finds a classic schema for progressive stages of development (awakening, purification, illumination, dark nights, and union) that is used diagnostically by spiritual mentors and guides (Underhill 1962). In contradistinction, Jewish spiritual texts focus much more on the dynamics of spiritual development than on stages or levels, although levels (albeit fluid) are assumed. The model for Jewish spirituality is one of *ratzo v'shov*, running and returning, or movement both close and away (Ezekiel 1:14), and the Jewish spiritual vocabulary is filled with expressions like *mohin d'katnut* and *mohin d'gadlut* (constricted and expanded consciousness); *yeridah l'tzorekh aliyah* (descent for the sake of ascent) and *yesh mai'ayin* (the emergence of existence from nothingness) (Lamm 1999, pp. 403–405).

  This Jewish language is extraordinarily helpful in guiding individuals as they reflect on changes in their spiritual lives over time and in providing support during times of spiritual confusion or alienation. At the same time, familiarity with descriptions of awakening, purification, illumination, dark nights and union will help Jewish educators and spiritual guides identify what may be happening in an individual's religious life and prescribe both spiritual practices and new images of God that will sustain and deepen the person's journey toward the divine. In providing a framework for Jewish spiritual directors' thinking about spiritual transformation, Breitman (2006) has offered a paradigm that attempts to combine both approaches using traditional Jewish tropes.

- **Tikkun ha-Middot—refinement of soul qualities.** When asked about the essence of Judaism, the Kotzker Rebbe replied that it is "working on oneself." *Tikkun Hamiddot,* the primary modality of Mussar, is a very direct and conscious way of doing that.

  Only recently has the active practice of Mussar (which includes text study, meditation, journaling, and spiritual companionship) been reintroduced into the non–Orthodox Jewish community. Stone (2007) is working on new translations with commentary of traditional Mussar works. Krumbein has produced an analysis of *Musar for Moderns* (2005), and Morinis has written a personal account of his introduction to the world and practice of Mussar (2002) and a guide for doing this work (2007). Having created a Mussar institute with web-based learning, <u>h</u>evruta study, and occasional regional conferences, Morinis is beginning to develop a network of Mussar teachers for the liberal community.

- **Changes in levels, states and structures of consciousness.** Transpersonal theory examines the higher reaches of human development, extending beyond Kegan's (1994) work on orders of consciousness into levels at which identity with the body-bounded ego-self is superceded and the self begins to identify with increasingly wider and more spiritual domains of experience (Sinnot 1992; Miller & Cook-Greuter 1994, 1999; Cortright 1997; Boucouvalas 1993). Both transpersonal psychologists who work from a model of Eastern spirituality (Wilber 1981, 1996) and those who follow a Western paradigm (Washburn 1994, 1995) build their models for self-transcendence on the prior consolidation of an established ego-self. But just because individuation is a step on the path of spiritual—as well as psychological—development, it is hardly its pinnacle. Higher states of consciousness loosen the strictures of the ego, leading to self-forgetful states that Jewish tradition refers to as *bitul ha-yesh* (abnegation of the ego) and *devekut* (cleaving to God).

  Repeated experiences of higher levels and states of consciousness may become integrated over time, leading to structural change in the way experience is perceived and processed. Although there are many accounts of dramatic, transformative experiences that change the individual "forever," even these require post-experience integrative work. The more common path of development is the slower one of spiritual discipline and practice: meditation, *davening*, the repetition of a sacred phrase (*gerushin*), text study, Nachman of Bratzlav's *hitbodedut*, etc. (see, for example, Buxbaum 1999; Slater, 2004; and Strassfeld, 2006).

- **Relationship with God.** While spiritual seekers may at first be content with episodic experiences of transcendence, spiritual development entails stabilizing and integrating those experiences, becoming increasingly open to intimations of *kedushah* or divine presence in the midst of daily life, feeling and perceiving oneself to be *in relationship* to God (although some Jews may avoid or even reject explicit God language). This relationship may be activated and expressed in prayer but also in study and *mitzvot,* both ritual and interpersonal. Cultivating ongoing attentiveness to God's presence and one's relationship to God is a primary purpose of spiritual practice. At the same time, experiences of God are illusive and generally perceived to be "gifts," something that we cannot create ourselves. Heschel taught that we can bring ourselves to the threshold of encounter with God but cannot cross over of our own will. Willingness, not willfulness, is the proper stance for being in relationship with the One (May 1982b). Green (1992) acknowledges that

  > In my own religious life, I have come to recognize the need for submission to God as a part of religious devotion. I fought long and hard against this aspect of religious life, but I now, perhaps with long delayed maturity, have come to accept it. I believe there is no room for God—however defined—in our lives until we can overcome our own willfullness. To thus submit, to "negate your will before God's will," is essential to accepting the covenant as I have described it, the readiness to serve as a channel for divine presence in the world....For myself, I recognize the

necessity of this link, the sense that religious awareness only becomes constant in life through the regularity of religious discipline (pp. 132–133).

Although each of these ways of understanding spiritual development has its own conceptual framework and vocabulary, each reflects our starting definitions of seeking connection with God (surrendering into Mystery) and striving to live a life of holiness appropriate to being in that relationship (letting go of one's narcissism). Because individuals' spiritual journeys take such varied forms, it is helpful for educators and spiritual mentors to have multiple ways—and language sets—for thinking and speaking about the nature of spiritual growth.

SPIRITUAL TYPES AND PATHS

Similarly, educators and guides need to be able to identify and work with different spiritual types and paths. The Seer of Lublin, when asked for one general way to serve God, replied:

> It is impossible to tell people what way they should take. For one way to serve God is through learning, another through prayer, another through fasting, and still another through eating. Everyone should carefully observe what way his heart draws him to, and then choose this way with all his strength (Buber 1961, 313).

While the Seer was speaking in the context of a halakhic community in which a fully observant life was assumed, he nevertheless recognized the reality of individual difference. Borowitz (1999 p. 11) distinguishes "four kinds of spirituality [all] amply attested to in Jewish tradition: the path of the *Tzaddik* (through deeds, both ritual and ethical), the path of the *Chacham* (through study), the path of the Psalmist (through the articulation of inwardly felt piety), and the path of the Kabbalist (through mysticism and direct experience). "These differences are reflected in Soncino's study of *Six Jewish Paths to God* (2002): acts of transcendence, study, prayer, meditation, ritual, relationships and good deeds.

Particularly illuminating are studies of spiritual types based on the Myers-Briggs typology (a system based on four sets of opposing proclivities: introversion vs. extroversion; sensate vs. intuitive ways of knowing; thinking vs. feeling ways of processing information; and perceiving vs. judging ways of relating to the external world) (Hirsh & Kise 1998) and on the Enneagram (a nine-type characterization of individuals' basic orientation to their experience and the world) (Maitri, 2000). Both systems are complex and highly nuanced, and the studies of their implications shaping and responding to an individual's spiritual path are often revelatory for a seeker and instructive for an educator or guide.

AGES, STAGES AND GENDER

Adult learning research has frequently focused on particular age segments (particularly college-age students and elders) or on gender—particularly women (Parks 1999, 2000; Tisdale 2000). In the Jewish community, congruent with Roof's research on the "generation of seekers" (1994), programs on spirituality primarily attract the 45–65-year-old population; two-thirds to three-quarters of the attendees are women. Programs of Jewish meditation attract a more balanced range of attendees—a larger percentage of men and both younger and older participants (Thal 2005). Schacter-Shalomi (1997) has developed formats for doing spiritual work and spiritualizing the status of elders, but little has been written yet about college students or generations X and Y. Grant (1999/2000) has written about the impact of adult bat mitzvah on women, but we know relatively little about the spiritual life or needs of Jewish men. A good beginning for such work can be found in Barden's monograph (2005) *Wrestling with Jacob and Esau: Fighting the Flight of Men: A Modern Day Crisis for the Reform Movement.*

THE ROLE OF NARRATIVE

An area of common interest for educators, students and researchers is that of narrative, the "Jewish journey" story. Students need to tell the story of their Jewish learning or spiritual growth as part of the transformative process, their way of articulating, reflecting upon, and integrating changes that may not be easy to name (Witherell & Noddings 1991). Educators attuned to the importance of personal meaning making frequently assign journaling or reflective papers (English & Gillen 2001; Kerka 1999). They may also include excerpts from spiritual autobiographies as part of their students' reading, for the very act of finding one's own experience reflected in the life and words of another may both initiate and confirm the transformative path. Similarly, researchers have moved away from quantitative research which used reported ritual practice, synagogue attendance, and/or in-marriage as signposts of Jewish identity to listening to interviewees' stories as a means of understanding the complex and changing nature of Jewish commitment (Cohen & Eisen 2000; Horowitz 2000; Schuster 2003; Grant et al. 2004). Moreover, they have witnessed the potentially transformative nature of the research process itself, as interviewees stop mid-sentence and reflect on their reflection (Thal 1999).

TEACHING AND TEACHERS

Although the teaching of new content, intellectual stimulation, and the development of critical thinking remain important, teaching toward a goal of spiritual meaning and development leans heavily on the use of affective, experiential forms of education. In addition to journaling and forms of spiritual autobiography, the literature emphasizes the use of metaphor and imagery (Tisdell 1999; Dirkx 1997), spiritual reading (Duncan 1995), meditation or contemplative exercises (Palmer 2003; Brown 2001; Miller 2005), body movement, art and poetry, and soul friends (English, Fenwick & Parsons 2003).

Most important for this kind of education, however, is the teacher. While it may be possible for a teacher to stimulate spiritual interest, seeking and even transformation without cultivating his or her own spiritual life, education that is *explicitly* spiritual can only be undermined by a teacher whose spiritual authenticity is in question. This need not mean that teachers must be spiritual masters. Evaluative research on the programs of the Institute for Jewish Spirituality (IJS) by Rosov (2001) highlighted the importance of the program's director being a "fellow traveler on the road."

We know little about these teachers. Those whose spiritual teaching is explicit have been seekers first and become teachers as a result of their own unfolding quest. They are repositories of tacit practical wisdom, selecting subject matter and developing their teaching styles based on an intuitive but unarticulated understanding of pedagogic content knowledge. Those teachers who work as an integrated faculty team that together determines a program's structure, content and tone have begun, to a greater or lesser degree, to have conversations about effective spiritual teaching. Work with these teams would be a particularly fruitful place to begin research. Moreover, Rosov's formative evaluation of the IJS's program enabled the team to further articulate and develop its storehouse of practical wisdom about education for spirituality.

Finally, for teachers in programs of adult learning that are not explicitly devoted to spiritual awakening or development, we should consider the kind of support and training that will further sensitize them to the way this subterranean theme is playing out in their classrooms and in their interaction with students—those "graced moments of teaching" of which Palmer writes. Adult learning literature provides adaptable examples (Doring 1997; Hopp 2001; Palmer 1998). It will also be important to anticipate the kinds of resistance we might expect to meet from faculty who are committed to creating "informed" but not necessarily spiritually engaged students.

MENTORING AND SPIRITUAL DIRECTION

With mentoring emerging as an important component of adult learning (Daloz 1999), religious educators are now exploring this form of education (Zeldin & Lee 1995; Thistlewaite & Carnes 1994; English 1998). Most visible in the Jewish community have been programs of private learning that may extend to personal mentoring offered by Chabad and Aish HaTorah.

A newer paradigm is emerging in the form of spiritual direction (Ochs & Olitzky 1997; Thal 2003, 2006; Addison & Breitman 2006). In spite of its name, this is a non-directive, contemplative form of spiritual guidance that provides safe and sacred space in which an individual may initiate, explore and deepen his or her spiritual life. To date, spiritual direction has not been explored by adult educators working in lay settings, although it is being adopted by a number of rabbinical seminaries, in particular the Reconstructionist Rabbinical College.

In addition to offering spiritual direction as an adjunct program at Kollels, this may be the one area of Jewish spirituality in which educators' practical wisdom has been articulated and published. Although Addison and Breitman's new anthology focuses on one-to-one or group spiritual direction, educators will find this to be the best writing available on Jewish spirituality, spiritual development, and spiritual guidance.

IMPLICATIONS AND POLICY RECOMMENDATIONS

GLEANING AND DISSEMINATING EXPERT TEACHERS' PRACTICAL WISDOM

There is enormous practical wisdom to be gleaned from those who teach in spiritually based programs and settings: retreat centers, institutes and training programs (Thal 2005). Much of this wisdom is unarticulated, particularly when instructors teach as individual agents rather than as part of a faculty that plans and deliberates together. In those relatively few instances in which faculties do meet regularly to discuss what they are learning as reflective practitioners, their wisdom remains limited to the particular group with which they work. By and large these teachers do not participate in the formal educational networks of the Jewish community; consequently their wisdom is unavailable to professional educators. Indeed, communication among teachers from various programs is limited to informal networks.

It would therefore be important to devise systems by which this wisdom can be made explicit and more widely available. This will require a combination of approaches, including:

- Creation of a series of facilitated working conferences that bring expert spiritual teachers together for structured conversation, presentations and response, shared study and learning sessions with each other and with educational professionals.

- Collaboration between teachers of existent programs and researchers in projects of action research that would help teachers learn to study and reflect on their practice and would engage researchers in a deeper understanding of spiritually focused learning.

- Creation of an Institute modeled on the Whizin Institute for Family Education that would further both the development and the dispersal of a growing body of knowledge about teaching for spiritual development.

SPIRITUAL DEVELOPMENT FOR TEACHERS

Given the two kinds of settings we have delineated—those with an explicit spiritual agenda and those in which spiritual concerns are an implicit but inherent part of Jewish learning—there need to be different forms of professional development opportunities available for teachers.

- The literature of adult learning will be useful in developing workshops and in-service learning for faculties of programs in which spiritual concerns remain implicit. This literature should be supplemented with the study and discussion of Jewish spiritual autobiographies and of articles on Jewish spirituality so that teachers feel comfortable helping students make a link between their spiritual questions and the tradition in which they are seeking to find direction. Teachers in these programs can learn to listen for, identify and name spiritual yearning and to help students find their way to sources that will speak directly to their spiritual concerns. They do not need, however, to become spiritual teachers per se.

- There will be Jewish teachers, however, who themselves identify with these yearnings and who, if encouraged and offered opportunities, will seek forms of spiritual learning and/or guidance for themselves, motivated both by their own desire for spiritual growth and by the felt need to address their students' search for meaning more directly. More intensive programs of spiritual learning and development for this group need to be designed and funded.

FUNDING

A central finding of "Rekindling the Jewish Soul" is that funders have little understanding of the ways in which the cultivation of spirituality is profoundly related to the communal agenda of Jewish continuity. Consequently, the case for funding programs of spirituality, let alone funding of research about them, will need to be clearly and convincingly articulated.

Critical to the success of such efforts will be the development of a positive discourse in the Jewish community and among Jewish educators about the importance of the spiritual component of Jewish life. The suspicion of spirituality as privatized, narcissistic, or even "not Jewish" will need to be overcome by developing greater clarity about what is meant by spirituality and by emphasizing the role of community and social responsibility as important aspects of Jewish spirituality. Leaders will need to defuse popular confusion—even fear—about both the separation and the interdependence of "religion" and "spirituality."

In addition to funding for initiatives such as those mentioned above, many already existing programs need support to ensure their ongoing survival. They constitute our most important resource for research and the development of the communal expertise that we currently lack.

RESEARCH QUESTIONS

The research we need at this stage is very basic. Suggested research questions include:

1. How do teachers of Jewish spirituality define, think about and identify signposts of spiritual development?

2. What practical wisdom do these teachers hold about teaching for spirituality?

3. How do students tell the stories that connect the change within themselves to the spiritual outcomes of their Jewish learning?

4. What forms of faculty development are effective in encouraging spiritual attentiveness and sensitivity in teachers?

5. What forms of education for spirituality are effective for educators who desire to grow personally and professionally?

6. What explanations of Jewish spirituality and its importance resonate with Jewish community leaders?

CONCLUSIONS

In this era, American Jews—and, increasingly, secular Israelis—are becoming aware of their deep spiritual longings. They seek meaning, purpose, connection and transcendence, and occasionally they explicitly seek God. Many feel lost, confused and conflicted by these powerful yearnings and the absence of spiritual perspectives in so much of the Jewish community's discourse. Others seek out study opportunities but struggle to make spiritual sense of what they are learning even in courses that explicitly address the learners' inner life. Still others need help in integrating new perspectives and practices into their lives. So far the Jewish community has considered these needs to be private and of little communal concern. However, Green, whose dedication to Jewish spirituality bridges the scholarly, the practical and the personal, claims that

> This exodus out of Judaism will continue unless we give [spirituality] an honored place on the American Jewish scene. We know that the majority of Jews are not affiliated. They want meaning....They will continue to go to other religions that honor spirituality and contemplative practice, even Christianity, if it is not central in Judaism. (Green in Thal 2005)

THE LARGER CONTEXT

This chapter highlights the fledgling state of the field of Jewish education for spiritual growth. Before we can marshal sufficient interest in and financial support for its development, the question of why Jewish spirituality is important at all must become more central to communal dialogue. Undergirding the continuity agenda that has motivated the Jewish community for the past twenty years lies the infrequently addressed question of *why* it is important for Jews and Judaism to survive. Our refusal to grant Hitler a posthumous victory is insufficient. Jews and Judaism have undeniable existential value, and the core of that value centers on spirituality, an encounter with the Ultimate, however that Ultimate is understood: as the Source of ethical values, as the Source of all creativity, as the Source of life itself. Jewish education, whether for adults or for children, whether explicitly or implicitly, needs to point toward this Ultimate.

ANNOTATED BIBLIOGRAPHY

Amann, P. (2007). *Journeys to a Jewish Life: Inspiring Stories from the Spiritual Journeys of American Jews.* Northvale, VT: Jewish Lights. Amann documents the "return to Judaism" journeys of individuals who have (re)discovered the importance of their attachment to Judaism. Her interviews are organized according to the many different pathways or portals through which adults re-enter the Jewish community, recommit to Jewish practice, and reengage in Jewish forms of meaning making.

Cohen, S. M. & Eisen, A. (2000). The *Jew Within: Self, Family and Community in America.* Bloomington: University of Indiana Press. Breaking with the pattern of investigating American Jewish life and identity through quantitative measures of affilation, practice, and in- or intermarriage, Cohen and Eisen conducted qualitative research with moderately affiliated Jews. They conclude that the construction of both meaning and identity is more private and individualistic than in previous generations. Their portraits of Jewish seekers will help educators understand the spiritual longings of the boomer generation.

Frankel, E. (2003). *Sacred Therapy: Jewish Spiritual Teachings on Emotional Healing and Inner Wholeness.* Boston: Shambhala. Frankel moves back and forth between psychological theory—generally depth psychology—and Jewish spiritual wisdom, looking for the commonalities but also noting differences in orientation. Her use of Hasidic and kabbalistic concepts, texts, and stories provides alternatives to psychological ways of understanding the movements of the soul without disparaging psychological wisdom.

Slater, J. (2004). *Mindful Jewish Living, Compassionate Practice.* New York: Aviv. Slater examines traditional Jewish sources—Hasidic texts, as well as liturgical, talmudic, and midrashic sources—and applies their teachings to the practices of mindfulness and meditation. The author demonstrates how Jewish teachings and practices, Shabbat and holidays can make us more aware of the spiritual essence of life.

Soncino, R. (2000). *Six Jewish Spiritual Paths: A Rationalist Looks at Spirituality.* Northvale, VT: Jewish Lights. Soncino has investigated what Jews mean when they talk about "spirituality." He delineates six Jewish spiritual paths and fills each chapter with both traditional texts and material from interviews he has conducted with contemporary teachers and practitioners of these paths.

REFERENCES

Addison, H. A. & Breitman, B. (2006). *Jewish Spiritual Direction: An Innovative Guide from Traditional and Contemporary Sources.* Woodstock, VT.: Jewish Lights.

Alexander, A. (2004). "Why Spirituality Deserves a Central Place in Liberal Education." *Liberal Education* 90 (2), 31–41.

Barden, D. (2005). *Wrestling with Jacob and Esau—Fighting the Flight of Men: A Modern Day Crisis for the Reform Movement.* New York: North American Federation of Temple Brotherhoods.

Borowitz, E. (1999). *Judaism After Modernity: Papers from a Decade of Fruition.* Lanham, MD: University Press of America.

Boucouvalas, M. (1993). Consciousness and Learning: New and Renewed Approaches. In S. B. Merriam (ed.), *An Update on Adult Learning Theory: New Directions for Adult and Continuing Education 57.*

Boyd, R. D. & J. G. Myers (1988). "Transformative Education." *International Journal of Lifelong Education* 7 (4) , 261–284.

Breitman, B. (2006).Spiritual Transformation: A Psychospiritual Perspective on Jewish Narratives of Journey. In H. A. Addison and B. Breitman (eds.), *Jewish Spiritual Direction: An Innovative Guide from Traditional and Contemporary Sources.* Woodstock, VT: Jewish Lights.

Brookfield, S. D. (1990). *The Skillful Teacher.* San Francisco: Jossey-Bass.

Brookfield, S. D. (1991). *Developing Critical Thinkers: Challenging Adults to Explore Alternative Ways of Thinking and Acting.* San Francisco: Jossey-Bass.

Brown, E. (2003). "An Intimate Spectator: Jewish Women Reflect on Adult Study." *Religious Education* 98 (1), 65–81.

Brown, M. H. (1997). "A Psychosynthesis Twelve-Step Program for Transforming Consciousness: Creative Explorations of Inner Space." *Information Analyses* 45 (2), 103–17.

Buber, M. (1961). *Tales of the Hasidim: The Early Masters*. Translated by Olga Marx. New York: Schocken Books.

Buxbaum, Y. (1999). *Jewish Spiritual Practices*. Northvale, NJ: Jason Aronson.

Cimino, R. & Lattin, D. (1998). *Shopping for Faith: American Religion in the New Millennium*. San Francisco: Jossey-Bass.

Cohen, S. M. & Eisen, A. (2000). *The Jew Within: Self, Family and Community in America*. Bloomington: University of Indiana Press.

Cranton, P. (1994). *Understanding and Promoting Transformative Learning: A Guide for Educators of Adults*. San Francisco: Jossey-Bass.

Daloz, L. (1999). *Mentor: Guiding the Journey of Adult Learners*. San Francisco: Jossey-Bass.

Dirkx, J. M. (1997). Nurturing Soul in Adult Learning. In P. Cranton (ed.). Transformative Learning in Action, *New Dirctions for Adult and Continuing Education* 74, 79–88.

Doring, A. (1997). "Faith Development of Teachers: A Pilot Study." *Journal of Research on Christian Education* 6, 49–64.

Duncan, J. C. (1995). Spiritual Reading and Its Effects on Human Growth. ERIC Research Report, ED386666.

Dykstra, C. (1986). What Is Faith: An Experiment in the Hypothetical Mode. In C. Dykstra and S. Parks (eds.), *Faith Development and Fowler* (45-64). Birmingham, Alabama: Religious Education Press.

English, L. (2001). "Reclaiming Our Roots: Spirituality as an Integral Part of Adult Learning." *Adult Learning* 12 (3), 2–3.

_____ (1998). *Mentoring in Religious Education*. Birmingham: Religious Education Press.

English, L. & Gillen, M. (2001). Journal Writing in Practice: From Vision to Reality. *New Directions for Adult and Continuing Education* 90, 87–94.

English, L., Fenwick, T. & Parsons, J. (2003). *Spirituality of Adult Education and Training*. New York: Kreiger.

Evans, D. (1992). *Spirituality and Human Nature*. Albany: SUNY Press.

Fowler, J.W. (1981). *Stages of Faith: The Psychology of Human Development and the Quest for Meaning*. New York: Harper & Row.

Gillman, N., as quoted in S. H. Blumberg, Jewish Spirituality: Toward My Own Definition. In C. Ochs, K. Olitzky, & J. Saltzman (eds.), *Paths of Faithfulness: Personal Essays on Jewish Spirituality* (1997). New York: KTAV.

Grant, L. D. (1999/2000). "Adult Bat Mitzvah: An American Rite of Continuity." *Courtyard* 1, 142–171.

Grant, L., Schuster, D. T., Woocher, M. & Cohen, S. M. (2004). *A Journey of Heart and Mind: Transformative Learning in Adulthood*. New York: Jewish Theological Seminary Press.

Green, A. (1992). *Seek My Face: Speak My Name*. Northvale, New Jersey: Jason Aronson.

Hirsh, S. K. & Kise, J. (1998). *Soul Types: Finding the Spiritual Path That Is Right for You*. New York: Hyperion.

Hopp, C. W. (2000). "Research Note: Transcendent Experiences and Teacher Transformation." *Journal of Curriculum and Supervision* 16 (3), 273–6.

Horowitz, B. (2000). *Connections and Journeys: Assessing Critical Opportunities for Enhancing Jewish Identity*. UJA-Federation of New York.

Hunt, C. et. al. (2001). *Is Your Journey Really Necessary?* Proceedings of the 31st Annual Standing Conference on University Teaching and Research in the Education of Adults. London: University of East London, 451–457.

Kegan, R. (1994). *In Over Our Heads*. Cambridge: Harvard University Press.

Kerka, S. (1999). *Journal Writing and Adult Learning*. ERIC Digest No. 174. ED399413.

Kristeller, Jean. (2005). "Cultivating Lovingkindnes: A Two-Stage Model of the Effects of Meditation on Empathy, Compassion and Altruism." *Zygon* 40 (2), 391–408.

Krumbein, E. (2005). *Musar for Moderns*. New York: KTAV.

Lamm, N. (1999). *The Religious Thought of Hasidism*. New York: Yeshiva University Press.

Lauzon, A. (2001). "The Challenges of Spirituality in the Everyday Practice of the Adult Educator: Blurring the Boundaries of the Personal and the Profesional." *Adult Learning* 12 (3), 4–6.

Lesser, E. (1999). *The New American Spirituality*. New York: Random House.

Maitri, S. (2000). *The Spiritual Dimension of the Enneagram: Nine Faces of the Soul*. New York: Jeremy Tarcher.

May, G. (1982 a). *Care of Mind, Care of Spirit: A Psychiatrist Explores Spiritual Direction*. San Francisco: Harper,

_____. (1982 b). *Will and Spirit: A Contemplative Psychology*. San Francisco: Harper.

Mezirow, J. (1991). *Transformative Dimensions of Adult Learning*. San Francisco: Jossey-Bass.

Mezirow, J. & Associates. (2000). *Learning as Transformation: Critical Perspectives on a Theory in Progress*. San Francisco: Jossey-Bass.

Miller, James P. (2005). *Holistic Learning and Spirituality in Education: Breaking New Ground*. Albany: SUNY Press.

Miller, John. P. (1994). *The Contemplative Practitioner: Meditation in Education and the Professions*. Westport, CT: Bergin and Garvey.

Miller, M. E. & Cook-Greuter, S. R. (1994). *Transcendence and Mature Thought in Adulthood: The Further Reaches of Adult Development*. Boston: Rowman and Little.

_____ (1999). *Creativity, Spirituality, and Transcendence: Paths to Integrity and Wisdom in the Mature Self*. Westport, CT: Ablex Publishing.

Morinis, A. (2002). *Climbing Jacob's Ladder*, New York: Broadway Books.

_____ (2007). *Everyday Holiness: The Jewish Spiritual Path to Mussar*, Boston: Trumpeter Books.

Ochs, C. & Olitzky, K. (1997). *Jewish Spiritual Guidance*. San Francisco: Jossey-Bass.

Palmer, P. (2003). "Education as Spiritual Formation." *Educational Horizons*, Fall, 55–67.

_____ (1998). *The Courage to Teach*. San Francisco: Jossey-Bass.

Parks, S. (2000). *Big Questions, Worthy Dreams: Mentoring Young Adults in Their Search for Meaning, purpose and faith*. San Francisco: Jossey-Bass.

_____ (1999). *The Critical Years*. San Francisco: Jossey-Bass.

Roof, W. C. (1999). *Spiritual Marketplace: Baby Boomers and the Remaking of American Religion*. Princeton: Princeton University Press.

_____ (1994). *A Generation of Seekers: The Spiritual Journeys of the Baby Boom Generation*. New York: Harper.

Rosov, W. (2001). Practicing the Presence of God: Spiritual Formation in an American Rabbincal School. Unpublished Dissertation, Stanford University.

Schacter-Shalomi, Z. & Miller, R. (1997). *From Age-ing to Sage-ing: A Profound Vision of Growing Older*. New York: Warner.

Schuster, D. T. (2003). *Jewish Lives, Jewish Learning: Adult Jewish Learning in Theory and Practice*. New York: UAHC Press.

Shulman, L. (1987). "Knowledge and teaching: Foundations of the new reform." *Harvard Educational Review* 57 (1), 1–22.

Sinnot, J. D. (1992). *Development and Yearning: Cognitive Aspects of Spiritual Development*. Paper presented at the Annual Convention of the American Psychological Association, Washington DC.

Slater, J. (2004). *Mindful Jewish Living: Compassionate Practice*. New York: Aviv Press.

Soncino, R. (2002). *Six Jewish Spiritual Paths: A Rationalist Looks at Spirituality*. Woodstock, VT: Jewish Lights.

Stone, I. (2007). *A Responsible Life: The Spiritual Path of Mussar*. New York: Aviv Press.

Strassfeld, M. (2006). *A Book of Life: Embracing Judaism as a Spiritual Practice*. Woodstock, VT: Jewish Lights.

Tacey, D. (2004). *The Spirituality Revolution: The Emergence of Contemporary Spirituality*. New York: Brunner-Routledge.

Thal, L. R. (1999). A Funny Thing Happened on the Way to This Forum: How Jewish Seekers and Researchers Tell the Stories of Adult Spiritual Journeys. Paper presented at the Association of Jewish Studies.

_____ (2003). Where Is God in This? Issues in the Emergence of Jewish Spiritual Direction. Unpublished Dissertation, Teachers College, Columbia University.

_____ (2005). Rekindling the Jewish Soul: Contemplative Judaism Takes on the Challenge, a study conducted for the Circle of Support for Contemplative Judaism within the Jewish Funders Network. *www.jfunders.org/knowledge_center*

_____ (2006). Creating Jewish Spiritual Direction: More Than an Act of Translation. In H. A. Addison & B. Breitman (eds.), *Jewish Spiritual Direction: An Innovative Guide from Traditional and Contemporary Sources*. Woodstock, VT: Jewish Lights.

Thistlewaite, S. & Cairns, J. (1994). *Beyond Theological Tourism: Mentoring as A Grassroots Approach to Theological Education*. Maryknoll, NY: Orbis Books.

Tisdell, E. (2003). *From Research to Practice: Toward a Spiritually Grounded and Culturally Relevant Pedagogy*. Paper delivered at the Pennsylvania Adult and Continuing Education Research Conference.

_____ (2001). *Spirituality in Adult and Higher Education*. ERIC Digest (ED459370).

_____ (2003). *Exploring Spirituality and Culture in Adult and Higher Education*. San Francisco: Jossey-Bass.

_____ (2000). "Spirituality and Emancipatory Adult Education in Women and Adult Educators for Social Change." *Adult Education Quarterly* 50 (4), 309–335.

_____ (1999). The Spiritual Dimensions of Adult Development. *New Directions for Adult and Continuing Education, 84,* 87–95.

Underhill, E. (1911/1962). *Mysticism*. New York: E.P. Dutton.

Vella, J. (2000). Sacred Epistemology. In L. English & M. Gillen (eds.), *Addressing the Spiritual Dimensions of Adult Learning: New Directions of Adult and Continuing Education 85,* 7–16.

Washburn, M. (1995). *The Ego and the Dynamic Ground* (2nd ed). Albany: SUNY Press.

_____ (1994). *Transpersonal Psychology in Psychoanalytic Perspective*. Albany: SUNY Press.

Wilber, K. (1981). No *Boundary: Eastern and Western Approaches to Personal Growth* Boulder, CO: Shambhala.

_____ (1996). *A Brief History of Everything*. Boston: Shambhala.

Witherell, C. & Noddings, N. (1991) (eds.), *Stories Lives Tell: Narrative and Dialogue in Education*. New York: Teachers College Press.

Wuthnow, R. (1998). *After Heaven: Spirituality in America Since the 1950's*. Berkeley: University of California.

Zeldin, M. & Lee, S. (1993) (eds.), *Touching the Future: Mentoring and the Jewish Professional*. Rhea Hirsch School of Education, Hebrew Union College—Jewish Institute of Religion.

Jewish Education and Adult Jewish Women

Shulamit Reinharz

In the United States the attraction of women to adult Jewish education is a current fact of life among the great variety of Jews. As Cohen and Davidson (2001) pointed out, women are more likely than men to be engaged in adult Jewish learning. In the Florence Melton Adult Mini-Schools and Me'ah, for example, two of the largest adult learning programs in North America, women comprise 60% of the students. We have to be careful not to over-generalize, however. In the liberal branches of Judaism women far out number men, while among the Orthodox it is the opposite. This heightened educational involvement among Jewish women, according to Joseph, represents a glorious new moment in Jewish history.

> "American Jewish women today have greater access to Jewish knowledge than any generation in history. Not only are women entering the halls of academe, they have also entered the *beis medrash*, the scene of intensive Torah study. Whether in co-educational environments, sex-segregated schools, or women-only study groups, as children or adults, women are amassing the tools and skills of Jewish scholarship. Ever so slowly the historically gender-restricted ideal of Torah study has become an egalitarian goal. Knowledge has become the membership card in every denomination...The history of the American Jewish community in the twentieth century, especially since 1950, has been marked by the education of its female members" (Joseph, pp. 221-222).

For others, women's interest in Jewish study is framed as a *problem*. As women's interest grows the fear is that women inadvertently are driving men away. Or, to put it differently, the more that women are involved, the less likely that men will want to participate. Thus, people believe a vicious cycle is established by the gender imbalance in adult Jewish learning: the more women, the fewer men, which drives away men even more. Only longitudinal qualitative and quantitative research will be able to demonstrate if this pattern actually exists and, if so, how it functions. If the pattern does exist, then research is needed to determine if it is a temporary or long-term phenomenon. Are men interested in Judaism only if they are in charge?

This concern about whether the Jewish community has reached a gendered "tipping point" in adult Jewish learning is common in the larger American community. According to Tavris, "a gendered tipping point reflects one of the oldest findings in the women's career choice literature. Young women often choose a career largely based on the number of women in it (perhaps a proxy for their feeling welcome and not deviant), but men on the field's economic promise, which declines as the proportion of women increases. There does seem to be a tipping point in many if not most occupations: it usually hovers at about 30% women. Higher than that, and men start leaving, and the status of the occupation declines (e.g., veterinarians, physicians, lawyers, psychologists)" (Tavris & Wade 2007).

On a completely different level, and possibly of greater concern, is the nature of gender differences themselves. Do women learn better than men as adults, or vice versa? Is there a women's "way of learning," unwittingly embedded by designers of adult Jewish education, that makes the learning opportunities more suited to women? More broadly, what do social scientists know about gender differences? Are men and women different, and if so, how? And, if there are no hard-wired differences, why does the idea about gender differences persist in our society (Tavris 1984)?

Since the 1970s, I have been deeply involved in studying these questions. Beginning at the University of Michigan and continuing at Brandeis University, my concentration has been on women's studies, including women's competence and feminist research methodology. A direct outgrowth of these activities has been the establishment of three projects at Brandeis: a graduate division within the Women's Studies Program, including the first graduate program in Jewish Women's Studies in the world (1992); the Hadassah-Brandeis Institute (HBI) (1997); and, most recently, the Women's Studies Research Center (WSRC), consisting of eighty researchers and artists (2001).

Rosalind Barnett, a leading social psychologist at the WSRC, has devoted her life to scientific research on possible gender differences. Capping a career including dozens of studies, Barnett recently published (with Caryl Rivers) *Same Difference: How Gender Myths Are Hurting our Relationships, Our Children and Our Jobs* (2004). In this volume Barnett demonstrates that "psychological studies have never been able to confirm differences in abilities or learning styles of men and women, although the public would like to think otherwise" (2004). Many meta-analyses and literature reviews substantiate this conclusion.

And yet books such as Erikson's *Identity and the Life Cycle* (1959); Gilligan's *In a Different Voice: Psychological Theory and Women's Development* (1982); Tannen's *You Just Don't Understand: Women and Men in Conversation* (1990); and Gray's *Men Are from Mars, Women Are from Venus* (1993) claim robust differences. It is important to note that none of these studies has withstood critical examination. Erikson has never shared the data about his observed play differences between young girls and boys so that they could be analyzed independently; Gilligan's interpretation of her own data has been shown to be forced; Gray's very credentials are dubious; and Tannen's study has been shown to be largely anecdotal. Belenky et al.'s, *Women's Ways of Knowing: The Development of Self, Voice and Mind* (1986) earned respect among researchers for its longitudinal analysis of the way some women learn, but it was not a comparative study and thus does not indicate if men learn the same way. The public has adopted the gender difference emphases of these books without recognizing that they do not correspond with the conclusions of careful social science. Former Harvard President Larry Summers fell into this trap when he was pilloried for having asserted—in front of a learned audience—that there are gender differences in scientific ability. Researchers of this topic know that this is not the case.

Facts on the ground also belie the myth of gender differences in learning. Were women to have demonstrable intellectual deficiencies and need for alternative teaching methods, women's colleges would not be able to produce skilled graduates, and women would be unable to compete effectively with men in all the other colleges, medical schools, business schools, law schools and more. Women would not be able to lead countries, serve as political analysts, build bombs, or plan cities. Nor would men be able to care effectively for children. None of this is the case. Gender differences in performance reflect opportunity, not biology or ability.

RECENT RESEARCH ON ATTITUDES TOWARD WOMEN'S LEARNING OVER TIME

Given the lack of scientific evidence for *innate* behavioral or cognitive differences between women and men, I turn to the past decade's historical and sociological studies in order to understand the *culturally* based gender differences that have characterized Jewish education throughout history. Women's access to Jewish "text study" as the key to understanding Jewish men's and women's behavior will serve as the case study. Text study is, after all, a foundation for being Jewish, whether one studies as a child or as an adult. The research demonstrates an unmistakable and profound ambivalence about Jewish women's access to text learning, with both points of view supporting the correctness of their position by turning to selected sacred passages. Whereas the Bible requires Jewish women's study of the law, the Rabbis distanced themselves from this attitude.

On the *pro-women's-learning side*, people refer to the Biblical command that women learn the law:

"And Moses wrote this law, and delivered it unto the priests the sons of Levi, that bore the Ark of the Covenant of the Lord, and unto all the elders of Israel. And Moses commanded them, saying: "At the end of every seven years, in the set time of the year of release, in the feast of tabernacles, when all Israel is come to appear before the Lord thy God in the place which He shall choose, thou shalt read this law before all Israel in their hearing. *Assemble the people, the men and the women and the little ones, and thy stranger that is within the gates, that they may hear, and that they may learn, and fear* the Lord your God, and observe to do all the words of this law; and that their children, who have not known, may hear, and learn to fear the Lord your God, as long as ye live in the land whither ye go over the Jordan to possess it" (Deuteronomy 31:9–13).

Clearly, this passage emphasizes that men, women and children are equal, and thus they must all hear the law and study it.

As the Jewish people left their nomadic, tribal desert existence and inhabited fixed homes within cities and towns in both the Holy Land and the diasporic communities, the Jewish woman became the heart of the home, which, in a sense, became her educational domain. Women participated in the services of the ancient synagogues, probably without a physical divider separating them from men. The learned woman was valued because she created the appropriate atmosphere within the home and was able to pass on her education to her children. Jewish women's education was thus much more instrumental than men's, which, by contrast represented study for its own sake. If the parent is supposed to teach the child, the parent must study first and be knowledgeable.

Reinforcing the virtue for women of being learned, the poem *Eishet Hayil* (Proverbs 31) praises the woman who has studied: "She opens her mouth with wisdom and a lesson of kindness is on her tongue." Thus it is not surprising that, as Shilo writes, even in the city of Jerusalem, where religious tradition prevailed in most matters, women emerged as educated leaders:

"[A]n in-depth study of contemporary sources reveals an impressive number of exceptional learned women in the Holy City community. The existence of 'learned women' or 'wise women' is a known phenomenon in the course of Jewish history, in general, and in the nineteenth century in particular...Within the Jewish community in Jerusalem, which numbered twenty thousand at the end of the century, we can enumerate more than thirty women, most of them Ashkenazic, who were knowledgeable in Hebrew and scriptures. Among them were three writers of pamphlets, which constitutes a unique Jerusalem phenomenon—Jewish women with Jewish education who published their writings" (Shilo 2005, 143).

On the other hand, in the Rabbinic period rabbis underscored the division of Jewish gender roles into male/public and female/private spheres by reference to text, specifically Psalms 45:15, which states that the "honor of the daughter of the king is within," or that women's achievements and goals should be within herself and her home, and not in the wider world. In other words, text was used against women's opportunity to engage in text study and thus to contest it (Joseph 1995, 207–209).

As Parush writes in her discussion of Jewish women's reading behaviors in 19th century Europe,

"The idea that Torah study was an exclusively male obligation and right was supported by an adage of Rabbi Eliezer, 'He who teaches his daughter Torah is teaching her promiscuity' (Talmud, Tractate Sotah 21b). This opaque statement was interpreted by many as forbidding the teaching of Torah to women, or at least as discouraging so doing" (2004, p. 62).

Baskin's *Midrashic Women* (2002) offers an extensive commentary on this statement by explaining that it relates to the conditions under which a woman's punishment for adultery would be delayed if she had learned Torah. Baskin comments that this startling accusation emerges from the dispute between Rabbi Eliezer and Ben Azzai (M. Sotah 3:4). Their argument about punishments for a lascivious woman goes as follows:

"If she had any merit, this (i.e., Torah study) holds her punishment in suspense. Certain merits may delay punishment for one year, others for two years, and others for three years; hence Ben Azzai says: A man ought to give his daughter a knowledge of the Law so that if she [is guilty and] drinks [the bitter water] she may know that the merit [that she acquired] will delay her punishment [but not prevent it]. R. Elizer says: If a man gives his daughter knowledge of the Law, it is as though he taught her lasciviousness" (quoted in Baskin, 81).

As Baskin notes, "Rabbi Eliezer's opposition to teaching Torah to girls and women became the dominant outlook in the Babylonian Talmud and in later Jewish tradition" (p. 81).

These scholars and others have documented that Jewish women's learning, characterized by its connection to the role of mother and wife, did not become widespread in terms of communal educational leadership. When men denied Jewish girls and women the opportunity to engage in study because of its interference with childbearing or economic activity, they were rendering women "special" in a negative way, less intellectually competent, primarily private, and in a sense, less fully Jewish (Millen 2004, p. 5).

The short story "Yentl the Yeshiva Boy" by Isaac Bashevis Singer (Yiddish, 1960; English, 1983) brought this problem into the contemporary Jewish imagination and redefined it not in terms of propriety but as a matter of "rights" (Anton 2005). Raised by her scholarly father, Yentl is a motherless girl who loves to study Talmud. Because of his love for his daughter and his lack of sons, he defies the norms of the day and teaches her surreptitiously. Her access to text study is linked entirely to the good will of one man, which makes it unstable. After her father's death Yentl leaves home, dresses as a man, takes her dead uncle's name and enters a Talmudic academy. Barbra Streisand's film *Yentl* (1983) became a favorite of American audiences and legitimated women's desire for free access to Jewish education.

An actual life analogue is Henrietta Szold, her rabbi father's favorite 'son,' according to biographer Shargel (1997, p. 6). "From her earliest days she had expedited his Hebrew scholarship, even conducted serious academic discussions with him at the table in German..." Szold went on to develop numerous extraordinary careers, the first being as secretary of the Jewish Publication Society, where she oversaw its most important projects.

At the time that text study was largely confined to men in the spirit of Rabbi Eliezer, Jewish women sought their education, entertainment and spiritual expression in other forms of literature and in other language, as Parush (2004) explains:

"Men acquired an ability to read texts in Hebrew, whereas women who learned to read, learned to read Yiddish. The literacy of both men and women made the Torah accessible to them, but men actively *studied* Torah, while women read Bible stories in Yiddish out of the Tseina Ur'eina on their own....Men prayed in Hebrew out of the prayer book, for the most part communally in the synagogue; their prayers followed an established order of service and a set schedule. By contrast, women read the tkhines written for women—in Yiddish, in their homes, at any time, and choosing whichever book of tkhines they preferred and whatever individual supplication they were drawn to from within the book" (p. 59).

Rabbi Mordechai M. Kaplan, like Henrietta Szold's father, had no sons. Influenced by witnessing a bat mitzvah in Italy (Francesconi 2007), he introduced the first public celebration of a bat mitzvah on March 18, 1922, at the Society for the Advancement of Judaism in New York City, for his daughter Judith. The now-accepted practice of bat mitzvah compels girls (and women who become b'not mitzvah as adults) to engage in preparation that includes text study. The adoption of egalitarian practices in all but the Orthodox branches of Judaism was abetted by the acceptance of bat mitzvah (two years after women got the vote in the U.S.). Nevertheless, Orthodox Judaism typically rejects the idea that a woman can read from the Torah or lead prayer services before mixed congregations. Rabbi Moshe Feinstein opposed anyone attending a bat mitzvah ceremony, as has the Sephardic rabbi René Samuel Sirat, Chief Rabbi of France. In other groups, compromises are found: Women do not read from the

Torah or lead prayer services but may lecture on a Jewish topic or recite the verses from other texts (such as the Book of Esther or the Book of Psalms) or prayers from the siddur.

The existence of strong, daring, and highly public teachers such as the U.S.–based Esther Jungreis and the late Israeli scholar Nechama Leibowitz, among the Orthodox, has contributed further to shattering old norms about the inappropriateness of women Torah scholars. Leibowitz is described frequently as one of the leading Torah teachers of the twentieth century and a role model for Orthodox women who are professional Jewish scholars and teachers. Until recently adult women's learning may have been directed toward a specific employment purpose, such as becoming an educator, or learning within an organizational context, such as a study group within Hadassah. Recently a new goal has arisen by which Jewish women engage in learning for the sake of becoming an adult bat mitzvah, for being able to participate more fully in a daughter's or son's becoming bar or bat mitzvah. Others now engage in learning for its own sake. Of particular note, interesting adult Jewish women's learning is undertaken by Orthodox women who explore Jewish law for the purpose of helping Jewish women cope with their Jewish legal problems, particularly around the difficulties incurred by the laws of Jewish divorce. Adult Jewish women's learning is also flourishing in Israel for the purpose of integrating communities in development towns and preparing women to take leadership roles.

The decrease in the birth rate that gives women more time for education, the move to the suburbs that propels women to find ways of exercising their talents and the increase in opportunities for secular education that began in late-19th-century America with the rise of women's colleges are all factors that contribute to Jewish women's high rates of involvement in Jewish learning. With regard to the latter, it is difficult, if not impossible, to rationalize barring women from Jewish education if these same women are neurosurgeons and astronauts! Ross (2004) offers an additional explanation: "Today's favorable attitude toward women's religious study is an[other] innovation that is sometimes based on the recognition that *in order to remain religiously committed in the modern world, women need to acquire an independent knowledge of sources*" (p. 54) [emphasis added].

WOMEN TEACHERS AND JEWISH WOMEN'S ORGANIZATIONS

My earlier research on women's community competence (Reinharz 1984) applies well to Jewish women's educational endeavors in groups. In the United States women have served both as consumers and as organizers of adult Jewish education. Among these, Rebecca Gratz of Philadelphia must be recognized as a key figure in the history of Jewish adult learning. Beginning in 1838 when she launched the Jewish Sunday school movement and insisted that its teachers be "young ladies," women had to be educated Jewishly in order to teach. "The annual exam [of the Sunday School] included a call to young women to join the society's 'labor of Love' and teach in the Sunday school. By 1861, twenty-five teachers served 250 students" (Ashton 2003, p. 29). In order to make the invitation even more attractive, Gratz assured the young women that they would "acquire while they impart a knowledge of the Laws and Customs and duties of our Holy religion as taught to Moses and our forefathers" (29). Gratz was one of the early motivators of women to move beyond their families—"not to the detriment of family life, but to improve the Jewish community and their own knowledge of their religion" (p. 29).

Sarna noted that "women founded the schools, directed them, taught in them and insisted that their daughters be free to attend them on a par with boys" (2000, p. 8). In fact, Sarna's overview of adult Jewish education in the United States leads one to conclude that women's engagement has been nearly continuous, and that the gender imbalance described today actually has a long history. As Sarna noted, in the late 19th and early 20th centuries, when there was not only an enormous influx of Jewish immigrants but also the founding of an extraordinary array of Jewish institutions and organizations, women took the lead, probably playing a "more active role than men" (p. 11). As Reinharz and Raider have shown (2005), this attitude toward learning applied as much to Jewish education as a whole as it later did to Zionist education.

Just as was true among non–Jews in the Progressive Era, Jewish women were considered the conscience of their communities; they were to serve as social housekeepers in tandem with keeping their own homes. And after the First Columbian Exposition in Chicago (1893) Jewish women began to organize single-sex organizations to be particularly effective. The National Council of Jewish Women (est. 1893) created a strong Jewish education program, a leadership position later taken over by Hadassah (1912) when NCJW changed its mission. Some women who taught in these schools were not treated with the respect and dignity they deserved (Feinberg 1999), an attitude applied to many working women. As recently as 1999, a study by Wertheimer showed that women fill the low-paid, under-trained supplementary-school teaching positions (1999). Jewish teachers' colleges (such as Gratz College in Philadelphia or the Hebrew Teachers College in Boston) were founded at the time in part to provide Jewish women with advanced and professional Jewish learning so they could be good teachers.

Nor were all efforts at adult Jewish education for women successful. Many were initiated only to fold or never got off the ground at all. For example, Lindheim, the third national president of Hadassah, proposed that Hadassah adopt "'the Gramsie Hour,' a mode of educating grandmothers to educate their grandchildren in Jewish learning." This idea became part of a larger proposal entitled "Operation Jewish Survival: A Preliminary Manual of Guidelines," which she pitched to the American Jewish Congress. That organization took her twenty-two-session syllabus and in 1966–67, through the Theodor Herzl Institute in New York, announced the opening of the School for Jewish Parent Education, a noble venture that failed for lack of students (Reinharz 1998).

Whereas the Jewish women's organizations alluded to above—Hadassah, the Women's Zionist Organization of America and the National Council of Jewish Women—integrated educational goals as *part* of their mission and plan of action, women now are creating organizations established solely for education. A prime example is the Florence Melton Adult Mini-School. This two-year adult Jewish learning program established in 1986 offers classes in sixty-two cities in North America, making it North America's largest pluralistic adult Jewish education program (Schiller 2007, p. 23). Although the program is available to men and women, it was the drive of a woman to become educated herself that established the Mini-School in the first place.

At a conference on "Gender Issues & Adult Jewish Education" sponsored by the Hadassah-Brandeis Institute (HBI) in 2000, Sarna stressed "the democratization of learning, Jewish learning belongs to the Jewish people as a whole, not just to the elite" (p. 2), a point also developed by Brown (2003). Jewish education for adult women and men has become commonplace in American society and takes many forms. Perhaps what is most striking about adult Jewish education is the large number of points of entry for learners and the lack of prior knowledge that is needed in order to participate. Bais Chana Women International writes in their website advertising "compelling Jewish study to confront the moral and spiritual challenges of the day. Unless otherwise indicated, all sessions are for women of any age. No Hebrew reading or previous Jewish education is required" (*http://www.baischana.org/content/view*).

One of the more dramatic changes took place in 1972 when the Reform Movement ordained Sally Priesand. Today males constitute only 33% of first-year rabbinical students at Hebrew Union College. This was followed in 1985 when the Conservative movement's Jewish Theological Seminary ordained Amy Eilberg. Now more than half of their students are women. What is most telling is the composition of the Talmud and Rabbinics faculty at the Jewish Theological Seminar. Of the eight full professors, one—Judith Hauptman—is a woman. Of the six assistant professors, three are women.

A few particularities in Jewish women's learning emerged in a recent study chaired by Wertheimer. The author found that Jewish women want their learning experiences to *focus on issues relevant to women*. After noting that Jewish women and girls enjoy unprecedented **access** to Jewish education, the study reported: "women still want more education **about Jewish women** for themselves and their children." In particular, they want Jewish education to include **gender analyses** of Jewish text, culture and history. The women seeking opportunities to learn believe that they must acquire Jewish knowledge and ritual skills in order to become credible as leaders (1999, p. 113) [emphases added].

Brown also studied Jewish women learners with a survey of fifteen questions to which respondents wrote answers (meaning that there were no probes). The thirty-two respondents included seventeen who identified as Orthodox, ten as Conservative, three as Reform, one as Reconstructionist, and one as unidentified with these branches. The age range was 20 through 71, with an average age of 47.5. Brown did not mention the kind of educational activities the women were engaged in or how their answers related to those settings. Her conclusions were that the women reported disdaining their childhood Jewish education as they returned to learn as adults in order to 1) connect with or educate their children, 2) find spiritual education, or 3) become able to fully participate in the Jewish community. Although the first and last goals were addressed and, in some cases, met, the second was not, much to the women's disappointment (2003).

Except in Orthodox circles, women are rabbis, cantors, mohalot, and other leaders of Jewish ritual, all of which require extensive Jewish learning as adults. At the same time, women are building institutions with an educational focus, just as they created the Sunday schools of the past. Examples include the three-year-old Mayyim Hayyim: Living Waters Community Mikveh and Education Center in Newton, Massachusetts. The purpose of Mayyim Hayyim is to bring women and men to a renewed appreciation of and involvement in Jewish ritual and education through the vehicle of a beautiful mikveh.

Many are aware that women are eager consumers of Jewish education today. But whether there will be a long-lasting gender imbalance, with women's presence creating a redefinition of Judaism as the domain of women, is open to debate. The May 2007 issue of *614: the HBI ezine (http://www.brandeis.edu/hbi/614/)* is devoted to this debate. Most of the contributors agree on two points—first, we have seen this gender imbalance before in American Jewish history, so we do not have to panic that men will desert Judaism forever. And second, we have to create men-only spaces just as we did womens-only educational spaces in the last few decades. Throughout history each debate has created a new resolution, which in turn becomes the genesis of a new reaction and debate. Gender concerns with regard to adult Jewish education are a telling example of this process.

IMPLICATIONS AND/OR POLICY RECOMMENDATIONS

The community implications of the research review are:

- Adult education should be offered in various formats, both single-sex and mixed-sex, because we have no definitive information that one format is right for all people.
- Women who embark on adult Jewish education should receive materials that explain the complications that existed in the past. They should learn about the trajectory toward democratization of which they now are a part. They should also learn about the women who preceded them as learners and teachers.
- All organizations and Jewish endeavors should include a strong educational component, making it possible for women to enter into their adult Jewish education in a variety of domains.

It is possible that we are currently witnessing the first phase of a strong renaissance of women's involvement in adult Jewish education. This phase may turn out to be a flash in the pan, a reflection more of curiosity than of commitment. If the endeavor is serious, however, then it will be necessary to see what kind of course sequence is best. In addition, if text study is the true core of Jewish learning, then provisions will have to be made for the study of Hebrew.

Finally, the presence of educated members of Jewish organizations will likely have an impact on how those organizations function. When organizational members need to make decisions, for example, they can draw on what they have learned in other contexts. An educated public will demand a lot from rabbis and other communal leaders. At the same time, communal organizations should be prepared to draw on the talents of newly educated Jewish women. They should be invited to give talks, to advise others, and to use their knowledge in other ways. New expectations can also be established as to how mothers of bar and bat mitzvah children should participate in the service.

ADDITIONAL RESEARCH QUESTIONS

- Comparative studies of the experience of men and women as adult Jewish learners should be undertaken. Only if we compare the sexes can we understand if there are significant differences.

- Longitudinal studies should attempt to assess the impact on men of women's engagement in adult Jewish learning. Two central areas are the impact on the male spouse and the impact on whether or not men participate in adult Jewish education.
- Comparative studies can also be made of women and men in single-sex or mixed-sex learning settings.
- Following the findings of Brown, it is important to understand what exactly the women are learning and how this impacts on their Jewish identity, Jewish practices and spirituality.
- There are extensive new developments in adult Jewish education in Israel, making it possible to conduct comparative research between Israel and the United States with regard to these questions.
- It is very important to differentiate between myth and reality in this field. Is there truly a Renaissance in adult Jewish learning? What are the indicators or metrics that would establish that this has occurred? Similarly, it is important not to rely on the self-promotional materials of organizations as the source of information.

FUTURE DIRECTIONS—PRACTICAL IDEAS FOR MOVING THE FIELD AHEAD

Information about Jewish women's interest in adult education is not readily available because it is spread among many different organizations: synagogues, book clubs, Me'ah, and rabbinical schools, to name only a few. Data from these various organizations are not synthesized to provide overall figures or figures by type of educational setting. We do not know, for example, if involvement in adult Jewish education is similar to the pattern found in visits to Israel; i.e., only about 15% American Jews have visited Israel, but these people go repeatedly, making it seem as if many American Jews visit. It may be possible for central agencies for Jewish education to begin to establish a meaningful and usable database that documents all the forms of adult Jewish education and their attendees.

Jewish Elderhostels may satisfy the desire of some adult women and men to study Jewish texts, with or without their partners, in a setting away from home. Other adult learning formats may need to focus on young mothers and fathers (see Ikkarim, in Boston), on single parents and on singles without children. Adult learning opportunities can also tie people to other organizations to enable them to become more involved with the community. But for all these possible innovations in adult Jewish learning, it is necessary not only to attract learners but also to train and hire teachers. The training of teachers for Jewish education may currently be focused exclusively on serving children and not adults.

HIGHLIGHTS

- Women outnumber men as consumers of Jewish education. People believe that men shy away from adult Jewish education because women predominate. We do not know if this is true.
- Scientists have not established any significant gender differences in abilities or learning styles, notwithstanding the popular books that claim otherwise.
- Sacred texts can be used either to bar women from or to include women in Jewish education.
- All the denominations, including the Orthodox, have extensive opportunities and leaders in Jewish women's education.
- Women have been and continue to be teachers as well as learners.
- Jewish women's organizations have consistently included an educational mission.
- Jewish adult learning has become democratic in the United States, meaning that it is open to all.

LARGER CONTEXT

Although Jewish women have participated in Jewish educational activities in the past, they are currently doing so in a way that changes the relations between the knowledge levels of Jewish men and women. As Jewish women increasingly become equal partners with men they will become ever more conscious of the possibility of taking leadership positions. As Bronznick, founding president of Advancing Women Professionals, suggests, Jewish organizations lag far behind the Fortune 500 in promoting women to top leadership positions and compensating them appropriately.

REFERENCES

614: the HBI ezine (*http://www.brandeis.edu/hbi/614*)

http://www.mayyimhayyim.org/

Anton, M. (2005). *Rashi's Daughters, Book One: Joheved*. Glendale, CA: Banot Press.

Ashton, D. (2003). The Lessons of the Hebrew Sunday School. In P. S. Nadell (ed.), *American Jewish Women's History: A Reader*. New York: New York University Press, 26–42.

Barnett, R. & C. Rivers (2004). *Same Difference: How Gender Myths Are Hurting Our Relationships, Our Children, and Our Jobs*. New York: Basic Books.

Baskin, J. R. (2002). *Midrashic Women: Formations of the Feminine in Rabbinic Literature*. Lebanon, NH: Brandeis University Press.

Belenky, M.F., Clinchy, B.M., Goldberger, N.R. & Tarule, J.M. (1986). *Women's Ways of Knowing: The Development of Self, Voice and Mind*. New York: Basic Books.

Brown, E. (2003). "An Intimate Spectator: Jewish Women Reflect on Adult Study." *Religious Education* 98 (1), 65–81.

Cohen, S. M. & Davidson, A. (2001). *Adult Jewish Learning in America: Current Patterns and Prospects for Growth*. New York: Heller/JCCA Research Center.

Erikson, E.H. (1959). *Identity and the Life Cycle*. New York: International Universities Press.

Feinberg, H. (1999). "Elsie Chomsky: A Life in Jewish Education." Donna Sudarsky Working Paper Series. Waltham: Hadassah-Brandeis Institute, available online at: *http://www.brandeis.edu/hbi/pubs/working_papers.html*

Francesconi, F. (2007). "Inside the Ghetto: Italian Jewish Women in Eighteenth-Century Modena," presentation at the Hadassah-Brandeis Institute.

Gilligan, C. (1982). *In A Different Voice: Psychological Theory and Women's Development*. Cambridge: Harvard University Press.

Gray, John. (1992). *Men Are from Mars, Women Are from Venus: A Practical Guide for Improving Communication and Getting What You Want from Your Relationships*. New York: Harper Collins.

Millen, R. L. (2004). *Women, Birth and Death in Jewish Law and Practice*. Lebanon, NH: Brandeis University Press.

Joseph, N. B. (1995) "Jewish Education for Women: Rabbi Moshe Feinstein's Map of America." *American Jewish History* 83 (2), 205–222.

Parush, I. (2004). *Reading Jewish Women: Marginality and Modernization in Nineteenth Century Eastern European Jewish Society*. Lebanon, NH: Brandeis University Press.

Reinharz, S. (1984). "Women as Competent Community Builders: The Other Side of the Coin," in A. Rickel, M. Gerrard and I. Iscoe (eds.), *Social and Psychological Problems of Women: Prevention and Crisis Intervention*. New York: Hemisphere, 19–43.

Reinharz, S. (1998). Irma 'Rama' Lindheim: An Independent American Zionist Woman. *Nashim: A Journal of Jewish Women's Studies & Gender Issues*, 1, 106–135.

Reinharz, S. & Raider, M. (eds.) (2005). *American Jewish Women and the Zionist Enterprise*. Lebanon, NH: University Press of New England.

Ross, T. (2004). *Expanding the Palace of Torah: Orthodoxy and Feminism*. Lebanon, NH: Brandeis University Press.

Sarna, J. (2000). "Adult Jewish Learning for Jews in the United States: Historical Perspectives." Paper presented at the conference Gender and Adult Jewish Education, Brandeis University.

Schiller, M. (2007). Back to the Books: Across the country, Jewish adults are returning to the classroom. *World Jewish Digest*. April, 23–27.

Shargel, B. R. (1997). *Lost Love: The Untold Story of Henrietta Szold*. Philadelphia, PA: Jewish Publication Society.

Shilo, M. (2005). *Princess or Prisoner? Jewish Women in Jerusalem, 1840-1914*. Lebanon, NH: Brandeis University Press.

Tannen, D. (1990). *You Just Don't Understand: Women and Men in Conversation*. New York: Morrow.

Tavris, C. (1992). *The Mismeasure of Woman: Why Women Are Not the Better Sex, the Inferior Sex, or the Opposite Sex*. New York: Simon and Schuster.

Tavris, C. (2007) personal communication.

Tavris, C. & Wade, C. (1984). *The Longest War: Sex Differences in Perspective*. New York: Harcourt Brace Jovanovich.

Wertheimer, J. (1999). Jewish Education in the United States: Recent Trends and Issues. *American Jewish Year Book*. New York: American Jewish Committee, 3–155.

Educators

Jewish Educational Personnel

Roberta Louis Goodman and Eli Schaap

Jewish educators are a critical component in providing quality Jewish educational experience to learners of all ages. Many professionals and lay leaders recognize the important role of the educators and are seeking new and innovative methodologies for investing in their growth, development and status (A Time to Act 1990; Goodman & Schaap 2006a). Among the numerous efforts to improve Jewish education over the last decade, those that were designed to address the needs of the professional educators were grounded in research as part of the implementation process. This general climate encouraged foundations to sponsor, academics to conduct, and policy makers and programmers to utilize research on the professional lives of Jewish educators as a component of their planning process.

The result of these research efforts changed perceptions about the shortage of qualified Jewish educators into an understanding that greater knowledge of the educators' backgrounds, their professional preparation and ongoing professional learning, and the process of recruitment and retention are key elements in addressing the overall concerns of the field. Some of the key questions that these studies addressed included: What do we know about the educators—their demographics, backgrounds, and levels of commitment? Why did they enter the field, and what factors will encourage them to remain—salaries, benefits, respect, status and/or *kavod*? How do we properly prepare them for success through pre-service and in-service professional development programs? What impact does the status of the educator have on the ability of the system to achieve success? The initial findings presented in this chapter compelled and propelled Jewish communal organizations, philanthropists, Jewish educational institutions, educators and lay leaders to take action and to embark on additional research initiatives.

Roberta Louis Goodman was on the research team that conducted the study of Jewish educational personnel as part of the Council for Initiatives in Jewish Education, an experience that changed her career path as a Jewish educator from practitioner in the field to researcher and evaluator. Subsequently she has been both a researcher of and advocate for issues related to personnel in Jewish education. Eli Schaap, as the associate director of CAJE, an organization interested in advocating for Jewish educators, focused much of his work on research aimed at bringing personnel related issues to the forefront of the larger Jewish community. The two researchers have collaborated on a number of key projects over the last five years.

CONTEXT

Personnel in Jewish education emerged as a priority issue in Jewish communal life as a key component of the Jewish continuity agenda in the late 1980s and early 1990s. The Commission on Jewish Education in North America, funded by philanthropist Mort Mandel, recommended raising the quality of personnel as one of its foundational centerpieces for improving Jewish education (A Time to Act 1990).

At the time, little was known about Jewish educators in terms of general characteristics or, more significantly, in terms of why they chose to work in Jewish education, their perception of themselves as professionals with a career, or why they remained in the field of Jewish education. A few studies in the decade prior to the 1990s existed, but they were either too limited in scope (the Aron and Bank study of supplementary school teachers in 1988) or were so broad and general in the information that they provided (the JESNA and Hebrew University census of Jewish schools in 1985) that they provided limited assistance in the planning process at the local and national levels.

The 1990s, on the other hand, were characterized by a number of studies that examined Jewish educators in the three formal educational settings—congregational schools, day schools, and early childhood programs—in order to help raise the quality of Jewish educators. Led by Mandel, who established the Council for Initiatives in Jewish Education (CIJE) to implement the recommendations proposed in *A Time to Act* (1990), the Lead Community project focused its resources on learning more about the educators in the three lead communities (Atlanta, Baltimore and Milwaukee) in order to help improve Jewish education on a community-wide basis. The CIJE project adapted Lortie's work on public school personnel (1975), which dealt with the nature and content of the teaching occupation, to better understand the sentiments and activities of Jewish educators. The CIJE study ("Policy Brief" 1994) included both a survey and interviews that provided insights into the professional lives of Jewish educators in terms of reasons for entering the field, career path, workplace conditions, satisfaction, professional development, and demographic characteristics. Subsequent studies incorporating similar questions in Cleveland (Tammivaara and Goodman 1996b) and Washington State (Tammivaara and Goodman 1996a) were used as planning tools for those communities.

In the first decade of the 21st century emphasis was placed on conducting studies, including action research, to inform policy, planning, programming, advocacy, and fundraising both nationally and locally. The emerging focus on early childhood Jewish education as a significant gateway for families into Jewish life was connected to several studies, including a national survey of early childhood Jewish educators (Vogelstein & Kaplan 2002), a study in Miami-Dade and Broward counties connected to a project to improve their salaries, benefits, and *kavod* (Goodman & Schaap 2006b) and Denver's planning effort to reach more Jewish families through its early childhood programs, which included examining its personnel (Center for Policy Research 2006a).

Early childhood was not the only delivery system targeted. The Central Agency for Jewish Education in St. Louis conducted a study of the perceptions of congregational educators by its major stakeholders—teachers, directors, rabbis, congregational board members, and federation board members—tied to the Jewish Education Recruitment and Retention Initiative (JERRI) of JESNA as a step toward addressing the status of local educators (Goodman & Schaap 2006a). A third study by Pomson (2000) examined in depth the working lives of graduates from the Jewish educational certification program for day schools, finding that teaching is connected closely to one's personhood.

On the continental level, Kelner et al. (2005), working on the assumptions that those individuals working in Jewish institutions are viewed as professionals and that the quality of institutions relies heavily on its personnel, surveyed full-time communal workers including Jewish educators in six communities. This study produced the first major comparisons of full-time Jewish educators in congregational and day school settings, including most day school teachers, to other Jewish communal professionals; early childhood Jewish educators were not included. On a more comprehensive level, the JESNA sponsored study of day and supplementary schools (Ben-Avie & Kress 2006) is aimed at identifying characteristics of these schools (School Registry) and educators' perceptions of the elements of school culture (Quality of Life). This study has the potential for creating educational change and raising the quality of Jewish education on the school, community, and national levels. Finally, the Reform movement is updating an earlier study of its congregational schools, now called "Portraits of Learning," including a section on teachers and education directors (Joseph 1997), in order to aid its planning for the future.

Despite the growth in the type, range, and number of personnel studies, they are limited primarily to Jewish educators in formal educational settings—that is, schools. Missing are significant studies of educators in informal settings, such as camps, youth movements and Israel experiences, and adult Jewish educators. In addition, there is little if any research on central agency for Jewish education staff, rabbis as educators, professors of Jewish education, Jewish studies faculty, and those working in Jewish educational roles in federations, national organizations, and private foundations. Another significant gap are those Jewish educators who have left the field or those who have considered entering the field but decided not to.

WHO ARE THE EDUCATORS?

Jewish education lacks a census of Jewish educators that would parallel the Jewish population studies, although the JESNA study (Ben-Avie & Kress, 2006) that is currently underway will hopefully fill this void in the near future. Most of the numbers about educators come from local sources, predominantly central agencies for Jewish education, that sometimes collect data on the number of Jewish educators in day schools, supplementary schools, and/or early childhood programs to aid their local planning. One attempt to estimate the number of Jewish educators was based on the 1999/2000 census of students conducted by ADCA (the Association of Directors of Central Agencies) and Schick's census of day school students. Goodman & Schaap (2002) extrapolated the number of educators using known teacher/student ratios. In 2000 they estimated that there were 22,000 day school teachers (including Judaic and general studies), 16,000 early childhood teachers and assistants and 28,000 congregational school teachers. These numbers do not account for those teachers who work in more than one type of setting. There are no similar estimates of the number of informal and adult educators.

The existing studies present information about teachers and administrators such as age, gender, Jewish identification, Jewish and general education, years in a setting, number of jobs in Jewish education, and career perceptions. The next section provides data and issues related to gender, Jewish identification, and Jewish and general education of Jewish educators in day schools, congregational schools, and early childhood programs.

GENDER

Most Jewish educators are female. That pattern is found in day schools, congregational schools and, most severely, early childhood education. Kelner (2005) reports that 77% of the educators in day schools, both teachers and administrators, are female. The St. Louis study of congregational school educators found that 79% of the Jewish educators, including both directors and teachers, are female. In early childhood Jewish education no less than 97% of the directors, teachers and aides are female, based upon the results of three studies, one national and two local (Vogelstein & Kaplan 2002; Goodman & Schaap 2006b; Center for Policy Research 2006a). Despite the preponderance of females, issues remain regarding gender equality in terms of positions, promotions, and salaries, which are related to status, power, and money. Kelner's study of Jewish communal professionals identified a gender gap affecting women's salaries for all positions (2005, p. 37). On a broader level, an issue facing the Jewish community is that of boys and men lacking role models for participation in Jewish life from the youngest ages through adulthood, of which little is known at present.

JEWISH IDENTIFICATION

Implicitly, regardless of the setting or program, Jewish education is expected to expose and convey Jewish knowledge, skills, and values, provide a context in which to experience Judaism and strengthen commitment to Judaism among its learners. While it might be anticipated that not all students in early childhood or day schools are Jewish, for a variety of reasons, what is less obvious is how prevalent non–Jewish staff are in both administration and teaching positions that include teaching about Judaism. The significance of having non–Jewish staff centers on the significance of staff serving as role models for how to live a Jewish life. When non–Jews serve in leadership roles, questions arise about their role in setting the Jewish vision and content for the programs.

Day schools often employ non–Jews in teaching and administrative roles, particularly in the area of general studies. However, with the growth of day school enrollment and the number of day schools, the supply of qualified Jewish educators has become strained. In 2005, 32% of general studies teachers and 11% of educational administrators, 20% of day school staff overall, were not Jewish, although almost all Judaic content teachers were Jewish (Kelner 2005). The significance of the percentage of non–Jewish general studies teachers varies as some schools prefer to split the curriculum between

Jewish and general studies while others favor an integration of Judaic and general studies. The issue is becoming more apparent and problematic in the upper-tier administrative positions, where many non–Jews have taken positions as head of school or principal, often because they are better qualified to administer a school in terms of credentials and experience than Jewish candidates. While having a non–Jewish head of school is in itself not necessarily a bad thing, it does present serious challenges for how Jewish schools create and sustain a compelling vision of Jewish life that is communicated through its educational system, since leadership is a key factor in this process. If the supply of qualified Jewish educators at all levels of the day school system continues to diminish, the very essence of the Jewish nature of the schools may come into question.

Early childhood Jewish education has the highest percentage of non–Jews serving in educational roles. The national study (Vogelstein & Kaplan 2002) showed that 31% of all early childhood Jewish educators were not Jewish, including 30% of the teachers. In Miami, as part of Project *Kavod*, the early childhood education directors provided information about the number of teachers on their staffs. The unpublished survey indicates that 38% of the teachers in Dade County and 27% in Broward County are not Jewish. The percentage of non–Jewish assistant teachers is 38% in Dade and 30% in Broward. These results are higher than in the "official" study of Jewish educational personnel (Goodman & Schaap 2006b) because a higher percentage of non–Jewish teachers did not respond to the survey. The numbers in Denver (Center for Policy Research 2006a) are similar, with 30% of the teachers and teacher aides not being Jewish. These numbers have changed dramatically since the CIJE study ("Policy Brief" 1994) conducted almost a decade earlier, which showed that 10% of the early childhood teachers were not Jewish, although in one of the three communities the percentage was 21%. As attention is drawn to early childhood Jewish education as a gateway to Jewish life, the preparedness of teachers and the program to foster those connections for the children and their families needs to be addressed.

EDUCATION: JEWISH AND GENERAL

The most desirable profile for a Jewish educator is to have degrees in both education and Judaic studies, as these constitute the two main fields from which Jewish education draws. The CIJE study ("Policy Brief" 1994) identified 19% of the teachers in Jewish schools as having credentials in both areas. An additional 35% had training in education, 12% in Judaic studies, and 34% in neither. More recent studies confirm that Jewish educators continue to lack appropriate credentials regardless of the setting (day school, congregational school, and early childhood), calling into question the preparedness and ability of these personnel to deliver high-quality Jewish education. As a result, there is a clear need for substantive professional growth opportunities in both Jewish learning and pedagogy to assist them in fulfilling their roles.

DAY SCHOOL EDUCATORS

The educational background of day school educators varies by position among administrators, Judaic studies teachers, and general studies teachers, according to the Kelner study (2005). Only 20% of the administrators and 23% of day school teachers received formal preparation in both Judaic studies and Jewish education, which is similar to the CIJE study ("Policy Brief" 1994), where 19% of the educators in the three school settings received training in both areas. A significant number of day school administrators and teachers hold no formal preparation in education. Only 76% of the administrators, 51% of the Judaica teachers, and 57% of the teachers with no Judaic responsibilities specified receiving formal training in education. In terms of Judaic studies, the picture is bleaker, with 32% of administrators, 42% of Judaic studies teachers, and 5% of the teachers with no specified Judaic responsibilities having formal training in Judaic studies. The good news is that approximately 31% of all day school teachers hold graduate degrees in Jewish or general education. Too many, however, lack the benefit of formal learning in education not to mention the preparation in Judaic studies, needed for their positions.

CONGREGATIONAL SCHOOL EDUCATORS

The St. Louis study (Goodman & Schaap 2006a) portrays congregational school educators as secularly well educated, with most having earned a bachelors degree, a noticeable percentage earning formal credentials in education, and demontrating a commitment to continuing adult Jewish learning and ongoing professional development, especially in pedagogy. Of the teachers 79% have earned a bachelors degree, 14% are enrolled in an undergraduate college program, and the remaining 7%, most of whom are older than 23, do not have a bachelors degree. Over one third of the teachers, 38%, hold a degree in general education. While many lack a degree in education, the study of Philadelphia's congregational teachers suggests that a much higher percentage have exposure to educational theory, with 79% indicating that they took at least one college level course in education (Rosenbaum & Tigay 2002). When we look at the number of teachers with credentials in both Judaic studies and education, the St. Louis study, which appears to be somewhat typical, indicates that only 1% of the teachers have earned credentials in both areas.

What is noticeable is the ongoing commitment to adult Jewish learning among the St. Louis educators (Goodman & Schaap 2006a). Seventy-five percent have participated in formal adult Jewish study, including 30% who have taken college level courses. While these numbers do not speak to either the quantity or quality of the adult Jewish learning experience, they do reflect that these teachers have studied Judaism as adults, are committed to courses, not just sporadic learning opportunities, and are willing to commit to lifelong learning experiences. Combined with the 24% who studied Judaism only as children, almost all, 99%, have received some formal Jewish education. This percentage distinguishes the preparation and commitment to learning of congregational teachers from early childhood educators in particular.

In terms of ongoing professional development, almost all teachers participated in a variety of professional development offerings, with 60% spending six hours or more in sessions or classes each year. Their participation speaks to the ability of congregations and central agencies to make professional development an expectation for this part-time work. The teachers' participation also indicates the potential for professional development to augment the effectiveness of congregational teachers and raise the quality of the congregational educational experience.

In Philadelphia there is a similar commitment to ongoing learning among the congregational school teachers (Rosenbaum & Tigay 2002) who come with strong backgrounds in Judaic studies, with 52% having taken college-courses in Judaica. Two thirds of the teachers surveyed expressed an interest in taking college level courses and another 14% in pursuing a degree in Jewish studies or education, although 70% indicated that a stipend is a necessary component to encourage them to pursue a degree in Jewish education. In both Philadelphia and St. Louis the central agencies for Jewish education—and in the case of Philadelphia, a local college of Jewish studies—actively encourage and support ongoing educator learning. These two communities demonstrate what is possible in terms of congregational school teachers' expectations and participation in ongoing professional development.

EARLY CHILDHOOD JEWISH EDUCATORS

Even though early childhood Jewish educators have slightly higher levels of secular education than their national counterparts (Center for Policy Research 2006a) compared to other Jewish educators who are either in day schools or congregational schools, they lack general as well as Jewish educational credentials. The three studies of early childhood Jewish teachers show a range in terms of earning a bachelors degree from a high of about two thirds in Denver (Center for Policy Research 2006) and nationally (Vogelstein & Kaplan 2002) to 43% in Miami (Goodman & Schaap 2006b). Not all of these bachelor degrees are in education much less early childhood education. While the Denver study points to the fact that most teachers have taken courses in early childhood education, it should be acknowledged that one can earn a CDA (Child Development Associate), a minimum certification, or fulfill state requirements for instruction in early childhood in many states without taking any university courses for credit. What is not known is whether the qualifications of the early childhood Jewish teachers studied in the past few years represent an increase in general educational qualifications or, as is the case among early childhood educators throughout the United States, a decline in educational qualifications from previous decades (Herzenberg 2005).

In addition to the lack of general education background, many early childhood Jewish educators have little if any formal Jewish education beyond early adolescence. Of the Jewish teachers in Miami, almost a third received no Jewish education as a child or adult. In the national study (Vogelstein & Kaplan 2002) 45% reported that their highest level of Jewish education was an afternoon Hebrew school. Very few early childhood teachers have participated in formal adult Jewish learning. In Denver 10% reported taking college-level Judaic classes and 25% adult Jewish education courses. While early childhood educators are generally required to participate in professional development as part of the licensing process of their institutions, it does not appear that schools are connecting required hours in professional development to studying Jewish topics.

A new development in many states is the movement to publicly supported educational programs for four-year-olds. As part of this change in the public availability of programs for four-year-olds, states are demanding higher educational levels for those teaching, with a bachelor's degree and credentials in the education of young children becoming the minimum standard, accompanied by increased salaries for those with proper credentials. If early childhood Jewish education does not keep pace in terms of the educational preparation of all personnel, they will lose their ability to remain competitive with these "free alternatives." Jewish early childhood programs will need to better match the salary and benefit levels of these publicly funded programs or risk losing their most qualified staff. At stake will be the ability of Jewish early childhood programs to compete with the publicly funded programs for students and for staff.

RECRUITMENT AND RETENTION

Recruitment and retention of qualified Jewish educational personnel is a serious problem. A high annual turnover rate characterizes Jewish educators in schools. Among the few results available from the Registry of Schools from the JESNA study (Ben-Avie & Kress 2006), it shows that a quarter of instructional staff members in day schools and supplementary schools were new to their positions in 2005/2006, for the most part replacing others and not as the result of new positions. In St. Louis it was estimated that 28% of the congregational teachers were new to their positions (Goodman & Schaap 2006a). These numbers reflect the pressure placed on schools to constantly find quality staff. On a national level 45% of day school directors and 50% of congregational school directors indicated that it is difficult or very difficult to find quality teachers (Ben-Avie & Kress 2006). According to many national studies, the first few years are the most critical for teachers' long-term retention. More focus on retaining educators will alleviate some of the recruitment needs.

Many Jewish educators stay in the field in all three school settings—day, congregational, and early childhood—long enough to make it worthwhile to invest in them. In terms of congregational school teachers, 50% in St. Louis worked in Jewish education five years or more, and in Philadelphia 63% worked six years or more, with nearly 50% teaching in the field for ten years or more. The early childhood Jewish educators in Miami (Goodman & Schaap 2006b) average seven years in their current positions and ten years in the field of Jewish education. In Denver (Center for Policy Research 2006b), early childhood Jewish teachers average 7.2 years working in their schools and 9.9 years working in early childhood Jewish education. Directors averaged only 4.3 years in their current positions in Denver. While Jewish educators on average show some longevity in the field, that is not necessarily true of their employment patterns in a particular school. Figuring out how to retain educators in their workplaces is a major challenge.

Investing in the career of a new teacher is viewed as a major strategy for retaining teachers in education. A major point of departure is often the first few years of teaching (Ingersoll 2001). The Rand Corporation's study of the research on teacher recruitment and retention found "Schools that provided mentor and induction programs especially related to collegial support had lower turnover of beginning teachers" (Guarino, Santebanez, Daley & Brewer 2004, p. x). One St. Louis congregational education director relates how her frustration with teacher turnover led her to develop a mentoring program for new teachers, essentially solving her problem (Goodman & Schaap 2006a). The whole area of teachers receiving support from directors or supervisors in the curricular guidelines given to them and their interaction with peers is something that needs to be addressed on a deeper level, as it affects both recruitment and retention as well as the quality of education provided (Goodman & Schaap 2006a).

This section on recruitment and retention considers four questions: 1) Where does one find Jewish educators? 2) What motivates an individual to become and remain a Jewish educator? 3) Are Jewish educators career or professionally oriented? 4) Do salaries and benefits matter?

WHERE TO FIND JEWISH EDUCATORS?

In many respects, the likely candidates to become Jewish educators are well identified—they are individuals who have continued their formal schooling beyond bar/bat mitzvah, participated in a youth group, attended a Jewish overnight or day camp, worked in Jewish education as a teen or college student, taken college-level Judaic or Hebrew courses and/or studied Judaism as an adult (Goodman & Schaap 2006a). In a study of individuals who participated in a recruitment program geared to college students, Schaap (2004) found that those who participated in a year-long Jewishly oriented program post-undergraduate were even more likely to enter a Jewish communal field. In addition, many young and older Jews come with the experience of having worked in Jewish education in one form or another that not only prepares them and shows them the rewards of being a Jewish educator, but also socializes them into living as a Jew within the Jewish community. These individuals have experienced the match among their values, skills, abilities and knowledge, which are key factors in the selection of any career (Goodman 2000). Some may lack an understanding of the possible career paths in Jewish education. Others need encouragement to enter the system either part-time or full-time.

While clearly not all Jews who share these characteristics become Jewish educators, these experiences lay the groundwork for learning about the field of Jewish education, socializing them into Jewish communal life, identifying meaningful and satisfying work, and developing some of the actual skills and knowledge that prepare one to be a Jewish educator.

WHAT MOTIVATES A PERSON TO BECOME AND REMAIN A JEWISH EDUCATOR?

The opportunity to work with children is a major factor attracting individuals into positions in Jewish education. Whether the study is of day school teachers (Pomson 2001), early childhood educators (Goodman & Schaap 2006b) or congregational school teachers (Goodman & Schaap, 2006a), working with children ranks highest as the reason that people are attracted to their work as Jewish educators. Pomson (2001) also found that serving the Jewish community was a value that brought people to the field. Goodman & Schaap (2006a) found that the ideal of serving the Jewish people was a significant factor in keeping men in the field.

Pomson's work suggests that as teachers become immersed in teaching, other factors unrelated to the act of teaching retain people in the field of Jewish education.

> When participants talked about the ongoing satisfactions and challenges in their work as well as their reasons for staying in the profession, they pointed to a set of factors that are neither intrinsic to the act of teaching nor contextual in a traditionally understood sense. Instead, they identified a set of rewards and discomforts that are experienced in deeply personal terms but that derive from within the school community and culture beyond the classroom (Pomson 2001 p. 9).

The factors that emerged were 1) cross-curricula partnerships, 2) a working life shaped by the rhythms of the Jewish year, 3) sharing a special language, 4) becoming a parent, and 5) dealing with parents. He sums up the importance of the factors as "an opportunity to connect and integrate many dimensions of selfhood" (Pomson 2001, p. 18).

In a related vein, Goodman & Schaap in their study of supplementary school teachers in St. Louis (2006a) found that many teachers valued the teaching, as it allowed them to be part of a congregational community, often the one that they belonged to. It provided a route to being involved in the congregation, known by and connected to others. As a retention strategy, fostering that sense of belonging, of feeling part of a community, can be achieved by building relationships among teachers as well as with parents, and connecting teachers to the larger life of the congregation.

Another important factor from the CAJE Schusterman study (Schaap & Goodman 2004) and earlier work that included the Lainer Interns for Jewish Education, two programs aimed at recruiting high school and college students into Jewish education (Goodman 2000), emerged in terms of identifying likely educators—namely, that of influentials. Most of the participants had significant influentials, either family members or others who were involved in Jewish education or communal life as professionals (63%) or volunteers (77%) in Jewish communal life exposing them to the value of contributing to Jewish communal life.

IS JEWISH EDUCATION VIEWED AS A CAREER?

Many Jewish educators consider themselves as having a career in Jewish education regardless of the setting, how many hours they work, or even if they are Jewish. The Miami data on early childhood Jewish educators showed that 83% of the Jews and 50% of the non–Jews—overall 75% of all the early childhood Jewish educators (Goodman & Schaap 2006b)—considered themselves as having a career. In some way, the amount of time that one is employed, full-time versus part-time, may be one significant factor affecting a person's view of whether or not Jewish education is a career. Given that most of the early childhood educators in Miami worked full-time (thirty-three hours a week or more), the high percentage of early childhood Jewish educators who consider themselves as having a career is not surprising, although the number of non–Jews who held this view was not anticipated. The Miami data on early childhood educators show that two-thirds entered the field as a second career. Other studies need to explore whether most Jewish educators enter the field as a second rather than first career, as it has implications for recruitment, continuing professional learning, and retention strategies.

Whether or not those working in Jewish education consider themselves as having a career, it does seem that Jewish educators are treated as if they were professionals and view themselves as professionals. Kelner (2005) asserts that "American Jewry has chosen a professionalized model for organizing Jewish life" (Kelner 2005, p. vii), including Jewish education, although, he primarily studied communal workers who are employed full-time. Most Jewish educators, especially those in congregational education, are employed part-time, although day school and early childhood education provide many opportunities for full-time employment. To some extent, the option of working full-time is connected to perceptions of professionalism. Most Jewish educators, part-time or full-time, are treated as professionals and view themselves as professionals. In the Philadelphia 2002 study of day school and congregational school educators (Rosenbaum & Tigay 2002), 63% of the congregational educators considered themselves to be professional educators, as compared to 33% who viewed themselves as avocational teachers. The authors speculate that since 56% of the congregational school teachers work full-time in addition to teaching in a congregational school, these teachers probably "apply the model of professionalism to their part-time work as well" (p. 197).

DO SALARY AND BENEFITS MATTER?

Perhaps the question of greatest concern is whether salaries and benefits from other sources make a difference in terms of who enters and remains in the field of Jewish education. Are Jewish educators able to work in the field because they are supported by well-paid Jewish spouses? Does the part-time pay for congregational school teachers matter? Overwhelmingly, on all accounts, the answer seems to be that salaries and benefits for Jewish educators do matter.

Day schools are a good example of how higher salary and benefit packages can raise satisfaction levels while lower, more modest salaries create dissatisfaction. Day school directors, along with clergy, are the two categories of communal Jewish staff members who are most highly satisfied with their salaries and benefits (Kelner 2005). In recent years, with the addition of new day schools and the growth of others along with the shortage of people who can fill those positions, packages have grown faster than the cost of living, as competition increases among the schools. A number of heads of schools have come from outside the Jewish community or switched from other professions to take these positions, another indication of their desirability. Yet during the same period of time, teachers experienced only modest increases in compensation, and their dissatisfaction level rates them among the least satisfied Jewish communal professionals (Kelner, 2005). Ingersoll (2001), who studied both public and private schools K–12, notes that while job satisfaction is often high among private school teachers, job turnover is also high, a factor that he attributes to low teacher compensation. Simply stated, "some teachers in small private schools depart because they cannot afford to remain" (Ingersoll 2001 p. 527).

Even though the average salary for an early childhood teacher is approximately $19,400 (Vogelstein & Kaplan 2002), most consider the income an important part of their livelihood. In Miami 90% indicated that it was a significant source of income, and for 28% it was the primary source, with nearly half (49%) of the educators reporting total family incomes of $45,000 or less. In Denver the situation was similar, with about half (48%) of the teachers and nearly 70% of the assistants reporting a total household income of less than $50,000 (Center for Policy Research 2006a). Educators in both Miami and Denver expressed dissatisfaction with their financial status, with 60% of the Miami educators sharing that they considered leaving the field because of their salaries (Goodman & Schaap 2006b).

The role of benefits in recruiting and retaining early childhood Jewish educators needs to be further developed, as substantiated by the CAJE 2006 study in Miami. Too often early childhood Jewish educators are not aware of what benefits are available to them or not able to afford them. While 76% of the programs in Miami have some form of major medical insurance available for their teachers, the enrollment restrictions and co-payments make it difficult for the teachers to avail themselves of this benefit. Thus, only 29% participate in the employer's major medical insurance. While others are covered through spouses, parents or other employers, 11% of early childhood Jewish educators in Miami indicate not having any medical insurance. For the retirement program, only 9% participate. In most cases the benefits plans are too costly relative to salaries, leading the teachers to not participate in the plans for medical insurance or pension even when offered. One benefit that directly affects recruitment is tuition support for educators' children to attend the school or summer camp or receive child care where they work. Many educators take their first position in early childhood (19%) when one of their children is in the program. "Overall, 45% indicated that their child(ren) attending a particular program was an important factor in their selection of a workplace" (Goodman & Schaap, 2006b, pp. 14–15).

While most congregational school teachers are part-time, salary matters for most, both for the individual and the school, based on the St. Louis experience (Goodman & Schaap 2006a). For some it was an incentive to teach rather than stay home. It changed the level of professionalism and the demands that the educator could place on the teachers in one school where they went from being volunteers to paid faculty. For others it is a significant part of their personal and household income.

> Forty-two percent indicated it was an important source, and for 4% it was the main source. Overall, 59% of the teachers have family incomes of $75,000 or less. Adjusting for the 14% of undergraduate college students ages 18–23, another 45% of the teachers fall into this economic bracket (Goodman & Schaap 2006a, page 32).

Salary also affects feelings about career. Almost half, 44% of those who consider themselves as having a career in Jewish education, indicated that increased salary was one of the most important factors that would improve their job. Another aspect of the salary levels is that approximately 22% of those teaching in congregational schools work in other segments of the Jewish community either part-time or full-time. In some way it appears that teaching is part of the way that they construct both a professional identity and reasonable incomes while serving the Jewish community.

IMPLICATIONS AND POLICY RECOMMENDATIONS

Knowledge about Jewish educators will guide and inform efforts to raise the qualifications and quality of personnel and ultimately the quality of Jewish education. Several implications and policy recommendations emerge from the existing studies of Jewish educational personnel.

- **Money matters**—Investment in salaries and benefits makes a significant difference in the tenure of most Jewish educators. Whether part-time or full-time, regardless of the setting, salaries and benefits stand out as a critical, if not the most important, factor in terms of educator retention in the field. Certain benefits, such as tuition reduction for school or camp attendance, both attract educators and help keep them in certain positions.

- **Professional development**—Serious professional development must become an integral component of the professionalization of the field. Many Jewish educators come without qualifications in either Judaic studies or education. Investing in the professional education of Jewish educators impacts the quality of Jewish education for many years, as most educators think of their involvement as a long-term career commitment.

- **The culture of institutions**—The institutional cultures that provide personal as well as professional support for Jewish educators must become a focus of community attention. Important issues such as *kavod* (respect and status), workplace conditions, meaningful curricular assistance, and clear school and institutional vision will significantly diminish the turnover rate of educators at all levels of the system.

- **Recruitment strategies**—Experience clearly indicates the backgrounds of people who are most likely to become Jewish educators. Designing initiatives that target groups and individuals who match the characteristics of successful Jewish educators—engagement in Jewish life, Jewish educational background, participation in youth group, camp, or Israel programs, and experience working in Jewish educational institutions—will benefit the community for years to come. Recruitment programs should target both first- and second-career individuals.

FUTURE RESEARCH QUESTIONS AND TOPICS

Current studies have expanded our understanding of Jewish educators in the three formal educational settings—days schools, congregational schools, and early childhood centers. But there is much more to be learned. Further research on issues relating to recruitment, retention, and professional learning will have direct impact on the quality of Jewish learning in the schools. Among the more important research questions and topics are:

- What is the connection between different types of professional development programs and excellence in the educational setting?

- What are the factors that affect educator longevity in an institution? In the field?

- What is the profile of Jewish educators in informal settings (camp, youth group, Israel experiences, retreats or trips, etc.), adult education, Judaic studies and Hebrew studies faculty, central agencies for Jewish education, and national organizations? How do they compare to one another and to formal Jewish educators?

- What factors link the career paths of Jewish educators across both formal and informal educational experiences?

- A longitudinal study of Jewish educator's experiences in the field, including tracking their career paths, will inform future initiatives for recruitment and retention of educators.

- What factors attract people to choose a second career in Jewish education and/or Jewish communal life? Are there certain experiences, such as participating in intensive Jewish study, fulfilling lay leadership roles in Jewish education, or traveling to Israel, that provide opportunities for future recruitment?

- What are the factors that contribute to educators successfully transitioning from the classroom to administrative roles?

FUTURE DIRECTIONS

Systemic change on the national, communal and institutional levels is required to attract, support, and retain outstanding Jewish educational personnel. Quality educators are essential in creating compelling Jewish educational visions for learners of all ages. In order to recruit and retain qualified educators, every aspect of the culture must become responsive to the needs and concerns of the educators, including levels of compensation, benefits, expectations and support for ongoing professional development, including degree and credential acquisition. Only then will the Jewish community feel comfortable and confident that it has done its best to prepare and support personnel who can deliver an excellent quality of Jewish education to all learners. Among the multitude of initiatives that should be at the top of the agenda are:

- With strong communal support, salaries and benefits must be increased significantly if we are to attract and retain quality personnel.
- Opportunities for quality and meaningful professional development for all Jewish educators in the areas of pedagogy and Jewish content must be offered at times and in venues where the educators will participate.
- Induction and mentoring programs for new teachers and Jewish educators in new positions must become standard in the Jewish community.
- Significant financial assistance must be provided for Jewish educators to obtain degrees and/or licenses in Judaic studies and in education to meet the standard of being credentialed in both.

CONCLUSION

While more studies of Jewish educators exist now than when *What We Know about Jewish Education* first appeared, gaps remain in what we know about Jewish educational personnel. Most recent studies focus predominantly on formal educators, leaving out the entire field of informal Jewish education. With the support of JESNA, a major national study is underway that will provide extensive data on the educators in day and congregational schools; however, early childhood educators, informal educators, and adult educators were not included in the study process. As part of their own planning process, several local communities are conducting studies of Jewish educators as an important step in making policy decisions designed to raise the quality of Jewish education. Without better data on both the local and national levels that crosses all venues of Jewish education, opportunities to create change that will impact the quality of the educational process will be severely limited. Despite this gap, it is clear that increased salaries and benefits, quality professional development, and increased standards for Jewish educators emphasizing degrees and licensure will raise the quality of Jewish educators and the field of Jewish education.

HIGHLIGHTS

- The range, variety, and number of personnel studies increased during the first decade of the 21st century, with most focusing on formal Jewish educators working with children.
- Significant numbers of Jewish educators view themselves as career-oriented professionals committed to advancing the quality of Jewish education in their settings.
- Salaries and benefits matter for educators in all three formal educational settings—day schools, congregational schools, and early childhood Jewish educational programs.
- Serious challenges have emerged as a result of an increasing number of non–Jews becoming teachers and educational leaders in early childhood Jewish education and in day schools, as they have direct responsibility for conveying Jewish content and cultivating a vision of Jewish life.
- The standard of having Jewish educators with credentials in both Judaic studies and education has not been achieved.
- Continuing professional development in pedagogy and Judaic studies (adult learning) is slowly becoming the norm for congregational school educators in a small number of communities.
- Early childhood Jewish educators fall far below day school and congregational school educators in terms of educational background, both Jewish and general, and compensation.
- With approximately 25% of all Jewish educators in day schools and congregations new to their positions each year, there is a significant need to establish effective recruitment and retention programs.

- As the majority of Jewish educators consider themselves professionals engaged in a meaningful long-term career, investment in their professional growth and development will have a positive impact on the quality of Jewish education.
- Most Jewish educators share a common background that makes them well suited for their roles: formal Jewish education as a child, teen and adult, participation in youth group and Jewish camp, travel to Israel, college-level Jewish studies classes, and employment in Jewish education as a teen or college student.
- The opportunity to work with children is the major reason that school personnel initially take positions in Jewish education.

LARGER CONTEXT

Jewish education is critical to the vitality and continuity of Jewish life. This means that the more Jewish education, the stronger the likelihood of one's connection to Jewish life. A strong educational system depends to a great extent on having a cadre of top-level Jewish educators (Bidol-Padva et al. 2007). Insights into the issues related to Jewish educational professionals are important to raising the quality of the field.

The studies of Jewish educators have helped provide a better understanding of who they are as a group. They have informed policies and program development that have helped to strengthen the qualifications and effectiveness of personnel. Yet these studies tend to be sporadic, often difficult to compare and they do not provide a complete picture of how many educators there are, much less a consistent and detailed characterization of all educators in both formal and informal education. The field would benefit from its own "National Jewish Educators Study" every five or ten years in order to provide a more complete picture, including a comparison to the overall Jewish population. Professional development programs for Jewish educators need to be evaluated for their impact on the quality of the education provided and how they affect the recruitment and retention of Jewish educators. More significantly, what is lacking is research that directly connects personnel studies and professional development programs to the quality of Jewish education. The current JESNA study of Jewish educators that connects their actions and attitudes to the culture of their institutions and educational change will be a powerful way of linking personnel studies to raising the quality of Jewish education, striving for excellence.

ANNOTATED BIBLIOGRAPHY

A Time to Act (1990). NY: The Report of the Commission on Jewish Education in North America. A report of the task force created by philanthropist Mort Mandel that focused on the importance of Jewish educators in raising the quality of Jewish education, thereby strengthening Jewish continuity.

Ben-Avie, M. & Kress, J. (2006). *The Educators in Jewish Schools Study: Preliminary Findings from a Registry of Day and Congregational/Supplemental Schools in North America.* New York: JESNA. Sponsored by JESNA, this study will be the first comprehensive study of day schools and congregational schools in the United States. The study is designed to provide information on the quality of life of Jewish educators that can lead to school change.

Kelner, S., Rabkin, M., Saxe, L. & Sheingold, C. (2005). *The Jewish Sector's Workforce: Report of a Six-Community Study. Professional Leaders Project*, Report No. 2. Waltham, MA: Cohen Center for Modern Jewish Studies, Brandeis University. Jewish educators are just one of the types of Jewish communal service workers investigated in this study allowing for comparisons within this larger field.

Lortie, D. (1975) *Schoolteacher.* Chicago: University of Chicago Press. Lortie's work on teachers is a classic. His work provides many theoretical constructs and concepts found in the work of several of the Jewish personnel studies.

Policy Brief: Background and Professional Training of Teachers in Jewish Schools (1994). NY: Council for Initiatives in Jewish Education. This study was the first "national" study of formal Jewish educators in day schools, congregational schools, and early childhood programs. It covered three communities: Atlanta, Baltimore, and Milwaukee, instead of one community, as was typical of the preceding studies. This study drew on the work of Dan Lortie in his portrayal of teachers in the public schools in the 1970s. Many of the questions in that study are utilized today in a wide range of studies of Jewish educators.

REFERENCES

A Time to Act (1990). New York, NY: The Report of the Commission on Jewish Education in North America.

Aron, I. (1988). "From Where Will the Next Generation of Jewish Teachers Come?" *Journal of Reform Judaism* 35, 51–66.

Ben-Avie, M. & Kress, J. (2006). *The Educators in Jewish Schools Study: Preliminary Findings from a Registry of Day and Congregational/Supplemental Schools in North America.* New York: JESNA.

Center for Policy Research (2006a). *Jewish Early Childhood Education in Denver and Boulder: Mapping the Field Final Report.* Denver, CO: Center for Policy Research.

Center for Policy Research (2006b). *Jewish Early Childhood Education in Denver and Boulder: Mapping the Field Executive Summary.* Denver, CO: Center for Policy Research.

Goodman, R., Padva, P.B. & Schaap, E. (2006). *Community Report on Early Childhood Jewish Educators: Culture of Employment 2004–2005 Miami-Dade and Broward Counties, Florida.* New York: CAJE.

Goodman, R., Schaap, E. & Ackerman, A. (2002). *What are the Numbers of Jewish Educators and Students in Formal Jewish Educational Settings?* http://www.caje-cbank.org/research-njps2.pdf

Goodman, R., & Schaap, E. (2006a). *Jewish Heroes Wanted: Inquire Within an Advocacy Campaign for the Recruitment and Retention of Congregational Teachers.* Report submitted to CAJE St. Louis.

Goodman, R., & Schaap, E. (2006b). CAJE St. Louis Project JERRI, Education Director Survey, Perceptions of Congregational Education and Educators.

Goodman, R. (2000). *Recruitment of College Students into the Field of Jewish Education: An Evaluation of Two Programs: CAJE Schusterman Program and JESNA's Lainer Interns for Jewish Education.* Tulsa, OK: Schusterman Foundation.

Guarino, C., Santebanez, L., Daley, G. & Brewer, D. (2004). *A Review of the Research Literature on Teacher Recruitment and Retention.* Santa Monica, CA: Rand Corporation.

Herzenberg, S., Price, M. & Bradley, D. (2005). *Losing Ground in Early Childhood Education: Declining Workforce Qualifications in an Expanding Industry 1979–2004.* Washington D.C.: Economic Policy Institute.

Ingersoll, R. M. (2001). "Teacher Turnover and Teacher Shortages: An Organizational Analysis". *American Educational Research Journal* 38 (3), 499–534.

Joseph, S. K. (1997). *Portraits of Schooling: A Survey and an Analysis of Supplementary Schooling in Congregations.* New York: UAHC Press.

Kelner, S., Rabkin, M., Saxe, L. & Sheingold, C. (2005). *The Jewish Sector's Workforce: Report of a Six-Community Study, Professional Leaders Project, Report No. 2.* Waltham, MA: Cohen Center for Modern Jewish Studies, Brandeis University.

Lortie, D. (1975). *Schoolteacher.* Chicago: University of Chicago Press.

Padva, P. B., Schaap, E. & Goodman, R. (2007). *Project Kavod. Executive Summary of the Final Report.* New York: CAJE.

Policy Brief: Background and Professional Training of Teachers in Jewish Schools (1994). New York, NY: Council for Initiatives in Jewish Education.

Pomson, A. (2001). *Between Calling and Career: A Study of the Working Lives of Jewish Day School Teachers.* Jerusalem, Israel: Paper presented at the 13th World Congress for Jewish Studies.

Rosenbaum, J. & Tigay, H. (2002). "Jewish Education in Philadelphia: Historic Precedents and New Observations." *Journal of Jewish Communal Service* 78, 187–203.

Schaap, E. & Goodman, R. (2004). *Recruitment of College Students into the Field of Jewish Education: A Study of the CAJE Schusterman College Program Alumni.* New York: CAJE.

Tammivaara, J., & Goodman, R. (1996a). Professional Lives of Jewish Educators in Washington State. In *Planning for Jewish Education in Washington State,* prepared for the Samis Foundation. Seattle, WA: The Jewish Education Council of the Jewish Federation of Greater Seattle.

Tammivaara, J. & Goodman, R. (1996b). *Professional Lives of Jewish Educators in Cleveland 1995–1996.* Cleveland, OH: Jewish Education Center of Cleveland.

Vogelstein, I. & Kaplan, D. (2002). *Jewish Early Childhood Education Study Highlights.* Baltimore: JECEP.

Learning to Teach

Sharon Feiman-Nemser

> How one frames the learning-to-teach question depends a great deal on how one conceives of what needs to be learned and how that learning might take place (Carter 1990, p. 307).

Each year thousands of Jewish teachers assume responsibility for the learning of Jewish children and youth in congregational schools, day schools, early childhood programs, camps, Israel programs and other educational settings. These teachers vary greatly in the knowledge, skills and experiences they bring and in the preparation they have for the challenging and consequential work of teaching. Some have a background in Jewish studies but little or no pedagogical training. Others have pedagogical training but limited subject matter knowledge. Few have access to serious induction support during their early years of teaching or to the kinds of ongoing professional learning opportunities that encourage retention and enable teachers to develop an effective and satisfying teaching practice. Most rely on images and strategies absorbed from their own Jewish education, gained through experience, and acquired through isolated workshops and seminars.

There are many reasons for these patterns—the part-time nature of the work, inadequate funding for professional education, low salaries, no coherent system of continuing education, the poor status of teachers in general and Jewish teachers in particular. Besides these structural factors, widely held beliefs about teaching and learning to teach work against the provision of adequate resources and opportunities for Jewish teacher learning. Many people believe that good teachers are born, not made, that people who know their subjects can teach them, that teaching is easy work learned mostly on the job. These naïve views may contain a grain of truth, but they also reflect a limited understanding of what teaching entails and how people learn to do it well.

We all know gifted teachers who seem to be "naturals," but we don't know how they became good teachers. We may know experts who are skilled at representing complex ideas in accessible ways, but we also know experts who have a very difficult time explaining what they know to others. People assume that teaching is easy because teachers have a short work day and a long summer vacation or because they equate teaching with telling and learning with listening. Would they also assume that conducting an orchestra is easy because it looks as if all a conductor does is stand in front of the musicians and wave his hands in time to the music? If those same people spent even one day trying to teach multiple subjects to a group of diverse learners, they would begin to appreciate that teaching is complex, multidimensional work that requires considerable knowledge and skill. While it is true that learning to teach depends on experience, practice alone does not make perfect. As John Dewey explained over a century ago, people learn not by doing, but by thinking about what they are doing. To learn well from experience, teachers need time, space and frameworks to analyze their teaching and its effects on students.

This chapter focuses on what we know about learning to teach and what it implies for the field of Jewish education. I addressed the same topic fifteen years ago in the predecessor to this volume (Feiman-Nemser 1992). During the intervening years teacher learning emerged as an important area of research, fueled by new developments in learning theory, new understandings of teaching, and a broad professionalization agenda. As Cochran-Smith and Fries (2005) point out in their history of empirical research on teacher education, between 1980 and 2000 "the concepts and language of 'learning to teach' more or less replaced the language of 'teacher training'." Higher standards for teachers appeared alongside higher standards for students. More ambitious teaching and learning required far more ambitious teacher education, since teachers could not be expected to teach what they themselves did not know and understand, or to teach in ways that they had never experienced or studied (National Commission on Teaching and America's Future 1996). This led to the creation of more coherent and intensive teacher education programs (Darling-Hammond 2000; Carroll et al. 2007), more robust professional development opportunities (Lieberman 1996; Little 1999) and more research on teacher education and teacher learning (Cochran-Smith and Zeichner 2005). In the current climate of accountability, researchers and policy makers want to know what teacher education contributes to teacher effectiveness and how teacher learning improves student learning.

While there is much that we do not know about learning to teach in general and learning to teach in Jewish educational settings, the research base is growing, and we have a more dependable basis for shaping programs and policies. This discussion is organized around three questions: (1) What do teachers need to learn? (2) How do teachers develop their practice? (3) What kinds of teacher education and professional development opportunities help teachers learn what they need to know and use it in their teaching? As these questions suggest, the phrase "learning to teach" requires a consideration of the content, processes, opportunities and contexts of teacher learning. After highlighting what research has to say about these matters, I consider key policy implications for Jewish education and pressing research questions.

WHAT DO TEACHERS NEED TO LEARN?

When we think of what teachers need to learn, we automatically think about subject matter knowledge. Clearly teachers need to understand the subjects they teach, and there has been important research in the past twenty years on what subject matter knowledge for teaching entails and what it consists of in particular subject areas.[1] But teachers need more than subject matter knowledge; in fact, they need more than knowledge. The quest to define the knowledge, skills and dispositions required for effective teaching has gone on for a long time, and no definitive consensus has emerged. Still, there is considerable overlap in recent efforts to outline what teachers need to know, care about and be able to do.[2]

I recently proposed a framework for learning to teach organized around four broad themes—learning to *think* like a teacher, learning to *know* like a teacher, learning to *feel* like a teacher, and learning to *act* like a teacher (see introduction to the section on "Teacher Learning" in Cochran-Smith et al. 2008; Feiman-Nemser 1983; 2001: Feiman-Nemser & Remillard 1996). This framework builds on findings from research on teaching and teacher learning and highlights the interactions between the content and processes of teacher learning.

The first theme—learning to think like a teacher—underscores the intellectual work of teaching and highlights the ways in which teachers' beliefs shape their actions and how they interpret experience. Learning to think like a teacher means moving beyond naïve theories—for example, that teaching involves the simple transfer of information from teacher to students—to embrace more defensible views of teaching and learning. It means learning to think pedagogically, connecting learning activities to learning outcomes. It means developing the capacity to think on one's feet and reflect on one's practice.

The second theme—learning to know like a teacher—points to the different kinds of knowledge that good teaching depends on. A recent effort to describe what teachers need to know, sponsored by the National Academy of Education, identifies three broad areas of knowledge for teaching, (1) knowl-

---

[1] Researchers have conceptualized the content knowledge and pedagogical content knowledge that teachers need to teach particular subjects (e.g., mathematics, writing, reading, history/social studies, science) to diverse learners. They have also shown that majoring in a subject does not guarantee that teachers have the requisite knowledge and understanding to teach that subject.

[2] There have been significant efforts to compile research on teaching and teacher education in a series of Handbooks of Research on Teaching and Handbooks of Research in Teacher Education. In addition, national organizations like the National Board for Professional Teaching Standards (NBPTS) and the New Teacher Assessment and Support Consortium (INTASC) have developed professional teaching standards that build on this research and on the wisdom of practice to describe what accomplished and beginning teachers need to know and be able to do in order to teach challenging content to diverse learners.

edge of learners and learning; (2) knowledge of curricular goals and content; and (3) knowledge of instruction, assessment and classroom organization (Darling-Hammond & Bransford 2005). In addition to knowledge *for* teaching, teachers need knowledge *of* teaching which can only be gained in the context of their work. This includes local knowledge of the community, curriculum, school norms and policies, and knowledge of particular students—who they are, what ideas, interests and life experiences they bring, what they find difficult or confusing. As Ball and Cohen (1999) explain: "Teaching occurs in particulars—particular students interacting with particular teachers over particular ideas in particular circumstances...no amount of knowledge can fully prescribe appropriate or wise practice" (p. 10). Although teachers may anticipate ahead of time what problems students may have, they cannot know ahead of time how individual students will make sense of their learning.

The third theme—learning to feel like a teacher—reminds us that teaching and learning to teach are deeply personal work rooted in teachers' emotions, values and identity. Beginning teachers form a professional identity by combining parts of their past, including their own experiences in school and in teacher preparation, with pieces of the present in their current school context, with images of the kind of teacher and colleague they want to become and the kind of classroom they want to create (Featherstone 1993). Often they struggle to reconcile competing images of their role as authority and friend, instructor and nurturer.

Ultimately teachers must integrate ways of thinking, knowing, feeling and acting into a principled and responsive practice. Inside the classroom teachers engage in a wide range of activities—explaining, listening, questioning, managing, demonstrating, assessing, inspiring. Out of the classroom teachers must plan for teaching, collaborate with colleagues, work with parents and administrators. The complex, uncertain, multidimensional nature of teaching exacerbates what Kennedy (1999) calls "the problem of enactment"—putting one's intentions into action.

To act like a teacher, a teacher needs a repertoire of skills, routines and strategies and the capacity to figure out what to do in changing circumstances. The normal busyness of classrooms requires the establishment of routines to make teaching manageable. At the same time, the unpredictability of teaching means that teachers are constantly taking in new information from their immediate surroundings and using it to inform their decisions and actions. So learning to act like a teacher means developing what cognitive scientists call "adaptive expertise" (Hatano & Oura 2003).

HOW DO TEACHERS DEVELOP THEIR PRACTICE?

New understandings about how people learn from cognitive science are exerting a profound influence on our understanding of how teachers learn to teach and develop their practice over time. These include theories about the active, situated nature of learning and about the development of expertise. Such ideas challenge the "naturalistic" view that teachers automatically absorb appropriate lessons from experience and the "training" view that teachers acquire knowledge and skills in courses and workshops that they then apply in the classroom.

In a review of research on learning to teach, Borko and Putman (1996) offer a succinct definition of learning from a cognitive science perspective. Learning is

> an active, constructive process that is heavily influenced by an individual's existing knowledge and beliefs and is situated in particular contexts...For knowledge to be useful for teaching, it must be integrally linked to, or situated in, the contexts in which it is to be used (pp. 674–675).

The definition highlights two key ideas. Learning is not a passive process of absorbing new information. Rather teachers, like all learners, construct new knowledge and understanding on the basis of what they already know and believe. What teachers learn is also influenced by the contexts where new knowledge is acquired and used. These ideas have important implications for the study and support of teacher learning and the improvement of teaching.

A significant body of research documents the beliefs that teachers hold and how they shape what teachers do and do not learn from teacher education and teaching (for a review, see Wideen et al. 1998). From their years of teacher watching and growing up in the culture, teachers form beliefs about what teaching is like, how children learn, what should be taught, etc. These beliefs serve as interpretive lenses, shaping what teachers learn from professional studies and teaching experience. Without an opportunity to examine critically their existing beliefs in light of new possibilities and understandings, teachers may ignore or distort new ideas and practices. Thus any effort to help teachers change their practice in significant ways must also help them acquire new knowledge and beliefs.

Research has also deepened our understanding of how social and cultural contexts influence learning (Brown, Collins & Duguid 1989; Lave & Wenger 1991). Socio-cultural theorists challenge the view that knowledge and skills exist independently of the contexts in which they are acquired. All knowledge, they claim, is socially mediated and situated in the contexts of its use. So, for example, we come to understand concepts like teaching, learning, content, and knowing through our interactions with others in the organizations and communities we participate in. The institutional norms and tools we encounter as part of these interactions shape what we can and cannot do and we, in turn, shape those norms and tools. The concept of "situated learning" helps explain why teachers may have difficulty transforming what they learn in university courses and professional development workshops for use in their teaching.

Socio-cultural perspectives are particularly helpful in longitudinal studies of learning to teach because they focus attention on how the various settings in which teachers learn—university courses, student teaching, schools and classrooms—enable and constrain their adoption and use of new knowledge and practices and their ongoing learning. In one study, for example, researchers (Grossman et al. 2000) followed a group of beginning elementary and secondary teachers from their last year of teacher education through their first three years of teaching. They found that the teachers used the reflective stance they had developed during their teacher education program to make sense of their teaching situation. Although some struggled as first-year teachers, by the second year most were able to use specific pedagogical tools (e.g., Writers Workshop) they had learned about in teacher education. The research team also identified particular aspects of the school and district context, including access to curricular materials and professional development opportunities, which dramatically affected teachers' on-the-job learning and their ability to use ideas and strategies introduced in teacher education. The researchers' conclusions emphasize the important role of teacher education in cultivating the skills and dispositions for continued learning:

> All of these teachers are off to a strong start in teaching…Although they are still very much learning to teach writing, teacher education provided these teachers with a set of tools with which to continue their learning and refine their practice. In the relatively brief time allotted for the professional preparation of teachers, providing tools that enable teachers to continue their development may be the most important legacy of all (p. 660).

Another area of cognitive science research that illuminates the process of learning to teach is the study of expertise and how it develops. Research comparing novice and expert teachers highlights the importance of having rich knowledge and well-rehearsed routines to manage classrooms, conduct lessons, interpret classroom events and act appropriately as well as the capacity to respond to unfamiliar problems with flexibility and innovation. Building on studies of expertise in other fields, Berliner (1986) proposes that teachers progress through five stages: novice, advanced beginner, competent, proficient and expert. This model is an important reminder that expertise in teaching is not acquired overnight and that it depends on teachers' developing the capacity to balance efficiency and innovation, a combination captured in the concept of "adaptive expertise" (Hatano and Oura 2003).

Growing interest in teachers as adaptive experts (Darling-Hammond & Bransford 2005) coincides with increasing attention to the idea of a continuum of teacher learning across the stages of preparation, induction and continuing career development (Feiman-Nemser 2001). Viewing teacher development in this way emphasizes the nature and timing of learning opportunities for teachers and highlights the absence of coordination and collaboration at key transition points along the continuum.

WHAT ARE THE IMPLICATIONS FOR TEACHER EDUCATION AND PROFESSIONAL DEVELOPMENT?

By and large, opportunities for teacher learning are not well aligned with what we know about teaching and learning to teach. Typically teacher education programs offer a collection of unrelated courses and field experiences. Until recently, most new teachers had to "sink or swim" on their own. And professional development consisted of inspirational lectures and one-shot workshops with no follow-up. Wilson and Berne (1999) summarize the state of affairs as follows: "Teacher learning has traditionally been a patchwork of opportunities, formal and informal, mandatory and voluntary, serendipitous and planned—stitched together into a fragmented and incoherent curriculum" (p. 174).

Since the late 1980s, however, teacher education reforms have led to more integrated and coherent programs of teacher preparation (Darling-Hammond 2000; Carroll et al. 2007). Concerns about teacher shortages and quality teaching have fueled a growing interest in mentoring and new teacher induction (Fideler & Haselkorn 2000; Johnson et al. 2003). And, professional development focused on teaching and learning, and situated in communities of practice, has been promoted by researchers and reformers (Little 1996; Lieberman 1999). Despite significant gaps in our knowledge of how teacher education and professional development lead to powerful teaching and learning, research suggests some design principles that seem to make a difference.

A continuum of learning opportunities. Learning to teach happens over time. It follows that teachers need access to professional learning opportunities geared to their stage of readiness. Teacher preparation can lay a critical foundation in knowledge, skills and commitments, including the capacity to learn from teaching. Beginning teachers need regular, supported opportunities to learn to teach in the company of more experienced colleagues. This includes opportunities to observe and be observed, to co-plan, to analyze student work and to reflect on their teaching. Experienced teachers also need opportunities to extend their subject matter knowledge, strengthen their repertoire, and gain the flexibility and depth that high-quality teaching entails.

Knowledge connected to practice. Teachers need to know about many things, including subject matter, learning, students, curriculum, and pedagogy. But such knowledge cannot remain in separate domains if it is going to be usable. Teachers need a conceptual map to help them understand how different kinds of knowledge fit together and how they relate to teaching performance. They also need a vision of good teaching to guide their work and direct their learning. Such a vision connects important values and goals to concrete classroom practices.

Transforming beliefs. Teachers' prior knowledge and beliefs play a paradoxical role in teacher learning—they are both an obstacle to change and a target of change. Prospective and practicing teachers need opportunities to uncover, examine and, in some cases, revise their taken-for-granted beliefs about teaching and learning lest those beliefs unconsciously shape what they do and how they make sense of their experiences.

Learning situated "in" practice. Experience is a powerful teacher in learning to teach, but it is not always a good teacher, often resulting in a perpetuation of the status quo. To learn effective ways of working with students, teachers need opportunities to see recommended practices, try them with guidance, and analyze the results. Powerful teacher learning can also be situated in records of practice such as classroom videotapes, instructional plans and assessments, and samples of student work, which do not evaporate like firsthand experience and which make it possible for teachers to study their teaching and its effects on students (Ball & Cohen 2000).

Critical colleagueship. There is growing evidence that improvements in teaching are most likely to occur in schools where teachers work together (Little 1999). Whether the focus is on novices learning to teach in the company of mentors or teachers at different career stages coming together to develop curriculum, discuss problems of practice or implement a new instructional program, researchers are demonstrating the power (some would say necessity) of collective activity to strengthen teaching and enhance student learning. Collaboration alone is not sufficient to improve teaching; rather, teachers need to adopt a critical stance toward teaching and develop norms that support questioning, respect for evidence, and openness to diverse perspectives.

IMPLICATIONS FOR JEWISH EDUCATION POLICY

In the field of Jewish education, a diverse group of people influence policies that affect the preparation, induction and continuing development of Jewish teachers. This includes philanthropists who decide whether and how to fund teacher development initiatives, educational leaders responsible for hiring and supporting teachers, heads of schools who allocate time, money and other resources for teacher development, professors of Jewish education who set standards and determine program requirements, and directors of communal, denominational and national organizations devoted to Jewish education. If this diverse group became advocates for serious Jewish teacher development, they could transform the quality of teaching and learning in Jewish educational settings. There are three policy implications that flow from our understanding of learning to teach and that support this goal.

I. EDUCATE LAY LEADERS AND PROFESSIONALS ABOUT THE CRITICAL RELATIONSHIP BETWEEN HIGH-QUALITY TEACHING AND HIGH-QUALITY PROFESSIONAL DEVELOPMENT.

What students learn is a function of what teachers teach, and what teachers teach is a function of what they know, care about and do. If we want more powerful and engaged learning on the part of Jewish children and youth, then we need to provide more powerful and engaged learning opportunities for their teachers. Lay and professional leaders may hold naïve views of learning to teach or underestimate the value of serious and sustained professional development. As they come to appreciate the centrality of teacher learning to the vitality of Jewish education, they will be more likely to advocate for policies that support teacher learning across career stages.

2. SUPPORT MULTIPLE PATHWAYS TO JEWISH TEACHING.

In order to insure an adequate supply of well-qualified teachers for Jewish schools and other educational settings, we need to create various pathways to teaching. Geared to the performance requirements of different educational settings, these pathways would support teachers' own Jewish journeys while enabling them to gain the kind of Judaic and professional knowledge and skills needed to create substantive and engaging learning opportunities for Jewish children and youth. No one who wants to become a Jewish educator or teach in a Jewish school should have to incur significant debt to acquire the necessary training.

3. PROVIDE CAREER-LONG TEACHER DEVELOPMENT ALIGNED WITH WHAT WE KNOW ABOUT GOOD TEACHING AND HOW IT CAN BE NURTURED.

The link between recruitment and retention in teaching is professional preparation and development. When Jewish schools hire teachers without preparation, they take on the added task of teacher development. Under the best circumstances, teachers with basic knowledge and skills would be inducted into a school culture that supports their continuing development. When Jewish schools create conditions that help new teachers thrive, they create a professional culture that enables all teachers to feel supported and stimulated in their work. All teachers need formal and informal opportunities inside and outside school to strengthen and extend their knowledge and skills and their commitment to the transformative work of Jewish teaching. Policies that promote the professional development of novice and veteran teachers contribute to teacher retention and renewal.

RESEARCH QUESTIONS

What we know about learning to teach derives from research in general education and public schooling. We have very little knowledge about the background, working conditions, career trajectories, professional development opportunities, and teaching practices of teachers in Jewish schools or of Jewish educators in other formal and informal settings. Below are some questions that require the serious attention of researchers interested in producing knowledge about the practice of teaching in Jewish educational settings and the learning of Jewish educators.

1. What do teachers need to know, care about and be able to do to perform the work of Jewish education in different settings? What do they need to know and be able to do to teach particular subjects to particular students in particular settings?

2. What professional learning opportunities are available for people who teach or who want to teach in Jewish educational settings? What do they cost? Who participates? What are their underlying views of teaching and learning to teach? To what extent do they reflect best practices in teacher education and professional development?

3. What do teachers actually learn from different professional development opportunities? To what extent do teachers use what they learn in their teaching? Under what conditions are teachers enabled to use or constrained from using knowledge and skills encountered in professional education in their work?

4. Do the working conditions in Jewish schools and other educational settings promote (or inhibit) teacher collaboration and teacher learning? What can we learn from studying schools with strong professional cultures about how to create working conditions that foster teacher learning?

5. How do teacher education and professional development for Jewish teachers affect student learning? Are there differences in the learning opportunities provided and the learning outcomes produced between teachers with different kinds of background, preparation and support?

Looking back at research programs and paradigms focused on teaching, Shulman (2002) notes that researchers took into account "the three C's of content, cognition and context" but ignored "the fourth C, consequences for students" (p. 251). This assessment applies to research on teacher learning that, until recently, focused on whether and how teacher education and professional development produce changes in teachers' knowledge, skills and dispositions. In the current climate of accountability, researchers are expected to consider the consequences, linking what teachers learn to what teachers do in their teaching and how that, in turn, influences what students learn. In Jewish education we still need to answer basic questions about each link in this chain of learning before we can tackle the question of how they fit together.

CONCLUSION

Learning to teach well takes time. According to most theories of teacher development, it takes three to five years to consolidate a teaching practice and five to seven years to achieve mastery. Unfortunately, a significant number of teachers leave the field before they achieve competence, let alone mastery. Furthermore, what teachers learn from teaching is powerfully shaped by the knowledge, understandings, skills and commitments they bring to their work, and by the professional culture and learning opportunities they encounter.

This chapter focuses on what we know about learning to teach and what this means for Jewish education. It is organized around the following questions: (1) What do teachers need to learn? (2) How do teachers develop their practice? (3) What kinds of teacher education and professional development opportunities help teachers learn what they need to know and use in their teaching? The chapter challenges "naïve" views of teaching and learning to teach, replacing them with more dependable views derived from research on teaching, learning and learning to teach. It argues for a continuum of professional learning opportunities geared to the changing needs of teachers at each stage in their career. It identifies research questions about Jewish teacher learning and outlines policy implications for Jewish education.

HIGHLIGHTS OF THE CHAPTER

- Teachers cannot teach what they do not know, nor can they teach in ways they have never seen or experienced.
- If we want more powerful learning on the part of Jewish children and youth, we need to provide more powerful learning opportunities for their teachers.

- Most opportunities for teacher learning do not reflect what we know about teaching and learning to teach.

- What links teacher recruitment and retention are teacher preparation, new teacher induction, and continuing professional development.

- Teachers need formal and informal opportunities both in and out of school to strengthen and extend their knowledge, skills and commitments and their vision of powerful teaching and learning.

- We have little systematic knowledge about who teaches in Jewish schools and other educating settings, what backgrounds they bring, how long they have taught and plan to stay in teaching, what they actually teach and what their students learn.

LARGER CONTEXT

The shortage of well-qualified teachers is a perennial problem in Jewish education and goes hand in hand with the practice of hiring teachers without professional preparation and/or Judaic background. If lay and professional leaders want to improve the quality of teaching and learning in Jewish schools and other educational settings, they must take the preparation, induction and ongoing development of Jewish educators seriously. This will require commitment, leadership and financial resources at national and community levels.

In general education, for example, educators and policy makers are starting to realize that serious support for beginning teachers is a critical component in a comprehensive approach to teacher development. For decades, new teachers were left to "sink or swim" on their own, with the result that up to 50% left teaching within the first three to five years on the job. and those who remained often clung to practices that helped them survive but did not represent "best practice." Educational leaders are beginning to acknowledge that new teachers, no matter what their background and preparation, are still learning to teach. Researchers are demonstrating that serious induction and mentoring can reduce teacher attrition and improve the quality of teaching. Across the country, states, districts and schools are providing some kind of induction support for beginning teachers, usually in the form of mentoring.

What would it take to extend the idea of new teacher induction to the non-system of Jewish education? First, lay and professional leaders would have to understand why new teachers need on-site support and guidance and what the costs and benefits were likely to be so that they could become advocates for such a policy and practice. Second, communities and institutions would have to develop cost-effective strategies for building capacity to promote new teacher learning. Third, it would be wise if funders supported design experiments to develop working models adapted to the differing realities of day schools, congregational schools, and early childhood programs. This coordination of policy, research and practice is often difficult to achieve in Jewish education.

Most people agree that good teachers can make an important difference in the lives and learning of students. There is no similar consensus about the influence of teacher education on the quality of teachers and teaching. Until we take teachers and their learning seriously, we are unlikely to get the kind of transformative education that Jewish children and youth deserve. We know enough about learning to teach and about the value of serious, content-rich, practice-centered, identity-forming teacher development to make this a priority in the operation of schools, the allocation of funds, and the support of research in Jewish education.

ANNOTATED BIBLIOGRAPHY

Darling-Hammond, L. & Bransford, J. (eds.) (2005). *Preparing Teachers for a Changing World: What Teachers Should Learn and Be Able to Do*. San Francisco: Jossey-Bass. Sponsored by the National Academy of Education, this book outlines core concepts and strategies that should inform initial teacher preparation in both traditional and nontraditional settings. It is intended primarily for those responsible for the preparation of teachers. The recommendations were developed through professional and scholarly consensus based on research about learning, teaching, teacher learning and teacher education.

Feiman-Nemser, S. (2001). From preparation to practice: Designing a continuum to strengthen and sustain teaching. *Teachers College Record*, 103(6), 1013–1055. Based on the reality that learning to teach well happens over time, this article proposes central tasks in teacher learning at the pre-service, induction and in-service stages. It also considers core challenges and promising practices in teacher education, new teacher induction and professional development.

Johnson, S. and the Project on the Next Generation of Teachers (2007). *Finders and Keepers: Helping New Teachers Survive and Thrive in Our Schools*. San Francisco, CA: Jossey-Bass. Based on a longitudinal study of fifty new teachers during their first years in the classroom, this book provides valuable insights about the challenges of beginning teaching and the impact of working conditions on new teachers' decisions to stay or move on to other schools or other lines of work. It underscores the importance of the school site and the crucial role that principals and experienced teachers play in the effective induction and development of new teachers.

REFERENCES

Ball, D. & Cohen, D. (1999). Developing practice, developing practitioners: Toward a practice-based theory of professional education.. In L. Darling-Hammond & G. Sykes (Eds.), *Teaching as the Learning Profession: Handbook of Policy and Practice*. San Francisco: Jossey-Bass, 3–32.

Berliner, D. (1986). In pursuit of the expert pedagogue. *Educational Researcher* 15 (7), 5–13.

Borko, H. & Putnam, R. (1996). Learning to teach. In D. Berliner & R. Calfee (eds.), *Handbook of Educational Psychology*. NY: Macmillan, 673–708

Brown, J.S., Collins, A. & Duguid, P. (1989). Situated cognition and the culture of learning. *Educational Researcher* 18 (1), 32–42.

Carroll, D., Featherstone, J., Featherstone, H., Feiman-Nemser, S. & Roosevelt, D. (eds.) (2007). *Transforming Teacher Education: Reflections from the Field*. Cambridge, MA: Harvard Education Press.

Carter, K. (1990). Teachers' knowledge and learning to teach. In W.R. Houston, M. Haberman, & J.P. Sikula (eds.), *Handbook of Research on Teacher Education*. New York: Collier Macmillan, 291–310.

Cochran-Smith, M. & Fries, K. (2005). Researching teacher education in changing times: Politics and paradigms. In M. Cochran-Smith & K. Zeichner (eds.), *Studying Teacher Education: The Report of the AERA Panel on Research and Teacher Education*. Mahwah, NJ: Lawrence Erlbaum, 69–109.

Cochran-Smith, M. & Zeichner, K. (2005) (eds.), *Studying Teacher Education: The Report of the AERA Panel on Research and Teacher Education*. Mahway, NJ: Lawrence Erlbaum.

Cochran-Smith, M., Feiman-Nemser, S. & McIntyre, J. (2008) (eds.), *Handbook of Research on Teacher Education: Enduring Issues in Changing Contexts*. Mahwah, NJ: Lawrence Erlbaum.

Darling-Hammond, L. (2000) (ed.), *Studies of Excellence in Teacher Education*. NY: National Commission on Teaching and America's Future.

Darling-Hammond, L. & Bransford, J. (eds.) (2005). *Preparing Teachers for a Changing World: What Teachers Should Learn and Be Able to Do*. San Francisco: Jossey-Bass.

Featherstone, H. (1993). "Learning from the first years of classroom teaching: The journey in, the journey out." *Teachers College Record* 95 (1), 93–112.

Feiman-Nemser, S. (1983). Learning to teach. In L. Shulman & G. Sykes (eds.), *Handbook of Teaching and Policy*. NY: Longma, 150–171.

Feiman-Nemser, S. (1992). Learning to teach. In S. Kelman (ed.). *What We Know about Jewish Education: A Handbook of Today's Research for Tomorrow's Jewish Education*. Los Angeles: Torah Aura, 51–57.

Feiman-Nemser, S. & Remillard, J. (1996). Perspectives on learning to teach. In F. Murray (ed.). *The Teacher Educator's Handbook: Building a Knowledge Base for the Preparation of Teachers*. Washington, DC: American Association of Colleges of Teacher Education, 63–91.

Feiman-Nemser, S. (2001). "From preparation to practice: Designing a continuum to strengthen and sustain teaching." *Teachers College Record* 103 (6), 1013–1055.

Fideler, E. & Haselkorn, D. (2000). *Learning the ropes: Urban Teacher Induction Practices in the United States*. Belmont, MA: Recruiting New Teachers, Inc.

Grossman, P., Valencia, S.W., Evans, K. Thompson, C., Martin, S. & Place, N. (2000). "Transition into teaching: Learning to teach writing in teacher education and beyond." *Journal of Literacy Research*, 32, 631–662.

Hatano, G. & Oura, Y. (2003). "Commentary: Reconceptualizing school learning using insight from expertise research." *Educational Researcher* 32 (8), 26–29.

Johnson, S. and the Project on the Next Generation of Teachers (2004). *Finders and Keepers: Helping New Teachers Survive and Thrive in Our Schools*. San Francisco: Jossey-Bass.

Kennedy, M. (1999). The role of preservice teacher education. In L. Darling-Hammond & G. Sykes (eds.), *Teaching as the Learning Profession: Handbook of Policy and Practice*. San Francisco: Jossey-Bass, 54–85.

Lave, J. & Wenger, E. (1991). *Situated Learning: Legitimate Peripheral Participation*. Cambridge, UK: Cambridge University Press.

Lieberman, A. (1996). Practices that support teacher development. In M.W. McLaughlin and I. Oberman (eds.), *Teacher Learning: New Policies, New Practices*. New York: Teachers College Press, 185–201.

Little, J.W. (1999). Organizing schools for teacher learning. In L.D. Hammond and G. Sykes (eds.), *Teaching as the Learning Profession: Handbook of Policy and Practice*. San Francisco: Jossey-Bass, 233–262.

National Commission on Teaching and America's Future (1996). *What Matters Most: Teaching for America's Future*. NY.

Shulman, L. (2002). "Truth and consequences: Inquiry and policy in research on teacher education." *Journal of Teacher Education* 53 (3), 248–253.

Wideen, M., Mayer-Smith, J. & Moon, J. (1998). A critical analysis of research on learning to teach: Making the case for an ecological perspective on inquiry. *Review of Educational Research* 68 (2), 130–178.

Wilson, S. & Berne, J. (1999). "Teacher learning and the acquisition of professional knowledge: An examination of research on contemporary professional development." *Review of Research in Education* 24, 173–209.

Supervision for Improving Teaching

Nehemia Ichilov

Somewhere there is a board of directors preparing a job description for an education director, with one of the many responsibilities being that of "supervision." What they mean this term to be, most committee members have no idea. What they want this term to mean is that this supervisor will manage the personnel in order to develop the best team of educators so that the students in turn can have the best learning experience.

What does it mean to supervise for improved teaching? To begin, one must clarify, almost redefine, the very term "supervision". In and of itself supervision has two basic functions; the first is the business-dominated act of "managing," "administrating," or even "organizing" the institution and its employees for the purpose of productivity and bottom-line outcomes. Alternatively, the second purpose grows out of the world of social service and human interaction, and is founded upon "caring for," "guiding," and "mentoring" the supervisee.

Successful supervision for improved teaching is found in the balance the supervisor achieves between these two worlds by managing and guiding the teacher to become the best that she can be while providing the students with the greatest opportunity to learn. Supervision for improved teaching, therefore, is built on the premise that, at the end of the day, success is measured according to the student's learning and not the teacher's instructional techniques.

As both a central agency director and a head of school, I have learned one undeniable truism: that successful supervision exists when a) the supervisor's feedback is specific, meaningful, and relevant to the supervisee; b) the supervisee expects and even demands the supervisor's input; and c) a supervisor clearly articulates what she understands the supervisee's role to be. Woven through this truism is an apparent understanding that successful supervision is achieved when the supervisor's primary motivation is to help the supervisee grow in her abilities as a teacher-educator.

Fullan (2001) exemplifies this idea when he writes about how all learning in the school, as both the institution and the individuals within the institution, is in a continual process of "making meaning". It is through an emphasis on relationships and values, rather than on structural changes, that we will find success in our educational institutions of tomorrow. Fullan (*ibid.*) identifies the "principals", these primary supervisors, as the "main agents" (or blockers) of this change process. By developing a reciprocal relationship with teachers, principals are able to exercise their authority to bring about the ultimate success with student learning in the classroom.

In many of today's schools we see the bulk of the supervisory burden unfairly placed on the teacher by building a foundation of supervision mainly on a mentoring-type program (Levin & Lee 2006). And although mentoring-type programs are critical for beginning and new teachers' success and retention (Glickman 2002; Sargent 2003; Levin & Lee 2006), we cannot stop there. What the institution often desperately needs is a supervisor to supervise complemented by an "induction program" to train the novice and inexperienced teachers (Wong 2002; 2004).

While significant data does not exist for teacher retention rates in Jewish education, the limited research that does exist suggests that teaching in Jewish schools is similar to that in the public sector.

With the recent JESNA study identifying that approximately 25% of teachers in both day schools and congregational schools leave their positions annually (2006), along with a national attrition rate for teachers in secular education reaching nearly 30% within the first three years and up to 50% within the first five years (Greiner & Smith 2006), it is not difficult to conclude that there exists an obvious lack of readiness for teachers to succeed in the classroom.

If Jewish schools expect to make a difference in the quality of the educational program, then teacher support is imperative and must become a high priority as a key tool for retaining the teachers entering the field (Greiner & Smith 2006). "The most important factor affecting individual student success in the schools is the classroom teacher" (Pollock 2007); and the expectations, demands, and wide-ranging skill sets necessary to survive as a teacher continue to grow. Without a trusted support system to scaffold the teachers through this foundational experience, we cannot presume that teachers will perform at the high levels the community expects.

Developing an induction program that consists of supervision through a variety of lenses such as the ones described in this chapter will not only produce improved learning outcomes for our students (through an enhanced teacher preparedness program), greater teacher retention (through improved job satisfaction) and ultimately, institutional advancement through reallocation of funds that would have otherwise gone to teacher recruitment, but it will also provide educational leaders for future generations (Wong 2004).

It is important to note that the *action* of supervision can and will continue to exist without taking all of these components into consideration. What will not exist, however, is the meaningful and consequential *reaction* of quality supervision that leads directly to improved student achievement.

Jewish tradition teaches us that you cannot ignore the human being when making a decision that may have a direct effect on another human being. The idea that supervision is an action and that decisions made are "not personal" but rather "business" is antithetical to a Jewish way of thinking. Everything is personal; in fact, some would even say that everything is Godly, and the very idea of removing the humanity from the thought process when making a decision is un-Godly in and of itself. Because of this fundamental Jewish approach to human interaction, meaningful and successful supervision in a Jewish institution can occur only when the supervisor perpetuates and lives these Jewish values by tapping into the humanity of her role and seeking to help the supervisee become better at his job through understanding who he is and what he needs to learn.

It is this perspective of blending the business and social service worlds from which this chapter speaks. It is my conjecture that there are three metaphoric roles for the supervisor, with each role forming a complex matrix with the others. Senge (1990) argues that one of the key problems with much that is understood and done in the name of management is that simplistic frameworks are generally applied to complex systems. Furthermore, he contends that supervision is complex, and supervision in education possibly even more so. The three metaphors below portray simple ideas specifically so that this complex system can become more easily discernable. According to one anonymous individual, "If a picture is worth a thousand words, then a metaphor is worth a thousand pictures."

Finally, each metaphor described in this chapter demonstrates a separate and unique scheme that best identifies the key components for successful supervision. It is important to note that these metaphors, if used alone, only portray a part of the picture; although these may provide useful perspectives on the overall role of the supervisor-educator, they will in fact fall short of providing a meaningful framework in which to better understand the complexities Senge (1990) describes. Together, however, these three metaphors (the supervisor as *parent*, *coach-evaluator*, and *servant-leader*) depict a model of supervision in education that is founded on building a nurturing, caring, supportive, and particularly effective learning environment, with successful student learning as its ultimate outcome.

METAPHOR I: SUPERVISOR AS PARENT

> "There is one thing a man cannot change...his parents."
> —David Ben Gurion

Every parent knows what his or her primary role is as the parent. The way one parent parents is likely to be different than the way another does. Parents may even disagree on what the final product of their parenting should look like. However, most parents will also agree that their role is to raise the child in order to ensure independence through providing opportunities for their successful growth and development...whatever that may mean to them.

Mogel (2001), on the other hand, "drills" down this parenting role even further and summarizes it as "making children into good people." She further explains that the role of parenting from a Jewish perspective is to raise children "to be self-reliant, compassionate, ethical adults" in order to "ensure that there will be people here to honor God after we are gone."

The Torah helps us to understand this role of Jewish parenting. In the text of the *Shema* (Deuteronomy 6:7), we read, "repeat them to your children and speak of them when you sit in your house, and when you go on your way, and when you lie down, and when you rise up." What is abundantly clear from this text is that there is no down time in parenting. A parent teaches, role-models, and supervises the child at all times, *even when the child is asleep*—a time traditionally viewed as when the child is under the direct care of God (Psalm 31:6).

However, there is another layer to the parent's role as stated in this text. Bringing us back to the truism identified earlier, the parent must provide feedback that is specific, meaningful, and relevant to the child. The actions described in the *Shema* are to be "repeated" and then "spoken". This very order demonstrates an active role-modeling of the behaviors followed by an explanation and teaching of why we need to take these actions.

No parent expects a child to be born walking, talking, reading, and writing. The parent's role is to help facilitate the child's learning of these actions. A parent has patience and understanding. Typically, walking follows crawling and precedes running. The child, however, learns these behaviors and actions by watching and by listening to words of encouragement, support, and explanation from the parent.

A parent nurtures a child in order to develop trust. A parent sets the child up for success. A parent provides opportunities for learning, for growth, and even for failure, knowing that one often learns more from failing than from succeeding. A parent wants the child to have everything that the parent did not have. There are even parents who take this idea to extremes and end up living their lives vicariously through their children.

On the other hand, confident parents are not jealous of their children. Caring parents do not focus solely on finding the errors in their children's ways. Trusting parents do not leave their children alone to figure things out for themselves. Compassionate parents do not take advantage of their children. Loving parents do not ask a child to do something beyond the child's understanding, ability, or level of maturity. And certainly selfless parents do not desert a child in times of trouble or danger.

The metaphor of supervisor as parent helps us understand the level of commitment, investment and connection between the supervisor and supervisee. It also helps us understand that teaching and role-modeling are only two aspects of a supervisor's role. Whether it is the principal, the education director, the head of a department or a team leader, being a supervisor is only one of their responsibilities. Just as parents care for the child and oversee the child's growth and development, so too do they do the shopping, earn a living, and manage the household, among many other tasks. In both cases, supervision does not negate other responsibilities, nor does it become a sole responsibility.

Of all the parenting responsibilities, probably the most important is to develop trust and encourage personal self-confidence. From the early stages of the parent–child relationship, trust is established through personal connection and tangible actions that tell the child *this person is here to help me survive*. Creating a safe environment in which to ask questions, to make mistakes and to eventually let the child go is all part of the relationship. Just as the child trusts the parent, so does the parent need to trust the child.

A parent may start by holding the child as it learns to walk. The parent will then shift to holding only one hand. But eventually the parent will let the child take its first steps alone, knowing the child will fall and not make it all the way across the room. However, the parent also trusts that the child, with hard work and effort, will learn this behavior. Letting go is never easy for the parent and requires the ultimate trust and confidence in the time invested in the relationship.

The development of trust is the core concept of the metaphor of the parent. It demonstrates the importance of a supervisor's open and honest feedback being specific, meaningful and relevant to the supervisee. Although Weber (1995) expresses this trust in her description of the mentor–mentoree relationship, she describes the "chemistry of reciprocal trust" as coming from a relationship similar to that of "a parent." It is only when such a relationship exists between the supervisor and supervisee that the novice, or even the veteran teacher, will achieve his or her full potential.

METAPHOR 2: SUPERVISOR AS COACH-EVALUATOR

> "Insanity is doing the same thing over and over and expecting different results."
> —Albert Einstein

A good coach is sought by his or her clients. While parents want the best for their child because of the personal connection, a coach wants the best for a client because it is professional. A coach's vested interest is in the client following the coach's recommendations. The client has the skills, and the coach is there to help develop, fine-tune, and bring together these skills.

Nowhere is the second component of supervision for improved teaching more evident than in this coaching relationship. It is here that the client/supervisee expects and even demands the coach/supervisor's input.

No more true was this than when Yitro (Moses' father-in-law) turned to Moses while he sat in daily judgment of the people's disagreements (Exodus 18:17–18) and counseled him to change his way of doing things. "What you're doing is no good," Yitro tells Moses. "You will surely wear away, both you and your people; for what you are doing is too much of a burden; you cannot continue to do this alone."

Certainly it was not an issue of Moses' not being able to do what Yitro was suggesting (we read of Moses' successful implementation of Yitro's recommendation later in the story); rather, it took someone on the outside looking in to realize that there was a better way for Moses to accomplish his goals, and to guide him through this change process. Although Yitro was not Moses' formal coach or evaluator, their relationship was built around open and honest communication. Moses looked to Yitro as one from whom he could learn, and Yitro looked to Moses as one who had great potential.

The coach sets goals, develops strategies, and motivates the client to push to his or her limits. The coach maintains momentum and provides accountability. The coach keeps the focus on the big picture while identifying areas needing attention. The coach delivers honest feedback to build on strengths and reduce the client's weaknesses. The coach is there at the will of the client, but the client knows that the coach is going to help make him/her better.

The coach is the client's development advisor. The coach's job is to assist the client to reach his/her greatest potential. It is the client who has the strengths; it is the client who has the skills; it is the client who has the talent. The coach's job is to draw out the best from within the client.

Without a coach, a client can only do what she or he knows. He or she will repeat the same things over and over and yet somehow expect different results. Lunenburg (1998), although less succinct than Einstein (see above quote), explains that in most cases teachers are given little direction on how to overcome specific weaknesses and are, therefore, unable to improve their performance; thus they will continue to repeat the same errors and mistakes. "Instructional supervision," Lunenburg (1998) explains, "has as its goal the professional development of teachers, with an emphasis on improving teachers' classroom performance."

Similarly, the coach's job is to constantly evaluate the client in order to provide the best outcome at the time of performance. How is the client doing during training? In what areas do we need to focus today, right now, this second? Is the client overusing certain strengths and downplaying others? What specific skills does this client need to develop? Coaching is by its very nature a process of relentless evaluation.

"A good evaluator should possess a variety of technical skills, must be good with people, should have a keen grasp of group dynamics and organizational functioning, should be ever-sensitive to political pitfalls and should conduct his/her business in an ethical, practical, trust-engendering manner." As wonderful as this anonymously attributed quote is, the author also admits that "At last count, there were three known persons in the Western Hemisphere possessing these attributes!"

So what is an educational supervisor-evaluator to do? A good supervisor will develop clear markers by which to evaluate the teachers, but a great supervisor will develop these markers with input from the teachers themselves. One of the first things this supervisor-evaluator needs to do is to develop an articulated plan for growth and development for which the supervisor will ultimately hold the teacher accountable. This basic premise stems from the notion that if it cannot be measured, it does not count!

Danielson & McGreal (2000) further elaborate on the creation of this professional development plan for teachers when they differentiate between the needs of novice and experienced teachers. "Teaching," they explain, "has a distinct life cycle; teachers at different stages in their careers have different needs and different levels of skill." The experienced supervisor-coach will therefore provide different assistance based upon a unique professional development plan to each of the teachers according to whether they fall into the "nontenured (probationary) teachers" or "tenured (career) teachers" status.

The development of such a plan should include an Individual Professional Development Program (IPDP). In their work on the Teacher Education Institute (TEI), Holtz, Dorph, and Goldring (1997) stated that "At the most straightforward level, educational leaders need to evaluate this enterprise; initiate, plan, develop and evaluate initiatives in their own institutions; work with their teachers to develop appropriate professional development plans; and work to advocate for particular programs that might best be offered across institutions or outside of the school, such as those that extend and deepen teachers' subject matter knowledge."

Ultimately the supervisor as coach-evaluator needs to clearly articulate the area being coached and to question how it will eventually be evaluated in order for the supervisee to grow and develop professionally. This entire relationship is based on the client's expectation that the coach will share his or her feedback often, immediately and in a way that will enable the client to grow.

The fundamental trait of this metaphor is that once the game begins, the coach retreats to the sidelines and simply observes his client in action. Although there may be an opportunity to communicate a needed adjustment or tweaking, the outcome is now in the hands of the client. In teacher supervision the same is true; once the teacher enters the classroom, the implementation of the supervisor's guidance is now in the supervisee's hands.

METAPHOR 3: SUPERVISOR AS SERVANT-LEADER

> "…Traditional autocratic and hierarchical modes of leadership are slowly yielding to a newer model—one that attempts to simultaneously enhance the personal growth of workers and improve the quality and caring of our many institutions through a combination of teamwork and community, personal involvement in decision making, and ethical and caring behavior. This emerging approach to leadership and service is called servant-leadership"
>
> —Larry Spears

A great supervisor must first serve others. The notion of the servant-leader, or in this case the "servant-supervisor," is not new. The term servant-leadership was coined by Robert Greenleaf in 1970 in his seminal essay "The Servant as Leader" (Greenleaf 1991).

The servant-leader is one who supervises from the position of shared responsibility, shared goals and shared ownership. Once the walls of the traditional model of authoritarian supervision are broken down, institutional purpose becomes transparent. When the supervisees understand and accept the true meaning of the institutional vision, mission, and objectives, their role in creating institutional evolution begins to function.

This transparency in thinking highlights the third component of successful supervision for improved teaching: that the supervisor clearly articulates the supervisee's role. In an institution with a clear (both figuratively and literally) driving vision, each person's role takes on a clear direction.

To get to this level of institutional advancement, however, Greenleaf identified that societal change was either *revolutionary* or *evolutionary* in nature. Revolutionary change is generally a quick, political, and usually short-lived process. Evolutionary change, however, lasts indefinitely because it occurs over an extended period of time and frequently involves change by individuals through personal growth and commitment. Servant-leadership, by its very nature, is organic, personal, and most certainly evolutionary.

In order to attain this meaningful and sustainable method of supervision, Spears suggests that the servant-leader needs to develop ten core skills that are built around nurturing personal relationships. These are in Spears' (2004) servant-leadership order, but for the purposes of this paper defined within the context of the "servant-educational-leader":

1. *Listening*—The servant-supervisor must be able to "hear" what the supervisee is saying. The supervisor needs to listen to ideas, suggestions, comments, and criticisms if the relationship is to grow. Additionally, the supervisor needs to "listen" to his/her inner voice and instinct. This core skill is critical in further developing the self-reflective practitioner.

2. *Empathy*—Having a sense of compassion and understanding for the supervisee enables the servant-supervisor to demonstrate respect for the individual. Glickman (2002) calls this empathic leadership the "nondirective interpersonal approach" where "the instructional leader's role is that of an active prober or a sounding board for the teacher to make his or her own decisions."

3. *Healing*—Growing out of a medical mindset, this skill assumes the ability of the supervisor to address the needs and conditions of the supervisee.

4. *Awareness*—Within the education framework this skill provides for both the supervisor and supervisee to enhance their self-reflective experiences. Greenleaf described this core skill as coming from a "holistic position."

5. *Persuasion*—By being able to influence, sway, or even argue a position without making it personal, the supervisor conveys alternative perspectives while encouraging and supporting supervisee growth and development. Spears expresses it best by describing it as the ability to "convince others, rather than coerce compliance."

6. *Conceptualization*—developing the skill to look beyond the day-to-day functions of the institution and to "conceptualize" perspectives that may not have been considered in the past.

7. *Foresight*—being able to develop and articulate a clear institutional vision that provides insight for achieving that vision.

8. *Stewardship*—holding the baton for the field of education until those entering the field are ready to assume their rightful place as mature teachers and leaders.

9. *Commitment to the growth of people*—demonstrating a positive motivation for supervision that interweaves all of the skills into promoting more effective teaching. This "commitment to growth" can be through direct interactions by the supervisor in supporting the faculty in their work, or through the supervisor's administrative actions, such as providing sufficient funding for the faculty to pursue professional development opportunities.

10. *Building community*—being a part of a dynamic process between supervisor and supervisee that creates strong, positive interactions throughout the institution.

Spears further demonstrates the servant-leadership position by showing how this obvious emphasis on personal development as a key to organizational effectiveness makes the servant-leader model align itself well with the theories, ideas, and approaches of Covey's (2004) *seven habits* and Goleman's (2006) *social intelligence* concepts. In addition, when comparing this model to other participatory models of organizational life, Greenleaf's servant-leadership aligns itself closely with Argyris and Schöen's (1996) as well as Senge's (1990) *learning organizations*, Blake and Mouton's (1985) *managerial grid*, and Deming's (1994) *quality movement*.

The supervisor as servant-leader in the educational setting is one who cares deeply about the students of tomorrow. For the servant-leader, supervising a Judaics teacher is not simply about whether the teacher is teaching the material in the classroom; rather, it is whether there will be a class for the children and grandchildren of these students in the future. This echos Mogel's (2001) perspective, considering what will be for our children's children once we decision makers of today are no longer here. However, caring about the students of tomorrow does not negate caring for those students here today; the servant-leader also wants to see this Judaics teacher teach the students to appreciate, understand, and care about the Torah and not just teach the subject of Torah.

Teachers who are nurtured by supervisors who follow this model are much more likely to last well beyond the statistical averages for teacher retention[1]. They are part of an evolutionary process that focuses on student achievement that is the direct result of long-term teacher stability, professional development, and improved quality of instruction.

This servant-supervisor metaphor is built on the transparency of the institution and the clearly defined roles of the professionals involved. The success of supervision for improved teaching comes from the supervisor clearly articulating the proper role of the supervisee.

THREE VISIONS, ONE PURPOSE

These three metaphors may at first appear to be contradictory, with the metaphors of "parent" and "coach" reinforcing a perception of a *top-down* chain of command and the servant-leader metaphor working with partnership empowerment and a *bottom-up* systemic approach to teacher development. But these metaphors in fact compliment and support each other more than contradict.

The similarity is not necessarily in the manner of communication, nor is it in the particular technique one type of supervisor may use compared to that of another; rather, the similarity is in the purpose of supervision. In all three metaphors the supervisor's impetus for change is guided by "service" rather than "self-interest."

For Feiman-Nemser and Floden (1986), intrinsic rewards for teachers of making a difference in students' lives far outweigh any extrinsic rewards. The same is true for coaches who desire that their clients produce that perfect swing of the bat or exhibit their greatest potential under pressure; how much more so for parents whose intrinsic rewards of parenthood infinitely surpass the extrinsic.

Block (1993) defines this selflessness and greater purpose as "stewardship," the notion that one supervises and leads others with an altruistic motivation for a greater good. "Stewardship is to hold something in trust for another," Block explains. "Stewardship was a means to protect a kingdom while those rightfully in charge were away, or more often, to govern for the sake of an underage king. The underage king for us is the next generation. We choose service over self-interest most powerfully when we build the capacity of the next generation to govern themselves."

What greater purpose is there than to develop meaningful relationships with other educators, whether direct reports or colleagues in the field? The goal, then, is for every Jewish educator to ensure the survival of our people for generations to come by promoting high quality professionals at every stage of their careers.

IMPLICATIONS & FUTURE DIRECTION

If quality supervision leads to improved teaching, then investment in this unbelievably complex and ostensibly impossible task is the logical approach to creating change in the endeavor of Jewish education. Medical education has long understood this importance—so much so that great care and concern are taken to establish environments ensuring thorough supervision during the medical practitioners' residency periods.

---

[1]According to the Project on the Next Generation of Teachers, Harvard Graduate School of Education, "...the key to addressing shortages lies...in schools and classrooms where teachers must find success and satisfaction. It is there they will decide whether or not to continue to teach."

At the Albert Einstein College of Medicine we see an example of this detailed supervisory process. It is here that a clinical communication skill strategy was developed to "help establish trust with the learner" (Milan et al. 2006). This skill strategy, known as "PEARLS"—*Partnership, Empathy, Apology, Respect, Legitimation, Support*—becomes the foundational building block for the doctor to establish a relationship of trust with the patient so that the patient will be able to "hear" what the doctor is saying and believe that the recommended treatment is ultimately in the patient's best interest (*ibid.*). The key to PEARLS success is that the supervisor is involved in the practitioner's learning process throughout, acting as mentor, role model, motivator, instructor, and much more.

Examples such as this help us understand that successful relationships, whether personal, professional, formal, or informal, are built first on trust, open communication, and an honest desire to achieve the common goal, though this is only the beginning. Good intentions and wonderful experiences can only take the affiliation so far.

Fortunately, it is a rare occurrence when a patient concludes that because he has experienced a certain medical procedure he suddenly has become qualified to perform this procedure on others. However, when it comes to supervision, there are an overwhelming number of supervisors with an assumed level of competency based completely on their experience of having been supervised.

In Jewish education, as in education in general, it is important for the purposes of training that we compare the supervisor to the surgeon. The surgeon studied countless hours, shadowed a mentor through numerous surgeries, and ultimately stepped into the role after thorough preparation, training, and experience. Similarly, we need to establish training programs through which the educational supervisor studies, becomes part of a mentorship experience, and finally steps into the role for which knowledge attainment and work experience will have prepared her. The supervisor possesses a different kind of "life," and until we admit that this life has equal value to the one in the operating room, we will continue to address the symptoms rather than the causes of our educational pain.

During the last fifteen years the Jewish community has started to recognize this need. Programs have been initiated at the graduate school level by both the Davidson Graduate School of Jewish Education at the Jewish Theological Seminary of America (JTSA) and the Rhea Hirsch School of Education at Hebrew Union College-Jewish Institute of Religion (HUC-JIR). There are master's-level courses that focus on "current theories of supervision such as developmental, clinical and peer coaching to the Jewish school and other educational settings" (JTSA) and "perspectives on the theory and practice of models of clinical supervision" (HUC-JIR), respectively. In addition, JTSA and HUC-JIR collaborated on the development of a grant to establish the Day School Leadership Training Institute (DSLTI) supported by the Avi Chai Foundation, with the primary purpose of preparing mid- and upper-level management to lead day schools. Incorporated in the program are sessions focused explicitly on the role and function of the educational leader supervising staff and faculty.

Outside of academic institutions, the Mandel Teacher Educator's Institute (MTEI) was an outgrowth of the Mandel Institute's response to *A Time to Act: Report of the Commission on Jewish Education in North America* (1990). The MTEI focuses on, among other activities, preparing educational leaders to assume greater responsibility for supervising teachers in the classroom. Additionally, and more recently, JESNA established the Jewish Educator Recruitment and Retention Initiative (JERRI) to "evaluate and leverage the national and community-wide recruitment and retention initiatives that currently exist as well as to plan and implement new programs and projects that will move the field forward." As part of this plan JERRI proposes to create a culture of support for Jewish educators within Jewish institutions through supportive and productive supervisor–educator relationships. Similarly, the DeLeT (Day School Leadership Through Teaching) program, housed on the East Coast at Brandeis University and on the West Coast at HUC-JIR, focuses on educators but does so in such a manner as to help them become more successful as supervisees by better understanding what their role is in the supervisor–educator relationship. Finally, a number of central agencies at the local level have established their own programs to train mentors, support educators and educational leaders and work closely with local schools to help develop their supervisor–educator relationships.

Yet with these new initiatives there remains a serious lack of trained personnel both at the community level and in the schools to properly supervise the large number of teachers in classrooms. What we have learned is that simply possessing a graduate degree in Jewish education, although certainly admirable, is not sufficient to provide the quantity and quality of supervision that the field requires. Additional training is necessary for the current supervisors to learn how to appropriately balance the responsibilities of the educational leader so that they will be able to provide proper supervision to their faculty. In this area the Jewish community falls short.

This shortcoming is further highlighted by the contrast between the inordinate number of well-intentioned, smart, passionate, involved, and eager teachers in classrooms who have little or no idea of how or what to teach (Levin & Lee 2006). Research tells us that teacher ineffectiveness has been linked to two particular areas of weakness: content knowledge and pedagogic knowledge (Torff & Sessions 2005). What we often overlook in Jewish education is how to help our teachers improve in both of these areas at the *causal* level rather than the *symptomatic*. Developing a comprehensive supervision program that takes into consideration the three metaphors mentioned earlier enables a supervisor to move beyond the peripheral classroom management, lesson plan, and discipline challenges (enabling these to be addressed as part of a teacher's induction program) in order to develop a mutually beneficial relationship that will help support and improve the teacher in his or her educational journey.

If student learning in both formal and informal Jewish education is the goal, then significant changes in the organizational system may be required. When our educational leaders have job descriptions that require them to serve as the visionary leaders to set the educational direction and institutional strategic plan in motion, as well as to implement and address the day-to-day functions for providing a quality educational experience on the ground level, then we are often asking the impossible from a single individual. Even Lee claims that "We could make a case for more consistent observation and supervision by the education director of the congregation, but there are so many demands of the job that adequate time for working with more than one teacher is scarce" (Levin & Lee 2006).

HIGHLIGHTS

- Three metaphors best demonstrate the role of the supervisor: the *parent*, the *coach*, and the *servant-leader*.
- Successful supervision exists when a) the supervisor's feedback is specific, meaningful, and relevant to the supervisee; b) the supervisee expects and even demands the supervisor's input; and c) a supervisor clearly articulates what she understands the supervisee's role to be.
- Successful supervision is measured when the supervisee is successful in her/his teaching duties and grows in her/his abilities as a teacher-educator.
- The supervisor as parent helps us understand the level of commitment, investment, and connection between the supervisor and supervisee.
- Like the coach providing the client advice on implementing a professional development plan, a supervisor needs to provide direction to the teacher on how to achieve his/her greatest potential.
- The effective supervisor will develop clear markers with which to evaluate teachers with input from the faculty themselves.
- The servant-leader is one who supervises from the position of shared responsibility, shared goals and shared ownership.
- Servant-leadership is organic, personal, and evolutionary.
- The ten core skills identified to form the foundation of servant-leadership are *listening*, *empathy*, *healing*, *awareness*, *persuasion*, *conceptualization*, *foresight*, *stewardship*, *commitment to the growth of people*, and *building community*.
- Schools need to develop an induction program as part of a beginning or new teacher's orientation to a school.

• Improved supervision provides opportunity for increased student learning, greater teacher retention, and enhanced institutional growth.

THE LARGER CONTEXT

Jewish tradition teaches that the community is greater than the sum of the individual parts. Servant-leadership is an approach to supervision that not only aligns itself with this Jewish moral, ethical, and value judgment, but also taps into human nature by urging us to be altruistic and transcend our personal self-interests for the benefit of others. However, supervision needs *tachles* (details) to complement the greater purpose in order to be meaningful and sustainable. Frequent feedback, well-articulated goals and objectives, regular and clear evaluations and assessments, and an open relationship built on trust, support, and shared commitment, are imperative for institutional growth and advancement.

As the American Jewish community reflects on the challenges of living Jewishly in the 21st century, the quality of the people who assume this most important role of teacher and educational leader is critical. By adopting a model built upon the three metaphors of parent, coach and servant-leader, the educational system will take on an evolutionary approach to a change process that focuses attention on student learning, growth and engagement in Jewish life in the future.

ANNOTATED BIBLIOGRAPHY

Block, P. (1993). *Stewardship: Choosing Service over Self-Interest*. San Francisco: Berrett-Koehler Publishers. Peter Block explains that organizations that practice stewardship will succeed in the marketplace by choosing service over self-interest through developing a broad redistribution of power, privilege, and wealth. Block shows his audience of corporate executives how to move from controlling and directing a staff toward his vision of shared governance, partnership, and the achievement of allegiance by team members to the overall business. Although this book was written for business executives, there is a relevance of human interaction, underlying values, and caring process that makes it the ideal model for the administrator supervising in the world of Jewish education.

Drago-Severson, E. (2004). *Helping Teachers Learn: Principal Leadership for Adult Growth and Development*. Thousand Oaks, CA: Corwin Press. Drago-Severson articulates a model for principal administrators to create a culture and model for continued professional development and learning. She labels this the "principal adult educator." We know that when professional development is done right and teachers are engaged in their own learning, student outcomes and motivation for learning improve. In this book Drago-Severson identifies four pillars that support this process: teaming, providing leadership roles, engaging in collegial inquiry, and mentoring. Any supervisor working in the world of Jewish education should take note of Drago-Severson's model as a demonstrated way of developing the staff while improving student outcomes.

Glatthorn, A. A. (1997). *Differentiated Supervision* (2nd ed.). Alexandria, VA: ASCD. Glatthorn espouses a form of supervision that enables the supervisor to spend significantly more time with the supervisees who are in greatest need. By enabling the supervisor to focus on the needs of the novice and inexperienced teachers, Glatthorn recognizes that the expert's time is best spent in building a faculty for the future. Veteran faculty are then guided to other forms of professional development and to creating collaborative teams among themselves to further their own growth. This approach empowers the supervisor to take back the evaluation process in a structured, methodical and disciplined manner to help provide the necessary feedback for teachers to succeed in the classroom.

Levin, N.P. & Lee, S. S. (2006). *Bridging the Gap: The Power of Mentor Teachers for Coaching Teaching Excellence*. Los Angeles: Hebrew Union College-Jewish Institute of Religion. Levin & Lee use their experiences from the *Creating Teaching Excellence in Congregational Education* project of the Rhea Hirsch School of Education of the Hebrew Union College-Jewish Institute of Religion to attempt to provide a "real" alternative to some of the challenging assumptions held in Jewish congregational education. This book provides a step-by-step process to develop a teacher-initiated mentorship program in the congregational school environment. It offers practical tools for teachers to dialogue and learn form one another, as well as to tap into each teacher's personal and professional skill sets in order for the faculty to grow as Jewish educators.

REFERENCES

Argyris, C., & Schöen, D. A. (1996). *Organizational Learning II: Theory, Method, and Practice*. Reading, MA: Addison-Wesley.

Ben-Avie, M., & Kress, J. (2006). *The Educators in Jewish Schools Study: Preliminary Findings from a Registry of Day and Congregational/Supplemental Schools in North America*. New York: JESNA.

Blake, R. R., & Mouton, J. S. (1985). *The Managerial Grid III*. Houston: Gulf Publishers Co.

Block, P. (1993). *Stewardship: Choosing Service over Self-Interest*. San Francisco: Berrett-Koehler Publishers.

Center for Policy Research (2006). *Jewish Early Childhood Education in Denver and Boulder: Mapping the Field Final Report*. Denver, CO: Center for Policy Research.

Covey, S. R. (2004). *The 7 Habits of Highly Effective People*. New York: Free Press.

Danielson, C. & McGreal, T. L. (2000). *Teacher Evaluation: To Enhance Professional Practice*. Alexandria, VA: ASCD.

Deming, W. E. (1994). *The New Economics: For Industry, Government, Education*. Cambridge, MA: Massachusetts Institute of Technology, Center for Advanced Engineering Study.

Feiman-Nemser, S. & Floden, R. (1986). "The Cultures of Teaching." *Handbook of Research on Teaching*, 3rd ed. New York: Macmillan.

Fullan, M. (2001). *The New Meaning of Educational Change*. New York: Teachers College Press.

Glickman, C. D. (2002). *Leadership for Learning: How to Help Teachers Succeed*. Alexandria, VA: ASCD.

Goleman, D. (2006). *Social Intelligence: The New Science of Human Relationships*. New York: Bantam Books.

Goodman, R. Bidol-Padva, P. & Schaap, E. (2006). *Community Report on Early Childhood Jewish Educators: Culture of Employment 2004–2005 Miami-Dade and Broward Counties, Florida*. New York: CAJE.

Greenleaf, R. K. (1991). *Servant as Leader*. Westfield, IN: Robert K. Greenleaf Center.

Greiner, C. S. & Smith, B. (2006). "Determining the Effect of Selected Variables on Teacher Retention." *Education* 126 (4), 653–659.

Holtz, B. W., Dorph, G. Z. & Goldring, E. B. (1997). "Educational Leaders as Teacher Educators: The Teacher Educator Institute—a Case from Jewish Education." *Peabody Journal of Education* 72 (2), 147–166.

Levin, N.P. & Lee, S. S. (2006). *Bridging the Gap: The Power of Mentor Teachers for Coaching Teaching Excellence*. Los Angeles: Hebrew Union College-Jewish Institute of Religion.

Lunenburg, F. C., (1998). "Techniques in the Supervision of Teachers: Preservice and Inservice Applications." *Education*, 118 (4), 521–525.

Milan, F. B., Parish, S. J. & Reichgott, M. J. (2006). "A Model for Educational Feedback Based on Clinical Communication Skills Strategies: Beyond the 'Feedback Sandwich'." *Teaching and Learning in Medicine* 18 (1), 42–47.

Mogel W. M. (2001). *The Blessing of a Skinned Knee*. London: Penguin Books Ltd.

Pollock, J. E. (2007). *Improving Student Learning: One Teacher at a Time*. Alexandria, VA: ASCD.

Sargent, B. (2003). "Finding Good Teachers—and Keeping Them." *Educational Leadership* 60 (8), 44–47.

Senge, P. M. (1990). *The Fifth Discipline: The Art and Practice of the Learning Organization*. London: Random House.

Spears, L. (2004). "Practicing Servant-Leadership." *Leader to Leader* 34, 7–11.

Torff, B. & Sessions, D. N. (2005). "Principals' Perceptions of the Causes of Teacher Ineffectiveness." *Journal of Educational Psychology* 97 (4), 530–537.

Weber, S. (1995). Mentoring, Gratification, Immortality, and Other Thoughts. In M. Zeldin & S. S. Lee (eds.), *Touching the Future: Mentoring and the Jewish Professional*. Los Angeles: HUC-JIR, 62–65.

Wong, H. K. (2002). "Induction: The Best Form of Professional Development." *Educational Leadership* 59 (6), 52–54.

Wong, H. K. (2004). "Producing Educational Leaders through Induction Programs." *Kappa Delta Pi Record* 106, 106–111.

Mentoring Jewish Educators

Renee Frank Holtz

Traditionally, schools are conceived of as places where students learn and teachers transmit. Yet research has shown that there are direct links between teacher learning and student learning (Platt et al. 2000). The more teachers learn, the better students learn. Having teachers learn more means that students may learn more, and one of the ways in which teachers can learn is from one another. Mentorship provides such an avenue for teacher learning.

According to one researcher of mentoring in a Jewish context, mentorship is defined as "the individual support, assistance, guidance, and challenge that one professional provides for another" (Aronson 2003, p. 654). How such an endeavor as mentorship can effect such sustenance to all participants and how it can be a Jewish endeavor is the subject of this chapter.

Many have begun their examination of some facet of mentoring with a restatement or reframing of the first Mentor (Crow & Matthews 1998; McCluskey et al. 2004). As the appointed guide for Odysseus' son Telemakhos, Mentor supports the boy in his growth to manhood and facilitates the formation of his adult identity. Such a contextual frame for the study of mentorship can be helpful in understanding the original intent of the relationship between mentor and mentee, but it is insufficient for depicting the full breadth of permutations of today's mentoring relationships. Mentorship in education, specifically in religious education, can be much greater than the parent-like interactions of Mentor and Telemakhos. The Catholic Church used formal mentorship programs to doctrinate new members and provide transmission from one generation to the next (Gonzalez 2006). As the rebbe mentored his pupils and partners in chevruta mentor each other, Judaism has long understood that some types of learning depend upon a partner, upon mentorship. Chevruta requires a partner, and so does the best of mentorship. How, then, do adults learn best? How and why can Jewish education use mentoring? What are its potential impacts?

Research into mentorship is voluminous, though by no means exhaustive; study of Jewish mentoring is startlingly sparse by comparison. Nonetheless, what clearly informs our understanding is the view that Judaism takes toward the concept of mentorship and toward adult learning as an entity. It is this lens that establishes the framework for the importance of mentorship endeavors.

CONTEXT

Teaching is not a simple, one-dimensional job, and schools are not uncomplicated places to work; in fact, they are increasingly complex (U.S. Department of Education 1998). Hiring and retaining qualified teachers is a struggle in nearly all contexts. In public schools it has been reported that 20% of new *teachers* leave the profession within their first three years (Association for Career and Technical Education 2000), and 30% to 50% leave within five years (Ballinger 2000). Mentoring improves these statistics. A study by the National Center for Educational Statistics found that 70% of new *teachers* who met with a mentor once a week said their instructional skills improved significantly (Association for Career and Technical Education 2000) and thus, they were more likely to stay in the field longer. According to some, 80% to 90% of teachers who undergo high-caliber induction programs (of which mentoring is a component) stay in the field for five years or more. Of the teachers who participated in a mentoring program at the University of California, 94% were still working in education seven years later (Hoff 2004). Mentorship impacts more than just the novice; veteran teachers also stay on the job longer if they feel honored and valued by their participation in mentoring programs.

Well-qualified teachers make a significant difference in student learning. Enabling teachers to become better qualified is frequently attempted through various types of teacher induction programs in a school (Evans et al. 2001). Mentorship is one of the best paths for learning the multifaceted tasks of teachers, and collaboration is a key to making it effective (Duckworth 1997; O'Brien & Christie 2005). Collaboration is a pivotal element of a good mentoring program. It enables the sharing of ideas on instruction; the breaking down of institutional barriers, the promotion of educational change (English 1998; Stigler & Hiebert 1999). Collaboration between teachers and administrators may "nurture the whole school culture" (Bartunek 1990).

According to Feiman-Nemser (1996), when teachers collaborate within mentorship, both mentors and mentees learn new ways of thinking and acting associated with new kinds of teaching. Collaborative contexts may be created when teachers take on active roles in their learning (Brause 2000). This is clearly a boon to a profession that is known for its isolation; a teacher is given a key to an empty classroom and encounters colleagues only by happenstance unless a mechanism is created for collaboration.

Traditionally, mentorship in teaching is the pairing of a veteran teacher (mentor) and a novice (mentee) for the purposes of induction of the mentee into the school and acclimation of the mentee into the culture of the institution; building of a professional community; provision of emotional support; and learning for all participants. Mentees are typically viewed as sponges; they absorb the information that the mentor provides. More recently, research (R. F. Holtz 2001) has shown that in many cases, mentees are providers of information that can foment knowledge for the mentors as well. In optimal mentorship interactions mentees are active participants in building community, offer affective support, and provide insights to their mentors.

RESEARCH

Significant research has contributed to the ways in which mentorship programs work and impact educational intuitions. The most salient of these examines how adults learn, how participants in a mentorship program "work" together, and considerations specific for Jewish contexts.

ADULT LEARNERS

Knowles, the father of adult learning theory, postulated that adults wish to direct their own learning (1980, 1984). Knowles' research preceded that of Maehl (2000), who discussed how the strong self-concept of most adults makes them want to direct their own learning. Adults may desire autonomy but may not have the skills or even the motivation to learn the same material in isolation (Cranton 1996). Adults may thus learn best when they can be "involved in planning, implementing, and evaluating their own learning" (Zachary 2000, p. 6) and when they can work with other adults in collaboration. It is the ways in which adults may direct their learning and at the same time collaborate that create such vibrant potential for learning.

Learning in a mentorship program is situated in social interactions. Vygotsky (1978) concluded that much of what we learn is learned in interaction with others. The Zone of Proximal Development is based on the belief that a teacher or peer can promote the development of others to a higher level. This assistance or guiding is known as mediation. The concept of mediation is central to Vygotsky's theory, and collaboration is a key concern (R. F. Holtz 2001). Accordingly, it is the collaboration that drives the learning.

If the intent of mentorship is for mentors and mentees to learn new ways of thinking and acting associated with new kinds of teaching, then a program must create collaborative contexts where mentors and novices can explore new approaches together (Feiman-Nemser 1996). Most adults have encountered mentors since our very first year as learners (Daloz 1999). We may have done so inadvertently or with intent, but mentors have guided us through the learning process in every stage. We change as we age (Daloz 1999), and we are transformed as we learn (Mezirow 1991), as we make meaning by building on or reinterpreting experiences. Collaboration can support this transformation.

Research into peer mentoring in most educational settings has discovered that adult learners are active "agents" in the learning process, not to be viewed as "empty vessels who are the passive recipients" of policy or information (Jones 2004). Collaboration makes it possible for mentors and mentees "to become both learners and teachers" (Skinner & Welch 1996, p. 154).

When adults are together in mentorship it is, at its heart, dialogue. According to Bakhtin, dialogue is inherently open-ended. Every word, every utterance is subject to interpretation by the speaker and by the listener. Dialogue is a reflection of the speakers, and it is the vehicle for new understandings (Bakhtin 1981; 1986). "Mentoring is made of language. Whether text or talk, discourse is central to the practice. It really *is* what we say that matters" (Garman 1995, p. 28). The manner of the dialogue, the style of the discourse, the selection of the language is a key to the way in which adults work together and learn together. It is within the dialogue that all participants are simultaneously teachers and students (Freire, cited in Bailey 2003). This is especially true within culture-rich settings such as Jewish life (Bekerman 2001).

With theories of adult learning as a guide, the role of the mentor shifts from that of one who transfers knowledge to that of a facilitator of learning for all (Zachary 2000, xv). The mentee and the mentor share responsibility for the setting of goals and priorities and for finding resources. In this regard, both are self-directed (Zachary 2000, p. 3).

It should not be ignored that in Jewish mentorship programs, adults are learners who are often encountering curriculum and concerns that are directly related to their settings. Religious settings are quite different from secular institutions, and adult learners may be uniquely directed when it comes to matters of religion (B. Holtz 1996). While the majority of the research on adult learners has shown that collaborative models are the modus of choice, when adults are learners in religious settings they may seek a more authoritative teacher figure. Whether or not this impacts programs of mentorship in Jewish institutions is not clear.

ROLES OF PARTICIPANTS

Like schools, mentorship is complex, typically occurring between people with "differing levels of experience and expertise which incorporates interpersonal or psychological development, career and/or educational development, and socialization" (Carmin. cited in O'Brien & Christie 2005). Today "mentoring relationships have changed from traditional and hierarchical to dynamic relationships that are contemporary, open, and flexible. Individuals can now learn…in reciprocal partnerships— they are both the giver and receiver of wisdom and information" (Kaye, Olevin & Ammerman, cited in Aronson 2003, pp. 656–657). Mentors are traditionally referred to as teachers (Feiman-Nemser 1996) and coaches (Kerka 1997; Showers & Joyce 1982, 1996), but mentors and mentees may occupy both of these roles. While the terms "teacher" and "coach" have much in common, they also emphasize differing perspectives, as noted in Figure 1 (R. F. Holtz 2001).

Figure 1: Mentor Roles

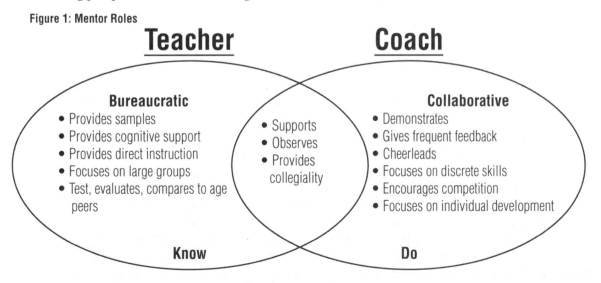

Teacher / Coach

Bureaucratic
- Provides samples
- Provides cognitive support
- Provides direct instruction
- Focuses on large groups
- Test, evaluates, compares to age peers

- Supports
- Observes
- Provides collegiality

Collaborative
- Demonstrates
- Gives frequent feedback
- Cheerleads
- Focuses on discrete skills
- Encourages competition
- Focuses on individual development

Know / Do

The terms teacher and coach overlap in their pedagogical processes. The contexts may differ; typically teachers work in more bureaucratic contexts than coaches. Teachers direct instruction for their partners to "learn new pedagogies and socialize them to new professional norms" and help promote standards and practices (Feiman-Nemser 1996, p. 1). Teachers observe their partners and discuss pedagogy with them, provide information and help learners construct their own knowledge (Kerka 1997, p. 4).

In contrast, coaching focuses more on the collaborative and affective nature of support and encouragement, with coaches facilitating the construction of learners' own knowledge. Peer coaching has long been used outside of the educational realm as the norm to tap into the expertise of professionals (Toto 2006). Coaches cheer their partners, demonstrating specific actions (Showers & Joyce 1996); then they observe the subsequent actions, providing encouraging, supportive, and constructive comments (Showers & Joyce 1982). Coaching "harnesses many of the elements...necessary for teacher change, including linkages among theory, demonstration [and] model[ing], practice, feedback, and follow-up assistance" (Friend & Cook 2000, p. 101).

Mentors and mentees may act as teachers or coaches for one another (R. F. Holtz 2001). As the mentee develops as a professional, he or she may support the mentor and help her develop new knowledge (Aronson 2003, p. 657). In this non-hierarchical model, mentor and mentee "collaborate to become both learners and teachers" (Skinner & Welch 1996, p. 154). This theory holds that all participants, new and veteran, benefit from inquiring, practicing, and reflecting with colleagues. They may be "a role model, nurturing, teaching, sponsoring, encouraging, counseling, befriending, and helping with professional and/or personal development" (Weasmer & Woods 2003, p. 175) for one another. Caccia (1996) reflected on his mentoring of new teachers: "I, for one, received as much benefit...as the new teachers did" (p. 19). Schaller (1996) explored mentoring as a means of promoting spiritual growth for women in a congregation and concluded that mentors in a mentorship program had as much to gain from the experience as mentees. Particularly in religious settings, mentors and mentees can "play complementary roles" in the mentoring process (English 1998). It has the potential to be a reciprocal relationship with a focus on learning (R. F. Holtz 2001; Zachary 2001; Fairbanks, Freedman & Kahn 2000).

CONSIDERATIONS FOR JEWISH EDUCATION

In 1988 Aron (1988) stated that "the most serious challenge facing Jewish education today is a severe shortage of skilled supplementary school teachers who combine Judaic knowledge and pedagogic experience with enduring personal dedication to Jewish teaching and learning" (p. 58) and commitment to the Jewish community. Five years later, research found that only 55% of supplementary school teachers had ever worked in general education, only 18% had certification in Jewish education, and only 12% had a degree in Jewish studies (Gamoran et al. 1994). With regard to day schools, recent reports show significantly higher rates of employment of teachers with three or fewer years of teaching experience (U.S. Department of Education 2003) than public schools.

How, then, do Jewish communities regard their teachers? "Communities often sabotage their efforts to recruit and retain Jewish teachers by not acknowledging and appreciating these dedicated individuals" (Aronson, 2003 p. 654). It is clear that mentorship is one path to integrating teachers into Jewish school systems, increasing learning and efficacy. According to English's research on mentoring in religious education (1998), mentoring programs do not only affect those directly participating, but they may also "revitalize the entire staff, even to spill over to the rest of the educational environment" (p. 24). As such, they may impact the entire educational community.

To be sure, community is an essential element of Jewish life and learning. Many of the Torah's commandments cannot be fulfilled privately, only communally. Numbers 14:27 states that in order to fulfill certain *mitzvot* one must have an "Assembly" of the people (Tanakh 1996). The Jewish people also have a communal obligation to teach, study, and practice the ideals of the Torah. One component of being part of a Jewish community is ensuring the transmission of Torah from one generation to the next. In Pirke Avot (1:1–3) it is written, "Moses received the Torah from Sinai, and he handed it down to Joshua, who handed it over to the elders, who handed it over to the prophets, who in turn handed it over to the members of the Great Assembly." This is a model for education; Jews are "obligated to be lifelong learners who never stop learning and teaching about the tradition" (Goldman, cited in Schuster 2003, p. 80). Pirke Avot 1:2a further states "They [the Elders of Israel] said three things: Be deliberate in judgment; develop many disciples; and make a protective fence around the Torah" (*Pirke Avot* 1989, p. 8). The command to "develop many disciples" asks that the teaching of Torah be spread to as many people as possible. This ensures that people are responsible not only for teaching Torah to others but for learning as well (R. F. Holtz, 2002). With regard to mentorship as a model for Torah study and communal life, many Jews are accustomed to viewing their rabbi as a mentor (Bechofer 1983) and to having that person be an integral part of the community.

Mentorship can, in fact, help to create such a community. In one study of mentorship in a supplementary school, participants viewed the mentorship community as directly connected to religion. They stated that "Judaism is a community religion" (Doris 2000) and that "I feel that the idea of a Jewish community was a factor in my participation in the [mentorship] program because I learned its importance and how to display that importance in my classroom" (Doris 2000; R. F. Holtz 2001).

In whatever context, teaching well is an ever-evolving process, one that is never finished or really even mastered. Research has shown that "quality learning experiences for students require[s] quality teachers" (Stronge, Tucker & Hindman 2004, p. 208). Improving teaching requires effective instruction and supervision, and that must be based on sound theory and good practice of building a community that supports the learning of teachers—with time, with money, with practice, and with culture. "Communities always exist, at least in part, because children need them as a place to learn to be adults. Thus, a 'school that learns,' wherever it is located and whatever form it takes, requires a community that fosters learning all around it" (Senge et al. 2000, p. 460). From the days of the one-room schoolhouse to today's monolithic structures, from our understanding of what made a Tanaaitic or Talmudic community to today's synagogues and Jewish agencies, the desire for communities that learn has remained unabated and, with the mindset and purpose as well as the grounding of theory and practice, such a desire may be achieved.

IMPLICATIONS AND/OR POLICY RECOMMENDATIONS

Mentorship needs funding. Formal mentorship programs are not free—they cost money, time, energy, resources, and a level of commitment that may not be present in some schools or other types of educational institutions. Mentorship may, in the end, save money for a school system. Research on new teachers in California found that providing $4,400 more in annual salary increased the chances that elementary school teachers would stay in their field by 17%. Teachers offered the opportunity to participate in mentoring programs, at a cost to the state of $3,370, were 26% more likely to stay in teaching (Associated Press, 2006). Still, many schools today may not have such resources to devote to mentorship. However, the research has shown that there are still significant benefits to mentoring, even in informal, unstructured situations (R. F. Holtz & Holtzer 2006). "Informal, spontaneous mentoring occurs during the natural course of events, when someone simply reaches out to give support or direction to another person" (Noller & Frey, cited in McCluskey et al. 2004). In much the same way that a formal mentor and mentee can be both teacher and coach to one another, an informally paired partner can be "a wise and trusted friend" (Smink 1999, p. 11) and even when the relationship is casually or informally developed, provide psychological support that makes the work environment more enjoyable and the work more rewarding. "If you ever need anything" can be understood as an outstretched hand that can be called upon, even months later, by colleagues seeking support. Such help can evolve into supportive relationships. Investigation is warranted into how to further implement informal mentorship programs in places where formal programs are not an option.

Mentorship needs more than the practice of pedagogy because practice alone cannot guide a teacher to his or her full potential. Research into student learning is based upon teacher reflection and willingness to change (Rodgers 2002). Research is not blind to the obstacles that teachers face in improving the quality of their teaching (Education Commission of the States 2000). The lack of openness of the learning community to include new members and the emphasis on achieving satisfactory performance (rather than excellence) has prevented many teachers from achieving their potential.

In New York regulations to improve the quality of teaching concentrate on how to address the "performance of teachers whose performance is evaluated as unsatisfactory" (Research and Educational Services 2003). The research supports the idea that interaction *can* increase job satisfaction (Marques & Luna 2005), but whether this translates to mentorship is not fully explored. Further research is needed to ascertain how best to assess mentorship programs and determine if they are indeed positively impacting teachers' performance, outlook, and learning.

Mentorship needs proximity. Jewish educational organizations have varying needs depending upon their purpose, their mission, their demographics, and their geographic location. Proximity, therefore, may have to come via a computer or a telephone. In 2003 the American Board of Certification of Teacher Excellence broadened its scope of programs by offering "virtual" mentoring for online discussions of classroom practice. One commentator described how important this might be to communities where it is difficult to find same-grade or same-subject mentors, especially those in rural communities (Blair 2003). Long-distance mentoring, in particular, may be a desire of many smaller Jewish communities or those in far-flung locales. To be sure, long-distance situations present unique challenges, including lack of common context, time differences that make conversations complicated to schedule (Zachary 2000), and difficulties in gauging feedback. The Leadership Institute for Congregational School Principals, co-sponsored by Hebrew Union College, The Jewish Theological Seminary, and UJA-Federation of New York, pairs seasoned professionals with those seeking mentors from many areas in the northeast. Participants create proximity in various fashions, much of it outside the face-to-face connections upon which more typical mentorship programs might thrive. Evaluations of such programs are essential for further development and exploration of the challenges faced by virtual mentoring.

Mentorship needs a common ground. Communities without sufficient Jewish resources or personnel may struggle with how to implement cross-cultural or cross-religious mentoring or with how to find a common ground. "Cross-cultural barriers consist of more than just language or semantic barriers…with how one sees the world as well as how one acts within it" (Zachary 2000, p. 38). Religion and culture both impact modes of expression, context, and participant expectations. This is not to say that cross-religious mentorship programs are not viable; rather, it is likely that disparate views must be considered.

Mentorship needs time. Time is also the most frequently expressed explanation for failure in a mentorship relationship (Zachary 2000). While theories of adult learning demand a degree of autonomy and self-direction by the participants, lack of consensus about time may be the downfall of a program. Is the need for time thought out in the planning? How will time be negotiated, watched, and kept in the program? Such considerations must be established prior to implementing a mentorship program. On several levels, time for programs of mentorship must be considered. It may require an overhaul of the structuring of the school day in order to allow teachers time away from classes and students to work with one another. "The mentor relationship is too important to be squeezed into the margins of an already busy workday" (Ballinger 2000, p. 33).

Mentorship needs to take a broad view of learning. Teachers need support if they are to grow in their practice and become more effective (Stronge Tucker & Hindman 2004). Using the characteristics of a professional learning community (Eaker, DuFour and DuFour 2000), schools can become places where *everyone* learns, teachers and students. This is in stark contrast to a classroom model where the students are viewed as acquirers of knowledge and teachers are the providers. In the traditional model, teachers may receive information, but their knowledge is assumed to have been acquired in teacher training programs. Such teacher knowledge is thus considered finite. Teachers are accountable for student learning but not for their own. In contrast, with the "progressive" model of schools as learning communities, learning is expected of everyone in the organization. This "progressive" model requires feedback that is designed to inform instruction (Danielson & McGreal 2000). If Jewish educational organizations create systems that are progressive, that view teachers as learners, mentorship may quickly become viewed as a natural entity that benefits teachers and students.

Mentorship needs administrative support. Teachers are not the only professionals who need to support programs of mentorship. Administrators, too, must value the relationships and learning that such programs may foster. They must promote collaboration, lobby for needed funds and incorporate time into the schedules of faculty members in order to foster successful mentorship (Jones & Pauley 2003). Administrators must appreciate the potential of mentorship and be skilled in guiding it to success for others and for themselves. They also need mentoring, but programs for them are still in their infancy.

ADDITIONAL RESEARCH QUESTIONS

- Mentoring has been shown to have a positive impact on teacher retention in public and private school settings. Does it have a similar benefit in congregational school settings where the challenges of locating and retaining personnel are significantly different than in a public or private school?

- Though mentorship programs have become increasingly common in school systems, there are no standards (Zachary 2006) or benchmarks for which to strive. What are appropriate benchmarks for mentorship programs in Jewish educational settings? How should they differ in such diverse educational settings as congregational schools and day schools?

- Teacher mentoring programs are "diverse in organization, administration, and implementation" (Teaching Music 2003). What are the variables that are most likely to succeed in Jewish institutions? Are there suggestions for organization, administration, or development that are most applicable to Jewish settings?

- What are the factors that determine the impact of the common mentoring activities (observations, discussions, journaling, lesson planning, curricular exchanges) on growth and learning?

- What is the role of religion in mentoring programs that reside within Jewish institutions? What roles do traditional Jewish study methods have in Jewish mentoring programs?

- What is the relationship between pedagogical learning and essential learning about "Torah" in its broadest sense that is important to mentorship in Jewish institutions?

FUTURE DIRECTIONS

- Financial resources for video-conferencing should be explored for teachers who mentor those in other institutions (Dorph & B. Holtz 2000). Investigation of the role of distance mentorship in secular education may clarify adaptations needed for the unique challenges in Jewish education. This study might clarify some of the ways that Jewish education might exploit practices in distance mentoring.

- If mentorship does have clear positive implications on teacher retention in Jewish settings, marketing such results may increase the implementation of such programs.

- School leaders "inspire, motivate, coordinate, supervise, and support teachers" (Grant 2004), but they may not be sufficiently skilled in how best to support their teachers within a mentorship program. Training of principals and other educational leaders on approaches to implementing mentorship programs must be fully developed, including the inculcation of a basic understanding of the theoretical underpinnings.

- Programs of mentorship for personnel other than teachers must be undertaken. Principals, agency heads, and other educational leaders will also benefit from mentoring. Such programs have recently been a focus in the secular realm (Archer 2006), and greater attention is warranted in Jewish education as well.

- Agencies and philanthropic organizations must begin to invest in sustainable leadership and mentoring programs. In forty-two schools in suburban counties outside of New York City, the Fairchester Fellows received a grant from the E. E. Ford Foundation to mentor new teachers. Modeled after a similar program in New York City, the program "supports twenty-five new teachers each year through weekly dinner meetings, classroom observations, journal writing, sample lessons, book reviewing, group discussions, and other forms of professional development" (Crane & Kelly 2005). Such an endeavor should be considered within the Jewish community.

CONCLUSION

As an entity, mentorship offers many potential benefits to educational institutions, to participants, and to the communities in which such programs take place. Jewish educational institutions are unique in their purpose and in their challenges, and mentorship has much to offer them. The collaboration that is essential for the success of mentoring is also vital to the creation of the community that is so important to Judaism. Still, much remains to be done as far as research and evaluation of existing programs, their mission, their methodology, and dimensions of their structure.

HIGHLIGHTS

- Learners' need for self-direction is consistent with adult learning theory in programs of mentorship.
- Mentorship is much more than one seasoned professional acting as a teacher for a novice who acts as a learner.
- Jewish educational programs will be positively impacted by mentoring programs.

LARGER CONTEXT

Better teachers make better students. The challenges of how to make better teachers, of teacher shortages and of retention are a struggle in nearly all school systems. Jewish educational institutions face additional hurdles in hiring and retaining effective teachers who possess both secular education and Judaic knowledge. Yet the challenge to create institutions in which all members are learners is even greater. Mentorship holds great potential for creating schools that are learning communities, in which novices and veteran faculty learn from one another. For many schools this purpose has become the pivotal rationale for mentorship that has as its primary byproduct increased teacher and student learning.

ANNOTATED BIBLIOGRAPHY

Eaker, R., DuFour, R. & DuFour, R. (2002). *Getting Started: Reculturing Schools to Become Professional Learning Communities*. Bloomington, IN: National Educational Service. This text offers many ideas for getting started in creating professional learning communities. It discusses aspects of school culture and faculty perspectives as well as how to make inroads in opening up and increasing receptivity to group learning. A case study of one school that made such a transition is a key feature of this book.

English, L. (1998). *Mentoring in Religious Education*. Birmingham: Religious Education Press. This text describes the stages of the mentoring process. Religious settings pose unique challenges and opportunities in the initiation of mentoring programs. English has designed an approach that administrators in all types of religious educational settings can use to develop their own programs.

Schuster, D. T. (2003). *Jewish Lives, Jewish Learning: Adult Jewish Learning in Theory and Practice*. NY: UAHC Press. Utilizing the experience of individuals to understand adult Jewish learners, this text addresses what creates the impetus for Jewish learning, how to create an embracing environment that will allow adults to feel safe in their study and how to encourage the pursuit of lifelong learning.

Zachary, L. J. (2000). *The Mentor's Guide: Facilitating Effective Learning Relationships*. San Francisco: Jossey-Bass. This text presents many practical and user-friendly ideas for implementing a mentorship program and facilitating a positive and effective learning environment. The information by Zachary is appropriate for all educational settings and beyond.

REFERENCES

Archer, J. (2006). "Mentoring for new principals gains policy attention." *Education Week* 26 (3), 10–11.

Aron, I. (1988). "From where will the next generation of Jewish teachers come?" *Journal of Reform Judaism* 35, 51–65.

Aronson, J. (2003). Partnering with a mentor. In N. Moskowitz (ed.), *The Ultimate Jewish Teachers Handbook*. Denver, CO: A.R.E. Publishing.

Associated Press (2006). "California study gauges methods for retaining new teachers." *Education Week* 25 (24), 30.

Association for Career and Technical Education (2000). "Mentoring may aid teacher retention." *Techniques: Connection Education & Careers* 75 (4), 9–13.

Bailey, T. (2003). "Analogy, dialectics, and lifelong learning." *International Journal of Lifelong Education* 22 (2) 132–146.

Bechofer, R. A. (1983). Judaism and counseling: Perspectives and comparisons. ED237826.

Bakhtin, M. M. (1981). *The Dialogic Imagination: Four Essays by M. Bakhtin,* C. Emerson & M. Holquist (eds.). Austin, TX: University of Texas Press.

Bakhtin, M. M. (1986). *Speech Genres and Other Late Essays,* C. Emerson & M. Holquist (eds.). McGee (Trans.). Austin, TX: University of Texas Press.

Ballinger, J. (2000). "Programs aim to stop teacher washout." *Journal of Staff Development* 21 (2), 28–33.

Bartunek, H. (1990). *The Classroom Teacher as Teacher Educator.* (ERIC Documents Reproduction Services No. ED 335 297).

Bekerman, Z. (2001). "Constructivist perspectives on language, identity, and culture: Implications for Jewish identity and the education of Jews." *Religious Education* 96 (4), 462–473.

Blair, J. (2003). "Critics question federal funding of teacher test." *Education Week* 23 (6), 1–2.

Brause, R. S. (2000). Theory building in professional development: The importance of personal stance on teaching/learning. In R. A. Connolly & D. A. Feola (eds.), *Teachers as learners: Multiple lenses on professional development,* 1–32.

Caccia, P. F. (1998). "Linguistic coaching: Helping beginning teachers defeat discouragement." *Educational Leadership* 53 (6), 17–21.

Crane, J. & Kelly, C. (2005). "Keeping new teachers." *Independent School* 64, (2), 76–79.

Cranton, P. (1996). *Professional Development as Transformative Learning.* San Francisco: Jossey-Bass.

Crow, G. M. & Matthews, L. J. (1998). *Finding One's Way.* Thousand Oaks, CA: Corwin Press.

Danielson, C. & McGreal, T. L. (2000). *Teacher Evaluation to Enhance Professional Practice.* Alexandria, VA: ASCD.

Daloz, L. A. (1999). *Mentor: Guiding the Journey of Adult Learners.* San Francisco: Jossey- Bass.

Doris I. (2000), Personal Communication with Renee Holtz.

Dorph, G. & Holtz, B. (2000). "Professional development for teachers: Why doesn't the model change?" *Journal of Jewish Education* 66 (1/2), 67–76.

Duckworth, E. (1997). *Teacher to Teacher.* New York: Teachers College Press.

Eaker, R., DuFour, R. & DuFour, R. (2002). *Getting Started: Reculturing Schools to Become Professional Learning Communities.* Bloomington, IN: National Educational Service.

English, L. (1998). *Mentoring in Religious Education.* Birmingham, AL: Religious Education Press.

Evans, C., Stewart, P.M., Mangin, M. & Bagley, C. (2001). "Teacher quality: Issues and research." *Education* 122 (1), 200–205.

Fairbanks, C. M., Freedman, D. & Kahn, C. (2000). "The role of effective mentors in learning to teach." *Journal of Teacher Education* 51 (2), 102–112.

Feiman-Nemster, S. (1996). *Teacher Mentoring: A Critical Review.* (ERIC Document Reproduction Service, ED 397 060)

Friend, M. & Cook, L. (2000). *Interactions: Collaboration Skills for School Professionals.* New York: Longman.

Gamoran, A., Goldring, E., Robinson, B., Tammivaara, J. & Goodman, R. (1998). *The Teachers Report: A Portrait of Teachers in Jewish Schools.* New York: Council for Initiatives in Jewish Education.

Garman, N. B. (1995). Mentoring as a discursive practice. In M. Zeldin & S. S. Lee (eds.), *Touching the Future: Mentoring and the Jewish Professional.* Los Angeles: HUC–JIR, 28–35.

Gonzalez, C. (2006). "When is a mentor like a monk?" *Academe* 92 (3), 29–33.

Grant, L. D. (2004). "Connection and caring: The role of educational leadership in adult Jewish learning." *Religious Education* 99 (2), 167–184.

Hoff, D. J. (2004). "Governors study teacher quality." *Education Week* 23(37), 24.

Holtz, B. W. (1996). "How do adults learn? The Catholic–Jewish colloquium and the possibilities for personal transformation." *Religious Education* 91 (4), 576–581.

Holtz, R. F. (2001). A mentoring program in a Jewish supplementary school (Doctoral dissertation, Fordham University, 2001). *Dissertation Abstracts International 62* (07), 2338A

Holtz, R. F. (2002). "One mentoring program—What really happened? Roles, process, and community." *Jewish Education News 23* (3), 53–55.

Holtz, R. F. & Holtzer, A. (2006). "Mentorship in a vacuum. *Jewish Education News 27*(3), 18–19.

Jones, I. (2004). Ways of learning from developments in policy." *Adults Learning 16* (2), 27.

Jones, M. S. & Pauley, W. F. (2003). "Mentoring beginning public school teachers." *Adult Learning 14* (1), 23–25.

Joyce, B. & Showers, B. (1983). "The coaching of teaching." *Educational Leadership* 40 (1), 4–10

Kerka, S. (1997). *Constructivism, Workplace Learning, and Vocational Education* (ERIC Document Reproduction Service No. ED 407 573).

Knowles, M. S. (1980). *The Modern Practice of Adult Education*. Chicago, IL: Association Press/Follett.

Knowles, M. S. (1984). *Andragogy in Action: Applying Modern Principles of Adult Learning*. San Francisco: Jossey-Bass.

Maehl, W. H. (2000). *Lifelong Learning at Its Best: Innovative Practices in Adult Education Programs*. San Francisco: Jossey-Bass.

Marques, J. F. & Luna, R. (2005). "Advising adult learners: The practice of peer partisanship." *Recruitment & Retention in Higher Education 19* (6), 5–7.

McCluskey, K. W., Noller, R. B., Lamoureux, K. & McCluskey, A. L. A. (2004). "Unlocking hidden potential through mentoring." *Reclaiming Children and Youth* 13 (2), 85–93.

Mezirow, J. (1991). *Transformative Dimensions of Adult Learning*. San Francisco: Jossey-Bass.

O'Brien, J. & Christie, F. (2005). "Characteristics of support for beginning teachers: Evidence from the new Teacher Induction Scheme in Scotland." *Mentoring and Tutoring* 13 (2), 189–203.

Platt, A. D., Tripp, C. E., Ogden, W. R., & Fraser, R. G. (2000). *The Skillful Leader: Confronting Mediocre Teaching*. Action, MA: Research for Better Teaching.

Research and Educational Services (2003). *Teacher Improvement Plan (TIP)*. New York: Research and Educational Services.

Robbins, P. & Alvy, H. (2004). Vision as the compass. In *The New Principal's Fieldbook: Strategies for Success.* . Alexandria, VA: ASCD, 1–13.

Rodgers, C. R. (2002). "Seeing student learning: Teacher change and the role of reflection." *Harvard Educational Review* 72 (2), 1–19.

Schaller, J. (1996). "Mentoring of women: Transformation in adult religious education." *Religious Education* 91 (2), 160–171.

Schuster, D. T. (2003). *Jewish Lives, Jewish Learning: Adult Jewish Learning in Theory and Practice*. New York: UAHC Press.

Senge, P., Cambron-McCabe, N., Lucas, T., Smith, B., Dutton, J. & Kleiner, A. (2000). *Schools That Learn*. New York: Doubleday.

Showers, B. & Joyce, B. (1996). "The evolution of peer coaching." *Educational Leadership* 53 (6), 12–16.

Skinner, M. E. & Welch, F. C. (1996). "Peer coaching for better teaching." *College Teaching* 44 (4), 153–156.

Smink, J. (1999). A training guide for mentors (ERIC Document Reproduction Service No. ED 430 125).

Stigler J.W. & Hiebert J. (1999). *The Teaching Gap*. NY: The Free Press.

Strong, J. H., Tucker, P. D. & Hindman, J. L. (2004). *Handbook for Qualities of Effective Teachers*. Alexandria, VA: ASCD.

Teaching Music (2003). FYI: "Mentor Programs for Beginning Teachers." *Teaching Music* 11 (2), 70.

Toto, J. (2006). "Untapped world of peer coaching." *ASTD* 4, 69–70.

U. S. Department of Education (1994). *Toward Better Teaching: Time for Professional Development*. Institute for Educational Sciences, National Center for Educational Statistics.

U. S. Department of Education (1998). *Time for Learning*. Teacher Survey on Professional Development.

U. S. Department of Education (2000). *Teacher Preparation and Professional Development: 2000.* Institute for Educational Sciences, National Center for Educational Statistics.

U. S. Department of Education (2003). *Contexts of Elementary and Secondary Education.* Institute for Educational Sciences, National Center for Educational Statistics.

Vygotsky, L.S. (1978). *Mind in Society.* Cambridge, MA: Harvard University Press.

Weasmer, J. & Woods, A. M. (2003). "The role of the host teacher in the student teaching experience." *Clearing House* 76 (4), 174–177.

Zachary, L. J. (2000). *The Mentor's Guide: Facilitating Effective Learning Relationships.* San Francisco: Jossey-Bass.

Zachary, L. J. (2001). "Lessons from a mentoring at Sinai." *Jewish Education News* 22 (3), 1–5.

Zachary, L. J. (2006). "Creating a mentoring culture." *Jewish Education News* 27 (3), 10–12.

Professional Development Requires a Discipline for Seeing Wholes

Cyd Weissman

A diploma in any field is only the invitation to participate. Experience, ongoing learning, reflection and support are the universities of experts. Professional development is the name of that university in the field of education. Teaching is a complex art that must respond to the changing goals, technology and curricula of schools; the developing nature, needs and attitudes of learners; and the varying expectations, support and involvement of communities. Becoming an expert in a field where shifting forces are often at odds with one another requires ongoing focused and intensive learning. To build the university of experts, the National Education Association (NEA) notes schools should be places where teachers learn as well as teach. "To improve student learning, we should improve teaching. To improve teaching, teachers must engage in learning continuously as an integral part of their job. Teacher learning cannot be relegated to special occasions, nor can the subject of that learning be divorced from the immediate learning needs of students" (NEA 2006). Professional development, rather than being an isolated initiative, must be an integral part of a school's overall plan, a smart part of a greater whole, for achieving student outcomes.

Jewish teachers work in a field as complex as general education, if not more so. Educational innovations and the expectations set by the Jewish community demand that teachers not only learn new skills and knowledge, but also re-conceptualize and re-invent the overall nature of their teaching so as to nurture learners of all ages in knowing, believing, living and belonging. Supporting teachers on such a trajectory requires the kind of ongoing, intensive and focused learning called for by the NEA. In response to this call, professionals in the field have begun to refer to professional development as professional learning. The use of the word learning instead of development signals the ongoing nature of the work and a shift away from focusing on teachers' deficits (Hirsh 2006). Despite these shifts, the prevailing model of professional learning in the Jewish community for approximately sixty-four thousand teachers in Jewish congregational schools, early childhood programs and day schools (Schapp, Goodman 2002) consists of sporadic generic workshops or college courses not related to classroom work (Dorph & Holtz 2000; Stodolsky et al. 2004). Fragmented, isolated learning for teachers has little impact on professional practice or student learning (Elmore 1997; Sparks & Hirsh 2000). A vast gap exists between the professional learning offered and what is needed.

When meeting the needs of Jewish education, leaders often look to the field of general education. Answers to the following four questions can help decision makers identify applicable and adaptable principles from general education for the unique needs of Jewish education.

1. What standards and practices established in the field of general education promote high quality professional learning?

2. What are recommended strategies to meet the specialized needs of beginning teachers in all forms of Jewish educational programs and schools?

3. What examples of professional learning in Jewish education reflect the standards and practices of general education?

4. What are the unique needs of Jewish teachers that may not be addressed by practices adopted from general education?

WHAT STANDARDS AND PRACTICES ESTABLISHED IN THE FIELD OF GENERAL EDUCATION PROMOTE HIGH QUALITY PROFESSIONAL LEARNING?

General education's current recommended standards and practices for professional learning are rooted in a systems approach that focuses on identifying and managing a wide range of factors that impact the desired goal of student outcomes. A systems approach requires a "discipline for seeing wholes" and stands in direct contrast to problem solving that attends to singular factors or causes (Senge et al. 2000). Wertheimer has labeled the need for seeing, planning and programming within a framework of "wholes" with the shorthand phrase "linking the silos" (2005). Reference to silos, he notes, is seen in the field of information technology and "characterizes the uni-dimensional manner in which institutions and fields of knowledge operate in isolation as vertically organized operations, divorced from constructive, horizontal interaction with others" (p. 2). When a systems approach is applied to professional learning, the answer to "How will teachers learn to support student outcomes?" is more complex than just "training." Leaders who practice a discipline for seeing wholes respond to that question by linking professional learning to a school's vision, goals and culture and to family engagement. To link the silos for professional learning, educational leaders need to attend to the *context, the process and the content* of what teachers *and* students experience.

The National Staff Development Council (NSDC)'s standards for professional development, established in 2001, focus on context, content and process, and have as their goal the improvement of all students. These standards are "generally recognized as one of the most comprehensive and judicious sets of professional development standards available today. In fact, many states have modeled their own standards on the NSDC's" (Schramm, 2005). The standards act as a guide, not a blueprint, adaptable by each school to create high-quality staff learning that improves teacher practice and student performance. They assure that professional learning will be results-driven and job-embedded. Educational leaders can use the NSDC standards as a map for seeing all of the factors to be addressed when designing learning for teachers that impacts the learning of students.

The necessity of standards in the field of general education arose "because for too long the professional development practices of too many school systems have led nowhere. Year after year, their staff development has amounted to little more than a disparate set of adult learning activities with few demonstrable results other than participants' mounting frustration" (Hord, Hirsh & Roy, p. 5). The NSDC standards were developed by representatives of the national education associations who reviewed research, discussed best practices, and reached consensus on the focus for the standards. Three questions guided the establishment of the standards:

- What are all students expected to know and be able to do?
- What must teachers know and do in order to ensure student success?
- Where must staff development focus to meet both goals?

A review of the NSDC standards follows, including three context standards, six process standards and three content standards. The NSDC standards are not the only rubric for high- quality professional development existing in general education. Many groups have adopted or based their standards on the work of the NSDC. Organizations that create their own rubric often justify the veracity of it by comparing it to the NSDC. For example, a rubric for professional development standards established by the University of Pennsylvania Graduate School of Education in 2003, although slightly different, assured the reader it was "consistent with the work of the NSDC" (Corcoran, McVay & Riordan, p. 5). Deeply rooted in current research, the NSDC standards should be considered a guide for creating high-quality professional learning as they enable educational leaders to see broadly and deeply. The NSDC standards enable professional development planners to practice a discipline for seeing wholes.

Three Context Standards focus on the set of circumstances that must surround professional learning: Professional Learning Communities, Leadership and Resources. Staff development that improves the learning of all students:

1. **Organizes adults into learning communities whose goals are aligned with the school and district.**

Professional Learning Communities (PLC) are formed when professional staff participates in regularized learning, planning, reflections, and observations as part of their daily teaching routine. This requires a total rethinking of the structure of schools and the time provided for focused and intentional professional learning (Sparks & Hirsh 2000). The gathering and learning of teachers is only considered elevated to the level of a true PLC when its work is focused on student outcomes, not the interest area of teachers, the products promoted by publishers, or new educational trends (Hord 1997).

2. **Requires skillful school and district leaders who guide continuous instructional improvement.**

   Leadership teams need to send the message that professional learning is a priority in a school environment where shifting demands and requirements can distract focus from teacher learning. To be the leaders of and the advocates for professional development, educational leaders require their own specifically designed professional development. Principals, in particular, can play, if supported with adequate learning, a key role in establishing a culture that values and integrates professional learning (Roy 2006).

3. **Requires resources to support adult learning and collaboration.**

   Resources need to be allocated to provide the time, money and materials for ongoing professional learning. Leaders need to share concrete data that demonstrate the link between professional learning and student outcomes to assure that decision makers see professional development not as an extra activity with few visible dividends, but as an important long-term investment in quality education.

Six Process Standards focus on essential steps in the creation of professional learning: Data-driven, Evaluation, Research-based, Design, Learning and Collaboration. Staff development that improves the learning of all students:

1. **Uses disaggregated student data to determine adult learning priorities, monitor progress and help sustain continuous improvement.**
   Data gathered from multiple sources on what students need to learn and have learned should drive a continuous loop of decision making, determining the focus of professional learning. Data-driven decision making contrasts with new-product–driven decision making that often occurs in education. Leaders need to develop the skills and knowledge to select and administer reliable tests and perform quality data interpretation (DuFour 1999).

2. **Uses multiple sources of information to guide improvement and demonstrate its impact.**
   Evaluation of clearly stated goals in terms of student and staff knowledge, skills, behaviors or attitudes needs to be established so that staff development programs and processes can be assessed. Evaluation answers the essential question: "Is professional learning enabling teachers to achieve student outcomes?"

3. **Prepares educators to apply research to decision making.**
   Research-based decision making requires leaders to have access to relevant research and to develop the skill of adapting and translating that research to meet the particular needs of teachers and students.

4. **Uses learning strategies appropriate to the intended goal.**
   Design of professional learning cannot be generic. Within a PLC, design strategies need to be carefully selected based on the learning needs of teachers (e.g., novice vs. experienced teachers) and students (e.g., learning to use computers requires different strategies than learning to write an essay).

5. **Applies knowledge about human learning and change.**
   Learning for adults should be self-directed, goal-oriented, and relevant to immediate needs, and should demonstrate respect for a learner's experience (Knowles, M. Holton, E. & Swanson, R. 1998). Attention should also be paid to managing forces of resistance that will most likely come when individuals are asked to develop new skills and knowledge.

6. Provides educators with knowledge and skills to collaborate

Collaboration is a learned skill. To work well in a PLC teachers need to learn how to build consensus, share ideas, and effectively listen to one another. Effective leaders need to foster common purpose, continuous inquiry, and shared practice if they are to create a collaborative environment (Leonard & Leonard 2003; Fullan 2004).

Three Content Standards on what subject areas teachers need to learn in quality professional development: Equity, Quality Teaching and Family and Communal Engagement. Staff development that improves the learning of all students:

1. Prepares educators to understand and appreciate all students, create safe, orderly and supportive learning environments, and hold high expectations for their academic achievement.

Equity for all learners irrespective of age, sexual orientation, gender, race, or other family background factors is expected and therefore requires that teachers meet the learning needs of their diverse student body. This includes, but is not limited to, knowing differentiated instruction, varied classroom management arrangements and ways of generating high expectations for all groups of students (Hord, Hirsh & Roy 2005).

2. Deepens educators' content knowledge, provides them with research-based instructional strategies to assist students in meeting rigorous academic standards, and prepares them to use various types of classroom assessments appropriately.

Quality teaching requires teachers to have deep content knowledge and the pedagogy and assessment specific to that content. As Joellen Killion writes, "What a teacher knows and does influences what a student learns" (2006, p. 1). Content, teaching strategies and evaluation all must be aligned to established student outcomes.

3. Provides educators with knowledge and skills to involve families and other stakeholders appropriately.

Family and communal involvement are necessary components for creating a partnership between the school, the home, and the community that enables students to achieve the best results. Principals and teachers, because of their unique roles, develop different kinds of relationships with the community and therefore need to learn different skills for engaging both parents and the community at large.

REASSURING, NOT OVERWHELMING

These standards are meant not to be overwhelming but to be a reassuring guide to linking context, content and process. Leaders use the standards to see the whole of what is needed for high-quality professional learning—to start with the end in mind—and then launch, over time, a continual series of initiatives. Each initiative, however, has to be designed, not as an end in itself, but as a smart-part of a greater whole. Smart-parts do the work set out by the standard *and* the work of revealing information, raising questions, and providing experiences that enable leaders to connect one standard to another, to link context, content and process. Eventually these smart-parts speak the language of shared purpose, working in their own ways to support common goals.

Schools take years to develop this approach. It is messy and complicated. To briefly illustrate this way of working, imagine, for example, a school that rearranges schedules so teachers can regularly learn together and observe one another (Context Standard: Professional Learning Communities [PLC]). Because leaders are working with a bigger picture in mind, they don't see the PLC as the end goal. Rather they use the PLC not only to bring teachers together, but also to provide information that will inform subsequent work, such as which teachers work well together and which teachers can take on leadership roles. Professional learning planners also listen for and work to address the questions raised by the PLC, such as "What should the PLC focus on? How do teachers translate the learning into the classroom?" (Content Standard: Quality Teaching). Then, when challenges arise among staff, professional learning leaders, guided by unfolding information and the standards, address a new question: "What are the best ways to help staff learn to work together?" (Process

Standard: Collaboration). Evolving over a two- to three-year period, requiring continual development in subsequent years, each step, naturally and by design, would lead to another standard. The NSDC Standards equip educational leaders to keep an eye on the whole while working on smart-part initiatives that, over time, create an integrated system transforming staff, culture, and learners.

WHAT ARE RECOMMENDED STRATEGIES TO MEET THE SPECIALIZED NEEDS OF BEGINNING TEACHERS?

One third of beginning teachers in public schools quit within the first three years. Continually recruiting, training and losing staff is a drain schools can ill afford. Beginning teachers, both novice and experienced, but newly hired, have special needs that, when met, can increase retention. Both require special attention. Novice teachers have an invitation to teach but lack the experience to translate what they have learned into effective action. Novice and experienced teachers need to learn the norms, practices and goals of a new school. Induction, a program specifically designed to "enculturate" and support new staff, should be considered a focused part of a school's established professional learning, not a program that can exist successfully in a school that has an unhealthy learning and teaching culture (Feiman-Nemser 2003).

Beginning teachers need emotional and personal support, task-problem focused support, and practice in critical reflection on teaching in order to achieve success and overcome the challenges of being new professionals. Stress, confusion, isolation and emotional discomfort are frequently the results when a new teacher does not receive these supports. Specific challenges include lesson planning, arranging parent–teacher conferences, responding to a disruptive student and deciding what materials are appropriate for a specific student with a particular need. These examples highlight the range of challenges that go from administrative details to classroom management to important educational decision making. Beginning teachers also need to develop an ability to reflect on their teaching, identify their challenges and act as independent educational problem solvers. This includes being able to prioritize challenges, consider alternative strategies to address them and then develop the confidence to take action. Clearly, induction programs need to offer multiple options of support if they are to carry out a sincere intent to respond to the wide variety of needs exhibited by new teachers.

Recognizing the importance of an induction program is the first step for a school to fulfill the wish to support new teachers. Only when educational leaders value the results that can be achieved with induction programs will resources be allotted. Additional strategies, specifically appropriate for beginning teachers, include mentoring, coaching, demonstration lessons, mini-courses for specific needs, and portfolio collection (gathering evidence of teaching for analysis). Each of these strategies requires learning for the beginning teacher and for the established staff. For example, when mentoring is a designated strategy, master teachers need to learn specific skills for how to support their protégés. Collecting and reflecting on teacher work also requires learned skills. By establishing a culture that promotes collaboration and learning, schools will support naturally occurring and thoughtfully designed opportunities for connecting the veteran and novice teachers, for regularizing reflection, planning and analysis and for deepening skills and content (Stansbury & Zimmerman 2001; Feiman-Nemser 2003). Focused, sustained commitment to supporting the unique needs of new teachers within a larger commitment to supporting the needs of all teachers will increase retention rates of staff and improve the quality of learning for students.

WHAT EXAMPLES OF PROFESSIONAL LEARNING IN JEWISH EDUCATION REFLECT THE STANDARDS AND PRACTICES OF SECULAR EDUCATION?

Today an increasing number of Jewish schools are discarding long-held, inadequate professional learning practices. Experiments in creating quality professional learning that ultimately impacts students are emerging in day schools, day care centers, congregational schools and early childhood schools across the country. "Congregational Schools Focus on Teacher Training" is the bold headline from the August 11, 2006 *Forward* article (Zeder) reporting that after decades of offering a smorgasbord of workshops for teachers that produced few results, communities are beginning to invest in serious, focused, and intensive professional development. However, high quality professional learning is far from the norm today. By sharing the stories of Jewish communities that are designing professional learning as smart-parts leading to a greater whole where context, content and process are being addressed, a new norm for quality Jewish professional learning can be established. Examples of these new initiatives include:

PROJECT ENGAJE! ENRICH NOURISH AND GROW THROUGH ADULT JEWISH EDUCATION, 2004–6

Creates a Professional Learning Community (NSDC Standard, Learning Communities); Deepens Educators Content Knowledge (NSDC Standard, Quality Teaching); Uses Learning Strategies Aligned to Intended Goals (NSDC Standard, Design); and Provides Teachers with Skills to Involve Families (NSDC Standard, Family Involvement).

Project ENGAJE, sponsored by UJA-Federation of New York, worked with two hundred and fifty early childhood teachers from the Metro New York community in a two year initiative to strengthen teacher knowledge and pedagogic skills. Eleven schools, including Jewish community centers, synagogues and a day care facility, participated in the program that was developed and administered by the Board of Jewish Education (BJE) of Greater New York and the Suffolk Association of Jewish Educational Services (SAJES). Teachers attended bi-monthly one-and-a-half-hour on-site sessions before or after the school day. Mentor teachers from settings of higher Jewish learning in the New York area led learning sessions on Jewish content and pedagogy. The mentor teachers were selected for their content knowledge and their ability to model adult commitment to ongoing Jewish learning. Teachers participated voluntarily, were paid a stipend for each year, and went on a group trip to Israel. By creating ongoing focused learning for teachers led by highly qualified instructors, Project ENGAJE laid the groundwork for establishing professional learning communities within each school.

The initial year of the project focused on enriching the Jewish knowledge of teachers. During the second year teachers worked to incorporate their personal learning into the classroom with the help of a newly created "integration specialist." Parents and families were also engaged in the second year through the development of a three-part series designed to enrich parents' Jewish learning.

Early results indicate that each site successfully created the beginnings of a PLC. Teachers reported increased feelings of being valued; increased use of Hebrew in the classroom and increased "liveliness" in the teaching of holidays and life cycle events. Additionally, planners recognized that subsequent versions of the project should address the larger school culture. Investing in how teachers work and think, it was reported, without a parallel investment in how the school works and thinks, minimized results (Meskin 2006). Hirsh, As Executive Director of the NSDC, notes, when you "put a good person in a bad system, the system will win every time" (2006). Based on the evaluation and gleaned insights, the next iteration of the project will keep many of the initial design elements with an added focus on the context for professional learning and a new focus on leadership, resources and vision. SAJES will administer an expanded version of Project ENGAJE with five new schools in 2007–9. In each of the participating schools a task force of lay and professional leaders will work to establish common vision and goals for the early childhood school. By creating a culture and governance that value and support early childhood education and teachers, the scope of professional learning will be expanded beyond what teachers need to know and do. This project began with smart-parts that have opened doors to additional standards that will further deepen professional learning in the schools engaged.

SHARSHERET: A PROGRAM FOR CONGREGATIONAL RELIGIOUS SCHOOL EXCELLENCE, 2005–PRESENT

Develops Skillful Leaders to Guide Continuous Professional Learning (NSDC Context Standard, Leadership); and Uses Learning Strategies Appropriate to Intended Goal (NSDC Process Standard, Design).

Sharsheret is a training program for seven congregational school principals to become instructional leaders who will create and lead professional development in their congregations. The initiative was created by the Center for the Advancement of Jewish Education (CAJE) in Miami with funding from the Greater Miami Jewish Federation. The program is in its second year of design and implementation and is being customized to the particular needs of each congregation. Principals spent the first year with NSDC and CAJE consultants learning and reflecting on the standards of the NSDC. They also worked to identify teaching strategies for implementation that were appropriate for congregational schools. In the second year, principals, with the help of an educational consultant from CAJE, are delivering individualized professional development plans that have as their ultimate goal improved student learning. In schools that do not have clearly defined goals or shared ownership of education, this initiative has spurred principals to engage their boards in answering key questions like "What does the ideal graduate of our school know, believe, and practice?" *Sharsheret's* Program Coordinators are open to continual revision, positioning themselves to respond to the evolving needs of principals. By focusing first on developing leaders who can create quality professional learning that is aligned to the specific needs of a particular school, this project recognizes that the time for generic professional learning has passed. The NSDC Standards and this project replace generic fragmented learning with professional learning designed to meet the specific needs of each school. Details of the progress of the program including evaluation reports are available at www.CAJE-Miami.org.

NESS—NURTURING EXCELLENCE IN SYNAGOGUE SCHOOLS, 2001–PRESENT

Develops Skillful Leaders to Guide Continuous Professional Learning (NSDC Context Standard, Leadership); Create a Professional Learning Community (NSDC Context Standard, Learning Communities); Uses Multiple Sources of Information to Guide Improvement and Demonstrate Its Impact (NSDC Process Standard, Evaluation); and Deepens Educators Content Knowledge (NSDC Content Standard, Quality Teaching).

NESS, a four year initiative for strengthening congregational schools in Greater Philadelphia, is funded jointly by private donors and Jewish Federation of Greater Philadelphia. The original NESS project was the creation of the Auerbach Central Agency for Jewish Education (ACAJE) in partnership with the University of Pennsylvania's School of Education and Foundations Inc., a national nonprofit organization that offers technical assistance to schools. Six schools participated in the first cohort of NESS (2002–6). Six additional schools have formed a new cohort (2006–2010).

NESS is a systemic initiative that addresses over time a school's professional learning, leadership, curriculum and culture. The project attends to the professional learning of the principals, the lay leaders and the teachers by providing them with twenty to thirty hours a year of learning for three years and reduced support in the fourth year. Teacher mentoring, up to twenty hours a year, is also provided. The content of the learning for all participants is primarily determined by the NESS curriculum and can be influenced by the results of an assessment tool administered in the first year of the project.

Early reports from JESNA's Berman Center for Research and Evaluation indicate that teachers are utilizing strategies learned through NESS in the classroom. The research report notes that teacher learning was relevant to classroom work, and teachers gained a new appreciation for ongoing professional learning. Early indicators are that students who participate in sessions led by NESS–trained teachers feel more positive about their Jewish identity and learning experiences (Tigay 2006). More information can be found at *http://www.acaje.org/content/ness/Ovrvw.shtml*

BOSTON MTEI-MANDEL TEACHER EDUCATION INSTITUTE 2002–2004

Develops Skillful Leaders to Guide Continuous Professional Learning (NSDC Context Standard, Leadership); Creates Professional Learning Community (NSDC Context Standard, Learning Communities); Provides Educators with the Knowledge and Skills to Collaborate (NSDC Process Standard, Collaboration)

Boston MTEI was a two-year initiative with eleven schools—three days schools, seven congregational schools and one after-school program—sponsored by the Mandel Foundation, the Mandel Center for Jewish Studies at Brandeis University, and the Bureau of Jewish Education of Greater Boston and supported by the Combined Jewish Philanthropies. MTEI created school-based teams that learned together for a year in order to design and implement learning for their schools. Educational teams including principals, department heads, lead teachers and/or individuals responsible for professional development met once a month for five hours with follow-up support from an advisor. Gail Dorph led the staff of advisors who worked with school teams to transfer the learning in the group seminars to a design of professional learning in the individual schools. Learning experiences for the teams were designed to model quality PLCs so that leaders would then create them in their own schools. Teams learned ways to increase collaboration among teachers on instruction through ongoing professional conversations, observations of one another and continued content learning that was relevant to the work in the classroom. Teams also learned ways to promote a culture of learning to be valued by all stakeholders.

After two years the Research Team of the Boston MTEI noted increased self-understanding in teachers, increased understanding of student learning, and an increased openness to thinking about teaching and learning. They also reported increased collaboration among teachers, and a sense of shared purpose. This project began with a primary focus on developing a context for ongoing professional development in each school so that process and content could be more fully developed in subsequent years. Following the two year funding cycle of Boston's MTEI, most schools have continued developing professional learning in their schools (Lieberman 2006).

Presently MTEI is working with a cohort of fourteen schools (early childhood, day schools and congregational schools) in the San Francisco area. Gail Dorph noted, "We try to achieve the greatest leverage from our project. Instead of working with a national cohort of individuals as we did initially, we are now seeking to work with communities. We want to create a tipping point where newly developed communal norms about professional learning are established" (2006).

For more detailed information about Boston MTEI see the project report at *http://www.brandeis. edu/centers/mandel/Mandel%20Documents/BMTEIprojectreport.pdf*

SMART-PART INITIATIVES LEAD TO INTEGRATING CONTEXT, CONTENT AND PROCESS

Although only one of these programs, *Sharsheret*, directly reported using the NSDC Standards as its guide, all of the programs are working to balance thoughtful first steps with keeping an eye on the big picture. Each program stated a clear expectation of expanding the scope of initial work over time. A *Sharsheret* director said, for example, "We understood that some schools may not have visions and goals but decided to begin with professional development, knowing we will have to address that when we come to it" (Mitrani, 2006). First steps in all of these initiatives are intentionally designed to open the pathways to next steps. Some projects are positioning themselves to respond to emerging needs. NESS, on the other hand, begins with a four-year plan to address many of the parts of the whole school. Either way, it is clear that the antidote to one-shot programs is not just a series of workshops.

Moving Jewish professional learning from one-shot workshops to becoming an integral part of a school's overall plan for achieving student outcomes will take sustained attention, resources and experimentation. It also requires leaders to expand their scope of attention from what traditionally is thought of as "what teachers need to know" to include attention to leadership, goals, governance and culture. As of now there are no established standards or recommendations for standards that are appropriate for the field (Dorph & Holtz 2000). It is yet to be determined if all of the NSDC standards are appropriate for Jewish education or what new standards need to be created to support the mission of Jewish education. Forums are needed to enable early experimenters with new models of professional learning to learn from one another's successes and misses. Consolidating and disseminating this work is essential if other communities are to join in the work of developing the context, process and content of professional learning in Jewish schools.

WHAT ARE THE UNIQUE NEEDS AND CIRCUMSTANCES OF JEWISH TEACHERS THAT MAY NOT BE ADDRESSED BY PRACTICES ADOPTED FROM SECULAR EDUCATION?

The Nature of Jewish Learning is different than general education and therefore may require standards, research and practices for professional learning that do not easily translate from the field of general education.

Research-based strategies are needed that align with the particular goals of Jewish education (e.g., faith development).

Teachers, according to the NSDC standards, should be trained to employ research-based strategies in their teaching. However, proven strategies of how to achieve the kind of goals promoted in Jewish education are poorly identified or known. A great deal of Jewish education strives to go beyond a learner's mind into a learner's heart, spirit and sense of self. Jewish schools aim to create life-long learners or makers of meaning who exhibit faith, identity, and commitment. Little research exists and/or has been translated for the field of Jewish education on how teachers can shape learning experiences that achieve these types of goals (Moore & Lippman 2005). Until the research is readily available for how to achieve goals such as the spiritual development of youth, Jewish teachers must be trained themselves as action researchers. Professional development for Jewish educators needs a "hothouse" emphasis where teachers can build on research in the field of faith and identity development and experiment with strategies to inform their own practice and contribute to a body of learning that can benefit the larger community.

SHORT-TERM EVALUATION FOR LONG TERM GOALS NEEDED IN ORDER TO DIRECT THE CONTENT OF PROFESSIONAL LEARNING

Quality professional learning, according to the NSDC standards, requires a feedback loop between what students are achieving and what teachers need to know. Data collected on student achievement should, in the best circumstances, direct the learning for teachers. But Jewish education is limited in its ability to evaluate its long-term goals. Long-term goals, often at the core of Jewish education, include outcomes like "love of Israel" or a "relationship with God." Short-term benchmarks for this kind of learning and ways to evaluate them need to be developed so schools can have a clear feedback loop between what students are gaining and what teachers need to learn. Without reliable means of evaluating the core outcomes of Jewish education that go beyond what a learner knows, teachers are swinging at a golf ball without ever knowing if they hit it or where it lands; there is no correction to the swing. The Jewish educational system requires more research on identifying short-term markers and ways of evaluating them for long-term goals such as increased faith development, identity building and applying learning to daily living. Established short-term benchmarks and the means for evaluating them would, in turn, inform appropriate professional learning strategies based on real, not imagined, data gathered from students.

DUGMA ISHIT—NEED TO NURTURE THE JEWISH JOURNEY OF TEACHERS SO THEY CAN DEEPLY UNDERSTAND AND MODEL WHAT THEY TEACH

Can a Jewish educator with little or no connection to God, Shabbat or prayer effectively teach others to be prayerful? Left as a rhetorical question, professional learning in Jewish life may well need to include a professional learning standard that addresses the need to nurture teachers' Jewish connections. Teachers need a clear framework of how to represent the difference between their own Jewish perspectives and the value of the host school/organization. The Jewish community needs more examples of how schools can not only develop teachers' content knowledge but also enrich teachers' personal relationship with what they teach. Schools that want their teachers to be living role models of lifelong learning and people striving to live what they learn will need to develop ways to support the Jewish journeys of their teachers.

The structure of Jewish education differs from that of general education. The part-time nature of congregational schools, the lack of unified standards and goals, the limited resources and the non-traditional settings for learning are unique conditions for how Jewish learning is structured and may require action not addressed by the NSDC standards.

UNDEFINED STANDARDS AND GOALS

Unlike public education where student outcomes are legislated, Jewish education often does not have clear student outcomes. Without clear goals for students there are no clear goals for teacher learning. Schools must develop clear visions, goals, and student outcomes so they can institute professional development plans that make a difference. In conjunction with clearly stated goals, Jewish schools need to work on clearly articulated points of view about theology, values and Jewish practices. The school's theology and values, not the belief system of individual teachers, should guide teacher practice and learning. Jewish schools will need complementary strategies for developing their visions, values and student outcomes so that professional learning is anchored in the belief system and goals of the school/organization.

RESOURCE-POOR

The part-time nature of staff and school schedules makes it difficult for individual schools to offer the quality professional learning that has been described by the NSDC. Difficult, however, does not equal impossible. Success stories of how schools and communities are creating new staffing structures, new scheduling and funding resources need to be shared so that the struggles and the successes of others can inform decision making. These stories can help Jewish educators and leaders believe that change is possible and necessary. Early experiments happening around the country (e.g., UJA-Federation of New York awarded grants to the Jewish Theological Seminary and Hebrew Union College and to The RE-IMAGINE Project of New York of the Experiment in Congregational Education to help congregations create professional learning that attends to content, context and process) will help establish an unchallenged assumption that a singular program, workshop or conference cannot achieve the change that is needed in professional learning.

Presently most of the educational support networks, such as central agencies and educational movement offices, are not staffed, trained or resourced to support the kind of professional learning prescribed by the NSDC standards. New expectations for quality professional learning will set new expectations for how educational support agencies work with congregations. Offering sporadic workshops will no longer be seen as acceptable. Initiatives such as the Coaches Training Institute sponsored by JESNA to re-envision how bureaus support educational innovation will be needed to create an educational infrastructure to support the adaptation of these standards to Jewish school settings.

LEARNING OUTSIDE THE SCHOOL MODEL

Today important Jewish learning is taking place at camp, in coffee houses, in homes and in museums for learners of all ages with varied needs. New models need to be developed that support both professional and avocational teachers in non-traditional settings for non-traditional learners.

STRIVING FOR ONENESS

Deeply rooted in Jewish tradition is a discipline for seeing wholes. Long before professional learning standards were established, Jews were practiced in a relationship to Oneness. Responsibility for identifying fragments, mending brokenness and creating wholeness is a Jewish standard for working in the world. A standard that informs the context, content and process of Jewish professional learning might read: *Professional learning that develops the Jewish knowing, believing, belonging and living of all learners nurtures educators' relationship to Oneness, enabling them to see and create an integrated-whole learning experience for teachers and students*

HIGHLIGHTS

- The significant gap that exists between the professional development offered in the Jewish community and what is needed to achieve educational goals can be addressed when educational planners develop a discipline for seeing and addressing the whole picture that impacts teacher knowledge and skills.
- The National Staff Development Council has identified twelve standards for high-quality professional development that address context, process and content.
- The NSDC Standards will help build a system that supports common goals for each school as opposed to fragmented and isolated workshops for teachers.
- Beginning teachers, new to the field and new to a school, will benefit from specifically designed professional learning known as induction and mentoring programs.
- A number of professional learning programs are emerging in the Jewish community as early experiments in applying current standards and practices in secular education to Jewish education.

- Jewish education has unique circumstances and needs that may require specially designed professional development that is yet to be created.

THE LARGER CONTEXT

Jewish learning is at the foundation of our tradition. Valuing teachers is at the core. And yet today we are still searching for ways to bring our traditions and values into alignment with the lives of learners. The broken pieces in the field of education litter our agendas with curriculum, professional development and family education as if they were separate entities. We are past the time of trying better programs. Departmentalized thinking has generated departmentalized actions. Systems thinking can direct systemic action that produces results for teachers and for students. This approach makes the difference we seek because whole vessels, not broken fragments, can carry our tradition in meaningful ways for learners of all ages.

ANNOTATED BIBLIOGRAPHY

Aron, I. (2000) *Becoming a Congregation of Learners*. Woodstock, VT: Jewish Lights Publishing. Identifies a process for making school/synagogue change in a systemic, not fragmented way. Principles and practices for change are illustrated through case studies of synagogues that have begun the work of holistic change.

Fullan, M. (2004). *Leading in A Culture of Change Personal Action Guide and Workbook*. San Francisco: Jossey-Bass. Educators who seek to develop a culture of innovation as the context for professional learning will benefit from identified leadership practices. Experimentation and journaling opportunities are provided in the companion workbook. Leadership practices include establishing moral purpose, understanding change, building relationships, knowledge building and coherence making.

National Staff Development Council Web site: http://www.nsdc.org/. This is an invaluable resource to people responsible for professional development. It includes a library of articles, projects and events sponsored by NSDC to support ongoing professional learning, a bookstore with relevant materials and in-depth discussion of the standards that support systemic professional learning. They offer a three-month free membership on the website to their journals, including "The Learning Principal" and "Tools for Schools".

Senge, P. (1999) *The Dance of Change: The Challenges to Sustaining Momentum in Learning Organizations*. New York: Doubleday. This book is written for leaders who are ready to go beyond the first steps of change and build smart-parts of a greater whole. It helps leaders move from first steps to generating profound change. It addresses the challenges of initiating change, sustaining transformation and developing new ways of working and thinking.

REFERENCES

Corcoran, T., McVay, S. & Riordan, K. (2003). Getting It Right: The MISE Approach to Professional Development, University of Pennsylvania School of Education. Retrieved from the World Wide Web August 2006, Cpre.org/publications/rr55.pdf

Dorph, G. (November, 2006) Personal Interview with the former Director of the Boston MTEI.

Dorph, G. & Holtz, B. (2000). "Why doesn't the model change?" *Journal of Jewish Education* 66 (1/2), 67–76.

DuFour, R. (1999, February). "Help Wanted: Principals who can lead professional learning communities." *NAASP Bulletin*.

Feiman-Nemser, S. (2003, May). "What New Teachers Need to Learn." *Educational Leadership* 60 (8), 25–29.

Fullan, M. (2004). *Leading in a Culture of Change Personal Action Guide and Workbook*. San Francisco: Jossey-Bass, 11–38.

Hirsh, S. (2006). Personal Presentation: Think Tank on Professional Learning, New York City. Organized by The RE-IMAGINE Project of the Experiment in Congregational Education and sponsored by UJA-Federation of New York.

Hord, S. (1997). Professional Learning Communities: Communities of Continuous Inquiry and Improvement. Southwest Educational Development Laboratory. Retrieved August 2006 from the World Wide Web: *http://www.sedl.org/pubs/change34/4.html*

Hord, S. Hirsh, S. & Roy, P. (2005). Moving NSDC's Staff Development Standards into Practice: Innovation Configurations, Vol. II. Southwest Educational Development Laboratory, NSDC.

Killion, J. (2002). *What Works in the Elementary School Results-Based Staff Development.* National Staff Development Council, Item #179.

The National Staff Development Council's Standards for Staff Development in Aciton, p. 5, Introduction).

Killion, J. February (2006). Students learn when the teacher knows. *Teachers Teaching Teachers,* National Staff Development Council.

Knowles, M., Holton E. & Swanson, R. (1998). *The Adult Learner,* 5ᵗʰ ed. Houston: Gulf Publishing Co,

Leonard, L. & Leonard, P. (2003). "The Continuing Trouble with Collaboration: Teachers Talk." *Current Issues In Education.* College of Education, Arizona State University, 6 (1).

Lieberman, J. (November 2006). Phone Interview with Jeff Lieberman, Associate Director, Boston Bureau of Jewish Education of Greater Boston.

Meskin, C. (2006). Personal interview with Director of Early Childhood Cheryl Meskin at the Board of Jewish Education of Greater New York.

Mitrani, V. (2006) Personal interview with Consultant Valerie Mitrani at CAJE-Miami.

Moore, K. & Lippman, L. (2005). *What Do Children Need to Flourish? Conceptualizing and Measuring Indicators of Positive Development.* Springer Science & Business Media. The Search Institute Series on Developmentally Attentive Community and Society.

National Education Association home page (2006). Retrieved from the World Wide Web August 2006 http://www.neafoundation.org/publications/engaging.htm#questions

National Staff Development Council website. Retrieved from the World Wide Web August 2006 *http://www.nsdc.org*

Roy, P. (2006). "The heart of instructional leadership: Developing quality teaching." *The Learning Principal* 1 (5), 1–3.

Schaap, E. & Goodman, R. (2002). Jewish Educators and the NJPS 2001 Demographic Study: Jewish Educators are Older, Better Educated, Less Well Paid Than Other Jews. Retrieved August 2006 from the World Wide Web caje-cbank.org

Schramm, R. (2005). An Analysis of The National Humanities Center's Teacher Professional Development Program and National Professional Development Standards National Humanities Center. Retrieved from the World Wide Web : http://www.nhc.rtp.nc.us:8080/pds/npdstandards.htm

Senge, P., Cameron-McCabe, N., Lucas, T., Smith, B. & Dutton, J. (2000). *A Fifth Discipline Resource: Schools that Learn.* New York: Doubleday Dell.

Sparks, D. & Hirsh, S. (2000). Strengthening professional development. *Education Week on the Web.* Retrieved August 2006 from the World Wide Web: *http://www.edweek.org/ew/articles/2000/05/24/37sparks.h19.html?qs=Sparks+Hirsh+professional_development+professional+development&levelId=1000&levelId=1000.*

Sparks, D. & Loucks-Horsley (1989). *Five Models of Professional Development.* North Central Regional Educational Library. Retrieved from the World Wide Web August 2006 http://www.ncrel.org/sdrs/areas/issues/educatrs/profdevl/pd2fimo.htm

Stansbury, K. & Zimmerman, J. (2001). Designing Support for the Beginning Teacher. West Ed. Retrieved from the World Wide Web: August 2006 *http://www.wested.org/online_pubs/tchrbrief.pdf*

Stodolsky, S., Dorph, G., Feiman-Nemser S. & Hecht, S. (2004). *Leading the Way to a New Vision for Teachers and Schools.* Retrieved August 2006 from the World Wide Web http://www.brandeis.edu/centers/mandel/Mandel%20Documents/BMTEIprojectreport.pdf#search=%22Boston%20MTEI%20Gail%20dorph%22

Tigay, H. (2006) Personal Interview with Helene Tigay, Executive Director, Auerbach Central Agency for Jewish Education, Philadelphia.

Wertheimer, J. (2005). Linking the Silos: How to Accelerate the Momentum in Jewish Education Today. Retrieved August 2006, from the World Wide Web: *http://www.avi-chai.org/Static/Binaries/Publications/Linking%20The%20Silos_0.pdf#search=%22linking%20the%20silos%22*

Zeder, Jeri (2006). Congregational Schools Focus on Teacher Training. *Forward.* Retrieved from the World Wide Web August 2006 *http://www.forward.com/articles/congregational-schools-focus-on-teacher-training/*

The Voice of the Principal

Elissa Kaplan

When I walked into my first job as a congregational principal over fifteen years ago I was passionate about children, proactive about running a quality school, and perplexed about how to do it. I was initially convinced that the principal improved the school by changing things. As I investigated principles of change I slowly came to realize that change was only one piece of the puzzle.

The big picture was really about leadership. What does educational leadership look like, and how does it operate in congregational schools? Three questions that frame the area of professional leadership are critical:

1. What are the leadership styles of principals of congregational schools?
2. How does the principal's leadership contribute to change?
3. How does the leadership style of the principal impact the school?

My research grew out of my own background—my reflective practice as the principal of four congregational schools. My hope is that this information will impact how we think of training principals for the future.

CONTEXT

Schoem (1992) cites that most adult American Jews reported that they received their education in congregational schools, and that they are greatly lacking in Jewish literacy. Indeed, Jews are highly assimilated into American culture, and many Jews are unlikely to identify as Jews in adulthood. "The responsibility for developing Jewish identity and instilling a commitment to Judaism...now rests primarily with education" (Gamoran et al. 1994, p. 1).

However, "synagogue education is itself a wild gamble: that children from diverse families who come for several hours a week to study Hebrew and learn about Judaism will take these matters to heart" (Reimer 1997, p. 184). "Of all the settings in Jewish education, that of the supplementary school has faced the most criticism and the greatest call for change" (Rosenblum 1993, p. 55). "Thirty years of research on the Jewish congregational school have documented that these schools are failing" (Schoem 1992, p. 163). In spite of the difficulty of providing a Jewish education, almost every synagogue has some kind of school associated with it.

Some people believe that educational leadership is missing in congregational schools. This chapter argues that the leader of a congregation school, i.e., the principal, is able to make the school successful. In some instances a single leader can turn a school around. If enough principals of congregational schools could turn their schools around, then a system that has been filled with problems would no longer be labeled a failure.

OVERVIEW OF RESEARCH

The need for educational change in the Jewish community is a response to events and their implications in both the Jewish community and the world at large.

When the 1990 National Jewish Population Survey reported that over 52% of Jews had married outside the faith (Zoll 2002), the Jewish world reacted strongly. Jewish education suddenly appeared on everyone's agenda. The American Jewish Committee (1999) took the challenge seriously by recommending the following initiatives: (a) allocate community resources to Jewish education, (b) target the entire family for Jewish education, and (c) make multiple models of Jewish education available to reach the largest possible audience. The congregational school as the primary provider of children's Jewish learning became a venue through which these initiatives could be implemented. However, to do so, new approaches would be necessary, and the role of the leader would take on a new importance. Central to this mission is the need to create change within the congregation and the school if success is to be achieved.

Fullan (1999) hypothesizes that change is more complex than a response to fix things. Schools actually benefit from problems; then they change things. Fullan notes, "We will see breakthroughs occur when we begin to think of conflict, diversity, and resistance as positive, essential forces for success" (1999, p. ix).

No matter how thoughtfully change is put into place, areas of conflict, diversity of populations and opinions, and resistance still exist on many levels. Fullan is adamant that "change cannot be managed. It can be understood and perhaps led, but it cannot be controlled" (2001, p. 33). He clarifies the complex change process with simple statements: "The goal is not to innovate the most; it is not enough to have the best ideas; appreciate the implementation dip; redefine resistance; reculturing is the name of the game; never a checklist, always complexity" (Fullan 2001, p. 34).

School leaders routinely face challenges of leadership, including change (Ackerman et al. 1996). Two critical differences emerge between principals of high-performing schools and principals of low-performing schools. Successful principals are able to act both as change agents and as problem solvers (Lopez 2003).

Organizational theorists and change experts from the business world agree with educational researchers that change is a constant (Easley & Alvarez-Pompilius 2004). Even managing change and problem solving are only partial tools. Organizations and their leaders need new paradigms to handle complex and chaotic environments. Leaders in schools as well as other organizations should look at what is possible, not only at what is wrong.

In 1972 a U.S. Senate study (Sergiovanni 1995) declared that the principal is the key player in school change. Leadership style is *the* determining factor that makes the principal the key player (Delaney 1997). Responsibility is an additional aspect of being a key player (Foster 1997). Successful principals especially need vision (Gardner 1990), with personal and organizational vision setting the principal apart from the rest of the staff in the school, including other administrators (Ercretin 1998). When the environment is challenging, dynamic, and highly political, the best principals provide unity of purpose (Davis 1997). Finally, the most successful principals initiate change rather than manage or respond to it (Stevens & Marsh 1987).

Ronneberg (2000) found that principals successfully create change when they demonstrate a particular set of critical elements of leadership: inspire a shared vision, focus on culture, challenge existing practices, model integrity, provide support, foster dialogue and learning, and develop leadership capacities. Ronneberg further discovered that principals who are successful as change agents must be able to build external support, establish partnerships, and find resources for generating, building, and maintaining change.

THE KEY PLAYER IN JEWISH EDUCATIONAL CHANGE IS THE PRINCIPAL.

Principals of congregational schools should demonstrate leadership models, seek research to help them develop more effective leadership skills, and be constantly aware of the culture in which they operate. Between 1990 and 2006 five major studies have addressed the issue of the principal as a leader of change in Jewish education.

In his study of congregational schools, Cohen (1992) visited schools in Florida, New Jersey and the Midwest. He observed the schools, interviewed a variety of people, discussed the programs, and evaluated the findings to learn about Jewish school management. Although all the settings were at the elementary level, Cohen proposed three major principles relating to school leadership:

1. All Jewish educational programs, whether in a synagogue or elsewhere in the Jewish community, should be coordinated to enhance mutual reinforcement and reduce the likelihood of duplication.

2. Educators should focus on the total ambiance of the Jewish school, not just on classes, to achieve maximum results.

3. Administrators of educational programs should help teachers learn and adapt new educational approaches that support the educational philosophy of the school and of the larger institution, i.e., the congregation (p. 11).

This study emphasized some of the same leadership traits that surfaced later in the Ronneberg (2000) study of three urban principals. Like Ronneberg, Cohen had previously identified the importance of a shared vision or coordination at all levels and the focus on the total ambiance or the culture in the school. Cohen also emphasized fostering dialogue and learning in the school when he called for helping teachers learn and use new educational approaches to further the school's educational philosophy.

Rosenblum (1993) gathered data from questionnaires and interviews with day school and congregational school educators throughout the United States to learn about and teach leadership skills. She employed the lens of transactional leadership and instructional leadership as defined in the 1980s, i.e., that good managers make good leaders. The cases involved top-down change imposed by the administration without consulting teachers, parents, or students or considering the upheaval or chaos of change. This study indicated that the successful principal was more a manager than a leader. In fact, most of her chapters started with the word *managing,* which suggests her perspective on the topic. None of the studies about principals in secular schools reached this conclusion. Harris (1997) spoke of vision, and Davis (1997) addressed unity of purpose in studies in the secular arena. Cohen (1992) also spoke of coordination and reinforcement, ambience, teacher training and educational philosophy as critical components of educational leadership.

Reimer's (1997) ethnographic study of one synagogue in the Boston area tells the story of congregational education through the context of its setting, the synagogue, again emphasizing the culture of the school. Reimer based his study on the 1983 study *Ethnic Survival in America (*Reimer 1997; Schoem 2001). He found the question of the connection of the school to the synagogue compelling but also found that connection missing in the earlier study. Schoem had concentrated on the goals, tasks, and support of the supplementary school without addressing its context. In his introduction to the Reimer study Woocher characterized Reimer's research as identifying one key variable in successful congregational education: "the extent to which the congregation provided a supportive and nurturing environment for the school" (p. xvi). Ronneberg (2000) identified the supportive and nurturing environment that builds external support as another critical factor of school leadership.

In addition to congregational support, Reimer summarized his findings as being "focused on social drama and ritual as cultural performance, for I believe that collective self-definition is a key to synagogue education" (p. 184). At the schools, the rabbis and educators defined the Judaism that they both taught and lived. The issues or social dramas, such as the mandatory Hebrew requirements at a congregation that stood for free choice, played out in the schools and helped to create the cultural identities of the schools and the communities. This finding in particular, and the study in general, left Reimer with yet another question. "The most significant question is the one I cannot answer: Will this Judaism, this religion-in-the-making, prove convincing and moving to their members? Will the children and adults whom I observed take this Judaism to heart and make it a living part of their lives? That, after all, is the ultimate educational question" (p. 185).

JESNA's Task Force on Congregational and Communal Jewish Education (2000) addressed concerns about congregational education. Three critical issues emerged: changing environment, new systems, and institutional vision. The task force report proposed seven strategies to set the agenda for the future of congregational education: (a) develop a clear vision, (b) build systemic linkages to strengthen Jewish education, (c) build broad community-wide support, (d) create effective, coordinated educational support systems, (e) develop new models for effective education, (f) strengthen systems for sharing knowledge and experience, and (g) identify and prepare high-quality personnel (Flexner & Berger 2000).

The task force completed its work despite the limited research available about congregational education. However, it stressed the need for career preparation and development of principals if we are to create successful programs.

Kaplan's (2007) review of the growing body of research about congregational schools found information available about students, teachers, the curriculum, and the milieu of these schools. Yet the voice of the principal was largely silent. Her cross-case study examined the leadership styles of three principals in congregational schools in the mid-Atlantic area. Through interviews, review of documentation, and observation of teachers, staff, and principals of the three schools, the principals' leadership styles emerged through their organizational leadership, educational leadership, and personal leadership.

The findings of this study demonstrated the similarities of the principals as change initiators, authority figures, demonstrators of unity of purpose, and problem solvers. Where they differed was in how they operated, how they communicated, and how they managed the schools. They faced different challenges within their settings, and they used different combinations of frameworks—structural, human resources, symbolic and political.

The important component of the study was its focus on the principal. It correlated strong leadership with successful congregational schools. Kaplan (2007) concluded that (a) strong leadership *does* exist in congregational schools, (b) commonalities exist among the principals, (c) being successful in this setting shares common elements with being successful in secular or independent school settings, and (d) training and development of principals of congregational schools is essential.

UNDERSTANDING LEADERSHIP THEORIES PRINCIPALS EMPLOY WILL LEAD TO ENHANCED TRAINING OF LEADERS

The field of leadership theory has produced an enormous amount of both research-based and anecdotal literature. In a 2002 review of the literature Lashway identified six areas of leadership: instructional, transformational, moral, participative, managerial, and contingent. However, information about these areas of leadership does not solve the daily challenges facing educational leaders. The principal's style as a key component remains central to how principals work around the system and move from management to leadership within the school setting. (Farkas et al. 2001).

Successful leadership in the congregational setting may be observed in three broad areas (Kaplan 2007). Leadership of the school as an organization requires understanding of *situational leadership*—leading in different situations, *transactional leadership*—being a good manager and *reframing organizations leadership*—seeing organizations through different lenses. Leadership of the school as an educational institution requires understanding of *instructional leadership*—functioning in an effective school and *learning organization leadership*—creating a community of learners. Leadership as a change agent requires understanding of *transformational leadership*—changing society and *moral leadership*—doing the right thing. Of the seven theories mentioned, each represents a response to the challenges of a certain context or environment. No theory of leadership is all-encompassing or could fit every situation. Yet by understanding which leadership theories principals of congregational schools employ, it is possible to enhance the training of leaders of Jewish congregational schools (Kaplan 2007).

Training toward successful school leadership is important for principals of congregational schools.

Researchers have examined principals of public schools in the context of their work situations with an eye toward improved training. They have identified four significant factors that influence the abilities of principals to perform their duties. Each is an important component of leadership training. 1) Structural factors include whether the school is an elementary, middle, or high school and the demographics of the students, teachers, and population of the local area (Grubbs et al. 2002). 2) Human resource factors include group collaboration, a culture of support, and a sense of success (Singh & McMillan 2002). 3) Political factors include the ability to make tough decisions, the willingness to put interests of children above all else, and the knack to communicate a clear educational vision and educational priorities (Farkas et al. 2001). 4) Symbolic factors include the willingness to do whatever is required to increase student learning (Singh & McMillan 2002).

Strong and effective leadership addresses issues about teachers, students, milieu, and curriculum in Jewish congregational schools.

TEACHER ISSUES

Lack of skilled teachers is one of the most important issues facing congregational schools (Aron et al. 1995; Feiman-Nemser 2002; Katzew 2001; Schiff 1982). Often principals hire teachers from Orthodox backgrounds even though the vast majority of congregational schools are Reform, Conservative or liberal in nature (Cohen 1992). Most teachers are not trained as Jewish educators (Gamoran et al. 1994). Congregational schools want teachers to be active in the congregation, serve as role models both inside and outside the classroom, bare their souls, and connect traditional values to modern situations (Artson 1993; Flexner 1995; Kaplan 1995; Mahrer & Rowe 1996). Finally, the part-time nature of congregational schools is a factor in hiring, retention, and cultivation of teachers (Rosenblum 1993).

Strong and effective leadership makes a difference with teachers. When a principal shows leadership by creating a learning organization, teachers develop greater capacities, with everyone benefiting. Successful congregational principals strengthen teaching and learning by providing on-going professional development for teachers through: 1) having a resource library on site, 2) making content classes and training sessions easily available for teachers, 3) providing monetary or other incentives, and 4) being a role model for learning. This approach to leadership addresses the traditional problems of teacher recruitment and retention.

STUDENT ISSUES

Student numbers in congregational schools have declined significantly in the last forty years. In 1962 540,000 students were enrolled in congregational schools. By 1988 the number of students enrolled had declined to 280,000. That number has remained constant, although a Wertheimer study reported in 2001 that there are now approximately 300,000 students (Schaap & Goodman 2002). However, even with these numbers and the significant increase in enrollment in day schools, less than half of all Jewish children enroll in any form of Jewish educational program (Cuban 1995), and many choose to do so only in time to prepare for the bar or bat mitzvah ceremony (Epstein 1999). Students in congregational schools also spend very little time in class, averaging about 200 hours per year. One of the reasons for the declining attendance and decreasing hours of class time is that student attendance in congregational education is voluntary at all ages (Woocher 1997). One of the results is a culture clash for the students as the content of the educational programs clashes with their lifestyles and values (Katzew 2001; Reimer 1997).

To reverse these negative aspects of congregational education, strong and effective leadership will make a difference for the students. When a principal shows leadership by transforming the school, students benefit. Strong leaders create programs for families as well as students, provide learning for populations with special needs, create bridges between early childhood and elementary school, change middle school programs from b'nai mitzvah factories into learning about service opportunities and giving back, and provide excellent learning, service, and leadership opportunities for high school students. Through their leadership, the traditional problems of attracting students before Grade 3 and keeping them after bar or bat mitzvah are more likely to disappear.

MILIEU ISSUES

The environment has a strong influence on the overall quality of the educational program. Students, teachers and families all respond to the nature of the physical facility and how it is maintained. This is especially true if the space is shared with another educational entity such as an early childhood center or day school (Cohen 1992; Reimer 1995; Rosenblum 1993). Even within the congregation where the school is a component of the larger institution, there is a critical symbolic message in the relationship between the two (Reimer 1995).

Strong and effective leadership makes a difference in the use of space and the creation of a powerful and creative milieu for the educational programs. When a principal demonstrates leadership by translating a vision for an attractive school into a beautiful and creative environment, it will serve as an attraction for new students and their families as well as for teachers. Whether the school is in spacious or tight quarters, strong leadership is manifested through an environment that is attractive, enriching, appropriate, and rich with resources.

CURRICULUM ISSUES

At the heart of every educational program is the curriculum that forms the basis of all of the activities within the school. Whether there is an existing curriculum with a clear vision or a new curriculum needs to be created, the principal is ultimately responsible for guiding the process (Friedenreich 1983). The serious reduction of hours that schools have experienced over the last quarter century has made the choices about what is to be taught and/or learned in the school increasingly difficult. This is especially important in the placement of Israel as a component of the history program (Chazan 1992) and in the nature of the Hebrew program, which is understood to be a core competency for most congregational schools (Dori 1992). Making these choices and guiding the leadership in developing a unified approach to Jewish learning that is relevant to the learners and their families is a strategic role for the principal.

Current research places the concept of the Educated Jew as the principal theme for curriculum development. The Mandel Foundation, in cooperation with Harvard's Philosophy and Education Research Center, created the Goals Project in the early 1990s to bring together the best minds in the Jewish community to explore the concept of what an Educated Jew should know. As there is no single perspective that all agreed upon, the six scholars who led the discussions each proposed his own approach to what an Educated Jew should know. Through a process that engaged educators and scholars, the six visions focusing on Jewish law, Zionist education, ultimate questions, Jewish values, Jewish language, and the value of learning were analyzed and critiqued (Fox et al. 2003). The result of the project raised the bar for curriculum in congregational schools as well as other educational settings.

Making the choices of what to teach is, however, only the beginning of the process. An effective principal and faculty will then need to adapt the content to the particular needs of the students. Creating a curriculum that begins with the youngest children in the early childhood years and progresses through to high school graduation in such a way that the students will remain with the program is the ultimate goal. Of equal importance is the ability of the leadership to create strategies that include experiential learning, multiple intelligences and other creative approaches to learning that fully engage the students. It is in this way that the principal demonstrates clear leadership by bringing together the right players within the congregation to build a strong curriculum for the educational programs.

IMPLICATIONS OR POLICY RECOMMENDATIONS/FUTURE DIRECTIONS

Training principals for congregational schools is vital to establishing the setting as a meaningful form of Jewish education. This requires that we prepare principals by providing them with the skills and knowledge to be more effective leaders. The following principles should guide the community in developing quality educational leaders:

1. Quality leaders who demonstrate strong leadership DO make a difference in the quality of the educational programs.

2. To have quality leaders, we must have quality training programs based on current research in leadership and learning theory.

3. Proper public recognition is critical to retaining educational leaders who continue to demonstrate their creativity and leadership.

4. Quality professional development opportunities must be created for congregational principals with mentoring, networking, study, and research as key components.

5. Research must be undertaken, with the results disseminated to academics, professionals and lay leaders, that continues to expand our knowledge and understanding of the impact that educational leaders have on their schools and how to properly prepare them for their important roles.

ADDITIONAL RESEARCH QUESTIONS

- What are the critical issues and concerns that are key to a quality professional training program for principals of congregational schools?
- What are the salient factors of principal training that would lead to increased capacity in teachers and improvement in student achievement?

CONCLUSION

This chapter examines the perception that leadership in Jewish congregational schools is based largely on outdated information and lays the foundation for an analysis of the leadership role of principals in congregational schools. Strong and successful congregational school leadership does exist, and that leadership is providing one way to face the challenges of the American Jewish community. The way to achieve strong leadership in congregational education is through research-based and carefully thought-out training programs.

HIGHLIGHTS

- The need for educational change in the Jewish community is a response to events in the Jewish community and the world at large.
- The key player in school change is the principal or educational leader.
- Understanding which leadership theories principals of congregational schools employ will lead to enhanced training of leaders.
- Training toward successful school leadership will lead to more effective schools. By adopting the thinking from the secular business and education worlds, we will be in a better position to prepare strong and effective educational leaders for congregational schools.
- Strong and effective leadership will address issues about teachers, students, milieu, and curriculum in congregational schools.

THE LARGER CONTEXT

Current research asks us to question our previous assessment of congregational education. Since the four commonplaces of teachers, students, milieu, and curriculum have been and continue to be rigorously studied, their issues and opportunities are well understood. What is underutilized is the information available from the world of business and education about leadership in organizations. If we listen to the voice of the successful principal, we will hear the sounds of the future of congregational education.

ANNOTATED BIBLIOGRAPHY

Bolman, L.G. & Deal, T.E. (2003). *Reframing Organizations: Artistry, Choice, and Leadership* (3rd ed.). San Francisco: Jossey-Bass. The authors provide the big picture of organizational leadership by describing the four frames of an organization: structure, human resources, politics, and symbolic. Principals and organizational leaders who are aware of this perspective understand how to recognize the frames, read the frames, and use the frames in their schools. This book helps principals see what they are up against and figure out what to do about it.

Fullan, M. (Introduction). (2000). *The Jossey-Bass Reader on Educational Leadership.* San Francisco: Jossey-Bass. This is a sampler of current scholarship on leadership theory and practice. Major topics on organizational leadership included are: principals, diversity and leadership, moral leadership, and shared leadership. Easy access is provided to the writings of Barth, Bolman and Deal, Evans, Fullan, Gardner, Marsh, Senge, Wheatley, and others.

Fullan, M. (2001). *Leading in a Culture of Change*. San Francisco: Jossey-Bass. Any book by Michael Fullan is a must-read for today's principal or organizational leader. Fullan believes that in a complex society change happens at a rapid pace and is unpredictable and nonlinear. Fullan offers guidelines about how to walk the tightrope of non-action that leads to extinction that could be fatal. Fullan encourages leaders to act quickly and strongly and to take risks while at the same time making meaning out of the chaos for others.

Hoy, W. K. & Miskel, C. G. (2001). *Educational Administration: Theory, Research, Practice* (6th ed.). Boston: McGraw Hill. This is both a practical guide and a theoretical primer that every principal should have close at hand. The information on school structure, culture and climate, power and politics, external environments, effective schools, decision making, communication, and leadership are presented in their theoretical bases and then discussed as practical matters. Case histories are included.

Sergiovanni, T. J. (2000). *Leadership for the Schoolhouse: How Is It Different? Why Is It Important?* San Francisco: Jossey-Bass. Sergiovanni is one of the leading voices for establishing a moral voice in the school. He argues for a shared agreement—in effect, a covenant of shared purposes, values, and beliefs. For Sergiovanni, the welfare of the community becomes more important than the welfare of the individual. Coming out of secular educational scholarship, this perspective fits nicely into Jewish educational values.

REFERENCES

Ackerman, R., Donaldson, G., Jr. & van der Bogert, R. (1996). *Making Sense as a School Leader: Persisting Questions, Creative Opportunities*. San Francisco: Jossey-Bass.

Aron, I., Lee, S. & Rossel, S. (eds.) (1995). *A Congregation of Learners: Transforming the Synagogue into a Learning Community*. New York: UAHC Press.

Artson, B. S. (1993). "Plunging in before the sea splits." *Jewish Education News* 14 (2), 28–29.

Chazen, B. (1992). What we know about...the teaching of Israel. In S. L. Kelman (ed.), *What We Know about Jewish Education: A Handbook of Today's Research for Tomorrow's Jewish Education*. Los Angeles: Torah Aura Productions, 242–252.

Cohen, B. I. (1992). *Case Studies in Jewish School Management: Applying Educational Theory to School Practice*. West Orange, NJ: Behrman House, Inc.

Cuban, L. (1995). Changing public schools and changing congregational schools. In I. Aron, S. Lee & S Rossel (eds.), *A Congregation of Learners: Transforming the Synagogue into a Learning Community*. NY: UAHC Press, 119–138.

Davis, S. H. (1997). "The principal's paradox: remaining secure in a precarious position." *NASSP Bulletin* 81 (592), 73–80.

Delaney, J. G. (1997). "Principal leadership: A primary factor in school-based management and school improvement." *NASSP Bulletin* 81 (586), 107–111.

Dori, R. (1992). What we know about...Hebrew language education. In S. L. Kelman (ed.), *What We Know about Jewish Education: A Handbook of Today's Research for Tomorrow's Jewish Education*. Los Angeles: Torah Aura Productions, 262–269.

Easley, C.A. & Alvarez-Pompilius, F. (2004). "A new paradigm for qualitative investigations: Towards an integrative model for evoking change." *Organization Development Journal* 22 (3), 42–59.

Epstein, J. M. (1999). "Jewish learning for Jewish living." *V'Aleh Hechadashot: News from The Jewish Educators Assembly*, 1, 4.

Ercretin, S. S. (1998). *Personal visions of the administrators in the Turkish elementary schools for the 21st century* (Clearinghouse No. EA 030535).

Farkas, S., Johnson, J., Duffett, A. & Foleno, T. (2001). *Trying to stay ahead of the game: Superintendents and principals talk about school leadership* (Clearinghouse No. ED 470932).

Feiman-Nemser, S. (2002). *Teachers are at the core of schools*. Retrieved November 30, 2003 from http://www.shma.com/mar02/nemser.htm.

Flexner, P. A. (1995). "The Jewish educator of the future." *Agenda* 6, 5–7.

Flexner, P.A. & Berger, H. (2000). Report of the task force on congregational and communal Jewish education: A vision for excellence. New York: Jewish Education Service of North America, Inc.

Foster, L. (1997). "Student images of the high school principal: Who's who and what's going on?" *NASSP Bulletin* 81 (589), 66–73.

Fox, S., Scheffler, I. & Marom, D. (eds.) (2003). *Visions of Jewish Education*. Cambridge, UK: Cambridge University Press.

Friedenreich, F. (1983). Curriculum development. In A. F. Marcus & R. A. Zwerin (eds.), *The Jewish Principals' Handbook*. Denver, CO: A.R.E. Publishing, Inc., 287–292.

Fullan, M. (1999). *Change Forces: The Sequel*. London: Falmer Press.

Fullan, M. (2001). *Leading in a Culture of Change*. San Francisco: Jossey-Bass.

Gamoran, A., Goldring, E., Goodman, R. L., Robinson, B. & Tammivaara, J. (1994). *Policy Brief: Background and Professional Training of Teachers in Jewish Schools*. New York: Council for Initiatives in Jewish Education.

Gardner, J. W. (1990). *On Leadership*. New York: The Free Press.

Grubbs, S., Leech, D., W., Gibbs, A. & Green, R. (2002). *Who's leading our South Georgia schools? A profile of principals* (ERIC Document Reproduction Service No. ED 475009).

Harris, S. (1997). "Five guidelines for a successful site-based administrator to follow." *NASSP Bulletin* 81 (588), 76–80.

Hoy, W. K. & Miskel, C. G. (2001). *Educational Administration: Theory, Research, Practice* (6th ed.). Boston: McGraw Hill.

Jewish Women's Archive (2004). This Week in History: August 29, 1976.

Kaplan, E. (1995). "The role of the Jewish family life educator." *Agenda* 6, 8–9.

Kaplan, E. (2007). Analysis of Leadership in Three Jewish Congregational Schools. Dissertation to be published in February 2007.

Katzew, J. (2001). Lifelong Jewish learning: The 2001 Jewish educational state of the union. Retrieved Deecember 2, 2003 from *http://uahc.org/educate/edstate/edstate01.shtml*.

Lashway, L. (2002). *Rethinking the principalship* (Clearinghouse No. EA 031544).

Lopez, M. (2003). The behaviors of effective urban school principals. *Dissertation Abstracts International, 64* (12), 4295.

Mahrer, L. N. & Rowe, D. M. (1996). *A Guide to Small Congregation Religious Schools*. New York: UAHC Press.

Reimer, J. (1995). When school and synagogue are joined. In I. Aron, S. Lee & S. Rossel (eds.), *A Congregation of Learners: Transforming the Synagogue into a Learning Community*. New York: UAHC Press, 93–118.

Reimer, J. (1997). *Succeeding at Jewish Education: How One Synagogue Made it Work*. Philadelphia: Jewish Publication Society.

Ronneberg, J. S. (2000). The urban school leader as change agent: Case studies of three urban principals. *Dissertation Abstracts International, 61* (01).

Rosenblum, Sheila (ed.) (1993). *Leadership Skills for Jewish Educators: A Casebook*. West Orange, NJ: Behrman House, Inc.

Rossel, S. & Lee, S. (1995). Introduction. In I. Aron, S. Lee & S Rossel (Eds.), *A Congregation of Learners: Transforming the Synagogue into a Learning Community*. NY: UAHC Press, 119–138

Schaap, E. & Goodman, R.G. (2002). *What Are the Numbers of Jewish Educators and Students in Formal Jewish Educational Settings?* New York: Coalition for the Advancement of Jewish Education.

Schiff, A. (1982). "The centrist Torah educator faces critical ideological and communal challenges." *Tradition* 19 (4), 275–289.

Schoem, D. (1992). "What we know about...the Jewish congregational school." In S. L. Kelman (ed.) *What We Know about Jewish Education: A Handbook of Today's Research for Tomorrow's Jewish Education*. Los Angeles: Torah Aura Productions, 163–168.

Schoem, D. (2001). *Who will support the reform of Jewish supplementary schools?* Retrieved December 24, 2004 at http://www.shma.com/mar02/david.htm.

Sergiovanni, T. J. (1995). *The Principalship: A Reflective Practice*. Boston: Allyn and Bacon.

Shevitz, S. L. (1992). What we know about...Changing Jewish schools or surf, don't pitch! In S. L. Kelman (ed.) *What We Know about Jewish Education: A Handbook of Today's Research for Tomorrow's Jewish Education*. Los Angeles: Torah Aura Productions, 205–220.

Shevitz, S. (1995). An organizational perspective on changing congregational education: What the literature reveals. In I. Aron, S. Lee & S. Rossel (eds.), *A Congregation of Learners: Transforming the Synagogue into a Learning Community*. New York: UAHC Press, 155–184.

Singh, J, & McMillan, J. H. (2002). *Staff Development Practices in Schools Demonstrating Significant Improvement on High-stakes Tests* (Clearinghouse No. ED 464103).

Stevens, W. & Marsh, D. D. (1987). *The role of vision in the life of elementary school principals.* Paper presented at the Annual Meeting of the American Educational Research Association, Washington, DC.

Woocher, J. (1997). Foreword. In J. Reimer. *Succeeding at Jewish Education: How One Synagogue Made It Work.* Philadelphia: Jewish Publication Society, xi-xviii.

Zoll, R. (2002). *Jewish population declining in U.S.* New York: Associated Press.

Curriculum

Hebrew Language Instruction

Lifsa Schachter & Adina Ofek

Many readers will recognize when part-time Jewish schools were called "Hebrew school" in recognition of the central role that Hebrew instruction in one form or another played in the education of Jewish youth. Given that centrality, it is surprising how little solid research exists around Hebrew instruction in these settings and how little serious attention has been paid to the dilemmas surrounding Hebrew instruction.

In her 1992 chapter "What We Know About Hebrew Language Education," Rivka Dori laments that "Hebrew language education doesn't seem to be an active issue in Jewish education in the United States today" (Dori 1992). This is no longer the situation.

- Significant studies of the state of Hebrew language instruction have been undertaken in recent years (Jewish Agency for Israel 2003; Memorial Foundation for Jewish Culture 2004).
- *Jewish Educational Leadership* devoted a recent print and online issue to teaching Hebrew (Fall 2005).
- Commercial and denominational publishers are producing new Hebrew language programs.
- The Internet has significantly expanded resources available to teachers and students.
- The National Center for the Hebrew Language provides extensive resources for teaching and experiencing Hebrew literature.
- The Memorial Foundation for Jewish Culture and the UJA Federation of Northern New Jersey have launched a pilot project called "Hebrew in America" to promote the study of Hebrew.
- Most unexpected is the recent proliferation of early childhood Hebrew language programs.

We can no longer say that Hebrew is not an active issue. Yet the confusion and frustration that Dori lamented in 1992 still characterize the field.

In this chapter we will map out the various fields that are encompassed by the term Hebrew language instruction, explore what we learn from general education research, examine current models of Hebrew language instruction from that perspective, identify some of the reasons for the continued confusion, and then present strategies we can take to move the field forward.

While there are considerable data surrounding Hebrew language learning (Ofek 1996; Shohamy 2000; Spolsky 1989 and others), we found little that illuminates pedagogic and curricular issues related to teaching Hebrew in the context of Jewish American schooling. When the *Journal of Jewish Education* (2003, 4:1) dedicated an issue to "Structuring Learning around Fundamental Concepts" they had to turn to the 1940s to find a comprehensive and relevant article based on the pedagogic and cultural realities of learning and teaching Hebrew (Rosen and Chomsky 1940, 2003).

A significant body of research into how languages are acquired, how second language learning differs from learning one's native language and the process of reading does exist, but very little of it is directly related to the realities of Hebrew language instruction. This research does have potential for clarifying issues related to Hebrew language instruction; however, it must be applied carefully. Hebrew language instruction often differs in significant ways from the fields on which the research is based. In addition, with controversies still characterizing the field of second language learning, the research frequently does not provide clear direction.

Our involvement in Hebrew language instruction comes from many years of work in Jewish education assisting teachers committed to teaching Hebrew. Ofek chaired the Hebrew Department at The Jewish Theological Seminary for eight years, where she also teaches courses on issues in teaching Hebrew as a second language and works with students preparing to become synagogue school directors and mentors. She served as academic chair for SAT II (Scholastic Assessment Tests), worked on the ACTFL (American Council for Teaching Foreign Languages) guidelines for Hebrew proficiency and is editor of the National Association of Hebrew Methodology Journal. Schachter has worked with teachers from preschool through high school and with students at the college level preparing to become Hebrew language instructors. For the past eight years she directed Moreshet, a program that advocates for Hebrew language in the community by training a new generation of Hebrew teachers for the synagogue and communal part-time school and provides in-service workshops for current teachers. In recent years Moreshet has also promoted the use of Hebrew in early childhood settings based on the Total Physical Response (TPR) approach (Asher 2000). Moreshet is housed at Siegal College of Judaic Studies in Cleveland and is co-sponsored by the Jewish Education Center of Cleveland.

DEFINING THE FIELD

Hebrew language instruction in North America is variously described as second language, foreign language, limited language for specific purposes, and more recently, with relevance to our concerns, heritage language (Fishman 2000). A heritage language is a language that preserves the language of an ethnic or cultural group. It overlaps with second language learning but is likely to also include older forms of the language no longer used in contemporary communication (Peyton et al. 2001). What all these approaches have in common is that they refer to languages acquired after a first language has been basically mastered (Spolsky 1989).

Therefore the term "Hebrew language instruction" is ambiguous. Until the modern period Hebrew language instruction's focus was primarily on preparing young (mostly male) Jews to participate fully in Jewish ritual life and secondarily to equip them to study classical Jewish texts. At the end of the 19th century and the beginning of the 20th century Hebrew language instruction began to include modern Hebrew, both oral and literary. Hebrew language instruction continues to mean different things to different people, including heritage language, second language and modern or foreign language. The balance between modern and traditional Hebrew depends on many factors, including world outlook, identification with Israel, the availability of teachers, the time allotted to studying Hebrew, and the goals of parents (Ofek 2001).

We can identify six basic types of Hebrew language instruction for students from the early childhood level through twelfth grade.

- Programs for early childhood settings for children from ages 3–6. These programs, developed locally and in Israel, appear in a variety of formats, including immersion and total physical response.

- A field popularly called "Siddur Hebrew," designed to teach children to decode Hebrew for liturgical purposes. These programs may be integrated in various degrees with teaching the meaning of prayer and its structure, sometimes with the acquisition of the meaning of some key words, roots and phrases.

- Programs for teaching modern Hebrew.
    - On the elementary level, these programs exist almost exclusively in the day school, where they generally involve a fusion of teaching modern Hebrew and classical texts.
    - High school programs have been an eclectic mix depending on whether the setting is a day school or an after-school program. This field has recently been energized by the introduction of the NETA program.
    - Modern Hebrew is also taught on the junior high and high school levels in approximately fifty public schools. These programs follow guidelines developed by state departments of education for all second languages.

- Classical Hebrew, to the exclusion of modern Hebrew, is still taught in some schools. Frequently these are schools that have a negative identification with the State of Israel. The Melton Biblical Hebrew program, while currently taught in only one school, is worth mentioning because of its potential for success (Riemer 2001; Aron 2004). Classical Hebrew is not treated in any of the literature reviewed in this paper and will therefore not be explored further.

- Many schools develop their own programs, creating a cottage industry of curricular materials enhanced by Internet technology. These programs and curricula are rarely based on any explicit theory or approach. They are not studied, are highly eclectic, and lead to little success (Shohamy 2000).

RESEARCH ON LANGUAGE LEARNING

The research we draw on for purposes of this exploration comes from many fields, including psycholinguistics, sociolinguistics, theoretical linguistics and motivation theory. We do not address research taking place in Israel, which is based on conditions where Hebrew is the learner's primary language. While Israel is a significant producer of curricula for the Diaspora, its products also suffer from an inadequate research base.

CURRENT BRAIN RESEARCH RELEVANT TO TEACHING HEBREW

Significant findings that come from what is popularly called brain research applied to acquiring languages include the following principles:

- The brain is wired for language learning.
- Positive emotions play an important role in learning.
- Much learning is subconscious and comes from peripheral stimuli.
- The mind is primed to seek meaning. Learning is enhanced when embedded in authentic situations. Decontextualized rote learning is problematic for most learners.
- New lexical items are stored in long-term memory only with sufficient rehearsal and timely review of new material.
- Motivation plays an important role in learning and is highest when studies are relevant to learners.
- The brain needs time and experience to consolidate new skills and down time for internal processing.
- Learning integrated with movement tends to be better integrated and retained.
- Student social interaction promotes learning.
- The brain learns best with moderate challenge and high feedback (Caine 1992; Dhority 1998; Genesee 2000).

These principles can easily be integrated into current learning contexts.

Research also claims that early exposure to multiple languages helps the brain grow, and that exposing children to multiple languages at young ages has many life-long benefits (Genesee 2000). It also supports providing students with oral language experiences prior to exposing them to printed matter and throughout the stages of language learning (Curtain 2004).

RESEARCH ON READING

The last decade has witnessed significant research on the reading process with relevance for teaching reading in second languages; i.e., Jewish educators who engage with Hebrew language instruction should take special note of the research as they develop their curriculum and how it is implemented in the classrooms.

The area of reading research that has gained the most attention in the past decade is phonemic awareness. An awareness of phonemes, the smallest sounds that a language can make, is necessary for grasping the alphabetic principle that is at the heart of reading. Some research suggests that phonemic awareness is the single most predictive factor in later success in learning, that it is critical to assess children's phonemic awareness at a young age and that phonemic awareness can be taught (Chard & Dickson 1999). But it must be stressed that principles related to phonemic awareness are developed around learning to read and cannot be applied automatically to programs that teach only decoding. The value of this research for teaching Hebrew decoding is limited for reasons that will be discussed in the section on Siddur Hebrew. Similarly, the considerable research taking place in Israel on language acquisition and Hebrew reading is based on reading Hebrew when it is one's native language.

RESEARCH ON TEACHING METHODOLOGY

There is no universally accepted approach to language learning. Recognized methods for teaching second, foreign, or traditional languages include the grammar translation approach, the audio-lingual method, the direct method, the natural approach, the silent way, immersion, and TPR. However, all of these methods have a weak theoretical basis. Because learning a second language is extremely complex, "any theory of second language learning that leads to a single method is obviously wrong" (Spolsky 1989). This reality will be better understood when we examine some of the other conditions relevant to language learning that transcend technique.

The major controversy in the field of language learning pits those who favor language acquisition approaches against those who promote formal instruction (Krashen 2002). Current thinking, backed by research, claims that, contrary to the once highly accepted notion that language should only be taught through natural language input, language instruction is most successful when it involves combining meaningful language with some emphasis on form. It asserts that grammar should be taught through meaning-based approaches and not through formal detached drills. "An internal grammar is built up via exposure to comprehensible, communicatively oriented input…As far as acquisition is concerned drills are simply unnecessary and at best a waste of time for the communicative language ability" (Long 1983; Wong & VanPatten 2003).

Met, Senior Research Associate and former director at the National Foreign Language Center at the University of Maryland, has effectively summarized the research on second language learning (2003). According to her analysis of the research, conditions that contribute to the most effective language teaching include adequate time, positive learner engagement (intensity), students' being exposed to comprehensible input, the presence of meaningful and purposeful communicative interaction, involvement with authentic tasks and purposes, and cultural understanding and empathy with the target language. There is considerable challenge in applying this research to the variety of Hebrew language programs.

CONDITIONS FOR LANGUAGE LEARNING

Spolsky (1989) also highlights the importance of social factors in language learning. While students learn as individuals, the social conditions, not only in the classroom but also in the family and the community in which languages are acquired, have both direct and indirect significance for language learning. Social conditions include the attitudes of the learners and their families toward other languages, their perceptions of the values embedded in those languages, and their rationales, goals and priorities with regard to the language. These attitudes and ideas lead to learners' expectations and perception of how much they can learn and determine the degree to which they take advantage of the learning situation. Attitude and motivation transcend innate capability and previous knowledge. We personally witnessed this when we observed Hebrew classes with the children of Refusniks in Russia. Non-professional teachers worked under the most primitive and limited conditions and had few resources. Yet the level of achievement was extraordinary and can only be attributed to the high level of motivation and the attitudes of the learners and their families.

RESEARCH ON THE ROLE OF TEACHERS

Most studies on the condition of Hebrew language instruction and its continuing problems point to issues around teacher background, subject matter competency, training, and attitudes (Shohamy

1994; Ofek 1996; Wohl 2005 and others). The background, training, and knowledge base of new teachers as well as of those currently teaching, while recognized as critical, remain largely unstudied.

The desirability of native vs. non-native speakers is a highly contested issue. The advantages of native speakers seem clear: They bring authentic live language into the classroom and a strong, if problematic, connection to Israel by the mere fact that they are here and not there. They often lack cultural familiarity with American children, their families, and the traditions of American Judaism.

Non-native speakers of Hebrew bring invaluable strengths, having themselves overcome the difficulties of learning the language. They understand the student and serve as role models and inspiration. Many American teachers also share the cultural milieu of the students and their parents; they understand the unique character of American religious life and readily become a part of the Jewish community where they teach. Yet most of the non-native teachers lack fluency, range of functional vocabulary, and sociolinguistic competency.

A critical research issue related to teachers lies in assessing the contributions of each group and in uncovering ways to support them with continuous professional development.

THE VARIOUS CONTEXTS

TEACHING HEBREW IN THE EARLY CHILDHOOD CONTEXT

While experiencing Hebrew on the early childhood level is seen as a value in and of itself (Simchovitch, personal communication, May 2005), many of its advocates see it as an experience that will "create positive attitudes, a fondness and sympathy for the Hebrew language, its culture and its speakers" (Nevo 2006). Hebrew immersion programs in early childhood did exist many decades ago. Currently Hebrew enters most early childhood settings only through ritual, songs, and prayer. In some settings modern Hebrew is used for some routines and classroom activities. Where Hebrew is a component of the curriculum, individual schools craft most programs with no explicit attention to theory. A number of privately run websites providing early childhood resources for Hebrew language exemplify this lack of attention to explicit theory.

This has recently changed with the development of several theory-based programs of childhood Hebrew language instruction. These programs include Aleh (BJE NY), *Nitzanim* (Melton Center, Hebrew University), *Maala* (JTS) and *Chalav u'Dvash* (Jewish Agency for Israel). Total Physical Response (TPR) has been adapted by a (small) number of Jewish preschools. The UJA of Northern New Jersey is piloting a study of early childhood Hebrew programs in fifty-four classes as part of its Hebrew in America initiative. Reports of these programs all describe learning environments that are joyful, with low threat and great excitement. However, these programs are still new, and there have as yet been no studies on long-range impact or of their impact on existing primary Hebrew language programs.

Three important questions related to Hebrew in the early childhood setting are: Is this an optimal age at which to expose children to another language? What is the impact on future development when young children are exposed to Hebrew language and culture? How important is it for students to continue their learning as they transition into kindergarten, whether in a day school or congregational school?

As in many areas of foreign or second language learning, there is no consensus on the optimal age for introducing another language. Research differentiates teaching a second language and teaching a foreign language. There is a belief that Hebrew is not a second language for the child in the Jewish early childhood setting. But neither is it entirely a foreign language. Depending on the setting, there is considerable support for Hebrew sounds, songs, phrases and ritual usage, making the situation move somewhat in the direction of second language learning. In the context of second language learning, research suggests that starting exposure at an early age is advantageous. Those who favor an instructional approach to learning foreign languages assert that it is important that the child reach the level of cognitive development when grammatical rules can be understood (Nevo 2006). Those who favor an acquisition model argue that the capacity of young children to learn languages is so great that they can master as many languages as they hear systematically and regularly at the same time (Curtis 1998).

TEACHING SIDDUR HEBREW

Although Siddur Hebrew programs use elements of Hebrew language, it is not clear that they can properly be called *language* instruction programs. Language instruction is generally defined as developing the capacity to communicate successfully and to read with comprehension. Siddur Hebrew achieves neither of these goals. Generally the aim of Siddur Hebrew is to develop the capacity to participate successfully in a Hebrew-based prayer service. It remains the dominant congregational school model (Memorial Foundation 2004). There is a certain irony in this. A recent Gallup Poll asserts that only 5% of non–Orthodox American Jews participate in weekly prayer services.

Siddur Hebrew is supported by a wide array of programs and curricular materials, including those that incorporate media and other technologies. They have become more interactive by addressing the different learning styles of students and their varying attendance patterns. Anecdotally, teachers report that they notice a difference in achievement in those students who engage with Hebrew technology at home. In recent years programs called Parent-Child Hebrew have been introduced. These are classes where children and parents learn together, almost always with an accompanying reduction in hours of instruction. The recent introduction of *Mitkadem (*URJ) is in large part a response to issues surrounding attendance patterns, learning styles and diverse levels of achievement.

While Siddur Hebrew programs attend to some aspects of brain research, they contain serious shortcomings, as indicated by current research. They provide no oral base for relating to Hebrew words and phrases; they confuse reciting with decoding, and decoding with reading. They ignore the relationship between personal relevance and learning and the power of motivation to further learning. They ignore the role of recitation and trope in acquiring Siddur skills and are frequently based on incorrect understandings of Hebrew (Schachter 2004).

There is increasing recognition in recent years that focusing exclusively on decoding Hebrew is insufficient for the acquisition of the desired prayerbook skills. As a result, there has been a reintroduction of Hebrew as a language into the published curricula for the congregational schools. But Siddur Hebrew remains the dominant approach to Hebrew in these schools (Aron, 2004).

TEACHING MODERN HEBREW

a. Elementary school

While there are a few congregational schools committed to retaining a modern Hebrew language program and a small number of public schools that include Hebrew as a foreign language, overwhelmingly communicative Hebrew on the elementary level is found in day schools. Only rarely do day schools attempt to integrate the teaching of communicative and classical Hebrew. The tension regarding Hebrew in the day school lies in finding the balance between communicative and modern language goals on the one hand and teaching Hebrew for mastering the sacred texts of the Jewish people on the other. Communicative language teaching is learner-centered and based on authentic, real-life situations.

Some schools continue with a strong Hebrew communicative language program through eighth grade. As they concentrate on Hebrew as a language, they generally spend less time on teaching texts. They approach language in a way similar to the "language across the subject areas" model (Wesby 2005), teaching Jewish content such as history, holidays, and Israel in Hebrew. Other schools, probably the majority of day schools, drop communicative Hebrew at fourth grade and focus thereafter on understanding texts through a read-and-translate methodology, with some attention to modern Hebrew, especially as it relates to Israel. This widely accepted view is attested to in the NETA promotional materials.

The reasons for this shift are numerous. In some cases teachers who can teach texts and maintain communicative Hebrew are not available. It is often claimed that the language level of the students makes it impossible for them to discuss in Hebrew the sophisticated concepts of the texts they are studying. A third claim is that maintaining a total Hebrew environment would lead to a sacrifice in the number of texts that can be learned by students.

Two recent Hebrew language curricula for day schools have been developed with explicit attention to learning theory. *Tal Am* is a program designed for grades 1–6 to integrate communicative language with the study of classical texts (Shimon 2006). It has had an enormous impact, and together with its predecessor program, *Tal Sela,* is used in approximately 350 schools in the United States and Canada. *Tal Am* explicitly attends to the "significance of the age variable, instructional design, methods of instruction, types of pedagogic materials, and the learning environment." It also attends to the "potential tension…between Hebrew as a communicative language and Hebrew as a heritage language."

Chaverim B'Ivrit is a second day school program with explicit attention to language theory (Litman, undated). Designed for elementary school children in grade 3 and above, it has a focus on the communicative aspects of language, integrates the four language skills, pays attention to the need to apply learning to new situations, and meets the interests and needs of diverse learners. Produced by the Union for Reform Judaism, it is a program designed for the more liberal day school. Although the program is relatively new, already a significant number of schools have adopted it for their Hebrew language programs.

While the authors of these programs have solicited feedback and evaluations, there is no public discussion of the findings. We are not aware of any rigorous research that examines the programs' assumptions or implementation.

b. High school.

Until the recent introduction of the NETA program, Hebrew on the high school level was an eclectic mix governed almost entirely by local curricula, often using what is known as the ulpan method and dominated by one textbook. NETA introduced a radical change. Created by Hebrew language curriculum specialists from the Hebrew University of Jerusalem, administered by the Hebrew College of Boston, and supported by The AVI CHAI Foundation, NETA has introduced a new professionalism into the high school Hebrew program. It seeks to provide a comprehensive linguistic and educational framework that will enable Jewish secondary school students to advance to high levels of Hebrew proficiency. Coming down squarely on the side of language instruction, it is based on a structured linguistic progression. It insists on training for teachers and accountability for student learning. It integrates modern Israeli culture, Jewish tradition and world knowledge. It includes clear and specific goals, time commitments and standardized tests.

c. Informal settings

Hebrew is increasingly taught in informal settings such as summer camps. This is another unstudied area.

IMPLICATIONS AND POLICY RECOMMENDATIONS

Hebrew language instruction has been taking place in America and in other Diaspora communities for a long time. While in recent years attention has been given to the conditions under which this instruction takes place, there is currently no significant body of research based on actual field realities that takes into account the distinctions among the various kinds of programs related to Hebrew language instruction and the classroom environment.

Based upon the lack of research, there are a series of critical issues related to teaching Hebrew that cross the various settings:

- Frequency and length of instruction
- Best methodologies linked to targeted purposes and goals
- Relationship among various kinds of Hebrew, such as modern communicative and classical texts
- Impact of the background of teachers on learning

- Most appropriate ages for instruction based on type of language
- How best to increase motivation for Hebrew study
- Interrelationship of each of the language skills
- Role of choice by families and students in language learning

Advocates for school improvement in general education assert that "confronting the brutal facts is the surest, fastest path" to improving learning in schools, that we cannot make significant change unless we really know what goes on in classrooms (Schmoker 2006). Equally, improvement in Hebrew language instruction must begin with studies of classroom realities. Because the very parameters of the field are unclear to many, we must begin the task by clarifying the distinctions among the various endeavors that are labeled "Hebrew language instruction." This will allow for more clarity in discussions about Hebrew language instruction and for identifying conditions and characteristics relevant to each type of instruction.

Research based on field realities is the necessary pre-condition for setting realistic expectations, selecting appropriate methodologies and structures for learning, and developing a research agenda appropriate for each type of Hebrew language instruction. Building a collective knowledge base, grounded in actual field realities and utilizing current research on language learning, is the key to moving our enterprise forward.

RESEARCH QUESTIONS

There is no aspect of Hebrew instruction that cannot benefit from significant research. This chapter alludes to the need for research in all of the commonplaces: research about the teachers and methodologies, the learner, the substance of the various kinds of Hebrew and effective milieus for learning languages. In addition we need to make better use of research in related fields. A sample of research questions for which we would like more data includes:

- Can learner choice be implemented as a strategy in currently existing contexts?
- Will learner and family choice increase success?
- What are the most effective ways for teaching decoding skills?
- How can prayer best be taught in ways that provide skill mastery and conceptual understanding?
- How do children studying Hebrew in various contexts understand the significance of acquiring Hebrew skills?
- How much Hebrew knowledge does a teacher need to be effective in a given language program?
- What are the benefits and disadvantages of teachers who are native speakers versus non-native speakers of Hebrew?
- How does teaching Hebrew in camps or other informal settings affect learning outcomes?

FUTURE DIRECTIONS

The field of Hebrew instruction in all sites and denominations seems to share a common flaw: Participants and leaders pay lip service to the importance of Hebrew language for Jewish identity and survival. Practice does not match the rhetoric.

We need to:

- Describe existing teaching practices and curricula honestly.
- Set clear, attainable goals.
- Involve all constituents in the decisions around Hebrew instruction.
- Create tracks and give choice related to the type and intensity of the Hebrew to be learned. Choice must be accompanied by agreements to devote the time and effort needed to succeed.
- Establish benchmarks for each type of Hebrew instruction with clear criteria and the means for evaluation.

HIGHLIGHTS OF THE CHAPTER

- Hebrew language instruction is an ambiguous term connoting a variety of interactions with Hebrew ranging from full language literacy to minimal exposure to Hebrew as a system of meaning.
- Jewish educators need to differentiate among the various approaches to Hebrew instruction and adapt methodologies based on goals and the needs of different age groups.
- Hebrew language instruction should make use of the significant research on learning, including significant research on learning to read—popularly called "brain research"—to design programs of language instruction.
- Educators need to face the challenges in applying the research on effective language learning and adapt the findings to the conditions under which Hebrew is taught.

ANNOTATED BIBLIOGRAPHY

The works described below are highlighted because of their significant contribution to the issues discussed in the chapter. They are recommended to those who would like to further their exploration of the issues related to Hebrew language instruction.

STUDIES ON THE STATE OF HEBREW LANGUAGE INSTRUCTION

Rodman, P. (2003). Israel and the Place of Modern Hebrew in Jewish Education: A Consultation about the Possibilities for Hebrew Language Instruction. Jerusalem: The Jewish Agency for Israel, Research and Development Unit, Department of Jewish Zionist Education.

Aron, I. (2004). Teaching Hebrew in the Congregational School. New York: Memorial Foundation for Jewish Culture.

These studies provide portraits of the current state of Hebrew language instruction. The Rodman study has a multinational focus and addresses multiple types of settings. Aron's focus is on the United States and the congregational school.

EXEMPLARY TEXTS ON TEACHING A SECOND LANGUAGE TO CHILDREN

Curtain, H. & Dahlber, C.A. (2004). *Languages and Children, Making the Match: New Languages for Young Learners* (3rd Ed.). Boston: Pearson. This book presents a comprehensive overview of the essential ingredients of a first-rate K–8 foreign language program with significant attention to early language programs. It integrates current standards, addresses the use of technology and advocates immersion programs.

Dhority, L. F. & Jensen, E. (1998). *Joyful Fluency: Brain Compatible Second Language Acquisition*. San Diego, CA: The Brain Store. This book applies general brain-compatible principles that are common to all teaching and learning to language teaching and advocates for language acquisition methodologies. Topics include paying attention to the environment, use of materials, music, good relationship and facilitation skills, maximizing first impressions, lesson planning, and active learning.

Richard-Amato, P. A. (2003). *Making It Happen: From Interactive to Participatory Language Teaching* (3rd Ed.). White Plains, NY: Longman. This text for language teachers provides a cyclic approach to theory and practice, reflecting the understanding that theory and practice constantly inform each other. It examines programs in action and fosters reflective teaching.

STANDARDS FOR LANGUAGE TEACHING

American Council on Teaching Foreign Languages. Standards for Foreign Language Leaning: Preparing for the 21st Century. Retrieved July, 2006 from *http://www.yearoflanguages.org/files/public/execsumm.pdf*. An eleven-member task force representing a variety of languages, levels of instruction, program models, and geographic regions was appointed to undertake the task of defining *content standards*—what students should know and be able to do—in foreign language education. The resulting document represents an unprecedented consensus among educators, business leaders, government, and the community on the definition and role of foreign language instruction in American education. ACTFL Guidelines have been developed for modern Hebrew.

RESEARCH ON LANGUAGE INSTRUCTION

Met, M. (2003). Best Practices in Pre-Collegiate Language Education: Models For Pipelines. Retrieved September, 2006 from *www.nlconference.org/docs/Met-paper.doc*. The best short summary available on research and issues related to second/foreign language instruction.

Teaching Hebrew as a Second/Foreign Language. *Jewish Educational Leadership: Focus on Hebrew Language Instruction* 4 (1). Retrieved August 2006 from *http://www.lookstein.org/retrieve.php?ID=3501176*. This issue of *Jewish Educational Leadership* is devoted to a broad discussion of the place of Hebrew language in Jewish life as well as a range of basic questions that surround Hebrew language instruction as it is currently presented in our schools. Contributors include long-time advocates of Hebrew language as well as cutting-edge practitioners, many of whom are discussed in this paper.

REFERENCES

Aron, I. (2004). *Teaching Hebrew in the Congregational School*. New York: Memorial Foundation for Jewish Culture.

Asher, J. J. (2000). *Learning Another Language through Actions: Total Physical Response* (6th Ed.). Los Gatos, CA: Sky Oaks Productions.

Caine, R. (1991). *Making Connections, Teaching and the Human Brain*. Alexandria, VA: ASCD.

Chard, D. J. & Dickson, S. V. (1999). "Phonological awareness: Instructional and assessment guideline". *Intervention in School and Clinic* 34, 261–270.

Curtain, H. & Dahlber C. (2004). *Languages and Children, Making the Match: New Languages for Young Learners* (3rd Ed.). Boston: Pearson/A and B.

Curtis, A. (1998). *A Curriculum for the Pre-school Child*. London: Routledge.

Dhority, L. F. & Jensen, E. (1998). *Joyful Fluency: Brain Compatible Second Language Acquisition*. San Diego, CA: The Brain Store.

Dori, R. (1992). What We Know About…..Hebrew Language Education. In *What We Know About Jewish Education*. Stuart Kelman (ed.). Los Angeles: Torah Aura Productions.

Diller, K.C. (1978). *The Language Teaching Controversy*. New York: Newbury House.

Fishman, J. A. (2000). 300-Plus Years of Heritage Language Education in the United States. In J. Kreeft Peyton, D. A. Ranard & S. McGinnis (eds.). *Heritage Languages in America: Preserving a National Resource*. Yonkers, NY: ACTFL, 81–97.

"Focus on: Hebrew Language Instruction" (2005). *Jewish Educational Leadership* 4 (1).

Genesee, F. (2000). Brain Research: Implications for Second Language Learning. Eric Digest ED447727. Retrieved July, 2006 from *http://www.ericdigests.org/2001-3/brain.htm*

Krashen, S. D. (2002). "Second Language Acquisition and Second Language Learning." Retrieved August 2005 from *http://sdkrashen.com/SL_Acquisition_and_Learning/index.html*

Litman, L. (undated) Introduction. Retrieved July, 2006 from *http://www.urjpress.com/resources/Chaverim_BIvrit_Essay_Eng.pdf*

Long, M. H. (1983). "Does Second Language Instruction Make a Difference? A Review of Research." *TESOL Quarterly* 17 (3).

Met, M. (2003). Best Practices in Pre-Collegiate Language Education: Models For Pipelines. Retrieved September 2006 from *www.nlconference.org/docs/Met-paper.doc*

Nevo, N. (1996).Teaching Hebrew in Early Childhood in the Diaspora: Reflections on the *Nitzanim* Program. Retrieved August 2006 from http:/'www.lookstein.org/outline_journal.

Ofek, A. (2001). A New Look a Old Hebrew Textbooks, Salient Features and Underlying Principles of Hebrew Textbooks: 1830–1930. In B. Cohen and A. Ofek (eds.), *Essays in Education and Judaism in Honor of Joseph S. Lukinsky*. New York: Jewish Theological Seminary Press.

Ofek, A. (1996). "The Making of a Hebrew Teacher: Preparing Hebrew Language Teachers for Jewish Day Schools." *Journal of Jewish Education* 62 (2), 21–28.

Peyton, J. K., Ranard, D. A. & McGinnis, S. (eds.) (2001). *Heritage Languages in America: Preserving a National Resource*. Delta Systems Co. Inc. Center for Applied Linguistics.

Riemer, J. (2001). *Succeeding at Jewish Education: How One Synagogue Makes it Work*. Philadelphia: Jewish Publication Society.

Robins, F. (undated), Monoligualism Can Be Cured. Retrieved August, 2006 from *http://www.ivrit.org/html/ why_hebrew/story_03.html*

Rodman, P. (2003). Israel and the Place of Modern Hebrew in Jewish Education: A Consultation about the Possibilities for Hebrew Language Instruction. Jerusalem: The Jewish Agency for Israel Research and Development Unit, Department of Jewish Zionist Education.

Rosen, B. & Chomsky, W. (2003). "Improving the Teaching of Hebrew in Our Schools." *Journal of Jewish Education 69 (1), 57–63.*

Schachter, L. (2004). "Teaching Hebrew Decoding: Principles and Strategies." *Gleanings* 6:2. Retrieved July 2006 from *http://www.jtsa.edu/davidson/melton/gleanings/v6n2.shtml#harvest1*

Shimon, T. & Peerless, S. (2006). *Tal Am*: A Natural Approach to Hebrew Language Acquisition. Retrieved August 2006 from *http://www.lookstein.org/online_journal.php?id=85*

Shohamy, E. (1999–2000). "Contextual and Pedagogical Factors for Learning and Maintaining Jewish Languages in the United States." *Journal of Jewish Education 65 (3), 21–29.*

Shmoker, M. (2006). *Results Now: How We Can Achieve Unprecedented Improvements in Teaching and Learning.* Alexandria VA: ASCD.

Wesby, C. (2005). "Language, Culture and Literacy." *The ASHA Leader,* 16–30.

Wohl, A. (2005). "Teaching Hebrew as a Second Foreign Language." *Jewish Educational Leadership* 4 (1). Retrieved August 2006 from *http://www.lookstein.org/retrieve.php?ID=3501176*

Wong, W. & Van Patten, B. (2003). "The Evidence is IN: Drills are OUT." *Foreign Language Annals 36,3.*

Teaching Jewish Texts

Jeffrey Schein

L'asok b'divrei Torah… to engage with words of Torah…to study sacred Jewish texts. Perhaps there is no single blessing in Jewish tradition that resonates as deeply for me as this one. Creating the conditions that allow myself and others to study Jewish texts is a great personal and professional joy. As a professor of Jewish education at Siegal College I have taught numerous courses about the teaching and learning of Jewish texts. As a member of my own Kol Halev congregation in Cleveland I relish every opportunity to both lead and participate in Jewish text study. As the senior consultant for the Lekhu Lakhem project for Jewish day camp directors of the JCCA I watch with wonder as Jewish professionals innocent of any previous encounters with Jewish text study begin to see its implications for their summer camps.

Yet I also recognize that this *brakhah* can easily become a *brakhah l'vatalah*, a problematic, even invalid blessing. Why? Teaching Jewish texts is ferociously complex. There are conceptual, educational, and theological challenges Jewish educators rarely acknowledge. Without such awareness the stroll through *Pardes*, the multi-leveled garden of Jewish text study, can be full of thorns, perhaps even snakes. In this article I will outline four of these challenges:

1. The role of the teacher as a Jewish human being in text study
2. The challenge of differing "frames" for describing and enacting the processes of Jewish text study
3. The development of a repertoire of practical skills for the Jewish educator engaged in Jewish text study
4. The relationship between text study and moral action

THE EDUCATIONAL VALUE OF A TEXT

Jewish educators regularly affirm that there is *kedushah* (uniqueness and holiness) in the act of Jewish study and in our sacred texts. Parker Palmer, an educator outside of our tradition, attributes extraordinary educational value to a text as completing the triangle of teacher-learner-text necessary for meaningful educational dialogue. In *To Know as We Are Known* he writes ,

> Where schools give students several hundred pages of text and urge them to learn speed reading, monks dwell on a page or a passage for hours and days at a time They call it *lectio divina*, sacred reading, and they do it at a contemplative pace. The method allows reading to open, not fill, our learning space.

> When all students in the room have read the same piece in a way that allows them to enter and occupy the text, a common space is created in which students, teachers, and subjects can meet. It is an open space since a good text will raise as many questions as it answers. It is bounded since the text itself dictates the limits of our mutual inquiry. It is a hospitable, reassuring space since everyone has walked around in it beforehand and become acquainted with its dimensions.

> Too often we fail to capitalize on this space-creating quality. We hold students individually accountable for what they read in texts, but seldom allow their reading to create a common space in which the group can meet in mutual accountability for their learning (1993).

In my experience this particular text serves as a wonderful mirror for Jewish educators, helping them name and analyze some of their greatest successes in teaching Jewish texts. Phrases like *space-creating quality, open-space,* and *bounded space* invite eloquent educational midrash.

The contemporary contexts for Jewish text study are important to understand. Traditionally, Jewish text study is associated with the *beit midrash,* the house of learning. A famous poem by Hayim Nahman Bialik written at the turn of the 20th century locates the secret to Jewish survival within the four walls of a house of study. Over the last twenty years there has been a remarkable broadening of the contexts in which Jewish text study occurs. In addition to the formal classroom, where lectures and discussions, sometimes in <u>h</u>evruta, take place, we have added informal retreats, Jewish camping and other venues as new contexts in which Jewish text study plays a prominent role.

CHALLENGE #1: THE ROLE OF THE JEWISH/HUMAN PERSON IN JEWISH TEXT STUDY: THE SPECTRUM FROM SWEET-SPOT TORAH STUDY AND THE INVERTED PYRAMID

The authority of an individual as a source of meaning in relationship to a Jewish text involves a spectrum of possibilities. By briefly describing the two ends of the spectrum we will assist teachers of Judaism to understand the need to find their own place along this spectrum in terms of the Jewish and educational presuppositions of each placement.

A member of my own community leads a weekly Torah study she calls "sweet-spot" Torah study. She believes that every portion has the capacity to evoke from the reader/student something of great existential meaning. Participants in sweet-spot Torah study engage in a slow, meditative reading of a selection from *parshat ha-shavua.* Then they begin to share in <u>h</u>evruta (study pairs) where the "sweet spot" was for each of them in the passage. No other mediation is required. Meaning ultimately resides within the individual learner and his/her encounter with the text.

Contrast this with the image of the "inverted pyramid" provided by Barry Holtz in *Back to the Sources* (1987). The apex of the inverted pyramid is often a single verse (or word) from Torah. The expanding levels above the apex represent the "great conversation" that has gone on over time and includes us through the traditions of commentary and interpretation.

To the eyes of the learner new to Jewish texts this inverted pyramid can be quite daunting. The learner can easily be crushed under its weight. Meaning can easily be construed as resting only with the cumulative, complex voices of tradition. Authority and meaning here lay outside the learner. At the very least the teacher must serve as a strong intermediary creating the scaffolding that would allow the learner to climb to any one point along the pyramid.

Ultimately Holtz does not intend this image of the inverted pyramid to function in such a dis-empowering way (actually, quite the opposite. His hope in writing *Back to the Sources* was to open up the textual treasures of Jewish tradition to Jews seeking greater literacy). But the contradistinction to the "sweet spot of Torah study" for heuristic and pedagogic reasons is clear. Everyone involved in promoting Jewish text study needs to be willing to reflect on his or her own position along this spectrum with regard to which voices (or combination of voices) has the final, authoritative word in Jewish text study.

CHALLENGE #2: CONCEPTUAL AND PEDAGOGIC FRAMES FOR JEWISH TEXT STUDY: IS 2, 9, 18 OR 72 ENOUGH?

Jewish text study is not one simple thing. Looking at it from two different perspectives highlights the complexity. Levenson suggests that we mean at least two very different things when we talk about teaching or learning Jewish texts (2002). Holtz identifies nine possible orientations of teaching Bible (2003). When we cross-reference these eighteen orientations (assuming that each of the nine orientations to Bible teaching suggested by Holtz could be taught through both of Levenson's modalities) with the traditional hermeneutical structures of the four-tiered PaRDeS (*peshat, remez, derash and sod),* which accounts for levels of understanding as well as different orientations along a horizontal plane, we are dealing with at least seventy-two educational/Jewish frames for teaching a Jewish text.

Levenson suggests that teachers of Jewish text consider the difference between *Jewish text study* and the *study of Jewish texts*. We typically conflate these two kinds of relationships with Jewish texts into a global rubric called text study, ultimately to our detriment, Levenson believes.

Jewish text study is the most traditional mode of Jewish study. It privileges depth over breadth. Its focus is micro. A whole year spent studying a single chapter of Bible (perhaps even a verse) is not only acceptable but desirable. The source of truth and authority for the text is a single voice believed to have derived from Sinai no matter how multi-vocal the voices of commentators might be in interpreting the text.

The *study of Jewish texts* is influenced more by contemporary Biblical scholarship and the disciplines of archaeology, linguistics, and historical analysis. Its focus is macro. Truth here is often conceived of contextually and drawn eclectically from a number of sources, including traditional sources. Breadth of knowledge is more critical than in *Jewish text study*.

In a recent test of my colleagues' assumptions in a year-long colloquium on Jewish texts we studied the weekly Torah portion from twin perspectives: the traditional Sephardic collection of Torah commentaries known as *Me'am Loez* (Kaplan 1988) and the recently published *New Jewish Study Bible* (2004). Like Levenson, I believe that there is great richness in blending these methodologies, a process he illustrates in discussing the origins of the Haggadah. By encouraging students to integrate these approaches, he finds they are able to reflect what is for them an authentic understanding of the purposes of Jewish text study.

Holtz explored this issue in greater depth in his volume *Textual Knowledge: Teaching the Bible in Theory and Practice* (2003). After observing and training hundreds of Bible teachers Holtz concludes that there are no less than nine different orientations. His names for these different orientations are the Contextual, Literary Criticism, Reader-Response, Parshanut—the Jewish Interpretive, Moralistic-Didactic, Personalization, Ideational, Bible Leads to Action, Decoding-Translating-Comprehension. According to Holtz, each of these orientations is part of the pedagogic content knowledge a teacher develops even before entering a given Jewish classroom to teach a particular Jewish text. At its best it reflects deep experience as a learner of these texts (content knowledge), a significant *tachlis* experience teaching these texts (pedagogic knowledge) and an artful blending of both dimensions into a creative rethinking of how to best teach the text in a given context (pedagogic content knowledge).

The details of these orientations are complex and described in depth in the book. For the purposes of this chapter, the overarching point is simply that the teaching of Jewish texts is a sophisticated art and craft requiring much thoughtfulness at many different levels. Educational directors and policy makers who push teachers into more Jewish text study because it is such an "authentic" mode of Jewish study ought to be aware of how much learning and professional development is necessary for that mode to be engaged in competently and creatively. Half tongue-in-cheek, there are seventy-two such modes. With greater certainty, there is a complexity to what is called, most simply and generically, Jewish text study.

CHALLENGE #3: THE SKILL SETS OF THE TEACHERS OF JEWISH TEXTS: MAKING THE STRANGE FAMILIAR AND THE FAMILIAR STRANGE

Given what has been discussed above, I believe the skills a Jewish educator needs to engage in the study of Jewish texts are both affective and cognitive. On the affective side, teachers need to know how to "make the strange familiar." Jewish texts can be quite intimidating. They speak in languages (linguistic and conceptual) quite strange to many Jewish learners. The effective teacher of Jewish texts needs to quiet the fears that come with this "strangeness", find ways of connecting the unfamiliar texts to familiar experiences of the learner and give the learner a sense of confidence about his/her ability to learn these new languages. Belenky et al. (1986) has called this process helping the learner discover her/his "voice" in relationship to the text.

Cognitively, a whole range of techniques that can effectively "problematize" the text are necessary. What looks like the plain meaning of the text has to be made (at least temporarily) unfamiliar, a matter of inquiry. One of the early and still one of the more sophisticated curricula written for Jewish text study of Bible—the Melton Bible curriculum—constantly challenges the learner with "Yes, that is what the text *says*, but what do you think it *means?*" (1966). Brown lists among his favorite questions: "What else might the text mean?" and "What does this text mean to YOU?" In a series of curricula about the Five Megillot called *Aytz Hayim We* (2000) I have used techniques of color-coding to help the learner interact with the text. Each color marker represents a different kind of interaction. The learner might underline with one color affirmations of deep values they want to affirm; a second color might underscore a question that the learner has about the text; a third, an "argument" the learner might want to have with the text.

There is no shortage of creative techniques for teaching Jewish texts in the cumulative repertoire of Jewish text teachers across the world. What is often lacking, in the first place, is effective inventorying and hence access to these skills. Second, training venues where new teachers can be mentored and coached about the proper use of these techniques are sparse. In the more traditional Jewish world these skills (often based on a more clearly defined and sharply delimited understanding of Talmudic hermeneutics) are acquired organically in yeshivot. For Jews on a journey, as Franz Rosensweig (1973) would have it, "from the periphery to the center of Jewish life," the skill sets for both the learner and the teacher seem to require more conscious cultivation.

CHALLENGE #4: WHAT IS THE PURPOSE OF JEWISH TEXT STUDY?

A famous *mahloket* (argument) in the Talmud pits the students of Rabbi Akiva against the students of Rabbi Tarfon (Kiddushin 40b). At stake: the great question whether *Talmud* (study) or *ma'aseh* (deeds/mitzvot) is of supreme importance. The resolution: *Talmud* is greater only if *Talmud* leads to *ma'asim* (deeds).

This is essentially the question of the purpose for studying Jewish texts. Consonant with what was said above about the space for inquiry, when teaching this text students are invited into the chambers of Nitza's house in Lydda, where the Talmud reports the debate occurred, and where they are asked to suspend judgment about the final outcome. By dividing the learning group into Akiva's and Tarfon's disciples and encouraging them to always speak *b'shem* (in the name of) Akiva or Tarfon, the best arguments for the primacy of study or action will occur.

There is a hidden agenda in doing this that is then revealed to the learner. There is much "lionizing" of *torah lishma* (learning for its own sake) and adult literacy in today's Jewish world. Over a decade ago Adin Steinsaltz noted that the rallying cry of the Jewish people in the 1970s to "Let My People Go" was with the Soviet Jewry movement, and now (then) the cry had changed to "Let My People Know," with a new focus on adult learning. If anything, the urgency (and occasional stridency) of that clamor for adult literacy has grown. As an example, Jewish literacy was the theme of the 2006 CAJE conference, which featured Rabbi Joseph Telushkin, author of the important book *Jewish Literacy* (1991).

In a scholarly vein, Elliot Dorff, Barry Chazan, and Joseph Riemer have each written about the study/moral action dialectic in Jewish education favoring Akiva's position in the archetypical Talmudic debate. In contrast—while professing my deep respect for Akiva's position (like Akiva, I started late in my journey toward Jewish literacy)—I advocate a new receptivity to Tarfon's focus on moral action.

My suspicion that Akiva might be off target in the context of American Jewry is drawn from the "pragmatic" thread of the philosophy of Mordecai Kaplan. Kaplan argues that a rationale for Jewish existence in an American context needs to be different than it might have been for such Jewish luminaries as Martin Buber, Herman Cohen or, in a more contemporary vein, Emanual Levinas, in the European context. The pragmatism of American life that draws from thinkers like John Dewey and William James suggests that study and action make a reciprocal dialectic. Sometimes the need and desire to act challenges us to act intelligently on the basis of knowledge and the wisdom of the past. This other side of the study/moral action dialectic is found most concretely in Jewish life when Jewish groups committed to *tikkun olam* (world prepare) precede or follow their work for the homeless or some other just cause with the study of Jewish texts. Here Jewish study deepens a previous disposition to act morally.

I raise this issue *l'mashal* (as an example) of a larger question to which there are a number of authentic different responses. It matters little in my mind how the shapers of Jewish educational policy and practical Jewish education weigh the balance of study and action (I have an intuition that both will always receive some weight). It matters a great deal, however, that one raises the issue of what is the ultimate rationale for a focus on Jewish text.

CONCLUSION

In the Talmud Yerushalmi a group of the students of Rabbi Yohanan spy a colleague, Rabbi Abbahu, from a distance. His face—even from a distance—is glowing *(afui nahirin)*. Yohanan and his disciples begin speculating about what might account for this near-preternatural glow coming from Abbahu. Undoubtedly it has something to do with the joy of Jewish learning, but Yohanan and the disciples incorrectly surmise that the glow comes from discovering something entirely new and earthshaking (an *oraita hadta shamata*). Abbahu corrects their straying speculations. His glow came from uncovering a small, ancient piece of learning *(tosefta atikta)*. The disciples then link this incident to a *pesuk* from Kohelet/Ecclessiastes, *hokhmat adam ta'ir panav*, a person's wisdom lights up his face.

Jewish text study has a powerful capacity to light up faces of Jewish learners. Yet I believe Jewish classrooms, camps, and synagogues are also filled with fallen faces, faces that have been blanched with embarrassment *(halvanat panim)* because Jewish texts have been poorly chosen and poorly taught. The centrality of Jewish texts in our tradition makes it clear that we have an exciting educational challenge: to shift the balance entirely in favor of the teaching/learning encounters where the end product is many faces that are *afui nahirim* (glowing) and where Yohanan's disciples might declare *hochmat adam tair panav*.

OTHER QUESTIONS FOR FURTHER RESEARCH

The four questions posed in this article naturally link to another set of questions related to the teaching and learning of Jewish texts:

- What is the "canon" of the most important Jewish texts for a "literate" adult Jew to study and learn?
- What would developmental stage theory suggest about which texts are most developmentally appropriate along this journey to Jewish textuality?
- What is meant by the term "master teacher" of Jewish texts?
- Would such a "master" be a generalist able to teach many different genres (Bible, Rabbinic, mystical, philosophical) or a specialist in the pedagogy of a particular genre?
- If there is a "master teacher" of Jewish texts, what does it mean to be a "master learner"?
- What role do the ideologies of different Jewish movements play in the way Jewish texts are taught?
- What would an inventory of "best practices" in the teaching of Jewish texts look like?

HIGHLIGHTS

- Jewish text study gives to those engaged both Jewish roots and wings.
- Jewish text study, however, is inherently complex, involving conceptual, Jewish and educational questions generally not posed by the practitioners of Jewish text.
- Four of the challenges emanating from the complexity include the role and authority of the individual in Jewish text study, the pedagogic content knowledge of the teacher, the expansion of a repertoire of creative techniques for the teacher, and the ultimate purposes of Jewish text study.

ANNOTATED BIBLIOGRAPHY

Adar, Z. (1969). *Humanistic Values in Teaching Bible.* Philadelphia: Reconstructionist Press. This volume by an outstanding Israeli educator is dated but still has considerable heuristic value for faculties looking to engage in a discussion about the purposes of teaching the Hebrew Bible. The first several chapters where Adar outlines the fundamental assumptions of the traditional, national, humanistic, and narrative schools of thought, make a good initial framework.

Aron, I. (2000). *Becoming a Congregation of Learners: Learning as a Key to Revitalizing Congregational Life.* Woodstock, VT: Jewish Lights. This volume focuses on the role of text study in shaping the process of becoming a congregation of learners. The wide range of resources is particularly useful in addressing issues of educational leadership.

Heilman, S. (1983). *People of the Book: Drama, Fellowship, and Religion.* Chicago: University of Chicago Press. For a variety of reasons, much of this book focused on the emerging phenomena of text study in the non–Orthodox world. Teachers and lay leaders operating in this non–Orthodox world, however, ought to appreciate the dynamics of traditional text study so well analyzed in this volume. The phenomena of becoming a learning community is particularly worthwhile.

Holtz, B. (1984). *Back to the Sources.* New York: Summit Books. This book broke new ground in terms of popularizing Jewish text study. Its exploration of the challenges of different genres of sources and literature is a very helpful introduction to the scholarly issues in understanding particular kinds of Jewish texts.

Holtz, B. (2003). *Textual Knowledge: Teaching the Bible in Theory and Practice.* New York: JTS Press. This volume is described within the article. It is perhaps the most sophisticated examination of teaching Bible presently available. The charts that lay out and analyze the nine teaching orientations are particularly valuable.

Meskin, N. (2006). *Text and Tradition: The Importance of Jewish Education and Educators.* New York: CAJE. This volume is devoted to advocacy for Jewish education but also models the role of Jewish texts in addressing important issues on the Jewish communal agenda.

Resnick, J. (1999). *Teaching Jewish Texts.* New York: CAJE. This journal addresses a wide range of issues in teaching a variety of Jewish texts. It poses challenges, but its great value is in inventorying some very successful experiments that intensify the focus on teaching Jewish texts in various Jewish educational settings.

Zion, N. (1994). *A Different Night, Teacher's Guide,* Jerusalem: Shalom Hartman Institute. This is essentially a Pesah Haggadah. The introduction, however, brilliantly lays out three different roles (priest, storyteller, and family educator) that a seder leader might take in relationship to the Haggadah. This makes for a "soft landing" in terms of appreciating the complexities of the teacher/leader's role in relationship to a given text.

_____ (2002, Spring). *Text and Context. The Reconstructionist* 66 (2). This issue contains the Alan Levenson paper referenced in the chapter. A paper by Jeffrey Schein on the "triangle" of teacher-text-learner shifts the discussion into a more conventional educational context. A paper by Rabbi Caryn Broitman explores four different sets of interpretive/hermeneutical assumptions drawn from quite sophisticated scholarship regarding textual interpretation in the Jewish and non–Jewish world. These three papers together constitute a solid intellectual core for an exploration of Jewish text study in non–Orthodox Jewish settings.

REFERENCES

Belenky, M.F., Clinchy, B.M., Goldberger, N.R. & Tarule, J.M. (1986). *Women's Ways of Knowing.* New York: Basic Books.

Berliner, A. & Brettler M. (2004), eds. *New Jewish Study Bible.* Oxford: Oxford University Press.

Brown, S. (2006). Lecture by Marc Kramer at Siegal College of Judaic Studies.

Kaplan, A. (1988). *Me'Am Loez.* New York: Moznayim Press.

Katz, E. & Schein, J. (2000). *Aytz Hayim We.* Philadelphia: Jewish Reconstructionist Federation .

Levenson, A. (2002, Spring). "Text Study vs. (and/or) The Study of Jewish Texts." *The Reconstructionist* 66 (2), 29–36.

Newman, L. (1966). *The Genesis Melton Bible Curriculum.* New York: United Synagogue Commission on Jewish Education.

Palmer, P. (1993). *To Know as We Are Known: Education as a Spiritual Journey.* San Francisco: Harper.

Rosenzweig, F. (1974). On the Opening of the Lehrhaus. In *On Jewish Learning.* New York: Schocken, 95–99.

Schein, J. (1991, Spring). "Moral Thought and Moral Action: Towards an Agenda for Future Research in Jewish Education." *Journal of Religious Education* 86 (2), 234–249.

Telushkin, J. (1991). *Jewish Literacy.* New York: W. Morrow.

Nurturing Jewish Values

Carol K. Ingall & Jeffrey S. Kress

How can Jewish schools actualize their goals for nurturing Jewish values and "making *ment-shen*"? What steps are important in laying the groundwork for students to develop positive Jewish values? The authors draw on their diverse backgrounds in the history and philosophy of education, research, consultation, and teacher training to answer these questions. Therefore, the chapter draws on knowledge from a variety of sources. We believe that this type of multifaceted approach is important for a comprehensive plan for nurturing Jewish values.

NURTURING JEWISH VALUES: OVERVIEW AND RECOMMENDATIONS

Values education has become the focal point of local and national attention, a tinderbox sparking fierce debate and relentless rancor. In both red and blue states, parents and teachers worry about similar issues: control vs. creativity, raising children who are autonomous yet connected to community, who are thoughtful individuals and still do the right thing. Everyone agrees that values education is important, but the question is "Whose values?" Values, whether religious or civic, have always been influenced by ideological, social, and economic factors.

The banal qualifier "*family* values" offers no clarification. Every family has its own family values, whether the family name is Soprano or Cleaver. What are Jewish values, and how do we as teachers nurture them? There is no simple answer to this question; it requires a thoughtful assessment of what Jewish schools can do and to whom they must answer. Jewish teachers must be the agents of the Jewish community while doing what all good teachers are supposed to do: help children individuate and find their places in an adult world.

Before we delve into the topic of nurturing Jewish values, we feel that some definitions are in order. We chose not to call our chapter "What We Know About Jewish Moral Education." David Nyberg observes, "Moral education may be a phrase like 'wet water.' Education is inherently moral in some respects, just as water is inherently wet. This is because any planned, deliberate education, whether in liberal arts or manual arts (or Jewish education—*added by the authors*), is always undertaken for the purpose of rendering the student, or the community in general, better off as a result of that education" (1990, p. 595). We both concur that nurturing Jewish values is not the same as providing children with a Jewish education. Teaching *b'rakhot*, whether by rote or through textual analysis, is going to produce Jewish cultural literacy, which, according to Nyberg's definition, is surely "good for the Jews" and the child. Teaching prayer is most certainly moral education because it socializes the child into the *mores* of the Jewish community, but it is not the same as teaching values, unless those values embedded in prayer, like humility, gratitude, and honor, are addressed explicitly.

A values-based Jewish education is therefore a subset of Jewish moral education, not a synonym for Jewish moral education. It begins with the selection of time-honored Jewish values and deliberately links them to desired outcomes. It is not identical to teaching *mitzvot*. *Mitzvot* encompass both ritual or theistic obligations (*bein adam l'Makom*) and societal obligations (*bein adam l'havero*); unfortunately, they are often taught through an apprenticeship of observation and modeling without any discussion of the Jewish values that are embedded in these actions.

By values we don't mean the personal preferences that made values clarification strategies of the seventies and eighties so *pareve*; we mean traditional Jewish virtues, *middot* or *ma'alot*. While "virtues" sounds like a throwback to the Victorian era, the word is from the Latin *vir* (man); to be virtuous means having the qualities that characterize someone as a *mentsh*. We are aware that these words have been co-opted and shaped by groups for their purposes; political conservatives appear to have a lock on "virtue," and traditional Jews have cornered the market on *middos*. A perfectly good Hebrew word, *ma'alot* (excellences or assets) seems to lack curb appeal.

Are we suggesting a Jewish version of character education that relies upon values/virtues and stresses a communitarian agenda? Yes, but with reservations. Character educators like Bennett, Ryan, and Lickona note that character comes from the Greek word meaning "etch" or "incise." Their approach, like that of *mussar* literature, is "outside-in" (Eisner 1985)—the teacher imposes values on a child who is imagined as either a *tabula rasa* or a willful, feral being who must be restrained. We prefer to think of the teacher's role as strengthening the goodness within the child and see ourselves as being more comfortable in the "inside-out" camp

Are we suggesting a Jewish approach to social and emotional learning that stresses social competence and emotional awareness? Again, yes, with reservations. The field of social and emotional learning (see Elias et al. 1997 for an overview) has traditionally been focused on the development of skills (such as self-control, decision making, and communication). Social and emotional learning has been less concerned with grounding these skills in standards that emanate from a particular moral or religious tradition. In summary, we are drawing from both of these approaches within the context of Jewish education.[1]

There is much merit for the goals of the values-based education Aristotle recommended in the Nicomachaean Ethics: to know the good, to love the good, and to do the good. A deliberate, planful curriculum must encompass a cognitive dimension, an affective dimension, and an experiential dimension. We all know that these areas cannot be neatly separated; we have all experienced the "cognitive emotions" Scheffler (1991) describes: the elation we feel when we solve a puzzle or understand a particularly difficult text. The distinctions are similarly blurred when we feel connected to others while performing an act of *hesed*, or are moved to action because of our admiration of a significant other. Despite its limitations, this description of the multi-faceted nature of values education provides a useful heuristic for infusing the curricular and co-curricular activities of a school or class with Jewish values.

A values-infused curriculum must first begin with deciding which values must be taught. Both of us are wary of the *middah*-of-the-month approach. Less is more; we prefer to choose Jewish values with "legs," those robust enough to integrate in text study, in literature, Jewish history or current events, and those adult Jewish activities that students can practice doing. An example of such a robust value is *hakhanassat orhim*. It is authentic, associated with Abraham, the father of the Jewish people, and reappears throughout Genesis and Exodus, the Biblical texts Jewish youngsters are most likely to encounter (Abraham and the angels, Rebekah and Abraham's steward, Joseph and his brothers in Pharaoh's court, and Jethro and Moses, to name but a few). Besides presenting opportunities for the study of *hakhnassat orhim*, teachers can imbue the value with an emotional valence by reading legends and folk tales about the rewards of hospitality and study U. S. immigration policy in social studies.

We recommend an approach that is at the same time spontaneous and deliberate. "Teachable moments" will arise in which a value might be addressed. A classmate's illness can be the jumping-off point for addressing *bikur holim*. The recent Katrina disaster moved many students to organize *tzedakah* drives. However, an approach that capitalizes on chance alone will not provide the consistency of reinforcement that is needed to move value education forward. A narrower, deeper and more deliberate focus will generate learning that lasts.

The remainder of our essay is a discussion of one such focused approach. Our organizing principle utilizes the Aristotelian definition of moral education discussed above (knowing, loving, and doing the good) and augments it with two other categories, "preparing for the good" and "reflecting on the good." While our recommendations are laid out in sections, we do not see them as linear or independent. The sequence in which we present these recommendations is not deterministic, and we

---

[1]In this way we are paralleling the convergence that is taking place in general education between character education and social and emotional learning (e.g., Novick, Kress, & Elias 2002).

see each aspect as interrelated with all others. Further, though we have framed the majority of this discussion in the language of "formal" Jewish education, we see the following principles as relevant to "informal" settings as well.

PREPARING FOR THE GOOD: CREATING CARING LEARNING ENVIRONMENTS

Preparing for the good is perhaps the only exception to our caveat regarding the non-hierarchical nature of our recommendations. A positive class climate and caring relationships among students and educators are not just a way of modeling values. Rather, these are essential to all the recommendations that follow. While issues of relationships within the class will recur throughout the process, nurturing values will be very difficult, if not impossible, in a setting marked by distrust, anxiety or feelings of vulnerability.

Before any educational experience, and particularly when addressing values, it is important to begin by building trust in the group. The teacher must get to know her students, have them get to know her, and help them to get to know one another. Social skills like respectful listening have to be taught, practiced, and reinforced. The teacher should establish, with input from the group, rules for group functioning and "check in" on these throughout the group's work together (see Charney 2002 for further information for group building and rule setting). She should greet students by name when they enter the class and follow up individually with any student who seems depressed, anxious, or afraid. Creating a caring community, as Noddings (1992) reminds us, is a challenge that all teachers must embrace.

KNOWING THE GOOD: DELIBERATION

Jewish education is context-dependent. When values clarification was all the rage in secular settings, it eventually made its way to Jewish schools, camps, and youth groups. The popularity of character education in general education during the eighties and nineties became *derekh eretz* programs in Jewish venues. During the seventies and eighties, when Kohlberg popularized moral dilemmas as a basis for deliberating about the right thing to do, Jewish educators followed suit. For a number of reasons, chiefly because of the untimely death of Kohlberg, but also because "knowing the good" did not automatically produce "doing the good," the cognitive dimension of moral education ceded the field to character education. Cognitive approaches have much to offer. Students can be presented with moral dilemmas and discuss how they would respond to them. Jewish texts can be used to highlight the values at stake. Unfortunately, many of these curricula are out of print, but teachers can design their own dilemmas based on real-life situations that students face. Or they can ask students to do the same, perhaps as part of a writing project. Teaching Torah presents any number of opportunities to point out ethical dilemmas. A teacher who wants to teach more than the bare bones of the story has any number of opportunities to lead the class in a discussion of the moral elements involved. Why do our forefathers and foremothers make the choices they make? What is at stake here? What were the consequences of their choices? What might have happened had they made different choices?

LOVING THE GOOD

Internalization and motivation to do the good are the jewels in the crown of values education. If our students engage with us in deliberation about values and participate with us in values behavior, *dayeinu*! If our students develop habits of values-behavior, *dayeinu*! But as in the *haggadah*, *dayeinu* is never enough. We want our students to embrace Jewish values, to incorporate them into their self-definitions and world views, so that when their values are called into question, and when teachers and parents aren't there to remind them, they have the strength to do the right thing.

Of Aristotle's three goals, "loving the good" is the one in which we can least measure our direct impact. However, this does not mean that we are not able to work with students to achieve this end. We do so by creating the fertile soil in which the seeds of "love" for the good can grow. In a way, all other recommendations in this chapter can be seen as serving this goal. Creating a positive classroom climate with warm relationships (discussed above) helps to ensure a positive affective tone for values-nurturing classroom discussions. Many students, unfortunately, have experienced the irony of a sarcastic, overly critical teacher haranguing the class about *sh'mirat ha-lashon* or *derekh eretz*. Working with students to understand and process their emotional experience while doing the good, and acknowledging how challenging doing the good is (discussed below), keeps them focused on values-improvements in the face of potentially negative experiences.

IMPORTANCE OF EXEMPLARS

The power of significant adults is a crucial element in loving the good. Young people want to emulate those they admire, like parents, adult relatives, and teachers. Children build a conscience by rehearsing their behavior in front of an internal audience. What would my father do in this situation? Ms. Goldberg? Rabbi Smith? Role models are those people whose behavior we've been able to see at close range. Heroes are more distant icons who fill another function. Through the stories we tell about them they turn abstract virtues into a direct appeal to our imagination. We learn about courage by reading about Hannah Senesh parachuting into enemy lines to gather information for the embattled Yishuv. We teach self-sacrifice when we teach the story of the blind Samson destroying the Philistine temple and himself in the process. Exemplars can be found in Jewish literature as well. Stories from the *aggadah*, like those told about Elijah, are full of values messages about *gemilut hasadim*. The Association of Jewish Libraries has a publication that highlights Jewish literature as a tool for teaching Jewish values (Karp & Frischer 1999) and a website, *www.ajljewishvalues.org/*.

"EXTENDING THE GOOD"

"Loving the good" will be further fostered to the extent that students see values behavior as "standard operating procedure" that extends beyond the classroom. Kress and Elias (1998) state, "It takes a *kehillah* to make a *mensch*". As educators, we have the "values deck" stacked against us. Contemporary culture deals our youth a hand that includes questionable values and behavior portrayed in the media and by sports and cultural icons. Students, and particularly teens (though increasingly younger children as well), exist under great academic pressures, with enormously structured schedules of school, work, and extra-curricular activities. They do not always have time to focus on values growth. Coordination of efforts is an important "ace in the hole" to assist educators in dealing a winning hand.

Coordination can take place on various levels, both within an educational setting and beyond. Curricula in math and reading are structured so that each year's efforts build on and expand those of the previous year. In the area of values education, such coordination is rare. In fact, teachers at one grade level are often unaware of the efforts of their peers at other grade levels. "Mitzvah project" requirements exist independently, not integrated into a progression of values behaviors. Students risk either redundancy (and many educators have heard the lament: "We heard this exact same thing, in the same way, and with the same project, last year") or omissions (values that might be among a school's goals that were never formally addressed).

School-based efforts must extend beyond the classroom so that reinforcement of values permeates the school experience. Administrators should link celebrations, assemblies and other school rituals to the value-themes being addressed by teachers. Staff throughout the school should be aware of the school's values goals, language and orientation, and develop ways to model and reinforce these values. A student who observes two teachers, secretaries, administrators, janitors (whoever!) gossiping in the hall may be learning a powerful but unintended lesson. It is important to note that one can err in the assumption that "We do not need to specifically address values; it is inherent in everything we do here!" Such a stance, even if it were true, assumes that students will simply pick up the values by osmosis or passive observation. As we have noted, there are many countervailing influences and many role models in a child's life that do not support these values. In order to make values stick, active preparation such as that described in this chapter is needed to complement school-wide infusion.

Finally, efforts should be made to enlist allies to further reinforce target values. Parents are, or course, key to this endeavor. Engaging parents as allies can be very rewarding to parents and educators alike. While parents might be hampered in their involvement in the school by limitations (perceived or real) in Hebrew or Judaic background, values enhancement allows school personnel to meet parents on common ground. Rather than seeing values as part of their home turf and not the school's province, parents will often be glad to know they have support for their efforts. Schools should inform parents about the values that will be taught and share the values-goals and language the children are learning. Together parents and educators should brainstorm opportunities to use this language and to reinforce values. The school can serve a valuable function troubleshooting difficulties that parents are having around their child's understanding of a given value.

Of course, others in the community can be a part of this extension and overlap as well. The rabbi of the synagogue (for a synagogue school) or a local rabbi can direct a sermon to address values, with specific mention of the work being done in the school. A youth group director can plan activities that help reinforce values being addressed in a school.

DOING THE GOOD

LAYING THE SOCIAL AND EMOTIONAL GROUNDWORK

The faculty should choose a value as a focal point. They are likely to select a value that will "pay dividends" in how the school functions, such as *derekh eretz* or *sh'mirat ha-lashon*. Perhaps they will decide to focus on how students relate to the broader community through *bikur holim* or *hakhnasat orhim*. Regardless of the specific value, they must consider the following question: What skills and abilities must one possess in order to successfully perform this particular value? What does *derekh eretz*, for example, look like?

Clearly Jewish values encompass complex expectations for social behaviors. Elsewhere (Kress & Elias 2001, 2003) we have shown that these behaviors call upon the skills of emotional intelligence (Goleman 1995), such as emotional awareness, empathy, communication, problem solving, self-monitoring, and self-control. In order to prepare students for actualizing values we must help them to build these underlying skill areas. While an in-depth analysis of each of these areas is beyond the scope of this chapter, a few examples of activities for building these skills are presented at the end of this article.

It is important to address underlying social and emotional intelligence skills in the service of actualizing Jewish values. Might a student's excitement over a juicy piece of gossip lead her to "spill the beans"? Might social anxieties make one give in to a friend's request for *lashon ha-ra*, regardless of any good intentions? Perhaps, but possessing the skills to manage such complex interactions will enable one to be more successful in following through with these intentions.

JUST DO IT!

Practicing underlying skills and deciding about correct moral actions lead up to actual use of the particular value. Opportunities to practice such values as *derekh eretz* and *sh'mirat ha-lashon* occur throughout the school day. While this provides many practice opportunities, it also presents a challenge by calling on students to break the flow of what might be long-established patterns of behavior. A first step is for students to alert themselves to situations in which the value will be called upon. To continue with the *sh'mirat ha-lashon* example, teachers can ask students questions such as "When in the course of the day do you find that the most gossip occurs?" or "What are, in general, the types of things you and your friends are most likely to gossip about?" Students often feel torn; they may know *lashon ha-ra* is wrong but are not confident in their ability to resist pressure to share gossip. Teachers should have students generate alternate responses for when they are put in such situations. What should the pressured student do? What should other students (the "bystanders") do to support the student? We recommend that they role-play these alternate behaviors.

Other values may occur naturally but may also be structured by educators. While the illness of a classmate provides opportunity for participation in *bikur holim*, so does a planned school visit to a nursing home. In either case, the situation may be unfamiliar. A similar role-play and problem-solving approach can be used in such cases to help students anticipate what the situation will be like, what the expectations are for appropriate behavior, what difficulties may arise, and how might these be handled. A visit to a hospital or nursing home may be accompanied by feelings of anxiety and awkwardness. If the prevailing emotional memory of the experience is overwhelmingly negative—full of confusion and self-doubt—it is unlikely that the student will seek to replicate it. Preparing for these situations will help give the child the support he or she needs to feel confident in his or her ability to be a competent participant in the experience.

In all of these role-plays and problem-solving discussions, teachers should be sure to call on the social and emotional skills that the students have been learning (see "Laying the Social and Emotional Groundwork" above) and to draw from the ethical discussion they have had (see "Knowing the Good" above).

Finally, educators should engage their students in service learning opportunities. Involvement in such projects is a way to build empathy that can help motivate behaviors that exemplify positive values.

REFLECTING ON THE GOOD

As John Dewey (1939) points out, reflection "is the heart of intellectual organization and of the disciplined mind" (p. 110). Reflection should occur as a part of all of the recommendations we have made. Educators should check in with students regarding their progress toward, and challenges with, actualizing values. Students should share, for example, their experiences with *sh'mirat ha-lashon* in the past week. How successful were they? What situations were difficult? Again, the group can problem-solve and rehearse how difficult situations can be handled and share strategies they used to achieve successes. This type of discussion should be undertaken regularly.

There are several benefits to reflection such as this. On the most pragmatic level, it helps students to anticipate the challenges and learn from the successes of their efforts toward enacting values. Students can learn not only from their own experiences, but also from the experiences, insights, and ideas of their peers. Further, these discussions help students develop the ability to self-monitor their behavior. Enacting Jewish values often involves inhibiting competing behaviors that may be so ingrained as to be almost habitual. The ability to track one's own behavior and to realize when a value is or is not being exhibited is a prerequisite for change. Finally, reflection sends the important message that Jewish values require persistence and practice, and that we are all on a journey of self-improvement in this regard.

In conclusion, Aristotle's formulation of "knowing the good, loving the good, and doing the good" highlights the idea that values enhancement must draw from the cognitive, emotional, social, and behavioral realms. For example, The Gideon Hausner Jewish Day School has a *tzedakah* program, *Avodah La-Olam*, which integrates the cognitive, the affective, and the experiential aspects of moral education. Rather than giving each other bar/bat mitzvah presents, the students create a *tzedakah* collective with these funds. After studying the mission statements of various charities, they direct their funds to those organizations whose work appeals to them. They are practicing an adult Jewish behavior with their heads, their hearts, and their hands.

While the importance of values enhancement is widely accepted, strong, sustained commitment to the type of recommendations we provide is less frequent. Educators face many demands for their time and attention. Values enhancement calls on educators to focus on their *"mentsh-*making missions" even in the face of competing demands for time and resources.

HIGHLIGHTS

- A values-infused curriculum begins with deciding which values must be taught. Choose Jewish values robust enough to integrate in text study, literature, Jewish history, or current events, and those students can enact.
- Lay the groundwork through creating a positive class climate with caring relationships among students and educators.
- Integrate cognitive, affective, social, and behavioral aspects of values-enhancement efforts.

- Attend to the cognitive dimension of moral education by presenting students with moral dilemmas and discuss how they would respond to them. Jewish texts can be used to highlight the values that are at stake.
- Help students "love the good" through a focus on exemplars, heroes, and building environments in which value behaviors are the norm.
- Prepare students to enact values by helping them develop the social and emotional competencies that underlie value behaviors.
- Provide opportunities for students to participate in social action activities.
- Add a dimension of reflection to all aspects of value-enhancement work.

ANNOTATED BIBLIOGRAPHY

Elias, M. J., Zins, J., Weissberg, R., Frey, K.S., Greenberg, M. T., Haynes, N, M. & Kessler, R. (1997). Promoting social and emotional learning: Guidelines for educators. Alexandria, VA: ASCD. Comprehensive guidelines and examples for developing and implementing programs to help students build their social and emotional skills.

Hansen, D. T. (1995). *The Call to Teach*. New York: Teachers College Press. An inspiring book that features portraits of teachers whose "expressive morality" (everyday goodness) permeates their classrooms.

Ingall, C. K. (1999). *Transmission and Transformation: A Jewish Perspective on Moral Education*. New York: JTS. An award-winning approach to teaching Jewish values that tries to operationalize Aristotle's dictum while recognizing the roles of responsibilities and rights.

Lickona, T. (1991). *Educating for Character: How Our Schools Can Teach Respect and Responsibility*. New York: Bantam Books. A fine handbook for teachers and principals advocating character education.

Novick, B., Kress, J. S. & Elias, M. J. (2002). *Building Learning Communities with Character: How to Integrate Academic, Social, and Emotional Learning*. Alexandria, VA: ASCD. A practical, step-by-step guide to implementing sustained social and emotional learning efforts that are integrated into the goals and activities of educational settings.

Sergiovanni, T. J. (1992). *Moral Leadership: Getting to the Heart of School Improvement*. San Francisco: Jossey-Bass. An exploration of the role of the principal as the critical factor in determining the moral climate of a school.

REFERENCES

Charney, R. S. (2002). *Teaching Children to Care (revised edition)*. Greenfield, MA: Northeast Foundation for Children.

Dewey, J. (1939). *Experience and Education*. New York: The Macmillan Company.

Eisner, E. (1985). *The Educational Imagination: On the Design and Evaluation of School Programs*. New York: Macmillan Publishing Company.

Elias, M. J., Zins, J., Weissberg, R., Frey, K.S., Greenberg, M. T., Haynes, N, M. & Kessler, R. (1997). Promoting social and emotional learning: Guidelines for educators. Alexandria, VA: ASCD.

Karp, H. & Frischer, R. (1999). Literature as a means of teaching values to children. New York: AJL.

Kress, J. S. & Elias, M. J. (1998). "It takes a kehilla to make a mensch: Building Jewish identity as part of overall identity." *Jewish Education News* 19 (2), 20–24.

Kress, J. S. & Elias, M. J. (2001). "Social and emotional learning in the Jewish classroom: Tools for a strong Jewish identity." *Journal of Jewish Communal Service* 77, 182–190.

Noddings, N. (1992). *The Challenge to Care in Schools*. New York: Teachers College Press.

Novick, B., Kress, J. S. & Elias, M. J. (2002). *Building Learning Communities with Character: How to Integrate Academic, Social, and Emotional Learning*. Alexandria, VA: ASCD.

Nyberg, D. (1990). "Teaching values in school: The mirror and the lamp." *Teachers College Record* 91 (4), 495–611.

Scheffler, I. (1991). *In Praise of the Cognitive Emotions and Other Essays in the Philosophy of Education*. Philadelphia: Routledge.

BUILDING EMOTIONAL INTELLIGENCE FOR NURTURING JEWISH VALUES: EXAMPLES FROM TWO SKILL AREAS

A. Emotional Awareness

a. Build emotional vocabulary by introducing Hebrew words for emotions.

b. Ask students to describe the emotional experience of biblical or literary characters and then describe situations in which they themselves might have felt this way.

c. Have students act out a biblical or literary scene, asking students to "stop action" to highlight the actors' expressions of emotions (or use a digital camera to photograph their expressions).

B. Self-control

a. Help students to identify bodily manifestations of stress in order to provide an early warning sign for lack of self-control.

b. Ask students to identify situations in which they are at particular risk for loosing control.

c. Teach a specific technique for calming down (e.g., deep breathing).

d. Have students role play use of this technique in drama related to a content area ("Let's act out the conflict of Cain and Abel. Now, let's think of how Cain could have reacted differently. Act this out using the calming technique we just learned").

e. Have students report back on when they used (or could have used) this skill in the past week.

f. Role play use of the self-control skill in the context of a target Jewish value ("Let's act out a situation in the lunchroom. Jenny, you were talking to Ruthie, and then you joined a group of your friends who asked you what you learned about Ruthie's romantic interest in your class-mate Matt. Act out how you can respond. How can our calming technique help?"). Use "stop action" to process Jenny's emotions as the drama unfolds. Ask the students to discuss why *sh'mirat ha-lashon* is so difficult.

Teaching Tefillah

Amy Walk Katz

> When Ma came in, Reverend Alden stood up and said they would all have the refreshment of prayer together before saying good night. They all knelt down by their chairs, and Reverend Alden asked God, Who knew their hearts and their secret thoughts, to look down on them there, and to forgive their sins and help them to do right. A quietness was in the room while he spoke. Laura felt as if she were hot, dry, dusty grass parching in a drought, and the quietness was a cool and gentle rain falling on her. It truly was refreshment. Everything was simple now that she felt so cool and strong. (Wilder, 1939, p. 218-219)

This text makes me envious. At times, I want to be Laura, so able to have an uplifting, rejuvenating prayer experience and so fortunate to have a religious leader who can offer her strength. At other times, I am envious of the Reverend Alden for knowing exactly what to say as a religious leader and how to lead the Ingalls family in a powerful prayer experience. As a rabbi, people often look to me to invoke prayer or make a prayer moment meaningful. I cannot imagine being able to do what Reverend Alden did.

The Wilder passage is an image of what I wish prayer was like for me, my family, my students, and my fellow Jews. In addition to being uplifting, prayer—a form of dialogue with God—should be meaningful and spiritually connecting.

And yet, often it is not.

ALIENATED BY TRADITION

Too often, for too many Jews, formal and communal prayer hinders spirituality. Worse, it can drive Jews away from worship or from Judaism. The Hebrew seems impenetrable, the rules too rigid, the references too obscure. Writing about the American Jew's encounter with traditional prayer, Wieseltier (1998) argues that, to many, prayer seems an "obscure and arduous practice" (p. vii).

Roger Kamenetz (1994) describes the plight of the typical contemporary liberal Jew who had some nominal Jewish education but knows nothing of Jewish ideology and is unfamiliar with Hebrew:

> In short, I'd grown up the typical liberal American Jew, loyal to his tribe and family, and very proud of the ethical heritage of the Jewish people. My Jewish identity was like a strong box, very well protected, but what was inside it?

> The interior meaning of being a Jew was indistinct, smuggled, inchoate—much like the Hebrew letters I could pronounce but not truly read. (p. 57)

Kamenetz writes about a modern Jew who is alienated by tradition. He has no sense of what Judaism is about but remains an identified Jew despite his ignorance.

Allegra Goodman (1998) offered a somewhat different insight. She described a Jewish man's alienation while sitting in services. The disconnect between a modern Jew and the traditional prayer experience is all too familiar:

> Nina was sitting with the children in the women's section, and Andras sat alone in the sanctuary among the hundreds who were fasting, alone, having eaten break-

fast that morning, and drunk his coffee black as usual. He sat, listening to the Rav, and the fast day was foreign to him, the community grieving together in this artificial way. The holiday couldn't move Andras, the day set aside for sadness, the reading of this poetry, all prescribed, as if grief could be expressed that way, as if mourning could be accomplished with these simple and unthinking acts and, at the end of it, put away. This is why he thinks these recitations and acts of prayer are for children—because they are so flat and simple, because magically they are intended to discharge infinite obligations. (p. 131)

For Andras, prayer was meaningless, uninspiring, and irrelevant. The notion that traditional services are alienating is critical for understanding the challenges to Jewish educators today. Goodman, Kamenetz, and Wieseltier are just a few whose stories can enhance such understanding

RELATING TO PRAYER

Prayers and praying are at the root of Judaism and still pervade traditional Judaism today. The tradition ordains prayer three times each day. Prayer also surrounds Jewish life-cycle events. Even daily activities—such as eating, rising in the morning, going to sleep, or going to the bathroom—are occasions for Jewish prayer. If modern, non-traditional Jews in ever-increasing numbers become alienated from these core Jewish practices, we face the very real possibility of losing important connections to our Jewish past, present, and future.

According to Jewish tradition, formal prayer is essential because it reinforces Jewish values and priorities. It also teaches that:

> It is never enough to pray for ourselves alone. Speaking as 'we,' the individual discovers, acknowledges, articulates the needs, desires, hopes, which he, though one man, shares with all men because he is not only a private self but a member of humanity. Besides when we are conscious of those with whom we stand, what we may have wanted to pray by ourselves is generally made less selfish, more humble, and therefore more appropriate for utterance before God. (Borowitz, 1977, pp. 59-65)

Despite its centrality and importance, many modern liberal Jews do not feel bound to pray regularly. Yet, when they do pray, many also want to garner meaning and understand the prayers. They want to be inspired. They want to reach a spiritual peak. A problem erupts when—like instant gratification in other aspects of life—some modern Jews expect instant nourishment from prayer. And yet, as Heschel explained, the meaning is hidden and has to be uncovered over time.

RECOGNIZING THE TENSION

I am a Jew and a rabbi. I pray. I teach prayers. I want to help people become pray-ers. Because, even as I envy Laura Wilder's ready access to the sublime, I have experienced the rejuvenating potential of Jewish prayer. Ironically—and frustrating to me in my role as spiritual leader—while prayer is central to Jewish life, little is understood about how to teach prayer or inspire praying. Teaching prayer and/or praying is difficult. Jewish educators are now responsible for teaching concepts and rituals that historically were learned at home and that derived meaning as a course of regular practice. From a purely practical perspective, teaching the skill and the meaning of prayer takes a lot of time—and time is scarce in an already packed curriculum with ever fewer hours for instruction. In addition, Jewish educators are challenged to interpret traditional ideas in a modern context.

Prayer should be a portal to religion, a point of connection, not disconnection, of attraction, not alienation. To derive true meaning from prayer, one must be able to appreciate the experience; to appreciate the experience, one must be able to understand the concepts; and to understand the concepts, one must be familiar with a Hebrew language foreign to most American Jews.

Educators are caught in a difficult cycle. Do we teach the ideas first and hope that they will inspire students to acquire the Hebrew skills? Or do we teach Hebrew so that eventually students are capable of participating in public worship? Rabbis and cantors face this dilemma when thinking about worship for adults. Do we engage the pray-er intellectually? Or do we seek to create meaningful spiritual experiences that will inspire congregants to study the ideas of the liturgy? When teaching prayer or creating meaningful worship services, most Jewish educators struggle to deal with these endemic and intractable challenges.

Ever since I began rabbinical school, I have devoted much thought to *tefillah*. I formally expressed my interest in this topic while studying for a doctorate in education at Michigan State University. My dissertation examined the challenges of teaching *tefillah* in a liberal congregational school setting. As a pulpit rabbi of a Conservative congregation, I continue to struggle with these questions. This essay gives rabbis, cantors and educators a brief summary of important factors that have shaped how we teach *tefillah*. They include: (1) how modernity has challenged the teaching of *tefillah*, and (2) how curricula writers have grappled with putting *tefillah* into the school curriculum.

TRADITIONAL PRAYERS AND THE LIBERAL JEW

One central theological challenge for liberal Jews involves the disjunction between our modern attitudes toward God and those who wrote or edited the prayer book. Holtz (1990) looks closely at *Nishmat Kol Hai* (The Breath of Every Living Thing), one of the central hymns of the Sabbath and festival morning service, as an example. Placing the hymn in context, Holtz cites scholar Joseph Heinemann, who claimed that the text was "the most exalted and eloquent prayer in the hymnic style to be found in the statutory liturgy" (p. 115).

Holtz describes *Nishmat Kol Hai* as a journey of self-discovery. First, the hymn establishes that God is "our King, our Redeemer, our Savior, our Deliverer in every time of trouble and distress." By describing God's omnipotence, the writer leads us to critical questions: If God is omnipotent and God is both the master and source of language, then who are we to praise God? And how will we find the proper words to bless God? Our inadequacy is overwhelming. But, as Holtz points out, the author of the hymn concludes that we can praise God because "it is God who has given us the ability to pray." By acknowledging that God enables us to pray, the individual becomes capable of praising God. Thus, in the third section it is no longer our limbs, but rather "the limbs which You have given us." It is not our tongue, but rather "the tongue which You have placed in our mouths." Holtz concludes that, according to *Nishmat*, we can pray because God allows us to. God is the source of prayer. God is the source of our strength. The perspective that the author of *Nishmat Kol Hai* assumes is difficult for the modern liberal Jew, who has confidence in humanity's abilities but has doubts and questions about God's existence.

In earlier times when Jews were struggling with prayer, they felt inadequate to pray to God but the liturgy does not suggest that they ever doubted God's existence. Their doubt focused on their ability to speak before their Creator. Before the modern era, prayer was an address to God, and God heard and responded. Modernity, Holtz asserts, is accompanied by doubt that makes prayer problematic. Modern Jews are troubled, for making a request of God assumes that God will answer our requests. Thanking God for something assumes that God is responsible for what happened. Praising God assumes that God exists. Such beliefs are not so easy to hold in the modern world.

Recently, much has been written about contemporary liberal Jews' struggle with traditional Jewish prayer (Dorff, 1992; Gillman, 1990; Hammer, 1994; Heschel, 1954; Holtz, 1993; Kamenetz, 1994; Wolpe, 1993). Wolpe (1990) describes the situation for contemporary liberal Jews:

> Questions of whether Judaism can stand without the God-Idea and attempts to redefine God in impersonal terms are part of a general struggle to understand anew the nature of Judaism. Is it a religion? Is it a people, a nationhood, a civilization? If Judaism is something more than a religion, can God be erased or ignored? Suspending definitional entanglements, we may simply ask: how central is God to Judaism?

> Many modern Jews will give an obligatory nod but insist that the centrality of Judaism lies elsewhere. Conceding that God was at one time the fulcrum of

> Judaism, they maintain that in our day the balance has shifted. Now the people of Israel are the true focus of Judaism...the land of Israel, revived by historical leg-erdemain and massive sacrifice...God is not central because, we are told in those hard dichotomies so beloved of people who come out on the right side, Judaism is a religion of action, not belief, centered in this world, not standing with its head thrust in clouds, that for all their loveliness, do obscure vision...
>
> While God is acknowledged as part of the redoubtable triad—God, Torah, and Israel—some are convinced that one leg can be removed and still the structure, in a neat twist of metaphysical carpentry, stays standing. (p. 4)

Wolpe suggests that the modern liberal Jew is struggling with the idea of God. Rather than acknowledging God as central to Judaism, some modern liberal Jews are wondering if Judaism can be redefined with Israel in the center, especially given the extraordinary historical circumstances that led to the founding of the state of Israel. Others are simply wondering if Israel can be redefined without God.

The liberal Jew is faced with many other theological questions. To whom does one pray? Does God hear prayers? If so, will God answer them? If prayer is not heard and answered by God, then why pray? Why would an omniscient God need us to articulate our prayers? Shouldn't God just know what we are thinking? These questions are not easily answered and often prevent a liberal Jew from praying (Dorff, 1992). Why are liberal Jews asking so many difficult questions? Why don't they have the faith in God their ancestors had?

There are several reasons for this erosion of faith. First, Western culture is grounded in scientific inquiry that depends upon knowledge, critical questioning, empirical data, and belief based upon evidence. Following Emancipation, Jews eagerly embraced opportunities to study secular subjects and pursue heretofore off-limits professional endeavors. They achieved notable success, but acceptance in the intellectual milieu of the university and the salon often required abandonment of belief based on faith, habit, religious tradition or accidents of circumstance. For many Jews, the logic behind forsaking obligations to an unproven God proved irresistible.

Perhaps one reason for this erosion of faith is that liberal American Jews live in a social and cultural milieu where faith does not uniformly play a major role. The environment of material abundance and popular culture do not lend themselves to faith. In addition, for liberal American Jews, attendance at college or university is the norm. The paradigm of the modern American university looks down upon determining one's beliefs about academic subjects based upon faith. That suspicion of unsupported beliefs can easily leak into one's personal life as well.

Yet another reason why contemporary liberal Jews struggle with these traditional images of God is because in traditional Judaism God is the King and the Jewish people are servants, obligated to fulfill God's commandment. The Enlightenment repudiated the divine right of kings. As a result, contemporary liberal Jews do not see themselves as servants but as individuals with rights. Traditional understandings of God reject this view of the world, claiming that God can be arbitrary, God is all powerful, and mortals have no way of understanding exactly what is God's will.

In the modern period, Jews have felt an increasing distance from the God described in the traditional liturgy: God as Creator, Revealer, and Redeemer. Scientific inquiry about how the world was created and how the universe functions raises questions about God for many modern liberal Jews.

A monumental challenge to traditional theology was the murder of six million Jews during the Second World War. Contemporary Jewish theologians have been forced to ask hard questions about God's role in history. How could a merciful God permit these unspeakable horrors? What was God's purpose for the mass murder of so many millions of innocent people?

Most contemporary liberal theologians reject the traditional notion of an active personal God who is responsible for reward and punishment. For example, the extreme view of one modern Jewish theologian, Richard Rubenstein (1966), is that God is dead. If God is not dead, at least belief in God is dead because there is no good answer to the vexing question, "Why did God not intervene to prevent the suffering?"

CURRICULAR MATERIALS FOR TEACHING TEFILLAH

Given the generally uneven professional preparation and the lack of subject-matter knowledge of teachers in both the day school and the congregational school worlds, (Aron, 1995; Aron and Bank, 1987; Aron and Phillips, 1990, Flexner, 2003) it is not surprising that prepared curricular materials for teaching *tefillah* have become invaluable. These materials support teachers by extending subject matter knowledge, providing new ideas about how to teach in meaningful and appropriate ways, dealing with students' weak understanding of Hebrew, and offering sensible curricular organization.

Prepared curricular materials reflect a tension in the teaching of prayers and praying, in the teaching of Hebrew language and the concepts of the prayers, and in teaching skills that might lead to cultivating a relationship with God (Katz, 2002).

Yet there is more to Jewish prayer than reciting the Hebrew liturgy, or even knowing what the prayers are about. Prayer is inextricably bound to belief in God (Dorff, 1992; Wolpe, 1990). To whom after all, does one pray, if not to God? It would seem then that a prayer curriculum must help learners understand Jewish ideas and concepts about God, while also helping them develop a personal relationship with God (Katz, 2002).

Curricular materials generally try and focus on three important aspects of teaching prayer: skills, knowledge, and disposition. By skills, I mean acquiring the necessary Hebrew skills to worship in Hebrew. By knowledge, I mean learning what the prayers are about, and by disposition, I mean developing a love of prayer and a relationship with God. Curriculum writers emphasize these three important areas differently. Some focus on skills, others on knowledge and still others on disposition (Katz, 2002).

These questions that modern curricula writers are asking and addressing are strikingly different than the question and topics that were being addressed in the beginning and middle of the 20th century. Until 1971, most Jewish educators focused on the acquisition of prayer skills and fluency in Hebrew reading. The situation has changed dramatically since then.

Historically, the emphasis was on children learning *how to pray,* not learning the meaning of the prayers. Greenberg (1938)) clearly describes the situation:

> …the prayer book was and remains to this day the dominant, almost the exclusive, subject of study for the pupil until he acquires a high proficiency in the ability to read its contents fluently…The pupil remembered his prayer-book period as a time when he read some meaningless passages with the teacher being obviously more bored than the pupil himself (pp. 28–29)

Describing what American Jews understood about the prayer book, Greenberg claimed that most Jews only knew how to read Hebrew and follow the order of the service. Prayer was taught by rote, and the teaching of prayer was not being used as an opportunity to teach important Jewish concepts or values. Greenberg argued that it was the unusual American Jew who had *any* knowledge of the contents of the prayers, and he articulated a need for a significant paradigm shift in the teaching of prayer.

The change in the American Jewish landscape was such that by the 1980s and 1990s curricula writers were hard at work trying to incorporate liturgical ideas into the teaching of prayer. Why, relatively suddenly, did so many Jewish educators begin to focus on the meaning of the prayers? In many ways, 1971 was a watershed year for the teaching of prayer. Saul Wachs completed his dissertation entitled, "An Application of Inquiry Teaching to the *Seedur"* (sic). In addition, Burt Jacobson published *Teaching the Traditional Liturgy.* Both of these publications assume there is much more to the teaching of prayer than memorizing Hebrew prayers and reciting liturgy by rote.

Wachs introduced the inquiry method to the study of the prayer book. He asserts that, "knowledge of the ideas in a prayer make possible a deeper and more sustained emotional response to the prayer than were such knowledge is lacking" (p. 69). Wachs believes that it is possible for students to grasp prayer concepts through class discussions. His dissertation describes an approach to the teaching of prayer that involves students actively uncovering the meaning of the prayers.

Wachs' dissertation describes the teacher's role "as a kind of orchestra conductor leading the class to discover what he has put before them" (p. 76).

While students are actively involved in the learning process, the teacher is the leader, directing and making strategic decisions about the nature of the discussion. Wachs acknowledges that there are novel situations when the student will offer an interpretation or an insight that is unknown to the teacher. "In this novel situation, the conductor lays down his baton and becomes a player, joining his fellow students in search for truth" (Wachs, 1970, p. 77).

Like Wachs, Jacobson also intends to teach the ideas of the prayers through classroom inquiry. The purpose of teaching prayer is to heighten "the student's ability to concretize and validate or correct his intuitive grasp of the prayer, and to allow him to learn the poetic tools that give depth to the meaning." Such a grasp, won by discovery, may give the student a deep sense of identity with the concerns of the traditional prayers. Jacobson says that the goals of teaching prayer are:

1. To uncover the common experiences that underlie the author's prayer in the interests of the students, and to thereby broaden the student's sensitivities so that he realizes there are common experiences that all men undergo; to understand the particularly Jewish symbolic framework within which this can be carried out.

2. To develop an understanding of an empathetic appreciation for the experiences and language of Jewish religious poets of the past.

3. To give the students the tools for literary analysis which they will be able to use in connection with any prayer or with poetry.

4. To show that the faith encountered with God is a genuine possible way of grappling with ultimate questions. (1971)

To achieve these goals, Jacobson assumes that the teacher will create a classroom environment that encourages students to be open and honest about their feelings and ideas. Teachers are expected to guide the classroom discussions, encourage students to think, and also be knowledgeable about the ideas of the prayer.

Notice both Jacobson and Wachs are suggesting that there is much more to the teaching of prayer than Hebrew reading skills. Both believe that an important part of the teaching of prayer is conceptual. Students need an opportunity to learn the big ideas of Jewish prayer. Rather than just reiterating Greenberg's point, both Jacobson and Wachs further the discussion of the teaching of prayer by creating curricular materials intended to teach key concepts of Jewish liturgy.

It is worth noting that both Jacobson and Wachs were working with the Melton Research Center of the Jewish Theological Seminary of America. The Center was influenced in the 1960's and 1970's by the work of Ralph Tyler and Jacob Schwab, two of the most prominent educational thinkers of that generation. As a result, both Jacobson and Wachs owe much to their ideas and approaches to education in general and to its application to their work.

Tyler cautioned the educators that it was critical to deliberate carefully before commissioning curricular projects. Schwab focused on the practical aspects of curriculum writing. He argued that the curriculum had to take into account what already existed in Jewish schools, being mindful of constraints and possibilities. In a newsletter of the Melton Research Center for Jewish Education (1977), we learn that both Tyler and Schwab

> ...warned that the products of the new curricular movement (the new math, the new physics, the new biology, etc.) had often been distorted in the classroom because materials being produced considered only one of the important aspects of curriculum, the subject matter. (p. 2)

They believed that it was important to consider four commonplaces when doing curriculum development. To this end, Schwab (1973) argued that

> ...defensible educational thought must take account of four commonplaces of equal rank: the learner, the teacher, the milieu, and the subject matter. None of these can be omitted without omitting a vital factor in educational thought and practice. (p. 371)

> Coordination, not superordination or subordination, is the proper relation of these four commonplaces...representatives of all four commonplaces must be included in the deliberating group from the start. Almost as obvious is the need that these representatives be men who are not overawed by the scholar. (p. 372)

In addition to the subject matter, curriculum writers must consider the child, the teacher, and the society in the curriculum-writing process. Notice Schwab is arguing that the curriculum-writing process must be conducted by capable individuals who are able to think critically about all of the commonplaces.

If not, Schwab feared, educators would identify subjects as important and perhaps even find new and exciting ways to develop the material only to have their efforts negated by later findings that the subject was not appropriate for children or the teachers are not able or willing to teach that particular subject. As a result of Tyler and Schwab's recommendations, the Melton curricula asked the following questions:

> In light of the limitations of time and money and considering the nature of our teachers, students, parents and the community, what is it that our children should learn? How should our teachers teach so that the ideas presented might be internalized and affect the thinking, feeling and behavior of our children? (Melton newsletter, 1977, p. 2)

It seems reasonable to argue that the intellectual milieu of the Melton Research Center influenced the work of both Jacobson and Wachs. While many educators had once assumed that the teaching of prayer should prepare children to recite Hebrew words clearly and quickly, Jacobson and Wachs—having encountered the ideas of educational luminaries like Schwab and Tyler—had to ask themselves questions like:

> How can we strike a balance between teaching understanding of the prayers and developing the skills to recite them properly? How can we prepare a child to become a member of a *tzibbur*, a praying community? (Melton newsletter, 1977, p. 1)

The insights and answers provided by Schwab and Tyler from the general education community, and from Jacobson and Wachs within Jewish education, have paved the way for today's Jewish educators to think much differently about the relationships between Hebrew recitation skills and liturgical understanding in the teaching of *tefillah*.

Notice that I have described the cognitive aspects of learning tefillah. Wachs and Jacobson focused on the ideas. It is not that they lacked concern for spirituality. They believed that if the students understood the ideas and had the skills, then the *tefillah* would become meaningful for the pray-ers and they would have religious experiences.

Since neither Jacobson nor Wachs directly considered the "spiritual" lives of their students, educators, in the past 10 to 15 years, have added the spiritual dimension to the teaching of *tefillah*. Recently several curriculum guides have been published which focus on creating spiritual experiences for students (Schein 1996; Hoffman & Cohen-Kiener 2000).

Most notably, Shire (1996) investigated what young people say about their own spirituality and how it is influenced by their Jewish educational programs. Ultimately Shire suggests three phases, Encounter, Reflection, and Instruction, which he believes will nurture spirituality.

First, Shire recognizes that the educator must set up an experience for a religious Encounter. This includes being sensitive to the moment and knowing when to speak and what to say. Of equal importance is choosing the right ritual, *bracha*, or routine. And, finally, the educator's choice of the right environment is key to the success or failure of the Encounter.

During the phase of Reflection, the educator asks questions of students, encouraging them to articulate their wonder and ask questions. He wants students to look back at their experiences and think about God. An example might be to ask students to recall how they felt at a significant moment in their life—a Bar/Bat Mitzvah, a family celebration, a tragedy of sorts? (Shire studied teen-agers so asking students about their Bar/Bat Mitzvah was natural.) Another moment of Reflection might be to ask students to talk about times in their lives when they experienced God. The educator creates an opportunity for open thoughtful Reflection. By asking probing questions, the student will eventually be able to express personal ideas in an open non-judgmental setting. Shire wants students to be able to look at their distant life experiences and feel God's presence. He also wants them to look at their more recent experiences as well. Ideally, Shire wants students to experience God in the moment.

Finally, Shire describes Instruction for religiosity. Here the educator provides answers to students' questions and poses new questions that lead to deeper thought. Naturally, students need to ask hard questions like "Where was God when the car accident happened?" The important thing in this phase is for educators to welcome the questions, find possible answers from within the Jewish tradition and encourage the student to be open for further Encounter and Reflection.

During the last 50 years there has been a tremendous shift in the teaching of *tefillah*. First curricular materials focused on skills. Students needed to learn to read Hebrew and recite prayers. Then educators began to realize that understanding the ideas of the liturgy would go a long way towards making prayer experiences meaningful. Most recently, educators have started to consider the spiritual lives of their students. Curricular materials are now at a point where they focus on the skills, the knowledge and the disposition of the students.

IMPLICATIONS FOR PRACTICE

There is no simple formula for the teaching of *tefillah*. Still, my experience as a teacher and my research demonstrates that there are important issues that must be considered. Educators will weigh the considerations differently depending upon their theology, their vision of what authentic *tefillah* might be like, and their educational philosophies. But ultimately all educators, rabbis, and cantors will have to consider the following factors as they prepare to teach *tefillah*.

- Hebrew language—Traditional prayer is in Hebrew and most liberal Jews are not facile in it. As a result, Hebrew is often a barrier as it excludes people who cannot read fluently. Those who are committed to prayer in Hebrew argue that it conveys a richer meaning, allowing the pray-er to identify with an ancient tradition and with Jews all over the world. Educators will need to decide how Hebrew will be taught. Will it be integrated into tefillot, or will it be a separate class? Is the purpose of tefillot to become fluent Hebrew readers? Or do students learn to read Hebrew fluently in Hebrew class?

- Goal of teaching tefillah—Related to this curricular question is the need to define the goal of teaching tefillah. Do we focus on learning to read Hebrew? Or, are the ideas of the liturgy most important? These are not the same. In the first, the focus is on skills acquisition. In the latter, the focus is on the knowledge of ideas. While both skills and knowledge would compliment one another, these two different curricular goals are achieved differently. How does Shire's research inform our thinking about prayer? How much attention is given to creating opportunities for an Encounter, Reflection, or Instruction on questions related to God?

- Keva versus kavannah—Jewish tradition recognizes that the individual will not always feel moved to pray. As a result, over time the Sages structured prayer by prescribing fixed times to pray and a fixed text to recite. This presents challenges because many liberal educators feel bound by the formal liturgy. Its value is recognized leading to a need to insure that students are comfortable with the formal liturgy. At the same time, many educators are eager to create moments of spontaneous prayer. Creating a balance between the formal liturgy which many feel is the only authentic prayer and spontaneous prayer which has deep biblical roots and touches both the heart and the soul of the pray-er is one of the greatest tensions in contemporary life.

Educators have to make very tough decisions as they examine prayer curricula. This study will guide them in their deliberations. The decision of how to direct any school or camp curriculum is difficult and any direction will—to a certain extent—be unsatisfying. If the curriculum emphasizes ideas, we will want our students to acquire more skills. If the curriculum emphasizes skills, we will want our students to understand the significant ideas that make Judaism a meaningful and compelling religion. And if there is no opportunity to explore spiritual questions, we will be neglecting an important aspect of prayer.

At the risk of oversimplifying, the tension focuses on a familiar educational dilemma: ought we teach the "basics" or ought we teach the ideas and concepts? There are no easy answers to this question. As educators go about choosing the appropriate curricula for their school, they need to consider who the students are, what life experiences they have, and how other activities can supplement what is being taught. No curriculum can cover all aspects of a particular subject. The challenge is for educators to be aware of the tension and to carefully consider the trade-offs of any resolution.

Each educator must consider how the home is contributing to the teaching of prayer. Are students living in homes where they see their parents pray regularly? Do they attend synagogue with their parents? Do their parents have rich spiritual lives? Depending upon how the home is supplementing the formal curriculum, educators can make curricular decisions.

Dewey (1938) provides the educator who is struggling to prepare students for adult prayer experiences with several interesting insights. He warns that it is important for the student to get

> ...out of his present experience all that there is in it for him at the time in which he has it. When preparation is made the controlling end, then the potentialities of the present are sacrificed to a suppositious future. When this happens, the actual preparation for the future is missed or distorted. The ideal of using the present simply to get ready for the future contradicts itself. It omits, and even shuts out, the very conditions by which a person can be prepared for the future. We always live at the time we live and not at some other time, and only by extracting at each present time the full meaning of each present experience are we prepared for doing the same thing in the future. This is the only preparation which in the long run amounts to anything. (p. 49)

Dewey argues that school experiences are critical and must be worthwhile in the moment. In terms of this chapter, in order that students' future encounters with prayer will be meaningful, their experiences must not *just* prepare them for the future but *must* be meaningful for the *present*. Dewey urges educators to recognize that the present can inform the future. And it is the responsibility of the educator to make responsible decisions that take both present conditions and future goals into consideration.

CONCLUSION

This chapter focused on (1) how modernity has challenged the teaching of tefillah and (2) how curriculum writers have grappled with putting tefillah into the school curriculum. While the examination focused on prepared curricula for congregational schools only, the issues uncovered are relevant for Jewish educators working in many different venues: day schools, camps, and youth groups. In addition, there is value for rabbis and cantors thinking about tefillah for their congregation to balance their congregants' need for skills, their need to understand the prayers and their need to have a Religious Encounter. Similarly, the theological tensions between traditional liturgy and the modern liberal Jewish home are applicable for all Jews who have embraced modernity and are encountering the traditional ideas of the prayer book.

This essay does not offer solutions for how to teach prayer. Rather, it provides a conceptual framework. It guides the educator, rabbi or cantor to think about what to consider when presenting *tefillot*.

ADDITIONAL RESEARCH

- How were adults who daven regularly taught to pray? Was the emphasis of their education on Hebrew skills, on conceptual ideas of the liturgy or on spiritual experiences? Were these individuals who are now comfortable in our synagogues taught to pray in classrooms or through prayer experiences? Is one's denominational affiliation a factor in the learning of Tefillah?

- How does the supplementary school fit into the congregational approach to worship. Is there a consistent philosophy that is reflected in the practice of the clergy, the educational director and the teachers? Do the teachers understand the clergy's vision for worship in the congregation?

FUTURE DIRECTIONS: PRACTICAL IDEAS FOR ADVANCING THE FIELD

- Create a school-wide service that assumes that each of the curricular traditions is valid if students are to have rich prayer experiences. At once, educators can teach students how to pray in Hebrew, discuss important ideas of the liturgy and create an environment which will allow students to experience an Encounter. Through strategic pedagogic decisions, meaningful spiritual experiences should be created for students of all ages.

- Create professional development opportunities for educators to learn the many approaches to teaching *Tefillah*. Provide educators with an overview of the important aspects of teaching *Tefillah* complete with discovering their own personal approaches to prayer.

LARGER CONTEXT

While adults often struggle with prayer, young children are often natural pray-ers. Their spontaneous prayers offer hope, trust and awe. We see this in the following letters to God

Dear God,
Please send Dennis Clark to a different camp this year.

       Peter

Dear God,
I think of you sometimes even when I'm not praying

       Elliott

Dear God,
I didn't think orange went with purple until I saw the sunset you made on Tue. that was <u>*cool*</u>*.*

       Eugene

Dear God,
I don't ever feel alone since I found out about you.

       Nora

As we lose our childhood innocence, something happens to our prayerful moments. Our own words to God feel awkward. We worry about the irrationality of prayer, or we fret over being hypocrites—at one moment rational, at another faith-full. For those who continue to attend services, the formal liturgy often totally replaces our spontaneous outbursts. We become machines reciting words. Within Judaism there is room for both spontaneous prayer and the formal liturgy. But experience suggests that many Jewish adults do not think of spontaneous prayers as authentic and have no sense of what the traditional liturgy has to offer.

ANNOTATED BIBLIOGRAPHY

Fowler, J. (1981) *Stages of Faith*. New York: Harper and Row.. The foundational work in the field of faith development. Highly readable and significant in its worldwide influence in the 1980s and 1990s.

Greenberg, S. (1938). "The Prayerbook in the Elementary Jewish School Curriculum." *Jewish Education*, 28-34. In this concise and important article, Simon Greenberg expresses a vision for teaching prayer that includes a commitment to skills, knowledge of the prayers and developing the student's spirituality.

Holtz, B.W. (1990). "Prayer and Praying: Teaching the Inner Life." *The Melton Journal, Autumn: 14*. In this concise but very thoughtful essay Holtz describes how liberal Jews struggle with traditional prayer. Faithful to the traditional texts, Holtz describes tools to use the Siddur, while embracing ideas of modernity.

Shire, M.J. (1987). "Faith Development and Jewish Education." *Compass*, July. This article provides a concise explanation and critique of Fowler's sages of faith for Jewish educators.

REFERENCES

_____. (1977). *Developing the Melton Curriculum*. New York: Melton Research Center Newsletter.

Aron, I. (1995). From the Congregational School to the Learning Congregation: Are We Ready for a Paradigm Shift? In I. Aron, S. Lee and S. Rossel. *A Congregation of Learners*. New York: Union of American Hebrew Congregations.

Aron, I. & Bank, A. (1987). "The Shortage of Supplementary School Teachers: Has the Time for Concerted Action Finally Arrived?" *Journal of Jewish Communal Service, 63*, 264-271.

Aron, I. & Phillips, B. (1990). *Findings of the Los Angeles Bureau of Jewish Education's Jewish Teacher Census*. Fourth Annual Conference on Research in Jewish Education, New York.

Borowitz, E. B. (1977). The Individual and the Community in Jewish Prayer. In L. A. Hoffman *Gates of Understanding*. New York: Union of American Hebrew Congregations.

Dewey, J. (1938). *Experience & Education*. New York: Collier Books.

Dorff, E. N. (1992). *Knowing God: Jewish Journeys to the Unknowable*. New Jersey: Jason Aronson.

Flexner, P.A. (2003). *Providing for the Jewish Future: Professional Recruitment, Development, Retention and Placement*. New York: JESNA

Gillman, N. (1990). "Why You Can't Pray and What You Can Do About It." *Moment Magazine, 15*, 48-55.

Goodman, A. (1998). *Kaaterskill Falls*. New York: The Dial Press.

Greenberg, S. 1938). "The Prayerbook in the Elementary Jewish School Curriculum." *Jewish Education 10* (Jan-Mar), 28-34.

Hammer, R. (1994). *Entering Jewish Prayer: A Guide to Personal Devotion and the Worship Service*. New York: Schocken Books.

Heschel, A. J. (1954). *Man's Quest for God*. New York: Charles Scribner's Sons.

Hoffman, J. & Cohen-Kiener, A. (2000). *Karov L'chol Korav For All Who Call: A Manuel for Enhancing the Teaching of Prayer*. New York: The Melton Research Center of the Jewish Theological Seminary of America.

Holtz, B.W. (1990). *Finding our Way: Jewish Texts and Lives We Lead Today*. New York: Schocken Books.

Holtz, B. W. (1993). "Prayer and Praying: Teaching the Inner Life." *The Melton Journal Autumn:14*.

Jacobson, B. (1971). *Teaching the Traditional Liturgy*. New York: The Melton Research Center.

Kamenetz, R. (1994). *The Jew in the Lotus*. San Francisco: Harper.

Katz, A. (2002). *Teaching Prayer in Liberal Supplementary School Settings: An Analysis of the Challenges*. Unpublished doctoral dissertation, Michigan State University.

Rubenstein, R. L. (1966). *After Auschwitz*. Indianapolis: Bobbs Merrill.

Schein, J. L., Ed. (1996). *Connecting Prayer and Spirituality Kol Haneshamah as a Creative Teaching and Learning Text*. Wyncote, PA: Reconstructionist Press.

Schwab, J. J. (1973). The Practical: Translation into Curriculum, *School Review 81*, 501-22, in *Science, Curriculum, and Liberal Education Selected Essays (1978)*. Chicago: The University of Chicago Press.

Shire, M. (1996). *Enhancing Adolescent Religiosity in Jewish Education: A Curriculum Inquiry*. Unpublished doctoral dissertation, Hebrew Union College.

Wachs, S. P. (1970). *An Application of Inquiry-Teaching in the 'Seedur'*. Unpublished doctoral dissertation, The Ohio State University.

Wieseltier, L. (1998). *Kaddish*. New York: Alfred A. Knopf.

Wilder, L. I. (1939). *By the Shores of Silver Lake*. New York: HarperCollins.

Wolpe, D.J. (1990). *The Healer of Shattered Hearts: A Jewish View of God*. New York: Henry Holt and Company.

Wolpe, D.J. (1993). *Teaching Your Children About God: A Modern Jewish Approach*. New York: Henry Holt and Company.

"Whad'Ya know?"
About Teaching the Holocaust:
Not Much, You?

Simone Schweber & Debbie Findling

It is significant that in Kelman's edition of *What We Know About Jewish Education*, the Holocaust was not granted a chapter. Published in 1992, that volume understandably aimed to decenter the Holocaust within Jewish education. As Israel had become a politically vexed issue, a bone of contention among American Jews, the Holocaust had rushed into the curricular vacuum left in its wake, forming a sort of interdenominational glue and becoming a prominent subject area, at least among most liberal denominations. Therefore, despite the fact that the teaching of the Holocaust in both Jewish schools (Sheramy, 2003) and public schools (Fallace, 2004) took place since the early 1950s and late 1970s respectively, it nonetheless held a disputed position among those intellectuals dedicated to shaping Jewish education. By the early 1990s, the Holocaust was viewed as not what Jewish education should be about. Jews are, after all, a people with a vast and various history, a forceful and formidable culture, beautiful and beguiling texts and a wide-ranging, wonderful diversity. A single-minded focus on Jewish victimization—which is what any Holocaust education necessarily risks—was thought to serve neither Jewish students nor the larger Jewish community. In short, many of those sitting at the helm of Jewish education begrudgingly acknowledged the Holocaust as important, but considered its ascendance in the Jewish school curriculum to be a trend worth actively resisting.

In 1994, the force of public culture at once confirmed, justified, and paradoxically dispelled any hesitations about the Holocaust that such intellectuals held. That year convinced most that the Holocaust would hold a place in the Jewish school curriculum regardless of the potential hazards of its teaching. In that year, both the U.S. Holocaust Memorial Museum and Steven Spielberg's *Schindler's List* opened, both to staggering audiences and widespread praise. A year later, a range of 50th anniversary events commemorating the end of World War II and the Holocaust peppered the calendar internationally. With the proceeds from *Schindler's List*, Spielberg seeded the Shoah Foundation dedicated in part to transforming Holocaust education worldwide. As a mark of the considerable uptick in Holocaust consciousness, the Holocaust became not only *a*— but *the*— dominant metaphor in American public discourse (Novick, 1999). So-called pro-life organizations as well as pro-choice organizations invoked the Holocaust in support of their causes, just as the National Rifle Association and People for the Ethical Treatment of Animals would later. Given its prominence in American public memory, the message for those involved in Jewish education was clear: the Holocaust was not about to be toppled from its standing as an all-important subject.

Despite the persistence of the hallowed status of the Holocaust for the last decade in American Jewish schools, surprisingly little is known about Holocaust education in that milieu. That is, surprisingly little research has been done to date on Holocaust education among Jews. Though there are voluminous materials available from well-intentioned authors advocating particular pedagogies and strategies or excoriating others (see, for example, Totten (2000) on simulations), very few publications or recommendations in this vast realm are actually research-based. Fewer still address Jewish school contexts. Put differently, very few scholars involved in Jewish education (or general education for that matter) have dedicated themselves to this realm. This makes sense, of course, for a whole host of reasons, of which the legitimate resistance among scholars of Jewish education is only one. Holocaust education sits uncomfortably between Holocaust studies and Jewish education. Within Holocaust studies, the vast majority of scholars tend to be interested in the humanities, specializing in history and literature, rather than social science. (This is not a disappointment as there are fascinating studies within those disciplines that hold important ramifications for us as educational researchers. See, as an example, Stier, 2005.) In addition and perhaps more importantly, Holocaust education simply has not been around for very long. Moreover, the Holocaust's curricular pre-eminence of late hardly guarantees nuanced study. Regardless of the explanations for this paucity of inquiry, though, it's clear that enduring questions about the enterprise loom large.

Before examining those questions that have been addressed and those that have yet to be answered, it's worth categorizing the arenas in which Holocaust education takes place, for this act in and of itself attests to the Holocaust's widespread coverage within Jewish educational realms. There are essentially four venues through which young people encounter the Holocaust within Jewish education. These include formal schooling arenas, informal arenas, museum-based activities—which are a sub-set of informal arenas—and commemorative events, locales or ceremonies. (A fifth arena, the Jewish home, is of course an educative institution, but it sits outside the scope of this overview.) By formal arenas, we mean primarily congregational, interdenominational and day school settings: places where the Holocaust will be offered as a unit of study, typically within a traditional classroom space. Within the category of informal arenas, we consider the Poland-Israel trips (such as March of the Living) to be especially intensive sites of Holocaust study. Museum trips—like those to the U.S. Holocaust Memorial Museum, Yad Vashem or to the huge number of smaller, state and local Holocaust organizations—are commonplace for students across grade levels. And, finally, commemorations of the Holocaust, whether they occur on Yom HaShoah, the 10th of Tevet, or in other spaces throughout the Jewish year, are also clear sites of Holocaust learning. We consider popular culture—such as filmic representations of the Holocaust aimed at young audiences—as being akin to a thread which runs intermittently through the fabric of these categories, for indeed films are often used, not only within the formal school classroom, but in commemorations and museum spaces. Indeed as the recent work of Wineburg et al (2001) attests, filmic representations of subject matter can play a powerful role in shaping how students perceive and interpret that which they learn in schools and in other contexts.

FORMAL JEWISH EDUCATION

Within the realm of formal Jewish education, a very modest, if impressive, group of studies exists. These include a lovely history of the Holocaust in American Jewish schools authored by Sheramy (2003), wherein she documents that early coverage of the Holocaust within Jewish history textbooks and other curricular materials stressed resistance and heroism rather than vulnerability and catastrophic loss. Until the Eichmann Trial in Jerusalem fostered awareness of victims' experiences, most Jewish children's Holocaust education would have centered on the Warsaw Ghetto uprising and Hannah Szenes; in the hopes of molding the "new Jew" and ideologically supporting the new state, Jewish education in the period between 1945 and 1960 tightly coupled the Holocaust and Israel. As this chapter illustrates, the Holocaust in American Jewish life (Novick, 1999) can be periodized along the fault-lines of Israeli history generally, and Sheramy's study is indeed excellent at mapping out the consistencies and disjunctures. Much more remains to be done, however, for not only are the production and reception of educational materials not necessarily commensurate, but this most recent decade—which exceeds the scope of Sheramy's research—raises a whole new set of questions. What does the so-called new wave of anti-Semitism mean for Holocaust education in Jewish schools and trips? What does the current state of Israeli politics mean for Holocaust education (and vice versa)?

In fact, many more basic questions about Holocaust education as practiced have yet to be answered. While it seems very likely that the Holocaust is currently taught in most if not all liberal Jewish schools, in what grades, with what frequency, using which "official" curricula, emphasizing which conceptions of the Holocaust, and with what results all remain basically uncharted territory. In our recently published, *Teaching the Holocaust* (Schweber and Findling, 2007), we organized the field by theme with each chapter beginning with an introduction illuminating the "big ideas" and key terms followed by innovative teaching ideas and resources for further learning. While comprehensive, the book is not exhaustive—clearly more teaching resources on the subject are needed. While initial studies have investigated the ages at which children are too young to be taught the Holocaust as part of the formal public school curriculum (Schweber, 2007), such studies don't actually answer the question of how old is old enough to learn about it and what difference a Jewish context makes in that determination. Dan Porat is currently investigating the teaching of the Shoah in Israel, building off earlier studies (Bar-On, 1999, 2004; Chaitin, 2000) that usefully focus on students' reception of that teaching. How does one's ethnicity as a Jew matter in learning about the Holocaust? How does one's personal connection to the Holocaust, religious, political and educational identities matter? While this work is exceedingly promising, much more needs to be done.

Anecdotally, it seems that teaching the Holocaust within the formal curriculum among the orthodox (and here we include the ultra-orthodox as a sub-category) has increased significantly in recent years. Not only are new curricula being published that specifically address the Shoah from orthodox viewpoints, but professional development opportunities for teachers in these communities are springing up among mainstream Holocaust education organizations. Yad VaShem, for example, held a conference on teaching the Shoah from within orthodox religious paradigms for the first time only a few years ago. And, organizations like Facing History and Ourselves, which claims to train 35,000 teachers per year, has instituted new liaisons to connect with religious communities. Nonetheless, very basic research questions linger about the treatment of the Holocaust in these worlds: where is it being taught, in which denominations, at what grades, by whom (by teachers in the religious or secular portions of the school day), and, always importantly, but often glossed over, with what results?

In a forthcoming article, Schweber wrote a portrait of the teaching of the Holocaust within an ultra-orthodox, Chabad girls' yeshiva. In that school, the Shoah was taught at the end of the eighth grade year as part of the secular history curriculum. The teacher was certified to teach in public schools and did not herself share the worldview of her mostly Lubavitch students. Her classroom observations and individual interviews revealed, though, that the Holocaust was taught and learned about as a highly religiously-laden topic in this environment. Like God, the Holocaust was shrouded in mystery, cloaked in unfathomability and perceived to be incomprehensible. Jewish victimization was so important as to allow no room for coverage of other victim groups, and the Jewish victims themselves were symbolically ultra-orthodox (Schweber, forthcoming). Though this single case seems to be theoretically generalizeable, it's not at all clear how. That is, the study begs far more questions than it answers, such as: How typical is such a treatment of the Holocaust in ultra-orthodox environments? In other ultra-orthodox denominations, what is included in the narrative presented? What is excluded? Who are the main characters, supporting characters and invisibles? How do Zionist and/or anti-Zionist notions affect perceptions of the Shoah? Do *haredi* boys perceive the Holocaust through the same lens as *haredi* girls? What does it even "mean" in this case for the Holocaust to have been taught in the secular curriculum? Has its position within the larger American culture enabled it to be wrenched from the long religious history of Jewish suffering? Among the orthodox, is the Holocaust unique or consistent with Jewish history?

INFORMAL JEWISH EDUCATION

In the area of informal Jewish education, the Holocaust is most often taught myopically through travel pilgrimages to Poland. While the most widely known and prolific of these travel programs is the March of the Living, (which claims to have brought more than 100,000 teenagers to Poland since 1988), it is certainly not the only program of its kind. Nearly every national Jewish youth movement, scores of Jewish community federations, Jewish community centers, synagogues and resident camps throughout North America offer programs that take teenagers (and now adults) to Poland—usually immediately followed by a trip to Israel. The programs have been criticized for presenting the Holocaust simplistically—polarizing Poland, and by extension all Poles, as the nexus of death and destruction on the one hand with Israel as the place of Jewish rebirth and renewal on the other. A handful of studies have looked at the educational impact of these trips, specifically to what extent trips to Poland strengthen participants' Jewish identity and increase their Jewish pride. However, scant research exists on what is learned about the Holocaust as a result of these programs. One of the few studies was conducted by Findling as part of her dissertation research that explored the "meaning making"—the take-home messages—that teenagers on the March of the Living gain through their experiences with Holocaust monuments and memorials in Poland, though significant additional research is needed in this arena (Findling, 2001).

MUSEUM EDUCATION

In terms of museum-based educational programs, too, very little is known. While institutions like the U.S. Holocaust Memorial Museum are instituting serious evaluations of their on-site programming, especially for teachers (and military and law-enforcement personnel), these evaluations are currently in the planning phases. Not only could much more be done to evaluate, assess and simply investigate teacher training on the Holocaust, but clearly, a richer picture of how students interact with, move through, and attend to exhibits on the Holocaust deserves greater attention. How do Jewish students as compared to Christian, Muslim, or Buddhist students think about the Holocaust and hence the Holocaust Museum differently? Ellsworth's (2002) fabulous studies of the ways in which the architecture of the U.S. Holocaust Memorial Museum positions visitors, its implied "pedagogical address," we hope, will usher in more studies of the same ilk, perhaps describing in nuanced ways the interactions of complex, lived Jewish identities with complex, projected Holocaust histories.

COMMEMORATIVE EDUCATION

The final category deserving of much more educational research is commemoration work, whether on the sites of actual events (as youth might experience during a trip to Poland) or in remote sites (in their home synagogues or community centers). Though commemoration is a distinctly different enterprise than education, the Venn diagram of their overlapping aims and experiences may be fruitful as an avenue of educational research. Given the repetitive nature of commemoration as a ritual activity, what educational impacts does it carry, with what students, under what conditions? How, for example, do different students "hear" lists of names of survivors or experience moments of silence? When are commemorations educative or not? What is it that they teach, politically, morally, religiously, personally? Here, too, the literature is scant, but developing. (See, for example, Ben-Amos & Bet-El, 1999.)

HIGHLIGHTS

What we know, in short, can be summarized by the following big ideas:

1. Students encounter the Holocaust as a part of their Jewish education primarily within the formal curricula of their congregational or day schools, within the informal educational experiences they may engage in such as trips to Poland or Israel, within dedicated Holocaust museums or exhibits, and during commemoration events.

2. The Holocaust remains a curricular powerhouse within liberal Jewish educational arenas, but how it is taught, when, using what materials and methods and most importantly, with what effects on students, their parents and communities, still needs to be investigated.

3. Holocaust education is in all likelihood spreading into new denominational terrain. Whereas once it was rarely taught among the ultra-orthodox, it seems likely that it is now being incorporated into the formal yeshiva curriculum. More work remains do be done on whether this is the case.

4. In all likelihood, too, there is the appearance that the Holocaust is being taught in younger and younger grades, but much more information about this trend is still needed.

LARGER CONTEXT

In sum, what we now know about Jewish education on the Holocaust is still rather small. The situation brings to mind a Midwestern radio show hosted by Michael Feldman entitled "Whad'Ya know?" In the segment that opens every show, Feldman yells out to the audience with a decidedly Midwestern twang, "Whad'Ya know?" As a chorus, they respond heartily, "Not much, you?" Though it may be safe to conclude that, as compared with the publication of Kelman's *What we know about Jewish education*, the field of Holocaust education has certainly grown, the answer to what we *now* know still seems to be "not much." We sincerely hope, though, that the next edition will bring us closer to being able to answer Feldman's query, heartily, with, "Plenty, you?"

REFERENCES

Bar-On, D., & Selah, O. (1991). "The 'vicious cycle' between current social and political attitudes and attitudes towards the Holocaust among Israeli youngsters." *Psychologia,* 2(2), pp. 126-138.

Ben-Amos, A. & Bet-El, I. (1999). "Holocaust Day and Memorial Day in Israeli schools: Ceremonies, education and history." *Israel Studies,* 4(1), 258-284.

Chaitin, J. (2000). "Facing the Holocaust in generations of families of survivors—the case of partial relevance and interpersonal values." *Contemporary Family Therapy,* 22(3), pp. 289-213

Ellsworth, Elizabeth Ann. (2002). "The U.S. Holocaust Museum as a scene of pedagogical address." *Symploke,* 10(1-2) 13-31

Fallace, T. D. (2004). *The construction of the American Holocaust curriculum.* Unpublished doctoral dissertation. University of Virginia.

Feldman, J. (2002). "Marking the boundaries of the enclave: Defining the Israeli collective through the Poland experience." *Israel Studies,* 7(2), p. 84-114.

Findling, D. (2001). *A hermeneutic exploration of the past as present and future: The march of the living as text.* Unpublished doctoral dissertation. University of San Francisco.

Lazar, A., Chitin, J., Gross, T. & Bar-On, D. (2004). "Jewish Israeli teenagers, national identity, and the lessons of the Holocaust." *Holocaust and Genocide Studies,* 18(2), pp. 188-204.

Novick, P. (1999). *The Holocaust in American life.* Boston: Houghton Mifflin.

Schweber, S. (2004). *Making Sense of the Holocaust: Lessons for Classroom Practice.* New York: Teachers College Press.

Schweber, S. (forthcoming, 2007). "'What happened to their pets?': Third graders encounter the Holocaust." New York: *Teachers College Record.*

Schweber, S. (forthcoming). "'Here there is no why': Holocaust education at a Lubavitch girls' yeshiva." Stanford University: *Jewish Social Studies.*

Schweber, S. & Findling, D. (2007). *Teaching the Holocaust.* Los Angeles: Torah Aura.

Sheramy, R. (2000). *Defining lessons: The Holocaust in American Jewish education. Unpublished doctoral dissertation.* Brandeis University.

Spielberg, S. (Director). (1993). *Schindler's List* [Motion picture]. US: Universal Studios.

Stier, O. B. (2005). "Different trains: Holocaust artifacts and the ideologies of remembrance." *Holocaust and Genocide Studies,* 19(1), 81-106.

Totten, S. (2000). "Diminishing the complexity and horror of the Holocaust: using simulations in an attempt to convey historical experiences." *Social Education,* 64(3), 170.

Wineburg, S., Mosborg, S., & Porat, D. (2001). ?What can *Forrest Gump* tell us about students' historical understanding?" *Social Education,* 65(1), p. 55.

Ed Linenthal, *Commemorating Tragedy, Preserving Memory: The Struggle to Create America's Holocaust Museum*

Technology and
Distance Learning

Peter Margolis

As a transnational people for the greatest part of our history, Jews have long used technology to distribute learning across distances. For our purposes, distance learning is defined as "the acquisition of knowledge and skills through mediated information and instruction, encompassing all technologies and other forms of learning at a distance." (USDLA, 2005) In practice, most distance learning is Internet-based, or "e-learning" and videoconferencing.

To better understand the role of distance learning in Jewish education, the key questions are:

- Is distance learning as good as traditional learning?
- How can distance learning serve the special needs of the Jewish community?
- How is distance learning currently being used in Jewish learning?
- What changes are required for Jewish education to take better advantage of distance learning technologies?
- What do emerging technologies suggest for the future of distance learning in Jewish education?

CONTEXT

In order for Judaism to survive, Jews must be knowledgeable about their civilization. This imperative places education at the center of Jewish communal priorities. With finite resources for education, the advent of educational technology coupled with computer communications in recent years—especially the popularity of the Internet since the mid-1990s—carries with it the promise of revitalizing Jewish education by making scarce resources and innovative, engaging teaching methods widely available. Today, while Internet-based and videoconferencing technologies have become part of the Jewish educational landscape, they remain under-utilized in Jewish learning, resulting in missed opportunities to engage the generation of "wired" Jews. This chapter will not provide a comprehensive listing of the websites and online distance learning endeavors designed to enhance Jewish teaching. Rather, we will examine the current state of distance learning in general and, by using representative examples, will extract ideas and directions for stakeholders to enhance its application to Jewish education for K-12, academic, and adult learning.

Central to any discussion of distance learning is the "no significant difference" phenomenon, named for the results of research indicating that the use of distance learning technology neither improves nor denigrates learning outcomes. While this may be dismaying news to those who look to distance learning as a magic cure for all that is wrong or ineffective in Jewish education, in reality it is a highly liberating concept that shifts the focus away from unrealistic expectations and onto the specific and realistic uses of technology.

The research on distance learning is virtually unanimous in finding that the "no significant difference" phenomenon applies regardless of the type of distance learning technology used (broadly referred to as Web-based or videoconferencing, but specifically including one-way video/two-way audio, two-way video conferencing, white boarding, interactive Web-based courses, asynchronous learning networks, e-learning and Web conferencing, and e-mail). The true task of using distance learning in Jewish education, therefore, lies in identifying and optimizing the ways in which technology can provide an edge. In a recent review of videoconferencing in education, Greenberg and Colbert (2004) identify the following advantages of distance learning technology:

- Increasing access to education: Expanding access to academic materials, to degree programs, and to learners and their families.

- Accommodating multiple learning styles: Using a "buffet" of learning technologies to reach the broadest variety of learners.

- Developing new instructional strategies: Matching the right "mix" of teaching tools and strategies to the subject and the audience.

- Maximizing benefits for invested resources: Centralizing the course development process, using distance learning materials in a wide variety of settings and applications, and enabling faculty members to share content and materials. (pp. 6-9)

Moreover, distance learning demands a holistic approach, since it typically involves a blend of technologies. For example, the WebStudy online learning software (http://www.webstudy.com) widely used in Jewish distance learning combines text, discussion boards, interactive assignments, Web links, e-mail, and several ways of implementing synchronous and asynchronous chat, voice and video in a single package; it can be deployed both for fully online learning and as an enhancement to the classroom. Properly understood, then, the correct question to ask about distance learning is: What is the appropriate mix of instructional strategies and distance learning technology to produce the desired learning outcome for the intended audience?

K–12 DISTANCE LEARNING

The recent study of Web-based distance learning in the K-12 sector by Cavanaugh et al (2004) is one of very few resources tracking its effectiveness and analyzing the contributory factors. Driven by the prevailing educational opinion regarding the need for school reform, the study recognizes both the promise of Web-based learning to improve the quality of education through innovation, and the lack of scientific studies of sufficient scope and quality to serve as a reliable basis for making policy decisions, largely owing to the newness of this educational medium. As the lack of research on Jewish distance learning in this (or any) age range is even more severe, the conclusions of the Cavanaugh study for Jewish education should be understood to reflect what can be reasonably expected after several years of implementation.

While recognizing the general benefit of accommodating greater choice of courses and learning styles, the study found, unsurprisingly, that the effect of distance learning is influenced by "the design of the distance learning system, the demands of the content, the abilities and disabilities of the student, and the quality of the teacher...as they are in conventional educational enterprises." The report goes on to state that "educators and other stakeholders can reasonably expect learning in a well-designed distance education environment to be equivalent to learning in a well-designed classroom environment." (Cavanaugh et al, 2004, p. 2) The implications of the study thus suggest the need for extensive teacher training if Jewish distance learning is to be successful. These points will be addressed below.

The Cavanaugh study emphasizes that, in order to realize the potential of K-12 distance learning and to enable program designers and managers to deliver more effective programs, "[w]e need to know how to make it more effective, what factors contribute most to effectiveness, and in what contexts the factors operate. Acquiring this knowledge requires consensus on a definition of effectiveness that goes beyond standardized tests, and a system for identifying and measuring factors that influence effectiveness." (Cavanaugh et al, 2004, p. 2)

The study identifies two factors of special importance in determining the effectiveness of K-12 distance learning:

- teacher quality
- the emergence of virtual (online) charter schools

Teacher quality was found to far outweigh other factors such as class size or demographics. Focused professional development for teachers engaged in distance learning should therefore be expected to improve student success. Stated bluntly, good teaching can compensate for a poor choice of technology, but technology will never save bad teaching. The second factor, the emergence of virtual charter schools, is an outgrowth of the charter school movement stimulated by the No Child Left Behind Act of 2001 allowing ailing public schools to be restructured as charter schools. We will return to the concept of virtual charter schools with regard to Jewish education in the section below. The Cavanaugh study concludes with a reminder that (as of its publication in 2004) there had been fewer than ten years' experience in K-12 distance learning, and reiterates the need for systematic research. (Cavanaugh et al, 2004, p. 20)

While the Cavanaugh study focused on Web-based K-12 distance learning, DeFord et al (2002) produced a literature review and policy issues review based on a 2002 conference on K-12 interactive videoconferencing, defined as "live, two-way audio and fullmotion (*sic*) video communication" (DeFord et al, 2002, p. 2). This study concurs with Cavanaugh about the need for teacher training and judicious integration of technology into the learning program. However, influenced by the greater effort and expense involved in design, production and implementation of interactive videoconferencing, it also devotes considerable space to the policy considerations that must accompany this (or any) technology decision:

- Technical Considerations
- Facilities and Budgetary Considerations
- Learner/Student Considerations
- Teacher/Curriculum Developer Considerations
- Assessment and Evaluation Considerations
- Management and Administration Considerations
- Marketing and Public Relations Considerations (Cavanaugh et al, 2004, pp. 20-25)

What are the implications of the Cavanaugh and DeFord studies for K-12 Jewish distance learning? By comparison to general K-12 distance learning, the use of these technologies in the Jewish classroom lags far behind. In the absence of systematic study, the causes of this can reasonably be attributed to well-known factors in the Jewish school: limited numbers of qualified teachers, lack of sufficient teacher training, limited infrastructure, and the like. Nevertheless, the study suggests several areas where a concentrated effort can make distance learning more effective in Jewish education:

TEACHER TRAINING AND RESOURCES FOR DISTANCE LEARNING

Extensive resources and training opportunities are available to guide teachers in applying distance learning technologies in Jewish education. Indeed, the proliferation of online opportunities constitutes a significant branch of Jewish distance learning. Moreover, training encompasses two distinct areas: teaching methods and the design of materials for distance learning delivery. Issues of teacher salaries, retention, and professional status, while clearly related to motivations to obtain training, are outside the scope of this discussion. The following represent a sample of the resources and organizations available to Jewish teachers.

- The Jewish Education Center of Cleveland, ORT/JECC Partnership for Technology in Education (*http://www.jecc.org/edres/medtech/ortjecc.htm#online*)
  Teacher education and sample curricula for Web-based learning
- United States Distance Learning Association (*http://www.usdla.org/*)
  Extensive discussions and links to information on all varieties and aspects of distanc e learning technology and their applications

- Gratz College (*http://www.gratz.edu*)
  Offers a graduate-level course titled "Using Computers in the Jewish Classroom" in both online and hybrid (online/in-class) formats.
- Preparing Tomorrow's Teachers to Use Technology (*http://www.pt3.org/*)
  Website of a Federally-funded grant program containing links to resources, strategies, tools, training opportunities, and research.

POLICY CONSIDERATIONS

Essential to any meaningful implementation of distance learning technology must be a commitment to transforming Jewish education and enhancing the professionalism and status of teachers. To that end, the Jewish community has embraced the concept of Jewish day schools which provide a much-needed framework to attain both goals. Indeed, the day school has become fertile ground for distance learning technologies. However, Jewish day schools cannot address the needs of the overwhelming majority of Jewish youth who, whether for reasons of expense or commitment, do not attend them and receive their Jewish education in congregational schools. The following concepts are applicable to both day and congregational schools, but are of greater significance for the improvement of the latter.[2]

- Virtual Charter schools—The charter school enables citizens to use communal resources to structure and govern their children's education in a way that combines choice and accountability. It is primarily implemented where conventional public education is perceived as a failure. The virtual charter school extends that idea by eliminating geographic limitations through the use of distance learning. Given the continued predominance of the Jewish congregational school and the widespread sense of its inadequacy, a bold experiment to create a virtual Jewish charter school could link attractive technology with innovative Jewish learning. Resources for further investigation include:

    The Pennsylvania Cyber Charter School (*http://www.wpccs.com/Class/gotoclass.aspx*)

    Learn Hebrew Online (*http://www.hebrewonline.co.il*)

    U.S Department of Education, Office of Innovation and Improvement, *Innovations in Education: Successful Charter Schools*. Washington, D.C. 2004. Available online: *http://www.ed.gov/admins/comm/choice/charter/index.html*

- Consortia—Implementing distance learning represents a large investment in the areas of financial and material resources, human and support resources, training and professional development, community support, and more. Consortia represent a way for combining resources and experience to help individuals, schools, other stakeholders, and the wider community embrace the potential and power of distance learning technology. The DeFord study (2002) on K-12 interactive videoconferencing referenced above draws on the experiences of schools linked in a regional consortium. A description of the thinking and planning behind this and other regional consortia is available in a U.S. Department of Education publication titled *Fulfilling the Promise of Technologies for Teaching and Learning Through the Support of the Regional Technology in Education Consortia Program: A Summary and Resource Guide*. (USDoE, 1998)

- Hybrid Learning—Hybrid learning combines traditional, face-to-face learning with distance learning technology. Because of the degree of attention devoted in recent years to this relatively new methodology, its significance to Jewish distance learning will be discussed in a separate section below.

ACADEMIC DISTANCE LEARNING

Distance learning has become a fixture in higher education. Two resources that illustrate this in abundant detail for general education are the Allen and Seaman (2003) and Tabs (2003) studies. A

---

[2] Many of the resources devoted to using distance learning technology were developed in response to the widespread inadequacies of public education in the United States. With regard to Jewish education, an analogous need for improvement renders these resources highly relevant, even as the general educational needs of most Jewish youth are well served.

very brief synopsis of these two studies indicates the extent of this phenomenon in higher education in the United States:

- In 2000-2001, 56% of all 2-year and 4-year degree-granting institutions in the United States offered distance education courses (Tabs, p. 3).

- 34% offered distance learning degree or certificate programs (Ibid, p. 10).

- The majority (90%) used asynchronous Internet courses as their primary delivery mode. Other modes included two-way video with two-way audio (51%); synchronous Internet instruction (43%); and one-way pre-recorded video (41%) (ibid, p. 11).

- 60% participated in some type of distance learning consortium (Ibid, p. 13).

- In 2003 over 90% of public institutions offered distance learning, compared to 54.5% of the private, non-profit institutions, and 44.9% of the for-profit institutions (Allen and Seaman, p. 7).

- Nearly half (48.9%) of the public institutions offered a distance learning degree, compared with just over one-fifth (20.2%) in the private, non-profit sector (Idem).

- While the largest schools predictably enroll the most distance learners, the smallest schools have the highest percentage of distance learners (8.7% for schools over 15,000 students, compared to 17.6% for schools with fewer than 1,500 students) (Ibid, p. 17).

Jewish academic distance learning is a relative latecomer to this field, and has different characteristics. For example, of eight academic institutions offering distance learning in Jewish education surveyed by Isaacs et al (2002), only one (Chico State University in California) was a large institution, which subsequently ceased operation with the departure of its founder. Indeed, even among large Israeli institutions where distance learning technology has been implemented by "top-down" government fiat, only one conventional large institution (Bar-Ilan University) offers a modest program of fully online Jewish Studies courses. Other Israeli universities use distance learning technology primarily in a limited, "web-facilitated" capacity, and only for small numbers of Jewish Studies courses.[1] Even the completely distance learning Open University of Israel uses distance learning technology as an "add-on" to its traditional correspondence courses in Jewish studies, rather than as a primary teaching method.

The main institutions offering Jewish academic distance learning are:

- Baltimore Hebrew University (not included in Isaacs et al, 2002) (http://www.bhu.edu)
- Gratz College (http://www.gratz.edu)
- Hebrew College (http://www.hebrewcollege.edu/html/hconline.htm)
- Hebrew Union College (http://www.huc.edu/academics/continuing/de.shtml)
- Jewish Theological Seminary (http://www.courses.jtsa.edu)
- Siegal College of Judaic Studies (videoconferencing only) (http://www.siegalcollege.edu/distance_intro.php)
- Spertus Institute of Jewish Studies (correspondence only) (http://www.spertus.edu/degreeprograms/jewishstudies/index.php)

Although Jewish academic distance learning lags behind its counterparts in general higher education, it has emerged as a serious factor at a time when current best practices recommend a blend of multiple technology tools and the use of hybrid online/in-class learning. This coincides with a time when, for many young Jews, university-level Jewish studies constitute their first serious encounter with Jewish learning. For them, studying in the presence of a Jewish scholar carries with it a range of affective meaning beyond the acquisition of an additional three credits. Moreover, students paying high tuitions in elite universities expect small classes and personal attention. This face-to-face intimacy is also part of the appeal of small colleges of Jewish studies. These factors must be considered when designing and marketing distance learning. Unfortunately, many Jewish studies faculty lack familiarity with the tools of online learning, and may indeed be antipathetic to using technol-

---

[1] For example, Bar Ilan University's "Bar-e-learn" program offers only six Jewish studies courses fully online, and the most (25+) hybrid courses in Jewish studies of any conventional Israeli institution. By comparison, the Hebrew University of Jerusalem offers only seven web-enhanced Jewish studies courses. This is due in part to the perception in Israeli academia (prevalent in the United States until the mid-to-late 1990s) that distance learning is not "real" education.

ogy. Typically, faculty development programs emphasize technical skills without a well-thought-out and systematic methodology for selecting and integrating the technology tools appropriate to the instructor's discipline and interests, thus doing little to remedy the situation.

Where academic distance learning has been most successfully implemented in Jewish studies, several factors are present. These, along with relevant and available resources, include:

- *Strong administrative support:* Shoemaker (1998) is one of very few guides to the skills necessary to lead an academic distance learning program.
- *Extensive marketing and concentrated programmatic focus:* Marketing and program design available through the *www.CollegeAnywhere.org* consortium
- *Careful selection of participating faculty members:* If in-house faculty are reluctant, adjunct faculty may be preferred. Advice on this is available from USDLA *www.usdla.org* and the *www.CollegeAnywhere.org* consortium.
- *Faculty preparation and support:* Faculty training guides like Moore at al (2001) *www.mhhe.com/ucanteachonline*
- Instructional design available through the *www.CollegeAnywhere.org* consortium. Course review like Maryland Online's Quality Matters project at *www.qualitymatters.org*

ADULT JEWISH DISTANCE LEARNING

The realm of adult education represents the greatest degree of innovation in Jewish distance learning. This may be the result of the recent growth in adult Jewish education which makes it a relatively new field and thus less obligated to entrenched shareholders than K-12 and academic education. It also may be more of a function of the initiative of inspired individuals, even if they are operating within existing organizations. Jewish adult distance learning succeeds when—and because—it is:

- Voluntary and non-coercive
- Responsive to the quest for Jewish knowledge of mature adults
- Capable of strengthening the values of community and family

The recent book by Goodman and Katz (2004) represents a comprehensive overview of adult learning in Jewish life and is the standard work on the subject at this time. It includes chapters on the adult learning process from such perspectives as learning and teaching theory, program planning and design, and professional development. As distance learning has much in common with traditional learning, the insights of these chapters transfer readily to distance learning, and the book is strongly recommended to readers. Of particular interest is the chapter by Levine (2004) on technology in adult Jewish learning. Levine's discussion covers the entire spectrum of technology: CD-ROMs and fax machines, videotapes and e-mail, Web searches and conference calls, online courses and videoconferencing. When referring to distance learning, she offers the following useful categories of adult learners which are quite different from what is associated with the younger generation of "wired" learners:

- "[T]hose who use technology for learning in their professional lives or for recreation"
- "[T]hose who are familiar with technologies like computers but are not using them in the context of learning"
- Those who "are not particularly proficient in using technology and do not use it on a regular basis" (Levine, 2004, pp. 235-6)

Like other resources cited above with regard to K-12 and academic distance learning, Levine stresses the need to select the appropriate technology and design and support the distance learning program according to the needs of the audience.

Examples of adult Jewish distance learning programs that illustrate the considerations of audience and mission as they have been applied to serve specific constituencies include:

- eAcademy of the Jewish Agency for Israel (*http://www.jacontact.org*). This is a program of Israel studies courses designed for technologically adept educators and individuals involved in Israel advocacy. The courses cover such topics as the land and history of Israel, Jerusalem, Israeli culture and the Middle East conflict. Predominantly asynchronous and completely online, they use a blend of chat, discussions, and on-demand pre-recorded video; the occasional synchronous chats are scheduled well in advance to accommodate the scheduling needs of students and workers.

- Makor (*http://www.makor.net/*). The non-profit Makor Jewish Learning Foundation was founded in 2002 by Saul Korin, a former Hillel program director. Its purpose is to build pluralistic Jewish communities in selected cities (Los Angeles, Chicago, and Baltimore at the time of this writing) through a hybrid program of online learning of sacred texts and monthly Shabbat dinners. It is directed at the 20-39 year old age group.

- Mishpacha—A Virtual Community for Real Jewish Families (*http://www.mishpacha.org*). A project of the Memorial Foundation for Jewish Culture, Mispacha creates virtual communities of 30 persons through a three-month online course in Jewish life using books supplied by the program, electronic texts, synchronous chats, and asynchronous discussions. The course covers beliefs, practices, holidays, lifecycle, community and parenting, and is directed at parents who feel their Jewish knowledge is inadequate for raising Jewish children.

- Virtual Beit Midrash of Yeshivat Har Etzion (*http://www.vbm-torah.org/*). The Virtual Beit Midrash provides the text of traditional lessons in Torah, Talmud, and the Weekly Portion in an e-mail based discussion list. Courses are available in English and Hebrew for beginning and advanced learners and include e-mail interaction with rabbis of Yeshivat Har Etzion.

Beyond the design and teaching considerations reflected in this sample of adult learning programs, the question must be asked: What are the implications of adult Jewish distance learning for successful implementation of distance learning in the K-12 and academic realms?

HYBRID LEARNING

A recurring motif throughout this chapter has been the idea of hybrid learning. A hybrid course is one where part of the instruction takes place in a traditional face-to-face setting and part takes place by distance learning technology. Hybrid learning moves a significant portion of learning out of the classroom and onto the Internet via the same online learning tools used in fully online learning. As is the case with all types of distance learning, course design and teacher training are of paramount importance in hybrid learning. Moreover, as the technology used for the Web-based component of hybrid learning becomes more sophisticated, a variety of voice and videoconferencing methods, both synchronous and asynchronous, can make the online system a true "virtual classroom." Of the various service providers offering online learning software that can be used for hybrid learning, WebStudy (*www.webstudy.com*) is widely used in Jewish education and has the ability to deliver Hebrew text.

At present, hybrid learning is primarily located in academia, where it is regarded as "the best of both worlds" and a significant addition to good educational practice. (Lindsay, 2004; Wingard, 2004) The Allen and Seaman study found that over half (55.6%) of all types of academic institutions delivered hybrid learning. (2004, p. 6) However, all projections about the future of education clearly indicate that the emergence and integration of new technologies will transform this blending of methodologies from a specific entity called "hybrid," to what will simply and axiomatically be known as "education." (USDoC, 2002)

In Jewish education, hybrid learning exists far more as potential than as actuality. As with all forms of distance learning, the uses of hybrid learning are limited only by the imagination. For example, hybrid learning lends itself to:

- Enriching the congregational school with attractive technology while retaining community involvement

- Creating the right mix of online and face-to-face activities for a Jewish charter school

- Enriching and extending adult education programs such as Me'ah or the Florence Melton Adult Mini School

- Adding resources and experiences to academic Jewish studies and Hebrew instruction

Given the special needs of Jewish education to both strengthen communal identification and impart knowledge, hybrid learning has great potential. In many ways, this is an educational revolution waiting to happen. As discussed above, all Israeli academic institutions now offer a Web component for the use of every course, although this remains poorly used in Jewish studies. The current spike in Jewish studies enrollments on American campuses is fueled by students discovering serious Jewish study for the first time; hybrid learning could satisfy their demand for access to high-quality resources and the intimacy of studying with a scholar. All of the design, training, and administrative issues discussed throughout this chapter apply to hybrid learning.

QUESTIONS FOR ADDITIONAL RESEARCH

- What is the degree of computer literacy among teachers of the three constituencies? among learners?

- What resources and incentives are made available for instructors to implement distance learning technology? To institutions? (For example: training, instructional design support, salary increases, tenure consideration, etc.)

- What research can be conducted to identify and target specific markets for distance learning?

- What is the feasibility and desirability of a global Jewish distance learning infrastructure initiative (including the delivery system, faculty training, and instructional design)?

- What creative technology blends lend themselves to Jewish education? For example, what are the issues, expenses, and feasibility associated with new technologies such as gaming?

- How do we measure the accomplishments of Jewish distance learning?

FUTURE DIRECTIONS

Almost daily, we are treated to the enticing possibilities of distance learning. (USDoC, 2002) Distance and computer-mediated learning must become permanent fixtures in Jewish life. This will only occur as the result of a changed attitude that recognizes distance learning technology as integral to Jewish education. Some strategies to accomplish this include:

- Institute a distance and computer-mediated learning requirement for teacher certification by central agencies for Jewish education.

- Institute required tracks in academic teacher education for both teaching and administration, taught with online and hybrid technologies.

- Mobilize stakeholders in federations, central agencies for Jewish education, universities, and the Israeli government to create a global infrastructure—analogous to the electric power grid—to make distance learning technologies available and affordable to all Jewish institutions.

- Create consortia to share resources and experience between educational institutions, central agencies for Jewish education and federations.

- Develop institution-appropriate professional incentives for instructors and faculty members such as salary increases or tenure considerations.

- Create bold, high profile pilot programs (such as a virtual charter school, a hybrid program of academic Jewish Studies or a distance learning component for the Florence Melton Adult Mini School) to demonstrate viability and raise visibility.

CONCLUSION

"The problem is not that we have expected too much from technology in education—it is that we have settled for too little."(USDoC, 2002) While referring to general education, these words might well have been written to describe the situation in Jewish education. At a time when new technologies are transforming organizations throughout society, Jewish education is still debating the usefulness of technology. Moreover, this situation unwittingly reinforces the perception for an entire generation of Jews—at a time of weakening Jewish identification—that Jewishness has little in common with the non-linear, postmodern virtual environment where they spend much of their time. This inability of Jewish education institutions to exploit the potential of distance learning results, in part, from a lack of teaching and administrative personnel who are comfortable in both technology and Jewish studies environments.

Fortunately, an abundance of robust and affordable technologies, and a wealth of expertise, are available to bring to bear on this problem. Moreover, the accelerating blending of digital technologies—resulting in a synthesis of synchronous and asynchronous learning using Web-based voice, text, and video—means that the application of technology is less fragmented and limited only by the imagination of the stakeholders. All of the necessary components are in place. It is now time to translate this opportunity into general awareness and to create a new educational reality.

CHAPTER HIGHLIGHTS

- Distance learning is underutilized at all levels of Jewish education.
- Appropriate use of distance learning is as effective as the best of traditional learning.
- Teaching is more important than technology.
- A wealth of applicable experience and resources is available from general education.
- Successful implementation of distance learning requires knowledge, vision, leadership, planning, resources, and communal commitment.
- Hybrid learning combines the best of traditional and distance learning.
- Technology will transform learning as much as it changes life in general.

THE LARGER CONTEXT

Despite stirring calls to action, little changes from year to year in the use of distance learning technology in Jewish education. Every passing year increases the urgency of integrating this into Jewish life, yet every year the field of Jewish education seemingly lacks the will to take full advantage of its potential. The challenge for our time is to stimulate a creative Jewish engagement with the contemporary world that embraces the challenges of globalization, networking, and instantaneous access to massive information resources, while strengthening Jewish identification and community. In its way, this represents a challenge to Jewish life as great as that faced by rabbinical Judaism after the destruction of the Second Temple. The response of the rabbis was to fearlessly create an enduring cultural edifice built on education. We must follow their example.

ANNOTATED BIBLIOGRAPHY

Anderson, T. & Elloumi, F. (Eds.). (2004). *Theory and Practice of Online Learning.* Retrieved from the World Wide Web March 2007, *http://cde.athabascau.ca/online_book/* This online book combines scholarship and research with practical information on teaching and learning online, as well as program administration.

Horton, W. (2006). *e-Learning by Design.* San Francisco: Pfeiffer.. This book systematically presents a methodology for addressing the many choices and decisions that go into creating distance learning. It draws upon numerous case studies using many varieties and combinations of online learning concepts and technologies.

Innovate Journal of Online Education. Retrieved from the World Wide Web March 2007, *http://innovateonline. info/.. Innovate* is an open access, bimonthly, peer-reviewed online periodical published by the *Fischler School of Education and Human Services at Nova Southeastern University.* The journal focuses on the creative use of information technology (IT) to enhance educational processes in academic, commercial, and governmental settings.

Oblinger, D. G. & Oblinger, J. L., (Eds.). *Educating the Net Generation.* Washington, D.C.: Educause, 2005. Retrieved from the World Wide Web March 2007, *http://www.educause.edu/books/educatingthenetgen/5989* A collection by educators and students examining the generation that has grown up with information technology and the ways institutions can accommodate them with regard to teaching, faculty development, and curriculum.

REFERENCES

This list, while making no claims to comprehensiveness, includes the studies referred to in the chapter. Note that all Web addresses were correct at the time of publication, although they are subject to change. The reader is encouraged to seek additional resources, both under Jewish and general auspices.

Allen, E. I. & Seaman, J. (2003). *Sizing the Opportunity: The Quality and Extent of Online Education in the United States, 2002 and 2003* Needham, MA: The Sloan Consortium. Retrieved from the World Wide Web March 2007, *http://www.aln.org/resources/sizing_opportunity.pdf*

Cavanaugh, C., Kathy J. G., et al., (2004). The Effects of Distance Education on K–12 Student Outcomes: A Meta-Analysis. Naperville, Illinois: Learning Point Associates. October, 2004. Retrieved from the World Wide Web March 2007, *http://www.unf.edu/~ccavanau/CavanaughIJET01.pdf*

CollegeAnywhere. Retrieved from the World Wide Web March 2007, *http://www.collegeanywhere.org*

DeFord, K., Dimock, K. V., Heath, M. J., et al., (2002). Interactive Videoconferencing: A Literature Review. K–12 National Symposium for Interactive Videoconferencing Dallas, Texas. . Retrieved from the World Wide Web March 2007, *http://neirtec.terc.edu/k12vc/resources/litpolicy.pdf*

Greenberg, A. & Colbert, R. (2004, February). Navigating the Sea of Research on Video Conferencing-Based Distance Education: A Platform for Understanding Research into Technology's Effectiveness and Value. Pleasanton, California: Polycom. Retrieved from the World Wide Web March 2007, *http://www.polycom. com/common/pw_cmp_updateDocKeywords/0%2C1687%2C2898%2C00.pdf*

Goodman, R. L., & Katz, B.D. (2004). *The Adult Jewish Education Handbook: Planning, Practice, and Theory.* Denver: A. R. E. Publishing.

Isaacs, L. W., Levine, C. N., Goldwater, R. (2002). Draft Survey of Distance Learning in Jewish Education. New York: JESNA, Jewish Education Service of North America. May, 2002. Retrieved from the World Wide Web March 2007, *http://archive.jesna.org/pdfs/mt_elearn.pdf*

Learn Hebrew Online. Retrieved from the World Wide Web March 2007, *http://www.hebrewonline.co.il*

Levine, C. N. (2004). Technology and Adult Jewish Learning. In Goodman, R. L., & Katz, B. D. *The Adult Jewish Education Handbook: Planning, Practice, and Theory.* (213-249) Denver: A. R. E. Publishing.

Lindsay, E. B. (2004). "The Best of Both Worlds: Teaching a Hybrid Class." *Academic Exchange Quarterly*, 8, 4. Retrieved from the World Wide Web March 2007, *http://rapidintellect.com/AEQweb/*

Moore, G. S., Winograd, K., & Lange, D. L. (2001). *You Can Teach Online: Building a Creative Learning Environment.* Boston: McGraw-Hill Higher Education. With companion website (Retrieved from the World Wide Web March 2007): *http://wwwmhhe.com/ucanteachonline*

Shoemaker, C. (1998). *Leadership in Continuing and Distance Education in Higher Education.* Needham Heights, MA: Allyn & Bacon.

Tabs, E. D. (2003). Distance Education at Degree-Granting Postsecondary Institutions: 200-2001. National Center for Education Statistics Washington, D.C.: US Department of Education. July, 2001.

The Jerusalem Archaeological Park. Retrieved from the World Wide Web March 2007, *http://www.archpark. org.il/index.asp*

The Pennsylvania Cyber Charter School (PCCS) (2005). Retrieved from the World Wide Web March 2007, *http://www.wpccs.com/Class/gotoclass.aspx*

U.S. Department of Commerce Technology Administration, Office of Technology Policy (USDoC). (2002) *2020 Visions: Transforming Education and Training Through Advanced Technologies.* Washington, D.C.

U.S. Department of Education (USDoE). (1998) *Fulfilling the Promise of Technologies for Teaching and Learning Through the Support of the Regional Technology in Education Consortia Program: A Summary and Resource Guide.* Critical authors: Rocap, Kevin, Cassidy, Sheila, and Connor, Catherine. Washington, D.C. October 26, 1998.

United States Distance Learning Association (USDLA). Retrieved from the World Wide Web March 2007, *http://www.usdla.org*

Wingard, R. C. (2004). "Classroom Teaching Changes in Web-Enhanced Courses: A Multi-Institutional Study." *Educause Quarterly, 1*, 26-35.

Early Childhood, Media, and Jewish Education

Lewis Bernstein

One of these things is not like the others.
One of these things just doesn't belong.
Can you tell which thing is not like the others
Before I finish my song?

If you answered media, you're absolutely right! Why is it that using media as a means for Jewish education is unnatural, uncommon, or, at least, institutionally ignored?

Makes no sense to me. But then again, I am biased. I am not a Jewish educator, but I am a product of a strongly religious Jewish home, Orthodox day school, Jewish camp, Jewish community, and "seven 'substantive' years" living in Israel. I have no Jewish educational credentials to speak of, although I am an educator who is proudly Jewish.

My professional career has been at *Sesame Street*. I am an informed, impassioned, and deeply committed educator, researcher, and producer who has used media as a means to reach and educate preschoolers in America and in one-hundred-and-twenty countries around the world, including Israel.

I was raised to believe that there were three great influences on a child: home, school, and church (in my case, synagogue). I know that the Jewish community believes in and supports two other significant influences on Jewish identity: Jewish camping and trips to Israel. I have personally benefited enormously from both.

But can the Jewish community continue to ignore a fourth powerful and pervasive influence on Jewish children: "screen media?" Here are some recent statistics about screen media use in the United States:

> "Young people today live media-saturated lives, spending an average of nearly six and a half hours a day with media…. and given that about a quarter (26%) of the time young people are using media, they're using more than one medium at a time (reading and listening to music, for example), they are actually exposed to the equivalent of 8½ hours a day (8:33) of media content, even though they pack that into less than 6½ hours of time" (Rideout, et.al., 2005).

And lest one think that only older kids are using screen media, Kaiser has issued a report on the use for children six and under. Children under the age of six spend over two hours a day in front of screen media, and even children under the age of one are spending over an hour a day in front of screens (Kaiser Foundation, 2003).

In 1961, Schramm, Lyle, and Parker estimated that by the time a child finishes high school, she or he will have spent over 15,000 hours viewing television (1961). Clearly, in our multi-media, multi-tasking world, it is safe to assume that most of our children will be spending more time in front of screen media than they will in their classrooms, after-school programs, synagogues, or (sadly) with their parents and friends.

Yet the Jewish community largely ignores the opportunities and potential that new media can offer for Jewish education. True, screen media is not 'the answer' to Jewish educational problems or deficiencies. It is, to paraphrase from Lesser's comments about television, "...only one element in a complex balancing act of simultaneous influences—peers, siblings, parents, and people in the neighborhood as well as television..."(1974, p. 244).

But at the same time, it should not be consistently ignored. Its potential for good and evil is too great. The late Lubavitcher Rebbe, Menachem Schneerson z"l, when accused of using the tainted medium of cable television to reach and teach Jews, said the following: "Is a knife a weapon? Actually a knife is really Pareve: true, it can be used to maim or kill, but it can equally be used to cut Challah on Shabbat. So too media: it can be used for the holy and/or the profane. It is up to us to use it positively and wisely." Ignoring the potential effects of screen media on children essentially relegates the knife to the weapon category; it is only when screen media is vigorously pursued as a positive educational influence on our children that it can indeed make a critical healthy educational difference in their lives.

My charge for this chapter is to use the research evidence from the world in which I work to extrapolate a case for utilizing media to address early childhood Jewish educational needs.

Let us first turn to the case for early childhood education. Does investing resources in education make the most sense when children are in preschool?

EARLY CHILDHOOD EDUCATION AND ITS IMPACT

"Careful the things you say/ Children will listen/ Careful the things you do/ Children will see/ And learn."—Stephen Sondheim

"Give me a child for the first 7 years and you may do what you like with him afterwards."—Anonymous

"Give me a child, and I'll shape him into anything"—B.F. Skinner

"Why begin teaching pre-school Jewish children 'Torat Kohanim' when they first begin to learn Torah? Let the holy children come and begin learning the laws of holiness...."—Rashi?

Elisha ben Avuyah declared in the Mishnah: "He who learns as a child may be compared to ink written on new paper." (Avot 4:25).

These epigrams (and lyrics) reflect a singular, powerful idea: begin educating children early when they are most impressionable, when their brains are most ready to learn, and when the impact on their lives and the societies they live in will be profound and long-lasting.

But what does research show about the long-term impact of early childhood education?

"Early interventions for disadvantaged children promote schooling, raise the quality of the workforce, enhance the productivity of schools, and reduce crime, teenage pregnancy and welfare dependency. They raise earnings and promote social attachment. Focusing solely on earnings gains, return to dollars invested [in early childhood education] are as high as 15–17%" (Heckman, 2006).

James Heckman is a Nobel Laureate in Economics at the University of Chicago. For the past several years, Heckman, his students, and several colleagues have been looking at data from early childhood interventions to analyze the cost benefits to society, as well as to the children themselves. Heckman and various other researchers have harvested studies on preschool children in the 1960s and tracked these children over time (into their 30s and 40s). Those who attended preschool education programs did remarkably well, and these effects lasted over time.

Heckman comments about the benefits of early educational intervention, claiming that "a large body of research in social science, psychology and neuroscience shows that skill begets skill; that learning begets learning… (p.2) motivation begets motivation. Early failure begets later failure… (p.3). The earlier the seed is planted and watered, the faster and larger it grows. There is substantial evidence of critical or sensitive periods in the lives of young children. Environments that do not stimulate the young and fail to cultivate both cognitive and non-cognitive skills, place children at an early disadvantage. Once a child falls behind, he or she is likely to remain behind. Remediation for impoverished early environments becomes progressively more costly the later it is attempted in the life cycle of the child. The track record for criminal rehabilitation, adult literacy and late teenage public job training programs is remarkably poor" (2006).

Heckman and others argue that experimental interventions that enrich early childhood environments produce more successful adults, and these interventions are not just successful because they introduce cognitive skills early. In fact, the non-cognitive abilities and motivational skills—like believing in one's own ability to succeed—are themselves determinants of socioeconomic success. Interestingly, many of the changes in test scores, abilities, and behaviors do not appear at the initial early childhood intervention. Rather, they appear over time, as children move into high school and the work force, and these changes are significant and dramatic.

Heckman correctly states that we in America believe in second chances, in "the possibility of redemption and renewal." However, the economic evidence proves that it is costly to teach skills at a late date to correct for missed opportunities.

Bottom line: the economic returns for early childhood educational interventions are significant and profound, and they have life-changing effects for the individual participants and society at large.

Do early Jewish educational experiences have similar benefits? I am not sufficiently literate in the relevant research in this field to fully address this question. I do know, however, that it is important to build on extant research findings and to expand the knowledge about what distinguishes quality early Jewish education from sub-quality early Jewish education. Important work needs to be done, even in the excellent Jewish day schools that my children attended and with which I am very familiar, to define objectives for preschoolers (and their families), to develop curriculum, and to create meaningful and reliable measures to assess success of both skill acquisition and of more illusive non-cognitive objectives, like the development of belief, wonder, and the stirrings of holiness.

What are the benefits of early interventions in Jewish education compared to later interventions, like Bar and Bat Mitzvah preparation, for example? Is there any research on this? If not, given the Heckman analysis, it seems an important question to explore.

Let's turn next to the case for media use in education. What do we know about the educational effects of media? Are they significant and meaningful, and, if so, do they last?

MEDIA AND EDUCATIONAL IMPACT

> "All television is educational television. The only question is, what is it teaching?" (Johnson, 1976)

Joan Ganz Cooney, the creator of *Sesame Street*, often paraphrased this remark when talking about the power of all forms of television (which I believe to be true for all forms of screen media) to entertain, model, inform, and teach. Children learn from entertainment television "regardless of a program's content—or purpose…" (Liebert, et.al., 1973).

What does the research show that they learn? A great deal of research was done in the 1960s, first on the effects of television violence on children's aggression, and later on pro-social messaging children learn from television modeling. For example:

> "Studies show… that exposure to the actions and values of others can change a child's willingness to aid others (Rosenhan & White, 1967) and his learning of language rules" (Liebert, Odom, Hill & Huff, 1969).

But it was the early summative research on *Sesame Street* that proved how much cognitive information young preschool children could actually learn from a television medium that, until then, was mainly used to sell products and to entertain.

Ball and Bogatz tested inner-city and middle class three-to-five-year-old preschoolers who watched *Sesame Street*. They found:

> "…first… that children who watched the most learned the most…. Second, the skills to which the program gave the most time and attention [literacy and numeracy skills] were, in almost every case, the skills best learned. Third, children viewing at home learned as much as children viewing in school under the supervision of a teacher. Fourth, the relationship of learning to amount of viewing held true across age, sex, geographical location, SES, mental age (measured by the Peabody Picture [vocabulary] test), and viewing at home or at school" (1970).

The Ball and Bogatz studies were the first of what would soon grow to over a thousand studies on record concerning *Sesame Street's* impact (see *G is for Growing*, Fish and Truglio, 2001 for some of the best of them).

Three studies are worth mentioning here, because, like the Heckman study mentioned above, they assemble a clear pattern of effects lasting beyond the preschool years.

In a three-year longitudinal study, entitled "the Early Window study," Wright et.al. found that *Sesame Street* viewing at ages two and three was positively associated with reading, math, vocabulary and school readiness at ages three and five. (2001)

Nicholas Zill reports that data from the 1993 National Household Educational Survey (NHES) found significant correlations between *Sesame Street* viewing and preschoolers' ability to recognize letters of the alphabet and tell connected stories.

Finally, and analogous to the Heckman study, various researchers re-contacted the preschool children whose *Sesame Street* viewing they had tracked ten to fifteen years earlier. The results of their studies showed that high school adolescents who had been frequent viewers of *Sesame Street* when they were preschoolers had significantly better grades in English, science and math; read more books for pleasure; perceived themselves as more competent in school; had higher motivation toward achievement; and expressed lower levels of aggressive attitudes.

How can we explain this? Here's what the researchers Huston, Anderson, et. al. say:

> "In fact it may be surprising to some that we found any association suggesting long-term effects of viewing. Obviously, watching *Sesame Street* cannot directly improve high school grades. High school examinations do not test students on number and letter identification or identifying which things are not like the others…. Rather, we believe that a related series of processes can be initiated by watching educational programs in the preschool years. Children who watch *Sesame Street* enter school not only with good academic skills, but also with a positive attitude toward education…. Early school success in turn fosters better learning and greater enthusiasm about school, leading to a trajectory of long-term achievement." (2001)

The evidence about lasting effects from an educational program delivered through screen media is similar to what Heckman found for quality early childhood non-media classroom interventions. And what do both of these preschool and educational media interventions have in common? "Skill begets skill…learning begets learning…motivation begets motivation…." And initiating young children early to a trajectory of learning has clear, measurable benefits.

And one more thing: what if quality educational interventions and quality educational media were combined and used in the classroom? Could that make a difference?

There is ample evidence that using "embedded multimedia"—that is, teaching methods that embed video content within teachers' lessons—can enhance learning. In fact Chambers, et. al. provide an overview worth sharing:

"For more than fifty years, educators and policymakers have been expectantly wait-ing for the video (DVD and CD as well) evolution in education. Indeed, research on educational programs such as *Sesame Street* (Bogatz & Ball, 1971; Fish & Truglio, 2001; Rice, Huston, Truglio, & Wright, 1990; Linebarger, Kosanic, Greenwood, & Doku, 2004) has shown positive effects of educational television for the reading and language development of young children. Yet video has remained a minor medium in the classroom, where it has been seen as a replacement for teacher in-struction rather than a tool for teachers.

In recent years, however, video has begun to appear in educational practice in a new form that has great potential for education reform. Video is one example of what Mayer calls "multimedia," instructional formats that combine words and pic-tures. Instead of replacing instruction, multimedia can be embedded in classroom instruction to enhance teachers' lessons. This "embedded multimedia" application is not widely known or used, but research on the practice has shown initial prom-ise." (2006).

Wouldn't the combination of powerful media used selectively in either the classroom or at home, together with strong educational interventions, potentially yield powerful effects for Jewish educa-tion? Shouldn't we apply the most successful lessons from general educational research data to Jewish education?

IMPLICATIONS FOR JEWISH EDUCATION: BARRIERS AND OPPORTUNITIES

Clearly, for me, these are rhetorical questions. Why wouldn't we take the best of what we have learned over the past forty years from early education and media research and apply it to Jewish education? What stands in the way? I'm not certain, but here are some hypotheses about barriers that need to be overcome:

First, it seems to me that Jewish institutions do not take either early preschool education or the potential of education via screen media seriously enough. We have seen that both have the potential to deliver cognitive and long-lasting messages to children and parents. The research is clear: media can supplement and supplant what children learn at home and/or what in-school caregivers teach judiciously and effectively in their classrooms.

Second, early Jewish preschool educational programs need to carefully plan what outcomes they want to deliver to the Jewish children in their care. Do the best of Jewish early childhood programs have curricular goals with measurable outcomes for their children? Early childhood Jewish educa-tion provides a unique entry-point to Jewish education and community, especially for unaffiliated Jewish parents and mixed couples. Why? Although this is an empirical question that a little market research could help answer, I venture that parents feel Jewish preschool education may offer more quality content compared to a general preschool program and is a relatively dogma-free introduction to Jewish heritage, language, culture and religion.

But how can we maximize this opportunity? Let's take one example that can benefit from the use of media, and greatly enhance the quality and marketability of Jewish preschools: the learning of Hebrew. Can the learning of Hebrew for Jewish children be made as attractive as, say, Chinese, or other second-language learning is for other American children? Can screen media-based programs help teach language skills? Is learning a second language helpful to learning general literacy skills and other languages? Yes, to all of the above.

Third, the Jewish educational community does not necessarily have the media skills to produce quality Jewish educational materials. However, these skills are not necessarily needed within the Jewish community; they can be found beyond it, and a partnership can be formed. *Sesame Street* was a shot-gun marriage between television producers with backgrounds in comedy, and educators and researchers with backgrounds in child development and psychology. As Tevye might have said: after twenty-five years, they learned to love each other! The challenge for the Jewish community is to form an independent, non-profit institution which can be creative and educational, pluralistic and self-sustaining, and free of fossilized thinking, while dedicated to the Jewish past, mindful about the Jewish present, and adventurous in educating about the Jewish future.

And that brings us to a fourth barrier: resources and structure. How will such an institution be funded and sustained? As one of my mentors, Eli Evans of the Revson Foundation, is wont to say, "If the vision is big enough and important enough, they will come." Unfortunately, that has not yet happened.

I remember the challenge faced by Joel Lurie Grishaver, a stellar media artist, at a CAJE conference over twenty years ago. He was showing his wonderful illustrations of Rashi's interpretations on "et Ha'Elokim hithalech Noach" –a hand extending from Heaven with a finger holding Noah's hand: an illustration of Joel's' creative rendering of Midrash for children. He needed support, encouragement, distribution help, and more. But there was too little support for his creativity using media back then for Jewish education. The Jewish community is fortunate that he chose a path to pursue publishing and his artistic creativity in other directions. But why did he have to?

The scope of this article is too narrow to appropriately explore this question. Suffice it to say that the Jewish community is too small to sustain a for-profit model to both produce, market, and distribute quality educational media. A project-by-project approach, like the successful *Shalom Sesame* series, is also not a sustainable model. More products are needed. An institution needs to have the resources to build on its success, to nurture creative talent, and to feed distribution outlets it has created. This does not mean specific projects should not be supported; rather, it means that something of greater significance is needed.

What I believe needs to be considered is a non–profit model, analogous perhaps to the one I know best: Sesame Workshop's model. The Workshop is a not-for-profit corporation which sustains itself with revenues from the following sources: non-restricted philanthropic grants and contributions; project specific restricted grants (e.g., funds to support *Rechov Sumsum* in Israel and *Shalom Sesame* in the U.S.); corporate sponsorship; revenues from broadcasters, licensing and product sales; and interest from an endowment it set up years ago. Such a model has allowed the Workshop to remain an independent educational presence in an ever-changing and competitive commercial media environment for close to forty years.

What would be the cost benefit of such an institution to the Jewish community? One only needs to consider the potential reach of media to know that cost of production and distribution can be amortized over large numbers of viewers/users. Early analyses of the cost benefits of *Sesame Street* in terms of initial dollars invested compared to numbers of children reached, showed the costs of the series to be pennies a day. Today, with versions of *Sesame Street* in China, India (with 150 million preschool children alone), and soon Indonesia, the reach and potential impact of an investment in media is greater still. Of course, the potential to reach a smaller Jewish population will certainly alter the cost benefit ratio, but media cuts across boundaries and can reach the affiliated and unaffiliated alike. It has tremendous potential to build critical bridges between Jews and people of other faiths and cultures, and this is especially true with new screen media opportunities.

What opportunities do new screen media offer Jewish education, and why is the time ripe today to address them?

In the world of media, there has been an explosion of new platforms on which to produce and distribute content to children and adults alike. There are the traditional platforms of Big Screen media (film, television, DVDs) and the ever-increasing smaller screen platforms (computers, handheld devices like iPods, handheld video games like the Xbox and Wii, cell phones). Content is often interchangeably available across platforms.

These new digital platform alternatives, especially broadband, allow for new opportunities for a Jewish educational media institution to reach affiliated and unaffiliated Jewish children throughout the country and throughout the world, without having to depend solely on large scale, big budget projects for film and television distribution.

Together with these new platforms comes an important shift in the way young people use media. Jenkins describes this shift as the creation of a participatory culture, in which children are no longer passive recipients of a one way flow of information from a media source. Instead, they are active "user-creators" of media. They respond and they initiate. They even create their own podcasts (2006).

In fact, new screen media can enable children to more deeply explore the rich tapestry of Jewish content and to become co-creators of materials. Now, with guidance, online or in the classroom, there is a unique opportunity to apply children's screen media experience to Jewish educational content.

For example:

- Children (and their parents) can learn Hebrew language skills interactively and at their own pace in order to communicate with each other;
- They can partake in inter-generational learning—
  - with young-adult mentors from the Birthright project who can teach from their first-hand Israel experience,
  - with older siblings, cousins, or friends who are studying for their Bar and Bat Mitzvah,
  - with grandparents, collecting stories about their personal Jewish histories;
- They can be presented with animated tales from the Midrash and be given the tools to interact with or create their own animated Midrashim—perhaps about Jewish futures—their visions of a world they want to live in, share with others and leave for kids like themselves;
- They can communicate with their peers in Israel, the Palestinian territories, Jordan or Egypt;
- They can learn, question and challenge each other about the core beliefs of Judaism, Islam and Christianity;
- They can be exposed to master storytellers and teachers who can convey values and challenge children to actively apply the values learned in a virtual world (or classroom) into real-life outreach programs.

The above ideas are just initial ramblings, but specific content ideas could be developed through an operational model similar to the one used successfully by Sesame Workshop for the past forty years. This model calls for some of the following:

- convening seminars—with content experts in Jewish education, teachers, and creative media producers
- attracting proven talent and nurturing new talent
- partnering and empowering educators, artists, and young technology mavens to co-create effective educational materials via media
- designing curriculum and testing outcomes
- researching experimentally produced materials through formative testing, to guarantee its appeal and comprehensibility, and summative testing to see if objectives are achieved.

In sum, the evidence is unassailable: the research is clear and consistent about the importance and life-long impact of both early childhood and educational media interventions. The time to systematically experiment with Jewish education through screen media could not be more opportune. The question now is one of will, imagination, and vision. Does the Jewish community have the desire to support such an endeavor?

In the second century C.E., Rabbi Yehuda Hanasi created a momentous "media" shift for Jewish education by redacting and writing the Mishna, which until then had been taught orally. If the rabbis who lived during the period of the redaction of the Mishna and Talmud were alive today, would they hesitate to use the media tools available to us for the education of future generations of our People? I doubt it.

As J. Robert Oppenheimer once said, "There are children playing in the streets who could solve some of my top problems in physics, because they have modes of sensory perception that I lost long ago." Indeed, children often have wisdom that we adults have lost, forgotten, or never had. If we give them the tools they need through the media they use, they may be able to not only solve our most difficult problems, but also inspire a new generation of creative, innovative, and impactful Jewish learning. Let's not miss this opportunity.

REFERENCES

Ball, S.J., & Bogatz, G.A. (1970). *The First Year of Sesame Street: An evaluation*. Princeton, N.J.: Educational Testing Service.

Ball, S.J. & Bogatz, G.A. (1971). *Sesame Street: A Continuing Evaluation*. *Princeton*, NJ: Educational Testing Service.

Chambers, B., Cheung, A.C.K., Madden, N.A., Slavin, R.E. & Gifford, R. (2006). "Achievement Effects of Embedded Multimedia in a Success for All Reading Program." *Journal of Educational Psychology*, 98, 1, 232-237

Fish, S.M.& Truglio, R.T. (2001). *"G" is for Growing: Thirty Years of Research on Children and Sesame Street*. Mahwah, NJ: Lawrence Erlbaum Associates, Inc.

Heckman, J. (2006) *Investing in Disadvantaged Young Children is an Economically Efficient Policy*. Paper presented at the Committee for Economic Development/The Pew Charitable Trusts/PNC Financial Services Group. Forum on "Building the Economic case for Investments in Preschool" New York.

Huston, A.C., Anderson, D.R., Wright, J.C., Linebarger, D.L., & Schmitt, K.L. (2001). Sesame Street Viewers as Adolescents: The Recontact Study. In S. M. Fish & R. T. Truglio (Eds.)., *"G" is for Growing: Thirty Years of Research on Children and Sesame Street*. Mahwah, NJ: Lawrence Erlbaum Associates. pp. 131-143

Jenkins, H. (2006). Confronting the Challenges of Participatory Culture: Media Education for the 21st Century. Chicago: MacArthur Foundation

Johnson, N. (1976). Quoted in Schramm, W. "The Second Harvest of Two Research-Producing Events: The Surgeon General's Inquiry and Sesame Street." *Proceedings of the National Academy of Education, 3*, pp 151–219.

Lesser, G., (1974). *Children and Television: Lessons from Sesame Street*. New York: Random House.

Liebert, R. M., Neale, J.M. & Davidson, E.S. (1973). *The Early Window: Effects of Television on Children and Youth*. New York: Pergamon Press.

Liebert, R.M., Odom, R.D., Hill, J.H. & Huff. R.L. (1969). "Effects of age and rule familiarity on the production of modeled language construction." *Developmental Psychology, 1, 2*, 108–112.

Linebarger, D. L., Kosanic, A. Z., Greenwood, C. R., & Doku, N. S. (2004). "Effects of viewing the television program Between the Lions on the emergent literacy skills of young children." *Journal of Educational Psychology, 96, 2*, 297–308.

Rice, M. L., Huston, A. C., Truglio, R., & Wright, L. C. (1990). "Words from Sesame Street: Learning vocabulary while viewing." *Developmental Psychology, 26, 3*, 421–428.

Rideout, V., Roberts, D. & Foehr, U. (2005). *Generation M: Media in the Lives of 8–18 year olds*. Washington, D.C.: Kaiser Family Foundation Study.

Rosenhan, D. & White. G,M, (1967). "Observation and rehearsal as determinants of pro-social behavior." *Journal of Personality and Social Psychology, 5, 4*, 424–431.

Schramm, W. (1976). "A Second Harvest of Two Research-Producing Events, the Surgeon General's Inquiry and *Sesame Street*." *The National Academy of Education, 3* 151–219.

Scramm, W., Lyle, J., & Parker, E.B. (1961). *Television in the Lives of Our Children*. Stanford, CA: Stanford University Press

_____ (2003). *Zero to Six: Electronic Media in the Lives of Infants, Toddlers, & Preschoolers*. Washington, D.C.: The Henry J Kaiser Foundation

Wright, J.C., Huston, A.C., Scantlin, R. & Kotler, J. (2001). The Early Window Project: Sesame Street Prepares Children for School. In S. M. Fish,. & R. T. Truglio (Eds.)., *"G" is for Growing: Thirty Years of Research on Children and Sesame Street*. Mahwah, NJ: Lawrence Erlbaum Associates. , pp. 97-114.

Zill, N. (2001). Does Sesame Street Enhance School Readiness? Evidence From a National Survey for Children. In S. M. Fish & R. T. Truglio (Eds.)., *"G" is for Growing: Thirty Years of Research on Children and Sesame Street*. Mahwah, NJ: Lawrence Erlbaum Associates., pp. 115-130.

Incorporating the Arts
in Jewish Education

Ofra Backenroth

The main challenge for introducing the arts into Jewish education is the fundamental belief that Jewish education is text-based. Traditionally it has been thought that teaching Jewish studies required text-reading and the mimetic learning of behavior. However, the ultimate goal of teaching does not end with transmission of knowledge and rituals, but entails cognitive objectives such as understanding and affective objectives such as transforming the spirit. Jewish schools want to contribute to students' spirituality as well as their knowledge and cultural literacy. The awareness of the power of the affect, attitudes, and emotions underscores the need for arts education as a crucial component of education for identity formation, spirituality, and a facilitator of better educational methods.

Expanding the arts curriculum in Jewish schools presents various challenges not only in terms of budget, space, scheduling time, and teacher hiring and training, but also raises questions about what an arts education in a Jewish environment should constitute. Should it be based on skills teaching, art appreciation or art history? What is the best way for the arts to be taught? Should they be taught in isolation as discrete disciplines or integrated into the Jewish studies curriculum? And, if the arts are integrated into the curriculum, how is this to be accomplished and what is the content?

This chapter will survey the most important recent research on the arts in general education and Jewish education including my own research of arts integration in Jewish education.

After completing a doctorate on the topic of the arts and Jewish education, my involvement in arts projects includes continuing research about educators who use the arts as a component of Jewish education. In addition to teaching graduate level courses, including one on the integration of the arts with Judaic studies, I am a member of a team that designs and contributes to MeltonArts.org, a website dedicated to the arts and Jewish education.

CONTEXTUALIZING THE ISSUE OF ARTS AND JEWISH EDUCATION

Through an exploration of the current research on the arts and Jewish education, this chapter will describe some of the challenges that Jewish education faces in its journey to introduce the arts within the educational systems, both formal and informal. Of particular importance will be the implication of using the arts in Jewish education and suggestions for future research.

Traditionally, the arts have been absent from the curricula, in Jewish schools or has been relegated to occasional visual art classes, choral music courses, or extra-curricular activities. Historically, Jewish day schools, overburdened by the extensive requirements of a dual curriculum, ignored the arts and many forms of experiential and creative learning as their focus was on the learning of texts and other core curriculum areas. Even in congregational schools and other after-school programs, the serious lack of time stood in the way of a meaningful arts education program. The demands of accomplishing all of the academic goals of the curriculum within the short time students are in schools require many decisions about what should be included in the curriculum and what should be discarded. Often, administrators see the arts only as an ancillary piece of the curricula and arts education such as visual art, music or drama are included only as discrete subjects and not as a means to teach content.

With the expansion of new Jewish day schools and research about the contributions of the arts to education in general, the arts are making their way back into Jewish schools and into the Jewish studies curriculum, both in day and congregational schools. This shift in attitude is not limited to the liberal Jewish circle. Atid, an orthodox education organization headed by Rabbi Chaim Brovender, is promoting the use of arts within the curriculum as an entry to Ahavat Hashem (Handelman and Saks, 2003).

Research in general education further informs us that the arts play a major role in helping schools surmount the challenges of a complex curriculum by becoming an integral part of the teaching process in every classroom. Consequently, Jewish policy makers are beginning to promote the inclusion of the arts as a valuable component in Jewish education in order to make Judaism and prayers more accessible to students and enhance Jewish studies with spirituality.

AN OVERVIEW OF RESEARCH IN GENERAL AND JEWISH EDUCATION

THE ARTS IN GENERAL EDUCATION

The ideas of child-centered education, creative expression, and the arts as integral to child development were introduced by the progressive education movement at the turn of the century by Dewey and reemerged during the seventies and eighties with the establishment of the American Council for the Arts, the John D. Rockefeller Education in the Arts Program, and the educational mandate of the National Endowment for the Arts. More recent research focuses even greater attention on the contributions of the arts to cognition, particularly in students' achievements, retention of knowledge, effective assessment, and better teaching methods.

The benefits of integrating the arts in education are well grounded in research. Project Zero, launched in 1967 at Harvard University culminating with the publishing of *Frames of Mind* by Gardner (1983), brought the use of the arts in education to public awareness by advancing the idea that the linguistic and the logical-mathematical abilities cannot be regarded as the only indicators of human intelligence. Gardner presented his theory of multiple intelligences which originally posited that there are seven intelligences: linguistic, logical-mathematical, spatial, bodily-kinesthetic, musical, interpersonal, and intrapersonal. He later added the naturalist and existential intelligences to bring the number to nine. Based upon this model of multiple intelligences, teachers are urged to legitimate the use of alternative methods of teaching including using art, music, and movement in class. By encouraging teachers to expand their current teaching repertoire to include a broader range of methods, material, and techniques, they will be able to reach an ever more diverse range of learners.

As interest in the arts grew and research in cognitive development and brain research found new evidence to support the value of teaching the arts (Eisner, 1998), new experimental programs were established motivated to use the theory as the foundation for new curricular materials for education. In 1985, Project Zero, based on the multiple intelligences theory collaborated with the Educational Testing Service in Pittsburgh to create Art Propel (http://www.pz.harvard.edu/Research/PROPEL.htm). The project was built on the conviction that the arts teach content and that they exercise not just the hand and heart, but the mind as well. The project's goal was to measure the impact of the arts on assessment in schools. A subsequent program, Project Spectrum (*http://www.pz.harvard.edu/Research/Spectrum.htm*), was based on the assumption that every child has the potential to develop strength in one or several content areas and that it is the responsibility of the educational system to discover and nurture these inclinations. Project Spectrum emphasizes identifying children's areas of strength and using this information as the basis for an individualized educational program. Spectrum researchers design assessment activities in seven different domains of knowledge: language, math, music, art, social understanding, science, and movement.

Blurring the lines between learning and assessment, grounding assessment in engaging real-life situations, applying assessment through different intelligences, and focusing on children's strengths rather than on weaknesses allows teachers to use hands-on activities in the domains of visual arts, music, dance, and drama, as well as on games, machinery, and physical activity.

Further research substantiates what the theorists suggest. Jensen (2001), surveying current brain research, argues that the arts enhance the process of learning. In addition to their effect on the sensory, cognitive, and motor capacities, the arts promote self-discipline and motivation, teach aesthetic awareness, and improve emotional expression. He further contends that music helps with recall and the ability to retrieve information. Creating artistic representations of texts promotes long-lasting learning, improves retention, and eliminates "fragile knowledge" (Perkins, 1993). Researchers claim that students' general attitudes towards learning and school improves as a result of a challenging but enjoyable activity, and that learning art skills forces mental 'stretching' useful to other areas of learning (Csikszentmihalyi, 1996).

Learning doesn't take place in isolation from feelings, which indicates that being emotionally literate is as important for learning as instruction in math and reading. Therefore, the emotions of students cannot be treated as irrelevant and intrusive in academic studies, but need to be incorporated into teaching. Recent studies have shown that there is a strong correlation between the cognitive and affective domains and that the arts contribute to the development of the affective domain (Jensen, 2001).

THE ARTS AND JEWISH EDUCATION

As a relatively new field, research on the use of the arts in Jewish education has focused mostly on the affective domain incorporating the teaching of Jewish studies and rituals through drama, music, visual art, and dance. The goal is to make old texts relevant to students' lives, to create personal connections to the sacred texts, and to enhance spirituality. This is different from the world of general education where the studies focus on the arts in terms of students' achievements and assessment.

Two studies explore the integration of the arts to the entire curriculum of Jewish studies in contrast to the use of a single art form within the curriculum. Epstein (2004) suggests that Jewish educators often too narrowly define the parameters of what counts as a text within the classroom maintaining that visual images such as a painting or a student-generated tableau can be read as textual commentary upon the Bible. Epstein underscores that teachers who use drama-related activities help students to more fully express themselves in conversations about the text. Similarly, Miller (1999) and Milgrom (1992) suggest that teaching art skills in conjunction with text skills enriches the way students interpret the text and helps them make a personal connection with Torah. Both demonstrate that art making is a legitimate strategy for traditional Jewish learning. The students are encouraged to work from an intellectual cognitive framework through succeeding stages in order to develop an understanding of the text through creative and affective responses. To keep students accountable for true understanding of the texts, they are asked to return to the text following the creative activity and re-visit and re-test their interpretations.

Hascal (2001) demonstrates how dance, as a learning-by-doing approach, provides an alternative way to help students recall and sequence events in the Bible. She further suggests that interpreting the events through dance allows the student to visualize the events and therefore gain better understanding. During the discussions that follow the students demonstrate abstract thinking, renewed interests in the texts, and the ability to ask new questions. The most important finding of the study is the students' ability to engage in hermeneutic methods of text study such as word analysis, juxtaposition, and filling the gaps in the text.

In a study on integration and the arts, Goldberg (2001) identifies learning with the arts and learning through the arts as two different models of integrating art and learning. The first is the theme-based unit that maintains the integrity of each of the disciplines with the arts used to convey and to intensify what was learned in the content-based subjects. The second model is an interdisciplinary model in which the arts are fully integrated into the school curriculum. In this case, the arts are studied not only as a distinct discipline which includes art history, appreciation, and making art, but are also used as facilitators in studying texts, history, rituals and other areas.

Backenroth (2004b) examined schools that integrate the study of the arts in Judaic studies identifying several models of teaching the arts in Jewish schools. First, most Jewish schools have art and music teachers who work in isolation and participate in school activities mostly during the Jewish holidays and celebrations. They depend on a few Judaic teachers who choose to work with the arts teachers or they have the necessary skills to create Jewish content and arts integrated units. A few high schools have an elaborate arts curriculum both during and after school hours that include chamber ensembles, bands, dance troupes, and an extensive visual art department; however, they mostly operate as isolated entities.

There are arts-based Jewish day schools where art activities are considered to be an integral component of the teaching methodology. In this model of teaching, the arts are utilized in all aspects of the curriculum from making connections with the texts to helping with emotional issues and nurturing spirituality. In addition to teaching art skills, the arts are used to teach Hebrew, Classical texts from Talmud to Bible, as well as the holidays and rituals. The arts are used to teach Israel, to shape Jewish identity, to promote spirituality and to enhance the experience of prayers. In addition, students learn about the arts as a body of knowledge on its own, where music, art, and dance are aspects of Jewish life in and outside of Israel.

Backenroth found that using the arts fulfills the needs of the school's population and provides a method of teaching, a way of learning, an outlet of expression, and creativity for the teachers as well as for students. She maintains that when the arts are embedded within the larger curriculum, they often serve as the glue that holds the secular and the Jewish curriculum together. Integration encompasses the entire curriculum and facilitates in highlighting the commonalities as well as the tensions between the Jewish and the secular world. Additionally, she maintains that the arts are a vehicle to deliver the "hidden curriculum." In every school there is an explicit goal to teach content, but at the same time, curriculum deals implicitly with other issues like self-expressiveness, creativity, spirituality, feminism, Jewish values and ethics, to name only a few. Using the arts, schools can subliminally articulate the importance of these issues within the education of its students.

IMPLICATIONS AND RECOMMENDATIONS

In the last few years, there has been an increase in the interest in the arts by policy makers. A few recent initiatives in the arts include the 2006 Jewish Educators Assembly annual conference which was dedicated to the arts, central agencies for Jewish Education that have held arts-focused seminars and professional development programs in the arts, graduate programs in Jewish education that offer classes in the arts and Jewish education, new Jewish camps founded on an arts theme, and an unprecedented surge in artist Beit Midrash, where scholars and visual artists team-teach Jewish texts and students create artistic interpretations of these texts. Two examples of the artist Beit Midrash are at the Skirball Center at Temple Emanuel, in New York City led by the artist Toby Kahn and Rabbi Leon Morris, and at Beth Shalom, in Teaneck NJ led by the artist Harriet Finck and Ann Lapidus Lerner.

However, it is also important to note that there is confusion about what arts and Jewish education means. Does it mean teaching art skills or appreciation? Does it mean teaching art history? Is arts education exclusively about the Jewish heritage and the study of ritual objects? Is it the study of Jewish artists, musicians, and dancers? Does it mean an occasional art project for the holidays? Or does it mean deepening text-understanding and enhancing spirituality? To move from the former to an integrated Jewish arts curriculum, a school or community may implement the following strategic approach:

- Establish a well-articulated vision for the creation of a strong arts-integrated curriculum
- Provide strong leadership from administrators and board members committed to the idea of teaching through the arts
- Support the faculty as they implement a successful arts-integrated curriculum.
- Provide resources for curriculum development through funding, writing, and testing a national curriculum for using the arts in Jewish education
- Create internal structures of support to assist schools as they implement an art-integrated curriculum which includes mentoring and continuous staff development.
- Enable teachers in cross discipline teams to create art-integrated units with the assistance of the arts specialists and visiting artists

Implementing an arts-integrated curriculum poses great challenges but it promises great rewards in terms of reaching the most important educational goals for Jewish education: enhancing spirituality, creating strong Jewish identity, building a foundation for future Jewish engagement as teens and adults, integrating Judaism into daily life, and creating a culture of knowledgeable and involved Jews.

ADDITIONAL RESEARCH QUESTIONS

Research on the arts and Jewish education is scarce. Additional research will enable the field to become more integrated into the mainstream of the Jewish educational arena by demonstrating the impact that the arts will have on creating stronger Jewish identity among our students. A few of the key issues that should guide the research include:

- What is the impact of a strong arts education program in engendering stronger Jewish identity formation?
- What is the impact of arts education in strengthening student attitudes towards Jewish studies?
- What is the impact of arts education on language acquisition?
- How will the use of the arts strengthen the overall educational programs?
- How will the use of arts education strengthen students understanding of Jewish texts and other aspects of Jewish knowledge?
- What is the impact of a strong arts education program on the attitudes of teachers?
- What types of professional development will create an integrated educational program that involves the arts?
- How will an arts education program impact the culture of the school, the synagogue and/or the family?

FUTURE DIRECTIONS

In order to underscore the importance of the arts in Jewish education there needs to be agreement on the following:

- Promoting the concept that the arts are a primary context for learning and sharing ideas
- Giving the arts an important role within the overall structure of the educational program
- Creating comprehensive educational programs in universities and colleges to prepare teachers to integrate the arts into their classrooms
- Establishing the importance of the arts in Jewish education for school professionals, volunteer leadership and parents
- Providing intensive professional development programs for teachers that combine arts education strategies with working in teams with other teachers
- Developing appropriate materials and curricula for use throughout the Jewish educational system
- Encouraging more research on arts and Jewish education

CONCLUSION

Research in general education highlights a strong correlation between experiences in the arts, students' and teachers' satisfaction, and students' achievement. It further shows that there is a correlation among the cognitive and the affective domains. Similar research in Jewish education demonstrates the merits that integration of the arts contributes to making deeper connections to Jewish texts and enriching Jewish spiritual life. Experiencing, observing, and engaging in the arts should be integrated into every school's curriculum. In so doing, recognition will be given to the importance that:

- Integration of the arts improves education in the cognitive and the affective realms
- Using the arts contributes to the spiritual life of individual Jews and of Jewish schools

- Using the arts improves school culture
- Implementing the arts requires articulated vision, strong leadership, teacher professional development and mentoring, and community support

LARGER CONTEXT

This chapter explores the way arts education is implemented in Jewish schools, what is being taught through the arts, and how it changes schools and teachers' practices. The issue of teaching through the arts is a subset of a larger issue of school change. Traditionally, art, music, dance, and drama teachers worked in isolation from the rest of the school faculty. The research explored in this chapter strongly indicates the merits of integrating the arts in the curriculum of the school, particularly in Jewish studies, as a valuable tool for establishing stronger Jewish schools and educating our youth to be more engaged in Jewish life.

ANNOTATED BIBLIOGRAPHY

Backenroth, O. A. (2004a). "Art and Rashi: A portrait of a Bible teacher." *Journal of Religious Education, 99*(2), 151–166. The article examines the practice of teaching content-based disciplines through visual art and how teaching through the arts acknowledges students diversity and helps them to make personal connections with the biblical texts.

Backenroth, O. A. (2004b). *The Blossom School: Teaching Judaism in an arts-based school.* Unpublished Doctoral dissertation, The Jewish Theological Seminary, New York. The study examines how the arts can be used to achieve the goals of Jewish education: knowledge of Jewish texts and culture, shaping Jewish identity, and enhancing spirituality through an arts-based, complex multi-disciplinary curriculum.

Brovender, C. (2003). Towards Ahavat Hashem: Art and the religious experience: issues and challenges in contemporary Torah education. In S. Handelman & J. Saks (Eds.), *Wisdom from all my teachers: Issues and challenges in Torah education.* Jerusalem: Atid/Urim Publications. The author argues that the arts serve as a means to improve engagement with Jewish rituals and prayer, and a gateway to learning Jewish texts.

Epstein, S. D. (2004). "Reimagining literacy practices: Creating living *midrash* from ancient texts through tableau." *Journal of Jewish education, 70* (1&2), 60–73. The author explores how participatory drama enabled students to actively question Bible and to grapple with the texts' complexities.

Hascal, L. (2001). *Dancing the Torah: The role of performance in extending understanding.* Unpublished Master of Education, York University, Toronto. The author maintains that teaching biblical texts through dance utilizes hermeneutics techniques similar to those employed by the Rabbis, helps in internalization of meaning, strengthens recall, and develops abstract and symbolic thinking.

Milgrom, J. (1992). *Handmade midrash.* Philadelphia: The Jewish Publication Society. The author presents her methodology of teaching Jewish texts through the arts. The innovative method does not assume art skills, but rather allows everyone to create an art-*midrash*.

Miller, H. (1999). "Visual reflective learning: A new framework for teaching art in Jewish Studies." *The Journal of Progressive Judaism, 13,* 67–78. The paper, based on the author's research on teaching biblical texts through the arts, suggests that teaching art skills and text skills improves students' understanding and retention of Jewish texts.

REFERENCERS

Brovender, C. (2003). Towards Ahavat Hashem: Art and the religious experience: issues and challenges in contemporary Torah education. In S. Handelman & J. Saks (Eds.), *Wisdom from all my teachers: Issues and challenges in Torah education.* Jerusalem: Atid/Urim Publications.

Czikszentmihalyi, M. (1996). *Creativity: Flow and the psychology of discovery and invention.* New York: Harper Collins Publishers.

Eisner, E. (1998). *The kind of schools we need.* Portsmouth, NH: Heinemann.

Gardner, H. (1983). *Frames of mind: The theory of multiple intelligences.* New York: BasicBooks.

Goldberg, M. (2001). *Arts and learning: An integrated approach to teaching and learning in multicultural and multilingual settings.* New York: Longman.

Hascal, L. (2001). *Dancing the Torah: The role of performance in extending understanding.* Unpublished Master of Education, York University, Toronto.

Jensen, E. (2001). *Art with the brain in mind.* Alexandria, Virginia: ASCD.

Milgrom, J. (1992). *Handmade midrash.* Philadelphia: The Jewish Publication Society.

Perkins, D. (1993). *Smart Schools.* New York: Simon and Schuster.

Experiential Jewish Education

Joseph Reimer & David Bryfman

For over a century Jewish education in North America has proceeded along two parallel tracks: instruction in schools and socialization through contexts such as settlement houses, summer camps and Israel experiences (Sarna, 2006). As the field has matured, Jewish educators adopted the terms "formal" and "informal" education to describe these parallel tracks.

In this new century, it is time to question this simplistic distinction. Schools no longer limit their educational work to formal instruction and contexts such as camps and Israel experiences employ many different methods to accomplish their educational goals. While it is vital that Jewish education continues to operate through these different contexts, it may no longer be wise to divide those contexts into two parallel tracks (Zeldin, 2006). Rather, a more complex descriptive matrix is needed to map the terrain of Jewish education.

This chapter is one small step in that direction. Our focus is on "experiential Jewish education" which we understand to be an approach that can be employed in all these different settings. True, we will cite examples from what we now call "informal" settings but only because those are the contexts that we know best. Professor Joseph Reimer is the Director for Informal Jewish Eductaion at Brandeis University. David Bryfman is a Doctoral student in Education and Jewish Studies at NYU focusing on the Jewish identity development of adolescents.

In principle what we are describing applies to any context in which educators seek to challenge participants to build Jewish knowledge and commitment from the basis of their experiences in this world. Ours is an integrative approach that asks what different contexts have in common and how Jewish educators who identify with those different contexts can learn from one another to promote experiential Jewish learning.

Experiential Jewish education is not a familiar phrase and our approach may be new for some readers. But we borrow freely from research and theory in a number of different domains to suggest that the time is ripe to rethink how we engage Jewish learners in discovering the power of Jewish concepts and practices to enrich the way they live their lives.

BEGINNING WITH INFORMAL JEWISH EDUCATION

There is a long oral tradition that defines informal educational practices in settings as diverse as Jewish camps, JCCs, youth movements, Hillel foundations and Israel experiences. But there has been a reluctance to commit that tradition to writing and to a systematic analysis of informal Jewish education. That reluctance has been overcome by Barry Chazan (2003), who has spelled out a clear, defensible philosophy of informal Jewish education. Building on the work of Bernard Reisman (1979), Chazan has developed these key points:

1. While informal Jewish education takes place in many distinctive settings and is identified with well-known methods of educational practice, it is best thought of as an approach to Jewish education rather than being identified with any particular settings or methods. It is this approach that unifies the field.

2. Informal Jewish education is poorly named because "informal" suggests both a high degree of informality and an opposition to formal education. Clearly many informal educators are

informal in their approach and would not choose to work in a school. But Chazan cautions against seeing those tendencies as defining the field.

3. Informal education is often identified with feeling rather than cognition and with fun rather than serious learning. While Chazan embraces the role that fun and feelings play in informal education, he also believes that serious cognitive learning has its place and would reject easy dichotomies between feeling and thinking, fun and learning.

4. Informal education is often thought of as taking place spontaneously as the educator seizes on a teachable moment to impress participants with his/her deep Jewish commitments. While informal educators do need the skills to seize upon such moments, Chazan emphasizes that much of the work of informal educators involves serious preparation to structure the environment so that the spontaneous can occur. What appears as magic moments result from good educational planning by seasoned professionals

At the heart of Chazan's approach is a fundamental commitment, derived from Dewey (1938), to learning from experience. Informal education begins with the learner's experiences. However, we are not talking about isolated experiences, but providing an overall blueprint of Jewish experiences that participants can anticipate as part of a well-planned informal Jewish educational program. Those planned experiences should take place in a stable, supportive educational environment whose very culture educates. It is a place where the participants can breathe in the air of Jewish values. In that environment participants should have as their role models holistic Jewish educators who teach by example and know how to shape the experience of others. These educators' genuine interest in the participants' lives and their openness to sharing their own commitments forms the soil from which the values of this educational approach grow.

It is hard to read Reisman and Chazan and not be impressed with the seriousness of their message. But while Chazan labels this approach "informal Jewish education," Reisman refers to the same approach as "Jewish experiential education." Chazan states that "informal Jewish education is rooted in a belief that the experience is central to the individual's Jewish development" (2003); but he does little to explain how "experience" is actually educative. By not tackling these knotty questions, both Reisman and Chazan have left this field in a bit of a conceptual bind.

DISTINGUISHING INFORMAL FROM EXPERIENTIAL JEWISH EDUCATION

In our view Chazan has made a significant contribution, but is off the mark in referring to this approach as a "philosophy of informal Jewish education." When we have looked at how the term "informal education" is used in the general education literature, it does not map well to Chazan's usage. Second, if we were to follow the logic of his argument, we would have to conclude that in practice most informal Jewish educators do not meet all of the criteria which he has set as integral for characterizing "informal Jewish education." It is self-defeating to set such lofty criteria for what constitutes "informal Jewish education" and we prefer to create a classification that is more inclusive of what we observe educators doing in their regular practice.

We therefore suggest that "informal Jewish education" be used as a broad umbrella term that refers to the familiar settings of Jewish education outside of schools. We will use "experiential Jewish education" as the term to describe what educators do to promote experientially-based Jewish learning. We hypothesize that experiential Jewish learning involves three distinct initiatives, each with its own set of goals:

- Recreation
- Socialization
- Challenge

> *Recreation—As recreation, experiential Jewish education aims to provide its participants with social comfort, fun and belonging in a Jewish context.* Experiential Jewish education operates primarily as a set of leisure-time activities. Participants voluntarily choose to participate in the programs that are offered. They must enjoy these activities or they will cease to attend. As recreation,

Jewish experiential education provides safe space for Jews to enjoy the company of other Jews in pursuing common cultural activities.

Socialization—*As socialization, experiential Jewish education aims to provide the knowledge, skills and attitudes to be an active member of the Jewish community.* When people feel part of a social unit, they begin to identify with its procedures, rules and world view. They want to belong and become an identifiable "member" of that unit. We call that process of identification "socialization." In the Jewish world, we encourage participants to identify with a Jewish group and to internalize those behaviors, attitudes and feelings that characterize members of that group. We also encourage their identifying with the Jewish people in some broader sense.

Challenge—*As experiential educators, Jewish educators aim to encourage participants to undertake the challenge of stretching themselves and growing towards a more complex participation in one's Jewish life.* Because there is a lot more to Judaism than participating skillfully in the activities of one's Jewish camp or youth movement, experiential educators need to motivate individuals to stretch beyond their comfort zone and creatively explore a variety of Jewish modes of expression. The goal is to deepen and personalize individuals' Jewish experiences so they feel they are on a Jewish journey and are not simply a member of a Jewish club.

To explore how these three initiatives might operate, let's take the example of a group's singing Jewish songs. How might teaching Jewish songs in an informal setting differ in terms of goals depending on which of these three initiatives is guiding the educator's practice?

At the *recreational level*, the primary goal is to create an environment in which all the participants are comfortable singing with one another. The song leader might choose songs that everyone knows and can enjoy. It does not really matter how well participants sing as long as they are enjoying singing with other Jews. It does not even matter if all the songs are Jewish songs, for singing popular American songs also works well when social togetherness and having fun define the primary goals of the event.

At the *socialization level*, the primary goal is to have the participants identify as Jews singing Jewish songs. The song leader might introduce some familiar songs from Israel. Here the words do matter for the goal is to identify with Israel. Singing the song will become enjoyable once the participants learn the words and music. Educators at this level usually aim for a balance between what is enjoyable and comfortable and what will help reinforce the Jewish identities of the members of the group.

At the level of *challenge*, exploration *is* the point. This can take many forms. Someone might introduce a more complex arrangement of an old, familiar song. Perhaps a song leader demands greater skill in learning how to sing a Jewish song in the "right way." Perhaps the group strives to sing with great spiritual intensity. All these moves involve greater concentration and learning; but when the participants rise to these challenges, they often feel more accomplished and satisfied.

We claim that each of these initiatives has its own integrity and value. We cannot imagine how any program in Jewish education could dispense with the recreational level or skip over the socialization level. All three initiatives are necessary aspects of a holistic Jewish education. At the same time we are privileging the level of challenge as most fully embodying the philosophic approach that Chazan spells out. We do so because we believe in the values of exploration and growth (Csikszentmihalyi, 1997) and want to see experiential Jewish education aim to challenge Jews to creatively engage with their Judaism (Kaplan, 1934).

EXPERIENTIAL JEWISH LEARNING

Some educators might object to our approach and say: "These are all examples of experiential Jewish education. Singing is an experiential act. The difference is in the degree of difficulty and challenge, but all singing is experiential."

That is a valid objection, but we are trying to distinguish having an experience from experiential learning. Singing around a camp fire can be a wonderfully rich experience. But is it designed to promote Jewish learning? We think not. The value and intention of such an experience is recreational: it builds good group feeling and social comfort. That is all for the good, but not the same as experiential Jewish learning. For learning involves exploration, risk and breaking new cognitive and emotional grounds.

It is much harder to distinguish between socialization and learning from challenge. Sociologists like Berger and Luckmann (1967) would argue the validity of our distinction. For socialization does involve new social-cognitive learning. An educator cannot get to the level of challenge without passing through socialization.

But we are following the psychologist L.S. Vygotsky (1978) who proposed that educators think of creating a "zone of proximal development" in which participants can be guided and supported to try out new learning that may move them towards the levels of their potential development. In simpler terms, we are distinguishing between when an educator is reinforcing what participants already know and value and when she is challenging what participants know and promoting their development towards a more complex understanding of and a deeper spiritual bond with their Judaism. *We view experiential Jewish education as more than reinforcing of existing commitments. It should aim as well to inspire participants to experience Jewish living at its creative best.*

In our view it is not enough for experiential Jewish education to provide "the Jewish air" that participants can breathe. That is a fine goal for Jewish socialization. But engaged Jewish youth will grow into the creative leaders of tomorrow's Jewish community only if today they learn to deal with complexity and risk. Experiential Jewish education is uniquely positioned to promote learning from challenge. Whether they are struggling with how to alleviate world hunger or bridge the gaps between diverse Jewish populations, engaged youth need to experience their Judaism as a serious arena for generating substantive responses to the deepest challenges their generation will face.

OVERVIEW OF RELATED RESEARCH

In a field that is conceptually underdeveloped, the scarcity of literature on informal and experiential Jewish education is not surprising. What surprises us is the lack of research which considers the variety of informal Jewish education contexts as constituting a single field. Very few researchers have recognized that the various informal educational settings constitute a singular field of experiential Jewish education.

Only the work of Chazan (2003), based on the earlier work of Reisman (1979), has attempted to define the field of informal Jewish education and articulate the elements that constitute this endeavor. A second attempt to explain experiential Jewish education is found in Reisman and Reisman (2002) which includes articles by various academics and practitioners that appeared previously in the May, 2001 edition of *Sh'ma*, entitled, "Informal Education: Practitioners' Perspectives."

In recent years, spurred largely by the findings of the 1990 National Jewish Population Survey, there has been an increased interest in the role in which informal Jewish education plays in the identity development of young Jews. The most ambitious of all experiential educational programs has been the Taglit-Birthright Israel programs, involving 100,000 young adult Jews. The most recent study of the Birthright Israel experience reports that the program is "achieving its fundamental goals of building Jewish identity, as a sense of Peoplehood, and a connection to Israel" (Saxe, Sasson, & Shahar, 2006, p.2). These findings have been echoed in the most recent works focusing on Jewish residential summer camps that analyze why the camping environment can have a powerful influence on the development of positive Jewish identity (Lorge & Zola, 2006; Sales & Saxe, 2004).

The theme of positive Jewish identity development also framed the chapter about the field in *What We Know About Jewish Education*. Sporadic articles have also appeared in popular publications that have largely focused on the contexts and their impact on Jewish identity rather than on the processes taking place as part of experiential Jewish education.

Given the impressive number of informal Jewish educational programs available, the lack of literature dedicated to this field is of significant concern. Yet more dollars than ever before are being spent on developing informal education programs in North America. This disparity is tempered somewhat by anecdotal evidence suggesting that informal Jewish education organizations are conducting internal evaluations of their programming. When done well, evaluation studies allow us to learn more about which factors contribute to educational effectiveness.

In recent years several institutions of higher learning have begun programs that deal specifically with the broader phenomenon on experiential Jewish education. These include Brandeis University, Hebrew Union College, the Jewish Theological Seminary and the American Jewish University. The Cohen Center at Brandeis University has taken a leading role in a wide variety of evaluation studies in the area of Israel experience and educational programs.

Given the lack of attention to experiential Jewish education as a whole, it is necessary to move beyond the limited research in the specific field and seek out other literature which informs the field. The publication of *Learning in Places: The Informal Education Reader*, edited by Bekerman, Burbules and Silberman-Keller (2006) is the most recent general education book which should influence experiential Jewish education. This book illustrates several ways in which informal education can transform current educational practices into more powerful learning experiences.

Looking further afield it is clear that many of the theoretical underpinnings and practical applications of other educational contexts resonate with experiential Jewish education. Three such fields are outdoor education, museum education and the use of technology in education. By highlighting core components of these fields we are able to broaden our understanding of experiential Jewish education and the various challenges which it faces.

In the United States the term experiential education is most commonly associated with outdoor education or adventure learning. In recent years Jewish summer camps have invested significant amounts of money in ropes courses, climbing towers, adventure equipment and the training that accompanies such activities. But while Jewish summer camps often offer these activities, these are not the only features which link adventure learning and Jewish summer camps. The outdoor education movement highlights physically challenging experiences, primarily within peer group frameworks as integral to the moral development of individual youth. While rarely relying on such survival challenges, experiential Jewish education has cultivated group experiences as a means of socializing individuals within a broader set of communal norms. While one would be hard-pressed to claim that rock climbing should be equated with the struggle to analyze a complex ethical dilemma, the concept of "challenge," albeit dependent on context, operates within both contexts. The young Jewish person who struggles to navigate his/her personal identity in the broader context of Jewish tradition at least metaphorically resembles the Boy Scout, who, with compass in hand, attempts to find his way back to base camp. For Jewish education to reach the level of experiential education espoused in outdoor education, it would need to elevate challenge as a fundamental goal and look to stretching learners beyond their comfort zones in many experiential activities.

A personal experience of learning is also the guiding philosophy behind a significant current movement within museum education. This philosophy advocates that the role of the exhibit is to actively engage patrons to construct their own knowledge based on the display rather than the museum providing all information for the learner. This is commonly adopted in the genre of children's and science museums which have become regular features in the lives of many young learners. In a recent visit to the Chabad-sponsored Jewish Children's Museum in Brooklyn, we saw scores of young children engaged in learning Jewish history, values and traditions through a hands-on approach to learning. They were laughing and smiling as they eagerly moved from exhibit to exhibit.

There is much that the experiential Jewish educator can learn from these museum displays. In the Children's Museum, the children are learning with the display, and not necessarily from it. This does not imply that the educator is absent from the learning experience. In both the interactive museum and classroom, the display and the educator are integral to both learning processes. Their role is to facilitate the learner's individual experience and not adopt a stance in which they are the purveyors of all knowledge. But the challenge for educators who develop museum exhibits is to consider what the child at the museum has learned from their interaction with the display and how the educator can help that learning advance and connect to other learning contexts.

Within experiential Jewish education the educator is sometimes referred to as a *madrich*, a word whose Hebrew root is "way." The implication being that the educator's role is to show the way for learners rather than direct them down a specific path. Just as the museum does not forsake content, the experiential Jewish educator must also strive to ensure that important knowledge is not forsaken even as the educator invests more in the process of learning and less on traditional means of assessing knowledge gained.

Experiential Jewish educators also need to pay greater attention to current trends in technology. Current advances in the digital age have tremendous potential to impact both the practical and theoretical aspects of the experiential Jewish world. Educators need to know about technology to remain relevant to the lives of the learner, but they also can take advantage of new theories and resources that new technology offers. The plethora of Jewish websites that fill the internet may disguise the fact that, in general, Jewish education has been slow to adopt new technologies. Only very recently have Jewish organizations begun to consider, for example, the benefits of iPods and "MySpace" style communities.

Current theories behind advances in the uses of technology can greatly benefit the experiential Jewish educator. For example, a recent discussion with an interactive designer revealed an innovative digital billboard game proposed to appear in Times Square. Using their cell phone key-pads, pedestrians will be able to uncover matching squares to reveal a potential prize from a major cosmetics company. This level of interactivity is new to the world of advertising but may be at the forefront of future marketing strategies. Interactivity has also been vital in the video game industry, which is predicated on a concept of *teleprescence*, the experience of being present in an environment by means of a communication medium that could improve learners' motivation and increase the meaningfulness and desire to be part of the learning environment (Winn & Jackson, 1999).

Edwin Schlossberg (1998) defines interactive design as that which involves the audience in a compositional or collaborative experience that has meaning. Whether it be playing a video game or interacting with a digital billboard, this level of interactivity is designed to allow learners to enter into a state of flow—learning which requires concentration, high skills, a sense of control and satisfaction, all of which enable the participant to become immersed in an activity (Csikszentmihalyi, 1997). The challenge for experiential Jewish educators will be to create sophisticated programming that can engage youth at that level of intensity in meaningful Jewish experiences.

In these examples of outdoor education, museum education and technology we can see how the field of experiential Jewish education can benefit from research conducted in other fields. These are by no means the only spheres of learning that experiential Jewish education can learn from. Studies within education, sociology, psychology, anthropology, to name only a few fields of research, should all contribute to our broader understanding of experiential Jewish education.

We are hopeful the day will come when experiential Jewish education will have a literature of its own. Ultimately, it is possible to imagine a time when the relationship would become reciprocal, with practices from the experiential Jewish education world also informing other fields within broader experiential education.

IMPLICATIONS AND/OR POLICY RECOMMENDATIONS

Experiential Jewish education has been plagued by a lack of definition resulting in vague goals being established for the field as a whole. As a result educators have trouble generating identifiable benchmarks by which to assess their accomplishments. Often they are left counting the number of attendees and the return rate to subsequent events. Those numbers surely matter, but they tell little about the educational value of a program.

Understanding that experiential educational programs operate on three distinct levels can help clarify the goals and effectiveness of these programs. One can ask about any given program:

  (a) On a recreational level, were the participants made to feel socially comfortable? Did they enjoy the company of others? Did they find the activities engaging and stimulating? Did they have fun coming to this event and are they likely to return for more?

(b) On a socialization level, did the participants begin to identify with this group of people? Might they want to deepen their connections to them? Was it clear to them that this was a Jewish event? Were there sufficient opportunities for them to engage with Jewish symbols, practices and values and begin to make them their own?

(c) On a challenge level, were there opportunities to try new ways of expressing one's Judaism? Were there new Jewish ideas or practices that some may have experienced for a first time? Were there other kinds of people to interact with and learn from? Was there time to reflect on what those Jewish experiences meant to participants?

Not every program needs to meet in equal measure all three levels; but every educator needs to be aware of what he or she is aspiring to and what success will look like. Surely, though, best practice in this field should be defined as meeting a variety of clear goals on all three levels.

- Experiential Jewish education has been short on challenge. Educators facing difficulties in marketing their programs often respond by focusing on recreation. They want to be sure that participants will have fun. But they fail to consider that there are so many ways to have fun in our culture that Jewish programming may do better by focusing on unique challenges that will draw niche markets. That is what museums and adventure education often do with positive results. Jewish educators need to reconsider their efforts to provide recreation where what they offer is not unique and instead develop niche areas where their offerings would be exceptionally attractive.

- A lack of professional preparation for experiential Jewish educators has resulted in many programs hiring unskilled amateurs who simply replicate what they experienced in their teens years in youth group or at camp. Nothing fails more consistently than recycling old programs for a new generation. This is a field that needs to prepare educators who understand all three levels and how they operate and interact with one another. Many of these educators also need to be comfortable innovating. Technology is but one prime example of needed innovation. This is a field where centers of innovation and diffusion are keys to success.

- Experiential Jewish education cannot be limited to the traditional contexts of informal education. While camps, JCC's, youth movements, Hillel foundations and Israel experiences will continue to be vital settings, the borders of this field need to be constantly expanding. We have already mentioned the newer areas of adventure, museums and virtual reality; but other areas already developing include Jewish film-making, drama, global travel, virtual reality and meditative practices. Funders and educators need to be looking to expand thoughtfully in these and other new directions.

- Schools need a greater share of quality experiential Jewish education. The boundaries between the formal and informal are rapidly falling in school education, both in day and congregational schools; but many school educators are not prepared to successfully incorporate experiential learning into their repertoire. Anyone can show a film, have a discussion and serve Jewish foods. But it takes considerable educational skill to move from "providing experiences" to "stimulating experiential learning." Considerable effort needs to be invested in helping school educators learn how to structure experiential moments that are rich in Jewish learning, as well as fun for their students.

ADDITIONAL RESEARCH QUESTIONS TO BE ADDRESSED

- What types of learning are taking place within experiential Jewish education? What are the processes involved in the learning and how do they compare with other educational experiences?

- What is being learned in experiential Jewish education? How does this compare to what is taking place in more formal educational settings?

- What types of research methodologies are best suited to studying the impact of experiential Jewish education?

- Who are the experiential Jewish educators? What skills, knowledge and dispositions should characterize these educators? How do we prepare educators to incorporate experiential Jewish education in their practice?
- What conditions need to be in place for experiential Jewish education to take place effectively within formal educational environments?
- Why are a minority of Jewish teens involved in experiential Jewish education and what can be done to attract and retain more teens?
- What relevance does the research on experiential Jewish education for youth have for other demographic cohorts including younger children, young adults and adults?

CONCLUSION

Getting beyond the simplistic distinctions between formal and informal education may encourage a surge of creativity from educators to explore the rich opportunities that each has for promoting experiential Jewish learning. We believe that a well-defined approach to experiential Jewish education is an important step in helping Jews to both re-commit to enduring Jewish values and to creatively explore how those values can guide meaningful living when facing the challenges that confront us all on this precious, but endangered planet.

HIGHLIGHTS OF THE ARTICLE

- There is a long tradition of informal education settings in North America, even though relatively little has been written about the field from a research or evaluation perspective.
- While the term "informal Jewish education" has often been used to describe many forms of Jewish education outside of schooling, we prefer to limit the usage to describe the familiar contexts such as summer camps, retreats, youth groups and Israel experiences.
- We prefer the term "experiential Jewish education" to describe what educators do to promote experiential Jewish learning in any educational context and with any age learners. We claim that experiential Jewish education involves three distinct initiatives: recreation, socialization and challenge. We call for experiential educators to learn how to use all three of these initiatives in their work.
- With little research literature about experiential Jewish education, turning to related fields—including outdoor education, museum education and technology—can be very instructive. Experiential Jewish educators must learn from related fields if they are to remain relevant.
- Experiential Jewish education currently stands in the paradoxical position of being recognized as a formidable force for shaping Jewish identities while also being seen as significantly underdeveloped in clarifying its principles and identifying the conditions that assure its educational success.

So much of Jewish education today aims to build a felt connection between youth and the Jewish world. But people can feel only those connections that they have experienced. Connection and identity are shaped by our thoughts, but fueled by our emotions. Experiential education—whether at home, in a group setting or via the media—is the best route to connection. Understanding how to effectively utilize experiential education for Jewish purposes is the urgent agenda for the whole Jewish community.

ANNOTATED BIBLIOGRAPHY

Bekerman, Z., N. C. Burbules & Silberman-Keller, D. (Eds.) (2006). *Learning in Places: The Informal Education Reader*. New York: Peter Lang. Useful for academics, professionals and lay leaders looking to transform education by adopting informal educational practices, Bekerman, et. al., incorporate multiple disciplines within a variety of global contexts. A series of articles by internationally recognized researchers contributes to understanding what informal education is and how it can be implemented in a variety of settings.

Csikszentmihalyi, M. (1996). *Creativity: Flow and the Psychology of Discovery and Invention*. New York: Harper Collins. Culminating 30 years of research Csikszentmihalyi, a professor in psychology, uses the interviews from 91 prominent respondents to answer the question of what makes these people creative. Written to appeal both to scholars and general readers Csikszentmihalyi helps us understand creativity, and the parameters necessary to establish learning environments that encourage discovery and invention.

Hein, G. E. (1998). *Learning in the Museum*. London: New York: Routledge. Hein addresses some of the recent popular trends in museum education, in particular audience-centered and informal museum learning. A compilation of current museum learning theory, Hein suggests that the constructivist museum is the ideal approach for museums to adopt. The writer looks specifically at the ways in which patrons make meaning of their museum visits.

Informal Education Website: http://www.infed.org. This continually updated web site, edited in Great Britain, is an excellent resource for different types of informal educators. With over 100 articles and original pieces, the encyclopedia provides a comprehensive survey of informal education and lifelong learning. This site also draws attention to the subtle yet important differences between the use of the term "informal education" in different cultural contexts.

Mayer, R.E. (2001). *Multimedia Learning*. Cambridge: Cambridge University Press. Multimedia presentations provide a situation where people can learn from both words and pictures. Mayer summarizes ten years of research looking at multimedia learning from a cognitive perspective. The design principles articulated provide the basis for much of our understanding of the current trends within cognitive learning as it is applied in technology and education.

Smith, T.E., Roland, C.C., Havens, M.D. & Hoyt, J.A., (1992). *The Theory and Practice of Challenge Education*. Dubuque, Iowa: Kendall/Hunt Publishing Company. Smith, et.al. offer a variety of perspectives that will assist anyone interested in understanding challenge education and implementing it within their educational framework. The perspectives are useful to practitioners and academics endeavoring to gain an overall perspective on challenge education.

ADDITIONAL REFERENCES

Bekerman, Z., N. C., Burbules, Silberman-Keller, D. (Eds.) (2006). *Learning in Places: The Informal Education Reader*. New York: Peter Lang

Berger, P. L. & Luckmann, T. (1966). *The social construction of reality; a treatise in the sociology of knowledge* ([1st ed.). Garden City, N.Y.,: Doubleday.

Chazan, B. (2003). The philosophy of informal Jewish education. *The encyclopedia of informal education* Retrieved September 1st, 2006, from *www.infed.org/informaleducation/informal_jewish_education.htm*

Csikszentmihalyi, M. (1997) *Finding Flow: The Psychology of Engagement with Everyday Life*. New York: Basic Books.

Dewey, J. (1938). *Experience and Education*. New York: The Macmillan Company.

Kaplan, M. M. (1934). *Judaism as Civilization: Toward a Reconstruction of American-Jewish Life*. New York: The Macmillan Company.

Lorge, M. & Zola, G., P. (Eds.). (2006). *A Place of Our Own: The Rise of Reform Jewish Camping*. Tuscaloosa, Alabama: University of Alabama Press.

Reisman, B. (1979). *The Jewish experiential book : the quest for Jewish identity*. New York: Ktav Pub. House.

Reisman, B. & Reisman, J. I. (2002). *The New Jewish Experiential Book* (2nd Edition ed.). Jersey City, NJ: KTAV Pub. House.

Sales, A. L. & Saxe, L. (2004). *"How goodly are thy tents": Summer camps as Jewish socializing experiences*. Lebanon, N.H.: Brandeis University Press in association with The Avi Chai Foundation, published by University Press of New England.

Sarna, J. (2006). The Crucial Decade in Jewish Camping. In G. P. Zola & M. Lorge (Eds.), *The Beginnings of Reform Jewish Camping in America*. Tuscaloosa, Alabama: University of Alabama Press.

Saxe, L., Sasson, T., & Shahar, H. (2006). *Taglit-birthright israel: Impact on Jewish Identity, Peoplehood, and Connection to Israel*: The Maurice and Marilyn cohen Center for Modern Jewish Studies, Brandeis University.

Schlossberg, E. (1998). *Interactive Excellence: Defining and Developing New Standards for the 21st Century*. New York: Ballantine Books.

Vygotsky, L., S. (1978). *Mind in society: the development of higher psychological processes*. Cambridge, MA: Harvard University Press.

Winn, W. D., & Jackson, R. (1999). "Fourteen propositions about educational uses of virtual reality." *Educational Technology, 39*(4), 5–14.

Zeldin, M. (2006). Making the Magic in Reform Jewish Summer Camps. In G.P. Zola, P. & M. Lorge (Eds.), *The Beginnings of Reform Jewish Camping in America*. Tuscaloosa, Alabama: University of Alabama Press.

The Cultures of Jewish Education

Judah M. Cohen & Leah Strigler

To many Jewish educators, culture may comprise curricular content meant for transmission in a classroom or other setting. Culture, from another perspective, might also refer to the character of the interactions that take place in a classroom, school, institution, or other educational context, usually mediated by educators and leaders. As we will describe in this chapter, however, culture has much more to offer Jewish education than just descriptions of setting and content; taken in its many capacities, culture as a concept can provide a pervasive and powerful means for understanding the rich variety of value systems that underlie the most basic ideas about Jewish education.

Social theorist Raymond Williams has described culture as "one of the two or three most complicated words in the English language" (1983 p. 87). Comprising a broad series of concepts in several different fields of study, and holding relevance to other discussions of identity, history, and theology, the idea of culture poses great challenges to what we think we know about Jewish education. Our consideration of culture in this volume thus starts with the assertion that we must approach it as more than a monolithic, self-fulfilling entity; rather, we must acknowledge culture as a multifaceted term that stands at the center of several important lines of discussion. Favoring one perspective while dismissing others will provide, at best, only a partial (and rather skewed) perspective. When treated with a sensitive knowledge of its interlacing meanings, however, culture can allow those involved in Jewish education to hook into a series of important discussions extending to all levels of the learning process, while providing well-developed tools for asking crucial questions about education's meaning, scope, agendas and purpose.

We hold to the tenet that "culture never stops to have its picture taken." To treat culture as an unchanging entity, in other words, would be to miss its constantly and organically changing nature, powered by endless surprise and human inventiveness. One need not look further than the case of Matisyahu, a Hassidic Reggae singer who became a top ten recording artist, to see this process at work. Some of the most initially incongruous innovations in Jewish life have turned out to have staying power—occasionally even becoming important parts of Jewish practice that replaced or complemented other activities (such as Miriam's cup). At the same time, however, such activities never hold fast, even when scrupulously documented and protected: interpretations and conceptual frameworks constantly slide around over time, making "culture" a set of phenomena in constant flux. Culture, from this perspective, thus emerges as the product of a constant human search for stability.

In this chapter, we will present five models for understanding the different ways culture can introduce realms for exploration within the context of Jewish education. With each model, we present recent illustrative studies that give some inroads into thinking about what it means to transmit certain values and actions deemed to be "Jewish" within a variety of settings. In all cases, however, these models hardly scratch the surface. We ultimately know little about the relationship between culture and Jewish education, save that, given the goals of Jewish education, educators tend to view the concept of promoting Jewish culture as an unmitigated good. We hope a more textured discussion of culture that looks deeply into what it *means* to consider culture within Jewish education, will help add further nuance to future studies and praxis.

A CULTURE AS A BOUNDED GROUP OF PEOPLE

The disciplines of anthropology and archeology historically gained much of their relevance by focusing on "other cultures." At first, these cultures represented remote, geographically bounded groups of people (often perceived as primitive) who, early researchers believed, held a shared lifestyle, language and value system. Early ethnographers such as Bronislaw Malinowski (1974) and Claude Levi-Strauss (1995) based their research on this preconception; Clifford Geertz gave a nod to the idea in the title of his book, *The Interpretation of Cultures* (1973). By the 1980s, social scientists such as Benedict Anderson (2006), Arjun Appadurai (1996), and Jonathan and Daniel Boyarin (2002) had begun to loosen the geographic boundedness of cultures by introducing concepts such as "imagined communities" and "transnational or diasporic communities." The centerpiece of these ideas, however—that a defined group of people equals "*a* culture"— remained as strong as ever.

In this most monolithic conception of culture, Judaism presents a conundrum. Jews all over the world have often thought of themselves as a "people" united by a shared history and religious faith tradition. The symbolic practices and rituals Jews have kept over time and across space have underscored this belief as a core principle. From another angle, however, Judaism represents scattered groups of people, related tangentially at best, who have developed unique, sometimes mutually exclusive practices they consider to be intrinsically "Jewish." One of the latest comprehensive histories of Judaism, for example, acknowledges the wide range of such practices by entitling itself *Cultures of the Jews* (Biale, 2002). How can we bring together these two formulations of Jewish culture? One possible solution is to look at Judaism as a series of *separate*, often independent groups of Jews who make *assumptions* about being similar to Jews all around the world: a case of Anderson's "imagined communities" (2006). Making these assumptions not only creates a stronger sense of community, but also proves crucial to Jewish education's tendency (and need?) to limit and universalize the issue of Jewish authenticity. From such perceptions, moreover, emerge a generally understood (if somewhat amorphously established) set of Jewish ritual practices and beliefs that all groups are believed to follow: hence the idea of "Jewish tradition."

Culture in this context can also delineate an agenda for or identification of collective identity, such as with the creation of differentiated "Israeli" and "American Jewish" cultures. These nationalized approaches to Jewish culture are based on certain criteria, delineated according to specific ideas of what "Israeli" and "American Jewish" are intended to represent. Much recent research about these different cultural ideas has incorporated the "Israel Experience," a touristic, intricately designed trip created mainly for young non-Israelis (though, as Grant has shown, adult tours also have a prominent place in this area [2001]). Typically consisting of visits to sites considered biblically, historically or Zionistically significant, while occasionally arranging for controlled interactions with members of the population, Israel trips aim to effect a maximal *impact* upon their participants. In addition to Kelner's work on youth trips to Israel (2002), one of the most significant recent works exploring this phenomenon is the tripartite study published as *The Israel Experience: Studies in Jewish Identity and Youth Culture.*(Goldberg, Heilman and Kirshenblatt-Gimblett, 2002) Two parts of the study involved ethnographic observation of youth Israel trips, conducted by anthropologist Goldberg and sociologist Heilman; the third part, by performance studies scholar Kirshenblatt-Gimblett, provided an analysis. Kirshenblatt-Gimblett's assertion that "[t]he ultimate destination in this voyage of discovery is not Israel, but the Jewish identity of each individual participant" (p. 321) offers an important gloss on these studies' approaches to culture, and on this category of culture in general: by carefully orchestrating and portraying the "culture" of a nation-state seen as central to Jewish identity, it might be possible to influence the "culture" of a group traditionally seen as the recipients of educational efforts—in this case, the youth.

CULTURE AS A SYSTEM OF BELIEF AND ACTION

In addition to defining a people, culture may also comprise the totality of what people *do*. Sociologists such as Goffman (1974) and Bauman (1999) have viewed culture as a form of interaction, *enacted* and *negotiated* within a given space. When applied to Jewish education, this approach to culture has meant focusing less on overarching cultural norms (as in the previous section), and more on the ways people establish their own concepts of self and group identity. There have been calls for *ethnographic* studies in Jewish education based on this approach since at least the early 1980s; but as of this writing, there has been only a limited response (Chazan, 1983).

The classroom serves as a wonderful example for illustrating this kind of approach. An instructor attempts to teach students certain ideas, perceptions and concepts, perhaps using a book or other published material, in a way that allows the students to internalize the material; the process holds expectations of changing the students both individually and communally. Yet as any educator knows, this transfer of information and emotion does not happen automatically. Rather, "learning" itself takes place through many *interactions* between teacher, students, and the environment in which they dwell. Culture, from this perspective, documents the patterns that emerge in the interactive process: how people communicate, what they value, and how they interpret and respond to the scene taking place. Such an approach does not necessarily place the material itself first, nor does it invest as deeply in measuring the *amount* of material learned. Instead, it offers an important insight into the deeper, often unnoticed layers of discourse that serve as the basis for these interactions.

Within the context of Jewish education, some of the most salient work on this level has been based around the classroom. Wolberger, for example, explored the ways members of a yeshiva Talmud study class raised and lowered their voices to create an effective context for their discussions (1993). Cohen also used ethnographic means to analyze a summer camp's songleading course, exploring how the interactions in that class helped young people situate themselves and the "youth" culture attributed to them within a life continuum of "Jewish" sound (2006). Reimer's ethnography of a liberal synagogue's educational system, meanwhile, captured interactions both within the classroom and without, including parent involvement, adult education and rabbinic leadership as aspects of his study (1997).

CULTURE AS A FORM OF "NON-RELIGIOUS" JUDAISM

Numerous studies of Jewish "culture" (no less in education than in the rest of Jewish studies scholarship) focus on religious activities. Yet another, coexisting strain of thought frames culture in *counterpoint* to religious life. Used both rhetorically and in scholarly realms, culture in this context serves as a way to differentiate and isolate the spiritual "elements" of Judaism from those that do not appear to require adherence to a specific theology.

Expressions of Judaism not explicitly related to religious practice or belief thus tend to appear under their own moniker of "Cultural Judaism"; and the generic statement "I'm a cultural Jew" became a popular substitute for "I'm not religious" in the 1990s. In 2003, however, groups associated with Humanistic Judaism and other non-religious forms of Jewish identification institutionalized these ideas, and established the Center for Cultural Judaism in New York City. One of the centerpieces of this center is education, supported by $50,000 grants from the Felix Posen Foundation to create college curricula framing Judaism as a *civilization* rather than as a religious group. Based on an assertion that many Jews in the United States recognize their Jewish identity but do not embrace Jewish religious practice, the group's agenda has led to the creation of a large bibliography (*http://www.culturaljudaism.org/ccj/bibliography*), a philosophy of education by Israeli Humanist Judaism proponent Yaakov Malkin (2002), and a collegiate network of scholars across the United States and Israel. Such activity has helped crystallize one idea of Jewish culture into a basis for ethnic identification and instruction.

Outside Cultural Judaism, parts of the collegiate realm, several forms of Yiddish studies, and certain forms of educational tourism (such as March of the Living and some providers of Birthright Israel experiences), much of the rest of the Jewish education constellation revolves around worldviews that tend to support—and be supported by—institutions and ideologies motivated at least in part by religious concerns. Jewish culture within this setting denotes a category of activity and knowledge that complements ritual or text study in an educational curriculum. Perhaps one of the central organs for discussing Jewish culture in a religious sense in the 1990s was the short-lived journal *Avar Ve'Atid: a Journal of Jewish Education, Culture and Discourse* (1994-1997), which provided a religiously pluralistic forum for exploring culture within a strong Zionistic and continuity-centered agenda. "Jewish culture" in this context could include the elements of Jewish ritual or belief; yet it also maintained its own categorization and space within the educational agenda.

By being more expansive in its catchments, "culture" in this sense serves to offer within the constructs of the Jewish community entry points for those uninterested in the religious dimension of Jewish life, or enhancements for those already engaged. In working towards the ultimate goal of ensuring the perpetuation of "Jewish tradition," this approach to representing the terrain of Jewish culture offers the benefit of including a wider array of participants in the activities associated with "Jewish life."

CULTURE AS CREATIVE EXPRESSION AND INTELLECTUAL REFINEMENT

On another front, culture has come to signify a catchall for different forms of artistic expression: dance, music, theater, film, visual art, poetry/literature, and to a great extent museum exhibits. Institutionalized through organizations such as the National Foundation for Jewish Culture and the Jewish Book Council, and actualized through everything from Hebrew school arts and crafts projects to meet-the-author programs in synagogues and Jewish Community Centers, culture from this perspective links creative activities with *de facto* commitment to Judaism through intellectual, emotional, self-motivated, and "artistic" experiences. Consequently, the cultural arts have insinuated themselves into Jewish educational curricula across the age spectrum: young children create symbolic objects to represent holidays, Bible stories or "Jewish" values; Jewish dramatic/musical "pageants" illustrating important events or values in Judaism have existed for well over a century; and instruction on "The Jew in Film," "Jewish Music," and "Israeli Dance," have been staples of many Jewish school curricula and summer camps (not to mention programs geared toward Jewish college students and adult learners).

The turn of the twenty-first century, however, has seen a particular resurgence of interest in promoting and funding Jewish culture among young adults, supplemented by commissioned studies exploring (and justifying) the need for creative culture as a kind of insurance policy for Generation X/Y's Jewish continuity. Phenomena such as the short film "The Tribe", JDub Records, and *Heeb Magazine* may not adhere to conventional visions of Jewish education, nor necessarily fulfill the criteria for "informal" Jewish education. Nonetheless, they address more broadly issues of transmitting Jewish identity and values—a kind of "alternative" education that deliberately uses culture as a vessel for engagement outside the established structures of the Jewish educational world. One only need look at the curricula created around rap songs such as Ross Filler/Remedy's 1998 "Never Again" (distributed by the Anti-Defamation League) and HaDag Nachash/David Grossman's 2004 "Sticker Song" to understand the interest this kind of material has generated, and the desire among Jewish educators to link it into a more overt educational project.

Organizations looking to creative culture as a way to "engage" young Jews are seeking ways to measure its success in order to support and further such funding choices. Studies such as *OMG! How Generation Y is Redefining Faith in the iPod Era* (2005), and its followup, *"Grande Soy Vanilla Latte with Cinnamon, No Foam": Jewish Identity and Community in a Time of Unlimited Choices* (2006) specifically target creative culture's ability to "convene an audience that allows for an experience of community" (p. 32)—a precondition for beginning in-depth discussions. Similarly, Cohen and Kelman's study *Cultural Events & Jewish Identities: Young Adult Jews in New York* (2006), commissioned jointly by the National Foundation for Jewish Culture and the UJA-Federation of New York Commission on Jewish Identity and Renewal, highlighted music and theater as important elements of Jewish "cultural" events, many of which aimed at "convey[ing] a set of messages about being Jewish in America" (p. 73). While somewhat tangential to the core field of Jewish education, these studies nonetheless address the relationship between creative arts and Jewish identity among a "vulnerable" age cohort seen as unconnected to Jewish congregational or educational settings; they therefore deserve coverage in this forum as they explore Jewish education among the institutionally independent.

CULTURE AS A SITE FOR CRITIQUE

At the broadest level, studies about culture look to the larger picture, asking questions about why concepts such as Jewish education exist in the first place. What do the current forms of Jewish education say about the values of the societies in which they operate? What does Jewish education actually attempt to *do*? And what underlying expectations, motivations, and biases do Jewish educational discourses profess? This most encompassing approach to culture has been taken up by Marcus and Fischer in their now classic *Anthropology as Cultural Critique* (1986). Anthropologists study groups of people, Marcus and Fischer suggest, not just to learn about culture, but also to cast light upon and engage in wider debates about the nature of society. Insights into culture, in other words, can help us see our own activities in educational settings in a different, and perhaps more critical, light.

University Jewish studies instructors have created the best developed literature on this topic. Jewish Studies, after all, must constantly negotiate its place within the scope of liberal education—justifying its existence alongside topics such as English and Biology, while at the same time receiving support largely from private donations. Before the 1930s, as Ritterband and Wechsler note, most professors dealing with Jewish topics found themselves in university Classics departments where they rounded out an institution's need to present foundational Hebrew texts. The 1960s incarnation of Jewish Studies, meanwhile, refashioned the field as a kind of "ethnic" studies, meant in part to address the intellectual needs of the increasing number of Jewish university students (1994). By the start of the twenty-first century, Jewish studies existed in many forms: departments and programs, chronologically organized and regionally organized, religious and secular. As evidenced by the 2006 forum published in the Association for Jewish Studies's newsletter, *AJS Perspectives*, undergraduate Jewish studies curricula comprised several philosophies across a range of colleges, each of which commented on the general state of both Judaism and higher education (Spring, 2006). The nature of Jewish education, these studies implied, resulted from sweeping ideas about how Jews could be portrayed in society and history. In turn, however, these programs consciously shaped new perspectives on how people *should* learn about Judaism within a liberal education environment.

Apart from academic pursuits of Jewish knowledge, explorations of "Jewish culture" also extend to the contemporary Jewish scene as it exists within the larger structures of mainstream society. Young Jews will ultimately construct their Jewish identities (if they choose to) based on their experiences both inside and outside controlled Jewish educational settings or situations. An awareness of this dynamic is evident in research on the college-age Jewish population, such as Saxe and Sales's *Particularism in the University: Realities and Opportunities for Jewish Life on Campus* (2006).

Culture also looms large in discussions of *power discourses*. Emphasized heavily by Marxist theorists such as Gramsci (1991), and thinkers connected with the Center for Contemporary Cultural Studies in Birmingham, England (also known as the Birmingham School – for more information on the School see http://jahsonic.com/CCCS.html), power discourses examine the means by which certain ideas tend to dominate in a cultural debate. Studies on these issues tend to critique the *status quo*, looking to reveal large-scale cultural marginalization, ideological slants, and oppression of alternate viewpoints. Within the context of Jewish education, this type of critique typically comes from groups or individuals that represent excluded populations. Attempts to show the unequal treatment of women in Jewish curricula and the education field itself, for example, became a central part of *The Ma'ayan Report* (which looked at education as only a part of a more sweeping study) (Cohen, T., 2005). Similar though less developed critiques have also begun to arise surrounding Sephardic Judaism—most prominently through the efforts and funding patterns of the Maurice Amado Foundation—and Jews of alternative sexualities, such as the recent film *Hineni: Coming Out in a Jewish High School* (Fayngold, 2005).

Actions of this sort suggest that "Jewish culture" often shapes and defines itself through struggle and negotiation, and that no one interpretation of Judaism is necessarily "correct." The funding and organizational structures dominating Jewish education, however, which tend to pool resources and reputations around the search for what *works* (hence this book), allow little space for heeding critiques of this sort. Nonetheless, an awareness of the political issues the organized Jewish world faces in constructing and defining "Jewish culture" could open discussions about the way Jewish education's institutions and power brokers promote and disseminate their particular ideas to teachers and students.

Finally, it is important to highlight Bekerman's recent efforts to link cultural studies and Jewish education more directly. Bekerman's project focuses on using cultural studies to *inform* discourses of Jewish education, thus aiming to recreate visions of the field. His "Constructivist Perspectives on Language, Identity and Culture: Implications for Jewish Identity and the Education of Jews," criticizes the Jewish education field as too much enthralled with Western enlightenment discourses (2001). Bekerman promotes instead a paradigm based around dialogue rather than "fact," encouraging studies of educational discourse rather than empiricism, and shifting the weight of Jewish education to a narrative-based format that encourages young people to participate in the educational process rather than merely receive. Although, like many cultural theorists, Bekerman's syntax tends toward the over-technical, it also engages with demanding mainstream academic writings on culture, and provides a rare glimpse into the possibilities of exploring Jewish education from a position that values depth of analysis for its own sake.

FUTURE IMPLICATIONS FOR CULTURE AND JEWISH EDUCATION

From one perspective, virtually everything published on Jewish education bears relevance to this chapter. After all, culture in its numerous forms has relevance to all factors associated with the acts of defining and transmitting a deep sense of Judaism. Yet the literature, in its search for impact and effect, can often neglect the larger picture—to ask what it means for people to *value* the forms education takes in Jewish life. Prevailing perceptions of the field thus far peg Jewish education as a means to an end: namely the preservation of the Jewish people. But Jewish education also evinces a constant search for what Judaism actually "is," accompanied by a similar struggle over how to express such ideas to others. Understanding those processes in a manner separate from pressured expectations for "success" could further develop the field in significant, foundational ways.

AREAS FOR FURTHER STUDY AND CONSIDERATION.

Orthodox Judaism: The vast majority of mainstream research in Jewish education has focused on liberal Judaism, in part because liberal Judaism has most readily looked to the West for its models and methods, and hooked into mainstream forms of distribution (such as scholarly publications). Orthodox Jewish groups, however, have cultivated large, complex, and sometimes overlooked systems of education, complete with equally deep conversations, theories, and models (as exchanged, for example, on the Lookstein Center for Jewish Education's LookJEd listserv). Viewing these studies as part of a Jewish educational continuum, rather than stereotyping them as intrinsically "different," could add important dimensions to the literature and provide significant, relevant insights into the broader purposes of Jewish education.

The Internet: It is a truism that the Internet has transformed the way communications take place within the Jewish world. Much discussion of the Internet in Jewish education circles, however, focuses on *using* it to enhance the learning process. Yet educators could also benefit from understanding what it *means* to use the Internet: How do students conceive of their on-line teachers? How does "Jewish" learning fit into broader Internet usage? How do educators gauge the reliability of what they find on the World Wide Web? And, most significantly, how does the Internet, like any form of technology, empower actual forms of learning that eventually make their way into Jewish education's latest paradigms?

Cultural-Generational Dissonance: People of different generations, national identities, and social groups represent diverse cultural backgrounds and sensibilities. How can this understanding help us explore educational moments as interactions between representatives of sometimes starkly different points of view? Studies of Jewish education currently come largely from the perspective of the teacher and make broad assumptions about the world of the students. Yet if we look at students as more than just "people learning how to function in the Jewish world," and explore the learning process as a power-laden dialogue between complex systems of value, our ideas of "Jewish" learning could enter new areas of depth.

What, then, do we know about culture and Jewish education? Not nearly enough. But the theory is there, the possibilities are rich and promising, and the opportunities to take advantage of them remain ever in our sights.

IMPLICATIONS AND RECOMMENDATIONS

This discussion of culture highlights its complex nature, particularly in relationship to Jewish education. In the current state of research, what we "know" about culture and Jewish education all too often emerges from the agendas of Jewish communal agencies, philanthropists, and self-interested educational institutions. These groups tend to base their research premises on cultural anxieties, most notably concerns about self-preservation; in the process they skim over deeper cultural contexts in favor of "solutions," "impact," and "saving" the Jewish people. The vast majority of studies done on Jewish culture thus look at it as a unitary item whose "use" could hurt or help the situation. While interest fuels research, *disinterested* research may well provide a way to move out of the one-dimensional discussion of "culture" in Jewish education and into a more vibrant approach that includes the very nature of why these studies are of interest in the first place.

The kind of research we advocate in this essay complements and challenges the current state of affairs, and may seem at first counterintuitive. Rather than trying to further the agendas of Jewish educational initiatives which are all too often swayed by insider speculations and desires, we wish to push for research that has a certain intellectual distance from the stated goals of Jewish education. By taking an intensive focus on the qualitative interactions that occur within the performance and production of Jewish education, such work can begin to break itself away from the constant crisis state and heightened expectations often associated with the nature of Jewish education. Doing so can also address important questions about the larger picture: How, in other words, have the concepts of Jewish education themselves been constructed and disseminated in recent years, and what does that say about the nature of Jewish communal life?

We suggest utilizing the frames of research, inquiry and reflection in an inductive mode. It is important to acknowledge that within Jewish education, as within many arenas of activity dependent on private funding, great pressure exists to focus on evaluation and proof of success. While we understand that these assessments are driven by limited resources and discussions over communal agendas and priorities, we feel it is important to recognize that culture is, in essence, a process, not a finite product, and certainly not a magic bullet. Understanding the ways people and organizations define "culture" as a central factor in Jewish educational initiatives, and exploring what it means to use culture as an envelope for transmitting Jewish knowledge and values, require different methodologies than are typically used in program evaluation and success studies. We hope this chapter will help to open up the possibility within the infrastructure of Jewish education for more open-ended inquiry along these lines.

HIGHLIGHTS

- Culture is a many-faceted and constantly evolving process—not a specific item
- Culture has many meanings of relevance for Jewish education, including a collectively identified group of people, a system of belief and action, a form of "non-religious" Judaism, a type of "high level" artistic production, and series of background values that underlie personal, communal and policy choices.
- Culture is a term that will help Jewish educators think about their work contexts in a way that is removed from their primary concerns about goals and objectives
- Fruitful, under considered areas for further investigation in the convergence between Jewish education and culture include education in orthodox Judaism, the meaning of Jewish education in light of new technologies (such as the Internet), and the meaning of educating Jews across generational and ethnic lines.

LARGER CONTEXT

The concept of "culture" holds a central place within several academic fields and appears commonly in general discourse. Therefore, it reaches Jewish educators and scholars of Jewish education from a number of different directions. Used in everyday discussion, the term's concurrent multiple meanings create a rich arena for sharing ideas. Recently, however, the term "culture" has appeared at the center of philanthropic and scholarly efforts to ameliorate Jewish communal concerns, particularly among young people. These uses have been far more problematic precisely because of their tendency to use culture as a means to an end while striving to promote an academic, authoritative voice. With the number of academically oriented post-graduate programs in Jewish education proliferating, and the increasing use of culture as a "new way" for addressing Jewish education, it is important to recognize that most scholarly disciplines still have heated debates over what culture actually *is*, let alone what it can *do*. Continuous reflection on what one means by the term "Jewish culture" can therefore help articulate an ever-renewing understanding of what it means to learn about Judaism and Jewish identity.

ANNOTATED BIBLIOGRAPHY

Bekerman, Z. (2001). "Constructivist perspectives on language, identity and culture: Implications for Jewish identity and the education of Jews." *Religious Education* 96 (4); 462–473 An essay that looks to theoretical developments around language, identity and culture and considers the potential insights they can offer to those interested in Jewish education and other parallel educational endeavors. Beckerman, an Israeli academic, differentiates between Jewishness and Israeliness in his analysis, both within the State of Israel and among Jewish communities elsewhere. His consideration of these theoretical framworks serves as a useful model for careful exploration of "culture" and its possible dimensions.

Biale, D. ed. (2002). *Cultures of the Jews*. New York: Schocken Books. A major multi-author work that re-examines Jewish history under the premise that Jews created their own senses of culture in different eras and locations (as opposed to the primacy of a continuous "Jewish" culture that had been used in previous sweeping histories). Also differs from previous histories, in that it includes several chapters focusing on Sephardic Jewry, supported by the Maurice Amado foundation.

Cohen, S. M. & Kelman, A. (2006). Cultural events and Jewish identities: Young adult Jews in New York. New York: National Foundation for Jewish Culture.. A study of "new" Jewish cultural events in New York City, created in part to assess the "impact" of culture-based programming among the city's 20s and 30s population. While the study inevitably supports the premise for its commission—namely that culture can be an important means to "reengage" a Jewish population widely seen to be at-risk—it also provides some important insights into the backgrounds and values of the young people who attend these cultural events.

Goldberg, H., Heilman, S. & Kirshenblatt-Gimblett, B. (2002). *The Israel experience: Studies in Jewish identity and youth culture*. Jerusalem: Kav-Graph. A publication based on a Bronfman-sponsored project to explore the meaning of youth trips to Israel. Comprising ethnographic studies of two contrasting youth Israel tours and one commentary essay—all by prominent social scientists—the work offers an impressive level of qualitative detail, research and analysis. The young people themselves, moreover, serve as the focus of the study.

Greenberg, A. (2006). 'Grande soy vanilla latte with cinnamon, no foam': Jewish identity and community in a time of unlimited choices. New York: Reboot. A Bronfman/Reboot-commissioned study examining the attitudes of Jews in their 20s and 30s based on the assumption that by knowing this population's values, Reboot could better engage them in Jewish-oriented discussion. A particularly significant example of a survey-based study with "hip" trappings that aims to use research as a means to an end.

Kelner, S. (2002). Almost pilgrims: Authenticity, identity and the extra-ordinary on a Jewish tour of Israel. Unpublished dissertation. City University of New York. Kelner's dissertation examines Taglit-Birthright Israel as an example of pilgrimage-tourism. The piece draws upon a variety of data, including ethnographic research, and contextualizes Birthright Israel in sociological discussions of "routine-shattering" situations, group experience and sacred encounters, in addition to recounting the historical development of the "Israel experience". This form of educational program, Kelner claims, figures prominently in the Jewish educational repertoire and has analogs in other "heritage" trips, to Eastern Europe and New York City's Jewish neighborhoods.

Reimer, J. (1997). *Succeeding at Jewish education: How one synagogue made it work*. Philadelphia: Jewish Publication Society. An ethnographic case-study of the educational programs at a large, urban Reform congregation. Reimer observed and describes such features as the afternoon Hebrew school program, adult education offerings, congregants' articulated experiences of learning in the synagogue setting and the rabbinic leadership's involvement with educational issues. This in-depth study provides a model for understanding how Jewish education functions within the context of a particular institutional culture.

REFERENCES

Anderson, B. (2006). *Imagined communities: Reflections on the origin and spread of nationalism*. (Rev. Ed.) London: Verso Publications.

Appadurai, A. (1996). *Modernity at large: Cultural dimensions of globalization*. St. Paul: University of Minnesota Press.

Association for Jewish Studies (2006), "A Forum on the Jewish Studies Undergraduate Major: What Do We Learn About the Field from How We Educate our Undergraduates?" *AJS Perspectives*, 8–29.

Avar v'atid: A journal of Jewish education, culture and discourse. (1994 – 1997)

Bauman, Z. (1999). *Culture as praxis*. Thousand Oaks, CA: Sage Publications.

Bekerman, Z. (2001). "Constructivist perspectives on language, identity and culture: Implications for Jewish identity and the education of Jews." *Religious Education* 96 (4); 462–473.

Biale, D. ed. (2002). *Cultures of the Jews*. New York: Schocken Books.

Boyarin, J. & Boyarin, D. (2002). *Powers of diaspora: Two essays on the relevance of Jewish culture*. St. Paul: University of Minnesota Press.

Chazan, B. (1983). *Studies in Jewish Education: Volume 1*. Jerusalem, Hebrew University.

Cohen, J. M. (2006). 'And the youth shall see visions…': Songleading, summer camps and identity among Reform Jewish teenagers." In Kok, R. & Boynton, S. eds. *Musical childhoods and the cultures of youth*. Middletown, CT: Wesleyan University Pres.

Cohen, S. M. & Kelman, A. (2006). Cultural events & Jewish identities: Young adult Jews in New York. New York: National Foundation for Jewish Culture.

Cohen, T. et al. (2005). Jewish Education. Chapter 6 in *Listen to her voice: The Ma'ayan report*, 113-122.

Fayngold, I. (2005). Coming out in a Jewish high school. Film. Keshet USA.

Geertz, C. (1973). *The interpretation of cultures*. New York: Basic Books.

Goffman, E. (1974). *Frame analysis: An essay on the organization of experience*. Boston: Northeastern University Press.

Goldberg, H., Heilman, S. & Kirshenblatt-Gimblett, B. (2002). *The Israel experience: Studies in Jewish identity and youth culture*. Jerusalem: Kav-Graph.

Gramsci, A. (1991). *Selections from cultural writings*. Cambridge: Harvard University Press.

Grant, L. D. (2001). "Planned and enacted curriculum stories on a congregational Israel trip." *Conservative Judaism* 53 (3).

Greenberg, A. (2005). OMG! How generation Y is redefining faith in the ipod era. New York: Reboot.

Greenberg, A. (2006). 'Grande soy vanilla latte with cinnamon, no foam': Jewish identity and community in a time of unlimited choices. New York: Reboot.

Kelner, S. (2002). Almost pilgrims: Authenticity, identity and the extra-ordinary on a Jewish tour of Israel. Unpublished dissertation. City University of New York.

Levi-Strauss, C. (1995). *Myth and meaning: Cracking the code of culture*. (New York: Schocken Books.

Malinowski, B. (1984). *Argonauts of the Western Pacific*. Prospect Heights, Illinois: Waveland Press.

Marcus, G. & Fischer, M. (1986). *Anthropology as cultural critique*. Chicago: University of Chicago Press.

Malkin, Y. (2002). An invitation to study Judaism as a culture. Tel Aviv: Meitar College.

Reimer, J. (1997). *Succeeding at Jewish education: How one synagogue made it work*. Philadelphia: The Jewish Publication Society.

Ritterband, P. & Wechsler, H. (1994). *Jewish learning in American universities: The first century*. Bloomington: Indiana University Press.

Saxe, L. & Sales, A. (2006). *Particularism in the University: Realities and Opportunities for Jewish Life on Campus.* New York: The Avi Chai Foundation.

Williams, R. (1983). *Keywords.* (Rev. Ed.) New York: Oxford University Press, 1983.

Wolberger, L. (1993). "Music of holy argument: The ethnomusicology of a Talmud study session." *Studies in Contemporary Jewry*, IX, 110–136.

Contexts

Central Agencies (Bureaus) of Jewish Education

Gil Graff

Early in the twentieth century Judah Magnes, rabbi at Temple Emanu-El and chairman of the short-lived Kehillah of New York, noted that "Hundreds of thousands of dollars and boundless energy and affection are expended each year on the education of the Jewish child, but it may be said that we have no Jewish educational system" (Bentwich 1953, p. 76). A century later Jack Wertheimer—whose historical perspective on Jewish education appears in this volume—observed that Jewish education comprises "a loose, barely connected network of autonomous educating institutions". In Wertheimer's view, the compelling contemporary challenge of Jewish education "is to link the silos, to build cooperation across institutional lines…" (2005, p. 2). There is, however, a key difference between these two reflections on system building. While Magnes imagined a centrally managed school district model, Wertheimer points to a service-oriented model. These alternative visions are reflected in the development of central agencies of Jewish education. The transformation of central agencies of Jewish education over the course of the twentieth century and current and emerging areas of their focus early in the twenty-first century are examined in this chapter. Having served as a professional educator at the Los Angeles Bureau of Jewish Education since the 1980s, I have directly observed many of the changes described in these pages.

It is, I believe, telling that *What We Know about Jewish Education*, written fifteen years ago, bore no entry on Bureaus of Jewish Education and that the present volume includes such a chapter; a partial explanation of this change will be advanced in these pages. That recognition of the important role that central agencies (known by such names as Bureau of Jewish Education, Board of Jewish Education, Jewish Education Committee, Central Agency for Jewish Education and Partnership for Jewish Life and Learning) can play in the advancement of Jewish education is only now re-emerging after a period of disregard accounts, perhaps, for the decided lack of research on "bureaus." As a Jerusalem Fellow in 1990–91 I devoted a year to researching central agencies for Jewish education and considering their future possibilities (Graff 1991). Little had been written on the subject to that point, and research in the ensuing years has not yet addressed this lacuna.

DEVELOPMENT OF BUREAUS OF JEWISH EDUCATION

Responding to a perceived crisis in Jewish education in New York City, the Kehillah of New York established a Bureau of Jewish Education in 1910, headed by Dr. Samson Benderly (Winter 1966). As part of the trend toward federated communal activity, Bureaus of Jewish Education were established in twenty communities in the U.S. by 1940 (Gannes 1954, p. 192). Early Bureaus functioned as "district offices" for community Talmud Torah networks. In this capacity they established teacher certification requirements, provided professional in-service training to educators and developed standardized curricula for affiliated community schools. These curricula—consistent with the cultural Zionist nationalism of their authors—were typically Hebrew-based and included Hebrew language and literature, Bible, festivals, Palestine as the source of Jewish creativity, selections from rabbinic literature, Jewish history and a degree of synagogue ritual familiarity (under the rubric "customs and ceremonies"). In New York and elsewhere the BJE assembled graduates of the various Talmud

Torahs—which generally provided ten to twelve hours of weekly instruction, Sunday morning and Monday through Thursday afternoons—and launched a Hebrew high school.

Though early Bureaus of Jewish Education operated or closely controlled Talmud Torah (communal supplementary school) programs, a shift in the setting of Jewish schooling was already underway in the 1920s and 1930s as Jews moved to areas of second and third settlement. In the generation 1910–1935 the percentage of children enrolled in Jewish schools whose education was synagogue-based rose from thirty-five percent to sixty percent. Alexander Dushkin, BJE Director in Chicago and later in New York, argued that communal Bureaus should be "trans-ideological," functioning as resource service agencies in support of all streams of Jewish education. Central agencies for Jewish education, he maintained, should not promote any particular ideology, nor should they operate schools. The number of Bureaus nearly doubled in the 1940s, as eighteen new BJEs were launched (Gannes 1954, p. 193). By 1957 eighty-five percent of children in Jewish schools studied under synagogue auspices, and Dushkin's view of Bureaus as resource service agencies had become the norm.

THE POST–WORLD WAR II GENERATION

In 1959 the American Association for Jewish Education published the "Report of the Commission for the Study of Jewish Education in the United States." The report estimated that forty to forty-five percent of Jewish children five to fourteen years of age were receiving Jewish schooling—though upwards of eighty percent were enrolled at some time during their elementary school years. It pegged the average stay at three to four years (Dushkin & Engleman, p. 44). The post–World War II baby boom, combined with escalating rates of synagogue membership and Jewish school attendance, resulted in a near trebling of the number of students enrolled in Jewish schools, from 200,000 in 1937 to 588,955 in 1962. The post–World War II generation also saw significant growth in the numbers of Orthodox day schools and in day school pupil enrollment and the emergence of Conservative (beginning 1950) and Reform (beginning 1970) day schools.

Commenting on the role of Bureaus of Jewish Education in the 1960s, Walter Ackerman wrote:

> As the embodiment of the community's stake in Jewish education, the bureau's function is to give disinterested technical assistance and guidance to the schools of the various ideological groupings in the locality it serves. Affiliated schools may avail themselves of the bureau's supervisory personnel, in-service seminars, central audio-visual and pedagogic libraries, testing programs, placement services, publications and a wide variety of educational activities. The standards set by an adequately staffed and financed bureau can determine the quality of Jewish education in the community (Ackerman 1973, p. 187).

Despite expanding Jewish educational opportunities, however, there was growing communal concern about "Jewish survival" in the mid-1970s. The 1971 National Jewish Population Survey had reported a startlingly high intermarriage rate of thirty-one percent, compared to seven percent in the 1950s. Based on analyses of survey data, two widely publicized studies released in 1975 and 1976 claimed to scientifically demonstrate that the minimum threshold of instructional hours of Jewish schooling required to impact adult Jewish identification was beyond what the vast majority of students experienced. It appeared that the Jewish education in which the overwhelming majority of school-age American Jews participated at one time or another was unlikely to make a difference in their lives.

BUREAUS AND THE "CONTINUITY CRISIS"

In response to rising concern about Jewish continuity—rendered all the more acute by the 1990 National Jewish Population Survey, which reported an intermarriage rate of fifty-two percent (a figure challenged by some as overstating a rate of "only" forty-three percent)—many Jewish federations established "Continuity Commissions." In a few communities, Bureaus of Jewish Education—always heavily dependent on Federation funding—were dismantled and replaced by freshly constituted communal Jewish educational entities with a "continuity" mandate (and a new name). In some communities Bureaus were viewed as appropriately suited to limited educational functions (e.g., services in support of congregational supplementary schools), and Federation-operated commissions assumed responsibility for Jewish educational initiatives outside the narrowly defined mandate of the BJE. In some cases BJE activity was strengthened—with Federation support—to address an expanded educational agenda.

Another outgrowth of the post-1990 continuity concern was the emergence of philanthropic foundations as major players in the arena of Jewish education. To return to the riddle of the lack of reference to central agencies/Bureaus in *What We Know about Jewish Education* (Kelman 1992) and an entry in this new version (2007), a partial answer rests in a pendulum shift occasioned by the entry of an expanding number of major donors and service providers into the domain of Jewish education. Mounting interest and investment in Jewish education by an escalating number of entities contributed to a growing sense of the need for some sort of connecting hub with broad, value-added knowledge of the Jewish educational whole. While earlier there was a widely held view that Bureaus of Jewish Education were relics of another era, by the early twenty-first century Bureaus were—in many communities (it can be reasonably averred that each community creates the Bureau it deserves)—perceived as having the expertise and relationships required to effectively advance Jewish education on a systemic basis. Moreover, if there is an institution in place that, to quote Wertheimer, can "build cooperation across institutional lines…and help families negotiate their way through the rich array of educational options" (Wertheimer 2005, p.2), it is surely a central agency for Jewish education.

THE LOS ANGELES BUREAU OF JEWISH EDUCATION: A CASE STUDY

The range of educational activity in which central agencies are engaged is broad. Their missions vary based on communities' institutional resources and needs; for example, some of the sixty Bureaus across the country may be heavily involved in providing, organizing or coordinating adult Jewish learning, while others may focus on the Jewish education of children and families. In some communities—particularly smaller communities—Bureaus are called upon to operate community-sponsored schools. Notwithstanding such functional variations, the vision and values of central Jewish education agencies are remarkably similar. By way of concrete example, the vision, mission and values of the Bureau of Jewish Education (BJE) of Greater Los Angeles are framed as follows:

VISION: Jewish learning is the foundation of vibrant Jewish living. The Bureau of Jewish Education, a center of excellence, will ensure present and future generations of knowledgeable Jews who are committed to their religious and cultural heritage and an enduring connection with Israel. Through promoting lifelong Jewish learning, the Bureau of Jewish Education will play a vital role in fostering meaningful Jewish continuity and strengthening contemporary American Jewish life.

MISSION: The mission of the Bureau of Jewish Education of Greater Los Angeles is to enhance quality, increase access, and encourage participation in Jewish education throughout the Jewish communities of greater Los Angeles. The Bureau independently and in collaboration with schools and other community institutions is an advocate, planner, catalyst, and creative leader for strengthening and advancing Jewish learning, with special emphasis on children and youth, early childhood through high school, their educators and parents.

VALUES: Jewish education matters; it is essential for the individual Jew.

Jewish education matters; it is essential to the Jewish community.

Jewish education should be available to all who seek it.

Jewish education of children is a collective Jewish responsibility.

Multiple visions of Jewish education are to be respected.

Jewish educational institutions are enhanced by interaction with each other.

The quality of Jewish education matters.

The institutional health of Jewish schools matters.

Learning is life long.

The Los Angeles BJE, like many others, has adopted a strategic plan—in consultation with stake-holders—identifying specific goals and objectives for the advancement of Jewish education in the community it serves. By way of demonstrating what Bureaus of Jewish Education can, in today's environment, contribute "to enhance quality, increase access, and encourage participation," an example of recent and current initiatives—one in each of these domains—follows. There is, of course, a symbiotic relationship between quality, access and heightened participation, and progress in any of these domains impacts the others.

ENHANCING QUALITY

In the two decades from 1945 to 1965 Los Angeles Jewry grew from 160,000 to 500,000 residents. This growth was accompanied by a proliferation of Jewish schools, and the community's BJE provided the array of educational services referenced by Ackerman. By the early 1990s nearly 30,000 students were enrolled in 150 day schools, supplementary religious schools and early childhood education centers. In considering how, strategically, to better achieve the goal of enhancing educational quality, the BJE decided to develop a process of school accreditation. Such a program would begin with comprehensive self-study, include a site visit by an outside team of educators and provide grant support for school improvement activities resulting from recommendations emerging from the process. Because the Bureau works closely with all school clusters, it was readily able (over the course of the 1993–94 school year) to engage (school-based) stakeholder groups to develop procedures of accreditation. In the case of day schools, the BJE partnered with regional and private school accrediting authorities to undertake joint accreditation (with the BJE naming an educator with expertise in Jewish education to each visiting team and attaching its self-study requirements to the standard protocol). In addition to offering the "carrot" of financial grants to address issues identified through the accreditation process, the "stick" was a BJE Board mandate that only schools that were accredited would qualify for communal funding. Schools were given a decade over which to meet the new standard. As an outgrowth of this "quality enhancement" agenda, all thirty-seven day schools successfully undertook BJE accreditation. Previously only one half of the day schools had been accredited by secular accrediting bodies, and those that were so accredited had not been called upon to invest the same level of attention to Jewish educational self-study as was now required. More than eighty percent of the community's supplementary schools met the BJE–established accreditation standard within a decade. For several such schools the process served as a vehicle for re-thinking, re-imagining and re-inventing a long-static educational program. School improvement grants helped all accredited schools implement concrete quality enhancement strategies emerging from self-study and professional review. The Bureau of Jewish Education published and disseminated information about the assorted school improvement initiatives in process at the various schools.

INCREASING ACCESS

By 2004 nearly 10,000 students were enrolled in the community's 37 day schools. The aggregate operating budgets of these schools were in the neighborhood of $130 million, and the gap between tuition income and operating expenses was $30 million annually. The BJE approached the L.A. Federation with a novel idea: funding an appropriate professional at the BJE who would be dedicated full-time to operational capacity building in the day school sector. Projected activities would range from group purchasing to disseminating operational "best practices," facilitating grant applications, strengthening pupil recruitment and retention and launching an endowment campaign to create an additional revenue stream for day schools. Not only did the Federation respond positively to the funding request, it made available a highly qualified senior Federation professional to "relocate" to the Bureau to take on this new role within the agency. The "yield," in two short years, has been extraordinary, including millions of dollars in grants for day schools from external sources, hundreds of additional pupils through strengthened recruitment and retention, joint (consortium) arrangements for a variety of services and planning toward a day school endowment campaign. These activities aim to create the capacity to make day school education more accessible to more people who seek it. The BJE has benefited not only from the support of its Federation but from close collaboration with the Partnership for Excellence in Jewish Education (PEJE)—an example of synergy with a funding group that recognizes the important role that central agencies can play in the advancement of Jewish education on the local level.

ENCOURAGING PARTICIPATION

Only recently did the Los Angeles BJE formally add to its historic "quality" and "access" mission the role of actively encouraging participation in Jewish education. Toward accomplishing this end the agency is conducting market research among Jewish families with children in early childhood education programs (under Jewish auspices and otherwise) as a starting point for developing appropriate strategies to promote engagement in Jewish education in any of its expressions. The BJE has developed a well-publicized website, *www.MyJewishResource.com*, at which it posts a variety of Jewish educational opportunities for persons of all ages. The Bureau will soon establish a CRM (Customer Relationship Management) system to help individuals and families navigate the expanding array of Jewish educational opportunities. A new initiative led by the Lippman Kanfer Institute at JESNA in collaboration with central agencies will further explore new approaches to "linking the silos," which will support the work of the Los Angeles BJE as it reaches further into the community to strengthen Jewish education.

ENHANCING QUALITY, INCREASING ACCESS AND ENCOURAGING PARTICIPATION

A recent service learning initiative—made possible by a three-year grant from the Covenant Foundation (an example of growing Foundation impact in sponsoring Jewish educational initiatives)—aimed at Jewish teens has met with success in achieving all three "prongs" of quality, access and participation. Recognizing the importance of reflecting on community service—service that has deep roots in Jewish life—and conscious of the reality that most teens today are in search of service opportunities to meet high school requirements, the Los Angeles BJE developed a multi-faceted approach to Teen Service Learning (see *www.SulamCenter.org*). By providing scores of "vetted" service opportunities appropriate for teens, developing and making available companion materials drawn from Jewish teaching and guiding personal reflection, training teachers/youth leaders in service learning and organizing group service learning opportunities, the Bureau has been able to:

(a) enhance the quality of Jewish education for those in the system;

(b) make access to Jewish educational opportunity readily available (while meeting the immediate need of the learner); and

(c) encourage participation in Jewish educational experiences both by meeting an ostensibly unrelated need (i.e., fulfilling a service requirement) and by facilitating interaction between Jewish teens with varying degrees of involvement in Jewish activities—interactions that sometimes, through peer connections, lead to expanded Jewish educational engagement.

EMERGING DIRECTIONS

As central agencies for Jewish education become centers of excellence in spheres of activity ranging from service learning to Hebrew language education, school accreditation, and the provision of special education support services, the desirability of disseminating best practices is evident. JESNA has strengthened its collaboration with central agencies with the aim of diffusing best practices. ADCA, the Association of Directors of Central Agencies (a professional network of central agency executive directors) undertakes—in collaboration with JESNA—to share information and approaches to meeting common challenges. As central agencies further their work in particular areas of service, there is growing reason to anticipate that the benefits of such success will be disseminated and adapted as appropriate.

The proliferation of philanthropic foundations interested in the advancement of Jewish education offers significant opportunities. Central agencies not only provide a value-added benefit in accomplishing particular outcomes; they provide enduring capacity to apply the learnings of their various initiatives on a continuing basis. The interest of many foundations in cutting-edge projects, however, combined with the trend toward designated giving in the world of federations, leaves some central agencies hard pressed to fund such activities as teacher referral, in-service teacher education, principals councils (for networking and professional growth) and other valuable but not cutting-edge services that don't necessarily appeal to idiosyncratic funders. Moreover, cutting-edge initiatives that establish their impact over a two- or three-year grant period cease—by dint of their proven track record—to be cutting-edge, posing a funding challenge. As with "rediscovering" Bureaus as essential Jewish educational hubs, it is hoped that vital activities at the heart of creating educational capacity will likewise be discovered as worthy of broad, continuing financial support. It is the responsibility of central agencies for Jewish education to effectively make the case for meeting essential long-term needs.

CONCLUSION

In most communities the era of marginalizing central agencies has passed as their value as hubs for enhancing quality, increasing access and encouraging participation is acknowledged. The "new Central Agency"—whether an independent agency or a department of a community's Jewish federation—is closely aligned with local federations, works to implement a well-conceived strategic plan and recognizes that Jewish education includes but is by no means limited to Jewish schools. It is committed to the pursuit of excellence and benefits from the partnership and shared vision of dedicated board leaders and skilled professionals. As foundations, federations and others interested in the advancement of Jewish education look to effect systemic change, the Central Agency represents an important vehicle for achieving significant outcomes in local communities, linking community institutions and individuals with one another and connecting local communities to national initiatives. As the late Professor Walter Ackerman, a keen observer and incisive commentator on the state of Jewish education in the United States, often remarked, "If Bureaus of Jewish Education didn't already exist, they would need to be invented."

There is every reason to anticipate that, should a third volume of this book appear fifteen years from now, its chapter on central agencies for Jewish education will chronicle substantial impact on Jewish educational activities and outcomes during an era of hitherto unparalleled possibility.

HIGHLIGHTS

- Central agencies for Jewish education, initiated in the generation 1910–1940 as central "district" offices of communally sponsored Jewish education, had, by mid-twentieth century, become service resources for autonomous (most typically, synagogue-sponsored) schools.

- Malaise about the efficacy of Jewish education as purveyed in the latter part of the twentieth century—in light of a "survival" crisis reflected in NJPS data—spawned Federation-sponsored Continuity Commissions in the 1980s and 1990s, sometimes marginalizing central agencies for Jewish education. Omission of central agencies in *What We Know about Jewish Education* (Kelman 1992) was symptomatic of the view that central agencies were "dinosaurs."

- By the early twenty-first century, particularly as mega-foundations undertook focused, substantial investment in Jewish education, the need for communal "hubs" of Jewish educational connection among and between the various institutions providing Jewish education, of encouraging participation in and offering counsel regarding Jewish educational opportunities to a broad public and of contributing expertise to Jewish educational initiatives on a community-wide basis was increasingly recognized. Central agencies for Jewish education are mechanisms capable of effectively meeting these needs.

- Central agencies for Jewish education are increasingly in contact with one another and with national Jewish educational initiatives, and it can be projected that dissemination of "best practices" through central agencies will become commonplace.

THE LARGER CONTEXT

With a proliferating array of Jewish educational experiences, educational institutions and funders of Jewish educational initiatives, the need for communal hubs of Jewish education connecting people and institutions, disseminating best practices and contributing value-added educational and operational expertise is increasingly recognized. Central agencies for Jewish education, launched in the first half of the twentieth century as operators of community Talmud Torahs and transformed by mid-century into educational service providers, are, at the beginning of the twenty-first century, uniquely poised to fill the role described by Jack Wertheimer as "linking the silos" and to nurture and strengthen communities' Jewish educational systems.

ANNOTATED BIBLIOGRAPHY

Ackerman, W. I. (1973). The Jewish School System in the United States, in D. Sidorsky (ed.), *The Future of the Jewish Community in America*. New York: Basic Books, 176-210. This critical look at the state of Jewish education in the U.S. one generation after World War II first appeared in the *American Jewish Year Book*, vol. 70 (1969), 3–36. I have referenced it as part of Sidorsky's volume, as the reader can find a number of significant articles of Jewish educational interest—in addition to Ackerman's (for example, Seymour Fox's "Toward a General Theory of Jewish Education")—in that work.

Gannes, A.P. (1954). *Central Community Agencies for Jewish Education*. Philadelphia: The Dropsie College for Hebrew and Cognate Learning. This volume explores the development of Bureaus of Jewish Education, 1910 until the early 1950s. It remains the only book-length treatment of the subject.

Graff, G. (2007). Jewish Education in the United States of America. *Encyclopedia Judaica,* second edition, vol. 6, 189–204. A broad look at developments in Jewish education in America from colonial times to the present. Examines the growing array of Jewish educational settings and concomitant proliferation of educational institutions.

Graff, G. (1991). Whither the BJE? Towards a Central Agency for Jewish Education. Unpublished paper presented to the Jerusalem Fellows. Summarizes historic roles of BJEs over the twentieth century and proposes a more comprehensive and essential role for the BJE of the future—a role that as the current chapter suggests, Bureaus are increasingly coming to play.

Krasner, J.B. (2005, 2006). "Jewish Education and American Jewish Education." *Journal of Jewish Education* 71:2, 121–178; 71:3, 279–318; 72:1, 29–76. This three-part series explores the central themes in articles appearing in the periodical *Jewish Education* (renamed *Journal of Jewish Education* in 1994), from its inception in 1929 to 1970. As many contributors to the periodical—and all of its editors—were professionals active in Bureaus of Jewish Education, Krasner's engaging synthesis and analysis of four decades of publications in the educational journal offers an excellent look at prevailing currents of thought and practice as seen through the eyes of central agency personnel.

Wertheimer, J. (2005) *Linking the Silos: How to Accelerate the Momentum in Jewish Education Today*. New York: Avi Chai. A research paper that argues that the field of Jewish education is today challenged to "link the silos"—i.e., connect Jewish educational entities operating in isolation—by building cooperation across institutional lines.

REFERENCES

Ackerman, W. I. (1973). The Jewish School System in the United States. In D. Sidorsky (ed.), *The Future of the Jewish Community in America*. New York: Basic Books, 176–210.

Bentwich, N. (1953). The Kehillah of New York, 1908–1922. In M. Davis (ed.), *Mordecai M. Kaplan Jubilee Volume*. New York: Jewish Theological Seminary of America, 73–85.

Dushkin, A. and Engleman, U. (1959). *Jewish Education in the United States*. New York: American Association for Jewish Education.

Gannes, A.P. (1954). *Central Community Agencies for Jewish Education*. Philadelphia: The Dropsie College for Hebrew and Cognate Learning.

Goren, A. A. (1970). *New York Jews and the Quest for Community*. New York: Columbia University Press.

Graff, G. (2007). Jewish Education in the United States of America. *Encyclopedia Judaica,* second edition, vol. 6, 189–204.

Graff, G. (1991) Whither the BJE? Towards a Central Agency for Jewish Education. Unpublished paper presented to the Jerusalem Fellows .

Jacoby, E. (1998). *Accreditation Manual for Jewish Schools*. Los Angeles: Bureau of Jewish Education of Greater Los Angeles.

Kelman, S. (1992) (ed.). *What We Know about Jewish Education*. Los Angeles: Torah Aura Productions.

Krasner, J.B. (2005,2006). "Jewish Education and American Jewish Education." *Journal of Jewish Education* 71:2, 121–178; 71:3, 279–318; 72:1, 29–76.

Wertheimer, J. (2005) *Linking the Silos: How to Accelerate the Momentum in Jewish Education Today*. New York: Avi Chai.

Winter, N.H. (1966). *Jewish Education in a Pluralist Society*. New York: New York University Press.

Early Childhood Jewish Education "If Not Now, When?" (Pirkei Avot I:14)

Ilene Vogelstein

Judaism considers children a great gift and sees them "as perhaps the purest form of being in God's image" (Shire 2006). The *brit milah* or *brit habat* welcomes a child into the world and signals to the parents and the community their responsibility to raise the child spiritually as well as physically. In addition to valuing children, our sacred texts cite the importance of early education.

> *Teach a child in the way he should go and he will not stray from it even when he gets older.*—Proverbs 22:6

> *What is learned in early childhood is absorbed in the blood.*—Avot de Rabbi Natan 24

> *The most important and decisive age in education is early childhood.*— Yesodot ha Chinuch.

> *Our children are our guarantors. For their sake I give the Torah to you.*—Shir Hashirim Rabbah, 1:24

For two decades leaders in early childhood Jewish education have maintained that this period of time is crucial for instilling a strong Jewish identity in children (Ravid & Ginsburg 1988) for engaging new parents (Feldman 1992) and for serving as a gateway for additional Jewish education and involvement in synagogue and community life (Holtz 1996). Current research in the field of early childhood Jewish education further corroborates these original findings (Beck 2002; Kotler-Berkowitz 2005; Auerbach CAJE 2005; Center for Policy Research 2006; Rosenblatt 2006; Wertheimer 2005; and Rosen 2006).

Research in the fields of child development and brain development validates the importance of focusing on the early years of life. Two of the key findings have profound implications for early childhood education. The first deals with the necessary conditions for proper brain development and the second with the role of interpersonal relationships.

Brain development is now understood to be a complex interaction between genetically timed periods of development (critical periods) and appropriate sensory experiences. "Every sight, sound, and thought leaves an imprint on specific neural circuits, modifying the way future sights, sounds, and thoughts will be registered" (Eliot 1999). This means the brain is literally molded by experiences. However, if the experience is not properly timed, some opportunities, such as vision and perfect pitch, are lost forever (Riken 2005; Kuhl et al. 2001). For example, children with innate musical skills never master perfect pitch if they aren't exposed to formal music education in the first six years of their lives. Furthermore, since the brain is molded by experiences, the earlier problems are identified, the earlier they can be addressed, enabling the brain to "rewire" itself during critical periods of development. This results in a greater chance for a positive impact on the child (Stegelin 2004).

Interpersonal relationships also play a role in brain development (Shiota et al. 2004). There is a growing body of research that finds that children who are reared in healthy, nurturing and responsive relationships have fewer behavior problems and more confidence and are more capable of positive social relationships (Zero to Three 2006). While parents are children's first, most important and most influential teachers, 61% of children in the United States under the age of six are in non-parental care on a regular basis (Federal Interagency Forum on Child and Family Statistics 2002). Consequently, caregivers have a significant impact on the child's development, especially the child's sense of emotional security and trust (Bruner 2004). Early childhood educators are as critical to a child's brain development as the child's experiences and the child's parents.

The ultimate objective of the Jewish community is to build Jewish identity in the next generation. Since the experiences young children have and the competency of the adults who care for them impact how children will behave as adults, the Jewish community should ensure that every Jewish child and every Jewish family with young children have the opportunity to experience authentic, engaging and meaningful Jewish experiences. Not investing in early childhood Jewish education compromises future investments at later ages.

This chapter will discuss early childhood Jewish education programs. It will review current student demographics, the state of early childhood Jewish education and educators, the impact of early childhood Jewish education on children and families, new initiatives, challenges facing the field and, finally, recommendations for strengthening early childhood Jewish education and for building a strong Jewish identity in children and their families.

STUDENT DEMOGRAPHICS

Documenting the number of Jewish children in the United States birth through five years of age is a complicated matter. Documenting the number of Jewish children in Jewish early childhood programs is even more difficult. It appears that there are currently 540,000 Jewish children birth through five years of age, approximately 90,000 per age cohort (Saxe et al. 2007). Of that number, approximately 78,000 (mostly three- and four-year-olds) are enrolled in early childhood programs affiliated with congregations (56,000), Jewish community centers (13,000) and independent schools (9,000) (Schaap 2004). Approximately thirty-two thousand four- and five-year-olds are enrolled in Jewish day schools (Schick 2005), and an additional seven thousand children under the age of four attend Jewish day school early childhood programs (Schick 2000). This data does not include children participating in congregational schools or in Jewish family (home-based) childcare. Enrollment in early childhood programs in congregational schools is generally stable and growing in some communities (Wertheimer 2007). Anecdotal information suggests there may be 13,000 children in congregational programs and several thousand in family home-based childcare. Therefore, the total number Jewish children in any kind of Jewish early childhood program is between 130,000 and 140,000. This is less than a quarter of the potential population.

ENROLLMENT OF CHILDREN FROM TWO TO FIVE YEARS OF AGE

Enrollment in the majority of Jewish early childhood programs begins at two years of age and peaks at four years of age (Vogelstein & Kaplan 2002). The Board of Jewish Education of Greater New York noted a significant increase in enrollment between children under two years of age and children two years of age every year since 2002 (Figure #1). Enrollment between two-year-old programs and four-year-old programs almost doubles, and there was a significant (approximately 50%) decrease in enrollment between the four-year-old program and the five-year-old program.

Figure 1: BJE of Greater NY Demographic Overview, Department of Early Childhood, 2006

Age	2002–2003	2003–2004	2004–2005	2005–2006
Mommy & Me	1,884	3,022	2,729	1,781
Less than 17 months	300	318	219	302
18 months to 2 years	469	737	540	830
2-year-olds	5,344	5,417	4,807	5,340
3-year-olds	8,288	8,818	7,900	8,337
4-year-olds	9,046	9,035	8,774	9,491
5-year-olds	4,512	4,648	3,939	5,096
Total	29,752	31,995	28,908	31,177

In Miami-Dade and Broward Counties in Florida there is little change in the enrollment in the early childhood programs between the two- (931), three- (1,185) and four- (1,110) year-old-programs, but they also noted a significant decrease in enrollment in their kindergarten programs (289) (Goodman, Bidol-Padva & Schaap 2006). Likewise, The St. Louis Community Study (2005) noted there were 205 children in their four-year-old programs and only 49 five-year-olds in Jewish early childhood programs, excluding day schools. This data raises three important questions. Where do the children go after their early childhood Jewish education? Where are the children birth through two years of age? And where are all the Jewish children who are not enrolled in Jewish early childhood programs?

According to Beck in *Jewish Preschools as Gateways to Jewish Life: A Survey of Jewish Preschool Parents in Three Cities* (2002), 72% of the children enrolled in Jewish early childhood programs leave to attend public kindergarten. In Miami-Dade and Broward County 47% attend public school after Jewish early childhood education, 43% continue on to day school, 9% attend private school and 1% are lost to follow-up. In New York City almost half of the children who complete a Jewish early childhood program at the age of five go on to attend public kindergartens, and the other half attend day school. A small percentage attend private non-sectarian schools (BJE NY 2005). Many Jewish early childhood programs offered kindergarten classes prior to the availability of public kindergartens. Now very few programs offer kindergarten; most Jewish kindergartens today are part of day schools, with a few in JCCs.

As public four-year-old programs become accessible there is a possibility that families will choose free public four-year-old programs over Jewish four-year-old programs. Tuitions for full-day programs range from approximately $6,000 to $20,000 (Baltimore and New York, respectively) and $4,000 (Atlanta) for half-day programs. This has the potential of significantly reducing the number of Jewish children enrolled in Jewish programs and reducing the number of children who continue on to day school and/or religious school education. Beck (2002) noted that 53% of the children who attend public school after completing a Jewish preschool continued their Jewish education in synagogue-based religious schools the year after completing an early childhood program, and 20% enroll in day schools. In the Miami-Dade and Broward County study, 69% percent of children completing Jewish early childhood education programs continued with some form of Jewish education; thirty-one percent did not (Goodman, Schaap & Bidol-Padva 2006).

JEWISH BABIES AND NEW JEWISH PARENTS

If the majority of children enrolled in Jewish early childhood programs are three- and four -year-olds, where are the Jewish babies? Fifty-seven percent of mothers in the United Stated with children birth to three years of age are in the labor force (National Academy of Sciences 2003). Seventy-three percent of children birth to three years of age in the United States spend time in non-parental care (Honig 2003). Fifty-five percent of women with infants under a year old are in the labor force (Gardner 2001). This number is declining for the first time in twenty-five years. Women who are college-educated and earn annual salaries of $50,000 and above are more likely to enroll their children in non-parental child care (Boushey 2003). At the same time, the decline in the percentage of women with infants in the work force is among "women who are white, married, over thirty and educated" (Gardner 2001). These figures suggest two things: first, that there are likely to be large numbers of Jewish children in non–Jewish childcare programs. Second, there may be an equally large number of young children at home with their mothers. The Denver study (2006) reported that the largest number of parent respondents with children enrolled in Jewish early childhood programs are home full-time (42%); 35% work part-time, and 24% work full-time. Nearly a third (28%) have full- or part-time nanny help. Only 13% of families have two parents working full-time with no nanny. The Board of Jewish Education of Greater New York reported 2,948 or 2.9% of the potential Jewish population of children two years of age or younger were enrolled in Jewish early childhood programs in the greater New York area during the 2004–2005 school year. This phenomenon raises a number of questions. Is the percentage of Jewish women in the workforce less than in the general population? Do families choose non–Jewish childcare centers over Jewish childcare centers? Is there a need for full- or part-time Jewish infant care? What is the Jewish community doing to reach out to and support stay-at-home moms/dads?

Three studies investigated the way communities identify and engage families with newborn babies (Rosen, Lorin & Bar-Yam 2004; Rosen 2005; and Rosen 2006). These studies indicated that there was no community-wide vision for this population. Different agencies within the federation system were offering programs to new parents but failed to collaborate with each other and were in fact unaware of each other's existence. Rosen recommended that communities become better organized, systematically find the babies and develop programs that meet new parents' needs. He stated, "This cycle of Jewish life has been largely ignored. New Jewish parents were looking to connect with other new Jewish parents, obtain information on child development and strengthen their parenting skills. Only a few parents are being welcomed in any significant and meaningful way by their communities" (2006). According to Mayer et al. (2001) in the American Jewish Identity survey, this may be due to the fact that more Jews are identifying themselves as secular than with any particular religious stream of American Judaism and are consequently outside the immediate reach of the Jewish community.

IMPACT OF EARLY CHILDHOOD JEWISH EDUCATION ON JEWISH LIFE

Numerous studies indicate that children's success in life is based on a foundation of relationships, experiences, and skills developed during the first three years of life (Dealy 2006). One of these skills is identity formation, a sense of self. Early childhood Jewish education appears to impact not only the identity of the child, but also the Jewish identity of the parents. This section will discuss the research demonstrating that participation in an early childhood Jewish education program impacts parents' ritual practices, impacts parents' decisions about continuing with Jewish education and facilitates non–Jewish spousal investment in Jewish life.

IMPACT ON FAMILY RITUAL BEHAVIORS

Several studies confirm that enrolling a child in a Jewish early childhood program has direct impact on the family as well as the child. Holtz noted that "young children influence family practice, early education programs become a 'mini-community' for families and early Jewish education acts as a feeder to the larger institution in which the program is housed" (1996). Beck demonstrated that while parents were not motivated to choose a school for its Jewish content and that the Jewish curriculum was often "ad-hoc and limited," parents felt overwhelmingly positive about their child's Jewish experience "Seventy percent of those interviewed were doing something different in terms of their Jewish observance or Jewish lifestyle as a result of their [children] attending a Jewish preschool" (2002, p. iv).

More recent research from three other community studies on early childhood Jewish education noted similar findings. The Auerbach Central Agency for Jewish Education in Philadelphia stated,

The impact of Jewish early childhood education on attitudes and family practices is immediate and powerful. An awareness of the Jewish calendar is developed and rituals are being practiced in the home as parents become interested in what Judaism can offer in terms of meaningful tools for living. Long-term effects of Jewish early childhood programs are also indicated. Parents frequently decide to join a synagogue and to continue their children's Jewish education (2005).

Rosenblatt (2006) and Center for Policy Research (Denver 2006) reports both noted a positive impact and increased engagement in the families' Jewish activities, parents' willingness to consider additional Jewish educational options for their children and an increased inclination to learn more about Judaism. Over 80% of the families in the Denver study changed their behavior as a result of their Jewish early childhood experience.

IMPACT ON FUTURE JEWISH EDUCATION

In addition to impacting Jewish family practice, participation in Jewish early childhood programs served as a catalyst for further Jewish education. Beck found that upon completing the Jewish early childhood programs, the overwhelming majority (76%) of the interviewed families continued their children's Jewish education the year after completing their early childhood experience. "Among the families who had not enrolled their child in a formal Jewish education program subsequent to completing preschool, 80% had specific plans to enroll their child in such a program within the next year or two" (2002, p. 13).

Wertheimer noted that children who attend a Jewish early childhood program were more likely to participate in many different forms of Jewish educational experiences than children who did not attend a Jewish early childhood program. Eighty-six percent of children who attended a Jewish early childhood program are currently enrolled in some form of Jewish education, and 60% of children who attended a Jewish early childhood program are actively involved in Jewish youth groups (2005, p. 15). It is important to note that the percentage of children continuing their Jewish education varies depending on the religious orientation of the early childhood program. Schaap, Goodman & Bidol-Padva (2006) noted that 84% of children in early childhood programs in day schools in Miami continue with their Jewish education compared to 64% and 56% respectively from Conservative and Reform congregation early childhood programs. Fifteen percent (15%) of children from JCC early childhood programs continue with their Jewish education.

These statistics strongly indicate that Jewish early childhood education makes a difference in both families' personal engagement with Jewish life and in their furthering their children's Jewish education. Early childhood Jewish education serves as a gateway for families to become involved in Jewish life (Kotler-Berkowitz 2005).

IMPACT ON INTERFAITH AND NON–JEWISH FAMILIES

An early childhood Jewish education experience also positively impacts non–Jewish spouses. A journalist for the Baltimore *Jewish Times* interviewed three non–Jewish mothers who were raising their children Jewish. They said the Jewish early childhood program welcomed them into the Jewish world and led to their thinking about becoming Jewish (Friedman 2006). One mother indicated that "This was the first place where I felt accepted as a non–Jew. I had to be accepted as a non–Jew before I could consider becoming a Jew." None of the three women intended to convert to Judaism, but learning with their children changed their minds. "You've got a preschooler that's demanding that you do something with the Shabbat basket, so you better do something!"

Interfaith families in San Francisco indicated that the early childhood program was their primary connection to the Jewish community (2006). The Denver study reported a positive impact on non–Jewish families (no Jewish adults in the household) who chose a Jewish early childhood program for their children. Sixty percent of the non–Jewish families said that their child's experience at a Jewish early childhood program has made them feel more positive about Judaism and the Jewish people (2006).

The evidence seems irrefutable. Early childhood Jewish education strengthens the Jewish identity and the Jewish ritual behaviors of parents and impacts parents' future Jewish education decisions. A Jewish early childhood experience serves as families' primary connection to the Jewish community for the majority of the parents and an important connection for many parents. Furthermore, an early childhood Jewish education experience has a positive impact on interfaith families. These studies suggest communities, federations and philanthropists should ensure that all Jewish children have the opportunity to attend an early childhood Jewish education program.

CREATING EXCELLENCE IN EARLY CHILDHOOD JEWISH EDUCATION

The importance of providing quality experiences for young children is now influencing pedagogic approaches and criteria for excellence in early childhood education in the secular world. Current accreditation programs have developed new core competencies and standards for excellence and many states are developing their own accreditation programs (Barnett 2005, NAEYC 2006). Research documenting the positive and powerful impact of an early Jewish education experience has had similar effect in the Jewish community. There have been several attempts to quantify excellence in Jewish early childhood programs. The *Best Practices Project in Early Childhood Jewish Education* (Holtz 1996) was one of the first to identify categories of best practice in Jewish early childhood programs. Four communities—Los Angeles, Chicago, Boston and Washington, DC—each developed Jewish accreditation programs that augment the National Associate for the Education of Young Children (NAEYC) accreditation standards. In 2004 the CAJE Early Childhood Department commissioned the Center for Applied Child Development at the Eliot Pearson Department of Child Development at Tufts University to develop a "Preliminary List of Quality Indicators" for early childhood Jewish education. The Tufts investigators began their work by interviewing Jewish early childhood teachers, many of whom felt that the primary criteria for excellence was cultivating Jewish identity in children and creating an emotionally based Jewish foundation that would either sustain ongoing Jewish education or coax their young students to return to Jewish life if they later chose to leave it. At this time there are no commonly accepted standards of excellence for early childhood Jewish education and no research on the pedagogic, curricular and/or organizational practices that would facilitate the replication of excellence when it occurs. There are, however, numerous independent and collaborative conversations around this topic.

The Jewish Early Childhood Education Initiative (JECEI) was established in 2005 specifically to focus on "creating a vision of excellence, embodied in the creation of vanguard centers using the best practices of early childhood, adult and family education, the most recent studies in brain development and social/emotional learning, and the accumulated lessons of organizational change efforts throughout the educational world." JECEI hopes "to create a vision of early childhood education framed by and embedded within foundational Jewish values that are meaningful and compelling to contemporary Jewish families seeking supportive communities for their families and the highest quality education for their children" (*www.jecei.org*).

Project Kavod, the Alliance for Jewish Early Education, the Coalition for the Advancement of Jewish Education, the United Synagogue of Conservative Judaism, the Union for Reform Judaism and the Jewish Community Center Association of North America are all addressing the issue of program standards and indicators of excellence for early childhood Jewish education programs.

PROFESSIONALS IN EARLY CHILDHOOD JEWISH EDUCATION

One of the primary factors for achieving excellence in early childhood programs is professionals. "Teacher quality is the single most important feature of the schools that drives student achievement" (Haskins and Loeb 2007). Two variables that have been identified as critical for staff quality are education and wages (Burchinal et al. 1996; Goelman et al. 2006; Whitebook 2003). All states require kindergarten teachers to have a minimum of a bachelor's degree, but few states require bachelor's degrees for early childhood teachers (Bell et. al. 2002). This is beginning to change. States are increasing their standards for early educators in light of research on the importance of interpersonal relationships and environments for young children (American Federation of Teachers 2002; Barnett et al. 2005) and the opening of state-financed pre-K programs. By 2010, BA degrees and early childhood training will be required of all National Association for the Education of Young Children accredited schools (NAEYC 2006).

Jewish early childhood education should be no different. Early childhood educators hold the key to quality in Jewish early childhood programs. "There is no place in Jewish education where personnel matters more than in early childhood Jewish education. The teachers' influence on young children is comparable to virtually no other area in Jewish education" (Holtz 1996). Unfortunately, most early childhood Jewish educators have limited Jewish knowledge (Gamoran et al. 1998), inadequate training in early childhood education (Goodman 2006) and are poorly compensated (Vogelstein & Kaplan 2002; Goodman 2006). (See Goodman & Schaap chapter on Jewish Education Personnel for an extensive discussion on early childhood Jewish educators.) The lack of training in child development is exacerbated by the lack of Judaic knowledge. Research studies on religious education suggest the lack of authenticity alienates children from their religion. Haskins and Loeb (2007) noted that older students do better when their teachers are of their own race. These research findings raise questions about the large number of non–Jewish teachers and Jewish educators with limited Jewish knowledge employed in Jewish early childhood programs (Krug & Schade 2004).

In an effort to address the lack of secular and Judaic training of early childhood professionals, two national organizations collaborated to create standards. The National Board of License for Teachers and Principals of Jewish Schools in North America and The Alliance for Jewish Early Education (a network of national organizations that provide services and/or advocacy for early childhood Jewish education) recently adopted professional standards for all educators working in Jewish early childhood programs. There are five levels. Level One requires 120 hours of training in child development and early childhood education integrated with Jewish values and concepts. Level Five requires a master's degree in Early Childhood Jewish Education.

But these standards are vacuous if central agencies of Jewish education and federations do not endorse these standards; if there are no incentives or requirements to fulfill and/or enforce them; if there are no programs for the approximately 16,000 early childhood educators to obtain certificates/degrees; and if there are no subsidies to enable the educators to participate in the certificate and degree programs. Currently only one Jewish institution of higher learning offers a master's degree in early childhood Jewish education, and it is in conjunction with a secular university. One Jewish institution of higher learning offers a bachelor's degree, and three Jewish institutions of higher learning offer certificates or courses in early childhood Jewish education. Two of these institutions offer courses online. In the summer of 2007 seven Jewish institutions of higher learning will meet to discuss the challenges facing educating the early childhood Jewish education workforce.

While fewer than one hundred early childhood educators are currently seeking degrees or certificates at Jewish institutions of higher learning, most early childhood educators participate in professional development programs, including workshops and conferences offered by central agencies for Jewish education, the Early Childhood Conference sponsored by the Coalition for the Advancement in Jewish Education (CAJE), The Union for Reform Judaism Annual Early Childhood Conference and secular conferences such as NAEYC. Research has clearly demonstrated that in order for professional development to actually improve teacher quality it must 1) be a multi-day program; 2) focus on subject matter instruction; and 3) have goals that are aligned with the goals and curriculum of the school (Haskins and Loeb 2007). Mentoring is also an effective technique for improving teacher quality. The Union for Reform Judaism, the United Synagogue of Conservative Judaism and the Jewish Community Center Association of North America each employ an early childhood consultant to serve their constituent schools.

SALARY AND COMPENSATION—CRISIS IN RECRUITING NEW PROFESSIONALS

Sufficient training programs that coincide with the new standards would still not solve the most pressing professional challenge—the recruitment of new professionals. The average age of early childhood educators in Jewish programs is 46. The majority of directors are in their 50s (Vogelstein & Kaplan 2002; Schaap 2004; Goodman, Bidol-Padva & Schaap 2006). The need to attract new educators to the field is critical. But, it is highly unlikely to attract and retain the best and the brightest with the current compensation packages. Early care and education has not been acknowledged as a part of the larger educational system in the United States. As such, early childhood teachers and care-givers are among the lowest-paying of all occupations (Barnett 2003). "Only 18 occupations out of 770 surveyed by the Bureau of Labor Statistics (2006) reported having lower mean wages than child care workers. Those who earned higher wages included service station attendants, bicycle repair-ers and locker room attendants" (Center for Childcare Workforce 2004). Rationales for maintaining low wages include the assumption that women are not the primary breadwinners of families and that this profession does not require great skill or education. Current research contradicts those as-sumptions. We unequivocally know that quality early education is dependent on skilled and knowl-edgeable educators (Bruner 2004) and that there is an increase in single women heading households (National Academy of Sciences 2003). Furthermore, salary is now the main source of income for 28% of early childhood teachers in Jewish early childhood programs and an important source of income for 91% of the teachers in Miami-Dade and Broward County, Florida (Goodman, Schaap & Bidol-Padva 2006).

An additional challenge to recruitment is the increasing demand for early childhood teachers in the public schools. As states mandate universal pre-K programs to boost kindergarten readiness, more early childhood teachers will be required. As public schools expand their programs and hire more trained early childhood teachers, the compensation levels will, of necessity, increase significantly. But will the Jewish early childhood programs be able to keep up? As a comparison, the national me-dian salary for a preschool teacher in 2004 was $20,980 and the national median for a kindergarten teacher ranged from $41,400–$45,370 plus benefits, with the top 10% earning between $66,240 and $71,370 (Bureau of Labor Statistics 2006). The national median salary for an early childhood educa-tor in a Jewish program in 2004 was $15,000, compared to $41,250 for day school educators working the same number of hours (Schaap 2004). Poor compensation and lack of incentives for additional educational training will severely threaten the quality of early childhood Jewish education in the coming decade.

NEW INITIATIVES

In her 1992 chapter in *What We Know about Jewish Education*, Feldman discussed the major is-sues facing early childhood Jewish education and suggested a four-part strategy for addressing those issues.

1. Conceptualize Jewish early childhood programs as Jewish family resource centers.
2. Relieve families of the financial pressure of an early childhood Jewish education by sharing the fiscal responsibility with a third party (e.g., federations, synagogues and/or JCCs).
3. Create mechanisms for training early childhood professionals.
4. Develop a curriculum that reflects a vibrant Judaism appropriate for young children.

Unfortunately, in the fifteen years since its publication, only a few of these strategies have been ad-dressed. As we look to the future, each of these policy recommendations remain high on the agenda if quality early childhood Jewish education is to be achieved. Several new initiatives have emerged to respond to challenges facing the field.

- An Ethical Start® is an innovative multimedia curriculum for early childhood educators and par-ents in Jewish Community Centers. The program is designed to teach Jewish values from *Pirkei Avot*. There are over twenty early childhood programs in Jewish community centers currently participating in An Ethical Start.
- Early Childhood Department at the Coalition for the Advancement of Jewish Education serves as the leading national advocate and the primary venue for research on early childhood Jewish education; it provides professional services for any early childhood educator and promotes ex-cellent and authentic Jewish educational experiences for children and their families. *www.caje. org/earlychildhood*.

- JECEI offers the field of Jewish early childhood education a vision of excellence embodied in the creation of vanguard centers using the best practices of early childhood, adult and family education, the most recent studies in brain development and social/emotional learning and the accumulated lessons of organizational change efforts throughout the educational world. JECEI's work signifies an important departure from the commonplace standards in the field toward a unique and vibrant vision of early childhood education. JECEI is framed by and embedded within foundational Jewish values that are meaningful and compelling to contemporary Jewish families seeking supportive communities for their families and the highest quality education for their children. JECEI is currently working in sixteen schools. (Retrieved from *http://www.jecei. org/vision.html* October, 2006.)

- The Jewish Community Centers of North America offers early childhood consultation services for early childhood programs associated with the JCCA.

- *Ma'alah* is a program model designed to promote excellence in teaching Hebrew by Immersion to three- and four-year-olds. It is now in twenty-six schools. *Ma'alah* was an initiative of The Jewish Theological Seminary's Melton Research Center for Jewish Education. The goal of the project is to build a strong Jewish identity and connection to Israel by acquiring Hebrew as a second language when children are most receptive to learning a new language. Research suggests second languages are more easily learned when children are under six years of age. (Retrieved from *http://learn.jtsa.edu/topics/kids/maalah.shtml* October, 2006.)

- The Florence Melton Adult Mini-School Parent Education Program (PEP) is an adaptation of the Adult Mini-School program specifically for parents whose children are in Jewish early childhood programs. PEP is designed to match the Jewish learning interests of the parents of young children. Texts and discussions are designed to show the learners how the concepts they learn in class are relevant and applicable to their lives as Jewish parents. One of the main objectives of PEP is to encourage the learners to take the conversation home. (Retrieved from *http://www. fmams.org.il/pep/pep.html* October, 2006.)

- PJ Library is a program that sends participating children a high-quality Jewish children's book or CD every month through age five. Each book and CD comes with helpful resources. The goals of the program are to create stronger Jewish homes by fostering children's curiosity about their Jewish heritage and to help families explore their Jewish identity. The program is currently serving nearly 1,500 families in 12 communities. The PJ Library is sponsored by the Harold Grinspoon Foundation. (Retrieved from *http://www.pjlibrary.org <http://www.pjlibrary.org/>* October, 2006.)

- Project ENGAJE is a two-year professional development program for 250 early childhood educators in eleven New York early childhood programs to enhance their Judaic knowledge through informal lectures, text learning, group discussions and a 10-day trip to Israel. The program was sponsored by UJA-Federation of New York in partnership with the Board of Jewish Education of Greater New York and the Suffolk Association of Jewish Educational Services. (Retrieved October, 2006 from *http://www.ujafedny.org/site/c.ggLUI0OzGpF/b.1886315/apps/s/content.asp?ct=2685933.*)

- Project Kavod is a three-year pilot project conducted in partnership with the Center for the Advancement of Jewish Education in Miami to improve the quality of Jewish education by addressing the recruitment and retention of Jewish education personnel and the culture of employment in which they work. (*http://www.caje.org/interact/ProjectKavod-index.html.*)

- The Union for Reform Judaism Department of Lifelong Jewish Learning provides a variety of services for the Jewish early childhood education community including development opportunities, publications and consultation services to existing and new programs. (*http://urj. org/educate/childhood/.*)

- The United Synagogue for Conservative Judaism Department of Education offers early childhood consultation services that provide active support for early childhood programs in USCJ congregations and Solomon Schechter day schools. (*http://uscj.org/About6767.html.*)

FUTURE IMPLICATIONS

It is clear an early childhood Jewish education experience has a powerful impact on the children and the families who participate in these programs. But the research is incomplete. Were the parents who chose early childhood Jewish education predisposed to identifying with and participating in Jewish education and therefore more likely to respond positively? Why don't more parents choose early childhood Jewish education programs? What is the impact of an early childhood Jewish education on the children and families who do not continue their Jewish education? Why don't more families continue with Jewish education when the early childhood experience is so positive? How do we capture the curricular and pedagogic practices that result in positive outcomes? In order for early childhood Jewish education to compete with other public and private early childhood programs it must meet, and preferably exceed, the current standards for early childhood education.

To achieve the ultimate objectives of instilling a strong Jewish identity in children, strengthening the Jewish identity of families, and serving as a key gateway to life long Jewish living and learning, the Jewish community needs to focus on engaging the families, strengthening the professionals, building excellent programs and creating local and national infrastructures.

POLICY IMPLICATIONS FOR ENGAGING FAMILIES

Communities need to

- Develop an effective infrastructure for finding and engaging new families.
- Develop programs to attract and retain parents with children from birth through age three.
- Provide incentives to families to choose Jewish early childhood programs over public and other private early childhood programs.
- Provide support to early childhood programs that are a part of a congregational school.
- Provide support to home-based family child care programs.
- Invite parents to participate as equal partners in creating and implementing the new vision.

Policy implications for professionals in early childhood Jewish education:

- Provide equitable compensation for early childhood Jewish educators.
- Create and support Jewish early childhood certification and degree programs.
- Provide stipends and salary incentives for early childhood educators to participate in certification and degree programs.

POLICY IMPLICATIONS FOR EARLY CHILDHOOD JEWISH EDUCATION PROGRAMS

- Build stronger relationships and infrastructures with host institution professionals, clergy and lay leadership.
- Conceptualize Jewish early childhood programs as Jewish family resource centers.
- Increase family engagement, family involvement and family education in the early childhood programs.
- Ensure every early childhood program has a clear vision.
- Assist families with post-early childhood Jewish education and adult Jewish education decisions.
- Make visible the positive impact of an early childhood Jewish education.
- Apply the latest research to create the highest quality Jewish early education practices.
- Develop standards or quality indicators specifically for early childhood Jewish education programs based on Jewish values and concepts.
- Assist schools in identifying outcomes and meeting performance evaluations.
- Increase the number of Hebrew immersion programs.
- Continue to research, document and evaluate the impact of the programs.

POLICY IMPLICATIONS FOR SYSTEMIC CHANGE

- Develop effective community infrastructures for addressing the challenges facing early childhood Jewish education.

- Centralize all early childhood Jewish education efforts within each community in order to minimize the "silo" effect.

- Make families with young children a communal and national priority.

- Strengthen the relationship between early childhood programs, day schools, religious schools, and congregations.

- Build communal institutional networks and collaborations.

- Support existing national institutional networks and collaborations.

- Provide support to early childhood programs that are a part of a congregational school

- Provide support to Jewish home-based family day care programs.

- Strengthen the relationship between early childhood programs and other communal Jewish institutions.

CONCLUSION

Among all forms of Jewish education, early childhood Jewish education holds one of the greatest potentials for the future viability of the North American Jewish community. It instills a Jewish identity in children, one that is permanently imprinted in their brains and that will remain with them throughout their lives. It strengthens the Jewish identity and practice of families, provides a significant venue for adults to connect with other Jewish adults and serves as a pivotal gateway into further involvement and commitment to Jewish life and the Jewish community. This opportunity is threatened by both present and future challenges. Poor compensation and insufficient child development and Jewish knowledge threaten the quality of the early childhood educator, the quality of the programs and the ability to inspire and engage families. Early childhood Jewish education is limited to a five-year window—from birth until the child enters kindergarten. All of the research indicates that these are critical years in the development of the child and engagement of the family. As with the critical periods of brain development, if this opportunity is missed, it may be lost forever.

REFERENCES

American Federation of Teachers (December 2002). *At the starting line: Early childhood education in the 50 states.* *http://www.aft.org/pubs-reports/downloads/teachers/EarlyChildhoodreport.pdf* (retrieved February, 2006).

Auerbach Central Agency for Jewish Education (2006). *Effects of Jewish early childhood programs on family engagement in Jewish life. www.acaje.org*

Barnett, S. (2003). *Low wages = low quality. Solving the real teacher preschool crisis.* New York: National Institute for Early Education Research *http://nieer.org/resources/factsheets/3.pdf* (retrieved May, 2006)

Barnett, W., Hustedt, J., Robin, K. & Schulman, M. (2005). *The state of preschool: 2005 State Preschool Yearbook.* New Jersey: National Institute for Early Education Research.

Beck, P. (2002). *Jewish preschools as gateways to Jewish life: A survey of Jewish parents in three cities.* New York: Ukeles, Inc. *http://caje.org/earlychildhood/JECEPFinalReporte11-11MK.pdf.* (Retrieved January, 2006)

Bell, D., Burtin, A., Whitebood, M., Broatch, I. & Young, M. (2002). *Inside the pre-K classroom: A study of staffing and stability in state funded pre-K programs.* Center for Childcare Workforce. Washington, D.C. *http://www.ccw.org/pubs/ccw_pre-k_10.4.02.pdf* (retrieved May, 2006).

Board of Jewish Education of Greater New York Demographic Overview 2005–2006 (2006). New York: Board of Jewish Education of Greater New York.

Boushey, H. (2003). *Who Cares? The Child Care Choices of Working Mothers.* Center for Economic and Policy Research *http://www.cepr.net/publications/child_care_2003.htm* (retrieved February, 2006)

Bruner, B. (2004). "Harvard Family Research Project. "*The Evaluation Exchange*, 2, 24–25.

Burchinal, M.R., Roberts, J. E., Nabors, L.A. & Bryant, D.M. (1996). "Quality of center child care and infant cognitive and language development." *Child Development* 67, 606–620.

Bureau of Labor Statistics, U.S. Department of Labor. *Occupational Outlook Handbook, 2006–07 Edition*, Teachers—Preschool, Kindergarten, Elementary, Middle, and Secondary, on the Internet at *http://www.bls.gov/oco/ocos069.htm* (retrieved October 31, 2006).

Center for the Child Care Workforce (2004). Current data on the salaries and benefits of the U.S. early childhood workforce. *http://ccw.cleverspin.com/pubs/2004Compendium.pdf* (retrieved February 2006).

Center for Policy Research (2006). *Jewish Early Childhood Education in Denver and Boulder: Mapping the Field.* Denver: Center for Policy Research.

Central Agency for Jewish Education in St. Louis (2005). School census: Early childhood through adult 2004–2005. St. Louis: Central Agency for Jewish Education.

Dealy, K. (2006). Foundations: How states can plan & fund programs for babies & toddlers. Ounce of Prevention Foundation. *www.ounceofprevention.org* (retrieved October 2006).

Eliot, L. (1999). *What's Going on in there? How the Mind Develops in the First Five Years of Life.* New York: Bantam Books.

Federal Interagency Forum on Child and Family Statistics. *America's Children: Key National Indicators of Well-Being,* 2002. Federal Interagency Forum on Child and Family Statistics, Washington, DC: U.S. Government Printing Office.

Feldman, R. (1992). *What We Know about Jewish Education.* Los Angeles: Torah Aura Productions, pp. 81–88.

Friedman, S. (2006, March 31). "Conversion of thought." *Baltimore Jewish Times,* pp. 34–35.

Gardner, M. (2001). *Mothers who choose to stay home. http://www.csmonitor.com/2001/1114/p13s1-lifp.html%0A* (retrieved April, 2007).

Gamoran, A. et al. (1998). *The Teachers Report: A Portrait of Teachers in Jewish Schools.* New York: Council for Initiatives in Jewish Education.

Goelman, H., Forger, B., Kershaw, P., Doherty, G., Lero, D. & LaGrange, A. (2006). "Towards a predictive model of quality in Canadian child care centers." *Early Childhood Research Quarterly 21,* 280–295.

Goodman, R., Bidol-Padva, P. & Schaap, E. (2006). *Project Kavod: Improving the culture of employment in Jewish education. http://caje.org/interact/projectkavod.pdf* (retrieved June, 2006).

Goodman, R., Schaap E. & Bidol Padva, P. (2006). *Community report on early childhood Jewish educators: Culture of employment 2005–2005.* New York: Coalition for the Advancement of Jewish Education.

Haskins, R. & Loeb, S. (2007). *A plan to improve the quality of teaching in American schools. The Future of Children. http://www.futureofchildren.org/usr_doc/FOC_Brief_Spring2007.pdf* (retrieved April, 2007).

Holtz, B. (1996). *Early childhood Jewish education.* New York: Council for Initiatives in Jewish Education.

Honig, A. (2003). *Research on quality in infant-toddler programs. ERIC Digest, http://www.ericdigests.org/2003-4/infant-toddler.html* (retrieved January, 2006).

Kotler-Berkowitz, L. (2005). *The Jewish Education of Jewish Children: United Jewish Communities Series on the NJPS 2000–01 Report 11.* New York. United Jewish Communities.

Kuhl, P. K, Tsao, F.M., Liu H.M., Zhang Y. & De Boer, B. (2001). "Language/culture/mind/brain. Progress at the margins between disciplines". *Annals of the New York Academy of Science.* 935:136–74.

Krug, C. & Schade, L. (2004). *Defining Excellence in Early Childhood Jewish Education.* Medford, MA: The Center for Applied Child Development Eliot-Pearson Department of Child Development Tufts University, *http://caje.org/earlychildhood/ec_define.pdf* (Retrieved January 2006).

Mayer, E., Kosmin, B. & Keysar, A. (2003). *American Jewish Identity Survey.* New York: The Center for Cultural Judaism.

National Academy of Sciences (2003). *Working Families and Growing Kids: Caring for Children and Adolescents.* Washington, DC.

National Association for the Education of Young Children (2006). *Standard 6: NAEYC Accreditation Criteria for Teachers Standard, http://www.naeyc.org/academy/standards/standard6/.* (Retrieved November 2006).

Hensch, T.K. (2005) Critical period plasticity in local cortical circuits. *Nature Reviews Neuroscience 6* (11), 877–888.

Ravid, R. & Ginsburg, M. (1988). *The relationship between Jewish early childhood education and family Jewish practices: Phase II.* Chicago: Board of Jewish Education of Metropolitan Chicago.

Rosen, M., Lorin, L. & Bar-Yam, N. (2004). *Raising Jewish Babies: Community Based Programs for New Jewish Parents*. Waltham, MA: Cohen Center for Modern Jewish Studies, *http://register.birthrightisrael.org/files/Raising%20Jewish%20Babies.December%202004c.pdf* (retrieved June 2006).

Rosen, M. (2005). *Beginning at the Beginning: What Should the Jewish Community Be Doing for New Jewish Parents?* Waltham, MA: Cohen Center for Modern Jewish Studies, *http://www.cmjs.org/index.cfm?page=229&IDResearch=111* (retrieved June 2006).

Rosen, M. (2006). *Jewish Engagement from Birth: A Blueprint for Outreach to First-Time Parents*. Waltham, MA: Cohen Center for Modern Jewish Studies, *http://www.brandeis.edu/cmjs/Publication.cfm?IDResearch=127* (retrieved June 2006).

Rosenblatt, S. (2006). *Jewish early childhood education in the San Francisco Federated Service Area: Description of sites, educators and families*. Unpublished report.

Saxe, L., Tighe, E., Phillips, B. & Kadushin, C. (2007). *Reconsidering the Size and Characteristics of the American Jewish Population*. http://www.brandeis.edu/cmjs/Publication.cfm?idresearch=137 (retrieved April 2007).

Schaap, E. (2004). *Early childhood Jewish education and profiles of its educators*. New York: Coalition for the Advancement of Jewish Education, *http://caje.org/earlychildhood/ec-survey04.pdf* (retrieved May 2006).

Schick, M. (2005). *Census of U.S. Day Schools 2003–04*. New York: Avi Chai Foundation.

Schick, M. (2000). *Census of Jewish Day Schools in the United States*. New York: Avi Chai Foundation.

Shiota, M., Campos, B., Keltner, D. & Hertenstein, M. (2004). *Positive emotion and the regulation of interpersonal relationships*. *http://www.mindandlife.org/si04_reading/soc.func.emo.final.pdf* (retrieved June 2006).

Shire, M. (2006). Learning to be righteous: A Jewish theology of childhood. In K. M. Yust, A. N. Johnson, S. E. Sasso & E. C. Roehlkepartain (eds.) *Nurturing Child and Adolescent Spirituality*. Lanham, MD. Rowman & Littlefield Group. pp. 43–53.

Stegelin, D. (2004). Early childhood education. In F.P. Schargel & J. Smink (eds.), *Helping students graduate: A strategic approach to dropout prevention*. Larchmont, NY (pp. 115–123).

Vogelstein, I. & Kaplan, D. (2002). *Untapped Potential: A status report of Jewish early childhood education in America*. Baltimore: Jewish Early Childhood Education Partnership, *http://caje.org/earlychildhood/UntappedPotential.pdf* (retrieved January 2006).

Wertheimer, J. (2005). *Linking the Silos: How to Accelerate the Momentum in Jewish Education Today*. New York: Avi Chai Foundation. *http://www.avi-chai.org/Static/Binaries/Publications/Linking%20The%20Silos_0.pdf*

Wertmeimer, J. (2007). *Recent Trends in Supplementary Jewish Education*. New York: Avi Chai Foundation.

Whitebook, M. (2003). *Early education quality: Higher teacher qualifications for better learning environments—A review of the literature*. California: Center for the Study of Child Care Employment.

Zero to Three. Response to *The Myth of the First Three Years*, http://www.zerotothree.org/ztt_parents.html (retrieved October 2006).

Congregational Education

Steve Kraus

Despite the rapid growth of day school education in North America, the majority of Jewish children between 5 and 18 years of age receive their formal Jewish education in a congregational/communal setting. While interest in this important form of Jewish education declined over the last two decades, renewed interest among funders and community agencies is now on the increase. Congregations, the primary deliverer of this form of Jewish education, are once again taking seriously their commitment to raising the standards by working actively with outside resources to address a number of the endemic issues that confront the nature of the educational programs.

Over the last fifteen years, since publication of *What We Know about Jewish Education,* interest in congregational education has translated into a national task force, local initiatives and a series of privately funded and university-based projects designed to raise the quality of education. There was no single beginning point; rather, there was a confluence of interest that recognized the weakness of the system that was primarily responsible for the education of Jewish children in America. While each of the initiatives approached the area from a different perspective, there were five critical questions that all were addressing as they engaged in their research and program development.

- What evidence is there that congregational education can make a difference in terms of identity and commitment?
- Are there promising models of congregational education that can be adapted by others?
- What change models are appropriate and effective in the field of congregational education?
- Are there new forms of "non-day school" education that should be investigated?
- Should congregational education focus more on the formal approach to learning or build a new system that incorporates greater levels of informal learning?

Congregational education is the most vulnerable area of Jewish education, as it appears to receive the least amount of support from the community and with the passage of time continues to demonstrate the least positive results. Based upon a study by Steven M. Cohen using the data of the NJPS 2000, there are three quantitative factors that lead to greater engagement in Jewish life once the child becomes an adult (Cohen & Kotler-Berkowitz 2004). They represent a combination of day school, congregational school and informal youth activities during the high school years. In every case, the actual number of years of engagement and/or the number of informal activities is what makes the difference. Cohen's analysis of the data suggests that:

- Attendance at a day school seven years or more exerts the most powerful positive impact upon Jewish identity—in-married, most/all Jewish friends, ritual scale, synagogue membership, being Jewish very important, very attached to Israel.
- Attendance at congregational/communal schools (meeting two or more days per week) for 7–12 years also exerts a discernible positive impact upon Jewish identity.
- The combination of the three forms of informal education—Israel travel, youth groups, and Jewish camping—is associated with rather significant levels of impact upon the Jewish identity indicators.

Based upon these findings, Cohen posits that there is an effective model for the congregational school system. Such a model would combine seven or more years of formal schooling with two or three forms of informal education. This model is well suited for strongly enhancing the Jewish identity of our youth whose families prefer schooling routes other than day schools. These recent findings confirm research that has been completed over the last thirty years, beginning with the studies in the 1970s by Bok and Himmelfarb.

The challenge facing Jewish educational leaders, based on this recurring research, is how to better integrate formal schooling with the three forms of informal Jewish education. Beginning with a Task Force on Congregational and Communal Jewish Education in the late 1990s, JESNA convened the key players in congregational education to study the field and develop a set of recommendations, which appears in the Task Force Report, *A Vision of Excellence* (Flexner 2000). The report outlined a set of strategic challenges and recommendations for enhancing the quality of congregational/communal education, which led to the development of a three-step process of

1. Reviewing the current literature and research related to congregational Jewish education;
2. Site visits to observe noteworthy "traditional" (meeting one or two weekdays after school and one weekend morning) and "non-traditional" schools and programs; and
3. A consultation in December 2002 with top theoreticians, practitioners, lay leaders and funders that focused on the questions of where we are and where we need to go in this field.

Growing out of this process were four strategic options for generating significant positive change in the quality of congregational education. While each of these options is significant in its own right and will have impact on the success of the educational programs, it is through combining them into an overall strategic process that real change will take place within the congregational setting. The four options are to:

1. Encourage and support institution-wide educational visioning and systemic change
2. Upgrade educational leadership
3. Improve the teaching/learning process through curriculum, professional development and training
4. Develop alternative structures and modalities (Kraus, 2002).

The single greatest key to a successful implementation of these strategies is time. The culture of the congregation is deeply set in the frameworks of the community, and the educational programs are embedded within that culture. To begin to change the culture of the congregation and their schools, a multifaceted process involving multiple partners, including the top volunteer and professional leadership of the institution, is required. Their engagement in a significant and meaningful process will eventually generate a ripple effect extending to all aspects of the congregation.

Change theory and change models are important philosophical underpinnings of these strategies. Beginning with Senge's *The Fifth Discipline* (1990), those involved in promoting change initiatives in Jewish education have grounded their work in that of the leading thinkers in the secular education and business worlds. Their approaches to change are connected to a wide range of overlapping ideas and theories that have become increasingly applied in the Jewish community. (For additional insights into their work, see Shevitz' chapter in this volume.)

FROM THE FIELD

Three models of congregational change have emerged in the last decade that demonstrate impact of the process described above. The first, the Experiment in Congregational Education (ECE), is a national model that has been through a number of pilot stages and is now being adopted as a community model for change. The others, LA'ATID: Synagogues for the Future and Nurturing Excellence in Synagogue Schools (NESS), are locally created and funded initiatives.

The Experiment in Congregational Education is a project of the Rhea Hirsch School of Education at the Hebrew Union College-Jewish Institute of Religion, Los Angeles. Founded in 1992, ECE is a multi-dimensional initiative whose mission is to strengthen congregations as critical centers of Jewish life in North America. The goal of the ECE is to transform congregations from membership service organizations to "communities of meaning" in which members are involved and engaged with Jewish living and learning and with one another. ECE seeks to create Congregations of Learners and Self-Renewing Congregations (Aron 1995, 2000, 2002).

ECE supports synagogues through an entire change process with knowledge, information, processes, consultations and tools for learning from other congregations. ECE currently works with congregations in community-based groups with support from local community benefactors and often in partnership with local central agencies for Jewish education. One of its programs, the RE-IMAGINE project, is an eighteen-month, five-stage process focused on alternative models. Thirty-three congregations in New York are participants in the RE-IMAGINE project.

Evaluation of the pilot cohort in New York has shown that:

- Congregations typically emerge ready to embark on new educational initiatives.
- Innovations have spread from educational programming into the realm of worship and community.
- ECE develops leadership skills and capacity within congregations.
- ECE congregations are better prepared to respond to challenges and opportunities and to work together in furthering their advancement toward a shared vision.

La'atid: *Synagogues for the Future* is a community-based initiative in Hartford, CT, launched in 1999 to engage the community's congregations in nurturing a strong sense of Jewish identity, increase Jewish knowledge and enrich Jewish living for their constituents of all ages. The initial pilot version of the program involved three congregations in an organizational change process that reflected and responded to each congregation's vision, culture and needs and assisted each congregation to advance toward its own goals. The overall structure for LA'ATID was grounded in a set of principles that were adopted by each of the congregations as part of their being accepted into the program. These are:

- To nurture and develop a strong sense of Jewish identity, knowledge and living in synagogue members of all ages.
- To increase the capacity of synagogue members and schools to look at themselves and creatively "re-engineer" their own unique vision, mission and experimental action plans.
- To strengthen and expand partnerships among a broad base of professionals and lay leaders in cooperative planning and decision making.
- To develop an organic interconnection of synagogue and school with a strengthened professional and lay leadership.
- To institutionalize the changes and collaborative processes into the fiber of the congregations within three to five years.
- To implement a new emphasis on congregational schools and develop professional learning communities (Kraus, 2006).

LA'ATID has expanded to eight congregations for the second cohort. Building on the groundwork for change established by the original three congregations, the current emphasis is on forging and strengthening the organic interconnection of congregation and school, with the school seen as central to the congregation's purpose, mission, goals and activities. As a result of the change process and with the assistance of a trained facilitator, the congregations have experienced the following outcomes:

- Each congregation learned to meet the distinctive needs and wishes of their congregants—to increase Jewish knowledge and thereby comfort at services.
- Support groups were established for study and celebratory programs for the congregants and families as well as for the professional staff.
- LA'ATID congregations were able to attract new members and involve previously uninvolved congregants.

- Congregants have found new and broader ways of collaboration and partnership between professionals and lay leaders, between school and synagogue, in decision making, in strategic planning, and in programming.
- Congregations have instituted substantive on-site staff development.
- Through ongoing evaluation and reflective practice the congregations developed mechanisms to evaluate programs and elicit participants' feedback (Kraus 2006).

Nurturing Excellence in Synagogue Schools (NESS) is a project of the Auerbach Central Agency for Jewish Education (ACAJE) in Philadelphia, Foundations, Inc. and the Jewish Federation of Greater Philadelphia. Established as a pilot project for six schools in 2002, the goal of NESS is to foster excellence in synagogue schools. The projected outcomes are to increase the retention rate of students in synagogue schools, to enhance the Jewish identity of students and their families, and to increase the students' connections to the Jewish community post-b'nai mitzvah.

This four-year project engages the entire staff of the central agency along with specified staff from Foundations, Inc. and is conducted on-site for selected schools. It is multifaceted and consists of:

- Assessment of a school's assets and limitations through a specifically designed standardized instrument (Jewish School Assessment School Improvement Process).
- Introduction of innovative teaching strategies and techniques through quality professional development.
- Consultation in the development of curricula at each site.
- Training of mentors who work with teachers in their classrooms.
- Leadership development for educational leaders.
- Lay leadership development.
- Guidance with organizational development designed to create a mission statement and action plan for school improvement.
- Continued engagement with each congregation and school for one year beyond the program to encourage continued growth and development.

An evaluation of Cohort 1 was conducted by JESNA's Berman Center for Research and Evaluation in July 2006. This evaluation of the first cohort of six schools indicated the positive impact of the program, including:

- Each congregation indicated heightened interest in and attention to Jewish education.
- The structures and systems of the education committees were strengthened and improved.
- Models of leadership development were generalized and applied in other arenas of congregational life.
- A consensus model for congregational decision making developed.
- The educational directors demonstrated enhanced skills and were accorded higher status in the congregations.
- Teachers became more engaged in higher quality professional development.
- Teachers were held to a higher level of accountability for their teaching.
- Congregational Jewish education became more professionalized (Isaacs, 2006).

The ECE, LA'ATID and NESS programs emerged from entirely different sets of needs and concerns, and yet they all learned that systemic change involved a set of principles that shared many of the same components. At the outset they realized that a set of strategies would need to be implemented with each institution that engaged the lay and professional leadership. Only after there was a significant buy-in from the leadership did the program actually begin. The next steps for every congregation involved in one of these programs highlighted four critical strategies necessary for success. These are:

1. Encourage and support institution-wide educational visioning and systemic change.
2. Upgrade educational leadership.

3. Improve the teaching/learning process through curriculum and professional development.

4. Develop alternative structures and modalities.

Of the three programs, NESS has developed the most extensive change process that incorporates all of these strategies and includes an extensive evaluation process. A critical result of the NESS program is the development of a list of nineteen Philosophical Underpinnings. These incorporate a strong set of Jewish values that are integrated into the ideas of the best of the thinkers in the secular worlds of education and business.

The nineteen Philosophical Underpinnings are (Tigay, 2005):

1. Synagogue schools can be successful.

2. Schools and synagogues are systems.

3. The school must be integrated into its synagogue.

4. Jewish organizations and change initiatives must be based on Jewish values.

5. Transformative change is about holistic, systemic change.

6. Collaboration leads to synergy; the whole is greater than the sum of its parts.

7. There is power in lay–professional relationships.

8. Teamwork should shape decision-making, because more wisdom and rationality result from effective group work than from the work of a single individual.

9. An effective change process proceeds through a democratic, not hierarchical, model.

10. Policy, structure, mission and all interventions on a system must be aligned.

11. Organizations have personalities and cultures in much the same way that people and families do.

12. Organizational processes are non-linear and often messy.

13. Genuine stakeholder buy-in must precede change.

14. Successful products and processes must be celebrated regularly.

15. All aspects of process and products must be directly connected to the mission.

16. Lay and professional leadership must be nurtured and trained.

17. Change must be institutionalized in order to maintain it.

18. "Trust the process."

19. Maintenance.

In addition to these three initiatives, there are a wide range of other initiatives involving congregational education change. To learn more about these initiatives the reader should reference the list of school-based, community-based and national initiatives, along with a rubric for helping institutions determine which program/initiative might be most suitable for local adaptation on JESNA's website at *http://www.jesna.org/sosland/searchres.asp?rid=692*

ALTERNATIVE STRUCTURES AND MODALITIES

The trend over the last few decades has been one of decreasing the number of hours of formal classes in congregational education. As indicated earlier, even with the best of congregational education programs, there is still a need to integrate the educational offerings with Israel trips, camping and youth groups, and home learning via technology. There is also much to be learned from Christian educators to see how they organize Christian education. Ammerman's *Pillars of Faith: American Congregations and Their Partners* (2005) is a sociological analysis of America's 300,000 congregations and how they organize and give meaning to their work. Ammerman singles out Jewish congregations for prioritizing religious education over other activities and for doing it differently than other religious traditions. Both religious factors and cultural expectations are at work when congregations make decisions about structuring activities, according to Ammerman.

Each of the programs described in this section works within specific institutions and has demonstrated promise in bringing about significant improvement in congregational education. At the same time, there is evidence of the growth of a trend of "consumer-based" education in which families are not relying on current Jewish institutions, primarily congregations, to provide Jewish education for their families. Instead they are creating their own individualized education plans. With the advent of the Internet and technology, with new approaches by Jewish outreach groups to teach students and families in their homes, offices, online or at any convenient location, a new series of options for Jewish education are being developed and offered. Home schooling and tutoring of small groups of students at convenient times, instead of attending congregational school, are being reported in several large Jewish communities. This phenomenon needs to be examined with data gathering, evaluation and longitudinal study.

ADDITIONAL RESEARCH QUESTIONS

- What are the demographics of congregational education?
- How many students are enrolled by grade, by movement, by region?
- What do the consumers, students and parents seek from a quality congregational education program?
- What changes need to be made in the curriculum, structures, time commitments and settings to properly respond to the needs as identified?

But these questions only beg the question. Until we have a systemic study of the entire system, including the attitudes and desires of the clients, the sponsoring congregations and the professionals engaged in congregational education, we will be unable to create a guide for proper improvement strategies that will permeate the entire system.

FUTURE DIRECTIONS

The challenges facing congregational education are not new. Many have been recognized for decades. What *is* new is that at both the community and national levels, increasingly sophisticated efforts have been mounted and proposed to address these challenges systemically.

Although there is no "magic bullet" that will transform congregational education immediately and decisively, there are strategies for significant and broad-based improvement that are tested, realistic and promising and that need and merit additional investment in order to realize their full potential.

Experience and research indicate that there are ten strategies that we believe chart the direction toward consistent excellence in congregational education. Many of these strategies can and should be used in combination with one another to achieve the kind of wide-scale improvement that is needed.

1. **Intensive, Vision-driven Change at the Individual Congregational Level.** For more than a decade the Experiment in Congregational Education (ECE) has guided congregations through intensive processes of revisioning and redesigning their educational programs. Although resource-intensive and time-consuming, this approach has helped many congregations re-think their educational goals, introduce a wide range of new programs and practices, and move closer to the ideal of being a "congregation of learners."

2. **Community-guided and -supported Comprehensive Improvement Programs**. Beginning with efforts in communities like Hartford, Washington and Philadelphia, initiatives spear-headed by central agencies for Jewish education to assist groups of congregations to work through a systematic, multi-dimensional improvement process have grown in sophistication. Today programs like NESS represent the state of the art in combining work with congregational leadership, school principals, and teachers to elevate a synagogue's educational program. NESS seeks to deal with all of the key elements that affect educational success: school vision, leadership support, curricular content, and teacher quality and effectiveness.

3. **Building Communal and Congregational Readiness for Change.** One of the key lessons learned over the past decade is that many congregations and communities are simply not

ready for the kinds of intensive improvement initiatives represented by ECE or NESS. A first stage of building readiness is critical if wide-scale improvement is to be embraced.

4. **Training Coaches to Guide Systemic Change.** One of the major barriers to more widespread and rapid improvement of congregational education is the dearth of individuals who are prepared to assist and guide congregations through the change process. To address this, the Coaches Training Institute was established by JESNA, in partnership with the central agencies for Jewish education, the three religious movements, the Experiment in Congregational Education and with substantial numbers of affiliated congregational schools, to recruit and train a cadre of expert coaches to work with congregational leadership both on intensive, congregation-wide improvement efforts and on more focused improvement projects.

5. **Preparing Rabbis to be Change Agents and Supporters.** Rabbis are key catalysts and supporters of or barriers to congregational educational change. Experience in pursuing improvement of congregational education emphasizes the importance of informed rabbinic involvement. Planning is underway to engage rabbinic leadership across denominations in learning about issues in congregational education, strategies for improving education in their congregations and the roles they can play in advancing this objective.

6. **New Approaches to Professional Development.** Part-time teachers, principals and educational directors who were often not specifically trained for these positions are key to creating successful congregational education programs. Preparing these professionals through high-quality professional development opportunities that are designed for their particular needs and roles is a critical component of the change process. Although a number of effective models (Boston and Cleveland, among others) have been established, much more is needed on both the local and national levels. Programs should range from intensive year-long programs to sophisticated on-site training, from the development of short-term courses designed to meet specific needs to the use of Internet and computer technology. The challenge is that large numbers of teachers and directors do not have access to or are not taking advantage of opportunities for quality professional development. Successes to date demonstrate that the Jewish community *can* design and implement excellent professional development on a broad basis.

7. **Bringing Innovative Programs to Congregations.** As in so many other aspects of Jewish education, the challenge of innovation in congregational educational programming is less one of availability than of distribution. A scan of the field uncovers dozens of innovative ideas for enriching the substance of congregational education—both in the school setting and beyond (thereby capturing additional learning time). However, many of these are being used in extremely limited ways, in only a handful of settings or not at all.

8. **Strengthening Religious Movement Initiatives.** The vast majority of congregations offering part-time educational programs are affiliated with one of three religious movements: Reform, Conservative or Reconstructionist. Each of these movements has provided educational support to, and in some cases set educational standards for, their affiliated congregations for decades. In recent years all have launched new initiatives to provide more systematic support for congregational educational improvement. Movement support is especially important for those congregations outside the catchment areas of central agencies for Jewish education.

9. **Continuum of Learning.** Congregational education and certainly congregational schools are not ends in themselves. They are vehicles for seeking to engage, inspire, and educate children—and, increasingly, their families—toward a lifelong involvement in Jewish learning and living. Indeed, many observers believe that congregational schooling by itself is inherently limited in its potential impact and should always be seen as only one element in a more encompassing framework of Jewish experiences for children and their families. We have the opportunity today, by working with existing institutions and frameworks and by developing new programs and products, to create far more engaging and powerful continua of Jewish educational experiences that will involve greater numbers of people in Jewish learning and ac-

tivity and have a greater impact on their developing Jewish identity and commitment. What is needed is a fundamental change in mind-set: a readiness to move beyond focusing on individual institutions and programs to thinking about and implementing a holistic, personalized educational "journey" that families and individuals can experience over time.

10. **Incentive Grants.** The state of the art in congregational educational improvement has advanced dramatically in the last decade. Nevertheless, there will always be a need for further experimentation and additional learning. With new ideas and approaches emanating from many sources, often from the grass roots, a national fund that would encourage creative new programs and initiatives by providing incentive grants to individuals, institutions and consortia in the area of congregational school change should be part of a comprehensive, systemic change strategy (Woocher, J. 2005).

CONCLUSION

More Jewish young people receive their basic Jewish education in congregational settings than in any other venue. At the same time, the education they receive is too often perceived by the students themselves, their parents, and educators as inadequate and ineffectual.

Piecemeal approaches—a new piece of curriculum here, a teacher training workshop there—have not proven to be effective in achieving significant improvement. In order to effect serious change, a new systemic approach that builds on existing local and national endeavors that have shown promise for achieving substantial change must be implemented.

These challenges are not new. Many have been recognized for decades. What *is* new is that at both the community and national levels, increasingly sophisticated efforts have been initiated and are beginning to demonstrate results. Although there is no "magic bullet" that will transform congregational education immediately and decisively, there are strategies for significant and broad-based improvement that are tested, realistic, and promising and that need and merit additional investment in order to realize their full potential.

HIGHLIGHTS

- Research shows that long-term attendance in congregational school, in conjunction with ongoing participation in informal educational activities such as Israel travel, youth groups and Jewish camping, increases the likelihood of a positive Jewish identity in adulthood.
- There are examples of promising, sophisticated, evaluated models of systemic congregational school change. The goal of all is to make these programs available in other communities.
- An unstructured, consumer-based and -driven form of non-day school education is emerging in large urban centers of Jewish life.
- Because of the diffuse nature of the field of congregational education, it is crucial that all national and local institutions work together in sharing information, piloting new projects and collaborating on research.

THE LARGER CONTEXT

For the foreseeable future, the majority of students who receive formal Jewish education will receive it in a congregational setting. There is renewed communal interest in not only changing the negative perception about this form of education, but also changing the results. The pockets of excellence that currently exist need to be expanded. Serious efforts at designing and implementing complex school improvement initiatives continue. The challenge of determining how to adapt promising models to large numbers of schools in different settings is being addressed. Cautious optimism is not only allowed, but appropriate.

ANNOTATED BIBLIOGRAPHY

Bolman, L. & Deal, T. (2003) *Reframing Organizations: Artistry, Choice and Leadership.* San Francisco: Jossey-Bass. Bolman & Deal encourage leaders to step *back* and re-examine the operation of their organization through the use of various frames or windows. These different lenses can bring organizational life into a different or clearer focus. They allow the leader to view the workplace from different images to make judgments, gather information and get things done.

Fullan, M. (2001). *Leading in a Culture of Change.* San Francisco: Jossey-Bass. Fullan offers new and seasoned leaders' insights into the dynamics of change and presents a unique and imaginative approach for navigating the intricacies of the change process. He shows how leaders in all types of organizations can accomplish their goals and become exceptional. He draws on the most current ideas and theories on the topic of effective leadership, incorporates case examples of large-scale transformation and reveals a remarkable convergence of powerful themes or, as he calls them, the five core competencies.

Kotler-Berkowitz, L. (2005). *The Jewish Education of Jewish Children: Formal schooling, Early Childhood Program and Informal Experiences.* New York: United Jewish Communities. This report examines the Jewish education of today's Jewish children. It provides population estimates of how many Jewish children participate in various types of Jewish education, including formal schooling, informal experiences and early childhood programs. The report focuses on the association between parents' characteristics—both demographic and Jewish—and children's Jewish education. A concluding section highlights key policy implications of the findings for the Jewish communal system.

Ravitch, S. (2002). *Engaging & Retaining Jewish Youth Beyond Bar/Bat Mitzvah: An Action Research Study.* Philadelphia, PA: The Auerbach Central Agency for Jewish Education. This study focused on youths' reflections on their synagogue school experiences before, during and after becoming bar/bat mitzvah. The initial goal was to use the findings to serve as a springboard for community-based post-b'nai mitzvah initiatives that would counter the high dropout rate. The findings, however, indicated that first more work needed to be done to improve synagogue school education before bar/bat mitzvah. This report was the catalyst for the creation of the NESS project.

Senge, P. (1990). *The Fifth Discipline: Art and Practice of the Learning Organization.* New York: Doubleday. *The Fifth Discipline* brings word of "learning organizations"—organizations where people continually expand their capacity to create the results they truly desire, where new and expansive patterns of thinking are nurtured, where collective aspiration is set free and where people are continually learning how to learn together. Five disciplines are described as the means of building learning organizations.

REFERENCES

Ammerman, N.T. (2005). *Pillars of Faith: American Congregations and Their Partners,* Berkeley and Los Angeles: University of California Press.

Aron, I. Lee, S. & Rossel, S. (1995). *A Congregation of Learners: Transforming the Synagogue into a Learning Community.* New York: UAHC Press.

Aron, I. (2000). *Becoming a Congregation of Learners.* Woodstock, VT: Jewish Lights Publishing.

Aron, I. (2002). *The Self-Renewing Congregation: Organizational Strategies for Revitalizing Synagogue Life.* Woodstock, VT: Jewish Lights Publishing.

Cohen, S.M. & Kotler-Berkowitz, L. (2004). *The Impact of Childhood Jewish Education on Adults' Jewish Identity: Schooling, Israel Travel, Camping and Youth Groups.* New York: United Jewish Communities (*http://www.ujc.org/content_display.html?ArticleID=118670*).

Flexner, P.A. (2000). *A Vision for Excellence.* New York: JESNA.

Isaacs, L. (2006). NESS Nurturing Excellence in Synagogue Schools Cohort 1: Final Report, New York: Berman Center for Research and Evaluation, JESNA. Retrieved from *http://www.acaje.org/assets/pdf/ness/NESSFinRep.pdf*

Kraus, S. (2002). Strategic Funding Options to Improve Congregational and Communal Jewish Education, Unpublished manuscript. New York: JESNA.

Kraus, S. (2006). *Synagogue/School Change Initiatives.* JESNA. Retrieved September 2006 from http://www.jesna.org/j/pdfs/coaches/Synagogue_Change.pdf

Senge, P. (1990). *The Fifth Discipline: Art and Practice of the Learning Organization.* New York: Doubleday.

Tigay, H. (2005). For JESNA's Coaches Training Institute, Philadelphia, PA: Auerbach Central Agency for Jewish Education. Retrieved from (*http://www.jesna.org/j/pdfs/coaches/Nineteen_Philosophical_Underpinnings.pdf*).

Woocher, J.S. (2005). Twelve Things We Can Do to Improve Congregational Education. Unpublished manuscript. New York: JESNA.

The Jewish Day School

Joshua Elkin & Bonnie Hausman

During the last decade day schools have received more attention than most other Jewish educational settings. Newspaper articles, magazine features, rabbinic seminars and conference sessions have focused increasingly on aspects of the day school experience. Questions abound. How large is the day school enterprise? What are some of the key challenges confronting day schools? Does a day school education make a difference in the long run? What about the cost of day school tuition?

This chapter will offer some answers to these questions. PEJE, the organization for which we both work, focuses exclusively on helping day schools in North America to grow and thrive. We have a unique continental perspective that we will incorporate as we explore the rapidly changing day school environment.

THE GROWTH OF JEWISH DAY SCHOOLS

Day schools have been growing and proliferating during the past four decades and figure prominently in most Jewish communities' educational visions and strategic plans. They are among the most powerful institutional forces working to ensure the future of Jewish life in America. This growth has been well documented in terms of the number and growth of new schools as well as the overall number of students in all schools, new and established (Schick 2005).

A quick scan of the North American day school world reveals that it is a decentralized network of over 700 schools across all denominations and many non-denominational or community schools. Excluding the approximately 200 mostly right-wing Orthodox schools located in Brooklyn, the other 500 schools include approximately 300 Orthodox, of which about 100 identify themselves as Modern Orthodox; another 120 Community (i.e., non-denominational, trans-denominational or pluralistic); 65 Conservative; and 18 Reform. They are located in 41 states and 5 Canadian provinces and range in age from brand new to over 70 years old. They receive financial support to a varying degree from their local federations, but all engage in aggressive annual fundraising, as tuition revenue falls short of covering the total per pupil costs. Within the last decade an unprecedented number of schools have engaged in building new facilities or refurbishing older ones. These projects have required substantial capital campaigns. This combination of annual fundraising and capital campaigning has led to an infusion of philanthropic resources at levels never before seen.

As the number of schools has increased, so has enrollment. Today the total day school enrollment is approximately 205,000, representing an increase of approximately 20,000 students since 1999. However, the range in school size varies greatly, from an enrollment of 30 in the smallest schools to well over 1,000. Schick (1999 and 2005), with the Avi Chai Foundation, published two census studies of Jewish day schools in the United States. These studies document an 11% increase ("an impressive figure") in kindergarten through 12th grade enrollment during this five-year period. Looking at enrollment patterns within the schools, the Avi Chai report documents a gradual decline in overall enrollment per grade level from first grade to the 12th grade (reflecting student attrition), although the degree of drop-off has also declined during the same five-year period. Of particular significance is that day school enrollment overall continued to grow during the 2000–2003 economic slowdown. Some of this growth may be attributed to enrollment increases at the high school level that have been documented in the PEJE Day School Peer Yardstick™ (Litman 2005). The observation that enrollment continues to grow suggests that day schools have become a more normative and growing segment of the Jewish educational landscape, including beyond the Orthodox community.

Growth notwithstanding, there have been a limited number of school closures, and some emerging schools whose leaders aborted plans to open. Generally schools fail for a number of reasons. Some school groups lack the experience in fundraising from a broad base of financial supporters, tending to rely on few donors or even a single one. Financial stress has played a role to some extent, but it is not the whole story. A review of closures in several locations by PEJE staff revealed several factors leading up to the closure: disagreement about the school's core mission and religious focus, lack of a critical mass of students, a failure to achieve sufficient grass-roots support in the community and competition from other day schools. Generally there is no single factor leading to school failure, but rather the accumulation of difficulties that result in declining enrollment and insufficient financial resources.

A very recent trend has been the merging, re-invention or transformation of an existing school or schools into a new entity. In a few instances this trend reflects an attempt to attract unaffiliated families as well as families across a broader range of denominations. More data need to be gathered before reaching any conclusions about the reasons and the value of this approach to maximizing enrollment.

SUPPORTIVE NETWORKS AND ORGANIZATIONS

Several organizations—Jewish and non–Jewish—have been involved in supporting efforts to increase day school enrollment and to ensure that Jewish day schools provide quality education.

Operating nationally, five organizations or support networks provide assistance to day schools: the Association of Modern Orthodox Day Schools (AMODS), the Jewish Community Day School Network (RAVSAK), which now has incorporated the North American Association of Jewish High Schools (NAAJHS), the Progressive Association of Reform Day Schools (PARDeS), the Solomon Schechter Day School Association (SSDSA), and Torah u'Mesorah. Each provides a variety of services and benefits to its membership, but most schools remain independent in such critical areas as the number of hours devoted to Judaic studies, educational philosophy, pedagogy, and curricular content. However, there is a recent trend, spearheaded by the network leadership, to guide and assist schools in working together to solve common problems and develop high-quality joint programming.

On the local level, federations and central agencies for Jewish education provide important support to day schools. Federations are devoting greater attention to day schools, both because of a growing recognition of their role in Jewish continuity and identity development and because the schools sometimes run into challenging times. Central agencies for Jewish education in some communities are engaging more with day schools to sharpen their focus and identity. However, other central agencies continue to respond to the communal pressure to address the needs of the majority of Jewish children who do not attend day school.

The newest players in the day school field from within the Jewish community are unquestionably the philanthropists and foundations. Following the lead of the Jim Joseph Foundation and the Avi Chai Foundation, several individuals and ad hoc groups have emerged to provide support for a wide range of programs to foster enrollment growth and improve school quality. Many donors have remained focused on their individual schools (usually capital needs) or on those schools within their own geographical area. In the case of Avi Chai, which has been a true leader for over two decades, the reach has been continental and the investment substantial and wide-ranging (see their Annual Report at avichaina.org).

In 1997 ten prominent philanthropists, Avi Chai and one federation collaborated to form the Partnership for Excellence in Jewish Education (PEJE). This new philanthropic entity created a pooled fund initially for investing in new elementary and middle day schools. PEJE has gradually evolved into a field-building organization with a mission to strengthen and grow all day schools through capacity-building initiatives. Some observers have commented that PEJE, working in collaboration with individual day school networks, has sparked a movement within the day school world, notwithstanding the continued autonomy of each school.

Jewish day schools have greatly benefited from a range of resources outside the Jewish community, especially from Independent School Management (ISM) and the National Association of Independent Schools (NAIS), as well as from the regional independent school organizations across the continent. These groups have provided expertise, research, and other materials to the growing number of Jewish day schools and their leaders. Though many day schools resist the identification as independent or private schools, they bear many similarities to such schools. Other organizations, such as the Association of Supervision and Curriculum Development (ASCD) and BoardSource, have resources and programs on professional development, curriculum, governance, and leadership that reach many schools.

RESEARCH ON DAY SCHOOL IMPACT

Despite all of the investment in Jewish day schools, only limited funds have been secured to investigate the impact of a day school education on students and families. Lipset (1994), Rimor and Katz (1993), Fishman and Goldstein (1993), and Schiff & Schneider (1994) have all attested to strong correlations between day school enrollment and strong adult Jewish identification. Some studies have focused on specific schools and communities (Kadimah 2004). One investigator (Phillips 1997) concluded that the positive impact of Jewish day school education may be over-stated. As we write there are two new studies being conducted that we expect will yield important findings about the impact of day schools. One, led by Ben-Avie at the Yale Child Study Center, will focus on the relationship between day schooling and quality of life; the other, sponsored by a consortium of donors convened by PEJE and conducted by Brandeis University's Cohen Center for Modern Jewish Studies/Steinhardt Social Research Institute, will investigate the impact of day schooling on college-aged alumni.

Several in-depth descriptive case studies have recently been completed that enrich our understanding of the challenges and benefits of the new community high schools. The case studies conducted by Hausman (2000) and Jacobs (2001), in which they interviewed pioneering graduates, have taught us about the strengths of these institutions as well as the challenges of maintaining the integrity of their mission. Pomson (2003) contributed greatly to our understanding of the impact of a new day school on the parent body and the broader community. Ingall (2006) provides an in-depth examination of three graduates of a Jewish teacher training program and their initial experiences in the classroom that highlights some of the serious issues of induction and mentoring of novice teachers. In the coming years we expect to see increased investment in research—both descriptive case studies and empirical work on day school alumni—that are designed to learn more about the impact of day schools on the students, their families and their communities.

TRENDS, ISSUES, CHALLENGES AND RECOMMENDATIONS

The current trends and realities within Jewish day schools point to a number of key issues and challenges worthy of particular attention:

A. **Vision**—Vision-driven schools have greater potential to excite an expanding group of parents to consider day school education. Unfortunately, many schools and their leadership rarely give themselves the opportunity to step back and reflect on their identities and project a vision of the future on such critical questions as Hebrew language, educational philosophy, and Israel. A welcome asset in support of conversations about vision is Fox, Scheffler and Marom's *Visions of Jewish Education* (2003). Six distinct visions are presented, along with overviews and a valuable case study. Pekarsky has added to the research on visioning in day schools with his recent case study *Vision at Work: The Theory and Practice of Beit Rabban* (2006). Senge (1990), Nanus (1992), Heifetz (1994) and Collins (2001) are four prominent writers on leadership who stress the vital role played by vision in an organization's growth and development.

B. **Governance and Leadership**—Day schools have become increasingly complex and expensive to run, requiring talented and adaptive lay and professional leadership. One of the great challenges for day schools is their difficulty in securing leadership who are prepared to govern. Toward that end, every school should establish a committee on trustees that is charged with identifying, cultivating and nurturing the next cadre of board members so that they are ready and capable of assuming the rewarding yet challenging task of governance. This same board must also support, nurture, and evaluate the head of school, ideally through a standing head support and evaluation committee. When necessary, this committee is responsible for effecting a smooth termination of employment, conducting a sound search, and engaging the services of a new head with the proper supports and feedback mechanisms in place. ISM, NAIS and BoardSource have all underscored these issues, while providing resources to address them.

C. **Access to Expertise**—The power of expert coaching to improve school performance cannot be emphasized enough. Because day school management is so complex, requiring enhanced skill sets to manage and govern, it is vitally important that school leaders access the expertise of former day school heads as well as experts in all aspects of non-profit management. Increasingly day school leaders are taking the risk of opening themselves to outside expertise in the hope of learning how best to strengthen their management and educational programs. The most frequently used expertise services include:

- Holistic institutional assessment
- Strategic planning
- Faculty professional development
- Responding to the needs of diverse learners
- Board retreats and overall board development
- Fundraising—annual, capital, and solicitation training
- Student recruitment and attrition prevention
- Marketing
- Financial management
- Evaluation of head and board performance
- Managing leadership transition

The rapid growth of the business consulting industry, followed by the burgeoning field of nonprofit management support, have created a climate conducive to the use of expertise, reflection and evaluation to promote solid organizational performance.

D. **Marketing**—Whether a school is experiencing enrollment growth, decline or status quo, the challenge of marketing the school is substantial. From the Avi Chai day school census and from new data emerging from the Day School Peer Yardstick™, we know that the day schools are reaching only a fraction of their potential audience. Schools need to focus on excellence in all facets (especially math and science, but also the arts, Hebrew, Judaic studies, character education, and physical education) and must find ways to communicate that excellence to a wider audience. Much expertise exists to help schools become more sophisticated in how they present themselves to prospective parents, and how they provide individual attention and response to diverse learning needs. With the help of market segmentation research, schools can learn to target their messages to reach a much wider audience (see the Lieberman Study at *www.peje.org* and the NAIS Marketing Handbook for further details).

E. **Cost**—Many researchers have focused on the high cost of day school education as a deterrent to growth. Providing any high quality educational program is expensive; with a full general and Judaic studies program, day schools are no exception. Our experience with grantee schools has taught us that in general, approximately one-third of prospective parents can pay the full cost; one-third have incomes that require significant tuition assistance (which the day schools, often together with federation and foundation support, already have in place); and one-third struggle to pay the full cost. The middle group is the most affected by the tuition levels. Though cost is a significant factor, issues of quality, ambivalence about Jewish life, fears of ghettoization, and competing priorities often play equally major or even more extensive roles in a family's decision making about Jewish day school enrollment (see the Lieberman Study for details). Schools would do well to strengthen their tuition assistance programs and to market them (see PEJE Peer Yardstick data), as well as to explore with their local federation and with other schools ways to create additional endowments to ensure that as much support as possible can be offered to families, coupled with somewhat moderated tuition increases. However, school leadership must be able to present a compelling case for their high-quality program as justification for the cost charged.

In some instances the grandparents of prospective or current students are key underwriters of day school tuition. They are the unsung supporters of day school education; their pivotal role needs to be celebrated and expanded by opening up discussion about their current and future support through tuition payments and through donations. Note that a recent Zogby International poll found that 55% of grandparents indicated that they contribute financially to the education of their grandchildren (MetLife Mature Market Institute and Zogby International 2006).

F.   **Assessment of Performance**—With a growing number of day schools accredited by their local independent school network, recognition grows that it is valuable to benchmark a school's performance against others. Schools learn from each other through accreditation visiting teams and at conferences, while peer benchmarking encourages deep and significant learning. The Day School Peer Yardstick™ (DSPY), developed by PEJE in collaboration with Measuring Success, began in 2004-2005 with data from 104 schools and had grown to 155 participating schools by the end of 2006. The DSPY represents a prime example of day school leaders investing in self-assessment referenced to peer institutions for the purpose of improving management performance. An institutional assessment by an outside professional (such as that offered by ISM or Fieldstone Consulting) can also provide invaluable peer reference points. Since 2004 PEJE has awarded grants to 20 schools for the purpose of providing a professional institutional assessment with follow-up coaching expertise to assist in the implementation of recommendations emanating from the assessment.

G.   **Professional Recruitment/Admission/Attrition Function**—Telling the day school story requires devoted professional time. (Rheua Stakely, a renowned expert on independent school recruitment, has made this point abundantly clear.) Heads are occupied with other responsibilities that compete with the vital admission function. Boards do not have time to devote to this very labor-intensive priority area. By professionalizing, even with a part-time dedicated position:

   • relationships can be cultivated with partner early childhood programs or middle schools;

   • admission criteria can be clarified (hopefully with increased awareness of a responsibility to address the needs of an increasingly diverse student population);

   • the number of visits can be dramatically increased; and

   • the conversion of visits to applicants and applicants to matriculated students can be increased substantially.

H.   **Fundraising—Annual/Capital/Endowment**—While tuition revenue from a growing student body is the largest source of income for any day school, the next largest is most often fundraising. Here, too, there is a significant value in having a resource development professional capable of organizing the efforts and keeping the school on track toward established goals. Critical to the success of any fundraising campaign is the ongoing training of board members and development committee members in the art and skill of solicitation. The professional cannot and should not be doing the asking (see Colson 1996). The case for support needs to be clear and understandable, and all potential contributors should have their giving history accurately recorded in a functional database. Many workshops, consultants and resources are available to help the lay and professional leadership of a day school grow their capacities for both annual and capital/endowment fundraising.

I. **External Relations and Collaborations**—Many communities are witnessing an increasing level of collaboration among day schools for the purpose of addressing common challenges such as marketing, recruitment, professional development, and community-wide endowment efforts. This represents a promising trend, but one that presents its own challenges in terms of time, perceived competition, and equity. Federations and central agencies are often playing and will continue to play key roles in this unfolding trend of day schools partnering with each other and with community-wide leadership.

LOOKING TO THE FUTURE: BUILDING A CULTURE OF EXPERTISE

To meet the multiple challenges facing day schools, PEJE, in collaboration with the day school networks, JESNA, and selected federations and central agencies, sees itself as a provider of expertise to day schools. The goal is to provide guidance in school leadership and management to enable schools to recognize their strengths, identify and address challenges, and capitalize on their opportunities. Through knowledge of promising practices disseminated via assessment, coaching, strategic convening, funding, and networks of professional peers, PEJE will continue to work with all who seek to grow and strengthen day schools for the next generation. An ever-widening movement of lay leaders, professionals, donors, federations, and central agencies, all accessing vetted expertise, will help ensure that day schools make progress in reaching their potential. PEJE is looking to a future where the capacity-building efforts of many philanthropists and the receptiveness of practitioners result in better outcomes: outstanding day schools, strong Jewish literacy, and vibrant communities rooted in a well-articulated set of values.

IMPLICATIONS AND/OR POLICY RECOMMENDATIONS

The state of the research, trends and challenges suggests a number of implications and policy recommendations. We note a profound lack of research on the day school phenomenon. We need to invest far more in learning about the impact of day schooling. One promising avenue is to provide incentives for front-line practitioners (administrators and teachers) to engage in action research with oversight and guidance from a professional researcher to help ensure the requisite rigor and design.

The trends and challenges also suggest a number of policy recommendations.

1. School leaders need time to devote to articulating cogent visions of a desired future. The pace of day-to-day school administration and governance works against reflective, vision-generating opportunities. We must create the space for this vital work, which drives the entire enterprise.

2. The challenge of leadership and governance means that each community must invest in developing its leadership, lay and professional. In cities or regions with more than one day school, leadership development institutes sponsored by the federation or central agency with ongoing one-on-one coaching will lead to learning being implemented successfully.

3. With regard to marketing, Boston and Philadelphia have both completed market segmentation studies. The two cities are remarkably similar, thereby suggesting that other communities across North America will learn from these studies and adapt the findings and the interpretations to their own communal realities (see the study of the Boston market by Lieberman Research Worldwide 2004).

4. Much more information is needed on the impact of price on day school matriculation. Given the strong record of day schools in providing financial aid, the role of this factor, while important, may be overplayed. There is a great need for hard quantitative research to supplement the anecdotal reporting. The entire financial profile of each school should receive high-level attention from school leaders as well as from outside consultants. We need to help schools compare themselves to peer institutions (e.g., by using PEJE's Day School Peer Yardstick) and to ensure that successful strategies are widely promulgated and adapted by other schools.

Day schools must be able to present themselves cogently as well-managed institutions with a range of efforts designed to keep them as accessible as possible.

5. Each day school should include funds in its budget for coaching and expertise. By maintaining a line item for this purpose, school leaders will become accustomed to accessing the requisite knowledge and best practices to address their most pressing needs, including resources to ensure that their educational program is outstanding and compelling.

6. With rising concerns over leadership transitions in day schools, we recommend that each school's board chair appoint a committee on trustees to support, evaluate, and nurture a strong Board, and a head support and evaluation committee to support, assess and nurture a head of school over a period of years (see DeKuyper 2003).

7. The easiest way to sustain strong enrollment is to reduce the attrition of existing students. A well-thought-through attrition-preventing protocol is vitally important in addressing student needs promptly, promoting greater parent satisfaction, and responding quickly to the first intimation that a particular child might leave the following year.

8. Day schools must build relationships with a wide number of organizations in the Jewish community, especially with personnel in the partner schools from which they draw their students and with rabbis in their local synagogues. Operating in self-imposed isolation reduces the awareness of the day school, prevents valuable collaborations from taking hold, and contributes to the perception of a parochialism that is one of the major barriers to day school enrollment growth.

ADDITIONAL RESEARCH QUESTIONS AND STRATEGIES

- What is the long-term impact of Jewish day school education?
- How well are Jewish day schools connecting with their alumni? What do schools need to do better? What are the fundraising implications for the schools that do it well?
- What marketing strategies have the greatest impact on recruiting students to a Jewish day school? What factors have the greatest impact on increasing enrollment? What factors impinge on enrollment?
- Encourage action research through grants to individual teachers and/or schools to test a hypothesis or conduct an internal experiment. Explore the outcomes of the educational process by engaging teachers as researchers.
- Establish a continuous flow of information and findings from these studies by working with the Network for Research in Jewish Education as well as education policy journals that publish and disseminate knowledge relevant to the day school field.

CONCLUSION

The growth of the day school enterprise in North America is clearly one of the more significant developments in Jewish education over the last few decades. This growth has been driven by multiple factors, including parents searching for educational quality and strong Judaic literacy and/or acculturation; greater communal recognition of the values and quality of an intensive formal Jewish educational setting; increased acceptance of non-public school educational options; and fluctuations in the quality of local public school options. The dramatic increase in the number of non–Orthodox high schools since 1990 came about in response to increased demand for continuation of day schooling generated by the earlier growth of elementary schools. Furthermore, many day schools have become increasingly sophisticated in communicating and marketing their programs, thereby reaching a larger audience.

This growth, coupled with a changing environment where educational excellence is receiving more attention, presents each day school with many challenges. School leaders must work simultaneously on multiple fronts:

- sharpening their future vision and current mission

- identifying and sustaining lay and professional leaders
- improving the quality of their program
- marketing to and reaching a wide range of parents beyond those already committed to day school
- accessing and funding needed expertise
- maintaining their accessibility to a wide range of families educationally, economically, religiously, and geographically
- securing the financial and communal support so vital to their long-term health.

The early part of the 21st century may indeed prove to be a crossroads for day schools. Successful meeting of these multiple challenges will strengthen and sustain the day school movement. Failure to tackle the challenges will likely keep day schools from reaching the next group of potential families, thereby limiting the impact of these schools beyond the Orthodox community.

HIGHLIGHTS OF THE ARTICLE

- Day schools are experiencing and projecting growth in enrollment, especially in the Orthodox sector, according to the Avi Chai census (Schick 2005), and at the high school level, according to the PEJE Day School Peer Yardstick™.
- Day schools are part of an extensive network of organizations both within and outside the Jewish community.
- There is a strong positive correlation between day school experience and positive Jewish involvement.
- Critical to day school success is the alignment of vision, board governance, and professional leadership.
- Successful marketing will acquaint more people with day schools.
- Cost is one factor among many that affects an individual family's decision about day school enrollment.
- Quality day schools engage in annual assessments of the performance of the board and head.
- Professionalizing the admissions process establishes proper relationships with all partners, especially in early childhood and/or middle school programs.
- Cultivating and soliciting leadership gifts is a prime function of the board.

LARGER CONTEXT

Jewish day school education is rapidly becoming one of the most important areas of Jewish education for the 21st century. It provides the students with a high-quality Jewish and secular education in an in-depth environment that cannot be matched in any other setting. However, a day school education alone is rarely sufficient to engender a life-long commitment to and involvement in Jewish life. To accomplish this goal, day schools must partner with synagogues, camps, informal educational experiences such as youth groups and meaningful trips to Israel. Through a multifaceted, multi-dimensional educational program, our Jewish youth will mature into active, involved members of the Jewish future.

ANNOTATED BIBLIOGRAPHY

Colson, H. (1996). *Philanthropy at Independent Schools*. Washington, DC: National Association of Independent Schools. This is the single best resource to guide a day school in setting up an effective annual campaign. Of particular note is the emphasis on the vital roles played by the board, its development committee, and the head of school.

DeKuyper, M.H. (2003). *The Trustee Handbook: A Guide to Effective Governance for Independent School Boards*. Washington, DC: National Association of Independent Schools. This 8th edition of the NAIS classic is comprehensive and readable. It covers key topics including the role of the trustee, board meeting agenda, committee structure, the crucial committee on trustees, and separating board–head roles.

Dickson, S. (2004). "Kadimah: The Pursuit of Scholastic Excellence and Religious Commitment." *Journal of Jewish Education* 69 (3), pp. 15–47. This study tracks Kadimah School alumni from 1964–1992 to explore the benefits of Jewish day school education. The research questions focus on alumni commitment to religious practice and their involvement in Jewish communal life.

Dym, B. (2004). *Leadership Transition*. Boston: Partnership for Excellence in Jewish Education. This research underscores how frequently day school leadership changes. The study focuses on heads of school, though lay leadership transition is certainly a key priority area. The author argues that better orientation and support of new heads can reduce the frequency of leadership transition; furthermore, when transition occurs, schools can learn how to handle such challenges more effectively.

Fox, S., Scheffler, I. & Marom, D. (2003). *Visions of Jewish Education*. Cambridge: Cambridge Press. A seminal work containing six well-developed visions of the educated Jew. The authors have produced a resource to propel school leaders forward in the work of visioning a better future for Jewish educational institutions by imagining the ideal graduates of our schools.

Lakey, B. (2000). *The Board Building Cycle*. Washington, DC: BoardSource. This classic highlights clearly the key work that must be performed by the committee on trustees that is charged with developing the board, including but not limited to recruiting, orienting, and evaluating board members. An accompanying disk allows a school the opportunity to customize valuable tools to enhance board performance.

Lieberman Research Worldwide (2004). *Understanding the Needs of Jewish Parents in Greater Boston to More Effectively Market Day Schools—A Report Prepared for the Day School Advocacy Forum of the Combined Jewish Philanthropies of Greater Boston*. Boston: Combined Jewish Philanthropies. This is a sophisticated market segmentation analysis of the attitudes of Jewish parents to day schools. The grouping of parents into five categories points to the need to tailor messages to different groups. The investigators also concluded that only two of the five groups are currently being addressed by day schools.

Litman, S. (2005). *Day School Peer Yardstick™ Generic Report*. Boston: PEJE, in cooperation with Measuring Success. A report based on data from 104 day schools and their performance on the leading indicators of enrollment growth conducted by Measuring Success for PEJE. The 2006–2007 Generic Reports can be downloaded from the PEJE website. Each school received a confidential customized school report in two parts, the first focusing on operational factors and the second on financial and fundraising indicators.

Pomson, A. (2003). "Parents Under the Influence: Thinking Differently about the Relationships Between Parents and Their Children's Schools" (unpublished). This study showcases the power of day school to create community even beyond the students, to include parents and entire families. The day school is portrayed as a builder of social capital and a dynamic force within the broader community. This phenomenon is not limited to North America; it appears to be more international. (A groundbreaking conference on the relationship of day school and community was held at the Melton Center for Jewish Education at the Hebrew University in Jerusalem in June, 2006.)

REFERENCES

Ben-Avie, M. & Kress, J. (2006). *The Educators in Jewish Schools Study: Preliminary Findings from a Registry of Day and Congregational/Supplemental Schools in North America*. New York: JESNA.

Collins, J. (2001). *Good to Great*. New York: Harper Collins.

Colson, H. (1996). *Philanthropy at Independent Schools*. Washington, DC: National Association of Independent Schools.

DeKuyper, M.H. (2003). *The Trustee Handbook: A Guide to Effective Governance for Independent School Boards*. Washington, DC: National Association of Independent Schools.

Dickson, S. (2004). "Kadimah: The Pursuit of Scholastic Excellence and Religious Commitment." *Journal of Jewish Education* 69 (3), pp. 15–47.

Fishman, S. B. & Goldstein, A. (1993). *When They Are Grown Up They Will Not Depart: Jewish Education and the Jewish Behavior of American Adults*. Waltham: Cohen Center for Modern Jewish Studies of Brandeis University and JESNA.

Fox, S., Scheffler, I. & Marom, D. (2003). *Visions of Jewish Education*. Cambridge: Cambridge Press.

Hausman, B. (2000). *Emerging Non-Orthodox Jewish High Schools: A Progress Report for Major Donors*. Boston: Partnership for Excellence in Jewish Education.

Heifetz, R. (1994). *Leadership without Easy Answers*. Cambridge, MA: Harvard University Press.

Ingall, C.K. (2006). *Down the Up Staircase: Tales of Teaching in Jewish Day Schools.* New York: Jewish Theological Seminary Press.

Jacobs, M. (2003). *The Jewish Academy of Metropolitan Detroit: The Experience of the Pioneering Graduating Class.* Boston: The Partnership for Excellence in Jewish Education.

Lieberman Research Worldwide (2004). *Understanding the Needs of Jewish Parents in Greater Boston to More Effectively Market Day Schools—A Report Prepared for the Day School Advocacy Forum of the Combined Jewish Philanthropies of Greater Boston.* Boston: Combined Jewish Philanthropies.

Lipset, S.M. (1994). *The Power of Jewish Education.* Jerusalem: Mandel Institute for the Advanced Study and Development of Jewish Education.

MetLife Mature Market Institute and Zogby International (2006). *The MetLife Grandparents Poll.* New York: Metropolitan Life Insurance Company.

Nanus, B. (1992). *Visionary Leadership.* San Francisco: Jossey-Bass.

Pekarsky, D. (2006). *Vision at Work: The Theory and Practice of Beit Rabban.* New York: Jewish Theological Seminary Press.

Phillips, B. (1997). *Re-examining Intermarriage: Trends, Textures and Strategies.* Boston: The Wilstein Institute of Jewish Policy Studies and the American Jewish Committee.

Pomson, A. (2003). *Parents Under the Influence: Thinking Differently about the Relationships between Parents and Their Children's Schools* (unpublished manuscript).

Rimor, M. & Katz, E. (1993). *Jewish Involvement of the Baby Boom Generation.* Jerusalem: Louis Guttman Israel Institute.

Schick, M. (1999 and 2005). *A Census of Jewish Day Schools in the United States 2004.* New York: Avi Chai (and previous census published in 1999).

Schiff, A. & Schneider, M. (1994). *The Jewishness Quotient of Jewish Day School Graduates: Studying the Effect of Jewish Education on Adult Jewish Behavior.* New York: Azrieli Graduate Institute.

Senge, P. M. (1990). *The Fifth Discipline: The Art & Practice of the Learning Organization.* New York: Doubleday.

Shahar, C. (1998). *The Jewish High School Experience: Its Implications for the Evolution of Jewish Identity in Young Adults.* Toronto: The Federation CJA.

CONTACT INFORMATION FOR ORGANIZATIONS MENTIONED

BoardSource—www.boardsource.org

Independent School Management— www.isminc.org

National Association of Independent Schools—www.nais.org

Summer Camps as
Jewish Socializing Experiences

Amy L. Sales & Leonard Saxe

Among the most exciting developments in Jewish education over the past decade is the increased recognition of summer camping as a valuable Jewish educational experience. A century-old movement, Jewish camping appears on the edge of a new Golden Age (Cohen 1993; Goldberg 1989; Joselit 1993; Sarna 2000). Residential camps are in growth mode with enrollment near capacity, a number of capital projects successfully completed, and plans for new camps underway. Some of this activity has been facilitated by the Foundation for Jewish Camping and its focus on raising the number of children attending Jewish camps in North America and by increased support from philanthropists and Jewish federations.

The activity is not just on the business and operational side but also includes renewed attention to the Jewish mission of camp (Sales & Saxe 2004). Camps provide children important developmental experiences with regard to independence, teamwork, and group living. Jewish camps also have the potential to give children the experience of life in a Jewish community and to teach them about Judaism. Interest in realizing this potential has been fueled in part by dismay over the congregational schools that are the primary educational setting for the majority of Jewish children (Wertheimer 2005). These schools have long been troubled institutions but in recent years have been further weakened by a reduced number of hours of instruction and, in some cases, the loss of the most committed families and talented teachers to day schools (Sales 2006). It is not surprising that community leaders and funders have come to see summer camp as an institution that might supplement the Jewish education received during the school year.

Unlike school, camps seem to work magic. Our study of Jewish summer camping was designed to deconstruct this magic and explain how camp transmits Jewish values, knowledge, and sentiments (Sales & Saxe 2004).[2] The research was a multi-year study (1999-2001) based on surveys and field observations. We conducted a census of Jewish-identified camps in the U.S. and later surveyed over 1,000 Jewish counselors and 4,000 Jewish college students who were not employed as camp counselors. The observational portion of the study was based on visits to 18 Jewish camps across the United States. These camps were selected to represent different regions of the country and represented a range of sponsors (the religious movements, Zionist organizations, communities, foundations, and private ownership). Camper characteristics vary by region, and sponsorship influences every aspect of camp related to Jewish life and learning, from the camp's philosophy to its daily practices, activities, staffing, and clientele.

In the aggregate, the data from our study describe the educational components of the Jewish summer camp—where they fall short and where they fulfill their great promise. They also suggest ways to improve, expand, or intensify the Jewish aspects of camp.

THEORY OF CAMP

Every camp's website, advertisements, and brochure emphasize similar themes: that the camp is safe and nurturing, that its campers have opportunities to grow and to make new friends, that camp is fun. In camp surveys parents say that the most important benefits their children derive from camp

---

[2]The research was supported by a generous grant from The Avi Chai Foundation.

are personal (increased self-confidence and self-esteem), social (new friends, learning how to get along with others), and recreational (an appreciation for nature and the outdoors, recreational skills) (Fine 2007; Marsh 2000; Philliber Research Associates 2005).

Camps that are intentional about promoting the personal benefits of camping and explicitly state so in their camp philosophy appear, in fact, to do a better job of helping children increase their self-confidence and self-esteem. And as the research consistently finds, this higher self-regard correlates with developmental outcomes—more positive relationships with peers and parents, greater satisfaction with life, higher academic achievement, more responsible attitude toward sexual behavior, and more positive adjustment during the middle school transition (Marsh 2000). Seen this way, camping does seem to have magical power.

CENTRALITY OF FUN

Personal growth objectives notwithstanding, the fundamental purpose of camp is to have fun. Fun, we would argue, is camp's greatest strength and the quality that most distinguishes it from formal educational institutions. Camp abounds with opportunities to take risks, experiment with new behaviors, make friends, and learn new skills. In the spirit of fun, campers are more likely to take advantage of these opportunities than they would be in a setting associated with achievement and evaluation. When campers have fun, they are thus more likely to enjoy the personal, social, and recreational benefits of camp.

But more importantly, when campers have fun they return the following summer. A high return rate has several benefits. It ensures that the camp can focus more on its program and less on advertising and marketing. It helps build the strong community that is key to the camp experience. And it provides multiple opportunities to affect a child's life trajectory. When successful, camps will have children not just two months for a summer, but two months every summer for eight to ten years, from when they enter as young campers in elementary school through the high school years, when they may become junior counselors, and into college, when they may become camp staff. Camp touches young people across multiple points in their development. Unlike an Israel experience, camp is not a transformative "aha" experience (Saxe et al. 2000). Rather, directors liken it to a seed that is planted so that it might grow with time.

SETTING AND COMMUNITY

The uniqueness of camp and a key to its magic is the setting and the community that form there. Camp is separate from home and removed from the rest of the world, isolated within the beauty of nature. It is an intense environment. Campers move almost immediately into camp mode when they arrive, and from that moment on they live in the here and now. A sense of community forms virtually overnight. This community is *intentional*, which means that attention is paid to fostering the relationships and spirit that make the camp a tightly knit whole. The bunk where campers live with their peers is a central social and organizational structure. It is this structure, probably more than anything else, that develops self-reliance and teamwork and teaches campers how to get along with others. Counselors who live in the bunks fulfill every adult role vis-à-vis the campers, from teacher to "cool" big brother or sister. Through bunk life and the intensity of camp, campers develop a deep intimacy with bunkmates, counselors, and other staff. These elements distinguish camp from religious school back home. With rare exception, religious schools pay scant attention to community building and group bonding, and they offer few opportunities in which these might occur spontaneously. Children's preference for camp over school may emanate from their strong affection for community, team spirit, and friendship.

The same ingredients that make camp work as a special place that furthers healthy development make it work as an institution that motivates and educates Jewishly. The fun of camp makes campers open to Jewish practices that they might scorn at home. The intensity of camp creates intensity around Jewish life. The separation of camp from the outside world and the close-knit quality of the camp community make it possible to live Judaism at camp in a holistic fashion. Judaism is lived at camp as a matter of course.

THE DESIGN OF JEWISH EDUCATION AT CAMP

The fundamental educational theory of Jewish summer camping is simple: If children associate Jewish life with sweetness—the smell of pine tress, the closeness of friends, laughter in the bunk—what they practice and learn at camp will remain with them for a lifetime. The approach is multi-fold: Shabbat observance, matters of daily life (e.g., song, mealtime rituals, prayer), formal study sessions, informal educational activities, and cues in the physical environment (Jewish symbols, sacred space, Hebrew language, etc.). Judaism is in the air at camp, but it is also transmitted with intentionality.

Each camp has its own goals for and approach to Jewish teaching. These are shaped by the camp's sponsorship, leadership, clientele, and history. Some camps primarily emphasize Torah learning or values (both Jewish and universal), while others emphasize Israel and Zionism, Jewish pride and respect, or Jewish friendships. Some camps have explicit Jewish education only one hour a week; others have daily lessons.

Jewish education at camp varies with regard to its integration into everyday life at camp or its compartmentalization into its own time and space. Where Jewish education is compartmentalized, it is seen as an activity like any other, fitted into the schedule along with swimming, rocketry, and arts and crafts. Where Jewish learning is infused into any and all activities, campers are as likely to encounter Jewish education on the high ropes course as they are in *limud* (Jewish study).

Jewish education at camp also varies in the degree to which it is a centralized or shared responsibility. In some camps Jewish education rests in the hands of specialists—rabbis, Jewish educators, Israeli *schlichim* (emissaries). This latter design may be inevitable in places where bunk counselors lack Judaic knowledge and are unprepared to take on any part of the educational mission. It also predominates in camps where there are disagreements about "how Jewish" the camp should be and what balance is desirable between personal growth goals and Jewish goals. When counselors cannot or will not assume part of the responsibility for education, Jewish learning remains confined to whatever box is allocated to the educator.

In other camps, responsibility for Jewish education is shared by specialists and bunk counselors. This design is possible in the denominational and Zionist camps, where counselors typically come up through the movement and assume their staff positions with some level of Judaic preparedness. Even in these camps, however, shared responsibility requires continuing education for counselors, teacher-friendly materials, and a supportive environment.

The third dimension along which Jewish education varies is the mix of formal and informal educational approaches. Both are found in all of the camps we studied, but the emphasis overall is on informal Jewish education. Such an approach entails experiential, sensory, and group-based experiences. A great deal of curricular experimentation is underway in this realm. Indeed, camps are ideal pilot sites for programming, since camp norms support creative thinking and experimentation. Moreover, an activity can be rerun multiple times with a large number of children of varied ages and backgrounds over a single season.

FOCUS ON STAFF

The field of Jewish camping is rife with opportunities to develop original curricula, to explore new ways of integrating Jewish education into everyday camp activities, and to refine the techniques of informal Jewish education. Programming, however, does not stand on its own but depends almost entirely on staff. Whether in leading activities, grasping a teachable moment, modeling Jewish values and behavior, or supporting children as they try on new behaviors, it is the staff members' knowledge, ability to relate to the campers, and facilitation and programming skills that are most critical to success.

Our survey of camp counselors found that the great majority had been active in Jewish youth groups, had attended or worked at a Jewish summer camp, and had traveled to Israel. More than three-fourths feel that they know enough to be Jewish role models for their campers. They are not just relying on what they learned in preparation for becoming b'nai mitzvah: Half of the Jewish staff at the summer camps in our study had taken a Judaics course during the previous two years.

Moreover, camp staff differ from the general population of American Jewish college students in terms of their high levels of Jewish involvement and in the greater emphasis they place on Jewish values—social action, support for Jewish organizations, spirituality, Shabbat observance and so on. They are suffused with Jewish pride. Almost everyone said that s/he is proud to be a Jew, and for virtually all of these respondents this is a statement with which they "strongly" agree. The young adults staffing camps also, by and large, feel comfortable and at home in Jewish settings and recognize a special connection with their Jewish friends.

On the other hand, one-fourth of the Jewish camp staff we surveyed lack these backgrounds and commitments. One-fourth described themselves in secular terms, as cultural Jews or as "just Jewish." One-fourth admitted that they do not know enough to be real Jewish role models. With the current configuration of hires, camps face the challenges of integrating diverse staff members into a coherent and vibrant Jewish community and of delivering a Jewish message that can be carried by only a portion of the staff.

Each year the camps see staff turnover at all levels and continually need to identify and recruit new staff. It is difficult to find young adults who are willing and able to spend a summer at camp, let alone to find those who are also Judaically sophisticated. If young people come up through a movement and have their own memories of summers at camp, the sale is easy. For these individuals the tug of camp is great, and they are eager to return each summer. These, however, are the "insiders," and their numbers are limited. For outside recruitment, the benefits that might entice are not there (e.g., money, recognition, college credit, access to future job opportunities). Camps face staffing challenges every step of the way—recruiting, hiring, training, and retaining high-quality counselors.

These challenges have inevitably led to staffing shortages, in evidence in several of the camps in our study. One of the camps was shy by fifteen counselors. Another permitted partial summer employment, taking counselors, unit heads, and specialists for whatever time period they were available. A third asked high school students in the CIT program to move into full counselor positions to fill a shortage after the first two-week session. One camp was making recruitment calls while we were there in early August, trying to find counselors for the last session.

Staffing shortages have pernicious effects on camps. They exacerbate the problem of staff stress and exhaustion. Camps that are understaffed need to limit time off to the extent that at one camp, the counselors' free time was "barely enough just to clear your head." Shortages also make it difficult for a camp to fire counselors who perform poorly, break camp rules, or otherwise violate the terms of their contract. Most importantly, perhaps, shortages mean fewer role models of Jewishly engaged counselors on staff—a serious threat to one of camp's best means to educate young children.

CHALLENGES

Although much of the Jewish educational programming at summer camps appears successful, the full potential of the camps to educate has hardly been realized. Despite the existence of excellent programs and experimentation, our study recorded many programming failures. Girls were more engaged than boys; there were moments of joy in learning but also moments of boredom; there were those who attend as expected and required and those who skip class; there were activities that ran well and others that were stopped due to disruptive behavior and lack of interest. In some places there was no Judaica simply because the specialist in charge had not considered the possibility, lacked knowledge or ideas, or was uncomfortable with the material. In other instances Jewish education fell short due to flawed program design, inadequate resources, or failure to capitalize on teachable moments.

Excellence in programming depends on having the right staff—people who are well trained, responsible, effective role models, teachers, and guides. The list of what qualified staff need to know is a long one: the general field of camping; specific information about the camp (from traditions, myths and songs to correct administrative and operating procedures); group work and counseling skills; youth work (e.g., how to discipline and set boundaries; how to deal with issues of intimacy, emotional distress, and homesickness); basics of programming; and Judaics.

These informational needs are a tall order that cannot readily be filled by a five-day orientation at the beginning of the season. The time for Judaics is especially limited. For reasons of health, safety, and accreditation, camps generally work on all the other aspects of a counselor's job before they get to those related to Jewish life and learning at camp. In some settings it is difficult to make up the time while camp is in session. Counselors' enthusiasm to pursue their own Jewish studies at camp is dampened by the demands of their jobs and by the fact that their primary motivation for being there has little to do with Jewish experiences and a great deal to do with fun and friends.

FUTURE DIRECTIONS

In the ideal world, the Jewish camps would move in the following directions:

- Counselors would regard themselves, and be seen by others, as informal Jewish educators. In operational terms, "Jewish educator" would become part of the counselor's job description and Jewish education incorporated into counselor training, supervision and evaluation. In cultural terms, camps would seek ways to decentralize Jewish education, create partnerships between Judaic experts and counselors, and push Jewish education down into the bunks.

- Jewish programming would be integrated so that Jewish learning would be infused throughout the camp and its myriad activities. There would be ongoing experimentation with programming that makes Judaism an organic part of everyday life. This experimentation would be done in the spirit of action research so that camps could continuously learn from their efforts and strive for higher quality in their programs.

- Camps would bring informal Jewish education to its full potential. Informal education is serious pedagogy with philosophical and theoretical underpinnings and a treasure house of methods and techniques. Staff would be taught about informal Jewish education, and camp leaders would, over time, master the skills that are needed to develop curricula, design activities, and lead sessions effectively.

- The result would be authentic Judaism and not "camp" Judaism. As much fun as the activities would be, the content would be serious and carefully rooted in Jewish text and teachings.

Our research makes clear that in order to move in this direction, camp leadership must feel a need to change. Some directors in our study believe that their camp has the correct blend of Jewish life and secular activities to suit the campers and their families. These directors do not want to risk current success by altering the Jewish nature of the camp. Others became interested in such change when they began to grow in their own Jewish knowledge and practice. Unless the new direction is fully embraced by the director, change will not occur. Camps are strongly hierarchical systems, and no change will take place unless it is driven by the director. We repeatedly found in our study that, for better or worse, the director's own Jewish journey is intertwined with that of the camp. Unless directors understand and value Jewish growth, they will not fully incorporate it into their camps' mission or program in a meaningful way.

The motivation to change Jewish life and learning at camp is but a first step. The camps must also overcome the forces that resist change—the strong culture and traditions that good camps establish, the recalcitrance of counselors and other staff, and the resistance of the camp's best customers, their long-time campers. When we look at camps that have tried to enrich their Jewish identities, we find that change comes slowly. Infusing camp with a deeper sense of Jewish life probably takes a "camp generation"; that is, the length of time it takes today's youngest campers to become counselors.

RECOMMENDATIONS

The recommendations identify key means by which camps could be assisted to deepen and broaden their Jewish educational impact.

1. **Expand the reach of Jewish camping.** One step to maximize the influence of Jewish camps is to expand their capacity by adding to existing facilities, opening satellite camps, converting secular settings into Jewish camps, or creating "camp" in other settings (e.g., on a ship at sea or on a college campus). Expansion also means greater promotion of Jewish camps in order to increase

the likelihood that families will make Jewish choices for their children's summer program. And it means a change in the fee structure along with revenue enhancement from private, foundation, and community funding to enable Jewish camps to attract and serve a greater range of children.

The Foundation for Jewish Camping (FJC), founded in 1998, has focused its mission on increasing the number of Jewish children attending Jewish camps. Its approach is simultaneously to create more demand and to increase capacity. The Grinspoon Institute for Jewish Philanthropy was established by the Grinspoon Foundation in 2004 to help Jewish nonprofit overnight camps increase their fundraising and leadership capacities. With a stronger financial base and the capacity to raise funds, it is hoped that camps will be able to purchase sites, renovate facilities, and, in the Foundation's words, "create an infrastructure that will bring the Jewish camping experience to new heights and to a broader spectrum of Jewish youth." As well, the Grinspoon Foundation and various local Jewish federations have begun offering stipends to families that choose Jewish educational camps for their children. These initiatives are the beginnings of a serious effort to expand the reach of Jewish camping.

2. **Make camp a model of Jewish education.** American culture is founded in individualism (cf. Bellah et al. 1985), and young people today are under enormous pressure for individual achievement. From state-mandated testing programs in elementary school to the competitive college admissions process, children learn early that individual success is paramount. Formal Jewish educational programs have largely been designed in this mold, paying scant attention to the relationships that form among children, the value of teachers as role models, the school as a caring community, and the possibility of filling the air with Jewish song and spirit. Camps, with their expertise in creating intentional communities, can be an instructive model for schools to emulate. To become such a model, however, they need to recognize themselves as educational settings, achieve consistent levels of excellence, and disseminate their accomplishments.

They also need to join the effort to professionalize informal Jewish education. The Institute for Informal Jewish Education at Brandeis University and the newly constituted JEXNET[3], among others, are promoting advanced education and training in the field, development and testing of innovative curricula, and recognition and support for those committed to informal educational approaches to Jewish learning. The camping field should position itself as a primary beneficiary and contributor to the theory, research, practice, and professional talent that emerge from these efforts.

3. **Prepare directors to move toward greater Jewish life at camp.** A third step to maximizing the influence of Jewish camps is to provide top-level training for directors, to open their minds to new ideas for Jewish life at camp and to help them plan and implement changes in their camps' Jewish practices. The past few years have seen the emergence of such efforts. The Foundation for Jewish Camping has instituted the Executive Leadership Institute, which works with experienced camp professionals on their business, management and leadership skills. These include, among others, marketing, recruitment, strategic planning, visioning, board development, and fundraising. Content is informed by Jewish values, informal education, and best practices in both the private and public sectors. Also targeting top camp leadership is *Tse Ul'mad*, a program funded by The Avi Chai Foundation and administered by the Foundation for Jewish Camping. The program provides matching grants for camp directors to take courses for their own Judaic enrichment. *Lekhu Lakhem*, a program of the JCCA, provides Jewish education for a select group of directors at Jewish community center camps and works with them on establishing and implementing a Jewish vision for their camps. These efforts are of critical importance. Our research makes clear that unless the director is interested in intensifying Jewish life and learning at camp, it will not happen.

4. **Focus on Jewish staff as a target group in their own right.** Jewish summer camps have inadvertently created the perfect environment for the development of the young adults who work there. Camp is an opportunity for them to live away from home, try out new things, make

---

[3]Editor's Note: JEXNET suspended its program operations in October, 2007.

friends, build a community, take on responsibility for others, and acquire valuable life skills. It is an ideal place for identity exploration. Importantly, it offers two months of living, teaching, and studying together in a Jewish community that is intentional about the Jewish environment it creates and the Jewish experiences and lessons it imparts.

For these benefits to be realized, the camp experience must be re-framed to be as much about the counselors as it is about the campers. It requires camps to place new emphasis on counselor education, supervision and mentoring, and on opportunities for personal growth and professional development. To do so, camps need to experiment with new models of pre-season training, to create in-service programs, and to increase staff support. Two questions should inform these efforts: (1) What do staff members need to know in order to further the Jewish mission of the camp? (2) What do they need to know in order to develop personally and professionally at camp?

A few recent efforts related to staff development are notable. The Cornerstone Fellowship, funded by the Avi Chai Foundation, was originally designed to incentivize counselors to return for a third year of service. Recognizing the value of these counselors as emerging Jewish leaders, the program soon added a four-day professional development seminar to the requirements for receiving a $500 incentive stipend. The seminar includes training in leadership and life skills. Participants are encouraged to see themselves as Jewish educators and to have confidence in their capacity to play this role. During the summer at camp, a senior staff member reinforces curricular concepts and helps Fellows implement the Jewish skills and programs they learned at the seminar.

The JCCA, through its TAG initiative, is developing programming units for infusing everyday camp life with Jewish values. These units are for counselors, many of whom have limited Judaic backgrounds. In order for camps to receive these programming materials, they must agree to have their counselors trained to use them. The training currently takes place at a regional seminar, but in 2008 it will shift to on-site training during staff orientation. The impetus for this shift came from directors who, through their participation in *Lekhu Lakhem,* became ready to advance the Jewish agenda at their camps. As the professional development press is coming simultaneously from the top and the bottom, it is hoped that it will lead to a camping system with increased motivation and capacity to be serious about its Judaism.

5. **Bring more Jewish counselors to camp.** In order to alter the profile of camp staff, there need to be more qualified Jewish candidates in the applicant pool. Recommendations for how to enlarge the pool include raising salaries and promoting the value of camp work. There is a need to expand recruitment efforts through stronger linkages with colleges, campus programs and organizations, Judaic studies programs, and Birthright Israel. In addition, youth groups, volunteer programs, and Israel trips could be turned into feeder programs that would produce staff that possess an understanding of informal Jewish education and an appreciation of the spirit that makes Jewish life at camp so joyous and memorable. To do so, however, these experiences must be not only educationally rich and highly motivating but also linked to camps. Bridges need to be built between a variety of teen programs and summer camps so that when the teens reach college age and beyond they will be primed to work as Jewish educational camp counselors.

6. **Conduct research to inform the field of Jewish camping and to ground its future development in reliable information.** Our study of Jewish summer camps provided an important starting point for research in a field that, until recently, has received little serious attention. Our inventory of Jewish camps has become a database maintained by the Foundation for Jewish Camping. Annually, information is gathered about the residential camps' programs and operations (e.g., capacity, staffing, budget, scholarships). Over time this information could provide trend analysis about growth and shifts in the field.

Our counselor survey was a first step in understanding the backgrounds and motivations of the young adults who find their way to camp in the summer. Through our studies of Birthright Israel (see Saxe et al. 2006) and Jewish life on college campuses (Sales & Saxe 2006) we are beginning to develop a knowledge base about this age cohort, but much remains to be done. More research is needed about this generation's social networks, connections to Judaism, identity explorations, and worldviews. Of particular interest is the influence of camp on the formation of each of these elements. Such research requires data collection from Jewish young adults who have worked at camp as well as those who have not. We need to understand the differences between these two groups and the possibilities for engaging more of the latter group in camp life.

Our recommendations call for greater innovation and experimentation at camp. All such efforts need to be accompanied by action research that measures the outcome of these initiatives (their impact on the camps, campers, and their families) but also their process. How do they effect change? Under what conditions are they most likely to succeed? What factors strengthen or weaken their impact? Such feedback is invaluable to a dynamic field, helping it to continuously learn from the important work that it does.

RESEARCH QUESTIONS

- How is Jewish summer camping changing with regard to the size, shape, and content of the field?

- Under what conditions are camps most likely to undertake an effort to amplify their Jewish educational mission, and under what conditions is this effort most likely to succeed?

- What influence does camp have on the Jewish lives of campers and their families? Under what conditions is it most likely to have a positive effect?

- What impact does a summer camp experience have on the young adult staff? How does the experience affect their social networks, connections to Judaism, identity explorations, and worldviews? What can be done to maximize that impact?

- How do programmatic innovations affect the camp, its campers and their families? Under what conditions are innovations most likely to succeed? What factors strengthen or weaken their impact?

CONCLUSION

In the past few years, since the publication of our research, the field of Jewish summer camping has been developing at a strong and rapid pace. It is benefiting from increased funding, capacity building, leadership, and educational sophistication. As we deconstructed the magic we were able to point to programmatic shortcomings and to interventions that might raise Jewish life and learning at camp to higher levels of excellence. We are now seeing those interventions become a reality, and the field is moving to new heights. Yet on a warm summer Friday night at camp, sitting under the stars with the air filled with music, it still feels like magic.

HIGHLIGHTS

- Summer camping is increasingly recognized as a valuable Jewish educational experience. New activity in the field includes capital projects, capacity enrollments, and renewed attention to the Jewish mission of camps.

- The approach to Jewish education at camp is multi-fold: Shabbat observance, matters of daily life, formal study sessions, informal educational activities, and cues in the physical environment. Explicit instruction varies with regard to the extent to which it is integrated into everyday life at camp or compartmentalized into its own time and space; the extent to which it is a centralized or shared responsibility; and the extent to which it relies on formal or informal educational approaches.

- The success of Jewish education at camp depends almost entirely on staff. Although the majority of counselors have been active in Jewish life, one-fourth lack Jewish backgrounds and commitments and admit that they do not know enough to be Jewish role models for their campers. Camps face continual challenges in recruiting, hiring, training, and retaining high-quality counselors.

- Overall, camps have not as yet realized their full educational potential. Jewish education falls short due to staff limitations, flawed program design, inadequate resources, and failure to capitalize on teachable moments.

- In the ideal world, counselors at the Jewish camps would be regarded as informal Jewish educators. Jewish programming would be integrated into camp life, and there would be a plethora of experimentation in programming. In order to move in this direction, however, camp directors must fully embrace the change and manage to overcome the strong forces that resist change at camp.

- If camps are to deepen and broaden their Jewish educational impact, it will be necessary to expand the reach of Jewish camping, making camp a model of Jewish education; to prepare directors to move toward greater Jewish life at camp, focus on Jewish staff as a target group in their own right, bring more Jewish counselors to camp, and conduct research to inform the field and to ground its future development in reliable information.

LARGER CONTEXT

The Jewish community excels at peak experiences for youth. It has invented Jewish camp, Israel, and retreat experiences that are intensive and often transformative. The community has fallen short, however, in creating everyday Jewish life experiences that similarly attract and inspire youth. Importantly, camp is a peak experience that endures over two months in the summer. It gives participants the experience of living in a Jewish community where Jewish life is practiced and enjoyed as a matter of course, seamlessly blended into the flow of everyday activities. Yet camp belongs to summer and cannot extend into the school year. It is precisely the time delimitation of peak experiences that give them much of their preciousness and potency.

Summer camping is normative in American culture, and choices abound among the thousands of camps on the landscape. Within this field there are over 200 camps that are perceived as "Jewish camps." Our research makes clear, however, that these camps vary widely with regard to the emphasis they place on Judaism and Jewish education, from those that are deeply committed to the Jewish enterprise to those that are only nominally Jewish. Moreover, unlike a bar/bat mitzvah celebration, a Jewish summer camp experience is far from universal, and in fact, the Jewish camps serve only a fraction of the Jewish youth population. The community thus faces two challenges: getting more families to choose Jewish summer camps that are serious about their Jewish mission, and getting more camps to intensify their Jewish purposes. Efforts are underway on both counts, with Jewish foundations and federations establishing funds to incentivize parents to make Jewish choices for their children's summer experience and organizations like the Foundation for Jewish Camping, the JCC Association, and the Grinspoon Foundation working to enhance the Jewish mission of camps.

We do not believe, however, that camp's potential impact is in becoming a year-round venture or in reaching the majority of Jewish youth. Rather, camp is likely to have its greatest impact as a laboratory for Jewish education. Camp is the ideal setting for experimenting with and learning about immersion experiences, group dynamics, implicit and explicit Jewish education, the melding of informal and formal educational approaches, and the instructional uses of everyday Jewish living. It is not unreasonable to expect that camps could fulfill this role. Each year the rabbis and teachers who work at camp return to their home institutions filled with camp's spirit of Jewish life and learning. Throughout the community, in both its secular and religious organizations, a disproportionate number of lay and professional leaders have a camp background. In the Reform world, much credit is given to the camps for their influence on the movement overall, particularly with regard to music, Hebrew language, education, and prayer (Lorge & Zola 2006).

In our recent work mapping the field of Jewish education we found the beginnings of new modes of operating that should increase experimentation and diffusion of innovation. The general format entails piloting and modeling, conducting evaluation research, aggregating results of studies to derive general principles, disseminating findings, and scaling up. A great deal of work remains to be done to perfect these modes of operating, but the vision and language for working in this way have already taken hold in many agencies and foundations (Sales 2006). Camp is a perfect laboratory for piloting and modeling. But for maximum impact, its creative output needs to be measured, documented, published and disseminated. Only in this way can lessons learned in one camp be transmitted to another and lessons from the camping field influence the rest of the Jewish education world.

ANNOTATED BIBLIOGRAPHY

Arnett, J.J. & Tanner, J.L. (eds.) (2006). *Emerging Adults in America: Coming of Age in the 21ˢᵗ Century*. Washington, DC: American Psychological Association. *Emerging Adults in America: Coming of Age in the 21st Century* portrays the lives of young Americans between adolescence and young adulthood, a distinct developmental stage referred to as "emerging adulthood." Chapters cover a range of topics including relationships with parents; views about love, sex, and marriage; experiences in college and in the workplace; religious beliefs; and beliefs about the concept of adulthood.

Eisner, M.D. (2005). *Camp*. NY: Warner Books. Eisner unabashedly describes this book as a "valentine" to camp. In this narrative of his, his father's, and his son's experiences at camp he addresses the question of why summer camp matters as an institution.

Lorge, M.M. & Zola, G.P. (Eds.). (2006). *A Place of Our Own: The Rise of Reform Jewish Camping*. Tuscaloosa, AL: The University of Alabama Press. The essays in *A Place of Our Own* place the Reform Jewish camps in historical context and examine specific dimensions of Reform Jewish camping—music, prayer, education and Hebrew language. The editors conclude that Reform Jewish camping had an unequivocal influence on the character of the Reform movement as a whole.

Sales, A.L. & Saxe, L. (2004). *"How Goodly Are Thy Tents": Summer Camps as Jewish Socializing Experiences*. Hanover, NH: University Press of New England. Based on an extensive study of Jewish summer camps, *How Goodly Are Thy Tents* presents rich ethnographic material gleaned from a participant-observation field study at twenty Jewish summer camps located throughout the United States, data from a national census of Jewish residential camps and their participants, organizational analyses of camps, and the results of surveys of the attitudes and motivations of the young adults who work at camp.

REFERENCES

Bellah, R.N., Madsen, R., Sullivan, W.M., Swidler, A. & Tipton, S.M. (1985). *Habits of the Heart: Individualism and Commitment in American Life*. Berkeley: University of California Press.

Cohen, D. (1993). A brief history of summer camp in the United States. In J.W. Joselit & K.S. Mittelman (eds.), *A worthy use of summer*. Philadelphia: National Museum of American Jewish History, 10–13.

Fine, S. (2007). *The generational research of the camp experience: Alumni perspectives*. Paper presented at the American Camp Association Research Symposium, Austin, TX.

Goldberg, E.C. (1989). "The beginnings of educational camping in the Reform movement." *Journal of Reform Judaism*, 36(4), 4–12.

Joselit, J.W. (1993). The Jewish way of play. In J.W. Joselit & K.S. Mittelman (eds.), *A Worthy Use of Summer*. Philadelphia: National Museum of American Jewish History, 15–28.

Lorge, M.M. & Zola, G.P. (eds.) (2006). *A Place of Our Own: The Rise of Reform Jewish Camping*. Tuscaloosa, AL: The University of Alabama Press.

Marsh, P.E. (2000). *What Does Camp Do for Kids?* Martinsville, IN: American Camp Association.

Philliber Research Associates and the American Camp Association (2005). *Directions: Youth Development Outcomes of the Camp Experience*. Martinsville, IN: American Camp Association.

Sales, A. (2006). *Mapping Jewish Education: The National Picture*. Retrieved February 1, 2007, from http://www.jimjosephfoundation.org/PDF/Brandeis%20Report%202.pdf

Sales, A.L. & Saxe, L. (2004). *"How Goodly Are Thy Tents": Summer Camps as Jewish Socializing Experiences*. Hanover, NH: University Press of New England.

Sales, A.L. & Saxe, L. (2006). *Particularism in the University: Realities and Opportunities for Jewish Life on Campus*. New York: The Avi Chai Foundation.

Sarna, J. (2000). *The Crucial Decade in Jewish Camping* (unpublished manuscript).

Saxe, L., Sasson, T. & Hecht, S. (2006). *Taglit-Birthright Israel: Impact on Jewish Identity, Peoplehood, and Connection to Israel* . Waltham, MA: Cohen Center for Modern Jewish Studies, Brandeis University.

Wertheimer, J. (2005). *Linking the Silos: How to Accelerate the Momentum in Jewish Education Today*. New York: The Avi Chai Foundation.

Jewish Education in the JCCs

Patricia Cipora Harte, Richard Juran & Alvin Mars

Following more than two decades of intensive Jewish educational growth, Jewish community centers throughout North America have come to see themselves as responsible for "inspiring Jewish journeys." These may be diverse journeys experienced by individuals, families, program participants or various other sub-communities; they also may include finessing transitions for JCC program "graduates"—toddlers in early childhood education, teen athletes in JCC Maccabi Games, etc.—to other programs in the JCC or elsewhere in the Jewish community, thereby facilitating seamless, continuous, positive Jewish journeys for all. Jewish community centers have taken their first name seriously, making great strides in creating Jewish spaces and places while helping JCC professionals see themselves as significant players in transmitting the Jewish mission of the JCC.

The central questions and issues characterizing Jewish education in JCCs today are:

- **THE CONTEXT:** What does it mean to engage in Jewish education in the JCC given its unique characteristics as an educational setting—i.e., ages ranging from early childhood to senior citizen, a non-normative approach to education, multiple modes of learning, and full staff involvement in fostering Jewish living as an integral component of the JCC mission?

- **THE PROFESSION:** Who is the JCC Jewish educator? What should constitute prerequisite training and experience? How should the job be configured? Are there multiple models for different agencies reflecting mission, program emphases, size, location or other variables? Should the educator's focus be on direct delivery of service or indirect impact as a resource to others? What defines the profession of the JCC Jewish educator? To what extent and in what ways can all JCC professionals see themselves as Jewish educators involved in the transmission of Jewish life?

- **THE CONTENT:** What is the content of "Jewish" within the JCC? Within the diversity of ages, interactions, and settings, what is the Jewish core of the JCC in both program and substance?

- **THE SUCCESS:** In a Jewish educational environment that is by definition welcoming, non-judgmental and non-prescriptive, what are the objectives and criteria for success?

These four issues are among the central challenges that JCCs face today as they emphasize their Jewish nature. Through their wide range of experiences in the JCC movement in North America and in Israel, in both formal and informal settings, the authors reveal insights into the state of Jewish education in the JCCs of North America today.

JEWISH EDUCATION IN THE JCCS
CONTEXT

At the continental level, the JCC Association is engaged in a myriad of contextual frameworks for Jewish living and learning. The consulting services, along with curriculum and program development, serve all ages and areas of Jewish life, ranging from the arts, culture and spirituality to health, fitness and recreation. They also focus on a wide range of formal and informal educational settings. JCCs have developed new contexts and strategies for building Jewish life in North America, ranging from the design of new physical spaces to a diverse menu of programs and services, from producing of innovative materials (print, audio-visual, electronic) to nurturing sub-communities among its members while serving as a resource to the community at large.

The JCC Association both leads and serves JCCs throughout North America in the quest to enhance Jewish living and learning. As full service agencies reaching all age groups throughout the community in a plethora of program areas, JCCs are uniquely positioned to bring Jewish living and learning to all in a non-threatening, pluralistic and creative manner. Each local JCC operates autonomously with a shared commitment to the "J" in JCC, which is at the core of its programs, activities and services.

RESEARCH

In *What is Jewish Education in the JCC?* Chazan (1996) provided an overview of the essential qualities of Jewish education in JCCs: associational, pluralistic, inter-generational, personally focused, interpersonal, experiential, cognitive and affective Jewish learning, ambiance, and values (*Klal Yisrael; Hesed, Tzedakah, Gemilut Hasadim;* Jewish life and practice, Israel) (pp. 13–20).

Cohen and Holtz (1996) described in *Jewish Education in JCCs* that "in the Center's day-to-day operation, the Jewish education specialist is the central figure in improving a Center's educational program," noting the range of roles that vary from programmer to resource, advocate, teacher and scholar (p. 16). They further point out that "the successful educators were people who understood that other *staff* of the JCC were as much their clients as were the members" (p. 17). In the course of analysis of Jewish education in the realms of early childhood education, summer camps, teen programs, and senior adults, Cohen and Holtz found that "in the six Centers that we examined closely, the most developed area of Jewish programming was in the area of adult education," which manifested itself in holiday workshops, libraries, cultural events, lectures and courses (p. 26).

Furthermore, they identified key elements of an educational philosophy for the JCC movement: Judaism can be enjoyable; introductory Judaism for the many, advanced Judaism for the few; the JCC as gateway; the new Jewish neighborhood; complementarity of the Center and the synagogue; and Israel as a special JCC opportunity (pp. 33–36). They noted three different approaches to aspects of intervention and confrontation vis-à-vis the Jewish educational agenda of JCCs: the classical "non-confrontational" stance favoring educational intervention while respecting individual autonomy, or in its more minimalist form, the JCC as Jewish neighborhood supplying Jewish oxygen in a safe setting; a more proactive model promoting Judaism and Jewish involvement without advocating any particular perspective; and a perhaps less prevalent stance extolling the need to "challenge the beliefs, values, life choices and religious practices of the people with whom they interact" (pp. 37–38). A critical issue for them is whether Jewish education within the inclusive, non-denominational JCC can be religious education or whether the JCC represents an alternative model (pp. 38–39).

Cohen and Holtz conclude by identifying conditions conducive to Jewish educational success: location in a strong Jewish community; a secure executive; reasonable financial security; a supportive local Jewish federation; and a sufficient size in terms of budget and staff (pp. 39–40). They pose a number of questions worthy of further analysis, including the need to focus on the appropriate constituency (whether JCC members or the general Jewish community); the worthiest targets (those accessible, amenable and/or in need); the Jewish identity and knowledge of the staff; the appropriate degree of intervention in the Jewish lives of the constituencies; whether to offer a supermarket of Jewish options or advocate a distinctive form of American Judaism; the ability of the JCC to produce replicable Jewish educational models; and characteristics of the larger surrounding community that supports the Jewish educational mission of its JCC (pp. 44–45).

In a subsequent monograph, *A Jewish Philosophy for the JCC Movement: An Invitation to a Discussion on Jewish Peoplehood, Pluralism, Living and Learning,* Chazan and Cohen (1999) argued in favor of articulating a Jewish philosophy that "would serve to lend structure and meaning to JCCs' Jewish educational enterprise, thereby further encouraging policy makers, practitioners and donors to support such efforts....to help shape Jewish educational programs in JCCs....to inform and influence the numerous day-to-day decisions taken by front-line and supervisory staff....to serve as verification to influential outsiders (other agencies, other Jewish communal leaders) of the sophistication and dedication of the JCC movement to the Jewish educational agenda....[and to afford] the opportunity (or, some may say, the responsibility) to advocate their particular approach to Jewish life, Judaism, and

Jewishness" (pp. 5–7). As indicated by the title, they proposed an ideology based on Jewish people-hood, pluralism, living and learning (pp. 8–13).

IMPLICATIONS AND/OR POLICY RECOMMENDATIONS

In their discussion of the potential of JCCs to build *Meaningful Jewish Community*, Cohen, Israel and Fine (2000) recommend they "engage around matters of Jewish content and purpose. Attempts to build Jewish community for the sole 'purpose' of building Jewish community fail to appreciate the importance of meaning-seeking among contemporary Americans, or of higher purpose in all successful Jewish communities. Accordingly, policy makers and practitioners need to further articulate the relationship of the JCCs to a variety of Jewish issues and purposes. These include Jewish learning, prayer, spirituality, Jewish peoplehood, Israel engagement in the larger society, social justice, philanthropy and other such matters that lay at the heart of historic Judaism in all its beauty, complexity, and diversity" (p. v).

In light of research findings and impressions of the state of Jewish education in North American JCCs today, it would seem imperative that JCCs take a fresh look at their Jewish educational vision, the strategy and methods currently in place to bring it to fruition, and the criteria for measuring success. It may not be necessary for all JCCs to adopt an identical vision or strategy, but each would be well served by grappling with available models, selecting the most appropriate one, and investing necessary resources to realize the chosen vision. Toward that end, JCCs should consider formulating appropriate Jewish educational benchmarks, which will take them beyond the important *Standards for Jewish Community Centers* issued in 2000.

Parallel to these efforts, the JCC Association should redouble its efforts to nurture the Jewish educational "conversation" among North American JCCs—executive directors, volunteer leaders and Jewish educators, if not the entire lay and professional network. After more than twenty years of investment, Jewish educators have become an integral part of the JCC, though there is still much to be done to create greater stability, professional identity and support for the remarkable Jewish educators and programmers found throughout the system.

ADDITIONAL RESEARCH QUESTIONS

Although the JCC Association has developed an extensive knowledge base of the Jewish education activities and agendas within the movement, many issues remain for further research:

- The relative prevalence and impact of Jewish education in various JCC departments (according to age groups, program areas, etc.).
- Further investigation of key variables associated with the presence, quality and impact of Jewish education in JCCs (e.g., support of the executive director, president and/or federation, the presence and status of Jewish educator, and the budget).
- In-depth look at Jewish educators in JCCs: their academic and professional experience, from whom they receive supervision, their terms of employment, the nature of their job assignment, their longevity in the position, and their perceived impact.
- The Jewish educational strategies currently employed by JCCs, an assessment of the extent to which they are reflected in programs and in agency priorities, and their impact on leadership, staff, members and the community.
- JCCs' Jewish educational objectives and criteria for measuring success.

Among the possible ways of moving the field forward:

- Provide consultation to local JCCs interested in reexamining their Jewish educational game plan and performance.
- Highlight Jewish education as the focus of JCC conferences and gatherings.
- Create a forum to nurture communication and professional development for JCC Jewish educators among themselves and in cooperation with their colleagues throughout the JCC.

- Sponsor Israel-based seminars for JCC lay and professional leaders to facilitate greater attention to the Jewish educational agenda of JCCs.
- Encourage writing and publishing of articles, essays, books and program materials related to Jewish education in JCCs.

CONCLUSION

Though JCCs have long seen Jewish education as part of their mission (*cf.* Janowsky 1948), the field has witnessed a genuine revolution since the report of the Commission on Maximizing Jewish Educational Effectiveness of Jewish Community Centers was issued in 1984. Many JCCs have explicitly incorporated Jewish education in their vision and mission statements as well as their programs and have hired talented Jewish educators who enhance this dimension of the agency in invaluable ways. JCCs are currently focused on facilitating Jewish journeys for those they serve, seeking to help each find suitable paths to meaningful Jewish life. Following these accomplishments, they may now set their sights on the next horizon as they seek to identify the elements of leadership, professionalism and content associated with the quality of Jewish education that they aspire to provide to their constituents and community.

HIGHLIGHTS

- JCCs have come to see themselves as responsible for "inspiring Jewish journeys," thereby facilitating seamless, continuous positive Jewish journeys for all.
- JCCs are uniquely positioned to bring Jewish living and learning to all in a non-threatening, pluralistic and creative manner.
- Successful JCC Jewish educators understand that other *staff* of the JCC are as much their clients as are members.
- The essential qualities of Jewish education in JCCs include associational, pluralistic, inter-generational, personally focused, interpersonal, experiential, cognitive and affective Jewish learning, ambiance, and values.
- The conditions conducive to Jewish educational success are location in a strong Jewish community, a secure executive; reasonable financial security, and a supportive local Jewish federation.

THE LARGER CONTEXT

In *The School and Society* Dewey posits the meaningless nature of an education that is disconnected from its society. Jewish educators face an even greater disconnect as they attempt to provide Jewish educational experiences, often without the existence of on enveloping Jewish milieu with which those experiences might be linked for meaning or relevance. The JCC movement has come to realize that one of its greatest Jewish educational strengths is its potential to create Jewish community and meaningful Jewish experience within that community.

Chazan (1994) begins his definition of informal Jewish education with the statement: "Informal Jewish education refers to an approach to Jewish education, the objective of which is to enable people to participate—usually with others—in a diverse series of Jewish life experiences for the inherent value in them." As such, JCCs are, indeed, centers of informal Jewish education. And the more reflective the JCC has been about its Jewish educational role over the past decades, the more attention it has devoted to its own Jewish educational development, the greater its potential impact on the entire field has become.

Informal education is not the exclusive possession of any one Jewish educational institution (even formal education has its informal, experiential elements); the research and educational developments at JCCs can be of importance to day schools, congregational schools, youth movements and senior centers , among others, as well as within JCCs themselves.

ANNOTATED BIBLIOGRAPHY

Charendoff, M. & Chazan, B. (1994). *Jewish Education and the Jewish Community Center.* Jerusalem: JCC Association. This anthology is a barometer for the emergence of Jewish education at Jewish community centers. It describes a variety of facets of Jewish education in the JCC and reflects the breadth and scope of the JCC Association and the Jewish Community Center movement. Its contributors include academics, executive directors, lay leaders, and reflective practitioners. Subjects covered include ideology, staffing, setting and the connection between Israel and the JCCs.

Cohen, S.M. (1998). *Religious Stability and Ethnic Decline: Emerging Patterns of Jewish Identity in the United States.* New York: The Florence G. Heller-Jewish Community Centers Association Research Center. This national survey of American Jews documents the emerging patterns of Jewish identity in the United States. Cohen describes the inherent difficulties in understanding Jewish identity. The results indicate that ethnicity remains a keystone of Jewish identity. Religiosity, on the other hand, while being stable as a frame for Jewish identity, is not growing. This study informs Jewish federations, synagogues, JCCs and others who can individually and collectively provide programs and services to help strengthen Jewish community and Jewish identity.

Fox, S. with Novak, W. (1997). *Vision at the Heart: Lessons from Camp Ramah on the Power of Ideas in Shaping Educational Institutions.* Jerusalem: The Mandel Institute and New York: The Council for Initiatives in Jewish Education. The authors examine the importance of having a clear and well-developed educational mission that guides future decisions at respective educational institutions. The vision must be dynamic and flexible, inspire educators, and help lay the groundwork for future institutions. Using Camp Ramah's vision as a guide, the authors outline five critical steps that will help Jewish educators make the leap from theoretical to practical implementation of the vision.

Fox, S., Scheffler, I. & Marom, D. (2003). *Visions of Jewish Education.* New York: Cambridge University Press, This volume offers six distinct visions of an ideal Jewish education and argues that powerful ideas and their skillful translation into practice are indispensable to successful education. The authors argue that a thoughtful and compelling vision can improve existing institutions and lead to the development of new ones. Such a vision can ignite the will of the community and its leaders, inspire the creativity of teachers, and motivate students to invest their passion and talents in the revitalization of Jewish life.

COMJEE II: Task Force on Reinforcing the Effectiveness of Jewish Educators in JCC's. New York: JCC Association, May 1995. This report of the COMJEE II (Commission on Maximizing Jewish Educational Effectiveness) task force marks the completion of eighteen months of exploration and deliberation. It signifies the continued commitment on the part of Jewish Community Center Movement leadership to shape JCCs in such a fashion that they become more effective instruments of creative Jewish learning and continuity. This report draws upon the work of the first commission and connects its own vision and recommendations.

REFERENCES

Bekerman, Z. & Chazan, B. (1994). *Towards Conceptualization of Informal Jewish Education.* Jerusalem: JCC Association.

Chazan, B. (1996). *What Is Jewish Education in the JCC?* New York: JCC Association.

Chazan, B. & Cohen, S.M. (1999) *A Jewish Philosophy for the JCC Movement—An Invitation to a Discussion on Jewish Peoplehood, Pluralism, Living, and Learning.* New York: JCC Association.

Cohen, S.M. & Holtz, B.W. *Jewish Education in JCCs, The Best Practices Project in Jewish Education* series. New York: Council for Initiatives in Jewish Education, 1996.

Cohen, S.M., Israel, S. & Fein, L. (2000). *Meaningful Jewish Community.* New York: Jewish Community Centers of North America.

Dewey, J. (1907). *The School and Society.* Chicago: University of Chicago Press.

Janowsky, O.I. (1948). *The JWB Survey.* New York: Dial Press.

Report: Commission on Maximizing Jewish Educational Effectiveness of Jewish Community Centers. (1984). Jewish Welfare Board (JWB).

Jewish Educational Travel

Shaul Kelner

There is at present no field of research that could properly be called Jewish educational travel studies. Scholarship on Jewish travel and tourism exists but has typically been undertaken in two non-intersecting research traditions. One branch consists of evaluations of Israel experience programs (IEPs), pilgrimages to Shoah-related sites, and political or volunteer missions. These studies conceive of the trips in explicitly educational terms but tend to be program-specific or destination-specific, not generalizing their findings to speak to the issue of Jewish travel writ large. In contrast, anthropological research has applied sophisticated conceptual frameworks to the study of Jewish travel and tourism but in most instances has shown little interest in the subject's practical bearing on Jewish education. Some work, such as Chazan's (2002) edited volume on IEPs, Feldman's (2000) doctoral thesis on Israeli high school trips to Poland, and my own research on *Taglit/Birthright Israel* (Kelner 2002; 2003–4), makes an effort to bridge the two literatures.

In this chapter I will review the anthropological literature to draw out its implications for Jewish education. This body of research, more than the evaluation studies, offers a theoretical groundwork that can help us to articulate a program of research in Jewish educational travel, broadly conceived. Its guiding questions—which I have reframed in a language that explicitly addresses education—ask the following:

- What are Jews using travel to educate about? What do Jewish tours and museums tell us about the ideologies and constructions of collective memory that underlie the educational enterprise?
- How do structural elements of travel *implicitly* construct knowledge?
- How are travel situations *explicitly* structured to facilitate education?

CONTEXTS

Jewish educational travel is not the heir of ancient Jewish pilgrimage traditions. Rather, it has sprung from developments in modern economics, politics and social organization. Economically, it was enabled by the emergence of a modern mass tourism industry that commoditized travel as a desirable, affordable and feasible leisure activity for a growing share of the population. Politically, Jewish statehood and the fall of the Iron Curtain granted easy access to Israel and Eastern Europe, helping transform them into two of Jewish educational travel's most popular destinations. Moreover, the concentration of Jews in the Western world provided an ample supply of tourists. Organizationally, Jewish communities in diaspora and Israel created institutions that systematized the work required to provide Jewish educational tours. This includes the development of Jewish education as a specialized career area. Professional educators have played a crucial role in reconceptualizing travel from a form of leisure into a medium of Jewish education (Kelner 2002).

Jewish educational travel now includes youth trips to a variety of destinations, including Israel, Holocaust sites, Western Europe, and across North America; pilgrimages to places of Jewish nostalgia such as the Lower East Side; international visits to homelands in Morocco, the former Soviet Union and elsewhere; fund-raising missions for Jewish non-profits; volunteer missions to places where Jews are in distress; volunteer service programs that serve largely non–Jewish populations; seminars convened in places that offer special resources for addressing particular topics (e.g., Washington, D.C. for seminars on political activism); study abroad programs; genealogical research tours; kosher cruises with scholars-in-residence; and a host of private sector tours that engage Jews in travel to destinations that speak to their identities as Jews. The list could go on.

Although such options have grown prodigiously in recent years, there is little evidence that educators consider travel to constitute a distinctive subfield of Jewish education. There is no Conference on Jewish Educational Travel. No professional association. No certificate program. Directors of IEPs have had mechanisms that link them as a network. Informal Jewish educators have articulated a professional identity that unites them under a single rubric. But Jewish educational travel as a field broader than IEPs and narrower than informal Jewish education has yet to coalesce, either intellectually or institutionally.

OVERVIEW OF RESEARCH

The anthropological research that can inform thought on the question of travel as a medium of Jewish education treats three major themes: ideology, the formal relationship of travel to knowledge, and structuring of travel education. (Here I depart from the explicit intentions of many of the authors in framing these issues as questions of Jewish education, but I do so in order to make the lines of connection explicit.)

THEME I: WHAT EDUCATIONAL MESSAGES DOES JEWISH TRAVEL ENCODE? WHAT DO TOURS AND MUSEUMS TELL US ABOUT THE IDEOLOGIES AND CONSTRUCTIONS OF COLLECTIVE MEMORY THAT UNDERLIE THE JEWISH EDUCATIONAL ENTERPRISE?

Research in this vein addresses two related and often overlapping sub-themes: a) collective memory and b) the politics of representation and display.

In *Rethinking Modern Judaism* Arnold Eisen described nostalgia as a modern Jewish *mitzvah*. If so, then tourism to Jewish heritage sites has become one of the important ways contemporary Jews fulfill this commandment. How can people feel nostalgia for things they never personally experienced? For this to occur, memory must be transformed from an individual phenomenon into a collective one. Studies of "collective memory" going back to Halbwachs, who coined the term, have inquired into the ways that groups represent the past and relate it to the present. Zerubavel's (1996) study of collective memory in Israel examined notable tourist destinations like Masada and demonstrated how the meanings attributed to important national sites have been shaped by the needs and interests of the people doing the remembering. The key insight in this line of research is that those who would use tourist sites to teach lessons must inevitably take a stand on the question of what the site means—a question that has an inescapable political dimension. Should Yavneh, for example, be used to represent the authority of rabbinic Judaism, a justification for religious reform, a diasporist counterpoint to Zionist negation of exile, or perhaps something else?

This potential for conflict over the meaning of sites indicates that more than nostalgia is at stake. Jewish educational travel has played an important role in shaping collective identity and asserting Jewish territorial claims not only in Israel, but also (on a more symbolic level) in Europe and the United States. Research on the history of *tiyul* (hiking) in the Zionist movement has examined how the meanings ascribed to the land of Israel helped inculcate a commitment to it and to the efforts to secure Jewish sovereignty over it (Almog 2000; Katriel 1995). *Tiyul*'s first practitioners were explicit in affirming that the hike was and should be a medium of nationalist education. Consider, for example, Zev Vilnay's 1948 essay "The *Tiyul* and Its Educational Value."

> The tiyul's purposes are to mold the character of our youth and to make it an organic, inseparable part of the landscape of the homeland; to plant in its heart and soul, and to inscribe in its flesh and sinews the healthy feeling of deep-rooted, unseverable, valiant communion with the land, with its stones, its waterways, its vegetation and with its entire history, as in the words of the poem, 'From the rock of the homeland were we born....' (Vilnay 1952 [1948]: 22).

Sometimes the meanings attributed to sites are so consensual that the political character of the ascription of meaning goes unnoticed. In charged political contexts, however, the "meaning" of a site can become a matter of pointed debate. One such debate is addressed in Feldman's (2000) study of Holocaust pilgrimages. The latest in a series of ethnographic studies of March of the Living and similar programs, the study shows that trips like these become a flashpoint for broader controversies over the politics of invoking Holocaust memory.

Both Masada and the Nazi-era sites are venues where conflict over the questions of "Who are we?" and "What lessons should we derive from history?" is quite fierce. A relative lack of overt conflict does not mean, however, that issues of memory and ideology are irrelevant. For American Jews, the Lower East Side has been transformed from a major Jewish population center into an important and seemingly consensual Jewish pilgrimage destination—a site of collective memory where people go to reflect on the American Jewish experience (Diner, Shandler & Wenger 2000). The way that the neighborhood has been used to construct the memory of this experience has changed over the decades, however. By observing the shifts in tourists' uses of the Lower East Side, researchers have been able to shed light on how American Jewish self-understanding has changed over the years.

Related to the theme of collective memory are research questions about the politics of representation and display. Sites used by Jewish educators to represent Jewish themes are often embedded in broader cultural contexts where Jews and non-Jews interact. Museums and heritage sites frequently address multiple constituencies, which can lead to contests over the meanings that they should encode. For both economic and cultural reasons, efforts at historical preservation of the Jewish Lower East Side have sometimes met with resistance from current residents (Diner et al. 2000). In Poland, locally produced memorials and monuments often tell the story of the Nazi era in a way different from that which Jewish educators and tourists would prefer. The conflicts over memorializing strategies may themselves become topics that educational travel tries to address (Feldman 2000).

Both the focus on representation and the interest in collective memory draw our attention to a particular aspect of Jewish educational travel that differentiates it from other forms of Jewish education. Travel occurs in physical space, and this spatiality frames the way that issues of ideology and values manifest themselves. The sites that educational tours would visit are often constructed by others—governments, businesses, agencies, and individuals—often with interests and values of their own. Moreover, the built environment of multiple eras and interest groups can accumulate in a single place, leaving a residue of possibly contradictory meanings. Ideological presuppositions shape educational travel, but the ideologies at work in tourism are not only those of the tour sponsors. The spatial nature of the enterprise almost ensures that other ideologies, interests and educational messages will be represented in the sites visited. These may affirm or subvert the intended educational messages of the tours.

THEME 2: HOW DO STRUCTURAL ELEMENTS OF TRAVEL IMPLICITLY CONSTRUCT KNOWLEDGE?

Research that examines the effects of the formal aspects of travel on learning and knowledge tends to approach the issue in three ways. One looks at how placing culture on display shapes the ways that people understand it. Another looks at how the traveler's presence makes learning not simply a matter of developing knowledge about the things being observed, but also involves elements of self-discovery. The third examines how the spatial and temporal dimensions of travel shape the educational process.

Tourism is largely a semiotic enterprise in which people treat places as objects of symbolic consumption. Tourists value Auschwitz, for example, because it serves as a medium through which they can meditate upon the Holocaust. Because of the importance of semiotics in tourism, questions of representation loom large in research. Perhaps the best book on the general subject of cultural representation is one that also devotes significant attention to the representation of Jews. Kirshenblatt-Gimblett's *Destination Culture* (1998) inquires into the meaning and effects of placing things on display. When cultures are represented to tourists, be they in museum displays or through the windows of a tour bus, the act of displaying detaches them cognitively and sometimes literally from their original contexts, transforming them into "exhibits of themselves" (pp. 18, 150–1). Instead of merely presenting what "is," representation creates new meanings. Consider, for example, the railcars at Yad Vashem and the United States Holocaust Memorial. Sometimes this detachment frames knowledge by providing context (which raises questions of ideology). Sometimes it impedes knowledge by distancing observer and observed.

In his study of IEPs, Kelner (2002) finds that the tourist situation implicitly represents the destination, Israel, as an embodiment of authentic culture. It does this by engaging tourists in a series of binary contrasts between themselves and their familiar home with the objectified, essentialized Israeli culture they have come to see. Authenticity can only be conceptualized if its opposite, inauthenticity, is also posited. Tourism posits both and locates cultural authenticity in the observed Other, the unfamiliar destination, rather than in the observing Self and familiar home. In contrast to Kirshenblatt-Gimblett, who examines tourists as consumers of representations produced by others, this approach focuses on the ways that tourists actively represent to themselves the places they visit.

Tourist situations do engage people not only in encounters with places and cultures, but also in active processes of self-exploration and identity construction. Travel education stimulates self-knowledge through bodily experiences that are felt rather than understood (Kirshenblatt-Gimblett 2002) and through acts of reflection on the relationship between site and self (Kelner 2002).

Self-knowledge also emerges through interaction with fellow tourists, guides and locals. Tourism's liminal character—its time out of time quality—fosters relationships that can grow very intense in a very short time. These "communitas" relationships (the term is Victor Turner's) are akin to shipboard romances but refer to a more generalized context of fellowship with members of the tour group.

Among the distinguishing features of travel education is the fact that it entails movement through space for a specific duration of time. Both the spatial and temporal dimensions of tourism influence the way that tourists develop understandings of the places they encounter. At the extreme, the touring context is a totally immersive environment that provides educators with a significant amount of control over the minute-to-minute experience of their charges (Feldman 2000; Kelner 2002).

Educators' control over space is exercised broadly through control over the itinerary. In an important piece articulating the educational rationale of Israel experience programs, Chazan (1994) offers a model of travel education in which curriculum design and itinerary planning will ideally interact. Sites used for pedagogical ends will often serve as embodiments of curricular themes or as stages on which non–site-specific educational programming is carried out.

Because the spatial location of sites is not determined by educators, however, logistical considerations such as geographic proximity will affect the planning of the itinerary (Kirshenblatt-Gimblett 2002). This has implications for curriculum design. A single site can be used to exemplify any number of themes. Will the Lower East Side be used to represent the working-class politics of Jewish socialists, cross-cultural encounters between Jewish and non–Jewish neighbors or something else? If sites are grouped together for logistical reasons, this juxtaposition may influence the decision about how the site should be thematized. Alternatively, a decision to use a site to treat a specific topic may lead to the decision to ignore a nearby attraction that does not happen to fit the curricular focus.

Themes are conveyed not only by the use of space, but also by the use of time. Feldman describes how the theme of "exile to destruction to redemption" is realized on Shoah trips through a cyclical movement that unfolds in real time and takes the pilgrims "from Israel to Poland and back" (2000, p. 175). Trips also unfold with a rhythm whose contrasts—between up-time and down-time, formal time and informal time, week time and Sabbath time—convey messages and structure attention (Feldman 2000). The rapid pace and frequent juxtaposition of unrelated or marginally related sites create a cumulative experience where recollections of individual places and lessons blur, leaving tourists with general impressions, sensations and feelings that they associate with the tour as a gestalt (Kelner 2003–4; Kirshenblatt-Gimblett 2002).

In practice, the vagaries of travel inevitably subvert a total thematization of places and time. Much of this results from the active agency of the travelers, who shape their own experience to a large degree. In addition, trip staff often diverge from written itineraries for a variety of reasons. They may encounter unforeseen logistical challenges; may adapt to students' interests and energy levels; may choose to seize opportunities that present themselves; or, if they themselves are not the curriculum planners, may deemphasize, undermine or ignore aspects of the curriculum that do not reflect their own educational goals.

THEME 3: HOW DO EDUCATORS EXPLICITLY STRUCTURE TRAVEL SITUATIONS TO FACILITATE LEARNING?

Efforts to structure the tourist environment for pedagogical purposes draw heavily on general principles of informal education, while remaining attuned to peculiar features of travel as an educational medium. In addition to the broad work of thematizing and arranging sites to produce curricular coherence in the itinerary, educators also focus on structuring the details of the tourist environment, including the experiences at particular sites, the logistics of travel education, the social environment, and the pre-trip and post-trip framing. This raises questions about spontaneity and individualization on mass-produced trips.

Research on the ways guides structure learning experiences at individual sites demonstrates that they regularly face dilemmas of cultural representation when leading groups. Tourism is an educational medium that engages multiple senses, but sites do not speak for themselves. Rather, they provide materials out of which meanings are constructed. Some of these meanings have been built into the physical environment by those who developed the sites. Much of the responsibility for making sites meaningful falls to the guides, however (Katriel 1997). Whereas some guides adopt a narrow conception of their role, acting as navigators through unfamiliar terrain and mediators between travelers and locals, Jewish educational travel has been influenced by a more expansive understanding of the guide's role. The Hebrew term *moreh derekh* ("teacher of the way") conveys clearly the notion of the guide as educator—teaching "the way" both in the sense of actively interpreting sites and also in the sense of acting as a role model for tourists to emulate (Cohen 1985; Katz 1985). As a role model, the tour guide's cultivation of a performative persona and strategic deployment of self become important resources in the discharge of his or her educational mission.

In a study of guiding practices in IEPs, Goldwater shows that guides integrate narrative and non-narrative strategies for representing sites to tourists (2002). In terms of their structure, narrative strategies frequently differ in the ways they invoke (or do not invoke) the surrounding physical environment and artifacts, in the ways they rhetorically position the guides themselves vis-à-vis the material, in the ways they adopt descriptive or prescriptive stances and in the ways they create distance or attachment between tourists and subject matter (see also Katriel 1997). Goldwater found non-narrative strategies were often invoked at the end of site visits as a means of engaging tourists not as passive listeners and observers, but as active agents of meaning-construction. Through group song, prayer, and ceremonies, site-specific themes were translated into non-discursive practices, which travelers affirmed to themselves and to each other through active performance.

The staff members of educational tours spend much of their time attending to logistical matters. Although the successful management of logistics tends to be invisible to participants, it has important consequences for staff's credibility and authority, for the creation of a cohesive learning community, and for the direction of participants' attention toward the educational program. Because so much of the pedagogy in educational travel occurs by moving people through structured narrations of sites, *morei derekh* devote considerable effort to plan the logistics of each stop along the way (Goldwater 2002). For example, when experienced guides think about where a group might comfortably congregate for a presentation, they attend to numerous minute considerations. Will the sun be in their eyes? Will there be other groups trying to occupy the same space? Can the group sit close enough together to allow all of them to hear the guide? Even the important educational decision of how to link space and narrative will lead guides to think about how to structure the group's movement through a place. If the story of a place will be related piecemeal, building to a climax, then where would it be best to tell each chapter of the story? How will the constraints presented by the geography of the site affect the way the tale is broken up?

In examining the ways that group dynamics are structured to further educational goals, researchers have focused on three sets of relationships: guide-tourist, tourist-tourist, and tourist-local. The role of guide as mentor has been discussed above. Overall, however, researchers have devoted little attention to the guide-tourist relationship. Research on the relationship among trip staff is also minimal, but to the extent that it exists, it highlights the potential for conflict brought on by cross-cultural differences in international tours, differing demands imposed by role, and struggles over authority (Chazan 2002).

Jewish travel educators devote significant energy to fostering group cohesion among participants (Chazan 2002; Feldman 2000; Kelner 2002). They accomplish this through group- building exercises, discussion circles, limitations on private time and space, uniform application of rules, systematic planning of sub-group formation (as when hotel rooms are assigned), and attentiveness to potentially disruptive factors. This *gibush,* or group crystallization, serves educational goals in several ways, not the least of which is by creating a cohesive group that models an idealized Jewish community. To the extent that Jewish education is intended to provide the socialization necessary for individuals to become functioning members of the Jewish group, the first-hand experience of Jewish community directly realizes this end. The cohesive groups offer a vision of what Jewish community can be. In the immediate context of the trips, *gibush* also serves educational ends by mobilizing peer pressure in support of the tours' official messages, and by repositioning each participant as a potential peer educator (Kelner 2002).

The tourist-local relationship can pose particular challenges to Jewish educational travel. The act of touring tends to establish barriers between observers and observed. Trapped in a "tourist bubble," visitors can easily objectify locals as essentialized representations of native culture. To the extent that Jewish educational travel seeks to build community between Jewish tourists and Jewish locals, it must work directly against this inherent characteristic of tourism. This challenge has been taken up primarily by IEPs, which have sought to overcome it through the institution of the *mifgash*—a structured encounter between diaspora Jewish tourists and Israeli locals. The most effective *mifgashim* appear to be those that integrate Israeli peers as tourists in the traveling group with the diaspora Jewish visitors (Bar-Shalom 1998).

The tour itself is increasingly recognized as only an intermediate moment in Jewish educational travel, nestled between the preparatory education that can occur before the trip and the follow-up education that can occur after it. In general, efforts to address pre-trip and post-trip education have been unsystematic, with little sharing of information across programs. There is not much of a general knowledge base about these issues.

One may wonder if such careful attempts to structure so many aspects of the tourist environment impede education by eliminating room for spontaneity and personalization. Kelner (2002) found that the rigid structuring and mass production of the educational program on IEPs were sometimes perceived as barriers to an "authentic" encounter with Israel. In this context, unstructured individual interactions with Israelis came to be highly valued. This "resistance," however, actually furthered the official educational goal, which was to encourage a feeling of personal connection to Israel.

POLICY RECOMMENDATIONS

Travel has emerged as an important medium of Jewish education, one that has attracted large numbers of participants and significant investment of communal resources. In spite of its extensive presence, the ability to develop it systematically as an educational field is hampered by fragmentation and isolation. For the field to be developed, those working in each particular form of travel education would have to recognize their common cause with educators working with its other forms. Whether through a conference, a website, an email list, or an interest group within an organization like CAJE, those working in the disparate areas of Jewish travel education should find ways to come together, to exchange knowledge, to form partnerships and to advocate collectively.

By articulating Jewish educational travel as a distinct area within Jewish education, new ways of utilizing the medium may be more easily identified. This can proceed from a variety of starting points, such as the adult education program thinking about incorporating a travel dimension, or the local federation establishing a task force on developing the city's Jewish community as a destination for Jewish heritage tourism. Once the field can be conceptualized, ideas that were once impossible to imagine become thinkable.

ADDITIONAL RESEARCH QUESTIONS

The research on Jewish educational travel has generally been conducted under paradigms that have subordinated questions of curriculum and learning to other concerns. Future research in this area will be most useful to Jewish education if it breaks with this tendency. Among the areas that might be placed front and center are the following:

- **Educators:** How does the training of *morei derech* affect their work as educators? How do guiding styles relate to learning outcomes? How does the work of *morei derech* support and/or subvert the educational goals of sponsoring agencies?

- **Learners:** Most of the research on learners in contexts of Jewish educational travel focuses on members of tour groups in programs of short duration. To what extent does learning differ for those who travel as individuals, or for longer periods of time, or in programs that combine tourism with other things like volunteer work, classroom study, or professional work? In addition, most of the research on learners focuses on teenagers and young adults. How does travel at other points in the life cycle affect learning?

- **Destinations:** To what extent do Jewish educational travel experiences to different destinations reinforce a master narrative of Jewish life? To what extent do they offer pluralistic understandings? How does the development of places as destinations for Jewish educational travel affect Jewish life in the communities that live in those places?

- **Ethics:** Tourist settings offer planners a great deal of control over immersive social environments. How do travel educators conceptualize and negotiate the ethical dilemmas that arise when wielding this potentially powerful medium for influencing how people think, feel and behave?

FUTURE DIRECTIONS

In order to realize the potential of Jewish educational travel, educators and other stakeholders need to recognize explicitly that it constitutes a distinctive form of Jewish education. The most significant activity that can be undertaken to set such a process in motion is to convene a conference of Jewish travel educators that will bring together a diverse group of people working in different areas of the field. Such a conference should have as its goals:

- Fostering a collective identity
- Exchanging best practices
- Identifying key challenges that can be addressed cooperatively
- Establishing ongoing mechanisms of communication, information exchange and collaboration
- Beginning to develop an advocacy agenda to strengthen the field

CONCLUSION

Today it is common to speak of fields such as informal Jewish education, lifelong Jewish learning, and Jewish family education. Several decades ago, none of these terms would have rolled familiarly from the tongue, nor would they have had institutional bases of support, nor clearly articulated statements of their educational philosophies, principles and missions. The recent history of Jewish education is a history of growing self-awareness among educators about the nature of their work, coupled with deliberate efforts to translate this self-awareness into programs of action that would realize nascent potentials. Jewish educational travel stands at the threshold of self-awareness, but has not yet crossed it. It is not clear that it will cross it, but it would be a significant development in Jewish life if it does.

HIGHLIGHTS

- Travel has emerged as an important medium of Jewish education. It represents a constructive form of Jewish discontinuity.

- "Jewish educational travel" as a field broader than Israel experience programs and narrower than informal Jewish education has yet to coalesce intellectually or institutionally.

- There is currently no field of research that could properly be called "Jewish educational travel studies." Anthropological work offers a theoretical basis for articulating a program of research.

- The unique spatial and temporal dimensions of travel make travel education different from other forms of informal education.

- The way that culture is placed on display shapes the ways that people understand it.

- Educators explicitly structure travel situations to facilitate learning. They treat sites as exemplars of educational themes, plan how sites will be used to tell desired stories, and attempt to create cohesive learning communities.

- In order to realize the potential of Jewish educational travel, educators and other stakeholders need to recognize explicitly that it constitutes a distinctive form of Jewish education. A conference on Jewish educational travel should be convened to this end.

LARGER CONTEXT

Over the years, Jewish education has been elaborated through the development and institutionalization of a variety of distinct subfields. Sometimes this has emerged through differentiation, as with Jewish early-childhood education or the more recent "Israel education." Other times, subfields have developed through a process of coalescence. The notion of "Jewish informal education" is perhaps the best example of this, forged by a recognition that youth groups, camps, Israel experience programs and other forms of Jewish educational programming all share certain core principles, approaches and interests. This chapter argues that similar processes of coalescence and differentiation could lead to a conception of "Jewish educational travel" as a distinct Jewish educational subfield, broader than Israel experience programs, but narrower than informal education. Such a process has not yet occurred and may not necessarily occur but would be of benefit to those who are engaging in the process, whether they recognize it or not.

ANNOTATED BIBLIOGRAPHY

Almog, O. (2000). The Stamp of His Country's Landscape. In *The Sabra: The Creation of the New Jew*. Trans. Haim Watzman. Berkeley: University of California Press. A history of the development of *tiyul* during the period of the Yishuv. Important for understanding the historical roots of contemporary Jewish educational travel, particularly on Israel experience programs.

Chazan, B. (1994). The Israel Trip: A New Form of Jewish Education. In *Youth Trips to Israel: Rationale and Realization*. New York: CRB Foundation and the Mandell L. Berman Jewish Heritage Center at JESNA. To the Israel experience program what Vilnay's essay is to *tiyul*. Perhaps the most coherent articulation of the educational rationale of Israel trips. Can serve as a model for thinking about other forms of Jewish travel education.

Feldman, J. (2000). It Is My Brothers Whom I Am Seeking: Israeli Youth Voyages to Holocaust Poland. Unpublished doctoral dissertation, Hebrew University of Jerusalem. An anthropologist accompanies Israeli students on high school trips to Holocaust sites in Poland and analyzes the way the Holocaust pilgrimage is used to reinforce Israeli Jewish identity.

Katriel, T. (1995). Touring the Land: Trips and Hiking as Secular Pilgrimages in Israeli Culture. *Jewish Folklore and Ethnology Review* 17 (1–2), 6–13. Similar to Almog, but examines the philosophies of *tiyul* during the period of the Yishuv and traces them through to the present. Important for understanding the historical roots of contemporary Jewish educational travel, particularly on Israel experience programs.

Kelner, S. (2002). Almost Pilgrims: Authenticity, Identity and the Extra-Ordinary on a Jewish Tour of Israel. Unpublished doctoral dissertation, Graduate School and University Center, City University of New York.

A sociologist accompanies American Jewish college students on Israel experience programs and analyzes how tourism serves as a medium of ethnic socialization.

_____ (2003–4). "The Impact of Israel Experience Programs on Israel's Symbolic Meaning." *Contemporary Jewry 24*, 124–54. Analyzes how Israel experience programs reinvigorate Israel as a sacred symbol for American Jews. The country comes to symbolize the experience of being on an Israel experience program.

Kirshenblatt-Gimblett, B. (1998). *Destination Culture: Tourism, Museums and Heritage.* Berkeley and Los Angeles, CA: University of California Press. A series of essays addressing what it means to place culture on display. A tour-de-force of erudition, packaged beautifully.

_____(2002) Learning from Ethnography: Reflections on the Nature and Efficacy of Youth Tours to Israel. In B. Chazan (ed.), *The Israel Experience: Studies in Jewish Identity and Youth Culture.* Jerusalem and New York: The Andrea and Charles Bronfman Philanthropies, 267–331. The author reflects on the findings of two ethnographic studies of summer-long Israel experience programs for teenagers. Concisely and eloquently raises many of the key philosophical issues that Jewish educators should consider if they are seeking to use travel to shape Jewish identity.

Vilnay, Z. *Ha-Tiyul Ve-'Erko Ha-Hinukhi: Tiyulim Ve-Siyurim be-Erets Yisrael.* (1952) (The Hike and Its Educational Value: Hikes and Tours in the Land of Israel). *She'alim*: Sifriyah Pedagogit Le-Madrikhim. Vol. 7. Jerusalem: World Zionist Organization, Youth and Hechalutz Department. For Hebrew readers. The classic statement of Jewish travel education. Originally published in 1948, its influence is still felt today on every Israel experience program. The unabashed romanticism of the language serves as a mirror through which educators can reflect on current discourses of Jewish travel education. How much has changed?

ADDITIONAL REFERENCES

Almog, O. (2000). The Stamp of His Country's Landscape. In *The Sabra: The Creation of the New Jew.* Trans. Haim Watzman. Berkeley: University of California Press.

Bar-Shalom, Y. (1998). Encounters with the Other: An Ethnographic Study of Mifgashim Programs for Jewish Youth, Summer 1997. Jerusalem: The Charles R. Bronfman Centre for the Israel Experience—Mifgashim.

Chazan, B. (1994). The Israel Trip: A New Form of Jewish Education. In *Youth Trips to Israel: Rationale and Realization.* New York: CRB Foundation and the Mandell L. Berman Jewish Heritage Center at JESNA.

Chazan, B. (ed.) (2002). *The Israel Experience: Studies in Jewish Identity and Youth Culture.* Jerusalem and New York: The Andrea and Charles Bronfman Philanthropies.

Cohen, E. (1985). "The Tourist Guide: The Origins, Structure and Dynamics of a Role." *Annals of Tourism Research 12*, 5–29.

Diner, H., J. Shandler & B. S. Wenger (eds.) (2000). *Remembering the Lower East Side: American Jewish Reflections.* Bloomington, IN: Indiana University Press.

Feldman, J. (2000). *It Is My Brothers Whom I Am Seeking: Israeli Youth Voyages to Holocaust Poland.* Unpublished doctoral dissertation, Hebrew University of Jerusalem.

Goldwater, C. (2002). *Constructing the Narrative of Authenticity: Tour Educators at Work in the Israel Experience.* Unpublished master's thesis, Hebrew University of Jerusalem.

Katriel, T. (1995). "Touring the Land: Trips and Hiking as Secular Pilgrimages in Israeli Culture." *Jewish Folklore and Ethnology Review 17* (1–2), 6–13.

Katriel, T. (1997). *Performing the Past: A Study of Israeli Settlement Museums.* Mahwah, NJ: Lawrence Erlbaum Associates.

Katz, S. (1985). "The Israeli Teacher-Guide: The Emergence and Perpetuation of a Role." *Annals of Tourism Research 12*, 49–72.

Kelner, S. (2002). *Almost Pilgrims: Authenticity, Identity and the Extra-Ordinary on a Jewish Tour of Israel.* Unpublished doctoral dissertation. Graduate School and University Center, City University of New York.

Kelner, S. (2003–4). "The Impact of Israel Experience Programs on Israel's Symbolic Meaning." *Contemporary Jewry 24*, 124–54.

Kirshenblatt-Gimblett, B. (1998). *Destination Culture: Tourism, Museums and Heritage.* Berkeley and Los Angeles, CA: University of California Press.

Kirshenblatt-Gimblett, B. (2002). Learning from Ethnography: Reflections on the Nature and Efficacy of Youth Tours to Israel. In B. Chazan (ed.), *The Israel Experience: Studies in Jewish Identity and Youth Culture*. Jerusalem and New York: The Andrea and Charles Bronfman Philanthropies. Pp. 267-331.

Vilnay, Z. *Ha-Tiyul Ve-`Erko Ha-Hinukhi: Tiyulim ve-siyurim be-Erets Yisrael* (1952) (The Hike and Its Educational Value: Hikes and Tours in the Land of Israel). *She'alim*: Sifriyah Pedagogit Le-Madrikhim. Vol. 7. Jerusalem: World Zionist Organization, Youth and Hechalutz Department.

Zerubavel, Y. (1995). *Recovered Roots: Collective Memory and the Making of Israeli National Tradition*. Chicago, IL: University of Chicago Press.

VEULAI—AND PERHAPS: Israel as a Place for Jewish Education

Barry Chazan

ABRAHAM'S "ISRAEL EXPERIENCE"

Travel to Israel has come a long way since the first "Israel trip" taken by Abraham to the Land of Canaan. From that time until today, "going to Israel" has been a significant thread within the fabric of the Jewish psyche. It has accompanied Jews over time and place, and it has surfaced in key rituals of Jewish life, in daily prayers, on Passover seder evenings and at wedding ceremonies. Indeed, if historian Paul Johnson is correct, Jews are the quintessential travelers, and "going to Israel" is the primal metaphor of that human experience (Johnson).

Jews have traveled to Israel over the ages for diverse reasons. For some Jews, going to Israel has been in response to a Divine command. For others it has been to a refuge from oppression and destruction. Some have traveled to Israel in search of spirituality, and others have traveled to be buried in Israel in anticipation of messianic days.

GOING TO ISRAEL IN THE TWENTIETH CENTURY

In the twentieth century, travel to Israel assumed three forms. The first form was *aliyah*—emigration to Israel—as the fulfillment of an ideological commitment to the rebuilding of the Homeland, to personal fulfillment, and to fulfillment of the Zionist world-view. The Zionist idea encompassed many dimensions, but *aliya* was and remains a central defining trait.

The second form of travel to Israel was emigration of masses of Jews who were victims of persecution or discrimination in mostly Middle Eastern Arab societies or refugees from the Holocaust. This form of travel, often denoted as "refugee" or "catastrophic" Zionism, is also denoted as *aliya* or sometimes *kibbutz galuyot,* and it has been a cornerstone of the shaping of the contemporary State of Israel.

These two forms of going to Israel have proven to be a great success story in Jewish history. By the end of the twentieth century millions of Jews had emigrated to and lived in Israel. Jews who lived in regimes and societies of oppression are today free citizens in a Jewish homeland. These new twentieth-century forms of "going to Israel" have dramatically changed the map of Jewish life in Israel and throughout the world.

Organized American Jewry participated in enabling these two forms of *aliya*, although for almost the totality of American Jews these two forms had no personal resonance or meaning. American Jewry did not accept the notion that going to Israel defined being a Zionist or a Jew, and American Jews did not believe that they needed a refuge or an escape from an oppressive regime. Thus the issue of teaching Israel in America has had unique complexities rooted in American Jewry's inherent rejection of the two prominent twentieth-century forms of "going to Israel."

VISITING ISRAEL: A NEW FORM OF JEWISH EDUCATION

With the establishment of the State, "going to Israel" began to assume another new role that was not related to either halutzic *aliyah* or catastrophic Zionism. This type of going to Israel was seen in the context of the journey toward deepening personal and collective Jewish identity and consciousness. Beginning in 1948, and particularly after 1967, the Israel trip emerged as a promising resource of world Jewry to educate and affect the Jewishness of young and old alike (Chazan 1994; Kelner 2003). It became recognized as a new form of Jewish education that offered new promise for enriching personal and collective Jewishness.

By the 1980s the visit to Israel had reached new heights (in 1987 a peak of 12,925 young people participated in Israel experience programs [Cohen 2000]). By that time, several hundred short- and long-term educational programs for teens were in place. The Jewish Agency had a full-fledged department (the Youth and Hehalutz Department) devoted to such programs. Several overseas organizations (UJA, CJF and JCCA) had established full-time offices in Israel. Major North American youth movements—NCSY, USY, Ramah, NFTY, Young Judea, JCCA—had programs and departments of Israel travel staffed by talented and committed professionals.

The sociology of these programs was strikingly homogeneous. For the most part, youngsters in these programs were of high school age and affiliated with at least one Jewish institution in their home country (a youth group, a camp, a school, a synagogue, or a JCC). Typically they came for a 4–8 week period, generally during the summer months. The typical group numbered 30–40 youngsters who participated in programs that combined touring the country with discussion, study, and group activities. For most young people, these trips constituted their first visit to Israel. The trips were conducted by committed and skilled educators—usually with sophisticated informal educational skills—and were almost always regarded as memorable and powerful Jewish experiences.

Over the years this field evolved educationally and became increasingly sophisticated and creative. In the 1980s the phrase used to describe visiting Israel changed from "the Israel trip" to "the Israel experience". The new phrase was knowingly or unknowingly influenced by John Dewey's notion that education is rooted in experiences, and it overtly affirmed that going to Israel was first and foremost a Jewish educational experience of great power. The change in name clearly reflected the commitment to Israel travel as a very important resource and experience in Jewish education and identity.

The educational richness of the Israel experience was enhanced in the 1980s through the work of several talented individuals working outside the mainstream of national organizations, synagogue movements and Jewish communal organizations, e.g., Charles Herman's Nesiya, Anne Lanski's Shorashim, Aharon Botzer's Livnot Ul'hibanot, and the Muss High School in Israel. These programs combined a personalized educational focus with unique emphases on such subjects as arts and culture, outdoors and spirituality, *mifgashim* and a regular high school semester in Israel. These groups never conquered the field numerically, but they introduced themes, educational vision and content that raised the bar significantly and were to ultimately have great impact on the field as a whole.

The other noteworthy development in this period was the emergence of year-long post high school, pre-university study programs in Israel for the Orthodox world as a norm. By the last years of the century a post-high school year in Israel became the default setting in the Orthodox educational community, constituting one of the unique achievements of Orthodoxy in Jewish education and in the Israel–Diaspora connection.

THE ECSTASY AND THE AGONY

By the end of the century a strange reality existed. The ecstasy was that American Jewry had succeeded in creating an extremely exciting new form of Jewish education that proved to have verifiable and long-term impact on Jewish identity (Chazan 2000).

The agony was that all of these trips were but a drop in the bucket. They affected a minimum of young Jews (in any one year 2% of the eligible age cohort would travel to Israel), and the only people they affected were those already affiliated with a synagogue or youth movement (moreover, even in the world of the affiliated, the majority of young people did not go to Israel in their teen years). Going to Israel was not something that mainstream, all-American Jewish teens did; it was a legacy of either the very Orthodox or highly committed Conservative or Reform Jews.

A BREAKTHROUGH

A significant development began in Montreal in the late 1980s and was to have profound impact on this story. At that time Charles Bronfman and his wife Andrea decided to establish a philanthropic foundation with a mandate to address the unity of the Jewish people. After much reflection and research, youth travel to Israel became one of their banner programs. For the first time the Israel experience as a significant form of Jewish education had powerful lay champions with substantial resources to effect change.

In the mid 1990s, influenced by the Bronfman impetus, several national and international organizations (CJF—the Council of Jewish Federations, predecessor to UJC; the UJA; the Jewish Agency; and the Israeli Ministry of Tourism) came together to create Israel Experience Inc., a national advocacy agency for educational travel to Israel. Their efforts established the groundwork for the major breakthrough that occurred when Charles Bronfman and Michael Steinhardt, an affluent American Jewish philanthropist, decided to dramatically up the ante and establish a new conception and a new partnership. In 1998 Birthright Israel was established (Saxe & Chazan, in press).

Birthright Israel quantitatively changed the state of youth travel to Israel, with over 120,000 young people experiencing Israel in person in the first six years (which included some of the most difficult years in the history of Israeli tourism). It changed the organizational structure of Israel educational travel and the default age group. It opened the market, broke the exclusive denominational monopoly, and aimed at a different age cohort, the college students and young adults as opposed to high school students. Birthright Israel broke with the sacrosanct 4–6 week summer trip, opting instead for ten days. It introduced legislated educational and logistical standards, with concomitant sanctions and penalties. Aside from everything else, Birthright Israel constituted what has become known as a paradigm shift in the way business is done.

WHAT WE CAN LEARN FROM SEVERAL DECADES OF THE ISRAEL EDUCATIONAL TRIP

This brief historical stroll leads to four important conclusions about the state of the field:

1) An Israel experience has emerged as an indisputably positive Jewish experience and as such constitutes an important new form of Jewish education. It is probably the most positive and enjoyable Jewish experience Jewish adolescents have, an experience whose impact has been documented repeatedly by the best Jewish social science research.

2) The Israel experience has been an arena for highly creative Jewish educators to engage in the most innovative educational work in contemporary Jewish education.

3) Broadening the Israel experience beyond the high school model will have significant impact on the power of an educational trip for the North American Jewish community. The possibilities of developing age and developmentally appropriate Israel experiences for groups such as young families, elementary students, college students, post-college young adults, special interest niche trips, and family trips are options not adequately pursued at the moment.

4) The state of the Israel experience has developed significantly in educational terms over the decades; however, its numerical impact and place in the DNA of American Jewish life still seems peripheral.

THE GOOD TRIP

The Israel experience is more than just a new form of Jewish education. It adds a qualitative change with new models of instruction and learning that has proven attractive, impactful and fun. Consequently, it is a valuable phenomenon that has implications for how we do Jewish education generally and how we teach about Israel in Jewish schools and informal programs specifically. In order to consider the potential educational lessons that might be culled from the Israel trip we need to examine what have emerged as the core characteristics of the good Israel trip.

1. **EXPERIENTIAL.** The Israel experience is first and foremost a paradigm of education through experience. According to Dewey, an educative experience is an engagement in an activity that flows from the life of the participants, reflects a message or an idea, and results in growth. The heart of learning in the Israel experience is through the direct and personal experiencing of ideas, sites, personalities, and events related to Jewish history, Jewish values, and contemporary Jewish life. These experiences may relate to ideas or events that students had vaguely heard about in their younger years, or they may be entirely new experiences. What is critical is that experiencing the place or event in person ignites a spark and interest. The essential element of experiential learning is that the young person physically "goes" someplace where something actually happened or is happening and participates, touches, and feels an event, place, or idea. This includes participating in a dig, being on the streets of Jerusalem as the Shabbat siren sounds, climbing Massada and then hearing the story, or listening to Rachel's poem "Perhaps" while sitting alongside her grave on the shores of the Sea of Galilee. The critical point is that experiential education engages learners and makes them active rather than passive.

2. **LEARNER-CENTERED.** The Israel experience is a learner-centered form of education. Its pedagogy focuses on the learner as much as on the subject matter. The leaner stands near the tour educator, asks questions and interacts directly with the site or event. The tour educators see his/her eyes and hear his/her voice. The rhythm of the program is determined as much by the reactions and response of the participant as by a fixed curriculum. The participants feel that this experience with Jewish education is about them as well as about Judaism.

3. **INTERACTIVE.** The Israel experience is rooted in interaction and dialogue rather than telling and "talking at". Tour educators answer questions and promote discussions as well as "tell the story". Participants talk to one another on buses, in cafes, and at dinner. They talk to their Israeli peers as well. The dialogic process plays a central pedagogic role in this type of education.

4. *MIFGASH.* The Israel experience offers the opportunity for intensive and meaningful cross-cultural exchange between young American Jews and young Jews in Israel. The meeting with Israelis becomes a "site" for deepening their understanding of the historical or religious venues. When implemented effectively, such *mifgashim* become windows into the psyche and soul of each other's culture, as well as a powerful force for creating or deepening the notion of the unity and oneness of the Jewish people (Wolf 2007).

5. **JOURNEY AS CURRICULUM.** Ultimately the curriculum of the Israel experience is the journey of young people on the pathway of Jewish life. The word "journey" implies movement, and the Israel trip is very much about physical movement. Groups travel on buses; they hike through deserts and forests; their educators are "tour guides". But it is also about movement in a spiritual and developmental sense, about movement toward a Jewish lifestyle. This is done through a continuum of carefully planned Jewish experiences, guided by "tour educators" and leading toward a personal Jewish journey. The journey—and not specific way-stations—is ultimately the goal of the Israel trip.

6. **CORE VALUES AND THEMES.** Israel experience trips have proven to be particularly effective in exposing young people to certain major values and themes of Jewish life:

    1) The roots of the Jewish people are in the Land of Israel.

    2) Contemporary Israel is intimately connected with the age-old masterpiece of the Jewish people and all humanity—the Bible.

    3) The Jewish people renewed itself by returning to its ancient land where is created a modern State.

4) Israel is a modern society that reflects and embodies the core values and lifestyles of Jewish tradition and civilization (Shabbat, *tikkun olam*, Jewish calendar).

5) Israel is a contemporary society combining general and Jewish cultures.

6) The State of Israel and the Hebrew language are intimately connected and together comprise important components of Jewish civilization.

Trips built on these values and themes work because young people can see, touch, feel and study them through a combination of on-site experiences and related texts. Thus the Biblical text becomes part of the excavations at the Western Wall. Yair's speech is read at Massada. Amichai's poem "Ecology of Jerusalem" is read at the very site on Paul Emile Botta Street near the King David Hotel where it was written. The trip affords a unique synergy between themes, places, and texts.

7. **PEOPLE, PLACES AND EVENTS AS "TEXTS".** The Israel trip introduces a broadened notion of "texts" into Jewish learning. Whereas most young Jews are familiar with books as "texts", the Israel trip expands this to encompass people, places, and events. Meetings with the ardent settler, the passionate leftist, the secularist, the ultra-Orthodox, the Jerusalemite, and the *Tel Aviva* are vivid sources for learning and understanding ideas and ideologies. Sde Boker, Kibbutz Degania, and Tzipori are places that teach messages. Rabin Square, Shabbat in Jerusalem, and Tisha B'Av are events that are as powerful as any written text. The Israel trip incorporates and expands the scope of the Jewish textual tradition.

8. **TEACHER AS *MOREH DEREKH*.** The Israel experience introduces a new kind of teacher—the teacher as *moreh derekh*—one who shows the way. The educator in the Israel experience conveys information, but he/she is as much guide, counselor, and role model as dispenser of knowledge. The Israel experience educator draws upon informal education, social work, and the helping professions in addition to history, sociology, and theology. The educator on Israel trips serves as an exemplar and model of desirable Jewish lifestyle. The Israel trip educator is ultimately a guide on the Jewish journey of the traveler.

9. **THE SOCIAL CONTEXT.** The experience of being together with a like-minded group of Jewish peers has proven to be one of the most significant dimensions of the Israel trip. This trip provides a unique—and sometimes first-time—experience of positive peer culture in a Jewish context. The social cohesion created by the group tour proves to be a valuable factor in enhancing individual Jewish identity. The group becomes not simply the framework in which the trip occurs, but also a most important pedagogic force in identity development. The group experience contributes to the development of the sense of *Klal Yisrael*—Jewish communality and unity. Being with other Jews contributes both to individual identity and to strengthening collective affiliation.

These nine factors essentially constitute a philosophy of Jewish education that focuses on core values, experiences, an interactive and experiential culture, and the teacher as *moreh derekh* rather than as encyclopedia. It implies an educational framework that has a curriculum, encompasses values as well as cognitive contents, significantly shifts the pedagogic framework to social context and interactive pedagogy, and that views teachers as holistic role models and spiritual guides rather than knowledge dispensers.

IMPLICATIONS AND POLICY RECOMMENDATIONS

This chapter has focused on the evolution of a successful new form of Jewish education. The implications and policy recommendations that flow from this new form of Jewish education will guide the field in expanding the importance of the Israel experience as an important approach to Jewish education in the future.

IMPLICATIONS

First, when a society, a people, or a community has discovered a successful new educational format with empirically demonstrated outcomes that meet the community's dreams, it should do everything at its disposal to incorporate the new format into the educational system. Put more starkly, American Jewish life has created what may be one of its most attractive and successful forms of Jewish education, but it has not turned it into a framework for all. If the community is truly committed to the Jewish identity goals it professes, one would assume the Israel experience would be on the highest rung of communal priority.

Second, the Israel experience has attracted some of the most talented and creative contemporary Jewish educators. The community must harness this talent and its thinking for visioning and programming over and beyond their success in Israel trips. This, too, has not happened.

Third, if this experience is so good, significant efforts should be invested in broadening its market, age range, focus, and sales. A successful product (like the iPod, for example) spawns a whole series of new products and accessories (as the iPod did). With the powerful exception of Birthright Israel—and it is powerful—this growth process has not happened in the Israel experience field or, more generally, in the Jewish community.

Fourth, there are six cornerstones of teaching Israel:

1) The roots of the Jewish people are in the Land of Israel. Not all of Jewish history is Israel-centered, but very important elements of it are (the idea of God, Torah, the Prophetic vision, the notion of Jewish peoplehood, and the beginnings of the Rabbinic tradition).

2) There is a direct connection between the Bible and contemporary Judaism. The Bible is more than a history of the origins of the Jewish people; it is an ideology of core Jewish values. This connection was developed in the old–new land called the State of Israel.

3) The Jewish people renewed itself by returning to its ancient land and creating a modern State. The story of the creation of a Jewish homeland in the land of Israel is a powerful saga about the human ability to change history and become masters of our own fate.

4) Israel embodies many core values and lifestyles of Jewish tradition and civilization: Shabbat, *tikkun olam*, the Jewish calendar, *kehilla*, Jewish customs, language, and holidays. It is a hothouse for seeing the possibilities for living and practicing the values held dear by our people.

5) The State of Israel is a contemporary society combining general and Jewish cultures. Being Jewish means living in two worlds, one shaped by Jewish culture, history, and sources and the other by general culture, history, and sources. Contemporary Israel is a laboratory for seeing how that experiment plays out.

6) The Hebrew language is an integral part of Israel and of Jewish civilization as a whole.

POLICY RECOMMENDATIONS

The policy recommendations are:

1. There needs to be a concentrated change in American Jewish life that makes visiting the State of Israel on an Israel experience a core Jewish experience on par with *brit milah, bar mitzvah*, and *ḥuppah*.

2. A set of clearly enunciated themes and values should underlie this enterprise.

3. The creative forces involved with the Israel experience should be co-opted to become key figures in the enrichment and enhancement of other, less attractive forms of American Jewish education.

4. Collateral programs to the Israel experience (summer camps, youth movements, and retreats) should be developed based on the experiential, person-centered, group process, value-focused and staffing philosophy that is at the core of most Israel experience programs.

5. In order to meet its highest priorities, the American Jewish community needs to place an Israel experience at the top of its educational priorities.

ADDITIONAL RESEARCH QUESTIONS

1. What aspects of Jewish identity does the Israel experience contribute to, and for what aspects has it proven less valuable?

2. Are there differences between the diverse organizers and programs of Israel experience or, once a minimal bar is reached, is the experience *per se* what matters?

3. What are the developmental outcomes of the Israel experience for participants at different ages?

4. Does Jewish schooling have any connection, relevance, or importance for the Israel experience, or are these two totally distinct worlds?

5. What standards, sanctions or accreditation procedures should be established to create a profession for Israel experience providers? Will this improve the quality of the experience?

6. Are post-trip activities essential to the impact of the Israel experience, or do Israel trips have independent value of their own?

THE ISRAEL TRIP AND THE LARGER CONTEXT OF JEWISH EDUCATION

The Israel trip—with some notable exceptions—is still in its infancy in terms of its relationship with the larger context of Jewish education. Schools, camps, day schools, youth movements, and young adult programs need to determine how to make the Israel experience part of a seamless, ongoing, educational continuum, rather than an isolated, disjunctive, one-time educational moment. At the moment, the report card on this relationship is not exemplary.

THE LARGER CONTEXT

For the Jewish community to find success in educating the next generation, the Israel experience is one of the key factors for every Jewish child and young adult. Learning about Israel through the themes, motifs, dimensions of contemporary Israel and its historical antecedents in a child's life beginning in the elementary years will create a milieu in which the Israel experience will take on significant importance in the life of the community.

Ultimately, the critical goal of presenting Israel in Jewish schools is to enable every child to visit Israel. It is then and only then that teaching Israel will take its rightful place in the Jewish educational system.

HIGHLIGHTS

1. The Israel experience has developed significantly over the past few decades. Today it is one of the most creative and successful forms of Jewish education.

2. The educational characteristics of a good Israel trip have been identified through actual experience and thorough research.

3. American Jewish education has not made the Israel experience a central educational priority, nor has it figured out how to relate it to the larger educational context.

4. Ultimately, the best way to teach Israel is to have our youth participate in a creative peer group trip.

5. If one wills it, it need not remain a dream.

ANNOTATED BIBLIOGRAPHY

Book, T. (2004). *For the Sake of Zion: Pride and Strength Through Knowledge: An Educator's Guide*. New York: BJE of New York and the World Zionist Movement. This is the clearest and best-set-out statement of a philosophy of teaching Israel and translation into eight lessons. It is appropriate for all schools and movements.

Segal, B. (1987). *Returning: The Land of Israel as a Focus in Jewish History*. Jerusalem: World Zionist Organization. This is a core reference book, rich with quotations and references, on the place Israel has played in Jewish life throughout the ages.

Gerber, K. & Mazor, A. (2003) *Mapping Israel Education: An Overview of Trends and Issues in North America.* Gilo Family Foundation. This is the most comprehensive review of the field up to 2003, encompassing what exists and what is needed. The educational materials distributed by the Bureau of Jewish Education of Greater Boston, while produced many years ago, remain accessible and pedagogically creative resources for schools and teachers.

REFERENCES

Book, T. (2004). *For the Sake of Zion: Pride and Strength Through Knowledge: An Educator's Guide.* New York: BJE of New York and the World Zionist Movement.

Chazan, B. & Cohen, S. (2001). "What We Know about American Jewish Youth and Young Adults: Some Implications for Birthright Israel." *Journal of Jewish Communal Service* 77 (2), 76–82.

Chazan, B. (1997). *Does the Teen Israel Experience Make a Difference?* New York: Israel Experience Inc.

Chazan, B. (ed.) (2000). *The Israel Experience: Studies in Jewish Identity and Youth Culture.* Jerusalem: CRB Foundation.

Chazan, B. (1994). The Israel Trip: A NewFor of Jewish Education. *Youth Trips to Israel: Rationale and Realization.* New York: CRB Foundation and the Mandell L. Berman Jewish Heritage Center at JESNA.

Cohen, E. H. & Cohen, E. (2000). *The Israel Experience* (Hebrew). Jerusalem: The Jerusalem Institute for Israel Studies.

Creating, Developing, and Sustaining a Relationship with Israel (2004). New York: The Reform Jewish Commission in Lifelong Jewish Learning.

Dewey, J. (1938) *Experience and Education.* New York: Collier.

Gerber, K. & Mazor, A. (2003) *Mapping Israel Education: An Overview of Trends and Issues in North America.* Gilo Family Foundation.

Isaacs, L. (1997). *AMSHI Project Evaluation.* New York: JESNA.

Johnson, P. (1988) *A History of the Jews.* New York: Harper Perennial.

Kelner, S., Saxe, L., Kadushin, C., Canar, R., Lindholm, M. et al. (2000). *Making Meaning: Participants Experience of Birthright Israel.* Waltham, MA: Cohen Center for Modern Jewish Studies, Brandeis University.

Kelner, S. (2003). "The Impact of Israel Experience Programs on Israel's Symbolic Meaning." *Contemporary Judaism 24,* 124–154.

Mittelberg, D. (1994). *The Israel Visit and Jewish Identification.* New York: American Jewish Committee.

Phillips, B. (1998). *Re-examining Intermarriage: Trends, Textures, Strategies.* New York: Wilstein Institute and American Jewish Committee.

Saxe, L., Sasson, T. & Hecht, S. (2006). *Taglit/Birthright Israel: Impact on Jewish Identity, Peoplehood, and Connection to Israel.* Waltham, MA: The Cohen Center for Modern Jewish Studies, Brandeis University.

Saxe, L. & Chazan, B. (in press). *The Story of Birthright Israel* Waltham: New England University Press.

Segal, B. (1987). *Returning: The Land of Israel as a Focus in Jewish History.* Jerusalem: World Zionist Organization.

Tobin, G. (1995). *Teen Trips to Israel: Cost, Price, and Marketing.* Waltham, MA: Cohen Center for Modern Jewish Studies, Brandeis University.

Wolf, M. (2007) *Negotiating the Boundary: Exploring Identities during Israel Experience Mifgashim.* Unpublished doctoral dissertation, Hebrew University, Jerusalem, Israel.

Jewish Education in Australia

Suzanne D. Rutland

Since 1945 the Jewish day school system in Australia has developed into what has been described by Rubinstein (1991) as the jewel in the crown of Australian Jewish life. Today it is estimated that 70–75% of Jewish children attend Jewish day schools in Melbourne and 62% in Sydney, while Jewish day schools also operate in the smaller centers of Perth, Adelaide, Brisbane and the Gold Coast. Zionist youth movements and visits to Israel organised by the Australasian Union of Jewish Students (AUJS) remain a strong feature of Jewish education in Australia, and in more recent years, adult Jewish education has developed. Yet, as will be shown, little serious research has been conducted into Jewish education in Australia, and most was done before 1990. Thus the key questions to address are why so little research has been undertaken to date, how effective Jewish day schools have been in securing Jewish identity, what type of identity the Jewish communal leadership is aiming to achieve, what the role and importance of experiential Jewish education is and how important adult Jewish education is. Since 1990, when I was appointed to the inaugural position of Jewish Education Coordinator for teacher preservice in Hebrew and Jewish Studies in the Faculty of Education at the University of Sydney, I have been involved in researching and writing about these questions.

THE CONTEXT

Australian Jewry is largely a pre– and post–*Shoah* community. In 1933 there were only 23,000 Jews living in Australia, concentrated in the two main centers of Sydney and Melbourne. Unlike English-speaking communities in the United States, Canada, Britain and South Africa, Australian Jewry was not reinforced by the mass migration from Eastern Europe between 1880 and 1920. By the 1930s the community was assimilated, highly anglicized and parochial, cut off from the mainstreams of Jewish thought and learning, with minimal levels of Jewish knowledge. In 1951 one observer described the Sydney Jewish community as:

> …a spiritual desert.. they have time… but for Hebrew education of their children, none whatsoever… it does not thirst for Jewish knowledge… it is turning its back on Jewish traditions, rejecting the spiritual heritage in favour of material gain…

All that was to change with the impact of the prewar and particularly postwar survivor migration. Between 1938 and 1961 the community more than doubled in size to 61,000. Many of the newcomers arrived with a strong commitment to Jewish continuity and Zionism, and they completely transformed the Jewish community. While many had come from centres of Jewish learning and were well steeped in Jewish tradition, a large number were no longer observant Jews. For them, G-d had died in Auschwitz.

In the middle of the nineteenth century two small Jewish schools were established in Sydney and Melbourne, but when government funding was withdrawn from denominational schooling in the 1870s and 1880s they closed, and from the turn of the century Jewish education was provided by part-time systems, with a weekly class offered during school hours in government schools combined with after-school and Sunday morning classes (Conyer 1998). The first twentieth-century Jewish day school was formed in the midst of the *Shoah*, opening officially as the North Bondi Jewish Day School and Kindergarten (later renamed Moriah College) in February 1943 in Sydney. It was only two decades later that other Jewish day schools emerged in Sydney with the foundation of Masada

College in Sydney's north in 1966, of the Yeshiva Chabad school system, also in 1966, and then Mount Sinai College, a primary school in Sydney's southeast in 1980 and the Emanuel School, the first full Progressive School (K to 12), in 1983. Jewish day schools in Sydney were slow to develop, however, and in 1970 only 17% of Jewish children attended them.

It was in Melbourne that the really strong and diverse Jewish day school system developed in the 1950s, reflecting the full spectrum of prewar Polish Jewish life from the *Haredi* Adass Israel (1952) to Chabad Schools Yeshiva College (1951) and Beth Rivka (1955), Yavneh College (1961), a Mizrachi School, and Mount Scopus College (1949), a modern Orthodox school. Later three more schools emerged, adding to the religious diversity: Bialik College (1962—building on the kindergarten already formed in 1942), a secular Zionist school devoted to Hebrew culture; Shalom Aleichem (1975), a Bundist, Yiddish primary school; and King David School (1978), a Progressive Jewish day school. In 1963 Mount Scopus had a student population of 1,300, and by the mid-1980s it had developed into the largest private Jewish day school in the world with a student population of 2,800.

Since the 1970s Jewish school population has further grown for a number of reasons. In the 1970s there was a general move from the government school system to private schools, most of which have a religious affiliation, and the Jewish schools have benefited from this trend. In addition, the introduction of some federal government funding on a needs-based system in the mid-1970s and the growth of multiculturalism encouraged by government policies contributed to their growth. This has also been reinforced by new waves of immigrants from Russia, Israel and particularly South Africa.

Commitment to Zionism has been a very important element in Jewish education in Australia. Not only have the Jewish schools run informal Zionist education programs for high school students as an integral part of their Jewish studies programs, including Year 10 programs in Israel, but they have also encouraged their graduates to spend time studying in Israel after school. As a result 70% of Jewish young people have visited Israel at least once, with many others visiting two or even three times. Given the distance of travel between the two countries with the resultant high costs, this is a significant proportion, especially compared with only 30% in the United States. The needs of Jewish children who do not attend Jewish schools continue to be serviced by Boards of Jewish Education, which exist in each of the main centers.

IMPORTANT RECENT RESEARCH IN JEWISH EDUCATION

Since the development of Jewish education is a recent phenomenon, only gaining momentum in the postwar period, and for Sydney only since the 1970s, there has been little serious research into the key issues facing Jewish education in Australia. The area where the most significant research has been done is in the history of the development of Jewish day school education (Conyer 1998; Ruth 1997; Rutland 2003; Tofler 2001). Given the community's strong Zionist identification, one would presume that its day schools would be at the forefront of teaching Israel Studies, yet this is not the case. The issue of the nature and effectiveness of Zionist or Israel education has been the subject of two studies (Rutland 1993/4; Bryfman 2000/1).

Bryfman delineates three possible areas of Israel education: what he calls "the separate approach, the integrated approach and the co-curricula approach". The "separate approach" is where Zionism/Israel studies are taught as a separate unit; the "integrated approach" is where they are incorporated into an overall Jewish history program; and the "co-curricula approach" is where separate activites in informal education are conducted. Bryfman stresses that "it is mainly in a Separate Approach that adequate attention can be given to the transmission of large quantities of knowledge" (2001, p. 17). These findings support the earlier research (Rutland 1994) that Israel education is not a separate strand in most school curricula, and that there is no systematic, consistent or overall approach. In addition, none of the schools teach contemporary Israel. While individual teachers believe that a more effective Israel program would enrich students' Jewish identity, they feel obliged to support the conventional wisdom that there is insufficient time to create a separate strand in a curriculum that already has so much to teach within the four main areas of Hebrew, *Tanach*, Judaism and Jewish history. While the "separate approach" is completely neglected in the Jewish schools, both studies showed that the integrated and co-curricula approaches, including the study tours to Israel and the Year 9 Zionist seminars, were much more successful. Until 2000, up to 50% of the pupils at Moriah College, Sydney, participated in the Israel Study Tour (IST), which has had a significant impact (Rutland 2003). However, as Bryfman has pointed out, "often the two aspects of education are run as completely separate entities within the respective schools with little or no consultation taking place" (Bryfman 2001, p. 37).

Both studies also investigated the teaching of the reality of Israel, including the Arab–Israeli conflict, as opposed to what Bryfman calls "mythical Israel," an idealised version of Israeli history. They have demonstrated that most schools take a very conservative approach to this issue, with only a minority choosing to broaden the syllabus to deal with the realities. Bryfman also highlights the fact that very few members of the teaching staff are formally trained in the subject matter, and most are ill-prepared to teach Israel education. The findings also demonstrated a lack of appropriate resources. Even where such materials exist, such as a new textbook on the Arab–Israeli conflict published in 1993, these were not being utilized effectively. In sum, the research into this key area of Jewish education and identification shows that the Australian Jewish schools have not fully realized the potential that Israel could play in the development of a strong Jewish identity. While in theory the communal leadership pays lip service to the vital importance of Israel, the classroom reality lags far behind this conceptual principle.

Another key area yet to be fully investigated is Hebrew teaching, which is seen as a central endeavor of the Jewish day schools. Again, classroom realities seem to lag behind publicized statements. During the 1990s efforts have been made to introduce more effective Hebrew curricula from overseas, with the Canadian-based Tal Am/Tal Selah program starting at Yavneh College in 1996, and now used by most Australian Jewish schools. Furthermore, in 2004 the high school NETA program (*Noah L'Tovat haIvrit*—Youth for the Benefit of Hebrew), developed by a writing team from the Hebrew University led by Hila Kobliner, working in conjunction with the Boston Hebrew College, was introduced. Yet to date, almost no research has been undertaken into school Hebrew teaching in Australia.

At the University of Sydney a major innovation in Hebrew teaching was introduced by the Modern Hebrew lecturer, Yona Gilead, in 2001. At that time the Modern Hebrew program in the Department of Hebrew, Biblical & Jewish Studies moved from pedagogy based on locally designed programs, which were thematic-topic-based, to adopting a graded and sequenced language-based curriculum with a communicative focus, developed in the Rothberg International School for Overseas Students at the Hebrew University Israel. These changes were implemented with two main objectives in mind. The first objective has been to bring the teaching of Modern Hebrew into line with pedagogy used in other international tertiary institutions in Israel and the United States. The second objective has been to ensure that the Modern Hebrew program is relevant and interesting to students, thus ensuring the continued existence of this small enrolment course at the University of Sydney (Gilead 2004).

Since 2001 student numbers have more than doubled, and this result, together with students' evaluations and lecturers' perspectives, indicates the success of this innovation. Ms. Gilead analyzes a number of reasons to explain why this change has been successful. She argues that the Rothberg programs are far superior to the locally devised programs previously used; they are based on a spiral curriculum with six levels of instruction and an effective placement test, ensuring that students start their Modern Hebrew studies at the appropriate level. The program is compatible with materials used previously; the necessary professional development had taken place as a precursor for change. The change was implemented slowly, and the improvement was readily discernable by all. She has also shown how this innovation has affected the teaching of Modern Hebrew at local secondary schools through the trickling down process. (Gilead in press) This study is the precursor for a much larger study of Modern Hebrew teaching and educational change at tertiary level.

Such a study itself is an innovation, as the whole question of research into the effectiveness of Jewish education in day schools and the need for curriculum innovation was a neglected area until recently. Leadership has continued to fear negative findings, not accepting that these could be important pointers for educational change. In addition, while the community overall understands the importance of Jewish schooling, there is still a lack of understanding of the importance of investing in Jewish educators at both the preservice and inservice levels and of supporting research at the tertiary level. Such programs are in their infancy and lack funding in both Melbourne and Sydney. In the last decade, however, there has been a major shift in attitudes regarding the importance of investing in Jewish educators and of supporting research at the tertiary level, with the establishment of tertiary Jewish education programs first at the University of Sydney and then at Monash University, Melbourne, contributing significantly to this shift.

The convening of major Jewish education conferences—the first of which was held in 1997, supported by the Zionist Federation—and the development of a more professional level amongst Jewish educators, inspired a number of Jewish educators who are now involved in undertaking research into different aspects of Jewish education, including a comparative study of the Melbourne Jewish school system with the Greek Orthodox system; an investigation of a pluralistic approach to Jewish day school education; the impact of a teacher's biography in the teaching of the *Shoah*; and factors needed for successful innovation in Hebrew teaching in Australia. Undoubtedly these present projects will lead to a greater knowledge and understanding of Jewish education in Australia in the next decade.

IMPLICATIONS AND/OR POLICY RECOMMENDATIONS

The Jewish day schools have attracted a very high proportion of Jewish children, and the number of young people who have undertaken programs in Israel is also extremely high. Judged by student numbers and matriculation results, the schools are very successful, but the Moriah College research revealed that there are serious issues to be addressed in terms of Jewish education. In 1992 a parent survey at Moriah College found that for the high school parents, the first priority motivating them to send their children to the College was its Jewish ethos, and their top priority for outcomes was a desire for "knowledge and appreciation of Jewish values and heritage". However, in the high school the greatest level of dissatisfaction of the parents was with Hebrew, 31%, followed by *Tanakh* (Bible) and French equally. As the survey pointed out, the main focus of the criticism was the standard of teaching in the Jewish Studies department, with the most common complaints being:

1. the employment of teachers who are not fluent in the English language;
2. the inability of "imported" teachers to control the classes;
3. large discrepancies in standards between one teacher and the next, and from one year to the next;
4. the apparent inability of the school to produce students who have mastered conversational Hebrew;
5. the minimal use of modern language methods for Hebrew;
6. the allocation of excessive time to *Tanach*, and not enough to current topical issues of Jewish philosophy and modern thought;
7. rapid turnover of teaching staff;
8. over-emphasis on ritual performance of religious activities and insufficient attention to explanation of rituals; and
9. compulsory Hebrew.

As the report commented in regard to the high school, "the commentary leaves little doubt that urgent and drastic attention is warranted." In the primary school the level of dissatisfaction with Hebrew was not as high, but the survey noted that "concern appears to grow as the given child progresses [up the school]" (Rutland 2003, pp. 277–278). The innovation introduced at the University of Sydney in 2001 has influenced seven high schools across Australia with their adoption of the Hebrew program, NETA. On the other hand, whilst the research on the teaching of Israel studies does have important implications for the schools, its results have not been widely disseminated, and there has not been any noticeable impact from these findings.

Further serious research is needed to investigate problem areas, including the issue of family education. The strongest recommendation is that the community begin to invest in Jewish educational research, as reflection on current practice will help to strengthen what is happening and ensure a stronger future for Jewish educational endeavours. The wide range of Jewish educational research, that needs to be undertaken is discussed below.

ADDITIONAL RESEARCH QUESTIONS TO BE ADDRESSED.

Assessment and evaluation in several areas is called for.

- Assessment of the effectiveness of curriculum reform that has taken place over the last decade in Hebrew and Jewish Studies teaching and learning, particularly with the introduction of the Tal Am/Tal Selah Hebrew/Jewish studies program in most primary schools, the introduction in 2004 of the NETA Hebrew program in the high school systems, and the development of a new Jewish Studies program at Moriah College.
- Assessment of Israel programs. At what age are they most likely to be successful—in Year 10 as part of a Jewish school program or in what has been called Year 13, after students complete their matriculation, before starting at university?
- What are the best methods of introducing educational innovation and change into the teaching and learning of Hebrew and Jewish studies at all levels of learning?
- How can one increase the number of students undertaking Hebrew and Jewish studies at university level?
- Strengths and weaknesses of informal Jewish education in Australia.
- Reasons for the lack of family Jewish education.
- Issues relating to pluralistic Jewish education.
- Advantages and disadvantages of employing non–Jewish principals.

CROSS-CULTURAL RESEARCH

Research undertaken in relation to some of these issues in other Diaspora communities is definitely relevant to the Australian scene, even though the community also faces different issues. A much higher proportion of Australian Jewish children attend Jewish schools, so the challenge is to maintain present enrolment levels and improve the quality of Jewish education, rather than to attract more students to the schools. The Australian Jewish community is more diversified because of the various waves of migrants since World War II, an issue that is less relevant in the North American Jewish schools, where a much higher proportion of children are third generation and more. Australian Jewry has developed a system of teacher education for Hebrew and Jewish studies within the mainstream secular universities, again something that is not relevant to North America, where York University, Toronto, is one of the few institutions with a similar system of teacher education. To date there have been no direct cross-cultural studies with Australia. In 1989 a volume on *Jewish Education Worldwide* included a long but dated chapter on Jewish Education in Australia (Solomon in Himmelfarb and DellaPergolia). There certainly are advantages in cross-cultural dialogue as Australian Jewry faces the challenges of maintaining Jewish identity, but first there needs to be more intensive local research to provide a basis for such a dialogue to take place.

FUTURE DIRECTIONS

- Ongoing process of curriculum development and evaluation in the fields of Hebrew and Jewish studies at all levels.
- More effective remedial and extension programs in Hebrew and Jewish studies.
- Maximizing opportunities for Jewish studies and Hebrew learning on the web by ensuring close cooperation with such developments in other parts of the Jewish world.
- Raising the profile of Israel education by holding a nationwide conference on the teaching of Israel in the twenty-first century and seeking ways to ensure that Israel studies is developed as a separate strand within the Jewish education structure. This would include developing an Israel curriculum framework for what can be taught in the Australian Jewish community.

- Development of an effective family education program, possibly by bringing in a team of experts to assist in establishing such programs.
- Creating a greater awareness of the importance of preservice and inservice for teachers.
- Creating more Jewish educational opportunities for non–Jewish day school students, including strengthening the work of the BJEs (both Orthodox and Progressive) across Australia.
- Finding ways of reaching out to the unaffiliated, particularly in the Russian and Israeli communities.
- Establishment of a foundation to assist parents who cannot pay the high school fees and work on other ways of ensuring that as many students as possible attend a Jewish day school.

CONCLUSION

The development of Jewish education in postwar Australia presents an exciting picture, with a large percentage of Jewish children receiving formal Hebrew and Jewish studies in Jewish schools. However, there are serious issues relating to the effectiveness of this schooling for Jewish knowledge and identity. These relate to inadequate curricula, the need to develop better programs of teacher preservice and inservice, to create a separate Israel studies strand in secondary schools, and to develop family education programs. In order to address these issues, much more effective research needs to be sponsored to analyze the strengths as well as the weaknesses and to make recommendations for improvement.

HIGHLIGHTS

- Provides the context for the development of postwar Jewish schools in Australia.
- Analyses the major research undertaken over the last decade, in regard to the history of day schools; strengths and weaknesses of Israel education, drawing on studies undertaken in 1993/4 and 2000/1; and research into innovation in Hebrew teaching at university level.
- Discusses the reason for the lack of research and suppression of data over the last two decades.
- Provides suggestions for future research and areas where change and development are needed.

LARGER CONTEXT

With its creation of a vibrant Jewish day school system, Australian Jewry can certainly serve as a model for world Jewry. Research into its strengths and weaknesses is, therefore, relevant within the international context. The issues and problems relating to curriculum development and evaluation, building effective Israel education programs, improving the teaching of Modern Hebrew, creating a more professional body of Jewish educators through preservice and inservice, and family education are issues that are relevant for Jewish education throughout the Diaspora.

ANNOTATED BIBLIOGRAPHY

Gilead, Y. (2004). Revival strategies: Modern Hebrew, the University of Sydney, in G. Wigglesworth (ed.), Proceedings of the Marking Our Difference Conference 2003, School of Languages, University of Melbourne, Melbourne, pp. 54–66. An innovative research paper, Yona Gilead analyses the factors in successful educational innovation, using the Hebrew program at the University of Sydney as a case study.

Rubinstein, W.D. (1991). *The Jews in Australia: A Thematic History*. Melbourne: Heinemann Australia. This is the second of two-volume history of Australian Jewry with a major chapter covering the development of Jewish education.

Rutland, S.D. (2000). "The State of Jewish Day School Education in Australia." *Australian Journal of Jewish Studies* 14, 78–100. This article analyses the main features of Jewish schools in Australia, utilizing data gathered from a nationwide survey conducted by the author in 1996.

REFERENCES

Bryfman, D. (2000/1). "The Current State of Israel Education for Jewish High School Students in NSW." Unpublished Master of Education thesis, Monash University, Melbourne.

Conyer, B.(1998). Social Phenomena in Jewish Australia and the Development of Jewish Education. *Australian Jewish Historical Society Journal* 14 (2), 322–344.

Gilead, Y. (2004). Revival Strategies: Modern Hebrew, the University of Sydney. In G. Wigglesworth (ed.), Proceedings of the Marking Our Difference Conference 2003, School of Languages, University of Melbourne, Melbourne, pp. 54–66

Rubinstein, W.D. (1991). *The Jews in Australia: A Thematic History.* Melbourne: Heinemann Australia.

Ruth, J. (1997). Jewish Secular Humanist Education in Australia. Unpublished doctoral dissertation, University of Melbourne.

Rutland, S.D. (1994). "The Challenges of Teaching Zionism and the Arab Israel Conflict in Jewish Schools." *Jewish Educators' Network Journal* IV (Part 1), 44–53.

Rutland, S.D. (2000). "The State of Jewish Day School Education in Australia." *Australian Journal of Jewish Studies* 14, 78–100.

Rutland, S.D. (2003). *If You Will It, It Is No Dream: The Moriah Story.* Sydney: Playright Publishing.

Solomon, G. (1989). Jewish Education in Australia. In H. S. Himmelfarb & S. DellaPergolia (eds.), *Jewish Education Worldwide: Cross-Cultural Perspectives, Studies in Judaism.* Lanham, MD and London: University Press of America, 395–443.

Tofler, O.B. (2000). *Forty Years On: A History of G. Korsunski Carmel School.* Perth: Sponsored publication.

Jewish Educational Israel Experiences

Susan Wall & Sally Klein-Katz

Over the last decade and more, organized Jewry has invested heavily in both short- and long-term Israel experiences. Traditionally these trips have been directed toward teens, Jewish professionals, families and adults and sponsored by community agencies, synagogues, youth movements, camps, etc. Newer initiatives such as Birthright Israel and MASA have dramatically increased the number of young people traveling to Israel.

Are these trips worth the investment? The research points to the enduring impact of these experiences on a wide variety of Jewish identity measures (Cohen 2006; Grant 2000; Kelner 2001/2002; Saxe 2004). Participants almost always rave about their experiences. Despite the large measure of customer satisfaction and the generally positive results of the studies, we know that some Israel trips work better than others and some participants are more heavily impacted than others.

What accounts for these variations? Why do some programs seem to make more of an educational impact? Why are some participants more strongly affected than others? What, in short, comprises a "good" Israel experience?

We have fifty years of experience in formal and informal Jewish education, studying how people learn and what leads to successful programs. For thirty-five of these years we have worked in educational Israel travel along with many wonderful colleagues. We have witnessed the power of carefully planned and thoughtfully implemented Jewish educational Israel experiences.

We believe that all Israel trips potentially have a significant and lasting impact if they integrate a more serious educational approach. To accomplish this, there must be careful planning and implementation of both the overall program and each site visit with creative elements of exploration, experimentation, reflection, processing and articulation in a supportive atmosphere. We believe that these educational practices will lead to a strengthening of the participant's Jewish personal narrative and Israel's place within it. This is worth the investment.

In order for the establishment to capitalize on the potential of Israel trips, we need a better understanding of how and why these trips work. Through a combination of existing research and collective empirical knowledge we will define the elements that enhance the impact an educational Israel experience has on North American travelers. The categories of learners addressed are adults, teachers/Jewish professionals, families, young adults, high school students and eighth graders.

The key questions that we address are:

1. Why do educational Israel experiences have so much potential for Jewish growth and learning?
2. How does the research about how people learn inform the development and implementation of Israel experience programs?
3. How do we realize the educational potential in building and implementing such programs?
4. How do basic educational principles apply to different types of groups?

WHY DO EDUCATIONAL ISRAEL EXPERIENCES HAVE SO MUCH POTENTIAL FOR JEWISH GROWTH AND LEARNING?

Travel opens up the individual to a transformational experience. In a very concrete and physical sense, travel temporarily shifts the focus from one's daily environs, routine and responsibilities. This freedom leaves the individual more open to experimentation as well as reflection on his/her own life: what there is to value, and what elements one might want to change or discard.

> *Participants…were engaged in a process whereby they…turned their gaze inward to reflect on their own lives. By piecing together selective elements of their own life histories…participants constructed personal narratives about their own Jewishness"* (Kelner 2001, p. 9).

Travel establishes a framework; travel to Israel provides the meaning.

Israel as a spiritual, national and physical center is a context for authentic Jewish experiences. The bulk of the biblical and early rabbinic narratives took place in the Land of Israel. One virtually enters into this time period when in Israel. Exposure to Israel's history connects with *our personal* story in very immediate and intimate ways. In the words of the Yiddish poet Yitzhak Yasinowitz, "One does not travel to Jerusalem, one returns."

In order for our participants to truly feel a sense of *returning*, to personally enter into the biblical Jewish narrative, we could, for example, begin an Israel trip at the Tayelet in Jerusalem. On this ridge Abraham might have stood with Isaac to look out upon Mt. Moriah. Here we open a Bible—the book that ties us to both our ancestors and one another—and read God's words to Abraham from Genesis 22. Here, within these physical surroundings, the words take on new meaning. Thus we link our participants' first journey to Israel with that of the first Jew's sojourn in the Land, preparing them for a personal Israel experience, contextualized within the story of their people.

Religious life of Diaspora Jews is intrinsically bound up with Israel through Tanakh, siddur and holidays. "Israel travel has heightened potential for American Jews, since it connects them back to their own past and their own sense of collective memory" (Grant 2000, p. 64). Bringing these connections to life in Israel creates powerful memories, deepening Jewish life back home. For example, Jews sing *Shir Ha-Ma'alot* (the Psalm of Ascent introducing grace after meals) on Shabbat and holidays everywhere in the world. Singing it while ascending the southern steps that led to the Temple, as did the Levites of old, enriches every recitation of *Shir Ha-Ma'alot* for our traveler from that day forward, including for those who are reciting it for the first time.

Such visceral memories can transform our rituals. Before they were words and motions; now they are filled with meaning and memories. One shared his powerful memory of a Shabbat in Jerusalem:

> [It] was the most interest[ing] Shabbat experience I've had, because I've been to Shabbat where people just light some candles, go to temple [and] come back…So many people there really, really were deep into the whole meaning of Shabbat, taking the commandment of honoring Shabbat…I just never had an experience where so many people were just so energized to be doing something on a Friday night that wasn't going out" (Kelner 2001, p. 6).

This confluence of travel, Israel and the possibility of integrating the experience back home is what gives the experience its potential. All Israel trips carry within them this possibility of changing/strengthening the mindset and behaviors of participants, which is the educational impact desired.

HOW DOES THE RESEARCH ABOUT HOW PEOPLE LEARN INFORM THE DEVELOPMENT AND IMPLEMENTATION OF ISRAEL EXPERIENCE PROGRAMS?

Research has emerged regarding different types of learners: their motivations to learn, individual strengths, different intelligences (Gardner 1993, 2000) and other cultural, sociological, and gender-related issues. Travel, as a holistic experience, inherently addresses more learning needs, styles, and intelligences than most participants' daily lives. Travel provides visual, auditory, and kinesthetic/tactile stimuli, for example: seeing (the sites themselves), reading (captions at the sites, sourcebooks), hearing (listening to the guide and surrounding sounds), speaking (sharing and talking with other participants and Israelis), movement and touch (walking the land, planting trees, touching the Kotel, climbing Massada, digging and crawling through ancient caves, etc.).

In today's world educators realize that learning involves much more than simply acquiring knowledge (Bloom 1984; Wiggins & McTighe 2005; National Research Council 2000). There is little benefit in the often endless series of facts thrown at Israel travelers. Real learning helps the individual understand facts and ideas in a conceptual framework. To learn, one must organize the information in a way that he/she can later retrieve and apply it.

Finally, participants must feel free to learn. Abraham Maslow's earlier research (Maslow 1962) shows us that only if their basic needs have been met can people reach a level of meaning making (in Maslow's word, self-actualization). His pyramid includes five levels, each level serving as the foundation for the next: physiological needs (food, water, physical comfort, rest), safety and security needs, belonging needs (friends, a sense of community), esteem needs (the respect of others, attention, appreciation) and finally self-actualization. Our goal is for the participants to reach a level of self-actualization–in our terms, becoming the most committed Jews that they can be. In order for this to be accomplished, an Israel experience must carefully provide for all of Maslow's foundational levels. For example, if participants feel overtired, hungry, unsafe, lonely or undervalued, we will not be able to accomplish our educational goals.

HOW DO WE REALIZE THE EDUCATIONAL POTENTIAL IN BUILDING AND IMPLEMENTING SUCH PROGRAMS?

Having taken into consideration travel's potential, the power of Jews visiting Israel and what we know about how people learn, we now turn to the trip itself. Every day needs to stand on its own merit in terms of content, enjoyment, and logistics. This is necessary, but not sufficient. Beginning with conception, through planning, pre-trip sessions, time in Israel and post-trip sessions, the transformational potential of every decision and every moment is key (Cohen & Wall 1994). The specifics of these elements and how they can be incorporated are beyond the scope of this chapter but are available elsewhere (Klein-Katz 2000). Here we will focus on the philosophical aspects that reflect a specific educational approach as to how one conceives of the trip and functions as the trip unfolds.

We maximize the educational potential for all ages, strengthening their Jewish identities and connecting them to their Jewish heritage when the programming includes reflection, empowering the learner, scaffolding, building a supportive community, the use of multiple modalities, alignment of expectations, attention to pace and timing, flexibility, themes, an educational approach to sites and people and staff who are educators.

Reflection is the foundation stone of Jewish educational Israel experiences. Asking questions and facilitating thoughtful challenges along with time for processing is critical. Opportunities for reflection to be formulated and articulated must happen while in Israel. This allows participants to look back and share their accomplishments and insights. Reflection should be a daily activity that provides time to think about that day and relate it to previous experiences. It is this reflection and articulation that facilitates the integration of the experience into thoughts, feelings, beliefs, personal narratives and lives. Kirshenblatt-Gimblett writes the following about youth programs, but it applies as well to other educational trips.

> A defining feature of The Israel Experience…is to make identity, and specifically Jewish identity, a reflexive project. The(y) are expected to examine their experiences and reflect on their Jewish identities through moderated group discussion, personal diaries, and a group journal….Tours…not only attempt to direct the process of securing a Jewish identity, but also socialize the youngsters into the very process of making an identity" (Kirshenblatt-Gimblett 2002, pp. 37–8).

Empowering the learner places the responsibility for learning on the participants, to the extent that this is possible. Conversely, infantilization will limit their potential for learning and growth. The program needs to activate the participants to ask, explore and make connections on their own.

This includes participants interviewing Israelis on the street, exploring the desert or a site on their own, recapping highlights of the day for the group, etc.

Tourists are usually open to experimentation. At the simplest level they try out new foods and physical challenges, which in and of themselves can be viewed as major accomplishments. However, empowerment should be expanded to the intellectual and educational spheres, including Jewish thought, ritual, texts and beyond. For example, one might reconstruct a Beit Midrash with participants taking the roles of the rabbis, empowering them to enter history and grapple with text.

Scaffolding in construction terms is what supports a structure while new building occurs. In educational terms, the program "should be designed to support the (learner) as (s/he) reaches and extends beyond…current safety range. They should provide the physical and psychological safety to learn something new and try it out without risking a fall" (Kelman, 1993). On an Israel trip scaffolding permits/encourages travelers to safely go beyond their comfort zones in trying new experiences and articulating new thoughts. For example, on the simplest level, most people are usually proficient at shopping. A shopping "game" where participants identify products as Western, Jewish or Israeli will lead to an important discussion of Jewish identity and assimilation.

A supportive community (however temporary) facilitates deeper reflection and learning within the group. The staff should facilitate the acquisition of shared language (jokes, terms, Hebrew, songs, prayers), shared rituals (both Jewish and travel-related), common stories and shared memories. Within this kind of atmosphere participants are more open to powerful experiences, spiritual moments and religious experimentation from which they draw personal meaning. Such a community requires planning and nurturing in order to establish a norm of positive energy, mutual support, tolerance for differences and safe space to explore and be oneself. To build such a community, one must attend to inclusiveness and discourage cliques. Asking participants to sit with different people on the bus and planning so as to actively include everyone in creative endeavors are only two of many approaches.

The use of multiple modalities in designing activities draws upon the participants' diverse abilities and interests. Activating the senses is critical for all ages and can be enhanced by: music/singing, drama (complete with costumes), movement, sketching, quiet contemplation, writing, and more.

> Simulation games can increase students' motivation, allow them to empathize with historical characters, show history as a process which had many possible outcomes, improve learning and memory, develop social skills and introduce variety into the educational experience (Cohen, E.H. 2004).

These creative techniques are not add-ons; they are an integral part of the experience. One needs to view the totality of the day to ensure a balance of modalities.

Alignment of expectations means ensuring that everyone is prepared for the actual program. This ranges from honest publicity regarding the nature of the trip to constantly repeating what the trip will be about—reiterating the vision—during pre-trip programs and throughout the trip itself. Will there be a strong religious/spiritual component? Will the trip be study-centered? Will Israeli song accompany the group throughout their journey? In addition, elements such as the pace of the trip and specific information as to places they will visit (and where not) must be clearly delineated before the group arrives in Israel so as to avoid frustration and disappointment. The customers need to feel comfortable with what they are buying in order to immerse themselves wholeheartedly in the experience.

The **pace and timing** distinguish Jewish educational Israel experiences from regular tours. Often regular trips pack as many sites as possible into each day to give customers a sense of getting their money's worth. An educational Israel experience is more focused on adequate time at each site for the participants to experience and think about the theme or content in order to promote real understanding. More time at each site allows the educator to go beyond the simple sharing of information to a level of meaning-making. This is the reason for more time at fewer stops—less is more!

Flexibility in the program and schedule must be in response to circumstances and people's needs. Teachers make over 5,000 decisions a day while teaching (Hunter, 1979). We can expect no less from the staff on educational Israel experiences. Flexibility is critical for all kinds of logistical and administrative circumstances on all Israel trips. However, in order to maximize the educational impact of the experience, the guide/leader needs to understand when it is time to stay with an issue, when to move on, when to be silent or when to change what was planned. The staff needs to be skilled in embracing the unplanned when it can enhance the thematic impact of any site visit or educational moment.

Themes, be they daily or meta, organize the program's content and help focus the participants. Themes are a critical component in allowing the participant to make meaning of the Israel experience. They determine where you go, whom you meet and what you do. Themes need to relate to context and hopefully be rich enough to relate to the participants' lives back home; for example, "Individuals Making a Difference," "Building a Society" or "Survival in the Face of Adversity."

Each site is related to as a text with an identified focus and articulated message or question relating to the larger themes of the trip. As in approaching any text lesson, we determine enduring understandings (lasting messages) and essential questions (issues to explore) as a basis for planning the experience at each site (Wiggins & McTighe 2005). There are often choices to be made at particular sites in terms of the themes to be explored or the messages to convey. At Masada, for example, one enduring understanding could be "Incorporating important values in our lives that necessitate personal sacrifice" (albeit of lesser drama than the story of Masada). Pointed questions such as "What do you treasure about your Jewishness?" and "Are there other aspects of Judaism you might want to take on, and if so, what might you have to give up in order for that to happen?" could lead participants to look beyond the time and place to make personal meaning.

"Textpeople," a term coined by Heschel, refers to the importance of the teacher as a personality becoming "the text that they [the pupils] will never forget." Just as the approach to sites can lead to a greater understanding, so choices of personalities the participants engage with during the trip will strengthen the learning and promote growth. *Textpeople* are contemporaries—the staff members, guest speakers, and other Israelis they meet. Through *Mifgashim* (multi-session cross-cultural encounters), talking with their beloved bus driver or having guides share personal stories, Israel comes alive. These conversations and stories, when contextualized and processed, become meaningful memories connecting them with Israel, Israelis and added dimensions of their personal Jewish narrative. In addition, the historical personalities who are brought to life through appropriate modalities (Devorah the Prophetess overlooking the battlefield, Rabban Gamliel in his Sanhedrin in Yavne, Yehuda HaNasi in Tzippori, Herzl at Har Herzl, etc.) also take on the significance of being *Textpeople* as the participants meet them in their own settings.

The **staff** person leading the group through an Israel educational experience needs to be an educator as well as a tour guide; not all guides are educators. The power that a professional educator brings to the experience is enormous. "They must have a view towards the long-term impact of the tour they lead, and not just provide short-term enjoyment" (Cohen 2002). Whether from Israel or abroad, staff members (trip leaders, guides, *madrikhim*) must share a common educational vision, lead the trip with passion and meet regularly to assess and adjust the program. These educators need to bring the best elements of formal and informal educational training as they plan for and take advantage of the "aha moments" inherent in every Israel experience. A staff that knows how to personalize the Israel experience and apply the educational elements cited throughout this chapter brings the potential of educational Israel experiences to fruition.

HOW DO BASIC EDUCATIONAL PRINCIPLES APPLY TO DIFFERENT TYPES OF GROUPS?

Basic educational principles as articulated above apply to *all* ages and types of groups. Highlighted in this section are the elements that are critical for certain groups in order to maximize the impact of the experience.

Adults are consumers who expect value and quality. Their lives are filled with multiple responsibilities, often including concern for elderly parents, their children's welfare and work. While they bring years of experience and professional competency, they may have limited experience and skills in reflecting, articulating, or sharing emotionally and spiritually with others. Being asked to be learners again can make adults feel particularly vulnerable. There also may be physical challenges in terms of the individual's stamina or the weather. Therefore, for adults we need to be particularly concerned with alignment of expectations, empowerment, scaffolding and pace.

Teachers/Jewish professionals usually are participants on subsidized trips. The sponsoring agencies have expectations such as deepening the participants' Jewish identity and knowledge, connecting them with Israel and developing ideas for enhancing their professional work. We believe that professionals should be treated like other adult learners, allowing the experience to be first and foremost a personal one. There is a danger in limiting the power of the experience by overly focusing on the professional application while missing the personal impact. Therefore we recommend that much of the transfer to classroom activities and other institutional roles take place toward the end of the trip (or perhaps in a retreat following the trip). Ongoing support after the trip is critical.

Families on an Israel experience should benefit from the best of what family education has to offer. The experience should challenge the family to grow Jewishly, allow for parents and children to teach and learn from one another and create common Jewish memories. The itinerary and programming will need careful attention so as to be age-appropriate for the children while providing adequate intellectual stimulation for the adults. This does not mean one program for the kids at the back of the bus with a separate program for their parents with the guide. Most programming should ideally be for the entire family, yet there are times when it may be valuable to divide the group by age-parallel activities (preferably involving the same theme) or provide additional games for the children on the bus or at certain sites. It is also important to remember that families are often very diverse in how they function, particularly under stress, which travel can engender. "For the majority of families, this will be the most intense time that they will spend together during the year. This requires sensitivity and insight on the part of staff as to when and to what extent to intervene" (Klein-Katz 2000).

Young adults (18- to 26-year-olds, such as on Birthright Israel trips) are at critical junctures in their lives and come with differing levels of maturity. Those on the younger end (just after high school) may be more susceptible to temptations of newfound independence and may exhibit behavior more typical of teenagers. Those in the later college and post-college years tend to be in flux both personally and professionally. They have yet to establish set patterns in their lives, which allows an Israel trip to be particularly impactful. They are open, looking for direction, and yet mature enough to be very serious and insightful. Many participants on these trips come knowing few of the other participants. They come willing to open themselves socially and to form community. When the tour educators or *madrikhim* are peers, they can be particularly influential.

High school students tend to be immersed in the social scene and can appreciate physical challenges (also true for young adults). Teenagers are also capable of high intellectual functioning and reflection if sufficiently motivated, which means that the theme/topic needs to be relevant to their lives and experiences. While this is true for all groups, younger people totally disengage if they do not find the content relevant. They also need "safe space". If this is not provided, they will shut down and neither share nor engage. *Madrikhim* who are strong, positive role models will also have an impact on them. The staff needs to keep in mind that teenagers often believe they are invincible, that if they break the rules they will not get caught and that if they do not drink enough water they will not dehydrate, etc.

Middle schoolers can be incredibly challenging, according to both parents and teachers. The contrast between their normal behavior and attitudes and that exhibited on Israel trips is often dramatic. They are far from familiar territory, and for some, this may be their first time away from home for a significant amount of time. The trip can be an empowering experience in terms of simple day-to-day life skills, which they will then associate with being Jewish and their time in Israel. Middle schoolers, given clear guidelines, will actually listen to adults on Israel trips. They can be very enthusiastic and willing to jump into activities, which should be highly active and hands-on. These young teens cover the full spectrum between concrete and abstract thinkers. With direction they can help one another learn higher-level thinking skills and reflection.

ADDITIONAL RESEARCH QUESTIONS

- What is the impact of the Israel experience in relation to other educational experiences on a person's active identification with Am Yisrael and Medinat Yisrael?
- What are effective methods of post-trip activities that enhance the impact of the Israel experience?
- What is the long-term impact of Jewish family educational experiences in Israel? For adults? For children?

FUTURE DIRECTIONS

- Educate those who fund, support or plan Israel experiences to realize the educational value of a positive educational Israel experience.
- Provide educational expertise for those planning such trips.
- Find ways for communal leadership to encourage and make educational Israel experiences for families and adults financially feasible, as it has for teens, young adults and Jewish professionals.
- What is the place of the Israel experience within the broader context of lifelong Jewish learning?

HIGHLIGHTS

- The proliferation of Israel experiences has met with overall success but resulted in trips of varying quality. The serious investment in such trips by the Jewish community demands stronger and more consistent outcomes.
- A serious educational approach to the planning and implementation of these trips will lead to greater impact for the individuals and the community.
- The educational potential of such experiences lies in the confluence of the power of travel, Israel as the repository of national memory and the possibility of connecting to one's Jewish life in the home community.
- Research on what it means to learn, what conditions are necessary for learning and individual learning styles sheds light on the planning and implementation of Israel experiences.
- Every decision in planning is critical; smooth functioning and high quality are necessary but not sufficient for educational excellence.
- Educational excellence demands that the trip be designed with daily and site themes that promote reflection, provide scaffolding, empower the learners, use multiple modalities, ensure adequate time at a limited number of sites and expose participants to historical or current personalities as role models.
- The staff members are educators who know how to implement the above design, create a supportive community and respond flexibly, as needed, to daily challenges and educational moments.

ANNOTATED BIBLIOGRAPHY

Chazan, B., Cohen, S. & Wall, S. (1994). *Youth Trips to Israel: Rationale and Realization*. New York: JESNA. Basic rationale and definitions for the Israel trip as a form of Jewish education for teens. The researchers followed several teen trips in an attempt to determine what elements constituted excellence in teen Israel travel.

Cohen, E.H. (2004). Preparation, Simulation and the Creation of Community: Exodus and the case of Diaspora Education Tourism. In T.E. Coles and D. J. Timothy (eds.), *Tourism, Diasporas and Space*. (pp. 124–138). London: Routledge. This study of the teen Exodus educational simulation on a ship to Israel analyzes what made the experience so powerful for participants and how and why it had such a significant impact on the subsequent time in Israel.

Cohen, E.H., Ifergan, M. & Cohen, E. (2002). «The Madrikh: A New Paradigm in Tour Guiding: Youth, Identity and Informal Education." *Annals of Tourism Research* 29 (4), 919–932. This "multi-dimensional analysis uncovered the structure of these characteristics [essential to guides leading these trips] and created a structure for an 'excellent' Israel Experience *madrikh*."

Grant, L. (2000). *Paradoxical Pilgrimage: American Jewish Adults on Congregational Israel Trip*. Unpublished doctoral dissertation, Jewish Theological Seminary of America. The author served as participant researcher on two congregational family Israel trips. Her focus was on the educational implications and applications of congregational Israel trips for adults.

Kelner, S. (2001). *Authentic Sights and Authentic Narratives on* Taglit. Paper presented at the 33rd Annual Meeting of the Association for Jewish Studies, Washington, D.C. This paper examines the use of tourism for the purposes of Jewish education through the Taglit/Birthright Israel program. The paper is available to download at http://cmjs.org/Publication.cfm?IDResearch=60

Kelner, S. (2002). *Almost Pilgrims: Authenticity, Identity and the Extra-Ordinary on a Jewish Tour of Israel*. Unpublished doctoral dissertation, Brandeis University. The author examines the case of Taglit/Birthright Israel, a ten-day educational pilgrimage-tour. Combining archival, ethnographic, survey and sociometric data, this work considers how meaning is produced in pilgrimage-tourism. The question of authenticity—both Israel's and the travelers'—is a central focus.

Kirshenblatt-Gimblett, B. (2002). Learning from ethnography: Reflections on the nature and efficacy of youth tours to Israel. In H. Goldberg, S. Heilman & B. Kirshenblatt-Gimblett, *The Israel Experience: Studies in Youth Travel and Jewish Identity* (pp. 267–331). Jerusalem: Studio Kavgraph. This is an ethnography of two youth trips (NFTY and Young Judea) from 1994 that presents a picture of the experience from the point of view of the participants as seen through the eyes of anthropologists. The author comments on the research, focusing on the nature of the experience and its impact on the participants.

Klein-Katz, S. (ed.) (2000). *The Ma Nishtana of Family Education Israel Trips*. Jerusalem: Melitz and Project Oren. A useful volume written as a handbook intended for anyone contemplating bringing family groups to Israel. It is the culmination of a two-year research and development project that included many pilot groups. In practical terms, it defines and lays out the elements of program planning, pre- and post-trip programming, staffing and more. It is available through Melitz in Jerusalem.

Olsen, D. and Timothy, D. (eds.) (2006). *Tourism, Religion & Spiritual Journeys*. UK: Routledge. A comprehensive assessment of the primary issues and concepts related to the intersection of tourism and religion, this revealing book gives a balanced discussion of both the theoretical and applied subjects that destination planners, religious organizations, scholars, and tourism service providers must deal with on a daily basis.

Saxe, L. et al. (2004). *Evaluating Birthright Israel: Longterm Impact and Recent Findings*. Waltham, MA: The Cohen Center for Modern Jewish Studies, Brandeis University. Since Birthright Israel's inception, the Cohen Center for Modern Jewish Studies has conducted a systematic evaluation of the program, in particular its impact on participants from the United States and Canada.

REFERENCES

Bloom, B. (ed.) (1984). *Taxonomy of Educational Objectives*. Book 1 Cognitive Domain. Reading, MA: Addison Wesley.

Chazan, B. (1992). "The Israel Trip as Jewish Education." *Agenda Jewish Education* 1 (1), 30–33.

Chazan, B. (1997). *What We Know About The Israel Experience*. New York: Israel Experience Inc.

Cohen, E. H. (2006). Excellence In Educational Youth Tourism: The Case of The Israel Experience Program. Paper delivered at the 24th EuroCHRIE (The Hospitality and Tourism Educators) Congress sponsored by The University of the Aegean, 25–28 October 2006.

Cohen, E. H. (2003). "Tourism and Religion. A Case Study: Visiting Students in Israeli Universities." *Journal of Travel Research*, 42 (1), 36–47.

Cohen, S. M. (1986). *Participation in Educational Programs in Israel: Their Decision to Join the Programs & Short-term Impact of Their Trips*. Jerusalem: Nativ Policy & Planning Consultants.

Cohen, S. M. & Wall, S. (1992). The good trip to Israel. In *The Israel Experience*. Jerusalem: CRB Foundation.

Gardner, H. (2000). *Intelligence Relearned: Multiple Intelligences for the 21st Century*. New York: Basic Books.

Gardner, H. (1993). *Frames of Mind: The Theory of the Multiple Intelligences*. New York: Basic Books.

Heschel, A. J. (1972). *The Insecurity of Freedom—Essays on Human Existence*. Philadelphia: Jewish Publication Society—"Textpeople," 237.

Hunter, M. (1979). "Teaching is Decision Making." *Journal of Educational Leadership* 37 (1), pp. 62–67.

Kelman, V. (1993). *Jewish Family Retreats: A Handbook*. New York and California: The Melton Research Center of the Jewish Theological Seminary of America and The Shirley and Arthur Whizin Institute for Jewish Family Life.

Maslow, A. (1962). *Toward a Psychology of Being*. New York: Van Nostrand.

Mittleberg, D. (1994). *The Israel Visit and Jewish Identification*. New York: Institute on American Jewish–Israeli Relations, American Jewish Committee.

Mittleberg, D. (1999). *The Israel Connection and American Jews*. Westport, CT: Praeger.

National Research Council (2000). *How People Learn: Brain, Mind, Experience and School*. Washington, DC: National Academy Press.

Wiggins, G. & McTighe, J. (2005). *Understanding by Design*. Alexandria, VA: The Association for Supervision and Curriculum Development.

Developments in Religious Education

John L. Elias

In the past few months scholars of religion have taken interest in the debate at Harvard University over the role of religion in the core curriculum for undergraduate students. Newspapers carried accounts that Harvard would require all undergraduate students to take a course entitled *Reason and Faith*. The course was proposed with the rationale that in today's world religious understanding was increasingly important for making sense of world events and in promoting religious understanding in a society where many religious faiths exist side by side. After a vigorous debate the Core Curriculum Committee decided to drop the requirement, pointing out that no stronger case could be made for religion than for many other aspects of society: class, race, gender, culture. However, a course on what it means to be human will be included in the core curriculum. This is a significant development, since what Harvard, does many others follow. What this debate suggests to all religious educators is that efforts by families and religious bodies have to be strengthened if we are to make religion an important aspect of individual behavior. In this context, learning what other religious groups do to educate their members becomes an even more pressing need.

Taking the book *Visions of Jewish Education* (Fox, Scheffler and Marom 1997) as a starting point, I will focus on developments in religious education among Christians as well as recent trends in school-based religious education in the English-speaking world that might be of interest to Jewish educators. This chapter will add to the impressive philosophical scholarship of the book and should influence discussions among all religious educators. The approaches to Jewish education revolve around the relative importance of classical texts, history and academic disciplines, and will present individual and social experiences and interests. I bring to this chapter over forty years of experience in religious education as a teacher of adults and youth, an administrator of religious education programs and a college and university teacher. I spent two years in Britain studying their systems of religious education where I taught and lectured at various universities and participated in meetings between Jewish and Christian educators.

TERMINOLOGY

The enterprise of education in religion is variously named among Christian educators. The oldest term, *Christian education*, has long been associated with Protestant theological orthodoxy or neo-orthodoxy, which places greatest emphasis on interpretations of classical Christian Scriptures. It is the term preferred today by evangelical Protestants. *Religious education* was introduced by liberal Protestant religious educators at the beginning of the twentieth century; in opposing the revivalist and emotional thrust of previous religious education, they established in 1903 the Religious Education Association, which has published the influential journal *Religious Education*. Among a large number of Roman Catholics, the preferred terminology is *Catechetics* (from the Greek *katecheo*, meaning echoing back responses), referring to education of believers by fellow believers. This term is widely used in official documents of the Roman Catholic Church and by Catholic religious educators throughout the world. Recently a hybrid term has been introduced, *Christian religious education*, that tries to establish an interdisciplinary field drawing not only on theological sources but also on the social sciences, especially educational theories (Groome 1999 [1980]; Astley 1994). The preferred term for English-speaking educators outside the United States where education in religion is part of the school curriculum is *religious education*.

NATURE OF THE ACADEMIC ENTERPRISE

Traditionally, the enterprise of religious education is viewed as a branch of *practical or pastoral theology*. In this viewpoint, Christian theology is the controlling discipline. Protestant seminaries organize their studies under biblical studies, doctrinal or systematic theology, church history and practical theology, which includes liturgy, pastoral care and counseling, social ministry, church administration and religious education. Catholics tend to use the language of pastoral theology, which focuses mainly on the role of priests as shepherds or leaders of their flock. Recently many efforts have been made to develop a more sophisticated understanding of practical theology (Browning 1996).

Some Christian educators have assigned a lesser role to theology and have preferred to describe the discipline as a social science discipline (Lee 1971) or a distinct interdisciplinary field in which theology is only one player (Moran 1994 [1971]). These draw primarily but not exclusively on philosophy, psychology, sociology, and anthropology.

THEORETICAL APPROACHES TO CHRISTIAN EDUCATION

It is not an easy task to identify and classify the various theoretical approaches to religious education among Christian writers. Sara Little (1993) has described the period since the mid-1960s as a time of critical reflection in Protestant religious education. One can add Catholic and Eastern Orthodox, which suggests that this is a time in which "there is no one clue, no dominant theory...but a spectrum of theories and divergent interests" (p. 20). Two leading Christian scholars have developed maps for the field of Christian religious education (Boys 1989; Seymour 1997).

There are four factors that are relevant in analyzing theoretical approaches to religious education, each of which is found in *Visions of Jewish Education* (Fox, Scheffler & Marom, 1997): the texts, history, experience of individuals and groups, and relevant academic disciplines. What attitude is taken toward the text, which may include the privileged Scriptures, tradition or later commentaries and writers? How is the history of the religious group to be mined for relevance to religious education? What role do human individual and social experience and needs play in the process of religious education? What academic disciplines are privileged in determining the meaning of human experience? Finally, what is the interrelationship among these factors?

ORTHODOX, DOCTRINAL AND NEO-ORTHODOX APPROACHES TO CHRISTIAN EDUCATION

Orthodox and Evangelical approaches privilege the text, which can be the Scriptures for evangelical Protestants, the doctrines of the Church for traditionalist Roman Catholics and early church writings for Eastern Orthodox Christians. Theology in these approaches is viewed as an ordered understanding of beliefs within a theological system. Criticism of the tradition itself is not usually an acceptable activity for theologians and educators who share this perspective.

Human experience in these approaches does not have significant internal theological meaning for these educators. Secular learning such as philosophy, psychology, and social sciences are valuable only in providing analogies for understanding the texts or systematic structures for understanding and structuring the texts. They may also be instrumental in providing a defense of religious truths.

The Protestant evangelical educator Kenneth O. Gangel (1978) outlines the basic principles of evangelical Christian education. It is committed to the authority of the Bible, which is considered contemporaneous in its understanding of the nature, source, discovery and dissemination of the truth. Christian education depends on a curriculum constructed on the centrality of the special revelation found in the Scriptures. A bibliocentric world view and life view is the ultimate end of Christian education.

In Roman Catholicism *a doctrinal approach* centering on the teachings of the church as found in catechisms has long been dominant. The texts are approved catechisms for adults and children that incorporate the Scriptures as interpreted by the church and the teachings of popes, church councils, and bishops. Today the *Catechism of the Catholic Church* (2003 [1992]) is the chief source for those committed to this approach. Memorization of important doctrinal statements is stressed, especially in the education of children. Individual and social experience enters the process as the starting point for understanding the doctrines or as the area to which the doctrines may be applied in real life. The academic disciplines of philosophy, psychology and sociology can be of service to a more effective catechizing in the faith by providing an understanding of human experience and help in determining methods of approach.

Eastern Orthodox Christian religious education privileges the text not only of the Scriptures, but also the teachings of the early councils of the church and the Christian writers of the first five centuries. Otherwise their approach to religious education is similar to the evangelical and doctrinal approaches described above. Anton Vrame (1999) has brought a high degree of sophistication to Orthodox Christian education by focusing on the use of icons to stimulate religious learning of Orthodox theology.

At the beginning of the 20th century Protestant and Catholic religious educators offered criticisms of these theoretical approaches on various grounds: lack of a critical approach to the sources, the dangers of mindless memorization, the authoritarianism entailed in the approach, unattractiveness of the question-and-answer approaches, too great reliance on obedience, and an unresponsiveness to the changes in the general culture.

After the liberal criticism of Protestant Orthodoxy and the education based on it (to be considered in the next section), Protestant theologians and educators developed *neo–Orthodox approaches* to theology and religious education. This is an effort to combine a liberal spirit with an Orthodox tradition as found in a revitalized biblical theology that harkened back to the work of the Apostle Paul, Augustine of Hippo, and Martin Luther. Rooted in the dominant theologies of Karl Barth, Rudolph Bultmann, and Paul Tillich, Protestant educators place a more sophisticated and complete interpretation of biblical revelation at the heart of education. They stress the kingdom of God as an otherworldly reality. The principal tenets of this approach are these: Individuals are to be confronted with the eternal gospel, respond to biblical revelation, view God as transcendent, recognize that one is justified by grace through faith, accept Jesus as the revelation and deed of God, face up to the tragic elements in human existence and live in hope for the end of times. These theologians and educators have attempted to balance the optimism of the liberal educators with awareness of human sinfulness (Elias 2002, 171–175).

Neo–Orthodox educators give a more prominent role to human experience and secular disciplines than do the earlier Orthodox and present-day evangelical educators. They are committed to scientific and historical methods of biblical criticism. They make substantial use of philosophy, psychology and the social sciences, which they subordinate to their biblical theology. However, they do charge liberals with largely abandoning theology for these secular disciplines.

A Roman Catholic form of neo–Orthodoxy appeared in the 1950s and 1960s in the form of a *kerygmatic* (meaning heralding, from the Greek for herald) theology and education. In this approach the primary text is not the doctrinal teachings of the church but a specific approach to the biblical literature, which was new for Roman Catholics when it was first introduced. *Kerygma* refers to proclaiming the central biblical teachings narrating the life, death and resurrection of Jesus in such a way that learners would be invited to respond in faith and works. This method thus moves beyond the traditional doctrinal approach utilized in schools and colleges, namely authoritative teaching of the church as presented through catechisms and textbooks.

This approach, which borrows heavily from Protestant and Catholic studies of the Christian Scriptures and liturgy, makes some use of the sciences of pedagogy and psychology, but the biblical message proclaimed in the texts of Scripture and celebrated in the liturgies of the church are central. New religion books that utilize this approach include stories, songs, prayers, and colorful pictures. The theology developed at the Second Vatican Council in the 1960s has lent authority to this approach. In the end, however, many voices have been raised to criticize not only its interpretation of the biblical literature but its failure to deal seriously with human individual and social experience.

The main criticisms of Orthodox approaches to religious education come from liberal religious educators. They charge that such theories do not have much to offer religious educators, since they do not deal adequately with human experience. They question whether or not such approaches actually enhance the religious lives of those involved with them. Liberals are also critical of neo–Orthodox approaches for not offering an adequate reevaluation and reconstruction of the theological tradition and its symbols. The lack of criticism of the tradition is also pointed out.

LIBERAL APPROACHES TO CHRISTIAN EDUCATION

Liberal theology and education developed among Protestants in this country at the very end of the 19th century and remained particularly strong for the first half of the 20th century. Liberal theologies and the educational approaches that relate to them tend to place greatest emphasis on individual and social experience. The liberal spirit is greatly committed to modern thought and especially to modern science. In addition, this spirit is more centered on human persons, views God in continuity with creation, emphasizes the ethical and social demands of religious calling and mission, and views the church as one of the many institutions that do good in the world. In many ways liberal theology is a child of the European Enlightenment. Liberal theology and education try to reconcile Christianity with the emerging modern world. It takes an evolutionary viewpoint on the world, accepts the application of modern historical methods to the study of the Bible and generally agrees with the positive assessment of human nature bequeathed by the Enlightenment. It elevates ethics over dogma and argues that Christians should work for a more just society.

With regard to Christian texts, theological liberals tend to give humanistic and social interpretations to many basic Christian teachings about humanity, salvation, Jesus Christ, ethics, the church, and Scriptures. Liberals stress those elements of the texts that promote a social Gospel, as seen in the classic works of George A. Coe (1917) and Sophia Fahs (1952), which subordinates the traditional goal of individual salvation to the broader aim of social reconstruction. Liberal educators are interested in the classic texts as expressions of religious experience and not as a definitive statement of eternal truths.

Individual and social experience is predominant in liberal religious education that allies itself with the progressive education movement, notably the work of John Dewey. It makes much of the disciplines of psychology and sociology and emphasizes learning through active experience, utilizing the interests of the learners, and forging a close connection between education and social change. Religious conversion as the goal of education always includes a commitment to the social reconstruction of society. Religious education is viewed as a process of creative discovery in which students deal with both their individual and social experiences. The content of religious education follows from the lives and experiences of students. Religious education has as its purpose the fostering of creativity, freedom, and discovery. Liberal educators tend to place emphasis on the present and future, not the past.

Liberal religious educators today differ from the 20th-century liberals in being less optimistic about the direction of society and less confident in the power of education to bring about social reconstruction. The liberal spirit in religious education found expression in Roman Catholicism in the work of Gabriel Moran. Moran began his career as a critic of the neo–Orthodox *kerygmatic* approach in his highly influential *Theology of Revelation* (1966a) and *Catechesis of Revelation* (1966b), which constituted his doctoral dissertation. In many writings since the early 1970s he has made a valiant effort to establish a broadly ecumenical field of religious education utilizing a penetration analysis of language, concepts, assumptions, and arguments situated at the intersection of religion, culture, and education (1979; 1981; 1997). It appears that Moran is the Christian educator who would be most appealing to Jewish educators because of his broadly ecumenical approach and his efforts to explicitly include Jewish education within his overall vision.

Like other approaches, these liberal approaches have their critics. They are criticized for their lack of attention to the religious tradition or for a selective reading of the tradition that fits their preconceived worldview. While orthodox approaches are charged with absolutizing the tradition, liberal approaches are criticized with absolutizing the situation. Many critics charge that liberal educators and theologians have so accommodated themselves to modernity that they have emptied the Christian faith of essential elements.

CRITICAL DIALOGICAL OR CO-RELATIONAL APPROACHES

In recent years attempts have been made by Christian theologians and educators to deal with both texts and human experience in a critical manner. These efforts include both a critical revision of the beliefs, values and faith of an authentic Christianity and a similar criticism of secular experience. These approaches attempt a critical correlation of Christian texts with the experience of individuals, with the ultimate goal being a decision to have one's actions in the world shaped by one's religious faith. These approaches come closer to the discipline of practical theology as described by Browning (1996).

The most influential proponent of this theoretical approach is Thomas Groome (1980; 1993), who has developed a sophisticated theory and practice for Christian education that emphasizes critical self-reflection. The theoretical basis for this approach lies in the critical social theory of Jurgen Habermas and the pedagogy of the oppressed of Paulo Freire. Groome's approach, called Shared Praxis, has five steps: (1) Individuals name their present action by reflecting on present events as well as the difference between what is and what should be; (2) participants share their stories and visions relating to present actions; (3) participants probe Christian texts (stories, sayings, traditions, etc.) that have a bearing on the chosen present events and experiences; (4) participants engage in a dialogue between their own stories and experiences and the Christian texts; (5) participants make decisions about what they should do to close the gap between their own experiences and the demands of the Christian texts.

The Shared Praxis model follows the lead of critical theory and critical theology in providing for criticism both of participants' experience and the texts or tradition. The Christian texts provide a criticism of participants' stories and a guide to future action. However, individuals' experiences and stories can critique the Christian texts and perhaps even lead to their revision. Thus this approach is called revisionist, since it is open to the possibility that interpretations of both texts and experiences may have to be revised as the result of educational processes. Mary Elizabeth Moore (1983; 1998) has proposed a similar model for religious education, which she calls "traditioning."

Underlying the critical approach to Christian religious education is the belief that neither the religious tradition nor any particular interpretation of human experience can be absolutized. True theological understanding must attend to the interconnection among the various spheres of human existence: personal, interpersonal, and political. People also have to come to some understanding of the normativeness of the tradition for their religious lives.

While one can see the value of correlational approaches for the theological education of clergy and educated adults, one can question whether these approaches are appropriate for church education. Also, does such an approach offer the opportunity for the ordered learning that is often lacking in religious education (Farley 1985)?

APPROACHES TO NON-CHURCH OR SCHOOL-BASED RELIGIOUS EDUCATION

For the past sixty years there have been debates in many European countries about approaches to teaching religion in state schools. It is interesting to note that such a debate is now taking place in countries that once were under the influence of the Soviet Union (Filipsone 2005). Until the sixties a confessional approach was predominant in countries in which Christianity was taught in the schools. The confessional approach to teaching Christianity was even enshrined in the 1943 law in Britain. As Britain and other countries became clearly multi-faith and multi-cultural, criticisms of the confessional approaches have given way to a number of other approaches that have been analyzed by Michael Grimmitt (2000) of Birmingham University, England.

LEARNING RELIGION—THE CONFESSIONAL APPROACH

In the confessional approach teachers and students are believers in the same religious faith. This is contrasted to teaching about religion. In this faith-based education, religion is taught from the inside, believer to believers. The stated purpose of learning religion is that students become believers or become more intelligent and committed believers. This situation exists in nations where there is a single dominant religious faith. Such was the situation in the United States until the mid-19th century when a generalized Protestantism was taught in the common schools of this country. The growing number of Catholic and Jewish immigrants in the second half of the century led to the virtual exclusion of religion from the curriculum and life of public schools. Today most Christians adhere to the confessional approach in schools that they sponsor at the elementary and secondary levels and in seminaries. At the college and university level the predominant approach is an objective study of religion.

Learning religion is especially valuable for a nation that has a strong anti-religious secular movement. When such a society becomes multicultural and multi-faith, the teaching of a single religion in schools meets serious challenges, as has happened in many European countries. One of two things usually occurs in such societies. Learning religion may be abandoned in the public or state schools of the nation, or parallel instruction may be given by teachers of particular religious faiths to members of their faith. Neither situation is desirable. In the first scenario students are denied any systematic education in religion, an important part of every culture. In the second students are denied a broad education in the various religions of the nation.

LEARNING ABOUT RELIGION

Religion can also be taught from the outside, as is permitted in public schools in the United States and other countries where the Bible can be taught as literature, not as a book of faith. Courses are also offered in comparative religions based on history or anthropology. At the college and university level such courses comprise religious studies. The approach to such teaching is descriptive and often historical. No effort is made to advocate any particular religion. Religion is thus taught like any other subject in the curriculum.

There is value in this approach to religious education, though it clearly does not satisfy the desires of many parents and leaders of religious bodies. Knowledge of various religions is a good in itself. Besides, it may alleviate prejudices against particular religions and promote a spirit of tolerance. Students may overcome uncritical beliefs about religious faith and eliminate some stereotypes. Learning about religion in schools where children come from different religious backgrounds or none at all may foster critical understanding and spill over into relationships among students.

The movement for teaching about religion in public schools in the United States is still a comparatively small one in comparison to the situation in other countries. Though the journal *Religion and Education* has kept this issue alive, most school districts try to steer clear of dealing with religion in the curriculum even though constitutionally it is legal to teach *about* religion. Small units on religion are found in social studies books. Courses in literature often contain religious literature.

The English experience presents another approach to teaching about religion; the phenomenological approach has been adopted by the city of Birmingham, with its large population of immigrants. Phenomenology describes the ways in which humans come to know and assumes that meaning, knowledge and truth depend on one's experience of the world. In studying religion phenomenologically, focus is placed on individuals' experience of symbols, ideals, buildings, and events. According to this approach, religion is taught neither to foster any particular religion nor to engender a critical understanding of religion. Rather, religion is taught in the context of secular ideologies by making comparisons and contrasts among various religious traditions and non-religious alternatives such as humanism and communism. Each religion is taught in a spirit of appreciation and inquiry. In this approach religion is taught from the outside with the purpose that students acquire an understanding of religious beliefs and thus be literate in the language of religion.

LEARNING FROM RELIGION

Some educators in Britain, unhappy with previously described alternatives, have proposed an approach where students will learn from religion (Grimmitt 2000). In this approach students are expected to participate in the beliefs and practices of the religion being taught. The focus in this approach is not so much on the religious content but on the life world of the students. This educational approach has as its principal objective the full human development of students by making a contribution to their moral and spiritual development.

From the perspective of the United States, it is interesting to note efforts in Britain and European countries to make the case for religious education in publicly funded state schools. It is almost impossible in a multi-faith society to make the case that the state should fund a confessional form of religious education. It is easier to justify teaching about religion, since religion can be a subject of study as valid as other subjects in the curriculum. In the United States, religious studies abound in publicly funded state colleges and universities and to a much lesser degree in public schools. It is clearly difficult to make the case for an approach in which students learn from religion. This form of religious education might be justified by the promotion of toleration for persons of other religious faiths and cultures. However, both parents and leaders of religious bodies might object to an approach that encourages children and young people to participate in any meaningful way in the religious practices and beliefs of religions not their own.

CONCLUSION

This is only a brief summary of developments in Christian education and in religious education in state schools in English-speaking countries. I cannot judge what Jewish educators might find instructive in this survey. One can really only know a religion and its activities from the inside. Over the years I have benefited greatly by reading such Jewish educators as Eugene Borowitz, Joseph Lukinsky, Hanan Alexander, Jack Spiro, Michael Rosenak, and Israel Scheffler. Many of these writers have shown a keen interest in and knowledge of religious education outside of Judaism. My presumption is that they have benefited from this knowledge.

I believe that it is true that we learn about ourselves and our endeavors by learning something about others and their endeavors. Religious education has been a large part of the life of Christian communities. Various approaches have been developed over the years. Jewish educators deal with many of these same issues and also have concerns that neither Christian educators nor state school religious educators face. Religious education is handing on a tradition in fidelity to classical expressions and contemporary understanding. Classic texts and authors, history of tradition, individual and social experience and academic disciplines all play their roles in the determination of aims and objectives, content and methods. Knowledge of how others have dealt with and continue to deal with these factors can have potential for broadening both theoretical perspectives and practical endeavors.

IMPLICATIONS

Jewish educators should be aware of the differences in terminology used among Christian educators. Often these distinguish Protestant, Catholic and Orthodox Christian educators. Terminology often reflects progressive or liberal theological positions as well.

Religious education among Christians is both a field of practice and an academic discipline. Some Christian educators have the academy as their primary focus; other have church bodies, while still others address the concerns of the wider public.

There are three major theoretical approaches to Christian religious education based on theological perspectives. The first group, orthodox or neo–Orthodox, places primary emphasis on chosen texts, either those of the first Christian Scriptures or writings from later periods in Christian church history. Liberal approaches place greater emphasis on the value of the human individual or social experience. Revisionist or critical approaches tend to correlate the data from texts and writings with individual and social experience in a mutually corrective manner.

Christian religious education as a school subject takes place in school settings throughout the world. At one time the curriculum was exclusively *learning religion*—in fact, the Christian religion. In the last forty years other approaches have emerged. Students *learn about religion,* which entails an objective study of various religions of the world. A most recent approach, pioneered in England by Grimmit (2000), is *learning from religion* by exposure to texts and practices of various religions and even secular alternatives.

ADDITIONAL RESEARCH QUESTIONS

- Research on the effectiveness of various approaches
- Research on the lasting influence of religious education
- Effective preparation of teachers and materials

FUTURE DIRECTIONS

- Explorations of methods besides classroom religious education
- Use of online learning in religious education
- Exploration of efforts in inter-religious religious education

ANNOTATED BIBLIOGRAPHY

Astley, J. (1994). *Philosophy of Christian Religious Education*. Birmingham, AL: Religious Education Press. This book, written by an Anglican priest, is the most thorough treatment of the philosophy of religious education. It reflects the British situation, where religious education is both a school subject and a church enterprise.

Groome, T. H. (1999 [1980]). *Christian Religious Education*. San Francisco: Jossey-Bass. Groome's book is the most sophisticated attempt at grounding an interdisciplinary approach to religious education. For twenty-five years this professor at Boston College has influenced professors and curriculum writers in Christian education.

Moran, G. (1981). *Interplay: A Theory of Religion and Education*. Winona, KS: St. Mary's Press.

Moran, G. (1997). *Showing How: The Act of Teaching*. Harrisburg, PA: Trinity Press International. Gabriel Moral, a professor for many years at New York University, has made a valiant attempt to develop an ecumenical approach to religious education. He manifests a deep appreciation for all religious traditions. His sensitivity to the use of language gives his work a precision not otherwise found in this field.

REFERENCES

Astley, J. (1994). *Philosophy of Christian Religious Education*. Birmingham, AL: Religious Education Press.

Boys, M. (1989). *Educating in Faith: Maps and Visions*. San Francisco: Harper and Row.

Browning, D. (1996). *A Fundamental Practical Theology*. Minneapolis, MN: Augsburg Fortress.

Catechism of the Catholic Church. 2003 [1995]. New York: Doubleday.

Coe, G. (1917). *A Social Theory of Religious Education*. New York: Scribner.

Elias, J L. (2002) *A History of Christian Education: Protestant, Catholic, and Orthodox Perspectives*. Malabar, FL: Krieger Publishing Co.

Fahs, S. L. (1952). *Today's Children and Yesterday's Heritage*. Boston: Beacon Press.

Farley, E. (1985). Can Church Education Be Theological Education? http://theologytoday.ptsem.edu/jul1985/v42-2-article1.htm

Filipsone, A. (2005). "Time of Uncertain Conversations: Religious Education in Public Schools of the Post-Soviet Latvia." *Religious Education* 100, (1), 52–66.

Fox, S., Scheffler, I. & Marom, D. (eds.) (2003). *Visions of Jewish Education*. New York: Cambridge University Press.

Gangel, K. (1978). "Christian Higher Education at the End of the Twentieth Century." *Bibliotheca Sacra*, 100–105.

Grimmitt, M. (2000). Contemporary Pedagogies of Religious Education: What Are They? In Michael Grimmitt, ed., *Pedagogies of Religious Education*. Great Wakering, England: McCrimmons.

Groome, T. H. (1999 [1980]). *Christian Religious Education*. San Francisco: Jossey-Bass.

Groome, T. H. (1993). *Sharing the Faith*. San Francisco: Harper.

Lee, J. M. (1971). *The Shape of Religious Education: A Social Science Approach*. Birmingham, AL: Religious Education Press.

Little, S. (1993). "The Clue to Religious Education." *Union Seminary Quarterly Review* 47, 7–21.

Moore, M. E. (1983). *Education for Continuity and Change: A New Approach for Christian Religious Education.* Nashville, TN: Abingdon Press.

Moore, M. E. (1998). *Teaching from the Heart: Theology and Educational Method.* Harrisburg, PA: Trinity Press International.

Moran, G. (1966a). *Theology of Revelation.* New York: Herder and Herder.

Moran, G. (1966b). *Catechesis of Revelation.* New York: Herder and Herder.

Moran, G. (1994 [1970]). *Design for Religion.* New York: Hyperion Books.

Moran, G. (1981). *Interplay: A Theory of Religion and Education.* Winona, KS: St. Mary's Press.

Moran, G. (1997). *Showing How: The Act of Teaching.* Harrisburg, PA: Trinity Press International.

Seymour, J. L. (1997). *Mapping Christian Education.* Nashville, TN: Abingdon Press.

Vrame, A. C. (1999). *The Educating Icon: Teaching Wisdom and Holiness in the Orthodox Way.* Brookline, MA: Holy Cross Orthodox Press.

Planning and Change

Informed and Passionate Dialogue: Transformative Community Change Initiatives

Patricia Bidol Padva

...and teach the people of Israel so that they may discuss, inquire and learn, becoming suf-ficiently knowledgeable to teach, in their own words, to others—ensuring that the chain of Jewish education will always continue (Deuteronomy 31:19).

The ultimate goal of Jewish education is to engage youth, families and adults in a pursuit of lifelong Jewish learning and affiliation with the community (Aron et al. 1995; Cohen 2006). In the Western world, the engagement of Jewish individuals in lifelong learning is a daunting task. Jewish individuals are able to participate freely in their country's educational, economic and social institutions with or without acknowledging either their individual Jewish identities or connections to a broader Jewish community (Sarna 2004; Padva 1991). The challenge is to create Jewish learning experiences that provide individuals and families with the breadth and depth of learning to enable them to live as Jews (Wertheimer 2007).

The dissemination of *A Time to Act* (Commission on Jewish Education of North America 1991), along with the 1990 National Jewish Population Study, influenced many federations to create "Commissions on Jewish Continuity". Most of these continuity commissions decided that their communities needed to provide quality formal and informal educational options. It was perceived that the net result of these educational experiences would be an increase in the number of individuals and families engaging in lifelong Jewish education. As a result, educational change projects in formal and informal Jewish education were funded.

The new educational options were not just an improvement in the status quo but were designed to create transitional change. A transitional change is a carefully designed "new way of doing" something that is different from what currently exists. The new educational options were carefully planned and implemented to be of high quality and to be aligned with the learning needs of individuals and families. They were not just a fine-tuning of existing options. They included both formal and informal educational options that often resulted in a temporary increase of involvement by those who participated in them. In most cases, the organization that was providing these new educational options did not perceive that they needed to change as part of the process.

Educational practitioners, researchers, professional leadership and lay leadership continue to perceive that transitional changes that result in incremental change in curriculum design are not resulting in a sustainable and significant increase in the number of Jews who choose to live a meaningful Jewish life. To achieve this result, it is essential to transform the quality of Jewish education and the entire educational system (Flexner 2000; Sarna 2004). Transformational change is "the fundamental shift from one state of being to another...a change so significant that it requires the organization to shift its culture and people's behavior and mindset to implement it successfully" (Ackerman & Anderson 2001, p. 4). If Jewish education is to deliver quality learning options that "link the silos" (Wertheimer 2005) between formal and informal education, there is a need for a compelling community-wide vision for Jewish education and a commitment to provide the resources needed to achieve it (Fox et al. 2003).

A community-wide Jewish educational vision that evokes excitement and commitment must be based on a consensus that is fashioned not just by the community's *machers* (leaders) but also by the diverse stakeholders that would be impacted by it (Bunker & Alban 2006; Susskind et al. 1999). In the last decade the leaders of many Jewish educational change initiatives have understood the need to provide meaningful opportunities for community participation to shape new educational directives. In *A Report of the Miami Commission on Jewish Continuity* (1994) the decision to create an effective instrument of change led the Commission to recognize

> the need to be inclusive of a wide range of viewpoints since solutions to the challenges of Jewish continuity are the responsibility of all parts of the Jewish community. As it was from its inception, the Commission has not been the voice of the Federation, the synagogues or any single element of the community, but a Commission of the entire Jewish community. While the Federation has provided financial and staff resources, others brought different perspectives, issues and resources to the community process.

Transformative change can only occur if the stakeholders who are impacted by and those who can implement the change jointly work together to create a compelling vision and execute it. Transformative change is systemic and affects the larger learning environment. *Recent Trends in Supplementary Jewish Education*, (Wertheimer 2007, p. 11) describes why improvement in synagogue education needs to be systemic change:

> Still another strategic question is whether the key effort for improvement should be directed toward the classroom or toward the larger learning environment. Systemic or holistic initiatives assume that such changes will have a limited impact, absent a sustained effort at organizational restructuring that gives power to a wide spectrum of so-called "stake-holders" and which opens the process of decision-making to transparency, mission-directed planning, and democratization. More broadly, the systemic approach looks beyond single programs to the mix of educational opportunities available to children and their families, and tries to create a synagogue-wide transformation, connecting the school to early childhood, teen experiences, adult education and family education. It seeks linkages, rather than strengthening the school in isolation from other educational venues.

This chapter will present an overview of transformative community change models and processes, how to create and implement transformative initiatives, the impact of transformative community change initiatives on the achievement of outcomes for Jewish education and implications of transformative change approaches for education, change and research. It reflects my perspectives as a seasoned scholar-practitioner with decades of international experience in all aspects of organizational and community change in Jewish and non–Jewish educational systems.

CHARACTERISTICS OF TRANSFORMATIONAL COMMUNITY INITIATIVES

> One cannot solve a problem from the same consciousness that created it.
>
> Albert Einstein

Systemic community change initiatives for Jewish education that compel stakeholders to create, implement and sustain a fundamental shift in the vision, mindsets, culture and protocols of the sponsoring organization (e.g., synagogue, school, JCC) and of the formal and informal educational options are transformational change efforts. They require a different way of thinking and engagement than other forms of educational change initiatives that fall under two other distinct headings: developmental and transitional (Ackerman & Anderson 2001; Cummings & Worley 2005). Most of the current examples of successful Jewish educational change projects have resulted in either developmental or transitional change. If the desire is to create transformative change, it is important to know the differences between three types of change approaches.

The focus of developmental change is an improvement in a specified area such as an existing curriculum. It is a fine-tuning of the status quo. The focus of a transitional change is a redesign of an organizational system, process, structure or work practices such as the redesign of the content and teaching style for an educational program. These types of projects are implemented by creating a strategic plan or a project plan that has specified tasks and timelines that ensure the achievement of incremental changes. Developmental and transitional change projects result in valuable improvements in specific aspects of Jewish education.

However, these types of educational changes, of and by themselves, do not result in sustainable changes to the community's total educational system. Only a transformational process will enable the system as a whole and its formal and informal educational components to create sustainable and deep-seated improvement in the quality of their educational options (Fullan 2005). An example of an educational transitional change project would be a program that provided excellent short-term professional development for existing educators but did not create a culture of excellence and the resources needed to sustain ongoing quality professional growth. Transformative change initiatives can be designed to systemically change education within an organization (e.g., a day school) or at community levels (e.g., a network of institutions or all of the day schools in a community or all of the stakeholders in the community).

The focus of transformational change in Jewish education is the creation of a powerful vision and the deep-seated reshaping of the mindset, values and behavior of professional and lay leaders about how Jewish education functions and how it relates to Jewish affiliation and lifelong learning. In other words, the entire nature of Jewish education is fundamentally changed. An example of this reshaping would be that the leaders understand that early childhood programs are not "babysitting" but are part of the educational continuum from early childhood through the teen years. It would also include an understanding that there is a need to reshape both early childhood educational programs and their interface with other formal and informal educational programs. This shift would include the acknowledgment that the culture of employment and *kavod* for early childhood educators should be the same as for day school educators, including the provision for quality professional development, salaries and benefits.

Transformation only occurs if a new reality for the substantive issues and stakeholder engagement is created. Due to the uncertainty and chaos that must occur to create a new reality, it is possible to know the desired outcomes but not exactly how to achieve them. Transformations create strong responses in those who are undergoing them. Since transformational change creates deep-seated shifts in the system's substantive matters and community change, it cannot be implemented by following a strategic implementation plan that identifies the exact sequence of action steps. Rather, transformative change processes must respond to emerging challenges and opportunities with carefully thought-out course corrections for both the action goals and implementation steps (Ackerman & Anderson 2001). Transformative change often seems to be chaotic and unpredictable. Through a conscious use of transformation principles such as building the transformative change strategy, roles for leading and implementing the strategy, course correction protocols and communication processes (Ackerman & Anderson 2001; Wheatley 1999), the chaos will be effectively addressed.

In order for a change in Jewish education to be transformative, the key stakeholders who share a common interest in the quality of Jewish education and the Jewish communal system will create a new vision based upon their jointly changing their mindsets, values and behaviors. In effect, these key stakeholders become partners in creating and implementing the change process. Depending on the nature or type of entity that is being changed, the key partners must represent the broad range of interests involved in the organization or community. Change processes are designed to enable existing and emerging parties to engage in "interactive think tank" opportunities to help shape a new vision, desired outcomes and implementation steps, all grounded within a system of Jewish values and wisdom.

CREATING AND IMPLEMENTING TRANSFORMATIVE COMMUNITY CHANGE INITIATIVES

Transformational change initiatives, whether in Jewish education or other areas of Jewish communal activity, must address three factors: 1) substantive areas to be changed (e.g., curriculum, organizational design, staffing patterns); 2) people (mindset, behaviors and cultural changes required to achieve the desired substantive changes); and 3) process (actions used to plan, design, implement and evaluate the substantive and people changes). These factors interweave with each other to create a set of concepts and approaches that mobilize organizations and the community and fit into the following categories: a Transformative Change Formula, a Change Process Model and Mobilizing Community Partners.

TRANSFORMATIVE CHANGE FORMULA

A transformative change formula illustrates what must be considered to effect real change in individuals, organizations and communities. The following DVF change formula is a version of the work of Richard Beckhard (Beckhard & Harris 1987). It was modified by Kathleen Dannemiller (Whole-Scale Change 2000) when she developed her Whole Scale Change. This transformative change approach is widely used to align the actions among hundreds of people to create powerful and successful processes for change (Holman et al. 2007).

The premises underlying the components of the DVF change formula are based on proven organizational change theories and approaches that are used in transformative change initiatives (Cummings & Worley 2005). The change formula is composed of the following four elements that describe the conditions necessary for a paradigm shift that supports the creation of a new reality.

$$D \times V \times F > R$$

(Dissatisfaction x Vision x First Steps > Resistance)

The first step in creating sustainable change is for individuals and the organization(s) to create dissatisfaction (D) with the current reality. The case for change can show that the current reality does not support the achievement of desired substantive change (i.e., educational change) or increase change competencies (capacity of community to implement the change initiative). The dissatisfaction with the current reality could be that youth do not continue with Jewish education after becoming bar/bat mitzvah.

The change partners use consensus decision-making tools to create a shared Case for Change database. It is essential that the data be gathered in a manner that allows in-depth dialogue to occur. The dialogue enables those who are creating the Case for Change to understand and appreciate each other's needs, interests and perspectives. It enables them to create a shared database that everyone accepts as the current reality and the reason why a transformative change is needed. These data can be gathered by means such as surveys, focus groups or trend analyses.

The second step in creating sustainable change is the creation of a consensus-based vision (V) that expresses a common yearning for the desired future state. The initial vision is often created by those who are sponsoring the change initiative. The sponsors are dissatisfied with the current reality and perceive that there is a need for a transformative change. In order to implement a transformative change, those who initially perceive the need for change need to reach out and engage other stakeholders in a joint exploration of the current reality and the creation of a future vision. As the change process unfolds, the vision needs to be jointly refined by those who initiated the change and those who are joining the effort.

After the dissatisfaction is identified and the initial vision is created, the change partners create the first (F) action steps to help the organization or community begin to actualize the vision. The outcomes from an effective transitional change project may be used as a foundation for some of the transformational initiative's s first steps. If any of the three forces (D or V or F) are not present, or if the combined presence of all three is low, the proposed change will not be able to overcome the resistance (R) that naturally arises during change efforts.

Resistance to change is normal and can occur at organizational, group, and individual levels. Resistance is an individual or sub-group's feeling that the proposed change is not what should be happening for them or for their organization. In transformational change, the change leaders use consensus-building approaches to understand what is causing the resistance and what purpose it is serving. When consensus-based thinking and decision-making tools are used, the commonalities between the individuals, organizations and members of the community are usually expanded without any part having to deny its core values and needs. The use of consensus approaches often results in changing the resistance into a shared commitment to the joint initiative. The change in perceptions that results in the parties working together to achieve the transformation is a paradigm shift, which is a new way of seeing the world that enables the change participants to "take the actions that that will begin to transform their shared vision into their shared reality" (Dannemiller Tyson Associates 2000).

To create the consensus conditions described in the Change Formula (D x V x F > R), a Change Process model is used to design the responses to the elements of the change formula.

CHANGE PROCESS MODELS

A change process model contains sequential phases that guide the creation, implementation and evaluation of a transformative community change initiative. Each of the phases has action steps that address the community change with substantive tasks. There are many change models being used to change Jewish education (Shevitz 1995; Woocher 1995; Ackerman & Anderson 2001; Fullan 2005).

A change process model provides change activists with the opportunity to understand why they want a change and to experience a deep-seated change in their mindset, values and behaviors. All transformative change process models include ways to address factors such as how to support inclusive engagement, enhance commitment, create consensus-based relationships and create supportive changes in mindset, values, behavior. The substantive tasks include ways to address factors such as how to create innovative and pragmatic systemic changes in structures, systems, processes or technology (Ackerman & Anderson 2001). These change models are implemented using consensus-based system thinking tools and deep dialogue approaches that include informed and passionate dialogue with advocating for one's views and a genuine inquiry into the views of others.

Transformational change process models (Ackerman & Anderson 2001; Fullan, M. 2001) have phases that are presented in a sequential manner that are similar to those found in traditional strategic planning. Change process strategies need to be carefully customized so they are aligned with the community's characteristics, the needs of the parties and the nature of the substantive issues and the desired outcomes. Transformative change process models can also be used with transitional change projects that involve several issues and impact several parties, especially those that are likely to support future transformative changes.

SIX-STAGE CHANGE PROCESS MODEL

One example of a transformative change process model that has been used to transform Jewish education is the Six-Stage Change Process Model. Project *Kavod*: Improving the Culture of Employment for Jewish Educators (Schaap et al. 2007) was created and implemented using this model. It is similar to other change process models (Dannemiller Tyson Associates 2000; Kotter 1996; Lippitt 1958; Nevis et al. 1996; Ackerman & Anderson 2001) that are used to create institutional and community systemic changes.

The Six-Stage Change Model and specific tools to implement it are in a manual that is on the website of The Coalition for the Advancement of Jewish Education (www.CAJE.org). Although the model's first stage must be the initial phase, the remaining stages are not always implemented in a linear fashion. In order to respond to emerging challenges and opportunities, the implementation of the stages is done in a fluid manner with a lot of back-and-forth movement between the stages. Earlier stages are re-addressed as the change partners grow in their understanding of the substantive issues related to the achievement of the initiative's desired outcomes. The six stages and the main actions that are included in each stage follow.

STAGE ONE: DECIDE TO ACT

During the first stage the initiative's formal leaders create the foundation that is necessary to successfully launch the change processes. The major tasks at this stage are:

- Identify the Case for Change by studying key internal and external indicators regarding the current reality of a given substantive condition (e.g., Jewish education).
- Create a team of change leaders (lay, staff and consultants). The change leaders need to understand that by launching a transformative change they will be creating a new reality for both the substantive issue and how it is delivered (e.g., creating a new culture of employment for early childhood Jewish educators). The team needs to include one or more members who are experts in transformative organizational and community change.
- Create an initial vision, guiding principles and desired initial outcomes for substantive issues and stakeholder engagement.
- Garner the resources needed for the initiative's change processes.

STAGE TWO: CREATE PARTNERSHIPS

In stage two the initiative's formal leaders share the case for change and the initial desired outcomes. Depending on the change initiative, the formal leaders could be a planning committee or a larger group of stakeholders. The major tasks to be accomplished are:

- Identify and activate an inclusive network of dedicated partners. Key stakeholders, organizational and individual, are contacted and asked to join in the initiative's consensus-decision making change mechanisms (e.g., task forces, project sites and study circles).
- Develop a common knowledge base and refined Case for Change that provide compelling data for motivating the change. Assessment processes are created to update the Case for Change or gather data in a more systemic manner (i.e., administering a Culture of Employment Survey to the community early childhood Jewish educators).
- Refine the vision through consensus-based system thinking and deep dialogue among the key stakeholders.
- Create a customized change process model.
- Acknowledge the needs of all partners.

STAGE THREE: DESIGN THE INITIAL DESIRED STATE

In the third stage the initiative's desired outcomes and vision are used to identify the actual future state that will be created. The design work is done using consensus-based decision-making approaches. The active engagement of the initiative's participants increases support for the desired outcomes. The major tasks are:

- Create an expanded shared purpose, values, final vision, and commitment to the achievement of the initiative's desired outcomes.
- Assess the current reality of the substantive issues and the success of the community change efforts.
- Create action recommendations and incorporate them into an adaptive strategic plan that is fluid enough to respond to key emerging challenges and opportunities.

STAGE FOUR: MOBILIZE THE ORGANIZATIONS AND/OR THE COMMUNITY

In the fourth stage the desired outcomes, case for change, vision and action recommendations are shared with the larger community in order to mobilize boarder support for the desired outcomes. The major tasks to be accomplished are:

- Identify and engage key community stakeholders (at organizational and/or community levels) so that they understand the need to achieve the desired outcomes.
- Identify potential funders (federation, foundations, grants and organizational).

- Garner feedback from the initiative's core participants and other impacted parties on how to enrich the proposed action recommendations and the partnership network.

STAGE FIVE: IMPLEMENT THE CHANGE

In the fifth stage the implementation plan is activated and carefully monitored. Modifications in the plan and its implementation are made to ensure that the desired outcomes are achieved and that the project continues to receive support from the community and/or stakeholders. Since transformation creates a qualitative difference in the outcomes projected and expected, the response of the community must be carefully addressed. The major tasks are:

- Create short-term gains by implementing the recommendations at a pilot site or by focusing on a few action goals.
- Assess the impact of the implementation and refine as needed.
- Use the success of the initial action steps to create more substantive changes and increase the participants' change competencies.

STAGE SIX: LEARN, MODIFY AND SUSTAIN THE CHANGE

In the sixth stage, continue to learn and reflect on the impacts of the change process in order to create course modifications. This will sustain the initiative's efforts to fully achieve the substantive changes and increase the change competencies. The major tasks include:

- Establish a system to continuously improve and sustain the initiative.
- Identify the cumulative impact of the change, including direct and indirect impacts, in order to continuously improve implementation process.
- Acknowledge and celebrate the short-term and long-term outcomes.

In summary, the use of a robust change model enables the partners to achieve their desired outcomes by connecting multiple current realties into a common case for change, creating a compelling vision and desired outcomes, and designing a mutually acceptable implementation plan.

MOBILIZING AND ORGANIZING COMMUNITY PARTNERS

Transformational change requires that the parties who have a direct impact on the achievement of the desired outcomes be mobilized during the creation and implementation of the vision, desired outcomes and implementation process. Community change initiatives have a continuum of participation levels that range from informing and educating to listening to the community to engaging in joint decision-making to creating consensus agreements (Creighton 2005). Each includes a set of core values that govern the creation and implementation of the engagement approaches. Although there is an inclusive engagement of stakeholders, the sponsoring entities of educational change (e.g., a school system, a synagogue, a federation or central agencies for Jewish education) retain the ultimate decision-making authority (Creighton 2005).

The core values and principles used for the mobilization of stakeholders in Jewish educational change are similar to those used in public sector education and community change. The International Association for Public Participation (IAPP 2000) was created to protect the integrity of public participation processes. With extensive international input, IAPP established the following core values that are aligned with the engagement needs of transformative change:

1. The pubic should have a say in decisions about actions that could affect their lives.
2. Public participation includes the promise that the public's contribution will influence the decision.
3. Public participation promotes sustainable decisions by recognizing and communicating the needs and interests of all participants, including decision-makers.
4. Public participation seeks out and facilitates the involvement of those potentially affected by or interested in a decision.
5. Public participation seeks input from participants in designing how they participate.

6. Public participation provides participants with the information they need to participate in a meaningful way.

7. Public participation communicates to participants how their input affected the decision.

TRANSFORMATIVE JEWISH EDUCATION CHANGE INITIATIVES

If you will it, it is no dream. Theodor Herzl

Transformational change initiatives for Jewish education are increasing in their number and their impact on formal and informal Jewish education. Several notable transformative initiatives are the Experiment in Congregational Education; Project Kavod: Improving the Culture of Employment in Jewish Early Childhood Education; La'atid: Synagogues for the Future; and Synagogue Transformation and Renewal (Issacs 2005).

An overview of two of the transformative change initiatives, La'atid and Project Kavod, will permit a more in-depth examination of the impacts of a transformative change initiative on the achievement of substantive changes and an increase in change competencies (capacity of community to change education). The description of the two cases is presented using excerpts (in italics) drawn from the executive summaries of the final reports. The descriptions of the two cases illustrate how each project used transformative change best practices to create a customized change approach that resulted in substantive Jewish education changes and enhanced the change competencies of those who participated in the initiative. The next section will present the implications and policy directions that have been drawn from these two cases and the research literature on community educational change initiatives.

LA'ATID: SYNAGOGUES FOR THE FUTURE'S EXECUTIVE SUMMARY

La'atid: Synagogues for the Future (Issacs, 2005) is the community-based initiative that was launched in 2000 by the Commission on Jewish Education of the Jewish Federation of Greater Hartford to help the community's congregations nurture a strong sense of Jewish identity, increase Jewish knowledge and enrich Jewish living in their constituents of all ages. La'atid was funded by the Jewish Federation of Greater Hartford, the Jewish Community Foundation of Greater Hartford, and the Commission on Jewish Education of the Jewish Federation of Greater Hartford. As with all effective change process models, the La-atid change processes provided the lay and professional leaders at each of the synagogues with opportunities to understand why they wanted a transformative change and to enable them to experience a deep-seated change in their mindset, values and behaviors. A report on La'atid is on the JESNA website.

Over an initial three-year period (2000–2003) the first cohort of three synagogues engaged in individual organizational change processes that reflected and responded to each congregation's vision, culture and needs and that helped each congregation advance toward its own goals. While each congregation was expected and encouraged to develop its own unique vision and goals, they all shared the project's common set of over-arching aims and definition of success. These included:

- involvement of a broad base of professional and lay stakeholders in congregational planning and decision-making;
- the organic interconnection of synagogue and school, with the school seen as central to the congregation's purpose, mission, goals and activities;
- strengthening and expanding partnerships among professionals and lay leaders;
- rethinking and visioning creative change opportunities in the school and synagogue;
- implementation of experimental action plans to bring congregations closer to their idealized visions of themselves;
- varied expressions of more positive Jewish identity by constituents of all ages;
- increased Jewish knowledge among constituents of all ages;
- strengthening professional and lay leadership; and

- institutionalization of the changes and participatory processes into the fiber of the congregations within three to five years.

The Commission on Jewish Education received additional funding in 2003 for a second phase of La'atid (Phase II) to:

- continue work with the first cohort of congregations (La'atid I) in order to maintain and extend the original congregational work in addition to integrating and deepening the effort by implementing a new emphasis on congregational schools and developing professional learning communities; and

- add two new congregations (La'atid II) using best practices learned from La'atid I and other national initiatives.

La'atid provides each congregation (from both cohorts) with ongoing support and guidance for congregational strategic visioning, planning and implementation by a highly experienced local facilitator and the project's educational director. Lay and professional leaders from each of the congregations enroll in relevant credit-bearing courses (e.g., Synagogue/School Renewal and Leadership) at the Hartford Institute of Jewish Studies: An Affiliate of Hebrew College. The La'atid Challenge Grants provide funding to support programmatic initiatives emanating from the strategic planning processes in each of the congregations. Annual conferences (e.g., "Reaching Out: Finding and Involving Young Families" in Spring 2005) exposed La'atid (as well as other community educational institutions) to knowledge and experience from field leaders and national models from outside the community.

PROJECT KAVOD'S EXECUTIVE SUMMARY

In 2004, the Coalition for the Advancement of Jewish Education (CAJE), with funding from the Covenant Foundation, launched a three-year pilot project to improve the culture of employment in Early Childhood Jewish Education in Miami-Dade, Florida (Schaap et al. 2007). The idea for this project was initiated by CAJE's Advocacy Commission.

Project Kavod: Improving the Culture of Employment in Early Childhood Jewish Education (ECJE) was implemented by CAJE in partnership with The Center for the Advancement of Jewish Education of Miami-Dade (CAJE-Miami), The Greater Miami Jewish Federation and the four project pilot sites of Bet Shira Congregation's Early Childhood Center, the Dave and Mary Alper Jewish Community Center's Early Childhood Center, the Hebrew Academy of Greater Miami's Early Childhood Center and Temple Beth Sholom's Early Childhood Center. The project was implemented using the Six-Stage Change Process Model. A report on the project and a change manual on its change processes are available on the Coalition for the Advancement of Jewish Education website (www.caje.org).

In addition to the partnership between CAJE the central agency, and the four synagogue pilot sites, a community task force was created whose members were also drawn from the partners and the general community. At the conclusion of the project a Project Kavod Community Leadership Forum was held. The forum was the largest event ever held for early childhood Jewish education and resulted in more stakeholders joining in the continuation of the project after it formally ended.

PROJECT KAVOD'S SUBSTANTIVE OUTCOMES

- Each of the four Project Kavod pilot sites significantly increased the salaries of their ECJE educators.

- Each of the four Project Kavod pilot sites raised the quality of their ECJE programs and the culture of ECJE employment through professional development and an assessment of their current program.

- Project Kavod's Community Task Force created a comprehensive set of eighteen action recommendations that addressed both the quality of ECJE and the culture of employment.

- The project partners and the Miami-Dade Jewish community increased their appreciation for quality ECJE and the need to improve the culture of employment.

- Project Kavod's Community Committee and Task Force now understand that there is a recruitment and retention crisis in Jewish education.
- Project Kavod's Community Committee and Task Force now understand that there must be an increased focus on the Jewish part of ECJE.
- Project Kavod's Community Committee and Task Force now understand the importance of ECJE to the future of the Jewish people.
- Project Kavod lay and staff leaders are collecting data on whether or not there is an increase in the number of children continuing to participate in Jewish education, whether at day schools, synagogues or JCCs.

PROJECT KAVOD COMMUNITY PARTNERSHIP OUTCOMES

- The community partners are now a committed and passionate network of informed lay leaders and professional staff.
- The sponsoring organizations and the change consultant engaged in ongoing contracting regarding their roles, responsibilities, and tasks and have created a deeper capacity to engage in national, communal and local site partnerships.
- Project Kavod created a data-based case for change using action research tools such as customized surveys, reviewing key documents, and identifying best standards that can be used as baseline data to continue the improvement of the culture of employment for ECJE educators.
- The project's partners, with the assistance of the project's change consultant, used state-of-the art consensus decision-making, dialogue, and systems thinking. They were taught how to select and use basic change tools for their future meetings.
- Project Kavod meetings supported the sharing of power and capacity to create mutually-acceptable recommendations and to continue to work in shared leadership settings.
- The partners learned that building partnerships and creating transformative change takes time. It is a process, not an event. The project's community partners and project staff took the time needed to create the case for change and create informed recommendations.
- The work of the project's partners was enhanced by the consultative team, who provided synergistic change consulting and evaluation support. The project's partners learned when they needed to have the assistance of technical and change process consultants and when they did not.
- At the beginning of each meeting the partners began by reflecting on text-based sources regarding the culture of employment in Jewish education, and a study guide, Text and Tradition: The Importance of Jewish Education and Jewish Educators, was created (Miskin 2006).

PERSPECTIVES ON TRANSFORMATIVE CHANGE APPROACHES

The two cases, La'atid and Project Kavod, illustrate the key actions that ensure the creation of a sustainable transformative initiative. Both cases enabled a community to achieve substantive Jewish educational outcomes and increased the individual, organizational and communal capacity to engage in complex consensus-based change. They were designed to promote synergistic interactions between a large number of key parties ranging from organizations to interest groups and individuals. The participants engaged in a variety of learning processes to ensure that they understood the substantive educational issues, consensus-based change approaches and the Jewish values related to Jewish education. The participants jointly created a vision, strategic and implementation plans and change process that were based on the community and organizational needs, values, interests and resources.

The foundations that funded these initiatives did so because they have a passionate commitment to achieve substantive educational goals. As a result, the foundation staff was engaged throughout the process and often helped respond to the challenges that arose when addressing the substantive issues and the change dynamics.

In both cases, several key messages and lessons learned emerged. The following overview may be used to design, refine and evaluate similar transformations. The factors directly related to the initiative's evaluation are presented in the following section on the evaluation of transformative change initiatives.

KEY MESSAGES AND LESSONS LEARNED

- *Complex Transformative Change Is a Long-term Process*. Both of the cases created significant accomplishments, but it will take several years and the allocation of significant resources to achieve long-term outcomes that are both systemic and sustainable.

- *Create Sustainable Partnership Funding*. Fiscal and leadership resources are required to achieve long-term changes. The resources for these systemic educational changes usually need to be garnered from multiple sources such as local sites, central agencies, federations and foundations.

- *Create Ongoing Learning Communities*. Both of the cases created learning communities where the participants expanded their understanding of the substantive issues in Jewish education, capacity to engage in informed and consensus-based change leadership, and awareness of Jewish values for education and community change. These learning communities occurred in different types of settings where lay and professional leaders learned together or where lay leaders and professional staff learned separately. The learning communities helped the participants create sound decisions that were data-based and pragmatic. The learning community processes also enable participants to accept and move beyond the normal frustrations that arise during participatory endeavors.

- *Create Change Strategies That Address Site-based and Community Change*. When the goal is to create systemic changes within a site and for the total community, it is essential that change processes are created at the site and community levels. Representatives of the sites and of the general community need to belong to the community-level committees or task forces in order to create a community consensus that "systemic Jewish education is needed and resources should be allocated to implement the changes". During the consensus-based meetings, it is important that traditional lay and professional "power brokers" view the other participants as peers. In order for this to occur, careful planning must be done to determine whether a decision is a recommendation to be considered or a decision to be implemented.

EVALUATING TRANSFORMATIVE CHANGE INITIATIVES

Evaluation of transformative change initiatives involves the ongoing collection and diagnosis of data that can be used to guide the creation of both quality systemic Jewish educational changes and participatory change strategy. This form of action research is based on an outcomes model that makes explicit the connection between initiative goals, inputs, activities, outputs and outcomes for the substantive issues and the change processes. Since transformations do not have detailed linear strategies, it is important that the evaluation approaches are not only based on traditional project evaluation tools but also use those that can accurately evaluate the emerging "realities" of systemic changes. Outcome evaluation for community transformation includes measuring changes in participants' knowledge, skills, behaviors, and values at individual, organizational and community levels.

In addition to evaluating the outcomes of the change initiative, research is also done during complex change initiatives. During Project Kavod the research efforts included a comprehensive survey of the ECJE educators regarding their perception of the culture of employment in their school, a fiscal analysis of the income, direct and indirect expenses and profit/loss for an ECJE site and a survey of ECJE directors. The results of the evaluations were used at the beginning to create the Case for Change and during the initiative to design action plans to enhance the culture of employment for ECJE educators and to identify what aspects of the ECJE programs needed to be addressed in order to improve the quality of the ECJE program.

CUSTOMIZED ACTION RESEARCH FOR EVALUATING TRANSFORMATIVE CHANGE

The research and evaluation approaches for Project Kavod and La'atid used a customized action research model that enabled the project evaluator and the change consultants to both garner key research and evaluation data and support the development of action goals by the change participants. Key features of a customized action research approach include the following:

- The sponsors, the change consultants and the evaluator/researcher jointly identify the research and evaluation questions of interest.

- The sponsors, the change consultants and the evaluator/researcher jointly develop the evaluation plan by using a customized logic model linking outcome goals, resources, activities, outputs, outcomes and the overall initiative impact on substantive issues and change leadership.

- The sponsors, the change consultants and the evaluator/researcher jointly develop a research plan to garner the data needed to determine the current state (case for change data) and to develop adaptive strategic goals and action steps.

- The sponsors, the change consultants and the evaluator/researcher develop appropriate methods to communicate the research findings to stakeholders (participants, funders, organizational sponsors).

- Participants use the research and evaluation information throughout the initiative because they believe the data is useful and credible and helps them to design ways to achieve their desired outcomes.

Goodman was the evaluator and researcher for Project Kavod. In the evaluation report on the project that she submitted to the funder (Covenant Foundation), she described her experience with Project Kavod. The following are excerpts of her report:

> The initial expectation of this evaluator was that she would serve as a "traditional" evaluator maintaining contact with the project throughout, perhaps a bit more intensely at first as goals were formalized, but doing most of the "assessment work" at the end. Since the initial diagnosis of this project clearly revealed that this was a complex multi-party and multi-issue project whose mandate was to do something that had not yet been done for early childhood Jewish education (ECJE), that model quickly became insufficient for the task at hand and an approach more akin to action research was utilized. Action research is "the study of a social situation, with a view to improving the quality of action within it" (Winter, p. 10). Action research involves the researcher working closely with project participants, sharing her expertise, acting when research or evaluation organically contributes to the project's goals. In the case of Project Kavod, that meant assisting in the change process to motivate lay leaders, professionals, parents, and funders to take action toward improving the culture of employment for early childhood Jewish educators. The evaluator served in fulfilling a goal of participatory research, namely, making "the evaluation process and its results relevant and useful to stakeholders for future actions" (W.K. Kellogg, p. 11). Her work was aimed at helping create a process and materials that could aid another community in undertaking a similar approach.

> In essence, the evaluator was a member of the consultative team who contributed to the project at all levels and throughout the process. This means that the "evaluative" component was not solely her work, nor solely her perceptions. As in participatory evaluation, "the evaluator's perspective is given no more priority than other stakeholders, including program participants" (W.K. Kellogg, p. 11). What the evaluator has to offer is technical expertise in how best to conduct evaluation drawing out the voices of the participants and engaging them in determining what is important to know and how to interpret data once it is offered. For example, the evaluator in writing up the report of the results from the early childhood Jewish educator survey did NOT offer recommendations. Not only did she work with the other staff members in synthesizing the findings into key messages and raising

questions related to the findings, she left the work of determining implications and recommendations to those who knew the community the best, those who were empowered to set policy and take action, the participants themselves.

This approach to evaluation helped overcome a problem associated with evaluation, namely that it is an intervention that can potentially negatively impact or impede a project. Since the evaluator was incorporated as a member of the consultative team, decisions on when to have her take stock of what was happening or be involved in any way, was sensitive to the main goal of engaging the stakeholders in improving the culture of employment and work conditions for early childhood Jewish education. Her involvement augmented rather than detracted from the process at all times (Goodman, 2007).

FUTURE DIRECTIONS

From the current evaluation reports, community partners and funders who use transformative change approaches are able to increase their capacity to implement systemic responses to Jewish educational challenges and to deliver demonstrable results and accountability. In order to address the fundamental issues that determine the long-term impacts of these changes, questions such as the following need to be addressed:

- How do you define a successful transformative community change initiative for Jewish education that includes multiple partners such as a partnership between local sites, communal organizations, national organizations and funders? What are the indicators of substantive and change competencies for each of the multiple partners?

- What will increase the willingness and the capacity of national and communal foundations, federations and central agencies to provide the fiscal resources needed to implement transformative community change initiatives for Jewish education?

- How can we improve our collective learning from the evaluation of transformative community change initiatives for Jewish education and translate that learning into action?

- What will help educational providers, funders and oversight agencies overcome the fractured manner in which the funding and delivery of education occurs when a "cloak of collaboration" is donned without fundamentally changing the ways that providers and funders do their work (Conner, & Kadel-Taras 2003)?

CONCLUSION AND HIGHLIGHTS

Compelling and systemic visions for Jewish education are more likely to be implemented if they are created by transformative community change strategies. This chapter described how to create transformational community change approaches that result in systemic changes in Jewish education for both the substantive educational issues and change leadership capacities. This chapter has shown that:

- In order for Jewish educational systems to deliver quality learning options and to create synergistic linkages between formal and informal educational options, there is a need for a compelling community-wide vision for Jewish education and the resources needed to achieve it.

- Compelling and systemic visions for Jewish education are more likely to be implemented if they are created by transformative community change strategies.

- Educational transformation change initiatives address three factors: 1) substantive areas to be changed; 2) people; and 3) process.

- Transformation change cannot be done unless the parties who have a direct or indirect influence on the achievement of the desired outcomes are mobilized during the creation and implementation of the vision, desired outcomes and implementation plan.

- Transformational change initiatives for Jewish education are increasing in their number and their impact on formal and informal Jewish education.

- A customized participatory evaluation model that is based on a program logic model is needed when evaluating the substantive and change leadership outcomes of a transformative change initiative.

ANNOTATED BIBLIOGRAPHY
TRANSFORMATIVE CHANGE

The following books are essentials texts for both change practitioners and organizational and community leaders who want to know how to effectively achieve meaningful and sustainable change in Jewish education.

Ackerman, L. & Anderson, D. (2001). *The Change Leader's Roadmap: How to Navigate Your Organization's Transformation*. San Francisco: Jossey-Bass.

Anderson, D. & Ackerman, L. (2001). *Beyond Change Management: Advanced Strategies for Today's Transformational Leaders*. San Francisco: Jossey-Bass. These books provide the theories, step-by-step change processes and leadership approaches needed to design and implement transformational change initiatives. The books include user-friendly worksheets, questionnaires, guidelines and assessment instruments.

Creighton, J. (2005). *The Public Participation Handbook*. San Francisco: Jossey-Bass. This book is a practical guide to designing and leading inclusive participatory projects and initiatives. It is a toolkit that includes practical advice, checklists, worksheets and illustrative examples.

Dannemiller Tyson & Associates (2000). *Whole Scale Change*. San Francisco: Berrett-Koehler Publishers. This book combines transformational change theories and system theory approaches in a proven, flexible approach that aligns the visions and actions among multiple stakeholders. It shows how to rapidly engage the whole system in meeting organizational and community needs. It includes both concepts and a description of step-by-step change processes.

LARGE GROUP CHANGE METHODS

Bunker, B. & Alban, B. (2006). *The Handbook of Large Group Methods: Creating Systemic Change in Organizations and Communities*. San Francisco: Jossey-Bass. This book is authored by two of the founders of the field of large group change interventions. The second edition of this book includes a comprehensive overview of large group change theories and methods including approaches such as Appreciative Inquiry, World Café, Future Search and Open Space. Case studies illustrate the use of the methods.

Holman, P., Devane, T. & Cady, S. (2007). *The Change Handbook: The Definitive Resource on Today's Best Methods for Engaging Whole Systems*. San Francisco: Berrett-Koehler. This extensively updated second edition of a classic on large group change describes sixty-one change methods by the foremost practitioners of methods such as Appreciative Inquiry, World Café, Future Search and Open Space Technology. It includes a comparative chart that helps readers determine which methods would work best for their situation. The book also provides guidance on how to customize the approaches.

EVALUATION OF TRANSFORMATIVE CHANGE INITIATIVES

Auspos, P. & Kubisch, A. (2004). *Building Knowledge about Community Change: Moving Beyond Evaluations*. New York: Aspen Institute. This publication shares what the Aspen Institute has learned about evaluating community-based initiatives and using that knowledge to enhance both the community-based change and how to increase learning in the future. *www.aspenroundtable.org*

GRANTMAKING FOR COMPREHENSIVE IMPACT

Connor, J. & Kadel-Taras, S. (2003). *Community Visions, Community Solutions: Grantmakng for Comprehensive Impact*. Saint Paul: Amherst Wilder Foundation. Based on five years of research and hands-on experience, the book includes fresh ideas, concrete strategies, compelling case studies and wisdom from the field on how to improve collaboration between organizations and the community who are working on transformative change initiatives. It presents bold steps that funders, providers and community partners can do to create effective cross-organization alliances between funders and providers, and institutional and community leaders.

REFERENCES

Ackerman, L. & Anderson, D. (2001). *The Change Leader's Roadmap: How to Navigate Your Organization's Transformation*. San Francisco: Jossey-Bass.

Aron, I., Lee, S. & Rossel, S. (eds.) (1995). *A Congregation of Learners: Transforming the Synagogue into a Learning Community*. New York: UAHC Press.

Beckhard, J. & Harris, R. (1987). *Organizational Transitions: Managing Complex Change*. New York: Addision-Wesley.

Bunker, B. & Alban, B. (2006). *The Handbook of Large Group Methods: Creating Systemic Change in Organizations and Communities*. San Francisco: Jossey-Bass.

A Time to Act: The Report of the Commission on Jewish Education in North America (1991). Lanham, MD: University Press of America.

Cohen, S.M. (2006). *A Tale of Two Jewries: The "Inconvenient Truth" for American Jews*. New York: Jewish Life Network/Steinhardt Foundation.

Connor, J. & Kadel-Taras, S. (2003). *Community Visions, Community Solutions: Grantmaking for Comprehensive Impact*. Saint Paul: Amherst Wilder Foundation.

Creighton, J. (2005). *The Public Participation Handbook*. San Francisco: Jossey-Bass.

Cummings, T.G. & Worley, C.G. (2005). *Organization Development & Change* (8th ed). Belmont, CA: Thomson Higher Education, South-Western.

Dannemiller Tyson & Associates (2000). *Whole Scale Change*. San Francisco: Berrett-Koehler Publishers.

Flexner, P.A. (2000). *A Vision for Excellence: Report of the Task Force on Congregational and Communal Jewish Education*. New York: JESNA.

Fox, S., Scheffler, I. & Marom, D. (eds.) (2003). *Visions of Jewish Education*. New York: Cambridge University Press.

Fullan, M. (2001). *Leading in a Culture of Change*. San Francisco: Jossey-Bass.

Fullan, M. (2005). *Leadship and Sustainability*. Thousand Oaks: Corwin Press.

Goodman, R. (2007). *Project Kavod Evaluation Report*. New York: The Coalition for the Advancement of Jewish Education (CAJE).

Greater Miami Jewish Federation (1994). *Report of the Miami Commission on Jewish Continuity*. Miami: Greater Miami Jewish Federation.

Holman, P., Devane, T. & Cady, S. (2007). *The Change Handbook: The Definitive Resource on Today's Best Methods for Engaging Whole Systems*. San Francisco: Berrett-Koehler.

IAPP (2000). *Core Values for the Practice of Public Participation*. Denver: International Association of Public Participation (www.Iap2.org).

Issacs, L. (2005). *La'atid: Synagogues for the Future Summary Evaluation*. New York: JESNA.

Kotter, J. (1996). *Leading Change*. Boston: Harvard Business School Press.

Lippitt, L. (1958). *Dynamics of Planned Change*. Westport: Harcourt & Brace.

Miskin, N. (2006). *Text and Tradition: The Importance of Jewish Education and Jewish Educators*. New York: The Coalition for the Advancement of Jewish Education (CAJE).

Nevis, E., Lancourt, J. & Vassallo, H. (1996) *Intentional Revolutions: A Seven-Point Strategy for Transforming Organizations*. San Francisco: Jossey-Bass.

Padva, P. (1991). *Attitudes toward Israel and Jewish Identity*. New York: The American Jewish Committee.

Schaap, E., Bidol Padva, P. & Goodman, R. (2007). *Project Kavod: Improving the Culture of Employment in Jewish Education*. New York: The Coalition for the Advancement of Jewish Education (CAJE).

Sarna, J. (2004). *American Judaism: A History*. New Haven: Yale University Press.

Shevitz, S. (1995). An Organizational Perspective on Changing Jewish Education: What the Literature Reveals. In I. Aron, S. Lee & S. Rossel (eds.), *A Congregation of Learners: Transforming the Synagogue into a Learning Community*. New York: UAHC Press.

Susskind, L., McKearan, S. & Thomas-Larmer, J. (1999). *The Consensus Building Handbook: A Comprehensive Guide to Reaching Agreement*. Thousand Oaks: Sage.

Wertheimer, J. (2005). *Linking the Silos: How to Accelerate the Momentum in Jewish Education Today*. New York: Avi Chai Foundation.

Wertheimer, J. (2007). *Recent Trends in Supplementary Jewish Education*. New York: Avi Chai Foundation.

Wheatley, M. (1999). *Leadership and the New Science: Discovering Order in a Chaotic World*. San Francisco: Berrett-Koehler.

W.K. Kellogg Foundation (1998). *Evaluation Handbook*.

Winter, R. (1989). *Learning from Experience: Principles and Practice in Action Research*. New York: The Falmer Press.

Woocher, J. S. (1995). Toward a "Unified Field Theory" of Jewish Continuity. In I. Aron, S. Lee & S. Rossel (eds.), *A Congregation of Learners: Transforming the Synagogue into a Learning Community*. New York: UAHC Press.

"Don't Conduct, Improvise!" New Approaches to Changing Congregational Schools

Susan Shevitz

Fifteen years ago, when I wrote the chapter on changing Jewish schools for the first version of this book (Shevitz 1992), I quoted a metaphor suggested by Thomas Sergiovanni in his work on changing schools. "Surf, don't pitch," Sergiovanni cautioned as he argued for a new mindset relevant to the hard work of improving schools:

> The idea is to ride the wave of the pattern until it unfolds, adjusting to the shifting circumstances. The pattern is made up of goals and circumstances that must be handled in a balanced way. Like surfing, schooling is hard to monitor and improve from a distance. It must be observed and coached up close. Crucial to success in surfing are the successive interrelated decisions the surfer makes as he or she responds to ever-changing situations. Improvement efforts are not designed to program what the surfer does but rather to inform the instincts and decisions that he or she makes (Sergiovanni 1989:3).

All these years later, *Passion for Action* (July 2006, Vol. 1, No. 3), the newsletter of MIT's Leadership Center, uses a metaphor based on Orlikowski's work to capture the dynamic nature of change. It advises leaders, "Don't conduct, improvise!"

> Although managers might see their role as conducting an orchestra, the conductor-led structure can be out of tune with rapid technological and market change… That's because surprises—both good and bad—pop up…. Organizations that stay flexible and collaborate, like a jazz combo, have a better chance of making the new technology work effectively in practice.

In conditions of high uncertainty, Orlikowski writes,

> The maestro's careful direction should give way to the ad hoc creativity of a group's accomplished practitioners, who *improvise within a set of rhythms and chord changes, but without a precise and predefined composition.*

While each metaphor captures the dynamic, indeterminate nature of change processes, the differences between them reveal ideas that have emerged over the last fifteen years about the challenges of rooting change in an organization, whether a school or a corporation. In the first metaphor an individual surfer interprets conditions and responds to them alone. If the surfer is sufficiently skilled, he or she will catch the wave and, presumably, ride it successfully to shore. Perhaps the waves and winds are fierce, and dangerous fish abound. Or perhaps the conditions are calm, and the shore is close by. The surfer must be ready for variable winds and currents. Though there may be other surfers with whom to share information, commiserate and plan, the surfer rides the wave alone.

The second metaphor features an interdependent group. Musicians with different expertise and roles look to each other and to a leader who sets the guiding framework. As "accomplished practitioners," each builds on what others do. At best there is collaboration and flexibility, attentiveness to the parts and to the whole. Musicians can play together or solo; a leader gives direction, yet moves aside when it is time for others to perform.

These metaphors illustrate how ideas about organizational change in general, and school change in particular, have developed from the 1990s to today.

THE CONTEXT

In 1992, coordinated efforts to change Jewish schools on local, regional and national levels were just getting underway. Breakthroughs of that era shaped what has happened since. Based on models of change from general education and organizational studies, the early efforts were framed by several concepts. First and foremost, based on research and theories that were counter-intuitive to people who were looking for clear road maps, some researchers and practitioners urged change agents (to use dated jargon) to see each Jewish school as part of larger systems rather than as a self-enclosed, independent unit (Shevitz 1992, 1995). Reimer's in-depth study (1997) of a congregational school "that succeeds" demonstrated the different relationships a school might have to its sponsoring congregation and how profoundly this influences its ability to improve.

Once advocates for change began to think of the congregation as a system, it was a small step to recognize that they needed to involve professionals and members active in other aspects of the congregation when they wanted to move in new ways. For that reason, almost all of the change projects of the 1990s required the involvement of a congregational team.

Another framing concept of that era was vision. Supported by the common-sense notion that "if you don't know where you're going, any path will lead you there" and by a plethora of management books that pointed to vision as a prime ingredient for achieving organizational excellence, change processes frequently required their planners to engage in some type of visioning—to imagine and then assert new directions. The best documented of these projects, the Experiment in Congregational Education (ECE) developed by Hebrew Union College's Rhea Hirsch School of Jewish Education, built an approach that was based on serious, guided efforts by the congregation to develop its vision for Jewish education and then an implementation plan to move toward its vision. This process has spawned several new models of congregational education.

Over the last fifteen years there has been considerable activity in this "change" arena, with millions of dollars supporting innovation. UJC's web-based newsletter *Hadashot (http://www.ujc.org/ content_display.html?ArticleID=138898)* identifies four national, twelve communal and four local initiatives, though it is likely this underestimates local initiatives. JESNA's website, *http://www.jesna. org/j/congregational.asp*, describes elements of these projects. Many have operated for years, and there certainly are reports of success. Even so, according to the author of this issue of *Hadashot,* the picture remains gloomy:

> There are pockets of excellence, but there is also a broad consensus that these programs [the many current supplementary schools that educate 71% of the Jewish students in North America that enroll in Jewish schools] must be improved if we are to successfully inspire a large proportion of these young Jewish people and their families to become and remain active, committed and knowledgeable Jews.

The article goes on to identify schools' vexing problems, though it is not obvious which are causes and which are effects: unclear, unrealistic goals; lukewarm commitment from parents and children; institutional ambivalence; awkward scheduling ; teachers and educational leaders not well trained; unengaging curricula; low post-bar/bat mitzvah retention.

Several of the change initiatives employed consultants with training as diverse as education, management, rabbinics, social work and planning to help the congregations move through change processes organized by denominations, central Jewish education agencies, federations, philanthropic foundations and individual schools and congregations (Shevitz and Cousens 2004).

LESSONS LEARNED OVER THE LAST FIFTEEN YEARS

Given all of this effort, there are some lessons from the congregational change initiatives and from the research on change in school settings that can help guide future efforts.

- **School and Congregational Change Processes Overlap.** It is difficult today to talk about the congregational school by itself; sometimes it even seems to have faded from view. One of the reasons is that during the school improvement efforts from the late 1980s into the 1990s some leaders, motivated by their frustrations, learned to think more systemically. To use one example: An early assumption about Jewish family education (JFE) was that it would be a catalyst to improving congregations more generally. But it soon became apparent that JFE could not succeed unless it had the backing of a wide range of congregational stakeholders, and most often, the congregation itself had to change; it needed to become "family friendly." If it wanted to attract young families to Sabbath services, for example, it needed to rethink scheduling, seating arrangements, length of different segments and other elements of the service. Congregants and procedures needed to be welcoming to families, and budget priorities needed to shift. In other words, without changes within the congregational system, JFE would be stymied (Banks and Wolfson 1998 [Parts IV and V]; Sales, Koren and Shevitz 2000; Shevitz 1994; Shevitz and Karpel 1995; Shevitz and Koren 2004). JFE advocates found they needed a perspective that was broader than parents, children and school. Many of them helped spearhead the "synagogue change" movement.[1] The overlap between school and congregational improvement is recognized by ECE's explicit goals: "1) To create *congregations of learners* in which congregants of all ages are actively engaged in learning throughout their lives; 2) To evolve *learning congregations* that practice shared leadership and have incorporated deliberation, reflection and ongoing assessment into all their activities" (Aron 2000:1).

  In addition, innovators soon realized that targeting the school alone only reinforced, to use the sociologist Marshall Sklare's phase, the post–World War II "pediatric Judaism" that helped cause the current woes. School change morphed into educational change and then into congregational change (see Sales 2006 for an overview of synagogue change efforts). It is today impossible to talk about congregational school change in isolation, and efforts to change the congregation most often involve some form of Jewish education. This means improving the Jewish school is more complex than originally assumed.

- **Congregational Schools Overshadowed by Other Educational Activities.** In the last two decades congregational schools seem to have faded from view, despite their enrolling approximately 70% of all children enrolled in Jewish education. Among the reasons is the often negative reputation that these schools have in the community. Due in part to widespread skepticism about the potential of the congregational school, attention on regional and national levels has shifted to other forms of Jewish education. One need only flip through the pages of this book to be reminded of the powerful role that people ascribe to Jewish camps, day schools, youth groups, family education, adult learning and the like. National foundations and academic centers to support these endeavors have emerged, including PEJE, the Foundation for Jewish Camping and the Institute for Informal Jewish Education. There is no similar advocacy and support for the congregational school, though this may very well be changing with JESNA's recent establishment of the Partnership for Congregational Education and the heightened attention that the Reform, Conservative and Reconstructionist movements, as well as some philanthropic foundations, are expressing.

- **Limited Information about Earlier Initiatives.** There has been too little systematic, impact-based research on these projects, whether on a broad scale or within individual schools. Research undertaken most often looks at participation, satisfaction and other factors and is generally proprietary and remains in the realm of funders and the sites. Without serious study of the different programs and evaluations of their impact, a coherent, usable body of knowledge cannot develop. We do have, however, some recent literature about congregational change processes that

---

[1] For example, the work of the Whizin Institute at the University of Judaism moved in this direction by extending the perspective of its Summer Institute from JFE narrowly defined to a systems-wide, congregational view; its leaders became involved with synagogue change and co-founded Synagogue 2000.

have relevant messages for people focusing on school or congregational change (Hoffman 2006; Herring 2001; Schwarz 2002; and Wolfson 2006). We still must turn to research and theory from other arenas for guidance about changing Jewish schools.

- **Questions about Congregations as Systems.** There are competing views, often expressed metaphorically, about the nature of the synagogue as a system, and these views shape the way school change is conceptualized and accomplished (Shevitz and Cousens 2004). A metaphor for some organizations, first used by Morgan (1993:63–89), is the spider plant that produces multiple offshoots, each connected to the main plant by a stem that eventually can (but needn't) become a separate plant. In this metaphor the school is one of several offshoots—units—within the congregation, and there is minimal integration among the units. It suggests an approach that relies on spawning many discrete services to meet members' different needs within a synagogue.[2] Another metaphor is that of a business where the consumers' needs and satisfaction drive the organization, perhaps allowing for a boutique approach. A third metaphor is the immune system: When a change addresses one part of the system but does not adequately take into account characteristics of the rest of the system, it will be rejected by the system or modified by it so that it will be more comfortable with how the synagogue actually works. This is akin to the observation made by Sarason that reforms are either rejected or become so watered down that they cannot significantly change the setting (Sarason, 1996). Each metaphor captures some aspect of congregational life and has implications for the preferred roles of professionals and members. Whatever the metaphor, there is consensus that as resource-poor environments (without enough time, energy or sometimes money), congregations pursuing change initiatives should have: 1) a person who will coordinate the effort, 2) a team involved that dedicates the necessary time over several years, 3) mechanisms for keeping records and disseminating information, and 4) tactics for gaining the necessary financial backing. Understanding this and other pre-implementation conditions has led to increasingly sophisticated tools to gauge "congregational readiness" (Shevitz and Cousens 2004).

- **Chaos Theory Applied to School Change Processes.** Organizational theorists, including those studying schools, have applied concepts from chaos theory to build a model of how schools operate. Fullan, whose evolving body of work informs much of the thinking about school change in general education, presents a helpful overview of this in *Change Forces: The Sequel*. His earlier book, *Change Forces,* was organized around eight guiding principles. It tried to move people from mechanistic, linear notions of change to a model built on early experimentation designed to uncover promising directions and to create reflection in (and on) action, to use the concept developed by Schon (1987). "Ready, fire, aim" expresses, in Fullan's words, the way change really happens. Through analysis and experimentation, groups discover and fine-tune their goals as well as approaches. From this perspective change is, as Fullan puts it, "a journey, not a blueprint." This approach also challenges initiatives to develop feedback loops and reflective practices so they can draw appropriate lessons from their experiments and experiences. Several Jewish school change initiatives took Fullan's advice to heart and struggled with the tension between process and product as well as people's unease with the ambiguity that is part of this experimental stance regarding change.

In the sequel, Fullan applies chaos theory to change processes and provides examples that are grounded in schools' actual experiences. The eight principles he presents are notable for how deeply they rely on educational principles; as he writes, "theories of education and theories of change need each other" (1999:20). Businesses, he notes, have begun to appreciate the need for moral purpose, and schools have seen how "ideas, knowledge creation and sharing are essential to solving learning problems in a rapidly changing society" (Fullan 2001: xi). This model is based on principles of living systems that have emerged from sciences such as biology and physics. When faced with major threats or opportunities, organisms move toward what Fullan, Senge (1990) and others call "the edge of chaos"; this "evokes higher levels of mutation and experimentation, and

---

[2] One participant called the groups *garinim*, comparing them to seeds that settle and build new life. Experimentation has demonstrated that such small groups can effectively bring the uninvolved into synagogue life, but that the synagogues require significant infrastructure—staff and materials—to maintain participation and to nourish the new baby plants.

fresh new solutions are likely to be found" (Fullan 2001:108). Much of Fullan's writing attempts to help people interested in reforming schools understand how to work at the edge of chaos, where opportunities for creative adaptations abound. Unforeseen events and consequences can be neither prevented nor managed. The key to successful change is to *"disturb* them in a manner that approximates the desired outcome" (Fullan 2001:109) and, based on the work of Lewin and then Schein, to create a safe enough environment for learning to take place.[3]

Significant change requires "re-culturing," and that, as Schein (1992, 1999), Deal and Peterson (1999) and others have taught, is difficult for individuals and groups to accomplish because it challenges their very assumptions about what things mean, not merely their notions of how to behave and do things. Change requires that both individuals and groups within the system review and revise or replace assumptions about how things are or ought to be—a sophisticated learning task. This, and the collaborations that are essential to change a complex system with multiple stakeholders, causes anxiety, another dynamic that must be considered during a change process (Schein 1992, 1999). In an environment of uncertainty, experimentation, anxiety and anticipation—at the edge of chaos—it is important to provide coherence and clarity (Fullan 1999). Lest this all remain theoretical, Fullan's *Leading in a Culture of Change* (2001) develops the ideas and demonstrates their use.

- **Schools as Learning Organizations.** Fullan's approach makes use of ideas developed in Senge's groundbreaking work *The Fifth Discipline: The Art and Practice of the Learning Organization* (1990). In an age of rapidly changing conditions we need "…organizations where people continually expand their capacity to create the results they truly desire, where new and expansive patterns of thinking are nurtured, where collective aspiration is set free, and where people are continually learning to see the whole together"(Senge, 1990:3).

With detailed theoretical and practical explanations, Senge presents five disciplines that he posits as central to developing learning organizations: systems thinking, personal mastery, mental models, shared vision and team learning (Kofman and Senge 2006). Senge and his collaborators have produced a growing set of practical and theoretical papers and books that further develop *The Fifth Discipline's* ideas (see especially, his *Schools that Learn: A Fifth Discipline Fieldbook for Educators, Parents and Everyone Who Cares about Education,* 2000). Concerned by the late 1990s that even well-resourced organizations have a hard time becoming learning organizations (though some succeeded), Senge now looks to biological systems for guidance, proposing tools that support self-organization and emergence (see Wheatley 1999). The challenge is to create a context in which "generative conversations and concerted actions" can take place, where "language functions as a device for connection, invention and coordination" (Kofman and Senge 16).

This brief summary does not do justice to the richness of Senge's work. The salient points for our inquiry are the emphasis on ongoing and deep learning that emerges from uncertainty and the engagement of people throughout the organization in the learning. Learning, in the context, involves exploring assumptions, developing new "mental models" and the ability of a group to learn from its new experiences. Several of the school (and synagogue) change projects have tried to make use of these ideas; see Aron (2002) for examples of how one change project draws on these concepts. Senge's more recent emphasis, like Fullan's, on how to use the system's own assets to organize might be appropriate for Jewish settings, specifically because participation is voluntary.

A compatible set of ideas has emerged in the field of professional development for educators. The naïveté of developing complex plans for school change and then assuming that after a few workshops the educators will be prepared to do their work differently has long been noted. Sarason first analyzed this in the 1971 edition of *The Culture of Schools and the Problem of Change.* There is growing awareness that serious professional development needs to be at the heart of attempts to change schools. In a recent book Fullan, Hill and Crevola put ongoing professional learning at the center of strategies they argue are poised to "break through" schools' inertia and to change their cultures (2006). From this perspective professional development must be organic; it must be

---

[3]The need for "psychological safety" during a change process was advanced by Kurt Lewin and elaborated by Edgar Schein.

integrated into the work of the educators. Inquiry, learning with and from each other and serious engagement with ideas is advocated by those who would change the culture of the schools by changing how its professionals relate to each other's work, their growth as professionals and, as Elmore and others point out, the nature of learning . Based on a body of research from general education, serious attempts to reconceptualize professional development in Jewish schools are beginning to take place, though the challenges of accomplishing this in the congregational school, with its severe time constraint, are numerous (see Weisman chapter in this volume for a fuller discussion of professional development).

- **New Ideas about Leadership.** These insights into systems and organizations developed hand in hand with new conceptualizations of leadership. Heifitz's *Leadership: No Easy Answers* (1994) is a seminal study. Building on the approaches of Schein, Argyris and Schon, Senge, Fullan and others, he distinguishes between technical and adaptive challenges to a system. Technical problems are routine, while adaptive ones require new thinking and approaches. The primary responsibility of a leader is to present adaptive challenges in ways that a community can accept without being overwhelmed, and to create conditions for the people to engage in developing the solutions. Understanding, holding and using the anxiety created by surfacing the problem is the leader's task, but the leader cannot, in this view, assume responsibility that is rightly the community's. Heifitz also demonstrates that people throughout a system, including those who do not have formal authority, are leaders without whom significant change cannot take place.

Even its supporters agree that the congregational school faces adaptive challenges, though there may also be some simple technical problems. Heifitz's approach challenges leaders to think about their work in new ways. Aron uses these ideas in her argument for "shared leadership" where the solution does not emerge from the official leaders (rabbi, educator) alone but instead from the group's investigation of what it wants Jewish education to be. But it also means that individuals such as teachers and parents, who are sometimes not taken into account when new ideas are developed, need to be cultivated as leaders who can make a difference in the system as well. This idea is consonant with the concept of "distributive leadership" applied to education by Elmore (2000), Gronn (2002), Spillane (2004), Hargreaves (2005) and others who argue that for improvements to be made in schools there needs to be continuous learning by the many people involved in the changes. Innovation must draw on the expertise distributed throughout a system instead of relying on role-based conceptions of leadership that assume compliance within a hierarchical system. People with different skills, knowledge and roles have to be supported in taking responsibility and leading within their spheres.[4]

This approach presents challenges to the ways professionals such as principals and rabbis have been taught to perform, though the approach is consonant with views of leadership that emerge from the tradition (see Lewis 2006, chapter 4, for a full discussion of shared power). Borowitz, drawing on Lurianic concepts, presented a model of shared leadership in his influential article *'Tzimtzum': A Mystical Model for Contemporary Leadership* in the earlier version of this book (Kelman 1992). In the new model, professionals are not the sole sources of solutions; instead, those affected by the solution have important roles. More in-depth studies of the practice of shared and distributive leadership in Jewish schools, as a way to help people understand and use the concepts, would be a welcome addition to the literature.

- **Innovations "Catching On": Dissemination and Acceptance.** Malcolm Gladwell's best-selling *The Tipping Point* (2000) provides a theory of the conditions that cause something new, whether shoes or social policy, to catch on. Basing his argument on an epidemiological model, Gladwell specifies circumstances that stimulate and support change and describes the roles different types of people play in making things happen. His model accounts for the messiness of the environment, with elements that are out of the planners' control, while at the same time suggesting that there are quite a few things that can be done to increase the factors that support change, such as promoting a "sticky message" that people quickly understand and use, finding small levers to

---

[4] This is an oversimplification of a position that draws on many empirical studies of school reform and is framed by an understanding of the culture of schools. See Elmore 2002 for a fuller treatment of the topic.

wide-scale change, and carefully involving the people he identifies as helping to disseminate a change: the "mavens," connectors and salesmen. Exploring what Gladwell's theory might mean for the Jewish school would be worthwhile.

IMPLICATIONS AND UNDERLYING QUESTIONS FOR CONGREGATIONAL EDUCATION

- **Questions of Purpose.** Schools often jump into change processes without thinking through fundamental questions. In the 21st century, with the changing nature of Jewish identity and identification in North America (Eisen and Cohen 2000; Horowitz 2000), questions about the purposes of Jewish education are especially important. To what extent is it literacy (and if so, what is a literate Jew?) or enculturation? Widespread use of the word "transformation" further obscures assumptions different people (and change initiatives) make about the endeavor itself. A 2002 issue of *Sh'ma* presented two distinct positions about congregational education. There are those who suggest that the congregational school is a relic of the past and cannot be made a relevant setting for Jewish education today (Schoem). They call for "transformation" as a total reinvention that might lead to something with no resemblance to a school. Others writing in the same issue of *Sh'ma* acknowledge the schools' difficulties but claim that under the right conditions they can become powerful educational settings (Koller-Fox, Aron, Lee and Weinberg). From this perspective the school might make use of camping and retreats, adult and family learning and cyberspace. (This is also called "transformation" by its proponents.) Greater clarity about what is being proposed will help both the initiatives and the schools that are attempting to improve. What are the schools' purposes? What is the context in which they operate? What are their families' realities? What should be the relationship to other Jewish educational opportunities within the congregation and the community? How can the school support and deepen Jewish identity? Positions about these basic questions should shape a school's strategic choices, which are too easily driven by an agency or foundation RFP.

- **Questions of Leadership: What is Needed?** Recent organizational literature presents challenging new approaches to leadership. As discussed in the section about new leadership models, Senge, Fullan, Heifitz and others assert that leadership is to be found—and needs to be nurtured—throughout the organization. In this view the role of those with formal authority—to return to the metaphor with which I started—is akin to the head of a jazz ensemble. His or her role is to create the conditions that allow for learning and experimentation to take place, to modulate the pace of the challenges and to recognize the contributions that others need to make in order to achieve success. At different times leaders, Senge asserts, function as designers, teachers and stewards (1999:339–363).

  These ideas, only partially described here, are not easily compatible with the hierarchical nature of many congregations or with the consumerist orientation of many congregants. Moving away from the symbolic role of clergy and other professionals, it calls for new ways of thinking about knowledge, collaboration and decision-making. Of course, these ideas are concepts to be tested and honed in action, and although their suitability to today's congregation and school seem clear to me, there is much to be learned about their application to our setting. What we do know is that the stance of professionals knowing and doing all or being "in control" puts members in a passive, disengaged role, which is the antithesis of an active and engaged community.

- **Questions about Effectiveness, Evaluation and Time.** The American Jewish community is hyperactive. Issues come into focus and are quickly forgotten. Funders frequently support new ideas but are not always ready to invest over the long time frame needed for new ideas to mature and be institutionalized. This raises questions: What will focus the community on the needs of the congregational school? Will it support changes for long enough periods for innovations to unfold and take hold? At what points is it appropriate to evaluate what is happening, and how will the information be used? How will the community be organized—whether locally or nationally—to learn from its efforts? These questions need to be addressed as new approaches are developed.

SOME PRACTICAL SUGGESTIONS

- **Develop Contexts for Learning from Experience.** It would benefit all those involved in school improvement, whether as funders, practitioners, planners, or researchers, if there were ways to share information about what is being learned as different initiatives proceed. Information that would be useful to everyone includes:

  - A regularly updated conceptual map showing what is happening nationally, regionally and locally;
  - Information about the dilemmas and new learning that emerge from different change initiatives;
  - Research protocols that can be adapted and shared by different initiatives so that their processes and results might be compared;
  - In-depth, systematic case studies of planning and implementation processes;
  - In-depth, systematic studies of different approaches to leadership embedded in different initiatives.

  We can imagine several ways to access this information, including annually convening the people most involved in this "change work" to examine the most pressing questions. The information gleaned would be made widely available electronically and in print and within a few years generate a body of usable knowledge. There could be special web-based sites that gather in-depth information from different projects. Whatever the mechanism for sharing information and resources, it will require a shift from a private, proprietary ethic to one of collaboration and a commitment to building a usable knowledge base.

- **Investigate the Essential Question: How Has/Have the Initiative/s Affected Participants' Learning and Their Lives?** If we are investing in the congregational school in order to deepen, extend, or otherwise improve the learning that takes place, with the expectation that this will have a positive effect on participants' Jewish identity, then we need to understand the extent to which we succeed in meeting these goals. The evaluative work has generally not addressed this most basic question; it looks instead at the process issues and at participants' satisfaction and affect. These are important. But unless we think that improved learning is a secondary goal, then we have to address conceptually and methodologically difficult questions about learning and improvement without reducing them to simplistic metrics akin to an achievement test. In the absence of agreed-upon standards, how is new learning to be measured? What is the proper time frame: the end of a student's year in school, graduation, adulthood? How does learning influence the student's emerging sense of Jewish identity? While difficult, these questions can be addressed. It would require a willingness to extend the evaluation capacity beyond an initiative's first few years and to develop sophisticated ways to conceptualize and measure Jewish education, learners, settings and impacts. Doing this is important, but not only from the perspective of the community's financial investment. It is important because of the nature of the work itself. If learning, as Ahad Ha'Am put it, is the secret to Jewish survival, then knowing more about conditions that support meaningful and enduring learning must be a cornerstone of our communal strategies for school improvement.

HIGHLIGHTS

This article has shown that:

- an impressive body of knowledge in general education and organizational studies has developed over the last fifteen years about wide-scale change in educational settings;
- significant change processes are messy, take place at the "edge of chaos," which is a potentially creative state, and require both adaptiveness and generativity;
- successful change requires a high degree of individual and group/organizational learning and "systems thinking," and
- there are practical implications in these concepts for planning and leading change processes.

Change initiatives in Jewish schools have been instigated over the last fifteen years. Many of these:

- are shaped, at least in part, by insights from organizational and educational theories;
- blend congregational and school change efforts;
- have not shared information in ways that can build a usable body of knowledge to guide future efforts.

While the sense that congregational schools are troubled endures, there is some indication that they are starting to receive more attention as the community recognizes that:

- most children who will receive some Jewish education in North America will attend a congregational school;
- there are a number of promising new models being developed.

Ongoing and future efforts should be:

- better conceptualized, especially in terms of the purposes of Jewish schooling in today's environment with the changing nature of Jewish identity;
- more aware of the organizational contexts in which they work;
- evaluated in terms of the improvements in Jewish learning, not only participation rates and/or immediate satisfaction;
- given sufficient time and resources to flourish.

THE LARGER CONTEXT

This chapter looks at planned change—i.e., deliberate attempts to improve something by developing new approaches. Yet if we take experience (our own and others') seriously, we know that trying to improve complex systems is difficult, and all too often the results of change initiatives disappoint. "The more things change, the more they stay the same." אֵין כָּל חָדָשׁ תַּחַת הַשָּׁמֶשׁ [ain kol ḥadash taḥat ha-shamesh]—"There is nothing new under the sun." "The only thing that likes change is a wet baby." Or, from a credit card advertisement, "Change is good." Ours is a fast-moving society that is enamored of change while simultaneously being skeptical and unrealistic about it. What we have discussed about changing Jewish schools is as relevant to effecting change in other Jewish educational enterprises.

ANNOTATED BIBLIOGRAPHY

ISA ARON AND COLLABORATORS

Aron, I., Lee, S. and Rossel, S. (1995) *A Congregation of Learners: Transforming the Synagogue into a Learning Community*. New York: UAHC Press.

Aron, I. (2000) *Becoming a Congregation of Learners: Learning as a Key to Revitalizing Congregational Life*. Woodstock, VT: Jewish Lights Publishing.

Aron, I. (2002) *The Self-Renewing Congregation: Organizational Strategies for Revitalizing Congregational Life*. Woodstock, VT: Jewish Lights Publishing.

I am grouping three books together because they show how the conception and implementation of school and congregational change efforts developed over time as the ECE went forward. Because careful documentation of the individual congregation's experience and the strategic plans of the overall project was part of the ECE from the start, the books that emerged are based on both theory and implementation experience. Assumptions about the meaning of such key concepts as Jewish, education, learning, knowledge, congregation, community, partnership, change and leadership are explored. The first volume presents papers that helped shape ECE's conceptual framework. The second and third volumes use what was learned from the experience of the ECE and its experimenting congregations to present theory-based, practical field guides for congregational change that focus on Jewish education. The methodology they develop can be widely adapted and used. Also see www.eceonline.com.

MICHAEL FULLAN AND COLLABORATORS

_____ (1993). *Change Forces: Probing the Depths of Educational Reform*. London and Bristol, PA: The Falmer Press.

_____ (1999) *Change Forces: The Sequel*. London and Bristol, PA: The Falmer Press.

_____ (2005) *Leadership and Sustainability: Systems Thinkers in Action*. Thousand Oaks, CA: Corwin Press.

Fullan, M., Hill, P. and Crevola, C. (2006). *Breakthrough*. Thousand Oaks, CA: Corwin Press.

Fullan, with his team of researchers and practitioners, is deeply involved in educational reform but draws on new thinking from related disciplines. His work has evolved over the years and helps people interested in changing schools understand the contexts of schools and develop ways to make change. He was one of the first to focus on the nonrational, non-linear forces at work in schools and to help people think more systemically about school reform. His most recent work is both pessimistic and optimistic: pessimistic because he recognizes that billions of dollars later, school reform has not accomplished all it needed to. He is optimistic because he believes the pieces are finally in place and are nearing the "tipping point."

Gladwell, M. (2000) *The Tipping Point: How Little Things Can Make a Big Difference*. Boston, MA: Little, Brown and Company. The content is summarized in the body of this essay. This book is not about the content of change; it focuses entirely on processes that cause some changes to take hold while others, equally interesting, quickly fade from view. It behooves groups attempting to sustain change in a school to think through Gladwell's model and apply the processes he describes in their setting.

Heifitz, R. (1994) *Leadership: Without Easy Answers*. Cambridge, MA: Harvard University Press. Based on a wide range of theoretical, historical, psychological and empirical studies, this highly influential book asserts that the leader's primary task is to mobilize the organization's adaptive work. Heifitz considers the leaders with authority—who are supposed "to lead" but often have their hands tied—and the others throughout the organization who are poised to lead without authority. The book is a helpful, engaging and nuanced view of leadership in an era of complexity and anxiety. While most of the cases he uses to illustrate his points are large-scale, historical cases (Martin Luther King and the civil rights movement, for example), there are other, more immediate cases as well. The accounts help the reader understand the theories and how they can be applied in schools and congregations, even though this is not Heifitz's audience.

Reimer, J. (1997) *Succeeding at Jewish Education: How One Synagogue Made It Work*. Philadelphia: Jewish Publication Society. This is an ethnographic study of a congregational school that attempted to develop a distinctive vision of Jewish life and education. This is simultaneously embraced and resisted by the congregants. The book provides an insider view of some of the complexities of making changes when there are diverse stakeholders and shows some of the blind spots as well as strengths its leadership exemplified.

Sarason, S. (1996) *Revisiting: The Culture of Schools and the Problem of Change*. New York: Teachers College Press. Although the examples are dated (the first edition was published in 1971), this remains a seminal book. Examining the question of why so few innovations take root in schools (or take root but in watered down versions), Sarason shifted the focus from teacher and administrator ineptitude or resistance to the cultural system of the school by identifying "regularities" of school cultures that need to be understood if initiatives are to be successful. Much of the attention to the process of school change and the organizational systems of schools emerges from Sarason's critique.

PETER SENGE AND COLLABORATORS

_____ (1990) *The Fifth Discipline: The Art and Practice of the Learning Organization*. New York: Doubleday.

_____ (1994) *The Fifth Discipline Fieldbook: Strategies and Tools for Building a Learning Organization*. New York: Doubleday.

_____ (1999) *The Dance of Change: The Challenges to Sustaining Momentum in Learning Organizations*. New York: Doubleday.

_____ (2002) *Schools That Learn*. New York: Doubleday.

_____ (2005) *Presence: An Exploration of Profound Change in People, Organizations, and Society*. New York: Currency.

Kofman, F. & Senge, P. (1005). Communities of Commitment: The Heart of Learning Organizations. In Cawla, S. and Renesch, J., *Learning Organizations: Developing Cultures for Tomorrow's Workplace*. Portland, OR: Productivity Press.

Disputing simplistic frameworks that management literature sometimes applies to complex systems, Senge makes the case that for organizations to succeed in today's challenging and dynamic environment, people throughout the organization need to continue to learn—to question assumptions and develop new ways of working together. He adopts a long-term view and delineates five basic disciplines that converge in innovative learning organizations: systems thinking, personal mastery, mental models, shared vision and team learning. The theoretical underpinnings of his work, with rich examples, are carefully laid out in *The Fifth Discipline,* and the other books (1994, 1999, 2000) provide practical applications and examples of the approach. More recently Senge has looked to living organisms and self-organizing systems for guidance (2004). Senge's work is complex and applicable for settings facing adaptive challenges.

Sh'ma: A Journal of Jewish Responsibility. Congregational Schools. (March 2002). In a series of short essays the volume lays out current thinking about the dilemmas and possibilities of congregational education. Different viewpoints are presented, from Feiman-Nemser's argument that teachers and their professional development should be at the heart of the school improvement approaches to Aron, Lee and Weinberg's approach that looks to new ideas and structures to revitalize the school and ultimately the congregation.

ADDITIONAL REFERENCES

Argyris, C. & Schon, D. (1982). *Theory in Practice: Increasing Professional Effectiveness.* San Francisco: Jossey-Bass.

Aron, I. (2000). *Becoming a Congregation of Learners: Learning as a Key to Revitalizing Congregational Life.* Woodstock, VT: Jewish Lights Publishing.

Aron, I. (2002). *The Self-Renewing Congregation: Organizational Strategies for Revitalizing Congregational Life.* Woodstock, VT: Jewish Lights Publishing.

Banks, A. & Wolfson, R. (1998) *First Fruit: A Whizin Anthology of Jewish Family Education.* Los Angeles: Whizin Institute for Jewish Family LIfe.

Borowitz, E. (1992). "Tzimtzum: A Mystic Model for Contemporary Leadership" in S. Kelman (ed.), *What We Know about Jewish Education: A Handbook of Today's Research for Tomorrow's Jewish Education.* Los Angeles: Torah Aura.

Deal, T. & Peterson, K. (1996). *Shaping School Culture: The Heart of Leadership.* San Francisco: Jossey-Bass.

Cohen, S.M. & Eisen, A. (2000). *The Jew Within: Self, Family, and Community in America.* Bloomington: Indiana University Press

Elmore, R. (2000). *Building New Structures for School Leadership.* Albert Shanker Institute.

Fullan, M. (1999). *Change Forces: The Sequel.* London and Bristol, PA: The Falmer Press.

_____ (2001). *Leading in a Culture of Change.* San Francisco: Jossey Bass.

Gladwell, M. (2000). *The Tipping Point: How Little Things Can Make a Big Difference.* Boston: Little, Brown and Company.

Gronn, P. (2002). Distributed Leadership. In K. Leithwood & P. Hallinger (eds.), *Second International Handbook of Educational Leadership and Administration: Part 2.* Great Britain: Dordrecht: Kluwer Academic Publishers.

Hargreaves, A. (2005). "Sustaining Educational Leadership" [Symposium]. *The Educational Forum* 69 (2).

Heifitz, R. (1994). *Leadership: Without Easy Answers.* Cambridge, MA: Harvard University Press.

Herring, H. (2001). Networked Judaism: A Fresh Look at the Organization of the American Jewish Community. In H. Herring, & B. Shrage, (eds.), *Networked Judaism: Linking People, Institutions, Community.* Newton, MA: Wilstein Institute.

Hoffman, L. (2006). *ReThinking Synagogues: A New Vocabulary for Congregational Life.* Woodstock, VT: Jewish Lights.

Horowitz, B. (2000). *Connections and Journeys: Assessing Critical Opportunities for Enhancing Jewish Identity.* New York: UJA-Federation of New York.

Kelman, S. (1992). *What We Know about Jewish Education: A Handbook of Today's Research for Tomorrow's Jewish Education.* Los Angeles: Torah Aura.

Kofman, F. and Senge, P. (1995). Communities of Commitment: The Heart of Learning Organizations. In S. Cawla, & J. Renesch, *Learning Organizations: Developing Cultures for Tomorrow's Workplace.* Portland, OR: Productivity Press.

Koren, A. & Shevitz, S. (2004). "'It Planted the Seeds': A Retrospective Account of Jewish Family Education." In *Jewish Education* 70 (3).

Lewis, H. (2006). *From Sanctuary to Boardroom: A Jewish Approach to Leadership.* Lanham, MD: Rowman and Littlefield Publishers.

Morgan, G. (1993). *Imaginization: The Art of Creative Management.* Newbury Park, CA: Sage.

Orlikowski, W.J. (2006, July) *Passion for Action,* the newsletter of MIT's Leadership Center, 1 (3).

Oshry, B. (1995). *Seeing Systems: Unlocking the Mysteries of Organizational Life.* San Francisco: Berrett-Koehler Publishers.

Reimer, J. (1997) *Succeeding at Jewish Education: How One Synagogue Made It Work.* Philadelphia: Jewish Publication Society.

Sales, A., Koren, A. & Shevitz, S. (2000). *Sh'arim: Building Gateways to Jewish Life and Community.* Waltham, MA: Cohen Center for Modern Jewish Studies, Brandeis University.

Sales, A. (2006). *Synergy: Mining the Research, Framing the Questions.* www. Cmjs.org//files/Synergy%20Precis. pdf.

Sarason, S. (1996). *Revisiting: The Culture of Schools and the Problem of Change.* New York: Teachers College Press.

Schein, E. (1992). *Organizational Culture and Leadership (2nd edition).* San Francisco: Jossey-Bass.

Schein, E. (1999). *The Corporate Culture Survival Guide.* San Francisco: Jossey-Bass.

Schein, E. *http://www.a2zpsychology.com/articles/kurt_lewin's_change_theory.htm*

Schon, D. (1983). *The Reflective Practitioner: How Professionals Think in Action.* New York: Basic Books.

Schon, D. (1987). *Educating the Reflective Practitioner.* San Francisco: Jossey-Bass.

Schwarz, S. (2002). *Finding a Spiritual Home: How a New Generation of Jews Can Transform the American Synagogue.* San Francisco: Jossey-Bass.

Senge, P. (1999). *The Dance of Change: The Challenges to Sustaining Momentum in Learning Organizations.* New York: Doubleday.

_____, (2000). *Schools That Learn: A Fifth Discipline Fieldbook for Educators, Parents and Everyone Who Cares about Education.* New York: Currency.

Serviovanni, T. (1989). What Really Counts in Improving Schools. In T. Sergiovanni, & J. Moore (eds.), *Schooling for Tomorrow: Directing Reforms to Issues that Count.* Boston: Allyn and Bacon.

Shevitz, S. (1992). "What We Learn about Changing Jewish Schools...Or, 'Surf, Don't Pitch!'" In S. Kelman (ed.), *What We Know About Jewish Education.* Los Angeles: Torah Aura Productions.

Shevitz, S. (1994). "An Orientation to Transformation in Congregational Settings." In *Creating an Environment to Transform Jewish Lives.* New York: Avi Chai Foundation.

Shevitz, S. (1995). "An Organizational Perspective on Changing Jewish Education: What the Literature Reveals." In I. Aron, S. Lee, S. & S. Rossel, *A Congregation of Learners: Transforming the Synagogue into a Learning Community.* New York: UAHC Press.

Shevitz, S. & Cousens, B. (2004). "Why Is This System Different Than All Other Systems?" Unpublished manuscript.

Shevitz, S. & Karpel, D. (1995). "Sh'arim Family Educator Initiative: An Interim Report of Programs and Populations." Boston: Bureau of Jewish Education.

Spillane, J. P. (2004). "Educational Evaluations and Policy Analysis." *Educational Leadership* 26 (2), 169–172.

Wertheimer, J. (2005). *Linking the Silos: How to Accelerate the Momentum in Jewish Education Today.* New York: Avi Chai Foundation.

Wheatley, M. (1999). *Leadership and the New Science.* San Francisco: Berreett-Koehler Publishers.

Wolfson, R. (2006). *The Spirituality of Welcoming: How to Transform Your Congregation into a Sacred Community.* Woodstock, VT: Jewish Lights.

Zeder, J. "Congregational Schools Focus on Teacher Training." *Forwards,* August 11, 2006.

Finding New Models: Alternatives to Religious School

Rob Weinberg

INTRODUCTION

The congregational religious school is an institution Jews love to hate. For over a century, educational professionals, lay leaders, parents, and students have been relentless in their critiques of the congregational school, complaining that the hours are inconvenient, the discipline lax, the teachers unprofessional, and the students bored. Responses to this situation have varied over time. In the 1970s, for example, the denominational movements created new curricula, and local central agencies for Jewish education launched initiatives to recruit and train teachers. In the 1980s and 1990s, in contrast, the congregational school suffered from benign neglect as communal leaders focused their attention on day schools, pre-schools, Israel trips, and other modes of informal Jewish education.

Today, however, leaders of the Jewish community realize that they cannot avoid dealing with congregational education in general and the congregational school in particular. The majority of Jewish children who receive a Jewish education are educated in congregational schools. While much of the conversation has centered on how to *improve* these schools, a few congregations have opted instead to fundamentally rethink children's Jewish education. These congregations have recognized that schooling itself is a paradigm subject to examination and change. Paradigms shift when the world changes and underlying needs to which they once presented a solution shift.

THE CONGREGATIONAL RELIGIOUS SCHOOLS IN HISTORICAL CONTEXT

When the grandparents and great-grandparents of today's congregational school students came to these shores starting in the late 19th century and the early decades of the 20th century, they sought to "modernize" Jewish education by modeling it after public schools. For these immigrant Jews seeking to become true Americans, the most patriotic thing they could do was to send their children to public schools. The creation of so-called "supplementary" Jewish schools made it possible for these new Americans to do the patriotic thing.

That model met their needs at the time. It enabled their children to learn the language of the new land and acclimate to the regularities of American life, even while living in very Jewish communities where the rhythms, the sights, and the sounds of Jewish life surrounded them.

But what was "supplementary" school intended to supplement? Not the child's secular education. It was designed to be a primarily cognitive instructional experience to *supplement* the Jewish learning and living that went on naturally within a home, a community, and a synagogue in which Judaism was woven into daily life. It assumed a cultural context in which Judaism permeated the air, the daily conversation and the daily, weekly, and seasonal routines.

Supplementary schools were designed to impart the **knowledge** and **information** that young Jews would need to participate fully in that active Jewish community while parents, extended families and the broader Jewish community took responsibility for the rest of a child's full enculturation into Jewish living.

Fast-forward to 2008. The society has changed, the needs of children and their families have changed, and yet the predominant paradigm of so-called supplementary Jewish schooling remains remarkably similar in structure. Weissman (2005) is fond of saying that when educators were supported by parents and the community, the tools of schools were enough. But today parents drop off their children at our synagogue schools and expect their kids, when they come out the other end, not only to **know** but also to **believe** and **belong**. If these are the goals and expectations, then the tools of schooling—the classroom, the textbook, the teachers, and the principal—are not enough.

Emerging new models of Jewish education either augment schooling with additional educational experiences or, in some cases, depart from the paradigm of schooling altogether.

RESEARCH INTO NEW MODELS

In 1992 the Rhea Hirsch School of Education at the Los Angeles campus of the Hebrew Union College created the Experiment in Congregational Education (ECE), of which the author is the current director. The ECE's goals are to create both **Congregations of Learners** (in which more people participate in richer and deeper learning) and **Self-Renewing Congregations** (which are reflective, ready to experiment and practice collaborative leadership). During the ECE's first decade fourteen congregations throughout North America worked intensively to develop the model. Over the last five years the ECE has expanded its activities in an effort to reach a larger number of congregations and to quicken the pace of their transformation. One of these efforts focuses on re-thinking and re-designing the congregational school.

Though there was little in the literature about alternative models of the congregational religious school, several new models grew out of the initial pilot congregations. To find additional models, interviews and site visits were conducted seeking answers to the following questions:

- What alternative models have been created, and how do they differ from conventional congregational school models?
- How did the innovators address the underlying issues that led to the development of these new models?
- What goals were they seeking to achieve?
- What type of change process is required to move from the conventional models to new ones?

ALTERNATIVE MODELS OF THE RELIGIOUS SCHOOL

In the research, close to a dozen alternative programs were identified that were grouped into five models, some of which augment or modify the conventional school model, while others break the mold entirely. These models are:

SHABBAT COMMUNITIES

In **Shabbat Communities** families learn, pray, and celebrate Shabbat together. Shabbat communities are not meant to be programs at which parents simply drop off their children. Rather, they emphasize the importance of regular participation in the life of the community by both parents and children. Powerful prayer experiences, meaningful learning, quality family time, and building community are the primary motivators that lead parents to choose a Shabbat community program over enrolling their children in a traditional school track. These programs involve parents and children equally and provide many opportunities for families to take leadership roles and contribute to the community.

Although programs within this model differ slightly in the details, the basic structure has families attend Shabbat Community programs for two to three hours on Shabbat morning or afternoon. The time spent at the congregation includes a prayer service, children's learning and parent learning. In some programs the parents and children study separately, while other programs involve all family members in joint study. In addition to Shabbat attendance, this model is supplemented with midweek Hebrew instruction for the appropriate age groups.

CONGREGANT-LED EXPERIENTIAL LEARNING

This model transforms the school into a congregation-wide learning experience in which adults and post-b'nei mitzvah-aged teens facilitate experiential, theme-based learning for their fellow congregants. Congregant-led experiential learning dramatically alters the traditional conception of the school as an educational program. Rather than following a set curriculum for each grade, this model involves the entire congregation in the process of exploring various thematic units over the course of the year. Each unit lasts from two to eight weeks and covers a particular topic, which could vary from biblical heroes to Jewish cooking, to the role of the moon in the Jewish calendar. Many of the learning activities through which themes are explored are designed to involve all congregants and emphasize the value of intergenerational learning. The teachers are congregants who volunteer to be members of teaching teams. The directors of the program carefully design teaching teams to draw upon the strengths of each of the team members. Prior to the introduction of a new thematic unit, volunteer teachers meet for an adult learning workshop where they explore the theme and are given precise instructions for implementation of the learning activities. The congregation-based structure of this program emphasizes community-building and identity formation. Congregants get to know one another both as fellow learners and as teachers. The relationships formed through communal learning provide congregants with an array of Jewish role models and opportunities to explore Jewish identity.

AFTER-SCHOOL CARE AND STUDY

Students in after-school care and study programs experience Jewish learning and community as part of their ongoing daily experience in the after-school program. The model is a unique hybrid of daycare and Jewish education. It provides students with the warm, caring environment of an after-school daycare facility accompanied by the curricular content of a religious school or Jewish camp. Students attend the program from a minimum of two afternoons a week to a maximum of five. Since students spend extended hours in the program, it is particularly important to make them feel at home and part of a community. Strong bonds form among participants and between staff and participants. The sense of community fostered by the after-school care and study model extends to the parents of the participants who gather for family programming and have taken the initiative to form parent study and support groups. Many children and their parents remark that this model provides them with a sense of family, both nuclear and extended. Beyond the social benefits of the extended hours of attendance, the daycare structure provides unique curricular opportunities. For example, extended attendance provides the opportunity to teach a Modern Hebrew curriculum that is reinforced by the use of Hebrew terms during social interactions. In addition to Hebrew, each week two Judaica themes are explored.

FLEXIBLE LEARNING OPTIONS

In this model learning is tailored to the schedules and interests of children and families. Not every student in every family can fit into a single time frame and a single learning structure. The programs included under this rubric, flexible learning options, were designed to accommodate students who need more individualized attention and/or those whose schedules preclude attending religious school at one of the set times. Programs in this model trade off time spent in grade-level classrooms for time spent studying at home, at camp, or as a family. There are three basic types of religious school options that offer flexible scheduling arrangements:

- Individualized Hebrew tutoring (at the synagogue or at home)
- Independent study projects
- Intensive day camp

RELIGIOUS SCHOOL ENHANCEMENTS

This model enhances the conventional school with additional learning opportunities for students and/or their families. Even congregations committed to a conventional school structure have found that their goals for Jewish education are more easily reached when they include elements of family education, informal education, intensive study, or arts education. The programs within this model augment the formal school with frequent family programs; weekend retreats, trips and special events; small-group intensive study; or by incorporating arts-based or project-based learning into their programs.

COMMON THREADS: SIGNIFICANT ISSUES AND GOALS

In analyzing the learning from the programs within all five of the models, as well as the innovation processes that led to their creation, four significant cross-cutting issues began to emerge. Although some issues figured more strongly into the program that emerged at one congregation or another, each congregation's innovators considered each of the issues. These issues highlight key aspects of what differentiates these models from a conventional congregational school:

1. How can we integrate Jewish learning and Jewish living more closely?
2. How can we involve parents more deeply in their children's Jewish education?
3. How can we create a stronger sense of community?
4. How do we create lasting Jewish memories?

INTEGRATING LEARNING AND LIVING

Students who learn *about* Judaism but live in a largely secular environment come to regard their Judaism as outside of or ancillary to their true selves. If, for example, students learn prayers and never go to services, or if they learn "how Jews celebrate Shabbat" and never celebrate it in their homes, their learning can easily be perceived as irrelevant. If, however, students learn something in school (e.g., prayers or Shabbat practice) and then integrate it into their lives (e.g., by going to services or making Shabbat at home), then their learning will not only be relevant but can also have a real impact on their lives.

For example, models like Shabbat communities and after-school care and study create an ongoing regularity to Jewish learning and practice. The former makes a child's Jewish education part and parcel of the family's weekly rhythm of Shabbat observance. Families learn about Shabbat by doing Shabbat. At after-school care and study children experience daily the **continual** reinforcement of Jewish rituals (e.g., daily prayer, food blessings, tzedakah). Learning and practice are intertwined.

PARENT INVOLVEMENT

As discussed above, supplementary schools originally were intended to augment what parents teach their children about Judaism at home and what they absorb from living in an active Jewish community. However, many Jewish children do not learn much about Judaism or experience much of Jewish life at home or in their community. The result is that all too often the congregational school becomes a replacement for—instead of a supplement to—a child's Jewish life.

A better education requires that the responsibility for a child's Jewish education be shared among parents, the synagogue or school, and the entire community. However, for whatever reason, the weight of this responsibility has fallen to the afternoon or weekend school—a weight it cannot possibly bear alone. This is further complicated by parents who face the challenge of not knowing enough about Judaism to teach their children.

Alternative models such as religious school enhancement and Shabbat communities incorporate elements of family learning—whether joint learning, where parents and children engage in activities together, or parallel learning, where parents and children learn separately but simultaneously, each at their own levels. Others, such as congregant-led experiential learning, involve parents as teachers and in other supportive roles.

Family learning leads to several important outcomes. First, when parents and children come to the synagogue to learn together, they develop a shared vocabulary that they can then incorporate into their lives, both in conversation and in practice. Perhaps the most powerful impact is that parents model their values—they "walk the walk" and not just "talk the talk" about the importance of Judaism. Parents send very different messages to children when they, too, are involved in Jewish learning instead of just dropping the children off. They convey to their children that Judaism matters, that it matters to them personally and that Jewish learning is a lifelong pursuit.

THE ROLE OF COMMUNITY

The role that community plays in alternative learning models is two-fold—the presence and support of community facilitates learning, and learning in these models becomes a vehicle to build stronger community ties.

Through the ages Jewish learning has been a communal activity. Although our tradition does not require a *minyan* for learning to take place, a traditional Jewish method of study is in *hevruta*, meaning with a partner. Discussion and debate, which are central to an authentically Jewish learning process, require the presence of another person—or of other people—to stimulate each person's thoughts.

Second, the act of learning builds community. Dialogue—the effort of two people to really listen and respond to each other—not only enriches each person's learning but forges connections among the learners. The act of studying together builds the community connections that so many Jews come to synagogue looking to find. Learning builds community, and Jews find community through learning. This is one strength of the after-school care and study model, since children who may attend different secular schools see one another daily after school and are able to make connections and form friendships. Flexible learning options and religious school enhancements—when they include multiple family education programs, retreats, and field trips—provide the possibility for community-building among children and families as well.

Finally, the two come together when students feel part of a community where what is learned is lived; it gives rich meaning and relevance to their learning, well beyond the acquisition of knowledge. Learning to recite Torah blessings is a dramatically different experience if you understand its purpose as preparing you for the day when you will be given an *aliyah*, thereby taking your place in a community where you have seen others chant the blessings and read Torah week in and week out. And being present for such a *simcha* deepens the connections among those who are part of that community and witness the fruit of the seeds that learning has planted. Shabbat community models excel in this respect by creating a regular, ongoing community of Jews who learn, pray, eat, and celebrate together.

LASTING JEWISH MEMORIES

Memories we have of Jewish experiences—and especially of our Jewish educational experiences—seem to have a significant impact on our affiliation and involvement later in life. Much has been written about the fact that many North American adults' personal growth as Jews was stunted at age thirteen when they dropped out of Hebrew school after bar or bat mitzvah, leaving them with a "pediatric" view of Judaism. Innovators of alternative Jewish educational models have sought to replace the "I hated Hebrew school…and so will you" memories with experiences that will produce more positive memories and replace the downward spiral with positive—even enthusiastic—generational cycles of Jewish memory and identification.

Among the ways that innovative models seek to create positive and lasting memories are:

- Creating exceptional moments that are embedded in very engaging programs (for example, through retreats or extended arts activities);
- Creating curricula that demonstrate in compelling ways how Judaism can help learners to respond to the real-life issues that they face personally and as part of a wider community;
- Employing a wide range of learning modalities, in recognition of the fact that students will connect differently with their education;
- Recruiting teachers who will be accessible role models and who will form strong bonds with their students, even if that means that these teachers require more in-house preparation and support.

In each case the intent is for participants to remember their Jewish education as not only creative, engaging and joyful, but also as something that helped them make and find meaning in their life.

FOSTERING CHANGE IN CONGREGATIONAL EDUCATION

Aron, Lee and Weinberg have written extensively about the kinds of processes required to bring about positive and lasting change in congregational schools and, more broadly, in congregational education (Aron, Lee and Rossel 1995; Aron 2000; Aron 2002; Weinberg and Aron 2002; Aron and Weinberg 2002; Weinberg 2005). The fact that congregational schools are embedded in larger synagogue systems is critical to keep in mind when looking to bring about significant change. Synagogues tend to be tradition-bound institutions, slow to change and led by congregants who often have difficulty distinguishing capital "T" Tradition—our immutable heritage—and small "t" traditions—the habits and customs we've created and passed down within our congregations. When you can't tell what is sacred and what is not, it is difficult to change anything. At the school level, many efforts at "school improvement" have sought to bring about change by revamping curricula or training teachers. But these efforts are necessarily limited in scope and impact because they do not address the entire system (see, e.g., Holtz 1993; *Agenda: Jewish Education* 2002; *Jewish Education News* 2006).

What's more, creating compelling congregational education is not a one-time effort. Experience with and research about congregations that have succeeded in transforming Jewish education indicate that congregations need to view change as an ongoing activity. The goal is not simply to disseminate a particular innovation, but rather to *create innovators* and to build a *culture of experimentation* and the congregational *capacity for ongoing change*.

Such change requires not only new models but new questions and assumptions, new partnerships, and new skills. Congregations that are innovating new models are able to do so because they have changed the conversation from one that only asks questions like "What information should students absorb?" "How many hours on how many days?" and "Will they be able to perform well at their bar or bat mitzvah service?" to a conversation that instead asks questions like "What is the function of Jewish education? Is it **instruction** or **enculturation**?" "How should what we learn in the synagogue relate to the way we live our lives day to day?" and "Who are the learners and who are the teachers?"

To succeed in a synagogue setting, the processes through which they ask these questions must be collaborative, vision-driven, infused with systemic thinking (Senge 1990; Senge et al. 1999; Kofman and Senge 1993) and informed by appreciative inquiry (see, e.g., Watkins and Mohr 2001) that builds on strength and possibility and honors the past, rather than seeking out deficiency and finding fault. No single educator, rabbi, or impassioned lay person alone can bring about this sort of change. It takes collaboration among rabbis, educational directors, teachers, parents and others, not only to come up with new models—creative educators could do that on their own—but to build ownership and a foundation of shared ownership. It takes investing the time to get to know one another, to come to trust one another and to commit together to a compelling future for Jewish learning in the congregation before anyone can have the courage and the stamina to make long-lasting, far-reaching, significant educational change.

And it takes new Jewish leadership skills. These are the skills to bring Jewish values to the table of decision making. These are the skills to build a community that can embrace change aligned with a compelling vision for the future: processes that model Jewish leadership skills and that build trust, community, vision, and energy. The medium—the way that change occurs—is the message. That kind of process builds strong cadres of support for new models and patience to let them evolve through experimentation and revision.

IMPLICATIONS FOR POLICY AND THE PRACTITIONER

The picture painted of alternative models and innovative processes to create them yields several implications for practitioners and policy-makers. Just as these models break the mold of conventional thinking, transforming congregational education will require that we alter conventional assumptions about what it takes and how to go about it.

First, the underlying goals must shift from improvement to transformation, from dissemination of innovations to creation and empowerment of innovators.

Second, alternative models can't be transplanted without careful attention to context. They evolved in particular settings in response to specific needs and in consonance with certain values affirmed by their communities. Each one owes its success, in large part, to a supportive congregational environment in which learning is considered a communal responsibility. That means departing from the assumption that the road to improvement is to find "best practices" and facilitate their replication. Repeated efforts at best practice dissemination in Jewish education have met with limited success. In the field of human resources within the business world, the best practice dissemination approach has been contrasted with the notion of "strategic fit" (Becker and Gerhart 1996)—that each organization must design and implement those practices that uniquely support its strategy or vision. The latter suggests that each congregation, with its unique culture, circumstances, and history, must fashion its own vision of its desired future and then adapt, mix and match, or draw inspiration from others' innovations to develop models that align with the congregation's own visions.

Third, although the expertise of national initiatives may be needed to start congregations on the road to innovation, local central agencies and movement-based educational resources must evolve into a new kind of network of support for congregations that are innovating. These agencies need to become well-informed about new models and well-equipped to help congregations bring their entire educational system into alignment with a new educational vision and new programmatic paradigms.

Finally, those who invest in educational transformation at the congregational level—whether through foundation or federation grants or individual gifts—need to recognize that congregations change slowly. If we want change to be long-lasting, far-reaching and significant, we must have patience to wait for those results and to fund evaluation efforts with similarly long time horizons.

QUESTIONS FOR ADDITIONAL RESEARCH

As research into the transformation of congregational education continues to develop, these questions bear consideration:

- How well are these emerging alternative models working? Each model has its own goals and must be evaluated on its own terms.

- What does it take to align the whole congregational and educational system around a well-articulated vision?

- What differentiates the congregations that are able to initiate and continually regenerate long-lasting, far-reaching, significant change from those that make small changes with vanishing effects?

FUTURE DIRECTIONS—PRACTICAL IDEAS TO MOVE THE FIELD AHEAD

- Those interested in innovation can begin the conversation in their own congregations by trying a little experiment. Start asking people what they think the goals are for the educational program. Ask them, "What do you think we are really trying to accomplish?" and "What kind of learning experiences would we really like our kids to have?" Ask the school principal. Ask the rabbi(s). Ask some teachers. Ask some parents. Ask some students. Ask some synagogue board members. It is likely that you will find a dizzying array of answers—many of them potentially conflicting—and an astounding level of uncertainty. When goals are not clear, a congregation's time, talent, and treasure get diffused in many directions. Once the lack of clarity and consensus is identified, the door may open to concerted discussion to forge a shared vision and goals.

- Change the vocabulary! As long as we frame the conversation as being about "religious school," we remain firmly implanted in the paradigm of schooling. Instead we need subtly to shift our language. Begin by talking about "Jewish education," although the word "education" for many

505

still carries connotations of school. If you reread this chapter, you will see that I often refer to "Jewish learning," which opens the door to many settings and modalities. To move ahead, we must be prepared to deconstruct part-time Jewish education to its elements and rebuild it with a variety of answers that don't necessarily add up to something that looks like schooling.

REFERENCES

Agenda: Jewish Education, #15 (Summer 2002). New York: JESNA.

Aron, I. (2000). *Becoming a Congregation of Learners: Learning as a Key to Revitalizing Congregational Life.* Woodstock, VT: Jewish Lights Publishing.

Aron, I. (2002) *The Self-Renewing Congregation: Organizational Strategies for Revitalizing Congregational Life.* Woodstock, VT: Jewish Lights Publishing.

Aron, I., Lee, S. & Rossel, S. (1995). *A Congregation of Learners.* New York: UAHC Press.

Aron, I. & Weinberg, R. (2002). "Learning as a Portal for Synagogue Revitalization." *Jewish Education News,* 23 (1), 21–23.

Becker, B., & Gerhart, B. (1996). "The Impact of Human Resource Management on Organizational Performance: Progress and Prospects." *The Academy of Management Journal,* 39 (4), 779–801.

Holtz, B.W. (1993). Best Practices Project: Supplementary Schools. New York: Council for Initiatives in Jewish Education.

Jewish Education News, 27, 1 (Winter 2006). New York: CAJE.

Kofman, F. & Senge, P. (1993). "Communities of Commitment: The Heart of Learning Organizations." *Organizational Dynamics,* 22 (2), 4–23.

Senge, P. (1990) *The Fifth Discipline: The Art and Practice of the Learning Organization.* New York: Doubleday.

Senge, P., Kleiner, A., Roberts, C., Ross, R. et al. (1999). *The Dance of Change: The Challenges to Sustaining Momentum in Learning Organizations.* New York: Doubleday.

Watkins, J. M. & Mohr, B. J. (2001). *Appreciative Inquiry: Change at the Speed of Imagination.* San Francisco: Jossey-Bass/Pfieffer.

Weinberg, R. (2005). "Creating and Enacting Shared Visions for Congregational Education." *Jewish Education News,* 26 (1), 19–22.

Weinberg, R. & and Aron, I. (2002). "Revitalizing Congregational Education: Lessons Learned in the Trenches." *Agenda: Jewish Education,* 15, 15–17.

Weissman, C. (2005). Private conversation.

Communal Planning—Continuity Efforts

Beth Cousens

"Would you tell me, please, which way I ought to go from here?"

"That depends a good deal on where you want to get to," said the Cat.

"I don't much care where—" said Alice.

"Then it doesn't matter which way you go," said the Cat.

"—so long as I get *somewhere*," Alice added as an explanation.

"Oh, you're sure to do that," said the Cat, "if you only walk long enough." (Carroll 1960)

Planning can be understood as the ongoing development of a strategy that will reach a specific end. In other words, as Alice and the Cheshire Cat imply, planning involves walking intentionally toward something, weighing options that arise, and then taking paths that will help one get to where one wants to go. One is always sure to wind up somewhere, the Cheshire Cat suggests. But only with intentionality, strategic thinking, and preparation—in other words, planning—can one achieve a desired result.

All Jewish communal organizations plan. In this chapter intentional, community-wide planning processes as they are used by federations and central agencies for Jewish education will be the primary focus. Such communal planning is designed to create change, streamline and create new projects, research and evaluate existing services, and generally strengthen the Jewish education that is offered within a community. Communal planning focuses broadly on all members of a community, with the participants in the planning process being a range of community stakeholders. Such planning is differentiated from educational planning, an activity that more narrowly relates to the specific tasks of education, such as choosing curricula, for example, which is conducted by those directly engaged in the act of education (Lauer 1992, fn l, p. 203). It refers to deliberate, premeditated planning as opposed to naturalistic planning, or the decisions that develop organically in daily events (Bean & Kuh 1984). Such planning is also similar to but differentiated from agency-based planning by a synagogue, Hillel, school, youth group, camp, or other, a-traditional organization responsible for an aspect of Jewish education, or from the national umbrella and issue-oriented organizations that also conduct similar types of planning in Jewish education.

Is planning worthwhile? In recent years a debate in *Curriculum Inquiry* posed this question. As its skeptic, Eisenberg (1995) argues that planning too often relies on specific situations in order to receive a desired outcome. But, he continues, life is never as expected; such specific situations rarely arise, and so attempting to control outcomes is somewhat futile. Floden (1996), on the other hand, suggests that planning is not a panacea and that plans cannot be seen as mandating a specific outcome (a perfectly balanced chocolate soufflé, for example). Still, he maintains that planning must continue, for absent it, we would begin the educational enterprise over again anew every day, pretending we are not building on our past and are not moving intentionally toward a goal. Jewish communal planning in education blends these ideas. Situations are rarely as we believe they will be, but we must still use planning to maximize our resources, build on our previous accomplishments and lessons and move carefully toward our goals. Planning must be a mix of art and science, of plotting, intuition, flexibility, rationality, and creativity. Implemented amid a work routine that is unpredictable, our plan will never take us exactly where we want to go. However, it will help us identify a destination, revisit the appropriateness of our destination as our situation shifts and move us toward that destination. Without a plan we will get somewhere—but it might be far from where we wanted to be.

This debate in *Curriculum Inquiry* understands educational planning to evolve out of empirical investigations of productive education; in other words, planning for education and research on education are always linked. In Jewish organizations and communities, planning is institutionalized. It often is not prompted by empirical research but by a problem facing a Jewish community. What, then, is the role of research in communal planning in Jewish education? When does planning occur, and why? And what does such planning accomplish, produce, and initiate?

Exploring these questions raises challenges. Little research about Jewish communal planning exists. Moreover, the extent to which planners in Jewish education consistently use any materials on planning is not clear. There are few established, well-known practices in this area, nor is there a clear set of work in the area of general planning that Jewish communal planners access. Internal documents that are created or used in Jewish educational planning are not distributed widely or readily. This leaves little documentation or research to inform communal planning in Jewish education or document specifically how planning is used.

In this chapter, then, I hope to collect available ideas about communal planning. An overview of the recent history of communal planning in Jewish education will provide an understanding of the documents that exist. Similarly, a review of the concepts and literature from the field will show what issues from general research impact the planning community. After examining these areas I will present an expanded research agenda for communal planning in Jewish education. Such an agenda can help us begin to understand communal planning not just theoretically, but systematically and practically.

Many of the ideas shared in this article grew during my tenure as the educational planner for the Jewish Federation of Greater Washington. In that position I had the privilege of working with lay and professional leaders on a wide range of planning projects related to Jewish education. We approached planning from the perspective of participants—from each age group and audience—and through an agency's lens. We sat through with stakeholders with expertise in different kinds of education and also explored actions that the federation could take toward strengthening Jewish education. We worked alongside central agency leadership, often discussing the federation/central agency relationship. We considered how community institutions could work together to enable the participation of any community member in Jewish education and Jewish life. These approaches characterize the diverse and layered realm of communal planning in Jewish education.

WHAT WE KNOW ABOUT COMMUNAL PLANNING

Jewish education has been described recently as existing in a kind of tension, acting as a "stepchild" of American Judaism, yet also producing a kind of "plastic moment" in which anything can happen (Sarna 1998). Communal planning can take a significant amount of responsibility for both circumstances. As a stepchild, Jewish education protests that it receives little attention and funds as it carries on with its numerous challenges. Often communal planning leads to acquiring funding for Jewish education and creating circumstances in which Jewish education can thrive. If Jewish education is a stepchild, it is in part because communal planning in Jewish education has not been a priority, or because such planning has not led to meaningful or measurable progress. At the same time, the plastic moment in Jewish education refers to the tremendous creativity that can be seen in this area nationally and in some communities. Emphases on families and teens, the Israel experience, informal education, educator recruitment, retention, and development, community day schools and campus services all indicate growth in services that stemmed in part from communal planning.

Communal planning in Jewish education, then, has a significant responsibility to develop Jewish education financially and creatively. A brief recent history illustrates the extent to which this has occurred.

CONTINUITY AND COMMISSIONS

In 1997 *Sh'ma: A Journal of Jewish Responsibility* devoted an issue to the period's emphasis on "Jewish continuity." In the issue one writer promoted one 1990 National Jewish Population Survey intermarriage statistic—that 52% of marriages between 1985 and 1990 were between a Jew and a Gentile—as launching the American Jewish community into "collective panic" (Brooks 1997). Another writer described the frenzy into which American Jewish organized life entered as "Operation Continuity" (Isaacs 1997). During the 1990s Jewish organizations entered into discussions of and efforts toward ensuring Jewish continuity. It seemed as though not a periodical could pass without mention of the continuity debate. The words "continuity," "identity," and "education" became nearly interchangeable.

In actuality, an emphasis on Jewish education as the strategy to promote the continuity of Judaism in America developed even before the National Jewish Population Survey data was released. The now-legendary intermarriage statistic of 52% merely let loose existing fear, panic, and hopes, turning what had been a slow interest in Jewish continuity into a ubiquitous emphasis on Jewish education. Nationally, the Commission on Jewish Education of North America began meeting in the late 1980s and issued its report, *A Time to Act*, in 1991. Many large federations, and some intermediate and small ones, sponsored "Commissions on Jewish Continuity" dedicated to communal planning in Jewish education, many of which began in the late 1980s. Such commissions often began by identifying the community's resources in the area of Jewish education and outlining current projects. They then addressed areas of potential growth and created a plan to achieve this growth. The commissions' work resulted in increasing funds for Jewish education, a focus on new areas of Jewish education, including Jewish family education and the Israel experience for teens, and new means of awarding grant funds. Through these grants new partnerships were developed that included non-traditional federation beneficiary agencies, collaborations among beneficiaries and sometimes federation or agency relationships with synagogues. Often grants were given if the receiving organization could match the grant for a limited number of years and/or for a descending grant amount in order to encourage the organization's financial investment in the project. The grant projects began to require a variety of monitoring mechanisms, and in some communities formal project evaluation was conducted or required for the first time. Because of their omnipresence, their impact, and their reliance on new ways of planning, these continuity commissions represent a significant planning endeavor in the American Jewish community.

Such commissions were supported and sometimes led by similar North American efforts. The Commission on Jewish Education in North America met under the leadership of the Mandel Associated Foundations, JCC Association, and JESNA, in collaboration with the former Council of Jewish Federations (*A Time to Act*, 1991). Several years later the North American commission on Jewish Identity and Continuity built on the efforts of the previous Commission (1995). Both membership bodies included professional and volunteer leaders of a wide variety of educating organizations, including central agencies of Jewish education, schools, community centers, Hillels, and synagogues, and researchers from colleges and universities. On both commissions sat leading rabbis, scholars and teachers as well as those involved in federations and national agencies. In crafting their recommendations the commissions relied on empirical research, long conversation and debate among stakeholders, and concrete programs and strategies to help achieve their outlined visions.

The national and local commissions' collective recommendations both echoed and strengthened the themes of the decade for communal planning in Jewish education. Target audiences of the varied planning projects included teens, young families, and adult learners. The commissions provided paradigms of the ways that planning should occur. The commissions also demonstrated the link between financial and personnel resources and planning; in other words, planners noted that their work in strengthening Jewish education required an investment in locating new financial resources and the professionalization of the field of Jewish education. In the ways that commissions then supported change in Jewish education, the work of the commissions established the ways that grants can initiate change in Jewish education; by asking participating organizations to match the commission funds and to evaluate grant projects, organizations receiving grants were required to incorporate planning into the projects being supported.

In the first years of the twenty-first century the talk about continuity has subsided, but Jewish education continues to change. New maps for communal planning emerged from the commissions and other national bodies such as JESNA during the late 1990s (Isaacs & Shluker 1995; Isaacs, Beckerman & Trachtenberg 2000). Communities used these maps in their ongoing planning work, learning from the strategies developed. Some community continuity commissions continue to create educational change through grant-making, research, and evaluation. The Lippman-Kanfer Institute of JESNA convenes national resources to imagine the larger context in which Jewish education operates, providing local organizations with vital information for planning. Projects such as the Experiment in Congregational Education, Synagogue Transformation and Renewal (STaR) Synagogue 2000 and the Leadership Development Institute of Combined Jewish Philanthropies of Greater Boston engage synagogues in a strategic planning process related to education and Jewish life, providing additional paradigms for planning while generating new data about the impact that planning can have on education. In all, spending on Jewish education has increased. The sponsors of and stakeholders in planning have expanded beyond central agencies and federations to include local and national foundations, Hillel, synagogues and the religious movements, new national organizations working to strengthen day schools, residential camping, informal education, adult education, and early childhood education. The Jim Joseph Foundation provides an excellent example of—and perhaps is the paradigm for—a private foundation engaged in Jewish communal planning. As it prepares to spend record sums annually on Jewish education, it has employed a number of visionaries and researchers to create public planning documents in Jewish education, using the documents to move purposefully toward a mission and goals. As technology has made the world smaller, Israel and Jewish communities around the globe have become closer, and new planning efforts related to Israel education have emerged. All of these changes reflect a different situation for communal planning in Jewish education, one with higher goals, bigger stakes, different and more numerous partners, and more potential.

Despite this evolving and expanded richness, planning efforts continue to be insular in sharing the lessons they have learned. Many documents related to continuity planning remain in the hands of the sponsoring organizations. An area of significant potential growth in communal planning in Jewish education lies in our ability to collect and analyze these documents, thereby creating a systematic understanding of what is known about the promise and impact of continuity planning and maximizing our efforts by learning effectively from each other's work.

JEWISH COMMUNAL IDEAS ABOUT PLANNING

While little is known about specific practices used in communal planning, many theories from general literature are invoked in discussions related to Jewish communal planning. Such theories have provided insight into how ideas are developed and executed and how intellectual change happens. They have become part of the communal planning lexicon, shaping conversations about how Jewish education can be influenced and developed.

The paradigm shift, explored by Thomas Kuhn in *The Structure of Scientific Revolutions* (1970), offered planners an opportunity to understand how to move from one fundamental way of viewing the world to another. A paradigm represents the beliefs and strategies that we attach to something; to create a shift, then, we must create change in those strategies, and also in our very beliefs about how something works. Toward the end of the 1990s, Malcolm Gladwell (2000) gave planning a way to accomplish a paradigm shift through his "tipping point," which describes the moment at which random incidents become a widespread phenomenon. They can occur accidentally or, as Gladwell demonstrates, they can be created deliberately. Applied by Barry Shrage in synagogue/federation relations (2002), the tipping point in Jewish education can represent the gathering of a "critical mass for change" and the creation of a new communal norm. The concept of building toward a tipping point offers a new way to understand the goal of planning and the creation of change in Jewish education.

Peter Senge provided additional language for planners, changing the way planning itself worked in some organizations (2000). Through his five "disciplines" Senge promoted ideas about ongoing reflection, arguing that a rich life grows from persistent personal, organizational, and communal learning. In addition to promoting the development of personal and organizational insight, Senge advances collaboration, collective inquiry, transparency, and interdependency as primary modes of operation, suggesting that these practices all lead to a community that is learning together about itself and its members. Projects such as the Experiment in Congregational Education (ECE) adapted Senge's materials for Jewish organizational use, particularly for synagogues. The ECE, and specifically Isa Aron, developed some of the richest materials available in Jewish communal planning for education, guiding synagogues in becoming "learning congregations" (Aron et al. 1995; Aron 2000; 2002). These materials are designed specifically for synagogues' educational enterprises but include values clarification and visioning exercises that any organization can adapt for communal planning in Jewish education. As organizations attempt to identify their priorities in the first stages of planning, these exercises can be particularly helpful in their identification of directions in which to work.

Some ideas about planning have come from the literature of organizational behavior. Bolman and Deal (1997) offer four "frames" through which organizations and communities can be understood. Often, as they demonstrate, we use only one frame to understand a situation, but reframing our view can lead to alternate perceptions that allow different strategies and plans. The four frames include (1) the structural, which sees the building blocks of organizations, (2) the human resource, which understands human interactions as the building blocks of organizational life, (3) the political, which appreciates agendas and negotiations as motivators of organizational interactions, and (4) the symbolic, which identifies rituals, myths, and metaphors as the definers of organizational culture. These frames have helped planners examine problems from different perspectives, seeing new opportunities and also recognizing obstacles. In addition, the very concept of reframing—the idea that we should take a different perspective to gain greater comprehension of our situation—has allowed alternatives and growth.

These ideas are clearly referenced in some communal planning conversations. But other than Aron's work, in which *Fifth Discipline* ideas can be seen clearly, little has been contributed by other researchers or planners to develop maps or other approaches for communal planning. While ideas and research are utilized in planning, more often, it seems, organizations use a "ready, fire, aim" approach to program implementation. Governed by budget realities and the ever-pressing need to strengthen Jewish life, organizations want to move quickly. They identify a target, an end toward which they want to work, and then implement the project, thinking afterward about the appropriateness of the path that they took toward their desired end.

Yet unlike Alice, Jewish organizations often know where they want to go. They have the intellectual and personnel resources to be sophisticated about the ways in which they use knowledge. They have the capacity to document the models that they use in planning, to explore the challenges of planning, and to discuss the nature of communal planning and how planning processes can be maximized. Creating real research in communal planning—documenting and describing productive and less constructive planning models, using research to launch conversations about planning—can help communal planning in Jewish education develop workable common practices that encourage organizations to plan concretely and thoroughly, aim before they fire and walk purposefully toward a desired end.

IMPLICATIONS: USING IDEAS TO GET WHERE WE WANT TO GO

The slate for such research on planning is not completely blank. Research in planning in general education often provides approaches to effective Jewish communal planning. Before suggesting a research agenda, I will share research that already exists related to project-based planning and to ongoing planning in Jewish education. The research reviewed here can provoke ideas about planning in Jewish education and can serve as diagrams for how research on communal planning might be conducted.

PROJECT-BASED PLANNING

You wake up in the middle of the night and realize that families must become involved in your organization, or you want to incorporate a retreat program into what you do, or you want to understand how you can raise the Jewish activities of teenagers through your organization. What happens next?

Project-based planning involves a number of activities: identifying a general purpose, gathering a committee, writing goals, learning about the planning problem, communicating with key stakeholders, clarifying the values of the committee, developing a strategy to respond to the planning problem, and finding resources for implementation. These activities raise challenges, including working as a team and bringing ideas together, garnering enough authority as an organization and team to implement your findings and becoming educated enough about the planning problem at hand to identify a strong set of conclusions. What specific challenges does each activity raise? How can they be managed? In a layered typology that integrates planning challenges and also confronts them, Bean and Kuh (1984, pp. 33–35) elaborate on these questions, making the specific challenges more concise. For example:

- A strong planning project has tight, unambiguous goals. However, different members of a planning project bring different goals to the project; similarly, members of a project can understand goals differently. How can goal consensus be accomplished? How can hidden goals be uncovered? How can the shifting definitions of goals be accounted for?

- Political considerations often dictate the selection of participants for a planning project. Yet the more diverse the participants, the harder it will be to reach goal consensus. How can political considerations be balanced with the need to manage diverse opinions on the project? What about when diverse opinions lead to conflict—how can disagreement be managed?

- Small meetings outside of the primary project meetings can ensure that conflict can be handled effectively. They can allow project members to be invested in the project and understand the goals and activities of the project. Finally, they can bring community stakeholders into the project who might not be members of the planning endeavor but are nevertheless related to the project. This entire process of working with participants in small meetings—project members and all those that the project impacts—should ensure that at the close of the process, the sponsoring organization can implement its findings. Yet too many meetings can distract from the task at hand, offering too many players a hand in the project. How can the need for communication, idea gathering, and information sharing be balanced with moving the project forward?

- Empirical data can help project members begin the planning process in a similar place, reviewing other projects around the country, reading similar studies in general education, and studying the developmental needs and religious attitudes of the population under discussion. How else can the planning project begin with a common and thorough understanding of the problem? How can project members be updated on the project in varied ways and often?

- Planning is costly—it needs resources, human and financial, to be maximized. When can planning be initiated if resources are not available? How does the sponsoring organization maintain credibility if it is planning without the capacity to implement?

By elaborating on these planning steps, Bean and Kuh demonstrate how planning can be studied, how its component parts and their challenges can be broken apart and examined systematically for all of their complexity. This adaptation, then, of their work to communal planning in Jewish education begins a research agenda for such planning; we, too, can study communal planning processes in Jewish education, the challenges that processes raise, and how challenges are handled.

ONGOING PLANNING: GETTING TO THE RIGHT PLACE

Peter Senge's five disciplines (2000, pp. 59–83) provide both a way of understanding how productive ongoing planning can occur in Jewish education and a way it can be studied. The disciplines that Senge and his team have developed rely on several key principles: continuing reflection, honest and transparent communication among partners, risk-taking, safety, and trust. The disciplines themselves are means of practice that individuals, organizations, and communities can study and adopt. They imply that ongoing planning is ongoing learning, the continuous assessment of one's status against one's broader ends. By working within the disciplines, planners can develop habits that allow them to learn from their work in an ongoing way and work toward the betterment of Jewish education in the broadest sense.

Briefly, the five disciplines are as follows:

- "Personal mastery" involves the extent to which one considers one's own vision and develops a clear, sharp idea of where one wants to go. Existing in tension between present and potential, it constantly but realistically moves oneself toward one's vision, offering opportunity to assess and reassess the value and place of one's vision and the skills one needs to develop to help accomplish one's vision.

- "Shared vision" helps individual visions to come together into a group commitment to planning and to a collective image of what can be.

- "Mental models" relate to our assumptions about the way that things work, demonstrating that whenever we learn new information, we sort it according to our existing mental models. In order to see things in a new way—to make a paradigm shift—we need to take apart our models and be flexible in how we see and understand things.

- "Team learning" helps those involved in planning make their mental models transparent, allowing the team to learn together. Such team learning is key to ongoing reflection, as it involves regular inquiry, check-in, and surfacing of agendas and group dynamics.

- "Systems thinking" describes the many possible systems in which planning work is involved. When we consider each institution and project related to our work, we are able to consider the implications of these interactions and what these interactions teach us.

In *Schools That Learn* (2000), Senge and his research team present dozens of exercises that help planners practice these disciplines and move toward habits of ongoing learning. These exercises evolved out of ongoing experimentation; they are well-tested and linked to creativity and to healthy planning dynamics. The five disciplines provide an example of how research can strengthen planning and provide communal planning in Jewish education with concrete ways to grow. Through testing exercises, strong planning models can be developed, as were the five disciplines. In addition, as planners increasingly apply the five disciplines to their ongoing work, these disciplines suggest a research agenda: How do the disciplines strengthen this kind of planning? What happens when the disciplines are translated to planning in Jewish education?

Senge's work also demonstrates how planning can generate research continually. Fifth discipline work is intended to help practitioners be more knowledgeable about what they do. By consistently analyzing mental models, by sitting together in teams to learn about and work toward a shared vision, planners document their practice and create knowledge—they do *research*—about what they do. Fifth discipline work results in groups—ideally of planners, scholars, and educators—together unpacking their assumptions and learning. Such groups can read existing research about Jewish education and discuss its implications, share their personal ideas about Jewish education and Jewish life, and become a true team working toward a common goal. Ongoing learning generates ideas for growth toward a common end; in this way ongoing learning as a team can facilitate the best ongoing planning for Jewish life.

BUILDING A RESEARCH AGENDA

Thus far, three potential areas have emerged as ripe for research about communal planning: study of continuity planning models and program evaluations used in the 1990s, documentation of how general planning practices and challenges arise in Jewish organizations, and ongoing reflection about Jewish education. A research agenda in communal planning for Jewish education is amplified by examining research ideas unique to the Jewish community. This agenda should include the following questions:

- What are the types of planning in which different organizations engage, and with what results? Grounded theory—observation and documentation of planning processes while letting hypotheses and conclusions emerge from observation—could help uncover models of planning and could link kinds of organizations and their resources with the planning models that they choose. Results could also be studied, and the extent to which various aspects of planning models facilitate different results could be revealed.

- Specifically, what are the roles of central agencies and of federations in planning? How do they work together, work side by side or duplicate efforts? How should central agencies and federations be structured to plan effectively? What are the different structures of central agencies, and how do they plan for strong systems of Jewish education?

- What empirical research is used in planning? How is this research used? For example, in recent years book-length studies of Jewish education have been made readily available. Are these texts bought and read? By whom? What do different groups do with what they learn?

- How can research be translated into usable knowledge for planners? How can research lead to stronger planning?

- What is the role of grassroots projects in planning? Do smaller, less mainstream organizations participate in planning? As the source of much creativity and novelty, it seems unhelpful that they be excluded—as players in a community come together to plan, when should all possible stakeholders be included? To what extent should there be boundaries between traditional communal agencies and newer agencies?

- How can ongoing reflection be institutionalized? What stops organizations and communities from being more reflective?

- What prevents planning from occurring? Moreover, what prevents good, productive planning from occurring? What happens to planning projects—do they accomplish what they set out to achieve, or are they stilted in some way? Included in this investigation will likely be the extent to which community agencies and stakeholders can act as partners, the challenges that are faced in the creation of change, and the weak connection that may exist between ideas and action and among planning, discussion, and implementation.

CONCLUSION

Working on this research agenda is not easy. American Jewish education is a voluntary system, one infused with choice at every opportunity (Ackerman 1975). Moreover, it is a system without a head; rather than a hierarchy of institutions with a common purpose, it is a matrix of overlapping institutions (Elazar 1975). They work toward the same general purpose but without direct interconnections, one source of authority, or even a common definition of what Jewish education should be. Communal planning, then, may never be one seamless endeavor, with all organizations fulfilling their prescribed purpose in a greater shared picture of Jewish life. At the same time, each institution that plans has the opportunity to sit with the other, to talk together, to fit projects together and to learn from the other. Despite their disparate existences, members of this voluntary system can share goals for planning, communicate and even argue, and be excited together about ideas. Organizations can be less proprietary about their individual work, sharing accomplishments and lessons that they have learned. They can wander, or they can walk purposefully toward a shared vision, together, maximizing efforts made in communal planning.

HIGHLIGHTS

- Continuity commissions have dominated planning in Jewish education in the late 1990s and provided a foundation for further planning..

- Little documentation exists of common practices in communal planning in Jewish education.

- To understand such planning, we need to learn from planning in general education and also begin to study communal planning in Jewish education empirically.

- A research agenda for such study is included here.

LARGER CONTEXT

As the body of research in Jewish education grows, planners and policy-makers can take a more significant role as the users of research—communal planning is best positioned to use findings from research. Similarly, as education research expands, communal planning in Jewish education has an increased opportunity to learn from the documented relationship between research and policy in general education. In this context, the relationship between research and planning should continue to be explored actively.

ANNOTATED BIBLIOGRAPHY

In addition to the texts referenced and reviewed in the article, some reviews of the state of Jewish education are very helpful in understanding issues in Jewish education and how they were handled. Such reviews include the following:

Ackerman, W. I. (1969). Jewish Education—For What? *American Jewish Yearbook*. New York: American Jewish Committee.

_____. (1989). Strangers to the Tradition: Idea and Constraint in American Jewish Education. In S. Della Pergooa, *Jewish Education Worldwide*. Lanham, MD: University Press of America.

Wertheimer, J. (1999) Jewish Education in the United States: Recent Trends and Issues. *American Jewish Yearbook*. New York: American Jewish Committee.

Several organizations have taken the task of communal planning in Jewish education quite seriously producing visioning documents that map the field and that are helpful for planning. Such resources include:

Sales, A. (2006). *Mapping Jewish Education: The National Picture*. Waltham, MA: Cohen Center for Modern Jewish Studies. This and other visioning papers can be found at www.jimjosephfoundation.org.

Wertheimer, J. (2005). *Linking the Silos: How to Accelerate the Momentum in Jewish Education Today*. New York: Avi Chai Foundation

REFERENCES

_____ (1995). *To Renew and Sanctify: A Call to Action. The Report of the North American Commission on Jewish Identity and Continuity*. New York: Council of Jewish Federations.

_____(1991). *A Time to Act: The Report of the Commission on Jewish Education in North America*. Lanham: University Press of America.

Ackerman, W. (1975). "The Americanization of Jewish Education." *Judaism* 24 (4), 416–435.

Aron, I. (2002). *The Self-Renewing Congregation: Organizational Strategies for Revitalizing Congregational Life*. Woodstock, VT: Jewish Lights.

_____ (2000). *Becoming a Congregation of Learners: Learning as a Key to Revitalizing Congregational Life*. Vermont: Jewish Lights.

Aron, I., Lee, S. & Rossel, S. (1995). *A Congregation of Learners: Transforming the Synagogue into a Learning Community*. New York: UAHC Press.

Bean, J.P. & Kuh, G. D. (1984). "A Typology of Planning Problems." *The Journal of Jewish Education 55 (1)*, 35–55.

Bolman, L. G. & Deal, T. E. (1997). *Reframing Organizations: Artistry, Choice, and Leadership*. San Francisco: Jossey-Bass.

Brooks, M. (1997). "The Jewish Continuity Agenda." *Sh'ma: A Journal of Jewish Responsibility 28 (2)*.

Carroll, L. (1960). *Alice's Adventures in Wonderland and Through the Looking-Glass*. New York: Signet Classics.

Eisenberg, J. (1995). "The Limits of Educational Research: Why Most Research and Grand Plans in Education Are Futile and Wasteful." *Curriculum Inquiry 25 (4)*, 367–380.

Elazar, D. J. (1975) *Community and Polity: The Organizational Dynamics of American Jewry.* Philadelphia: Jewish Publication Society.

Floden, R. E. (1996). "Educational Research: Limited, but Worthwhile, and Maybe a Bargain." *Curriculum Inquiry, 26 (2),* 193–197.

Gladwell, M. (2000). *The Tipping Point: How Little Things Can Make a Big Difference.* Boston: Little, Brown and Company.

Isaacs, L.W. (1997). "The Jewish Continuity Agenda." *Sh'ma: A Journal of Jewish Responsibility 28 (3).*

Isaacs, L.W. & Shluker, D. (1995). *Planning for Jewish Continuity: A Handbook.* New York: JESNA.

Isaacs, L.W., Beckerman, A.F. & Trachtenberg, C. (eds.) (2000). *Beyond "Continuity": Taking the Next Steps: A Handbook for Jewish Renaissance and Renewal.* New York: JESNA.

Kuhn, T. (1970). *The Structure of Scientific Revolutions.* Chicago: The University of Chicago Press.

Lauer, C. (1992). What We Know about…Communal Planning in S. Kelman *What We Know about Jewish Education.* Los Angeles: Torah Aura Productions.

Sarna, J.D. (1998). American Jewish Education in Historical Perspective. *Journal of Jewish Education 64 (1–2),* 8–18.

Shrage, B. (2002). *Sacred Communities at the Heart of Jewish Life: Twenty Years of Federation/Synagogue Collaboration and Change in Boston.* Boston: Combined Jewish Philanthropies.

Senge, P. et al. (2000). *Schools That Learn: A Fifth Discipline Fieldbook for Educators, Parents, and Everyone Who Cares About Education.* New York: Doubleday.

Program Evaluation in Jewish Education

Wendy J. Rosov & Leora W. Isaacs

Question:
How many evaluators does it take to change a lightbulb?

Answer:
one to do a needs assessment
one to do a feasibility study
one to do a qualitative study to find out what bulb to change
one to empower the bulb to change
one to tender a contract for further study
one to write performance indicators for success
one to do a cost benefit analysis to determine the best bulb to buy
one to do a meta-evaluation showing that all previous studies have left everyone in the dark

SO…how many evaluators does it take?
None, actually. Evaluators don't change bulbs. That's an implementation problem!

So what *do* program evaluators do? How is program evaluation currently viewed and utilized by the Jewish community? What are some of the challenges facing program evaluators in Jewish education, and what are some of the most promising areas for growth? These are the central questions that are addressed in this chapter.

WHAT IS PROGRAM EVALUATION?

The first question is "What is the difference between evaluation and social science research?" The purpose and uses of evaluation differ from those of social science research, even though evaluators utilize many of the same quantitative and qualitative methods as social science researchers. The fundamental difference between program evaluation and research lies in the purpose of data collection—basic scientific research is undertaken to discover new knowledge, test theories, establish some truth and/or generalize across time and space. Program evaluation is undertaken to inform decisions, clarify options, identify improvements and provide information about programs and policies within contextual boundaries of time, place, values and politics (Patton 1997). Cronbach and Suppes (1969) characterize research as "conclusion-oriented inquiry" and evaluation as "decision-oriented inquiry."

Within the field, definitions of program evaluation also vary significantly, and consequently lead to a range of very different foci, approaches and uses. For example, one traditional view defines evaluation simply as assessing the extent to which a program achieves its stated goals. But others define program evaluation by its methodology and its usage:

> The systematic collection of information about the activities, characteristics and outcomes of programs to make judgments about the program, improve program effectiveness, and/or inform decisions about future programming. Utilization-focused program evaluation is evaluation done for and with specific, intended primary users for specific, intended uses. (Patton 1997)

Adherents of this definition (including the authors of this chapter) see program evaluation as a powerful way to determine what works, understand why and under what conditions it works (or doesn't), suggest ways to improve current programs, and guide decisions about future comparable endeavors.[1]

This chapter is about program evaluation in the Jewish community, particularly evaluation of informal educational and identity-building programs. We take authors' prerogative to focus on program evaluation both because of its noteworthy growth over the past several decades, and because that is what we do. JESNA's Berman Center for Research and Evaluation in Jewish Education has completed well over 150 program evaluations since the early 1990's.

A BRIEF HISTORY OF PROGRAM EVALUATION

Although historians note examples of planful social evaluation as early as 2200 B.C.E., and document instances of program monitoring throughout the last 200 years, the widespread practice of using empirically derived data to inform decision-making is relatively new even in the secular world. It was not until the 1960s and 1970s that massive federal expenditures for social services and education led to a demand for accountability and for systematic empirical data about if and how the many programmatic changes introduced through the Great Society initiatives made a real difference. With insufficient funding to do all the things that needed to be done, evaluation provided a pragmatic way to figure out what works and is worth funding. Needless to say, grantees were initially very leery about evaluation and were threatened by the prospect of losing funding based on negative evaluations (Shadish, W.R., Jr., Cook, T.D. & Leviton, L.C. 1991).

The field of program evaluation burgeoned and matured over time. By the early 1970s evaluations were regularly required of health, education and welfare programs. As experts such as Patton (1997) and Shadish et al. (1991) note, at first there were few clear, agreed-upon criteria for judging the worth of social services, what constituted improvement in social welfare or education or ways to assess program impact. Practitioners of program evaluation initially borrowed concepts and practices from the fields in which they had been trained, particularly academic social science disciplines. As experience with program evaluation accumulated, evaluators adapted these concepts and methods, invented others, and combined them in new ways that broadened and sophisticated the practice of evaluation.

Whereas the earliest evaluations were designed purely to guide funding decisions, over time a new role emerged: helping improve programs as they were implemented. Evaluators were called on not only to offer final judgments about the overall effectiveness of programs, but to gather process data and provide feedback to help solve programming challenges along the way. Evaluators such as Stufflebeam advocated that the primary purpose of evaluation is to improve rather than merely to prove (1971, 2000).

---

[1]It should be noted that *educational assessment* that includes such areas as personnel performance and student achievement is its own specialized field. The project to develop standards and benchmarks for teaching and learning of TaNaKh in Jewish day schools that is currently being conducted by the William Davidson Graduate School of Jewish Education at the Jewish Theological Seminary of America and the Melton Research Center for Jewish Education with partnership and support from the AVI CHAI is an example of ground-breaking work in this area that is intended to lead to school-based assessment tools. PEJE (The Partnership for Excellence in Jewish Education) is encouraging day schools to use The Day School Peer Yardstick™ to measure and track their performance in key areas of school operations including enrollment, attrition, financial aid, etc. The Yardstick is designed to improve schools' planning process by introducing data into decision-making discussions. However, with few other examples of comparable endeavors in the field of educational assessment, this area has not been developed in the Jewish education world. Therefore, we will not address the area of educational assessment in this chapter.

CURRENT TRENDS IN PROGRAM EVALUATION

Over the past ten to fifteen years the field of program evaluation has expanded and evolved in many ways. Patton (2002), a noted field leader in contemporary program evaluation, identifies four "breakthrough ideas" that have characterized the field during this time: (1) a focus on process (evaluating what happens throughout, not just after a program; a focus on learning and capacity building, not just on findings; and, a focus on utilization by working with primary evaluation users to identify and help them reach intended uses); (2) a significant increase in evaluation choices (there are over one hundred possible approaches); (3) the demise of the qualitative-quantitative debate (acceptance of the benefits of mixed methods and an attention to best-suited approaches); and (4) a growing awareness of cross-cultural issues and contexts. To sum up: Program evaluation in this most recent period has been characterized by its keen attention to matters of utility, participation, and empowerment, along with the increasing use of mixed methods. A brief review of recent and emerging trends/practices in program evaluation in the general not-for-profit sector will help us better contextualize current practices in program evaluation in the Jewish communal/educational sector.

Of most significance in the general field is the near-ubiquitous adoption/adaptation of Patton's Utilization-Focused approach to evaluation (Patton 1997). This approach "begins with the premise that evaluations should be judged by their utility and actual use...Use concerns how real people in the real world apply evaluation findings and experience the evaluation process." This approach, pioneered in the mid-1970s and refined through the 1980s and early 1990s, has informed several kindred approaches to evaluation, chief among them Participatory Evaluation (PE) and Empowerment Evaluation (EE). In PE the evaluator, organization, staff, clients, and board members are all involved in deciding what to ask as well as collecting, analyzing, and writing up data. The central goal of PE is to "democratize" the research process and increase utility of the findings to stakeholders and future actions (Upshur, C.C. & Barreto-Cortez, E. 1995). In this way Participatory Evaluation aims to:

- be practical by responding to the needs of users;
- be useful by disseminating findings in ways that can be used;
- be formative by improving program outcomes rather than summative in evaluating overall impact.

Empowerment Evaluation pushes Participatory Evaluation to its logical limits by giving evaluation tools to program staff and participants and making evaluation a part of the planning and operation of the program or organization. Like Participatory Evaluation, Empowerment Evaluation is not defined by a particular methodology but is its collaborative way of using methods (Wandersman, A. and Snell-Johns, J. 2005).

Another powerful influence on the field of program evaluation has been a significant shift in the philanthropic and programmatic sectors toward outcomes-based planning and accountability. First evident in the work of national social service agencies in the mid-1990s (e.g., United Way 1996), this development has, in turn, necessitated a response from professionals in the program evaluation field. Logic modeling, the basic tool or methodology, enables the evaluator, along with program stakeholders, to develop an image of how a program works. At its core it connects outcomes with program interventions based on the program's theories and assumptions. Benefits of logic modeling include:

- better focus on outcomes;
- clarity of linkages between short-term and long-term outcomes;
- highlighting of program assumptions and keeping them at the fore;
- identification of the intended path of change and what adjustments may be made while program is operating;
- better focused evaluation work.

The process of developing a logic model is beneficial due to its elicitation of a logical and participative discussion that necessarily identifies the various components and any missing pieces. Logic modeling is particularly beneficial for looking at programs with intangible outcomes or long-term outcomes that may not come into effect for many years by identifying interim outcomes (W.K. Kellogg Foundation 2001).

More recently the field of program evaluation has witnessed a swing toward the use of more narrative methods, which includes the now oft-cited "appreciative inquiry" approach. Appreciative inquiry is a form of action research whose goal is to create new theories and/or ideas to help in "the developmental change of a system." As a method, appreciative inquiry is constituted by systematically collecting people's stories of something at its best and using them to generate discussion about ideas that will help developmental change. Proponents of narrative methods observe that "Program evaluation progressed into an epistemological approach and a wider use of qualitative and mixed research methods, participatory and empowerment action research and interpretive and constructivist approaches. Yet, the field remains largely empirical" (McClintock, C. 2004). The author suggests that the field of program evaluation ought to borrow the skills that are stressed in organization development, such as effective communication, diagnosis, negotiation, motivation, and change dynamics. Training ought to combine these skills with the already emphasized research know-how to produce a "scholar practitioner." In this way narrative methods are offered as a bridge to connect the fields of program evaluation and organization development.

THE EMERGENCE AND HISTORY OF PROGRAM EVALUATION IN THE NORTH AMERICAN JEWISH COMMUNITY

In the North American Jewish community, 1990 was a landmark year for program evaluation comparable to the sea change that occurred in the 1960s in American society in general. Alarmed by precipitously declining affiliation rates, rapidly increasing intermarriage rates, and indicators of weakening Jewish identity reported in the *1990 National Jewish Population Study (1991)*, Jewish communities across North America quickly responded by establishing commissions on Jewish continuity and identity to find ways to combat these trends. Most North American Jewish communities raised and/or earmarked considerable funds (sometimes through special campaigns) for new and innovative programs designed to strengthen Jewish identity and continuity. Many of these communities established grants programs to support initiatives in specific areas or for particular populations who were deemed pivotal (e.g., those who were particularly vulnerable or who could be highly influential). The RFPs (requests for proposals) typically sought innovative programs for those in interfaith relationships, families (especially those with very young children), teens, college students or adult Jewish learning, with the grants generally designed to fund projects for three years.

Initially the grant processes did not include any provision for evaluation, and most communities rejected the notion of including provision or funds for evaluation on the grounds that a) the situation was of crisis proportion and all of the available funding would be better utilized addressing the issues directly through programming, and b) success would be self-evident, making formal evaluation superfluous. However, as in the general world, by the end of the first grant cycle Jewish communal leaders began to demand accountability (what *had* worked?) and to recognize the need for more systematic evaluation processes. That is how JESNA as a national agency for Jewish education as well as numerous individual researchers entered the "business" of program evaluation.

There were considerable challenges, however. Most programs had not clearly articulated measurable goals or developed a "logic model" to delineate how their program was aligned with their goals. Few if any programs had collected baseline data, which made it difficult to track changes in relevant indicators (behaviors, attitudes, skills and/or knowledge) that might have taken place since the beginning of the programs. The durations of the grants were generally very short (three years or less), limiting the ability to measure the impact. Program providers required significant amounts of time to plan, implement and refine programs that were selected *because* they were innovative and untried.

As a result of these various limitations, reliably measuring *impact* of specific programs on highly ambitious (but vague) goals such as strengthening Jewish identity or increasing Jewish affiliation was impossible. Some program providers became frustrated because promising ideas were falling flat in implementation, with little understanding as to why. Initially few funders or program providers shared a common understanding of the goals and purposes of evaluation, knowledge about the range of possible approaches or methodologies or awareness of how to use the evaluation data they received. As a result, much of the initial (and current) work done by program evaluators in the Jewish community necessarily included building an "evaluative culture"—enlightening funders and program providers about the uses (and limitations) of evaluation findings for decision making and programming, enabling them to be better partners in planning and implementing evaluations, and building their capacities to use evaluation data effectively.

CURRENT TRENDS IN PROGRAM EVALUATION IN THE NORTH AMERICAN JEWISH COMMUNITY[2]

FROM THE PERSPECTIVE OF GRANT-MAKERS AND PHILANTHROPISTS

Despite many promising advances and increased interest, the field and practice of program evaluation in the Jewish community is still in its infancy. While there is growing awareness of the potential benefits, most funders (foundations and federations) are just beginning to explore how they might use evaluative thinking and techniques to advance their work—with only a very limited number in the first stages of developing systematic approaches to evaluation.

PRIMARY EVALUATION QUESTIONS

As a rule, federations and foundations are primarily interested in assessing the impact of programs on participants (end users) and ensuring accountability. Whereas foundations often tend to specify their interest in terms of impact relative to the stated goals of the programs, federations often primarily focus on fiscal accountability. Few foundations are concerned with questions of program implementation or understanding the underlying factors leading to the success of particular programs (and the obstacles impeding others).

PRIMARY USES FOR EVALUATION

Foundations and federations that fund programs in the Jewish sector primarily use evaluation findings from grantees to ensure accountability (primarily fiscal) and/or to inform funding decisions, particularly whether to re-fund particular programs. Few use research and evaluation data to inform their initial granting decisions or to inform their foundation/federation funding agendas, although some leading funders are beginning to do so—or have started thinking about how to. A few funders of programs in the Jewish community have followed the lead of funders in the general sector by using findings from implementation-focused and process-focused evaluations to guide mid-course corrections and to inform their work with grantees to achieve their longer-term goals or outcomes (i.e., using evaluation to improve, rather than simply to prove).

EVALUATION REQUIREMENTS

While most foundations and federations in the Jewish sector monitor their grants and require periodic reports as a condition of funding, few have formal evaluation requirements for their grantees and rarely have specific forms for progress reports. However, this situation seems to be changing as additional foundations (including some community foundations that are closely aligned with local federations) have initiated processes for developing more systematic, grounded approaches and requirements for program evaluation. A few leading foundations have initially adopted a "targeted" approach: They select significant projects for external evaluation and/or commission research related to specific projects.

In general, foundations and federations that only require periodic reports and monitoring do not require grantees to consult with outside evaluators, while those that require more formal evaluations generally require the program providers to engage outside evaluators. The foundations that have selected particular projects to be evaluated have engaged the evaluators directly, with the evaluators reporting to the funders (as opposed to the program providers).

[2]The following characterization of current trends in program evaluation in the North American Jewish community is based on the authors' twenty-five cumulative years of experience in the field supported by data from interviews with program officers from leading foundations, community endowment funds and federations (n=10) as well as professional evaluators who have extensive experience in the the North American Jewish community (n=6).

Funders (from both federations and foundations) generally believe that evaluations must include quantitative methodology to be credible, although there is widespread preference for a mixed model including both qualitative and quantitative methodology. This mixed model provides funders with hard numeric data as well as examples and quotes that, when combined, readily and convincingly communicate the key findings and issues highlighted in the research. Funders who require formal evaluations from their grantees (and who have more sophisticated, systematic evaluation plans and requirements) are also most likely to understand that the methodology employed depends on the project and must be consistent with the evaluation questions to be addressed.

SUPPORT FOR EVALUATION

Funders rarely provide specific or sufficient funding for evaluation, even when they expect grantees to provide evaluative data as part of periodic reports. Even organizations that require formal evaluation and provide funding for that purpose as part of their grants tend to underestimate evaluation costs, both in terms of external costs (outside evaluators' fees, costs associated with data collection, analysis and reporting) and internal costs (program staff time). For example, whereas conventional wisdom from the field suggests that a well-designed evaluation costs an amount equivalent to 8–12% of the total program budget, funders of programs in the Jewish community allot a percentage or flat fee that is as low as 5% of the budget, which is inadequate.

In addition to financial support, grantees need help in building their capacity through training modules to include evaluation processes in their planning, to conduct basic evaluative and monitoring tasks, and to use evaluation findings to improve their programs. Several federations have recently introduced workshops and training programs to increase the evaluation capacity of their beneficiary agencies.

FROM THE PERSPECTIVE OF PROFESSIONAL EVALUATORS

PROGRAM TYPES

Professional program evaluators working in the Jewish communal sector are being asked to assess all types of programs, with a significant focus on "Jewish identity-building" programs for teens and young adults, as well as in the area of outreach. Evaluators are working in all arenas of Jewish education, including such domains as day school, congregational school, and camping and across the developmental spectrum (from early childhood through family and adult education). They are evaluating national, regional, and community-based programs that focus on educator recruitment, induction, and professional development—everything from start-up initiatives to well-established programs. They are being asked to evaluate school and synagogue change initiatives and, in a few cases, are being asked by funders to evaluate their grantmaking processes.

KEY ISSUES

Evaluators' work spans a wide continuum of issues. Sometimes the work is more developmental in nature (clarifying goals and outcomes, building logic models, building internal capacity for evaluation), while at other times it is more formative toward the goal of information feedback to improve implementation and/or work out kinks in new programmatic initiatives. As noted earlier, many evaluations are solely impact-oriented, including the development of post-intervention measures of Jewish feeling and behavior. Increasingly, as funders and Jewish communities are becoming more attuned to the benefits of "data-driven" decision making, evaluators are being asked to plan and carry out needs assessment studies (an evaluative activity) as well as gathering data that help inform the decision-making processes that lead people to select specific Jewish educational options. From time to time evaluators are called upon to conduct goal-free/exploratory evaluation and to consult with foundation and federation leaders on informing grant procedures. Rarely if ever are evaluators asked to do cost-benefit analyses or policy-informing evaluations for any sector of the Jewish community (see Rosov 2006).

METHODOLOGY

As has been the case in the general field of program evaluation, evaluators working in the Jewish communal arena employ mixed methods in their work. Whether employing survey research (both online and more traditional pen and paper), face-to-face and phone interviewing, focus groups, observations and site visits (whether of the limited or more detailed ethnographic variety) or document review, evaluators seek to ensure that method is driven by the central questions one is seeking to have answered in the evaluation process. With few exceptions the vast majority of current evaluation work in the Jewish communal world is non-experimental in design, with the possible exception of work done by evaluators situated in academic/research settings who tend toward quasi-experimental design (e.g., control group). Often small sample sizes, poor record keeping and engagement late in the process preclude this type of design. Furthermore, some evaluation projects (particularly those focused on implementation rather then impact) do not lend themselves to quasi-experimental designs.

EVALUATION CLIENTS

On the whole, the vast majority of evaluation "clients" are funders (family and community foundations, federations), national organizations (e.g., STAR, URJ, CAJE, Birthright, PANIM, etc.) and individual program providers who receive grants that require outside evaluation and include funding for that express purpose. The individuals in these organizations with whom evaluators work ranges from seasoned education and foundation professionals to social entrepreneurs and, in many cases, novices. They vary widely in their sophistication and/or understanding of program evaluation, its processes, its products, and its uses.

CHALLENGES AND IMPLICATIONS

The field of program evaluation in Jewish education has made huge advances over the past fifteen years. From the increase in the number and quality of professionals doing the work to the growing sophistication of program providers and funders in terms of their understanding of the overall importance and utility of evaluation, the field of program evaluation in the Jewish communal endeavor has grown significantly. Yet with all that has been accomplished as a community of funders, programmers and professional evaluators, there are a number of key challenges and implications remaining prior to making evaluation an integral part of the Jewish communal agenda.

- Funders and program providers struggle to articulate measurable goals for their projects. Similarly, there is a lack of clear operational definitions for concepts like "Jewish identity," which translates into a lack of reliable (tested and validated) measures.

- Although more funders and program providers understand the importance and utility of evaluation, they still grossly underestimate the time and resources (human, financial, and intellectual) necessary to conduct quality evaluations. Small organizations often do not have the staff time, capacity and/or support to attend to evaluation activities even when funders provide the financial resources and outside evaluators. On a related note, many program providers do not recognize that evaluation is *part of* the work, as opposed to *on top of/in addition to* the work.

- Data gathering efforts (even when funded and fully supported) are often hampered by poor record keeping, difficulty in obtaining access to people to survey or interview, institutional politics, and evaluators with limited understanding of the full content and/or context of the program.

- There is a paucity of opportunities for knowledge sharing, due in large measure to the limited, program-specific emphases of contracted evaluation work and the resistance of those commissioning evaluations to share instruments, data and findings. Even as they decry the lack of sharing, most funders and program providers overwhelmingly view evaluations of their programs as proprietary and are reluctant to share reports, findings or instruments with others.

HIGHLIGHTS

- The Jewish community started to fund and encourage program evaluation in the early 1990s when community leaders sought data on the effectiveness of the multitude of continuity initiatives that were spawned in the wake of the 1990 National Jewish Population Study.

- The predominant emphasis among funders in the Jewish community is on accountability (particularly fiscal accountability), with increasing focus on outcomes relative to goals. Mixed methodology is gaining acceptability, although there remains a strong interest in the quantitative approach for verifying program success.

- With increasing awareness of the benefits of evaluation as a tool for program improvement and excellence, leading funders within the Jewish community are exploring and developing systematic evaluation approaches and requirements for their grantees.

- Although more funders and program providers understand the importance and utility of program evaluation, they still grossly underestimate the time and resources (human, financial, and intellectual) necessary to achieve the results that are desired.

- Many organizations do not have the staff, skills and knowledge to undertake and benefit from evaluative activities. Several forward-thinking funders (foundations and federations) are now investing in building local evaluation capacity to enable their grantees to become fully engaged as beneficiaries and participants in the evaluation process.

- There is a paucity of opportunities for knowledge sharing due in large measure to the limited, program-specific emphases of contracted evaluation work and the resistance of those commissioning evaluations to share instruments, data and findings.

THE LARGER CONTEXT

Evaluation is a powerful tool for program effectiveness and improvement. The Jewish community has made significant progress in commissioning and utilizing evaluations in the last two decades. Building on this foundation, the community must develop mechanisms to expand the understanding of evaluation and evaluative thinking among funders, program providers and decision-makers. The pool of professional evaluators who combine content, context and technical knowledge must be expanded. We must create a culture that values knowledge sharing and develop better mechanisms for that to occur. In so doing we will build the capacity of foundations, federations, communal organizations, program providers and end users to be better consumers and partners in evaluation—and to improve and enhance Jewish education programs in the coming decades.

ANNOTATED BIBLIOGRAPHY

W.K. Kellogg Foundation (2001). *Logic Model Development Guide.* The *W.K. Kellogg Foundation Logic Model Development Guide.* A companion publication to the Foundation's *Evaluation Handbook,* focuses on the development and use of the program logic model for program planning, implementation, evaluation, and dissemination of results. The guide provides a clear orientation to the underlying principles of logic models, as well as clear and directive steps and worksheets that enable practitioners to develop logic models.

Patton, M. Q. (1997). *Utilization-Focused Evaluation: The New Century Text (3rd ed.).* Newbury Park, CA: Sage. This comprehensive text reviews and integrates the literature on program evaluation use and practice and makes the case for why and how program evaluation must be utilization focused. Each chapter begins with a literature review that introduces practical case studies and practice guides.

Rosov, W. (2006). "Towards a Culture of Accountability." *Contact.* New York: JLN/Steinhardt Foundation. Rosov makes the case for developing a culture of accountability for educational and identity-building programs in the Jewish community and makes specific recommendations regarding how to achieve this goal.

Stufflebeam, D.L. & Madaus, T.K. (2000). *Evaluation Models: Viewpoints on Educational and Human Services Evaluation.* Boston: Kluwer Academic Publishers. Organized in three sections, this work includes a historical perspective on the growth of evaluation theory and practice as well as comparative analyses of the various alternative perspectives on evaluation. It describes and discusses the Standards for Program Evaluation and the reformation of program evaluation.

REFERENCES

Cronbach, L.J. & Suppes, P. (1969). *Research for Tomorrow's Schools: Disciplined Inquiries for Education*. New York: MacMillan.

Logic Model Development Guide (2001). W.K. Kellogg Foundation.

McClintock, C. (2004). The Scholar-Practitioner Model. In A. DiStefano, K. E. Rudestam & R. J. Silverman (eds.), *Encyclopedia of Distributed Learning* Thousand Oaks, CA: Sage, 393–396.

Measuring Program Outcomes: Training Kit. United Way of America, 1996.

National Jewish Population Study 1989–90. New York: Council of Jewish Federations, 1991.

Patton, M. Q. (1997). *Utilization-Focused Evaluation: The New Century Text (3rd ed.)*. Newbury Park, CA: Sage.

Patton, M. Q. (2002). A Conversation with Michael Quinn Patton. *The Evaluation Exchange, 7 (1)*, 10-11.

Rosov, W. (2006). "Towards a Culture of Accountability." *Contact*, New York: JLN/Steinhardt Foundation.

Shadish, W.R., Jr., Cook, T.D. & Leviton, L.C. (1991). *Foundations of Program Evaluation: Theories of Practice*. Newbury Park, CA: Sage, 19-35.

Stufflebeam, D.L. & Foley, W.J., Gephart, W.J., Hammond, L.R., Merriam, H.O. & Provus, M.M. (1971). *Evaluation and Decision-making in Education*. Itasca, IL: Peacock.

Stufflebeam, D.L. & Madaus, T.K. (2000). *Evaluation Models: Viewpoints on Educational and Human Services Evaluation*. Boston: Kluwer Academic Publishers.

Upshur, C.C. & Barreto-Cortez, E. (1995). "What Is Participatory Evaluation (P.E.)? What Are Its Roots?" *The Evaluation Exchange*, I, 3/4.

Wandersman, A. & Snell-Johns, J. (2005). "Empowerment Evaluation: Clarity, Dialogue, and Growth." *American Journal of Evaluation*, 26 (3), 421–428.

Creating an Effective Lay Leadership

Samuel K. Joseph

Any visit to a Barnes and Noble, Borders, or the Internet will reveal the huge volume of books, materials and websites about how to be the "most effective", "best", "most artful", "caring", "capable", "mission based", "strategic", "successful", "responsible", and "excellent" board of a not-for-profit organization. A myriad of associations and consultants exist to support these boards as they attempt to govern. Colleges and universities have centers to study issues related to not-for-profit leadership. Organizations with their volunteer and professional leadership issues are big business.

Simultaneously, the even larger volume of work related to leading in the for-profit sector spills over into the not-for-profit world. The lessons learned (or not) in the business community are frequently applied to volunteer organizations. On a practical level, board members in not-for-profits assume their roles with their business, educational and professional backgrounds and experience. They believe that one contribution they can make is to ensure that their favorite not-for-profit operates in a businesslike manner and achieves its goals and purposes. It often does not enter their thinking that measuring the success of their not-for-profit organization is a primary function of their role and differs significantly from for-profit organizations.

This we do know. The concerns and challenges facing not-for-profit boards coalesce around three core issues: 1) the board's responsibility for the mission and the vision of the organization; 2) the board's responsibility for the finances of the organization; and 3) the board's responsibility for selecting and supporting the senior professional of the organization.

However, not all not-for-profit organizations are the same; the boards often have many different roles and responsibilities based on the history, context, cultural realities and mandates. In Jewish education, whether full-time or part-time, formal or informal, some of the practice and research is germane and some is not. While there is research about and wisdom from Jewish organizations, the secular and other religious not-for-profits are far richer in their resources. Taken as a complete body of knowledge, what we know about lay leadership gives us direction toward understanding the opportunities and challenges facing lay leaders governing Jewish education institutions. Clearly, being a lay leader in a Jewish context is a complex role. Of course, this may have historical roots. One of our quintessential leaders, Moses, sat atop Mt. Sinai receiving the Ten Commandments while his "lay leaders" were rebelling and building the golden calf below.

During the past twenty-five years I have worked with professionals, lay leaders and parents in both the congregational and day school settings. Key areas have included strategic planning, team building, transformational change processes and leadership development and assessment. Countless times I have heard the saying that "we need board members who fulfill at least two if not three of the 'W Criteria'—wealth, wisdom, and work—for nomination to the board". Board membership is much more complex and nuanced than simply giving money, working hard for the welfare of the schools and sharing one's advice. The W Criteria may have worked in an earlier age, but not in today's fast-paced, competition-filled times.

THE COMPLEXITIES OF LAY LEADERSHIP

Jewish education is not a monolithic system where all schools and programs have a similar structure. Although there are many different models, the system generally breaks down into two general systems: full-time day schools and part-time congregational programs, including both the formal schools and the informal youth experiences. Each has its own challenges that involve issues of staffing, funding, and planning. But these are institutional in nature. There is a fourth issue that relates specifically to the board itself: the need to recruit, develop, maintain and retain members of the board, the lay leadership. Since the two systems differ in many dramatic ways, we will explore the nature of lay leadership in each separately.

THE CONGREGATIONAL PROGRAMS

In the typical not-for-profit, the relationship between the board and the chief professional is generally complicated. In the congregation, how much the more so when that chief professional is a rabbi, and other staff, including the educational director, do not report directly to either the board or the chief professional. Furthermore, the educational programs have their own lay leadership structures, which are officially committees of the board but often operate with a high level of independence from the board. In the typical congregation the board is responsible for, among other items, the budget of the organization as a whole, including the educational programs. However, education budgets are the products of educational professionals and education committees and, with rare exception, are deficit budgets with the balance to be covered by the organization as a whole. How does this affect the dynamic between the board and the education committees and their professionals?

On a different level, the board is responsible for the congregation's mission and vision. How does this filter down to the education committees that have responsibility for guiding the curriculum of the school and other education programs? Whose responsibility is it to make sure that the curriculum of the educational programs is aligned with the values, mission and vision of the congregation?

Some of the key questions for lay leaders in congregations relating to the Jewish educational programs are:

- What is the role of the lay leaders? How does it differ for members of the board and members of the education committees? What are the responsibilities of board and committee members?
- What are the elements of an excellent congregational education committee or youth experiences committee?
- How do the education committees renew themselves by recruiting new members? What criteria are used for nomination or selection to the committee? What types of orientation and/or training are provided to the new as well as the continuing members of the committees?
- What makes for a successful relationship between the chief education officer, the youth professionals, the chief executive officer (rabbi), the education committees and board? How do they build a strong collaborative relationship?

One of the great challenges for congregations is that there is little substantive research relating to the dynamics between lay leadership and professionals. Most individual congregations operate as independent entities and rarely look to their counterparts within either their communities or their movements for advice and guidance on the best systems for building a strong institution. Rather, they rely on their own experiences and what little they pick up or transfer from other organizations where they serve as volunteer or professional leaders.

THE JEWISH DAY SCHOOL

The Jewish day school community, in contrast, is rich with practice and research data, supporting associations and consultants. Even with this support it pales compared to the not-for-profit and general private school boards. The National Association of Independent Schools and the Independent Schools Association of the Central States have over forty monographs on their websites detailing all aspects of board leadership in the full-time school setting (*http://www.nais.org* and *http://isacs.org*). Since Jewish day schools operate in the same vein as private, independent schools, the research and resources connected with independent schools are applicable, in many instances. In addition, the Partnership for Excellence in Jewish Education (PEJE) is fully dedicated to the growth and development of all facets of Jewish day schools, including substantive resources for lay leaders (*http://peje.*

org). Of particular importance are materials for leadership and governance, which includes links to pages with the collective wisdom gleaned from the PEJE schools.

In the vast majority of Jewish day schools, lay leaders serve on the board of trustees of the school. These boards are similar to boards of trustees of most independent schools and similar to boards of many not-for-profit institutions and organizations. For this reason day school boards frequently seek wisdom and practice from other settings for guidance and support.

In both the general and the Jewish not-for-profit communities, materials that are available on the web, in books, or through consultations include exercises and activities to judge the effectiveness of the board. Notable examples include "BoardSource: Building Effective Nonprofit Boards," a major consulting and web-based firm. They have developed their expertise through extensive work with important not-for-profit organizations. Their website offers background information on the roles and functions of good board operations as well as a number of quality self-assessment tools (*http://www.boardsource.org*). The "Corporate Nonprofit Board Self-Assessment Kit" is another well-known and highly used instrument (*http://www.thecorporatefund.org/board_self_assessment_kit.asp*). Board Café also works extensively with not-for-profit boards. On the web they have articles and instruments that help guide a board through an assessment process (*http://compasspoint.org/boardcafe/index.php*).

BEST PRACTICES AND BOARD EFFECTIVENESS

Many not-for-profit boards report using these various materials on effectiveness and find them useful. At the same time, the body of systematic research related to the validity of these materials and ideas is quite new and very recently done (Millesen and Lakey 1999). Beginning in 1990s and beyond, several researchers, such as Abzug (1996), Bradshaw et al. (1992) and Herman (1997) looked at board processes, board members' skills, functions of a board and board recruitment and training. The implication was that these various processes and aspects of "boardsmanship" and board functioning are connected to a board's effectiveness. Researchers wanted to find out if there was a positive relationship between the perception of board effectiveness and widely accepted notions of how a not-for-profit board of directors should operate (Bradshaw et al. 1992).

An overarching issue that bridges both the general not-for-profit world and the Jewish educational world of lay leadership is the nature of board effectiveness. Herman and Renz claim that "…important in the study of nonprofit organizational and board effectiveness is the manner in which effectiveness should be conceived—is it as a real characteristic of a board or organization, or as socially constructed judgments reached by multiple constituencies" (1997). Put differently, are there outside, external, objective measures that inform an organization that its board is effective? Herman and Renz suggest that the effectiveness of the board may actually be determined by all the board's (organization's) stakeholders. If the stakeholders believe the board is effective, they know more than the criteria listed on some instrument that is created from the outside.

One of the problems with these "boilerplate" instruments a board may use to determine its effectiveness is that they may be so general in nature that they really do not help or measure a particular board's effectiveness. This view of board effectiveness implies that there may be no such thing as independent real board or organizational effectiveness. Effectiveness is constructed (Scott 1995).

Board effectiveness is also quite related to the thinking about best practices and whether there are such benchmarks for boards and lay leadership. There are many resources that list best practices. For example, Green and Griesinger created a list based on their study of sixteen social service organization boards to assess the degree to which board attention to the duties and responsibilities prescribed in the normative literature is related to organizational effectiveness (Green & Griesinger 1996).

"The Nonprofit Good Practice Guide" of the Dorothy A. Johnson Center for Philanthropy and Nonprofit Leadership has a novel way of nuancing the issue of best practice. Their term is "preferred practices" for not-for-profit governance (*http://www.npgoodpractice.org* and *http://www.gvsu.edu/jcp*). What makes this list a bit more compelling than an externally created and shared best practice list is that it was prepared by practitioners in the field, most of whom are active lay leaders serving on boards. By making it possible for the list to be continually expanded by the practitioners, it becomes an ongoing conversation. As it grows, the concerns, challenges and opportunities facing lay leaders on these boards become more evident. There is also the implicit message that best practice is not a set of ideals that exist in the heavens but is an ever-growing and expanding body of knowledge based on actual experience.

The value of having a board look at its effectiveness in relation to a list of criteria or capacities for board effectiveness, or by studying its practice in relation to best practices, is that it provides a set of criteria to assess the performance of the board.

As indicated earlier, board effectiveness research is relatively new. The earlier literature is very practitioner-oriented and prescriptive. It offers advice on how to improve a board's effectiveness (Bhardwaj & Vuyyuri 2005); see also Houle 1989, and Chait, Holland & Taylor 2004). This literature draws heavily upon the experience and anecdotes of its authors. Many times the work becomes a handbook for improving board effectiveness. An important benefit is that many boards recognize that they are not fulfilling their responsibilities. Through this self-reflection process board members seek to function in a better, more effective manner and to realize that there are certain practices and processes that will help them become more effective (Herman & Renz 1997; see also Axelrod 1994).

The hypothesis that board effectiveness is related to prescribed board practices is supported by recent research (Bhardwaj & Vuyyuri 2005; see also Millessen & Lakey 1999; Herman & Renz 2000). Board involvement in strategic planning, meaningful and engaging board meetings and low conflict among board members leads to the chief professional perceiving that the board is effective (Bradshaw & Wolpin 1992). Research finds a positive relationship between the perception of board effectiveness and widely accepted notions of how a nonprofit board of directors should operate. This includes development of the organization's mission and strategic planning, together with participation at meetings and in committees. All contribute to the perception that the board has had a positive impact on the overall organizational performance (Millesen & Lakey 1999).

Our focus thus far has been about board effectiveness. Best practice provided the criteria. Researchers identified boards that were labeled as effective and distilled the practices of these boards. Thus effectiveness and practice were linked.

Yet the connection between best practice and effectiveness may only be an assumption. That is, it is assumed that highly effective boards use best practices. Are there objective criteria for board effectiveness? How is effectiveness measured? The prescriptive literature suggests that boards that use more of the recommended board practices will be more effective (Herman & Renz 1997). The problem is that a lack of consistency in board effectiveness judgments makes testing very, very difficult.

Research indicates a positive relationship, rather than a direct link, between best practice and organizational effectiveness and includes such factors as involvement in policy/mission formation, strategic planning, program review, board development, resource procurement, financial planning and control and dispute resolution (Green & Griessinger 1996). Other researchers write that best practice and effectiveness include raising funds to ensure the fulfillment of the mission, involvement in strategic planning, program review and board capacity building (Millesen & Lakey 1999).

Ultimately most people accept as true that best practice and board effectiveness go hand in hand. When studying boards of organizations thought of as effective and comparing them to boards of organizations thought of as less effective, many of the practices are the same. The primary differences are that the more effective boards practice board self-evaluation, have written expectations about giving contributions and have a chief executive who is involved in the nominations process (Herman & Renz 1997).

"The position taken in the literature is that a nonprofit board of directors can and should be used to enhance organizational effectiveness…Boards of directors are seen as ultimately responsible for establishing organizational direction and can add value by broadening the organization's perspective. They can help management recognize the major opportunities and challenges that are likely to affect the organization's future. Also they may need to serve as the ultimate court of appeals in resolving conflicting claims on organizational resources, and through their diverse perspectives, they may identify blind spots that can potentially inhibit chief executives from properly assessing the need, direction and speed of change" (Millesen & Lekey 1999).

LAY LEADERSHIP FOR JEWISH EDUCATION

In 1991 the Commission on Jewish Education in North America singled out as vital for Jewish education that "top community leaders must be recruited" if we are to make a difference in the quality of Jewish education. Through the publication of *A Time to Act* the commission issued a call to arms that Jewish education needed lay leaders to create a positive environment for Jewish education, put Jewish education on the top of the communal agenda and provide increased funding for Jewish education.

Pearl Beck, building on the ideas contained in *A Time to Act* recommended five major actions for lay boards governing Jewish educational enterprises (Beck 1999). These actions stem from what Beck found as lacking in Jewish educational lay leadership settings and systems. The first recommendation is to convince laity of the importance of Judaism and Jewish education. Beck's research revealed that many potential lay leaders had very little Jewish knowledge and "admit to being Jewishly ignorant." To be effective, a board member must live with Judaism and Jewish identity as core to his or her being. Second, boards need to recruit prestigious, creative and interesting people to serve because people with cachet will ultimately help the cause. Third, educational institutions need people to design long-term vision through on-going strategic planning. Fourth, boards need professional standards, which often reduce the size of the board, and must provide clear job definitions, extensive orientation for new members and evaluation of members' job performance. Finally, Beck recommended that boards schedule regular lay leadership development programs that enable them to be more effective in their work and in understanding the big picture.

For Jewish day schools, the Partnership for Excellence in Jewish Education (PEJE) is an excellent resource for lay leaders. Building on outstanding research from not-for-profit agencies, independent schools and Jewish day schools, PEJE advocates for and consults with Jewish day schools to develop the highest quality lay leadership. According to PEJE, the best school boards are those that display excellence in five primary areas:

1. Mission and Vision—The board reflects the vision of the school as it articulates, safeguards, models and promotes its organizational values, especially in the area of Judaic studies.

2. Committee on Trustees—The board ensures outstanding leadership in the present and the future by selecting, educating and evaluating the performance of trustees.

3. Financial resources—The board is responsible for fiscal oversight and uses a proactive, multi-year approach to ensure that the school has adequate resources to achieve its mission.

4. Policy and Planning—The board sets the direction for the school.

5. Board–Head Collaboration—The board hires, evaluates, and works cooperatively with the professional head of the school. The relationship between the board chair and the head of the school is the key dyad (*PEJE Newsletter*, December 2002, page 2).

Similar to PEJE, RAVSAK, The Jewish Community Day School Network, is committed to a set of benchmarks to which all board members should aspire. Their recommendation is to follow the National Association of Independent Schools' "2006 Governance Survey". Included are specific recommendations regarding who should sit on the board, proper methods of identifying and selecting board members, whether the head of school should serve on the nominating committee and issues relating to board effectiveness in the face of conflict.

In congregational and other forms of part-time Jewish education there is virtually no research on lay leadership or the establishment of proper standards. Since most of these schools and related programs reside within either a synagogue or a communal agency, it is the board of trustees of the larger organization that has the ultimate responsibility. In most cases there are education committees (with a variety of names) that assume responsibility under the leadership of the board for setting policy, overseeing the budget, developing the curriculum goals with the staff and other areas as assigned by the board. Due to their secondary role within the organization, membership on the committee generally lacks a formal review process, appropriate leadership development programs are a rarity and the understanding of the overall vision and policies of the central organization is often lacking (Alpert 2002).

The little research that does exist focuses on the relationship between the education committee and the congregation's board. This research emanates from synagogue transformation projects such as the Experiment in Congregational Education (ECE), which began with a series of position papers and a consultation in May 1993. Looking at best practice from organizational life and greatly affected by the writing and research of such people as Peter Senge and Michael Fullan, ECE looked to a number of Jewish and non–Jewish researchers and thinkers to reflect upon how to improve learning within the synagogue. When Aron, Shevitz and Reimer looked at congregational education, they noted that when lay and professional leadership connected, all of the education within the synagogue as an entire entity improved systemically. "The synagogue as a learning community" or "school and synagogue joined" is how they labeled their findings (Aron et al. 1995).

The research indicates that congregational schools cannot be "fixed" without looking at the entire system of the congregation. In other words, Jewish education does not live by itself inside the synagogue. Thus while the education committee(s) and the board of directors have different responsibilities, they must establish a common set of goals and outcomes and work collaboratively to achieve them.

In order to accomplish this complex set of goals, the lay leadership of the entire congregation must be dedicated to creating a congregational culture of learning (Aron 2002). Lifelong Jewish learning is the current language and must become pervasive throughout the entire congregation. The board and committees must engage in Jewish study as part of their meetings. New opportunities for expanded adult Jewish learning should be sponsored by the congregation itself, or through a collaboration with other congregations and agencies in the community, with an expectation that a majority of adults in the congregation are involved in learning. Of greatest importance is the need for families to participate together in Jewish learning. These learning opportunities should be connected to the larger value system of the congregation, including its social action agenda and the worship experiences. Thus the mission, values and vision of the congregation become aligned around learning as the core driving force behind congregational vibrancy and participation.

ADDITIONAL RESEARCH QUESTIONS

The level of understanding based upon serious research relating to lay leadership in Jewish education, whether in Jewish day schools, congregational schools or other forms of formal and informal Jewish education, is seriously lacking. Only through an active observation of specific leadership groups are we able to extrapolate general principles that can be applied to specific boards. Generally these relate to planning, financing and governance. (For purposes of these questions, we will use the term 'board' to refer to both the board of the larger organization, day school or congregation and the individual committees that oversee various aspects of the educational program.) A few of the more important research questions include:

- What do we know about the reasons why a person accepts a leadership role in Jewish education? How does this affect the manner in which board members are chosen?
- How do we distinguish between the leader's perception of his or her role and the reality of being a board member?
- What types of board orientation are most effective? Does this differ for the different types of boards? When does this orientation begin?
- Will a mentoring program for new board members aid them in learning their role and contribute to their being more effective? If so, what should be included in the training and preparation of the mentors?
- What characteristics lead to more effective leadership for board chairs? How should chairs be selected and/or trained for their roles?
- What are the elements that contribute to a good meeting? What types of evaluation should a board engage in to determine if their meetings are productive and meaningful, i.e., good meetings?

- What is the role and responsibility of a good lay leader? What are the boundaries, and how are they determined?
- What are the factors that contribute to a positive relationship between the lay leaders and the professional head of the educational program?
- What level of Judaic background contributes to more effective board members?
- What is the place of evaluation for the board, both in relationship to the institution/educational program and to its own role as a governing body?
- What factors should be taken into consideration as new board members are recruited?

FUTURE DIRECTIONS

Erica Brown, in a recent issue of the *Journal of Jewish Communal Service*, suggests that inspired leaders are the key to effective organizations (Brown 2005). She contends that leadership development programs fail to connect leaders' sources of inspiration with their life's purposes and their roles as board members. Brown admits that very little research has been done on the importance of inspiration as part of leadership training. As the new generation of lay leaders move into their roles, it is clear that they seek to make a difference in the future of the Jewish community, particularly through outreach to marginalized Jews. If these leaders are able to see the integration of what generates passion in their lives with their volunteer experiences, our organizations will benefit.

This is an interesting take on the problem of lay leadership in the 21st century. Given that people are busier than ever, given that Jews have more choices of where to exercise their voluntary leadership, why should someone decide to be on a Jewish day school board or the congregation's education committee? Even more, when and if they do decide to serve, how do we use their time and talents best for the betterment of school and educational programs? How do we guarantee that they feel they are making a real contribution and not wasting their time and energy?

Hopefully, there are people who are ready to assume leadership roles that will grow and strengthen the boards and committees primarily entrusted with the governance of our children's educational institutions. The ultimate goal is apparent: a higher-quality, more effective Jewish education program for our children and their families.

HIGHLIGHTS

- There is little if any research relating to lay leadership engaged in Jewish education.
- We must turn to research from the secular community, especially non–Jewish private schools and/or the general world of not-for-profit boards, to guide our efforts in lay leadership development.
- What we learn from the not-for-profit world is generally prescriptive rather than research-based.
- The most common belief about best practices for boards includes developing mission/vision and strategic planning, program review, resource procurement, financial planning and oversight, dispute resolution, and board development.
- Collaboration, in the best sense, between the board and the senior educational professional is seen as vital.
- It is unclear how, if at all, Jewish knowledge and Jewish living contribute to the effectiveness of a board member.
- For a congregational Jewish education program to succeed, it must be embedded in a synagogue where learning is pervasive.

CONCLUSION

It should be self-evident that excellence in leadership for both Jewish day schools and congregations is the deep commitment to Jewish learning and education of the lay leaders. They are learners themselves. They see their volunteer leadership time as an extension of this commitment to learning. As such, they are dedicated to an understanding of how their leadership can best be effectuated.

These lay leaders must advocate for research that is specific to their roles as leaders in various Jewish educational environments.

ANNOTATED BIBLIOGRAPHY

Aron, I., Lee, S. & Rossel, S. (eds.) (1995). *A Congregation of Learners*. New York: Union of American Hebrew Congregations. Containing the "thought papers" that laid the foundation for congregational transformation experiments, namely ECE, this book is especially rich in both looking at Jewish learning systemically in an institution and as a lever for change. Especially noteworthy are essays by Isa Aron on the learning congregation, Susan Shevitz on organizational perspectives on congregational education and Joseph Reimer on joining synagogue and school. The book also includes case studies.

Aron, I. (2000). *Becoming a Congregation of Learners* and (2002) *The Self-Renewing Congregation*. Woodstock, VT: Jewish Lights. Both of these books include strategies used by congregations as they planned for diffusing Jewish learning as the core value of a congregation throughout the entire system. There are dozens of activities that can be immediately used by lay leaders.

Holland, T. & Hester, D. (2002). *Building Effective Boards for Religious Organizations*. San Francisco: Jossey-Bass. A handbook for lay leaders, this book contains concrete ideas related to improving board performance. Each chapter is written in a very thoughtful manner, so the theory and practice ideas are joined.

The Nonprofit Good Practice Guide, *http://www.npgoodpractice.org/*, from the Dorothy A. Johnson Center for Philanthropy and Nonprofit Leadership. The website contains a wealth of downloadable materials for lay leadership looking to improve their practice.

National Association of Independent Schools, *http://www.nais.org/*. This website is full of materials and resources to assist the Jewish day school. The organization also publishes a regular magazine for a subscription fee. Their resource database is searchable from the web.

The Partnership for Excellence in Jewish Education, http://www.peje.org/. PEJE is one of the main addresses for day school concerns, opportunities, and issues today. Their web site contains much information plus links to other important sites related to full-time Jewish schools.

The Nonprofit Board Self-Assessment Kit. The Corporate Fund, *http://www.thecorporatefund.org/board_self_assessment_kit.asp*. This material is fully downloadable and immediately usable by a board looking toward discussion and reflection on everything from roles and responsibility to evaluation of board work.

REFERENCES

Abzug, R. (1996). "The Evolution of Trusteeship in the United States: A Roundup of Findings from Six Cities." *Nonprofit Management and Leadership 7 (1)*, 101–111.

Alpert, K. (2002). Rethinking Jewish Education: The Role of the Education Committee. New York: Union for Reform Judaism.

Aron, I., Lee, S. & Rossel, S. (eds.) (1995). *A Congregation of Learners*. New York: Union of American Hebrew Congregations.

Aron, I. (2000). *Becoming a Congregation of Learners*. Woodstock, VT: Jewish Lights.

Aron, I. (2002). *The Self-Renewing Congregation*. Woodstock, VT: Jewish Lights.

Axelrod, N. (1994). *Handbook on Nonprofit Leadership and Management*. San Francisco: Jossey-Bass.

Beck, P. (1991). "Leadership in Jewish Education." *Journal of Jewish Communal Service 75 (4)*, 210–223.

Bhardwa, S. & Vuyyuri, S. (2005). "Analysis of Board Effectiveness in Nonprofit Organizations in India." *Journal of Social Science 10 (1)*, 29–36.

Bradshaw, P., Murray, V. & Wolpin, J. (1992). "Do Nonprofit Boards Make a Difference?" *Nonprofit and Voluntary Sector Quarterly, 21*, 227–249.

Brown, E. (2005). "Making Inspired Leaders: New Approaches to Jewish Leadership Development." *Journal of Jewish Communal Service 81 (1–2)*, 63–72

Chait, R.P., Holland, T. & Taylor, B. (2004). *Governance as Leadership: Reframing the Work of Nonprofit Boards*. New York: Wiley and Sons.

Green, J. C. & Griesenger, D.W. (1996). "Board Performance and Organizational Effectiveness in Nonprofit Social Service Organizations." *Nonprofit Management and Leadership, 6*.

Herman, R. & Renz, D. (2000). "Board Practices of Especially Effective and Less Effective Local Nonprofit Organizations." *American Review of Public Administration* 30 (2), 146–160.

Herman, R. & Renz, D. (1997). Board Practices of Especially Effective and Less Effective Local Nonprofit Organizations. Paper presented to Annual Meeting of the Association for Research on Nonprofit Organizations and Voluntary Action, Indianapolis, IN, December 4, p. 2.

Holland, T. & Hester, D. (2002). *Building Effective Boards for Religious Organizations*. San Francisco: Jossey-Bass.

Houle, C. (1989). *Governing Boards*, San Francisco: Jossey-Bass.

Millesen, J. & Lakey, B. (1999). The Nonprofit Board Self-Assessment Process: Lessons Learned from the Field. Association for Research on Nonprofit Organizations and Voluntary Action. Paper presented to National Meeting, Washington, DC, pp. 3–4

Scott, W. (1995). *Institutions and Organizations*. Thousand Oaks, CA: Sage.

Philanthropic Funding
for Jewish Education:
Unlimited Potential, Questionable Will

Sandy Cardin & Yossi Prager

Amid all of the changes that have taken place within the American Jewish community during the past fifteen years, few are as striking and significant as those in the fields of Jewish philanthropy and Jewish education. These two areas have experienced fundamental shifts, independently and in relationship to each other, and both are now regarded as among the most dynamic aspects of Jewish communal life.

Lying at the heart of the recent transformations in both fields are three overarching trends: (a) the assimilation of substantial numbers of Jews into the larger American society, resulting in the abandonment of behaviors and social interactions that had long been the hallmark of the Jewish community; (b) the emergence of increased funding for a broad array of Jewish education programs and institutions as a response to that abandonment; and (c) a growing interest in research by Jewish educators, policymakers and philanthropists seeking to ascertain the extent to which various kinds of Jewish educational experiences actually strengthen Jewish identity and lead to greater participation in Jewish life.

While these trends are helping to reshape the current landscape of the organized Jewish community in a positive manner, the prospects for a truly vibrant American Jewish community in the years ahead will depend on the degree to which Jewish communal leaders, philanthropists and researchers are able to reinforce and sustain their current efforts by attracting significantly greater resources for effective Jewish educational programming.

*   *   *

During the past two decades momentum in the field of Jewish philanthropy has shifted away from centralized fundraising and allocations through the Jewish federation system toward private philanthropists funding independently or in small groups. To some degree this shift from communal action to atomized funding mirrors a trend in American philanthropy generally (Blum 2005; *Business Week*, Oct. 6, 1997). As sociologist Gary A. Tobin has noted, there has been an "Americanization of Jewish philanthropy" resulting from the significant integration of Jews into American society, and thus Jewish philanthropic trends are likely to track philanthropy in America generally (Tobin 2001; Panepento 2005).

The shift in momentum toward private Jewish philanthropy also reflects factors and challenges that are unique to the American Jewish community. For years the Jewish federation system was widely and justifiably recognized as a fundraising juggernaut. It was the self-proclaimed "central address" of Jewish giving; the largest federations collected and allocated tens of millions of dollars each year through a well-choreographed, consensus-driven, and deliberative process in which volunteer leadership typically worked very closely with their professional counterparts[1] (Raphael 1977). By the

---

[1] That perception of the federation system was captured by Marc Lee Raphael in a 1977 book review for *Commentary*: "Philanthropy in Judaism is not so much an individual as a collective project, and has become even more of one in recent American Jewish life. The federated Jewish philanthropies in this country, which have acquired greater and greater control over welfare, social-service, and Israel-related programs in the past decades, have also come to identify themselves as the chief public representatives of the Jewish community" (*Commentary*, September 1977 p. 84). The same point is made more pithily in the punch line to a popular joke about two men (one of whom is Jewish) stranded on a deserted island. The Jew is unconcerned for his future, secure in

1990s the effectiveness of the federations had dimmed. Overall giving to federations did not nearly keep pace with the fantastic economic growth, and the average age of federation donors rose (Popper 2004; D.N. Cohen 2005; NJPS 2000-2001 2004, p. 9).[2]

The decline in federation fundraising was partially explained by the findings of the National Jewish Population Survey 1990 (NJPS 1990), which showed large numbers of American Jews opting out of engagement with Jewish life, including federation giving. This Judaic abandonment, represented most vividly by the infamous finding of a 52% rate of intermarriage, (Kosmin et al. 1991, p. 14), led many to suggest that a dramatic change in the priorities of the federated system would be required to inspire, engage and educate a new generation of American Jews. Indeed, after heated communal debate, federations began reducing their allocations to the State of Israel in favor of domestic giving (D.N. Cohen 2004). Many federations established "continuity commissions," and there was much talk about the need to devote more resources to Jewish education and identity programs.

At the same time as the federation system began to grapple with these challenges, a significant number of existing and potential donors with substantial personal wealth and influence began to take greater interest in the future of the American Jewish community. Many of these philanthropists and foundations turned to the federation system for guidance and partnership as they commenced their own philanthropic journeys through personal giving, family foundations or donor-advised funds.

With a few notable exceptions, what these philanthropists discovered about the federation world did not impress them. They found a system responding to the situation in a slow, bureaucratic fashion, failing to recognize the true extent of the problem at hand. According to Edelsberg, "Frankly, federations' abiding commitment to process too often collides headlong with a new, donor-driven agenda that requires federations to focus on outcomes, efficiency and effectiveness" (2005). Unwilling to either delegate the initiative to the federation system or altogether abandon the Jewish community, many of the philanthropists began working outside the system to develop Jewish educational institutions and programs they believed would be more effective in the struggle to reverse the troubling trends reported in NJPS 1990.

In addition to their willingness to pour millions of dollars into programs designed to promote "Jewish continuity" or a "Jewish renaissance," private Jewish philanthropists introduced a much more bottom line, businesslike approach to Jewish philanthropy than had existed in the past. They represented the Jewish "new" or "venture" philanthropists, terms that gained prominence in the late 1990s to describe funders who engaged in their giving in much the same manner as venture capitalists invested their money (Letts et al. 1997). Those characteristics most often associated with venture philanthropists are: (a) an interest in reviewing relevant research and performing other due diligence before making a grant; (b) a willingness to act quickly and nimbly, either alone or in partnership with others who shared their social objectives; (c) a desire to be personally involved in the development and implementation of the programs they choose to fund; (d) a commitment to evaluation; and (e) a dispassionate, results-oriented approach to making funding decisions (Billitteri 2000, 2002).

Today an uneasy alliance exists in Jewish philanthropy. Still reeling from the conditions that led to the merger creating the United Jewish Communities (UJC) in 1999[3] (Bubis & Windmueller 2005), local federations are nonetheless trying to find a way to work with venture philanthropists. One challenge is that the philanthropists often come to the table with specific goals and approaches, while federations are consensus-driven communal institutions responsible to help maintain basic local agencies such as family services and the home for the aged and to contribute to causes in Israel. Recognizing the need for cooperation, many foundations and individual philanthropists are explor-

---

the knowledge that the fundraisers at the United Jewish Appeal will find him.

[2] NJPS 2000–01, commissioned and published by the United Jewish Communities, is cited sparingly here because the survey was marred by questions about its reliability. In general it indicated a kind of polarization within the American Jewish community between the affiliated and the unaffiliated, and between those who were in-married and those who were intermarried. The affiliated were substantially more likely to engage in a range of behaviors, including ritual practice and enrolling both themselves and their children in Jewish education (NJPS 2000–01, p. 27).

[3] Until the merger in 1999, the four legs of the North American Jewish federation system were the United Jewish Appeal (UJA), the United Israel Appeal (UIA), the Council of Jewish Federations (CJF) and all of the local federations serving Jewish communities throughout the United States and Canada. The three national umbrella organizations were then merged to become the UJC.

ing ways of partnering with the federation system without forsaking their independence or ability to act quickly.[4]

For the sake of the future of the American Jewish community, and especially for the field of Jewish education, it is important that both of the partners in this philanthropic dance continue to search for meaningful and effective ways to work together. Estimates of Jewish charitable resources are breathtakingly large; the value of the endowment funds held by the federation system as a whole is over $10 billion,[5] while Jewish family and independent foundations are said to have more than $25 billion in combined assets (Charendoff 2002). Even more remarkable is what the future holds. According to researchers at Boston College, the projected intergenerational transfer of American wealth through 2052 is in excess of $41 *trillion*, a disproportionate amount of which will likely end up in Jewish hands (Havens & Schervish 1999, 2003).

* * *

As staggering as Jewish philanthropic capabilities may be now and in the future, the extraordinary potential and financial needs of Jewish education have become equally evident over the past fifteen years.

Today Jewish education is a multi-billion-dollar enterprise, the vast majority of which is covered by tuitions (day schools), synagogue membership dues (supplementary education), fees (summer camps), dues (youth groups) and philanthropy. Assuming an average cost of $10,000 per student for approximately 200,000 students, the current annual operating cost of the American Jewish day school system alone is $2 billion (Wertheimer 2001). It seems likely that the cost for the full Jewish education system easily exceeds $3 billion annually.

Along with the growth of the educational system, there has been an expansion of the concept of Jewish education. Barry Chazan, a widely respected Jewish educator, explained the shift:

> Older notions of Jewish education saw it as aimed at children, housed in schools, and focused on either cognitive transmission or communal solidarity. Newer notions see it as lifelong, taking place on a campus that extends beyond classroom, and focused on shaping the total, holistic self. The clients of Jewish education are, increasingly, Jews of all ages—from preschoolers and their parents, to adolescents, university students and young adults, to adults and senior citizens. The venues of Jewish education are, increasingly, not just in school buildings in the local community, but in the larger Jewish world—learning takes place in day and supplementary schools, Jewish community centers, summer camps, college campuses, and on trips to Europe and Israel. The emerging aim of Jewish education, regardless of age level or setting, is to touch the inner soul and affect the Jew within (Chazan 2002).

While all of these types of Jewish experience have long existed, it is only in the past 15 years that the community has come to view them as part of a systemic whole. This new holistic view of Jewish education has generated a renewed sense of optimism within the Jewish educational community.

Although much of the growth in Jewish education stems from the grassroots efforts of local donors and professionals,[6] a small group of philanthropists operating on both the national and international levels have played a crucial role in making the case for increased funding of Jewish education in general and in stimulating much of the experimentation taking place in the field. These philanthropists, some of the more active and well-known of whom are routinely identified as "mega-donors," have also financed many of the research and evaluation projects undertaken in an effort to collect the kind

---

[4] In this context it is important to recognize the efforts of the Covenant Foundation, which is a joint program of the Crown Family Foundation and the Jewish Education Service of North America (JESNA), a national federation-affiliated agency. For more than fifteen years the Covenant Foundation has worked to honor outstanding Jewish educators and support creative approaches to Jewish educational programming.

[5] The 2005 Survey of Federation Endowment Development reported $10.2 billion dollars in total endowment assets owned by Jewish federations/community foundations (information obtained from UJC). However, not all of these funds are necessarily destined for Jewish causes or federation-affiliated programs. In 2005 more than half of these endowment assets were held in supporting foundations or in local donor-advised funds, vehicles that, depending on the rules of the local federation, enable donors to recommend allocations to both Jewish and secular organizations.

[6] In this context it is important to recognize the efforts of the Wexner Heritage Foundation, whose inspirational programming for local lay leaders seems to have stimulated significant grassroots activity.

of data necessary to measure the effectiveness of educational programs and, quite often, to attract new sources of funding for the field.

As a direct result of those efforts, a significant body of research about Jewish education has emerged over the past fifteen years to suggest that certain kinds of Jewish educational experiences have greater impact than others on the Jewish identities of those who participate in them. Not surprisingly, and quite appropriately, this data is being used to raise additional and much-needed philanthropic resources for those initiatives that research suggests are the most effective in accomplishing their educational goals.

Perhaps nowhere is that phenomenon more evident than in the area of Jewish day schools. Long a province almost exclusively of Orthodox Jewry, day schools had until the 1990s received the attention of only one major philanthropy, The Gruss Life Monuments Fund, which offers an impressive range of programs. Today, however, day school education has emerged as an area of significant interest and activity for the entire Jewish community (Ellenson & Zeldin 2004).

In 1993 the Jerusalem-based Louis Guttman Israel Institute of Applied Social Research issued a provocative report based on the findings of NJPS 1990 confirming that "Jewish day schools are the best vehicle for implementing Jewish involvement." Equally significant, the report found that "At least nine years of Jewish education mark the most significant upward jump in Jewish involvement" (Louis Guttman Israel Institute of Applied Social Research 1993).

The Guttman report convinced The Avi Chai Foundation, which had commissioned the study, to shift its philanthropic focus to the day school field, with a focus on high schools. The Guttman report and others that followed lent significant credibility to the effort by Michael Steinhardt and Rabbi Irving "Yitz" Greenberg to create an $18 million philanthropic partnership specifically for the purpose of expanding the number of Jewish day and high schools in North America. The first meeting of the **Partnership for Excellence in Jewish Education (PEJE)** took place in 1997, and under the able leadership of Rabbi Joshua Elkin, it is now recognized as a valuable resource center for innovation and growth.[7] Inspired by the success of PEJE, Bay-area philanthropist Laura Lauder joined with several other major philanthropists to create **DeLeT (Day-school Leadership through Teaching)**, a $6 million national fellowship program created in 2002 and designed to attract, train, inspire and retain top-quality educators for day schools.[8] In 2004 a group of anonymous donors in Boston banded together and pledged $45 million to enhance the fourteen local day schools, with three of the schools to receive a total of $30 million from the gift (Paulson 2004).

Research conducted in 1998 and again in 2003 by Dr. Marvin Schick, the pre-eminent scholar of the day school system, suggests that Jewish day schools represent both a stunning success (measured by growth to date) and unrealized potential (measured by the percentage of non–Orthodox Jews enrolled) as a communal response to advancing assimilation. Dr. Schick found that day school enrollment grew by nearly 30% in the years between 1992–93 and 2003–04, with the larger percentage of growth in the non–Orthodox sector. The most obvious development has been among non–Orthodox high schools. While there were five such schools in 1990, today there are approximately thirty-five throughout the United States (Schick 2005).

This growth is remarkable given the pressure rising tuition costs are placing on many families. The need to raise tuition levels simply to continue providing what already exists compels Jewish educational institutions to charge high prices while at the same time offering a product that is not nearly as strong as it needs to be to engage larger numbers of American Jews. As was stated in a report issued in 2003 by The Continental Council for Jewish Day School Education, an initiative spearheaded by the UJC and the Jewish Education Service of North America (JESNA):

---

[7] The original partners in PEJE were The Abramson Family Foundation, Avi Chai, The Andrea & Charles Bronfman Philanthropies, Edgar M. Bronfman, The Harold Grinspoon Foundation, The Jesselson Family, Jim Joseph, Morton Mandel, Charles and Lynn Schusterman, Michael Steinhardt/Jewish Life Network, the UJA Federation of New York and Leslie H. Wexner. A list of the current partners and a wealth of additional material can be found at peje.org.

[8] There are a number of teacher recruitment and training programs ranging from the Beth Jacob seminaries, to universities such as JTS and Hebrew College, to newer programs such as the Pardes Educators Program in Israel and a similar program involving the Hartman Institute in Jerusalem and Tel Aviv University. In 2004 the Jewish Education Service of North America (JESNA) convened a Jewish Education Leadership Summit, one outcome of which was the creation of JERRI: the Jewish Educator Recruitment and Retention Initiative. Among the more successful JESNA ventures in this area is the Lainer Interns for Jewish Education program, one that gives self-selected North American college students spending a year in Israel the opportunity to learn about careers in Jewish education and provides mentorships upon their return. According to an internal JESNA study on early participants in the program, approximately 60% of them are now Jewish communal professionals,

Schools are caught in the quandary of balancing affordability and quality. They will only attract students if they provide high quality, state-of-the-art Jewish and general education that requires ongoing continual updating of facilities, technology, curricular materials, professional development, co-curricular offerings, and more. At the same time, escalating costs of providing quality education make tuition prohibitive to large segments of the population (JESNA 2003).

A July 2003 report by the Cohen Center for Modern Jewish Studies at Brandeis University put it even more succinctly: "Balancing tuition costs with the needs for funds to ensure breadth and depth in school offerings is the essential challenge" (Cohen Center for Modern Jewish Studies 2003, unpublished).

The fact that high tuitions pose both a financial struggle for day school parents and a barrier to entry for prospective parents has been recognized for more than a decade. In an analysis of a study of Conservative synagogue members in 1995, Cohen found that day school enrollment was lowest in middle-income households ($75,000–99,000) (S. M. Cohen 1995). This makes intuitive sense; upper-income families can better afford tuition, while lower-income families qualify for scholarships, leaving the middle-income households to struggle the most with tuition.[9]

This data prompted Avi Chai to experiment with a voucher program in Atlanta and Cleveland. The program offered a $3,000 voucher per year for four years, but only for children in second grade and up who did not have an older sibling in day school. The program was an experiment to test the impact of cost reduction on day school enrollment as well as an attempt to demonstrate to the Jewish community the potential impact of a government voucher program.

Over two years (1997–98 and 1998–99) 213 children were recruited to day school through the voucher program. Extensive research conducted by the Cohen Center for Modern Jewish Studies at Brandeis University ("the Cohen Center") accompanied the program (Cohen Center for Modern Jewish Studies 2003, unpublished). One significant finding was that while tuition is not the single most important factor in parental decision making about their children's Jewish education,[10] it can be the "tipping point," particularly if parents disagree about the proper setting for their children's education.[11]

Independent of the Avi Chai program, the Samis Foundation in Seattle experimented with another form of tuition reduction. From 1997 to 2001 Samis made a grant to the only Jewish high school in Seattle to reduce tuition for all students from $7,200 to $3,000 (subsequently tuition rose but was still highly subsidized). In the ensuing years the school's enrollment grew from 56 to over 130.[12]

Both the Avi Chai and Samis programs served as models for subsequent philanthropic efforts, and new ideas were developed as well. The Continental Council for Jewish Day School Education, a JESNA/UJC initiative, assembled a report in June 2003 collecting information on twelve different tuition reduction programs, including a Schusterman Family Foundation-supported "fair share" tuition abatement program pegged to household income that is still in use at Heritage Academy in Tulsa, Oklahoma. The report listed the lessons learned for the benefit of communities and philanthropists seeking to adopt or adapt any of the programs (JESNA 2003). Recently the Solomon Schechter and Agnon schools in Cleveland introduced an across-the-board tuition reduction that will be partially funded as part of a major federation campaign that will fund day schools, among many other communal agencies.[13]

In much the same way as the leading funders of day school education have used research to inform their work in that field, a growing number of Jewish philanthropists are beginning to rely more

---

[9] Results would likely be different among Orthodox families, where day school enrollment is the norm for virtually all families.

[10] In fact, as many as 40% of the parents reported that they either "would have" or "might have" switched their children to day school even without the voucher. The credibility of these statements must be weighed against the low historic rate of transfer into the participating schools from second grade and up.

[11] Having proven the value of a voucher program in attracting new parents as well as the complexity involved in parental decision making, Avi Chai did not renew the experimental program. It viewed follow-up as a task for the local communities, one of which (see below) has picked up the challenge.

[12] In subsequent years SAMIS modified the program when it became apparent that the foundation was becoming the single largest source of revenue for the school, a position SAMIS viewed as unhealthy for the school.

[13] In March 2005, the Torah Academy in Minneapolis also announced a program that will provide vouchers decreasing over time for children transferring from public or non–Jewish private schools.

on evaluations and other studies to guide their philanthropic activities. In most cases, rather than research driving funding, research is following the money as philanthropists seek to assess the value of their efforts.

One question remains unanswered by the research to date: the extent of additional funding needed to provide the range of Jewish educational programming required to counteract the Judaic abandonment with which the American Jewish community continues to struggle. In the case of day schools, Wertheimer (2001) has suggested that adding 100,000 day school students to the system would entail capital costs of $1.35 billion and $250 million to prepare the necessary teachers. Moreover, it is likely that expanding the day school population in this way would necessitate tuition incentives that would require raising hundreds of millions in scholarship dollars annually.

Given that realizing the full potential of day schools alone may require the investment of billions of dollars, the total cost for providing a full range of quality Jewish educational experiences for American Jews of every age appears daunting. Fortunately, the last fifteen years have witnessed a substantial infusion of new money into the field. Among the other Jewish educational initiatives receiving significant funding, most of which benefit from a healthy interaction between philanthropy and research, are the following.

1. Trips to Israel. Although much anecdotal information about the educational value of an Israel experience existed for years, data from NJPS 1990, 2000–01 and other studies (E. Cohen 1999; S.M. Cohen & Kotler-Berkowitz 2004) finally confirmed the generally-accepted wisdom that trips to Israel correlate with increased Jewish involvements. In 1999 a coalition of philanthropists led by Michael Steinhardt and Charles Bronfman persuaded the State of Israel and the UJC to join them in establishing the $210 million **Birthright Israel** program, which recently brought its 120,000[th] participant to Israel. Longitudinal studies conducted by the Cohen Center of more than 70,000 Birthright alumni reveal that this free ten-day educational experience in Israel for 18–26-year-olds has significantly strengthened the participants' Jewish identities and their sense of connection to Israel and has led to an increase in their Jewish involvement when they return to their home communities (Cohen Center for Modern Jewish Studies 2004, 2006). A recent study of the **March of the Living** program for high school students produced similar findings (Helmreich 2005).

   Hoping to capitalize on the success of **Birthright Israel** and other Israel experiences, the government of Israel joined with the Jewish Agency for Israel (JAFI) in December 2004, to launch the MASA Program. According to a press release issued by JAFI, "the MASA project (meaning "journey")…aims to provide 20,000 young Jews from around the world each year with a semester to year-long program of studying and volunteering in Israel" (JAFI, 2004). The budget for MASA is expected to rise to $100 million, based on equal contributions from the government of Israel and a JAFI-led partnership that will include private philanthropists by the time the goal of 20,000 students/year is reached (Kraft 2005). Approximately 6,800 people attended MASA-approved programs in 2005–06 (MASA 2006).

2. Campus Programming: The annual budget of **Hillel: The Foundation for Jewish Campus Life** was $18 million in 1990; today it is $60 million and climbing (Hillel internal documents). This impressive increase is a direct result of a communal decision in 1995 to make the campus a focal point of Jewish investment, one supported by both the mega-donors (led by Edgar Bronfman) and the federations (Council of Jewish Federations 1995). During the past fifteen years—with Richard Joel at the helm for most of them—Hillel has successfully implemented a multi-faceted fundraising strategy that has attracted more than 250,000 new donors and resulted in the construction of more than 25 new buildings for the approximately 350,000 young Jews on college campuses each year. As in the case of trips to Israel, the overall effect of Hillel's work is difficult to measure and the precise percentage of students Hillel reaches is uncertain. However, the first effort to measure Jewish life on campus was recently undertaken by researchers from the Cohen Center. Based on interviews and surveys at 20 campuses throughout North America, approximately 45% percent of all Jewish students on campus spend some time at Hillel or other Jewish-affiliated clubs or organizations (Sales & Saxe 2005,

p. 12). A similar percentage of all Jewish students on the campuses included in that survey take at least one Jewish studies class by the time they graduate (*Ibid.*, p. 21). Further, Hillel, after undertaking a strategic planning process, in 2006 developed a five-year plan to dramatically increase the number of students involved in Jewish life and having meaningful Jewish experiences. Wayne Firestone, recently promoted internally to be Hillel's new president, leads the organization in the implementation of the new plan.

3. Summer Camping. One of the informal educational experiences studied most heavily during the past decade has been Jewish overnight camping (see *www.jewishcamping.org*). Multiple studies, from NJPS to specific research on Camp Ramah (Keysar & Kosmin, 2004), have shown the link between Jewish camping and subsequent Jewish engagement. In 2000, the Cohen Center undertook a comprehensive programmatic study of overnight camps and developed programmatic recommendations for a field they described as "an ideal venue for informal Jewish education that gives children the experience of life in a Jewish community and teaches them about Judaism" (Sales & Saxe 2002, p. 3). Energized and validated by findings about the Jewish impact of summer camps, the **Foundation for Jewish Camping**, formed by Rob and Elisa Bildner in 1998, has become the central, though not exclusive, address for national efforts on behalf of summer camping. The foundation has initiated programs to train camp directors and counselors, has advocated effectively for summer camping within the Jewish funding community and has guided camps in the areas of marketing, growth and strategic planning.

4. Adult Education: The National Jewish Population Survey (NJPS) 2000 reported that a surprising 24% of the 4.3 million more-involved Jews said that they had participated in an adult Jewish education class in the year prior to the survey. While some question the validity of this finding and note that this figure includes people who attended as little as one lecture, the optimistic finding is supported by increases in participation in three national adult education programs: (1) the **Florence Melton Mini-School,** now in 60 communities, enrolling 5,500 participants annually; (2) the **Me'ah** program, sponsored by the Hebrew College and the Combined Jewish Philanthropies of Boston, offered in six states in 2005–06 with an enrollment of 1,300 students; and (3) the Jewish Learning Institute of Chabad, with an enrollment in 2005 of 20,500 participants in 150 cities.

The Melton program has been extensively studied by Grant, Schuster, Woocher and Cohen (2004). In a summary of the research Grant and Schuster described a series of impacts of the Melton program. According to the researchers, the key impact "has to do with how the learning enriches and shapes the meaning participants derive from their Jewish lives. While relatively few outward changes in religious behaviors can be observed, learners' inner Jewish lives appear profoundly changed" (Grant & Schuster 2003).

Further evidence of philanthropic support for Jewish adult education is the significant growth of a myriad of Jewish websites, including **MyJewishLearning.com** and offerings from **Jewish Family and Life**.

5. Youth Groups: One of the most neglected areas of Jewish life during the past two decades, youth groups and programming for Jewish teens, has recently started to attract the attention of some American Jewish philanthropists at both the local and national levels. Locally, more than thirty-seven community-wide initiatives for Jewish teens like the Baltimore-based **Meyerhoff Teen Initiative** have been created in recent years. Nationally, BBYO is exploring creative and dynamic ways to engage under-affiliated teens in Jewish life by leveraging technology and addressing the core needs of American Jewish teens. At the same time, the major youth groups in North America, including BBYO, B'nei Akiva, NFTY, NCSY, Noar Hadash, USY and Young Judaea, have joined together in collaborative initiatives such as the Jewish Teen Leadership Summit and J-Serve, the Jewish Teen Day of Service, in an effort to reach out to the 80% of Jewish teens who are not currently involved in a youth movement. Sponsored by the Schusterman Family Foundation and spearheaded by PANIM: The Institute for Jewish Leadership and Values and the Jewish Coalition for Service, these projects

aim to find substantive ways for Jewish teens to work together across denominational lines and to involve their Jewish peers of all backgrounds in meaningful Jewish experiences inside and outside the youth group framework. Engaging Jewish young people during the teenage years is of critical importance, particularly as a recently released report by the Cohen Center indicates that 52% of Jewish communal workers began their work for the community while still in high school or college, typically working as camp counselors, religious school teachers, and youth group advisors, indicating the importance of these experiences to the Jewish community (Kelner et al. 2005, pp. 20–21).

6. Congregational Education: Another important area of Jewish education that has failed to receive adequate consideration is congregational education. Given the large numbers of Jewish children who will continue to be enrolled in congregational schools,[14] this is an aspect of Jewish education our community can no longer afford to overlook. Inspired and challenged by traditionally negative feelings toward congregational Hebrew schools, (Kadushin et al. 2001, p. 24; Kosman & Keysar 2000, 2004), the **Experiment in Congregational Education** (**ECE**) project of the Rhea Hirsch School of Education at the Hebrew Union College-Jewish Institute of Religion/Los Angeles and **Nurturing Excellence in Public Schools** (**NESS**) of the Auerbach CAJE in Philadelphia are working to enhance the effectiveness of synagogue-based education programs. Reimer of Brandeis University has also been engaged in an effort to target the various Hebrew high schools across the country through the Institute for Informal Jewish Education. Curricularly, both the Union for Reform Judaism and the United Synagogue for Conservative Judaism have recently released new curricula and other kinds of support for congregational education (see *http://urj.org/chai/samplelessons* and http://www.uscj.org/Project_Etgar_2005205964.html). In addition to the new curricula, the schools have benefited over the past five years from BabagaNewz, a Jewish values-based co-curricular suite of products that reaches over 30,000 congregational school students via school subscriptions. BabagaNewz is produced by **Jewish Family & Life**, with support from Avi Chai.

In the last decade there have been two new and very different initiatives in congregational education. Chabad is becoming a significant provider of congregational education, a development that bears further attention. In a different vein, the Goldring/Woldenberg Institute of Southern Jewish Life has taken upon itself to aid congregational schools in communities too small to have a rabbi and/or professional educator. The Institute provides a standard curriculum as well as visiting educators and a national conference.

The newest development to benefit the field of congregational education is the formation of the **Partnership for Congregational Education** announced in 2006. This partnership, led by a group of philanthropists and involving the professional staffs at the Jewish Education Service of North America and the Jewish Funders Network (JFN), seeks to spearhead the improvement of congregational education in North America.

Currently the state of research into congregational education is weak, and serious questions remain about the efficacy of these once- or twice-weekly schools. However, the new energy and resources invested in the field are likely to produce richer and more comprehensive information in the coming years. According to one estimate, it would take only $60 million annually to significantly strengthen the congregational system in 200 communities across the country (Wertheimer 2001, p. 14).

7. Early Childhood Education. Spurred by recent research in the general field of child development as well as in this specific aspect of Jewish life (Beck 2002; Vogelstein & Kaplan 2002), in 2005 several philanthropists banded together to create the **Jewish Early Childhood Education Initiative** (**JECEI**). This effort will spend $5 to $7 million over three years to create mod-

---

[14] There is no reliable data on the number of students in congregational schools, though there is much anecdotal evidence that supplementary school enrollment has declined over time. For example, in a forthcoming paper Wertheimer notes that over the past 3–5 years supplementary school enrollment in Philadelphia, Los Angeles and Cleveland has dropped precipitously—5.5%, 10% and 10.6%, respectively. However, enrollment in day schools and yeshivot has increased significantly over the last 20 years, leading the NJPS 2000–01 to conclude: "In short, over the past two decades, day school and yeshiva enrollments have grown dramatically, largely at the expense of supplementary Jewish schooling" (NJPS 2000–01, p. 15).

els of excellence in Jewish early childhood education, increase the number of families with children attending quality Jewish early childhood centers and raise the number of families continuing to engage in Jewish learning and living after pre-school.

*　　*　　*

While these initiatives and many other comparable programs reflect positive trends in the fields of Jewish philanthropy and Jewish education, the sad truth is that no current data exist indicating a broad-based reversal of the Judaic abandonment sketched by NJPS 1990. To the extent the findings of the NJPS 2000–01 are reliable, they confirm the enduring impact of Jewish education, indicate that a larger number (albeit still a minority) of affiliated Jews are participating in Jewish education programs and show that the *increase* in the intermarriage rate has slowed. Overall, however, the Jewish community is not growing, enrollment in supplementary schools continues to decline and there are more American Christians than ever before who have at least one Jewish parent (Phillips 2004). Other studies report that when compared to the American Jewish community of 1990, Jews today are less likely to have large numbers of Jewish friends, identify less with the State of Israel and feel less responsible for other Jews (Cohen & Werthiemer 2006).

Evidence of a distressing lack of progress can also be found in the day school world. As successful as the effort to increase day school enrollment has been on a percentage basis during the past ten years, the total number of Jewish students in day schools remains very low. In fact, it is estimated that only some 40,000 non–Orthodox children attend day schools (Schick 2005), a figure that represents less than 10% of the total non–Orthodox student population).

Perhaps the most disturbing statistics of all, however, are those that plainly reveal the extent to which the organized Jewish community has yet to demonstrate the ability to raise the resources necessary to help the field of Jewish education stem the tide of assimilation despite the awesome wealth controlled by Jewish families and foundations. Indeed, recent studies reveal that the vast majority of Jewish philanthropists continue to direct significantly more of their philanthropy to secular causes and organizations than to Jewish ones.

In 1998 Wertheimer studied the 232 foundations in America that self-identified as giving at least $200,000 to Jewish causes and found that even these foundations gave nearly two-thirds of their funding—$487 million—to non-sectarian causes (unpublished). A 2003 report by Tobin and colleagues examined the 865 philanthropic gifts of $10 million or more made by American donors between 1995 and 2000 (Tobin, Solomon & Carp 2003). While nearly 25% (188 gifts totaling $5.3 billion) of the mega-grants were made by Jews, fewer than 10% of the gifts made by Jewish philanthropists were directed to Jewish or Israeli organizations. While these two studies do not represent the full panoply of Jewish giving—most of which is by individuals giving much less than $10 million—it seems likely that the data accurately capture the overall thrust of philanthropic giving by Jews.

There are multiple ironies in this situation. First, most Jews view the openness of American culture as America's greatest gift to the Jews; it has allowed us to succeed academically, socially and economically to the degree that Jews can be significant philanthropists. That very same integration into society has proven to be a double-edged sword, however, for many of these wealthy American Jews often no longer feel the ethnic or religious ties that have traditionally encouraged Jews to give to Jewish causes. Tobin captured this phenomenon when he wrote, "Jews are now so integrated into the American mainstream that *tzedakah* has taken on more of the character of American philanthropy, and will continue to do so, representing less the religious tradition of Jews and more the civil tradition of philanthropy in the United States"[15] (2003). Further evidence for the impact of assimilation is evident in the debate about whether all philanthropy—from supporting Jewish institutions to the opera—is "Jewish" if the donor identifies as a Jew.

Second, too many donors who have some attachment to the Jewish community argue that Jewish institutions do not deserve support because they fail to deliver excellence. While some Jewish edu-

---

[15] The evolution of Jewish philanthropy also reflects the emergence of several trends in American philanthropy generally—the decline of centralized or "umbrella" giving, the heightened demand by donors for increased accountability, an increased number of women of wealth, the need to nurture the "next generation" of donors and the staggering number of new not-for-profit organizations and foundations created each year.

cational institutions fall short in this regard for non-financial reasons, others are caught in a philanthropic Catch-22: the only thing standing between them and excellence is a lack of resources! The Jewish "cost of living" is already high and growing higher every year; congregational dues are rising, school tuitions are increasing and camping fees are climbing (Wertheimer 2001). Jewish institutions cannot strive for excellence if funders do not first ensure that the institutions can afford to keep their doors open.

In a sense, the organized Jewish community and those Jewish philanthropists dedicated to strengthening the entire field of Jewish education face two shared challenges. The first is finding ways to persuade those Jewish donors currently directing the vast majority of their giving to museums, universities and hospitals to make comparably sized grants to Jewish education. The second is making sure that Jewish education remains a top priority of the federation system. In addition to contending with the lure of secular institutions, supporters of Jewish education must also find a way to compete successfully with powerful advocates within the organized Jewish community for all kinds of other important causes—social services, seniors, Israel, culture, social action, public policy and more—to ensure that sufficient resources of all kinds are devoted to strengthening this critical element of Jewish life.[16]

Two recent programs, one initially launched by Avi Chai and the Jewish Funders Network and one by the Schusterman Family Foundation, may provide a small measure of hope. By offering matching grants to new donors to Jewish education (or to donors increasing their largest prior gift by 500%), the initial Avi Chai/JFN program induced over 80 donors to contribute a total of $3.4 million (which the program matched with an equal amount) to Jewish educational causes of their choice.

The program, now named MATCH, was repeated in 2005–2006, having been adopted by five philanthropists joining together to create a $5 million pool to match $10 million in new gifts to day school education on a 1:2 basis (see *www.dayschoolmatch.org* for a list of funders). PEJE also joined the program as an operating partner. The program was dramatically oversubscribed, yielding 334 applications for the benefit of 177 schools representing new gifts of more than $22 million. To avoid having to reject eligible applicants, the five initial donors increased their commitments and were subsequently joined by a group of PEJE partners and anonymous donors, bringing the pool of matching funds to $7.8 million. This was sufficient to match on a 1:2 basis the 296 eligible donors to 155 schools and eight day-school-related projects, a total of $18.1 million (gifts over $100,000 were matched at the maximum $50,000). The hope is that many of these new donors become ongoing supporters of Jewish education.

In 2004, and as an inducement for the federation system to raise more money for the Taglit/Birthright Israel program, the Charles and Lynn Schusterman Family Foundation issued a challenge to every federation in the United States and Canada. The foundation promised to give each federation $1 in unrestricted funds for every $2 by which that federation increased its funding for Taglit/Birthright Israel in the 2004–2005 fiscal year beyond its commitment in 2003-2004. According to the terms of the challenge grant, the new funds raised by federations could come either from their regular allocation or from individual donors in their communities. As a result of that challenge, the federation system contributed $7,200,000 to Taglit/Birthright Israel in 2004–2005, an increase of $2,700,000 over the $4,500,000 allocated in 2003-2004. The challenge grant was so successful, in fact, that the United Jewish Communities recently requested that each federation in its system increase its allocation to the Taglit/Birthright program by 50% over its commitment in 2005–2006, a step that would increase the total allocation from federations from approximately $5,000,000 to $7,500,000 per year.

Two additional philanthropic rays of hope for the field of Jewish education include the funding of the San Francisco-based Jim Joseph Foundation and the nascent Fund for Our Jewish Future.

---

[16] According to a 1999 report issued by the UJC/JESNA Task Force on Jewish Day Schools, "there are responsible leaders, including members of the Task Force, who believe that the high priority we urge for increasing financial resources for day school education justifies reallocating funds from worthy, but less urgent communal endeavors. We believe that this is a decision best made locally in light of specific conditions. But under no circumstances will reallocation of resources alone meet the need for significant expansion of funding for day schools, Jewish education in general, as well as the broad array of important communal needs."

In February 2006 the Jim Joseph Foundation received a bequest of $500 million from the estate of its founder and announced that it was "preparing to become the largest Jewish philanthropy exclusively focused on Jewish education of youth and children" (Gordon 2006). According to Alvin T. Levitt, longtime attorney and friend of Mr. Joseph, the late philanthropist felt that "developing programs for youth and children...would in the future strengthen the Jewish community in the United States" (Strom 2006).

In November 2003, speaking in Jerusalem at a plenary session of the UJC's General Assembly, Michael Steinhardt proposed "the creation of a Fund for Our Jewish Future devoted entirely to our next generation....[that] would invigorate the most important outlets of Jewish identity-formation from early childhood to days schools, camps and college programs." Steinhardt went on to say that he was "prepared to start [the Fund] with a gift of $10 million whose [sic] only condition is that it be no more than 10% of the fund" (Steinhardt 2003). While the Fund has yet to be established, a group of philanthropists have expressed interest in the concept and are committed to assuring its realization.

As useful as these programs may be, the financial resources involved are a pittance in the context of a multi-billion-dollar educational system. The only real chance to raise the money needed to maintain and enhance the system is for philanthropists and others who care about Jewish education to trumpet the field by articulating a compelling vision that captures the imagination of the most influential leaders of the Jewish community, the federations, the mega-donors and everyone else concerned about the Jewish future.

Once that occurs, the next step will be the formulation and implementation of targeted fundraising strategies designed to optimize the dollars raised from large and small contributors alike, ranging from very specialized appeals to mega-givers of both genders and young donors to broad-based giving programs. These strategies must be research-based and research-oriented, steeped with evaluative data proving the efficacy of the Jewish educational programs for which resources are being sought. When developing these strategies, both the immediate and long-terms needs of the Jewish institutions involved must be taken into account and adequately addressed.

Finally, every one of these efforts must also take into account the decentralized nature of the American Jewish community. To paraphrase the famous Thomas ("Tip") O'Neill comment about politics, all Jewish education is local, and the success of the field over the long run will depend on its ability to meet local needs primarily with local funding, both from the federation and from other sources.

*   *   *

The following policy implications and recommendations emerge from this review of Jewish educational philanthropy since 1990.

1. **Sustainability of Funding:** The mutual ferment in the Jewish educational and philanthropic communities has yielded significant progress in the past fifteen years. However, few of the new programs or educational enhancements (e.g., Birthright Israel, PEJE, DeLeT) have thus far developed sufficiently broad bases of support to ensure long-term continuity. As a result, there is a risk that if the current funders lose interest or capacity, the progress in the field could dissipate. To some degree, this is a built-in weakness of the entrepreneurial style of philanthropy as compared with the slower consensus-building approach. Funders, federations, schools and organizations should work together to build endowments and fundraising capacities within both Jewish educational institutions and the new non-profit organizations that have been established to support them. The current generation of donors should also seek to engage younger funders in the programs so that the programs outlive the mega-donors who have been fixtures in our community in the past two decades.

2. **Expanding the Circle of Funders for Jewish Education:** As noted earlier, Jewish education in all of its forms requires the support of a larger number of philanthropists. However, bemoaning the problem is not likely to solve it. The immediate need is to understand the thinking of donors not yet committed to Jewish education and to construct arguments for Jewish educa-

tion using language and ideas that are more responsive to the concerns of these donors. There should be more settings in which Jewish education philanthropists collaborate with other givers so that there can be more peer-to-peer marketing. The Jewish Funders Network can be helpful here; another useful model may be found in Natan, a New York-based network of funders under forty-five whose funding is focused in the areas of Jewish education and identity.

There also remains a need for advocacy within the federation system, particularly to the lay and professional leaders responsible for guiding the use of endowment funds. Many of the endowments are in the form of donor-advised funds or supporting foundations, and advocates (especially alumni) of powerful Jewish educational experiences on the local level should join with federation to educate the donors and their children about the important opportunities in Jewish education philanthropy.

3. **Quantifying the Need**: While it is evident to all that the underfunding of Jewish education is in large part responsible for deficiencies in both quality and recruitment, there has not yet been a comprehensive effort to quantify the need. What will it cost to offer at an accessible price a full range of high-quality Jewish education programming—day schools, camps, Israel trips, campus programming, summer camping, youth groups, adult education, congregational schools and early childhood education? This kind of quantification is necessary for both planning and advocacy.

4. **Government Support:** For decades the organized Jewish community stood firmly behind a high wall between church and state in America, arguing against any kind of government support for Jewish education. In recent years there has been a shift in the thinking in some circles, with the result that support for voucher or tax credit programs for the benefit of Jewish day schools has become a mainstream, if still minority, position. (It may be a majority position among day school advocates.) Government programs of one kind or another exist in Milwaukee, Cleveland, Florida, Arizona and Pennsylvania. Issues of both policy and law continue to be debated and litigated. In light of the difficulties to date in attracting a dramatically larger group of funders to support Jewish education and the critical need for strong Jewish education to ensure the continuity of American Jewry, the issue of government support should be revisited. The fundamental question, framed from the narrow Jewish perspective, is whether Jews have more to fear from limited, even-handed government support for religious education than from the Judaic abandonment resulting from the limited enrollments in Jewish schools.

5. **Federations and the Future:** Will federations continue to be dominant features of Jewish life in the coming decades, or will the energy of private philanthropy lead to the continuing decline in both resources and influence of the federated system? While some would not mourn the demise of the federated system, federations play a critical role in raising funds for the general operating expenses of the range of low-visibility yet essential Jewish institutions such as homes for the aged and Jewish family service providers. Because these institutions are critical to Jewish life, philanthropists who practice "venture philanthropy" should also be helping to plan for the future organization of an American Jewish community that is capable of supporting these institutions. Similarly, as Edelsberg has argued, federations must imagine a future that is both more participatory and focused on achieving outcomes. This future would include "a rich tapestry of nationally networked donor advised funds, giving circles, youth philanthropies, social venture partners, women's foundations and supporting organization" (2004, p. 36).

6. **Linkages:** Most of the programs described in this report hone in on one or another type of Jewish education, with some projects for day schools, others for camps and yet others for Israel trips. Similarly, the Jewish educational institutions see themselves autonomously. A new report from a research team led by Wertheimer, entitled *Linking the Silos: How to Accelerate the Momentum in Jewish Education Today* (2005), argues compellingly that the community should have the overarching agenda of linking the different types of Jewish education both vertically and horizontally. This is because all of the data show that participation in multiple Jewish

education experiences is far more likely to generate enduring Jewish commitment. Vertically, families sending their children to Jewish pre-schools should be encouraged to continue on to Jewish elementary schools, and bar/bat mitzvahs should be encouraged toward Jewish high schools (day or supplementary). Horizontally, Jewish children should be encouraged and perhaps even provided incentives to participate in all of—not just one of—the modalities: summer camps, youth groups and Israel trips. Adult education programs should inform parents of the benefits of giving their children comprehensive Jewish experiences. Linking the different Jewish educational institutions in this way runs contrary to long-standing culture and will require the use of financial leverage as well as advocacy and training.

★   ★   ★

As noted above, the dramatic expansion of Jewish educational philanthropy, much of which has been accompanied by evaluation and research, has yielded an enormous amount of quantitative and qualitative data. Currently, even where the research is in the public domain, the sheer volume and complexity of the material makes it difficult for funders and educational institutions to draw appropriate lessons from past experience. The fragmented nature of the American Jewish community also creates substantial informational challenges. Wertheimer has noted the absence of "a clearinghouse of information, let alone a sustained process for gathering data on the field"[17] (2001, p.3; Prager, 2005). Without a better system for making current and new data useful, there is a great risk that critical information will gather dust on shelves.

There is another concern. Much of the research being conducted today is commissioned by philanthropists in connection with funded programs. However subtly, researchers no doubt feel pressure to support the philanthropists' desires. We should ensure that research is based on a need to know rather than a need to prove and that the findings receive critical scrutiny.

Finally, there are many studies showing that Jewish education enhances Jewish identity, and that more intensive experiences and those of longer duration have a greater impact than lesser ones (Cohen & Kotler-Berkowitz 2004, p. 18). However, we lack basic data about enrollment (other than in day schools), faculty turnover, training, and compensation, institutional finances and participant/family motivation for much of our educational system. The field requires a group, or an academic discipline, that conducts primary research on the essential facts about Jewish education in order to ensure that both philanthropists and professional leaders make wise decisions based on actual facts.

The Jewish community today has many strengths—energy, financial wealth, and creativity. The question is whether these resources can be harnessed for a compelling marketing and fundraising campaign that will provide the capital needed to secure a vibrant and first-rate Jewish educational system to educate the next generation of American Jews. This is surely the most critical question facing the Jewish community today.

ANNOTATED BIBLIOGRAPHY

Edelsberg, C. (2004). "Federation Philanthropy for the Future." *Journal of Jewish Communal Service* 80 (1), 31–38. In this article Edelsberg, formerly the vice president and director of endowments and foundations at the Jewish Community Federation of Cleveland and currently the executive director of the San Francisco-based Jim Joseph Foundation, addresses the need for federations to become as effective at grantmaking as they have historically been in raising money for the Jewish community.

Saxe, L., Sasson, T. & Hecht, S. (2006). *Taglit-Birthright Israel: Impact on Jewish Identity, Peoplehood and Connection to Israel*. Waltham, MA: Brandeis University, The Maurice and Marilyn Cohen Center for Modern Jewish Studies. This work is the latest in a series of longitudinal studies of the Taglit-Birthright Israel program, one of the most rigorously evaluated programs in the Jewish world. According to the authors, the findings in this report, like those in earlier studies, "are dramatic in the extent to which they suggest nearly universal positive evaluations."

---

[17] The new Steinhardt Social Research Institute at Brandeis University will collect, analyze, and disseminate data about the Jewish community in the United States and plans to address this void in the Jewish community. Similarly, the North American Jewish Data Bank is attempting to collect all quantitative Jewish research studies undertaken in North America, to make the research reports and data sets available on the Internet.

Tobin, G. A. (2001). *The Transition of Communal Values and Behavior in Jewish Philanthropy*. San Francisco, CA: Institute for Jewish & Community Research. Tobin is widely recognized as one of the most astute observers of the trends in Jewish philanthropy, especially insofar as the largest donors and private foundations are concerned. This work explores "the guiding principles, beliefs and myths that define the [Jewish] philanthropic system" and suggests how that system should reorient itself in order to attract greater financial support for Jewish causes and institutions.

Tobin, G. A., Solomon, J. R. & Karp, A. C. (2003). *Mega-Gifts in American Philanthropy*, San Francisco, CA: Institute for Jewish & Community Research. Starting with the definition of a "mega-gift" as one of $10 million or more, the authors examine the giving patterns of "mega-donors" in both the Jewish and general communities during the period between 1995 and 2000. Among their findings was that only a few mega-gifts from Jewish mega-donors went to Jewish organizations or institutions during that period. Anecdotal evidence suggests that while the amount of mega-philanthropy in the Jewish world has improved since that time, Jewish mega-donors still give an overwhelming proportion of their mega-gifts to secular organizations, especially to institutions of higher education and medical research.

Wertheimer, J. (2001). *Talking Dollars and Sense About Jewish Education*. New York: American Jewish Committee and Avi Chai. This paper begins the process of quantifying the needs in the fields of day schools, supplementary education and some forms of informal education by gathering existing data and projecting costs for expanding and enhancing the field.

Wertheimer, J. (2005). *Linking the Silos: How to Accelerate the Momentum in Jewish Education Today*, New York: Avi Chai. This summary synthesizes the results of a multi-part research project examining family decision-making about Jewish education. It argues that "leaders concerned with Jewish education must find ways to build institutional linkages between various formal and informal educational programs, between families and schools, between educators in various venues, [and] between the key communal agencies engaged in support of Jewish education." The reports from the individual research studies will be collected in a forthcoming book.

REFERENCES

Beck, P. (200), Jewish PreSchools as Gateways to Jewish Life: A Survey of Jewish PreSchool Parents in Three Cities. New York: Ukeles Associates, Inc.

Billitteri, T. J. (2000, June 1). "Venturing a Bet on Giving." *Chronicle of Philanthropy*, Vol. 12.

_____, *Venture Philanthropy 2002*. Community Wealth Ventures Inc., available at *www.vppartners.org*

Blum, D. (2005, April 14). "Held to a New Standard," *The Chronicle of Philanthropy*.

Bubis, G. & Windmueller, S. (2005) *Predictability to Chaos? How Jewish Leaders Reinvented Their National Communal System*. Baltimore: Baltimore Hebrew University, Center for Jewish Communities Studies.

Business Week (1997, October 6). "The New Face of Philanthropy."

Charendoff, M. (2002, November 15). "Challenge for Family Funds: Spending Down the Wealth," *The Forward*.

Chazan, B. (2002) *A Mega-Experiment in Jewish Education: The Impact of Birthright*. Waltham, MA: Cohen Center for Modern Jewish Studies, Brandeis University, iii.

Cohen Center for Modern Jewish Studies, Brandeis University (2003). *Increasing Enrollment at Day Schools and Jewish High Schools: Lessons from the Avi Chai Voucher Incentive Program*, 4 (unpublished).

Cohen, D. N. (2004, November 24). "U.S. Jewish Groups Ponder How Much Money to Send to Israel," *The Chronicle of Philanthropy*.

Cohen, D. N. (2005, February 17). "Merger of Jewish Groups Fails to Meet Expectations, Report Finds," *The Chronicle of Philanthropy*.

Cohen, E. H. (1999) "Prior Community Involvement and 'Israel Experience' Educational Tours," *Evaluation and Research in Education*, 13 (2), 76–91.

Cohen, S.M. (1995) "Day School Parents in Conservative Synagogues" in *Jewish Identity and Religious Commitment*, New York: Jewish Theological Seminary, 22.

Cohen, S. M. & Kotler-Berkowitz, L. (2004). The Impact of Childhood Jewish Education on Adults' Jewish Identity: Schooling, Israel Travel, Camping, and Youth Groups. New York: United Jewish Communities.

Cohen, S.M. & Wertheimer, J. (2006, June). "Whatever Happened to the Jewish People," *Commentary*, 121 (6), 33–37.

Council of Jewish Federations (1995). Report of the Working Group on Funding Jewish University Student Services. New York.

Edelsberg, C. (2004). "Federation Philanthropy for the Future." *Journal of Jewish Communal Service*, 80 (1), 31–38.

Edelsberg, C. (2005) "More than Money: A Covenant Model of Federation Philanthropic Effectiveness." *Journal of Jewish Communal Service*, 81 (1–2), 107–114.

Ellenson, D. & Zeldin, M. (2004, August 20). "Day Schools for Reform Jews, Too." *New York Jewish Week*.

Gordon, A.L. (2006, February 15). "Jim Joseph Foundation to Become Largest Jewish Philanthropy," *The New York Sun*.

Grant, L.D. & Schuster, D.T. (2003). *The Impact of Adult Jewish Learning in Today's Jewish Community, A Report to the UJC Renaissance and Renewal Pillar*. New York: United Jewish Communities.

Grant, L.D., Schuster, D.T., Woocher, M. & Cohen, S. M. (2004). *A Journey of Heart and Mind: Transformative Jewish Learning in Adulthood*. New York: Jewish Theological Seminary Press.

Havens, J.J. & Schervish, P.G. (1999). *Millionaires and the Millennium: New Estimates of the Forthcoming Wealth Transfer and the Prospects for a Golden Age of Philanthropy*. Boston: Boston College, Social Welfare Research Institute.

_____ (2003). "Why the $41 Trillion Wealth Transfer is Still Valid: A Review of Challenges and Questions." *The Journal of Gift Planning*, 7 (1), 11–15, 47–50.

Helmreich, W. B. (2005). "Long-Range Effects of the March of the Living on Participants." Available on the March of the Living website: *http://mol2005.org*.

Jewish Agency for Israel (2004, December 20). "Press Releases," *http://www.jafi.org.il/press/2004/dec/dec20.htm*

JESNA (1999). "Report of the Task Force on Jewish Day Schools" (available at *www.jesna.org*)

JESNA, Continental Council for Jewish Day School Education (2003). *Day School Tuition Subvention, Reduction and Scholarship Programs* (available at *www.jesna.org*)

Kadushin, C, Kelner, S. Saxe, L., Adamczyk, A., Stern, R. & Brodsky, A. (2001). *Being a Jewish Teenager in America: Trying to Make It*. Waltham, MA: Brandeis University, Cohen Center for Modern Jewish Studies.

Kelner, S., Rabkin, M., Saxe, L. & Sheingold, C. (2005). *The Jewish Sector's Workforce: Report of a Six-Community Study*. Waltham, MA: Brandeis University, Cohen Center for Modern Jewish Studies, Fisher Bernstein Institute for Jewish Philanthropy and Leadership.

Keysar, A. & Kosmin, B. A. (2004). *Research Findings on the Impact of Camp Ramah*. New York: The National Ramah Commission, Inc.

Kosmin, B. A., Goldstein, S., Waksberg, J., Lerer, N., Keysar, A., & Scheckner, J. (1991). *Highlights of the CJF 1990 National Jewish Population Survey*. New York: Council of Jewish Federations.

Kosmin, B. A. & Keysar, A. (2000). *"Four Up"—The High School Years 1995–1999, The Jewish Identity Development of the of the B'nai Mitzvah Class of 5755*. New York: Ratner Center for the Study of Conservative Judaism).

Kosmin, B. A. & Keysar, A. (2004). *"Eight Up"—The College Years: The Jewish Engagement of Young Adults Raised in Conservative Synagogues, 1995–2003*. New York: Ratner Center for the Study of Conservative Judaism

Kraft, D. (2005, May 30). "Israel Hoping Long-Term Stays by Diaspora Youth Will Pay Dividends." Jewish Telegraphic Agency.

Letts, C. W., Ryan, W. & Grossman, A. "Virtuous Capital: What Foundations Can Learn from Venture Capitalists." *Harvard Business Review*, 75 (2), 36–44.

Louis Guttman Israel Institute of Applied Social Research (1993). Jewish Involvement of the Baby Boom Generation: Interrogating The 1990 National Jewish Population Survey.

MASA website, *http://www.masaisrael.org.il/masa/english/*, July 14, 2006.

The National Jewish Population Survey 2000–2001 (2004, January). *Strength, Challenge and Diversity in the American Jewish Population*. New York: United Jewish Communities (available at *www.ujc.org*) .

Panepento, P. (2005, March 31). "Connecting with Generation X." *The Chronicle of Philanthropy*.

Paulson, M. (2004, October 10). "Jewish Day Schools Given $45m Gift," *The Boston Globe*.

Phillips, B. (2004). The 2001 National Jewish Population Study: Its Implications for Reform Judaism. *Hebrew Union College Chronicle* #64.

Popper, N. (2004, August 24). "UJC Faces Questions as Rieger Takes Helm," *The Forward*.

Prager, Y. (2005). "Jewish Giving—Keep the Faith Alive." *Philanthropy*, The Philanthropy Roundtable (May/June).

Raphael, M. L. (1977) Review: Why They Give, by Milton Golden. *Commentary*, 64 (3).

Sales, A. L. & Saxe, L. (2002). *Limud by the Lake: Fulfilling the Educational Potential of Jewish Summer Camps*. Waltham, MA: Cohen Center for Modern Jewish Studies, Brandeis University.

Sales, A. L. & Saxe, L. (2005). *Particularism in the University: Realities and Opportunities for Jewish Life on Campus*. New York: Avi Chai Foundation.

Saxe, L., Kadushin, C., Hecht, S., Rosen, M.I., Phillips, B. & Kelner, S. (2004). *Evaluating Birthright Israel: Long-Term Impact and Recent Findings*. Waltham, MA: Cohen Center for Modern Jewish Studies, Brandeis University.

Schick, M. (2005). *A Census of U.S. Day Schools 2003–04*. New York: Avi Chai Foundation.

Steinhardt, M. Address by Michael Steinhardt at the 2003 General Assembly of the UJC, *http://www.ujc.org/content_display.html?ArticleID=95482*.

Strom, S. (2006, February 15). "Foundation for Jewish Youth Gets Founder's $500 Million." *New York Times*.

Tobin, G. A. (2001). *The Transition of Communal Values and Behavior in Jewish Philanthropy*. San Francisco, CA: Institute for Jewish & Community Research.

Tobin, G. A., Solomon, J. R. & Karp, A. C. (2003). *Mega-Gifts in American Philanthropy*. San Francisco, CA: Institute for Jewish & Community Research.

Vogelstein, I. & Kaplan, D. (2002). "Untapped Potential: The Status of Jewish Early Childhood Education in America." New York: Jewish Early Childhood Education Partnership.

Wertheimer, J. (1999) Jewish Education in the United States: Recent Trends and Issues, *American Jewish Year Book*, 3-115

Wertheimer, J. (2001). *Talking Dollars and Sense about Jewish Education*. New York: American Jewish Committee and Avi Chai.

Wertheimer, J. (2005). *Linking the Silos: How to Accelerate the Momentum in Jewish Education Today*. New York: Avi Chai.

Closure

Jewish Awakening
and Jewish Education

Gerald Bubis

AN "EVER-DYING PEOPLE"

We Jews have seen ourselves as the "ever-dying people" for many centuries, and certainly, depending upon how one views Jewish history, the "lachrymose" approach held by so many would make that case. There have been others, including the present day transformationalists, who see naught but cloudless and sunny skies awaiting Jews in the twenty-first century. Before formulating some responses to dealing with the hemorrhaging of Jewish affiliation and physical continuity, a few reminders from the past might be helpful to provide a context for our concerns.

Demographers have reminded us that we probably constituted one-tenth of the population of the Roman Empire, some three million strong, and thus a significant percentage of the "civilized" world at that time.

From the beginning of the first millennium of the common era to the beginning of the nineteenth century, we escalated in number to an estimated high of six million, having first fallen to an estimated low of three-quarters of a million in the sixteenth century.

As we know all too well, our ranks had swelled to a high of eighteen million by the time of our grievous nightmare and the loss of six million in the Shoah.

The first point to remember, then, is that we have never been as countless as the stars but have remained, with oscillations, a relatively insignificant group when measured quantitatively.

In the 1920s Ruppin estimated that had there been no autos-da-fé, forced conversions or voluntary assimilation, we would have numbered some 250 million.

The blandishments of assimilation are thus not new, and no hermetical sealant will work in stopping the "leakage" problem. That admission price for Jews as a collective far outweighs in number those unwilling to "pay" by reaping the benefits of the society. We therefore must begin with the premise that stepping away from our heritage and betraying ourselves physically can be an option chosen only by a few. Therefore, strategies born of our goal and objectives to continue as a people must focus on how to more effectively achieve a better ratio of success to failure in our efforts to maintain a dynamic community into the twenty-first century.

We must face the reality that we are today much more the choosing people than the chosen people and have entered fully and, I would argue, willingly into the period of volitional Judaism. Thus threats about the consequences of inter-dating and intermarriage, and strictures to hear and obey God's commandments, are doomed to fail for all but a small percentage of Jews in the Western world.

The laudable and desirable—some would say imperative—Jewish teachings that emphasize interdependence and boundary-setting of self and community behaviors were born of commandments and God's path. They often seem to have little effect upon people's behavior. The sociological realities are such that the blandishments and potential the Western world offers to Jews are too available and beneficial in material ways to be counterbalanced by the threat of Jewish extinction or God's wrath.

Simon Herman has demonstrated to us repeatedly that we are all products of, and producers of, many identities. We are male or female, single or married, parent or child, and sometimes all simultaneously. For many, we are shaped by our vocations, our jobs; for others, our class defines us. For yet others it is nationality or age. We possess a multiplicity of identities that wax and wane depending on the appropriateness of that identity to our existential realities. And these identities can be combined. Thus, for example, at any given moment or period, being a Jewish feminist will manifest itself in its importance and attractiveness by the time and place in which one finds oneself. How often have we seen men put on *kipot* after getting on an El Al plane bound for Israel and watched them disappear as the plane landed in New York?

Have we noted that language itself may change, depending on where we find ourselves? Herman demonstrated that those in Israel who spoke their "mother tongue" in the home with their children "slipped" into Hebrew as they got closer to the school their children were attending.

Herman's premise was that the dominance and attractiveness of an identity had to be nourished and encouraged by the communal environment created by those for whom the continuity of identity was important.

Remember, identity is ultimately the sorting-out of who we are, and identification is the way we manifest our identity or identities. Perhaps it will be clearer than it is now that Jewish institutions—the family included—must be shaped and reshaped to offer attractive and desirable ways of being Jews. (It is an irony of language that we speak of Jewish identity—Jew-like identity—rather than the identification with Jews and Jews' institutions, so that we are more intensively Jews rather than more Jewish… Jewing identity, perhaps?).

A careful and thoughtful application of Herman's theories of identity (drawn from Kurt Lewin) can help guide those who shape institutions and their responses to Jews at the beginning of the twenty-first century.

In our collective and often faddish rush to respond to the need for Jewish continuity, too few of us give careful thought to what it is we are responding to. I suggest that building upon Herman's premises, a further step can be taken by educators *before* the bandwagon effect traps all thinking and action.

To my mind, there are eight components to Jewish identity formation. In each instance the child (or often, more importantly, the adult) can have strong affinity for one or more of these components, but those affinities can be negative rather than positive.

Let me first identify these components, describe them and later discuss the implications for educators in developing both formal and informal approaches to educational practice.

I cast the components in gerund form so as to underline my strong opinion that each one must be seen in action terms. The eight dimensions are 1) remembering, 2) feeling, 3) proving, 4) creating, 5) behaving, 6) belonging, 7) believing, and 8) hoping.

REMEMBERING

Essential to any attempt to form positive identity is the need for Jewish memory bank building. The family, all manner of community events and institutions, and the individual's experiences result in a reservoir to be drawn upon. If the desire exists within the family there is early recognition that a partnership between family and school, community center, and synagogue evolves. This partnership is interactive, feeding upon and folding upon the other. From the first days a family creates a Jewish environment in the home, at the table, in the books, and with the music and language the child hears, memory banking is being created.

It is imperative to note that a shared experience is no rejection of how one will react when evoking memory. More of this later.

FEELING

This strand of identity seems to be the most widely held. Many of us "feel" Jewish. In many instances there is no intention of doing anything about the feeling. For such Jews negative news from Israel can make them feel concerned. Positive news from Israel or about Jews in general can result in a feeling of great pride. Identifying with Jews elsewhere thus affects this strand of identity.

It must be the intent of those who want to enhance the intensification of identity to help Jews feel good about themselves as Jews. The goal cannot be xenophobia nor feelings of superiority. Rather, it is to help evolve a sense of one's self as a Jew that is wholesome, pleasant and positive, and ultimately provides a sense of communality that binds and bonds Jews to other Jews.

For others this aspect of identity is sometimes manifested in feelings of self-hatred. Whatever the cause or reason, the point is that each of these dimensions is capable of being expressed in positive or negative terms.

KNOWING

Knowledge is a potentially potent component of identity. The premise abounds that somehow intensive Jewish education is a cure-all for the disease of assimilation. Sequential learning geared to the levels and abilities of students is inherent in good education. The acquisition of knowledge as self-evident is also grounded in experiential learning in formal and informal settings, inside and outside the classroom, in camps, in friendship groups, in the family, through websites, books, TV, CD-ROMs, travel. In short, in living. (The caution for those who get on the day school bandwagon is two-fold: 1) Knowing is but one of eight components of identity, and 2) Many anti–Semites know or knew Jewish history, language, and text.) Having said that, the goal of any educator must continue to be to help produce knowledgeable Jews.

CREATING

Inherent in any expansion of positive Jewish identity is the need for expression born of Jewish inspiration, calendar, or environment. It is for the educator to grasp those opportunities, to channel them in all ways—formal and informal—for the children, for the families, for the communities. We, as past generations, stand on the shoulders of those who preceded us. We can weave past, present, and future through creative processes. We must be confident that as we make use of previous legacies of the past that have come to us in all manner and form that, if we are thoughtful and purposeful, our generations can leave such legacies for those who will follow us.

BEHAVING

Dennis Prager has often asked his audiences a probing question: "If people followed you around each day, how would they know you are Jewish?" Jews who are positively oriented toward being Jews manifest this through behaviors. These behaviors are manifested and range from the obvious, such as what we wear (a mezuzah, a *kipah*), to what we read, eat, listen to, discuss, and involve ourselves in socially and for socially beneficial reasons.

In more subtle ways it might include how we treat animals, other human beings, and the environment. The value we place on secular education is now so manifest it has come to be identified as a Jewish value. In reality, as we have embraced secular education to the degree we have (a Jewish dropout is said to have a master's degree) that we often are more ambivalent about the Jewish behaviors related to Jewish study.

BELONGING

The Dali Lama met with Jews because he wanted to know why Jews belong or feel they belong one to the other, and certainly in time past, one for the other.

Daniel Elazar was invited to India to help him understand the secrets of the Jewish Diaspora's relationship and sense of belonging with, if not to, Israel.

Classically, Jewish ritual behavior is cast in the context of group. We can't recite the full blessing after a meal without three being present; we often must pass on the recital of Kaddish without a quorum. (Rabbi David Aronson noted that nine chief rabbis don't make a minyan.)

The hoary joke notes that the Jew stranded on a desert isle quickly builds two synagogues so s/he'll have one s/he won't attend. To be a Jewish hermit is to commit an unnatural act.

BELIEVING

It is my contention that the thoughtful Jew believes, albeit sometimes in unconventional ways; for some it is belief in a personal God, for others the concept of predicate theology emphasizing the belief in goodliness rather than Godliness. Yet others draw strength in Imitateo Deo with some inescapable belief that imitating the attributes of a just God (even one s/he does not believe in) will somehow hasten that mysterious, elusive Messianic era. For others, the pursuit of social justice as personified by the belief in *tikkun olam* is the driving belief.

The pursuit of a belief system is at the heart of an authentic Jewish educational experience.

HOPING

For me, last but not least, a Jew must be optimistic. This is seen as near impossible, and yet at the bleakest and blackest moments, hope has sustained and despair has betrayed.

The late Rabbi Hugo Gryn of Great Britain was an Auschwitz survivor. He often recounted how his father came into possession of a half kilo of butter. Instead of using the butter to make the stale bread more palatable, or trade for other food or tobacco, he celebrated Chanukah, using it for the Chanukiah instead. He pointed out to his then-fourteen-year-old son at Chanukah 1944 that the human can live for many days without food but cannot last ten minutes without hope.

Every educator must make every effort to escape conveying the conventional lachrymose approach to exploring Jewish history in order to emphasize the grandeur of the Jewish adventure.

I have used the word "components" in this part of my introduction precisely to emphasize the complexity involved in defining what it means to be Jewish. Therefore, my premises are:

1) All that happened to and is happening to Jews is to be seen as shaping the definition of what is Jewish. Historical events, theological perceptions (and misperceptions), legal prescriptions and proscriptions, and contemporary realities, all impinge upon, shape, and influence the psyche and the very life of the Jew today, *even as every Jew in all places through time was so influenced*, negatively or positively, by the components mentioned above.

To be as specific as possible, an example may suffice. The "enlightened" Jew in Germany who decided to convert to Christianity was responding to his Jewish condition with what to him was appropriate behavior. Other Jews evolved radical new Jewish forms or Reforms alongside still other Jews who drew inward from the newly observed society in order to escape its negative effects. All three responses were by Jews engaging in appropriate behavior from their respective points of view. This leads to the next point.

2) Jewish experiences can be viewed negatively or positively depending upon the perspective of the times and the person.

The Holocaust was, to put it much too mildly, a horrendously negative experience for the Jewish people (and, of course, millions of others). However, the lesson drawn from this experience by its survivors is highly variable. Some survivors renewed their lives as Jews with a fervor that bespoke their thanks to God for having lived through the unspeakable horror. For some, the opportunity to give testimony against man's bestiality was and is seen as an opportunity to serve God in ever more pietistic, ritualistic, traditional terms.

A hypothesis enunciated by other Jews said that Jews throughout the ages were persecuted for being different. As a result, some tried to become like everyone else—e.g., to assimilate, as many did in Germany. Their reasoning, however, was that Hitler punished the grandchildren of the assimilated as Jews *because* they had become *too* much like the Germans and in the process had diluted the purity of the "master" race. Other Jews felt they had been damned for being different from others and damned for being the same as others. They concluded they would celebrate being Jews regardless of what the world said or felt about them.

Yet others concluded that the problem for the Jew in the Holocaust related to his not having disappeared enough. This group, fortunately small, has removed itself from Jewish life, changing names and sometimes physiognomy, moving to places distant from other Jews, all in the hope of saving themselves and their progeny the pain of being labeled Jew.

From this analysis grows the next premise.

3) The components we call Jewish are multifaceted and must be understood as a context for identity development. They include the political, sociological, psychological, theological, cultural, and ideological.

What Jews believed and believe shapes the least religious among us even as it guides the most devout. A Jewish atheist does not really earn that label unless he understands, as Hillel prescribed, that which he is against. However, to define being a Jew *only* in theological terms would do a great disservice to the historical definitions of Judaism. It provides a simplistic definition that has led to a false syllogism on the part of many of our young. Judaism is a religion, goes the argument. I am not religious; therefore, I am not a Jew. The Drew study of college freshmen in the early part of the 1990s found 17% of the Jewish respondents indicating that their parents were Jews but they themselves were not, because they did not believe in God.

The ideological approach for some does not encompass the theological. A generation of Marx-inspired Zionists has successfully (to their satisfaction) fused a modern ideology to an ancient dream and proudly identify as Jews even as the name of God has been expunged from their Jewish practices. Even they, in studying the Bible, admit that whether or not God exists, the Jews of ancient (and some would say recent) times have lived as if He did. That belief, however misplaced, has produced if not a God-intoxicated people, then a good-intoxicated people.

For still others, the connection with Jewish reality resulted in a Zionist ideology with messianic and universalistic overtones shareable with the most traditional among us. As they espouse the hope for normalcy in Israel when Jews there will be as people everywhere, they are alongside the fervent pray-ers for the Messianic period when all people shall be as one in preparation for the acceptance of the One God.

There are yet others for whom the cultural components of Jewish life are more than matters of theology and/or ideology. The artifacts, stories, legends, language, music, food (almost all of which, in truth, represent borrowings and transmutations from other peoples in whose midst the Jew has dwelled) provide comfort, nourishment, familiarity and kinship as a frame for living. At its crassest, lox, bagels, and cream cheese on Sunday mornings may be nearly the last but not least remnant of a culture that is taken in physical nourishment even as the Mickey Katz record is played for nostalgic reasons before or after the *2013-Year-Old Man*. That sense of culture can also manifest itself through Milhaud's opera *Moses and Aron*, Bernstein's *Jeremiah Symphony*, a painting by Chagall, a story by Kafka, or a poem by Shapiro. Disraeli's identification with his ancestors even as he spoke as a convert to Christianity has some of the ironic contradictions and inconsistencies I'm trying to identify.

The psychological and the sociological also define the Jewish components. Many seek psychological comfort in being Jews and are affiliated and engage in Jewish practices not out of obedience to God's strictures, but out of a search for their own need for psychic ease. It feels good to be Jewish and do Jewish things with other Jews. It even feels good for lots of Jews to do "non–Jewish" things with fellow Jews. The golf courses and theaters are peopled by small clusters of humans. Upon analysis they would be seen, more often than not, to be discreetly identifiable groups of ethnically homogenized people. There they find comfort in engaging in shared activities that are a function of their socio-economic position and are best enjoyed with others of like socio-economic *and* ethnic background.

Most Jews today would deny theological imperatives even as they select from the 613 commandments those that comfort them most or with which they find the most satisfaction. The recent upsurge in Jewish practice on a personal and communal level often grows out of this search for Jewish adjustment as much as it may manifest a way to return to a belief in God.

The sociology of the times encourages this. Ethnicity is at its height. Group membership has been labeled acceptable by all manner of sage and seer. Within the group called Jews there is succor possible for the eternally marginal people. Sometimes anomalies are created wherein the group is expected to act in public in a manner that is incongruent with individual behavior. Jews who relish the "forbidden" foods may be horrified with the same menu they enjoy in the privacy of their homes or restaurants when it is served at a public Jewish function.

Just as importantly, the Jew's public actions might also grow out of what the general community might think or do. "What will the Gentiles say?" has had its ebb and flow through history as a guide for the public behavior of Jews.

The geopolitical realities are no less important a facet of Jewish identity. Washington watches the level of Jewish giving in America as one way to measure the wavering or growing sense of the oneness of Jews. Can Israel's response to Diaspora Jewry as a sometime full partner to life in Israel not then be seen as an expression of the brutal reality of political clout and trade-offs? How can 2% of the population maintain a relationship with Congress and an administration that will result in sympathetic responses to requests and at the same time feel free to criticize the same people when the legitimate interests of non–Jews are being ignored or subverted? Does anyone truly believe anything could be done to help Israel, or Jews here and elsewhere, if there were not coalitions of understanding made and continued with all manner of other groups? Will poor ethnics sit still for the return of high-priced gas in America because Israel gets fuel guaranteed by America unless Jews agree to help those poor ethnics with their own economic and political concerns? Time will answer the question.

IMPLICATIONS FOR EDUCATORS

I am not one who believes in cookbooks for educators. For me, the challenge is to set a framework for use and application. Each educator faces different students, different ages, different time frames for teaching, and different expectations by the institution in which s/he works.

The model I have put forth sets a frame of reference for serious expansion of teaching and learning opportunities. It is for the teacher to plan activities, events, simulations, readings, discussions, and projects that actively weave together the eight strands of identity into a rope. This will help keep the student tied to the Jewish world for a life-long expanding series of experiences that ever expand the opportunities for growth and learning.

It is not enough to teach prayer or mastery of Hebrew. It is insufficient to keep education focused on the past. Those teachers who are doing the best kind of educating engage students in today's issues, writings, and events. Jewish civics comes to life in the classroom as appropriate. So do opportunities to celebrate the possibility of becoming a Jewish educator, a Jewish communal service worker, and a rabbi.

As the student is older, the learning opportunities must gain sophistication. Zionism in its latter-day forms, the realities of present-day Israel, and other Diaspora communities can be explored through song, story, exchange of videos, e-mail, letters…cross-fertilizing experiences that need expanding.

The political realities of Jews, the way Jewish life works, the realities of today's Jewish families all beg for exploration in the context of today's Jewish education.

The goal must be to have all that takes place cast in a positive frame. Kids must end up liking Jewish school at whatever level they experience it.

It is not an easy time to compete for Jews' time and make Jewish time holy. No one said it would be easy. Nevertheless, we have never had access to as many tools as we have today. The opportunities have never been greater, and neither have the consequences.

In a world where we now choose to be Jews more frequently than we see ourselves as chosen Jews, education has never been more important. Neither have teachers.

We are not an ever-dying people. We are an ever-renewing people and would not do this without teachers. All honor to them.

Shaping a Research Agenda By Building On What We Now Know.

Linda Dale Bloomberg

The past informs the future, as history continues to show us. We learn from those who have gone before us, and in so doing we, in turn, pass on new lessons to future generations. Educational research is about looking at what works and what doesn't, understanding how educational experiences can be enhanced, and developing a broader awareness of what others have learned. Jewish educational research does all this and more. Based on the widely held belief that increasing Jewish literacy and learning will lead to more meaningful participation in Jewish practices and communal life, Jewish education is about supporting and deepening Jewish identity, thereby strengthening Jewish life as we know it in order to ensure its very continuity. As such, the stakes are high; the social responsibility immense.

The urgency of the continuity question was powerfully demonstrated by the findings of the 1990 National Jewish Population Study, in particular increasing rates of intermarriage and assimilation and declining levels of identification among younger Jews. In response to these alarming trends, communal leaders and funders focused more acutely on questions of Jewish identity. What emerged strongly was an emphasis on Jewish education as *the* strategy to promote the continuity of Judaism. Many federations established Continuity Commissions to strengthen local programs connected to Jewish identity-formation, and funders conceived of a series of new initiatives to reach under-served populations and Jews at risk.

What We Know about Jewish Education, published in 1992, was a response to the identified need for increased knowledge and understanding that would enhance our ability to address the many challenges facing Jewish education. That edition has certainly played a valuable role in expanding the knowledge base and in stimulating much critical debate in the field. Over the past two decades much has transpired in the Jewish educational world. With ongoing innovation, the entry of new funders, and more firmly established connections between Jewish education and the quality of Jewish life, research and evaluation have become an integral part of decision making, planning, programming, and funding. It is these developments, and the current discourse around Jewish educational issues, that the current volume seeks to capture and address.

This chapter provides an overview of the lessons learned as well as an agenda for further research. In seeking to identify emergent themes regarding the current state of Jewish educational research, and those foci that are deserving of further attention, the author analyzed the chapters of this volume through a process of coding, sorting, and categorizing data. The findings of this qualitative analysis highlight a number of key themes pertaining to the practical and conceptual challenges that lie ahead. Proposed themes include:

(a) Need for ongoing commitment to research and evaluation.

(b) Incorporating research and theory from other arenas serves to inform Jewish educational research.

(c) Recognizing and reaching the diversity of Jewish educational contexts.

(d) Importance of continuing to address the broader purposes of Jewish education.

(e) Importance of conceptualizing research as a collaborative effort.

What follows is an overview of each of these emergent themes, substantiated by illustrative verbatim quotations taken from this volume's chapters. Following this overview the author provides an integrative synthesis vis-à-vis the implications of the research to date, and suggestions for moving the research agenda forward. A few words must be said about the way in which this chapter was conceptualized and structured. Rather than make use of a representative sample of quotations in order to shed light on what has emerged from the data and substantiate the researcher's claims (as would be the case in a traditional qualitative research study) the intention to include the broad selection of quotations from this volume's chapters was (a) to establish connections within and among the identified themes by drawing this volume's authors into a conversation *with one other* around research issues, and (b) through that conversation vividly illuminate for the reader the underlying *nuances and subtleties* (in terms of both similarities and differences) of their opinions, perspectives, and insights surrounding the issues under review.

OVERVIEW

(A) ONGOING COMMITMENT TO RESEARCH AND EVALUATION

In every generation, the key objectives in Jewish education have shifted in line with the changing needs and interests of students, community and society. As the chapters of this volume suggest, these needs and interests continue to change creating both new demands on education as well as providing new opportunities. The vast range of educational opportunities that is currently available poses a series of questions about the purposes, processes, and programs that fall within the broad rubric of what we call "Jewish learning." What we know from current research, as is evident in so many chapters of this volume, is that Jewish learning embodies the potential to strengthen identity, enhance Jewish values, engender Jewish connections, and transform the lives and outlooks of individual Jews, thereby positively impacting Jewish communal life.

Jewish education has certainly developed in many new directions, and the infrastructure of educational programs, both formal and informal, has attained a new level of maturity, offering learners of all ages a range of attractive options. Alongside these developments and the many opportunities that these developments bring with them, Jewish identity and the ways in which Jews conceive of and express their diverse ways of being Jewish inevitably pose new challenges and constraints for Jewish education. What is called for thus is a more nuanced and richer understanding of who our Jewish learners are, how they learn, where they learn, as well as the nature and impact of the Jewish educational experiences that are currently available. This knowledge is imperative to guide strategic planning and policy development.

Over a decade ago Stuart Kelman noted that the field of Jewish Education suffered from a paucity of published research-based literature (1992, p. 10). As is evident from an analysis if this volume's chapters, contemporary writers and researchers of Jewish education tend to concur, with the majority pointing out what we know, and acknowledging too what we don't yet know about, but should. Great strides have indeed been made, but to date there are still gaps in our knowledge base. Additional research is needed across all the dimensions upon which this volume is structured; educators, learners, curriculum, context, and planning and change.

First, it is abundantly clear that further empirical research is needed regarding all those who participate in Jewish educational programs—educators, leadership, as well as the learners:

It is commonly accepted that Jewish educators are a critical component in providing quality Jewish educational experiences. However despite that, there is still much we need to learn about our educators, particularly around issues of demographics, recruitment and retention, as well as how teacher education and professional development impact teaching and learning.

Goodman and Schaap point out that while studies of Jewish educators have informed policy and program development and have contributed to strengthening the qualification of personnel, these studies tend to be sporadic and do not provide a complete picture. As these authors explain:

"Missing are significant studies of informal Jewish educators and adult Jewish educators that could help grow these fields. Other personnel who are understudied or not studied at all are central agency for Jewish education staff, rabbis as educators, professors of Jewish education, Jewish studies faculty, and those working in Jewish educational roles in federations, national organizations both primarily Jewish educational organizations and those with a Jewish educational component, and private foundations. Another significant gap is that there is little known about Jewish educators who have left the field or about those who have considered entering the field but decided not to."

Feiman Nemser's chapter sheds light on the need for increased knowledge about teaching practices in Jewish educational settings. She explains that while the research base is growing and while we have a more dependable basis for shaping programs and policies, there is still much we need to know about how educators develop their practice, and what kinds of professional development opportunities help them learn what they need to know to enhance their teaching. Similarly, as Weissman explains:

"The Jewish community needs more research and examples of how schools can not only develop teachers' content knowledge but also enrich teachers' personal relationship with what they teach. Schools who want their teachers to be living role models of life-long learners and people striving to live what they learn will need to develop ways to support the Jewish journeys of their teachers."

In addition to the necessity for additional research pertaining to Jewish educators, more research is clearly needed to shed light on leadership development—the very core of the Jewish educational initiative. Kaplan talks of the need for further research to better understand the professional leadership styles of school principals, and how these leadership styles might impact educational change. It is clear too that that there is little substantive research on the roles and responsibilities of lay leadership in various educational environments. As Joseph, puts it:

"The level of understanding based upon serious research relating to lay leadership in Jewish education, whether in Jewish day schools, congregational schools or other forms of formal and informal Jewish education, is seriously lacking."

Aside from gaps in our knowledge base regarding Jewish educators and leaders, there is a dearth of information regarding Jewish learners of all ages:

Vogelstein points to the need for additional research surrounding our youngest learners, whose learning in turn has far reaching implications for family education and communal involvement. As she explains, " While it is clear an early childhood Jewish education experience has a powerful impact on families, these studies also suggest a need for additional research."

As Goldwater points out, given that more than 80% of Jewish young people between the ages of 18 and 25 spend at least three years in an institution of higher education, and despite the growth of Jewish communal interest in this population over the past decade, "we still know remarkably little about the Jewish education that goes on during the college years."

With regard adult learners, Grant and Schuster emphasize areas as yet untapped, pointing out,

"Presently, research is needed about specific learning populations…and the long-term impact of adult Jewish learning on learners, family members, or communal institutions. Such information will assist communal leaders in making more informed decisions about how to meet the needs of Jewish adults and how to increase the literacy and intellectual well-being of the contemporary Jewish adult population."

More specifically, issues pertaining to adult spiritual development also warrant attention. Thal highlights the very fledgling state of the field of Jewish education for spiritual growth:

"...there is a great gap in our research-based knowledge about what we might call Jewish religious education or Jewish spiritual formation. To date, there are only a few studies that examine programs of Jewish learning in which spirituality is the focus of either the teaching or the research."

In an attempt to assess the impact of engagement in adult Jewish learning on women, and to shed light on the nature of potential gender differences, Reinharz calls for longitudinal studies, explaining that,

"Comparative studies of the experience of men and women as adult Jewish learners should be undertaken...it is important to understand what exactly the women are learning, and how this impacts on their Jewish identity, Jewish practices and spirituality. There are extensive new developments in adult Jewish education...It is very important to differentiate between myth and reality in this field—is there truly a Renaissance in adult Jewish learning? What are the indicators or metrics that would establish that this has occurred?"

The second major area in need of further systematic research is that which encompasses modes of instruction, curriculum, and program development. It is indeed apparent that there are pockets of excellence. However, there is also a broad consensus that many current pedagogical approaches, curricula, and programs could be improved, and that continuous improvement is contingent upon ongoing and systematic research and evaluation:

As Vogelstein, writing about early childhood curriculum, points out:

"The Jewish Early Childhood Education Initiative (JECEI) was established in 2005... However, at this time, there are no commonly accepted standards of excellence and no research on the pedagogic, curricular and organizational practices that would facilitate the replication of excellence when it occurs."

Schachter and Ofek point to the central role that Hebrew instruction in one form or another plays in the education of Jewish youth. However, as these authors note:

"...Given that centrality, it is surprising how little solid research exists around Hebrew instruction in these settings and how little serious attention has been paid to the dilemmas surrounding Hebrew instruction."

Despite the recent resurgence of Holocaust consciousness, as Schweber and Findling point out, surprisingly little is known about Holocaust education. As they write:

"Though there are voluminous materials available from well-intentioned authors advocating particular pedagogies and strategies...very few publications or recommendations in this vast realm are actually research-based. Fewer still address Jewish school contexts...Regardless of the explanations for this paucity of inquiry, though, it's clear that enduring questions about the enterprise loom large."

In recent years, there has been an increased interest in the role in which informal and experiential Jewish education plays in the identity development of young Jews. Informal and experiential Jewish education currently stands in the paradoxical position of being recognized as a formidable force for shaping Jewish identities while also being seen as significantly underdeveloped in clarifying its principles and identifying the conditions that assure its educational success. That relatively little has been written about the field from a research or evaluation perspective is of significant concern. As Reimer and Bryfman explain:

"In a field that is conceptually underdeveloped, the scarcity of literature on informal and experiential Jewish education is not surprising. What surprises us is the lack of research which considers the variety of informal Jewish education contexts as constituting a single field."

Third, there is consensus around the lack of systematic, impact-based research on educational initiatives and projects within particular contexts. Research that has been undertaken most often examines levels of participation, satisfaction, and other factors, and is generally proprietary, remaining in the realm of funders and specific sites. As Shevitz describes it:

> "If we are investing in Jewish education in order to deepen, extend, or otherwise improve the learning that takes place, with the expectation that this will have a positive effect on participants' Jewish identity, then we need to understand the extent to which we succeed in meeting these goals. The evaluative work has generally not addressed this most basic question…While difficult, these questions can be addressed. It would require a willingness to extend the evaluation capacity beyond an initiative's first few years and to develop sophisticated ways to conceptualize and measure Jewish education, learners, settings and impacts."

The phenomenon concerning the paucity of research extends throughout the gamut of contexts in which Jewish learning occurs:

Given that during the last decade, day schools have received more attention than most other Jewish educational settings, and are supposedly among the most powerful institutional forces working to ensure the future of Jewish life in America, Elkin and Hausman note a profound paucity of research on the day school phenomenon, calling for empirical research to supplement the anecdotal reporting, and claiming that "We need to invest far more in learning about the impact of day schooling."

There has been increased recognition of summer camping as a valuable Jewish educational experience, and as an educational institution in its own right, camping has developed at a strong and rapid pace, benefiting from increased funding, capacity building, leadership, and educational sophistication. However, research in this field has until recently received little serious attention. As Sales and Saxe note:

> "Work in this area is just beginning…But much remains to be done. More research is needed about this generation's social networks, connections to Judaism, identity explorations, and worldviews… Our recommendations call for greater innovation and experimentation at camp. All such efforts need to be accompanied by action research that measures the outcome of these initiatives but also their process."

Over the past decade there have been heavy investments in both short and long-term Israel experiences, and research points to the enduring impact of these experiences on a wide variety of Jewish identity measures. Yet many unanswered questions remain. In terms of the Israel experience being so integral to Jewish identity development, as pointed out by Chazan as well as Wall and Klein Katz, additional research will be essential to ensure careful planning and implementation of programs.

Aside from research and evaluation of the impact of programs and projects within particular contexts, further research is also needed within the broader contexts that are responsible for directing, guiding, and controlling large-scale educational programming and planning initiatives. Graff calls for ongoing research into central agencies for Jewish education and their future possibilities. As he states:

> "Little had been written on the subject up until 1991, in response to rising concern about Jewish continuity—rendered all the more acute by the 1990 National Jewish Population Survey which reported high intermarriage rates, and research in the ensuing years has not sufficiently addressed this lacuna."

Cousins, talking more broadly about communal planning, explains:

> "Little research about Jewish communal planning exists. Moreover, the extent to which planners in Jewish education consistently use any materials on planning is not clear. There are few established, well-known practices in this area, nor is there a clear set of work in the area of general planning that Jewish communal planners access. Internal documents that are created or used in Jewish educational planning

are not distributed widely or readily. This leaves little documentation or research to inform communal planning in Jewish education or document specifically how planning is used."

Cardin and Prager point out that while the many initiatives that are currently in place reflect positive trends in the fields of Jewish philanthropy and Jewish education, "the sad truth is that no current data exists indicating a broad-based reversal of the Judaic abandonment sketched by NJPS 1990..." Therefore a serious question that remains unanswered by the research to date, and which needs still to be addressed is the extent of additional funding needed to provide the range of Jewish educational programming that is needed to counteract the Judaic abandonment that characterizes the American Jewish community. As these authors stress,

> "The field requires a group, or an academic discipline, that conducts primary research on the essential facts about Jewish education in order to ensure that both philanthropists and professional leaders make wise decisions based on actual facts."

This is indeed a critical consideration for Jewish education as funders are increasingly turning to and relying upon research and evaluation studies to guide their philanthropic activities.

SECTION SUMMARY AND IMPLICATIONS FOR FURTHER RESEARCH

Over the past two decades, the quantity and quality of substantive research in all aspects of Jewish education has increased significantly. Every arena and domain has captured the attention of serious academics and practitioners. Recent years have seen a broadening of research methods in the field of Jewish education, including qualitative approaches such as ethnography, case study, and action research, as well as a variety of quantitative data collection techniques. While a body of knowledge has certainly developed, across the board however, chapter authors are of the mind that many critical questions still exist, and that ongoing systematic research and evaluation efforts are necessary.

It is clear that ongoing evaluation and research is needed in order to provide deeper insights into the different types of Jewish learning activities that are currently available, the learners and the educators who are participating and the communities that are involved in these activities, the instructional philosophies and curricula that support these activities, and the long-term impacts on learners and communities. In addition, more in-depth, systematic case studies of planning and implementation processes are needed both within individual schools, as well as on a broader scale. Without serious study of all of these interlocking areas, a coherent, usable body of knowledge cannot develop. The consensus is that it is only by way of ongoing research and evaluation that Jewish education will discover new ways to enhance its impact and effectiveness. Additional data will indeed enable us to re-craft and refine our programs and pedagogy accordingly as we strive for educational excellence.

(B) RESEARCH AND THEORY FROM OTHER ARENAS INFORMS JEWISH EDUCATION.

An analysis of this volume's chapters highlights the usefulness of incorporating research and theory from secular education as a means to inform Jewish educational research and practice. Having noted the paucity of empirical research in Jewish education, what emerges is that the ever-increasing body of knowledge in general education and organizational studies can be useful for our purposes. This notion is attested by the following selection of comments:

> "Training toward successful school leadership will lead to more effective schools. By adopting the thinking from the secular business and education worlds, we will be in a better position to prepare strong and effective educational leaders...What is underutilized is the information available from the world of business and education about leadership in organizations." (Kaplan on Leadership in Congregations)

> "Given the lack of attention to experiential Jewish education as a whole, it is necessary to move beyond the limited research in the specific field and seek out other literature which informs the field...With little research literature about experiential

Jewish education, turning to related fields—including outdoor education, museum education and technology—can be very instructive. Experiential Jewish educators must learn from related fields if they are to remain relevant." (Reimer & Bryfman on Experiential Education)

"What we know about learning to teach derives from research in general education and public schooling. We have very little knowledge about the background, working conditions, career trajectories, professional development opportunities, and teaching practices of teachers in Jewish schools or of Jewish educators in other formal and informal settings." (Feiman Nemser on Learning to Teach)

"Hebrew language instruction should make use of the significant research on learning, including significant research on learning to read, popularly called 'brain research' to design programs of language instruction...Educators need to face the challenges in applying the research on effective language learning and adapt the findings to the conditions under which Hebrew is taught." (Schachter & Ofek on Hebrew Language Instruction)

"Jewish education has only reluctantly, at best, learned from the country's educational change initiatives. Yet, the great debates about education and how to translate research findings into educational practice are taking place within the initiatives." (Ben Avie on Adolescent Education)

"While little is known about specific practices used in communal planning, many theories from general literature often are invoked in discussions related to Jewish communal planning. Such theories have provided insight into how ideas are developed and executed and how intellectual change happens. They have become part of the communal planning lexicon, shaping conversations about how Jewish education can be influenced and developed." (Cousins on Communal Planning)

"...those involved in promoting change initiatives in Jewish education have grounded their work in that of the leading thinkers in the secular education and business worlds. Their approaches to change are connected to a wide range of overlapping ideas and theories that have become increasingly applied in the Jewish community." (Kraus on Congregational Education)

"...what we know about lay leadership from secular not-for-profits, from the church world and from the Jewish world gives us direction toward understanding the opportunities and challenges facing lay leaders governing Jewish education institutions." (Joseph on Lay Leadership)

"Shouldn't we apply the most successful lessons from general educational research data to Jewish education? ...Why wouldn't we take the best of what we have learned over the past forty years from early education and media research and apply it to Jewish education?" (Bernstein on Screen Media)

SECTION SUMMARY AND IMPLICATIONS FOR FURTHER RESEARCH

Many of us who are researching issues in Jewish education continue to incorporate theoretical and conceptual models that have been developed in other arenas. While we are no doubt on the way to developing a sound body of literature pertaining to various contexts and issues vis-à-vis Jewish education, we can certainly benefit from drawing from theory and practice in other arenas and settings to broaden our scope and guide us in our quest for further knowledge. Research in secular or general education, as well as interdisciplinary models and theories can indeed inform us, and it is apparent that there is much to be learned about their application to our setting. Moreover, it is possible to imagine a time when the relationship would become reciprocal, with practices from the Jewish education world informing other fields within general education. Jewish education is a nascent (albeit growing) field of inquiry, and it is largely the case that Jewish education follows in the wake of trends in general education. Yet, interestingly, as Daniel Pekarsky notes, research in Jewish education is indeed in some ways ahead of, and may already be influencing work in general education.

(C) RECOGNIZING AND REACHING THE DIVERSITY OF JEWISH EDUCATIONAL CONTEXTS.

As so many of this volume's authors point out the idea of attending to the settings or contexts within which education takes place is key. However, as is commonly acknowledged, contexts are fluid, changing, and emergent. Along with the growth of the educational system, there has been an expansion of the very concept of Jewish education. No longer is Jewish education aimed just at children, housed in schools, and focused on cognitive transmission of knowledge. It is a commonly accepted notion that Jewish education is lifelong, taking place inside the classroom, but also extending beyond the classroom walls.

The venues of Jewish education are, increasingly, situated within the larger Jewish world; learning takes place in Jewish community centers, summer camps, college campuses, and on trips to Europe and Israel. But education is increasingly taking place outside of traditional educational domains too: The internet continues to expand access to knowledge exponentially. Newspapers, social justice activities, music, films, museums, camping and retreats, and all manner of cultural events and pursuits provide the venue for learners of all ages with varied needs to express their Jewish interest and, as such, engage in Jewish learning and Jewish education. Weissman describes what she calls *Learning outside the school model*. As she sees it, "New models need to be developed that support both professional and avocational teachers in non-traditional settings for non-traditional learners."

As contexts continue to evolve and diversify it is imperative that we acknowledge and pay close attention to emergent, non-traditional, and radically changing domains, not least of which is distance education. In our quest to understand and enhance all types of Jewish educational experiences, distance learning programs in the Jewish educational world demand greater attention from educational researchers as we continue to develop a more complete understanding of both the limitations and the possibilities brought about by new communications and computing technologies. As Margolis describes it:

> "...the use of distance learning technology neither improves nor denigrates learning outcomes...in reality this is a highly liberating concept that shifts the focus away from unrealistic expectations and onto the specific and realistic uses of technology... The true task of using distance learning in Jewish education, therefore, lies in identifying and optimizing the ways in which technology can provide an edge."

As many of this volume's authors emphasize, it is important that we understand how and in what ways learning is occurring within and across contexts, and that we remain aware of the subtle underlying nuances that operate there. Feiman Nemser calls for a deepened understanding of how social and cultural contexts influence learning, explaining that,

> "[knowledge] is socially mediated and situated in the contexts of its use. So, for example, we come to understand concepts like teaching, learning, content, and knowing through our interactions with others in the organizations and communities we participate in."

Reimer and Bryfman adopt an integrative approach that asks what different contexts have in common, and how Jewish educators who identify with those different contexts can learn from one another to promote experiential Jewish learning. These authors point out that as the field has matured, Jewish educators have adopted the terms "formal" and "informal" education to describe these parallel tracks, but they caution that it is time to question this simplistic distinction. As they explain it:

"Schools no longer limit their educational work to formal instruction and contexts such as camps and Israel experiences employ many different methods to accomplish their educational goals. While it is vital that Jewish education continues to operate through these different contexts, it may no longer be wise to divide those contexts into two parallel tracks. Rather, a more complex descriptive matrix is needed to map the terrain of Jewish education."

These comments echo the sentiments of Sales and Saxe who see the Jewish summer camping experience as a mix of formal and informal educational approaches. As they explain:

"Where Jewish learning is infused into any and all activities, campers are as likely to encounter Jewish education on the high ropes course as they are in *limud*."

Weinberg, writing about change efforts within the congregational education context explains that understanding the very specific nature of different contexts is key:

"Alternative models can't be transplanted without careful attention to context… Repeated efforts at best practice dissemination in Jewish education have met with limited success. In the field of Human Resources, within the business world, the best practice dissemination approach has been contrasted with the notion of "strategic fit" —that each organization must design and implement those practices that uniquely support its strategy or vision. The latter suggests that each congregation, with its unique culture, circumstances, and history, must fashion its own vision of its desired future, and then adapt, mix and match, or draw inspiration from others' innovations to develop models that align to the congregation's own visions."

Kelner, in proposing the significant implications of Jewish educational travel as a context for Jewish education explains:

"The research on Jewish educational travel has generally been conducted under paradigms that have subordinated questions of curriculum and learning to other concerns. Future research in this area will be most useful to Jewish education if it breaks with this tendency."

SECTION SUMMARY AND IMPLICATIONS FOR FURTHER RESEARCH.

While day schools, congregational schools, synagogues, camps, Jewish community centers, youth movements, Hillel foundations, and Israel experiences continue to be vital settings, the borders of the field of Jewish education are constantly in flux. As such, researchers and funders need to be looking to expand in new and as yet untapped directions. Moreover, in our endeavor to understand and research the myriad of contexts in which Jewish education plays out, we should also remember, as Wertheimer (2005) points out, that education is not a separate and disconnected sphere of Jewish life; rather, it is integral to how American Jews live today. Learners, parents, members of extended families, synagogue congregants, peer groups, educators, and communal leaders all interact with one another in the interconnected activities and experiences that make up Jewish education.

In our endeavor to strengthen Jewish identification and community the challenge facing us is to honor the richness of our past, while at the same time embrace change and creatively stimulate engagement with the realities of the contemporary world. Today's learners expect learning experiences that are relevant, meaningful, and authentic. Be this the *age of Google* (Woocher, this volume), or the *world of web 2.0* (Amkraut, this volume), what are required are the skills and knowledge that will enable success in a world that is increasingly global and constantly evolving. Jewish education will be ready to meet these requirements only if leadership engages its collective imagination and energy in working toward delivering the type of learning that meets the needs of *every* learner.

Almost a century ago, in *The School and Society*, John Dewey posited the meaningless nature of an education that is disconnected from its society. In line with this educational philosophy, to be truly effective and to ensure the potential impact of Jewish education on the future of Judaism, we must ensure that we are attending to all educational realities, both old and new; that we are reaching each and every learner where she or he is at; that we are designing, developing, and delivering the best possible learning experiences in every context in which Jewish learners are engaged; and that we are doing so thoughtfully and purposively. And to achieve excellence in our practice, it is imperative that we engage in ongoing research and critical evaluation in all the contexts in which learning takes place.

(D) ADDRESSING THE BROADER PURPOSES OF JEWISH EDUCATION

Many hard questions remain about the purposes and scope of Jewish education, and the potential impact of learning on Jewish identity and engagement in Jewish communal life. These questions are raised over and again as shifts in Jewish life require us to rethink our understanding of how Jewish education works—and *ought to work*. Indeed, now, more than ever before, with the changing nature of Jewish identity and Jewish communal identification questions about the "Why?" of Jewish education become especially important. To move toward a clear understanding and conceptualization of the very purposes of Jewish education, as Daniel Pekarsky so eloquently points out, we need to work toward establishing well-articulated visions that will guide meaningful Jewish living in face of the challenges that confront us. We will also need the commitment to provide the resources necessary to realize and achieve those visions.

As attested by many of the chapter authors of this volume, we need to engage in dialogue around matters not only of Jewish content and process, but those pertaining to *purpose*. Accordingly, researchers, policy makers and practitioners of today need to articulate the relationship of Jewish education to a broader base of Jewish social and cultural issues. These issues include Jewish Peoplehood, Israel engagement in the larger society, social justice, spirituality, faith development, philanthropy and other such matters that lie at the heart of Judaism in all its complexity and diversity. Addressing purpose in Jewish education is no doubt a challenging task comprised of multifarious issues, as attested by Cousins who states:

> "Working on this research agenda is not easy. American Jewish education is a voluntary system, one infused with choice at every opportunity. Moreover, it is a system without a head; rather than a hierarchy of institutions with a common purpose, it is a matrix of overlapping institutions. They work toward the same general purpose but without direct interconnections, one source of authority, or even a common definition of what Jewish education should be."

The following selection of comments gleaned from this volume's chapters illustrate the many subtleties and nuances inherent in the very meaning of Jewish education, in identifying goals and defining outcomes, and in measuring success:

> "…proven strategies of how to achieve the kind of goals promoted in Jewish education are poorly identified or known. A great deal of Jewish education strives to go beyond a learner's mind into a learner's heart, spirit and sense of self. Jewish schools aim to create life-long learners, or makers of meaning, who exhibit faith, identity, and commitment…Without reliable means of evaluating the core outcomes of Jewish education that go beyond what a learner knows, teachers are swinging at a golf ball without ever knowing if they hit it or where it lands; there is no correction to the swing. The Jewish educational system requires more research on identifying short-term markers and ways of evaluating them for long-term goals such as increased faith development, identity building and applying learning to daily living." (Weissman on Professional Development)

> "The first [challenge] is definitional: we lack clear, operational definitions for concepts like "Jewish identity" and, therefore, reliable (tested and validated) measures for them. In the same vein, many funders and program provides alike struggle

to articulate measurable goals for their projects." (Rosov & Isaacs on Program Evaluation)

> "We ultimately know little about the relationship between culture and Jewish education, save that, given the goals of Jewish education, educators tend to view the concept of promoting Jewish culture as an unmitigated good. We hope a more textured discussion of culture that looks deeply into what it means to consider culture within Jewish education will help add further nuance to future studies and praxis... Culture can allow those involved in Jewish education to hook into a series of important discussions extending to all levels of the learning process, while providing well-developed tools for asking crucial questions about education's meaning, scope, agendas and purpose...We wish to push for research that has a certain intellectual distance from the stated goals of Jewish education...Doing so can also address important questions about the larger picture." (Cohen & Strigler on Jewish Culture)

A commonly held assumption is that an overriding goal of Jewish Education is to impact values, beliefs, and practices in significant and enduring ways. It is generally accepted that Jewish educational experiences enhance a sense of Jewish identity. As expressed by Ben Avie:

> "One notable desired developmental outcome of Jewish education is the formation of a strong relationship with the Jewish people, past and present. The outcome of this relationship is membership in the Jewish group, as expressed by the knowledge that we have learned and continue to learn, the attitudes we have developed and continue to develop, the emotional arousal we experienced and continue to experience when learning, and our continual partaking in the life of the community."

While many would undoubtedly agree with this view, there are various issues that need to be addressed, not least among them the question of identity itself; what it is, what it means, and its implications in today's postmodern society. We must also consider that there are vast differences in what we understand as the desired outcomes of Jewish education, acknowledging that there are often conflicting forces involved. Goldwater, with regard the university context points out for instance:

> "The academic discipline of Jewish studies is focused on the intellectual and the "objective", while the non-academic Jewish activities on campus are concerned with Jewish growth, transformative experiences, and Jewish leadership. This inherent tension has led to a lack of integration and sometimes even tension between the academic and the non-academic Jewish worlds on campus."

The comments of Reimer and Bryfman lend support to the ongoing tensions surrounding the purposes of Jewish education, casting the net further into the broader social arena:

> "In our view it is not enough for experiential Jewish education to provide "the Jewish air" that participants can breathe. That is a fine goal for Jewish socialization. But engaged Jewish youth will grow into the creative leaders of tomorrow's Jewish community only if today they learn to deal with complexity and risk. Experiential Jewish education is uniquely positioned to promote learning from challenge. Whether they are struggling with how to alleviate world hunger or bridge the gaps between diverse Jewish populations, engaged youth need to experience their Judaism as a serious arena for generating substantive responses to the deepest challenges their generation will face."

In terms of the power of affect, intuition, and emotion, Jewish education must, according to some, also foster spiritual development in addition to enhancing knowledge and cultural literacy. As Thal points out:

573

"Most adult education programs define their mission in terms of Jewish literacy with resultant commitment to Jewish identity and communal participation rather than spiritual or religious growth… Before we can marshal sufficient interest in and financial support for its [spiritual] development, the question of why Jewish spirituality is important at all must become more central to communal dialogue. Deeper, even, than the continuity agenda that has motivated the Jewish community for the past twenty years is the question of *why* is it important for Jews and Judaism to survive."

Backenroth, writing about the Arts, contends that,

"The ultimate goal of teaching does not end with transmission of knowledge and rituals, but entails cognitive objectives such as understanding and affective objectives such as transforming the spirit."

While some, like Backenroth, view Jewish learning as having the capacity to be transformative (Kay and Rotstein refer to "transformative Jewish family education", and Grant and Schuster talk about how "learning may transform the meaning of Judaism"), still others feel that "transformation" is too severe a term. As Shevitz provocatively points out:

"In the 21st century, with the changing nature of Jewish identity and identification in North America, questions about the purposes of Jewish education are especially important. To what extent is it literacy (and if so, what is a literate Jew?) or enculturation? Widespread use of the word "transformation" further obscures assumptions different people (and change initiatives) make about the endeavor, itself."

SECTION SUMMARY AND IMPLICATIONS FOR FURTHER RESEARCH

While we have begun to develop a sound knowledge base of the range of content offered in a wide variety of programs and settings and of what constitutes "good" teaching, as attested by many of this volume's authors, Jewish communal leaders have to date not sufficiently articulated the scope and purposes of Jewish learning. Many questions abound regarding the philosophical considerations of Jewish existence in our time as reflected in Jewish education, its alternative visions, the values it should serve, and the personal and social character it ought to foster.

Understandably, we each represent different conceptions of the goals of Jewish education, and the way in which these goals are likely to be achieved. However we do need to think more deeply about the broader purposes of education and the relevance of such purposes vis-à-vis educational planning and practice. Unlike public education where student outcomes are legislated, Jewish education does not have clear-cut student outcomes. But every Jewish educator does need to be aware of what she or he is aspiring to, and what success will look like. Ongoing discourse around what is being proposed as the vision or very purpose of Jewish education—and research around those issues—will bring greater clarity with regard our responsibilities as Jewish educators, and will inform Jewish leadership as to how best prepare its educators to respond to the challenges of the 21st century.

(E) CONCEPTUALIZING RESEARCH AS A COLLABORATIVE EFFORT

Stuart Kelman stated a decade and a half ago that the research that was being conducted then represented a microscopic view through individual lenses, noting that "missing is a macroscopic view of the whole" and that "chapters reveal holes in systemic thinking about particular subjects" (1992, pp. 10-11). In carrying out the analysis in preparation for writing this chapter the preponderance of the words such as *cooperation, coordination, collaboration, dialogue, discourse, linkages, synthesis, partnerships, knowledge dissemination, and information sharing* was indeed astonishing and inspiring.

Systemic awareness and ongoing collaboration are necessary for framing some of the key rubrics and issues that all of us—educators, researchers, policymakers and funders—will need to consider as we move forward in our efforts. Adopting a holistic view will involve greater numbers of people in Jewish learning and activity, and help us better understand the "big picture" by opening and expanding conversation about the field in all of its rich and varied facets. As Bidol Padva reminds us, transformative change is, of necessity, a systemic endeavor. As such, there is a clear need for ongoing conversations around pertinent issues in Jewish education, and for the development of opportunities to reflect collectively on the impact and implications of existing programs and initiatives. As of now it appears, however, that we have not sufficiently shared information and experiences in ways that can build a usable body of knowledge to guide future efforts, and we have yet to build the infrastructure that will make research and evaluation more useful. As Rosov and Isaacs explain:

> "...the absolute paucity of opportunities for knowledge sharing, in large measure the result of limited, program-specific emphases of contracted evaluation work... Another form of education that we must purse is building internal evaluation capacity among the many, many organizations devoted to the enterprise of Jewish education. This, as well, would do so much toward alleviating many of the challenges that we face in doing our work...We need—as a community—to establish a culture for sharing and disseminating our learnings..."

As new approaches are developed, many of this volume's authors point to the need to find ways to share information about all those who are learning, what is being learned, and how that learning is taking place. The following selection of quotations illustrate this need:

> "The field can grow through more sharing of information among those involved in adult learning, parent education, family education, and teacher education." (Katz & Parker on Parent Education)

> "Dialogue among scholars, practitioners, curriculum writers, program planners, and policy makers will help to clarify objectives and values." (Grant & Schuster on Adult Learners)

> "Information about Jewish women's interest in adult education is not so readily available, because it is divided into many different organizations...Data from these various organizations are not synthesized...It may be possible for Bureaus of Jewish Education in various towns or cities to begin to cooperate by locating all the forms of adult Jewish education within them."(Reinharz on Women as Learners)

> "We need to develop and share ways in which they have adapted or created programs and strategies for teaching Hebrew, Tanach, and other Judaic studies." (Miller Jacobs on Special Learning Needs)

> "To succeed in a synagogue setting, the processes through which they ask these questions must be collaborative, vision-driven, infused with systemic thinking and informed by appreciative inquiry... It takes collaboration among rabbis, educational directors, teachers, parents and others, not only to come up with new models—creative educators could do that on their own—but to build ownership and a foundation of shared ownership." (Weinberg on Synagogues)

> "Because of the diffuse nature of the field of congregational education, it is crucial that all national and local institutions work together in sharing information, piloting new projects, and collaborating on research." (Kraus on Congregational Education)

> "There is a need to expand and collaborate on qualitative and quantitative efforts to understand these [university] students, their interests, their needs, and what is already working well for them... In addition more research should be commissioned, perhaps by a central body that can coordinate the interests of all the interested parties, in order to develop further research questions and to facilitate collaboration in the use of the data." (Goldwater on University Students)

> "Camps, with their expertise in creating intentional communities, can be an instructive model for schools to emulate. To become such a model, however, they need to recognize themselves as educational settings, achieve consistent levels of excellence, and disseminate their accomplishments." (Sales & Saxe on Camping)

> "Foundations interested in Jewish education should partner with local Jewish communities to do small scale studies on Jewish education…Jewish education research in the 21st century will depend upon local studies." (Phillips on Demography)

As attested by the following comments, there is clear need to share knowledge regarding all those who participate in Jewish educational programs; not only the learners, but also our educators:

Kaplan writing about educational leadership in congregations explains:

> "Research must be undertaken with the results disseminated to academics, professionals and lay leaders that continues to expand our knowledge and understanding of the impact that educational leaders have on their schools and how to properly prepare them for their important roles."

Weissman, in promoting professional development, calls for Jewish educators to be trained to employ action research based strategies in their teaching, and to share and disseminate that knowledge with other educators. As she puts it:

> "Forums are needed to enable early experimenters with new models of professional learning to learn from one another's successes and misses. Consolidating and disseminating this work is essential if other communities are to join in the work of developing the context, process and content of professional learning in Jewish schools…The broken pieces in the field of education litter our agendas with curriculum, professional development and family education as if they were separate entities. We are past the time of trying better programs. Departmentalized thinking has generated departmentalized actions. Systems thinking can direct systemic action that produces results for teachers and for students."

Feiman Nemser talks about "critical colleagueship" as an important factor in examining the issue of learning to teach. She suggests that,

> "There is growing evidence that improvements in teaching are most likely to occur in schools where teachers work together. Whether the focus is on novices learning to teach in the company of mentors or teachers at different career stages coming together to develop curriculum, discuss problems of practice or implement a new instructional program, researchers are demonstrating the power (some would say necessity) of collective activity to strengthen teaching and enhance student learning."

In addition, there is a clear need for the sharing of information among funders as explained by Cardin and Prager who write:

> "Jewish education in all of its forms requires the support of a larger number of philanthropists…The immediate need is to understand the thinking of donors not yet committed to Jewish education and construct arguments for Jewish education using language and ideas that are more responsive to the concerns of these donors. There should be more settings in which Jewish education philanthropists collaborate with other givers, so that there can be more peer-to-peer marketing."

In addition to sharing information on learners, educators and leadership, so that we can begin to build a usable body of knowledge to guide future efforts, we also need to engage in ongoing sharing of knowledge, skills, and ideas about the specific contexts and settings in which Jewish education takes place, as well as about extant curricula and programs:

Thal, writing about spirituality and spiritual development, calls for

"Collaboration between teachers of existent programs and researchers in projects of action research which would help teachers learn to study and reflect on their practice and would engage researchers in a deeper understanding of spiritually focused learning."

As Kelner notes:

"Travel has emerged as an important medium of Jewish education, one that has attracted large numbers of participants and significant investment of communal resources. In spite of its extensive presence, the ability to develop it systematically as an educational field is hampered by fragmentation and isolation. For the field to be developed, those working in each particular form of travel education would have to recognize their common cause with educators working with its other forms... Those working in the disparate areas of Jewish travel education should find ways to come together, to exchange knowledge, to form partnerships and to advocate collectively."

Elkin and Hausman explain that,

"An ever widening movement of lay leaders, professionals, donors, federations, and central agencies, all accessing vetted expertise, will help ensure that day schools make progress in reaching their potential."

Moreover, these authors raise the issue of inter-institutional collaboration, stating that,

"Day schools must build relationships with a wide number of organizations in the Jewish community... Operating in self-imposed isolation reduces the awareness of the day school, prevents valuable collaborations from taking hold, and contributes to the perception of a parochialism which is one of the major barriers to day school enrollment growth."

Similarly, many of this volume's authors' comments suggest that aside from collaboration among colleagues within related fields, there is a strong need for coordinated efforts at the organizational level. This raises the issue of the need for "systems" approach whereby "cellular" institutions will come to recognize that they are part of a larger network, and that interaction with each other is more beneficial than working in isolation. In this regard, Ben Avie, writing about adolescents, comments:

"The camp, youth group, school, and synagogue need to make a coordinated effort. Moreover, the most effective way to develop this coordinated effort is through promoting complementary educational systems."

Likewise, as Kay and Rotstein on family education explain:

"Collaboration within institutions must also be encouraged. Supporting the growth and development of Jewish families must be seen as the work of all Jewish professionals. Partnership and team work can bring together the talent, skills and resources needed for this visionary work."

Graff views central agencies for Jewish education uniquely poised to fill the role described by Jack Wertheimer as "linking the silos" and to nurture and strengthen communities' Jewish educational systems. He explains:

"As foundations, federations and others interested in the advancement of Jewish education look to effect systemic change, the Central Agency represents an important vehicle for achieving significant outcomes in local communities, linking community institutions and individuals with one another and connecting local communities to national initiatives...With a proliferating array of Jewish educational experiences, educational institutions and funders of Jewish educational initiatives, the need for communal hubs of Jewish education connecting people and institutions, disseminating best practices and contributing "value added" educational and operational expertise is increasingly recognized."

The majority of contributors to this volume emphasize the need to support and encourage greater cooperation, collaboration, and synergy between the myriad of Jewish educational venues. The essential idea here is that knowledge, information, research, expertise, resources, and educational developments should not be considered the exclusive possession of any one Jewish educational institution; that sharing these would be mutually beneficial. As Cousins describes it:

"Despite this evolving and expanded richness, planning efforts continue to be insular in sharing the lessons they have learned. Many documents related to continuity planning remain in the hands of the sponsoring organizations. An area of significant potential growth in communal planning in Jewish education lies in our ability to collect and analyze these documents together, thereby creating a systematic understanding of what is known about the promise and impact of the continuity planning efforts and maximizing our efforts by learning effectively from each other's work."

Bidol Padva, writing more broadly about how to create and implement transformative initiatives, likewise calls attention to the importance of collaborative efforts, stating that,

"Transformative change can only occur if the stakeholders who are impacted by and those who can implement the change jointly work together to create a compelling vision and execute it."

What is needed is an apparent readiness to move beyond focusing on individual institutions and programs toward thinking more holistically. It must be acknowledged that changing the mindset of one of separateness to one of increased collaboration will not be without challenges. If a systems approach is to take root and grow, organizations will indeed have to become less proprietary about their individual work, and more open to sharing accomplishments and lessons learned. As Shevitz explains:

"Whatever the mechanism for sharing information and resources, it will require a shift from a private, proprietary ethic to one of collaboration and a commitment to building a usable knowledge-base."

Similarly, Cardin and Prager caution that,

"...Linking the different Jewish educational institutions in this way runs contrary to long-standing culture and will require the use of financial leverage as well as advocacy and training.

SECTION SUMMARY AND IMPLICATIONS FOR FURTHER RESEARCH

A thread running through much of the literature contained in this volume is that for the Jewish educational endeavor to be truly effective it must *of necessity* be a collaborative effort. In many arenas we continue to hear about the benefits of collaboration: In Jewish education we hear talk of "cutting the seams" (Schatten, 2004), "linking the silos" (Wertheimer, 2005), "striving for oneness" (Weissman, this volume), and "building bridges" (Sales & Saxe, this volume). In the fields of general education and organizational development we hear about "communication webs" (Capra, 2002), "interconnected networks" (Wheatley, 1999), "culture of connectedness" (Bloomberg, 2005), and "partners in thought" (John-Steiner, 2000). This same organic and holistic approach is described differently using different metaphors, but all carry the same message: Collaboration is a powerful engine for change. As many of this volume's authors emphasize, change efforts run the risk of remaining limited in scope and impact if they do not endeavor to address the *entire* system.

Rather than conceive of the Jewish educational enterprise as a series of cellular institutions, it should be experienced as *one synergistic system* with each of its individual components being interconnected with those that surround them. Now that it has become conventional wisdom that participation in multiple Jewish education experiences is far more likely to generate enduring Jewish commitment, we must situate the field of Jewish education within its broader social, communal, and familial contexts. Aside from collaboration among colleagues within related fields, there is a strong call for broader coordinated efforts to share resources and experience at the organizational level between institutions, bureaus of Jewish education, and federations. Increased attention to collaborative work will facilitate the identification of key challenges, the exchange of best practices, and the pooling of resources. Working collaboratively will also enable us to exchange ideas pertaining to research and the policy implications of that research, to publicize these ideas to a wider audience, and to establish ongoing mechanisms of communication, information exchange, and dialogue.

SYNTHESIS

The chapters that comprise this volume attest to the dynamism of the field and its responsiveness to an ever-changing community. The past decade has seen the emergence of a growing interest in evaluation and research by Jewish educators, policymakers, and philanthropists seeking to ascertain the extent to which various kinds of Jewish educational experiences will serve to impact learning, strengthen Jewish identity, and engender more meaningful engagement in Jewish life.

There have been enormous strides made in researching Jewish education in all its multiple vicissitudes. We have developed a deeper understanding of who our learners are, and how and in what ways different teaching methods and pedagogical approaches impact learning. We have learned much about established curricula, programs and materials, as well as about more recent innovations. We have information about contexts and settings that have existed for some time, and we are continuing to gather more information about emergent and as yet underdeveloped contexts in which Jewish learning occurs. We have collected valuable information that sheds light on "Jewish demography", and that informs Jewish education on both national and local levels.

The body of knowledge that has emerged is being used to raise additional and much-needed philanthropic resources for those initiatives that research and evaluation suggests are the most effective in accomplishing their educational goals. As a result of these efforts a significant infrastructure of schools and programs has been put in place, and a wealth of new ideas has emerged to improve the design and delivery of Jewish education. There has been an unprecedented surge in the types of Jewish education available, with learners of all ages now having access to Jewish learning in a broad range of contexts—formal as well as informal, real as well as virtual.

The field of Jewish education has certainly worked hard to address the new realities of the American Jewish community. And for all the important strides taken by the field, those who work tirelessly—every planner, every teacher, every researcher, and every funder—should be commended. While we have much reason to celebrate our achievements, multiple challenges continue to confront Jewish education. Not least among these, as pointed out by Steven M. Cohen, is the significant decline in Jewish ethnicity and collective Jewish identity. As such, Jewish education as a field of practice as well as an object of academic study must remain a matter of critical significance.

The times we live in challenge us not to rest on the good efforts of the past, or to assume that what worked then will still work now. As attested by this volume's chapters, no matter what the focus of interest or field of practice, for Jewish education to be meaningful and significant, and to have the kind of impact that we hope for, there is a clear call for ongoing sustained research and evaluation, and for increased attention to building collaborative networks through which we can share insights, understanding, and lessons learned. With the emergence and development of a myriad of educational opportunities, there are many areas of Jewish education that are deserving of further systematic exploration. Not only is there a need for more detailed information about the range and types of learning experiences, we also need to understand more about their nature and quality, as well as their impact on engagement in Jewish life and more specifically on Jewish identity.

As we continue to weave the rich tapestry of Jewish education we need to fully understand its current state, its future, and the challenges it faces. Toward this end, research must continue to address issues regarding the learners, the educators, the pedagogy, the educational contexts, as well as the more philosophical questions regarding the very purposes of Jewish education. Moreover, we need to create channels and opportunities to share what we know across contexts and practice areas, and in so doing make what we have learned educative, relevant, and meaningful to others. This volume offers a forum for expanding the rich emerging conversation regarding an ideal Jewish education for our times and beyond. The sequel to this volume will hopefully contribute to the ongoing discourse by capturing and further expanding upon the fruits of the research and evaluation efforts of the years that lie ahead.

REFERENCES

Capra, F. (2002). *The hidden connections: Integrating the biological, cognitive, and social dimensions of life into a science of sustainability.* New York: Doubleday.

Bloomberg, L. D. (2005). *Action Learning: A profoundly connected experience.* Unpublished paper presented to AEGIS Doctoral Program, Teachers College, Columbia University New York.

Dewey, J. (1960). *The school and society* (2nd ed.). Chicago: Centennial Publications University of Chicago Press. (Originally published 1915)

John-Steiner, V. (2000). *Creative collaboration.* New York: Oxford University Press.

Schatten, J. (2004). A seamless Jewish educational plan. *Jewish Education News, Winter 2005. http://www.caje. org/learn/fs_jen.html*

Wertheimer, J. (2005). *Linking the silos: How to accelerate the momentum in Jewish education today.* New York: Avi Chai Foundation. *http://www.avi-chai.org/Static/Binaries/Publications/Linking%20The%20Silos_0.pdf*

Wheatley, M. J. (2006). Leadership lessons for the real world. *Leader to Leader Magazine. http://www.margaret-wheatley.com/articles/leadershiplessons.html*

Jewish Education and the Jewish Future

Paul A. Flexner

Recently a group of senior Jewish educators engaged in a heated discussion about the burning issues of Jewish education in America. Some spoke about the lack of real commitment of many parents. Others spoke about the need for creativity and imagination. A few suggested that there was a severe lack of quality teachers and professional leaders. As the conversation delved deeper into the issues there was a general consensus that these were superficial symptoms of the need for a consistent community-wide vision for Jewish education.

Even within this group of knowledgeable and experienced educators there were very different views about the end game or outcome of the Jewish educational experience. Some spoke about knowledge and understanding, while others focused on engagement with the tradition; some spoke about the need to create a new generation of active, involved Jewish adults, and others added the need for a life-long system of learning and doing. All agreed that our current system of Jewish education only partially fulfills their dream of a dynamic Jewish community actively engaged in transmitting Jewish values and ideals.

This vignette never took place in real time. It is the result of an internal dialogue that has been ruminating in my mind over the past year as I have read and re-read the chapters included in this volume. The authors never met formally, although many are colleagues and close friends. They did not compare notes as they penned their chapters. Only a few sought outside opinions before making their submission. However, the result of the combined thinking of some of America's and Israel's leading and emerging thinkers in Jewish education is enlightening and challenging both to themselves and to the community as a whole.

We are, as the saying goes, a community blessed with great minds, creative thinkers, and deeply committed people who constantly strive to build a strong and vital Jewish community for all of our children and grandchildren. The writers of these chapters have each approached their slice of the system with an expertise and understanding that will enlighten the community as it strives to educate current and future generations.

As we bring this volume to a close, it is time to reflect on this conversation and to initiate a broader, more profound dialogue. The issues in Jewish education are multifaceted and highly complex. They cross every line. They reflect the different movements, the different philosophies of education, and the different perspectives on Judaism. Despite these differences, there is a high level of consensus that what we are doing today is not good enough; that we can do better if only we put our talents to better use; that we have the resources, both human and capital; and that the Jewish people will, as a community, find the right tools and motivation to create a better system.

This volume is in many ways a portrait of our commonalities, an insider's view of what we believe and understand about ourselves. But it is more than just a portrait. The words of the authors offer a challenge to the Jewish community. It begins with the understanding that our success is grounded in a deeper understanding of who we are, which in turn is built upon our having the knowledge that serious research provides. To this end the authors have set an agenda for future research in their specific fields and for the community as a whole. It is this agenda that will guide the future of Jewish educational research.

TODAY'S REALITY

In the years since the appearance of *What We Know about Jewish Education* there have been significant changes in the nature of Jewish life in America. A brief review of four of these changes will highlight the world view that our authors now bring to their work as researchers and thinkers about the future of Jewish life in America.

New Initiatives—The level of interest in Jewish education has increased dramatically over recent decades commencing with the 1990 National Jewish Population Study. New initiatives and innovative organizations confronting the real issues of our time have sprouted up everywhere. Examples include national organizations that focus on day schools, camping, youth initiatives, early childhood and, most recently, congregational education. Entrepreneurs are creating start-ups to engage teens, adults and almost any other subgroup that can be identified. All are founded on innovative ideas, and all are receiving support from across the community.

New Resources—The Jewish people have flourished in America. We have benefited greatly from the openness that has welcomed us as no other society has throughout our history. The result is that we are one of the wealthiest sub-populations within American society. This wealth has provided us with tremendous opportunities to support causes that benefit everyone in America as well as our own people.

Over the last two decades a new generation of Jewish philanthropists has taken the lead, accepting the challenge of addressing the needs of the Jewish people. This is clearly demonstrated by the establishment of Birthright Israel, the opening of new Jewish day schools, especially at the secondary level, and the expansion of Jewish camping. None of this would be possible if the private philanthropists had not directed their foundations to think Jewish and to plan for the future of the Jewish people.

New Ideas—The most imaginative and creative ventures are sometimes the product of a simple idea in the mind of a single individual. In the last fifteen years we have seen many of these ideas become reality and flourish. Their success, however, has also been the result of careful observations made by trained researchers and evaluators.

This combination of experimentation and evaluation combined with serious analysis of new data and careful observation of the programs as they grew and matured has led to a greater appreciation of what can be done to make a real difference. This ranges from simple program evaluation initiated by early funders to the more expansive research conducted by the Cohen Center for Modern Jewish Studies at Brandeis University and the Avi Chai Foundation, to name two. We now know much more about our educational programs than in any previous generation. Now we will be able to drive a new agenda aimed at strengthening the Jewish community for future generations by building on this knowledge and understanding.

New Partnerships—Creating new bridges that bring Jews together to learn, celebrate and engage in Jewish life is at the heart of the new agenda. Within individual institutions cross generational programming is spreading. On a larger scale, initiatives like Synagogue 3000 and STaR bring multiple institutions together for joint programming designed to create vibrant experiences for Jews of all ages. In many communities, joint ventures between the federation, the JCC and congregations are establishing a new kind of Jewish community. In others, new models are being introduced that bring Jews together, creating a new kind of organizational structure around Jewish values like tikkun olam and limmud. Philanthropists have joined with innovators to provide the resources that bring Jews together to celebrate, to learn and to live active and engaging Jewish lives. It is only through this combination of the best of the new ideas, new investment and the energy of the innovators that we will open new avenues for living Jewish lives in 21st century America. These are the values, the ideals and the directions that will establish a new dynamic for the Jewish community of the future.

CRITICAL ISSUES

Throughout these pages the authors highlight over and over three ideas that when taken together weave a foundation upon which the entire enterprise of Jewish education is based. In presenting these ideas as we bring this volume to a close, we are focusing new attention on the critical directions that research will take in the coming decade.

BUILDING COMMUNITY

The Jewish people have long been known for their sense of humor. The jokes start with a single Jew needing two congregations—the one he attends and the one he never sets foot in. In many ways, this is typical of the Jewish community as a whole. We have long divided ourselves into small groups that are connected by family structure, neighborhood alliances, or particular philosophies. However, over the last half century, many of these natural divisions have melted away as life in America has been transformed from small neighborhoods centered on ethnic groups to the sprawl of the modern city. By virtue of our general acceptance into the fabric of American life, many new opportunities have opened for living arrangements and the redesign of our institutional frameworks. The result is that we no longer have the natural connections that linked us to one another in the past.

This changing reality is reflected by the life of the typical member of the Jewish community, who has fewer and fewer Jewish friends, no longer lives in close proximity to other Jews or close relatives, has a greater likelihood of finding a non–Jewish partner and in general is less and less engaged with Judaism and the Jewish community. This new reality poses one of the great challenges to every Jewish institution: the ability to create community among its members. It all begins with the smallest unit, the family, which may be tight and close when the children are young but splits in multiple directions as the children grow. This is as true within the institutions themselves as it is for the family members within the general society. Whereas activities and programming were once designed to bring families together as clusters, today each individual picks and chooses where to become involved, and most institutions, especially within the Jewish community, plan for individuals to interact with other like-minded and similarly-aged individuals, and not in family groupings.

We see this most clearly within our teen community, where the pressures to interface with their peers crosses all lines of activity, both within the Jewish community and within their educational and social circles outside of the Jewish environment. We offer both formal and informal activities to build deeper connections with their Jewish peers, but these are always in conflict with the pressures to be involved elsewhere. In our open society the choices that our teens make are often to seek their connections on the wider stage. This is driven by the pressures to build a strong résumé designed to gain admission to the finest universities, a pressure that comes naturally to a Jewish community that has long placed the highest value on education and learning.

On the other hand, our institutions (synagogues, JCCs, federations and others) continue to struggle with discovering new ways to build their communities and constituencies. The natural systems that were their foundation from the 1930s to the 1980s no longer meet the needs of people in the age of Google and Web 2.0. New venues that bring small groups together around common interests instead of within the large complexes of the modern organization may be one of the answers. Utilizing the new technologies and building on the nascent interests in spirituality and seeking greater understanding of the self, the institutions need to discover new ways to build connections and build community around Jewish themes. This will require a new way of thinking, planning, and organizing; a new way of reaching the individuals as individuals and within their family units and the creation of a Jewish way of life that reflects the life patterns of today's Jewish community.

CREATING A SYSTEMS APPROACH

"Linking the silos" became the phrase of the moment when Jack Wertheimer published his monograph in 2005. With this one document the Jewish community woke up to what many had been saying for years. The individual pods of Jewish life and Jewish education were not achieving success. Children and families were buying into Jewish life as consumers by purchasing those pieces that had appeal to them at the moment. When they tired of that piece or they had completed that portion of their education they moved on to something new. This is as true of parents buying an early childhood Jewish experience as it is for adults who attend a semester- or year-long study seminar. Once it is over and they have received the benefit of the program, they move on to something new, which may or may not be a continuation of a Jewish learning experience.

We all know the shortcomings of the current system. Some reference the three times in a child's life when he or she is likely to drop out—after the early childhood program, after becoming bar/bat mitzvah and after college. The reality is that it is significantly harder to bring people back once they have left than to maintain their involvement once they are in. Despite our knowledge of this reality, few communities or institutions have seriously invested in a solid systems approach to Jewish engagement. There are a few models, but they do not represent a clear direction for the community. The language is clear; we can talk the talk; but the reality is also present. We have yet to walk the walk.

HAVING THE RIGHT PERSONNEL

Jewish organizational life is a people business. For over 3,000 years we have looked to the people for our leaders and thinkers. We have long recognized those whose insights and abilities will set the path for others to follow. In the 20th century America's Jews demonstrated their appreciation of their best leaders with honors and awards, with compensation and with a level of respect unmatched in much of American life. But not everyone is one of our "best" leaders; not everyone received the recognition that serving the Jewish people so richly deserves. In fact, many of those who devote significant years of their lives to serving the community, either as paid staff or as volunteers, receive little to show that the community values their service.

Jewish education, not unlike the education community in general, is a prime example. Research continually indicates that many people who lead our programs and guide our students are among the least prepared and least compensated individuals within the community. They perform their duties to the best of their abilities out of a love for Judaism and a love for the Jewish people. Their devotion and commitment is a model for all, and yet remuneration and respect are frequently missing.

It is not just the teachers and educators who fall into this category. Those who serve in a volunteer role also receive little in exchange for their efforts. They operate, often in their first volunteer leadership role, with little guidance or understanding of their responsibilities. Although highly educated in the worlds of science and the humanities, many have little understanding of what a vision for Jewish education should look like. Their passion is unmatched by an understanding or knowledge of the product that they are deeply committed to creating and supporting. Their ability to make the important decisions about the future of the Jewish people is limited by their own lack of background. Their need to learn, to be mentored and guided and to develop an understanding of the educational process is critical to creating the new communities for the future and to building systems that will serve the Jewish people for generations to come.

The message is clear. Those who are actively engaged in every pursuit of Jewish education—from classroom teachers, youth workers and camp counselors to the directors of the schools and programs, rabbis and the diverse population of volunteer leaders—require extensive learning opportunities themselves in Judaica, educational practice and theory, and systems thinking. If we as a community believe that our learners, children and adults, deserve only the best, then it is incumbent upon the community to use its resources to recruit and prepare the best to serve at all levels as our professional and volunteer leaders. Once they have been recruited and prepared, we need to mentor and nurture them as they develop the skills appropriate for their roles and to treat them with the respect and trust that they so richly deserve.

BUILDING FOR TOMORROW

This portrait grows out of the research contained in these pages of a Jewish community that is far different from the one that emerged in 20th-century America. Beginning with an immigrant population centered in small, tight-knit enclaves in large and small cities, we grew and spread into the suburbs and integrated into the fabric of American life. We developed institutions and patterns of behavior that supported our goal to become a part of this great country. Our success leaves us with a new challenge to create a new type of Jewish life that will meet the needs of the new generation and a new century. This is what the research suggests and, specifically, what our writers have highlighted in their recommendations for future research.

JEWISH EDUCATION TO BECOME JEWISH LEARNING

We begin with a process that has already begun. Over the last fifteen years the conversation has broadened to focus on Jewish learning rather than Jewish education. The systems that were created in the 20th century no longer meet the needs of a widely diverse population that is subject to the overwhelming demands and influences of a modern, technologically advanced society.

The Judaism that was centered on synagogues and centers, on rabbis, educators and program directors tied to institutions and buildings, no longer serves a population that chooses to not identify with physical structures. Much of today's Jewish education is institutionally based, time-centered and focused on the daily rigors of Jewish living. This form of Jewish life has already lost touch with significant segments of the Jewish people. A new direction, a new structure and a new vision are what the researchers tell us we need if the Jewish community is to remain a vital component of the American landscape.

This new Judaism is grounded in the new culture of America. It builds on the search that our youth, as well as their parents and grandparents, are pursuing to find meaning and spirituality in their lives. Learning to read Hebrew and to observe the rituals or sitting through experiences that follow an old script no longer engages the hearts and souls of our community. They, like many of their contemporaries, are seekers; they want to find meaning in their lives and to understand how to make choices. To accomplish this, a new definition of Jewish education is called for. By redefining the educational process to focus on deep learning, on exploring the meanings of life grounded within the traditional literature of the Jewish people, we will begin to focus on the learner as seeker.

Our research indicates that not every member of the Jewish community is necessarily a seeker at every stage of his or her life. It also indicates that there are times in everyone's life when purpose and meaning take on greater importance. Laying a positive foundation in the early years for Jewish texts and Jewish learning will provide each learner with the tools and skills necessary when the need arises. To accomplish this goal, an ongoing process of redefining Jewish education to be Jewish learning in its deepest sense is critical.

JEWISH LEARNING AND THE JEWISH FUTURE

In essay after essay the writers are clear that a new vision for Jewish education begins with the people who are at the center of the system—the Jewish educators themselves. They are dedicated, knowledgeable and committed individuals working at every level of the system. They continue to devote their lives, in part or in full, to the future of the Jewish people. They value their own Judaism and desire to share it with the next generation or their peers in this generation. They believe deeply that their approaches are grounded in a system of learning that will accomplish these results.

However, as I have already indicated, the system itself is not fulfilling the needs of today's youth or adults. By reconceptualizing the field, adapting the approaches utilized in the classrooms and re-thinking the goals of Jewish education, we will be in a better position to provide the type of learning that addresses the issues of today's learners. The research is clear; new approaches and new curricula are the keys to creating a new form of Jewish learning.

The need to start the process of redesigning the enterprise of Jewish education is suggested by the current body of research. The _hiddush_ of this volume is the clarity of the message, the understanding that Jewish education as we know it must find new ways of reaching learners. Through a process of weaving these themes into a multifaceted approach designed to address the issues of Jewish education and Jewish learning, we will move a step closer to achieving our goals.

As we add this volume to the ever-expanding literature of Jewish education, we have to ask ourselves if we are capable of creating real change in a system that is the heart and soul of the Jewish people. Are we capable of building learning communities that operate as synergistic systems? These are communities where each of the individual components is connected to those that surround them; where the people who have committed themselves to the enterprise have the tools to create the most exciting learning opportunities; where the various visions of Jewish education and Jewish life interweave with each other to create a strong fabric that holds the community together, despite our differences.

This is the challenge that this book places before the American Jewish community. This is the challenge that the community planners, the philanthropists, the volunteer leaders, the academics, the rabbis and the educators must continually struggle with as they design the new face of Jewish education. For it is only through the combined efforts of all that we will create a Jewish educational system to meet the new and exciting challenges of the 21st century.

May we all go from strength to strength.

Afterword

Where To From Here?

The chapters that comprise this volume speak to what Jewish education has been, what it currently is, what it should be, and what it may be going forward. It would be equally valid to say that an "attribute" of what makes Jewish education, Jewish education, is what it cannot or should not be; that is a definition of Jewish education by constraint. Many hard questions abound regarding the philosophical considerations of Jewish existence in our time as reflected in alternative visions of Jewish education, the values Jewish education should serve, and the personal and social character Jewish education should foster. Such questions—and new ones—will undoubtedly be raised over and again, as shifts in Jewish life require us to rethink our understanding of how Jewish education works—and ought to work. It somehow seems easier and more comforting to define what Jewish education is than what it is not. Flipping on its side the question of what Jewish education has been, is, can be, and ought to be—with the caveat not to neglect conversations around what Jewish education is not—calls for further exploration. This will allow for a deeper probing around critical issues, and will certainly shed light on as yet undiscovered potentialities and eventualities.

We know with some certainty that Jewish education is critical to the vitality, quality, and continuity of Jewish life. We also know that with the field undergoing major transformation over the past two decades, shifting social trends have altered the landscape of Jewish communal life, complicating the task of designing and delivering Jewish education. What we have yet to learn more about is the gap between what Jewish educational programs seek to impart and actual engagement in and commitment to Jewish life—remembering that these terms are variably defined and understood. In an era of constructivist learning, multiple intelligences, and diverse interests, skills, and learning styles, Jewish education must keep pace with an educational environment that is rapidly generating new types of materials and curricula, and new modes of teaching and learning. This vast range of educational opportunities will no doubt continue to pose a series of new questions about the purposes, processes, and programs that fall within the broad rubric of what we call "Jewish learning". Notably, "learning" is one of the threads that bind all of our work together. Hopefully as we continue to develop ways to help organizations and systems in education and beyond, we, as Jewish educators, can support both individual and organizational learning in the pursuit of quality and effectiveness.

The current challenge is to work toward accelerating the development of collaborative networks among the disparate institutions that make up Jewish education. As the majority of this volume's authors suggest, it is imperative that we build linkages within communities between formal and informal education, between educators in various venues, between families and the network of educational programs, and between the key communal agencies engaged in support of Jewish education. It is also imperative that we attend to and actively practice ways to address knowledge dissemination and diffusion, so that what we have learned and continue to learn can become useful and educative to others. Becoming more systemically aware means stepping away from the immediate context and viewing it in terms of its parts and the connections among them that make it a whole. To work effectively in this stance, and to generate the kind of synergy needed to move forward, we must be willing to listen attentively, to critically examine our own assumptions in order to understand different perspectives, and thereby be prepared to let go of our own certainties. In so doing we will succeed in establishing a professional learning community through which we will be able share what we are learning, and nurture our common interests and concerns.

Of significance is that as we work together toward creating and developing purposeful and meaningful forms of engagement with Jewish education, we acknowledge that Jewishness and being Jewish in contemporary society epitomizes an era of personal choice. As educators, it is our responsibility to actively instill the choice, the will, and the commitment to be not just Jews but Jewish, today, tomorrow, and forever. In so doing we will each play a vital role in nurturing and sustaining a Jewish heritage for our children, and our children's children. As Gerald Bubis (this volume) poignantly puts it:

> "We, as past generations, stand on the shoulders of those who preceded us. We can weave past, present, and future through creative processes. We must be confident that as we make use of previous legacies of the past which have come to us in all manner and form that, if we are thoughtful and purposeful, our generations can leave such legacies for those who will follow us."

Ours is a technologically driven world that defies predictability. Twenty-first century Judaism will continue to be shaped by social and historic forces presently unseen, unknown, and unexpected. The future poses great challenges. But it also promises great opportunities in terms of reaching the most important goals for Jewish education that affect all aspects of living and learning.

Linda Dale Bloomberg
Atlanta, Georgia
Shavuot 5767

Biographies

THE EDITORS

Linda Dale Bloomberg is an adjunct faculty member in the department of Adult and Organizational Learning Program at Teachers College, Columbia University, where she teaches qualitative research, serves as dissertation advisor, and leads various initiatives for program planning and curriculum development. In addition, she is an adjunct assistant professor of Jewish education at Cleveland's Siegal College of Judaic Studies, where she is an academic advisor in the distance learning master's program. With master's degrees in counseling psychology, organizational psychology, and Jewish education and a doctorate in adult education from Columbia University, she has practiced as a psychologist, career counselor, and educational and business consultant and has held research, teaching, and advisory positions at various institutes in South Africa and the United States. In 2005, together with Roberta Goodman, she founded Goodman Bloomberg Associates, specializing in educational evaluation and organizational development. Dr. Bloomberg is the author of numerous publications in the fields of qualitative research, organizational leadership development, Jewish education, adult education, and distance learning. Her latest accomplishments include *Completing Your Qualitative Dissertation: A Roadmap from Beginning to End* (Sage 2008), and *Coaching the Coach: Professionalizing the Field of Leadership Development* (forthcoming).

Paul A. Flexner has devoted his career to Jewish education and the Jewish people, where he has been the principal of congregational schools, executive director of central agencies for Jewish education, a national consultant with JESNA and an instructor of Jewish educators. With a doctorate from Teachers College Columbia University, he serves as an instructor in the School of Education at Georgia State University, the Siegal College of Judaic Studies, and Baltimore Hebrew University. Together with Teachers College Innovations he is establishing the New Teacher Academy, a teacher induction program for public and private school teachers. His articles and essays have appeared in numerous journals and news media for over three decades. Of particular note are *A Vision for Excellence: Report on the Task Force on Congregation and Communal Jewish Education* (2000) and *Providing for the Jewish Future: Report of the Task Force on Professional Recruitment, Development, Retention and Placement* (2003), which resulted from extensive research by lay and professional leadership at JESNA.

Roberta Louis Goodman is the Director of Research and Standards for JECEI (Jewish Early Childhood Education Initiative) and an adjunct associate professor of Jewish education for Siegal College of Judaic Studies, where she teaches through two-way interactive video conferencing. She conducted empirical studies in Jewish education for all of her degrees, receiving a master's in Jewish Education from the Rhea Hirsch School of Education, HUC-JIR, where she was a student of Stuart Kelman's, and a doctorate in adult education from Teachers College Columbia University. Much of her research is in the areas of personnel, institutional and community-wide educational change, family education, early childhood education, and other topics, including a day school feasibility study. She continues to do evaluation, research, and organizational development with Linda Bloomberg as part of Goodman Bloomberg Associates. Goodman's publications include curricula, student materials, and articles in the areas of faith development and spirituality, research and evaluation, adult education, distance learning, Jewish educational personnel, grant writing, and other topics. Her books include *Head Start on Holidays* with Andye Honigman-Zell (ARE 1991), *Teaching about God and Spirituality*, co-edited with Sherry Blumberg (ARE 2002), and *The Adult Jewish Education Handbook: Planning, Practice, and Theory* with Betsy Dolgin Katz (ARE 2004).

THE AUTHORS

Brian Amkraut, Provost and Professor of Judaic Studies at the Laura and Alvin Siegal College of Judaic Studies in Cleveland, OH. Received B.A. from Columbia University; M.A. and Ph.D. from New York University in European history and Judaic Studies. He has served as Visiting Assistant Professor of Jewish Studies at Oberlin College and at Northeastern University. His first book, titled Between Home and Homeland: Youth Aliyah from Nazi Germany, was published by the University of Alabama Press in June 2006.

Patricia Bidol Padva, Ph.D., is a seasoned scholar-practitioner with decades of international experience in all aspects of organizational and community change in Jewish and non–Jewish educational systems. She has provided change consultations and evaluation services for Jewish entities at the national, communal and site levels. She is on faculty of the American University—NTL Master's in Organization Development program in Washington, DC.

Michael Ben-Avie, Ph.D., appears in the federal government's Registry of Outcome Evaluators. He is an academic psychologist with postdoctoral work in child neuropsychiatric disorders and research and co-editor of six books on student learning and development with colleagues at the Yale School Development Program. Dr. Ben-Avie has conducted numerous research studies, including the Educators in Jewish Schools Study (EJSS), a national study of educators in congregational and day schools sponsored by JESNA. He is a research affiliate at the Yale Child Study Center and co-directs the Learning and Development Initiative for Jewish Educational Change and the Impact Analysis & Strategies Group.

Ofra Arieli Backenroth is the Assistant Dean of WM Davidson Graduate School of Jewish Education at The Jewish Theological Seminary. Her recent publications (in collaboration) include Bringing the Text to Life and Into Our Lives: Jewish Education and the Arts (*Journal of Religious Education* 2006), and *Introduction to Open It Up! Integrating the Arts into Jewish Education* (Springfield, NJ: A.R.E., 2006).

Lewis Bernstein has worked for Sesame Workshop, the creators of *Sesame Street*, for over 30 years. He has served as Executive Producer of both *Sesame Street* and of the Israeli/Palestinian version of the show. Dr. Bernstein is currently the Executive Vice President of Education, Research and Outreach for Sesame Workshop, where he is responsible for establishing the educational agenda for all Workshop productions and creative executions.

David Bryfman has worked in formal and informal Jewish educational institutions in Australia, Israel and North America. A graduate of Melbourne University and the Senior Educators program a Hebrew University, David is currently a Wexner Fellow and doctoral student in education and Jewish studies at NYU, focusing on Jewish adolescent identity development in formal and informal settings.

Gerald Bubis is the Founding Director of the School of Jewish Communal Service and Alfred Gottschalk Professor Emeritus of Jewish Communal Studies at Hebrew Union College in Los Angeles. Professor Bubis is currently Vice President and a Fellow at the Jerusalem Center for Public Affairs. Bubis is the author of twelve books and monographs and over 175 articles, including the latest with co-author Steven Windmueller, "From Predictability to Chaos: How Jewish Leaders Re-Invented Their Communal System, Center for Jewish Community Studies, Baltimore, 2005.

Sandy Cardin serves as Executive Director for the Charles and Lynn Schusterman Family Foundation, which is a strong proponent of Jewish education, especially in the field of informal Jewish education for teens and college-age adults.

Judah M. Cohen is the Lou and Sybil Mervis Professor of Jewish Culture and an assistant professor of folklore and ethnomusicology at Indiana University. He has taught and published widely on American Jewish music and has authored *Through the Sands of Time: A History of the Jewish Community of St. Thomas, U.S. Virgin Islands*.

Steven M. Cohen, a sociologist of American Jewry, is Research Professor of Jewish Social Policy at HUC-JIR and Director of the Florence G. Heller / JCCA Research Center. With Arnold Eisen he wrote *The Jew Within: Self, Family and Community in America,* and co-authored with Charles Liebman *Two Worlds of Judaism: The Israeli and American Experiences.*

Beth Cousens is the Director for Campus Advancement for Hillel: The Foundation for Jewish Campus Life. She is a Ph.D. candidate and Wexner Graduate Fellow studying the sociology of Jewish education at Brandeis University (graduation anticipated Fall 2007). Prior to her academic career she spent five years as the educational planner for The Jewish Federation of Greater Washington. Her dissertation research (in progress) is titled "Texts in the City: The Jewish Growth of Adults in Their 20s and 30s."

John L. Elias is Professor of religion studies and education at Fordham University. His most recent books are *Philosophical Foundations of Adult Education,* 3rd Edition (2005) and *A History of Christian Education: Protestant, Catholic and Orthodox Perspectives* (2002).

Joshua Elkin is the Executive Director of the Partnership for Excellence in Jewish Education (PEJE), an organization devoted to growing day school enrollment through capacity-building initiatives. Prior to PEJE, Josh served as Head of the Solomon Schechter Day School of Greater Boston for twenty years.

Sharon Feiman-Nemser is a leading scholar of teacher education. Since coming to Brandeis University to fill the Mandel Chair in Jewish Education, she launched the DeLeT Program, which prepares day school teachers, and founded the Mandel Center for Studies in Jewish Education, which supports research on teaching and learning in Jewish educational settings.

Debbie Findling earned a doctorate from the University of San Francisco, graduate degrees in education and Hebrew letters from the University of Judaism, and a bachelor's degree in women's studies from the University of Colorado. She has published widely, including *Teaching the Holocaust* with Simone Schweber, and has contributed chapters to *The Ultimate Jewish Teacher's Handbook* and *All the Women Followed Her: A Collection of Writings on Miriam the Prophet and the Women of Exodus.*

Clare Goldwater is currently the Director of the Joseph Meyerhoff Center for Jewish Learning at the Charles and Lynn Schusterman International Center for Hillel: the Foundation for Jewish Campus Life in Washington, DC. An informal educator and Israeli tour educator, she was born in the UK and made aliyah to Israel in 1991. She holds an M.A. in Jewish education from the Hebrew University of Jerusalem, a B.A. from Oxford University and is a graduate of the Mandel Jerusalem Fellows program.

Paul Golin is the associate executive director of the Jewish Outreach Institute and the author of numerous op/ed pieces that have appeared in various publications, including *The Jerusalem Post* and the (New York) *Jewish Week.* He is also author of the report *The Coming Majority: Suggested Action on Intermarried Households for the Organized Jewish Community* and most recently co-author with Dr. Olitzky of *20 Things for Grandparents of Interfaith Grandchildren to Do (and Not Do) to Nurture Jewish Identity in Their Grandchildren.*

Gil Graff, Executive Director of the Bureau of Jewish Education of Greater Los Angeles, is the author of a book and numerous articles in the fields of Jewish history and Jewish education. Gil, whose academic background includes a master's degree in educational administration, a J.D. and a Ph.D. in Jewish history, has served as an adjunct faculty member at the University of Judaism, Hebrew Union College, Touro College and AJR-California. Prior to joining the BJE he was a teacher and administrator at Jewish day and supplementary schools as well as director of Camp Ramah in New England.

Patricia Cipora Harte, Vice President, Program Services, has worked in the Jewish communal service field for over twenty-five years in a number of varied positions many of which focused on the Jewish living and learning aspect of the organization. She joined JCC Association in 1999 as Coordinator of Jewish education and has since taken on responsibilities for consulting to JCCs on adult programs as well as arts and culture and social action. She has held positions at CAJE, NYANA, JTS and the Educational Alliance.

She has an MSW from Wurzweiler School of Social Work and has a certificate in not-for-profit management through a joint program with UJA-Fed NY and Columbia University.

Bonnie Hausman is Senior Program Officer, Research and Evaluation at the Partnership for Excellence in Jewish Education (PEJE). In addition to her professional work as an educational evaluator and researcher prior to PEJE, Bonnie served as the founding president of Gann Academy—the New Jewish High School of Greater Boston.

Renee Frank Holtz, Ph.D. is currently the Coordinator of Academic Support for the middle school at the Solomon Schechter School of Westchester (NY) and is an adjunct professor at various graduate schools in New York. Her doctoral dissertation about what occurs between partners during the mentorship relationship was the beginning of a continued interest into the best practices of mentorship. She is the author of *Hineni, the Family Companion*, published by Behrman House; is a co-author of a chapter in *The Ultimate Jewish Teacher's Handbook*, published by A.R.E.; is an author of *Family Shabbat Table Talk*; and has written various articles, several about mentoring.

Nehemia Ichilov, Executive Director of SAJE and the Head of School for the Jerome Lippman Jewish Community Day School, Akron, OH, is also an Adjunct Professor of Jewish education at Siegal College of Jewish Studies. He presents a definition of supervision that clarifies the educational professional's role and helps institutions grow through developing a culture of empowerment, trust, and motivation.

Carol K. Ingall is the Dr. Bernard Heller Professor of Jewish Education at the Jewish Theological Seminary. Her book *Transmission and Transformation: A Jewish Perspective on Moral Education* won the National Jewish Book Award in Education in 1999.

Samuel K. Joseph is Professor of Jewish Education and Leadership Development at Hebrew Union College in Cincinnati, where he teaches in the rabbinical school. His special interest is how Jewish institutions and organizations, from schools to synagogues to national groups, can be most excellent as they seek to fulfill their mission and vision. Rabbi Joseph consults with rabbis, educators, administrators, communal leaders and lay leaders, supporting them as they lead their institutions and organizations. He is the author of four books and more than fifty articles in the area of education and leadership.

Richard Juran, Regional Vice-President and Israel Office Director, joined the JCC Association Israel Office in 1989 and has served as its director since 1997. He received his M.A. in Contemporary Jewry at the Hebrew University, specializing in Jewish education for the Diaspora. His major areas of academic interest include processes of identity formation and Israel for Jewish education. Since moving to Israel in 1977, Richie has served as educational coordinator of the Jerusalem Fellows, director of community affairs at the American Zionist Youth Foundation in New York, Director of the Hadassah Youth Center and Young Judaea Programs in Israel, and educational coordinator and teacher at the Institute for Diaspora Youth Leaders. He resides in Jerusalem.

Jo Kay is Director of HUC-JIR's New York School of Education. She has worked in day school and congregational school education, created the PACE model of family education, and is faculty for the Consortium for the Future of the Jewish Family. She is a CAJE vice president and is a 2001 Covenant Award recipient.

Shaul Kelner is Assistant Professor of Sociology and Jewish Studies at Vanderbilt University. He studies diaspora Jewish travel to Israel and is currently writing a book on the topic.

Sally Klein-Katz served for twelve years in Jewish education in the U.S.A. and, since making aliyah in 1985, has been educator/consultant/coordinator of a variety of Israel experiences for all ages. A Jerusalem Fellow, Sally worked at Melitz, JESNA, OSRUI Camp Institute and is on the faculty of HUC-JIR in Jewish education since 1991.

Rachel Korazim is the Academic Director of Distance Learning programs at The Jewish Agency for Israel's (JAFI) Department of Education. Born in Israel, she is a graduate of Haifa University. She headed the JAFI delegation to Canada (1985–1988). Since her return she has been deeply involved with Jewish education in the Diaspora, creating and implementing in-service training programs for educators, writing educational materials, counseling and teaching.

Steven Kraus is the Director of Day School, Congregational and Communal Education Initiatives for the Jewish Education Service of North America (JESNA). He is also the director of JESNA's Center for Excellence in Congregational Education. Before coming to JESNA he served as a teacher or administrator in early childhood, day school, congregational education, family education, youth and adult education and served as a congregational education director for nineteen years.

Jeffrey S. Kress, Ph.D., is Assistant Professor of Jewish Education and Senior Research Associate at the William Davidson Graduate School of Jewish Education, Jewish Theological Seminary of America. He holds a degree in clinical psychology from Rutgers, The State University of New Jersey.

Peter Margolis is a doctoral candidate at the Institute of Contemporary Jewry of the Hebrew University of Jerusalem, writing on the influence of the Internet in American Jewry. He also designs general and Jewish studies e-learning courses and teaches in the Philadelphia branch of the Florence Melton Adult Mini School.

Alvin Mars, Ph.D., Director, Mandel Center for Jewish Education, previously has served as headmaster of the American Hebrew Academy, executive vice president of the Brandeis-Bardin Institute, vice president for academic affairs and dean of the Fingerhut Graduate School of Education at the University of Judaism, director of Camp Ramah in California and headmaster of the Solomon Schechter Day Schools of Philadelphia. He was also on the founding faculty of the Reconstructionist Rabbinical College and founding director of its Department of Education. Dr. Mars received his Ph.D. in education from the Dropsie College and rabbinic ordination from Metivta of Los Angeles.

Sandy Miller-Jacobs serves as Director of Special Education Services at the Bureau of Jewish Education for Greater Boston. In this role she consults to congregational/community, day, and preschools to initiate and expand programs for children with special needs and provides professional development for teachers. A professor emerita in special education at Fitchburg State College, she taught and supervised undergraduate and graduate students, served as chairperson of the Special Education Department, interim vice president for academic affairs and interim dean for academic personnel.

Kerry M. Olitzky, an ordained rabbi, is Executive Director of the Jewish Outreach Institute in New York, the only independent national organization dedicated to reaching interfaith families and their children as well as the unaffiliated. Dr. Olitzky is the author of many inspiring books that bring the Jewish wisdom tradition into everyday life. Among his most recent works is *Jewish Holidays: A Brief Introduction for Christians* (with Dan Judson). Previously he served on the faculty and administration of Hebrew Union College-Jewish Institute of Religion, New York, where he directed its School of Education and graduate studies program.

Daniel Pekarsky is a professor and former chairperson in the Department of Educational Policy Studies at the University of Wisconsin-Madison, and he is currently the director of the Mosse/Weinstein Center for Jewish Studies. He also serves as a consultant on Jewish education to the Mandel Foundation.

Bruce Phillips is Professor of Sociology and Jewish communal service at Hebrew Union College. He served on the National Technical Advisory Committee for the 1990 and 2000 National Jewish Population studies and has conducted a dozen local Jewish population studies. He is currently writing a book about intermarriage.

Yossi Prager serves as North American Executive Director of The Avi Chai Foundation, which devotes its resources in North America primarily for the benefit of Jewish day schools and summer camps. As insiders to the history outlined in this chapter, the authors acknowledge the possibility that their perspective is colored by their experience. They also gratefully recognize the substantial assistance of Rabbi Ellen Flax in preparing the chapter.

Joseph Reimer is the Director of the Institute for Informal Jewish Education (IJE) at Brandeis University, where he is also an associate professor in the Hornstein Program.

Dr. Evie Rotstein is the Director of the Leadership Institute for Congregational School Principals, a joint project of HUC-JIR and JTS. A congregational educator for twenty-six years, she has developed programs for faculty development, teen mentoring, and parent education. She is an adjunct professor at Hebrew Union College and the Jewish Theological Seminary.

Suzanne D. Rutland (M.A. (Hons) Ph.D., Dip.Ed.), is an Associate Professor and Chair of the Department of Hebrew, Biblical & Jewish Studies, University of Sydney. She has published on Australian Jewish history, *Shoah*, Israel and Jewish education. Her latest book is *The Jews in Australia* (Cambridge University Press, 2005). She received the Medal of the Order of Australia in 2008, in recognition for her contributions to Jewish Higher Education.

Amy L. Sales is the Associate Director of the Cohen Center for Modern Jewish Studies at Brandeis University, the director of the Fisher-Bernstein Institute for Jewish Philanthropy and Leadership, and Associate Professor in Hornstein: The Jewish Professional Leadership Program. Trained as a social psychologist, she conducts research on Jewish institutions and their role in creating Jewish life and community.

Eli Schaap is a consultant focusing on transforming Jewish education through consensus decision-making, action research, and other elements of change organizing. Previously he served as the Associate Executive Director of CAJE. He received his training in a Ph.D. program in ecology and evolution at SUNY at Stony Brook. He has conducted action research and published several articles on the culture of employment, recruitment and retention of Jewish educators, early childhood Jewish education, and institutional finances, comparing them to the goals of an institution. He has frequently presented his research at the Conference of the Network for Research in Jewish Education.

Lifsa Schachter is Professor of Jewish Education and Director of Professional Development at the Siegal College of Judaic Studies. Previously she served as the director of the college's Center for Jewish Education and as dean of the college. Her interests include the study and teaching of Hebrew language, developing the skills of educators at all levels and studying and teaching Bible.

Susan Shevitz is Associate Professor at Brandeis University, where she directed and taught in the Hornstein Program in Jewish Communal Service for over two decades. Her research and consulting has focused on change in the congregational setting, especially on the characteristics that make significant long-term change difficult. She is currently involved with several evaluations of innovations in Jewish life as well as a study of pluralism in Jewish education. With a doctorate in educational planning and policy from Harvard, Shevitz remains fascinated by change processes.

Jeffrey Schein is Professor and Director of the Department of Jewish Education at Siegal College of Judaic Studies. He has served as a senior consultant for the Jewish Reconstructionist Foundation and the Mandel Center for Jewish Education of the JCCs.

Diane Tickton Schuster, consultant and writer, serves as a visiting faculty member at HUC-JIR, Brandeis University, and the American Jewish University. Her book *Jewish Lives, Jewish Learning* was a finalist for the 2004 National Jewish Book Award in education. With Lisa Grant she is conducting a long-term study of adult learning in several Long Island communities.

Simone Schweber is the Goodman Professor of Education and Jewish Studies at the University of Wisconsin-Madison, where she teaches courses on Holocaust history and representation and American Jewish identity. She is author of the book *Making Sense of the Holocaust: Lessons from Classroom Practice* (Teachers College Press 2004), co-author of *Teaching the Holocaust* (Torah Aura 2007) and along with Debbie Findling she is at work on an edited volume about the experience of abortion during the Bush era.

Ilene Vogelstein is currently the Director of the Alliance for Jewish Early Education and a consultant for JECEI. Prior to assuming these positions Ilene was the director of *Machon L'Morim: Bereshit* (an intensive professional development program for Jewish early childhood educators), the founding director of JECEP (Jewish Early Childhood Education Partnership), and the founding director of the Early Childhood Department at CAJE. She is the co-author of "Untapped Potential: The Status of Jewish Early Childhood Education in America" (2002).

Amy Walk Katz is a rabbi at Congregation Beth Shalom in Overland Park, KS. She was ordained at the Jewish Theological Seminary of America, has an M.A. in Jewish education from the University of Judaism and received her Ph.D. in education from Michigan State University. Amy has been an educator in a variety of settings, working with adults and children in both formal and informal settings.

Rob Weinberg, Ph.D., is Director of the Experiment in Congregational Education (ECE), an initiative of the Rhea Hirsch School of Education, HUC-JIR/Los Angeles. He wishes to acknowledge the efforts of many members of the ECE staff—current and former—upon whose collective work this chapter draws.

Cyd B. Weissman is the Director of the New York RE-IMAGINE Project of the Experiment in Congregational Education. Sponsored by UJA-Federation of New York, this project supports over thirty congregations in the New York area, across denominations, to re-imagine congregational education. The RE-IMAGINE Project is launching a professional development pilot with three congregations in New York to align teacher learning with new educational visions, goals and structures. Previously, she was the director of education at Congregation Beth Am Israel, where she was part of a team that created a Shabbat-centered community model of education for adult and child learners. Her master's thesis was on a systems approach to professional development.

Jack Wertheimer is the Joseph and Martha Mendelson Professor of American Jewish History at the Jewish Theological Seminary. He is the editor of *Family Matters: Jewish Education in an Age of Choice* and has published a number of essays and reports on Jewish education, including *Linking the Silos: How to Accelerate the Momentum in Jewish Education Today* and *Recent Trends in Jewish Supplementary Education*.

Jonathan S. Woocher is Chief Ideas Officer of JESNA and heads its Lippman Kanfer Institute: An Action-oriented Think Tank for Innovation in Jewish Learning and Engagement. He served for twenty years as JESNA's chief professional officer before assuming his new position this year. JESNA fosters excellence in Jewish education by providing the field with the knowledge and know-how it needs in order to thrive. Prior to coming to JESNA in 1986 Dr. Woocher served on the faculties of Carleton College in Minnesota and Brandeis University, where he taught in the Benjamin S. Hornstein Program in Jewish Communal Service. Dr. Woocher is the author of *Sacred Survival: The Civil Religion of American Jews* and numerous articles on Jewish education, community, and religious life. He earned a B.A., summa cum laude, from Yale University, and a Ph.D. in religion from Temple University.